# TOP TITLES
## FOR THE ENTHUSIAST

**WORLD AIRLINE FLEETS NEWS**
Published monthly, World Airline Fleets News brings you the latest news and photographs from around the world. Available as single copies or on subscription, WAF News provides an excellent photographic record of the ever changing airliner scene. A high quality PVC binder, holding 12 issues, is also available (see order form for details).

**BOEING 747 - THE FIRST 20 YEARS**
Details and fleet lists of all past and present Boeing 747 operators are contained in this invaluable reference book, together with a full production list providing roll-out and  flight dates. Also included is an illustrated historical background and details of constructi  and the numerous variants (including the 747-400), plus 16 pages of colour photographs.
SPECIAL OFFER - NOW ONLY £7-50 (was £14-95)

**AN ILLUSTRATED HISTORY OF BRITISH EUROPEAN AIRWAYS**
A consise and interesting history by all accounts, this beautifully illustrated 192-page book contains a wealth of historical information following the airline from its formation in 1946 to its eventual merger with BOAC and the formation of British Airways in 1972. Photographic coverage is evident from 1946 to 1972, illustrating all types operated by BEA and the various liveries carried. Route maps and service details are featured throughout, together with an all-time fleet list, including disposal details and remarks.
SPECIAL OFFER - NOW ONLY £8-00 (was £15-95)

**WORLD AIRLINE COLOURS (VOLS. 2, 3 and 4)**
World Airline Colours provides the ultimate collection of airline colourschemes in four fabulous colour volumes, each featuring the liveries of 148 airlines The most comprehensive airline recognition guide currently available and a fascinating record to look back on in years to come.(152 pages - A5 hard).
SPECIAL OFFER - NOW ONLY £6-00 (Previously £11-95) PER VOLUME.

**BIZ JET 1991**
The new completely updated edition of the world's leading executive jet listing. Biz Jet covers all the world's business jets - including for each individual aircraft, registration, type, construction number, owner/operator and all previous identities.

**HIGH IN THE SKY**
The complete airband radio guide for VHF and HF listeners. Includes details on the type of airband receivers available, how to understand radio communications, call-signs and frequencies used etc. Also includes airline three-letter designators and SELCAL/registration tie-ups. (136 pages - A5)

**JET AIRLINER PRODUCTION LIST**
Now the standard production reference for the enthusiast, Jet Airliner Production List contains complete production details covering all western-built jet airliners - past and present. Listed in construction number order, each individual entry includes first flight and delivery dates, model number, full service history with lease, acquisition and write-off dates and all registrations and names carried by the aircraft.

**TURBOPROP AIRLINER PRODUCTION LIST**
Sister volume to the Jet Airliner Production List detailed above, the turboprop edition provides complete production details of all turboprop airliners - past and present. Manufacturers include Aerospatiale/Aeritalia, Armstrong Whitworth, Avro, Beech, British Aerospace, Bristol, Canadair, CASA, Convair, de Havilland Canada, Dornier, Embraer, Fairchild, Fokker, GAF, Grumman, Handley Page, HAL, IAI, Lockheed, NAMC, Nord, Saab, Saunders, Shorts and Vickers.

**AIRLINES '91**
Published by T.H.A.S., Airlines '91 contains fleet lists for all the world's airlines in a handy portable format with optional lay-flat opening. Each airline entry includes; head office address, flight codes, fleet - by registration, type, c/n, line number and previous identity, together with individual aircraft names and lease/order details. Available in lay-flat or bound formats, Airlines '91 comes highly recommended for anyone seeking an up to date fleet list for the summer season. (Published April 1991)

**1991 JET & PROPJET CORPORATE DIRECTORY**
All the world's executive jet and turboprop aircraft have been combined into one pocket-size directory, offering a convenient and cost-effective way of keeping track of all corporate-owned aircraft; listed in country order by registration, type, c/n, registered owner and previous identity. (Published February 1991)

Please add the following for postage and packing.
**UK:** Add 10% to the value of your order (minimum charge £1-50)
**EUROPE:** Add 20% (minimum charge £2-00)
**OUTSIDE EUROPE (surface):** Add 20% (minimum charge £2-00)
**OUTSIDE EUROPE (airmail):** Add 20% (minimum charge £6-00)

## ORDER FORM

| | | | |
|---|---|---|---|
| **Airlines '91** | | £7-50 | |
| **Jet and Propjet Corporate Directory** | | £10-50 | |
| **Biz Jet 1991** | | £8-95 | |
| **Jet Airliner Production List** | | £8-9 | |
| **Turboprop Airliner Production List** | | £8-95 | |
| **World Airline Colours Vol. 2** | NOW | £6-00 | |
| **World Airline Colours Vol. 3** | NOW | £6-00 | |
| **World Airline Colours Vol. 4** | NOW | £6-00 | |
| **High in the Sky** | | £4-25 | |
| **Boeing 747 - The first 20 years** | NOW | £7-50 | |
| **Illustrated history of British European Airways** | NOW | £8-00 | |
| **World Airline Fleets News (single copy)** | | £2-50 | |
| **annual subscription 12 issues** | UK | £26-00 | |
| | Europe | £30-00 | |
| | Outside Europe | £35-00 | |
| **World Airline Fleets News Binder** | | £6-00 | |

Plus many new titles and special offers for 1991 - further details available on request.

How to pay: Cheques made payable to 'Browcom Publishing', Credit Card, Postal Order, International Money Order, Foreign Cheque payable on a UK Bank. All payments must be in pounds sterling.

**Name:**_____

**Address:**_____

_____

_____

 total enclosed: £ _____     Credit Card type: _____

Card No. _____     Exp. date: _____

Send your order to:
**BROWCOM PUBLISHING,**
**Browcom House, Browells Lane, Feltham, Middlesex, TW13 7EQ, England.**

# Monthly news & aircraft movements throughout the UK

Over 500 pages every year, packed with regular national UK movement reports, airline news, military aviation and overflight listings. Add the most comprehensive Heathrow movement lists available, a full UK register update and illustrate with photographs and you have the best magazine of its type. All this for just £12.00 per year.

To commence membership from January 1991 send £12.00 to SAS (CAM Offer), 271 Birchanger Lane, Birchanger, Bishop's Stortford, Herts, CM23 5QP. Or to join during the year, simply send £1 per month of 1991 remaining. As well as postal subscription to the magazine you will also be entitled to discounts at the Society shop (open Sundays at Stansted Airport) which stocks current registers, books, postcards, kits and models.

**Stansted Aviation Society**

NEWS 12/01

Artist's impression of the proposed BAe 146-NRA, alongside a -200 series. (PHOTO: BRITISH AEROSPACE)

January 1991

Volume 12 Number 1

The essential magazine for the aircraft enthusiast

**Just £12 p.a.**

# Contents

This forty-second edition published 1991

ISBN 0 7110 1969 X

Published by Ian Allan Ltd, Shepperton, Surrey;
and printed by Ian Allan Printing Ltd at their works
at Coombelands in Runnymede, England.

*Cover Overall:* This Shorts Belfast of HeavyLift Cargo Airlines is registered G-BFYU. *HeavyLift*

*Cover Inset:* A Lufthansa Boeing 737-200 on final approach to Heathrow. *Allan Burney*

# CIVIL AIRCRAFT MARKINGS 1991

## ALAN J. WRIGHT

**LONDON**

**IAN ALLAN LTD**

# Introduction

The 'G' prefixed four letter registration system was adopted in 1919 after a short-lived spell of about three months with serial numbers beginning at K-100. Until July 1928 the UK allocations were in the G-Exxx range, but as a result of further International agreements, this series was ended at G-EBZZ, the replacement being G-Axxx. From this point the registrations were issued in a reasonably orderly manner through to G-AZZZ, reached in July 1972. There were two exceptions. To avoid possible confusion with signal codes, the G-AQxx sequence was omitted, while G-AUxx was reserved for Australian use originally. In recent years however, an individual request for a mark in the latter range has been granted by the Authorities.

Although the next logical sequence was started at G-Bxxx, it was not long before the strictly applied rules relating to aircraft registration began to be relaxed. Permission was readily given for personalised marks to be issued incorporating virtually any four letter combination, while re-registration has also become a common feature, a practice almost unheard of in the past. In this book, where this has taken place at some time, the previous UK civil identity appears in parenthesis after the owner's/operator's name. An example of this is One-Eleven G-BBMG which originally carried G-AWEJ.

Some aircraft have also been allowed to wear military markings without displaying their civil identity. In this case the serial number actually carried is shown in parenthesis after the type's name. For example Mosquito G-ASKH flies as RR299 in RAF colours. As an aid to the identification of these machines, a military conversion list is provided.

Other factors caused a sudden acceleration in the number of registrations allocated by the Civil Aviation Authority in the early 1980s. The first surge came with the discovery that it was possible to register plastic bags and other items even less likely to fly, on payment of the standard fee. This erosion of the main register was checked in early 1982 by the issue of a special sequence for such devices commencing at G-FYAA. Powered hang-gliders provided the second glut of allocations as a result of the decision that these types should be officially registered. Although a few of the early examples penetrated the normal in-sequence register, the vast majority were given marks in other special ranges, this time G-MBxx, G-MGxx, G-MJxx, G-MMxx, G-MNxx, G-MTxx, G-MVxx, G-MWxx, G-MYxx and G-MZxx. At first it was common practice for microlights to ignore the requirement to carry their official identity. However the vast majority now display their registration somewhere on the structure, the size and position depending on the dimensions of the component to which it is applied.

Throughout the UK section of this book, there are many instances where the probable base of the aircraft has been included. This is positioned at the end of the owner/operator details preceded by an oblique stroke. It must of course be borne in mind that changes do take place and that no attempt has been made to record the residents at the many private strips. The base of airline equipment has been given as the company's headquarter's airport, although frequently aircraft are outstationed for long periods.

Non-airworthy preserved aircraft are shown with a star after the type.

The three-letter codes used by airlines to prefix flight numbers are included for those carriers appearing in the book. Radio frequencies for the larger airfields/airports are also listed.

## Acknowledgements

Once again thanks are extended to the Registration Department of the Civil Aviation Authority for their assistance and allowing access to their files. The comments and amendments flowing from Wal Gandy have as always proved of considerable value, while Ian Checkley, Duncan Cummins, Howard Curtis and Kenneth Nimbley also contributed useful facts. The help given by numerous airlines or their information agencies has been much appreciated. The work of A. S. Wright and C. P. Wright during the update of this edition must not go unrecorded, since without it, deadlines would probably become impossible. **AJW**

# International Civil Aircraft Markings

| | |
|---|---|
| A2- | Botswana |
| A3- | Tonga |
| A5- | Bhutan |
| A6- | United Arab Emirates |
| A7- | Qatar |
| A9- | Bahrain |
| A40- | Oman |
| AP- | Pakistan |
| B- | China/Taiwan |
| C-F, C-G | Canada |
| C2- | Nauru |
| C3 | Andora |
| C5- | Gambia |
| C6- | Bahamas |
| C9- | Mozambique |
| CC- | Chile |
| CCCP-* | Soviet Union |
| CN- | Morocco |
| CP- | Bolivia |
| CS- | Portugal |
| CU- | Cuba |
| CX- | Uruguay |
| D- | Germany |
| D2- | Angola |
| D4 | Cape Verde Islands |
| D6- | Comores Islands |
| DQ- | Fiji |
| EC- | Spain |
| EI- | Republic of Ireland |
| EL- | Liberia |
| EP- | Iran |
| ET- | Ethiopia |
| F- | France, Colonies and Protectorates |
| G- | United Kingdom |
| H4- | Solomon Islands |
| HA- | Hungarian People's Republic |
| HB- | Switzerland and Liechtenstein |
| HC- | Ecuador |
| HH- | Haiti |
| HI- | Dominican Republic |
| HK- | Colombia |
| HL- | Korea (South) |
| HP- | Panama |
| HR- | Honduras |
| HS- | Thailand |
| HV- | The Vatican |
| HZ- | Saudi Arabia |
| I- | Italy |
| J2- | Djibouti |
| J3- | Grenada |
| J5- | Guinea Bissau |
| J6- | St Lucia |
| J7- | Dominica |
| J8- | St Vincent |
| JA- | Japan |
| JY- | Jordan |
| LN- | Norway |
| LV- | Argentine Republic |
| LX- | Luxembourg |
| LZ- | Bulgaria |
| MI- | Marshall Islands |
| N- | United States of America |
| OB- | Peru |
| OD- | Lebanon |
| OE- | Austria |
| OH- | Finland |
| OK- | Czechoslovakia |
| OO- | Belgium |
| OY- | Denmark |
| P- | Korea (North) |
| P2- | Papua New Guinea |

| | |
|---|---|
| P4- | Aruba |
| PH- | Netherlands |
| PJ- | Netherlands Antilles |
| PK- | Indonesia and West Irian |
| PP-, PT- | Brazil |
| PZ- | Surinam |
| RDPL- | Laos |
| RP- | Philippine Republic |
| S2- | Bangladesh |
| S7- | Seychelles |
| S9- | São Tomé |
| SE- | Sweden |
| SP- | Poland |
| ST- | Sudan |
| SU- | Egypt |
| SX- | Greece |
| T2 | Tuvalu |
| T3- | Kiribati |
| T7- | San Marino |
| TC- | Turkey |
| TF- | Iceland |
| TG- | Guatemala |
| TI- | Costa Rica |
| TJ- | United Republic of Cameroon |
| TL- | Central African Republic |
| TN- | Republic of Congo (Brazzaville) |
| TR- | Gabon |
| TS- | Tunisia |
| TT- | Chad |
| TU- | Ivory Coast |
| TY- | Benin |
| TZ- | Mali |
| V2- | Antigua |
| V3- | Belize |
| V5- | Namibia |
| V8- | Brunei |
| VH- | Australia |
| VN- | Vietnam |
| VP-F | Falkland Islands |
| VP-LMA/LUZ | Montserrat |
| VP-LVA/LZZ | Virgin Islands |
| VQ-T | Turks & Caicos Islands |
| VR-B | Bermuda |
| VR-C | Cayman Islands |
| VR-G | Gibraltar |
| VR-H | Hong Kong |
| VT- | India |
| XA-, XB-, XC-, | Mexico |
| XT- | Burkina Faso |
| XU- | Kampuchea |
| XY-, XZ- | Burma |
| YA- | Afghanistan |
| YI- | Iraq |
| YJ- | Vanuatu |
| YK- | Syria |
| YN- | Nicaragua |
| YR- | Romania |
| YS- | El Salvador |
| YU- | Yugoslavia |
| YV- | Venezuela |
| Z- | Zimbabwe |
| ZA- | Albania |
| ZK- | New Zealand |

* Cyrillic letters for SSSR.

| | | | |
|---|---|---|---|
| ZP- | Paraguay | 6O- | Somalia |
| ZS- | South Africa | 6V- | Senegal |
| 3A- | Monaco | 6Y- | Jamaica |
| 3B- | Mauritius | 7O- | Democratic Yemen |
| 3C- | Equatorial Guinea | 7P- | Lesotho |
| 3D- | Swaziland | 7Q- | Malawi |
| 3X- | Guinea | 7T- | Algeria |
| 4R- | Sri Lanka | 8P- | Barbados |
| 4U | United Nations Organisation | 8Q- | Maldives |
| 4W- | Yemen Arab Republic | 8R- | Guyana |
| 4X- | Israel | 9G- | Ghana |
| 4YB | Jordanian-Iraqi Co-op Treaty | 9H- | Malta |
| 5A- | Libya | 9J- | Zambia |
| 5B- | Cyprus | 9K- | Kuwait |
| 5H- | Tanzania | 9L- | Sierra Leone |
| 5N- | Nigeria | 9M- | Malaysia |
| 5R- | Malagasy Republic (Madagascar) | 9N- | Nepal |
| 5T- | Mauritania | 9Q- | Zaïre |
| 5U- | Niger | 9U- | Burundi |
| 5V- | Togo | 9V- | Singapore |
| 5W- | Western Samoa (Polynesia) | 9XR- | Rwanda |
| 5X- | Uganda | 9Y- | Trinidad and Tobago |
| 5Y- | Kenya | | |

# Aircraft Type Designations

(eg PA-28 Piper Type 28)

| | | | |
|---|---|---|---|
| A. | Beagle, Auster | GY | Gardan |
| AA- | American Aviation, Grumman American | H | Helio |
| | | HM. | Henri Mignet |
| AB | Agusta-Bell | HP. | Handley Page |
| AS | Aérospatiale | HR. | Robin |
| A.S. | Airspeed | H.S. | Hawker Siddeley |
| A.W. | Armstrong Whitworth | IL | Ilyushin |
| B. | Blackburn, Bristol Boeing, Beagle | J. | Auster |
| | | L. | Lockheed |
| BAC | British Aircraft Corporation | L.A. | Luton |
| BAe | British Aerospace | M. | Miles, Mooney |
| BAT | British Aerial Transport | MBB | Messerschmitt-Bölkow-Blohm |
| B.K. | British Klemm | MJ | Jurca |
| BN | Britten-Norman | M.S. | Morane-Saulnier |
| Bo | Bolkow | NA | North American |
| Bu | Bucker | P. | Hunting (formerly Percival), Piaggio |
| CAARP | Co-operative des Ateliers Aer de la Région Parisienne | PA- | Piper |
| | | PC. | Pilatus |
| CCF | Canadian Car & Foundry Co | QAC | Quickie Aircraft Co |
| C.H. | Chrislea | R. | Rockwell |
| CHABA | Cambridge Hot-Air Ballooning Association | S. | Short, Sikorsky |
| | | SA., SE, SO. | Sud-Aviation, Aérospatiale, Scottish Aviation |
| CLA | Comper | SC | Short |
| CP. | Piel | SCD | Side Cargo Door |
| D. | Druine | S.R. | Saunders-Roe, Stinson |
| DC- | Douglas Commercial | ST | SOCATA |
| D.H. | de Havilland | T. | Tipsy |
| D.H.C. | de Havilland Canada | TB | SOCATA |
| DR. | Jodel (Robin-built) | Tu | Tupolev |
| EMB | Embraer | UH. | United Helicopters (Hiller) |
| EoN | Elliotts of Newbury | UTA | Union de Transports Aérien |
| EP | Edgar Percival | V. | Vickers-Armstrongs, BAC |
| F. | Fairchild, Fokker | V.S. | Vickers-Supermarine |
| FH | Fairchild-Hiller | WAR | War Aircraft Replicas |
| G. | Grumman | W.S. | Westland |
| GA | Gulfstream American | Z. | Zlin |
| G.A.L. | General Aircraft | | |
| G.C. | Globe | | |

| Reg. | Type (†False registration) | Owner or Operator | Notes |
|------|----------------------------|-------------------|-------|
| G-EACN | BAT BK23 Bantam (K123) ★ | Shuttleworth Trust/O. Warden | |
| G-EAGA | Sopwith Dove | R. H. Reeves | |
| G-EASQ | Bristol Babe (replica) (BAPC87)★ | Bomber County Museum/Hemswell | |
| G-EAVX | Sopwith Pup (B1807) | K. A. M. Baker | |
| G-EBHX | D.H.53 Humming Bird | Shuttleworth Trust/O. Warden | |
| G-EBIA | S.E.5A (F904) | Shuttleworth Trust/O. Warden | |
| G-EBIB | S.E.5A (F939) ★ | Science Museum | |
| G-EBIC | S.E.5A (F938) ★ | RAF Museum | |
| G-EBIR | D.H.51 | Shuttleworth Trust/O. Warden | |
| G-EBJE | Avro 504K (E449)★ | RAF Museum | |
| G-EBJG | Parnall Pixie III ★ | Midland Aircraft Preservation Soc | |
| G-EBJO | ANEC II ★ | Shuttleworth Trust/O. Warden | |
| G-EBKY | Sopwith Pup (N5180) | Shuttleworth Trust/O. Warden | |
| G-EBLV | D.H.60 Cirrus Moth | British Aerospace/Hatfield | |
| G-EBMB | Hawker Cygnet I ★ | RAF Museum | |
| G-EBNV | English Electric Wren | Shuttleworth Trust/O. Warden | |
| G-EBQP | D.H.53 Humming Bird ★ | Russavia Collection | |
| G-EBWD | D.H.60X Hermes Moth | Shuttleworth Trust/O. Warden | |
| G-EBYY | Cierva C.8L ★ | Musée de l'Air, Paris | |
| G-EBZM | Avro 594 Avian IIIA ★ | Greater Manchester Museum of Science & Technology | |
| G-EBZN | D.H.60X Moth | I. B. Grace (G-UAAP) | |
| G-AAAH | D.H.60G Gipsy Moth (replica) | Hilton Hotel/Gatwick (BAPC 168) ★ | |
| G-AAAH | D.H.60G Gipsy Moth ★ | Science Museum | |
| G-AACN | H.P.39 Gugnunc ★ | Science Museum/Wroughton | |
| G-AADR | D.H.60GM Moth | H. F. Moffatt | |
| G-AAHY | D.H.60M Moth | M. E. Vaisey | |
| G-AAIN | Parnall Elf II | Shuttleworth Trust/O. Warden | |
| G-AAMX | D.H.60GM Moth | R. J. Parkhouse | |
| G-AAMY | D.H.60M Moth | R. M. Brooks | |
| G-AAMZ | D.H.60G Moth | C. C. & J. M. Lovell | |
| G-AANG | Blériot XI | Shuttleworth Trust/O. Warden | |
| G-AANH | Deperdussin Monoplane | Shuttleworth Trust/O. Warden | |
| G-AANI | Blackburn Monoplane | Shuttleworth Trust/O. Warden | |
| G-AANJ | L.V.G.-C VI (7198/18) | Shuttleworth Trust/O. Warden | |
| G-AANL | D.H.60M Moth | D. & P. Ellis | |
| G-AANM | Bristol 96A F.2B (D7889) | Aero Vintage Ltd | |
| G-AANO | D.H.60GMW Moth | A. W. & M. E. Jenkins | |
| G-AANV | D.H.60G Moth | R. I. Souch | |
| G-AAOK | Curtiss Wright Travel Air 12Q | Shipping & Airlines Ltd/Biggin Hill | |
| G-AAOR | D.H.60G Moth (EM-01) | J. A. Pothecary/Shoreham | |
| G-AAPZ | Desoutter I (mod.) ★ | Shuttleworth Trust/O. Warden | |
| G-AAUP | Klemm L.25-1A | J. I. Cooper | |
| G-AAVJ | D.H.60GMW Moth | Proteus Petroleum Aviation Ltd/ Goodwood | |
| G-AAWO | D.H.60G Gipsy Moth | N. J. W. Reid & L. A. Fenwick | |
| G-AAXK | Klemm L.25-1A | C. C. Russell-Vick | |
| G-AAYX | Southern Martlet | Shuttleworth Trust/O. Warden | |
| G-AAZP | D.H.80A Puss Moth | R. P. Williams | |
| G-ABAA | Avro 504K (H2311) ★ | Greater Manchester Museum of Science & Technology | |
| G-ABAG | D.H.60G Moth | Shuttleworth Trust/O. Warden | |
| G-ABDW | D.H.80A Puss Moth (VH-UQB) ★ | Museum of Flight/E. Fortune | |
| G-ABDX | D.H.60G Moth | M. D. Souch | |
| G-ABEE | Avro 594 Avian IVM (Sports) ★ | Aeroplane Collection Ltd | |
| G-ABEV | D.H.60G Moth | Wessex Aviation & Transport Ltd | |
| G-ABLM | Cierva C.24 ★ | Mosquito Aircraft Museum | |
| G-ABLS | D.H.80A Puss Moth | R. C. F. Bailey | |
| G-ABMR | Hart 2 (J9941) ★ | RAF Museum | |
| G-ABNT | Civilian C.A.C.1 Coupe | Shipping & Airlines Ltd/Biggin Hill | |
| G-ABNX | Redwing 2 | J. Pothecary (stored) | |
| G-ABOI | Wheeler Slymph ★ | Midland Air Museum | |
| G-ABOX | Sopwith Pup (N5195) | Museum of Army Flying/Middle Wallop | |
| G-ABSD | D.H.60G Moth | M. E. Vaisey | |
| G-ABTC | CLA.7 Swift | P. Channon (stored) | |

| Notes | Reg. | Type | Owner or Operator |
|---|---|---|---|
| | G-ABUS | CLA.7 Swift | R. C. F. Bailey |
| | G-ABUU | CLA.7 Swift | H. B. Fox |
| | G-ABVE | Arrow Active 2 | J. D. Penrose |
| | G-ABWP | Spartan Arrow | R. E. Blain/Barton |
| | G-ABXL | Granger Archaeopteryx ★ | Shuttleworth Trust/O. Warden |
| | G-ABZB | D.H.60G-III Moth Major | R. E. & B. A. Ogden |
| | G-ACBH | Blackburn B.2 ★ | R. Coles |
| | G-ACCB | D.H.83 Fox Moth | I. B. Grace |
| | G-ACDA | D.H.82A Tiger Moth | R. J. Biddle |
| | G-ACDC | D.H.82A Tiger Moth | Tiger Club Ltd/Headcorn |
| | G-ACDJ | D.H.82A Tiger Moth | P. Henley & J. K. Moorhouse |
| | G-ACEJ | D.H.83 Fox Moth | J. I. Cooper |
| | G-ACET | D.H.84 Dragon | M. C. Russell |
| | G-ACFM | Avro 631 Cadet | R. I. Souch |
| | G-ACGT | Avro 594 Avian IIIA ★ | Yorkshire Light Aircraft Ltd/Leeds |
| | G-ACIT | D.H.84 Dragon ★ | Science Museum/Wroughton |
| | G-ACLL | D.H.85 Leopard Moth | D. C. M. & V. M. Stiles |
| | G-ACMA | D.H.85 Leopard Moth | S. J. Filhol/Sherburn |
| | G-ACMD | D.H.82A Tiger Moth | J. A. Pothecary/Shoreham |
| | G-ACMN | D.H.85 Leopard Moth | H. D. Labouchere |
| | G-ACOJ | D.H.85 Leopard Moth | M. J. Abbott |
| | G-ACOL | D.H.85 Leopard Moth | M. J. Abbott |
| | G-ACSP | D.H.88 Comet | Saltair Ltd/Staverton |
| | G-ACSS | D.H.88 Comet | Shuttleworth Trust/Hatfield |
| | G-ACTF | CLA.7 Swift ★ | Brooklands Museum of Aviation/ Weybridge |
| | G-ACUS | D.H.85 Leopard Moth | T. P. A. Norman/Panshanger |
| | G-ACUU | Cierva C.30A (HM580)★ | G. S. Baker/Duxford |
| | G-ACUX | S.16 Scion (VH-UUP) ★ | Ulster Folk & Transport Museum |
| | G-ACVA | Kay Gyroplane★ | Glasgow Museum of Transport |
| | G-ACWM | Cierva C.30A ★ | International Helicopter Museum/ Weston-s-Mare |
| | G-ACWP | Cierva C.30A (AP507) ★ | Science Museum |
| | G-ACXB | D.H.60G-III Moth Major | I. B. Grace |
| | G-ACXE | B.K.L-25C Swallow | J. C. Wakeford |
| | G-ACYK | Spartan Cruiser III ★ | Museum of Flight (front fuselage)/ E. Fortune |
| | G-ACZE | D.H.89A Dragon Rapide | Wessex Aviation & Transport Ltd (G-AJGS)/Henstridge |
| | G-ADAH | D.H.89A Dragon Rapide ★ | Greater Manchester Museum of Science & Technology |
| | G-ADCG | D.H.82A Tiger Moth | D. A. Lowe (stored) |
| | G-ADEV | Avro 504K (H5199) | Shuttleworth Trust (G-ACNB)/ O. Warden |
| | G-ADFO | Blackburn B.2 ★ | R. Cole |
| | G-ADFV | Blackburn B.2 ★ | Humberside Aircraft Preservation Soc |
| | G-ADGP | M.2L Hawk Speed Six | R. I. Souch |
| | G-ADGT | D.H.82A Tiger Moth | D. R. & Mrs M. Wood |
| | G-ADGV | D.H.82A Tiger Moth | K. J. Whitehead |
| | G-ADHA | D.H.83 Fox Moth | Wessex Aviation & Transport Ltd |
| | G-ADHD | D.H.60G-III Moth Major | M. E. Vaisey |
| | G-ADIA | D.H.82A Tiger Moth | M. F. W. B. Maunsell/Goodwood |
| | G-ADJJ | D.H.82A Tiger Moth | J. M. Preston |
| | G-ADKC | D.H.87B Hornet Moth | L. E. Day/Carlisle |
| | G-ADKK | D.H.87B Hornet Moth | C. P. B. Horsley & R. G. Anniss |
| | G-ADKL | D.H.87B Hornet Moth | A. de Cadenet |
| | G-ADKM | D.H.87B Hornet Moth | L. V. Mayhead |
| | G-ADLY | D.H.87B Hornet Moth | Proteus Petroleum Aviation Ltd/ Goodwood |
| | G-ADMT | D.H.87B Hornet Moth | M. A. Livett |
| | G-ADMW | M.2H Hawk Major (DG590) ★ | Museum of Army Flying/Middle Wallop |
| | G-ADND | D.H.87B Hornet Moth | Shuttleworth Trust/O. Warden |
| | G-ADNE | D.H.87B Hornet Moth | R. Twisleton-Wykeham Fiennes/ Biggin Hill |
| | G-ADNZ | D.H.82A Tiger Moth | C. A. Pullan |
| | G-ADOT | D.H.87B Hornet Moth ★ | Mosquito Aircraft Museum |
| | G-ADPJ | B.A.C. Drone | N. H. Ponsford |
| | G-ADPR | P.3 Gull | Shuttleworth Trust Jean/O. Warden |
| | G-ADPS | B.A. Swallow 2 | Wessex Aviation & Transport Ltd |
| | G-ADRA | Pietenpol Air Camper | A. J. Mason & R. J. Barrett |
| | G-ADRC | K. & S. Jungster J-1 | J. J. Penney & L. R. Williams |

| Notes | Reg. | Type | Owner or Operator |
|---|---|---|---|
| | G-ADRG† | Mignet HM.14 (replica) (BAPC77) ★ | Cotswold Aircraft Restoration Group |
| | G-ADRH | D.H.87B Hornet Moth | I. M. Callier |
| | G-ADRR | Aeronca C.3 | D. S. Morgan |
| | G-ADRY† | Mignet HM.14 (replica) (BAPC29) ★ | Brooklands Museum |
| | G-ADUR | D.H.87B Hornet Moth | Wessex Aviation & Transport Ltd |
| | G-ADWO | D.H.82A Tiger Moth | Wessex Aviation Soc |
| | G-ADXS | Mignet HM.14 ★ | Thameside Aviation Museum/E. Tilbury |
| | G-ADXT | D.H.82A Tiger Moth | R. G. Hanauer/Goodwood |
| | G-ADYS | Aeronca C.3 | B. C. Cooper |
| | G-AEBB | Mignet HM.14 ★ | Shuttleworth Trust/O. Warden |
| | G-AEBJ | Blackburn B-2 | British Aerospace PLC/Brough |
| | G-AEDB | B.A.C. Drone 2 | M. C. Russell |
| | G-AEDT | D.H.90 Dragonfly | Wessex Aviation & Transport Ltd |
| | G-AEDU | D.H.90 Dragonfly | T. Norman |
| | G-AEEG | M.3A Falcon | Skysport Engineering Ltd |
| | G-AEEH | Mignet HM.14 ★ | RAF Museum/St Athan |
| | G-AEFG | Mignet HM.14 (BAPC75) ★ | N. Ponsford |
| | G-AEFT | Aeronca C.3 | C. E. Humphreys & ptnrs/Henstridge |
| | G-AEGV | Mignet HM.14 ★ | Midland Aircraft Preservation Soc |
| | G-AEHM | Mignet HM.14 ★ | Science Museum/Wroughton |
| | G-AEJZ | Mignet HM.14 (BAPC120) ★ | Bomber County Museum/Hemswell |
| | G-AEKR | Mignet HM.14 (BAPC121) ★ | S. Yorks Aviation Soc |
| | G-AEKV | Kronfeld Drone ★ | Brooklands Museum of Aviation/Weybridge |
| | G-AELO | D.H.87B Hornet Moth | S. N. Bostock |
| | G-AEML | D.H.89 Dragon Rapide | Proteus Petroleum Ltd/Goodwood |
| | G-AENP | Hawker Hind (K5414) (BAPC78) | Shuttleworth Trust/O. Warden |
| | G-AEOA | D.H.80A Puss Moth | P. & A. Wood/O. Warden |
| | G-AEOF† | Mignet HM.14 (BAPC22) ★ | Aviodome/Schiphol, Holland |
| | G-AEOF | Rearwin 8500 | Shipping & Airlines Ltd/Biggin Hill |
| | G-AEOH | Mignet HM.14 ★ | Midland Air Museum |
| | G-AEPH | Bristol F.2B (D8096) | Shuttleworth Trust/O. Warden |
| | G-AERV | M.11A Whitney Straight ★ | Ulster Folk & Transport Museum |
| | G-AESB | Aeronca C.3 | D. S. & I. M. Morgan |
| | G-AESE | D.H.87B Hornet Moth | J. G. Green/Redhill |
| | G-AESZ | Chilton D.W.1 | R. E. Nerou |
| | G-AETA | Caudron G.3 (3066) ★ | RAF Museum |
| | G-AEUJ | M.11A Whitney Straight | R. E. Mitchell |
| | G-AEVS | Aeronca 100 | A. J. E. Smith |
| | G-AEVZ | B. A. Swallow 2 | J. R. H. Ealand |
| | G-AEXD | Aeronca 100 | Mrs M. A. & R. W. Mills |
| | G-AEXF | P.6 Mew Gull | J. D. Penrose/Old Warden |
| | G-AEXT | Dart Kitten II | A. J. Hartfield |
| | G-AEXZ | Piper J-2 Cub | Mrs M. & J. R. Dowson/Leicester |
| | G-AEYY | Martin Monoplane ★ | Martin Monoplane Syndicate/Hatfield |
| | G-AEZF | S.16 Scion 2 ★ | Southend Historic Aircraft Soc |
| | G-AEZJ | P.10 Vega Gull | R. N. Goode & C. R. Wilson |
| | G-AEZX | Bucker Bu133C Jungmeister | A. J. E. Ditheridge |
| | G-AFAP† | C.A.S.A. C.352L ★ | Aerospace Museum/Cosford |
| | G-AFAX | B. A. Eagle 2 | J. G. Green |
| | G-AFBS | M.14A Hawk Trainer ★ | G. D. Durbridge-Freeman (G-AKKU)/Duxford |
| | G-AFCL | B. A. Swallow 2 | A. M. Dowson/O. Warden |
| | G-AFDO | Piper J-3F-60 Cub | R. Wald |
| | G-AFDX | Hanriot HD.1 (75) ★ | RAF Museum |
| | G-AFEL | Monocoupe 90A | Fortune Holdings Ltd/Barton |
| | G-AFFD | Percival Q-6 ★ | B. D. Greenwood |
| | G-AFFH | Piper J-2 Cub | M. J. Honeychurch |
| | G-AFFI | Mignet HM.14 (replica) (BAPC76) ★ | Yorkshire Air Museum/Elvington |
| | G-AFGC | B. A. Swallow 2 | H. Plain |
| | G-AFGD | B. A. Swallow 2 | A. T. Williams & ptnrs/Shobdon |
| | G-AFGE | B. A. Swallow 2 | G. R. French |
| | G-AFGH | Chilton D.W.1. | M. L. & G. L. Joseph |
| | G-AFGI | Chilton D.W.1. ★ | J. E. McDonald |
| | G-AFGM | Piper J-4A Cub Coupé | A. J. P. Marshall/Carlisle |
| | G-AFGZ | D.H.82A Tiger Moth | I. B. Grace (G-AMHI) |
| | G-AFHA | Mosscraft M.A.1. ★ | C. V. Butler |
| | G-AFIN | Chrislea Airguard ★ | Aeroplane Collection Ltd |

# JAVIATION
## *VHF/UHF AIRBAND SPECIALISTS*

**A**s specialists in the VHF & UHF airbands we can offer unbiased, professional advice and information on all the various receivers and scanners available suitable for airband listening. With equipment from Yupiteru, Fairmate, AOR, Icom, Signal, Sony, Win, Uniden, Black Jaguar, Tandy/Realistic & others we offer one of the widest ranges of receivers and scanners along with accessories available to the enthusiast.

*If you would like further information please feel free to give us a call, as fellow aviation enthusiasts we would be happy to talk with you or if you would like a catalogue please send a large (A5+ size) SAE.*

### FREQUENCY LISTS

**O**ur VHF & UHF frequency lists are recognised as two of the most accurate and informative airband frequency guides available, they are both updated regularly and contain a consderable amount of information not found in any other publications including squawk codes, ICAO 3 letter airline decodes, airline callsigns, stud numbers, range frequencies & adjacent European agencies.

### ACCESSORIES

**W**e carry a wide range of accessories for all types of receivers, spare battery packs, aerials - both mobile and "homebase" for improved performance, carry cases, mains adaptors, crystals and ₊with a wide range of publications on receivers & airband listening.

### SECONDHAND EQUIPMENT

**A**s part exchanges are welcome we usually have a selection of secondhand equipment, as this obviously changes all the time please call us for the latest details on what is we have available.

## JAVIATION
**Carlton Works, Carlton Street,**
**BRADFORD. West Yorkshire. BD7 1DA**
Telephone: 0274-732146.     Facsimile: 0274-722627

| Notes | Reg. | Type | Owner or Operator |
|---|---|---|---|
| | G-AFIU | Parker C.A.4 Parasol ★ (LA-3 Minor) | Aeroplane Collection Ltd/Warmingham |
| | G-AFJA | Watkinson Dingbat ★ | K. Woolley |
| | G-AFJB | Foster-Wikner G.M.1. Wicko (DR613) ★ | K. Woolley |
| | G-AFJR | Tipsy Trainer 1 | M. E. Vaisey (Stored) |
| | G-AFJV | Mosscraft MA.2 | C. V. Butler |
| | G-AFLW | M.17 Monarch | N. I. Dalziel/Biggin Hill |
| | G-AFNG | D.H.94 Moth Minor | T. E. G. Buckett/White Waltham |
| | G-AFNI | D.H.94 Moth Minor | B. M. Welford |
| | G-AFOB | D.H.94 Moth Minor | Wessex Aviation & Transport Ltd |
| | G-AFOJ | D.H.94 Moth Minor | R. M. Long |
| | G-AFPN | D.H.94 Moth Minor | J. W. & A. R. Davy/Carlisle |
| | G-AFPR | D.H.94 Moth Minor | J. A. Livett |
| | G-AFRZ | M.17 Monarch | R. E. Mitchell (G-AIDE) |
| | G-AFSC | Tipsy Trainer 1 | R. V. & M. H. Smith |
| | G-AFSV | Chilton D.W.1A | R. Nerou |
| | G-AFSW | Chilton D.W.2 ★ | R. I. Souch |
| | G-AFTA | Hawker Tomtit (K1786) | Shuttleworth Trust/O. Warden |
| | G-AFTN | Taylorcraft Plus C2 | Leicestershire County Council Museums |
| | G-AFUP | Luscombe 8A Silvaire | Trust Me Airtours |
| | G-AFVE | D.H.82 Tiger Moth | R. J. F. Parker/Denham |
| | G-AFVN | Tipsy Trainer 1 | W. Callow & ptnrs |
| | G-AFWH | Piper J-4A Cub Coupé | J. R. Edwards & D. D. Smith |
| | G-AFWI | D.H.82A Tiger Moth | N. E. Rankin & ptnrs |
| | G-AFWT | Tipsy Trainer 1 | J. S. Barker/Redhill |
| | G-AFYD | Luscombe 8E Silvaire | J. D. Iliffe |
| | G-AFYO | Stinson H.W.75 | R. N. Wright |
| | G-AFZA | Piper J-4A Cub Coupé | J. R. Joiner & M. L. Ryan |
| | G-AFZE | Heath Parasol | K. C. D. St Cyrien |
| | G-AFZK | Luscombe 8A Silvaire | M. G. Byrnes |
| | G-AFZL | Porterfield CP.50 | P. G. Lucas & ptnrs/White Waltham |
| | G-AFZN | Luscombe 8A Silvaire | A. L. Young/Henstridge |
| | G-AGAT | Piper J-3F-50 Cub | Wessex Aviation & Transport Ltd |
| | G-AGBN | G.A.L.42 Cygnet 2 ★ | Museum of Flight/E. Fortune |
| | G-AGEG | D.H.82A Tiger Moth | T. P. A. Norman |
| | G-AGFT | Avia FL.3 | P. A. Smith |
| | G-AGHY | D.H.82A Tiger Moth | P. Groves |
| | G-AGIV | Piper J-3C-65 Cub | P. C. & F. M. Gill |
| | G-AGJG | D.H.89A Dragon Rapide | M. J. & D. J. T. Miller/Duxford |
| | G-AGLK | Auster 5D | W. C. E. Tazewell |
| | G-AGMI | Luscombe 8A Silvaire | Bluegale Ltd |
| | G-AGNJ | D.H.82A Tiger Moth | B. P. Borsberry & ptnrs |
| | G-AGNV | Avro 685 York 1 (MW100) ★ | Aerospace Museum/Cosford |
| | G-AGOH | J/1 Autocrat | Leicestershire County Council Museums |
| | G-AGOS | R.S.4 Desford Trainer (VZ728) | Museum of Flight/E. Fortune |
| | G-AGOY | M.48 Messenger 3 (U-0247) | P. A. Brooks |
| | G-AGPG | Avro 19 Srs 2 ★ | Brenzett Aviation Museum |
| | G-AGPK | D.H.82A Tiger Moth | P. D. Castle |
| | G-AGRU | V.498 Viking 1A ★ | Aerospace Museum/Cosford |
| | G-AGSH | D.H.89A Dragon Rapide 6 | Venom Jet Promotions Ltd/ Bournemouth |
| | G-AGTM | D.H.89A Dragon Rapide 6 (NF875) | Russavia Ltd |
| | G-AGTO | J/1 Autocrat | M. J. Barnett & D. J. T. Miller/Duxford |
| | G-AGTT | J/1 Autocrat | R. Farrer |
| | G-AGVG | J/1 Autocrat | S. J. Riddington/Leicester |
| | G-AGVN | J/1 Autocrat | S. Thursfield & K. E. Eld/Leicester |
| | G-AGVV | Piper J-3C-65 Cub | P. R. Lewis |
| | G-AGWE | Avro 19 Srs 2 ★ | Phoenix Aviation Museum |
| | G-AGXN | J/1N Alpha | I. R. Walters/Cranwell |
| | G-AGXT | J/1N Alpha ★ | Nene Valley Aircraft Museum |
| | G-AGXU | J/1N Alpha | R. J. Guess/Sibson |
| | G-AGXV | J/1 Autocrat | B. S. Dowsett |
| | G-AGYD | J/1N Alpha | P. Herring & ptnrs/Dishforth |
| | G-AGYH | J/1N Alpha | W. R. V. Marklew |
| | G-AGYK | J/1 Autocrat | D. A. Smith |
| | G-AGYL | J/1 Autocrat ★ | Military Vehicle Conservation Group/ Havant |
| | G-AGYT | J/1N Alpha | P. J. Barrett |
| | G-AGYU | DH.82A Tiger Moth (DE208) | Amalgamated Investments Ltd |

16

| Notes | Reg. | Type | Owner or Operator |
|---|---|---|---|
| | G-AGYY | Ryan ST.3KR | D. S. & I. M. Morgan |
| | G-AGZZ | D.H.82A Tiger Moth | G. P. L. Shea-Simonds/Netheravon |
| | G-AHAL | J/1N Alpha | Wickenby Flying Club Ltd |
| | G-AHAM | J/1 Autocrat | P. J. Stock/Goodwood |
| | G-AHAN | D.H.82A Tiger Moth | A. J. Clarry & S. F. Bancroft/Redhill |
| | G-AHAP | J/1 Autocrat | V. H. Bellamy |
| | G-AHAU | J/1 Autocrat | B. W. Webb |
| | G-AHAV | J/1 Autocrat | C. J. Freeman/Headcorn |
| | G-AHBL | D.H.87B Hornet Moth | Dr Ursula H. Hamilton |
| | G-AHBM | D.H.87B Hornet Moth | P. A. & E. P. Gliddon |
| | G-AHCK | J/1N Alpha | P. A. Woodman/Shoreham |
| | G-AHCR | Gould-Taylorcraft Plus D Special | D. E. H. Balmford & D. R. Shepherd/Dunkeswell |
| | G-AHEC | Luscombe 8A Silvaire | P. & M. Chamberlain |
| | G-AHED | D.H.89A Dragon Rapide (RL962) ★ | RAF Museum Storage & Restoration Centre/Cardington |
| | G-AHGD | D.H.89A Dragon Rapide (Z7258) | M. R. L. Astor/Booker |
| | G-AHGW | Taylorcraft Plus D (LB375) | C. V. Butler/Coventry |
| | G-AHGZ | Taylorcraft Plus D | P. N.Cooke |
| | G-AHHH | J/1 Autocrat | H. A. Jones/Norwich |
| | G-AHHP | J/1N Alpha | D. J. Hutcheson (G-SIME) |
| | G-AHHT | J/1N Alpha | A. C. Barber & N. J. Hudson |
| | G-AHHU | J/1N Alpha ★ | L. Groves & I. R. F. Hammond |
| | G-AHIP | Piper J-3C-65 Cub | R. E. Nerou/Coventry |
| | G-AHIZ | D.H.82A Tiger Moth | C.F.G. Flying Ltd/Cambridge |
| | G-AHKX | Avro 19 Srs 2 | British Aerospace PLC/Woodford |
| | G-AHKY | Miles M.18 Series 2 | Museum of Flight/E. Fortune |
| | G-AHLI | Auster 3 | G. A. Leathers |
| | G-AHLK | Auster 3 | E. T. Brackenbury/Leicester |
| | G-AHLT | D.H.82A Tiger Moth | R. C. F. Bailey |
| | G-AHMJ | Cierva C.30A (K4235) ★ | Shuttleworth Trust/O. Warden |
| | G-AHMN | D.H.82A Tiger Moth (N6985) | Museum of Army Flying/Middle Wallop |
| | G-AHNH | Bucker Bu181 Bestmann | R. A. Anderson |
| | G-AHNR | Taylorcraft BC-12D | M. L. Balding & J. M. Oakins/Biggin Hill |
| | G-AHOO | D.H.82A Tiger Moth | G. W. Bisshopp |
| | G-AHRI | D.H.104 Dove 1 ★ | Newark Aviation Museum |
| | G-AHRO | Cessna 140 | R. H. Screen/Kidlington |
| | G-AHSA | Avro 621 Tutor (K3215) | Shuttleworth Trust/O. Warden |
| | G-AHSD | Taylorcraft Plus D | A. Tucker |
| | G-AHSO | J/1N Alpha | W. P. Miller |
| | G-AHSP | J/1 Autocrat | D. S. Johnstone & ptnrs |
| | G-AHSS | J/1N Alpha | P. J. Wenman/Denham |
| | G-AHST | J/1N Alpha | C. H. Smith |
| | G-AHTE | P.44 Proctor V | J. G. H. Hassell |
| | G-AHTW | A.S.40 Oxford (V3388) ★ | Skyfame Collection/Duxford |
| | G-AHUF | D.H.82A Tiger Moth | D. S. & I. M. Morgan |
| | G-AHUG | Taylorcraft Plus D | D. Nieman |
| | G-AHUI | M.38 Messenger 2A ★ | Berkshire Aviation Group |
| | G-AHUJ | M.14A Hawk Trainer 3 (R1914) | — |
| | G-AHUN | Globe GC-1B Swift | A. G. Craig |
| | G-AHUV | D.H.82A Tiger Moth | W. G. Gordon |
| | G-AHVU | D.H.82A Tiger Moth (T6313) | Foley Farm Flying Group |
| | G-AHVV | D.H.82A Tiger Moth | R. Jones |
| | G-AHWJ | Taylorcraft Plus D (LB294) | Museum of Army Flying/Middle Wallop |
| | G-AHXE | Taylorcraft Plus D (LB312) | J. Pothecary/Shoreham |
| | G-AIBE | Fulmar II (N1854) ★ | F.A.A. Museum/Yeovilton |
| | G-AIBH | J/1N Alpha | M. J. Bonnick |
| | G-AIBM | J/1 Autocrat | D. G. Greatrex |
| | G-AIBR | J/1 Autocrat | A. A. Marshall |
| | G-AIBW | J/1N Alpha | W. E. Bateson/Blackpool |
| | G-AIBX | J/1 Autocrat | Wasp Flying Group |
| | G-AIBY | J/1 Autocrat | D. Morris/Sherburn |
| | G-AICX | Luscombe 8A Silvaire | R. V. Smith/Henstridge |
| | G-AIDL | D.H.89A Dragon Rapide 6 | Snowdon Mountain Aviation Ltd |
| | G-AIDS | D.H.82A Tiger Moth | K. D. Pogmore & T. Dann |
| | G-AIEK | M.38 Messenger 2A (RG333) | J. Buckingham |
| | G-AIFZ | J/1N Alpha | C. P. Humphries |
| | G-AIGD | J/1 Autocrat | R. B. Webber & P. K. Pike |
| | G-AIGF | J/1N Alpha | A. R. C. Mathie |
| | G-AIGM | J/1N Alpha | Wickenby Flying Club Ltd |
| | G-AIGT | J/1N Alpha | P. R. & J. S. Johnson |

| Reg. | Type | Owner or Operator | Notes |
|------|------|-------------------|-------|
| G-AIGU | J/1N Alpha | N. K. Geddes | |
| G-AIIH | Piper J-3C-65 Cub | J. A. de Salis | |
| G-AIJI | J/1N Alpha ★ | C. J. Baker | |
| G-AIJM | Auster J/4 | N. Huxtable | |
| G-AIJR | Auster J/4 | B. A. Harris/Halfpenny Green | |
| G-AIJS | Auster J/4 ★ | stored | |
| G-AIJT | Auster J/4 srs 100 | Aberdeen Auster Flying Group | |
| G-AIJZ | J/1 Autocrat | stored | |
| G-AIKE | Auster 5 | C. J. Baker | |
| G-AIPR | Auster J/4 | MPM Flying Group/Booker | |
| G-AIPV | J/1 Autocrat | W. P. Miller | |
| G-AIPW | J/1 Autocrat | B. Hillman | |
| G-AIRC | J/1 Autocrat | A. G. Martlew/Barton | |
| G-AIRI | D.H.82A Tiger Moth | E. R. Goodwin (stored) | |
| G-AIRK | D.H.82A Tiger Moth | R. C. Teverson & ptnrs | |
| G-AISA | Tipsy B Srs 1 | J. W. Thomson & R. P. Aston | |
| G-AISC | Tipsy B Srs 1 | Wagtail Flying Group | |
| G-AISS | Piper J-3C-65 Cub | K. W. Wood & F. Watson | |
| G-AIST | V.S.300 Spitfire IA (AR213) | Proteus Petroleum Ltd/Goodwood | |
| G-AISX | Piper J-3C-65 Cub | V. Luck | |
| G-AITB | A.S.10 Oxford (MP425) ★ | RAF Museum/Cardington | |
| G-AIUA | M.14A Hawk Trainer 3 | P. A. Brook | |
| G-AIUL | D.H.89A Dragon Rapide 6 | I. Jones | |
| G-AIXA | Taylorcraft Plus D | A. A. & M. J. Copse | |
| G-AIXD | D.H.82A Tiger Moth | Sark International Airways/Guernsey | |
| G-AIXN | Benes-Mraz M.1c Sokol | A. J. E. Smith | |
| G-AIYG | SNCAN Stampe SV-4B | J. F. Hopkins/Old Sarum | |
| G-AIYR | D.H.89A Dragon Rapide | C. D. Cyster & ptnrs | |
| G-AIYS | D.H.85 Leopard Moth | Wessex Aviation & Transport Ltd | |
| G-AIZE | F.24W Argus 2 ★ | RAF Museum/Henlow | |
| G-AIZF | D.H.82A Tiger Moth ★ | stored | |
| G-AIZG | V.S. Walrus 1 (L2301) ★ | F.A.A. Museum/Yeovilton | |
| G-AIZU | J/1 Autocrat | C. J. & J. G. B. Morley | |
| G-AIZZ | J/1 Autocrat | M. J. Murphy | |
| G-AJAD | Piper J-3C-65 Cub | R. A. C. Hoppenbrouwers | |
| G-AJAE | J/1N Alpha | M. G. Stops | |
| G-AJAJ | J/1N Alpha | R. B. Lawrence | |
| G-AJAM | J/2 Arrow | D. A. Porter | |
| G-AJAO | Piper J-3C-65 Cub | P. L. Jones | |
| G-AJAP | Luscombe 8A Silvaire | R. J. Thomas | |
| G-AJAS | J/1N Alpha | C. J. Baker | |
| G-AJCP | D.31 Turbulent | B. R. Pearson | |
| G-AJDW | J/1 Autocrat | D. R. Hunt | |
| G-AJDY | J/1 Autocrat | Truck Panels Ltd | |
| G-AJEB | J/1N Alpha ★ | Aeroplane Collection Ltd/Warmingham | |
| G-AJEE | J/1 Autocrat | A. R. C. De Albanoz/Bournemouth | |
| G-AJEH | J/1N Alpha | J. T. Powell-Tuck | |
| G-AJEI | J/1N Alpha | W. P. Miller | |
| G-AJEM | J/1 Autocrat | J. C. Greenslade | |
| G-AJES | Piper J-3C-65 Cub (330485) | P. Crawford | |
| G-AJGJ | Auster 5 (RT486) | S. C. Challis | |
| G-AJHJ | Auster 5 | stored | |
| G-AJHS | D.H.82A Tiger Moth | Machine Music Ltd/Blackbushe | |
| G-AJHU | D.H.82A Tiger Moth | R. Jones | |
| G-AJIH | J/1 Autocrat | T. Boyd & A. H. Diver | |
| G-AJIS | J/1N Alpha | K. J. Slattery | |
| G-AJIT | J/1 Kingsland Autocrat | A. J. Kay | |
| G-AJIU | J/1 Autocrat | W. Greenhalgh & Son Ltd/Doncaster | |
| G-AJIW | J/1N Alpha | N. A. Roberts | |
| G-AJJP | Jet Gyrodyne (XJ389) ★ | Aerospace Museum/Cosford | |
| G-AJJS | Cessna 120 | L. G. Sharkey | |
| G-AJJT | Cessna 120 | P. M. Hallett & J. S. Robson | |
| G-AJJU | Luscombe 8E Silvaire | L. C. Moon | |
| G-AJKB | Luscombe 8E Silvaire | A. F. Hall & P. S. Hatwell/Ipswich | |
| G-AJOA | D.H.82A Tiger Moth (T5424) | F. P. Le Coyte | |
| G-AJOC | M.38 Messenger 2A ★ | Ulster Folk & Transport Museum | |
| G-AJOE | M.38 Messenger 2A | Cotswold Aircraft Restoration Group | |
| G-AJON | Aeronca 7AC Champion | A. Biggs & J. L. Broad/Booker | |
| G-AJOV† | Sikorsky S-51 ★ | Aerospace Museum/Cosford | |
| G-AJOZ | F.24W Argus 2 ★ | Lincolnshire Aviation Museum | |
| G-AJPI | F.24R-41a Argus 3 | M. R. Keen/Liverpool | |
| G-AJPZ | J/1 Autocrat ★ | Wessex Aviation Soc | |

| Notes | Reg. | Type | Owner or Operator |
|---|---|---|---|
| | G-AJRB | J/1 Autocrat | S. C. Luck/Sywell |
| | G-AJRC | J/1 Autocrat | S. W. Watkins & ptnrs |
| | G-AJRE | J/1 Autocrat (Lycoming) | T. A. Hodges |
| | G-AJRH | J/1N Alpha | Leicestershire County Council Museums |
| | G-AJRS | M.14A Hawk Trainer 3 (P6382) | Shuttleworth Trust/O. Warden |
| | G-AJTW | D.H.82A Tiger Moth (N6965) | J. A. Barker |
| | G-AJUD | J/1 Autocrat | C. L. Sawyer |
| | G-AJUE | J/1 Autocrat | P. H. B. Cole |
| | G-AJUL | J/1N Alpha | M. J. Crees |
| | G-AJVE | D.H.82A Tiger Moth | P. A. Layzell |
| | G-AJXC | Auster 5 | J. E. Graves |
| | G-AJXV | Auster 4 (NJ695) | P. C. J. Farries/Leicester |
| | G-AJXY | Auster 4 | G. B. Morris |
| | G-AJYB | J/1N Alpha | P. J. Shotbolt |
| | | | |
| | G-AKAA | Piper J-3C-65 Cub | G. J. C. Ball |
| | G-AKAT | M.14A Magister (T9738) | A. J. E. Smith |
| | G-AKAZ | Piper J-3C-65 Cub | A. W. Oakes & M. J. Espin |
| | G-AKBM | M.38 Messenger 2A ★ | Bristol Plane Preservation Unit |
| | G-AKBO | M.38 Messenger 2A | B. du Cros |
| | G-AKDN | D.H.C. 1A Chipmunk 10 | M. F. Newman |
| | G-AKEL | M.65 Gemini 1A ★ | Ulster Folk & Transport Museum |
| | G-AKER | M.65 Gemini 1A ★ | Berkshire Aviation Group |
| | G-AKEZ | M.38 Messenger 2A (RG333) | P. G. Lee |
| | G-AKGD | M.65 Gemini 1A ★ | Berkshire Aviation Group |
| | G-AKGE | M.65 Gemini 3C ★ | Ulster Folk & Transport Museum |
| | G-AKHP | M.65 Gemini 1A | P. G. Lee |
| | G-AKHW | M.65 Gemini 1A | P. G. Lee |
| | G-AKHZ | M.65 Gemini 7 ★ | Berkshire Aviation Group |
| | G-AKIB | Piper J-3C-90 Cub (480015) | M. C. Bennett |
| | G-AKIF | D.H.89A Dragon Rapide | Airborne Taxi Services Ltd/Booker |
| | G-AKIN | M.38 Messenger 2A | R. Spiller & Sons/Sywell |
| | G-AKIU | P.44 Proctor V | J. N. Sharman |
| | G-AKKB | M.65 Gemini 1A | J. Buckingham |
| | G-AKKH | M.65 Gemini 1A | M. C. Russell/Duxford |
| | G-AKKR | M.14A Magister (T9707) ★ | Greater Manchester Museum of Science & Technology |
| | G-AKKY | M.14A Hawk Trainer 3 (L6906) (BAPC44) ★ | Berkshire Aviation Group/Woodley |
| | G-AKLW | SA.6 Sealand 1 ★ | Ulster Folk & Transport Museum |
| | G-AKOE | D.H.89A Dragon Rapide 4 | J. E. Pierce/Chirk |
| | G-AKOT | Auster 5 ★ | C. J. Baker |
| | G-AKOW | Auster 5 (TJ569) ★ | Museum of Army Flying/Middle Wallop |
| | G-AKPF | M.14A Hawk Trainer 3 (V1075) | P. A. Brook |
| | G-AKPI | Auster 5 (NJ703) | B. H. Hargrave/Doncaster |
| | G-AKRA | Piper J-3C-65 Cub | W. R. Savin |
| | G-AKSZ | Auster 5 | A. R. C. Mathie |
| | G-AKTH | Piper J-3C-65 Cub | A. L. Wickens |
| | G-AKTI | Luscombe 8A Silvaire | N. C. W. N. Lester |
| | G-AKTK | Aeronca 11AC Chief | R. J. & F. A. Fox |
| | G-AKTM | Luscombe 8F Silvaire | D. J. Christy |
| | G-AKTN | Luscombe 8A Silvaire | L. S. Johnson |
| | G-AKTO | Aeronca 7AC Champion | D. C. Murray |
| | G-AKTP | PA-17 Vagabond | L. A. Maynard |
| | G-AKTR | Aeronca 7AC Champion | C. & G. Fielder |
| | G-AKTS | Cessna 120 | B. A. Bower |
| | G-AKTT | Luscombe 8A Silvaire | S. J. Charters |
| | G-AKUE | D.H.82A Tiger Moth | D. F. Hodgkinson |
| | G-AKUF | Luscombe 8A Silvaire | R. D. Jones |
| | G-AKUG | Luscombe 8A Silvaire | P. & L. A. Groves |
| | G-AKUH | Luscombe 8E Silvaire | I. M. Bower |
| | G-AKUI | Luscombe 8E Silvaire | M. A. Watts |
| | G-AKUJ | Luscombe 8E Silvaire | D. Delaney & C. L. Cooper |
| | G-AKUK | Luscombe 8A Silvaire | Leckhampstead Flying Group |
| | G-AKUL | Luscombe 8A Silvaire | E. A. Taylor |
| | G-AKUM | Luscombe 8F Silvaire | R. J. Willies |
| | G-AKUN | Piper J-3F-65 Cub | W. A. Savin |
| | G-AKUO | Aeronca 11AC Chief | A. C. Cassidy/White Waltham |
| | G-AKUP | Luscombe 8E Silvaire | R. J. Williams |
| | G-AKUR | Cessna 140 | P. Power & L. P. Z. Yelland |
| | G-AKUW | C.H.3 Super Ace | D. R. Bean |
| | G-AKVF | C.H.3 Super Ace | P. V. B. Longthorp/Bodmin |
| | G-AKVM | Cessna 120 | C120 Group/Norwich |

| Reg. | Type | Owner or Operator | Notes |
|------|------|-------------------|-------|
| G-AKVN | Aeronca 11AC Chief | J. S. R. Lancaster | |
| G-AKVO | Taylorcraft BC-12D | R. J. Whybrow & S. R. Roberts | |
| G-AKVP | Luscombe 8A Silvaire | D. G. Anderson | |
| G-AKVZ | M.38 Messenger 4B | Shipping & Airlines Ltd/Biggin Hill | |
| G-AKWS | Auster 5-160 | J. E. Homewood | |
| G-AKWT | Auster 5 ★ | Loughborough & Leicester Aircraft Preservation Soc | |
| G-AKXP | Auster 5 | F. E. Telling | |
| G-AKXS | D.H.82A Tiger Moth | P. A. Colman | |
| G-AKZN | P.34A Proctor 3 (Z7197) ★ | RAF Museum/St Athan | |
| G-ALAH | M.38 Messenger 4A (RH377) ★ | RAF Museum/Henlow | |
| G-ALAX | D.H.89A Dragon Rapide ★ | Durney Aeronautical Collection/ Andover | |
| G-ALBJ | Auster 5 | P. N. Elkington | |
| G-ALBK | Auster 5 | S. J. Wright & Co (Farmers) Ltd | |
| G-ALBN | Bristol 173 (XF785) ★ | RAF Museum/Henlow | |
| G-ALCK | P.34A Proctor 3 (LZ766) ★ | Skyfame Collection/Duxford | |
| G-ALCS | M.65 Gemini 3C ★ | Stored | |
| G-ALCU | D.H.104 Dove 2 ★ | Midland Air Museum/Coventry | |
| G-ALDG | HP.81 Hermes 4 ★ | Duxford Aviation Soc (Fuselage only) | |
| G-ALEH | PA-17 Vagabond | A. D. Pearce/Redhill | |
| G-ALFA | Auster 5 | Alpha Flying Group | |
| G-ALFM | D.H.104 Devon C.2 | C. Charalambous | |
| G-ALFT | D.H.104 Dove 6 ★ | Snowdon Mountain Aviation Museum | |
| G-ALFU | D.H.104 Dove 6 ★ | Duxford Aviation Soc | |
| G-ALGA | PA-15 Vagabond | M. J. Markey/Biggin Hill | |
| G-ALGT | V.S.379 Spitfire 14 (RM689) | Rolls-Royce Ltd | |
| G-ALIJ | PA-17 Vagabond | RFC Flying Group/Popham | |
| G-ALIW | D.H.82A Tiger Moth | D. I. M. Geddes & F. Curry/Booker | |
| G-ALJF | P.34A Proctor 3 | J. F. Moore/Biggin Hill | |
| G-ALJL | D.H.82A Tiger Moth | C. G. Clarke | |
| G-ALNA | D.H.82A Tiger Moth | P. D. Castle | |
| G-ALND | D.H.82A Tiger Moth (N9191) | J. T. Powell-Tuck | |
| G-ALNV | Auster 5 ★ | stored | |
| G-ALOD | Cessna 140 | J. R. Stainer | |
| G-ALRH | EoN Type 8 Baby (AST) | P. D. Moran/Chipping | |
| G-ALRI | D.H.82A Tiger Moth (T5672) | Wessex Aviation & Transport Ltd | |
| G-ALSP | Bristol 171 (WV783) Sycamore ★ | RAF Museum/Henlow | |
| G-ALSS | Bristol 171 (WA576) Sycamore ★ | E. Fortune | |
| G-ALST | Bristol 171 (WA577) Sycamore ★ | N.E. Aircraft Museum/Usworth | |
| G-ALSW | Bristol 171 (WT933) Sycamore ★ | Newark Air Museum | |
| G-ALSX | Bristol 171 (G-48-1) Sycamore ★ | International Helicopter Museum/ Weston-s-Mare | |
| G-ALTO | Cessna 140 | J. P. Bell | |
| G-ALTW | D.H.82A Tiger Moth ★ | A. Mangham | |
| G-ALUC | D.H.82A Tiger Moth | D. R. & M. Wood/Shipdham | |
| G-ALVP | D.H.82A Tiger Moth ★ | V. & R. Wheele (stored) | |
| G-ALWB | D.H.C.1 Chipmunk 22A | M. L. & J. M. Soper/Perth | |
| G-ALWF | V.701 Viscount ★ | Viscount Preservation Trust RMA Sir John Franklin/Duxford | |
| G-ALWS | D.H.82A Tiger Moth ★ | Air Service Training Ltd/Perth | |
| G-ALWW | D.H.82A Tiger Moth | F. W. Fay & ptnrs | |
| G-ALXT | D.H.89A Dragon Rapide ★ | Science Museum/Wroughton | |
| G-ALXZ | Auster 5-150 | B. J. W. Thomas & R. A. E. Witheridge | |
| G-ALYB | Auster 5 (RT520) ★ | S. Yorks Aircraft Preservation Soc | |
| G-ALYG | Auster 5D | A. L. Young/Henstridge | |
| G-ALYW | D.H.106 Comet 1 ★ | RAF Exhibition Flight (fuselage converted to Nimrod) | |
| G-ALZE | BN-1F ★ | M. R. Short/Southampton Hall of Aviation | |
| G-ALZO | A.S.57 Ambassador★ | Duxford Aviation Soc | |
| G-AMAW | Luton LA-4 Minor | R. H. Coates | |
| G-AMBB | D.H.82A Tiger Moth | J. Eagles | |
| G-AMCA | Dakota 3 | Air Atlantique Ltd/Coventry | |
| G-AMCK | D.H.82A Tiger Moth | V. S. E. Norman | |
| G-AMCM | D.H.82A Tiger Moth | G. C. Masterton | |
| G-AMDA | Avro 652A Anson 1 (N4877)★ | Skyfame Collection/Duxford | |
| G-AMEN | PA-18 Super Cub 95 | A. Lovejoy & W. Cook | |
| G-AMHF | D.H.82A Tiger Moth | A. J. West | |
| G-AMHJ | Dakota 6 | Air Atlantique Ltd/Coventry | |
| G-AMIU | D.H.82A Tiger Moth | R. & Mrs J. L. Jones | |

| Notes | Reg. | Type | Owner or Operator |
|---|---|---|---|
| | G-AMKU | J/1B Aiglet | Southdown Flying Group (stored) |
| | G-AMLZ | P.50 Prince 6E ★ | J. F. Coggins/Coventry |
| | G-AMMS | J/5F Aiglet Trainer | V. Long |
| | G-AMOG | V.701 Viscount ★ | Aerospace Museum/Cosford |
| | G-AMOU | D.H.82A Tiger Moth | Fortress Wastecare (Spa) Ltd |
| | G-AMPG | PA-12 Super Cruiser | R. Simpson |
| | G-AMPI | SNCAN Stampe SV-4C | J. Hewett |
| | G-AMPO | Dakota 4 | Air Atlantique Ltd/Coventry |
| | G-AMPP | Dakota 3 (G-AMSU) ★ | Dan-Air Preservation Group/Lasham |
| | G-AMPY | Dakota 4 | Air Atlantique Ltd/Coventry |
| | G-AMPZ | Dakota 4 | Air Atlantique Ltd/Coventry |
| | G-AMRA | Dakota 6 | Air Atlantique Ltd/Coventry |
| | G-AMRF | J/5F Aiglet Trainer | A. I. Topps/E. Midlands |
| | G-AMRK | G.37 Gladiator 1 (N2308) | Shuttleworth Trust/O. Warden |
| | G-AMSG | SIPA 903 | S. W. Markham |
| | G-AMSV | Dakota 4 | Air Atlantique Ltd/Coventry |
| | G-AMTA | J/5F Aiglet Trainer | H. J. Jauncey/Rochester |
| | G-AMTD | J/5F Aiglet Trainer | G. M. New |
| | G-AMTK | D.H.82A Tiger Moth | S. W. McKay & M. E. Vaisey |
| | G-AMTM | J/1 Autocrat | R. Stobo & D. Clewley |
| | G-AMUF | D.H.C.1 Chipmunk 21 | Redhill Tailwheel Flying Club Ltd |
| | G-AMUI | J/5F Aiglet Trainer | M. J. & A. A. Copse |
| | G-AMVD | Auster 5 | R. F. Tolhurst |
| | G-AMVP | Tipsy Junior | A. R. Wershat |
| | G-AMVS | D.H.82A Tiger Moth | J. T. Powell-Tuck |
| | G-AMXP | D.H.104 Sea Devon C.20 | M. A. Knowles |
| | G-AMXT | D.H.104 Sea Devon C.20 | W. Gentle & P. C. Gill |
| | G-AMYA | Zlin Z.381 | D. M. Fenton |
| | G-AMYD | J/5L Aiglet Trainer | G. H. Maskell |
| | G-AMYJ | Dakota 6 | Air Atlantique Ltd/Coventry |
| | G-AMYL | PA-17 Vagabond | P. J. Penn-Sayers/Shoreham |
| | G-AMZI | J/5F Aiglet Trainer | J. F. Moore/Biggin Hill |
| | G-AMZT | J/5F Aiglet Trainer | D. Hyde & J. W. Saull/Cranfield |
| | G-AMZU | J/5F Aiglet Trainer | J. A. Longworth & ptnrs |
| | G-ANAF | Dakota 3 | Air Atlantique Ltd/Coventry |
| | G-ANAP | D.H.104 Dove 6 ★ | Brunel Technical College/Lulsgate |
| | G-ANCF | B.175 Britannia 308 ★ | —/Weybridge |
| | G-ANCS | D.H.82A Tiger Moth (R4907) | P. G. Wright |
| | G-ANCX | D.H.82A Tiger Moth | D. R. Wood/Biggin Hill |
| | G-ANDE | D.H.82A Tiger Moth | The Vintage Aeroplane Co Ltd |
| | G-ANDM | D.H.82A Tiger Moth | J. G. Green |
| | G-ANDP | D.H.82A Tiger Moth | A. H. Diver |
| | G-ANDX | D.H.104 Devon C.2 | L. Richards |
| | G-ANEC | D.H.82A Tiger Moth ★ | (stored) |
| | G-ANEF | D.H.82A Tiger Moth (T5493) | RAF College Flying Club Co Ltd/ Cranwell |
| | G-ANEH | D.H.82A Tiger Moth ★ | A. Topen/Cranfield |
| | G-ANEL | D.H.82A Tiger Moth (N9238) | Chauffair Ltd |
| | G-ANEM | D.H.82A Tiger Moth | P. J. Benest |
| | G-ANEW | D.H.82A Tiger Moth | A. L. Young |
| | G-ANEZ | D.H.82A Tiger Moth | C. D. J. Bland & T. S. Warren/Sandown |
| | G-ANFC | D.H.82A Tiger Moth (DE363) | H. J. Jauncey |
| | G-ANFH | Westland S-55 ★ | International Helicopter Museum/ Weston-s-Mare |
| | G-ANFI | D.H.82A Tiger Moth (DE623) | D. H. R. Jenkins |
| | G-ANFL | D.H.82A Tiger Moth | R. P. Whitby & ptnrs |
| | G-ANFM | D.H.82A Tiger Moth | S. A. Brook & ptnrs/Booker |
| | G-ANFP | D.H.82A Tiger Moth ★ | Mosquito Aircraft Museum |
| | G-ANFU | Auster 5 (NJ719)★ | N.E. Aircraft Museum |
| | G-ANFV | D.H.82A Tiger Moth (DF155) | R. A. L. Falconer |
| | G-ANFW | D.H.82A Tiger Moth | G. M. Fraser/Denham |
| | G-ANGK | Cessna 140A | D. W. Munday |
| | G-ANHK | D.H.82A Tiger Moth | J. D. Iliffe |
| | G-ANHR | Auster 5 | C. G. Winch |
| | G-ANHS | Auster 4 | Tango Uniform Group |
| | G-ANHU | Auster 4 | D. J. Baker |
| | G-ANHX | Auster 5D | D. J. Baker |
| | G-ANHZ | Auster 5 | D. W. Pennell |
| | G-ANIE | Auster 5 (TW467) | S. J. Partridge |
| | G-ANIJ | Auster 5D (TJ672) | H. A. Jones |
| | G-ANIS | Auster 5 | J. Clarke-Cockburn |
| | G-ANJA | D.H.82A Tiger Moth (N9389) | J. J. Young |

| Reg. | Type | Owner or Operator | Notes |
|------|------|-------------------|-------|
| G-ANJD | D.H.82A Tiger Moth | H. J. Jauncey/(stored) | |
| G-ANJK | D.H.82A Tiger Moth | A. D. Williams | |
| G-ANJV | W.S.55 Whirlwind 3 (VR-BET) ★ | International Helicopter Museum/ Weston-s-Mare | |
| G-ANKK | D.H.82A Tiger Moth (T5854) | Halfpenny Green Tiger Group | |
| G-ANKT | D.H.82A Tiger Moth (T6818) | Shuttleworth Trust/O. Warden | |
| G-ANKZ | D.H.82A Tiger Moth (N6466) | R. Stephens | |
| G-ANLD | D.H.82A Tiger Moth | K. Peters | |
| G-ANLH | D.H.82A Tiger Moth | The Aeroplane Co (Hamble) Ltd | |
| G-ANLS | D.H.82A Tiger Moth | P. A. Gliddon | |
| G-ANLU | Auster 5 | S. C. Challis & G. Guinn | |
| G-ANLW | W.B.1. Widgeon (MD497) ★ | Wilkie Museum Collection/Blackpool | |
| G-ANLX | D.H.82A Tiger Moth | B. J. Borsberry & ptnrs | |
| G-ANMO | D.H.82A Tiger Moth | E. Lay | |
| G-ANMV | D.H.82A Tiger Moth (T7404) | J. W. Davy/Cardiff | |
| G-ANMY | D.H.82A Tiger Moth | D. J. Elliott | |
| G-ANNB | D.H.82A Tiger Moth | Cormack (Aircraft Services) Ltd/ Glasgow | |
| G-ANNK | D.H.82A Tiger Moth | P. J. Wilcox/Cranfield | |
| G-ANNN | D.H.82A Tiger Moth | T. Pate | |
| G-ANOA | Hiller UH-12A ★ | Redhill Technical College | |
| G-ANOD | D.H.82A Tiger Moth | D. R. & M. Wood | |
| G-ANOH | D.H.82A Tiger Moth | D. H. Parkhouse & ptnrs/White Waltham | |
| G-ANOK | Saab S.91C Safir ★ | A. F. Galt & Co (stored) | |
| G-ANOM | D.H.82A Tiger Moth | P. A. Colman | |
| G-ANON | D.H.82A Tiger Moth (T7909) | A. C. Mercer/Sherburn | |
| G-ANOO | D.H.82A Tiger Moth | R. K. Packman | |
| G-ANOR | D.H.82A Tiger Moth | C. L. Keith-Lucas & Aero Vintage Ltd | |
| G-ANOV | D.H.104 Dove 6 ★ | Museum of Flight/E. Fortune | |
| G-ANPE | D.H.82A Tiger Moth | I. E. S. Huddleston (G-IESH) | |
| G-ANPK | D.H.82A Tiger Moth | The D. & P. Group | |
| G-ANPP | P.34A Proctor 3 | C. P. A. & J. Jeffery | |
| G-ANRF | D.H.82A Tiger Moth | C. D. Cyster | |
| G-ANRM | D.H.82A Tiger Moth | C. A. Currie & D. G. Relf/Goodwood | |
| G-ANRN | D.H.82A Tiger Moth | J. J. V. Elwes | |
| G-ANRP | Auster 5 (TW439) | C. T. K. Lane | |
| G-ANRX | D.H.82A Tiger Moth ★ | Mosquito Aircraft Museum | |
| G-ANSM | D.H.82A Tiger Moth | J. L. Bond | |
| G-ANTE | D.H.82A Tiger Moth | T. I. Sutton & B. J. Champion/ Chester | |
| G-ANTK | Avro 685 York ★ | Duxford Aviation Soc | |
| G-ANTS | D.H.82A Tiger Moth (N6532) | J. G. Green | |
| G-ANUO | D.H.114 Heron 2D | Avtech Ltd/Biggin Hill | |
| G-ANUW | D.H.104 Dove 6 ★ | (stored)/Stansted | |
| G-ANWB | D.H.C.1 Chipmunk 21 | G. Briggs/Blackpool | |
| G-ANWO | M.14A Hawk Trainer 3 ★ | P. A. Brook | |
| G-ANWX | J/5L Aiglet Trainer | L. P. Mullins | |
| G-ANXB | D.H.114 Heron 1B ★ | Newark Air Museum | |
| G-ANXC | J/5R Alpine | C. J. Repek & ptnrs | |
| G-ANXR | P.31C Proctor 4 (RM221) | L. H. Oakins/Biggin Hill | |
| G-ANYP | P.31C Proctor 4 (NP184) | R. A. Anderson | |
| G-ANZJ | P.31C Proctor 4 (NP303) ★ | A. Hillyard | |
| G-ANZT | Thruxton Jackaroo | D. J. Neville & P. A. Dear | |
| G-ANZU | D.H.82A Tiger Moth | P. A. Jackson/Sibson | |
| G-ANZZ | D.H.82A Tiger Moth | Structure Flex Ltd | |
| G-AOAA | D.H.82A Tiger Moth | Rollason Aircraft & Engines Ltd/ Shoreham | |
| G-AOAR | P.31C Proctor 4 (NP181) ★ | Historic Aircraft Preservation Soc | |
| G-AOBG | Somers-Kendall SK.1 ★ | stored | |
| G-AOBH | D.H.82A Tiger Moth (T7997) | D. S. & I. M. Morgan | |
| G-AOBJ | D.H.82A Tiger Moth | I. B. Grace | |
| G-AOBO | D.H.82A Tiger Moth | P. A. Brook | |
| G-AOBU | P.84 Jet Provost ★ | Shuttleworth Trust/Loughborough | |
| G-AOBV | J/5P Autocar | P. E. Champney | |
| G-AOBX | D.H.82A Tiger Moth | M. Gibbs/Redhill | |
| G-AOCP | Auster 5 ★ | C. Baker (stored) | |
| G-AOCR | Auster 5D | J. M. Edis | |
| G-AOCU | Auster 5 | S. J. Ball/Leicester | |
| G-AODA | Westland S-55 Srs 3 | Bristow Helicopters Ltd | |
| G-AODT | D.H.82A Tiger Moth | A. H. Warminger | |
| G-AOEH | Aeronca 7AC Champion | M. Weeks & ptnrs/Eglinton | |
| G-AOEI | D.H.82A Tiger Moth | C.F.G. Flying Ltd/Cambridge | |

| Notes | Reg. | Type | Owner or Operator |
|-------|------|------|-------------------|
| | G-AOEL | D.H.82A Tiger Moth (N9510) ★ | Museum of Flight/E. Fortune |
| | G-AOES | D.H.82A Tiger Moth | A. Twemlow & G. A. Cordery |
| | G-AOET | D.H.82A Tiger Moth | Venom Jet Promotions Ltd/ Bournemouth |
| | G-AOEX | Thruxton Jackaroo | A. T. Christian |
| | G-AOFE | D.H.C.1 Chipmunk 22A | R. J. F. Parker/Denham |
| | G-AOFM | J/5P Autocar | N. P. Beaumont |
| | G-AOFS | J/5L Aiglet Trainer | P. N. A. Whitehead |
| | G-AOGA | M.75 Aries ★ | Irish Aviation Museum (stored) |
| | G-AOGE | P.34A Proctor 3 | N. I. Dalziel/Biggin Hill |
| | G-AOGI | D.H.82A Tiger Moth | W. J. Taylor |
| | G-AOGR | D.H.82A Tiger Moth (T6099) | M. I. Edwards |
| | G-AOGV | J/5R Alpine | R. E. Heading |
| | G-AOHL | V.802 Viscount ★ | British Air Ferries (Cabin Trainer)/ Southend |
| | G-AOHM | V.802 Viscount | British Air Ferries Viscount Sir George Edwards/Southend |
| | G-AOHT | V.802 Viscount | British Air Ferries (withdrawn)/Southend |
| | G-AOHY | D.H.82A Tiger Moth | C. R. Hardiman |
| | G-AOHZ | J/5P Autocar | P. H. Yarnold |
| | G-AOIL | D.H.82A Tiger Moth | T. C. Lawless |
| | G-AOIM | D.H.82A Tiger Moth | C. R. Hardiman/Shobdon |
| | G-AOIR | Thruxton Jackaroo | L. H. Smith |
| | G-AOIS | D.H.82A Tiger Moth | V. B. & R. G. Wheele/Shoreham |
| | G-AOIY | J/5G Autocar | C. N. Towers |
| | G-AOJC | V.802 Viscount ★ | Wales Aircraft Museum/Cardiff |
| | G-AOJH | D.H.83C Fox Moth | Proteus Petroleum Aviation Ltd/ Goodwood |
| | G-AOJJ | D.H.82A Tiger Moth (DF128) | E. Lay |
| | G-AOJK | D.H.82A Tiger Moth | P. A. de Courcy Swoffer |
| | G-AOJS | D.H.C.1 Chipmunk 22A | R. H. Cooper |
| | G-AOJT | D.H.106 Comet 1 ★ | Mosquito Aircraft Museum |
| | G-AOKH | P.40 Prentice 1 | J. F. Moore/Biggin Hill |
| | G-AOKL | P.40 Prentice 1 (VS610) | D. L. Claydon |
| | G-AOKO | P.40 Prentice 1 | J. F. Coggins/Coventry |
| | G-AOKZ | P.40 Prentice 1 (VS623) ★ | Midland Air Museum |
| | G-AOLK | P.40 Prentice 1 | Hilton Aviation Ltd/Southend |
| | G-AOLU | P.40 Prentice 1 (VS356) ★ | — |
| | G-AORB | Cessna 170B | Eaglescott Parachute Centre |
| | G-AORG | D.H.114 Heron 2 | Duchess of Brittany (Jersey) Ltd |
| | G-AORW | D.H.C.1 Chipmunk 22A | V. P. Butler/Biggin Hill |
| | G-AOSK | D.H.C.1 Chipmunk 22 | A. M. S. Cullen |
| | G-AOSO | D.H.C.1 Chipmunk 22 | Earl of Suffolk & Berkshire & J. Hoerner |
| | G-AOSU | D.H.C.1 Chipmunk 22 (Lycoming) | RAFGSA/Bicester |
| | G-AOSY | D.H.C.1 Chipmunk 22 (WB585) | Franbrave Ltd |
| | G-AOTD | D.H.C.1 Chipmunk 22 (WB588) | Shuttleworth Trust/O. Warden |
| | G-AOTF | D.H.C.1 Chipmunk 23 (Lycoming) | RAFGSA/Bicester |
| | G-AOTI | D.H.114 Heron 2D | Avtech Ltd/Biggin Hill |
| | G-AOTK | D.53 Turbi | The T. K. Flying Group/Hatfield |
| | G-AOTR | D.H.C.1 Chipmunk 22 | Ulster Chipmunk Club/Newtownards |
| | G-AOTY | D.H.C.1 Chipmunk 22A (WG472) | West London Aero Services Ltd/ White Waltham |
| | G-AOUJ | Fairey Ultra-Light ★ | International Helicopter Museum/ Weston-s-Mare |
| | G-AOUO | D.H.C.1 Chipmunk 22 (Lycoming) | RAFGSA/Bicester |
| | G-AOUP | D.H.C.1 Chipmunk 22 | Wessex Flying Group |
| | G-AOUR | D.H.82A Tiger Moth ★ | Ulster Folk & Transport Museum |
| | G-AOVF | B.175 Britannia 312F ★ | Aerospace Museum/Cosford |
| | G-AOVT | B.175 Britannia 312F ★ | Duxford Aviation Soc |
| | G-AOVW | Auster 5 | B. Marriott/Cranwell |
| | G-AOXG | D.H.82A Tiger Moth (XL717) | FAA Museum/Yeovilton |
| | G-AOXN | D.H.82A Tiger Moth | S. L. G. Darch |
| | G-AOYG | V.806 Viscount | British Air Ferries Viscount Sir Peter Masefield/Southend |
| | G-AOYL | V.806 Viscount | British Air Ferries Viscount Churchill/ Southend |
| | G-AOYN | V.806 Viscount | British Air Ferries/Southend |
| | G-AOYP | V.806 Viscount | British Air Ferries/Southend |
| | G-AOYR | V.806 Viscount | British Air Ferries/Southend |
| | G-AOZH | D.H.82A Tiger Moth (K2572) | V. B. & R. G. Wheele/Shoreham |
| | G-AOZL | J/5Q Alpine | E. A. Taylor/Southend |

| Reg. | Type | Owner or Operator | Notes |
|------|------|-------------------|-------|
| G-AOZP | D.H.C.1 Chipmunk 22 | M. E. Darlington | |
| G-AOZU | D.H.C.1 Chipmunk 22A | R. H. Cooper | |
| G-APAA | J/5R Alpine ★ | L. A. Groves (stored) | |
| G-APAF | Auster 5 | J. E. Allen (G-CMAL) | |
| G-APAH | Auster 5 | N. A. Ali | |
| G-APAL | D.H.82A Tiger Moth (N6847) | P. S. & R. A. Chapman | |
| G-APAM | D.H.82A Tiger Moth | R. P. Williams | |
| G-APAO | D.H.82A Tiger Moth | F. J. Longe | |
| G-APAP | D.H.82A Tiger Moth | R. A. Slade | |
| G-APAS | D.H.106 Comet 1XB ★ | Aerospace Museum/Cosford | |
| G-APBE | Auster 5 | C. W. Wilkinson/Panshanger | |
| G-APBI | D.H.82A Tiger Moth (EM903) | R. Devaney & ptnrs/Audley End | |
| G-APBO | D.53 Turbi | T. W. Harris | |
| G-APBW | Auster 5 | N. Huxtable | |
| G-APCB | J/5Q Alpine | M. J. Wilson/Redhill | |
| G-APCC | D.H.82A Tiger Moth | L. J. Rice/Henstridge | |
| G-APDB | D.H.106 Comet 4 ★ | Duxford Aviation Soc | |
| G-APEG | V.953C Merchantman | Air Bridge Carriers Ltd (withdrawn)/ E. Midlands | |
| G-APEJ | V.953C Merchantman | Air Bridge Carriers Ltd Ajax/E. Midlands | |
| G-APEK | V.953C Merchantman | Air Bridge Carriers Ltd Dreadnought/ E. Midlands | |
| G-APEM | V.953C Merchantman | Air Bridge Carriers Ltd/DHL Agamemnon/E. Midlands | |
| G-APEP | V.953C Merchantman | Air Bridge Carriers Ltd Superb/ E. Midlands | |
| G-APES | V.953C Merchantman | Air Bridge Carriers Ltd Swiftsure/ E. Midlands | |
| G-APET | V.953C Merchantman | Air Bridge Carriers Ltd Temeraire/ E. Midlands | |
| G-APEY | V.806 Viscount | British Air Ferries/Southend | |
| G-APFA | D.54 Turbi | A. Eastelow & F. J. Keitch/Dunkeswell | |
| G-APFG | Boeing 707-436 ★ | Cabin water spray tests/Cardington | |
| G-APFJ | Boeing 707-436 ★ | Aerospace Museum/Cosford | |
| G-APFU | D.H.82A Tiger Moth | Mithril Racing Ltd/Goodwood | |
| G-APGL | D.H.82A Tiger Moth | B. H. Strudwick | |
| G-APHV | Avro 19 Srs 2 (VM360) ★ | Museum of Flight/E. Fortune | |
| G-APIE | Tipsy Belfair B | P. A. Smith | |
| G-APIH | D.H.82A Tiger Moth (R5086) | C. R. Kirby | |
| G-APIK | J/1N Alpha | N. D. Voce | |
| G-APIM | V.806 Viscount ★ | Brooklands Museum of Aviation/ Weybridge | |
| G-APIT | P.40 Prentice 1 (VR192) ★ | WWII Aircraft Preservation Soc/Lasham | |
| G-APIU | P.40 Prentice 1 ★ | J. F. Coggins/Coventry | |
| G-APIY | P.40 Prentice 1 (VR249) ★ | Newark Air Museum | |
| G-APIZ | D.31 Turbulent | M. J. Whatley/Booker | |
| G-APJB | P.40 Prentice 1 (VR259) ★ | City Airways/Coventry | |
| G-APJJ | Fairey Ultra-light ★ | Midland Aircraft Preservation Soc | |
| G-APJO | D.H.82A Tiger Moth | D. R. & M. Wood | |
| G-APJZ | J/1N Alpha | P. G. Lipman | |
| G-APKH | D.H.85 Leopard Moth | I. Lemanski & ptnrs (G-ACGS) | |
| G-APKM | J/1N Alpha | D. E. A. Huggins | |
| G-APKN | J/1N Alpha | Felthorpe Auster Group | |
| G-APKY | Hiller UH-12B | D. A. George (stored) | |
| G-APLG | J/5L Aiglet Trainer | G. R. W. Brown | |
| G-APLO | D.H.C.1 Chipmunk 22A (WD379) | Channel Islands Aero Holdings Ltd | |
| G-APLU | D.H.82A Tiger Moth | The Intrepid Flying Group | |
| G-APMB | D.H.106 Comet 4B ★ | Gatwick Handling Ltd (ground trainer) | |
| G-APMH | J/1U Workmaster | R. E. Neal & E. R. Stevens/Leicester | |
| G-APML | Dakota 6 | Air Atlantique Ltd | |
| G-APMM | D.H.82A Tiger Moth (K2568) | R. K. J. Hadlow | |
| G-APMX | D.H.82A Tiger Moth | For rebuild | |
| G-APMY | PA-23 Apache 160 ★ | NE Wales Institute of Higher Education (instructional airframe)/Clwyd | |
| G-APNJ | Cessna 310 ★ | Chelsea College/Shoreham | |
| G-APNS | Garland-Bianchi Linnet | Paul Penn-Sayers Model Services Ltd | |
| G-APNT | Currie Wot | J. W. Salter | |
| G-APNZ | D.31 Turbulent | Tiger Club (1990) Ltd/Headcorn | |
| G-APOA | J/1N Alpha | J. S. M. Norman | |
| G-APOD | Tipsy Belfair | L. F. Potts | |
| G-APOI | Saro Skeeter Srs 8 ★ | Wilkie Museum Collection/Blackpool | |
| G-APOL | D.31 Turbulent | A. Gregori & S. Tinker | |

| Notes | Reg. | Type | Owner or Operator |
|---|---|---|---|
| | G-APPA | D.H.C.1 Chipmunk 22 | G. Cormack/Glasgow |
| | G-APPL | P.40 Prentice 1 | S. J. Saggers/Biggin Hill |
| | G-APPM | D.H.C.1 Chipmunk 22 | Freston Aviation |
| | G-APRF | Auster 5 | R. Giles & ptnrs/Clacton |
| | G-APRJ | Avro 694 Lincoln B.2 ★ | Charles Church Displays Ltd/Cranfield |
| | G-APRL | AW.650 Argosy 101 ★ | Midland Air Museum |
| | G-APRR | Super Aero 45 | R. H. Jowett |
| | G-APRT | Taylor JT.1 Monoplane | G. E. Valler |
| | G-APSA | Douglas DC-6A | Instone Air Line Ltd/Coventry |
| | G-APSR | J/1U Workmaster | D. & K. Aero Services Ltd/Shobdon |
| | G-APTH | Agusta-Bell 47J | A. M. Parkes |
| | G-APTP | PA-22 Tri-Pacer 150 | R. J. & F. A. Fox |
| | G-APTR | J/1N Alpha | C. J. & D. J. Baker |
| | G-APTS | D.H.C.1 Chipmunk 22A | Wycombe Air Centre Ltd |
| | G-APTU | Auster 5 | B. G. F. King |
| | G-APTW | W.B.1 Widgeon ★ | Cornwall Aero Park/Helston |
| | G-APTY | Beech G.35 Bonanza | G. E. Brennand & ptnrs |
| | G-APTZ | D.31 Turbulent | B. E. Francis |
| | G-APUD | Bensen B.7M (modified) ★ | Greater Manchester Museum of Science & Technology |
| | G-APUE | L-40 Meta Sokol | S. E. & M. J. Aherne |
| | G-APUK | J/1 Autocrat | P. L. Morley |
| | G-APUP | Sopwith Pup (N5182) (replica)★ | RAF Museum/Hendon |
| | G-APUR | PA-22 Tri-Pacer 160 | G. A. Allen & ptnrs |
| | G-APUW | J/5V-160 Autocar | Anglia Auster Syndicate |
| | G-APUY | D.31 Turbulent | C. Jones & ptnrs/Barton |
| | G-APUZ | PA-24 Comanche 250 | N. Parkinson & W. Smith |
| | G-APVF | Putzer Elster B (97+04) | K. P. Rusling |
| | G-APVG | J/5L Aiglet Trainer | C. M. Daggett/Cranfield |
| | G-APVN | D.31 Turbulent | R. Sherwin/Shoreham |
| | G-APVS | Cessna 170B | N. Simpson |
| | G-APVY | PA-25 Pawnee 150 | KK Aviation |
| | G-APVZ | D.31 Turbulent | H. R. Oldland |
| | G-APWJ | HPR-7 Herald 201 ★ | Duxford Aviation Soc |
| | G-APWN | WS-55 Whirlwind 3 ★ | Midland Air Museum |
| | G-APWR | PA-22 Tri-Pacer 160 | G. L. Ranscombe/Goodwood |
| | G-APWY | Piaggio P.166 ★ | Science Museum/Wroughton |
| | G-APWZ | EP.9 Prospector ★ | Museum of Army Flying/Middle Wallop |
| | G-APXJ | PA-24 Comanche 250 | T. Wildsmith/Netherthorpe |
| | G-APXM | PA-22 Tri-Pacer 160 | R. J. Chinn |
| | G-APXR | PA-22 Tri-Pacer 160 | A. Troughton |
| | G-APXT | PA-22 Tri-Pacer 150 (modified) | J. W. & I. Daniels |
| | G-APXU | PA-22 Tri-Pacer 125 | C. G. Stone/Biggin Hill |
| | G-APXW | EP.9 Prospector ★ | Museum of Army Flying/Middle Wallop |
| | G-APXX | D.H.A.3 Drover 2 (VH-FDT) ★ | WWII Aircraft Preservation Soc/Lasham |
| | G-APXY | Cessna 150 | Merlin Flying Club Ltd/Hucknall |
| | G-APYB | Tipsy T.66 Nipper 3 | B. O. Smith |
| | G-APYD | D.H.106 Comet 4B ★ | Science Museum/Wroughton |
| | G-APYG | D.H.C.1 Chipmunk 22 | E. J. I. Musty & P. A. Colman |
| | G-APYI | PA-22 Tri-Pacer 135 | G. K. Hare/Fenland |
| | G-APYN | PA-22 Tri-Pacer 160 | W. D. Stephens |
| | G-APYT | Champion 7FC Tri-Traveller | B. J. Anning |
| | G-APYW | PA-22 Tri-Pacer 150 | Fiddian Ltd |
| | G-APZJ | PA-18 Super Cub 150 | Southern Sailplanes |
| | G-APZK | PA-18 Super Cub 95 | W. T. Knapton |
| | G-APZL | PA-22 Tri-Pacer 160 | R. T. Evans |
| | G-APZR | Cessna 150 ★ | Engine test-bed/Biggin Hill |
| | G-APZS | Cessna 175A | G. A. Nash/Booker |
| | G-APZX | PA-22 Tri-Pacer 150 | Applied Signs Ltd |
| | G-ARAD | Luton LA-5A Major | W. T. Sproat |
| | G-ARAM | PA-18 Super Cub 150 | Clacton Aero Club (1988) Ltd |
| | G-ARAN | PA-18 Super Cub 150 | A. P. Docherty/Redhill |
| | G-ARAO | PA-18 Super Cub 95 (607327) | R. T. Bennett & N. Tyler |
| | G-ARAS | Champion 7EC Traveller | B. W. Webb |
| | G-ARAT | Cessna 180C | Eaglescott Parachute Centre |
| | G-ARAU | Cessna 150 | S. Lynn/Sibson |
| | G-ARAW | Cessna 182C Skylane | P. Channon |
| | G-ARAX | PA-22 Tri-Pacer 150 | S. J. Kew/Booker |
| | G-ARAZ | D.H.82A Tiger Moth (R4959) | Proteus Petroleum Aviation Ltd/Goodwood |
| | G-ARBE | D.H.104 Dove 8 | A. Freeman & T. Howe |

| Reg. | Type | Owner or Operator | Notes |
|------|------|-------------------|-------|
| G-ARBG | Tipsy T.66 Nipper 2 | Felthorpe Tipsy Group | |
| G-ARBN | PA-23 Apache 160 | H. Norden & H. J. Liggins | |
| G-ARBO | PA-24 Comanche 250 | D. M. Harbottle & I. S. Graham/ Goodwood | |
| G-ARBP | Tipsy T.66 Nipper 2 | F. W. Kirk | |
| G-ARBS | PA-22 Tri-Pacer 160 (modified to PA-20 Pacer 160) | S. D. Rowell | |
| G-ARBV | PA-22 Tri-Pacer 150 | Piper Flyers/Biggin Hill | |
| G-ARBZ | D.31 Turbulent | D. G. H. Hilliard/Bodmin | |
| G-ARCC | PA-22 Tri-Pacer 150 | RFC Flying Group/Popham | |
| G-ARCF | PA-22 Tri-Pacer 150 | R. E. Ryan | |
| G-ARCH | Cessna 310D ★ | Instructional airframe/Perth | |
| G-ARCS | Auster D6/180 | E. A. Matty/Shobdon | |
| G-ARCT | PA-18 Super Cub 95 | M. J. Kirk | |
| G-ARCV | Cessna 175A | R. Francis & C. Campbell | |
| G-ARCW | PA-23 Apache 160 | D. R. C. Reeves | |
| G-ARCX | AW Meteor 14 ★ | Museum of Flight/E. Fortune | |
| G-ARDB | PA-24 Comanche 250 | R. A. Sareen/Booker | |
| G-ARDD | CP.301C1 Emeraude | R. M. Shipp | |
| G-ARDE | D.H.104 Dove 6 | R. J. H. Small/Cranfield | |
| G-ARDG | EP.9 Prospector ★ | Museum of Army Flying/Middle Wallop | |
| G-ARDJ | Auster D.6/180 | RN Aviation (Leicester Airport) Ltd | |
| G-ARDO | Jodel D.112 | W. R. Prescott | |
| G-ARDP | PA-22 Tri-Pacer 150 | G. M. Jones | |
| G-ARDS | PA-22 Caribbean 150 | D. V. Asher/Leicester | |
| G-ARDT | PA-22 Tri-Pacer 160 | M. Henderson | |
| G-ARDV | PA-22 Tri-Pacer 160 | B. R. Griffiths | |
| G-ARDY | Tipsy T.66 Nipper 2 | M. J. Mann | |
| G-ARDZ | Jodel D.140A | M. J. Wright | |
| G-AREA | D.H.104 Dove 8 | British Aerospace/Hatfield | |
| G-AREB | Cessna 175B Skylark | R. J. Postlethwaite & ptnrs/ Wellesbourne | |
| G-AREE | PA-23 Aztec 250 | W. C. C. Meyer/Biggin Hill | |
| G-AREF | PA-23 Aztec 250 ★ | Southall College of Technology | |
| G-AREH | D.H.82A Tiger Moth | T. Pate | |
| G-AREI | Auster 3 (MT438) | R. Alliker & ptnrs/Bodmin | |
| G-AREJ | Beech 95 Travel Air | D. Huggett/Stapleford | |
| G-AREL | PA-22 Caribbean 150 | H. H. Cousins/Fenland | |
| G-AREO | PA-18 Super Cub 150 | Scottish Gliding Union Ltd | |
| G-ARET | PA-22 Tri-Pacer 160 | D. T. Daniels | |
| G-AREV | PA-22 Tri-Pacer 160 | Spatrek Ltd/Barton | |
| G-AREX | Aeronca 15AC Sedan | R. J. Middleton-Turnbull & P. Lowndes | |
| G-AREZ | D.31 Turbulent | J. St. Clair-Quentin/Shobdon | |
| G-ARFB | PA-22 Caribbean 150 | C. T. Woodward & ptnrs | |
| G-ARFD | PA-22 Tri-Pacer 160 | P. C. Hambilton & G. F. Martin/Blackpool | |
| G-ARFG | Cessna 175A Skylark | R. J. Fray/Sibson | |
| G-ARFH | PA-24 Comanche 250 | L. M. Walton | |
| G-ARFI | Cessna 150A | J. H. Fisher | |
| G-ARFL | Cessna 175B Skylark | Garflair Group | |
| G-ARFN | Cessna 150A ★ | Instructional airframe/Perth | |
| G-ARFO | Cessna 150A | Moray Flying Club Ltd | |
| G-ARFT | Jodel DR. 1050 | R. Shaw | |
| G-ARFV | Tipsy T.66 Nipper 2 | C. G. Stone/Biggin Hill | |
| G-ARGB | Auster 6A ★ | C. Baker (stored) | |
| G-ARGG | D.H.C.1 Chipmunk 22 (WD305) | Willpower Garage Ltd | |
| G-ARGO | PA-22 Colt 108 | B. E. Goodman/Liverpool | |
| G-ARGV | PA-18 Super Cub 150 | Deeside Gliding Club (Aberdeenshire) Ltd/Aboyne | |
| G-ARGZ | D.31 Turbulent | J. C. Mansell | |
| G-ARHC | Forney F-1A Aircoupe | A. P. Gardner/Elstree | |
| G-ARHF | Forney F-1A Aircoupe | R. A. Nesbitt-Dufort | |
| G-ARHI | PA-24 Comanche 180 | W. H. Entress/Swansea | |
| G-ARHL | PA-23 Aztec 250 | J. J. Freeman & Co Ltd/Headcorn | |
| G-ARHM | Auster 6A | D. Hollowell & ptnrs/Finmere | |
| G-ARHN | PA-22 Caribbean 150 | D. B. Furniss & A. Munro/Doncaster | |
| G-ARHP | PA-22 Tri-Pacer 160 | W. Wardle | |
| G-ARHR | PA-22 Caribbean 150 | J. A. Hargraves/Fairoaks | |
| G-ARHT | PA-22 Caribbean 150 ★ | Moston Technical College | |
| G-ARHU | PA-22 Tri-Pacer 160 | B. L. Newbold & ptnrs | |
| G-ARHW | D.H.104 Dove 8 | Proteus Petroleum Aviation Ltd/ Goodwood | |
| G-ARHZ | D.62 Condor | M. J. Groome & ptnrs | |
| G-ARID | Cessna 172B | A. Taylor | |

| Notes | Reg. | Type | Owner or Operator |
|---|---|---|---|
| | G-ARIE | PA-24 Comanche 250 | W. Radwanski (stored)/Coventry |
| | G-ARIF | Ord-Hume O-H.7 Minor Coupé | N. H. Ponsford |
| | G-ARIH | Auster 6A (TW591) | India Hotel Ltd |
| | G-ARIK | PA-22 Caribbean 150 | C. J. Berry |
| | G-ARIL | PA-22 Caribbean 150 | G. N. Richardson Motors/Shobdon |
| | G-ARIV | Cessna 172B | G-ARIV Group |
| | G-ARIW | CP.301B Emeraude | P. J. Marsh |
| | G-ARJB | D.H.104 Dove 8 ★ | J. C. Bamford (stored) |
| | G-ARJC | PA-22 Colt 108 | F. W. H. Dulles |
| | G-ARJE | PA-22 Colt 108 | C. I. Fray |
| | G-ARJF | PA-22 Colt 108 | M. J. Collins |
| | G-ARJH | PA-22 Colt 108 | Isabella Properties |
| | G-ARJR | PA-23 Apache 160G ★ | Instructional airframe/Kidlington |
| | G-ARJS | PA-23 Apache 160G | Bencray Ltd/Blackpool |
| | G-ARJT | PA-23 Apache 160G | Hiveland Ltd |
| | G-ARJU | PA-23 Apache 160G | Chantaco Ltd/Biggin Hill |
| | G-ARJV | PA-23 Apache 160G | Photractive Ltd |
| | G-ARJW | PA-23 Apache 160G | stored/Bristol |
| | G-ARJZ | D.31 Turbulent | N. H. Jones |
| | G-ARKG | J/5G Autocar | C. M. Milborrow |
| | G-ARKJ | Beech N35 Bonanza | Mouldrite Products Ltd |
| | G-ARKK | PA-22 Colt 108 | A. T. J. Hyatt |
| | G-ARKM | PA-22 Colt 108 | B. V. & E. A. Howes/Earls Colne |
| | G-ARKN | PA-22 Colt 108 | R. A. & N. L. E. Dupee |
| | G-ARKP | PA-22 Colt 108 | C. J. & J. Freeman/Headcorn |
| | G-ARKR | PA-22 Colt 108 | J. Fell |
| | G-ARKS | PA-22 Colt 108 | J. Dickenson |
| | G-ARLG | Auster D.4/108 | Auster D4 Group |
| | G-ARLK | PA-24 Comanche 250 | M. Walker & C. Robinson |
| | G-ARLO | A.61 Terrier 1 ★ | stored |
| | G-ARLP | A.61 Terrier 1 | A. P. Twort & N. A. M. Pelling |
| | G-ARLR | A.61 Terrier 2 | W. H. Dyozinski |
| | G-ARLU | Cessna 172B Skyhawk ★ | Instructional airframe/Irish AC |
| | G-ARLV | Cessna 172B Skyhawk | P. D. Lowdon |
| | G-ARLW | Cessna 172B Skyhawk | S. Lancashire Flyers Ltd/Barton |
| | G-ARLX | Jodel D.140B | Shipping & Airlines Ltd/Biggin Hill |
| | G-ARLZ | D.31A Turbulent | R. S. Hatwell & A. F. Hall |
| | G-ARMA | PA-23 Apache 160G ★ | Instructional airframe/Kidlington |
| | G-ARMB | D.H.C.1 Chipmunk 22A (WB660) | P. A. Layzell/Goodwood |
| | G-ARMC | D.H.C.1 Chipmunk 22A (WB703) | West London Aero Services Ltd/ White Waltham |
| | G-ARMD | D.H.C.1 Chipmunk 22A ★ | K. & L. Aero Services (stored) |
| | G-ARMG | D.H.C.1 Chipmunk 22A | Chipmunk Preservation Group Ltd/ Wellesbourne |
| | G-ARML | Cessna 175B Skylark | R. C. Convine |
| | G-ARMN | Cessna 175B Skylark ★ | Southall College of Technology |
| | G-ARMO | Cessna 172B Skyhawk | G. R. E. Evans & D. J. Clark |
| | G-ARMR | Cessna 172B Skyhawk | Sunsaver Ltd/Barton |
| | G-ARMW | H.S. 748 Srs 1 | Dan-Air Services Ltd |
| | G-ARMZ | D.31 Turbulent | J. E. M. B. Millns |
| | G-ARNA | Mooney M.20B | R. Travers/Blackpool |
| | G-ARNB | J/5G Autocar | R. F. Tolhurst |
| | G-ARND | PA-22 Colt 108 | A. Cambridge |
| | G-ARNE | PA-22 Colt 108 | T. D. L. Bowden/Shipdham |
| | G-ARNI | PA-22 Colt 108 | P. R. Monk & A. C. Savage |
| | G-ARNJ | PA-22 Colt 108 | Colt Flying Group/Denham |
| | G-ARNK | PA-22 Colt 108 | J. R. Colthurst/Biggin Hill |
| | G-ARNL | PA-22 Colt 108 | J. A. & J. A. Dodsworth/White Waltham |
| | G-ARNO | A.61 Terrier 1 | M. B. Hill |
| | G-ARNP | A.109 Airedale | S. W. & M. Isbister |
| | G-ARNY | Jodel D.117 | D. J. Lockett |
| | G-ARNZ | D.31 Turbulent | N. J. Mathias |
| | G-AROA | Cessna 172B Skyhawk | D. E. Partridge |
| | G-AROE | Aero 145 | Panther Aviation |
| | G-AROF | L.40 Meta-Sokol | G. D. H. Crawford |
| | G-AROJ | A.109 Airedale ★ | D. J. Shaw (stored) |
| | G-AROM | PA-22 Colt 108 | J. R. Colthurst |
| | G-ARON | PA-22 Colt 108 | R. W. Curtis |
| | G-AROO | Forney F-1A Aircoupe | W. J. McMeekan/Newtownards |
| | G-AROW | Jodel D.140B | Kent Gliding Club Ltd/Challock |
| | G-AROY | Boeing Stearman A.75N.1 | W. A. Jordan |
| | G-ARPD | H.S.121 Trident 1C ★ | CAA Fire School/Teesside |

| Reg. | Type | Owner or Operator | Notes |
|------|------|-------------------|-------|
| G-ARPH | H.S.121 Trident 1C ★ | Aerospace Museum, Cosford | |
| G-ARPK | H.S.121 Trident 1C ★ | Manchester Airport Authority | |
| G-ARPL | H.S.121 Trident 1C ★ | British Airports Authority/Edinburgh | |
| G-ARPN | H.S.121 Trident 1C ★ | British Airports Authority/Aberdeen | |
| G-ARPO | H.S.121 Trident 1C ★ | CAA Fire School/Teesside | |
| G-ARPP | H.S.121 Trident 1C ★ | British Airports Authority/Glasgow | |
| G-ARPR | H.S.121 Trident 1C ★ | CAA Fire School/Teesside | |
| G-ARPW | H.S.121 Trident 1C ★ | CAA Fire School/Teesside | |
| G-ARPX | H.S.121 Trident 1C ★ | Airwork Services Ltd/Perth | |
| G-ARPZ | H.S.121 Trident 1C ★ | RFD Ltd/Dunsfold | |
| G-ARRD | Jodel DR.1050 | C. M. Fitton | |
| G-ARRE | Jodel DR.1050 | A. Luty & M. P. Edwards/Barton | |
| G-ARRF | Cessna 150A | Electrical Engineering Services | |
| G-ARRL | J/1N Alpha | G. N. Smith & C. Webb | |
| G-ARRM | Beagle B.206-X ★ | Shoreham Airport Museum | |
| G-ARRS | CP.301A Emeraude | E. H. Booker | |
| G-ARRT | Wallis WA-116-1 | K. H. Wallis | |
| G-ARRU | D.31 Turbulent | P. Buchan & M. J. Brooman/Plymouth | |
| G-ARRW | H.S. 748 Srs 1 | British Independent Airways Ltd/Lydd | |
| G-ARRX | Auster 6A | J. E. D. Mackie | |
| G-ARRY | Jodel D.140B | R. C. Partridge & M. J. Oliver/Ipswich | |
| G-ARRZ | D.31 Turbulent | G. L. Winterbourne/Redhill | |
| G-ARSB | Cessna 150A | B. T. White/Andrewsfield | |
| G-ARSG | Roe Triplane Type IV replica | Shuttleworth Trust/O. Warden | |
| G-ARSJ | CP.301-C2 Emeraude | R. J. Lewis | |
| G-ARSL | A.61 Terrier 2 | R. A. Hutchinson & P. T. M. Hardy | |
| G-ARSP | L.40 Meta-Sokol | R. E. Carpenter | |
| G-ARSU | PA-22 Colt 108 | P. C. Riggs | |
| G-ARSW | PA-22 Colt 108 | Sierra Whisky Flying Group/Sibson | |
| G-ARSX | PA-22 Tri-Pacer 160 | A. W. F. Richards | |
| G-ARTD | PA-23 Apache 160 | Dr. D. A. Jones | |
| G-ARTF | D.31 Turbulent | J. R. D. Bygraves | |
| G-ARTG | Hiller UH-12C ★ | White Hart Inn/Stockbridge | |
| G-ARTH | PA-12 Super Cruiser | A. Horsfall/Sherburn | |
| G-ARTJ | Bensen B.8 ★ | Museum of Flight/E. Fortune | |
| G-ARTL | D.H.82A Tiger Moth (T7281) | P. A. Jackson | |
| G-ARTT | M.S.880B Rallye Club | R. N. Scott | |
| G-ARTW | Cessna 150B ★ | Instructional airframe/Perth | |
| G-ARTX | Cessna 150B ★ | Instructional airframe/Perth | |
| G-ARTY | Cessna 150B ★ | Instructional airframe/Perth | |
| G-ARTZ | McCandless M.4 Gyrocopter | W. E. Partridge (stored) | |
| G-ARUG | J/5G Autocar | D. P. H. Hulme/Biggin Hill | |
| G-ARUH | Jodel DR.1050 | PFA Group/Denham | |
| G-ARUI | A.61 Terrier | A. C. Ladd | |
| G-ARUL | Cosmic Wind | P. G. Kynsey | |
| G-ARUO | PA-24 Comanche 180 | Uniform Oscar Group/Elstree | |
| G-ARUR | PA-28 Cherokee 160 | The G-ARUR Group/Redhill | |
| G-ARUV | CP.301A Emeraude | J. Tanswell | |
| G-ARUY | J/1N Alpha | D. L. Webley | |
| G-ARUZ | Cessna 175C Skylark | Cardiff Skylark Group | |
| G-ARVM | V.1101 VC10 ★ | Aerospace Museum/Cosford | |
| G-ARVO | PA-18 Super Cub 95 | Mona Aviation Ltd | |
| G-ARVS | PA-28 Cherokee 160 | Skyscraper Ltd/Stapleford | |
| G-ARVT | PA-28 Cherokee 160 | Leon Smith Helicopter Services | |
| G-ARVU | PA-28 Cherokee 160 | D. J. Hockings/Biggin Hill | |
| G-ARVV | PA-28 Cherokee 160 | G. E. Hopkins | |
| G-ARVZ | D.62B Condor | C. Watson & W. H. Cole/Redhill | |
| G-ARWB | D.H.C.1 Chipmunk 22 (WK611) | L. J. Willcocks | |
| G-ARWH | Cessna 172C Skyhawk ★ | — | |
| G-ARWM | Cessna 175C | J. Taylor & S. E. Ellcome | |
| G-ARWO | Cessna 172C Skyhawk | J. R. Woolford | |
| G-ARWR | Cessna 172C Skyhawk | The Devanha Flying Group Ltd | |
| G-ARWS | Cessna 175C Skylark | E. N. Skinner | |
| G-ARWW | Bensen B.8M | B. McIntyre | |
| G-ARXD | A.109 Airedale | D. Howden | |
| G-ARXG | PA-24 Comanche 250 | I. M. Callier | |
| G-ARXH | Bell 47G | A. B. Searle | |
| G-ARXP | Luton LA-4A Minor | W. C. Hymas | |
| G-ARXT | Jodel DR.1050 | CJM Flying Group | |
| G-ARXU | Auster 6A | M. Pocock & ptnrs | |
| G-ARXW | M.S.885 Super Rallye | M. A. Jones | |
| G-ARXX | M.S.880B Rallye Club | M. A. Watts | |
| G-ARYB | H.S.125 Srs 1 ★ | British Aerospace PLC/Hatfield | |

| Notes | Reg. | Type | Owner or Operator |
|---|---|---|---|
| | G-ARYC | H.S.125 Srs 1 ★ | The Mosquito Aircraft Museum |
| | G-ARYD | Auster AOP.6 (WJ358) ★ | Museum of Army Flying/Middle Wallop |
| | G-ARYF | PA-23 Aztec 250B | I. J. T. Branson/Biggin Hill |
| | G-ARYH | PA-22 Tri-Pacer 160 | Filtration (Water Treatment Engineers) Ltd |
| | G-ARYI | Cessna 172C | J. Rhodes |
| | G-ARYK | Cessna 172C | J. H. Emery |
| | G-ARYR | PA-28 Cherokee 180 | R. J. Gerrard & C. S. Wilkinson/Booker |
| | G-ARYS | Cessna 172C Skyhawk | R. S. Morgan |
| | G-ARYV | PA-24 Comanche 250 | Ilford Business Machines Ltd |
| | G-ARYZ | A.109 Airedale | J. D. Reid |
| | G-ARZB | Wallis WA-116 Srs 1 | K. H. Wallis |
| | G-ARZE | Cessna 172C ★ | Parachute jump trainer/Cockerham |
| | G-ARZM | D.31 Turbulent | Tiger Club (1990) Ltd/Headcorn |
| | G-ARZN | Beech N35 Bonanza | D. W. Mickleburgh/Leicester |
| | G-ARZP | A.109 Airedale | G. B. O'Neill (stored)/Booker |
| | G-ARZW | Currie Wot | J. H. Blake |
| | G-ARZX | Cessna 150B | Woodside Flying Group |
| | | | |
| | G-ASAA | Luton LA-4A Minor | R. J. Moore |
| | G-ASAI | A.109 Airedale | K. R Howden & ptnrs |
| | G-ASAJ | A.61 Terrier 2 (WE569) | S. J. B. White & V. M. Howard |
| | G-ASAK | A.61 Terrier 2 | Rochford Hundred Flying Group/ Southend |
| | G-ASAL | SAL Bulldog 120 | British Aerospace PLC/Prestwick |
| | G-ASAM | D.31 Turbulent | Tiger Club (1990) Ltd/Headcorn |
| | G-ASAN | A.61 Terrier 2 | D. R. Godfrey |
| | G-ASAT | M.S.880B Rallye Club | M. Cutovic |
| | G-ASAU | M.S.880B Rallye Club | T. C. & R. Edwards |
| | G-ASAX | A.61 Terrier 2 | G. Strathdee |
| | G-ASAZ | Hiller UH-12E4 | P. A. Boitel-Gill |
| | G-ASBA | Currie Wot | M. A. Kaye |
| | G-ASBB | Beech 23 Musketeer | D. Silver/Southend |
| | G-ASBH | A.109 Airedale | D. T. Smollett |
| | G-ASBY | A.109 Airedale | R. Skingley |
| | G-ASCC | Beagle E.3 AOP Mk 11 | Old Training Plane Co |
| | G-ASCM | Isaacs Fury II (K2050) | D. S. T. Eggleton |
| | G-ASCU | PA-18A Super Cub 150 | Farm Aviation Services Ltd |
| | G-ASCZ | CP.301A Emeraude | Hylton Flying Group/Newcastle |
| | G-ASDF | Edwards Gyrocopter ★ | B. King |
| | G-ASDK | A.61 Terrier 2 | M. L. Rose |
| | G-ASDL | A.61 Terrier 2 | T. J. Rilley & C. E. Mason |
| | G-ASDO | Beech 95-A55 Baron ★ | No 2498 Sqn ATC/Jersey |
| | G-ASDY | Wallis WA-116/F | K. H. Wallis |
| | G-ASEA | Luton LA-4A Minor | G. C. Jones |
| | G-ASEB | Luton LA-4A Minor | S. R. P. Harper |
| | G-ASEG | A.61 Terrier (VF548) | R. S. O. B. Evans & J. P. P. A. Midgley |
| | G-ASEO | PA-24 Comanche 250 | Planetalk Ltd |
| | G-ASEP | PA-23 Apache 235 | Arrowstate Ltd/Denham |
| | G-ASEU | D.62A Condor | W. Grant & D. McNicholl |
| | G-ASFA | Cessna 172D | The Dakota Flying Club/Cranfield |
| | G-ASFD | L-200A Morava | M. Emery/Bournemouth |
| | G-ASFK | J/5G Autocar | R. W. & M. Struth |
| | G-ASFL | PA-28 Cherokee 180 | D. F. Ranger/Popham |
| | G-ASFR | Bo.208A1 Junior | S. T. Dauncey |
| | G-ASFX | D.31 Turbulent | E. F. Clapham & W. B. S. Dobie |
| | G-ASGC | V.1151 Super VC10 ★ | Duxford Aviation Soc |
| | G-ASHA | Cessna F.172D | R. Soar & ptnrs |
| | G-ASHB | Cessna 182F | Sport Parachute Centre Ltd/Tilstock |
| | G-ASHD | Brantly B-2A ★ | International Helicopter Museum/ Weston-s-Mare |
| | G-ASHH | PA-23 Aztec 250 | Leicestershire Thread & Trimming Manufacturers Ltd/Sibson |
| | G-ASHS | SNCAN Stampe SV-4B | Three Point Flying Ltd |
| | G-ASHT | D.31 Turbulent | C. W. N. Huke |
| | G-ASHU | PA-15 Vagabond | G. J. Romanes |
| | G-ASHV | PA-23 Aztec 250B | R. J. Ashley & G. O'Gorman |
| | G-ASHX | PA-28 Cherokee 180 | Sunsaver Ltd |
| | G-ASIB | Cessna F.172D | G-ASIB Flying Group |
| | G-ASII | PA-28 Cherokee 180 | T. R. Hart & Natocars Ltd |
| | G-ASIJ | PA-28 Cherokee 180 | Precision Products Ltd & D. Beadle |
| | G-ASIL | PA-28 Cherokee 180 | N. M. Barker & ptnrs/Leicester |
| | G-ASIS | Jodel D.112 | E. F. Hazel |

| Reg. | Type | Owner or Operator | Notes |
|------|------|-------------------|-------|
| G-ASIT | Cessna 180 | A. & P. A. Wood | |
| G-ASIY | PA-25 Pawnee 235 | RAFGSA/Bicester | |
| G-ASJC | BAC One-Eleven 201AC | British Air Ferries Ltd/Southend | |
| G-ASJL | Beech H.35 Bonanza | Robert Hinton & Ptnrs Ltd | |
| G-ASJM | PA-30 Twin Comanche 160 ★ | Via Nova Ltd (stored) | |
| G-ASJO | Beech B.23 Musketeer | M. Corbett & B. Hamilton | |
| G-ASJV | V.S.361 Spitfire IX (MH434) | Nalfire Aviation Ltd/Duxford | |
| G-ASJY | GY-80 Horizon 160 | Horizon Flyers Ltd/Denham | |
| G-ASJZ | Jodel D.117A | J. M. Gough/Barton | |
| G-ASKC | D.H.98 Mosquito 35 (TA719) ★ | Skyfame Collection/Duxford | |
| G-ASKH | D.H.98 Mosquito T.3 (RR299) | British Aerospace PLC/Chester | |
| G-ASKJ | A.61 Terrier 1 | N. K. & M. D. Freestone | |
| G-ASKK | HPR-7 Herald 211 ★ | Norwich Aviation Museum | |
| G-ASKL | Jodel D.150A | J. M. Graty | |
| G-ASKP | D.H.82A Tiger Moth | Tiger Club (1990) Ltd/Headcorn | |
| G-ASKS | Cessna 336 Skymaster | M. J. Godwin | |
| G-ASKT | PA-28 Cherokee 180 | A. Mattacks & T. Hood | |
| G-ASKV | PA-25 Pawnee 235 | Southdown Gliding Club Ltd | |
| G-ASLF | Bensen B.7 | S. R. Hughes | |
| G-ASLH | Cessna 182F | R. W. Boote | |
| G-ASLK | PA-25 Pawnee 235 | Bristol Gliding Club (Pty) Ltd/ Nympsfield | |
| G-ASLL | Cessna 336 ★ | stored/Bournemouth | |
| G-ASLR | Agusta-Bell 47J-2 | Leeds & Manchester Group Ltd | |
| G-ASLV | PA-28 Cherokee 235 | C.S.E. Aviation Ltd/Kidlington | |
| G-ASLX | CP.301A Emeraude | K. C. Green/Panshanger | |
| G-ASMA | PA-30 Twin Comanche 160 C/R | B. D. Glynn/Redhill | |
| G-ASMC | P.56 Provost T.1. | W. Walker (stored) | |
| G-ASME | Bensen B.8M | D. A. Farnworth | |
| G-ASMF | Beech D.95A Travel Air | Hawk Aviation Ltd | |
| G-ASMJ | Cessna F.172E | J. E. Tribe & Z. W. Jakubowski/ Audley End | |
| G-ASML | Luton LA-4A Minor | R. L. E. Horrell | |
| G-ASMM | D.31 Tubulent | G. E. Arthur | |
| G-ASMO | PA-23 Apache 160G ★ | Aviation Enterprises/Fairoaks | |
| G-ASMS | Cessna 150A | K. R. & T. W. Davies | |
| G-ASMT | Fairtravel Linnet 2 | A. F. Cashin | |
| G-ASMU | Cessna 150D | Telepoint Ltd/Barton | |
| G-ASMV | CP.1310-C3 Super Emeraude | P. F. D. Waltham/Leicester | |
| G-ASMW | Cessna 150D | Yorkshire Light Aircraft Ltd/Leeds | |
| G-ASMY | PA-23 Apache 160H | Hanseviter Aviation/Ipswich | |
| G-ASMZ | A.61 Terrier 2 (VF516) | R. C. Burden | |
| G-ASNB | Auster 6A (VX118) | M. Pocock & ptnrs | |
| G-ASNC | D.5/180 Husky | Peterborough & Spalding Gliding Club/ Boston | |
| G-ASND | PA-23 Aztec 250 | Commercial Air (Woking) Ltd/ Fairoaks | |
| G-ASNE | PA-28 Cherokee 180 | J. L. Dexter | |
| G-ASNH | PA-23 Aztec 250B | J. Hoerner & The Earl of Suffolk & Berkshire | |
| G-ASNI | CP.1310-C3 Super Emeraude | D. Chapman | |
| G-ASNK | Cessna 205 | Justgold Ltd | |
| G-ASNU | H.S.125 Srs. 1 | Flintgrange Ltd | |
| G-ASNW | Cessna F.172E | J. A. Gibbs | |
| G-ASNY | Bensen B.8M | D. L. Wallis | |
| G-ASNZ | Bensen B.8M | W. H. Turner | |
| G-ASOC | Auster 6A | J. A. Rayment/Finmere | |
| G-ASOH | Beech 95-B55A Baron | GMD Group | |
| G-ASOI | A.61 Terrier 2 | D. I. H. Johnstone | |
| G-ASOK | Cessna F.172E | Okay Flying Group/Denham | |
| G-ASON | PA-30 Twin Comanche 160 | Follandbeech Ltd | |
| G-ASOO | PA-30 Twin Comanche 160 | K. H. Acketts | |
| G-ASOP | Sopwith F.1 Camel (B6291) | K. C. D. St Cyrien/Middle Wallop | |
| G-ASOX | Cessna 205A | Border Parachute Centre | |
| G-ASPF | Jodel D.120 | W. S. Howell | |
| G-ASPI | Cessna F.172E | Icarus Flying Group/Rochester | |
| G-ASPK | PA-28 Cherokee 140 | Westward Airways (Lands End) Ltd/ St Just | |
| G-ASPP | Bristol Boxkite replica | Shuttleworth Trust/O. Warden | |
| G-ASPS | Piper J-3C-90 Cub | A. J. Chalkley/Blackbushe | |
| G-ASPU | D.31 Turbulent | I. Maclennan | |
| G-ASPV | D.H.82A Tiger Moth | B. S. Charters/Shipdham | |
| G-ASRB | D.62B Condor | T. J. McRae & H. C. Palmer/Shoreham | |

| Notes | Reg. | Type | Owner or Operator |
|---|---|---|---|
| | G-ASRC | D.62B Condor | J. Knight |
| | G-ASRF | Jenny Wren | G. W. Gowland (stored) |
| | G-ASRH | PA-30 Twin Comanche 160 | Island Aviation & Travel Ltd |
| | G-ASRI | PA-23 Aztec 250B ★ | Graham Collins Associates Ltd |
| | G-ASRK | A.109 Airedale ★ | R. Skingley |
| | G-ASRO | PA-30 Twin Comanche 160 | D. W. Blake |
| | G-ASRR | Cessna 182G | M. A. Hales |
| | G-ASRT | Jodel D.150 | H. M. Kendall |
| | G-ASRW | PA-28 Cherokee 180 | Astro Electrical & Heating Ltd/ Shoreham |
| | G-ASSB | PA-30 Twin Comanche 160 | J. D. Crinnan |
| | G-ASSE | PA-22 Colt 108 | J. B. King/Goodwood |
| | G-ASSF | Cessna 182G Skylane | Burbage Farms Ltd/Lutterworth |
| | G-ASSP | PA-30 Twin Comanche 160 | P. H. Tavener |
| | G-ASSR | PA-30 Twin Comanche 160 | Rangebury Ltd |
| | G-ASSS | Cessna 172E | D. H. N. Squires & P. R. March/Bristol |
| | G-ASST | Cessna 150D | F. R. H. Parker |
| | G-ASSU | CP.301A Emeraude | R. W. Millward (stored)/Redhill |
| | G-ASSW | PA-28 Cherokee 140 | C. J. Plummer/Biggin Hill |
| | G-ASTA | D.31 Turbulent | R. N. Steel |
| | G-ASTH | Mooney M.20C ★ | E. Martin (stored) |
| | G-ASTI | Auster 6A | M. Pocock |
| | G-ASTL | Fairey Firefly 1 (Z2033) ★ | Skyfame Collection/Duxford |
| | G-ASTP | Hiller UH-12C ★ | International Helicopter Museum/ Weston-s-Mare |
| | G-ASTV | Cessna 150D (tailwheel) ★ | stored |
| | G-ASUB | Mooney M.20E Super 21 | P. K. Pemberton |
| | G-ASUD | PA-28 Cherokee 180 | S. E. Hobbs & Co Ltd |
| | G-ASUE | Cessna 150D | D. Huckle/Panshanger |
| | G-ASUG | Beech E18S ★ | Museum of Flight/E. Fortune |
| | G-ASUI | A.61 Terrier 2 | K. W. Chigwell & D. R. Lee |
| | G-ASUL | Cessna 182G Skylane | Parafreight Ltd/Halfpenny Green |
| | G-ASUP | Cessna F.172E | GASUP Air/Cardiff |
| | G-ASUR | Dornier Do 28A-1 | Sheffair Ltd |
| | G-ASUS | Jurca MJ.2B Tempete | D. G. Jones/Coventry |
| | G-ASVG | CP.301B Emeraude | K. R. Jackson |
| | G-ASVM | Cessna F.172E | A. P. D. Hynes & ptnrs/Cambridge |
| | G-ASVN | Cessna U.206 Super Skywagon | British Skysports/Sibson |
| | G-ASVO | HPR-7 Herald 214 | British Air Ferries Ltd/Southend |
| | G-ASVP | PA-25 Pawnee 235 | Aquila Gliding Club Ltd |
| | G-ASVZ | PA-28 Cherokee 140 | P. Hatton |
| | G-ASWB | A.109 Airedale | C. Gene & G. Taylor/Teesside |
| | G-ASWH | Luton LA-5A Major | R. T. Callow |
| | G-ASWJ | Beagle 206 Srs 1 (8449M) ★ | RAF Halton |
| | G-ASWL | Cessna F.172F | Bagby Aviation Flying Group |
| | G-ASWN | Bensen B.8M | D. R. Shepherd |
| | G-ASWP | Beech A.23 Musketeer | H. Mendelssohn & ptnrs/Edinburgh |
| | G-ASWW | PA-30 Twin Comanche 160 | Bristol & Wessex Flying Club Ltd |
| | G-ASWX | PA-28 Cherokee 180 | A. F. Dadds |
| | G-ASXC | SIPA 901 | M. K. Dartford |
| | G-ASXD | Brantly B.2B | Lousada PLC |
| | G-ASXI | Tipsy T.66 Nipper 3 | P. F. J. Wells |
| | G-ASXJ | Luton LA-4A Minor | J. S. Allison/Halton |
| | G-ASXR | Cessna 210 | T. W. King & A. Schofield |
| | G-ASXS | Jodel DR.1050 | R. A. Hunter |
| | G-ASXU | Jodel D.120A | G. W. Worley |
| | G-ASXX | Avro 683 Lancaster 7 (NX611) ★ | Lincolnshire Aviation Heritage Centre/ E. Kirkby |
| | G-ASXY | Jodel D.117A | P. A. Davies & ptnrs/Cardiff |
| | G-ASXZ | Cessna 182G Skylane | P. M. Robertson/Perth |
| | G-ASYD | BAC One-Eleven 670 | British Aerospace |
| | G-ASYG | A.61 Terrier 2 ★ | stored/Hinton-in-the-Hedges |
| | G-ASYJ | Beech D.95A Travel Air | Crosby Aviation (Jersey) Ltd |
| | G-ASYK | PA-30 Twin Comanche 160 | M. S. Harvell |
| | G-ASYL | Cessna 150E | D. Mallinson |
| | G-ASYP | Cessna 150E | Henlow Flying Group |
| | G-ASYW | Bell 47G-2 | Bristow Helicopters Ltd |
| | G-ASYZ | Victa Airtourer 100 | N. C. Grayson |
| | G-ASZB | Cessna 150E | W. A. Smale/Exeter |
| | G-ASZD | Bo 208A2 Junior | A. J. Watson & ptnrs/O. Warden |
| | G-ASZE | A.61 Terrier 2 | P. J. Moore |
| | G-ASZJ | S.C.7 Skyvan 3A-100 | GEC Avionics Ltd/Luton |
| | G-ASZR | Fairtravel Linnet | H. C. D. & F. J. Garner |

| Reg. | Type | Owner or Operator | Notes |
|------|------|-------------------|-------|
| G-ASZS | GY.80 Horizon 160 | J. M. B. Duncan | |
| G-ASZU | Cessna 150E | T. H. Milburn | |
| G-ASZV | Tipsy T.66 Nipper 2 | R. L. Mitcham/Elstree | |
| G-ASZX | A.61 Terrier 1 | C. A. Bailey | |
| G-ATAD | Mooney M.20C | C. Ridout | |
| G-ATAF | Cessna F.172F | S. Lancashire Flyers Ltd | |
| G-ATAG | Jodel DR.1050 | R. J. Keyte | |
| G-ATAI | D.H.104 Dove 8 | L. A. Wootton/France | |
| G-ATAS | PA-28 Cherokee 180 | E. J. Titterrell | |
| G-ATAT | Cessna 150E | The Derek Pointon Group (stored) | |
| G-ATAU | D.62B Condor | M. A. Peare/Redhill | |
| G-ATAV | D.62C Condor | The Condor Syndicate | |
| G-ATBF | F-86E Sabre 4 (XB733) ★ | T. Bracewell (stored) | |
| G-ATBG | Nord 1002 (17) | L. M. Walton | |
| G-ATBH | Aero 145 | P. D. Aberbach | |
| G-ATBI | Beech A.23 Musketeer | R. F. G. Dent/Staverton | |
| G-ATBJ | Sikorsky S-61N | British International Helicopters Ltd | |
| G-ATBL | D.H.60G Moth | J. J. V. Elwes | |
| G-ATBP | Fournier RF-3 | Dishforth Flying Group | |
| G-ATBS | D.31 Turbulent | D. R. Keene & J. A. Lear | |
| G-ATBU | A.61 Terrier 2 | P. R. Anderson | |
| G-ATBW | Tipsy T.66 Nipper 2 | Stapleford Nipper Group | |
| G-ATBX | PA-20 Pacer 135 | G. D. & P. M. Thomson | |
| G-ATBZ | W.S.58 Wessex 60 ★ | International Helicopter Museum/ Weston-s-Mare | |
| G-ATCC | A.109 Airedale | J. F. Moore & ptnrs/Biggin Hill | |
| G-ATCD | D.5/180 Husky | Oxford Flying & Gliding Group/Enstone | |
| G-ATCE | Cessna U.206 | J. Fletcher & D. Hickling/Langar | |
| G-ATCI | Victa Airtourer 100 | B. & C. Building Materials (Canvey Island) Ltd | |
| G-ATCJ | Luton LA-4A Minor | R. M. Sharphouse | |
| G-ATCL | Victa Airtourer 100 | A. D. Goodall | |
| G-ATCN | Luton LA-4A Minor | J. C. Gates & C. Neilson | |
| G-ATCR | Cessna 310 ★ | ITD Aviation Ltd/Denham | |
| G-ATCU | Cessna 337 | University of Cambridge | |
| G-ATCX | Cessna 182H Skylane | K. J. Fisher/Bodmin | |
| G-ATDA | PA-28 Cherokee 160 | Global Aircraft Services Ltd | |
| G-ATDB | Nord 1101 Noralpha | J. B. Jackson/Prestwick | |
| G-ATDN | A.61 Terrier 2 (TW641) | S. J. Saggers/Biggin Hill | |
| G-ATDO | Bo 208C Junior | H. Swift | |
| G-ATEF | Cessna 150E | Swans Aviation | |
| G-ATEG | Cessna 150E | A. W. Woodward/Biggin Hill | |
| G-ATEK | H.S. 748 Srs 2B | STH Sales Ltd | |
| G-ATEM | PA-28 Cherokee 180 | Chiltern Valley Aviation Ltd | |
| G-ATEP | EAA Biplane ★ | E. L. Martin (stored)/Guernsey | |
| G-ATES | PA-32 Cherokee Six 260 ★ | Parachute jump trainer/Ipswich | |
| G-ATET | PA-30 Twin Comanche 160 | P. W. Bayliss | |
| G-ATEV | Jodel DR.1050 | B. A. Mills & G. W. Payne | |
| G-ATEW | PA-30 Twin Comanche 160 | Air Northumbria Group/Newcastle | |
| G-ATEX | Victa Airtourer 100 | Medway Victa Group | |
| G-ATEZ | PA-28 Cherokee 140 | J. A. Burton/E. Midlands | |
| G-ATFD | Jodel DR.1050 | V. Usher | |
| G-ATFF | PA-23 Aztec 250C | Neatspin Ltd | |
| G-ATFG | Brantly B.2B ★ | Museum of Flight/E. Fortune | |
| G-ATFK | PA-30 Twin Comanche 160 | D. J. Crinnon/White Waltham | |
| G-ATFM | Sikorsky S-61N | British International Helicopters Ltd/ Aberdeen | |
| G-ATFR | PA-25 Pawnee 150 | R. R. Harris | |
| G-ATFU | D.H.85 Leopard Moth | A. H. Carrington & C. D. Duthy-James | |
| G-ATFV | Agusta-Bell 47J-2A | Alexander Warren & Co Ltd | |
| G-ATFW | Luton LA-4A Minor | C. Kirk | |
| G-ATFX | Cessna F.172G | Isabella Properties Ltd | |
| G-ATFY | Cessna F.172G | H. Bennett & P. McCabe | |
| G-ATGE | Jodel DR.1050 | J. R. Roberts | |
| G-ATGH | Brantly B.2B | Helihire Ltd | |
| G-ATGN | Thorn Coal Gas balloon | British Balloon Museum | |
| G-ATGO | Cessna F.172G | M. Scott | |
| G-ATGP | Jodel DR.1050 | N. J. Heaton/Sherburn | |
| G-ATGY | GY.80 Horizon | P. W. Gibberson/Birmingham | |
| G-ATGZ | Griffiths GH-4 Gyroplane | G. Griffiths | |
| G-ATHA | PA-23 Apache 235 ★ | Brunel Technical College/Bristol | |
| G-ATHD | D.H.C.1 Chipmunk 22 (WP971) | Spartan Flying Group Ltd/Denham | |

| Notes | Reg. | Type | Owner or Operator |
|-------|------|------|-------------------|
| | G-ATHF | Cessna 150F ★ | Lincolnshire Aircraft Museum |
| | G-ATHG | Cessna 150F | Humberside Police Flying Club |
| | G-ATHI | PA-28 Cherokee 180 ★ | *Instructional airframe*/Dublin |
| | G-ATHK | Aeronca 7AC Champion | A. Corran |
| | G-ATHM | Wallis WA-116 Srs 1 | Wallis Autogyros Ltd |
| | G-ATHN | Nord 1101 Noralpha | E. L. Martin (*stored*)/Guernsey |
| | G-ATHR | PA-28 Cherokee 180 | Britannia Airways Ltd/Luton |
| | G-ATHT | Victa Airtourer 115 | H. C. G. Munroe |
| | G-ATHU | A.61 Terrier 1 | J. A. L. Irwin |
| | G-ATHV | Cessna 150F | P. Cooper |
| | G-ATHX | Jodel DR. 100A | A. D. Massey & R. C. Hibberd |
| | G-ATHZ | Cessna 150F | E. & R. D. Forster |
| | G-ATIA | PA-24 Comanche 260 | L. A. Brown |
| | G-ATIC | Jodel DR.1050 ★ | *stored* |
| | G-ATID | Cessna 337 | M. R. Tarrant/Bourn |
| | G-ATIE | Cessna 150F ★ | *Parachute jump trainer*/Chetwynd |
| | G-ATIG | HPR-7 Herald 214 | Janes Aviation Ltd/Blackpool |
| | G-ATIN | Jodel D.117 | D. R. Upton & J. G. Kay/Barton |
| | G-ATIR | AIA Stampe SV-4C | N. M. Bloom |
| | G-ATIS | PA-28 Cherokee 160 | S. Boon |
| | G-ATIZ | Jodel D.117 | R. Frith & ptnrs |
| | G-ATJA | Jodel DR.1050 | Bicester Flying Group |
| | G-ATJC | Victa Airtourer 100 | D. G. Palmer & D. C. Giles/Glasgow |
| | G-ATJG | PA-28 Cherokee 140 | Royal Aircraft Establishment Dept/ Thurleigh |
| | G-ATJL | PA-24 Comanche 260 | M. J. Berry/Blackbushe |
| | G-ATJM | Fokker DR.1 replica (152/17) | R. Lamplough/Duxford |
| | G-ATJN | Jodel D.119 | R. F. Bradshaw |
| | G-ATJR | PA-E23 Aztec 250C | W. A. G. Willbond/Bourn |
| | G-ATJT | GY.80 Horizon 160 | P. J. Stephenson |
| | G-ATJV | PA-32 Cherokee Six 260 | SMK Engineers Ltd |
| | G-ATKF | Cessna 150F | A. F. G. Clutterbuck |
| | G-ATKH | Luton LA-4A Minor | H. E. Jenner |
| | G-ATKI | Piper J-3C-65 Cub | J. H. Allistone/Booker |
| | G-ATKS | Cessna F.172G | Blois Aviation Ltd |
| | G-ATKT | Cessna F.172G | P. J. Megson |
| | G-ATKU | Cessna F.172G | Heatherlake Ltd |
| | G-ATKX | Jodel D.140C | A. J. White & G. A. Piper/Biggin Hill |
| | G-ATKZ | Tipsy T.66 Nipper 2 | M. W. Knights |
| | G-ATLA | Cessna 182J Skylane | Shefford Transport Engineers Ltd/ Luton |
| | G-ATLB | Jodel DR.1050-M1 | G. A. P. Barlow |
| | G-ATLC | PA-23 Aztec 250C ★ | Alderney Air Charter Ltd (*stored*) |
| | G-ATLG | Hiller UH-12B | Bristow Helicopters Ltd |
| | G-ATLM | Cessna F.172G | Air Fotos Aviation Ltd/Newcastle |
| | G-ATLP | Bensen B.8M | C. D. Julian |
| | G-ATLT | Cessna U-206A | Army Parachute Association/ Netheravon |
| | G-ATLV | Jodel D.120 | W. H. Greenwood |
| | G-ATLW | PA-28 Cherokee 180 | Lima Whisky Flying Group |
| | G-ATMC | Cessna F.150F | C. J. & E. J. Leigh |
| | G-ATMG | M.S.893 Rallye Commodore 180 | D. R. Wilkinson & T. Coldwell |
| | G-ATMH | D.5/180 Husky | Devon & Somerset Gliding Club Ltd |
| | G-ATMI | H.S.748 Srs 2A | Dan-Air Services Ltd/Gatwick |
| | G-ATMJ | H.S.748 Srs 2A | Dan-Air Services Ltd/Gatwick |
| | G-ATML | Cessna F.150F | B. A. Pickers |
| | G-ATMM | Cessna F.150F | B. Powell |
| | G-ATMT | PA-30 Twin Comanche 160 | D. H. T. Bain/Newcastle |
| | G-ATMU | PA-23 Apache 160G | P. K. Martin & R. W. Harris |
| | G-ATMW | PA-28 Cherokee 140 | Bencray Ltd/Blackpool |
| | G-ATMX | Cessna F.150F | Action Aviation Ltd/Dunkeswell |
| | G-ATMY | Cessna 150F | C. F. Read/Doncaster |
| | G-ATNB | PA-28 Cherokee 180 | R. F. Hill |
| | G-ATNE | Cessna F.150F | J. & S. Brew |
| | G-ATNJ | Cessna F.150F ★ | *Instructional airframe*/Perth |
| | G-ATNK | Cessna F.150F | Pegasus Aviation Ltd |
| | G-ATNL | Cessna F.150F | S. M. Kemp & ptnrs |
| | G-ATNV | PA-24 Comanche 260 | B. S. Reynolds & P. R. Fortescue/Bourn |
| | G-ATNX | Cessna F.150F | P. Jenkins |
| | G-ATOA | PA-23 Apache 160G | K. White |
| | G-ATOD | Cessna F.150F | R. N. R. Bellamy & ptnrs/St Just |
| | G-ATOE | Cessna F.150F | S. Armstrong |
| | G-ATOF | Cessna F.150F ★ | *Instructional airframe*/Perth |

| Reg. | Type | Owner or Operator | Notes |
|------|------|-------------------|-------|
| G-ATOG | Cessna F-150F ★ | *Instructional airframe*/Perth | |
| G-ATOH | D.62B Condor | L. S. Thorne | |
| G-ATOI | PA-28 Cherokee 140 | O. & E. Flying Ltd/Stapleford | |
| G-ATOJ | PA-28 Cherokee 140 | Firefly Aviation Ltd/Glasgow | |
| G-ATOK | PA-28 Cherokee 140 | J. R. Hewitt & P. Marlow | |
| G-ATOL | PA-28 Cherokee 140 | L. J. Nation & G. Alford | |
| G-ATOM | PA-28 Cherokee 140 | R. P. Synge & R. W. Mason/Kidlington | |
| G-ATON | PA-28 Cherokee 140 | R. G. Walters | |
| G-ATOO | PA-28 Cherokee 140 ★ | *Instructional airframe*/Moston Centre | |
| G-ATOP | PA-28 Cherokee 140 | P. R. Coombs/Blackbushe | |
| G-ATOR | PA-28 Cherokee 140 | D. Palmer & V. G. Whitehead | |
| G-ATOS | PA-28 Cherokee 140 | Matthews Air Trading Services | |
| G-ATOT | PA-28 Cherokee 180 | J. B. Waterfield & G. L. Birch | |
| G-ATOU | Mooney M.20E Super 21 | P. R. & M. R. Parr | |
| G-ATOY | PA-24 Comanche 260 ★ | Museum of Flight/E. Fortune | |
| G-ATOZ | Bensen B.8M | J. Jordan | |
| G-ATPD | H.S.125 Srs 1B | G. M. Kay | |
| G-ATPM | Cessna F.150F | Dan-Air Flying Club/Lasham | |
| G-ATPN | PA-28 Cherokee 140 | M. F. Hatt & ptnrs/Southend | |
| G-ATPT | Cessna 182J Skylane | Western Models Ltd/Redhill | |
| G-ATPV | JB.01 Minicab | B. Jones | |
| G-ATRA | LET L.13 Blanik | Blanik Sydincate | |
| G-ATRC | Beech B.95A Travel Air | P. J. Simmons | |
| G-ATRG | PA-18 Super Cub 150 | Lasham Gliding Soc Ltd | |
| G-ATRI | Bo 208C Junior | Chertwood Ltd | |
| G-ATRK | Cessna F.150F | J. Rees & F. Doncaster | |
| G-ATRL | Cessna F.150F | S. S. Delwarte/Shoreham | |
| G-ATRO | PA-28 Cherokee 140 | 390th Flying Group | |
| G-ATRR | PA-28 Cherokee 140 | Manx Flyers Aero Club Ltd | |
| G-ATRW | PA-32 Cherokee Six 260 | Pictex Ltd | |
| G-ATRX | PA-32 Cherokee Six 260 | J. W. Stow | |
| G-ATSI | Bo 208C Junior | D. L. Swallow | |
| G-ATSL | Cessna F.172G | D. Le Cheminant/Guernsey | |
| G-ATSM | Cessna 337A | Tremlett (Skicraft) Ltd | |
| G-ATSR | Beech M.35 Bonanza | Alstan Aviation Ltd | |
| G-ATSU | Jodel D.140B | B. M. O'Brien & P. J. Sellar | |
| G-ATSX | Bo 208C Junior | R. J. C. Campbell & M. H. Goley | |
| G-ATSY | Wassmer WA41 Super Baladou IV | Baladou Flying Group | |
| G-ATTB | Wallis WA-116-1 (XR944) | D. A. Wallis | |
| G-ATTD | Cessna 182J Skylane | K. M. Brennan & ptnrs | |
| G-ATTF | PA-28 Cherokee 140 | D. H. Fear | |
| G-ATTG | PA-28 Cherokee 140 | Arrow Air Services Engineering Ltd/ Shipdham | |
| G-ATTI | PA-28 Cherokee 140 | Parry & Co/Bristol | |
| G-ATTK | PA-28 Cherokee 140 | G-ATTK Flying Group/Southend | |
| G-ATTM | Jodel DR.250-160 | R. W. Tomkinson | |
| G-ATTP | BAC One-Eleven 207AJ | Dan-Air Services Ltd/Gatwick | |
| G-ATTR | Bo 208C Junior 3 | S. Luck | |
| G-ATTU | PA-28 Cherokee 140 | Lion Flying Group/Elstree | |
| G-ATTV | PA-28 Cherokee 140 | D. R. Winder | |
| G-ATTX | PA-28 Cherokee 180 | Ipac Aviation Flying Group | |
| G-ATTY | PA-32 Cherokee Six 260 | F. J. Wadia | |
| G-ATUB | PA-28 Cherokee 140 | R. H. Partington & M. J. Porter | |
| G-ATUD | PA-28 Cherokee 140 | E. J. Clempson | |
| G-ATUF | Cessna F.150F | A. R. Hawes/Ipswich | |
| G-ATUG | D.62B Condor | C. B. Marsh & D. J. R. Williams | |
| G-ATUH | Tipsy T.66 Nipper 1 | A. R. Lemmon | |
| G-ATUI | Bo 208C Junior | A. W. Wakefield | |
| G-ATUL | PA-28 Cherokee 180 | H. M. Synge | |
| G-ATVF | D.H.C.1 Chipmunk 22 | RAFGSA/Dishforth | |
| G-ATVH | BAC One-Eleven 207AJ | Dan-Air Services Ltd/Gatwick | |
| G-ATVK | PA-28 Cherokee 140 | JRB Aviation Ltd/Southend | |
| G-ATVL | PA-28 Cherokee 140 | West London Aero Services Ltd/White Waltham | |
| G-ATVO | PA-28 Cherokee 140 | Firefly Aviation Ltd/Glasgow | |
| G-ATVP | F.B.5 Gunbus (2345) ★ | RAF Museum/Hendon | |
| G-ATVS | PA-28 Cherokee 180 | I. J. & M. Foster-Thorne | |
| G-ATVW | D.62B Condor | J. P. Coulter & J. Chidley/Panshanger | |
| G-ATVX | Bo 208C Junior | G. & G. E. F. Warren | |
| G-ATWA | Jodel DR.1050 | Jodel Syndicate | |
| G-ATWB | Jodel D.117 | W. Bampton & ptnrs | |
| G-ATWE | M.S.892A Rallye Commodore | D. I. Murray | |

| Notes | Reg. | Type | Owner or Operator |
|-------|------|------|-------------------|
| | G-ATWJ | Cessna F.172F | C. J. & J. Freeman/Headcorn |
| | G-ATWP | Alon A-2 Aircoupe | H. Dodd & I. Wilson |
| | G-ATWR | PA-30 Twin Comanche 160B | Lubair (Transport Services) Ltd E. Midlands |
| | G-ATXA | PA-22 Tri-Pacer 150 | R. C. Teverson |
| | G-ATXD | PA-30 Twin Comanche 160B | Jet Heritage Ltd/Bournemouth |
| | G-ATXF | GY-80 Horizon 150 | D. C. Hyde |
| | G-ATXJ | H.P.137 Jetstream 300 ★ | British Aerospace (display mock-up)/ Prestwick |
| | G-ATXM | PA-28 Cherokee 180 | J. Khan/Ipswich |
| | G-ATXN | Mitchell-Proctor Kittiwake | C. Dews |
| | G-ATXO | SIPA 903 | M. Hillam/Sherburn |
| | G-ATXZ | Bo 208C Junior | J. Dyson & M. Hutchinson |
| | G-ATYM | Cessna F.150G | J. F. Perry & Co |
| | G-ATYN | Cessna F.150G | Skegness Air Taxi Services Ltd |
| | G-ATYS | PA-28 Cherokee 180 | R. V. Waite |
| | G-ATZA | Bo 208C Junior | Skyward Services Ltd/Jersey |
| | G-ATZG | AFB2 gas balloon | Flt Lt S. Cameron Aeolis |
| | G-ATZK | PA-28 Cherokee 180 | R. W. Nash & J. A. Gibbs/Kidlington |
| | G-ATZM | Piper J-3C-65 Cub | R. W. Davison |
| | G-ATZS | Wassmer WA41 Super Baladou IV | G. R. Outwin & D. P. Bennett |
| | G-ATZY | Cessna F.150G | P. P. D. Howard-Johnston/Edinburgh |
| | G-ATZZ | Cessna F.150G | Matthews Air Trading Services/Southend |
| | G-AVAA | Cessna F.150G | LAR Aviation Ltd/Shoreham |
| | G-AVAK | M.S.893A Rallye Commodore 180 | W. K. Anderson (stored)/Perth |
| | G-AVAP | Cessna F.150G | Seawing Flying Club Ltd/Southend |
| | G-AVAR | Cessna F.150G | J. A. Rees & F. Doncaster |
| | G-AVAU | PA-30 Twin Comanche 160B | L. Batin/Fairoaks |
| | G-AVAW | D.62B Condor | Avato Flying Group |
| | G-AVAX | PA-28 Cherokee 180 | J. J. Parkes |
| | G-AVBG | PA-28 Cherokee 180 | Transknight Group |
| | G-AVBH | PA-28 Cherokee 180 | T. R. Smith (Agricultural Machinery) Ltd |
| | G-AVBP | PA-28 Cherokee 140 | Bristol & Wessex Aeroplane Club |
| | G-AVBS | PA-28 Cherokee 180 | G. W. Atkins/St Just |
| | G-AVBT | PA-28 Cherokee 180 | P. O. Hire & D. J. Spicer/Denham |
| | G-AVBZ | Cessna F.172H | M. G. Hill |
| | G-AVCE | Cessna F.172H | A. Surr |
| | G-AVCM | PA-24 Comanche 260 | F. Smith & Sons Ltd/Stapleford |
| | G-AVCS | A.61 Terrier 1 | A. Topen/Cranfield |
| | G-AVCT | Cessna F.150G | Shobdon Aircraft Maintenance |
| | G-AVCU | Cessna F.150G | P. R. Moss/Alderney |
| | G-AVCV | Cessna 182J Skylane | University of Manchester Institute of Science & Technology/Woodford |
| | G-AVCX | PA-30 Twin Comanche 160B | T. Barge |
| | G-AVCY | PA-30 Twin Comanche 160B | R. C. Pugsley/Cardiff |
| | G-AVDA | Cessna 182K Skylane | J. W. Grant |
| | G-AVDF | Beagle Pup 100 ★ | Shoreham Airport Museum |
| | G-AVDG | Wallis WA-116 Srs 1 | K. H. Wallis |
| | G-AVDT | Aeronca 7AC Champion | D. Cheney & J. G. Woods |
| | G-AVDV | PA-22 Tri-Pacer 150 (modified to Pacer) | S. C. Brooks/Slinfold |
| | G-AVDW | D.62B Condor | Essex Aviation/Andrewsfield |
| | G-AVDY | Luton LA-4A Minor | D. E. Evans & ptnrs |
| | G-AVEB | Morane MS 230 (157) | T. McG. Leaver |
| | G-AVEC | Cessna F.172H | W. H. Ekin (Engineering) Co Ltd |
| | G-AVEF | Jodel D.150 | Tiger Club (1990) Ltd/Headcorn |
| | G-AVEH | SIAI-Marchetti S.205 | B. Thaler/Booker |
| | G-AVEM | Cessna F.150G | P. Brown |
| | G-AVEN | Cessna F.150G | N. J. Budd/Aberdeen |
| | G-AVEO | Cessna F.150G | H. I. Matthews/Southend |
| | G-AVER | Cessna F.150G | Telepoint Ltd/Manchester |
| | G-AVET | Beech 95-C55A Baron | Westways Developments Ltd |
| | G-AVEU | Wassmer WA.41 Baladou | Baladou Flying Group |
| | G-AVEX | D.62B Condor | Cotswold Roller Hire Ltd/Long Marston |
| | G-AVEY | Currie Super Wot | A. Eastelow/Dunkeswell |
| | G-AVEZ | HPR-7 Herald 210 ★ | Rescue Trainer/Norwich |
| | G-AVFB | H.S.121 Trident 2E ★ | Duxford Aviation Soc |
| | G-AVFE | H.S.121 Trident 2E ★ | Belfast Airport Authority |
| | G-AVFG | H.S.121 Trident 2E ★ | Ground handling trainer/Heathrow |
| | G-AVFH | H.S.121 Trident 2E ★ | Mosquito Aircraft Museum (Fuselage only) |

| Reg. | Type | Owner or Operator | Notes |
|------|------|-------------------|-------|
| G-AVFK | H.S.121 Trident 2E ★ | Metropolitan Police Training Centre/ Hounslow | |
| G-AVFM | H.S.121 Trident 2E ★ | Brunel Technical College/Bristol | |
| G-AVFP | PA-28 Cherokee 140 | H. D. Vince Ltd/Woodvale | |
| G-AVFR | PA-28 Cherokee 140 | VFR Flying Group/Newtownards | |
| G-AVFS | PA-32 Cherokee Six 300 | Comed Aviation Ltd/Blackpool | |
| G-AVFU | PA-32 Cherokee Six 300 | Couesnon Ltd/Biggin Hill | |
| G-AVFX | PA-28 Cherokee 140 | D. J. Young & H. Weldon | |
| G-AVFY | PA-28 Cherokee 140 | D. R. Davidson/Bournemouth | |
| G-AVFZ | PA-28 Cherokee 140 | R. S. Littlechild & V. B. G. Childs | |
| G-AVGA | PA-24 Comanche 260 | C. Matthews & V. R. Dennay | |
| G-AVGB | PA-28 Cherokee 140 | D. J. Hill/Fowlmere | |
| G-AVGC | PA-28 Cherokee 140 | P. A. Hill | |
| G-AVGD | PA-28 Cherokee 140 | S. & G. W. Jacobs | |
| G-AVGE | PA-28 Cherokee 140 | H. H. T. Wolf | |
| G-AVGH | PA-28 Cherokee 140 | Phoenix Aviation Services Ltd | |
| G-AVGI | PA-28 Cherokee 140 | D. G. Smith & C. D. Barden | |
| G-AVGJ | Jodel DR.1050 | S. T. Gilbert & D. J. Kirkwood | |
| G-AVGK | PA-28 Cherokee 180 | S. Crowden & J. Atkinson/Liverpool | |
| G-AVGP | BAC One-Eleven 408EF | Birmingham European Airways Ltd City of Coventry | |
| G-AVGV | Cessna F.150G | Bagby Aviation Flying Group | |
| G-AVGY | Cessna 182K Skylane | Clifford F. Cross (Wisbech) Ltd/Fenland | |
| G-AVGZ | Jodel DR.1050 | D. C. Webb | |
| G-AVHH | Cessna F.172H | M. J. Mann & J. Hickinbotom | |
| G-AVHL | Jodel DR.105A | G. L. Winterbourne/Redhill | |
| G-AVHM | Cessna F.150G | A. G. Wintle & J. Knight/Elstree | |
| G-AVHN | Cessna F.150F ★ | Brunel Technical College/Bristol | |
| G-AVHT | Auster AOP.9 (WZ711) | M. Somerton-Rayner/Middle Wallop | |
| G-AVHY | Fournier RF.4D | R. Swinn & J. Conolly | |
| G-AVIA | Cessna F.150G | Cheshire Air Training School (Merseyside) Ltd/Liverpool | |
| G-AVIB | Cessna F.150G | D. W. Horton/Humberside | |
| G-AVIC | Cessna F.172H | Pembrokeshire Air/Haverfordwest | |
| G-AVID | Cessna 182J | T. D. Boyle | |
| G-AVIE | Cessna F.172H | M. P. Parker | |
| G-AVII | AB-206A JetRanger | Bristow Helicopters Ltd | |
| G-AVIL | Alon A.2 Aircoupe | D. W. Vernon/Blackpool | |
| G-AVIN | M.S.880B Rallye Club | R. Wilcock | |
| G-AVIO | M.S.880B Rallye Club | H. Plain/Exeter | |
| G-AVIP | Brantly B.2B | P. J. Troy-Davies | |
| G-AVIS | Cessna F.172H | R. T. Jones/Rochester | |
| G-AVIT | Cessna F.150G | Shropshire Aero Club Ltd/Sleap | |
| G-AVIZ | Scheibe SF.25A Motorfalke | D. C. Pattison & D. A. Wilson | |
| G-AVJE | Cessna F.150G | P. R. Green & ptnrs/Booker | |
| G-AVJF | Cessna F.172H | J. A. & G. M. Rees | |
| G-AVJG | Cessna 337B | P. R. Moss/Bournemouth | |
| G-AVJI | Cessna F.172H | M. A. Kempson | |
| G-AVJJ | PA-30 Twin Comanche 160B | A. H. Manser | |
| G-AVJK | Jodel DR.1050 M.1 | G. Wylde | |
| G-AVJO | Fokker E.III Replica (422-15) | Personal Plane Services Ltd/Booker | |
| G-AVJV | Wallis WA-117 Srs 1 | K. H. Wallis (G-ATCV) | |
| G-AVJW | Wallis WA-118 Srs 2 | K. H. Wallis (G-ATPW) | |
| G-AVKB | MB.50 Pipistrelle | R. A. Fairclough | |
| G-AVKD | Fournier RF.4D | Lasham RF4 Group | |
| G-AVKE | Gadfly HDW.1 ★ | International Helicopter Museum/ Weston-s-Mare | |
| G-AVKG | Cessna F.172H | P. E. P. Sheppard | |
| G-AVKI | Slingsby T.66 Nipper 3 | J. Fisher | |
| G-AVKJ | Slingsby T.66 Nipper 3 | J. M. Greenway | |
| G-AVKK | Slingsby T.66 Nipper 3 | C. Watson | |
| G-AVKN | Cessna 401 | Law Leasing Ltd | |
| G-AVKP | A.109 Airedale | D. R. Williams | |
| G-AVKR | Bo 208C Junior | C. W. Grant | |
| G-AVKY | Hiller UH-12E | Agricopters Ltd/Chilbolton | |
| G-AVKZ | PA-23 Aztec 250C | AEW Engineering Co Ltd/Norwich | |
| G-AVLB | PA-28 Cherokee 140 | J. A. Overton Ltd/Andrewsfield | |
| G-AVLC | PA-28 Cherokee 140 | F. C. V. Hopkins/Swansea | |
| G-AVLD | PA-28 Cherokee 140 | WLS Flying Group/White Waltham | |
| G-AVLE | PA-28 Cherokee 140 | Video Security Services/Tollerton | |
| G-AVLF | PA-28 Cherokee 140 | G. H. Hughesdon | |
| G-AVLG | PA-28 Cherokee 140 | R. Friedlander & D. C. Raymond | |
| G-AVLH | PA-28 Cherokee 140 | P. Preece/Goodwood | |

| Notes | Reg. | Type | Owner or Operator |
|---|---|---|---|
| | G-AVLI | PA-28 Cherokee 140 | J. V. White |
| | G-AVLJ | PA-28 Cherokee 140 | E. Berks Boat Company Ltd |
| | G-AVLN | B.121 Pup 2 | C. A. Thorpe |
| | G-AVLO | Bo 208C Junior | J. A. Webb & K. F. Barnard/Popham |
| | G-AVLR | PA-28 Cherokee 140 | Group 140/Panshanger |
| | G-AVLT | PA-28 Cherokee 140 | R. W. Harris & ptnrs/Southend |
| | G-AVLU | PA-28 Cherokee 140 | London Transport (CRS) Sports Association Flying Club/Fairoaks |
| | G-AVLW | Fournier RF-4D | F. Mumford |
| | G-AVLY | Jodel D.120A | G-AVLY Flying Group |
| | G-AVMA | GY-80 Horizon 180 | B. R. Hildick |
| | G-AVMB | D.62B Condor | J. C. Mansell |
| | G-AVMD | Cessna 150G | Bagby Aviation Flying Group |
| | G-AVMF | Cessna F. 150G | J. F. Marsh & M. J. Oliver |
| | G-AVMH | BAC One-Eleven 510ED | British Airways *County of Cheshire*/Manchester |
| | G-AVMI | BAC One-Eleven 510ED | British Airways *County of Merseyside*/Manchester |
| | G-AVMJ | BAC One-Eleven 510ED | British Airways *Strathclyde Region*/Manchester |
| | G-AVMK | BAC One-Eleven 510ED | British Airways *County of Kent*/Manchester |
| | G-AVML | BAC One-Eleven 510ED | British Airways *County of Surrey*/Manchester |
| | G-AVMM | BAC One-Eleven 510ED | British Airways *County of Antrim*/Manchester |
| | G-AVMN | BAC One-Eleven 510ED | British Airways *County of Essex*/Manchester |
| | G-AVMO | BAC One-Eleven 510ED | British Airways *Lothian Region*/Manchester |
| | G-AVMP | BAC One-Eleven 510ED | British Airways *Bailiwick of Jersey*/Manchester |
| | G-AVMR | BAC One-Eleven 510ED | British Airways *County of Tyne & Wear*/Manchester |
| | G-AVMS | BAC One-Eleven 510ED | British Airways *County of West Sussex*/Manchester |
| | G-AVMT | BAC One-Eleven 510ED | British Airways *County of Berkshire*/Manchester |
| | G-AVMU | BAC One-Eleven 510ED | British Airways *County of Dorset*/Manchester |
| | G-AVMV | BAC One-Eleven 510ED | British Airways *Greater Manchester County*/Manchester |
| | G-AVMW | BAC One-Eleven 510ED | British Airways *Grampian Region*/Manchester |
| | G-AVMX | BAC One-Eleven 510ED | British Airways *County of East Sussex*/Manchester |
| | G-AVMY | BAC One-Eleven 510ED | British Airways *County of Derbyshire*/Manchester |
| | G-AVMZ | BAC One-Eleven 510ED | British Airways *County of Lancashire*/Manchester |
| | G-AVNC | Cessna F.150G | J. Turner |
| | G-AVNE | W.S.58 Wessex Mk 60 Srs 1 ★ | International Helicopter Museum/Weston-s-Mare |
| | G-AVNN | PA-28 Cherokee 180 | B. Andrews & C. S. Mitchell |
| | G-AVNO | PA-28 Cherokee 180 | Allister Flight Ltd/Stapleford |
| | G-AVNP | PA-28 Cherokee 180 | R. W. Harris & ptnrs |
| | G-AVNR | PA-28 Cherokee 180 | W. A. Webb & Co Ltd/Biggin Hill |
| | G-AVNS | PA-28 Cherokee 180 | I. J. Smith & B. S. Tufnell |
| | G-AVNU | PA-28 Cherokee 180 | Falcon Flying Services/Biggin Hill |
| | G-AVNW | PA-28 Cherokee 180 | Len Smith's School & Sports Ltd |
| | G-AVNX | Fournier RF-4D | Nymphsfield RF-4 Group |
| | G-AVNY | Fournier RF-4D | M. P. Dentith/Biggin Hill |
| | G-AVNZ | Fournier RF-4D | Aviation Special Developments (ASD) Ltd/Biggin Hill |
| | G-AVOA | Jodel DR.1050 | D. A. Willies/Cranwell |
| | G-AVOD | D.5/180 Husky | M. E. Taylor |
| | G-AVOH | D.62B Condor | D. F. Ranger/Popham |
| | G-AVOM | Jodel DR.221 | M. A. Mountford/Headcorn |
| | G-AVON | Luton LA-5A Major | G. R. Mee |
| | G-AVOO | PA-18 Super Cub 150 | London Gliding Club Ltd/Dunstable |
| | G-AVOZ | PA-28 Cherokee 180 | J. R. Winning/Booker |
| | G-AVPC | D.31 Turbulent | J. Sharp (*stored*) |

| Reg. | Type | Owner or Operator |
|------|------|-------------------|
| G-AVPD | D.9 Bebe | S. W. McKay (stored) |
| G-AVPH | Cessna F.150G | W. Lancashire Aero Club/Woodvale |
| G-AVPI | Cessna F.172H | R. W. Cope |
| G-AVPJ | D.H.82A Tiger Moth | C. C. Silk |
| G-AVPK | M.S.892A Rallye Commodore | B. A. Bridgewater/Halfpenny Green |
| G-AVPM | Jodel D.117 | J. Houghton/Brighton |
| G-AVPN | HPR-7 Herald 213 | British Air Ferries Ltd/Southend |
| G-AVPO | Hindustan HAL-26 Pushpak | J. C. Rimell |
| G-AVPR | PA-30 Twin Comanche 160B | Cold Storage (Jersey) Ltd |
| G-AVPS | PA-30 Twin Comanche 160B | J. M. Bisco/Staverton |
| G-AVPT | PA-18 Super Cub 150 | Tiger Club (1990) Ltd/Headcorn |
| G-AVPV | PA-28 Cherokee 180 | Robert Hinton & Partners Ltd |
| G-AVRK | PA-28 Cherokee 180 | S. R. Culley Developments Ltd & Macdillens Ltd |
| G-AVRN | Boeing 737-204 | Britannia Airways Ltd Capt James Cook/Luton |
| G-AVRP | PA-28 Cherokee 140 | T. Hiscox |
| G-AVRS | GY-80 Horizon 180 | Air Venturas Ltd |
| G-AVRT | PA-28 Cherokee 140 | R. S. Stopp |
| G-AVRU | PA-28 Cherokee 180 | G-AVRU Partnership/Clacton |
| G-AVRW | GY-20 Minicab | Kestrel Flying Group/Tollerton |
| G-AVRY | PA-28 Cherokee 180 | Brigfast Ltd/Blackbushe |
| G-AVRZ | PA-28 Cherokee 180 | Mantavia Group Ltd |
| G-AVSA | PA-28 Cherokee 180 | E. Barrow & J. Walker/Barton |
| G-AVSB | PA-28 Cherokee 180 | White House Garage Ashford Ltd |
| G-AVSC | PA-28 Cherokee 180 | Medidata Ltd |
| G-AVSD | PA-28 Cherokee 180 | Landmate Ltd |
| G-AVSE | PA-28 Cherokee 180 | Yorkshire Aeroplane Club Ltd/Leeds |
| G-AVSF | PA-28 Cherokee 180 | Monday Club |
| G-AVSI | PA-28 Cherokee 140 | CR Aviation Ltd |
| G-AVSP | PA-28 Cherokee 180 | Devon School of Flying/Dunkeswell |
| G-AVSR | D.5/180 Husky | A. L. Young |
| G-AVTC | Slingsby T.66 Nipper 3 | M. K. Field |
| G-AVTJ | PA-32 Cherokee Six 260 | Fly By Night Corporation Ltd |
| G-AVTK | PA-32 Cherokee Six 260 | Mannix Aviation Ltd/E. Midlands |
| G-AVTP | Cessna F.172H | BJJ Aviation |
| G-AVTT | Ercoupe 415D | Wright's Farm Eggs Ltd/Andrewsfield |
| G-AVTV | M.S.893A Rallye Commodore | D. B. Meeks |
| G-AVUD | PA-30 Twin Comanche 160B | F. M. Aviation/Biggin Hill |
| G-AVUG | Cessna F.150H | Skyways Flying Group/Netherthorpe |
| G-AVUH | Cessna F.150H | G-AVUH Group |
| G-AVUS | PA-28 Cherokee 140 | R. Groat/Glasgow |
| G-AVUT | PA-28 Cherokee 140 | Bencray Ltd/Blackpool |
| G-AVUU | PA-28 Cherokee 140 | A. Jahanfar & ptnrs/Southend |
| G-AVUZ | PA-32 Cherokee Six 300 | Ceesix Ltd/Jersey |
| G-AVVC | Cessna F.172H | Kestrel Air Ltd/Swansea |
| G-AVVE | Cessna F.150H ★ | R. Windley (stored) |
| G-AVVF | D.H.104 Dove 8 | K. R. Mitchell |
| G-AVVI | PA-30 Twin Comanche 160B | G. G. Long |
| G-AVVJ | M.S.893A Rallye Commodore | Herefordshire Gliding Club Ltd/ Shobdon |
| G-AVVL | Cessna F.150H | N. E. Sams/Cranfield |
| G-AVVO | Avro 652A Anson 19 (VL348) ★ | Newark Air Museum |
| G-AVVV | PA-28 Cherokee 180 | Courtrun Ltd/Redhill |
| G-AVVX | Cessna F.150H | Hatfield Flying Club |
| G-AVWA | PA-28 Cherokee 140 | Incipient Stall Co/Elstree |
| G-AVWD | PA-28 Cherokee 140 | M. P. Briggs |
| G-AVWE | PA-28 Cherokee 140 | W. C. C. Meyer (stored)/Biggin Hill |
| G-AVWG | PA-28 Cherokee 140 | Bencray Ltd/Blackpool |
| G-AVWH | PA-28 Cherokee 140 | P. Elliott/Biggin Hill |
| G-AVWI | PA-28 Cherokee 140 | L. M. Veitch |
| G-AVWJ | PA-28 Cherokee 140 | M. J. Steer/Biggin Hill |
| G-AVWL | PA-28 Cherokee 140 | P. J. Pratt/Dunkeswell |
| G-AVWM | PA-28 Cherokee 140 | P. E. Preston & ptnrs/Southend |
| G-AVWN | PA-28R Cherokee Arrow 180 | Vawn Air Ltd/Jersey |
| G-AVWO | PA-28R Cherokee Arrow 180 | P. D. Cahill/Biggin Hill |
| G-AVWR | PA-28R Cherokee Arrow 180 | D. A. Howe |
| G-AVWT | PA-28R Cherokee Arrow 180 | D. A. J. Maiden |
| G-AVWU | PA-28R Cherokee Arrow 180 | Arrow Flyers Ltd |
| G-AVWV | PA-28R Cherokee Arrow 180 | Mapair Ltd/Birmingham |
| G-AVWY | Fournier RF-4D | ASD Formaero Ltd/Biggin Hill |
| G-AVXA | PA-25 Pawnee 235 | S. Wales Gliding Club Ltd |

| Notes | Reg. | Type | Owner or Operator |
|---|---|---|---|
| | G-AVXC | Slingsby T.66 Nipper 3 | A. Horsfall |
| | G-AVXD | Slingsby T.66 Nipper 3 | D. A. Davidson |
| | G-AVXF | PA-28R Cherokee Arrow 180 | JDR Arrow Group |
| | G-AVXI | H.S.748 Srs 2A | Civil Aviation Authority/Stansted |
| | G-AVXJ | H.S.748 Srs 2A | Civil Aviation Authority/Stansted |
| | G-AVXV | Bleriot XI (BAPC 104) ★ | Bleriot Aeronautique Ltd |
| | G-AVXW | D.62B Condor | A. J. Cooper/Rochester |
| | G-AVXX | Cessna FR.172E | Hadrian Flying Group/Newcastle |
| | G-AVXY | Auster AOP.9 (XK417) ★ | R. Windley (on rebuild)/Leicester |
| | G-AVXZ | PA-28 Cherokee 140 ★ | ATC Hayle (instructional airframe) |
| | G-AVYB | H.S.121 Trident 1E-140 ★ | SAS training airframe/Hereford |
| | G-AVYE | H.S.121 Trident 1E-140 ★ | Test airframe/Hatfield |
| | G-AVYK | A.61 Terrier 3 | A. R. Wright/Booker |
| | G-AVYL | PA-28 Cherokee 180 | Cherokee G-AVYL |
| | G-AVYM | PA-28 Cherokee 180 | Carlisle Aviation (1985) Ltd/Crosby |
| | G-AVYP | PA-28 Cherokee 140 | T. D. Reid (Braids) Ltd/Newtownards |
| | G-AVYR | PA-28 Cherokee 140 | D.R. Flying Club Ltd/Staverton |
| | G-AVYS | PA-28R Cherokee Arrow 180 | D. H. Saunders/Ipswich |
| | G-AVYV | Jodel D.120 | Long Mountain Aero Group |
| | G-AVYX | AB-206A JetRanger | Mightycraft Ltd |
| | G-AVZB | Aero Z-37 Cmelak ★ | Science Museum/Wroughton |
| | G-AVZI | Bo 208C Junior | C. F. Rogers |
| | G-AVZM | B.121 Pup 1 | ARAZ Group/Elstree |
| | G-AVZN | B.121 Pup 1 | V. B. Wheele/Shoreham |
| | G-AVZO | B.121 Pup 1 ★ | Thameside Aviation Museum/E. Tilbury |
| | G-AVZP | B.121 Pup 1 | T. A. White |
| | G-AVZR | PA-28 Cherokee 180 | W. E. Lowe/Halfpenny Green |
| | G-AVZU | Cessna F.150H | R. D. & E. Forster/Swanton Morley |
| | G-AVZV | Cessna F.172H | B. Schreiber |
| | G-AVZW | EAA Biplane Model P | R. G. Maidment & G. R. Edmundson/Goodwood |
| | G-AVZX | M.S.880B Rallye Club | J. T. Hicks |
| | G-AWAA | M.S.880B Rallye Club | P. A. Cairns/Dunkeswell |
| | G-AWAC | GY-80 Horizon 180 | R. D. Harper |
| | G-AWAD | Beech 95-D55 Baron | Aero Lease Ltd/Bournemouth |
| | G-AWAH | Beech 95-D55 Baron | B. J. S. Grey |
| | G-AWAI | Beech 95-D55 Baron | Alibear Ltd/Booker |
| | G-AWAJ | Beech 95-D55 Baron | Standard Hose Ltd/Leeds |
| | G-AWAT | D.62B Condor | Tarwood Ltd/Redhill |
| | G-AWAU | Vickers F.B.27A Vimy (replica) (F8614) ★ | Bomber Command Museum/Hendon |
| | G-AWAW | Cessna F.150F | P. Brown |
| | G-AWAZ | PA-28R Cherokee Arrow 180 | Telepoint Ltd/Manchester |
| | G-AWBA | PA-28R Cherokee Arrow 180 | March Flying Group/Stapleford |
| | G-AWBB | PA-28R Cherokee Arrow 180 | H. G. Orchin |
| | G-AWBC | PA-28R Cherokee Arrow 180 | M. J. Blanchard |
| | G-AWBE | PA-28 Cherokee 140 | B. E. Boyle |
| | G-AWBG | PA-28 Cherokee 140 | D. Rowe |
| | G-AWBH | PA-28 Cherokee 140 | R. C. A. Mackworth |
| | G-AWBJ | Fournier RF-4D | The BJ Group/Biggin Hill |
| | G-AWBL | BAC One-Eleven 416EK | Birmingham European Airways Ltd City of Birmingham |
| | G-AWBM | D.31 Turbulent | A. D. Pratt |
| | G-AWBN | PA-30 Twin Comanche 160B | Stourfield Investments Ltd/Jersey |
| | G-AWBP | Cessna 182L Skylane | Bournemouth Aviation |
| | G-AWBS | PA-28 Cherokee 140 | W. London Aero Services Ltd/White Waltham |
| | G-AWBT | PA-30 Twin Comanche 160B ★ | Instructional airframe/Cranfield |
| | G-AWBU | Morane-Saulnier N (replica) (M.S.50) | Personal Plane Services Ltd/Booker |
| | G-AWBV | Cessna 182L Skylane | Aerofilms Ltd/Elstree |
| | G-AWBW | Cessna F.172H ★ | Brunel Technical College/Bristol |
| | G-AWBX | Cessna F.150H | D. F. Ranger |
| | G-AWCM | Cessna F.150H | Cheshire Air Training School (Merseyside) Ltd/Liverpool |
| | G-AWCN | Cessna FR.172E | LEC Refrigeration Ltd |
| | G-AWCP | Cessna F.150H (tailwheel) | C. E. Mason/Shobdon |
| | G-AWCW | Beech E.95 Travel Air | H. W. Astor/White Waltham |
| | G-AWDA | Slingsby T.66 Nipper 3 | J. A. Cheesebrough |
| | G-AWDD | Slingsby T.66 Nipper 3 | T. D. G. Roberts/Inverness |
| | G-AWDI | PA-23 Aztec 250C | (stored) |
| | G-AWDO | D.31 Turbulent | E. J. Lloyd |

| Reg. | Type | Owner or Operator | Notes |
|------|------|-------------------|-------|
| G-AWDP | PA-28 Cherokee 180 | B. H. & P. M. Illston/Shipdham | |
| G-AWDR | Cessna FR.172E | B. A. Wallace | |
| G-AWDU | Brantly B.2B | G. E. J. Redwood | |
| G-AWEF | SNCAN Stampe SV-4B | Tiger Club (1990) Ltd/Headcorn | |
| G-AWEI | D.62B Condor | Snowhit Ltd | |
| G-AWEL | Fournier RF-4D | A. B. Clymo/Halfpenny Green | |
| G-AWEM | Fournier RF-4D | B. J. Griffin/Wickenby | |
| G-AWEN | Jodel DR.1050 | L. G. Earnshaw & ptnrs | |
| G-AWEP | JB-01 Minicab | J. A. Stewart & S. N. Askey | |
| G-AWER | PA-23 Aztec 250C | H. McC. Clarke/Ronaldsway | |
| G-AWET | PA-28 Cherokee 180 | Broadland Flying Group Ltd/ Shipdham | |
| G-AWEV | PA-28 Cherokee 140 | Broxbow Ltd | |
| G-AWEX | PA-28 Cherokee 140 | R. Badham | |
| G-AWEZ | PA-28R Cherokee Arrow 180 | C. H. Elliott | |
| G-AWFB | PA-28R Cherokee Arrow 180 | Luke Aviation Ltd/Bristol | |
| G-AWFC | PA-28R Cherokee Arrow 180 | K. A. Goodchild/Southend | |
| G-AWFD | PA-28R Cherokee Arrow 180 | A. L. Irwin | |
| G-AWFF | Cessna F.150H | Shobdon Aircraft Maintenance | |
| G-AWFJ | PA-28R Cherokee Arrow 180 | D. C. E. Davies | |
| G-AWFK | PA-28R Cherokee Arrow 180 | J. A. Rundle (Holdings) Ltd/Kidlington | |
| G-AWFN | D.62B Condor | R. James | |
| G-AWFO | D.62B Condor | T. A. Major | |
| G-AWFP | D.62B Condor | Blackbushe Flying Club | |
| G-AWFR | D.31 Turbulent | L. W. Usherwood | |
| G-AWFT | Jodel D.9 Bebe | W. H. Cole | |
| G-AWFW | Jodel D.117 | F. H. Greenwell | |
| G-AWFZ | Beech A23 Musketeer | R. Sweet & B D. Corbett | |
| G-AWGA | A.109 Airedale ★ | stored/Sevenoaks | |
| G-AWGD | Cessna F.172H | Aero Marine Technology Ltd | |
| G-AWGJ | Cessna F.172H | J. & C. J. Freeman/Headcorn | |
| G-AWGK | Cessna F.150H | G. R. Brown/Shoreham | |
| G-AWGM | Arkle Kittiwake 2 | A. F. S. Caldecourt | |
| G-AWGN | Fournier RF-4D | R. H. Ashforth/Staverton | |
| G-AWGP | Cessna T.210H | S. Harcourt/Elstree | |
| G-AWGR | Cessna F.172H | P. Bushell/Liverpool | |
| G-AWGZ | Taylor JT.1 Monoplane | A. Hill | |
| G-AWHB | C.A.S.A. 2-111D (6J+PR) | Aces High Ltd/North Weald | |
| G-AWHV | Rollason Beta B.2A | D. M. J. Jones | |
| G-AWHX | Rollason Beta B.2 | J. J. Cooke/White Waltham | |
| G-AWHY | Falconar F.11-3 | J. R. Riley-Gale (G-BDPB) | |
| G-AWIF | Brookland Mosquito 2 | —/Husbands Bosworth | |
| G-AWII | V.S.349 Spitfire VC (AR501) | Shuttleworth Trust/Duxford | |
| G-AWIP | Luton LA-4A Minor | J. Houghton | |
| G-AWIR | Midget Mustang | K. E. Sword/Leicester | |
| G-AWIT | PA-28 Cherokee 180 | Ashley Gardner School of Flying Ltd | |
| G-AWIV | Airmark TSR.3 | C. J. Jesson (stored)/Redhill | |
| G-AWIW | SNCAN Stampe SV-4B | R. E. Mitchell | |
| G-AWIY | PA-23 Aztec 250C | B. Anderson/Belfast | |
| G-AWJC | Brighton gas balloon | P. D. Furlong Slippery William | |
| G-AWJE | Slingsby T.66 Nipper 3 | T. Mosedale | |
| G-AWJF | Slingsby T.66 Nipper 3 | R. Wilcock/Shoreham | |
| G-AWJI | M.S.880B Rallye Club | D. V. Tyler/Southend | |
| G-AWJV | D.H.98 Mosquito TT Mk 35 (TA634) ★ | Mosquito Aircraft Museum | |
| G-AWJX | Zlin Z.526 Akrobat | Aerobatics International Ltd | |
| G-AWJY | Zlin Z.526 Akrobat | Elco Manufacturing Co/Redhill | |
| G-AWKB | M.J.5 Sirocco F2/39 | G. D. Claxton | |
| G-AWKD | PA-17 Vagabond | A. T. & M. R. Dowie/ White Waltham | |
| G-AWKM | B.121 Pup 1 | D. M. G. Jenkins/Swansea | |
| G-AWKO | B.121 Pup 1 | P. A. Brook/Redhill | |
| G-AWKP | Jodel DR.253 | R. C. Chandless | |
| G-AWKT | M.S.880B Rallye Club | D. C. Strain | |
| G-AWLA | Cessna F.150H | Royal Artillery Aero Club Ltd/ Middle Wallop | |
| G-AWLE | Cessna F.172H | H. Mendelssohn & H. I. Shott | |
| G-AWLF | Cessna F.172H | Osprey Air Services Ltd | |
| G-AWLG | SIPA 903 | S. W. Markham | |
| G-AWLI | PA-22 Tri-Pacer 150 | J. S. Lewery/Shoreham | |
| G-AWLL | AB-206B JetRanger 2 | Base Helicopters Ltd | |
| G-AWLM | Bensen B.8MS | C. J. E. Ashby | |
| G-AWLO | Boeing Stearman E.75 | N. D. Pickard/Shoreham | |

| Notes | Reg. | Type | Owner or Operator |
|-------|------|------|-------------------|
| | G-AWLP | Mooney M.20F | Petratek Ltd |
| | G-AWLR | Slingsby T.66 Nipper 3 | C. F. O'Neill |
| | G-AWLS | Slingsby T.66 Nipper 3 | Stapleford Nipper Group |
| | G-AWLZ | Fournier RF-4D | E. V. Goodwin & C. R. Williamson |
| | G-AWMD | Jodel D.11 | N. R. Windley & P. G. Haines |
| | G-AWMF | PA-18 Super Cub 150 (modified) | Booker Gliding Club Ltd |
| | G-AWMI | Glos-Airtourer 115 | Airtourer Group 86/Cardiff |
| | G-AWMK | AB-206B JetRanger | Bristow Helicopters Ltd |
| | G-AWMM | M.S.893A Rallye Commodore 180 | D. P. & S. White |
| | G-AWMN | Luton LA-4A Minor | R. E. R. Wilks |
| | G-AWMP | Cessna F.172H | Blois Aviation Ltd |
| | G-AWMR | D.31 Turbulent | C. F. Kennedy |
| | G-AWMT | Cessna F.150H | R. V. Grocott/Sleap |
| | G-AWMZ | Cessna F.172H ★ | Parachute jump trainer/Cark |
| | G-AWNA | Boeing 747-136 | British Airways Colliford Lake/Heathrow |
| | G-AWNB | Boeing 747-136 | British Airways Llangorse Lake/Heathrow |
| | G-AWNC | Boeing 747-136 | British Airways Lake Windermere/Heathrow |
| | G-AWND | Boeing 747-136 | British Airways Coniston Water/Heathrow |
| | G-AWNE | Boeing 747-136 | British Airways Derwent Water/Heathrow |
| | G-AWNF | Boeing 747-136 | British Airways Blagdon Lake/Heathrow |
| | G-AWNG | Boeing 747-136 | British Airways Rutland Water/Heathrow |
| | G-AWNH | Boeing 747-136 | British Airways Devoke Water/Heathrow |
| | G-AWNJ | Boeing 747-136 | British Airways Bassenthwaite Lake/Heathrow |
| | G-AWNL | Boeing 747-136 | British Airways Ennerdale Water/Heathrow |
| | G-AWNM | Boeing 747-136 | British Airways Ullswater/Heathrow |
| | G-AWNN | Boeing 747-136 | British Airways Lowes Water/Heathrow |
| | G-AWNO | Boeing 747-136 | British Airways Grafton Water/Heathrow |
| | G-AWNP | Boeing 747-136 | British Airways Hanningfield Water/Heathrow |
| | G-AWNT | BN-2A Islander | Aerofilms Ltd/Elstree |
| | G-AWOA | M.S.880B Rallye Club | M. Craven & ptnrs/Barton |
| | G-AWOE | Aero Commander 680E | J. M. Houlder/Elstree |
| | G-AWOF | PA-15 Vagabond | J. K. Davies |
| | G-AWOH | PA-17 Vagabond | The High Flats Flying Group |
| | G-AWOT | Cessna F.150H | J. M. Montgomerie & J. Ferguson |
| | G-AWOU | Cessna 170B | S. Billington/Denham |
| | G-AWOX | W.S.58 Wessex 60 ★ | Sykes Aviation Ltd (stored) |
| | G-AWPH | P.56 Provost T.1 | J. A. D. Bradshaw |
| | G-AWPJ | Cessna F.150H | W. J. Greenfield |
| | G-AWPN | Shield Xyla | T. Brown |
| | G-AWPP | Cessna F.150H | D. Williams |
| | G-AWPS | PA-28 Cherokee 140 | M. Shipley |
| | G-AWPU | Cessna F.150J | Light Planes (Lancashire) Ltd/Barton |
| | G-AWPW | PA-12 Super Cruiser | J. E. Davies/Sandown |
| | G-AWPX | Cessna 150E | Starline Helicopters Ltd/Biggin Hill |
| | G-AWPY | Bensen B.8M | J. Jordan |
| | G-AWPZ | Andreasson BA-4B | J. M. Vening |
| | G-AWRK | Cessna F.150J | Southern Strut Flying Group/Shoreham |
| | G-AWRL | Cessna F.172H | B. Welsh |
| | G-AWRS | Avro 19 Srs. 2 ★ | N. E. Aircraft Museum |
| | G-AWRY | P.56 Provost T.1 (XF836) | Slymar Aviation & Services Ltd |
| | G-AWRZ | Bell 47G-5 | Hammond Aerial Spraying Ltd |
| | G-AWSA | Avro 652A Anson 19 (VL349) ★ | Norfolk & Suffolk Aviation Museum |
| | G-AWSD | Cessna F.150J | British Skysports |
| | G-AWSL | PA-28 Cherokee 180D | Fascia Ltd/Southend |
| | G-AWSM | PA-28 Cherokee 235 | S. J. Green |
| | G-AWSN | D.62B Condor | J. Leader |
| | G-AWSP | D.62B Condor | R. Q. & A. S. Bond/Wellesbourne |
| | G-AWSS | D.62C Condor | G. Bruce/Inverness |
| | G-AWST | D.62B Condor | Humberside Aviation/Doncaster |
| | G-AWSV | Skeeter 12 (XM553) | Maj. M. Somerton-Rayner/Middle Wallop |
| | G-AWSW | D.5/180 Husky (XW635) | RAF College Flying Club/Cranwell |

| Reg. | Type | Owner or Operator | Notes |
|------|------|-------------------|-------|
| G-AWSY | Boeing 737-204 | Britannia Airways Ltd *General James Wolfe*/Luton | |
| G-AWTA | Cessna E.310N | Heliscott Ltd | |
| G-AWTJ | Cessna F.150J | Metropolitan Police Flying Club/Biggin Hill | |
| G-AWTL | PA-28 Cherokee 180D | D. M. Bailey | |
| G-AWTS | Beech A.23 Musketeer | M. Corbett & ptnrs | |
| G-AWTV | Beech A.23 Musketeer | A. Johnston/Blackbushe | |
| G-AWTW | Beech 95-B55 Baron | R. W. Davies/Staverton | |
| G-AWTX | Cessna F.150J | R. D. & E. Forster | |
| G-AWUB | GY-201 Minicab | H. P. Burrill | |
| G-AWUE | Jodel DR.1050 | S. Bichan | |
| G-AWUG | Cessna F.150H | P. P. D. Howard-Johnston/Edinburgh | |
| G-AWUH | Cessna F.150H | Airtime (Hampshire) Ltd | |
| G-AWUJ | Cessna F.150H | W. Lawton/Doncaster | |
| G-AWUL | Cessna F.150H | Alderquest Ltd | |
| G-AWUN | Cessna F.150H | Northamptonshire School of Flying Ltd/Sywell | |
| G-AWUO | Cessna F.150H | Air Fenland Ltd | |
| G-AWUS | Cessna F.150J | Recreational Flying Centre (Popham) Ltd | |
| G-AWUT | Cessna F.150J | E. Phillips & P. Reddy | |
| G-AWUU | Cessna F.150J | D. G. Burden | |
| G-AWUW | Cessna F.172H | B. Stewart/Panshanger | |
| G-AWUX | Cessna F.172H | D. K. Brian & ptrs | |
| G-AWUZ | Cessna F.172H | G. F. Burling | |
| G-AWVA | Cessna F.172H | M. S. Medden | |
| G-AWVB | Jodel D.117 | D. J. R. Chapple | |
| G-AWVC | B.121 Pup 1 | J. H. Marshall & J. J. West | |
| G-AWVE | Jodel DR.1050M.1 | E. A. Taylor/Southend | |
| G-AWVF | P.56 Provost T.1 (XF877) | Pulsegrove Ltd/Shoreham | |
| G-AWVG | AESL Airtourer T.2 | C. J. Schofield & G. M. Gearing | |
| G-AWVN | Aeronca 7AC Champion | Bowker Air Services Ltd/Rush Green | |
| G-AWVZ | Jodel D.112 | D. C. Stokes | |
| G-AWWE | B.121 Pup 2 | J. M. Randle/Coventry | |
| G-AWWF | B.121 Pup 1 | N. M. Morris & Keef & Co Ltd/Denham | |
| G-AWWI | Jodel D.117 | J. C. Hatton | |
| G-AWWM | GY-201 Minicab | J. S. Brayshaw | |
| G-AWWN | Jodel DR.1051 | T. W. M. Beck & ptnrs | |
| G-AWWO | Jodel DR.1050 | Whiskey Oscar Group/Barton | |
| G-AWWP | Aerosport Woody Pusher III | M. S. Bird & R. D. Bird | |
| G-AWWT | D.31 Turbulent | M. A. Sherry & J. Tring/Redhill | |
| G-AWWU | Cessna FR.172F | Westward Airways (Lands End) Ltd | |
| G-AWWW | Cessna 401 | Air Charter & Travel Ltd | |
| G-AWWX | BAC One-Eleven 509EW | Dan-Air Services Ltd/Gatwick | |
| G-AWXA | Cessna 182M | P. Cannon | |
| G-AWXO | H.S.125 Srs. 400B | Twinjet Aircraft Sales Ltd/Luton | |
| G-AWXR | PA-28 Cherokee 180D | J. D. Williams | |
| G-AWXS | PA-28 Cherokee 180D | Rayhenro Flying Group/Shobdon | |
| G-AWXU | Cessna F.150J | B. B. Burtenshaw & ptnrs | |
| G-AWXV | Cessna F.172H | BAe (Warton) Flying Club/Blackpool | |
| G-AWXX | W.S.58 Wessex 60 Srs. 1 | Sykes Group Co Ltd/Bournemouth | |
| G-AWXY | M.S.885 Super Rallye | Sussex Spraying Services Ltd/Shoreham | |
| G-AWXZ | SNCAN Stampe SV-4C (D88) | Personal Plane Services Ltd/Booker | |
| G-AWYB | Cessna FR.172F | C. W. Larkin/Southend | |
| G-AWYF | G.159 Gulfstream 1 | Ford Motor Co Ltd/Stansted | |
| G-AWYJ | B.121 Pup 2 | H. C. Taylor | |
| G-AWYL | Jodel DR.253B | M. J. McRobert | |
| G-AWYO | B.121 Pup 1 | B. R. C. Wild/Popham | |
| G-AWYR | BAC One-Eleven 501EX | British Airways *County of Suffolk* | |
| G-AWYS | BAC One-Eleven 501EX | British Airways *County of Norfolk* | |
| G-AWYT | BAC One-Eleven 501EX | British Airways *County of Gwynedd* | |
| G-AWYU | BAC One-Eleven 501EX | British Airways *County of Avon* | |
| G-AWYV | BAC One-Eleven 501EX | British Airways *County of Powys* | |
| G-AWYX | M.S.880B Rallye Club | J. M. L. Edwards/Exeter | |
| G-AWYY | T.57 Camel replica (B6401) | FAA Museum/Yeovilton | |
| G-AWZE | H.S.121 Trident 3B ★ | *Instructional airframe*/Heathrow | |
| G-AWZI | H.S.121 Trident 3B ★ | Surrey Fire Brigade (*instructional airframe*)/Reigate | |
| G-AWZJ | H.S.121 Trident 3B ★ | British Airports Authority/Prestwick | |
| G-AWZK | H.S.121 Trident 3B ★ | *Ground trainer*/Heathrow | |
| G-AWZM | H.S.121 Trident 3B ★ | Science Museum/Wroughton | |
| G-AWZN | H.S.121 Trident 3B ★ | Cranfield Institute of Technology | |

| Notes | Reg. | Type | Owner or Operator |
|-------|------|------|-------------------|
| | G-AWZO | H.S.121 Trident 3B ★ | British Aerospace PLC/Hatfield |
| | G-AWZP | H.S.121 Trident 3B ★ | Greater Manchester Museum of Science & Technology (*nose only*) |
| | G-AWZR | H.S.121 Trident 3B ★ | CAA Fire School/Teesside |
| | G-AWZU | H.S.121 Trident 3B ★ | British Airports Authority/Stansted |
| | G-AWZX | H.S.121 Trident 3B ★ | BAA Fire Services/Gatwick |
| | G-AWZZ | H.S.121 Trident 3B ★ | Airport Fire Services/Birmingham |
| | G-AXAB | PA-28 Cherokee 140 | Bencray Ltd/Blackpool |
| | G-AXAK | M.S.880B Rallye Club | R. L. & C. Stewart |
| | G-AXAN | D.H.82A Tiger Moth (EM720) | M. E. Carrell |
| | G-AXAO | Omega 56 balloon | P. D. Furlong |
| | G-AXAS | Wallis WA-116T | K. H. Wallis (G-AVDH) |
| | G-AXAT | Jodel D.117A | P. S. Wilkinson |
| | G-AXAU | PA-30 Twin Comanche 160C | Bartcourt Ltd (*derelict*)/Bournemouth |
| | G-AXAW | Cessna 421A | London European Airways PLC/Luton |
| | G-AXAX | PA-23 Aztec 250D | Woodvale Aviation Co Ltd |
| | G-AXBF | D.5/180 Husky | C. H. Barnes |
| | G-AXBH | Cessna F.172H | Photoair Ltd/Sibson |
| | G-AXBJ | Cessna F.172H | Bravo Juliet Group/Leicester |
| | G-AXBW | D.H.82A Tiger Moth (T5879) | R. Venning |
| | G-AXBZ | D.H.82A Tiger Moth | D. H. McWhir |
| | G-AXCA | PA-28R Cherokee Arrow 200 | D. T. Wright |
| | G-AXCG | Jodel D.117 | Charlie Golf Group/Andrewsfield |
| | G-AXCI | Bensen B.8M ★ | Loughborough & Leicester Aircraft Museum |
| | G-AXCL | M.S.880B Rallye Club | L. A. Christie & D. P. Barclay |
| | G-AXCM | M.S.880B Rallye Club | Avcom Developments Ltd/Denham |
| | G-AXCN | M.S.880B Rallye Club | J. E. Compton |
| | G-AXCX | B.121 Pup 2 | R. S. Blackman/Elstree |
| | G-AXCY | Jodel D.117 | C. Smith |
| | G-AXDB | Piper J-3C-65 Cub | J. R. Wraight |
| | G-AXDC | PA-23 Aztec 250D | N. J. Lilley/Bodmin |
| | G-AXDE | Bensen B.8 | T. J. Hartwell |
| | G-AXDI | Cessna F.172H | M. F. & J. R. Leusby/Conington |
| | G-AXDK | Jodel DR.315 | Delta Kilo Flying Group/Sywell |
| | G-AXDM | H.S.125 Srs 400B | GEC Ferranti Defence Systems Ltd/ Edinburgh |
| | G-AXDN | BAC-Sud Concorde 01 ★ | Duxford Aviation Soc |
| | G-AXDU | B.121 Pup 2 | J. R. Clegg |
| | G-AXDV | B.121 Pup 1 | C. N. G. Hobbs & J. J. Teagle |
| | G-AXDW | B.121 Pup 1 | Cranfield Institute of Technology |
| | G-AXDY | Falconar F-II | J. Nunn |
| | G-AXDZ | Cassutt Racer Srs IIIM | A. Chadwick/Little Staughton |
| | G-AXEB | Cassutt Racer Srs IIIM | G. E. Horder/Redhill |
| | G-AXEC | Cessna 182M | H. S. Mulligan & E. R. Wilson |
| | G-AXED | PA-25 Pawnee 235 | Wolds Gliding Club Ltd/Pocklington |
| | G-AXEH | B.121 Pup ★ | Museum of Flight/E. Fortune |
| | G-AXEI | Ward Gnome ★ | Lincolnshire Aviation Museum |
| | G-AXEO | Scheibe SF.25B Falke | Newcastle & Tees-side Gliding Club Ltd |
| | G-AXES | B.121 Pup 2 | P. A. G. Field/Nairobi |
| | G-AXEV | B.121 Pup 2 | M. L. Sargeant |
| | G-AXFG | Cessna 337D | Skyborne Ltd |
| | G-AXFH | D.H.114 Heron 1B/C | — |
| | G-AXFN | Jodel D.119 | D. J. Williams & H. R. Leafe |
| | G-AXGC | M.S.880B Rallye Club | Ian Richard Transport Services Ltd |
| | G-AXGE | M.S.880B Rallye Club | R. P. Loxton |
| | G-AXGG | Cessna F.150J | A. R. Nicholls |
| | G-AXGP | Piper J-3C-65 Cub | W. K. Butler |
| | G-AXGR | Luton LA-4A Minor | B. Thomas |
| | G-AXGS | D.62B Condor | R. J. Hirst |
| | G-AXGT | D.62B Condor | G. M. Bradley & C. W. N. Huke |
| | G-AXGV | D.62B Condor | R. J. Wrixon |
| | G-AXGZ | D.62B Condor | Lincoln Condor Group/Sturgate |
| | G-AXHA | Cessna 337A | G. Evans |
| | G-AXHC | SNCAN Stampe SV-4C | W. R. Pointer |
| | G-AXHE | BN-2A Islander | NW Parachute Centre/Cark |
| | G-AXHI | M.S.880B Rallye Club | J. M. Whittard (*stored*)/Sandown |
| | G-AXHO | B.121 Pup 2 | L. W. Grundy/Stapleford |
| | G-AXHP | Piper J-3C-65 Cub | T. Coote |
| | G-AXHR | Piper J-3C-65 Cub (329601) | I. S. Hodge |
| | G-AXHS | M.S.880B Rallye Club | B. & A. Swales |
| | G-AXHT | M.S.880B Rallye Club | D. M. Leonard/Teesside |

| Reg. | Type | Owner or Operator | Notes |
|------|------|-------------------|-------|
| G-AXHV | Jodel D.117A | D. M. Cashmore | |
| G-AXHX | M.S.892A Rallye Commodore | D. W. Weever | |
| G-AXIA | B.121 Pup 1 | Cranfield Institute of Technology | |
| G-AXIE | B.121 Pup 2 | G. A. Ponsford/Goodwood | |
| G-AXIF | B.121 Pup 2 | T. G. Hiscock & R. G. Knapp | |
| G-AXIG | B.125 Bulldog 104 | George House (Holdings) Ltd | |
| G-AXIO | PA-28 Cherokee 140B | W. London Aero Services Ltd/ White Waltham | |
| G-AXIR | PA-28 Cherokee 140B | M. F. L. Purse/Weston Zoyland | |
| G-AXIT | M.S.893A Rallye Commodore 180 | South Wales Gliding Club Ltd | |
| G-AXIW | Scheibe SF.25B Falke | Mendip Falke Flying Group | |
| G-AXIX | Glos-Airtourer 150 | J. C. Wood | |
| G-AXIY | Bird Gyrocopter | Motor Museum/Chudleigh | |
| G-AXJB | Omega 84 balloon | Hot-Air Group Jester | |
| G-AXJH | B.121 Pup 2 | J. S. Chillingworth | |
| G-AXJI | B.121 Pup 2 | Cole Aviation Ltd/Southend | |
| G-AXJJ | B.121 Pup 2 | J. H. Askew & B. Ward | |
| G-AXJK | BAC One-Eleven 501EX | British Airways County of Hereford | |
| G-AXJM | BAC One-Eleven 501EX | British Airways County Durham | |
| G-AXJN | B.121 Pup 2 | D. M. Jenkins & D. F. Jenvey/Shoreham | |
| G-AXJO | B.121 Pup 2 | J. A. D. Bradshaw | |
| G-AXJR | Scheibe SF.25B Falke | D. R. Chatterton | |
| G-AXJV | PA-28 Cherokee 140B | Mona Aviation Ltd | |
| G-AXJX | PA-28 Cherokee 140B | Patrolwatch Ltd | |
| G-AXJY | Cessna U-206D | Hereford Parachute Club Ltd/Shobdon | |
| G-AXKD | PA-23 Aztec 250D | Levenmere Ltd/Norwich | |
| G-AXKH | Luton LA-4A Minor | M. E. Vaisey | |
| G-AXKI | Jodel D.9 Bebe | M. R. M. Welch | |
| G-AXKJ | Jodel D.9 Bebe | P. Hooker | |
| G-AXKK | Westland Bell 47G-4A | Alan Mann Helicopters Ltd/Fairoaks | |
| G-AXKO | Westland-Bell 47G-4A | Alan Mann Helicopters Ltd/Fairoaks | |
| G-AXKR | Westland Bell 47G-4A | F. C. Owen | |
| G-AXKS | Westland Bell 47G-4A ★ | Museum of Army Flying/Middle Wallop | |
| G-AXKW | Westland-Bell 47G-4A | C. J. Evans | |
| G-AXKX | Westland-Bell 47G-4A | Alan Mann Helicopters Ltd/Fairoaks | |
| G-AXKY | Westland Bell 47G-4A | L. Goddard | |
| G-AXLG | Cessna 310K | Smiths (Outdrives) Ltd | |
| G-AXLI | Slingsby T.66 Nipper 3 | N. J. Arthur/Finmere | |
| G-AXLL | BAC One-Eleven 523FJ | British Airways County of Yorkshire | |
| G-AXLS | Jodel DR.105A | E. Gee/Southampton | |
| G-AXLZ | PA-18 Super Cub 95 | J. C. Quantrell/Shipdham | |
| G-AXMA | PA-24 Comanche 180 | Tegrel Products Ltd/Newcastle | |
| G-AXMB | Slingsby T.7 Motor Cadet 2 | I. G. Smith/Langar | |
| G-AXMD | Omega O-56 balloon ★ | British Balloon Museum | |
| G-AXMN | J/5B Autocar | A. Phillips | |
| G-AXMP | PA-28 Cherokee 180 | B. Stewart | |
| G-AXMW | B.121 Pup 1 | DJP Engineering (Knebworth) Ltd | |
| G-AXMX | B.121 Pup 2 | Susan A. Jones/Cannes | |
| G-AXNC | Boeing 737-204 | Britannia Airways Ltd Isambard Kingdom Brunel/Luton | |
| G-AXNJ | Wassmer Jodel D.120 | Clive Flying Group/Sleap | |
| G-AXNK | Cessna F.150J | Fowler Aviation Ltd/Leavesden | |
| G-AXNL | B.121 Pup 1 | Northamptonshire School of Flying Ltd/ Sywell | |
| G-AXNM | B.121 Pup 1 | J. & F. E. Green | |
| G-AXNN | B.121 Pup 2 | Gabrielle Aviation Ltd/Shoreham | |
| G-AXNP | B.121 Pup 2 | J. W. Ellis | |
| G-AXNR | B.121 Pup 2 | S. T. Raby & ptnrs | |
| G-AXNS | B.121 Pup 2 | Derwent Aero/Netherthorpe | |
| G-AXNW | SNCAN Stampe SV-4C (E6452) | C. S. Grace | |
| G-AXNX | Cessna 182M | Cast High Ltd | |
| G-AXNZ | Pitts S.1C Special | W. A. Jordan | |
| G-AXOG | PA-E23 Aztec 250D | R. W. Diggens/Denham | |
| G-AXOH | M.S.894 Rallye Minerva | Bristol Cars Ltd/White Waltham | |
| G-AXOI | Jodel D.9 Bebe | P. R. Underhill | |
| G-AXOJ | B.121 Pup 2 | Pup Flying Group | |
| G-AXOL | Currie Wot | R. G. Boyes | |
| G-AXOR | PA-28 Cherokee 180D | Oscar Romeo Aviation | |
| G-AXOS | M.S.894A Rallye Minerva | D. R. C. Bell | |
| G-AXOT | M.S.893 Rallye Commodore 180 | P. Evans & J. C. Graves | |
| G-AXOV | Beech 95-B55A Baron | S. Brod/Elstree | |

| Notes | Reg. | Type | Owner or Operator |
|---|---|---|---|
| | G-AXPB | B.121 Pup 1 | C. N. Carter |
| | G-AXPF | Cessna F.150K | Y. Newell/Booker |
| | G-AXPG | Mignet HM-293 | W. H. Cole (stored) |
| | G-AXPM | B.121 Pup 1 | M. J. Coton |
| | G-AXPN | B.121 Pup 2 | D. J. Elbourn & ptnrs |
| | G-AXPZ | Campbell Cricket | W. R. Partridge |
| | G-AXRC | Campbell Cricket | K. W. Hayr (stored) |
| | G-AXRK | Practavia Sprite 115 | E. G. Thale |
| | G-AXRL | PA-28 Cherokee 160 | T. W. Clark/Headcorn |
| | G-AXRO | PA-30 Twin Comanche 160C | S. M. Bogdiukiewicz & W. B. Glastonbury |
| | G-AXRP | SNCAN Stampe SV-4C | C. C. Manning |
| | G-AXRR | Auster AOP.9 (XR241) | The Aircraft Restoration Co/Duxford |
| | G-AXRT | Cessna FA.150K (tailwheel) | W. R. Pickett/Southampton |
| | G-AXRU | Cessna FA.150K | Arrival Enterprises Ltd/Denham |
| | G-AXSC | B.121 Pup 1 | T. R. Golding & C. Spencer |
| | G-AXSD | B.121 Pup 1 | A. C. Townend |
| | G-AXSF | Nash Petrel | Nash Aircraft Ltd/Lasham |
| | G-AXSG | PA-28 Cherokee 180 | Shropshire Aero Club Ltd/Sleap |
| | G-AXSI | Cessna F.172H | S. M. Burrows & R. I. Chantrey (G-SNIP) |
| | G-AXSM | Jodel DR.1051 | C. Cousten/White Waltham |
| | G-AXSV | Jodel DR.340 | Leonard F. Jollye Ltd/Panshanger |
| | G-AXSW | Cessna FA.150K | Furness Aviation Ltd/Walney Island |
| | G-AXSZ | PA-28 Cherokee 140B | Kilo Foxtrot Group/Sandown |
| | G-AXTA | PA-28 Cherokee 140B | P. Barry & I. Cameron/Shoreham |
| | G-AXTC | PA-28 Cherokee 140B | B. Mellor & J. Hutchinson |
| | G-AXTD | PA-28 Cherokee 140B | G. R. Walker/Southend |
| | G-AXTH | PA-28 Cherokee 140B | W. London Aero Services Ltd/ White Waltham |
| | G-AXTI | PA-28 Cherokee 140B | London Transport (CRS) Sports Association Flying Club/Fairoaks |
| | G-AXTJ | PA-28 Cherokee 140B | A. P. Merrifield/Stapleford |
| | G-AXTL | PA-28 Cherokee 140B | Jenrick Flying Group |
| | G-AXTO | PA-24 Comanche 260 | J. L. Wright |
| | G-AXTP | PA-28 Cherokee 180 | E. R. Moore/Elstree |
| | G-AXTX | Jodel D.112 | J. J. Penney |
| | G-AXUA | B.121 Pup 1 | F. R. Blennerhassett & ptnrs |
| | G-AXUB | BN-2A Islander | Headcorn Parachute Club |
| | G-AXUC | PA-12 Super Cruiser | J. J. Bunton |
| | G-AXUE | Jodel DR.105A | L. Lewis |
| | G-AXUF | Cessna FA.150K | Bostonair Ltd/Humberside |
| | G-AXUI | H.P.137 Jetstream 1 | Cranfield Institute of Technology |
| | G-AXUJ | J/1 Autocrat | R. G. Earp & J. W. H. Lee/Sibson |
| | G-AXUK | Jodel DR.1050 | D. MacCallum |
| | G-AXUM | H.P.137 Jetstream 1 | Cranfield Institute of Technology |
| | G-AXUW | Cessna FA.150K | Coventry Air Training School |
| | G-AXVB | Cessna F.172H | C. Gabbitas/Staverton |
| | G-AXVC | Cessna FA.150K | V. F. Lynn/Sibson |
| | G-AXVK | Campbell Cricket | L. W. Harding |
| | G-AXVM | Campbell Cricket | D. M. Organ |
| | G-AXVN | McCandless M.4 | W. R. Partridge |
| | G-AXVS | Jodel DR.1050 | D. T. J. Harwood |
| | G-AXVV | Piper J-3C-65 Cub | J. MacCarthy |
| | G-AXVW | Cessna F.150K | J. M. R. Layton & A. Grant/Elstree |
| | G-AXWA | Auster AOP.9 (XN437) | M. L. & C. M. Edwards/Biggin Hill |
| | G-AXWB | Omega 65 balloon | A. Robinson & M. J. Moore Ezekiel |
| | G-AXWH | BN-2A Islander | Midland Parachute Centre Ltd |
| | G-AXWP | BN-2A Islander | Isles of Scilly Skybus Ltd/St Just |
| | G-AXWR | BN-2A Islander | Isles of Scilly Skybus Ltd/St Just |
| | G-AXWT | Jodel D.11 | R. C. Owen |
| | G-AXWV | Jodel DR.253 | J. R. D. Bygraves/O. Warden |
| | G-AXWZ | PA-28R Cherokee Arrow 200 | E. J. M. Kroes |
| | G-AXXV | D.H.82A Tiger Moth (DE992) | J. I. Hyslop |
| | G-AXXW | Jodel D.117 | A. Szep/Netherthorpe |
| | G-AXYD | BAC One-Eleven 509EW | Dan-Air Services Ltd/Gatwick |
| | G-AXYK | Taylor JT.1 Monoplane | T. W. M. Beck & M. J. Smith |
| | G-AXYY | WHE Airbuggy | R. A. A. Chiles |
| | G-AXYZ | WHE Airbuggy | W. B. Lumb |
| | G-AXZA | WHE Airbuggy | B. Gunn |
| | G-AXZB | WHE Airbuggy | D. R. C. Pugh |
| | G-AXZD | PA-28 Cherokee 180E | M. D. Callaghan & ptnrs |
| | G-AXZF | PA-28 Cherokee 180E | E. P. C. & W. R. Rabson/Southampton |
| | G-AXZK | BN-2A Islander | M. E. Mortlock/Pampisford |

| Reg. | Type | Owner or Operator | Notes |
|------|------|-------------------|-------|
| G-AXZM | Slingsby T.66 Nipper Srs 3 | G. R. Harlow | |
| G-AXZO | Cessna 180 | Brinkley Light Aircraft Services | |
| G-AXZP | PA-E23 Aztec 250D | Computaplane Ltd/Glasgow | |
| G-AXZT | Jodel D.117 | H. W. Baines | |
| G-AXZU | Cessna 182N | Earthlogic Ltd | |
| G-AYAA | PA-28 Cherokee 180E | Alpha-Alpha Ltd | |
| G-AYAB | PA-28 Cherokee 180E | J. A. & J. C. Cunningham | |
| G-AYAC | PA-28R Cherokee Arrow 200 | Fersfield Flying Group | |
| G-AYAL | Omega 56 balloon ★ | British Balloon Museum | |
| G-AYAR | PA-28 Cherokee 180E | V. Dowd | |
| G-AYAT | PA-28 Cherokee 180E | P. J. Messervy/Norwich | |
| G-AYAU | PA-28 Cherokee 180E | Tiarco Ltd | |
| G-AYAV | PA-28 Cherokee 180E | Tee Tee Aviation Ltd/Biggin Hill | |
| G-AYAW | PA-28 Cherokee 180E | Wizard Air Services Ltd/Coventry | |
| G-AYBD | Cessna F.150K | F. A. Fox/Southampton | |
| G-AYBG | Scheibe SF.25B Falke | D. J. Rickman | |
| G-AYBO | PA-23 Aztec 250D | Twinguard Aviation Ltd/Elstree | |
| G-AYBP | Jodel D.112 | G-AYBP Group | |
| G-AYBR | Jodel D.112 | R. N. Wright | |
| G-AYBU | Western 84 balloon | D. R. Gibbons | |
| G-AYBV | Chasle YC-12 Tourbillon | B. A. Mills | |
| G-AYCC | Campbell Cricket | D. J. M. Charity | |
| G-AYCE | CP.301C Emeraude | R. A. Austin/Bodmin | |
| G-AYCF | Cessna FA.150K | E. J. Atkins/Popham | |
| G-AYCG | SNCAN Stampe SV-4C | N. Bignall/Booker | |
| G-AYCJ | Cessna TP.206D | H. O. Holm/Bournemouth | |
| G-AYCN | Piper J-3C-65 Cub | W. R. & B. M. Young | |
| G-AYCO | CEA DR.360 | G. T. Birks/Booker | |
| G-AYCP | Jodel D.112 | D. J. Nunn | |
| G-AYCT | Cessna F.172H | Charlie Tango Flying Group | |
| G-AYDG | M.S.894A Rallye Minerva | R. P. Coplestone | |
| G-AYDI | D.H.82A Tiger Moth | R. B. Woods & ptnrs | |
| G-AYDR | SNCAN Stampe SV-4C | A. J. Mcluskie | |
| G-AYDV | Coates SA.II-1 Swalesong | J. R. Coates/Rush Green | |
| G-AYDW | A.61 Terrier 2 | A. Topen/Cranfield | |
| G-AYDX | A.61 Terrier 2 | G. W. & M. M. Bisshopp | |
| G-AYDY | Luton LA-4A Minor | T. Littlefair & N. Clark | |
| G-AYDZ | Jodel DR.200 | F. M. Ward/Sherburn | |
| G-AYEB | Jodel D.112 | M. A. Watts | |
| G-AYEC | CP.301A Emeraude | R. S. Needham | |
| G-AYED | PA-24 Comanche 260 | G. N. Snell | |
| G-AYEE | PA-28 Cherokee 180E | D. J. Beale | |
| G-AYEF | PA-28 Cherokee 180E | S. R. J. Attwood | |
| G-AYEG | Falconar F-9 | T. J. Wilkinson | |
| G-AYEH | Jodel DR.1050 | D. L. Riley/Barton | |
| G-AYEI | PA-31 Turbo Navajo | Stewart McDonald & Co | |
| G-AYEJ | Jodel DR.1050 | J. M. Newbold | |
| G-AYEK | Jodel DR.1050 | P. Cawkwell/Sherburn | |
| G-AYEN | Piper J-3C-65 Cub | P. Warde & C. F. Morris | |
| G-AYET | M.S.892A Rallye Commodore 150 | A. D. Lovell-Spencer | |
| G-AYEU | Brookland Hornet | M. G. Reilly | |
| G-AYEV | Jodel DR.1050 | L. G. Evans/Headcorn | |
| G-AYEW | Jodel DR.1051 | Taildragger Group/Halfpenny Green | |
| G-AYEY | Cessna F.150K | W. J. Moyse | |
| G-AYFA | SA Twin Pioneer 3 | Flight One Ltd/Shobdon | |
| G-AYFC | D.62B Condor | R. A. Smith/Redhill | |
| G-AYFD | D.62B Condor | B. G. Manning | |
| G-AYFE | D.62C Condor | J. Abbess/Andrewsfield | |
| G-AYFF | D.62B Condor | A. F. S. Caldecourt | |
| G-AYFG | D.62C Condor | W. A. Braim | |
| G-AYFJ | M.S.880B Rallye Club | P. J. Linney | |
| G-AYFP | Jodel D.140 | S. K. Minocha/Sherburn | |
| G-AYFT | PA-39 Twin Comanche 160 C/R | Subtec Aviation Ltd/Shoreham | |
| G-AYFV | Crosby BA-4B | A. R. C. Mathie/Norwich | |
| G-AYFZ | PA-31 Turbo Navajo | WLC Ltd | |
| G-AYGA | Jodel D.117 | R. L. E. Horrell | |
| G-AYGB | Cessna 310Q ★ | *Instructional airframe*/Perth | |
| G-AYGC | Cessna F.150K | Alpha Aviation Group/Barton | |
| G-AYGD | Jodel DR.1051 | B. A. James | |
| G-AYGE | SNCAN Stampe SV-4C | The Hon A. M. J. Rothschild/Booker | |
| G-AYGG | Jodel D.120 | G-AYGG Group | |
| G-AYGK | BN-2A Islander | Pathcircle Ltd/Langar | |

| Notes | Reg. | Type | Owner or Operator |
|---|---|---|---|
| | G-AYGN | Cessna 210K | J. W. O'Sullivan/Jersey |
| | G-AYGX | Cessna FR.172G | A. Douglas & J. K. Brockley |
| | G-AYHA | AA-1 Yankee | Elstree Emus Flying Group |
| | G-AYHI | Campbell Cricket | J. F. MacKay/Inverness |
| | G-AYHX | Jodel D.117A | L. J. E. Goldfinch |
| | G-AYHY | Fournier RF-4D | P. M. & S. M. Wells |
| | G-AYIA | Hughes 369HS ★ | G. D. E. Bilton/Sywell |
| | G-AYIF | PA-28 Cherokee 140C | The Hare Flying Group/Elstree |
| | G-AYIG | PA-28 Cherokee 140C | Snowdon Mountain Aviation Ltd |
| | G-AYII | PA-28R Cherokee Arrow 200 | Devon Growers Ltd & A. L. Bacon/ Exeter |
| | G-AYIJ | SNCAN Stampe SV-4B | K. B. Palmer/Headcorn |
| | G-AYIO | PA-28 Cherokee 140C | Frontline Aviation Ltd |
| | G-AYIT | D.H.82A Tiger Moth | Ulster Tiger Group/Newtownards |
| | G-AYJA | Jodel DR.1050 | G. I. Doake |
| | G-AYJB | SNCAN Stampe SV-4C | F. J. M. & J. P. Esson/Middle Wallop |
| | G-AYJD | Alpavia-Fournier RF-3 | E. Shouler |
| | G-AYJE | BN-2A-26 Islander | M. E. Mortlock/Pampisford |
| | G-AYJP | PA-28 Cherokee 140C | RAF Brize Norton Flying Club Ltd |
| | G-AYJR | PA-28 Cherokee 140C | RAF Brize Norton Flying Club Ltd |
| | G-AYJT | PA-28 Cherokee 140C | Jennifer M. Lesslie/Leicester |
| | G-AYJU | Cessna TP-206A | P. W. Yates |
| | G-AYJW | Cessna FR.172G | R. T. Burton |
| | G-AYJY | Isaacs Fury II | A. V. Francis |
| | G-AYKA | Beech 95-B55A Baron | Walsh Bros (Tunnelling) Ltd/Elstree |
| | G-AYKD | Jodel DR.1050 | B. P. Irish |
| | G-AYKF | M.S.880B Rallye Club | R. N. Preston/Cranfield |
| | G-AYKJ | Jodel D.117A | Juliet Group/Shoreham |
| | G-AYKK | Jodel D.117 | D. M. Whitham |
| | G-AYKL | Cessna F.150L | M. A. Judge |
| | G-AYKS | Leopoldoff L-7 | C. E. & W. B. Cooper |
| | G-AYKT | Jodel D.117 | G. Wright/Sherburn |
| | G-AYKW | PA-28 Cherokee 140C | A. G. Hopwood |
| | G-AYKX | PA-28 Cherokee 140C | M. J. Garland & ptnrs/Woodford |
| | G-AYKZ | SAI KZ-8 | R. E. Mitchell/Coventry |
| | G-AYLA | Glos-Airtourer 115 | R. E. Parker |
| | G-AYLB | PA-39 Twin Comanche 160 C/R | Penny (Mechanical Services) Ltd |
| | G-AYLE | M.S.880B Rallye Club | G-AYLE Syndicate |
| | G-AYLF | Jodel DR.1051 | A. C. Frost & ptnrs/Cranfield |
| | G-AYLL | Jodel DR.1050 | B. R. Cornes |
| | G-AYLP | AA-1 Yankee | D. Nairn & E. Y. Hawkins |
| | G-AYLV | Jodel D.120 | M. R. Henham |
| | G-AYLX | Hughes 269C | J. Lloyd |
| | G-AYLY | PA-23 Aztec 250C | —/Shoreham |
| | G-AYME | Fournier RF-5 | R. D. Goodger/Biggin Hill |
| | G-AYMG | HPR-7 Herald 213 | Channel Express PLC/Bournemouth |
| | G-AYMK | PA-28 Cherokee 140C | The Piper Flying Group |
| | G-AYML | PA-28 Cherokee 140C | Devon School of Flying/Dunkeswell |
| | G-AYMO | PA-23 Aztec 250C | RFS Transport Ltd |
| | G-AYMP | Currie Wot Special | H. F. Moffatt |
| | G-AYMR | Lederlin 380L Ladybug | J. S. Brayshaw |
| | G-AYMT | Jodel DR.1050 | Merlin Flying Club Ltd/Hucknall |
| | G-AYMU | Jodel D.112 | M. R. Baker |
| | G-AYMV | Western 20 balloon | G. F. Turnbull & ptnrs Tinkerbelle |
| | G-AYMW | Bell 206A JetRanger 2 | Dollar Air Services Ltd/Coventry |
| | G-AYMZ | PA-28 Cherokee 140C | T. H. & M. G. Weetman/Prestwick |
| | G-AYNA | Currie Wot | J. M. Lister |
| | G-AYNC | W.S. 58 Wessex 60 Srs 1 ★ | International Helicopter Museum/ Weston-s-Mare |
| | G-AYND | Cessna 310Q | Source Premium & Promotional Consultants Ltd/Fairoaks |
| | G-AYNF | PA-28 Cherokee 140C | W. S. Bath |
| | G-AYNJ | PA-28 Cherokee 140C | Lion Flying Group Ltd/Elstree |
| | G-AYNN | Cessna 185B Skywagon | Bencray Ltd/Blackpool |
| | G-AYNP | W.S.55 Whirlwind Srs 3 | Bristow Helicopters Ltd |
| | G-AYOD | Cessna 172 | E. N. Simmons |
| | G-AYOM | Sikorsky S-61N Mk 2 | British International Helicopters Ltd/ Aberdeen |
| | G-AYOP | BAC One-Eleven 530FX | British Airways County of Humberside |
| | G-AYOW | Cessna 182N Skylane | C. H. Royal |
| | G-AYOY | Sikorsky S-61N Mk 2 | British International Helicopters Ltd/ Aberdeen |
| | G-AYOZ | Cessna FA.150L | Exeter Flying Club Ltd |

| Reg. | Type | Owner or Operator | Notes |
|------|------|-------------------|-------|
| G-AYPD | Beech 95-B55A Baron | Sir W. S. Dugdale/Birmingham | |
| G-AYPE | Bo 209 Monsun | Papa Echo Ltd/Biggin Hill | |
| G-AYPF | Cessna F.177RG | S. J. Westley | |
| G-AYPG | Cessna F.177RG | D. Davies | |
| G-AYPH | Cessna F.177RG | W. J. D. Tollett | |
| G-AYPI | Cessna F.177RG | Cardinal Aviation Ltd/Guernsey | |
| G-AYPJ | PA-28 Cherokee 180 | Mona Aviation Ltd | |
| G-AYPM | PA-18 Super Cub 95 | N. H. Chapman | |
| G-AYPO | PA-18 Super Cub 95 | A. W. Knowles | |
| G-AYPR | PA-18 Super Cub 95 | J. W. Hollingsworth/Blackpool | |
| G-AYPS | PA-18 Super Cub 95 | Tony Dyer Television | |
| G-AYPT | PA-18 Super Cub 95 | P. Shires | |
| G-AYPU | PA-28R Cherokee Arrow 200 | Alpine Ltd/Jersey | |
| G-AYPV | PA-28 Cherokee 140D | R. J. & J. M. Charlton | |
| G-AYPZ | Campbell Cricket | A. Melody | |
| G-AYRF | Cessna F.150L | D. T. A. Rees | |
| G-AYRG | Cessna F.172K | W. I. Robinson | |
| G-AYRH | M.S.892A Rallye Commodore 150 | J. D. Watt | |
| G-AYRI | PA-28R Cherokee Arrow 200 | E. P. Van Mechelen & Delta Motor Co (Windsor) Sales Ltd/White Waltham | |
| G-AYRM | PA-28 Cherokee 140D | E. S. Dignam/Biggin Hill | |
| G-AYRN | Schleicher ASK.14 | T. M. Austin/Lasham | |
| G-AYRO | Cessna FA.150L Aerobat | Thruxton Flight Centre | |
| G-AYRR | H.S.125 Srs 403B | Duke of Westminster | |
| G-AYRS | Jodel D.120A | K. Heeley | |
| G-AYRT | Cessna F.172K | K. W. J. & A. B. L. Hayward | |
| G-AYRU | BN-2A-6 Islander | Joint Service Parachute Centre/ Netheravon | |
| G-AYSA | PA-23 Aztec 250C | N. Parkinson & W. Smith | |
| G-AYSB | PA-30 Twin Comanche 160C | R. K. Buckle/Booker | |
| G-AYSD | Slingsby T.61A Falke | R. G. G. English/Rufforth | |
| G-AYSH | Taylor JT.1 Monoplane | C. J. Lodge | |
| G-AYSJ | Bucker Bu133 Jungmeister LG+O1) | Patina Ltd/Duxford | |
| G-AYSK | Luton LA-4A Minor | M. P. Lobb | |
| G-AYSX | Cessna F.177RG | N. Green & D. G. Lewendon/ Bournemouth | |
| G-AYSY | Cessna F.177RG | H. J. Bendikson | |
| G-AYSZ | Cessna FA.150L | E. J. Miller/Dubai | |
| G-AYTA | M.S.880B Rallye Club | Kemps Corrosion Services Ltd Foxair/Perth | |
| G-AYTJ | Cessna 207 Super Skywagon | P. G. Hall & R. F. Jessett *Prometheus* | |
| G-AYTN | Cameron O-65 balloon | P. J. Hall | |
| G-AYTR | CP.301A Emeraude | Gp Capt A. S. Knowles | |
| G-AYTT | Phoenix PM-3 Duet | Tempete Group/Barton | |
| G-AYTV | MJ.2A Tempete | J. H. Wood & J. S. Knight | |
| G-AYTY | Bensen B.8 | Brook & Churches (Sales) Ltd | |
| G-AYUB | CEA DR.253B | M. S. Bayliss/Coventry | |
| G-AYUH | PA-28 Cherokee 180F | Andrewsfield Flying Club Ltd | |
| G-AYUI | PA-28 Cherokee 180 | S. W. Cross & M. A. Farrelly | |
| G-AYUJ | Evans VP-1 Volksplane | D. M. Butcher | |
| G-AYUL | PA-23 Aztec 250E | Hereward Flying Group/Sibson | |
| G-AYUM | Slingsby T.61A Falke | C. W. Vigar & R. J. Watts | |
| G-AYUN | Slingsby T.61A Falke | Cranwell Gliding Club | |
| G-AYUP | Slingsby T.61A Falke | W. A Urwin | |
| G-AYUR | Slingsby T.61A Falke | R. R. McKinnon & A. D. Lincoln/ Southampton | |
| G-AYUS | Taylor JT.1 Monoplane | R. Norris | |
| G-AYUT | Jodel DR.1050 | Snowdon Mountain Aviation Ltd/ Caernarfon | |
| G-AYUV | Cessna F.172H | | |
| G-AYUW | BAC One-Eleven 476FM★ | AIM Aviation Ltd (*cabin water spray tests*)/Bournemouth | |
| G-AYUY | Cessna FA.150L Aerobat | J. R. Bell | |
| G-AYVA | Cameron O-84 balloon | A. Kirk *April Fool* | |
| G-AYVO | Wallis WA120 Srs 1 | K. H. Wallis | |
| G-AYVP | Woody Pusher | J. R. Wraight | |
| G-AYVT | Brochet MB.84 ★ | Dunelm Flying Group (*stored*) | |
| G-AYVU | Cameron O-56 balloon | Shell-Mex & B.P. Ltd *Hot Potato* | |
| G-AYWA | Avro 19 Srs 2 ★ | Strathallan Aircraft Collection | |
| G-AYWD | Cessna 182N | Trans Para Aviation Ltd | |
| G-AYWE | PA-28 Cherokee 140 | N. Roberson | |
| G-AYWH | Jodel D.117A | D. Kynaston & J. Deakin | |

| Notes | Reg. | Type | Owner or Operator |
|---|---|---|---|
| | G-AYWM | Glos-Airtourer Super 150 | The Star Flying Group/Staverton |
| | G-AYWT | AIA Stampe SV-4C | B. K. Lecomber/Denham |
| | G-AYXO | Luton LA-5A Major | A. C. T. Broomcroft |
| | G-AYXP | Jodel D.117A | G. N. Davies |
| | G-AYXS | SIAI-Marchetti S205-18R | J. J. Barnett/Old Sarum |
| | G-AYXT | W.S. 55 Whirlwind Srs 2 | Wilkie Museum Collection/Blackpool |
| | G-AYXU | Champion 7KCAB Citabria | Kent Gliding Club Ltd |
| | G-AYXV | Cessna FA.150L | *Wreck*/Popham |
| | G-AYXW | Evans VP-1 | J. S. Penny/Doncaster |
| | G-AYYD | M.S.894A Rallye Minerva | P. D. Lloyd & ptnrs |
| | G-AYYF | Cessna F.150L | D. T. A. Rees |
| | G-AYYK | Slingsby T.61A Falke | Cornish Gliding & Flying Club Ltd/ Perranporth |
| | G-AYYL | Slingsby T.61A Falke | C. Wood |
| | G-AYYO | Jodel DR.1050/M1 | Bustard Flying Club Ltd/Old Sarum |
| | G-AYYT | Jodel DR.1050/M1 | Sicile Flying Group/Sandown |
| | G-AYYU | Beech C23 Musketeer | P. Peck |
| | G-AYYW | BN-2A Islander | RN & R. Marines Sport Parachute Association/Dunkeswell |
| | G-AYYX | M.S.880B Rallye Club | J. Turnbull & P. W. Robinson |
| | G-AYYY | M.S.880B Rallye Club | T. W. Heffer/Elstree |
| | G-AYZE | PA-39 Twin Comanche 160 C/R | J. E. Palmer/Staverton |
| | G-AYZH | Taylor JT.2 Titch | P. J. G. Goddard |
| | G-AYZI | SNCAN Stampe SV-4C | W. H. Smout & C. W. A. Simmons |
| | G-AYZJ | W.S. 55 Whirlwind Srs 2 (XM685) ★ | Newark Air Museum |
| | G-AYZK | Jodel DR.1050/M1 | G. Kearney & D. G. Hesketh |
| | G-AYZN | PA-23 Aztec 250D | D. J. Sewell/Nigeria |
| | G-AYZS | D.62B Condor | P. E. J. Huntley & M. N. Thrush |
| | G-AYZU | Slingsby T.61A Falke | The Falcon Gliding Group/Enstone |
| | G-AYZW | Slingsby T.61A Falke | J. A. Dandie & R. J. M. Clement |
| | G-AZAB | PA-30 Twin Comanche 160B | T. W. P. Sheffield/Humberside |
| | G-AZAD | Jodel DR.1051 | J. S. Paget & ptnrs/Bodmin |
| | G-AZAJ | PA-28R Cherokee Arrow 200B | J. McHugh & ptnrs/Stapleford |
| | G-AZAV | Cessna 337F | J. R. Surbey |
| | G-AZAW | GY-80 Horizon 160 | Horizon Flyers Ltd/Denham |
| | G-AZAZ | Bensen B.8M ★ | FAA Museum/Yeovilton |
| | G-AZBA | T.66 Nipper 3 | I. McKenzie |
| | G-AZBB | MBB Bo 209 Monsun 160FV | G. N. Richardson/Staverton |
| | G-AZBC | PA-39 Twin Comanche 160 C/R | Tenison Air Ltd |
| | G-AZBE | Glos-Airtourer Super 150 | F. B. Miles |
| | G-AZBH | Cameron O-84 balloon | — |
| | G-AZBI | Jodel D.150 | T. A. Rawson & W. H. Milner |
| | G-AZBK | PA-23 Aztec 250E | ATS Aircharter Ltd/Blackbushe |
| | G-AZBL | Jodel D.9 Bebe | West Midlands Flying Group |
| | G-AZBN | AT-16 Harvard 2B (FT391) | J. N. Carter |
| | G-AZBT | Western O-65 balloon | D. J. Harris *Hermes* |
| | G-AZBU | Auster AOP.9 | K. H. Wallis |
| | G-AZBY | W.S.58 Wessex 60 Srs 1 ★ | International Helicopter Museum/ Weston-s-Mare |
| | G-AZBZ | W.S.58 Wessex 60 Srs 1 ★ | International Helicopter Museum/ Weston-s-Mare |
| | G-AZCB | SNCAN Stampe SV-4C | M. J. Cowburn/Redhill |
| | G-AZCI | Cessna 320A Skyknight | Landsurcon (Air Survey) Ltd |
| | G-AZCK | B.121 Pup 2 | Martyn Balm Life & Pensions Ltd |
| | G-AZCL | B.121 Pup 2 | E. G. A. Prance |
| | G-AZCP | B.121 Pup 1 | Pup Group 87/Elstree |
| | G-AZCT | B.121 Pup 1 | N. J. Hall |
| | G-AZCU | B.121 Pup 1 | A. A. Harris |
| | G-AZCV | B.121 Pup 2 | N. R. W. Long/Elstree |
| | G-AZCZ | B.121 Pup 2 | P. R. Moorehead |
| | G-AZDA | B.121 Pup 1 | G. H. G. Bishop/Shoreham |
| | G-AZDD | MBB Bo 209 Monsun 150FF | Double Delta Flying Group/Biggin Hill |
| | G-AZDE | PA-28R Cherokee Arrow 200B | Electro-Motion UK (Export) Ltd/ E. Midlands |
| | G-AZDF | Cameron O-84 balloon | K. L. C. M. Busemeyer |
| | G-AZDG | B.121 Pup 2 | D. J. Sage/Coventry |
| | G-AZDK | Beech 95-B55 Baron | D. J. Nock |
| | G-AZDX | PA-28 Cherokee 180F | M. Cowan |
| | G-AZDY | D.H.82A Tiger Moth | J. B. Mills |
| | G-AZEE | M.S.880B Rallye Club | P. L. Clements |
| | G-AZEF | Jodel D.120 | J. R. Legge |

| Reg. | Type | Owner or Operator | Notes |
|------|------|-------------------|-------|
| G-AZEG | PA-28 Cherokee 140D | Ashley Gardner Flying Club Ltd | |
| G-AZER | Cameron O-42 balloon | M. P. Dokk-Olsen & P. L. Jaye | |
| G-AZEU | B.121 Pup 2 | P. Tonkin & R. S. Kinman | |
| G-AZEV | B.121 Pup 2 | G. P. Martin/Shoreham | |
| G-AZEW | B.121 Pup 2 | K. Cameron | |
| G-AZEY | B.121 Pup 2 | G. Huxtable/Elstree | |
| G-AZFA | B.121 Pup 2 | K. F. Plummer | |
| G-AZFC | PA-28 Cherokee 140D | M. L. Hannah & A. Seymour | |
| G-AZFF | Jodel D.112 | C. R. Greenaway | |
| G-AZFI | PA-28R Cherokee Arrow 200B | G-AZFI Ltd/Sherburn | |
| G-AZFM | PA-28R Cherokee Arrow 200B | Linco Poultry Machinery Ltd/Biggin Hill | |
| G-AZFP | Cessna F.177RG | Allen Aviation Ltd/Goodwood | |
| G-AZFR | Cessna 401B | Westair Flying Services Ltd/Blackpool | |
| G-AZFZ | Cessna 414 | Redapple Ltd/Fairoaks | |
| G-AZGA | Jodel D.120 | G. B. Morris | |
| G-AZGC | SNCAN Stampe SV-4C (No 120) | V. Lindsay | |
| G-AZGE | SNCAN Stampe SV-4A | M. R. L. Astor/Booker | |
| G-AZGF | B.121 Pup 2 | K. Singh | |
| G-AZGI | M.S.880B Rallye Club | J. & S. Cattle/Newcastle | |
| G-AZGJ | M.S.880B Rallye Club | P. Rose | |
| G-AZGL | M.S.894A Rallye Minerva | The Cambridge Aero Club Ltd | |
| G-AZGY | CP.301B Emeraude | J. R. Riley-Gale | |
| G-AZGZ | D.H.82A Tiger Moth | F. R. Manning | |
| G-AZHB | Robin HR.100-200 | C. & P. P. Scarlett/Sywell | |
| G-AZHC | Jodel D.112 | J. A. Summer & A. Burton/Netherthorpe | |
| G-AZHD | Slingsby T.61A Falke | J. Sentance | |
| G-AZHH | SA 102.5 Cavalier | D. W. Buckle | |
| G-AZHI | Glos-Airtourer Super 150 | H. J. Douglas/Biggin Hill | |
| G-AZHJ | S.A. Twin Pioneer Srs 3 | Flight One Ltd/Staverton | |
| G-AZHK | Robin HR.100/200B | D. J. Sage (G-ILEG) | |
| G-AZHR | Piccard Ax6 balloon | G. Fisher | |
| G-AZHT | Glos-Airtourer T.3 | D. G. Palmer & D. C. Giles/Glasgow | |
| G-AZHU | Luton LA-4A Minor | W. Cawrey/Netherthorpe | |
| G-AZIB | ST-10 Diplomate | Diplomate Group | |
| G-AZID | Cessna FA.150L | Exeter Flying Club Ltd | |
| G-AZII | Jodel D.117A | J. S. Brayshaw | |
| G-AZIJ | Jodel DR.360 | Rob Airway Ltd/Guernsey | |
| G-AZIK | PA-34-200 Seneca II | C.S.E. Aviation Ltd/Kidlington | |
| G-AZIL | Slingsby T.61A Falke | D. W. Savage | |
| G-AZIO | SNCAN Stampe SV-4C (Lycoming) ★ | /Booker | |
| G-AZIP | Cameron O-65 balloon | Dante Balloon Group *Dante* | |
| G-AZJC | Fournier RF-5 | J. J. Butler/Biggin Hill | |
| G-AZJE | Ord-Hume JB-01 Minicab | J. B. Evans/Sandown | |
| G-AZJI | Western O-65 balloon | W. Davison *Peek-a-Boo* | |
| G-AZJN | Robin DR.300/140 | Wright Farm Eggs Ltd | |
| G-AZJV | Cessna F.172L | J. A. & A. J. Boyd/Cardiff | |
| G-AZJW | Cessna F.150L | S. S. Delwarte/Shoreham | |
| G-AZJY | Cessna FRA.150L | G. Firbank | |
| G-AZJZ | PA-23 Aztec 250E | Encee Services Ltd/Cardiff | |
| G-AZKC | M.S.880B Rallye Club | L. J. Martin/Redhill | |
| G-AZKD | M.S.880B Rallye Club | P. Feeney/Kidlington | |
| G-AZKE | M.S.880B Rallye Club | B. S. Rowden & W. L. Rogers | |
| G-AZKK | Cameron O-56 balloon | Gemini Balloon Group *Gemini* | |
| G-AZKN | Robin HR.100/200 | Sussex Flying Group/Goodwood | |
| G-AZKO | Cessna F.337F | Crispair Aviation Services Ltd | |
| G-AZKP | Jodel D.117 | J. Lowe | |
| G-AZKR | PA-24 Comanche 180 | P. I. Kempsey & S. McGovern | |
| G-AZKS | AA-1A Trainer | B. W. Wells & Burbage Farms Ltd | |
| G-AZKV | Cessna FRA.150L | Penguin Flight/Bodmin | |
| G-AZKW | Cessna F.172L | J. C. C. Wright | |
| G-AZKZ | Cessna F.172L | R. D. & E. Forster/Swanton Morley | |
| G-AZLE | Boeing N2S-5 Kaydet | Parker Airways Ltd/Denham | |
| G-AZLF | Jodel D.120 | M. S. C. Ball | |
| G-AZLH | Cessna F.150L | Skegness Air Taxi Service Ltd/Boston | |
| G-AZLL | Cessna FRA.150L | Air Service Training Ltd/Perth | |
| G-AZLM | Cessna F.172L | J. F. Davis | |
| G-AZLN | PA-28 Cherokee 180F | Liteflite Ltd/Kidlington | |
| G-AZLO | Cessna F.337F | *Stored*/Bourn | |
| G-AZLV | Cessna 172K | B. L. F. Karthaus | |
| G-AZLY | Cessna F.150L | Cleveland Flying School Ltd/Tees-side | |
| G-AZLZ | Cessna F.150L | Exeter Flying Club Ltd | |
| G-AZMB | Bell 47G-3B | Trent Air Services Ltd/Cranfield | |

| Notes | Reg. | Type | Owner or Operator |
|---|---|---|---|
| | G-AZMC | Slingsby T.61A Falke | Essex Gliding Club Ltd |
| | G-AZMD | Slingsby T.61C Falke | R. A. Rice |
| | G-AZMF | BAC One-Eleven 530FX | British Airways *County of Northumberland* |
| | G-AZMH | Morane-Saulnier M.S.500 (ZA+WN) | Wessex Aviation & Transport Ltd |
| | G-AZMJ | AA-5 Traveler | R. T. Love/Bodmin |
| | G-AZMK | PA-23 Aztec 250E | Devon School of Flying/Dunkeswell |
| | G-AZMN | Glos-Airtourer T.5 | W. Crozier & I. Young/Glasgow |
| | G-AZMX | PA-28 Cherokee 140 ★ | NE Wales Institute of Higher Education (*Instructional airframe*)/Clwyd |
| | G-AZMZ | M.S.893A Rallye Commodore 150 | P. J. Wilcox/Cranfield |
| | G-AZNA | V.813 Viscount | British Air Ferries Ltd/Southend |
| | G-AZNF | AIA Stampe SV-4C | H. J. Smith/Shoreham |
| | G-AZNK | SNCAN Stampe SV-4A | R. H. Reeves/Barton |
| | G-AZNL | PA-28R Cherokee Arrow 200D | P. L. Buckley Ltd |
| | G-AZNO | Cessna 182P | M&D Aviation/Bournemouth |
| | G-AZNT | Cameron O-84 balloon | N. Tasker |
| | G-AZOA | MBB Bo 209 Monsun 150FF | R. P. Wilson |
| | G-AZOB | MBB Bo 209 Monsun 150FF | G. N. Richardson/Staverton |
| | G-AZOE | Glos-Airtourer 115 | R. J. Zukowski |
| | G-AZOF | Glos-Airtourer Super 150 | D. C. Macdonald |
| | G-AZOG | PA-28R Cherokee Arrow 200D | J. G. Collins/Cambridge |
| | G-AZOH | Beech 65-B90 Queen Air | Grange Aviation & General Investments Ltd/Shoreham |
| | G-AZOL | PA-34-200 Seneca II | M. T. Vaile & A. L. Howell/ Bournemouth |
| | G-AZON | PA-34-200 Seneca II | Willowvale Electronics Ltd/Elstree |
| | G-AZOO | Western O-65 balloon | Southern Balloon Group *Carousel* |
| | G-AZOR | MBB Bo 105D | Bond Helicopters Ltd/Bourn |
| | G-AZOS | Jurca MJ.5-F1 Sirocco | O. R. B. Dixon/Barton |
| | G-AZOT | PA-34-200 Seneca II | G. S. Jenkins & M. R. C. Smerald |
| | G-AZOU | Jodel DR.1051 | Horsham Flying Group/Slinfold |
| | G-AZOZ | Cessna FRA.150L | Seawing Flying Club Ltd/Southend |
| | G-AZPA | PA-25 Pawnee 235 | Black Mountain Gliding Co Ltd |
| | G-AZPC | Slingsby T.61C Falke | B. C. Dixon |
| | G-AZPF | Fournier RF-5 | R. Pye/Blackpool |
| | G-AZPH | Craft-Pitts S-1S Special | N. M. Bloom |
| | G-AZPV | Luton LA-4A Minor | J. Scott/(*Stored*) |
| | G-AZPX | Western O-31 balloon | Eugena Rex Balloon Group |
| | G-AZPZ | BAC One-Eleven 515FB | British Airways *Dumfries and Galloway Region* |
| | G-AZRA | MBB Bo 209 Monsun 150FF | Alpha Flying Ltd/Denham |
| | G-AZRD | Cessna 401B | Morbaine Ltd |
| | G-AZRG | PA-23 Aztec 250D | Woodgate Aviation (IOM) Ltd/ Ronaldsway |
| | G-AZRH | PA-28 Cherokee 140D | Newcastle-upon-Tyne Aero Club Ltd |
| | G-AZRI | Payne balloon | G. F. Payne *Shoestring* |
| | G-AZRK | Fournier RF-5 | Thurleigh Flying Group |
| | G-AZRL | PA-18 Super Cub 95 | B. J. Stead |
| | G-AZRM | Fournier RF-5 | A. R. Dearden & R. Speer/Shoreham |
| | G-AZRN | Cameron O-84 balloon | C. A. Butter & J. J. T. Cooke |
| | G-AZRP | Glos-Airtourer 115 | B. F. Strawford |
| | G-AZRR | Cessna 310Q | Routarrow Ltd/Norwich |
| | G-AZRS | PA-22 Tri-Pacer 150 | T. W. R. Case |
| | G-AZRV | PA-28R Cherokee Arrow 200B | Designed for Sound Ltd |
| | G-AZRW | Cessna T.337C | R. C. Frazle/Southend |
| | G-AZRX | GY-80 Horizon 160 | P. S. Cottrell/Sherburn |
| | G-AZRZ | Cessna U.206F | Cyprus Combined Services Parachute Club/Akrotiri |
| | G-AZSA | Stampe SV-4B | J. K. Faulkner/Biggin Hill |
| | G-AZSC | AT-16 Harvard IIB | Machine Music Ltd/Fairoaks |
| | G-AZSD | Slingsby T.29B Motor Tutor | R. G. Boynton |
| | G-AZSF | PA-28R Cherokee Arrow 200D | W. T. Northorpe & R. J. Mills/Coventry |
| | G-AZSG | PA-28 Cherokee 180E | Aero Group 78/Netherthorpe |
| | G-AZSH | PA-28R Cherokee Arrow 180 | C. R. Hayward |
| | G-AZSK | Taylor JT.1 Monoplane | R. R. Lockwood |
| | G-AZSN | PA-28R Cherokee Arrow 200 | Jetstream Air Couriers Ltd/Bristol |
| | G-AZSU | H.S.748 Srs 2A | Aberdeen Airways Ltd |
| | G-AZSW | B.121 Pup 1 | Northamptonshire School of Flying Ltd/Sywell |
| | G-AZSZ | PA-23 Aztec 250D | Strata Surveys Ltd |

| Reg. | Type | Owner or Operator | Notes |
|------|------|-------------------|-------|
| G-AZTA | MBB Bo 209 Monsun 150FF | R. S. Perks/Elstree | |
| G-AZTD | PA-32 Cherokee Six 300D | Presshouse Publications Ltd/Enstone | |
| G-AZTF | Cessna F.177RG | J. Bolson & Son Ltd/Bournemouth | |
| G-AZTI | MBB Bo 105D | Bond Helicopters Ltd | |
| G-AZTK | Cessna F.172F | C. O. Simpson | |
| G-AZTO | PA-34-200 Seneca II | Bulldog Aviation Ltd | |
| G-AZTR | SNCAN Stampe SV-4C | P. G. Palumbo/Booker | |
| G-AZTS | Cessna F.172L | J. F. Morgan/Humberside | |
| G-AZTV | Stolp SA.500 Starlet | G. R. Rowland | |
| G-AZTW | Cessna F.177RG | R. M. Clarke/Leicester | |
| G-AZUK | BAC One-Eleven 476FM | Ryanair Europe PLC/Luton | |
| G-AZUM | Cessna F.172L | Thatched Cottage Audio Ltd | |
| G-AZUO | Cessna F.177RG | C. W. Hall | |
| G-AZUP | Cameron O-65 balloon | R. S. Bailey & ptnrs | |
| G-AZUT | M.S.893A Rallye Commodore 180 | Rallye Flying Group | |
| G-AZUV | Cameron O-65 balloon ★ | British Balloon Museum | |
| G-AZUX | Western O-56 balloon | M. W. H. Henton | |
| G-AZUY | Cessna E.310L | Stagecoach (Holdings) Ltd | |
| G-AZUZ | Cessna FRA.150L | D. J. Parker/Netherthorpe | |
| G-AZVA | MBB Bo 209 Monsun 150FF | K. H. Wallis | |
| G-AZVB | MBB Bo 209 Monsun 150FF | P. C. Logsdon/Dunkeswell | |
| G-AZVE | AA-5 Traveler | G-AZVE Flying Group/Rochester | |
| G-AZVF | M.S.894A Rallye Minerva | P. D. Lloyd | |
| G-AZVG | AA-5 Traveler | G. Phillips | |
| G-AZVH | M.S.894A Rallye Minerva | Bristol Cars Ltd/White Waltham | |
| G-AZVI | M.S.892A Rallye Commodore | Shobdon Flying Group | |
| G-AZVJ | PA-34-200 Seneca II | Skyfotos Ltd/Lydd | |
| G-AZVL | Jodel D.119 | Forest Flying Group/Stapleford | |
| G-AZVM | Hughes 369HS | Diagnostic Reagents Ltd | |
| G-AZVP | Cessna F.177RG | R. G. Saunders/Biggin Hill | |
| G-AZVT | Cameron O-84 balloon | Sky Soarer Ltd *Jules Verne* | |
| G-AZWB | PA-28 Cherokee 140 | Skyscraper Ltd | |
| G-AZWD | PA-28 Cherokee 140 | BM Aviation (Winchester) | |
| G-AZWE | PA-28 Cherokee 140 | Devon School of Flying/Dunkeswell | |
| G-AZWF | SAN Jodel DR.1050 | J. S. Hill | |
| G-AZWS | PA-28R Cherokee Arrow 180 | J. E. Shepherd & C. A. Douglas | |
| G-AZWT | Westland Lysander IIIA (V9441) | Strathallan Aircraft Collection | |
| G-AZWW | PA-23 Aztec 250E | Phoenix Aviation (Bedford) Ltd/Cranfield | |
| G-AZWY | PA-24 Comanche 260 | Keymer Son & Co Ltd/Biggin Hill | |
| G-AZXA | Beech 95-C55 Baron | F.R. Aviation Ltd/Bournemouth | |
| G-AZXB | Cameron O-65 balloon | R. J. Mitchener & P. F.Smart | |
| G-AZXC | Cessna F.150L | S. Redfearn/Netherthorpe | |
| G-AZXD | Cessna F.172L | Birdlake Ltd/Wellesbourne | |
| G-AZXG | PA-23 Aztec 250D | N. J. Le Fevre & M. J. Leeder/Norwich | |
| G-AZXR | BN-2A-9 Islander | Stanton Aircraft Management Ltd | |
| G-AZYA | GY-80 Horizon 160 | T. Poole & ptnrs/Sywell | |
| G-AZYB | Bell 47H-1 ★ | International Helicopter Museum/Weston-s-Mare | |
| G-AZYD | M.S.893A Rallye Commodore | Buckminster Gliding Club Ltd/Saltby | |
| G-AZYF | PA-28 Cherokee 180 | J. C. Glynn/E. Midlands | |
| G-AZYM | Cessna E.310Q | Kingswinford Engineering Co Ltd | |
| G-AZYS | CP.301C-1 Emeraude | F. P. L. Clauson | |
| G-AZYU | PA-23 Aztec 250E | L. J. Martin/Biggin Hill | |
| G-AZYV | Burns O-77 balloon | B. F. G. Ribbans *Contrary Mary* | |
| G-AZYY | Slingsby T.61A Falke | J. A. Towers | |
| G-AZYZ | WA.51A Pacific | Yankee Zulu Ltd/Biggin Hill | |
| G-AZZG | Cessna 188 Agwagon | N. C. Kensington | |
| G-AZZH | Practavia Pilot Sprite 115 | K. G. Stewart | |
| G-AZZK | Cessna 414 | D. O. McIntyre | |
| G-AZZO | PA-28 Cherokee 140 | R. J. Hind/Elstree | |
| G-AZZP | Cessna F.172H | M. Bell & ptnrs/Exeter | |
| G-AZZR | Cessna F.150L | J. B. Small/Swansea | |
| G-AZZS | PA-34-200 Seneca II | Robin Cook Aviation/Shoreham | |
| G-AZZT | PA-28 Cherokee 180 ★ | *Ground instruction airframe*/Cranfield | |
| G-AZZV | Cessna F.172L | Century Composites Ltd | |
| G-AZZW | Fournier RF-5 | Aviation Special Developments | |
| G-AZZX | Cessna FRA.150L | J. E. Uprichard & ptnrs/Newtownards | |
| G-AZZZ | D.H.82A Tiger Moth | S. W. McKay | |
| G-BAAD | Evans Super VP-1 | R. A. Martin | |
| G-BAAF | Manning-Flanders MF1 replica | Aviation Film Services Ltd/Booker | |

53

| Notes | Reg. | Type | Owner or Operator |
|---|---|---|---|
| | G-BAAH | Coates SA.III Swalesong | J. R. Coates |
| | G-BAAI | M.S.893A Rallye Commodore | R. D. Taylor/Thruxton |
| | G-BAAK | Cessna 207 | Border Parachute Centre |
| | G-BAAL | Cessna 172A | Rochester Aviation Ltd |
| | G-BAAP | PA-28R Cherokee Arrow 200 | Shirley A. Shelley/Biggin Hill |
| | G-BAAT | Cessna 182P Skylane | A. H. Hunt/St Just |
| | G-BAAU | Enstrom F-28C-UK | M. Upton |
| | G-BAAW | Jodel D.119 | K. J. Cockrill/Ipswich |
| | G-BAAX | Cameron O-84 balloon | The New Holker Estate Co Ltd *Holker Hall* |
| | G-BAAZ | PA-28R Cherokee Arrow 200D | A. W. Rix/Guernsey |
| | G-BABB | Cessna F.150L | Seawing Flying Club Ltd/Southend |
| | G-BABC | Cessna F.150L | Suffolk Aero Club Ltd/Ipswich |
| | G-BABD | Cessna FRA.150L | C. J. Hopewell |
| | G-BABE | Taylor JT.2 Titch | P. D. G. Grist/Sibson |
| | G-BABG | PA-28 Cherokee 180 | S. J. Mather & N. P. Tyne |
| | G-BABH | Cessna F.150L | Skyviews & General Ltd/Leeds |
| | G-BABK | PA-34-200 Seneca II | D. F. J. & N. R. Flashman/Biggin Hill |
| | G-BABY | Taylor JT.2 Titch | R. E. Finlay |
| | G-BACB | PA-34-200 Seneca II | London Flight Centre (Stansted) Ltd |
| | G-BACC | Cessna FRA.150L | C. M. & J. H. Cooper/Cranfield |
| | G-BACE | Fournier RF-5 | R. W. K. Stead/Perranporth |
| | G-BACH | Enstrom F-28A | M. & P. Food Products Ltd |
| | G-BACJ | Jodel D.120 | Wearside Flying Association/Newcastle |
| | G-BACL | Jodel D.150 | M. L. Sargeant/Biggin Hill |
| | G-BACN | Cessna FRA.150L | Air Service Training Ltd/Perth |
| | G-BACO | Cessna FRA.150L | W. R. Burgess & ptnrs/Sibson |
| | G-BACP | Cessna FRA.150L | B. A. Mills |
| | G-BADC | Luton Beta B.2A | H. M. Mackenzie |
| | G-BADH | Slingsby T.61A Falke | Falke Flying Group |
| | G-BADI | PA-23 Aztec 250D | W. London Aero Services Ltd/ White Waltham |
| | G-BADJ | PA-E23 Aztec 250E | CKS Air Ltd/Southend |
| | G-BADK | BN-2A-8 Islander | CB Helicopters |
| | G-BADL | PA-34-200 Seneca II | Cartographical Services (Southampton) Ltd/Birmingham |
| | G-BADM | D.62B Condor | D. P. Trimm-Allen |
| | G-BADO | PA-32 Cherokee Six 300E | B. J. Haylor & ptnrs/Southampton |
| | G-BADP | Boeing 737-204 | Britannia Airways Ltd *Sir Arthur Whitten Brown*/Luton |
| | G-BADR | Boeing 737-204 | Britannia Airways Ltd *Capt Robert Falconer Scott*/Luton |
| | G-BADU | Cameron O-56 balloon | J. Philp *Dream Machine* |
| | G-BADV | Brochet MB-50 | P. A. Cairns/Dunkeswell |
| | G-BADW | Pitts S-2A Special | R. E. Mitchell/Coventry |
| | G-BADZ | Pitts S-2A Special | Tiger Club (1990) Ltd/Headcorn |
| | G-BAEB | Robin DR.400/160 | P. D. W. King |
| | G-BAEC | Robin HR.100/210 | Robin Travel |
| | G-BAED | PA-23 Aztec 250C | Advanced Airship Corp. Ltd/Jurby |
| | G-BAEE | Jodel DR.1050/M1 | J. B. Randle |
| | G-BAEF | Boeing 727-46 | Dan-Air Services Ltd/Gatwick |
| | G-BAEM | Robin DR.400/125 | M. A. Webb/Booker |
| | G-BAEN | Robin DR.400/180 | B. T. & L. M. Spreckley/Shoreham |
| | G-BAEP | Cessna FRA.150L (modified) | A. M. Lynn |
| | G-BAER | Cosmic Wind | R. S. Voice/Redhill |
| | G-BAET | Piper J-3C-65 Cub | C. J. Rees |
| | G-BAEU | Cessna F.150L | Skyviews & General Ltd |
| | G-BAEV | Cessna FRA.150L | N. J. Wiszowaty/Blackbushe |
| | G-BAEW | Cessna F.172M | Northamptonshire School of Flying Ltd/ Sywell |
| | G-BAEY | Cessna F.172M | R. Fursman/Southampton |
| | G-BAEZ | Cessna FRA.150L | E. Bannister |
| | G-BAFA | AA-5 Traveler | C. F. Mackley/Stapleford |
| | G-BAFD | MBB Bo 105D | Bond Helicopters Ltd/Aberdeen |
| | G-BAFG | D.H.82A Tiger Moth | J. E. & P. J. Shaw |
| | G-BAFH | Evans VP-1 | C. M. Gibson |
| | G-BAFI | Cessna F.177RG | Grandsystem Ltd/Bristol |
| | G-BAFL | Cessna 182P | Threshold Ltd |
| | G-BAFM | AT-16 Harvard IIB (FS728) | Parker Airways Ltd/Denham |
| | G-BAFP | Robin DR.400/160 | A. S. Langdale & J. Bevis-Lawson/ Shoreham |
| | G-BAFS | PA-18 Super Cub 150 | M. D. Morris/Sandown |
| | G-BAFT | PA-18 Super Cub 150 | Cambridge University Gliding Trust Ltd/ Duxford |

| Reg. | Type | Owner or Operator | Notes |
|------|------|-------------------|-------|
| G-BAFU | PA-28 Cherokee 140 | R. C. Saunders/Gamston | |
| G-BAFV | PA-18 Super Cub 95 | P. Elliott | |
| G-BAFW | PA-28 Cherokee 140 | Foxtrot Whisky Aviation | |
| G-BAFX | Robin DR.400/140 | Nicholas Advertising Ltd | |
| G-BAGB | SIAI-Marchetti SF.260 | British Midland Airways Ltd/ E. Midlands | |
| G-BAGC | Robin DR.400/140 | Hempalm Ltd/Headcorn | |
| G-BAGF | Jodel D.92 Bebe | G. R. French | |
| G-BAGG | PA-32 Cherokee Six 300E | Hornair Ltd | |
| G-BAGI | Cameron O-31 balloon | D. C. & S. J. Boxall | |
| G-BAGL | SA.341G Gazelle Srs 1 | Autokraft Ltd | |
| G-BAGN | Cessna F.177RG | R. W. J. Andrews | |
| G-BAGO | Cessna 421B | Thorntons PLC/E. Midlands | |
| G-BAGR | Robin DR.400/140 | F. C. Aris & J. D. Last/Mona | |
| G-BAGS | Robin DR.400/180 2+2 | Headcorn Flying School Ltd | |
| G-BAGT | Helio H.295 Courier | B. J. C. Woodall Ltd | |
| G-BAGU | Luton LA-5A Major | J. Gawley | |
| G-BAGV | Cessna U.206F | Scottish Parachute Club/Strathallan | |
| G-BAGX | PA-28 Cherokee 140 | D. S. W. Wells | |
| G-BAGY | Cameron O-84 balloon | P. G. Dunnington *Beatrice* | |
| G-BAHD | Cessna 182P Skylane | G. G. Ferriman | |
| G-BAHE | PA-28 Cherokee 140 | A. H. Evans & A. O. Jones/Sleap | |
| G-BAHF | PA-28 Cherokee 140 | S. J. Green/Halfpenny Green | |
| G-BAHG | PA-24 Comanche 260 | Friendly Aviation (Jersey) Ltd | |
| G-BAHH | Wallis WA-121 | K. H. Wallis | |
| G-BAHI | Cessna F.150H | A. G. Brindle/Blackpool | |
| G-BAHJ | PA-24 Comanche 250 | K. Cooper | |
| G-BAHL | Robin DR.400/160 | R. E. Thorns & G. W. Dimmer/Old Sarum | |
| G-BAHN | Beech 95-58TC Baron | AM Aviation Ltd | |
| G-BAHO | Beech C.23 Sundowner | G-ATJG Private Aircraft Syndicate Ltd | |
| G-BAHP | Volmer VJ.22 Sportsman | J. F. Morris | |
| G-BAHS | PA-28R Cherokee Arrow 200-II | A. A. Wild & ptnrs | |
| G-BAHU | Enstrom F-28A | Allen Timpany Racing | |
| G-BAHX | Cessna 182P | A. Dunkerley & ptnrs/Blackpool | |
| G-BAHZ | PA-28R Cherokee Arrow 200-II | J. H. Reynolds | |
| G-BAIA | PA-32 Cherokee Six 300E | Langham International (Aircraft) Ltd/ Southend | |
| G-BAIB | Enstrom F-28A | GB Air Academy Ltd/Goodwood | |
| G-BAIH | PA-28R Cherokee Arrow 200-II | G. J. Williamson | |
| G-BAII | Cessna FRA.150L | Air Service Training Ltd/Perth | |
| G-BAIL | Cessna FR.172J | G. Greenall | |
| G-BAIK | Cessna F.150L | Wickenby Aviation Ltd | |
| G-BAIM | Cessna 310Q | Air Service Training Ltd/Perth | |
| G-BAIN | Cessna FRA.150L | Air Service Training Ltd/Perth | |
| G-BAIP | Cessna F.150L | W. D. Cliffe & J. F. Platt/Wellesbourne | |
| G-BAIR | Thunder Ax7-77 balloon | P. A. & Mrs M. Hutchins | |
| G-BAIS | Cessna F.177RG | A. J. Everex & T. W. Goodall | |
| G-BAIW | Cessna F.172M | Humber Aviation Ltd | |
| G-BAIX | Cessna F.172M | R. A. Nichols/Elstree | |
| G-BAIY | Cameron O-65 balloon | Budget Rent A Car (UK) Ltd | |
| G-BAIZ | Slingsby T.61A Falke | Falke Syndicate | |
| G-BAJA | Cessna F.177RG | Don Ward Productions Ltd/Biggin Hill | |
| G-BAJB | Cessna F.177RG | K. D. Horton/Staverton | |
| G-BAJC | Evans VP-1 | J. R. Clements/Rochester | |
| G-BAJE | Cessna 177 Cardinal | J. E. Cull | |
| G-BAJN | AA-5 Traveler | Janacrew Flying Group | |
| G-BAJO | AA-5 Traveler | J. R. Howard/Blackpool | |
| G-BAJR | PA-28 Cherokee 180 | Chosen Few Flying Group/ Newtownards | |
| G-BAJW | Boeing 727-46 | Dan-Air Services Ltd/Gatwick | |
| G-BAJY | Robin DR.400/180 | F. Birch & K. J. Pike/Sturgate | |
| G-BAJZ | Robin DR.400/125 | Rochester Aviation Ltd | |
| G-BAKD | PA-34-200 Seneca II | Andrews Professional Colour Laboratories/Elstree | |
| G-BAKH | PA-28 Cherokee 140 | Woodgate Air Services (IoM) Ltd/ Ronaldsway | |
| G-BAKJ | PA-30 Twin Comanche 160B | M. F. Fisher & W. R. Lawes/Biggin Hill | |
| G-BAKK | Cessna F.172H ★ | *Parachute jump trainer*/Coventry | |
| G-BAKL | F.27 Friendship Mk 200 | Air UK Ltd/Norwich | |
| G-BAKM | Robin DR.400/140 | MKS Syndicate | |
| G-BAKN | SNCAN Stampe SV-4C | M. Holloway | |
| G-BAKO | Cameron O-84 balloon | D. C. Dokk-Olsen *Pied Piper* | |

| Notes | Reg. | Type | Owner or Operator |
|---|---|---|---|
| | G-BAKR | Jodel D.117 | A. B. Bailey/White Waltham |
| | G-BAKS | AB-206B JetRanger 2 | Dollar Air Services Ltd/Coventry |
| | G-BAKV | PA-18 Super Cub 150 | Pounds Marine Shipping Ltd/ Goodwood |
| | G-BAKW | B.121 Pup 2 | The KW Group/Shoreham |
| | G-BAKY | Slingsby T.61C Falke | G. A. Schulz & A. Jones/Leicester |
| | G-BALF | Robin DR.400/140 | F. A. Spear/Panshanger |
| | G-BALG | Robin DR.400/180 | R. Jones |
| | G-BALH | Robin DR.400/140B | J. D. Copsey |
| | G-BALI | Robin DR.400 2+2 | R. A. Gridley |
| | G-BALJ | Robin DR.400/180 | D. A. Bett & D. de Lacey-Rowe |
| | G-BALK | SNCAN Stampe SV-4C | L. J. Rice |
| | G-BALM | Cessna 340 | KK Demel Ltd |
| | G-BALN | Cessna T.310Q | O'Brien Properties Ltd/Shoreham |
| | G-BALS | T.66 Nipper 3 | L. W. Shaw |
| | G-BALT | Enstrom F-28A | Codnor Pet-Aquatics |
| | G-BALX | D.H.82A Tiger Moth (N6848) | Toadair |
| | G-BALY | Practavia Pilot Sprite 150 | A. L. Young |
| | G-BALZ | Bell 212 | B.E.A.S. Ltd/Redhill |
| | G-BAMB | Slingsby T.61C Falke | Bambi Aircraft Club |
| | G-BAMC | Cessna F.150L | D. F. Smith |
| | G-BAME | Volmer VJ-22 Sportsman | A. McLeod |
| | G-BAMF | MBB Bo 105D | Bond Helicopters Ltd/Bourn |
| | G-BAMG | Avions Lobet Ganagobie | J. A. Brompton |
| | G-BAMJ | Cessna 182P | A. E. Kedros |
| | G-BAMK | Cameron D-96 airship | D. W. Liddiard |
| | G-BAML | Bell 206B JetRanger 2 | Heliscott Ltd |
| | G-BAMM | PA-28 Cherokee 235 | G-BAMM Group |
| | G-BAMR | PA-16 Clipper | H. Royce |
| | G-BAMS | Robin DR.400/160 | G-BAMS Ltd/Headcorn |
| | G-BAMU | Robin DR.400/160 | The Alternative Flying Group/Sywell |
| | G-BAMV | Robin DR.400/180 | Rochester Aviation Ltd |
| | G-BAMY | PA-28R Cherokee Arrow 200-II | G. R. Gilbert & ptnrs/Birmingham |
| | G-BANA | Robin DR.221 | G. T. Pryor |
| | G-BANB | Robin DR.400/180 | Time Electronics Ltd/Biggin Hill |
| | G-BANC | GY-201 Minicab | J. T. S. Lewis & J. E. Williams |
| | G-BAND | Cameron O-84 balloon | Mid-Bucks Farmers Balloon Group Clover |
| | G-BANE | Cessna FRA.150L | Falcon Flight Training Ltd/Eglinton |
| | G-BANF | Luton LA-4A Minor | W. McNally |
| | G-BANG | Cameron O-84 balloon | R. F. Harrower |
| | G-BANK | PA-34-200 Seneca II | Cleveland Flying School Ltd/Teesside |
| | G-BANS | PA-34-200 Seneca II | Stapleford Flying Club Ltd |
| | G-BANT | Cameron O-65 balloon | M. A. Dworski & R. M. Bishop |
| | G-BANU | Wassmer Jodel D.120 | C. E. McKinney |
| | G-BANV | Phoenix Currie Wot | K. Knight |
| | G-BANW | CP.1330 Super Emeraude | P. S. Milner |
| | G-BANX | Cessna F.172M | D. Sharp |
| | G-BAOB | Cessna F.172M | Bulldog Aviation Ltd/Earls Colne |
| | G-BAOG | M.S.880B Rallye Club | G. W. Simpson |
| | G-BAOH | M.S.880B Rallye Club | R. J. Humphries |
| | G-BAOJ | M.S.880B Rallye Club | BOJ Group/Andrewsfield |
| | G-BAOM | M.S.880B Rallye Club | D. H. Tonkin |
| | G-BAOP | Cessna FRA.150L | M. K. Field |
| | G-BAOS | Cessna F.172M | F. W. Ellis & ptnrs |
| | G-BAOU | AA-5 Traveler | C. J. Earle & R. C. S. Evans |
| | G-BAOV | AA-5A Cheetah | A. Kerridge |
| | G-BAOW | Cameron O-65 balloon | P. I. White Winslow Boy |
| | G-BAOY | Cameron S-31 balloon | Shell-Mex BP Ltd New Potato |
| | G-BAPA | Fournier RF-5B Sperber | S. T. Evans & ptnrs |
| | G-BAPB | D.H.C.1 Chipmunk 22 | R. C. P. Brookhouse/Redhill |
| | G-BAPC | Luton LA-4A Minor | Midland Aircraft Preservation Soc |
| | G-BAPF | V.814 Viscount | Hot Air/British Air Ferries/Southend |
| | G-BAPG | V.814 Viscount | Ali Finance Ltd/Southend |
| | G-BAPI | Cessna FRA.150L | Industrial Supplies (Peterborough) Ltd/ Sibson |
| | G-BAPJ | Cessna FRA.150L | M. D. Page/Manston |
| | G-BAPK | Cessna F.150L | Andrewsfield Flying Club Ltd |
| | G-BAPL | PA-23 Turbo Aztec 250E | Medici Spa Marine & Exploration Ltd |
| | G-BAPM | Fuji FA.200-160 | R. P. Munday/Biggin Hill |
| | G-BAPP | Evans VP-1 | K. McNaughton |
| | G-BAPR | Jodel D.11 | R. G. Marshall |
| | G-BAPS | Campbell Cougar ★ | International Helicopter Museum/ Weston-s-Mare |

| Reg. | Type | Owner or Operator | Notes |
|------|------|-------------------|-------|
| G-BAPV | Robin DR.400/160 | J. D. & M. Millne | |
| G-BAPW | PA-28R Cherokee Arrow 180 | Papa Whisky Flying Group | |
| G-BAPX | Robin DR.400/160 | M. A. Musselwhite | |
| G-BAPY | Robin HR.100/210 | Gloria Baby Aviation Ltd | |
| G-BARB | PA-34-200 Seneca II | S. Wood | |
| G-BARC | Cessna FR.172J | G. N. Hopcraft | |
| G-BARD | Cessna 337C | Jadealto (Sales & Marketing) Ltd | |
| G-BARF | Jodel D.112 Club | C. D. Sword & A. G. V. McLintock | |
| G-BARG | Cessna E.310Q | Sally Marine Ltd | |
| G-BARH | Beech C.23 Sundowner | D. Wall | |
| G-BARJ | Bell 212 | Autair International Ltd/Panshanger | |
| G-BARN | Taylor JT.2 Titch | R. G. W. Newton | |
| G-BARP | Bell 206B JetRanger 2 | S.W. Electricity Board/Bristol | |
| G-BARS | D.H.C.1 Chipmunk 22 | T. I. Sutton/Chester | |
| G-BARV | Cessna 310Q | Old England Watches Ltd/Elstree | |
| G-BARZ | Scheibe SF.28A Tandem Falke | J. A. Fox & ptnrs/Dishforth | |
| G-BASB | Enstrom F-28A | The Big Chopper Co (Helicopters) Ltd | |
| G-BASD | B.121 Pup 2 | C. C. Brown/Leicester | |
| G-BASG | AA-5 Traveler | ASG Aviation/Glenrothes | |
| G-BASH | AA-5 Traveler | J. J. Woodhouse | |
| G-BASJ | PA-28 Cherokee 180 | ABS Building & Roofing Services Ltd | |
| G-BASL | PA-28 Cherokee 140 | Air Navigation & Trading Ltd/Blackpool | |
| G-BASM | PA-34-200 Seneca II | Poplar Aviation/Ipswich | |
| G-BASN | Beech C.23 Sundowner | M. F. Fisher | |
| G-BASO | Lake LA-4 Amphibian | R. J. Willies | |
| G-BASP | B.121 Pup 1 | Northamptonshire School of Flying Ltd/ Sywell | |
| G-BASX | PA-34-200 Seneca II | J. W. Anstee & Anstee & Ware Ltd | |
| G-BATC | MBB Bo 105D | Bond Helicopters Ltd/Swansea | |
| G-BATJ | Jodel D.119 | E. G. Waite/Shobdon | |
| G-BATM | PA-32 Cherokee Six 300E | Patgrove Ltd/Bolney | |
| G-BATN | PA-23 Aztec 250E | Marshall of Cambridge Ltd | |
| G-BATR | PA-34-200 Seneca II | Aerohire Ltd/Halfpenny Green | |
| G-BATS | Taylor JT.1 Monoplane | J. Jennings | |
| G-BATT | Hughes 269C | Fairglobe Ltd | |
| G-BATV | PA-28 Cherokee 180D | J. N. Rudsdale | |
| G-BATW | PA-28 Cherokee 140 | C. R. Lambert/Earls Colne | |
| G-BATX | PA-23 Aztec 250E | Tayside Aviation Ltd/Dundee | |
| G-BAUA | PA-23 Aztec 250D | David Parr & Associates Ltd/Shobdon | |
| G-BAUC | PA-25 Pawnee 235 | Southdown Gliding Club Ltd | |
| G-BAUD | Robin DR.400/160 | E. J. A. Woolnough | |
| G-BAUE | Cessna 310Q | A. J. Dyer/Elstree | |
| G-BAUH | Jodel D.112 | G. A. & D. Shepherd | |
| G-BAUI | PA-23 Aztec 250D | SFT Aviation Ltd/Bournemouth | |
| G-BAUJ | PA-23 Aztec 250E | S. J. & C. J. Westley/Cranfield | |
| G-BAUK | Hughes 269C | Curtis Engineering (Frome) Ltd | |
| G-BAUR | F.27 Friendship Mk 200 | Air UK Ltd *Robert Louis Stevenson*/ Norwich | |
| G-BAUV | Cessna F.150L | Skyviews & General Ltd | |
| G-BAUW | PA-23 Aztec 250E | R. E. Myson | |
| G-BAUY | Cessna FRA.150L | The PMM Group/Glenrothes | |
| G-BAUZ | SNCAN NC.854S | W. A. Ashley & D. Horne | |
| G-BAVB | Cessna F.172M | T. J. Nokes & T. V. Phillips | |
| G-BAVC | Cessna F.150L | Butler Associates (Aviation) Ltd | |
| G-BAVH | D.H.C.1 Chipmunk 22 | Portsmouth Naval Gliding Club/ Lee-on-Solent | |
| G-BAVL | PA-23 Aztec 250E | Seraph Aviation/Shoreham | |
| G-BAVO | Boeing Stearman N2S (26) | J. Charles | |
| G-BAVR | AA-5 Traveler | E. R. Pyatt | |
| G-BAVS | AA-5 Traveler | V. J. Peake/Headcorn | |
| G-BAVU | Cameron A-105 balloon | J. D. Michaelis | |
| G-BAVX | HPR-7 Herald 214 | British Air Ferries Ltd/Southend | |
| G-BAVZ | PA-23 Aztec 250E | Ravenair/Manchester | |
| G-BAWB | PA-23 Aztec 250C | Emberden Ltd/Biggin Hill | |
| G-BAWG | PA-28R Cherokee Arrow 200-II | Solent Air Ltd | |
| G-BAWI | Enstrom F-28A-UK | M. & P. Food Products Ltd | |
| G-BAWK | PA-28 Cherokee 140 | Newcastle-upon-Tyne Aero Club Ltd | |
| G-BAWN | PA-30 Twin Comanche 160C | P. A. Greenhalgh | |
| G-BAWR | Robin HR.100/210 | Yarmouth Marine Service/Sandown | |
| G-BAWU | PA-30 Twin Comanche 160B | CCH Aviation Ltd | |
| G-BAWW | Thunder Ax7-77 balloon | M. L. C. Hutchins *Taurus*/Holland | |
| G-BAXD | BN-2A Mk III Trislander | Aurigny Air Services/Guernsey | |
| G-BAXE | Hughes 269A | Reethorpe Engineering Ltd | |

| Notes | Reg. | Type | Owner or Operator |
|---|---|---|---|
| | G-BAXF | Cameron O-77 balloon | R. D. Sargeant & M. F. Lasson |
| | G-BAXH | Cessna 310Q | D. A. Williamson |
| | G-BAXJ | PA-32 Cherokee Six 300B | UK Parachute Services/Ipswich |
| | G-BAXK | Thunder Ax7-77 balloon | T. J. Orchard & A. R. Snook |
| | G-BAXP | PA-23 Aztec 250E | Ashcombe Ltd |
| | G-BAXS | Bell 47G-5 | Helicopter Supplies & Engineering Ltd/ Bournemouth |
| | G-BAXT | PA-28R Cherokee Arrow 200-II | P. R. Phealon/Old Sarum |
| | G-BAXU | Cessna F.150L | W. Lancs Aero Club Ltd/Woodvale |
| | G-BAXY | Cessna F.172M | N. A. Ali |
| | G-BAXZ | PA-28 Cherokee 140 | H. Martin & D. Norris/Halton |
| | G-BAYC | Cameron O-65 balloon | D. Whitlock & R. T. F. Mitchell |
| | G-BAYL | Nord 1203/III Norecrin | D. M. Fincham |
| | G-BAYO | Cessna 150L | Cheshire Air Training School (Merseyside) Ltd/Liverpool |
| | G-BAYP | Cessna 150L | Three Counties Aero Club Ltd/ Blackbushe |
| | G-BAYR | Robin HR.100/210 | Gilbey Warren Co Ltd/Stapleford |
| | G-BAYV | SNCAN 1101 Noralpha (1480)★ | Booker Aircraft Museum |
| | G-BAYZ | Bellanca 7GCBC Citabria | Cambridge University Gliding Trust Ltd/ Gransdon |
| | G-BAZB | H.S.125 Srs 400B | Short Bros PLC/Sydenham |
| | G-BAZC | Robin DR.400/160 | Southern Sailplanes |
| | G-BAZG | Boeing 737-204 | Britannia Airways Ltd *Florence Nightingale*/Luton |
| | G-BAZH | Boeing 737-204 | Britannia Airways Ltd *Sir Frederick Handley Page*/Luton |
| | G-BAZJ | HPR-7 Herald 209 ★ | Guernsey Airport Fire Services |
| | G-BAZM | Jodel D.11 | Bingley Flying Group/Leeds |
| | G-BAZS | Cessna F.150L | Sherburn Aero Club Ltd |
| | G-BAZT | Cessna F.172M | M. Fraser/Exeter |
| | G-BAZU | PA-28R Cherokee Arrow 200 | S. C. Simmons/White Waltham |
| | G-BBAE | L.1011-385 TriStar 100 | Caledonian Airways *Loch Earn*/ Gatwick |
| | G-BBAF | L.1011-385 TriStar | British Airways *Babbacombe Bay*/ Heathrow |
| | G-BBAG | L.1011-385 TriStar | British Airways *Bridgwater Bay*/ Heathrow |
| | G-BBAH | L.1011-385 TriStar | British Airways *Lyme Bay*/Heathrow |
| | G-BBAI | L.1011-385 TriStar | Caledonian Airways *Loch Inver*/Gatwick |
| | G-BBAJ | L.1011-385 TriStar 100 | Caledonian Airways *Loch Rannoch*/ Gatwick |
| | G-BBAK | M.S.894A Rallye Minerva | R. B. Hemsworth & C. L. Hill/Exeter |
| | G-BBAW | Robin HR.100/210 | Scoba Ltd/Goodwood |
| | G-BBAX | Robin DR.400/140 | S. R. Young |
| | G-BBAY | Robin DR.400/140 | Rothwell Group |
| | G-BBAZ | Hiller UH-12E | Copley Farms Ltd |
| | G-BBBC | Cessna F.150L | W. J. Greenfield |
| | G-BBBI | AA-5 Traveler | G. P. Williams |
| | G-BBBK | PA-28 Cherokee 140 | Bencray Ltd/Blackpool |
| | G-BBBM | Bell 206B JetRanger 2 | Express Newspapers PLC |
| | G-BBBN | PA-28 Cherokee 180 | BT Flying Group |
| | G-BBBO | SIPA 903 | J. S. Hemmings & C. R. Steer |
| | G-BBBW | FRED Series 2 | D. L. Webster/Sherburn |
| | G-BBBX | Cessna E310L | Atlantic Air Transport Ltd/Coventry |
| | G-BBBY | PA-28 Cherokee 140 | J. L. Yourell/Luton |
| | G-BBCA | Bell 206B JetRanger 2 | E. Wootton |
| | G-BBCB | Western O-65 balloon | M. Westwood *Cee Bee* |
| | G-BBCC | PA-23 Aztec 250D | Dorglen Ltd/Coventry |
| | G-BBCD | Beech 95-B55 Baron | L. M. Tulloch |
| | G-BBCH | Robin DR.400/2+2 | Headcorn Flying School Ltd |
| | G-BBCI | Cessna 150H | N. R. Windley |
| | G-BBCK | Cameron O-77 balloon | R. J. Leathart *The Mary Gloster* |
| | G-BBCN | Robin HR.100/210 | K. T. G. Atkins/Teesside |
| | G-BBCP | Thunder Ax6-56 balloon | J. M. Robinson *Jack Frost* |
| | G-BBCS | Robin DR.400/140 | J. A. Thomas |
| | G-BBCW | PA-23 Aztec 250E | JDT Holdings Ltd/Sturgate |
| | G-BBCY | Luton LA-4A Minor | D. C. Stokes |
| | G-BBCZ | AA-5 Traveler | P. J. Kember |
| | G-BBDB | PA-28 Cherokee 180 | T. D. Strange/Newtownards |
| | G-BBDC | PA-28 Cherokee 140 | C. Doggett & A. Dunk |
| | G-BBDD | PA-28 Cherokee 140 | Midland Air Training School |

| Reg. | Type | Owner or Operator | Notes |
|------|------|-------------------|-------|
| G-BBDE | PA-28R Cherokee Arrow 200-II | R. L. Coleman & A. E. Stevens | |
| G-BBDG | Concorde 100 ★ | British Aerospace PLC/Filton | |
| G-BBDH | Cessna F.172M | P. S. C. & B. J. Comina | |
| G-BBDJ | Thunder Ax6-56 balloon | S. W. D. & H. B. Ashby *Jack Tar* | |
| G-BBDK | V.808C Viscount Freightmaster | British Air Ferries *Viscount Linley/* Southend | |
| G-BBDL | AA-5 Traveler | D. G. Hopkins & W. Woods/Coventry | |
| G-BBDM | AA-5 Traveler | D. J. & P. L. Hazell | |
| G-BBDN | Taylor JT.1 Monoplane | T. Barnes | |
| G-BBDO | PA-23 Turbo Aztec 250E | R. Long/Bristol | |
| G-BBDP | Robin DR.400/160 | Robin Lance Aviation Associates Ltd | |
| G-BBDT | Cessna 150H | U. K. Mercer & J. K. Sibbald | |
| G-BBDV | SIPA S.903 | W. McAndrew | |
| G-BBEA | Luton LA-4A Minor | W. E. R. Jenkins | |
| G-BBEB | PA-28R Cherokee Arrow 200-II | R. D. Rippingale/Thruxton | |
| G-BBEC | PA-28 Cherokee 180 | C. F. Bishop/Clacton | |
| G-BBED | M.S.894A Rallye Minerva 220 | Sky-Ad Ltd/Birmingham | |
| G-BBEF | PA-28 Cherokee 140 | Air Navigation & Trading Co Ltd/ Blackpool | |
| G-BBEI | PA-31 Turbo Navajo | BKS Surveys Ltd/Exeter | |
| G-BBEL | PA-28R Cherokee Arrow 180 | G. R. Cole & A. Grimshaw/Ronaldsway | |
| G-BBEN | Bellanca 7GCBC Citabria | C. A. G. Schofield | |
| G-BBEO | Cessna FRA.150L | R. H. Ford | |
| G-BBEV | PA-28 Cherokee 140 | Comed Aviation Ltd/Blackpool | |
| G-BBEX | Cessna 185A Skywagon | Westward Airways (Lands End) Ltd | |
| G-BBEY | PA-23 Aztec 250E | Cormack (Aircraft Services) Ltd/ Glasgow | |
| G-BBFC | AA-1B Trainer | T. F. Shorter/Lydd | |
| G-BBFD | PA-28R Cherokee Arrow 200-II | CR Aviation Ltd | |
| G-BBFL | GY-201 Minicab | D. B. Busfield | |
| G-BBFS | Van Den Bemden gas balloon | A. J. F. Smith *Le Tomate* | |
| G-BBFV | PA-32 Cherokee Six 260 | A. L. Burton/Netherthorpe | |
| G-BBFZ | PA-28R Cherokee Arrow 200-II | Larkfield Garage (Chepstow) Ltd | |
| G-BBGB | PA-E23 Aztec 250E | Eurodynamics Systems PLC/Luton | |
| G-BBGC | M.S.893E Rallye Commodore 180 | A. Somerville | |
| G-BBGE | PA-23 Aztec 250D | B. Jones | |
| G-BBGH | AA-5 Traveler | L. W. Mitchell & D. Abbiss | |
| G-BBGI | Fuji FA.200-160 | J. J. Young/Seething | |
| G-BBGJ | Cessna 180 | R. C. Chapman | |
| G-BBGL | Baby Great Lakes | F. Ball | |
| G-BBGR | Cameron O-65 balloon | M. L. & L. P. Willoughby | |
| G-BBGX | Cessna 182P Skylane | WOC Hire Ltd | |
| G-BBGZ | CHABA 42 balloon | G. Laslett & ptnrs | |
| G-BBHB | PA-31 Turbo Navajo | Photomap (Jersey) Ltd | |
| G-BBHC | Enstrom F-28A | Blades Helicopters Ltd/Goodwood | |
| G-BBHD | Enstrom F-28A | R. E. Harvey | |
| G-BBHF | PA-23 Aztec 250E | Bevan Lynch Aviation Ltd/Birmingham | |
| G-BBHG | Cessna E310Q | Delta Aviation Ltd/Elstree | |
| G-BBHI | Cessna 177RG | T. W. Dean/Biggin Hill | |
| G-BBHJ | Piper J-3C-65 Cub | R. V. Miller & J. Stanbridge | |
| G-BBHK | AT-16 Harvard IIB (FH153) | Bob Warner Aviation/Exeter | |
| G-BBHL | Sikorsky S-61N Mk II | Bristow Helicopters Ltd *Glamis* | |
| G-BBHM | Sikorsky S-61N Mk II | Bristow Helicopters Ltd *Braemar* | |
| G-BBHW | SA.341G Gazelle 1 | McAlpine Aviation Ltd/Hayes | |
| G-BBHX | M.S.893E Rallye Commodore | JKP Aviation | |
| G-BBHY | PA-28 Cherokee 180 | Air Operations Ltd/Guernsey | |
| G-BBIA | PA-28R Cherokee Arrow 200-II | A. G. (Commodities) Ltd/Stapleford | |
| G-BBIC | Cessna 310Q | H. Bollmann Manufacturers Ltd | |
| G-BBID | PA-28 Cherokee 140 | M. & J. M. McCormac | |
| G-BBIF | PA-23 Aztec 250E | Northern Executive Aviation Ltd/ Manchester | |
| G-BBIH | Enstrom F-28A-UK | Pyramid Precision Engineering Ltd | |
| G-BBII | Fiat G-46-3B | A. L. Lindsay & ptnrs/Booker | |
| G-BBIL | PA-28 Cherokee 140 | D. Arlette/Stapleford | |
| G-BBIN | Enstrom F-28A | Southern Air Ltd/Shoreham | |
| G-BBIO | Robin HR.100/210 | R. A. King/Headcorn | |
| G-BBIT | Hughes 269B | Contract Development & Projects (Leeds) Ltd (*stored*) | |
| G-BBIV | Hughes 269C | Pyramid Precision Engineering Ltd | |
| G-BBIX | PA-28 Cherokee 140 | Sterling Contract Hire Ltd | |
| G-BBJB | Thunder Ax7-77 balloon | St Crispin Balloon Group *Dick Darby* | |
| G-BBJI | Isaacs Spitfire (RN218) | A. N. R. Houghton & ptnrs | |

| Notes | Reg. | Type | Owner or Operator |
|-------|------|------|-------------------|
| | G-BBJU | Robin DR.400/140 | J. C. Lister |
| | G-BBJV | Cessna F.177RG | Pilot Magazine/Biggin Hill |
| | G-BBJX | Cessna F.150L | Yorkshire Flying Services Ltd/Leeds |
| | G-BBJY | Cessna F.172M | J. Lucketti/Barton |
| | G-BBJZ | Cessna F.172M | Burks, Green & ptnrs |
| | G-BBKA | Cessna F.150L | R. Hall & L. W. Scattergood |
| | G-BBKB | Cessna F.150L | Shoreham Flight Simulation/ Bournemouth |
| | G-BBKC | Cessna F.172M | W. F. Hall |
| | G-BBKE | Cessna F.150L | Wickenby Aviation Ltd |
| | G-BBKF | Cessna FRA.150L | Compton Abbas Airfield Ltd |
| | G-BBKG | Cessna FR.172J | Sech Services Ltd |
| | G-BBKI | Cessna F.172M | C. W. & S.A . Burman |
| | G-BBKL | CP.301A Emeraude | R. Wells & H. V. Hunter |
| | G-BBKR | Scheibe SF.24A Motorspatz | P. I. Morgans |
| | G-BBKU | Cessna FRA.150L | LAR Aviation Ltd/Shoreham |
| | G-BBKX | PA-28 Cherokee 180 | RAE Flying Club Ltd/Farnborough |
| | G-BBKY | Cessna F.150L | Telair Manchester Ltd |
| | G-BBKZ | Cessna 172M | Exeter Flying Club Ltd |
| | G-BBLA | PA-28 Cherokee 140 | Woodgate Aviation Co Ltd/Woodvale |
| | G-BBLE | Hiller UH-12E | Agricopters Ltd/Chilbolton |
| | G-BBLH | Piper J-3C-65 Cub | Shipping & Airlines Ltd/Biggin Hill |
| | G-BBLL | Cameron O-84 balloon | University of East Anglia Hot-Air Ballooning Club *Boadicea* |
| | G-BBLM | SOCATA Rallye 100S | M. & J. Grafton |
| | G-BBLP | PA-23 Aztec 250D | Donnington Aviation Ltd/E. Midlands |
| | G-BBLS | AA-5 Traveler | V. C. Gover/Prestwick |
| | G-BBLU | PA-34-200 Seneca II | F. Tranter/Manchester |
| | G-BBMB | Robin DR.400/180 | J. T. M. Ball/Biggin Hill |
| | G-BBME | BAC One-Eleven 401AK | Birmingham European Airways Ltd (G-AZMI)/*City of Nottingham* |
| | G-BBMF | BAC One-Eleven 401AK | Birmingham European Airways Ltd (G-ATVU)/*City of Leicester* |
| | G-BBMG | BAC One-Eleven 408EF | Birmingham European Airways Ltd (G-AWEJ)/*Stratford upon Avon* |
| | G-BBMH | EAA. Sports Biplane Model P.1 | K. Dawson |
| | G-BBMJ | PA-23 Aztec 250E | Tindon Ltd/Little Snoring |
| | G-BBMK | PA-31 Turbo Navajo | Steer Aviation Ltd/Biggin Hill |
| | G-BBMN | D.H.C.1 Chipmunk 22 | R. Steiner/Panshanger |
| | G-BBMO | D.H.C.1 Chipmunk 22 | Holland Aerobatics Ltd |
| | G-BBMR | D.H.C.1 Chipmunk T.10 ★ (WB763) | Southall Technical College |
| | G-BBMT | D.H.C.1 Chipmunk 22 | V. F. J. Falconer & W. A. Lee/Dunstable |
| | G-BBMV | D.H.C.1 Chipmunk 22 (WG348) | P. J. Morgan (Aviation) Ltd |
| | G-BBMW | D.H.C.1 Chipmunk 22 (WK628) | Mike Whisky Group/Shoreham |
| | G-BBMX | D.H.C.1 Chipmunk 22 | A. L. Brown & P. S. Murchison |
| | G-BBMZ | D.H.C.1 Chipmunk 22 | Wycombe Gliding School Syndicate/ Booker |
| | G-BBNA | D.H.C.1 Chipmunk 22 (Lycoming) | Coventry Gliding Club Ltd/Husbands Bosworth |
| | G-BBNC | D.H.C.1 Chipmunk T.10 ★ (WP790) | Mosquito Aircraft Museum |
| | G-BBND | D.H.C.1 Chipmunk 22 (WD286) | A. J. Organ/Bourn |
| | G-BBNG | Bell 206B JetRanger 2 | Helicopter Crop Spraying Ltd |
| | G-BBNH | PA-34-200 Seneca II | Lawrence Goodwin Machine Tools Ltd Coventry |
| | G-BBNI | PA-34-200 Seneca II | Channel Aviation (UK) Ltd |
| | G-BBNJ | Cessna F.150L | Sherburn Aero Club |
| | G-BBNN | PA-23 Aztec 250D | J. W. B. Wimble |
| | G-BBNO | PA-23 Aztec 250E | Hedley & Ellis Ltd/Conington |
| | G-BBNR | Cessna 340 | Morris Cohen (Underwear) Ltd |
| | G-BBNT | PA-31-350 Navajo Chieftain | Northern Executive Aviation Ltd/ Manchester |
| | G-BBNV | Fuji FA.200-160 | G. C. Thomas/Kidlington |
| | G-BBNX | Cessna FRA.150L | General Airline Ltd |
| | G-BBNY | Cessna FRA.150L | Air Tows Ltd/Lasham |
| | G-BBNZ | Cessna F.172M | Anchor Plastics (UK) Ltd |
| | G-BBOA | Cessna F.172M | J. W. J. Adkins/Southend |
| | G-BBOC | Cameron O-77 balloon | J. A. B. Gray |
| | G-BBOD | Thunder O-45 balloon | B. R. & M. Boyle |
| | G-BBOE | Robin HR.200/100 | Aberdeen Flying Group |
| | G-BBOH | Pitts S-1S Special | Venom Jet Promotions Ltd/ Bournemouth |

| Reg. | Type | Owner or Operator | Notes |
|------|------|-------------------|-------|
| G-BBOI | Bede BD-5B | Heather V. B. Wheeler | |
| G-BBOJ | PA-23 Aztec 250E ★ | *Instructional airframe*/Cranfield | |
| G-BBOL | PA-18 Super Cub 150 | Lakes Gliding Club Ltd | |
| G-BBOO | Thunder Ax6-56 balloon | K. Meehan *Tigerjack* | |
| G-BBOR | Bell 206B JetRanger 2 | Land Air Ltd | |
| G-BBOX | Thunder Ax7-77 balloon | R. C. Weyda *Rocinante* | |
| G-BBOY | Thunder Ax6-56A balloon | N. C. Faithfull *Eric of Titchfield* | |
| G-BBPJ | Cessna F.172M | B. W. Aviation Ltd/Cardiff | |
| G-BBPK | Evans VP-1 | G. D. E. Macdonald | |
| G-BBPM | Enstrom F-28A | D. Newman | |
| G-BBPN | Enstrom F-28A | Selecting Ltd | |
| G-BBPO | Enstrom F-28A | Southern Air Ltd/Shoreham | |
| G-BBPS | Jodel D.117 | A. Appleby/Redhill | |
| G-BBPU | Boeing 747-136 | British Airways *Virginia Water*/ Heathrow | |
| G-BBPW | Robin HR.100/210 | D. H. Smith | |
| G-BBPX | PA-34-200 Seneca II | Richel Investments Ltd/Guernsey | |
| G-BBPY | PA-28 Cherokee 180 | T. Ogden | |
| G-BBRA | PA-23 Aztec 250D | Mainable Ltd/White Waltham | |
| G-BBRB | D.H.82A Tiger Moth (DF198) | R. Barham/Biggin Hill | |
| G-BBRC | Fuji FA.200-180 | W. & L. Installations & Co Ltd/Fairoaks | |
| G-BBRH | Bell 47G-5A | Helicopter Supplies & Engineering Ltd | |
| G-BBRI | Bell 47G-5A | Camlet Helicopters Ltd/Fairoaks | |
| G-BBRN | Procter Kittiwake | Vari-Prop (GB) Ltd/Exeter | |
| G-BBRV | D.H.C.1 Chipmunk 22 | HSA (Chester) Sports & Social Club | |
| G-BBRX | SIAI-Marchetti S.205-18F | A. L. Cogswell & R. C. West | |
| G-BBRZ | AA-5 Traveler | C. P. Osbourne | |
| G-BBSA | AA-5 Traveler | K. Lynn | |
| G-BBSB | Beech C23 Sundowner | Sundowner Group/Manchester | |
| G-BBSC | Beech B24R Sierra | Beechcombers Flying Group | |
| G-BBSM | PA-32 Cherokee Six 300E | R. Robson/Biggin Hill | |
| G-BBSS | D.H.C.1A Chipmunk 22 | Coventry Gliding Club Ltd/ Husbands Bosworth | |
| G-BBSU | Cessna 421B | Holding & Barnes PLC/Southend | |
| G-BBSV | Cessna 421B | Ashcombe Ltd | |
| G-BBSW | Pietenpol Air Camper | J. K. S. Wills | |
| G-BBTB | Cessna FRA.150L | Compton Abbas Airfield Ltd | |
| G-BBTG | Cessna F.172M | D. H. Laws | |
| G-BBTH | Cessna F.172M | S. Gilmore/Newtownards | |
| G-BBTJ | PA-23 Aztec 250E | Grange Aviation & General Investments Ltd/Shoreham | |
| G-BBTK | Cessna FRA.150L | Air Service Training Ltd/Perth | |
| G-BBTL | PA-23 Aztec 250C | Air Navigation & Trading Co Ltd/ Blackpool | |
| G-BBTS | Beech V35B Bonanza | P. S. Bubbear & J. M. Glanville | |
| G-BBTU | ST-10 Diplomate | P. Campion/Stapleford | |
| G-BBTX | Beech C23 Sundowner | K. Harding/Blackbushe | |
| G-BBTY | Beech C23 Sundowner | TY Club/Biggin Hill | |
| G-BBTZ | Cessna F.150L | Woodgate Air Services Ltd | |
| G-BBUD | Sikorsky S-61N Mk II | British International Helicopters Ltd/ Aberdeen | |
| G-BBUE | AA-5 Traveler | S. J. Southwell-Gray/Blackpool | |
| G-BBUF | AA-5 Traveler | W. McLaren | |
| G-BBUG | PA-16 Clipper | J. Dolan | |
| G-BBUJ | Cessna 421B | Merlin Marine Aviation Ltd | |
| G-BBUL | Mitchell-Procter Kittiwake 1 | R. Bull | |
| G-BBUT | Western O-65 balloon | G. F. Turnbull | |
| G-BBUU | Piper J-3C-65 Cub | O. J. J. Rogers | |
| G-BBVA | Sikorsky S-61N Mk II | Bristow Helicopters Ltd *Vega* | |
| G-BBVE | Cessna 340 | Beechair Ltd/Biggin Hill | |
| G-BBVF | SA Twin Pioneer III ★ | Museum of Flight/E. Fortune | |
| G-BBVG | PA-23 Aztec 250C | R. F. Wanbon & P. G. Warmerdan/ Panshanger | |
| G-BBVI | Enstrom F-28A ★ | *Ground trainer*/Kidlington | |
| G-BBVJ | Beech B24R Sierra | J. G. Kelwick/Gamston | |
| G-BBVM | Beech A.100 King Air | Northern Executive Aviation Ltd/ Manchester | |
| G-BBVO | Isaacs Fury II (S1579) | C. M. Barnes | |
| G-BBVP | Westland-Bell 47G-3B1 | CKS Air Ltd/Southend | |
| G-BBWM | PA-E23 Aztec 250E | Guernsey Air Search Ltd | |
| G-BBWN | D.H.C.1 Chipmunk 22 (WZ876) | D. C. Budd | |
| G-BBXB | Cessna FRA.150L | M. L. Swain/Bourn | |
| G-BBXG | PA-34-200 Seneca II | London Flight Centre (Stansted) Ltd | |

| Notes | Reg. | Type | Owner or Operator |
|---|---|---|---|
| | G-BBXH | Cessna FR.172F | H. H. Metal Finishing (Wales) Ltd |
| | G-BBXK | PA-34-200 Seneca II | Mona Travel Ltd |
| | G-BBXL | Cessna E310Q | Chatsworth Studios Ltd/Newcastle |
| | G-BBXO | Enstrom F-28A | Southern Air Ltd/Shoreham |
| | G-BBXS | Piper J-3C-65 Cub | M. J. Butler (G-ALMA)/Langham |
| | G-BBXU | Beech B24R Sierra | B. M. Russell/Coventry |
| | G-BBXW | PA-28-151 Warrior | Shropshire Aero Club Ltd |
| | G-BBXX | PA-31-350 Navajo Chieftain | Natural Environment Research Council |
| | G-BBXY | Bellanca 7GCBC Citabria | J. Turner/Shoreham |
| | G-BBXZ | Evans VP-1 | J. D. Kingston |
| | G-BBYB | PA-18 Super Cub 95 | Tiger Club (1990) Ltd/Headcorn |
| | G-BBYE | Cessna 195 | Profile Productions Ltd & TAC Productions Ltd |
| | G-BBYH | Cessna 182P | Sanderson (Forklifts) Ltd |
| | G-BBYK | PA-23 Aztec 250E | Kraken Air/Cardiff |
| | G-BBYL | Cameron O-77 balloon | Buckingham Balloon Club *Jammy* |
| | G-BBYM | H.P.137 Jetstream 200 | British Aerospace PLC (G-AYWR)/Warton |
| | G-BBYO | BN-2A Mk III Trislander | Aurigny Air Services (G-BBWR)/Guernsey |
| | G-BBYP | PA-28 Cherokee 140 | R. A. Wakefield |
| | G-BBYS | Cessna 182P Skylane | I. M. Jones |
| | G-BBZF | PA-28 Cherokee 140 | J. A. Havers & ptnrs/Elstree |
| | G-BBZH | PA-28R Cherokee Arrow 200-II | Zulu Hotel Club |
| | G-BBZI | PA-31-310 Turbo Navajo | Air Care (South West) Ltd |
| | G-BBZJ | PA-34-200 Seneca II | Sentry Courier Ltd/Blackbushe |
| | G-BBZK | Westland-Bell 47G-3B1 | Autair Helicopters Ltd/Cranfield |
| | G-BBZN | Fuji FA.200-180 | J. Westwood & P. D. Wedd |
| | G-BBZO | Fuji FA.200-160 | Melton Concrete Floors Ltd |
| | G-BBZS | Enstrom F-28A | Southern Air Ltd/Shoreham |
| | G-BBZV | PA-28R Cherokee Arrow 200-II | Unicol Engineering/Kidlington |
| | G-BCAC | M.S.894A Rallye Minerva 220 | R. S. Rogers/Cardiff |
| | G-BCAH | D.H.C.1 Chipmunk 22 (WG316) | V. B. Wheele/Shoreham |
| | G-BCAN | Thunder Ax7-77 balloon | Wessex Hot-Air Team |
| | G-BCAP | Cameron O-56 balloon | S. R. Seager |
| | G-BCAR | Thunder Ax7-77 balloon | T. J. Woodbridge/Australia |
| | G-BCAT | PA-31-310 Turbo Navajo | Hubbardair Ltd |
| | G-BCAZ | PA-12 Super Cruiser | A. D. Williams |
| | G-BCBD | Bede BD-5B | Brockmore-Bede Aircraft (UK) Ltd/Shobdon |
| | G-BCBG | PA-23 Aztec 250E | M. J. L. Batt/Booker |
| | G-BCBH | Fairchild 24R-46A Argus III | Bluegale Ltd/Biggin Hill |
| | G-BCBJ | PA-25 Pawnee 235 | Deeside Gliding Club (Aberdeenshire) Ltd |
| | G-BCBK | Cessna 421B | Robinson Publications Ltd |
| | G-BCBL | Fairchild 24R-46A Argus III (HB751) | Dega Ltd |
| | G-BCBM | PA-23 Aztec 250C | S. Lightbrown & M. Kavanagh |
| | G-BCBR | AJEP/Wittman W.8 Tailwind | D. A. Hood |
| | G-BCBW | Cessna 182P | Teesside Aero Club Ltd |
| | G-BCBX | Cessna F.150L | J. Kelly/Newtownards |
| | G-BCBY | Cessna F.150L | Scottish Airways Flyers (Prestwick) Ltd |
| | G-BCBZ | Cessna 337C | J. J. Zwetsloot |
| | G-BCCB | Robin HR.200/100 | M. J. Ellis |
| | G-BCCC | Cessna F.150L | Donington Aviation Ltd/E. Midlands |
| | G-BCCD | Cessna F.172M | Austin Aviation Ltd |
| | G-BCCE | PA-23 Aztec 250E | Falcon Flying Services/Biggin Hill |
| | G-BCCF | PA-28 Cherokee 180 | J. T. Friskney Ltd/Skegness |
| | G-BCCG | Thunder Ax7-65 balloon | N. H. Ponsford |
| | G-BCCK | AA-5 Traveler | Prospect Air Ltd/Barton |
| | G-BCCR | CP.301A Emeraude (modified) | I. G. & M. Glenn |
| | G-BCCX | D.H.C.1 Chipmunk 22 (Lycoming) | RAFGSA/Dishforth |
| | G-BCCY | Robin HR.200/100 | Bristol Strut Flying Group |
| | G-BCDA | Boeing 727-46 | Dan-Air Services Ltd/Gatwick |
| | G-BCDB | PA-34-200 Seneca II | A. & G. Aviation Ltd/Bournemouth |
| | G-BCDC | PA-18 Super Cub 95 | Cotswold Aero Club Ltd/Staverton |
| | G-BCDJ | PA-28 Cherokee 140 | C. Wren/Southend |
| | G-BCDK | Partenavia P.68B | Truman Aviation Ltd/Tollerton |
| | G-BCDL | Cameron O-42 balloon | D. P. & Mrs B. O. Turner *Chums* |
| | G-BCDN | F.27 Friendship Mk 200 | Air UK/Norwich |
| | G-BCDO | F.27 Friendship Mk 200 | Air UK *Lord Butler*/Norwich |

| Reg. | Type | Owner or Operator | Notes |
|------|------|-------------------|-------|
| G-BCDR | Thunder Ax7-77 balloon | W. G. Johnston & ptnrs *Obelix* | |
| G-BCDY | Cessna FRA.150L | Air Service Training Ltd/Perth | |
| G-BCEA | Sikorsky S-61N Mk II | British International Helicopters Ltd/ Aberdeen | |
| G-BCEB | Sikorsky S-61N Mk II | British International Helicopters Ltd/ Penzance | |
| G-BCEC | Cessna F.172M | United Propedent Ltd/Manchester | |
| G-BCEE | AA-5 Traveler | Echo Echo Ltd/Bournemouth | |
| G-BCEF | AA-5 Traveler | Forest Aviation Ltd/Guernsey | |
| G-BCEN | BN-2A Islander | Atlantic Air Transport Ltd/Coventry | |
| G-BCEO | AA-5 Traveler | Manville Ltd/Southampton | |
| G-BCEP | AA-5 Traveler | D. V. Reynolds | |
| G-BCER | GY-201 Minicab | D. Beaumont/Sherburn | |
| G-BCEU | Cameron O-42 balloon | Entertainment Services Ltd *Harlequin* | |
| G-BCEX | PA-23 Aztec 250E | Weekes Bros (Welling) Ltd/Biggin Hill | |
| G-BCEY | D.H.C.1 Chipmunk 22 | D. O. Wallis | |
| G-BCEZ | Cameron O-84 balloon | Anglia Aeronauts Ascension Association *Stars and Bars* | |
| G-BCFB | Cameron O-77 balloon | J. J. Harris & P. Pryce-Jones *Teutonic Turkey* | |
| G-BCFC | Cameron O-65 balloon | B. H. Mead *Candy Twist* | |
| G-BCFD | West balloon ★ | British Balloon Museum *Hellfire* | |
| G-BCFF | Fuji FA-200-160 | G. W. Brown & M. R. Gibbons | |
| G-BCFN | Cameron O-65 balloon | W. G. Johnson & H. M. Savage | |
| G-BCFO | PA-18 Super Cub 150 | Portsmouth Naval Gliding Club/ Lee-on-Solent | |
| G-BCFR | Cessna FRA.150L | J. J. Baumhardt/Southend | |
| G-BCFW | Saab 91D Safir | D. R. Williams | |
| G-BCFY | Luton LA-4A Minor | J. Knight | |
| G-BCGB | Bensen B.8 | A. Melody | |
| G-BCGC | D.H.C.1 Chipmunk 22 (WP903) | Culdrose Gliding Club | |
| G-BCGG | Jodel DR.250 Srs 160 | C. G. Gray (G-ATZL) | |
| G-BCGH | SNCAN NC.854S | T. J. N. H. Palmer & G. W. Oliver | |
| G-BCGI | PA-28 Cherokee 140 | A. Dodd/Redhill | |
| G-BCGJ | PA-28 Cherokee 140 | J. Miller & J. L. Hunter/Edinburgh | |
| G-BCGL | Jodel D.112 | J. Harris | |
| G-BCGM | Jodel D.120 | D. N. K. & M. A. Symon | |
| G-BCGN | PA-28 Cherokee 140 | Oxford Flyers Ltd/Kidlington | |
| G-BCGS | PA-28R Cherokee Arrow 200 | F. A. Ford | |
| G-BCGT | PA-28 Cherokee 140 | T. D. Bugg | |
| G-BCGW | Jodel D.11 | G. H. & M. D. Chittenden | |
| G-BCGX | Bede BD-5A/B | R. Hodgson | |
| G-BCHK | Cessna F.172H | E. Yorks Aviation Ltd | |
| G-BCHL | D.H.C.1 Chipmunk 22A (WP788) | Shropshire Soaring Ltd | |
| G-BCHM | SA.341G Gazelle 1 | Bristol Helicopters Ltd/Yeovil | |
| G-BCHP | CP.1310-C3 Super Emeraude | R. F. Sothcott (G-JOSI) | |
| G-BCHT | Schleicher ASK.16 | D. E. Cadisch & K. A. Lillywhite/ Dunstable | |
| G-BCHU | Dawes VP-2 | G. Dawes | |
| G-BCHV | D.H.C.1 Chipmunk 22 | N. F. Charles/Sywell | |
| G-BCHX | SF.23A Sperling | R. L. McClean/Rufforth | |
| G-BCID | PA-34-200 Seneca II | Comanche Air Services Ltd/Lydd | |
| G-BCIE | PA-28-151 Warrior | J. A. & J. V. Bridger/Exeter | |
| G-BCIF | PA-28 Cherokee 140 | Fryer-Robins Aviation Ltd/E. Midlands | |
| G-BCIH | D.H.C.1 Chipmunk 22 (WD363) | J. M. Hosey/Stansted | |
| G-BCIJ | AA-5 Traveler | I. J. Bond & D. J. McCooke | |
| G-BCIK | AA-5 Traveler | S. F. Lister/Tollerton | |
| G-BCIN | Thunder Ax7-77 balloon | P. G & R. A. Vale | |
| G-BCIO | PA-39 Twin Comanche 160 C/R | F. Duckworth | |
| G-BCIR | PA-28-151 Warrior | C. S. R. Steel | |
| G-BCIT | CIT/A1 Srs 1 | Cranfield Institute of Technology | |
| G-BCIW | D.H.C.1 Chipmunk 22 (WZ868) | Chipmunk G-BCIW Syndicate/Duxford | |
| G-BCJF | Beagle B.206 Srs 1 | A. A. Mattacks/Biggin Hill | |
| G-BCJH | Mooney M.20F | P. B. Bossard | |
| G-BCJM | PA-28 Cherokee 140 | Top Cat Aviation Ltd | |
| G-BCJN | PA-28 Cherokee 140 | A. J. Steed/Goodwood | |
| G-BCJO | PA-28R Cherokee Arrow 200 | Tomcat Aviation/Norwich | |
| G-BCJP | PA-28 Cherokee 140 | K. E. Tolliday & C. E. Jones | |
| G-BCJS | PA-23 Aztec 250C ★ | *derelict*/Ronaldsway | |
| G-BCKF | SA.102.5 Cavalier | K. Fairness | |
| G-BCKN | D.H.C.1A Chipmunk 22 | RAFGSA/Cranwell | |
| G-BCKO | PA-23 Aztec 250E | Planning & Mapping Ltd | |
| G-BCKP | Luton LA-5A Major | J. Horovitz & ptnrs | |

| Notes | Reg. | Type | Owner or Operator |
|---|---|---|---|
| | G-BCKS | Fuji FA.200-180 | J. T. Hicks/Goodwood |
| | G-BCKT | Fuji FA.200-180 | Littlewick Green Service Station Ltd/ Booker |
| | G-BCKU | Cessna FRA.150L | Air Service Training Ltd/Perth |
| | G-BCKV | Cessna FRA.150L | Air Service Training Ltd/Perth |
| | G-BCLC | Sikorsky S-61N | Bristow Helicopters/HM Coastguard |
| | G-BCLD | Sikorsky S-61N | Bristow Helicopters Ltd |
| | G-BCLI | AA-5 Traveler | Albemotive Ltd |
| | G-BCLJ | AA-5 Traveler | E. A. A. A. Wiltens |
| | G-BCLL | PA-28 Cherokee 180 | K. J. Scamp |
| | G-BCLS | Cessna 170B | C. W. Proffitt-White/Shotteswell |
| | G-BCLT | M.S.894A Rallye Minerva 220 | S. Clough |
| | G-BCLU | Jodel D.117 | N. A. Wallace |
| | G-BCLW | AA-1B Trainer | E. J. McMillan |
| | G-BCMD | PA-18 Super Cub 95 | R. G. Brooks/Dunkeswell |
| | G-BCMJ | SA.102.5 Cavalier (tailwheel) | R. G. Sykes/Shoreham |
| | G-BCMT | Isaacs Fury II | M. H. Turner |
| | G-BCNC | GY.201 Minicab | J. R. Wraight |
| | G-BCNP | Cameron O-77 balloon | M. L. J. Ritchie |
| | G-BCNR | Thunder Ax7-77A balloon | S. J. Miliken & ptnrs |
| | G-BCNT | Partenavia P.68B | Welsh Airways Ltd |
| | G-BCNX | Piper J-3C-65 Cub | K. J. Lord/Ipswich |
| | G-BCNZ | Fuji FA.200-160 | J. Bruton & A. Lincoln/Manchester |
| | G-BCOB | Piper J-3C-65 Cub | R. W. & Mrs J. W. Marjoram |
| | G-BCOE | H.S.748 Srs 2B | British Airways Glen Livet/Glasgow |
| | G-BCOF | H.S.748 Srs 2B | British Airways Glen Fiddich/Glasgow |
| | G-BCOG | Jodel D.112 | C. Hughes & W. K. Rose/Kidlington |
| | G-BCOH | Avro 683 Lancaster 10 (KB976) | Charles Church (Spitfires) Ltd |
| | G-BCOI | D.H.C.1 Chipmunk 22 | D. S. McGregor & A. T. Letham |
| | G-BCOJ | Cameron O-56 balloon | T. J. Knott & M. J. Webber |
| | G-BCOL | Cessna F.172M | Calros Ltd |
| | G-BCOM | Piper J-3C-65 Cub | Dougal Flying Group/Shoreham |
| | G-BCOO | D.H.C.1 Chipmunk 22 | T. G. Fielding & M. S. Morton/Blackpool |
| | G-BCOP | PA-28R Cherokee Arrow 200-II | E. A. Saunders/Halfpenny Green |
| | G-BCOR | SOCATA Rallye 100ST | D. Wright & R. J. Doughton |
| | G-BCOU | D.H.C.1 Chipmunk 22 (WK522) | P. J. Loweth |
| | G-BCOX | Bede BD-5A | H. J. Cox |
| | G-BCOY | D.H.C.1 Chipmunk 22 | Coventry Gliding Club Ltd/ Husbands Bosworth |
| | G-BCPB | Howes radio-controlled model free balloon | R. B. & Mrs C. Howes Posbee 1 |
| | G-BCPD | GY-201 Minicab | A. H. K. Denniss/Halfpenny Green |
| | G-BCPE | Cessna F.150M | Andrewsfield Flying Club Ltd |
| | G-BCPF | PA-23 Aztec 250D | Chapman Commercials Ltd |
| | G-BCPG | PA-28R Cherokee Arrow 200-II | Roses Flying Group/Liverpool |
| | G-BCPH | Piper J-3C-65 Cub (329934) | I. R. March |
| | G-BCPJ | Piper J-3C-65 Cub | P. Turton |
| | G-BCPK | Cessna F.172M | Skegness Air Taxi Services Ltd |
| | G-BCPN | AA-5 Traveler | B.W. Agricultural Equipments Ltd |
| | G-BCPO | Partenavia P.68B | H. Russell |
| | G-BCPU | D.H.C.1 Chipmunk T.10 | P. Waller/Booker |
| | G-BCPX | Szep HFC.125 | A. Szep/Netherthorpe |
| | G-BCRB | Cessna F.172M | Specialised Laboratory Equipment Ltd |
| | G-BCRE | Cameron O-77 balloon | A. R. Langton |
| | G-BCRH | Alaparma Baldo B.75 | A. L. Scadding/(stored) |
| | G-BCRI | Cameron O-65 balloon | V. J. Thorne Joseph |
| | G-BCRJ | Taylor JT.1 Monoplane | S. Wolstenholme |
| | G-BCRK | SA.102.5 Cavalier | S. B. Churchill |
| | G-BCRL | PA-28-151 Warrior | F. N. Garland/Biggin Hill |
| | G-BCRN | Cessna FRA.150L | Air Service Training Ltd/Perth |
| | G-BCRP | PA-E23 Aztec 250E | ReFair/Sibson |
| | G-BCRR | AA-5B Tiger | ReFair/Sibson |
| | G-BCRT | Cessna F.150M | Suffolk Aero Club Ltd/Ipswich |
| | G-BCRX | D.H.C.1 Chipmunk 22 | J. R. Chapman & ptnrs |
| | G-BCSA | D.H.C.1 Chipmunk 22 | RAFGSA/Kinloss |
| | G-BCSB | D.H.C.1 Chipmunk 22 (Lycoming) | RAFGSA/Cosford |
| | G-BCSL | D.H.C.1 Chipmunk 22 | Jalawain Ltd/Barton |
| | G-BCSM | Bellanca 8GCBC Scout | B. T. Spreckley/Southampton |
| | G-BCST | M.S.893A Rallye Commodore 180 | P. J. Wilcox/Cranfield |
| | G-BCSX | Thunder Ax7-77 balloon | A. T. Wood Whoopski |
| | G-BCSY | Taylor JT.2 Titch | T. Hartwell & D. Wilkinson |
| | G-BCTA | PA-28-151 Warrior | T. G. Aviation Ltd/Manston |

| Reg. | Type | Owner or Operator | Notes |
|------|------|-------------------|-------|
| G-BCTF | PA-28-151 Warrior | Premier Plane Leasing Co Ltd | |
| G-BCTI | Schleicher ASK.16 | Tango India Syndicate/Cranfield | |
| G-BCTJ | Cessna 310Q | S. E. Clark/Biggin Hill | |
| G-BCTK | Cessna FR.172J | C. Wellington & M. Slattery/Blackbushe | |
| G-BCTR | Taylor JT.2 Titch | D. L. Riley/Barton | |
| G-BCTT | Evans VP-1 | B. J. Boughton | |
| G-BCTU | Cessna FRA.150M | J. H. Fisher & N. D. Hall | |
| G-BCUB | Piper J-3C-65 Cub | A. L. Brown & G. Attwell/Bourn | |
| G-BCUF | Cessna F.172M | G. H. Kirke Ltd | |
| G-BCUH | Cessna F.150M | Heathgrange Ltd/Elstree | |
| G-BCUI | Cessna F.172M | Hillhouse Estates Ltd | |
| G-BCUJ | Cessna F.150M | T. Hayselden (Doncaster) Ltd | |
| G-BCUL | SOCATA Rallye 100ST | C. A. Ussher & Fountain Estates Ltd | |
| G-BCUW | Cessna F.177RG | S. J. Westley | |
| G-BCUY | Cessna FRA.150M | S. R. Cameron | |
| G-BCVA | Cameron O-65 balloon | J. C. Bass & ptnrs *Crepe Suzette* | |
| G-BCVB | PA-17 Vagabond | A. T. Nowak/Popham | |
| G-BCVC | SOCATA Rallye 100ST | A. P. Lawson-Tancred | |
| G-BCVE | Evans VP-2 | D. Masterson & D. B. Winstanley | |
| G-BCVF | Practavia Pilot Sprite | D. G. Hammersley | |
| G-BCVG | Cessna FRA.150L | Air Service Training Ltd/Perth | |
| G-BCVH | Cessna FRA.150L | Yorkshire Light Aircraft Ltd/Leeds | |
| G-BCVI | Cessna FR.172J | R. M. Savage | |
| G-BCVJ | Cessna F.172M | D. S. Newland & J. Rothwell/Blackpool | |
| G-BCVW | GY-80 Horizon 180 | P. M. A. Parrett/Dunkeswell | |
| G-BCVY | PA-34-200T Seneca II | C.S.E. Aviation Ltd/Kidlington | |
| G-BCWA | BAC One-Eleven 518 FG | Dan-Air Services Ltd (G-AXMK)/ Gatwick | |
| G-BCWB | Cessna 182P | G. McCabe | |
| G-BCWF | S.A. Twin Pioneer 1 | Flight One Ltd (G-APRS)/Staverton | |
| G-BCWH | Practavia Pilot Sprite | R. Tasker/Blackpool | |
| G-BCWI | Bensen B.8M | C. J. Blundell | |
| G-BCWK | Alpavia Fournier RF-3 | D. I. Nickolls & ptnrs | |
| G-BCWL | Westland Lysander III (V9281) | Wessex Aviation & Transport Ltd | |
| G-BCWM | AB-206B JetRanger 2 | Dollar Air Services Ltd/Coventry | |
| G-BCWR | BN-2A-21 Islander | Pilatus BN Ltd/Bembridge | |
| G-BCXB | SOCATA Rallye 100ST | A. Smails | |
| G-BCXE | Robin DR.400/2+2 | Headcorn Flying School Ltd | |
| G-BCXF | H.S.125 Srs 600B | Beecham International Aviation Ltd/ Heathrow | |
| G-BCXH | PA-28 Cherokee 140F | Devon School of Flying/Dunkeswell | |
| G-BCXJ | Piper J-3C-65 Cub (413048) | W. F. Stockdale/Compton Abbas | |
| G-BCXN | D.H.C.1 Chipmunk 22 (WP800) | G. M. Turner/Duxford | |
| G-BCXO | MBB Bo 105D | Bond Helicopters Ltd/Bourn | |
| G-BCXR | BAC One-Eleven 517FE | Dan-Air Services Ltd (G-BCCV)/Gatwick | |
| G-BCYH | DAW Privateer Mk. 2 | D. B. Limbert | |
| G-BCYI | Schleicher ASK-16 | J. Fox & J. Harding/Lasham | |
| G-BCYJ | D.H.C.1 Chipmunk 22 (WG307) | R. A. L. Falconer | |
| G-BCYK | Avro CF.100 Mk 4 Canuck (18393) ★ | Imperial War Museum/Duxford | |
| G-BCYM | D.H.C.1 Chipmunk 22 | C. R. R. Eagleton/Headcorn | |
| G-BCYR | Cessna F.172M | Donne Enterprises | |
| G-BCZH | D.H.C.1 Chipmunk 22 (WK622) | A. C. Byrne & D. Featherby/Norwich | |
| G-BCZI | Thunder Ax7-77 balloon | R. G. Griffin & R. Blackwell | |
| G-BCZM | Cessna F.172M | Cornwall Flying Club Ltd/Bodmin | |
| G-BCZN | Cessna F.150M | Mona Aviation Ltd | |
| G-BCZO | Cameron O-77 balloon | W. O. T. Holmes *Leo* | |
| G-BDAB | SA.102.5 Cavalier | A. H. Brown | |
| G-BDAC | Cameron O-77 balloon | D. Fowler & J. Goody *Chocolate Ripple* | |
| G-BDAD | Taylor JT.1 Monoplane | G-BDAD Group | |
| G-BDAE | BAC One-Eleven 518FG | Dan-Air Services Ltd (G-AXMI)/Gatwick | |
| G-BDAG | Taylor JT.1 Monoplane | R. S. Basinger | |
| G-BDAH | Evans VP-1 | A. M. Carter | |
| G-BDAI | Cessna FRA.150M | A. Sharma | |
| G-BDAK | R. Commander 112A | S. E. Boyles | |
| G-BDAL | R. 500S Shrike Commander | Quantel Ltd | |
| G-BDAM | AT-16 Harvard IIB (FE992) | N. A. Lees & E. C. English | |
| G-BDAO | SIPA S.91 | A. L. Rose | |
| G-BDAP | AJEP Tailwind | J. Whiting | |
| G-BDAR | Evans VP-1 | R. B. Valler | |
| G-BDAS | BAC One-Eleven 518FG | Dan-Air Services Ltd (G-AXMH)/ Gatwick | |

| Notes | Reg. | Type | Owner or Operator |
|---|---|---|---|
| | G-BDAT | BAC One-Eleven 518FG | Dan-Air Services Ltd (G-AYOR)/ Gatwick |
| | G-BDAV | PA-23 Aztec 250C | Acketts Ltd |
| | G-BDAX | PA-23 Aztec 250C | P. G. Lawrence |
| | G-BDAY | Thunder Ax5-42A balloon | T. M. Donnelly *Meconium* |
| | G-BDBD | Wittman W.8 Tailwind | E. D. Bond |
| | G-BDBF | FRED Srs 2 | R. G. Boyton |
| | G-BDBH | Bellanca 7GCBC Citabria | Inkpen Gliding Club Ltd/Thruxton |
| | G-BDBI | Cameron O-77 balloon | C. A. Butter & J. J. Cook |
| | G-BDBJ | Cessna 182P | H. C. Wilson |
| | G-BDBL | D.H.C.1 Chipmunk 22 | R. J. Fox |
| | G-BDBP | D.H.C.1 Chipmunk 22 | Proteus Petroleum Aviation Ltd/ Goodwood |
| | G-BDBS | Short SD3-30 | Short Bros PLC/Belfast City |
| | G-BDBU | Cessna F.150M | Andrewsfield Flying Club Ltd |
| | G-BDBV | Jodel D.11A | Seething Jodel Group |
| | G-BDBZ | W.S.55 Whirlwind Srs 2 ★ | *Ground instruction airframe*/Kidlington |
| | G-BDCB | D.H.C.1 Chipmunk 22 (WP835) | R. F. Tolhurst |
| | G-BDCC | D.H.C.1 Chipmunk 22 | Coventry Gliding Club Ltd/ Husbands Bosworth |
| | G-BDCD | Piper J-3C-85 Cub (480133) | Suzanne C. Brooks/Slinfold |
| | G-BDCE | Cessna F.172H | Lord Valentine William Cecil |
| | G-BDCI | CP.301A Emeraude | D. L. Sentance |
| | G-BDCL | AA-5 Traveler | J. Crowe |
| | G-BDCK | AA-5 Traveler | Northfield Garage Ltd |
| | G-BDCM | Cessna F.177RG | P. R. Gunnel/Gamston |
| | G-BDCO | B.121 Pup 1 | K. R. Knapp |
| | G-BDCS | Cessna 421B | British Aerospace PLC/Warton |
| | G-BDCU | Cameron O-77 balloon | H. P. Carlton |
| | G-BDDA | Sikorsky S-61N | British International Helicopters Ltd |
| | G-BDDD | D.H.C.1 Chipmunk 22 | RAE Aero Club Ltd/Farnborough |
| | G-BDDF | Jodel D.120 | Sywell Skyriders Flying Group |
| | G-BDDG | Jodel D.112 | A. J. Daley & J. A. Sumner/Burnaston |
| | G-BDDJ | Luton LA-4A Minor | D. D. Johnson |
| | G-BDDS | PA-25 Pawnee 235 | Vale of Neath Gliding Club |
| | G-BDDT | PA-25 Pawnee 235 | Boston Aviation Services |
| | G-BDDX | Whittaker MW.2B Excalibur ★ | Cornwall Aero Park/Helston |
| | G-BDDZ | CP.301A Emeraude | V. W. Smith & E. C. Mort |
| | G-BDEA | Boeing 707-338C | Anglo Cargo Airlines Ltd/Gatwick |
| | G-BDEC | SOCATA Rallye 100ST | A. Mitrega |
| | G-BDEF | PA-34-200T Seneca II | Haylock Son & Hunter |
| | G-BDEH | Jodel D.120A | EH Flying Group/Bristol |
| | G-BDEI | Jodel D.9 Bebe | P. M. Bowden/Barton |
| | G-BDEN | SIAI-Marchetti SF.260 | A. R. Graves |
| | G-BDET | D.H.C.1 Chipmunk 22 | R. T. Heinen/Shoreham |
| | G-BDEU | D.H.C.1 Chipmunk 22 (WP808) | A. Taylor |
| | G-BDEV | Taylor JT.1 Monoplane | D. A. Bass |
| | G-BDEW | Cessna FRA.150M | Compton Abbas Airfield Ltd |
| | G-BDEX | Cessna FRA.150M | Compton Abbas Airfield Ltd |
| | G-BDEY | Piper J-3C-65 Cub | Ducksworth Flying Club |
| | G-BDEZ | Piper J-3C-65 Cub | D. V. Wallis |
| | G-BDFB | Currie Wot | J. Jennings |
| | G-BDFC | R. Commander 112A | R. Fletcher |
| | G-BDFG | Cameron O-65 balloon | N. A. Robertson *Golly II* |
| | G-BDFH | Auster AOP.9 (XR240) | R. O. Holden/Booker |
| | G-BDFI | Cessna F.150M | LAR Aviation Ltd/Shoreham |
| | G-BDFJ | Cessna F.150M | T. J. Lynn/Sibson |
| | G-BDFM | Caudron C.270 Luciole | G. V. Gower |
| | G-BDFR | Fuji FA.200-160 | A. Wright |
| | G-BDFS | Fuji FA.200-160 | R. W. Struth & A. H. Biggs |
| | G-BDFU | Dragonfly MPA Mk 1 ★ | Museum of Flight/E. Fortune |
| | G-BDFW | R. Commander 112A | W. P. Simpson |
| | G-BDFX | Auster 5 | G.R. Mills & C. Fielder |
| | G-BDFY | AA-5 Traveler | Edinburgh Flying Club Ltd |
| | G-BDFZ | Cessna F.150M | Skyviews & General Ltd |
| | G-BDGA | Bushby-Long Midget Mustang | J. R. Owen |
| | G-BDGB | GY-20 Minicab | D. G. Burden |
| | G-BDGH | Thunder Ax7-77 balloon | R. J. Mitchener & P. F. Smart |
| | G-BDGM | PA-28-151 Warrior | B. Whiting |
| | G-BDGN | AA-5B Tiger | C. Zantow |
| | G-BDGO | Thunder Ax7-77 balloon | International Distillers & Vintners Ltd |
| | G-BDGP | Cameron V-65 balloon | Warwick Balloons Ltd |
| | G-BDGY | PA-28 Cherokee 140 | R. E. Woolridge/Staverton |

| Reg. | Type | Owner or Operator | Notes |
|------|------|-------------------|-------|
| G-BDHB | Isaacs Fury II | D. H. Berry | |
| G-BDHJ | Pazmany PL.1 | C. T. Millner | |
| G-BDHK | Piper J-3C-65 Cub (329417) | A. Liddiard | |
| G-BDHL | PA-23 Aztec 250E | Cheshire Flying Services Ltd/ Manchester | |
| G-BDIC | D.H.C.1 Chipmunk 22 | Woodvale Aviation Co Ltd | |
| G-BDIE | R. Commander 112A | C. A. Ringrose & N. B. Morgan | |
| G-BDIG | Cessna 182P | D. P. Cranston & Bob Crowe Aircraft Sales Ltd/Cranfield | |
| G-BDIH | Jodel D.117 | N. D. H. Stokes | |
| G-BDIJ | Sikorsky S-61N | Bristow Helicopters Ltd | |
| G-BDIM | D.H.C.1 Chipmunk 22 | Historic Flying Ltd/Cambridge | |
| G-BDIX | D.H.106 Comet 4C ★ | Museum of Flight/E. Fortune | |
| G-BDIY | Luton LA-4A Minor | M. A. Musselwhite | |
| G-BDJB | Taylor JT.1 Monoplane | J. F. Barber | |
| G-BDJC | AJEP W.8 Tailwind | J. H. Medforth | |
| G-BDJD | Jodel D.112 | Drem Sport Aviation Group | |
| G-BDJF | Bensen B.8MV | R. P. White | |
| G-BDJG | Luton LA-4A Minor | A. W. Anderson & A. J. Short | |
| G-BDJN | Robin HR.200/100 | Northampton School of Flying Ltd/ Sywell | |
| G-BDJP | Piper J-3C-90 Cub | J. M. Pothecary (stored)/Shoreham | |
| G-BDJR | SNCAN NC.858 | R. F. M. Marson & P. M. Harmer | |
| G-BDKB | SOCATA Rallye 150ST | N. C. Anderson | |
| G-BDKC | Cessna A185F | Bridge of Tilt Co Ltd | |
| G-BDKD | Enstrom F-28A | TR Bitz | |
| G-BDKH | CP.301A Emeraude | P. G. & F. M. Morris | |
| G-BDKJ | SA.102.5 Cavalier | H. B. Yardley | |
| G-BDKK | Bede BD-5B | A. W. Odell (stored)/Headcorn | |
| G-BDKM | SIPA 903 | S. W. Markham | |
| G-BDKU | Taylor JT.1 Monoplane | C. M. Harding & J. Ball | |
| G-BDKV | PA-28R Cherokee Arrow 200-II | H. Wilson/Bristol | |
| G-BDKW | R. Commander 112A | Denny Bros Printing Ltd | |
| G-BDLO | AA-5A Cheetah | S. & J. Dolan/Denham | |
| G-BDLR | AA-5B Tiger | MAGEC Aviation Ltd/Luton | |
| G-BDLS | AA-1B Trainer | P. W. Vaughan & M. D. Harling/ Andrewsfield | |
| G-BDLT | R. Commander 112A | Wintergrain Ltd/Exeter | |
| G-BDLY | SA.102.5 Cavalier | P. R. Stevens/Southampton | |
| G-BDMB | Robin HR.100/210 | R. J. Hitchman & Son | |
| G-BDMM | Jodel D.11 | P. N. Marshall | |
| G-BDMO | Thunder Ax7-77A ballon | G. C. Elson | |
| G-BDMS | Piper J-3C-65 Cub | A. T. H. Martin & K. G. Harris | |
| G-BDMW | Jodel DR.100 | R. O. F. Harper | |
| G-BDNC | Taylor JT.1 Monoplane | G. A. Stanley | |
| G-BDNF | Bensen B.8M | W. F. O'Brien | |
| G-BDNG | Taylor JT.1 Monoplane | D. J. Phillips/Lasham | |
| G-BDNO | Taylor JT.1 Monoplane | W. R. Partridge | |
| G-BDNP | BN-2A Islander ★ | Ground parachute trainer/Headcorn | |
| G-BDNR | Cessna FRA.150M | Cheshire Air Training School Ltd/ Liverpool | |
| G-BDNT | Jodel D.92 | Countryman Flying Group | |
| G-BDNU | Cessna F.172M | C. H. P. Bell | |
| G-BDNW | AA-1B Trainer | T. D. Saveker | |
| G-BDNX | AA-1B Trainer | R. M. North | |
| G-BDNY | AA-1B Trainer | M. R. Langford/Doncaster | |
| G-BDNZ | Cameron O-77 balloon | I. L. McHale | |
| G-BDOC | Sikorsky S-61N Mk II | Bristow Helicopters Ltd | |
| G-BDOD | Cessna F.150M | Latharp Ltd/Booker | |
| G-BDOE | Cessna FR.172J | Rocket Partnership | |
| G-BDOF | Cameron O-56 balloon | New Holker Estates Co Fred Cavendish | |
| G-BDOG | SA Bullfinch Srs 2100 | D. C. Bonsall/Netherthorpe | |
| G-BDOH | Hiller UH-12E (Soloy) | D. A. H. Jack | |
| G-BDOI | Hiller UH-12E | T. J. Clark | |
| G-BDOL | Piper J-3C-65 Cub | U. E. Allman & M. C. Jordan/Shoreham | |
| G-BDON | Thunder Ax7-77A balloon | J. R. Henderson & ptnrs | |
| G-BDOR | Thunder Ax6-56A balloon | M. S. Drinkwater & G. Fitzpatrick | |
| G-BDOW | Cessna FRA.150M | Scottish Airways Flyers (Prestwick) Ltd | |
| G-BDPA | PA-28-151 Warrior | Noon (Aircraft Leasing) Ltd/ Shoreham | |
| G-BDPC | Bede BD-5A | P. R. Cremer | |
| G-BDPF | Cessna F.172M | Semloh Aviation Services/Andrewsfield | |
| G-BDPK | Cameron O-56 balloon | Rango Balloon & Kite Co | |

| Notes | Reg. | Type | Owner or Operator |
|-------|------|------|-------------------|
| | G-BDPV | Boeing 747-136 | British Airways *Blea Water*/Heathrow |
| | G-BDRB | AA-5B Tiger | I. G. Harrison |
| | G-BDRC | V.724 Viscount ★ | Fire School/Manston |
| | G-BDRD | Cessna FRA.150M | Air Service Training Ltd/Perth |
| | G-BDRF | Taylor JT.1 Monoplane | B. R. Ratcliffe |
| | G-BDRG | Taylor JT.2 Titch | D. R. Gray |
| | G-BDRJ | D.H.C.1 Chipmunk 22 (WP857) | J. C. Schooling |
| | G-BDRK | Cameron O-65 balloon | D. L. Smith *Smirk* |
| | G-BDSB | PA-28-181 Archer II | Testair Ltd/Blackbushe |
| | G-BDSD | Evans VP-1 | J. E. Worthington |
| | G-BDSE | Cameron O-77 balloon | British Airways *Concorde* |
| | G-BDSF | Cameron O-56 balloon | A. R. Greensides & B. H. Osbourne |
| | G-BDSH | PA-28 Cherokee 140 | BCF Roofing Ltd |
| | G-BDSK | Cameron O-65 balloon | Southern Balloon Group *Carousel II* |
| | G-BDSL | Cessna F.150M | Cleveland Flying School Ltd/Tees-side |
| | G-BDSM | Slingsby T.31B Cadet III | J. A. L. Parton |
| | G-BDSN | Wassmer WA.52 Europa | Sierra November Group (G-BADN) |
| | G-BDSO | Cameron O-31 balloon | Budget Rent-a-Car *Baby Budget* |
| | G-BDSP | Cessna U.206F Stationair | J. E. Leakey/Biggin Hill |
| | G-BDTB | Evans VP-1 | S. Pearl |
| | G-BDTL | Evans VP-1 | A. K. Lang |
| | G-BDTN | BN-2A Mk III-2 Trislander | Aurigny Air Services Ltd/Guernsey |
| | G-BDTU | Omega III gas balloon | G. F. Turnbull |
| | G-BDTV | Mooney M.20F | J. P. McDermott & ptnrs/Biggin Hill |
| | G-BDTW | Cassutt Racer | B. E. Smith & C. S. Thompson/Redhill |
| | G-BDTX | Cessna F.150M | A. A. & R. N. Croxford/Southend |
| | G-BDUI | Cameron V-56 balloon | D. C. Johnson |
| | G-BDUJ | PA-31-310 Turbo Navajo | Club Air (Europe) Ltd |
| | G-BDUL | Evans VP-1 | J. T. Taylor |
| | G-BDUM | Cessna F.150M | SFG Ltd/Shipdham |
| | G-BDUN | PA-34-200T Seneca II | G-BDUN Ltd |
| | G-BDUO | Cessna F.150M | Sandown Aero Club |
| | G-BDUX | Slingsby T.31B Cadet III | J. C. Anderson/Cranfield |
| | G-BDUY | Robin DR.400/140B | J. M. Dean & A. L. Jubb |
| | G-BDUZ | Cameron V-56 balloon | Zebedee Balloon Service |
| | G-BDVA | PA-17 Vagabond | I. M. Callier |
| | G-BDVB | PA-15 (PA-17) Vagabond | B. P. Gardner |
| | G-BDVC | PA-17 Vagabond | A. R. Caveen |
| | G-BDVG | Thunder Ax6-56A balloon | R. F. Pollard *Argonaut* |
| | G-BDVS | F.27 Friendship Mk 200 | Air UK *Eric Gandar Dower*/Norwich |
| | G-BDVU | Mooney M.20F | Uplands Video Ltd/Stapleford |
| | G-BDWA | SOCATA Rallye 150ST | H. Cowan/Newtownards |
| | G-BDWE | Flaglor Scooter | D. W. Evernden |
| | G-BDWG | BN-2A Islander | Wilsons Transport Ltd |
| | G-BDWH | SOCATA Rallye 150ST | M. A. Jones |
| | G-BDWJ | SE-5A replica (F8010) | S. M. Smith/Booker |
| | G-BDWK | Beech 95-58 Baron | Cammac Coal Ltd |
| | G-BDWL | PA-25 Pawnee 235 | Peterborough & Spalding Gliding Group |
| | G-BDWM | Mustang ⅔ scale replica | D. C. Bonsall |
| | G-BDWO | Howes Ax6 balloon | R. B. & Mrs C. Howes *Griffin* |
| | G-BDWP | PA-32R Cherokee Lance 300 | W. M. Brown & B. J. Wood/Birmingham |
| | G-BDWV | BN-2A Mk III-2 Trislander | Aurigny Air Services Ltd/Guernsey |
| | G-BDWX | Jodel D.120A | J. P. Lassey |
| | G-BDWY | PA-28 Cherokee 140 | Comed Aviation Ltd/Blackpool |
| | G-BDXA | Boeing 747-236B | British Airways *City of Peterborough*/ Heathrow |
| | G-BDXB | Boeing 747-236B | British Airways *City of Liverpool*/ Heathrow |
| | G-BDXC | Boeing 747-236B | British Airways *City of Manchester*/ Heathrow |
| | G-BDXD | Boeing 747-236B | British Airways *City of Plymouth*/ Heathrow |
| | G-BDXE | Boeing 747-236B | British Airways *City of Glasgow*/ Heathrow |
| | G-BDXF | Boeing 747-236B | British Airways *City of York*/Heathrow |
| | G-BDXG | Boeing 747-236B | British Airways *City of Oxford*/ Heathrow |
| | G-BDXH | Boeing 747-236B | British Airways *City of Elgin*/ Heathrow |
| | G-BDXI | Boeing 747-236B | British Airways *City of Cambridge*/ Heathrow |
| | G-BDXJ | Boeing 747-236B | British Airways *City of Birmingham*/ Heathrow |

| Reg. | Type | Owner or Operator | Notes |
|------|------|-------------------|-------|
| G-BDXK | Boeing 747-236B | British Airways *City of Canterbury*/ Heathrow | |
| G-BDXL | Boeing 747-236B | British Airways *City of Winchester*/ Heathrow | |
| G-BDXM | Boeing 747-236B | British Airways *City of Derby*/Heathrow | |
| G-BDXN | Boeing 747-236B | British Airways *City of Stoke-on-Trent*/ Heathrow | |
| G-BDXO | Boeing 747-236B | British Airways *City of Bath*/Heathrow | |
| G-BDXP | Boeing 747-236B (SCD) | British Airways *City of Salisbury*/ Heathrow | |
| G-BDXX | SNCAN NC.858S | J. R. Rowell & J. E. Hobbs/Sandown | |
| G-BDXY | Auster AOP.9 (XR269) | B. A. Webster | |
| G-BDYC | AA-1B Trainer | N. F. Whisler | |
| G-BDYD | R. Commander 114 | SRS Aviation | |
| G-BDYF | Cessna 421C | City Flight Ltd/Gatwick | |
| G-BDYG | P.56 Provost T.1 (WV493) | Museum of Flight/E. Fortune | |
| G-BDYH | Cameron V-56 balloon | B. J. Godding | |
| G-BDYM | Skysales S-31 balloon | Miss A. I. Smith & M. J. Moore *Cheeky Devil* | |
| G-BDYZ | MBB Bo 105D | Bond Helicopters Ltd/Bourn | |
| G-BDZA | Scheibe SF.25E Super Falke | Norfolk Gliding Club Ltd/Tibenham | |
| G-BDZB | Cameron S-31 balloon | Kenning Motor Group Ltd *Kenning* | |
| G-BDZD | Cessna F.172M | Three Counties Aero Club Ltd/ Blackbushe | |
| G-BDZF | G.164 Ag-Cat B | CKS Air Ltd | |
| G-BDZS | Scheibe SF.25A Super Falke | A. D. Gubbay/Panshanger | |
| G-BDZU | Cessna 421C | Page & Moy Ltd & ptnrs/Leicester | |
| G-BDZX | PA-28-151 Warrior | E. Shipley | |
| G-BDZY | Phoenix LA-4A Minor | P. J. Dalby | |
| G-BEAA | Taylor JT.1 Monoplane | R. C. Hobbs/Bembridge | |
| G-BEAB | Jodel DR.1051 | C. Fitton | |
| G-BEAC | PA-28 Cherokee 140 | D. J. Hockings/Biggin Hill | |
| G-BEAD | WG.13 Lynx ★ | *Instructional airframe*/Middle Wallop | |
| G-BEAG | PA-34-200T Seneca II | C.S.E. Aviation Ltd/Kidlington | |
| G-BEAH | J/2 Arrow | W. J. & Mrs M. D. Horler | |
| G-BEAK | L-1011-385 TriStar 50 | British Airways *Carmarthen Bay* | |
| G-BEAL | L-1011-385 TriStar 50 | British Airways *Cardigan Bay* | |
| G-BEAM | L-1011-385 TriStar 50 | British Airways *Swansea Bay* | |
| G-BEAU | Pazmany PL.4A | B. H. R. Smith | |
| G-BEBC | W.S.55 Whirlwind 3 (XP355) ★ | Norwich Aviation Museum | |
| G-BEBE | AA-5A Cheetah | Denham School of Flying Ltd | |
| G-BEBF | Auster AOP.9 | M. D. N. & Mrs A. C. Fisher | |
| G-BEBG | WSK-PZL SDZ-45A Ogar | The Ogar Syndicate | |
| G-BEBI | Cessna F.172M | Calder Equipment Ltd/Hatfield | |
| G-BEBL | Douglas DC-10-30 | British Airways *Forest of Dean*/Gatwick | |
| G-BEBM | Douglas DC-10-30 | British Airways *Sherwood Forest*/ Gatwick | |
| G-BEBN | Cessna 177B | Anglia Aviation Ltd & Mondial Software Ltd | |
| G-BEBO | Turner TSW-2 Wot | The Turner Special Flying Group | |
| G-BEBR | GY-201 Minicab | A. S. Jones & D. R. Upton | |
| G-BEBS | Andreasson BA-4B | J. S. Mortimer | |
| G-BEBT | Andreasson BA-4B | A. Horsfall | |
| G-BEBU | R. Commander 112A | M. Rowland & J. K. Woodford | |
| G-BEBZ | PA-28-151 Warrior | Goodwood Terrena Ltd/Goodwood | |
| G-BECA | SOCATA Rallye 100ST | A. J. Frost & M. D. Hackworth | |
| G-BECB | SOCATA Rallye 100ST | A. J. Trible | |
| G-BECC | SOCATA Rallye 150ST | Golf Charlie Group/Booker | |
| G-BECD | SOCATA Rallye 100ST | A. J. Liddle | |
| G-BECF | Scheibe SF.25A Falke | D. A. Wilson & ptnrs | |
| G-BECG | Boeing 737-204ADV | Britannia Airways Ltd *Amy Johnson*/ Luton | |
| G-BECH | Boeing 737-204ADV | Britannia Airways Ltd *Viscount Montgomery of Alamein*/Luton | |
| G-BECJ | Partenavia P.68B | Covex PLC | |
| G-BECK | Cameron V-56 balloon | D. W. & P. Allum | |
| G-BECN | Piper J-3C-65 Cub (480480) | R. C. Partridge & M. Oliver | |
| G-BECO | Beech A.36 Bonanza | Euro Aviation Ltd/ Conington | |
| G-BECT | C.A.S.A.1.131 Jungmann | Shoreham 131 Group | |
| G-BECW | C.A.S.A.1.131 Jungmann | N. C. Jensen/Redhill | |
| G-BECZ | CAARP CAP.10B | Aerobatic Associates Ltd | |
| G-BEDA | C.A.S.A.1.131 Jungmann | M. G. Kates & D. J. Berry | |

| Notes | Reg. | Type | Owner or Operator |
|-------|------|------|-------------------|
| | G-BEDB | Nord 1203 Norecrin | B. F. G. Lister |
| | G-BEDD | Jodel D.117A | A. T. Croy/Kirkwall |
| | G-BEDE | Bede BD-5A | Biggin Hill BD5 Syndicate |
| | G-BEDF | Boeing B-17G-105-VE (485784) | B-17 Preservation Ltd/Duxford |
| | G-BEDG | R. Commander 112A | L. E. Blackburn |
| | G-BEDI | Sikorsky S-61N | British International Helicopters Ltd |
| | G-BEDJ | Piper J-3C-65 Cub (44-80594) | D. J. Elliott |
| | G-BEDK | Hiller UH-12E | Agricopters Ltd/Chilbolton |
| | G-BEDL | Cessna T.337D | R. Masterman |
| | G-BEDV | V.668 Varsity T.1 (WJ945) ★ | D. S. Selway/Duxford |
| | G-BEDZ | BN-2A Islander | Loganair Ltd/Glasgow |
| | G-BEEE | Thunder Ax6-56A balloon | I. R. M. Jacobs *Avia* |
| | G-BEEG | BN-2A Islander | D. W. Higgins |
| | G-BEEH | Cameron V-56 balloon | B. & N. V. Moreton |
| | G-BEEI | Cameron N-77 balloon | C. R. H. Cobbold |
| | G-BEEJ | Cameron O-77 balloon | DAL (Builders Merchants) Ltd *Dal's Pal* |
| | G-BEEL | Enstrom 280C-UK-2 Shark | Manchester Helicopter Sales Ltd |
| | G-BEEO | Short SD3-30 | Shorts Aircraft Leasing Ltd |
| | G-BEEP | Thunder Ax5-42 balloon | Mrs B. C. Faithful/Holland |
| | G-BEER | Isaacs Fury II | J. C. Lister |
| | G-BEEU | PA-28 Cherokee 140E | Berkshire Aviation Services Ltd |
| | G-BEEV | PA-28 Cherokee 140E | M. J. Groom |
| | G-BEEW | Taylor JT.1 Monoplane | K. Wigglesworth/Breighton |
| | G-BEFA | PA-28-151 Warrior | Firmbeam Ltd/Booker |
| | G-BEFC | AA-5B Tiger | Portway Aviation/Shobdon |
| | G-BEFF | PA-28 Cherokee 140 | C. Haymes & G. M. Thurlow/Shipdham |
| | G-BEFP | BN-2A Mk III-2 Trislander | Air Sarnia Ltd/Guernsey |
| | G-BEFR | Fokker DR.1/(replica) (2009) | R. A. Bowes & P. A. Crawford |
| | G-BEFT | Cessna 421C | Actioncall Ltd |
| | G-BEFV | Evans VP-2 | D. A. Cotton |
| | G-BEFY | Hiller UH-12E | Copley Farms Ltd |
| | G-BEGA | Westland-Bell 47G-3B1 | Flight 47 Ltd |
| | G-BEGG | Scheibe SF.25E Super Falke | G-BEGG Flying Group |
| | G-BEGV | PA-23 Aztec 250F | Flamex Ltd |
| | G-BEHH | PA-32R Cherokee Lance 300 | SMK Engineering Ltd/Leeds |
| | G-BEHJ | Evans VP-1 | K. Heath |
| | G-BEHM | Taylor JT.1 Monoplane | H. McGovern |
| | G-BEHS | PA-25 Pawnee 260C | Sussex Spraying Services Ltd/Shoreham |
| | G-BEHV | Cessna F.172N | P. P. D. Howard-Johnston/Edinburgh |
| | G-BEHW | Cessna F.150M | W. Lancashire Aero Club Ltd/Woodvale |
| | G-BEHX | Evans VP-2 | G. S. Adams |
| | G-BEIA | Cessna FRA.150M | Air Service Training Ltd/Perth |
| | G-BEIB | Cessna F.172N | Sheltons of Wollaston (Garages) Ltd |
| | G-BEIC | Sikorsky S-61N | British International Helicopters Ltd/ Aberdeen |
| | G-BEIE | Evans VP-2 | F. G. Morris |
| | G-BEIF | Cameron O-65 balloon | C. Vening |
| | G-BEIG | Cessna F.150M | Herefordshire Aero Club Ltd/Shobdon |
| | G-BEII | PA-25 Pawnee 235D | Burn Gliding Club Ltd |
| | G-BEIL | SOCATA Rallye 150T | The Rallye Flying Group |
| | G-BEIP | PA-28-181 Archer II | M. Ferguson Ltd/Newtownards |
| | G-BEIS | Evans VP-1 | P. J. Hunt |
| | G-BEJA | Thunder Ax6-56A balloon | P. A. Hutchins *Jackson* |
| | G-BEJB | Thunder Ax6-56A balloon | International Distillers & Vinters Ltd |
| | G-BEJD | H.S.748 Srs 1 | Dan-Air Services Ltd/Gatwick |
| | G-BEJE | H.S.748 Srs 1 | Dan-Air Services Ltd/Gatwick |
| | G-BEJK | Cameron S-31 balloon | Rango Balloon & Kite Co |
| | G-BEJL | Sikorsky S-61N | British International Helicopters Ltd/ Aberdeen |
| | G-BEJM | BAC One-Eleven 423ET | Ford Motor Co Ltd/Stansted |
| | G-BEJP | D.H.C.6 Twin Otter 310 | Loganair Ltd/Glasgow |
| | G-BEJV | PA-34-200T Seneca II | C.S.E. Aviation Ltd/Kidlington |
| | G-BEJW | BAC One-Eleven 423ET | Ford Motor Co Ltd/Stansted |
| | G-BEKA | BAC One-Eleven 520FN | Dan-Air Services Ltd/Gatwick |
| | G-BEKC | H.S.748 Srs 1 ★ | Airport Fire Service/Manchester |
| | G-BEKE | H.S.748 Srs 1 | Dan-Air Services Ltd/Gatwick |
| | G-BEKG | H.S.748 Srs 1 | British Independent Airways Ltd (G-VAJK)/Lydd |
| | G-BEKL | Bede BD-4E | H. B. Carter |
| | G-BEKM | Evans VP-1 | G. J. McDill/Glenrothes |
| | G-BEKN | Cessna FRA.150M | RFC (Bourn) Ltd |

| Reg. | Type | Owner or Operator | Notes |
|------|------|-------------------|-------|
| G-BEKO | Cessna F.182Q | Tyler International | |
| G-BEKR | Rand KR-2 | A. N. Purchase | |
| G-BELF | BN-2A Islander | Flying Tigers Ltd/Goodwood | |
| G-BELP | PA-28-151 Warrior | M. S. Choksey | |
| G-BELR | PA-28 Cherokee 140 | H. M. Clarke | |
| G-BELT | Cessna F.150J | Yorkshire Light Aircraft Ltd (G-AWUV)/ Leeds | |
| G-BELX | Cameron V-56 balloon | P. A. & N. J. Foot | |
| G-BEMB | Cessna F.172M | Stocklaunch Ltd | |
| G-BEMD | Beech 95-B55 Baron | A. G. Perkins | |
| G-BEMM | Slingsby T.31B Motor Cadet | M. N. Martin | |
| G-BEMU | Thunder Ax5-42 balloon | I. J. Liddiard & A. Merritt | |
| G-BEMW | PA-28-181 Archer II | Charta Furniture Ltd/Goodwood | |
| G-BEMY | Cessna FRA.150M | L. G. Sawyer/Blackbushe | |
| G-BEND | Cameron V-56 balloon | Dante Balloon Group *Le Billet* | |
| G-BENJ | R. Commander 112B | R. C. Wilcox/Blackbushe | |
| G-BENK | Cessna F.172M | Graham Churchill Plant Ltd | |
| G-BENN | Cameron V-56 balloon | S. H. Budd | |
| G-BENT | Cameron N-77 balloon | N. Tasker | |
| G-BEOD | Cessna 180 | Avionics Research Ltd/Cranfield | |
| G-BEOE | Cessna FRA.150M | J. R. Nicholls/Sibson | |
| G-BEOH | PA-28R-201T Turbo Arrow III | Larksfell Ltd | |
| G-BEOI | PA-18 Super Cub 150 | Southdown Gliding Club Ltd | |
| G-BEOK | Cessna F.150M | Seawing Flying Club Ltd/Southend | |
| G-BEOO | Sikorsky S-61N Mk. II | British International Helicopters Ltd | |
| G-BEOX | L-414 Hudson IV (A16-199) ★ | RAF Museum/Hendon | |
| G-BEOY | Cessna FRA.150L | R. W. Denny | |
| G-BEOZ | A.W.650 Argosy 101 ★ | Aeropark/E. Midlands | |
| G-BEPB | Pereira Osprey II | J. J. & A. J. C. Zwetsloot/Bourn | |
| G-BEPC | SNCAN Stampe SV-4C | J. A. Bridger & A. J. Foan | |
| G-BEPD | SA.102.5 Cavalier | P. & Mrs E. A. Donaldson | |
| G-BEPE | SC.5 Belfast | HeavyLift Cargo Airlines Ltd (G-ASKE) (*withdrawn*)/Southend | |
| G-BEPF | SNCAN Stampe SV-4A | L. J. Rice | |
| G-BEPH | BN-2A Mk III-2 Trislander | Aurigny Air Services Ltd/Guernsey | |
| G-BEPI | BN-2A Mk III-2 Trislander | Aurigny Air Services Ltd/Guernsey | |
| G-BEPO | Cameron N-77 balloon | G. Camplin & V. Aitken | |
| G-BEPS | SC.5 Belfast | HeavyLift Cargo Airlines Ltd/Stansted | |
| G-BEPV | Fokker S.11-1 Instructor | M. F. Newman | |
| G-BEPY | R. Commander 112B | Emin Aviation Ltd/Biggin Hill | |
| G-BEPZ | Cameron D-96 hot-air airship | D. W. Liddiard | |
| G-BERA | SOCATA Rallye 150ST | Surrey & Kent Flying Club (1982) Ltd/ Biggin Hill | |
| G-BERC | SOCATA Rallye 150ST | Severn Valley Aero Group | |
| G-BERD | Thunder Ax6-56A balloon | M. J. Betts | |
| G-BERI | R. Commander 114 | K. B. Harper/Blackbushe | |
| G-BERN | Saffrey S-330 balloon | B. Martin *Beeze* | |
| G-BERT | Cameron V-56 balloon | Southern Balloon Group *Bert* | |
| G-BERW | R. Commander 114 | C. D. Allison | |
| G-BERY | AA-1B Trainer | R. H. J. Levi | |
| G-BESO | BN-2A Islander | Isles of Scilly Skybus Ltd/St Just | |
| G-BESS | Hughes 369D | Fairview Securities Ltd | |
| G-BETD | Robin HR.200/100 | R. A. Parsons/Bourn | |
| G-BETE | Rollason B.2A Beta | T. M. Jones/Tatenhill | |
| G-BETF | Cameron 'Champion' balloon | Balloon Stable Ltd *Champion* | |
| G-BETG | Cessna 180K Skywagon | T. P. A. Norman/Panshanger | |
| G-BETI | Pitts S-1D Special | P. Metcalfe/Tees-side | |
| G-BETL | PA-25 Pawnee 235D | Boston Aviation Services | |
| G-BETM | PA-25 Pawnee 235D | Crop Aviation (UK) Ltd/Wyberton | |
| G-BETO | M.S.885 Super Rallye | B. Carter | |
| G-BETP | Cameron O-65 balloon | J. R. Rix & Sons Ltd | |
| G-BETT | PA-34-200 Seneca II | Andrews Professional Colour Laboratories Ltd/Headcorn | |
| G-BETV | HS.125 Srs 600B | Rolls-Royce PLC/Filton | |
| G-BETW | Rand KR-2 | T. A. Wiffen | |
| G-BEUA | PA-18 Super Cub 150 | London Gliding Club (Pty) Ltd/ Dunstable | |
| G-BEUD | Robin HR.100/285R | E. A. & L. M. C. Payton/Cranfield | |
| G-BEUI | Piper J-3C-65 Cub | M. J. Whatley | |
| G-BEUK | Fuji FA.200-160 | D. F. Ranger/Popham | |
| G-BEUL | Beech 95-58 Baron | Foyle Flyers Ltd/Eglinton | |
| G-BEUM | Taylor JT.1 Monoplane | M. T. Taylor | |
| G-BEUN | Cassutt Racer IIIm | R. S. Voice/Redhill | |

| Notes | Reg. | Type | Owner or Operator |
|---|---|---|---|
| | G-BEUP | Robin DR.400/180 | A. V. Pound & Co Ltd |
| | G-BEUR | Cessna F.172M | M. E. Moore/Compton Abbas |
| | G-BEUS | AIA Stampe SV-4C | G-BEUS Flying Group |
| | G-BEUU | PA-18 Super Cub 95 | F. Sharples/Sandown |
| | G-BEUV | Thunder Ax6-56A balloon | Silhouette Balloon Group |
| | G-BEUX | Cessna F.172N | Ladel Ltd |
| | G-BEUY | Cameron N-31 balloon | M. W. A. Shemilt |
| | G-BEVA | SOCATA Rallye 150ST | The Rallye Group |
| | G-BEVB | SOCATA Rallye 150ST | R. B. Tope & C. M. Blanchard |
| | G-BEVC | SOCATA Rallye 150ST | B. W. Walpole |
| | G-BEVG | PA-34-200T-2 Seneca | D. R. Davidson |
| | G-BEVI | Thunder Ax7-77A balloon | The Painted Clouds Balloon Co Ltd |
| | G-BEVO | Sportavia-Pützer RF-5 | T. Barlow |
| | G-BEVP | Evans VP-2 | P. N. Haley |
| | G-BEVS | Taylor JT.1 Monoplane | D. Hunter |
| | G-BEVT | BN-2A Mk III-2 Trislander | Aurigny Air Services Ltd/Guernsey |
| | G-BEVW | SOCATA Rallye 150ST | P. C. Goodwin |
| | G-BEWJ | Westland-Bell 47G-3B1 | Ropeleyville Ltd |
| | G-BEWM | Sikorsky S-61N Mk II | British International Helicopters Ltd |
| | G-BEWN | D.H.82A Tiger Moth | H. D. Labouchere |
| | G-BEWO | Zlin Z.326 Trener Master | Nimrod Group Ltd/Staverton |
| | G-BEWR | Cessna F.172N | Cheshire Air Training School Ltd/ Liverpool |
| | G-BEWX | PA-28R-201 Arrow III | A. Vickers |
| | G-BEXK | PA-25 Pawnee 235D | Howard Avis (Aviation) Ltd |
| | G-BEXN | AA-1C Lynx | Scotia Safari Ltd/Prestwick |
| | G-BEXO | PA-23 Apache 160 | B. Burton/Bournemouth |
| | G-BEXR | Mudry/CAARP CAP-10B | R. P. Lewis/Booker |
| | G-BEXS | Cessna F.150M | Firecrest Aviation Ltd |
| | G-BEXW | PA-28-181 Archer II | P. F. Larkins |
| | G-BEXX | Cameron V-56 balloon | K. A. Schlussler |
| | G-BEXY | PA-28 Cherokee 140 | G. J. Jenkins & D. L. James |
| | G-BEXZ | Cameron N-56 balloon | D. C. Eager & G. C. Clark |
| | G-BEYA | Enstrom 280C Shark | Manchester Helicopter Centre/Barton |
| | G-BEYB | Fairey Flycatcher (replica) (S1287) | John S. Fairey/Duxford |
| | G-BEYD | HPR-7 Herald 401 | *Stored*/Southend |
| | G-BEYF | HPR-7 Herald 401 | Channel Express (Air Services) PLC/ Bournemouth |
| | G-BEYK | HPR-7 Herald 401 | Janes Aviation Ltd/Blackpool |
| | G-BEYL | PA-28 Cherokee 180 | B. G. & G. Airlines Ltd/Jersey |
| | G-BEYN | Evans VP-2 | C. D. Denham |
| | G-BEYO | PA-28 Cherokee 140 | L. D. Johnston |
| | G-BEYT | PA-28 Cherokee 140 | H. Foulds |
| | G-BEYV | Cessna T.210M | Forth Engineering Ltd |
| | G-BEYW | Taylor JT.1 Monoplane | R. A. Abrahams/Barton |
| | G-BEYY | PA-31 Turbo Navajo | Subtec Aviation Ltd/Shoreham |
| | G-BEYZ | Jodel DR.1051/M1 | M. J. McCarthy & S. Aarons/ Biggin Hill |
| | G-BEZA | Zlin Z.226T Trener | L. Bezak |
| | G-BEZC | AA-5 Traveler | P. N. & S. E. Field |
| | G-BEZE | Rutan Vari-Eze | J. Berry |
| | G-BEZF | AA-5 Traveler | G. A. Randall/Exeter |
| | G-BEZG | AA-5 Traveler | B. A. & P. G. Osburn/Biggin Hill |
| | G-BEZH | AA-5 Traveler | H. & L. Sims Ltd |
| | G-BEZI | AA-5 Traveler | BEZI Flying Group/Cranfield |
| | G-BEZJ | MBB Bo 105D | Bond Helicopters Ltd/Bourn |
| | G-BEZK | Cessna F.172H | Zulu Kilo Flying Group |
| | G-BEZL | PA-31-310 Turbo Navajo C | Filemart Ltd |
| | G-BEZM | Cessna F.182Q | Fletcher Group Holdings Ltd (G-WALK) |
| | G-BEZO | Cessna F.172M | Staverton Flying Services Ltd |
| | G-BEZP | PA-32 Cherokee Six 300D | Falcon Styles Ltd/Booker |
| | G-BEZR | Cessna F.172M | Kirmington Aviation Ltd |
| | G-BEZS | Cessna FR.172J | R. E. Beeton & M. R. Cavinder |
| | G-BEZV | Cessna F.172M | Insch Flying Group/Aberdeen |
| | G-BEZY | Rutan Vari-Eze | R. J. Jones |
| | G-BEZZ | Jodel D.112 | G-BEZZ Jodel Group |
| | G-BFAA | GY-80 Horizon 160 | Mary Poppins Ltd |
| | G-BFAB | Cameron N-56 balloon | Phonogram Ltd *Phonogram* Southend |
| | G-BFAC | Cessna F.177RG | J. J. Baumhardt/Southend |
| | G-BFAF | Aeronca 7BCM (7797) | D. C. W. Harper/Finmere |

| Reg. | Type | Owner or Operator |
|------|------|-------------------|
| G-BFAH | Phoenix Currie Wot | N. Hamlin-Wright |
| G-BFAI | R. Commander 114 | D. S. Innes/Guernsey |
| G-BFAK | M.S.892A Rallye Commodore 150 | M. C. Aireton/Alderney |
| G-BFAM | PA-31P Pressurised Navajo | Ashcombe Ltd |
| G-BFAN | H.S.125 Srs 600F | British Aerospace (G-AZHS)/Hatfield |
| G-BFAO | PA-20 Pacer 135 | J. Day & ptnrs/Goodwood |
| G-BFAP | SIAI-Marchetti S.205-20R | A. O. Broin |
| G-BFAR | Cessna 500-1 Citation | Club Air (Europe) Ltd |
| G-BFAS | Evans VP-1 | A. I. Sutherland |
| G-BFAW | D.H.C.1 Chipmunk 22 | R. V. Bowles |
| G-BFAX | D.H.C.1 Chipmunk 22 (WG422) | B. Earl/Biggin Hill |
| G-BFBA | Jodel DR.100A | A. Brown & R. Wood |
| G-BFBB | PA-23 Aztec 250E | Dollar Air Services Ltd/Coventry |
| G-BFBC | Taylor JT.1 Monoplane | D. Oxenham |
| G-BFBD | Partenavia P.68B | Calmsafe Ltd |
| G-BFBE | Robin HR.200/100 | T. Keeley |
| G-BFBF | PA-28 Cherokee 140 | Marnham Investments Ltd |
| G-BFBM | Saffery S.330 balloon | B. Martin *Beeze II* |
| G-BFBR | PA-28-161 Warrior II | Lowery Holdings Ltd/Fairoaks |
| G-BFBU | Partenavia P.68B | W. Holmes & Son Ltd |
| G-BFBX | PA-25 Pawnee 235D | Oglesby Aviation Ltd/Bardney |
| G-BFBY | Piper J-3C-65 Cub | L. W. Usherwood |
| G-BFCT | Cessna TU.206F | Cecil Aviation Ltd/Cambridge |
| G-BFCZ | Sopwith Camel (B7270) ★ | Brooklands Museum Trust Ltd/ Weybridge |
| G-BFDC | D.H.C.1 Chipmunk 22 | N. F. O'Neill/Newtownards |
| G-BFDE | Sopwith Tabloid (replica) (168) ★ | RAF Museum Storage & Restoration Centre/Cardington |
| G-BFDF | SOCATA Rallye 235E | J. H. Atkinson/Skegness |
| G-BFDG | PA-28R-201T Turbo-Arrow III | Richard Pearson Ltd |
| G-BFDI | PA-28-181 Archer II | Truman Aviation Ltd/Tollerton |
| G-BFDK | PA-28-161 Warrior II | C.S.E. Aviation Ltd/Kidlington |
| G-BFDL | Piper J-3C-65 Cub (454537) | P. B. Rice & A. White |
| G-BFDM | Jodel D.120 | Worcestershire Gliding Ltd |
| G-BFDN | PA-31-350 Navajo Chieftain | Grange Aviation & General Investments Ltd/Shoreham |
| G-BFDO | PA-28R-201T Turbo Arrow III | M. I. & D. G. Goss |
| G-BFDZ | Taylor JT.1 Monoplane | H. R. Leefe |
| G-BFEB | Jodel D.150 | D. Aldersea & ptnrs/Sherburn |
| G-BFEC | PA-23 Aztec 250F | P. V. Naylor-Leyland |
| G-BFEE | Beech 95-E55 Baron | Interair (Aviation) Ltd/Bournemouth |
| G-BFEF | Agusta-Bell 47G-3B1 | R. I. C. Huxtable/Exeter |
| G-BFEH | Jodel D.117A | C. V. & S. J. Philpott |
| G-BFEI | Westland-Bell 47G-3B1 | Trent Air Services Ltd/Cranfield |
| G-BFEK | Cessna F.152 | Staverton Flying Services Ltd |
| G-BFER | Bell 212 | Bristow Helicopters Ltd |
| G-BFEV | PA-25 Pawnee 235 | B. Walker & Co (Dursley) Ltd |
| G-BFEW | PA-25 Pawnee 235 | B. Walker & Co (Dursley) Ltd |
| G-BFEX | PA-25 Pawnee 235 | CKS Air Ltd/Southend |
| G-BFEY | PA-25 Pawnee 235 | Howard Avis Aviation Ltd |
| G-BFFB | Evans VP-2 | D. Bradley |
| G-BFFC | Cessna F.152-II | Yorkshire Flying Services Ltd/Leeds |
| G-BFFE | Cessna F.152-II | Doncaster Aero Club |
| G-BFFG | Beech 95-B55 Baron | B. Walker & Co (Dursley) Ltd |
| G-BFFJ | Sikorsky S-61N Mk II | British International Helicopters Ltd/ Aberdeen |
| G-BFFK | Sikorsky S-61N Mk II | British International Helicopters Ltd/ Aberdeen |
| G-BFFP | PA-18 Super Cub 150 (modified) | Booker Gliding Club Ltd |
| G-BFFT | Cameron V-56 balloon | R. I. M. Kerr & D. C. Boxall |
| G-BFFW | Cessna F.152 | Mercia Aircraft Leasing & Sales Ltd/ Coventry |
| G-BFFY | Cessna F.150M | Northside Aviation Ltd/Liverpool |
| G-BFFZ | Cessna FR.172 Hawk XP | H. H. Elder |
| G-BFGD | Cessna F.172N-II | Falcon Flying Services/Biggin Hill |
| G-BFGF | Cessna F.177RG | Victree (V.M.) Ltd/Birmingham |
| G-BFGG | Cessna FRA.150M | Air Service Training Ltd/Perth |
| G-BFGH | Cessna F.337G | T. Perkins/Sherburn |
| G-BFGK | Jodel D.117 | B. F. J. Hope |
| G-BFGL | Cessna FA.152 | Yorkshire Flying Services Ltd/Leeds |
| G-BFGO | Fuji FA.200-160 | Gt Consall Copper Mine Co Ltd |

| Notes | Reg. | Type | Owner or Operator |
|---|---|---|---|
| | G-BFGP | D.H.C.6 Twin Otter 310 | BAC Leasing Ltd |
| | G-BFGS | M.S.893E Rallye 180GT | K. M. & H. Bowen |
| | G-BFGW | Cessna F.150H | J. F. Morgan |
| | G-BFGX | Cessna FRA.150M | Air Service Training Ltd/Perth |
| | G-BFGZ | Cessna FRA.150M | Air Service Training Ltd/Perth |
| | G-BFHG | C.A.S.A. C.352L (VK+AZ) | Aces High Ltd/North Weald |
| | G-BFHH | D.H.82A Tiger Moth | P. Harrison & M. J. Gambrell/Redhill |
| | G-BFHI | Piper J-3C-65 Cub | J. M. Robinson |
| | G-BFHP | Champion 7GCAA Citabria | T. A. Holding |
| | G-BFHR | Jodel DR.220/2+2 | R. J. Fray |
| | G-BFHS | AA-5B Tiger | P. H. Johnson |
| | G-BFHT | Cessna F.152-II | Riger Ltd/Luton |
| | G-BFHU | Cessna F.152-II | Deltair Ltd/Chester |
| | G-BFHV | Cessna F.152-II | Aerohire Ltd |
| | G-BFHX | Evans VP-1 | P. Johnson |
| | G-BFIB | PA-31 Turbo Navajo | Mann Aviation Ltd/Fairoaks |
| | G-BFID | Taylor JT.2 Titch Mk III | G. Hunter |
| | G-BFIE | Cessna FRA.150M | RFC (Bourn) Ltd |
| | G-BFIF | Cessna FR.172K XPII | Falcon Flight Training Ltd/Eglinton |
| | G-BFIG | Cessna FR.172K XPII | Tenair Ltd |
| | G-BFIJ | AA-5A Cheetah | J. H. Wise/Redhill |
| | G-BFIN | AA-5A Cheetah | I. W. Lewis & ptnrs |
| | G-BFIP | Wallbro Monoplane 1909 replica | K. H. Wallis/Swanton Morley |
| | G-BFIR | Avro 652A Anson 21 (WD413) | G. M. K. Fraser (*stored*)/Arbroath |
| | G-BFIT | Thunder Ax6-56Z balloon | J. A. G. Tyson |
| | G-BFIU | Cessna FR.172K XP | B. M. Jobling |
| | G-BFIV | Cessna F.177RG | Kingfishair Ltd/Blackbushe |
| | G-BFIX | Thunder Ax7-77A balloon | E. Sowden Ltd |
| | G-BFJA | AA-5B Tiger | Sentry Courier Ltd/Blackbushe |
| | G-BFJH | SA.102-5 Cavalier | B. F. J. Hope |
| | G-BFJI | Robin HR.100/250 | M. A. Egerton |
| | G-BFJJ | Evans VP-1 | M. J. Collins |
| | G-BFJK | PA-23 Aztec 250F | R. Marsden & P. E. T. Price |
| | G-BFJN | Westland-Bell 47G-3B1 | Howden Helicopters |
| | G-BFJR | Cessna F.337G | Mannix Aviation/E. Midlands |
| | G-BFJV | Cessna F.172H | Southport & Merseyside Aero Club Ltd |
| | G-BFJW | AB-206B JetRanger | European Aviation Ltd |
| | G-BFJZ | Robin DR.400/140B | Forge House Restaurant Ltd/Biggin Hill |
| | G-BFKA | Cessna F.172N | D. J. A. Seagram |
| | G-BFKB | Cessna F.172N | R. E. Speigel |
| | G-BFKC | Rand KR.2 | L. H. S. Stephens & I. S. Hewitt |
| | G-BFKD | R. Commander 114B | M. D. Faiers |
| | G-BFKF | Cessna FA.152 | Klingair Ltd/Conington |
| | G-BFKG | Cessna F.152 | Luton Flight Training Ltd |
| | G-BFKH | Cessna F.152 | T. G. Aviation Ltd/Manston |
| | G-BFKL | Cameron N-56 balloon | Merrythought Toys Ltd *Merrythought* |
| | G-BFKY | PA-34-200 Seneca II | S.L.H. Construction Ltd/Biggin Hill |
| | G-BFLH | PA-34-200T Seneca II | C.S.E. Aviation Ltd/Kidlington |
| | G-BFLI | PA-28R-201T Turbo Arrow III | Cowley (Recruitment) Ltd |
| | G-BFLK | Cessna F.152 | N. A. Ali |
| | G-BFLL | H.S.748 Srs 2A | Aberdeen Airways Ltd |
| | G-BFLM | Cessna 150M | Cornwall Flying Club Ltd/Bodmin |
| | G-BFLN | Cessna 150M | Sherburn Aero Club Ltd |
| | G-BFLO | Cessna F.172M | W. A. Cook & ptnrs/Sherburn |
| | G-BFLP | Amethyst Ax6 balloon | K. J. Hendry *Amethyst* |
| | G-BFLU | Cessna F.152 | Inverness Flying Services Ltd |
| | G-BFLV | Cessna F.172N | Cheshire Air Training School (Merseyside) Ltd/Liverpool |
| | G-BFLX | AA-5A Cheetah | Abraxas Aviation Ltd/Denham |
| | G-BFLZ | Beech 95-A55 Baron | Subtec Aviation Ltd/Shoreham |
| | G-BFMC | BAC One-Eleven 414FG | Ford Motor Co Ltd/Stansted |
| | G-BFME | Cameron V-56 balloon | Warwick Balloons Ltd |
| | G-BFMF | Cassutt Racer Mk IIIM | P. H. Lewis |
| | G-BFMG | PA-28-161 Warrior II | Bailey Aviation Ltd |
| | G-BFMH | Cessna 177B | Span Aviation Ltd/Newcastle |
| | G-BFMK | Cessna FA.152 | RAF Halton Aeroplane Club Ltd |
| | G-BFMM | PA-28-181 Archer II | Bristol & Wessex Aeroplane Club Ltd |
| | G-BFMR | PA-20 Pacer 125 | B. C. & J. I. Cooper |
| | G-BFMX | Cessna F.172N | Colton Aviation Aero Spraying Ltd |
| | G-BFMY | Sikorsky S-61N | Bristow Helicopters Ltd |
| | G-BFMZ | Payne Ax6 balloon | G. F. Payne |
| | G-BFNC | AS.350B Ecureuil | Dollar Air Services Ltd/Coventry |

| Reg. | Type | Owner or Operator | Notes |
|------|------|-------------------|-------|
| G-BFNG | Jodel D.112 | M. Lomax/Booker | |
| G-BFNI | PA-28-161 Warrior II | C.S.E. Aviation Ltd/Kidlington | |
| G-BFNJ | PA-28-161 Warrior II | C.S.E. Aviation Ltd/Kidlington | |
| G-BFNK | PA-28-161 Warrior II | C.S.E. Aviation Ltd/Kidlington | |
| G-BFNM | Globe GC.1 Swift | Nottingham Flying Group/Tatenhill | |
| G-BFNU | BN-2B Islander | Isle of Scilly Sky Bus Ltd/St Just | |
| G-BFOD | Cessna F.182Q | G. N. Clarke | |
| G-BFOE | Cessna F.152 | B. W. Wells & Burbage Farms Ltd | |
| G-BFOF | Cessna F.152 | Staverton Flying School Ltd | |
| G-BFOG | Cessna 150M | K. J. Steele & D. J. Hewitt | |
| G-BFOJ | AA-1 Yankee | A. J. Morton/Bournemouth | |
| G-BFOL | Beech 200 Super King Air | Bristow Helicopters Ltd | |
| G-BFOM | PA-31-325 Turbo Navajo C | Herbison Air Services Ltd | |
| G-BFOP | Jodel D.120 | R. J. Wesley & G. D. Western/Ipswich | |
| G-BFOS | Thunder Ax6-56A balloon | N. T. Petty | |
| G-BFOU | Taylor JT.1 Monoplane | G. Bee | |
| G-BFOV | Cessna F.172N | Gooda Walker Ltd/Shoreham | |
| G-BFOX | D.H.83 Fox Moth (replica) | R. K. J. Hadlow | |
| G-BFOZ | Thunder Ax6-56 balloon | R. L. Harbord | |
| G-BFPA | Scheibe SF.25B Super Falke | Yorkshire Gliding Club (Pty) Ltd/ Sutton Bank | |
| G-BFPB | AA-5B Tiger | Guernsey Aero Club | |
| G-BFPH | Cessna F.172K | J. M. Reid | |
| G-BFPJ | Procter Petrel | S. G. Craggs | |
| G-BFPL | Fokker D.VII (replica) (4253/18) | A. E. Hutton/North Weald | |
| G-BFPM | Cessna F.172M | N. R. Havercroft | |
| G-BFPO | R. Commander 112B | J. G. Hale Ltd | |
| G-BFPP | Bell 47J-2 | J. F. Kelly | |
| G-BFPS | PA-25 Pawnee 235D | Kent Gliding Club Ltd/Challock | |
| G-BFPX | Taylor JT.1 Monoplane | E. A. Taylor | |
| G-BFPZ | Cessna F.177RG | R. P. Nash/Norwich | |
| G-BFRA | R. Commander 114 | Sabre Engines Ltd/Bournemouth | |
| G-BFRD | Bowers Flybaby 1A | F. R. Donaldson | |
| G-BFRF | Taylor JT.1 Monoplane | E. R. Bailey | |
| G-BFRI | Sikorsky S-61N | Bristow Helicopters Ltd | |
| G-BFRL | Cessna F.152 | J. J. Baumhardt/Southend | |
| G-BFRM | Cessna 550 Citation II | Marshall of Cambridge (Engineering) Ltd | |
| G-BFRO | Cessna F.150M | Skyviews & General Ltd/Carlisle | |
| G-BFRR | Cessna FRA.150M | Interair Aviation Ltd/Bournemouth | |
| G-BFRS | Cessna F.172N | Poplar Toys Ltd | |
| G-BFRV | Cessna FA.152 | Rogers Aviation Ltd/Cranfield | |
| G-BFRX | PA-25 Pawnee 260 | Yorkshire Gliding Club (Pty) Ltd/ Sutton Bank | |
| G-BFRY | PA-25 Pawnee 260 | B. Walker & Co (Dursley) Ltd | |
| G-BFSA | Cessna F.182Q | Clark Masts Ltd/Sandown | |
| G-BFSB | Cessna F.152 | Seal Executive Aircraft Ltd/E. Midlands | |
| G-BFSC | PA-25 Pawnee 235D | Farm Aviation Services Ltd/Enstone | |
| G-BFSD | PA-25 Pawnee 235D | Deeside Gliding Club Ltd/Aboyne | |
| G-BFSK | PA-23 Apache 160 ★ | Oxford Air Training School/Kidlington | |
| G-BFSR | Cessna F.150J | Lamwood Aviation | |
| G-BFSS | Cessna FR.172G | Minerva Services | |
| G-BFSY | PA-28-181 Archer II | Downland Aviation/Goodwood | |
| G-BFTC | PA-28R-201T Turbo Arrow III | D. Hughes/Sherburn | |
| G-BFTF | AA-5B Tiger | F. C. Burrow Ltd/Leeds | |
| G-BFTG | AA-5B Tiger | BLS Aviation Ltd/Elstree | |
| G-BFTH | Cessna F.172N | J. L. Drinkell | |
| G-BFTT | Cessna 421C | P&B Metal Components Ltd/Manston | |
| G-BFTX | Cessna F.172N | E. Kent Flying Group | |
| G-BFTY | Cameron V-77 balloon | Regal Motors (Bilston) Ltd *Regal Motors* | |
| G-BFTZ | MS.880B Rallye Club | R. & B. Legge Ltd | |
| G-BFUB | PA-32RT-300 Lance II | Jolida Holdings Ltd | |
| G-BFUD | Scheibe SF.25E Super Falke | S. H. Hart | |
| G-BFUG | Cameron N-77 balloon | Headland Services Ltd | |
| G-BFUZ | Cameron V-77 balloon | Skysales Ltd | |
| G-BFVB | Boeing 737-204ADV | Britannia Airways Ltd *Sir Thomas Sopwith*/Luton | |
| G-BFVF | PA-38-112 Tomahawk | Ipswich School of Flying | |
| G-BFVG | PA-28-181 Archer II | G-BFVG Flying Group/Blackpool | |
| G-BFVH | D.H.2 Replica (5894) | Russavia Collection | |
| G-BFVI | H.S.125 Srs 700B | Bristow Helicopters Ltd | |
| G-BFVM | Westland-Bell 47G-3B1 | Pilotmoor Ltd | |
| G-BFVO | Partenavia P.68B | Travelair UK Ltd | |

| Notes | Reg. | Type | Owner or Operator |
|---|---|---|---|
| | G-BFVP | PA-23 Aztec 250F | R. H. Bicker |
| | G-BFVS | AA-5B Tiger | S. W. Biroth & T. Chapman/Denham |
| | G-BFVU | Cessna 150L | Thruxton Flight Centre Ltd |
| | G-BFVV | SA.365 Dauphin 2 | Bond Helicopters Ltd |
| | G-BFVW | SA.365 Dauphin 2 | Bond Helicopters Ltd |
| | G-BFWB | PA-28-161 Warrior II | C.S.E. Aviation Ltd/Kidlington |
| | G-BFWD | Currie Wot | F. E. Nuthall |
| | G-BFWE | PA-23 Aztec 250E | Air Navigation & Trading Co Ltd/ Blackpool |
| | G-BFWK | PA-28-161 Warrior II | Woodgate Air Services (IoM) Ltd |
| | G-BFWL | Cessna F.150L | Telair Manchester Ltd |
| | G-BFWW | Robin HR.100/210 | Willingair Ltd |
| | G-BFXC | Mooney M.20C | Kent Engraving Ltd |
| | G-BFXD | PA-28-161 Warrior II | C.S.E. Aviation Ltd/Kidlington |
| | G-BFXE | PA-28-161 Warrior II | C.S.E. Aviation Ltd/Kidlington |
| | G-BFXF | Andreasson BA.4B | A. Brown/Sherburn |
| | G-BFXG | D.31 Turbulent | S. Griffin |
| | G-BFXH | Cessna F.152 | Aerohire Ltd/Halfpenny Green |
| | G-BFXI | Cessna F.172M | Thanet Electronics/Manston |
| | G-BFXK | PA-28 Cherokee 140 | G. S. & Mrs M. T. Pritchard/Southend |
| | G-BFXL | Albatross D.5A (D5397/17) | FAA Museum/Yeovilton |
| | G-BFXM | Jurca MJ.5 Sirocco | R. Bradbury & A. R. Greenfield |
| | G-BFXO | Taylor JT.1 Monoplane | A. S. Nixon |
| | G-BFXR | Jodel D.112 | R. E. Walker & M. Riddin/Netherthorpe |
| | G-BFXS | R. Commander 114 | Keats Printing Ltd |
| | G-BFXW | AA-5B Tiger | Crosswind Aviation Ltd/Leeds |
| | G-BFXX | AA-5B Tiger | M. J. Porter |
| | G-BFYA | MBB Bo 105D | Veritair Ltd |
| | G-BFYB | PA-28-161 Warrior II | C.S.E. Aviation Ltd/Kidlington |
| | G-BFYC | PA-32RT-300 Lance II | A. A. Barnes |
| | G-BFYE | Robin HR.100/285 ★ | stored/Sywell |
| | G-BFYI | Westland-Bell 47G-3B1 | M&D Transport (Weston) Ltd |
| | G-BFYJ | Hughes 369HE | Krystle Aviation |
| | G-BFYL | Evans VP-2 | A. G. Wilford |
| | G-BFYM | PA-28-161 Warrior II | C.S.E. Aviation Ltd/Kidlington |
| | G-BFYN | Cessna FA.152 | Phoenix Flying Services Ltd/Glasgow |
| | G-BFYO | Spad XIII (replica) (S3398) ★ | FAA Museum/Yeovilton |
| | G-BFYP | Bensen B.7 | A. J. Philpotts |
| | G-BFYU | SC.5 Belfast | HeavyLift Cargo Airlines Ltd/Stansted |
| | G-BFZB | Piper J-3C-85 Cub | Zebedee Flying Group/Shoreham |
| | G-BFZD | Cessna FR.182RG | R. B. Lewis & Co/Sleap |
| | G-BFZG | PA-28-161 Warrior II | C.S.E. Aviation Ltd/Kidlington |
| | G-BFZH | PA-28R Cherokee Arrow 200 | K. E. Miles |
| | G-BFZL | V.836 Viscount | British Air Ferries Ltd/Southend |
| | G-BFZM | R. Commander 112TC | Rolls-Royce Ltd/Filton |
| | G-BFZN | Cessna FA.152 | Falcon Flying Services/Biggin Hill |
| | G-BFZO | AA-5A Cheetah | Heald Air Ltd/Manchester |
| | G-BFZT | Cessna FA.152 | One Zero One Three Ltd/Guernsey |
| | G-BFZU | Cessna FA.152 | R. T. Love |
| | G-BFZV | Cessna F.172M | R. Thomas |
| | G-BGAA | Cessna 152 II | PJC Leasing Ltd |
| | G-BGAB | Cessna F.152 II | TG Aviation Ltd/Manston |
| | G-BGAD | Cessna F.152 II | Redhill School of Flying Ltd |
| | G-BGAE | Cessna F.152 II | Klingair Ltd/Conington |
| | G-BGAF | Cessna FA.152 | Suffolk Aero Club Ltd/Ipswich |
| | G-BGAG | Cessna F.172N | Andrewsfield Flying Club Ltd |
| | G-BGAH | FRED Srs 2 | G. A. Harris |
| | G-BGAJ | Cessna F.182Q II | Ground Airport Services Ltd/Guernsey |
| | G-BGAK | Cessna F.182Q II | Safari World Services Ltd |
| | G-BGAU | Rearwin 9000L | T. G. Ratsey-Woodroffe/Sandown |
| | G-BGAX | PA-28 Cherokee 140 | Devon School of Flying/Dunkeswell |
| | G-BGAY | Cameron O-77 balloon | S. W. C. & P. C. A. Hall |
| | G-BGAZ | Cameron V-77 balloon | Cameron Balloons Ltd Silicon Chip |
| | G-BGBA | Robin R.2100A | D. Faulkner/Redhill |
| | G-BGBB | L.1011-385 TriStar 200 | British Airways Bridlington Bay/ Heathrow |
| | G-BGBC | L.1011-385 TriStar 200 | British Airways St Andrews Bay/ Heathrow |
| | G-BGBE | Jodel DR.1050 | J. A. Wootton & ptnrs |
| | G-BGBF | D.31A Turbulent | S. Haye |
| | G-BGBG | PA-28-181 Archer II | Harlow Printing Ltd/Newcastle |
| | G-BGBI | Cessna F.150L | Herefordshire Aero Club Ltd/Shobdon |

| Reg. | Type | Owner or Operator | Notes |
|------|------|-------------------|-------|
| G-BGBK | PA-38-112 Tomahawk | F. Marshall & R. C. Priest/Netherthorpe | |
| G-BGBN | PA-38-112 Tomahawk | Carter Aviation Ltd/Leavesden | |
| G-BGBP | Cessna F.152 | Stapleford Flying Club Ltd | |
| G-BGBR | Cessna F.172N | Falcon Flying Services/Biggin Hill | |
| G-BGBU | Auster AOP.9 (XN435) | P. Neilson | |
| G-BGBW | PA-38-112 Tomahawk | Truman Aviation Ltd/Tollerton | |
| G-BGBX | PA-38-112 Tomahawk | Ipswich School of Flying | |
| G-BGBY | PA-38-112 Tomahawk | Ravenair Ltd/Manchester | |
| G-BGBZ | R. Commander 114 | R. S. Fenwick/Biggin Hill | |
| G-BGCG | Douglas C-47A | on rebuild | |
| G-BGCL | AA-5A Cheetah | AIG Air Services Ltd | |
| G-BGCM | AA-5A Cheetah | Pacific Associates Ltd/Blackbushe | |
| G-BGCO | PA-44-180 Seminole | J. R. Henderson | |
| G-BGCX | Taylor JT.1 Monoplane | G. M. R. Walters | |
| G-BGCY | Taylor JT.1 Monoplane | M. T. Taylor | |
| G-BGDA | Boeing 737-236 | British Airways *River Tamar*/Heathrow | |
| G-BGDB | Boeing 737-236 | British Airways *River Tweed*/Heathrow | |
| G-BGDC | Boeing 737-236 | British Airways *River Humber*/Heathrow | |
| G-BGDD | Boeing 737-236 | British Airways *River Tees*/Heathrow | |
| G-BGDE | Boeing 737-236 | British Airways *River Avon*/Heathrow | |
| G-BGDF | Boeing 737-236 | British Airways *River Thames*/Heathrow | |
| G-BGDG | Boeing 737-236 | British Airways *River Medway*/Heathrow | |
| G-BGDH | Boeing 737-236 | British Airways *River Clyde*/Heathrow | |
| G-BGDI | Boeing 737-236 | British Airways *River Ouse*/Heathrow | |
| G-BGDJ | Boeing 737-236 | British Airways *River Trent*/Heathrow | |
| G-BGDK | Boeing 737-236 | British Airways *River Mersey*/Heathrow | |
| G-BGDL | Boeing 737-236 | British Airways *River Don*/Heathrow | |
| G-BGDN | Boeing 737-236 | British Airways *River Tyne*/Heathrow | |
| G-BGDO | Boeing 737-236 | British Airways *River Usk*/Heathrow | |
| G-BGDP | Boeing 737-236 | British Airways *River Taff*/Heathrow | |
| G-BGDR | Boeing 737-236 | British Airways *River Bann*/Heathrow | |
| G-BGDS | Boeing 737-236 | British Airways *River Severn*/Heathrow | |
| G-BGDT | Boeing 737-236 | British Airways *River Forth*/Heathrow | |
| G-BGDU | Boeing 737-236 | British Airways *River Dee*/Heathrow | |
| G-BGEA | Cessna F.150M | Agricultural & General Aviation Ltd | |
| G-BGED | Cessna U.206F | Peterborough Parachute Centre Ltd/ Sibson | |
| G-BGEE | Evans VP-1 | D. P. Byatt | |
| G-BGEF | Jodel D.112 | G. G. Johnson & S. J. Davies | |
| G-BGEH | Monnet Sonerai II | A. Dodd | |
| G-BGEI | Baby Great Lakes | I. H. Seach-Allen | |
| G-BGEK | PA-38-112 Tomahawk | Cheshire Flying Services Ltd/ Manchester | |
| G-BGEL | PA-38-112 Tomahawk | Ravenair Ltd/Manchester | |
| G-BGEM | Partenavia P.68B | Meridian Air Services Ltd/Staverton | |
| G-BGEN | D.H.C.6 Twin Otter 310 | Loganair Ltd/Glasgow | |
| G-BGEP | Cameron D-38 balloon | Cameron Balloons Ltd | |
| G-BGES | Currie Wot | K. E. Ballington | |
| G-BGEW | SNCAN NC.854S | R. A. Yates | |
| G-BGEX | Brookland Mosquito 2 | R. T. Gough | |
| G-BGFC | Evans VP-2 | A. C. Gray | |
| G-BGFF | FRED Srs 2 | F. Bolton/Blackpool | |
| G-BGFG | AA-5A Cheetah | Fletcher Aviation Ltd/Biggin Hill | |
| G-BGFH | Cessna F.182Q | Mindon Engineering (Nottingham) Ltd/ Tollerton | |
| G-BGFI | AA-5A Cheetah | I. J. Hay & A. Nayyar/Biggin Hill | |
| G-BGFJ | Jodel D.9 Bebe | C. M. Fitton | |
| G-BGFK | Evans VP-1 | I. N. M. Cameron | |
| G-BGFT | PA-34-200T Seneca II | C.S.E. Aviation Ltd/Kidlington | |
| G-BGFX | Cessna F.152 | A. W. Fay/Cranfield | |
| G-BGGA | Bellanca 7GCBC Citabria | I. N. Jennison | |
| G-BGGB | Bellanca 7GCBC Citabria | M. D. Cowburn | |
| G-BGGC | Bellanca 7GCBC Citabria | R. P. Ashfield & J. P. Stone | |
| G-BGGD | Bellanca 8GCBC Scout | Bristol & Gloucestershire Gliding Club/Nympsfield | |
| G-BGGE | PA-38-112 Tomahawk | M. B. Calvert/Tollerton | |
| G-BGGF | PA-38-112 Tomahawk | Truman Aviation Ltd/Tollerton | |
| G-BGGG | PA-38-112 Tomahawk | C.S.E. (Aircraft Services) Ltd/Kidlington | |
| G-BGGI | PA-38-112 Tomahawk | Truman Aviation Ltd/Tollerton | |
| G-BGGL | PA-38-112 Tomahawk | Pan-Air Ltd/Leavesden | |
| G-BGGM | PA-38-112 Tomahawk | Pan-Air Ltd/Leavesden | |

| Notes | Reg. | Type | Owner or Operator |
|-------|------|------|-------------------|
| | G-BGGN | PA-38-112 Tomahawk | Domeastral Ltd/Elstree |
| | G-BGGO | Cessna F.152 | E. Midlands Flying School Ltd |
| | G-BGGP | Cessna F.152 | E. Midlands Flying School Ltd |
| | G-BGGT | Zenith CH.200 | P. R. M. Nind |
| | G-BGGU | Wallis WA-116R-R | K. H. Wallis |
| | G-BGGV | Wallis WA-120 Srs 2 | K. H. Wallis |
| | G-BGGW | Wallis WA-112 | K. H. Wallis |
| | G-BGGY | AB-206B Jet Ranger ★ | Instructional airframe/Cranfield |
| | G-BGHE | Convair L-13A | J. Davis/USA |
| | G-BGHF | Westland WG.30 ★ | International Helicopter Museum/ Weston-s-Mare |
| | G-BGHI | Cessna F.152 | Taxon Ltd/Shoreham |
| | G-BGHK | Cessna F.152 | Wilson Leasing/Biggin Hill |
| | G-BGHM | Robin R.1180T | H. Price |
| | G-BGHP | Beech 76 Duchess | J. J. Baumhardt Ltd |
| | G-BGHS | Cameron N-31 balloon | W. R. Teasdale |
| | G-BGHT | Falconar F-12 | C. R. Coates |
| | G-BGHU | NA T-6G Texan (115042) | C. E. Bellhouse |
| | G-BGHV | Cameron V-77 balloon | E. Davies |
| | G-BGHW | Thunder Ax8-90 balloon | Edinburgh University Balloon Group |
| | G-BGHY | Taylor JT.1 Monoplane | R. A. Hand |
| | G-BGHZ | FRED Srs 2 | A. Smith |
| | G-BGIB | Cessna 152 II | Mona Aviation Ltd |
| | G-BGIC | Cessna 172N | T. R. Sinclair |
| | G-BGID | Westland-Bell 47G-3B1 | M. J. Cuttell |
| | G-BGIG | PA-38-112 Tomahawk | Scotia Safari Ltd/Prestwick |
| | G-BGIH | Rand KR-2 | G. & D. G. Park |
| | G-BGII | PA-32 Cherokee Six 300E | Rosefair Electronics Ltd/Elstree |
| | G-BGIK | Taylor JT.1 Monoplane | L. A. Davies |
| | G-BGIO | Bensen B.8M | C. G. Johns |
| | G-BGIP | Colt 56A balloon | J. G. N. Perfect |
| | G-BGIU | Cessna F.172H | Metro Equipment (Chesham) Ltd/ Panshanger |
| | G-BGIV | Bell 47G-5 | Trent Air Services Ltd/Cranfield |
| | G-BGIX | H.295 Super Courier | C. M. Lee/Andrewsfield |
| | G-BGIY | Cessna F.172N | P. R. Small/Glasgow |
| | G-BGIZ | Cessna F.152 | Creaton Aviation Services Ltd |
| | G-BGJB | PA-44-180 Seminole | Oxford Management Ltd |
| | G-BGJE | Boeing 737-236 | British Airways River Wear/Gatwick |
| | G-BGJF | Boeing 737-236 | British Airways River Axe/Gatwick |
| | G-BGJG | Boeing 737-236 | British Airways River Arun/Gatwick |
| | G-BGJH | Boeing 737-236 | British Airways River Lyne/Gatwick |
| | G-BGJI | Boeing 737-236 | British Airways River Wey/Gatwick |
| | G-BGJJ | Boeing 737-236 | British Airways River Swale/Gatwick |
| | G-BGJK | Boeing 737-236 | British Airways River Cherwell/Gatwick |
| | G-BGJM | Boeing 737-236 | British Airways River Ribble/Gatwick |
| | G-BGJU | Cameron V-65 Balloon | S. B. Sperring |
| | G-BGJV | H.S.748 Srs 2B | British Airways Glen Avon/Glasgow |
| | G-BGJW | GA-7 Cougar | Lambill Ltd |
| | G-BGKA | P.56 Provost T.1 (XF690) | D. W. Mickleburgh |
| | G-BGKC | SOCATA Rallye 110ST | J. H. Cranmer & T. A. Timms |
| | G-BGKD | SOCATA Rallye 110ST | W. G. G. Lowe |
| | G-BGKE | BAC One-Eleven 539GL | British Airways County of West Midlands |
| | G-BGKF | BAC One-Eleven 539GL | British Airways County of Warwickshire |
| | G-BGKG | BAC One-Eleven 539GL | British Airways County of Staffordshire |
| | G-BGKJ | MBB Bo 105C | Bond Helicopters Ltd |
| | G-BGKM | SA.365C-3 Dauphin | Bond Helicopters Ltd |
| | G-BGKO | GY-20 Minicab | R. B. Webber |
| | G-BGKS | PA-28-161 Warrior II | Woodgate Air Services (IoM) Ltd |
| | G-BGKT | Auster AOP.9 (XN441) | K. H. Wallis |
| | G-BGKU | PA-28R-201 Arrow III | Caplane Ltd |
| | G-BGKV | PA-28R-201 Arrow III | R. Haverson & R. G. Watson |
| | G-BGKW | Evans VP-1 | I. W. Black |
| | G-BGKY | PA-38-112 Tomahawk | MSF Aviation |
| | G-BGKZ | J/5F Aiglet Trainer | R. C. H. Hibberd |
| | G-BGLA | PA-38-112 Tomahawk | Norwich School of Flying |
| | G-BGLB | Bede BD-5B | W. Sawney |
| | G-BGLE | Saffrey S.330 balloon | C. J. Dodd & ptnrs |
| | G-BGLF | Evans VP-1 Srs 2 | M. Hartigan/Fenland |
| | G-BGLG | Cessna 152 | Skyviews & General Ltd/Bourn |
| | G-BGLH | Cessna 152 | Deltair Ltd/Chester |
| | G-BGLI | Cessna 152 | Luton Flying Club (stored) |
| | G-BGLK | Monnet Sonerai II | N. M. Smorthit |

| Reg. | Type | Owner or Operator | Notes |
|------|------|-------------------|-------|
| G-BGLN | Cessna FA.152 | Bournemouth Flying Club | |
| G-BGLO | Cessna F.172N | A. H. Slaughter/Southend | |
| G-BGLS | Super Baby Great Lakes | J. F. Dowe | |
| G-BGLW | PA-34-200 Seneca | P. C. Roberts | |
| G-BGLX | Cameron N-56 balloon | Sara A. G. Williams | |
| G-BGLZ | Stits SA-3A Playboy | B. G. Ell | |
| G-BGMA | D.31 Turbulent | G. C. Masterton | |
| G-BGMB | Taylor JT.2 Titch | E. M. Bourne | |
| G-BGME | SIPA S.903 | M. Emery (G-BCML)/Redhill | |
| G-BGMJ | GY-201 Minicab | S. L. Wakefield & ptnrs | |
| G-BGMN | H.S.748 Srs 2A | — | |
| G-BGMO | H.S.748 Srs 2A | — | |
| G-BGMP | Cessna F.172G | S. G. Hoole/Bourn | |
| G-BGMR | GY-201 Minicab | J. R. Large & ptnrs | |
| G-BGMS | Taylor JT.2 Titch | M. A. J. Spice | |
| G-BGMT | MS.894E Rallye 235GT | M. E. Taylor | |
| G-BGMU | Westland-Bell 47G-3B1 | V. L. J. & V. English | |
| G-BGMV | Scheibe SF.25B Falke | Wolds Gliding Club Ltd/Pocklington | |
| G-BGNB | Short SD3-30 Variant 100 | Celtic Airways Ltd *Celtic Warrior* | |
| G-BGND | Cessna F.172N | Stansted Fluid Power (Products) Ltd | |
| G-BGNG | Short SD3-30 | Fairflight Leasing Ltd | |
| G-BGNH | Short SD3-30 | Fairflight Leasing Ltd | |
| G-BGNM | SA.365C-1 Dauphin 2 | Bond Helicopters Ltd | |
| G-BGNR | Cessna F.172N | Bevan Lynch Aviation Ltd/Birmingham | |
| G-BGNT | Cessna F.152 | Klingair Ltd/Conington | |
| G-BGNV | GA-7 Cougar | R. W. Fairless/Southampton | |
| G-BGNZ | Cessna FRA.150L | Paysure Ltd/Edinburgh | |
| G-BGOD | Colt 77A balloon | C. Allen & M. D. Steuer | |
| G-BGOF | Cessna F.152 | Falcon Flying Services/Biggin Hill | |
| G-BGOG | PA-28-161 Warrior II | W. D. Moore & M. Sear | |
| G-BGOI | Cameron O-56 balloon | S. H. Budd | |
| G-BGOL | PA-28R-201T Turbo Arrow III | Clark Aviation Services Ltd | |
| G-BGOM | PA-31-310 Turbo Navajo | Oxford Aero Charter Ltd/Kidlington | |
| G-BGON | GA-7 Cougar | Walsh Aviation | |
| G-BGOO | Colt 56 SS balloon | British Gas Corporation | |
| G-BGOP | Dassault Falcon 20F | Nissan (UK) Ltd/Heathrow | |
| G-BGOR | AT-6D Harvard III | M. L. Sargeant | |
| G-BGOX | PA-31-350 Navajo Chieftain | Woodgate Aviation (IoM) Ltd | |
| G-BGPA | Cessna 182Q | R. A. Robinson | |
| G-BGPB | CCF T-6J Texan (20385) | Aircraft Restorations Ltd/Duxford | |
| G-BGPD | Piper J-3C-65 Cub | P. D. Whiteman | |
| G-BGPH | AA-5B Tiger | A. J. Dales | |
| G-BGPI | Plumb BGP-1 | B. G. Plumb | |
| G-BGPJ | PA-28-161 Warrior II | W. Lancs Warrior Co Ltd | |
| G-BGPK | AA-5B Tiger | Ann Green Manufacturing Co Ltd/ Elstree | |
| G-BGPL | PA-28-161 Warrior II | T. G. Aviation Ltd/Manston | |
| G-BGPM | Evans VP-2 | M. G. Reilly | |
| G-BGPN | PA-18 Super Cub 150 | Clacton Aero Club (1988) Ltd | |
| G-BGPT | Parker Teenie Two | K. Atkinson | |
| G-BGPU | PA-28 Cherokee 140 | Air Navigation & Trading Co Ltd/ Blackpool | |
| G-BGPZ | M.S.890A Rallye Commodore | J. A. Espin/Popham | |
| G-BGRA | Taylor JT.2 Titch | J. R. C. Thompson | |
| G-BGRC | PA-28 Cherokee 140 | Arrow Air Centre Ltd/Shipdham | |
| G-BGRE | Beech A200 Super King Air | Martin-Baker (Engineering) Ltd/ Chalgrove | |
| G-BGRG | Beech 76 Duchess | Arrows Aviation Co Ltd/Manchester | |
| G-BGRH | Robin DR.400/2+2 | Rochester Aviation Ltd | |
| G-BGRI | Jodel DR.1051 | B. Gunn & K. L. Burnett | |
| G-BGRK | PA-38-112 Tomahawk | Goodwood Terrena Ltd | |
| G-BGRL | PA-38-112 Tomahawk | Goodwood Terrena Ltd | |
| G-BGRM | PA-38-112 Tomahawk | Goodwood Terrena Ltd | |
| G-BGRN | PA-38-112 Tomahawk | Goodwood Terrena Ltd | |
| G-BGRO | Cessna F.172M | Northfield Garage Ltd/Prestwick | |
| G-BGRR | PA-38-112 Tomahawk | MSF Aviation Ltd/Manchester | |
| G-BGRS | Thunder Ax7-77Z balloon | W. & J. Evans | |
| G-BGRT | Steen Skybolt | Roding Air Flying Ltd | |
| G-BGRX | PA-38-112 Tomahawk | Willis Aviation Ltd | |
| G-BGSA | M.S.892E Rallye 150GT | Colin Draycott Group Ltd/Leicester | |
| G-BGSG | PA-44-180 Seminole | D. J. McSorley | |
| G-BGSH | PA-38-112 Tomahawk | Scotia Safari Ltd/Prestwick | |

| Notes | Reg. | Type | Owner or Operator |
|-------|------|------|-------------------|
| | G-BGSI | PA-38-112 Tomahawk | Cheshire Flying Services Ltd/ Manchester |
| | G-BGSJ | Piper J-3C-65 Cub | W. J. Higgins/Dunkeswell |
| | G-BGSM | M.S.892E Rallye 150GT | D. H. Rider & P. Curley |
| | G-BGSN | Enstrom F-28C-UK-2 | Spirit Busy Ltd |
| | G-BGSO | PA-31-310 Turbo Navajo | B. Butler |
| | G-BGST | Thunder Ax7-65 balloon | J. L. Bond |
| | G-BGSV | Cessna F.172N | Wickenby Flying Club Ltd |
| | G-BGSW | Beech F33 Debonair | Marketprior Ltd/Swansea |
| | G-BGSX | Cessna F.152 | B. W. Wells & Burbage Farms Ltd |
| | G-BGSY | GA-7 Cougar | Van Allen Ltd/Guernsey |
| | G-BGTB | SOCATA TB.10 Tobago ★ | D. Pope *(stored)* |
| | G-BGTC | Auster AOP.9 (XP282) | P. T. Bolton/Tollerton |
| | G-BGTF | PA-44-180 Seminole | New Guarantee Trust Properties Ltd |
| | G-BGTG | PA-23 Aztec 250F | R. J. Howard/Sherburn |
| | G-BGTI | Piper J-3C-65 Cub | A. P. Broad |
| | G-BGTJ | PA-28 Cherokee 180 | Serendipity Aviation/Staverton |
| | G-BGTK | Cessna FR.182RG | Kestrel Air Services Ltd/Denham |
| | G-BGTL | GY-20 Minicab | A. K. Lang |
| | G-BGTP | Robin HR.100/210 | J. C. Parker |
| | G-BGTR | PA-28 Cherokee 140 | Liverpool Flying School Ltd |
| | G-BGTT | Cessna 310R | Aviation Beauport Ltd/Jersey |
| | G-BGTU | BAC One-Eleven 409AY | Turbo Union Ltd/Filton |
| | G-BGTX | Jodel D.117 | Madley Flying Group/Shobdon |
| | G-BGUA | PA-38-112 Tomahawk | Rhodair Maintenance Ltd/Cardiff |
| | G-BGUB | PA-32 Cherokee Six 300E | R. Howton |
| | G-BGUY | Cameron V-56 balloon | J. L. Guy |
| | G-BGVA | Cessna 414A | Mansfield Television Holdings Ltd |
| | G-BGVB | Robin DR.315 | Cedric P. Jones Ltd/Blackbushe |
| | G-BGVE | CP.1310-C3 Super Emeraude | J. D. Snell |
| | G-BGVH | Beech 76 Duchess | Velco Marketing |
| | G-BGVI | Cessna F.152 | Stapleford Flying Club Ltd |
| | G-BGVK | PA-28-161 Warrior II | R. L. Brucciani |
| | G-BGVL | PA-38-112 Tomahawk | R. A. Crook/Norwich |
| | G-BGVN | PA-28RT-201 Arrow IV | Essex Aviation Ltd/Stapleford |
| | G-BGVR | Thunder Ax6-56Z balloon | A. N. G. Howie |
| | G-BGVS | Cessna F.172M | P. D. A. Aviation Ltd/Tollerton |
| | G-BGVT | Cessna R.182RG | Barnes Olson Aeroleasing Ltd |
| | G-BGVU | PA-28 Cherokee 180 | Cheshire Flying Services Ltd/ Manchester |
| | G-BGVV | AA-5A Cheetah | A. H. McVicar |
| | G-BGVW | AA-5A Cheetah | Jetbonus Ltd/Biggin Hill |
| | G-BGVY | AA-5B Tiger | Porter Bell Ltd/Goodwood |
| | G-BGVZ | PA-28-181 Archer II | Midland Aircraft Leasing Ltd/ Birmingham |
| | G-BGWA | GA-7 Cougar | Lough Erne Aviation Ltd |
| | G-BGWC | Robin DR.400/180 | E. F. Braddon & D. C. Shepherd/ Rochester |
| | G-BGWF | PA-18 Super Cub 150 | D. B. Meeks |
| | G-BGWH | PA-18 Super Cub 150 | Clacton Aero Club (1988) Ltd |
| | G-BGWI | Cameron V-65 balloon | Army Balloon Club/Germany |
| | G-BGWJ | Sikorsky S-61N | British Executive Air Services Ltd |
| | G-BGWK | Sikorsky S-61N | Bristow Helicopters Ltd |
| | G-BGWM | PA-28-181 Archer II | Thames Valley Flying Club Ltd |
| | G-BGWN | PA-38-112 Tomahawk | Frontline Aviation Ltd/Teesside |
| | G-BGWO | Jodel D.112 | A. J. Court |
| | G-BGWS | Enstrom 280C Shark | I. J. & G. J. Wooldridge |
| | G-BGWU | PA-38-112 Tomahawk | R. J. Howard |
| | G-BGWV | Aeronca 7AC Champion | RFC Flying Group/Popham |
| | G-BGWW | PA-23 Turbo Aztec 250E | Ski Air Ltd/Biggin Hill |
| | G-BGWY | Thunder Ax6-56Z balloon | J. G. O'Connel |
| | G-BGWZ | Eclipse Super Eagle ★ | FAA Museum/Yeovilton |
| | G-BGXA | Piper J-3C-65 Cub (329471) | K. Nicholls |
| | G-BGXB | PA-38-112 Tomahawk | Signtest Ltd/Cardiff |
| | G-BGXC | SOCATA TB.10 Tobago | N. N. Tullah/Cranfield |
| | G-BGXD | SOCATA TB.10 Tobago | Selles Dispensing Chemists Ltd |
| | G-BGXJ | Partenavia P.68B | Cecil Aviation Ltd/Cambridge |
| | G-BGXK | Cessna 310R | Air Service Training Ltd/Perth |
| | G-BGXL | Bensen B.8MV | B. P. Triefus |
| | G-BGXN | PA-38-112 Tomahawk | Panshanger School of Flying Ltd |
| | G-BGXO | PA-38-112 Tomahawk | Goodwood Terrena Ltd |
| | G-BGXP | Westland-Bell 47G-3B1 | Ace Motor Salvage (Norfolk) |
| | G-BGXR | Robin HR.200/100 | J. P. Kistner |

| Reg. | Type | Owner or Operator | Notes |
|------|------|-------------------|-------|
| G-BGXS | PA-28-236 Dakota | Bawtry Road Service Station Ltd | |
| G-BGXT | SOCATA TB.10 Tobago | County Aviation Ltd/Halfpenny Green | |
| G-BGXU | WMB-1 balloon | C. J. Dodd & ptnrs | |
| G-BGXZ | Cessna FA.152 | Alouette Flying Club Ltd/Biggin Hill | |
| G-BGYG | PA-28-161 Warrior II | C.S.E. Aviation Ltd/Kidlington | |
| G-BGYH | PA-28-161 Warrior II | C.S.E. Aviation Ltd/Kidlington | |
| G-BGYJ | Boeing 737-204 | Britannia Airways Ltd *Sir Barnes Wallis*/Luton | |
| G-BGYK | Boeing 737-204 | Britannia Airways Ltd *R. J. Mitchell*/Luton | |
| G-BGYL | Boeing 737-204 | Britannia Airways Ltd *Jean Batten*/Luton | |
| G-BGYN | PA-18 Super Cub 150 | A. G. Walker | |
| G-BGYR | H.S.125 Srs 600B | British Aerospace/Warton | |
| G-BGYT | EMB-110P1 Bandeirante | Business Air Travel/Skyrover Ltd | |
| G-BGYV | EMB-110P1 Bandeirante | Business Air Travel | |
| G-BGZC | C.A.S.A. 1.131 Jungmann | J. E. Douglas/Andorra La Vella | |
| G-BGZF | PA-38-112 Tomahawk | Cambrian Flying Club/Swansea | |
| G-BGZJ | PA-38-112 Tomahawk | W. R. C. M. Foyle | |
| G-BGZK | Westland-Bell 47G-3B1 | Dawnville Ltd | |
| G-BGZL | Eiri PIK-20E | D. I. Liddell-Grainger | |
| G-BGZN | WMB.2 Windtracker balloon | S. R. Woolfries | |
| G-BGZO | M.S.880B Rallye Club | G-BGZO Flying Group | |
| G-BGZR | Meagher Model balloon Mk.1 | S. C. Meagher | |
| G-BGZS | Keirs Heated Air Tube | M. N. J. Kirby | |
| G-BGZW | PA-38-112 Tomahawk | Ravenair Ltd/Manchester | |
| G-BGZY | Jodel D.120 | M. Hale | |
| G-BGZZ | Thunder Ax6-56 balloon | J. M. Robinson | |
| G-BHAA | Cessna 152 | Herefordshire Aero Club Ltd/Shobdon | |
| G-BHAC | Cessna A.152 | Herefordshire Aero Club Ltd/Shobdon | |
| G-BHAD | Cessna A.152 | Shropshire Aero Club Ltd/Sleap | |
| G-BHAF | PA-38-112 Tomahawk | Notelevel Ltd | |
| G-BHAG | Scheibe SF.25E Super Falke | British Gliding Association/Lasham | |
| G-BHAI | Cessna F.152 | P. P. D. Howard-Johnston/Edinburgh | |
| G-BHAJ | Robin DR.400/160 | Rowantask Ltd | |
| G-BHAL | Rango Saffery S.200 SS | A. M. Lindsay *Anneky Panky* | |
| G-BHAM | Thunder Ax6-56 balloon | D. Sampson | |
| G-BHAR | Westland-Bell 47G-3B1 | E. A. L. Sturmer | |
| G-BHAT | Thunder Ax7-77 balloon | C. P. Witter Ltd *Witter* | |
| G-BHAV | Cessna F.152 | Iceni Leasing | |
| G-BHAW | Cessna F.172N | Jet Support Flying Centre/Manston | |
| G-BHAX | Enstrom F-28C-UK-2 | Southern Air Ltd/Shoreham | |
| G-BHAY | PA-28RT-201 Arrow IV | Alpha Yankee Group/Newcastle | |
| G-BHBA | Campbell Cricket | S. M. Irwin | |
| G-BHBB | Colt 77A balloon | S. D. Bellew/USA | |
| G-BHBE | Westland-Bell 47G-3B1 (Soloy) | T. R. Smith (Agricultural Machinery) Ltd | |
| G-BHBF | Sikorsky S-76A | Bristow Helicopters Ltd | |
| G-BHBG | PA-32R Cherokee Lance 300 | R. W. F. Warner | |
| G-BHBI | Mooney M.20J | B. K. Arthur/Exeter | |
| G-BHBL | L.1011-385 TriStar 200 | British Airways *Largs Bay*/Heathrow | |
| G-BHBM | L.1011-385 TriStar 200 | British Airways *Poole Bay*/Heathrow | |
| G-BHBN | L.1011-385 TriStar 200 | British Airways *Bideford Bay*/Heathrow | |
| G-BHBO | L.1011-385 TriStar 200 | British Airways *St Magnus Bay*/Heathrow | |
| G-BHBP | L.1011-385 TriStar 200 | British Airways *Whitesand Bay*/Heathrow | |
| G-BHBR | L.1011-385 TriStar 200 | British Airways *Bude Bay*/Heathrow | |
| G-BHBS | PA-28RT-201T Turbo Arrow IV | B. C. Oates/Barton | |
| G-BHBT | Marquart MA.5 Charger | R. G. & C. J. Maidment/Shoreham | |
| G-BHBZ | Partenavia P.68B | T. Hayselden (Doncaster) Ltd | |
| G-BHCC | Cessna 172M | T. Howard | |
| G-BHCE | Jodel D.112 | D. M. Parsons | |
| G-BHCF | WMB.2 Windtracker balloon | C. J. Dodd & ptnrs | |
| G-BHCM | Cessna F.172H | The English Connection Ltd/Panshanger | |
| G-BHCP | Cessna F.152 | Sherburn Aero Club Ltd | |
| G-BHCW | PA-22 Tri-Pacer 150 | B. Brooks | |
| G-BHCX | Cessna F.152 | A. S. Bamrah/Biggin Hill | |
| G-BHCZ | PA-38-112 Tomahawk | J. E. Abbott | |
| G-BHDD | V.668 Varsity T.1 (WL626) ★ | Historic Flight/E. Midlands | |

| Notes | Reg. | Type | Owner or Operator |
|-------|------|------|-------------------|
| | G-BHDE | SOCATA TB.10 Tobago | A. A. Dooley/Popham |
| | G-BHDH | Douglas DC-10-30 | British Airways *Benmore Forest* /Gatwick |
| | G-BHDI | Douglas DC-10-30 | British Airways *Forest of Ae*/Gatwick |
| | G-BHDJ | Douglas DC-10-30 | British Airways *Glen Cap Forest*/Gatwick |
| | G-BHDK | Boeing B-29A-BN (461748) ★ | Imperial War Museum/Duxford |
| | G-BHDM | Cessna F.152 II | Tayside Aviation Ltd/Dundee |
| | G-BHDP | Cessna F.182Q II | R. J. D. Rimmer/Elstree |
| | G-BHDR | Cessna F.152 II | Tayside Aviation Ltd/Dundee |
| | G-BHDS | Cessna F.152 II | Tayside Aviation Ltd/Dundee |
| | G-BHDT | SOCATA TB.10 Tobago | W. R. C. Foyle/Luton |
| | G-BHDU | Cessna F.152 II | Falcon Flying Services/Biggin Hill |
| | G-BHDV | Cameron V-77 balloon | P. Glydon |
| | G-BHDW | Cessna F.152 | Tayside Aviation Ltd/Dundee |
| | G-BHDX | Cessna F.172N | R. P. A. Onslow |
| | G-BHDZ | Cessna F.172N | J. B. Roberts |
| | G-BHEC | Cessna F.152 | W. R. C. Foyle |
| | G-BHED | Cessna FA.152 | TG Aviation Ltd/Manston |
| | G-BHEG | Jodel D.150 | P. R. Underhill |
| | G-BHEH | Cessna 310G | Witham (Specialist) Vehicles Ltd |
| | G-BHEK | CP.1315-C3 Super Emeraude | D. B. Winstanley/Barton |
| | G-BHEL | Jodel D.117 | J. F. Dowe |
| | G-BHEM | Bensen B.8M | A. M. Sands |
| | G-BHEN | Cessna FA.152 | Leicestershire Aero Club Ltd |
| | G-BHEO | Cessna FR.182RG | M. C. Costin |
| | G-BHEP | Cessna 172 RG Cutlass | Proteus Petroleum Aviation Ltd/ Goodwood |
| | G-BHER | SOCATA TB.10 Tobago | Vale Aviation Ltd |
| | G-BHET | SOCATA TB.10 Tobago | Claude Hooper Ltd |
| | G-BHEU | Thunder Ax7-65 balloon | M. H. R. Govett |
| | G-BHEV | PA-28R Cherokee Arrow 200 | E. & G. H. Kelk |
| | G-BHEX | Colt 56A balloon | A. S. Dear & ptnrs *Super Wasp* |
| | G-BHEZ | Jodel D.150 | D. R. Elpick/O. Warden |
| | G-BHFC | Cessna F.152 | T. G. Aviation Ltd/Manston |
| | G-BHFE | PA-44-180 Seminole | Grunwick Ltd/Elstree |
| | G-BHFF | Jodel D.112 | P. J. Swain |
| | G-BHFG | SNCAN Stampe SV-4C (45) | A. L. Lindsay/Booker |
| | G-BHFH | PA-34-200T Seneca II | Hendefern Ltd/Goodwood |
| | G-BHFI | Cessna F.152 | BAe (Warton) Flying Group/Blackpool |
| | G-BHFJ | PA-28RT-201T Turbo Arrow IV | T. L. P. Delaney |
| | G-BHFK | PA-28-151 Warrior | Ilkeston Car Sales Ltd |
| | G-BHFM | Murphy S.200 balloon | M. Murphy |
| | G-BHFR | Eiri PIK-20E-1 | J. MacWilliam & T. Dalrymple-Smith |
| | G-BHFS | Robin DR.400/180 | Flair (Soft Drinks) Ltd/Shoreham |
| | G-BHGA | PA-31-310 Turbo Navajo | Heltor Ltd |
| | G-BHGC | PA-18 Super Cub 150 | D. E. Schofield |
| | G-BHGF | Cameron V-56 balloon | P. J. Smart |
| | G-BHGJ | Jodel D.120 | Q. M. B. Oswell |
| | G-BHGK | Sikorsky S-76A | Bond Helicopters Ltd |
| | G-BHGM | Beech 76 Duchess | T. Hayselden |
| | G-BHGO | PA-32 Cherokee Six 260 | Sydney House Communities/Manston |
| | G-BHGP | SOCATA TB.10 Tobago | C. Flanagan |
| | G-BHGX | Colt 56B balloon | M. N. Dixon |
| | G-BHGY | PA-28R Cherokee Arrow 200 | V. Humphries/Gamston |
| | G-BHHB | Cameron V-77 balloon | R. Powell & K. G. Betts |
| | G-BHHE | Jodel DR.1051/M1 | P. Bridges |
| | G-BHHG | Cessna F.152 | Northamptonshire School of Flying Ltd/ Sywell |
| | G-BHHH | Thunder Ax7-65 balloon | C. A. Hendley (Essex) Ltd |
| | G-BHHI | Cessna F.152 | Andrewsfield Flying Club Ltd |
| | G-BHHK | Cameron N-77 balloon | S. Bridge & ptnrs |
| | G-BHHN | Cameron V-77 balloon | Itchen Valley Balloon Group |
| | G-BHHU | Short SD3-30 | Celtic Airways Ltd |
| | G-BHHX | Jodel D.112 | C. F. Walter |
| | G-BHHZ | Rotorway Scorpion 133 | L. W. & O. Usherwood |
| | G-BHIA | Cessna F.152 | W. H. Wilkins/Stapleford |
| | G-BHIB | Cessna F.182Q | Gogood Ltd |
| | G-BHIC | Cessna F.182Q | General Building Services Ltd/Leeds |
| | G-BHIH | Cessna F.172N | Merlin Marine Aviation (Jersey) Ltd |
| | G-BHII | Cameron V-77 balloon | R. V. Brown |
| | G-BHIJ | Eiri PIK-20E-1 | R. W. Hall & ptnrs/Swanton Morley |
| | G-BHIK | Adam RA-14 Loisirs | L. Lewis |
| | G-BHIN | Cessna F.152 | P. Skinner/Netherthorpe |

| Reg. | Type | Owner or Operator | Notes |
|------|------|-------------------|-------|
| G-BHIR | PA-28R Cherokee Arrow 200 | Cheshire Flying Services Ltd/ Manchester | |
| G-BHIS | Thunder Ax7-65 balloon | Hedgehoppers Balloon Group | |
| G-BHIT | SOCATA TB.9 Tampico | Air Touring Services Ltd/Biggin Hill | |
| G-BHIY | Cessna F.150K | Westfield Flying Group | |
| G-BHJA | Cessna A.152 | Cornwall Flying Club Ltd/Bodmin | |
| G-BHJB | Cessna A.152 | E. E. Fenning & Son | |
| G-BHJF | SOCATA TB.10 Tobago | D. G. Dedman/Leavesden | |
| G-BHJI | Mooney M.20J | Christian Newman Aviation | |
| G-BHJK | Maule M5-235C Lunar Rocket | P. F. Hall & R. L. Sambell/Coventry | |
| G-BHJN | Fournier RF-4D | S. C. Cattlin | |
| G-BHJO | PA-28-161 Warrior II | Nairn Flying Services Ltd/Inverness | |
| G-BHJS | Partenavia P.68B | Tewin Aviation/Panshanger | |
| G-BHJU | Robin DR.400/2+2 | Harlow Transport Services Ltd/ Headcorn | |
| G-BHJZ | EMB-110P2 Bandeirante | Jersey European Airways/Exeter | |
| G-BHKA | Evans VP-1 | M. L. Perry | |
| G-BHKE | Bensen B.8MV | V. C. Whitehead | |
| G-BHKH | Cameron O-65 balloon | D. G. Body | |
| G-BHKJ | Cessna 421C | Bob Crowe Aircraft Sales Ltd/Cranfield | |
| G-BHKR | Colt 12A balloon ★ | British Balloon Museum | |
| G-BHKT | Jodel D.112 | M. L. & P. J. Moore | |
| G-BHKV | AA-5A Cheetah | Alouette Flying Club Ltd/Biggin Hill | |
| G-BHKX | Beech 76 Duchess | Jetstream Air Couriers Ltd | |
| G-BHKY | Cessna 310R II | Air Service Training Ltd/Perth | |
| G-BHLE | Robin DR.400/180 | L. H. Mayall | |
| G-BHLF | H.S.125 Srs 700B | MAGEC Aviation Ltd/Luton | |
| G-BHLH | Robin DR.400/180 | Trinecare Ltd/Southend | |
| G-BHLJ | Saffery-Rigg S.200 balloon | I. A. Rigg | |
| G-BHLK | GA-7 Cougar | Autair Ltd | |
| G-BHLT | D.H.82A Tiger Moth | P. J. & A. J. Borsberry | |
| G-BHLU | Fournier RF-3 | M. C. Roper | |
| G-BHLW | Cessna 120 | D. K. Frampton | |
| G-BHLX | AA-5B Tiger | Tiger Aviation (Jersey) Ltd | |
| G-BHLY | Sikorsky S-76A | Bristow Helicopters Ltd | |
| G-BHMA | SIPA 903 | H. J. Taggart | |
| G-BHMC | M.S.880B Rallye Club | The G-BHMC Group | |
| G-BHMD | Rand KR-2 | W. D. Francis | |
| G-BHME | WMB.2 Windtracker balloon | I. R. Bell & ptnrs | |
| G-BHMG | Cessna FA.152 | Tiger Air Ltd | |
| G-BHMI | Cessna F.172N | W. Lancashire Aero Club Ltd (G-WADE)/ Blackpool | |
| G-BHMJ | Avenger T.200-2112 balloon | R. Light *Lord Anthony 1* | |
| G-BHMK | Avenger T.200-2112 balloon | P. Kinder *Lord Anthony 2* | |
| G-BHML | Avenger T.200-2112 balloon | L. Caulfield *Lord Anthony 3* | |
| G-BHMM | Avenger T.200-2112 balloon | M. Murphy *Lord Anthony 4* | |
| G-BHMO | PA-20M Cerpa Special (Pacer) | A. B. Holloway & ptnrs | |
| G-BHMR | Stinson 108-3 | D. Holliday | |
| G-BHMT | Evans VP-1 | P. E. J. Sturgeon | |
| G-BHMU | Colt 21A balloon | J. R. Parkington & Co Ltd | |
| G-BHMW | F.27 Friendship Mk 200 | Air UK *Amy Johnson*/Norwich | |
| G-BHMX | F.27 Friendship Mk 200 | Air UK *Fred Truman*/Norwich | |
| G-BHMY | F.27 Friendship Mk 200 | Air UK/Norwich | |
| G-BHMZ | F.27 Friendship Mk 200 | Air UK *R. J. Mitchell*/Norwich | |
| G-BHNA | Cessna F.152 | Sheffield Aero Club Ltd/Netherthorpe | |
| G-BHNC | Cameron O-65 balloon | D. & C. Bareford | |
| G-BHND | Cameron N-65 balloon | Hunter & Sons (Wells) Ltd | |
| G-BHNE | Boeing 727-2J4 | Dan-Air Services Ltd/Gatwick | |
| G-BHNF | Boeing 727-2J4 | Dan-Air Services Ltd/Gatwick | |
| G-BHNL | Jodel D.112 | P. E. Barker | |
| G-BHNM | PA-44-180 Seminole | Cearte Tiles Ltd/Coventry | |
| G-BHNN | PA-32R-301 Saratoga SP | S. S. Bernholt/Elstree | |
| G-BHNO | PA-28-181 Archer II | Davison Plant Hire Co/Compton Abbas | |
| G-BHNP | Eiri PIK-20E-1 | M. Astley/Husbands Bosworth | |
| G-BHNU | Cessna F.172N | B. Swindell (Haulage) Ltd/Barton | |
| G-BHNW | Westland-Bell 47G-3B1 | Leyline Helicopters Ltd | |
| G-BHNX | Jodel D.117 | R. V. Rendall | |
| G-BHNY | Cessna 425 | Eclipsol Oil Ltd/Birmingham | |
| G-BHOA | Robin DR.400/160 | Ferguson Aviation Ltd | |
| G-BHOF | Sikorsky S-61N | Bristow Helicopters Ltd | |
| G-BHOG | Sikorsky S-61N | Bristow Helicopters Ltd | |
| G-BHOH | Sikorsky S-61N | Bristow Helicopters Ltd | |

| Notes | Reg. | Type | Owner or Operator |
|-------|------|------|-------------------|
| | G-BHOL | Jodel DR.1050 | D. G. Hart |
| | G-BHOM | PA-18 Super Cub 95 | C. H. A. Bott |
| | G-BHOO | Thunder Ax7-65 balloon | D. Livesey & J. M. Purves *Scraps* |
| | G-BHOP | Thunder Ax3 balloon | B. Meeson |
| | G-BHOR | PA-28-161 Warrior II. | Oscar Romeo Flying Group/Biggin Hill |
| | G-BHOT | Cameron V-65 balloon | Dante Balloon Group |
| | G-BHOU | Cameron V-65 balloon | F. W. Barnes |
| | G-BHOW | Beech 95-58PA Baron | Anglo-African Machinery Ltd/ Coventry |
| | G-BHOZ | SOCATA TB.9 Tampico | M. Brown |
| | G-BHPJ | Eagle Microlite | G. Breen/Enstone |
| | G-BHPK | Piper J-3C-65 Cub (236800) | H. W. Sage/Sywell |
| | G-BHPL | C.A.S.A. 1.131E Jungmann | M. G. Jeffries |
| | G-BHPM | PA-18 Super Cub 95 | P. I. Morgans |
| | G-BHPN | Colt 14 balloon | Colt Balloons Ltd |
| | G-BHPO | Colt 14A balloon | C. J. Boxall |
| | G-BHPS | Jodel D.120A | C. J. Francis/Swansea |
| | G-BHPT | Piper J-3C-65 Cub | J. A. Hubner |
| | G-BHPX | Cessna 152 | J. A. Pothecary/Shoreham |
| | G-BHPY | Cessna 152 | Christopher Lunn & Co |
| | G-BHPZ | Cessna 172N | O'Brian Properties Ltd/Redhill |
| | G-BHRA | R. Commander 114A | P. A. Warner |
| | G-BHRB | Cessna F.152 | Light Planes (Lancashire) Ltd/ Barton |
| | G-BHRC | PA-28-161 Warrior II | Sherwood Flying Club Ltd/Tollerton |
| | G-BHRD | D.H.C.1 Chipmunk 22 (WP977) | A. J. Dunstan & P. R. Joshua/Kidlington |
| | G-BHRH | Cessna FA.150K | Merlin Flying Club Ltd/Hucknall |
| | G-BHRI | Saffery S.200 balloon | N. J. & H. L. Dunnington |
| | G-BHRM | Cessna F.152 | Aerohire Ltd/Halfpenny Green |
| | G-BHRN | Cessna F.152 | P. P. D. Howard-Johnston/Edinburgh |
| | G-BHRO | R. Commander 112A | John Raymond Transport Ltd/Cardiff |
| | G-BHRP | PA-44-180 Seminole | Walsh Aviation |
| | G-BHRR | CP.301A Emeraude | T. W. Offen |
| | G-BHRW | Jodel DR.221 | J. D. Hunter & M. A. Britton |
| | G-BHRY | Colt 56A balloon | A. S. Davidson |
| | G-BHSA | Cessna 152 | Skyviews & General Ltd/Sherburn |
| | G-BHSB | Cessna 172N | Saunders Caravans Ltd |
| | G-BHSD | Scheibe SF.25E Super Falke | Lasham Gliding Soc Ltd |
| | G-BHSE | R. Commander 114 | 604 Sqdn Flying Group Ltd |
| | G-BHSL | C.A.S.A. 1.131 Jungmann | Cotswold Flying Group/Badminton |
| | G-BHSN | Cameron N-56 balloon | I. Bentley |
| | G-BHSP | Thunder Ax7-77Z balloon | G. J. Bell & ptnrs |
| | G-BHSS | Pitts S-1C Special | C. I. Fray |
| | G-BHST | Hughes 369D | Acme Jewellery Ltd |
| | G-BHSU | H.S.125 Srs 700B | Shell Aircraft Ltd/Heathrow |
| | G-BHSV | H.S.125 Srs 700B | Shell Aircraft Ltd/Heathrow |
| | G-BHSW | H.S.125 Srs 700B | Shell Aircraft Ltd/Heathrow |
| | G-BHSY | Jodel DR.1050 | S. R. Orwin & T. R. Allebone |
| | G-BHTA | PA-28-236 Dakota | Stenloss Ltd/Sywell |
| | G-BHTC | Jodel DR.1050/M1 | D. Masterson & ptnrs/Blackpool |
| | G-BHTD | Cessna T.188C AgHusky | ADS (Aerial) Ltd/Southend |
| | G-BHTG | Thunder Ax6-56 balloon | F. R. & Mrs S. H. MacDonald |
| | G-BHTH | T-6G Texan (2807) | A. Reynard/Kidlington |
| | G-BHTI | SA.102.5 Cavalier | R. Cochrane |
| | G-BHTJ | H.S.125 Srs 700B | British Aerospace PLC (G-BRDI/G-HHOI) |
| | G-BHTM | Cameron 80 Can SS balloon | BP Oil Ltd |
| | G-BHTR | Bell 206B JetRanger 3 | Huktra (UK) Ltd |
| | G-BHTT | Cessna 500 Citation | Paycourt Ltd |
| | G-BHTV | Cessna 310R | Brenair Ltd/Cardiff |
| | G-BHUB | Douglas C-47A (315509) ★ | Imperial War Museum/Duxford |
| | G-BHUE | Jodel DR.1050 | M. J. Harris |
| | G-BHUG | Cessna 172N | Property Maintenance File |
| | G-BHUI | Cessna 152 | Cheshire Air Training School Ltd |
| | G-BHUJ | Cessna 172N | Three Counties Aero Club Ltd/ Blackbushe |
| | G-BHUM | D.H.82A Tiger Moth | S. G. Towers |
| | G-BHUN | PZL-104 Wilga 35 | W. Radwanski/Lasham |
| | G-BHUO | Evans VP-2 | D. Harker |
| | G-BHUP | Cessna F.152 | Stapleford Flying Club Ltd |
| | G-BHUR | Thunder Ax3 balloon | B. F. G. Ribbons |
| | G-BHUU | PA-25 Pawnee 235 | Scanrho Aviation |
| | G-BHUV | PA-25 Pawnee 235 | Farmwork Services (Eastern) Ltd |
| | G-BHVB | PA-28-161 Warrior II | Bobbington Air Training School Ltd/ Halfpenny Green |

| Reg. | Type | Owner or Operator | Notes |
|------|------|-------------------|-------|
| G-BHVC | Cessna 172RG Cutlass | Ian Willis Publicity Ltd/Panshanger | |
| G-BHVE | Saffery S.330 balloon | P. M. Randles | |
| G-BHVF | Jodel D.150A | C. A. Parker & ptnrs/Sywell | |
| G-BHVN | Cessna 152 | Three Counties Aero Club Ltd/ Blackbushe | |
| G-BHVP | Cessna 182Q | Air Tows/Lasham | |
| G-BHVR | Cessna 172N | Air Tows/Blackbushe | |
| G-BHVT | Boeing 727-212 | Dan-Air Services Ltd/Gatwick | |
| G-BHVV | Piper J-3C-65 Cub | A. E. Molton | |
| G-BHVZ | Cessna 180 | R. Moore/Blackpool | |
| G-BHWA | Cessna F.152 | Wickenby Aviation Ltd | |
| G-BHWB | Cessna F.152 | Wickenby Aviation Ltd | |
| G-BHWE | Boeing 737-204ADV | Britannia Airways Ltd/ *Sir Sidney Camm*/Luton | |
| G-BHWF | Boeing 737-204ADV | Britannia Airways Ltd/ *Lord Brabazon of Tara*/Luton | |
| G-BHWG | Mahatma S.200SR balloon | H. W. Gandy *Spectrum* | |
| G-BHWH | Weedhopper JC-24A | G. A. Clephane | |
| G-BHWK | M.S.880B Rallye Club | Arrow Flying Group | |
| G-BHWN | WMB.3 Windtracker 200 balloon | C. J. Dodd & G. J. Luckett | |
| G-BHWS | Cessna F.152 | Stapleford Flying Club | |
| G-BHWW | Cessna U.206G | Fife Airport Management Ltd/ Glenrothes | |
| G-BHWY | PA-28R Cherokee Arrow 200-II | C. J. Harty | |
| G-BHWZ | PA-28-181 Archer II | I. R. McCue | |
| G-BHXD | Jodel D.120 | K. B. Sutton & N. Poole | |
| G-BHXK | PA-28 Cherokee 140 | GXK Flying Group | |
| G-BHXL | Evans VP-2 | T. W. Woolley | |
| G-BHXN | Van's RV.3 | P. R. Hing | |
| G-BHXS | Jodel D.120 | I. R. Willis | |
| G-BHXT | Thunder Ax6-56Z balloon | Ocean Traffic Services Ltd | |
| G-BHXU | AB-206B JetRanger 3 | Castle Air Charters Ltd | |
| G-BHXV | AB-206B JetRanger 3 | Compass Aviation Ltd (G-OWJM) | |
| G-BHXY | Piper J-3C-65 Cub (44-79609) | D. T. J. Harwood & A. L. Jubb | |
| G-BHYA | Cessna R.182RG II | Stainless Steel Profile Cutters Ltd | |
| G-BHYB | Sikorsky S-76A | British International Helicopters Ltd/Beccles | |
| G-BHYC | Cessna 172RG Cutlass | T. G. Henshall | |
| G-BHYD | Cessna R.172K XP II | Sylmar Aviation Services Ltd | |
| G-BHYE | PA-34-200T Seneca II | C.S.E. Aviation Ltd/Kidlington | |
| G-BHYF | PA-34-200T Seneca II | C.S.E. Aviation Ltd/Kidlington | |
| G-BHYG | PA-34-200T Seneca II | C.S.E. Aviation Ltd/Kidlington | |
| G-BHYI | SNCAN Stampe SV-4A | P. A. Irwin | |
| G-BHYN | Evans VP-2 | D. Cromie | |
| G-BHYO | Cameron N-77 balloon | C. Sisson | |
| G-BHYP | Cessna F.172M | G-BHYP Flying Group/Blackpool | |
| G-BHYR | Cessna F.172M | Alumvale Ltd/Stapleford | |
| G-BHYV | Evans VP-1 | L. Chiappi/Blackpool | |
| G-BHYW | AB-206B JetRanger | Gleneagles Helicopter Services (Scotland) Ltd | |
| G-BHYX | Cessna 152 II | Stapleford Flying Club Ltd | |
| G-BHZE | PA-28-181 Archer II | Northfield Garage Ltd | |
| G-BHZF | Evans VP-2 | P. Jenkins | |
| G-BHZH | Cessna F.152 | Havelet Leasing Ltd | |
| G-BHZK | AA-5B Tiger | N. K. Margolis/Elstree | |
| G-BHZM | Jodel DR.1050 | G. H. Wylde/Manchester | |
| G-BHZO | AA-5A Cheetah | Scotia Safari Ltd/Prestwick | |
| G-BHZU | Piper J-3C-65 Cub | J. K. Tomkinson | |
| G-BHZV | Jodel D.120A | J. G. Munro/Perth | |
| G-BHZX | Thunder Ax7-65A balloon | S. C. Kinsey & G. E. Harns | |
| G-BHZY | Monnet Sonerai II | C. A. Keech | |
| G-BIAA | SOCATA TB.9 Tampico | T. Smith | |
| G-BIAB | SOCATA TB.9 Tampico | H. W. A. Thirlway | |
| G-BIAC | SOCATA Rallye 235E | Anpal Finance Ltd & Aerial Facilities Ltd/ Biggin Hill | |
| G-BIAH | Jodel D.112 | D. Mitchell | |
| G-BIAI | WMB.2 Windtracker balloon | I. Chadwick | |
| G-BIAK | SOCATA TB.10 Tobago | Trent Combustion Components Ltd/ Tollerton | |
| G-BIAL | Rango NA.8 balloon | A. M. Lindsay | |
| G-BIAO | Evans VP-2 | P. J. Hall | |

| Notes | Reg. | Type | Owner or Operator |
|---|---|---|---|
| | G-BIAP | PA-16 Clipper | I. M. Callier & P. J. Bish/White Waltham |
| | G-BIAR | Rigg Skyliner II balloon | I. A. Rigg |
| | G-BIAU | Sopwith Pup Replica (N6452) | FAA Museum/Yeovilton |
| | G-BIAV | Sikorsky S-76A | British International Helicopters Ltd |
| | G-BIAW | Sikorsky S-76A | British International Helicopters Ltd |
| | G-BIAX | Taylor JT.2 Titch | G. F. Rowley |
| | G-BIAY | AA-5 Traveler | M. D. Dupay & ptnrs |
| | G-BIBA | SOCATA TB.9 Tampico | Impatex Computer Systems Ltd |
| | G-BIBB | Mooney M.20C | Gloucestershire Flying Club/Staverton |
| | G-BIBC | Cessna 310R | Air Service Training Ltd/Perth |
| | G-BIBD | Rotec Rally 2B | A. Clarke |
| | G-BIBG | Sikorsky S-76A | Bristow Helicopters Ltd |
| | G-BIBJ | Enstrom 280C-UK-2 Shark | Tindon Ltd/Little Snoring |
| | G-BIBK | Taylor JT.2 Titch | T. C. Horner |
| | G-BIBN | Cessna FA.150K | P. H. Lewis |
| | G-BIBO | Cameron V-65 balloon | I. Harris |
| | G-BIBP | AA-5A Cheetah | Scotia Safari Ltd/Prestwick |
| | G-BIBS | Cameron P-20 balloon | Cameron Balloons Ltd |
| | G-BIBT | AA-5B Tiger | Fergusons (Blyth) Ltd/Newcastle |
| | G-BIBU | Morris Ax7-77 balloon | K. Morris |
| | G-BIBV | WMB.3 Windtracker balloon | P. B. Street |
| | G-BIBW | Cessna F.172N | Deltair Ltd/Chester |
| | G-BIBX | WMB.2 Windtracker balloon | I. A. Rigg |
| | G-BIBY | Beech F33A Bonanza | Baythorne Ltd/Fairoaks |
| | G-BIBZ | Thunder Ax3 balloon | F. W. Barnes |
| | G-BICB | Rotec Rally 2B | J. D. Lye & A. P. Jones |
| | G-BICC | Vulture Tx3 balloon | C. P. Clitheroe |
| | G-BICD | Auster 5 | J. A. S. Baldry & ptnrs |
| | G-BICE | AT-6C Harvard IIA (41-33275) | C. M. L. Edwards/Ipswich |
| | G-BICG | Cessna F.152 | Falcon Flying Services/Biggin Hill |
| | G-BICJ | Monnet Sonerai II | D. J. Willison |
| | G-BICM | Colt 56A balloon | Avon Advertiser Balloon Club |
| | G-BICN | F.8L Falco | R. J. Barber |
| | G-BICP | Robin DR.360 | Bravo India Flying Group/Woodvale |
| | G-BICR | Jodel D.120A | Beehive Flying Group/White Waltham |
| | G-BICS | Robin R.2100A | J. E. Cummings |
| | G-BICT | Evans VP-1 | A. S. Coombe & D. L. Tribe |
| | G-BICU | Cameron V-56 balloon | J. M. S. Instone |
| | G-BICW | PA-28-161 Warrior II | T. W. Aisthorpe/Exeter |
| | G-BICX | Maule M5-235C Lunar Rocket | A. T. Jeans & I. Best-Devereux/Old Sarum |
| | G-BICY | PA-23 Apache 160 | A. M. Lynn/Sibson |
| | G-BIDD | Evans VP-1 | J. E. Wedgbury |
| | G-BIDE | CP.301A Emeraude | D. Elliott |
| | G-BIDF | Cessna F.172P | J. J. Baumhardt/Southend |
| | G-BIDG | Jodel D.150A | D. R. Gray/Barton |
| | G-BIDI | PA-28R-201 Arrow III | LBE Contract Tooling Ltd |
| | G-BIDJ | PA-18A Super Cub 150 | AB Plant (Bristol) Ltd |
| | G-BIDK | PA-18 Super Cub 150 | Scottish Gliding Union Ltd |
| | G-BIDM | Cessna F.172H | D. A. Mortimore/Humberside |
| | G-BIDO | CP.301A Emeraude | A. R. Plumb |
| | G-BIDP | PA-28-181 Archer II | H. S. Elkins/Bristol |
| | G-BIDU | Cameron V-77 balloon | E. Eleazor |
| | G-BIDV | Colt 14A balloon | International Distillers & Vintners (House Trade) Ltd |
| | G-BIDW | Sopwith 1½ Strutter replica (A8226) ★ | RAF Museum/Hendon |
| | G-BIDX | Jodel D.112 | H. N. Nuttall & R. P. Walley |
| | G-BIDY | WMB.2 Windtracker balloon | D. M. Campion |
| | G-BIEC | AB-206A JetRanger 2 | Autair Helicopters Ltd |
| | G-BIEF | Cameron V-77 balloon | D. S. Bush |
| | G-BIEH | Sikorsky S-76A | Bond Helicopters Ltd/Bourn |
| | G-BIEJ | Sikorsky S-76A | Bristow Helicopters Ltd |
| | G-BIEK | WMB.4 Windtracker balloon | P. B. Street |
| | G-BIEN | Jodel D.120A | Echo November Flight/Bristol |
| | G-BIEO | Jodel D.112 | Woodside Flying Group |
| | G-BIEP | PA-28-181 Archer II | Bickerton Aerodromes Ltd |
| | G-BIER | Rutan LongEz | V. Mossor |
| | G-BIES | Maule M5-235C Lunar Rocket | William Proctor Farms |
| | G-BIET | Cameron O-77 balloon | G. M. Westley |
| | G-BIEY | PA-28-151 Warrior | J. A. Pothecary/Shoreham |
| | G-BIFA | Cessna 310R-II | E. A. Pitcher |
| | G-BIFB | PA-28 Cherokee 150 | C. J. Reed/Elstree |
| | G-BIFC | Colt 14A balloon | Colt Balloons Ltd |

| Reg. | Type | Owner or Operator | Notes |
|------|------|-------------------|-------|
| G-BIFD | R. Commander 114 | D. F. Soul | |
| G-BIFH | Short SD3-30 | Fairflight Leasing Ltd/Gill Air | |
| G-BIFK | Short SD3-30 | Fortis Aviation Group/Gill Air | |
| G-BIFN | Bensen B.8M | B. Gunn | |
| G-BIFO | Evans VP-1 | D. J. Rees | |
| G-BIFP | Colt 56C balloon | J. Philp | |
| G-BIFT | Cessna F.150L | Colton Aviation Ltd | |
| G-BIFV | Jodel D.150 | J. H. Kirkham/Barton | |
| G-BIFY | Cessna F.150L | Colton Aviation Ltd | |
| G-BIFZ | Partenavia P.68C | ALY Aviation Ltd/Henstridge | |
| G-BIGD | Cameron V-77 balloon | D. L. Clark *Frog* | |
| G-BIGF | Thunder Ax7-77 balloon | M. D. Stever & C. A. Allen | |
| G-BIGH | Piper J-3C-65 Cub | W. McNally | |
| G-BIGJ | Cessna F.172M | Clacton Aero Club (1988) Ltd | |
| G-BIGK | Taylorcraft BC-12D | H. L. M. & G. R. Williams | |
| G-BIGL | Cameron O-65 balloon | P. L. Mossman | |
| G-BIGM | Avenger T.200-2112 balloon | M. Murphy | |
| G-BIGN | Attic Srs 1 balloon | G. P. Nettleship | |
| G-BIGP | Bensen B.8M | R. H. S. Cooper | |
| G-BIGR | Avenger T.200-2112 balloon | R. Light | |
| G-BIGU | Bensen B.8M | J. R. Martin | |
| G-BIGX | Bensen B.8M | P. R. Moore & M. B. Stone | |
| G-BIGY | Cameron V-65 balloon | Dante Balloon Group | |
| G-BIGZ | Scheibe SF.25B Falke | K. Ballington | |
| G-BIHD | Robin DR.400/160 | Alexander Howden Group Sports & Social Club/Biggin Hill | |
| G-BIHE | Cessna FA.152 | Inverness Flying Services Ltd | |
| G-BIHF | SE-5A (replica) (F943) | K. J. Garrett *Lady Di*/Booker | |
| G-BIHG | PA-28 Cherokee 140 | T. M. Plewman | |
| G-BIHI | Cessna 172M | J. H. Ashley-Rogers | |
| G-BIHN | Skyship 500 airship | Airship Industries Ltd/Cardington | |
| G-BIHO | D.H.C.6 Twin Otter 310 | Brymon Aviation Ltd/Plymouth | |
| G-BIHP | Van Den Bemden gas balloon | J. J. Harris | |
| G-BIHT | PA-17 Vagabond | G. H. Cork/Burnaston | |
| G-BIHU | Saffery S.200 balloon | B. L. King | |
| G-BIHX | Bensen B.8M | C. C. Irvine | |
| G-BIHY | Isaacs Fury | P. C. Butler | |
| G-BIIA | Fournier RF-3 | T. M. W. Webster | |
| G-BIIB | Cessna F.172M | Civil Service Flying Club (Biggin Hill) Ltd | |
| G-BIID | PA-18 Super Cub 95 | 875 (Westhill) Squadron ATC/Aberdeen | |
| G-BIIE | Cessna F.172P | Shoreham Flight Simulation Ltd/ Bournemouth | |
| G-BIIF | Fournier RF-4D | J. A. Bridges & J. A. Taylor (G-BVET)/ Biggin Hill | |
| G-BIIG | Thunder Ax-6-56Z balloon | Chiltern Flyers Ltd | |
| G-BIIJ | Cessna F.152 | Leicestershire Aero Club Ltd | |
| G-BIIK | M.S.883 Rallye 115 | Chiltern Flyers Ltd | |
| G-BIIL | Thunder Ax6-56 balloon | G. W. Reader | |
| G-BIIT | PA-28-161 Warrior II | Tayside Aviation Ltd/Dundee | |
| G-BIIV | PA-28-181 Archer II | Stratton Motor Co Ltd | |
| G-BIIX | Rango NA.12 balloon | Rango Kite Co | |
| G-BIIZ | Great Lakes 2T-1A Sport Trainer | J. R. Lindsay/Booker | |
| G-BIJB | PA-18 Super Cub 150 | Essex Gliding Club/North Weald | |
| G-BIJD | Bo 208C Junior | K. Cameron | |
| G-BIJE | Piper J-3C-65 Cub | R. L. Hayward & A. G. Scott | |
| G-BIJS | Luton LA-4A Minor | I. J. Smith | |
| G-BIJT | AA-5A Cheetah | Mid-Sussex Timber Co Ltd | |
| G-BIJU | CP.301A Emeraude | Eastern Taildraggers Flying Group (G-BHTX)/Southend | |
| G-BIJV | Cessna F.152 II | Falcon Flying Services/Biggin Hill | |
| G-BIJW | Cessna F.152 II | Civil Service Flying Club (Biggin Hill) Ltd | |
| G-BIJX | Cessna F.152 II | Civil Service Flying Club Ltd/ Biggin Hill | |
| G-BIKA | Boeing 757-236 | British Airways *Dover Castle*/ Heathrow | |
| G-BIKB | Boeing 757-236 | British Airways *Windsor Castle*/ Heathrow | |
| G-BIKC | Boeing 757-236 | British Airways *Edinburgh Castle*/ Heathrow | |
| G-BIKD | Boeing 757-236 | British Airways *Caernarvon Castle*/ Heathrow | |
| G-BIKE | PA-28R Cherokee Arrow 200 | R. V. Webb Ltd/Elstree | |

| Notes | Reg. | Type | Owner or Operator |
|-------|------|------|-------------------|
| | G-BIKF | Boeing 757-236 | British Airways *Carrickfergus Castle*/ Heathrow |
| | G-BIKG | Boeing 757-236 | British Airways *Stirling Castle*/ Heathrow |
| | G-BIKH | Boeing 757-236 | British Airways *Richmond Castle*/ Heathrow |
| | G-BIKI | Boeing 757-236 | British Airways *Tintagel Castle*/ Heathrow |
| | G-BIKJ | Boeing 757-236 | British Airways *Conway Castle*/ Heathrow |
| | G-BIKK | Boeing 757-236 | British Airways *Eilean Donan Castle*/ Heathrow |
| | G-BIKL | Boeing 757-236 | British Airways *Nottingham Castle*/ Heathrow |
| | G-BIKM | Boeing 757-236 | British Airways *Glamis Castle*/ Heathrow |
| | G-BIKN | Boeing 757-236 | British Airways *Bodiam Castle*/ Heathrow |
| | G-BIKO | Boeing 757-236 | British Airways *Harlech Castle*/ Heathrow |
| | G-BIKP | Boeing 757-236 | British Airways *Enniskillen Castle*/ Heathrow |
| | G-BIKR | Boeing 757-236 | British Airways *Bamburgh Castle*/ Heathrow |
| | G-BIKS | Boeing 757-236 | British Airways *Corfe Castle*/ Heathrow |
| | G-BIKT | Boeing 757-236 | British Airways *Carisbrooke Castle*/ Heathrow |
| | G-BIKU | Boeing 757-236 | British Airways *Inverary Castle*/ Heathrow |
| | G-BIKV | Boeing 757-236 | British Airways *Raglan Castle*/ Heathrow |
| | G-BIKW | Boeing 757-236 | British Airways *Belvoir Castle*/ Heathrow |
| | G-BIKX | Boeing 757-236 | British Airways *Warwick Castle*/ Heathrow |
| | G-BIKY | Boeing 757-236 | British Airways *Leeds Castle*/ Heathrow |
| | G-BIKZ | Boeing 757-236 | British Airways *Kenilworth Castle*/ Heathrow |
| | G-BILA | Daletol DM.165L Viking | R. Lamplough (*stored*) |
| | G-BILB | WMB.2 Windtracker balloon | B. L. King |
| | G-BILE | Scruggs BL.2B balloon | P. D. Ridout |
| | G-BILF | Practavia Sprite 125 | G. Harfield |
| | G-BILG | Scruggs BL.2B balloon | P. D. Ridout |
| | G-BILI | Piper J-3C-65 Cub (454467) | G–BILI Flying Group |
| | G-BILJ | Cessna FA.152 | Shoreham Flight Simulation Ltd/ Bournemouth |
| | G-BILK | Cessna FA.152 | Exeter Flying Club Ltd |
| | G-BILL | PA-25 Pawnee 235 | Pawnee Aviation |
| | G-BILR | Cessna 152 | Skyviews & General Ltd |
| | G-BILS | Cessna 152 | Skyviews & General Ltd |
| | G-BILU | Cessna 172RG | T. E. Abell |
| | G-BILZ | Taylor JT.1 Monoplane | A. Petherbridge |
| | G-BIMK | Tiger T.200 Srs 1 balloon | M. K. Baron |
| | G-BIMM | PA-18 Super Cub 150 | Clacton Aero Club (1988) Ltd |
| | G-BIMN | Steen Skybolt | C. R. Williamson |
| | G-BIMO | SNCAN Stampe SV-4C | R. A. Roberts |
| | G-BIMT | Cessna FA.152 | Staverton Flying Services Ltd |
| | G-BIMU | Sikorsky S-61N | Bristow Helicopters Ltd |
| | G-BIMX | Rutan Vari-Eze | A. S. Knowles |
| | G-BIMZ | Beech 76 Duchess | Barrein Engineers Ltd/Lulsgate |
| | G-BINA | Saffery S.9 balloon | A. P. Bashford |
| | G-BINB | WMB.2A Windtracker balloon | S. R. Woolfries |
| | G-BINF | Saffery S.200 balloon | T. Lewis |
| | G-BING | Cessna F.172P | J. E. M. Patrick |
| | G-BINH | D.H.82A Tiger Moth | Arrow Air Services (Engineering) Ltd (*stored*)/Felthorpe |
| | G-BINI | Scruggs BL.2C balloon | S. R. Woolfries |
| | G-BINL | Scruggs BL.2B balloon | P. D. Ridout |
| | G-BINM | Scruggs BL.2B balloon | P. D. Ridout |
| | G-BINO | Evans VP-1 | A. M. S. Liggat |

| Reg. | Type | Owner or Operator | Notes |
|------|------|-------------------|-------|
| G-BINR | Unicorn UE.1A balloon | Unicorn Group | |
| G-BINS | Unicorn UE.2A balloon | Unicorn Group | |
| G-BINT | Unicorn UE.1A balloon | Unicorn Group | |
| G-BINU | Saffery S.200 balloon | T. Lewis | |
| G-BINX | Scruggs BL.2B balloon | P. D. Ridout | |
| G-BINY | Oriental balloon | J. L. Morton | |
| G-BINZ | Rango NA.8 balloon | T. J. Sweeting & M. O. Davies | |
| G-BIOA | Hughes 369D | Colin Draycott Group Ltd | |
| G-BIOB | Cessna F.172P | Aerofilms Ltd/Elstree | |
| G-BIOC | Cessna F.150L | Seawing Flying Club/Southend | |
| G-BIOE | Short SD3-30 | Fairflight/Gill Air/Newcastle | |
| G-BIOI | Jodel DR.1051M | H. F. Hambling | |
| G-BIOJ | R. Commander 112TCA | A. T. Dalby | |
| G-BIOK | Cessna F.152 | Tayside Aviation Ltd/Dundee | |
| G-BIOM | Cessna F.152 | Falcon Flying Services/Biggin Hill | |
| G-BION | Cameron V-77 balloon | Elliott's Pharmacy Ltd | |
| G-BIOO | Unicorn UE.2B balloon | Unicorn Group | |
| G-BIOP | Scruggs BL.2D balloon | J. P. S. Donnellan | |
| G-BIOR | M.S.880B Rallye Club | Aircraft Dept. Royal Aircraft Establishment/Farnborough | |
| G-BIOU | Jodel D.117A | M. S. Printing & Graphics Machinery Ltd/Booker | |
| G-BIOW | Slingsby T.67A | A. B. Slinger/Sherburn | |
| G-BIOX | Potter Crompton PRO.1 balloon | G. M. Potter | |
| G-BIPA | AA-5B Tiger | J. Campbell/Barrow | |
| G-BIPH | Scruggs BL.2B balloon | C. M. Dewsnap | |
| G-BIPI | Everett Blackbird Mk 1 | G. C. Webber & N. V. de Candole | |
| G-BIPJ | PA-36-375 Brave | G. B. Pearce/Shoreham | |
| G-BIPK | Saffery S.200 balloon | P. J. Kelsey | |
| G-BIPM | Flamboyant Ax7-65 balloon | Pepsi Cola International Ltd/S. Africa | |
| G-BIPN | Fournier RF-3 | S. N. Lawrence | |
| G-BIPO | Mudry/CAARP CAP.20LS-200 | BIPO Aviation Ltd/Booker | |
| G-BIPS | SOCATA Rallye 100ST | McAully Flying Group/Little Snoring | |
| G-BIPT | Jodel D.112 | C. R. Davies | |
| G-BIPV | AA-5B Tiger | A. C. Gradidge | |
| G-BIPW | Avenger T.200-2112 balloon | B. L. King | |
| G-BIPY | Bensen B.8 | W. J. Pope | |
| G-BIPZ | McCandless Mk 4-4 | B. McIntyre | |
| G-BIRA | SOCATA TB.9 Tampico | Goldangel Ltd/Swansea | |
| G-BIRB | M.S.880B Rallye 100T | E. Smith | |
| G-BIRD | Pitts S-1C Special | CB Helicopters Ltd | |
| G-BIRE | Colt 56 Bottle balloon | Hot Air Balloon Co Ltd | |
| G-BIRH | PA-18 Super Cub 135 (R-163) | I. R. F. Hammond/Lee-on-Solent | |
| G-BIRI | C.A.S.A. 1.131E Jungmann | M. G. & J. R. Jeffries | |
| G-BIRK | Avenger T.200-2112 balloon | D. Harland | |
| G-BIRL | Avenger T.200-2112 balloon | R. Light | |
| G-BIRM | Avenger T.200-2112 balloon | P. Higgins | |
| G-BIRO | Cessna 172P | M. C. Grant | |
| G-BIRP | Arena Mk 17 Skyship balloon | A. S. Viel | |
| G-BIRS | Cessna 182P | John E. Birks & Associates Ltd (G-BBBS) | |
| G-BIRT | Robin R.1180TD | W. D'A. Hall/Booker | |
| G-BIRV | Bensen B.8MV | R. Hart | |
| G-BIRW | M.S.505 Criquet (F+IS) ★ | Museum of Flight/E. Fortune | |
| G-BIRY | Cameron V-77 balloon | J. J. Winter | |
| G-BIRZ | Zenair CH.250 | S. R. Porter | |
| G-BISB | Cessna F.152 II | Sheffield Aero Club Ltd/Netherthorpe | |
| G-BISF | Robinson R-22 | Compuster Ltd | |
| G-BISG | FRED Srs 3 | R. A. Coombe | |
| G-BISH | Cameron O-42 balloon | Zebedee Balloon Service | |
| G-BISI | Robinson R-22 | Sloane Helicopters Ltd/Luton | |
| G-BISJ | Cessna 340A | Bobbington Air Training School Ltd | |
| G-BISK | R. Commander 112B ★ | P. A. Warner | |
| G-BISL | Scruggs BL.2B balloon | P. D. Ridout | |
| G-BISM | Scruggs BL.2B balloon | P. D. Ridout | |
| G-BISS | Scruggs BL.2C balloon | P. D. Ridout | |
| G-BIST | Scruggs BL.2C balloon | P. D. Ridout | |
| G-BISV | Cameron O-65 balloon | Hylyne Rabbits Ltd | |
| G-BISW | Cameron O-65 balloon | G. J. Barton | |
| G-BISX | Colt 56A balloon | J. R. Gore | |
| G-BISZ | Sikorsky S-76A | Bristow Helicopters Ltd | |
| G-BITA | PA-18 Super Cub 150 | J. & S. A. S. McCullough | |

| Notes | Reg. | Type | Owner or Operator |
|---|---|---|---|
| | G-BITE | SOCATA TB.10 Tobago | M. A. Smith & R. J. Bristow/Fairoaks |
| | G-BITF | Cessna F.152 | Bristol & Wessex Aeroplane Club |
| | G-BITH | Cessna F.152 | Bristol & Wessex Aeroplane Club |
| | G-BITK | FRED Srs 2 | D. J. Wood |
| | G-BITL | Horncastle LL-901 balloon | M. J. Worsdell |
| | G-BITM | Cessna F.172P | D. G. Crabtree/Barton |
| | G-BITO | Jodel D.112D | A. Dunbar/Barton |
| | G-BITR | Sikorsky S-76A | Bristow Helicopters Ltd |
| | G-BITS | Drayton B-56 balloon | M. J. Betts |
| | G-BITW | Short SD3-30 | Shorts Aircraft Financing Ltd (G-EASI) |
| | G-BITY | FD.31T balloon | A. J. Bell |
| | G-BIUL | Cameron 60 SS balloon | D. C. Patrick-Brown |
| | G-BIUM | Cessna F.152 | Sheffield Aero Club Ltd/ Netherthorpe |
| | G-BIUP | SNCAN NC.854S | C. M. Mogg |
| | G-BIUU | PA-23 Aztec 250D ★ | G. Cormack/Glasgow |
| | G-BIUV | H.S.748 Srs 2A | Dan-Air Services Ltd (G-AYYH)/ Gatwick |
| | G-BIUW | PA-28-161 Warrior II | D. R. Staley |
| | G-BIUY | PA-28-181 Archer II | Maidenhead Electrical Services Ltd/ White Waltham |
| | G-BIVA | Robin R.2112 | Cotswold Aero Club Ltd/Staverton |
| | G-BIVB | Jodel D.112 | D. H. Anderson |
| | G-BIVC | Jodel D.112 | M. J. Barmby/Cardiff |
| | G-BIVF | CP.301C-3 Emeraude | J. Cosker |
| | G-BIVK | Bensen B.8 | J. G. Toy |
| | G-BIVL | Bensen B.8 | R. Gardiner |
| | G-BIVT | Saffery S.80 balloon | L. F. Guyot |
| | G-BIVU | AA-5A Cheetah | Lowlog Ltd |
| | G-BIVV | AA-5A Cheetah | W. Dass |
| | G-BIVY | Cessna 172N | Goodwood Aircraft Management Services Ltd |
| | G-BIVZ | D.31A Turbulent | I. Maclennan |
| | G-BIWB | Scruggs RS.5000 balloon | P. D. Ridout |
| | G-BIWC | Scruggs RS.5000 balloon | P. D. Ridout |
| | G-BIWD | Scruggs RS.5000 balloon | D. Eaves |
| | G-BIWF | Warren balloon | P. D. Ridout |
| | G-BIWG | Zelenski Mk 2 balloon | P. D. Ridout |
| | G-BIWJ | Unicorn UE.1A balloon | B. L. King |
| | G-BIWK | Cameron V-65 balloon | I. R. Williams & R. G. Bickerdike |
| | G-BIWL | PA-32-301 Saratoga | Harwoods of Essex Ltd |
| | G-BIWN | Jodel D.112 | C. R. Coates |
| | G-BIWP | Mooney M.20J | J. K. McWhinney |
| | G-BIWR | Mooney M.20F | C. W. Yarnton & J. D. Heykoop/Redhill |
| | G-BIWU | Cameron V-65 balloon | J. T. Whicker & J. W. Unwin |
| | G-BIWW | AA-5 Traveler | B&K Aviation/Cranfield |
| | G-BIWX | AT-16 Harvard IV (FT239) | A. E. Hutton/White Waltham |
| | G-BIWY | Westland WG.30 ★ | *Instructional airframe*/Sherborne |
| | G-BIXA | SOCATA TB.9 Tampico | WPS Aviation/Staverton |
| | G-BIXB | SOCATA TB.9 Tampico | Kitchen Bros/Little Snoring |
| | G-BIXH | Cessna F.152 | Cambridge Aero Club Ltd |
| | G-BIXI | Cessna 172RG Cutlass | J. F. P. Lewis/Sandown |
| | G-BIXJ | Saffery S.40 balloon | T. M. Pates |
| | G-BIXK | Rand KR.2 | R. G. Cousins |
| | G-BIXL | P-51D Mustang (472216) | R. Lamplough/North Weald |
| | G-BIXM | Beech C90 King Air | Veritair Airways Ltd (G-SALV)/Cardiff |
| | G-BIXN | Boeing A.75N1 Stearman | I. L. Craig-Wood & ptnrs |
| | G-BIXR | Cameron A-140 balloon | Skysales Ltd |
| | G-BIXS | Avenger T.200-2112 balloon | M. Stuart |
| | G-BIXT | Cessna 182R | M. L. J. Warwick |
| | G-BIXV | Bell 212 | Bristow Helicopters Ltd |
| | G-BIXW | Colt 56B balloon | J. R. Birkenhead |
| | G-BIXX | Pearson Srs 2 balloon | D. Pearson |
| | G-BIXZ | Grob G-109 | V. J. R. Day |
| | G-BIYG | Short SD3-30 | Fairflight/Gill Air/Newcastle |
| | G-BIYH | Short SD3-30 | Celtic Airways Ltd |
| | G-BIYI | Cameron V-65 balloon | Sarnia Balloon Group |
| | G-BIYJ | PA-18 Super Cub 95 | S. Russell |
| | G-BIYK | Isaacs Fury | R. S. Martin/Dunkeswell |
| | G-BIYM | PA-32R-301 Saratoga SP | Pinta Investments Ltd |
| | G-BIYO | PA-31-310 Turbo Navajo | Northern Executive Aviation Ltd/ Manchester |
| | G-BIYP | PA-20 Pacer 135 | R. J. Whitcombe |

| Reg. | Type | Owner or Operator | Notes |
|------|------|-------------------|-------|
| G-BIYR | PA-18 Super Cub 135 | Delta Foxtrot Flying Group/ Dunkeswell | |
| G-BIYT | Colt 17A balloon | A. F. Selby | |
| G-BIYU | Fokker S.11.1 Instructor (E-15) | H. R. Smallwood & A. J. Lee/ Denham | |
| G-BIYW | Jodel D.112 | J. D. Bysh & P. Franzini | |
| G-BIYX | PA-28 Cherokee 140 | A. Gowlett/Blackpool | |
| G-BIYY | PA-18 Super Cub 95 | A. E. & W. J. Taylor/Ingoldmells | |
| G-BIZF | Cessna F.172P | R. S. Bentley/Bourn | |
| G-BIZG | Cessna F.152 | M. A. Judge | |
| G-BIZI | Robin DR.400/120 | Headcorn Flying School Ltd | |
| G-BIZK | Nord 3202 | A. I. Milne/Swanton Morley | |
| G-BIZL | Nord 3202 | —/Liverpool | |
| G-BIZM | Nord 3202 | Magnificent Obsessions Ltd | |
| G-BIZN | Slingsby T.67A | Condor Aeroplane Co | |
| G-BIZO | PA-28R Cherokee Arrow 200 | Ellis & Co (Restoration & Building) Ltd | |
| G-BIZR | SOCATA TB.9 Tampico | R. M. Shears (G-BSEC) | |
| G-BIZT | Bensen B.8M | J. Ferguson | |
| G-BIZU | Thunder Ax6-56Z balloon | S. L. Leigh | |
| G-BIZV | PA-18 Super Cub 95 (18-2001) | S. J. Pugh & M. Risdale | |
| G-BIZW | Champion 7GCBC Citabria | G. Read & Son | |
| G-BIZY | Jodel D.112 | C. R. A. Wood | |
| G-BJAD | FRED Srs 2 | C. Allison | |
| G-BJAE | Lavadoux Starck AS.80 | D. J. & S. A. E. Phillips/Coventry | |
| G-BJAF | Piper J-3C-65 Cub | P. J. Cottle | |
| G-BJAG | PA-28-181 Archer II | K. F. Hudson & D. J. Casson/Sherburn | |
| G-BJAJ | AA-5B Tiger | A. H. McVicar/Prestwick | |
| G-BJAL | C.A.S.A. 1.131E Jungmann | R. H. Reeves/Barton | |
| G-BJAN | SA.102-5 Cavalier | J. Powlesland | |
| G-BJAO | Bensen B.8M | G. L. Stockdale | |
| G-BJAP | D.H.82A Tiger Moth | J. A. Pothecary | |
| G-BJAR | Unicorn UE.3A balloon | Unicorn Group | |
| G-BJAS | Rango NA.9 balloon | A. Lindsay | |
| G-BJAU | PZL-104 Wilga 35 | Anglo Polish Sailplanes Ltd | |
| G-BJAV | GY-80 Horizon 160 | B. R. Hildick | |
| G-BJAW | Cameron V-65 balloon | G. W. McCarthy | |
| G-BJAX | Pilatus P2-05 (U-108) | P. Warren Wilson & ptnrs | |
| G-BJAY | Piper J-3C-65 Cub | K. L. Clarke/Ingoldmells | |
| G-BJBI | Cessna 414A | Borfin Ltd/Manchester | |
| G-BJBK | PA-18 Super Cub 95 | M. S. Bird/Old Sarum | |
| G-BJBM | Monnet Sonerai II | J. Pickerell & B. L. Sims/Southend | |
| G-BJBO | Jodel DR.250/160 | C. C. Gordon | |
| G-BJBP | Beech A200 Super King Air | All Charter Ltd (G-HLUB)/ Bournemouth | |
| G-BJBS | Robinson R-22 | R. L. G. Vine | |
| G-BJBV | PA-28-161 Warrior II | C.S.E. Aviation Ltd/Kidlington | |
| G-BJBW | PA-28-161 Warrior II | C.S.E. Aviation Ltd/Kidlington | |
| G-BJBX | PA-28-161 Warrior II | C.S.E. Aviation Ltd/Kidlington | |
| G-BJBY | PA-28-161 Warrior II | C.S.E. Aviation Ltd/Kidlington | |
| G-BJBZ | Rotorway Executive 133 | P. J. D. Kerr | |
| G-BJCA | PA-28-161 Warrior II | D. M. & J. E. Smith | |
| G-BJCD | Bede BD-5BH | Brockmoor-Bede Aircraft (UK) Ltd | |
| G-BJCF | CP.1310-C3 Super Emeraude | K. M. Hodson & C. G. H. Gurney | |
| G-BJCI | PA-18 Super Cub 150 (modified) | The Borders (Milfield) Aero-Tour Club Ltd | |
| G-BJCJ | PA-28-181 Archer II | Wilsam Ltd | |
| G-BJCP | Unicorn UE.2B balloon | Unicorn Group | |
| G-BJCR | Partenavia P.68C | Nullifire Ltd/Coventry | |
| G-BJCT | Boeing 737-204ADV | Britannia Airways Ltd *The Hon C. S. Rolls*/Luton | |
| G-BJCU | Boeing 737-204ADV | Britannia Airways Ltd *Sir Henry Royce*/Luton | |
| G-BJCV | Boeing 737-204ADV | Britannia Airways Ltd *Viscount Trenchard*/Luton | |
| G-BJCW | PA-32R-301 Saratoga SP | Viscount Chelsea/Kidlington | |
| G-BJDE | Cessna F.172M | S. Lynn/Sibson | |
| G-BJDF | M.S.880B Rallye 100T | W. R. Savin & ptnrs | |
| G-BJDI | Cessna FR.182RG | Sunningdale Aviation Services Ltd/ Blackpool | |
| G-BJDJ | H.S.125 Srs 700B | Consolidated Contractors International Ltd/Heathrow | |
| G-BJDK | European E.14 balloon | Aeroprint Tours | |

| Notes | Reg. | Type | Owner or Operator |
|---|---|---|---|
| | G-BJDM | SA.102-5 Cavalier | J. D. McCracken |
| | G-BJDO | AA-5A Cheetah | Border Transport/Southampton |
| | G-BJDT | SOCATA TB.9 Tampico | Tampico Group/Old Sarum |
| | G-BJDW | Cessna F.172M | Suffolk Aero Club Ltd/Ipswich |
| | G-BJEI | PA-18 Super Cub 95 | H. J. Cox |
| | G-BJEL | SNCAN NC.854 | N. F. & S. G. Hunter |
| | G-BJEN | Scruggs RS.5000 balloon | N. J. Richardson |
| | G-BJEO | PA-34-220T Seneca III | D. W. Clark Land Drainage Ltd (G-TOMF) |
| | G-BJES | Scruggs RS.5000 balloon | J. E. Christopher |
| | G-BJEU | Scruggs BL.2D-2 balloon | G. G. Kneller |
| | G-BJEV | Aeronca 11AC Chief | R. F. Willcox |
| | G-BJEX | Bo 208C Junior | G. D. H. Crawford/Thruxton |
| | G-BJFB | Mk 1A balloon | Aeroprint Tours |
| | G-BJFC | European E.8 balloon | P. D. Ridout |
| | G-BJFE | PA-18 Super Cub 95 | W. E. & C. E. Cooper |
| | G-BJFI | Bell 47G-2A1 | Helicopter Supplies & Engineering Ltd/ Bournemouth |
| | G-BJFK | Short SD3-30 | Shorts Aircraft Financing Ltd |
| | G-BJFL | Sikorsky S-76A | Bristow Helicopters Ltd |
| | G-BJFM | Jodel D.120 | M. L. Smith & ptnrs/Popham |
| | G-BJGC | Mk IV balloon | Windsor Balloon Group |
| | G-BJGD | Mk IV balloon | Windsor Balloon Group |
| | G-BJGE | Thunder Ax3 balloon | K. A. Williams |
| | G-BJGF | Mk 1 balloon | D. & D. Eaves |
| | G-BJGG | Mk 2 balloon | D. & D. Eaves |
| | G-BJGK | Cameron V-77 balloon | A. Simpson & R. Bailey |
| | G-BJGL | Cremer balloon | G. Lowther |
| | G-BJGM | Unicorn UE.1A balloon | D. Eaves & P. D. Ridout |
| | G-BJGO | Cessna 172N | Stratair Ltd/Wellesbourne |
| | G-BJGW | M.H.1521M Broussard (92) | The Aircraft Restoration Co/Duxford |
| | G-BJGX | Sikorsky S-76A | Bristow Helicopters Ltd |
| | G-BJGY | Cessna F.172P | Lucca Wines Ltd |
| | G-BJHA | Cremer balloon | G. Cape |
| | G-BJHB | Mooney M.20J | Zitair Flying Club Ltd/Redhill |
| | G-BJHC | Swan 1 balloon | C. A. Swan |
| | G-BJHD | Mk 3B balloon | S. Meagher |
| | G-BJHK | EAA Acro Sport | D. Calabritto |
| | G-BJHL | Osprey 1C balloon | E. Bartlett |
| | G-BJHN | Osprey 1B balloon | J. E. Christopher |
| | G-BJHO | Osprey 1C balloon | G. G. Kneller |
| | G-BJHP | Osprey 1C balloon | N. J. Richardson |
| | G-BJHS | S.25 Sunderland V | Sunderland Ltd |
| | G-BJHT | Thunder Ax7-65 balloon | A. H. & L. Symonds |
| | G-BJHU | Osprey 1C balloon | G. G. Kneller |
| | G-BJHV | Voisin Replica | M. P. Sayer/O. Warden |
| | G-BJHW | Osprey 1C balloon | N. J. Richardson |
| | G-BJIA | Allport balloon | D. J. Allport |
| | G-BJIB | D.31 Turbulent | N. H. Lemon |
| | G-BJIC | Dodo 1A balloon | P. D. Ridout |
| | G-BJID | Osprey 1B balloon | P. D. Ridout |
| | G-BJIF | Bensen B.8M | H. Redwin |
| | G-BJIG | Slingsby T.67A | B. R. Chapman/Redhill |
| | G-BJIR | Cessna 550 Citation II | Gator Aviation Ltd |
| | G-BJIV | PA-18 Super Cub 150 (modified) | Yorkshire Gliding Club (Pty) Ltd/ Sutton Bank |
| | G-BJJE | Dodo Mk 3 balloon | D. Eaves |
| | G-BJJN | Cessna F.172M | Ospreystar Ltd (stored)/Stapleford |
| | G-BJJO | Bell 212 | British Executive Air Services Ltd |
| | G-BJJP | Bell 212 | British Executive Air Services Ltd |
| | G-BJJW | Mk B balloon | S. Meagher |
| | G-BJJX | Mk B balloon | S. Meagher |
| | G-BJJY | Mk B balloon | S. Meagher |
| | G-BJKA | SA.365C Dauphin 2 | Bond Helicopters Ltd |
| | G-BJKB | SA.365C Dauphin 2 | Bond Helicopters Ltd |
| | G-BJKF | SOCATA TB.9 Tampico | Manor Promotion Services Ltd/Booker |
| | G-BJKW | Wills Aera II | J. K. S. Wills |
| | G-BJKY | Cessna F.152 | Westair Flying Services Ltd/Blackpool |
| | G-BJLB | SNCAN NC.854S | M. J. Barnaby |
| | G-BJLC | Monnet Sonerai IIL | P. J. Robins & R. King/Sywell |
| | G-BJLE | Osprey 1B balloon | I. Chadwick |
| | G-BJLF | Unicorn UE.1C balloon | I. Chadwick |
| | G-BJLG | Unicorn UE.1B balloon | I. Chadwick |

| Reg. | Type | Owner or Operator | Notes |
|------|------|-------------------|-------|
| G-BJLH | PA-18 Super Cub 95 (K-33) | D. S. Kirkham | |
| G-BJLK | Short SD3-30 | Shorts Aircraft Financing Ltd | |
| G-BJLO | PA-31-310 Turbo Navajo | Linco (Poultry Machinery) Ltd/ Biggin Hill | |
| G-BJLU | Featherlight Mk 3 balloon | T. J. Sweeting & N. P. Kemp | |
| G-BJLV | Sphinx balloon | L. F. Guyot | |
| G-BJLX | Cremer balloon | P. W. May | |
| G-BJLY | Cremer balloon | P. Cannon | |
| G-BJMA | Colt 21A balloon | Colt Balloons Ltd | |
| G-BJMG | European E.26C balloon | D. Eaves & A. P. Chown | |
| G-BJMI | European E.84 balloon | D. Eaves | |
| G-BJMJ | Bensen B.8M | J. I. Hewlett | |
| G-BJML | Cessna 120 | D. F. Lawlor/Inverness | |
| G-BJMO | Taylor JT.1 Monoplane | R. C. Mark | |
| G-BJMR | Cessna 310R | J. McL. Robinson/Sherburn | |
| G-BJMU | European E.157 balloon | A. C. Mitchell | |
| G-BJMV | BAC One-Eleven 531FS | Dan-Air Services Ltd/Gatwick | |
| G-BJMW | Thunder Ax8-105 balloon | G. M. Westley | |
| G-BJMX | Jarre JR.3 balloon | P. D. Ridout | |
| G-BJMZ | European EA.8A balloon | P. D. Ridout | |
| G-BJNA | Arena Mk 117P balloon | P. D. Ridout | |
| G-BJND | Osprey Mk 1E balloon | A. Billington & D. Whitmore | |
| G-BJNF | Cessna F.152 | Exeter Flying Club Ltd | |
| G-BJNG | Slingsby T.67A | D. F. Ranger | |
| G-BJNL | Evans VP-2 | K. Morris | |
| G-BJNN | PA-38-112 Tomahawk | Scotia Safari Ltd/Prestwick | |
| G-BJNP | Rango NA.32 balloon | N. H. Ponsford | |
| G-BJNX | Cameron O-65 balloon | B. J. Petteford | |
| G-BJNY | Aeronca 11CC Super Chief | P. I. & D. M. Morgans | |
| G-BJNZ | PA-23 Aztec 250F | Leavesden Flight Centre Ltd (G-FANZ) | |
| G-BJOA | PA-28-181 Archer II | Channel Islands Aero Holdings (Jersey) Ltd | |
| G-BJOB | Jodel D.140C | T. W. M. Beck & M. J. Smith | |
| G-BJOD | Hollman HA-2M Sportster | W. O'Riordan | |
| G-BJOE | Jodel D.120A | Forth Flying Group | |
| G-BJOI | Isaacs Special | J. O. Isaacs | |
| G-BJOP | BN-2B Islander | Loganair Ltd/Glasgow | |
| G-BJOT | Jodel D.117 | E. Davies | |
| G-BJOV | Cessna F.150K | W. H. Webb & P. F. N. Burrow | |
| G-BJOZ | Scheibe SF.25B Falke | P. W. Hextall | |
| G-BJPB | Osprey Mk 4A balloon | C. B. Rundle | |
| G-BJPI | Bede BD-5G | M. D. McQueen | |
| G-BJPJ | Osprey Mk 3A | K. R. Bundy | |
| G-BJPL | Osprey Mk 4A balloon | M. Vincent | |
| G-BJPM | Bursell PW.1 balloon | I. M. Holdsworth | |
| G-BJPV | Haigh balloon | M. J. Haigh | |
| G-BJPW | Osprey Mk 1C balloon | P. J. Cooper & M. Draper | |
| G-BJRA | Osprey Mk 4B balloon | E. Osborn | |
| G-BJRB | European E.254 balloon | D. Eaves | |
| G-BJRC | European E.84R balloon | D. Eaves | |
| G-BJRD | European E.84R balloon | D. Eaves | |
| G-BJRF | Saffery S.80 balloon | C. F. Chipping | |
| G-BJRG | Osprey Mk 4B balloon | A. de Gruchy | |
| G-BJRH | Rango NA.36 balloon | N. H. Ponsford | |
| G-BJRI | Osprey Mk 4D balloon | G. G. Kneller | |
| G-BJRJ | Osprey Mk 4D balloon | G. G. Kneller | |
| G-BJRK | Osprey Mk 1E balloon | G. G. Kneller | |
| G-BJRL | Osprey Mk 4B balloon | G. G. Kneller | |
| G-BJRP | Cremer balloon | M. Williams | |
| G-BJRS | Cremer balloon | P. Wallbank | |
| G-BJRT | BAC One-Eleven 528FL | British Airways *County of South Glamorgan* | |
| G-BJRU | BAC One-Eleven 528FL | British Airways *County of West Glamorgan* | |
| G-BJRV | Cremer balloon | M. D. Williams | |
| G-BJRW | Cessna U.206G | A. I. Walgate & Son Ltd | |
| G-BJRY | PA-28-151 Warrior | Routair Aviation Services Ltd/ Southend | |
| G-BJRZ | Partenavia P.68C | Air Kilroe Ltd/Manchester | |
| G-BJSA | BN-2A Islander | Foxair/Glasgow | |
| G-BJSC | Osprey Mk 4D balloon | N. J. Richardson | |
| G-BJSD | Osprey Mk 4D balloon | N. J. Richardson | |
| G-BJSE | Osprey Mk 1E balloon | J. E. Christopher | |

| Notes | Reg. | Type | Owner or Operator |
|-------|------|------|-------------------|
| | G-BJSF | Osprey Mk 4B balloon | N. J. Richardson |
| | G-BJSG | V.S.361 Spitfire LF.IXE (ML417) | Patina Ltd/Duxford |
| | G-BJSI | Osprey Mk 1E balloon | N. J. Richardson |
| | G-BJSK | Osprey Mk 4B balloon | J. E. Christopher |
| | G-BJSL | Flamboyant Ax7-65 balloon | Pepsi Cola International Ltd |
| | G-BJSP | Guido 1A Srs 61 balloon | G. A. Newsome |
| | G-BJSR | Osprey Mk 4B balloon | C. F. Chipping |
| | G-BJSS | Allport balloon | D. J. Allport |
| | G-BJST | CCF Harvard 4 | V. Norman & M. Lawrence |
| | G-BJSU | Bensen B.8M | J. D. Newlyn |
| | G-BJSV | PA-28-161 Warrior II | R. Gilbert & J. Cole |
| | G-BJSW | Thunder Ax7-65 balloon | Sandicliffe Garage Ltd |
| | G-BJSX | Unicorn UE-1C balloon | N. J. Richardson |
| | G-BJSZ | Piper J-3C-65 Cub | H. Gilbert |
| | G-BJTA | Osprey Mk 4B balloon | C. F. Chipping |
| | G-BJTB | Cessna A.150M | Clacton Aero Club (1988) Ltd |
| | G-BJTG | Osprey Mk 4B balloon | M. Millen |
| | G-BJTH | Kestrel AC Mk 1 balloon | R. P. Waller |
| | G-BJTK | Taylor JT.1 Monoplane | E. N. Simmons (G-BEUM) |
| | G-BJTN | Osprey Mk 4B balloon | M. Vincent |
| | G-BJTO | Piper J-3C-65 Cub | K. R. Nunn |
| | G-BJTP | PA-18 Super Cub 95 (115302) | J. T. Parkins |
| | G-BJTV | M.S.880B Rallye Club | E. C. Hender |
| | G-BJTW | European E.107 balloon | C. J. Brealey |
| | G-BJTY | Osprey Mk 4B balloon | A. E. de Gruchy |
| | G-BJUB | BVS Special 01 balloon | P. G. Wild |
| | G-BJUC | Robinson R-22 | Northern Helicopters Ltd |
| | G-BJUD | Robin DR.400/180R | Lasham Gliding Soc Ltd |
| | G-BJUE | Osprey Mk 4B balloon | M. Vincent |
| | G-BJUG | SOCATA TB.9 Tampico | R. A. Stockdale |
| | G-BJUI | Osprey Mk 4B balloon | B. A. de Gruchy |
| | G-BJUK | Short SD3-30 | Shorts Aircraft Leasing Ltd (G-OCAS) |
| | G-BJUR | PA-38-112 Tomahawk | Truman Aviation Ltd/Tollerton |
| | G-BJUS | PA-38-112 Tomahawk | Panshanger School of Flying |
| | G-BJUU | Osprey Mk 4B balloon | M. Vincent |
| | G-BJUV | Cameron V-20 balloon | Cameron Balloons Ltd |
| | G-BJUW | Osprey Mk 4B balloon | C. F. Chipping |
| | G-BJUX | Bursell balloon | I. M. Holdsworth |
| | G-BJUZ | BAT Mk II balloon | A. R. Thompson |
| | G-BJVA | BAT Mk I balloon | B. L. Thompson |
| | G-BJVC | Evans VP-2 | W. E. King |
| | G-BJVF | Thunder Ax3 balloon | A. G. R. Calder & F. J. Spite |
| | G-BJVH | Cessna F.182Q | A. R. G. Brooker Engineering Ltd/ Wellesbourne |
| | G-BJVJ | Cessna F.152 | Cambridge Aero Club Ltd |
| | G-BJVK | Grob G-109 | B. Kimberley/Enstone |
| | G-BJVM | Cessna 172M | Mercia Aircraft Leasing & Sales Ltd |
| | G-BJVS | CP.1310-C3 Super Emeraude | A. E. Futter/Norwich |
| | G-BJVT | Cessna F.152 | Cambridge Aero Club Ltd |
| | G-BJVU | Thunder Ax6-56 balloon | G. V. Beckwith |
| | G-BJVV | Robin R.1180 | Medway Flying Group Ltd/Rochester |
| | G-BJVX | Sikorsky S-76A | Bristow Helicopters Ltd |
| | G-BJVZ | Sikorsky S-76A | Bristow Helicopters Ltd |
| | G-BJWC | Saro Skeeter AOP.12 (XK 482)★ | J. E. Wilkie |
| | G-BJWD | Zenith CH.300 | D. Winton |
| | G-BJWH | Cessna F.152 | Biggin Hill School of Flying |
| | G-BJWI | Cessna F.172P | Shoreham Flight Simulation Ltd/ Bournemouth |
| | G-BJWJ | Cameron V-65 balloon | R. G. Turnbull & S. G. Forse |
| | G-BJWO | BN-2A-8 Islander | Chapman Aviation Ltd (G-BAXC)/ Biggin Hill |
| | G-BJWR | D.H.82A Tiger Moth | D. R. Whitby & ptnrs |
| | G-BJWT | Wittman W.10 Tailwind | J. F. Bakewell & R. A. Shelley |
| | G-BJWV | Colt 17A balloon | D. T. Meyes |
| | G-BJWW | Cessna F.172N | Shireburn Carpets Ltd |
| | G-BJWX | PA-18 Super Cub 95 | A. Haig-Thomas |
| | G-BJWY | S-55 Whirlwind HAR.21 (WV198) | J. E. Wilkie |
| | G-BJWZ | PA-18 Super Cub 95 | G. V. Harfield/Thruxton |
| | G-BJXA | Slingsby T.67A | Comed Aviation Ltd/Blackpool |
| | G-BJXB | Slingsby T.67A | Light Planes (Lancs) Ltd/Barton |
| | G-BJXJ | Boeing 737-219 | Britannia Airways Ltd *The O'Neill Hereditary King of Ulster*/Luton |
| | G-BJXK | Fournier RF-5 | G-BJXK Syndicate/Cardiff |

| Reg. | Type | Owner or Operator | Notes |
|------|------|-------------------|-------|
| G-BJXO | Cessna 441 | Hatfield Executive Aviation Ltd | |
| G-BJXP | Colt 56B balloon | Birmingham Broadcasting Ltd | |
| G-BJXR | Auster AOP.9 (XR267) | Cotswold Aircraft Restoration Group | |
| G-BJXU | Thunder Ax7-77 balloon | S. M. Vardey | |
| G-BJXX | PA-23 Aztec 250E | Aztec Euro Ltd | |
| G-BJXZ | Cessna 172N | T. M. Jones | |
| G-BJYC | Cessna 425 | Carters Aviation Ltd/E. Midlands | |
| G-BJYD | Cessna F.152 II | Cleveland Flying School Ltd/ Teesside | |
| G-BJYF | Colt 56A balloon | Hot Air Balloon Co Ltd | |
| G-BJYG | PA-28-161 Warrior II | Browns of Stoke Ltd | |
| G-BJYK | Jodel D.120A | T. Fox & D. A. Thorpe | |
| G-BJYL | BAC One-Eleven 515FB | Dan-Air Services Ltd (G-AZPE)/Gatwick | |
| G-BJYM | BAC One-Eleven 531FS | Dan-Air Services Ltd/Gatwick | |
| G-BJYN | PA-38-112 Tomahawk | Panshanger School of Flying Ltd (G-BJTE) | |
| G-BJZA | Cameron N-65 balloon | A. D. Pinner | |
| G-BJZB | Evans VP-2 | J. A. Macleod | |
| G-BJZC | Thunder Ax7-65Z balloon | Greenpeace (UK) Ltd/S. Africa | |
| G-BJZD | Douglas DC-10-10 | — (G-GFAL) | |
| G-BJZE | Douglas DC-10-10 | — (G-GSKY) | |
| G-BJZF | D.H.82A Tiger Moth | C. A. Parker/Sywell | |
| G-BJZK | Cessna T.303 | Landlink Ltd | |
| G-BJZL | Cameron V-65 balloon | S. L. G. Williams | |
| G-BJZN | Slingsby T.67A | A. Shuttleworth | |
| G-BJZR | Colt 42A balloon | C. F. Sisson | |
| G-BJZT | Cessna FA.152 | Biggin Hill School of Flying | |
| G-BJZX | Grob G.109 | Oxfordshire Sport Flying Ltd/Enstone | |
| G-BJZY | Bensen B.8MV | D. E. & M. A. Cooke | |
| G-BKAC | Cessna F.150L | Seawing Flying Club Ltd/Southend | |
| G-BKAE | Jodel D.120 | M. P. Wakem | |
| G-BKAF | FRED Srs 2 | L. G. Millen | |
| G-BKAG | Boeing 727-217 | Dan-Air Services Ltd/Gatwick | |
| G-BKAM | Slingsby T.67M Firefly | A. J. Daley & R. K. Warren | |
| G-BKAN | Cessna 340A | Arrows Aviation Co Ltd/Manchester | |
| G-BKAO | Jodel D.112 | R. Broadhead | |
| G-BKAR | PA-38-112 Tomahawk | 1st European (Leasing & Finance) Ltd | |
| G-BKAS | PA-38-112 Tomahawk | 1st European (Leasing & Finance) Ltd | |
| G-BKAT | Pitts S-1C Special | I. M. G. Senior & J. G. Harper | |
| G-BKAY | R. Commander 114 | The Rockwell Group | |
| G-BKAZ | Cessna 152 | Skyviews & General Ltd | |
| G-BKBB | Hawker Fury replica (K1930) | A. L. Lindsay ptnrs/Booker | |
| G-BKBD | Thunder Ax3 balloon | D. L. Clark *Tow-Rite* | |
| G-BKBF | M.S.894A Rallye Minerva 220 | M. S. Wright | |
| G-BKBK | SNCAN Stampe SV-4A | Freshname No77 Ltd | |
| G-BKBN | SOCATA TB.10 Tobago | Cross Bros Ltd/Andrewsfield | |
| G-BKBO | Colt 17A balloon | J. Armstrong & ptnrs | |
| G-BKBP | Bellanca 7GCBC Scout | H. G. Jefferies & Son | |
| G-BKBR | Cameron Chateau 84 SS balloon | Forbes Europe Ltd/France | |
| G-BKBS | Bensen B.8MV | Construction & Site Administration Ltd | |
| G-BKBV | SOCATA TB.10 Tobago | R. M. Messenger | |
| G-BKBW | SOCATA TB.10 Tobago | P. Murphy/Blackbushe | |
| G-BKCB | PA-28R Cherokee Arrow 200 | Bristol & Wessex Aeroplane Club Ltd | |
| G-BKCC | PA-28 Cherokee 180 | Hitachi Credit (UK) PLC | |
| G-BKCD | H.S.125 Srs 600B | MAGEC Aviation Ltd (G-BDOA)/Luton | |
| G-BKCE | Cessna F.172PII | M. Askanoglu | |
| G-BKCF | Rutan LongEz | I. C. Fallows | |
| G-BKCH | Thompson Cassutt | S. C. Thompson/Redhill | |
| G-BKCI | Brügger MB.2 Colibri | E. R. Newall | |
| G-BKCJ | Oldfield Baby Great Lakes | S. V. Roberts/Sleap | |
| G-BKCK | CCF Harvard IV (P5865) | E. T. Webster/North Weald | |
| G-BKCL | PA-30 Twin Comanche 160C | J. & J. Cannings (G-AXSP) | |
| G-BKCN | Currie Wot | S. E. Tomlinson | |
| G-BKCR | SOCATA TB.9 Tampico | Surrey & Kent Flying Club (1982) Ltd/ Biggin Hill | |
| G-BKCT | Cameron V-77 balloon | Quality Products General Engineering (Wickwat) Ltd | |
| G-BKCV | EAA Acro Sport II | M. J. Clark | |
| G-BKCW | Jodel D.120A | A. Greene & G. Kerr/Dundee | |
| G-BKCX | Mudry CAARP CAP.10 | Mahon & Associates/Booker | |
| G-BKCY | PA-38-112 Tomahawk II | Wellesbourne Aviation Ltd | |
| G-BKCZ | Jodel D.120A | M. R. Baker/Shoreham | |

| Notes | Reg. | Type | Owner or Operator |
|---|---|---|---|
| | G-BKDC | Monnet Sonerai II | K. McBride |
| | G-BKDD | Bell 206B JetRanger | Dollar Air Services Ltd/Coventry |
| | G-BKDE | Kendrick I Motorglider | J. K. Rushton |
| | G-BKDF | Kendrick II Motorglider | J. K. Rushton |
| | G-BKDH | Robin DR.400/120 | Wiltshire Aeroplane Club/Old Sarum |
| | G-BKDI | Robin DR.400/120 | Cotswold Aero Club Ltd/Staverton |
| | G-BKDJ | Robin DR.400/120 | Wiltshire Aeroplane Club/Old Sarum |
| | G-BKDK | Thunder Ax7-77Z balloon | A. J. Byrne |
| | G-BKDP | FRED Srs 3 | M. Whittaker |
| | G-BKDR | Pitts S.1S Special | T. R. G. Barnby & ptnrs/Redhill |
| | G-BKDT | S.E.5A (replica) (F943) | J. H. Tetley & W. A. Sneesby/Sherburn |
| | G-BKDX | Jodel DR.1050 | Delta X-Ray Group |
| | G-BKEK | PA-32 Cherokee Six 300 | Flyfast Ltd |
| | G-BKEM | SOCATA TB.9 Tampico | C. J. Burt/Biggin Hill |
| | G-BKEP | Cessna F.172M | R. Green/Glasgow |
| | G-BKER | SE-5A replica (F5447) | N. K. Geddes |
| | G-BKET | PA-18 Super Cub 95 | J. A. Wills/Inverness |
| | G-BKEU | Taylor JT.1 Monoplane | R. J. Whybrow & J. M. Springham |
| | G-BKEV | Cessna F.172M | One Zero One Three Ltd |
| | G-BKEW | Bell 206B JetRanger 3 | N. R. Foster |
| | G-BKEX | Rich Prototype glider | D. B. Rich |
| | G-BKEY | FRED Srs 3 | G. S. Taylor |
| | G-BKEZ | PA-18 Super Cub 95 | G. V. Harfield |
| | G-BKFA | Monnet Sonerai IIL | R. F. Bridge |
| | G-BKFC | Cessna F.152 II | Sulby Aerial Surveys Ltd |
| | G-BKFG | Thunder Ax3 balloon | P. Ray |
| | G-BKFI | Evans VP-1 | F. A. R. de Lavergne |
| | G-BKFK | Isaacs Fury II | G. C. Jones |
| | G-BKFM | QAC Quickie | A. J. Briggs |
| | G-BKFN | Bell 214ST | Bristow Helicopters Ltd |
| | G-BKFP | Bell 214ST | Bristow Helicopters Ltd |
| | G-BKFR | CP.301C Emeraude | C. R. Beard |
| | G-BKFV | Rand KR-2 | F. H. French/Swansea |
| | G-BKFW | P.56 Provost T.1 (XF597) | Slymar Aviation & Services Ltd |
| | G-BKFX | Colt 17A balloon | Colt Balloons Ltd |
| | G-BKFY | Beech C90 King Air | Corgi Investments Ltd |
| | G-BKFZ | PA-28R Cherokee Arrow 200 | Shacklewell Flying Group/Leicester |
| | G-BKGA | M.S.892E Rallye 150GT | B. F. Hill |
| | G-BKGB | Jodel D.120 | R. W. Greenwood |
| | G-BKGC | Maule M.6-235 | Stol-Air Ltd/Sibson |
| | G-BKGD | Westland WG.30 Srs 100 | British International Helicopters Ltd (G-BKBJ)/Aberdeen |
| | G-BKGL | Beech 18 (1164) | The Aircraft Restoration Co/Duxford |
| | G-BKGR | Cameron O-65 balloon | S. R. Bridge |
| | G-BKGT | SOCATA Rallye 110ST | Long Marston Flying Group |
| | G-BKGW | Cessna F.152-II | Leicestershire Aero Club Ltd |
| | G-BKGX | Isaacs Fury | I. L. McMahon |
| | G-BKGZ | Bensen B.8 | C. F. Simpson |
| | G-BKHA | W.S.55 Whirlwind HAR.10 (XJ763) | C. J. Evans |
| | G-BKHC | W.S.55 Whirlwind HAR.10 (XP328) | Flight C Helicopters Ltd |
| | G-BKHD | Oldfield Baby Great Lakes | P. J. Tanulak |
| | G-BKHE | Boeing 737-204 | Britannia Airways Ltd Sir Francis Chichester/Luton |
| | G-BKHF | Boeing 737-204 | Britannia Airways Ltd Sir Alliot Verdon Roe/Luton |
| | G-BKHG | Piper J-3C-65 Cub (479766) | K. G. Wakefield |
| | G-BKHL | Thunder Ax9-140 balloon | R. Carr/France |
| | G-BKHP | P.56 Provost T.1 (WW397) | M. J. Crymble/Lyneham |
| | G-BKHR | Luton LA-4 Minor | A. C. P. de Labat |
| | G-BKHT | BAe 146-100 | Dan-Air Services Ltd/Gatwick |
| | G-BKHV | Taylor JT.2 Titch | P. D. Holt |
| | G-BKHW | Stoddard-Hamilton Glasair SH.2RG | N. Clayton |
| | G-BKHX | Bensen B.8M | D. H. Greenwood |
| | G-BKHY | Taylor JT.1 Monoplane | M. C. Holmes & A. Shuttleworth |
| | G-BKHZ | Cessna F.172P | Warwickshire Flying Training Centre Ltd |
| | G-BKIA | SOCATA TB.10 Tobago | D. H. Barton/Redhill |
| | G-BKIB | SOCATA TB.9 Tampico | A. J. Baggerley & F. D. J. Simmons/Goodwood |
| | G-BKIC | Cameron V-77 balloon | C. A. Butler |
| | G-BKIF | Fournier RF-6B | G. G. Milton |

| Reg. | Type | Owner or Operator | Notes |
|------|------|-------------------|-------|
| G-BKII | Cessna F.172M | M. S. Knight/Goodwood | |
| G-BKIJ | Cessna F.172M | V. Speck | |
| G-BKIK | Cameron DG-10 airship | Airspace Outdoor Advertising Ltd | |
| G-BKIM | Unicorn UE.5A balloon | I. Chadwick & K. H. Turner | |
| G-BKIN | Alon A.2A Aircoupe | P. A. Williams/Blackbushe | |
| G-BKIR | Jodel D.117 | R. Shaw & D. M. Hardaker/Sherburn | |
| G-BKIS | SOCATA TB.10 Tobago | Ospreystar Ltd | |
| G-BKIT | SOCATA TB.9 Tampico | D. G. Bligh/Ipswich | |
| G-BKIU | Colt 17A balloon | Robert Pooley Ltd | |
| G-BKIV | Colt 21A balloon | Colt Balloons Ltd | |
| G-BKIX | Cameron V-31 balloon | G. Stevens | |
| G-BKIY | Thunder Ax3 balloon | A. Hornak | |
| G-BKIZ | Cameron V-31 balloon | A. P. Greathead | |
| G-BKJB | PA-18 Super Cub 135 | Cormack (Aircraft Services) Ltd/Glasgow | |
| G-BKJD | Bell 214ST | Bristow Helicopters Ltd | |
| G-BKJE | Cessna 172N | The G-BKJE Group/Burnaston | |
| G-BKJF | M.S.880B Rallye 100T | Nova Flying Group | |
| G-BKJR | Hughes 269C | March Helicopters Ltd/Sywell | |
| G-BKJS | Jodel D.120A | S. Walmsley | |
| G-BKJT | Cameron O-65 balloon | K. A. Ward | |
| G-BKJW | PA-23 Aztec 250E | Alan Williams Entertainments Ltd | |
| G-BKKI | Westland WG.30 Srs100 | Westland Helicopters Ltd/Yeovil | |
| G-BKKN | Cessna 182R | R A. Marven/Elstree | |
| G-BKKO | Cessna 182R | B. & G. Jebson Ltd/Crosland Moor | |
| G-BKKP | Cessna 182R | ISF Aviation Ltd/Leicester | |
| G-BKKR | Rand KR-2 | D. Beale & S. P. Gardner | |
| G-BKKS | Mercury Dart Srs 1 | B. A. Mills | |
| G-BKKZ | Pitts S-1D Special | G. C. Masterton | |
| G-BKLB | R. S2R Thrush Commander | Ag-Air | |
| G-BKLC | Cameron V-56 balloon | M. A. & J. R. H. Ashworth | |
| G-BKLJ | Westland Scout AH.1 ★ | J. E. Wilkie | |
| G-BKLM | Thunder Ax9-140 balloon | Aerial Promotions Balloon Club | |
| G-BKLO | Cessna F.172M | Stapleford Flying Club Ltd | |
| G-BKLP | Cessna F.172N | Holmes Rentals | |
| G-BKLT | SA.341G Gazelle 1 | Specialist Flying Training Ltd/Carlisle | |
| G-BKMA | Mooney M.20J Srs 201 | Clement Garage Ltd/Stapleford | |
| G-BKMB | Mooney M.20J Srs 201 | W. A. Cook & ptnrs/Sherburn | |
| G-BKMD | SC.7 Skyvan Srs 3 | London Skydiving Centre Ltd/Cranfield | |
| G-BKME | SC.7 Skyvan Srs 3 | Flightspares PLC (G-AYJN)/Southend | |
| G-BKMG | Handley Page O/400 replica | M. G. King | |
| G-BKMH | Flamboyant Ax7-65 balloon | Pepsi-Cola International Ltd/S. Africa | |
| G-BKMI | V.S.359 Spitfire HF VIII (MV154) | Aerial Museum (North Weald) Ltd | |
| G-BKMK | PA-38-112 Tomahawk | D. W. Higgins/Glasgow | |
| G-BKMM | Cessna 180K | M. Kirk | |
| G-BKMN | BAe 146-100 | Dan-Air Services Ltd (G-ODAN)/Gatwick | |
| G-BKMR | Thunder Ax3 balloon | B. F. G. Ribbons | |
| G-BKMT | PA-32R-301 Saratoga SP | Severn Valley Aviation Group | |
| G-BKMX | Short SD3-60 | Manx Airlines Ltd/Ronaldsway | |
| G-BKNA | Cessna 421 | Young Investments Ltd | |
| G-BKNB | Cameron V-42 balloon | S. A. Burnett | |
| G-BKND | Colt 56A balloon | Flying Colours Balloon Group | |
| G-BKNH | Boeing 737-210 | Dan-Air Services Ltd/Gatwick | |
| G-BKNI | GY-80 Horizon 160D | A. Hartigan & ptnrs/Fenland | |
| G-BKNL | Cameron D-96 airship | Drawarm Ltd | |
| G-BKNN | Cameron Minar E Pakistan balloon | Forbes Europe Ltd/France | |
| G-BKNO | Monnet Sonerai IIL | J. K. Cook | |
| G-BKNX | SA.102.5 Cavalier | G. D. Horn | |
| G-BKNY | Bensen B.8M-P-VW | D. A. C. MacCormack | |
| G-BKNZ | CP.301A Emeraude | R. Evernden/Barton | |
| G-BKOA | SOCATA M.S.893E Rallye 180GT | B. Conway & P. J. Clegg | |
| G-BKOB | Z.326 Trener Master | W. G. V. Hall | |
| G-BKOR | Barnes 77 balloon | Robert Pooley Ltd | |
| G-BKOS | P.56 Provost T.51 (178) | Sylmar Aviation & Services Ltd | |
| G-BKOT | Wassmer WA.81 Piranha | B. D. Deubelbeiss | |
| G-BKOU | P.84 Jet Provost T.3 (XN637) | A. Topen/Cranfield | |
| G-BKOV | Jodel DR.220A | Merlin Flying Club Ltd/Hucknall | |
| G-BKOW | Cameron 77A balloon | Hot Air Ballon Co Ltd | |
| G-BKPA | Hoffman H-36 Dimona | A. Mayhew | |
| G-BKPB | Aerosport Scamp | E. D. Burke | |

| Notes | Reg. | Type | Owner or Operator |
|---|---|---|---|
| | G-BKPC | Cessna A.185F | Black Knights Parachute Centre |
| | G-BKPD | Viking Dragonfly | E. P. Browne & G. J. Sargent |
| | G-BKPE | Jodel DR.250/160 | J. S. & J. D. Lewer |
| | G-BKPG | Luscombe Rattler Strike | Luscombe Aircraft Ltd/Lympne |
| | G-BKPH | Luscombe Valiant | Luscombe Aircraft Ltd/Lympne |
| | G-BKPK | John McHugh Gyrocopter | J. C. McHugh |
| | G-BKPM | Schempp-Hirth HS.5 Nimbus 2 | J. L. Rolls |
| | G-BKPN | Cameron N-77 balloon | R. H. Sanderson |
| | G-BKPS | AA-5B Tiger | Eyewitness Ltd/Southampton |
| | G-BKPT | M.H.1521M Broussard (192) | R. M. Johnston |
| | G-BKPV | Stevex 250.1 | A. F. Stevens |
| | G-BKPW | Boeing 767-204 | Britannia Airways Ltd *The Earl Mountbatten of Burma*/Luton |
| | G-BKPX | Jodel D.120A | N. H. Martin |
| | G-BKPY | Saab 91B/2 Safir (56321)★ | Newark Air Museum Ltd |
| | G-BKPZ | Pitts S-1T Special | A. J. Whitehead |
| | G-BKRA | NA T-6G Texan (51-15227) | A. D. M. Edie/Shoreham |
| | G-BKRB | Cessna 172N | Saunders Caravans Ltd |
| | G-BKRD | Cessna 320E | Jadealto Ltd |
| | G-BKRF | PA-18 Super Cub 95 | K. M. Bishop |
| | G-BKRG | Beechcraft C-45G | Aces High Ltd/North Weald |
| | G-BKRH | Brügger MB.2 Colibri | M. R. Benwell |
| | G-BKRI | Cameron V-77 balloon | J. R. Lowe & R. J. Fuller |
| | G-BKRJ | Colt 105A balloon | Owners Abroad Group PLC |
| | G-BKRK | SNCAN Stampe SV-4C | J. M. Alexander & ptnrs/Aberdeen |
| | G-BKRL | Chichester-Miles Leopard | Chichester-Miles Consultants Ltd |
| | G-BKRM | Boeing 757-236 | Air 2000 Ltd/Manchester |
| | G-BKRN | Beechcraft D.18S ★ | S. Topen/Cranfield |
| | G-BKRR | Cameron N-56 balloon | S. L. G. Williams |
| | G-BKRS | Cameron V-56 balloon | D. N. & L. J. Close |
| | G-BKRT | PA-34-220T Seneca III | Paucristar Ltd |
| | G-BKRU | Ensign Crossley Racer | M. Crossley |
| | G-BKRV | Hovey Beta Bird | A. V. Francis |
| | G-BKRW | Cameron O-160 balloon | Bondbaste Ltd |
| | G-BKRX | Cameron O-160 balloon | Bondbaste Ltd |
| | G-BKRZ | Dragon 77 balloon | J. R. Barber |
| | G-BKSB | Cessna T.310Q | Offshore Express Ltd |
| | G-BKSC | Saro Skeeter AOP.12 (XN351) | R. A. L. Falconer |
| | G-BKSD | Colt 56A balloon | M. J. & G. C. Casson |
| | G-BKSE | QAC Quickie Q.2 | M. D. Burns |
| | G-BKSH | Colt 21A balloon | T. A. Gilmour |
| | G-BKSJ | Cameron N-108 balloon | Cameron Balloons Ltd |
| | G-BKSO | Cessna 421C | Aviation Beauport Ltd/Jersey |
| | G-BKSP | Schleicher ASK.14 | J. H. Bryson & E. A. H. Boyle |
| | G-BKSR | Cessna 550 Citation II | Moseley Group (PSV) Ltd/E. Midlands |
| | G-BKSS | Jodel D.150 | D. H. Wilson-Spratt/Ronaldsway |
| | G-BKST | Rutan Vari-Eze | R. Towle |
| | G-BKSX | SNCAN Stampe SV-4C | C. A. Bailey & J. A. Carr |
| | G-BKSZ | Cessna P.210N | Kenbal Properties Ltd |
| | G-BKTA | PA-18 Super Cub 95 | K. E. Chapman/Southend |
| | G-BKTH | CCF Hawker Sea Hurricane IB (Z7015) | Shuttleworth Trust/Duxford |
| | G-BKTM | PZL SZD-45A Ogar | Ogar Syndicate |
| | G-BKTR | Cameron V-77 balloon | G. F. & D. D. Bouten |
| | G-BKTS | Cameron O-65 balloon | C. H. Pearce & Sons (Contractors) Ltd |
| | G-BKTT | Cessna F.152 | Stapleford Flying Club Ltd |
| | G-BKTU | Colt 56A balloon | E. Ten Houten |
| | G-BKTV | Cessna F.152 | London Flight Centre Ltd/Stansted |
| | G-BKTW | Cessna 404 Titan II | Aberdeen Airways Ltd (G-WTVE) |
| | G-BKTY | SOCATA TB.10 Tobago | E. J. H. Morgan/Alderney |
| | G-BKTZ | Slingsby T.67M Firefly | Trent Air Services Ltd (G-SFTV)/Cranfield |
| | G-BKUE | SOCATA TB.9 Tampico | W. J. Moore/Kirkbride |
| | G-BKUI | D.31 Turbulent | R. F. Smith |
| | G-BKUJ | Thunder Ax6-56 balloon | R. J. Bent |
| | G-BKUR | CP.301A Emeraude | P. Gilmour/Perth |
| | G-BKUS | Bensen B.8M | G. F. Gardener |
| | G-BKUT | M.S.880B Rallye Club | Rallye Aircraft Flyers |
| | G-BKUU | Thunder Ax7-77-1 balloon | City of London Balloon Group |
| | G-BKUY | BAe Jetstream 3102 | British Aerospace PLC/Prestwick |
| | G-BKUZ | Zenair CH.250 | K. Morris |
| | G-BKVA | SOCATA Rallye 180T | T. Miller |
| | G-BKVB | SOCATA Rallye 110ST | Martin Ltd/Biggin Hill |

| Reg. | Type | Owner or Operator | Notes |
|------|------|-------------------|-------|
| G-BKVC | SOCATA TB.9 Tampico | Martin Ltd/Biggin Hill | |
| G-BKVE | Rutan Vari-Eze | H. R. Rowley (G-EZLT) | |
| G-BKVF | FRED Srs 3 | N. E. Johnson | |
| G-BKVG | Scheibe SF.25E Super Falke | G-BKVG Ltd | |
| G-BKVJ | Colt 21A balloon | Colt Balloons Ltd | |
| G-BKVK | Auster AOP.9 (WZ662) | J. D. Butcher | |
| G-BKVL | Robin DR.400/160 | The Cotswold Aero Club Ltd/Staverton | |
| G-BKVM | PA-18 Super Cub 150 | D. G. Caffrey | |
| G-BKVN | PA-23 Aztec 250F | B. A. Eastwell/Shoreham | |
| G-BKVO | Pietenpol Air Camper | G. H. & M. G. A. Phillipson | |
| G-BKVP | Pitts S-1D Special | P. J. Leggo | |
| G-BKVR | PA-28 Cherokee 140 | D. P. Alexander | |
| G-BKVS | Bensen B.8M | V. Scott | |
| G-BKVT | PA-23 Aztec 250E | L. G. Culverwell (G-HARV) | |
| G-BKVV | Beech 95-B55 Baron | L. Mc. G. Tulloch | |
| G-BKVW | Airtour 56 balloon | L. D. & H. Vaughan | |
| G-BKVX | Airtour 56 balloon | E. G. Woolnough | |
| G-BKVY | Airtour 31 balloon | Airtour Balloon Co Ltd | |
| G-BKVZ | Boeing 767-204 | Britannia Airways Ltd *Sir Winston Churchill*/Luton | |
| G-BKWA | Cessna 404 Titan | Aberdeen Airways Ltd (G-BELV) | |
| G-BKWB | EMB-110P2 Bandeirante | Alexandra Aviation Ltd (G-CHEV)/ Gatwick | |
| G-BKWD | Taylor JT.2 Titch | E. Shouler | |
| G-BKWE | Colt 17A balloon | Hot-Air Balloon Co Ltd | |
| G-BKWG | PZL-104 Wilga 35A | Anglo-Polish Sailplanes Ltd | |
| G-BKWI | Pitts S-2A | R. A. Seeley/Denham | |
| G-BKWP | Thunder Ax7-77 balloon | G. V. Beckwith | |
| G-BKWR | Cameron V-65 balloon | D. H. Usill | |
| G-BKWW | Cameron O-77 balloon | A. M. Marten | |
| G-BKWY | Cessna F.152 | Cambridge Aero Club | |
| G-BKXA | Robin R.2100 | G. J. Anderson & ptnrs | |
| G-BKXC | Cameron V-77 balloon | P. Sarretti | |
| G-BKXD | SA.365N Dauphin 2 | Bond Helicopters Ltd/Bourn | |
| G-BKXE | SA.365N Dauphin 2 | Bond Helicopters Ltd/Bourn | |
| G-BKXF | PA-28R Cherokee Arrow 200 | P. L. Brunton | |
| G-BKXG | Cessna T.303 | Wilton Construction Ltd | |
| G-BKXL | Cameron Bottle 70 balloon | Cameron Balloons Ltd | |
| G-BKXM | Colt 17A balloon | R. G. Turnbull | |
| G-BKXN | ICA IS-28M2A | British Aerospace PLC/Filton | |
| G-BKXO | Rutan LongEz | P. J. Wareham | |
| G-BKXP | Auster AOP.6 | B. J. & W. J. Ellis | |
| G-BKXR | D.31A Turbulent | M. B. Hill | |
| G-BKXT | Cameron D-50 airship | Cameron Balloons Ltd | |
| G-BKXX | Cameron V-65 balloon | A. J. Legg & C. H. Harbord | |
| G-BKYA | Boeing 737-236 | British Airways *River Derwent*/ Heathrow | |
| G-BKYB | Boeing 737-236 | British Airways *River Stour*/Heathrow | |
| G-BKYC | Boeing 737-236 | British Airways *River Wye*/Heathrow | |
| G-BKYD | Boeing 737-236 | British Airways *River Conway*/ Heathrow | |
| G-BKYE | Boeing 737-236 | British Airways *River Laggan*/Heathrow | |
| G-BKYF | Boeing 737-236 | British Airways *River Spey*/Heathrow | |
| G-BKYG | Boeing 737-236 | British Airways *River Exe*/Heathrow | |
| G-BKYH | Boeing 737-236 | British Airways *River Dart*/Heathrow | |
| G-BKYI | Boeing 737-236 | British Airways *River Waveney*/ Heathrow | |
| G-BKYJ | Boeing 737-236 | British Airways *River Neath*/Heathrow | |
| G-BKYK | Boeing 737-236 | British Airways *River Foyle*/Heathrow | |
| G-BKYL | Boeing 737-236 | British Airways *River Isis*/Heathrow | |
| G-BKYM | Boeing 737-236 | British Airways *River Cam*/Heathrow | |
| G-BKYN | Boeing 737-236 | British Airways *River Ayr*/Heathrow | |
| G-BKYO | Boeing 737-236 | British Airways *River Kennet*/ Heathrow | |
| G-BKYP | Boeing 737-236 | British Airways *River Ystwyth*/ Heathrow | |
| G-BKZA | Cameron N-77 balloon | University of Bath Students Union | |
| G-BKZB | Cameron V-77 balloon | A. J. Montgomery | |
| G-BKZC | Cessna A.152 | Montaguis Ltd/Kuwait | |
| G-BKZE | AS.332L Super Puma | British International Helicopters/ Aberdeen | |
| G-BKZF | Cameron V-56 balloon | G. M. Hobster | |

| Notes | Reg. | Type | Owner or Operator |
|-------|------|------|-------------------|
| | G-BKZG | AS.332L Super Puma | British International Helicopters/ Aberdeen |
| | G-BKZH | AS.332L Super Puma | British International Helicopters/ Aberdeen |
| | G-BKZI | Bell 206B JetRanger 2 | Heliwork Services Ltd/Thruxton |
| | G-BKZJ | Bensen B.8MV | J. C. Birdsall |
| | G-BKZT | FRED Srs 2 | A. E. Morris |
| | G-BKZV | Bede BD-4A | A. L. Bergamasco/Headcorn |
| | G-BKZY | Cameron N-77 balloon | W. Counties Automobile Co Ltd |
| | G-BLAA | Fournier RF-5 | A. D. Wren/Southend |
| | G-BLAC | Cessna FA.152 | Ladel Ltd |
| | G-BLAD | Thunder Ax7-77-1 balloon | V. P. Gardiner & I. K. Turner |
| | G-BLAF | Stolp SA.900 V-Star | J. R. Ware |
| | G-BLAG | Pitts S-1D Special | C. M. Evans |
| | G-BLAH | Thunder Ax7-77-1 balloon | T. Donnelly |
| | G-BLAI | Monnet Sonerai IIL | T. Simpson |
| | G-BLAM | Jodel DR.360 | B. F. Baldock |
| | G-BLAT | Jodel D.150 | R. Bennett/Ipswich |
| | G-BLAW | PA-28-181 Archer II | Luton Flight Training |
| | G-BLAX | Cessna FA.152 | Shoreham Flight Simulation Ltd/ Bournemouth |
| | G-BLAY | Robin HR.100/200B | B. A. Mills |
| | G-BLCA | Bell 206B JetRanger 3 | R.M.H. Stainless Ltd |
| | G-BLCC | Thunder Ax7-77Z balloon | P. Hassell Ltd |
| | G-BLCF | EAA Acro Sport 2 | M. J. Watkins & ptnrs |
| | G-BLCG | SOCATA TB.10 Tobago | Charlie Golf Flying Group (G-BHES)/ Shoreham |
| | G-BLCH | Colt 56D balloon | Balloon Flights Club Ltd |
| | G-BLCI | EAA Acro Sport | M. R. Holden |
| | G-BLCK | V.S.361 Spitfire F.IX (TE566) | Historic Aircraft Collection Ltd |
| | G-BLCM | SOCATA TB.9 Tampico | Repclif Aviation Ltd/Liverpool |
| | G-BLCT | Jodel DR.220 2+2 | H. W. Jemmett |
| | G-BLCU | Scheibe SF.25B Falke | B. Lumb/Rufforth |
| | G-BLCV | Hoffman H-36 Dimona | Charlie Victor Motor Glider Group |
| | G-BLCW | Evans VP-1 | K. D. Pearce |
| | G-BLCY | Thunder Ax7-65Z balloon | Thunder Balloons Ltd |
| | G-BLDB | Taylor JT.1 Monoplane | C. J. Bush |
| | G-BLDC | K&S Jungster 1 | A. W. Brown |
| | G-BLDD | WAG-Aero CUBy AcroTrainer | C. A. Laycock |
| | G-BLDE | Boeing 737-2E7 | Dan-Air Services Ltd/Gatwick |
| | G-BLDG | PA-25 Pawnee 260C | Ouse Gliding Club Ltd/Rufforth |
| | G-BLDH | BAC One-Eleven 475EZ | McAlpine Aviation Ltd/Luton |
| | G-BLDK | Robinson R-22 | R. H. Cleare & Co Ltd |
| | G-BLDL | Cameron Truck 56 balloon | Cameron Balloons Ltd |
| | G-BLDM | Hiller UH-12E | G. & S. G. Neal (Helicopters) Ltd |
| | G-BLDN | Rand KR-2 | R. Y. Kendal |
| | G-BLDP | Slingsby T.67M Firefly | Cavendish Aviation Ltd/Netherthorpe |
| | G-BLDY | Bell 212 | Bristow Helicopters Ltd |
| | G-BLEB | Colt 69A balloon | I. R. M. Jacobs |
| | G-BLEC | BN-2B-27 Islander | LEC Refrigeration PLC (G-BJBG) |
| | G-BLEJ | PA-28-161 Warrior II | Eglinton Flying Club Ltd |
| | G-BLEL | Price Ax7-77-245 balloon | T. S. Price |
| | G-BLEP | Cameron V-65 balloon | D. Chapman |
| | G-BLES | Stolp SA.750 Acroduster Too | T. W. Harris |
| | G-BLET | Thunder Ax7-77-1 balloon | Servatruc Ltd |
| | G-BLEW | Cessna F.182Q | Interair Aviation Ltd/Bournemouth |
| | G-BLEY | SA.365N Dauphin 2 | Bond Helicopters Ltd |
| | G-BLEZ | SA.365N Dauphin 2 | Bond Helicopters Ltd |
| | G-BLFE | Cameron Sphinx SS balloon | Forbes Europe Inc |
| | G-BLFF | Cessna F.172M | Air Advertising UK Ltd |
| | G-BLFJ | F.27 Friendship Mk 100 | Air UK Ltd (G-OMAN/G-SPUD)/Norwich |
| | G-BLFT | P.56 Provost T.1 (WV686) | B. W. H. Parkhouse |
| | G-BLFW | AA-5 Traveler | Grumman Club |
| | G-BLFY | Cameron V-77 balloon | A. N. F. Pertwee |
| | G-BLFZ | PA-31-310 Turbo Navajo C | Huktra UK Ltd |
| | G-BLGB | Short SD3-60 | Loganair Ltd/Glasgow |
| | G-BLGH | Robin DR.300/180R | Booker Gliding Club Ltd |
| | G-BLGI | McCullogh J.2 | R. J. Everett |
| | G-BLGM | Cessna 425 | John Hanson Services Ltd |
| | G-BLGN | Skyhawk Gyroplane | S. M. Hawkins |
| | G-BLGO | Bensen B.8M | F. Vernon |
| | G-BLGR | Bell 47G-4A | Base Helicopters Ltd |

| Reg. | Type | Owner or Operator | Notes |
|------|------|-------------------|-------|
| G-BLGS | SOCATA Rallye 180T | Lasham Gliding Society Ltd | |
| G-BLGT | PA-18 Super Cub 95 | T. A. Reed/Dunkeswell | |
| G-BLGV | Bell 206B JetRanger | Base Helicopters Ltd | |
| G-BLGW | F.27 Friendship Mk 200 | Air UK Ltd *Louis Marchesi*/Norwich | |
| G-BLGX | Thunder Ax7-65 balloon | Harper & Co (Glasgow) Ltd | |
| G-BLHA | Thunder Ax10-160 balloon | Thunder Balloons Ltd | |
| G-BLHB | Thunder Ax10-160 balloon | Thunder Balloons Ltd | |
| G-BLHD | BAC One-Eleven 492GM | Twinjet Aircraft Sales Ltd/Luton | |
| G-BLHF | Nott-Cameron ULD-2 balloon | J. R. P. Nott | |
| G-BLHH | Jodel DR.315 | G. G. Milton | |
| G-BLHI | Colt 17A balloon | Thunder & Colt Ltd | |
| G-BLHJ | Cessna F.172P | P. P. D. Howard-Johnston/Edinburgh | |
| G-BLHK | Colt 105A balloon | Hale Hot-Air Balloon Club | |
| G-BLHM | PA-18 Super Cub 95 | N. M. Bloom | |
| G-BLHN | Robin HR.100/285 | H. M. Bouquiere/Biggin Hill | |
| G-BLHR | GA-7 Cougar | Fotex Aviation Ltd | |
| G-BLHS | Bellanca 7ECA Citabria | J. W. Platten & E. J. Timmins | |
| G-BLHW | Varga 2150A Kachina | D. M. Jagger | |
| G-BLHZ | Varga 2150A Kachina | MLP Aviation Ltd/Elstree | |
| G-BLID | D.H.112 Venom FB.50 (J-1605) | P. G. Vallance Ltd | |
| G-BLIE | D.H.112 Venom FB.50 | R. J. Everett | |
| G-BLIG | Cameron V-65 balloon | W. Davison | |
| G-BLIH | PA-18 Super Cub 135 | I. R. F. Hammond | |
| G-BLIK | Wallis WA-116/F/S | K. H. Wallis | |
| G-BLIP | Cameron N-77 balloon | L. A. Beardall & G. R. Hunt | |
| G-BLIT | Thorp T-18 CW | A. J. Waller | |
| G-BLIV | Cameron O-105 balloon | A. M. Thompson | |
| G-BLIW | P.56 Provost T.51 (177) | Pulsegrove Ltd (*stored*)/Shoreham | |
| G-BLIX | Saro Skeeter Mk 12 (XL809) | A. P. Nowicki | |
| G-BLIY | M.S.892A Rallye Commodore | A. J. Brasher & K. R. Haynes | |
| G-BLIZ | PA-46-310P Malibu | Bachs Ltd | |
| G-BLJD | Glaser-Dirks DG.400 | P. A. Hearne & ptnrs | |
| G-BLJE | AB-206B JetRanger | Nexgen Ltd | |
| G-BLJF | Cameron O-65 balloon | C. Dupernex & L. Kindley | |
| G-BLJG | Cameron N-105 balloon | J. W. Cato | |
| G-BLJH | Cameron N-77 balloon | Phillair | |
| G-BLJI | Colt 105A balloon | Colt Balloons Ltd | |
| G-BLJJ | Cessna 305 Bird Dog | P. Dawe | |
| G-BLJK | Evans VP-2 | R. R. Pierce | |
| G-BLJM | Beech 95-B55 Baron | Elstree Aircraft Hire Ltd | |
| G-BLJN | Nott-Cameron ULD-1 balloon | J. R. P. Nott | |
| G-BLJO | Cessna F.152 | Redhill School of Flying Ltd | |
| G-BLJP | Cessna F.150L | F. & S. E. Horridge/Lasham | |
| G-BLJX | Bensen B.8M | R. Snow | |
| G-BLJY | Sequoia F.8L Falco | K. Morris | |
| G-BLKA | D.H.112 Venom FB.54 (WR410) | A. Topen/Cranfield | |
| G-BLKB | Boeing 737-3T5 | Britannia Airways Ltd/Luton | |
| G-BLKC | Boeing 737-3T5 | Britannia Airways Ltd/Luton | |
| G-BLKD | Boeing 737-3T5 | Britannia Airways Ltd/Luton | |
| G-BLKE | Boeing 737-3T5 | Britannia Airways Ltd/Luton | |
| G-BLKF | Thunder Ax10-160 balloon | Thunder Balloons Ltd | |
| G-BLKG | Thunder Ax10-160 balloon | Thunder Balloons Ltd | |
| G-BLKH | Thunder Ax10-160 balloon | Thunder Balloons Ltd | |
| G-BLKI | Thunder Ax10-160 balloon | Thunder Balloons Ltd | |
| G-BLKJ | Thunder Ax7-65 balloon | D. T. Watkins | |
| G-BLKK | Evans VP-1 | R. W. Burrows | |
| G-BLKL | D.31 Turbulent | D. L. Ripley | |
| G-BLKM | Jodel DR.1051 | T. C. Humphreys | |
| G-BLKP | BAe Jetstream 3102 | British Aerospace PLC/Warton | |
| G-BLKU | Colt 56 SS balloon | Hot-Air Balloon Co Ltd | |
| G-BLKY | Beech 95-58 Baron | Kebbell Holdings Ltd/Leavesden | |
| G-BLKZ | Pilatus P2-05 | Autokraft Ltd | |
| G-BLLA | Bensen B.8M | K. T. Donaghey | |
| G-BLLB | Bensen B.8M | D. H. Moss | |
| G-BLLD | Cameron O-77 balloon | D. C. Strange | |
| G-BLLE | Cameron 60 Burger King SS balloon | Burger King UK Ltd | |
| G-BLLH | Jodel DR.220A 2+2 | D. R. Scott-Longhurst & V. D. Stotter | |
| G-BLLM | PA-23 Aztec 250E | C. & M. Thomas (G-BBNM)/Cardiff | |
| G-BLLN | PA-18 Super Cub 95 | Felthorpe Flying Group Ltd | |
| G-BLLO | PA-18 Super Cub 95 | D. G. & M. G. Marketts | |
| G-BLLP | Slingsby T.67B | Devon School of Flying/Dunkeswell | |
| G-BLLR | Slingsby T.67B | Trent Air Services Ltd/Cranfield | |

| Notes | Reg. | Type | Owner or Operator |
|-------|------|------|-------------------|
| | G-BLLS | Slingsby T.67B | Trent Air Services Ltd/Cranfield |
| | G-BLLT | AA-5B Tiger | Alpha Welding & Engineering Ltd |
| | G-BLLU | Cessna 421C | Bumbles Ltd |
| | G-BLLV | Slingsby T.67B | R. L. Brinklow |
| | G-BLLW | Colt 56B balloon | J. C. Stupples |
| | G-BLLY | Cessna 340A | Thunder & Colt Ltd |
| | G-BLLZ | Rutan LongEz | G. E. Relf & ptnrs |
| | G-BLMA | Zlin 326 Trener Master | G. P. Northcott/Shoreham |
| | G-BLMC | Avro 698 Vulcan B.2A (XM575) ★ | Aeropark/E. Midlands |
| | G-BLME | Robinson R-22 | Skyline Helicopters Ltd |
| | G-BLMG | Grob G.109B | K. & A. Barton |
| | G-BLMI | PA-18 Super Cub 95 | B. J. Borsberry |
| | G-BLMN | Rutan LongEz | G-BLMN Flying Group |
| | G-BLMP | PA-17 Vagabond | M. Austin/Popham |
| | G-BLMR | PA-18 Super Cub 150 | W. J. J. Kamper |
| | G-BLMT | PA-18 Super Cub 135 | I. S. Runnalls |
| | G-BLMV | Jodel DR.1051 | S. Windsor |
| | G-BLMW | T.66 Nipper 3 | S. L. Millar |
| | G-BLMX | Cessna FR.172H | A. J. Fuller & ptnrs/Felthorpe |
| | G-BLMZ | Colt 105A balloon | M. J. Hutchins |
| | G-BLNB | V.802 Viscount | British Air Ferries (G-AOHV)/Southend |
| | G-BLNJ | BN-2B-26 Islander | Loganair Ltd/Glasgow |
| | G-BLNO | FRED Srs 3 | L. W. Smith |
| | G-BLNW | BN-2B-27 Islander | Loganair Ltd/Glasgow |
| | G-BLOA | V.806 Viscount Freightmaster II | British Air Ferries Ltd (G-AOYJ) *Viscount Jock Bryce OBE*/Southend |
| | G-BLOB | Colt 31A balloon | Jacques W. Soukup Ltd |
| | G-BLOC | Rand KR-2 | F. Woodhouse |
| | G-BLOE | PA-31-350 Navajo Chieftain | PW Cleaning Services Ltd (G-NITE) |
| | G-BLOG | Cameron O-77 balloon | M. W. A. Shemilt |
| | G-BLOJ | Thunder Ax7-77 Srs 1 balloon | J. W. Cato |
| | G-BLOK | Colt 77A balloon | D. L. Clark *Spritsa* |
| | G-BLOL | SNCAN Stampe SV-4A | Skysport Engineering Ltd |
| | G-BLOO | Sopwith Dove Replica | Skysport Engineering Ltd |
| | G-BLOR | PA-30 Twin Comanche 160 | Aeros Flying Club Ltd/Staverton |
| | G-BLOS | Cessna 185A (also flown with floats) | E. Brun |
| | G-BLOT | Colt Ax6-56B balloon | H. J. Anderson |
| | G-BLOU | Rand KR-2 | D. Cole |
| | G-BLOV | Colt Ax5-42 Srs 1 balloon | Thunder & Colt Ltd |
| | G-BLPA | Piper J-3C-65 Cub | G. A. Card |
| | G-BLPB | Turner TSW Hot Two Wot | J. R. Woolford & K. M. Thomas |
| | G-BLPE | PA-18 Super Cub 95 | A. Haig-Thomas |
| | G-BLPF | Cessna FR.172G | A. C. McKay & A. H. McVicar |
| | G-BLPG | J/1N Alpha (16693) | P. G. & A. Valentine (G-AZIH) |
| | G-BLPH | Cessna FRA.150L | New Aerobat Group/Shoreham |
| | G-BLPI | Slingsby T.67B | W. F. Hall |
| | G-BLPK | Cameron V-65 balloon | A. J. & C. P. Nicholls |
| | G-BLPM | AS.332L Super Puma | Bristow Helicopters Ltd |
| | G-BLPN | M.S.894E Rallye 220GT | Midair Services Ltd |
| | G-BLPP | Cameron V-77 balloon | L. P. Purfield |
| | G-BLRB | D.H.104 Devon C.2 (VP962) | D. Liddell-Grainger |
| | G-BLRC | PA-18 Super Cub 135 | Grays (Pakefield) Ltd |
| | G-BLRD | MBB Bo.209 Monsun 150FV | M. D. Ward |
| | G-BLRF | Slingsby T.67C | Bristow Helicopters Ltd/Redhill |
| | G-BLRG | Slingsby T.67B | Devon School of Flying/Dunkeswell |
| | G-BLRH | Rutan Long Ez | G. L. Thompson |
| | G-BLRJ | Jodel DR.1051 | M. P. Hallam |
| | G-BLRL | CP.301C-1 Emeraude | R. A. Abrahams/Barton |
| | G-BLRM | Glaser-Dirks DG.400 | D. J. Barke |
| | G-BLRN | D.H.104 Dove 8 (WB531) | C.W. Simpson/Exeter |
| | G-BLRP | FMA IA.58-A Pucara | R. J. H. Butterfield |
| | G-BLRW | Cameron 77 Elephant balloon | Forbes Europe Inc |
| | G-BLRX | SOCATA TB.9 Tampico | Wiselock Ltd/Elstree |
| | G-BLRY | AS.332L Super Puma | Bristow Helicopters Ltd |
| | G-BLRZ | SOCATA TB.9 Tampico | Aldred Associates Ltd |
| | G-BLSC | Consolidated PBY-5A Catalina (JV928) | J. P. Warren Wilson/Duxford |
| | G-BLSD | D.H.112 Venom FB.54 (J-1758) | Aces High Ltd/North Weald |
| | G-BLSF | AA-5A Cheetah | J. P. E. Walsh (G-BGCK) |
| | G-BLSH | Cameron V-77 balloon | C. N. Luffingham |
| | G-BLSI | Colt A5-56 airship | G. F. Turnbull |
| | G-BLSJ | Thunder Ax8-90 balloon | Thunder Balloons Ltd |

| Reg. | Type | Owner or Operator | Notes |
|------|------|-------------------|-------|
| G-BLSK | Colt 77A balloon | Solarmoor Ltd | |
| G-BLSM | H.S.125 Srs 700B | Dravidian Air Services Ltd/Heathrow | |
| G-BLSN | Colt AS-56 airship | Flying Pictures (Balloons) Ltd | |
| G-BLSO | Colt AS-42 airship | Huntair Ltd | |
| G-BLSR | Everett autogyro | R. J. Everett | |
| G-BLST | Cessna 421C | Cecil Aviation Ltd/Cambridge | |
| G-BLSU | Cameron A-210 balloon | Skysales Ltd | |
| G-BLSX | Cameron O-105 balloon | B. J. Petteford | |
| G-BLSY | Bell 222A | Wilkes Asset Management Ltd | |
| G-BLTA | Thunder Ax7-77A | K. A. Schlussler | |
| G-BLTC | D.31 Turbulent | G. P. Smith & A. W. Burton | |
| G-BLTF | Robinson R-22A | Forest Dale Hotels Ltd | |
| G-BLTG | WAR Sea Fury (WJ237) | A. N. R. Houghton & D. H. Nourish | |
| G-BLTK | R. Commander 112TC | B. Rogalewski/Denham | |
| G-BLTM | Robin HR.200/100 | R. Houghton | |
| G-BLTN | Thunder Ax7-65 balloon | J. A. Liddle | |
| G-BLTP | H.S.125 Srs 700B | Dravidian Air Services Ltd/Heathrow | |
| G-BLTR | Scheibe SF.25B Falke | V. Mallon/Germany | |
| G-BLTS | Rutan LongEz | R. W. Cutler | |
| G-BLTT | Slingsby T.67B | Devon School of Flying/Dunkeswell | |
| G-BLTU | Slingsby T.67B | The Neiderhein Powered Flying Club/ Germany | |
| G-BLTV | Slingsby T.67B | Slingsby Aviation PLC/Kirkbymoorside | |
| G-BLTW | Slingsby T.67B | Slingsby Aviation PLC/Kirkbymoorside | |
| G-BLTZ | SOCATA TB.10 Tobago | Martin Ltd/Biggin Hill | |
| G-BLUA | Robinson R-22 | J. R. Budgen | |
| G-BLUE | Colting Ax7-77A balloon | M. R. & C. Cumpston | |
| G-BLUI | Thunder Ax7-65 balloon | S. Johnson | |
| G-BLUJ | Cameron V-56 balloon | J. N. W. West | |
| G-BLUK | Bond Sky Dancer | J. Owen | |
| G-BLUL | Jodel DR.1051/M1 | J. Owen | |
| G-BLUM | SA.365N Dauphin 2 | Bond Helicopters Ltd | |
| G-BLUN | SA.365N Dauphin 2 | Bond Helicopters Ltd | |
| G-BLUO | SA.365N Dauphin 2 | Bond Helicopters Ltd | |
| G-BLUP | SA.365N Dauphin 2 | Bond Helicopters Ltd | |
| G-BLUV | Grob G.109B | Go-Grob Ltd | |
| G-BLUX | Slingsby T.67M | Slingsby Aviation Ltd/Kirkbymoorside | |
| G-BLUY | Colt 69A balloon | The Balloon Goes Up Ltd | |
| G-BLUZ | D.H.82B Queen Bee (LF858) | B. Bayes | |
| G-BLVA | Airtour AH-56 balloon | Airtour Balloon Co Ltd | |
| G-BLVB | Airtour AH-56 balloon | Airtour Balloon Co Ltd | |
| G-BLVC | Airtour AH-31 balloon | Airtour Balloon Co Ltd | |
| G-BLVG | EMB-110P1 Bandeirante | Alexandra Aviation Ltd (G-RLAY) | |
| G-BLVI | Slingsby T.67M | Slingsby Aviation Ltd/Kirkbymoorside | |
| G-BLVK | CAARP CAP-10B | E. K. Coventry/Earls Colne | |
| G-BLVL | PA-28-161 Warrior II | C.S.E. Aviation Ltd/Kidlington | |
| G-BLVN | Cameron N-77 balloon | B. Hodge | |
| G-BLVS | Cessna 150M | W. Lancashire Aero Club Ltd/Woodvale | |
| G-BLVU | Pitts S-2A | A. J. E. Ditheridge | |
| G-BLVV | Bell 206B JetRanger | Bristow Helicopters Ltd | |
| G-BLVW | Cessna F.172H | R. & D. Holloway Ltd | |
| G-BLVY | Colt 21A balloon | Colt Balloons Ltd | |
| G-BLWB | Thunder Ax6-56 balloon | S. A. Simington | |
| G-BLWD | PA-34-200T Seneca | C.S.E. Aviation Ltd/Kidlington | |
| G-BLWE | Colt 90A balloon | Huntair Ltd | |
| G-BLWF | Robin HR.100/210 | N. G. P. Evans | |
| G-BLWG | Varga 2150A Kachina | W. M. Patterson | |
| G-BLWH | Fournier RF-6B-100 | Gloster Aero Club Ltd/Staverton | |
| G-BLWM | Bristol M.1C replica (C4994) ★ | RAF Museum/Hendon | |
| G-BLWP | PA-38-112 Tomahawk | A. Dodd/Booker | |
| G-BLWR | Currie Wot | H. Moffat | |
| G-BLWT | Evans VP-1 | C. J. Bellworthy | |
| G-BLWV | Cessna F.152 | Redhill Flying Club | |
| G-BLWW | Taylor Mini Imp Model C | M. K. Field | |
| G-BLWX | Cameron N-56 balloon | W. Evans | |
| G-BLWY | Robin 2161D | A. Spencer & D. A. Rolfe | |
| G-BLWZ | M.S.883 Rallye 115 | J. H. Betton | |
| G-BLXA | SOCATA TB.20 Trinidad | R. A. McCarthy | |
| G-BLXF | Cameron V-77 balloon | D. I. Gray-Fisk | |
| G-BLXG | Colt 21A balloon | Balloon & Airship Co Ltd | |
| G-BLXH | Fournier RF-3 | A. Rawicz-Szczerbo | |
| G-BLXI | CP.1310-C3 Super Emeraude | RAE Bedford Flying Club | |
| G-BLXK | Agusta-Bell 205 | Autair Helicopters Ltd | |

| Notes | Reg. | Type | Owner or Operator |
|---|---|---|---|
| | G-BLXO | Jodel D.150 | P. R. Powell |
| | G-BLXP | PA-28R Cherokee Arrow 200 | A. M. Bailey |
| | G-BLXR | AS.332L Super Puma | Bristow Helicopters Ltd |
| | G-BLXS | AS.332L Super Puma | Bristow Helicopters Ltd |
| | G-BLXT | RAF SE-5A (B4863) | Museum of Army Flying/Middle Wallop |
| | G-BLXX | PA-23 Aztec 250F | ABR Aviation Ltd (G-PIED) |
| | G-BLXY | Cameron V-65 balloon | Gone With The Wind Ltd |
| | G-BLYB | Beech B200 Super King Air | Alfred McAlpine Aviation Ltd |
| | G-BLYC | PA-38-112 Tomahawk | R. I. Tatlock |
| | G-BLYD | SOCATA TB.20 Trinidad | Air Touring Services Ltd/Biggin Hill |
| | G-BLYE | SOCATA TB.10 Tobago | R. C. Watts |
| | G-BLYJ | Cameron V-77 balloon | E. E. Clark & J. A. Lomas |
| | G-BLYK | PA-34-220T Seneca III | P. G. Somers |
| | G-BLYM | B.121 Pup 2 | D. J. Sage |
| | G-BLYP | Robin 3000/120 | Lydd Air Training Centre Ltd |
| | G-BLYR | Airtour AH-77B balloon | Airtour Balloon Co Ltd |
| | G-BLYT | Airtour AH-77 balloon | Airtour Balloon Co Ltd |
| | G-BLYU | Airtour AH-31 balloon | Airtour Balloon Co Ltd |
| | G-BLYV | Airtour AH-56 balloon | Airtour Balloon Co Ltd |
| | G-BLYY | PA-28-181 Archer II | A. C. Clarke |
| | G-BLZA | Scheibe SF.25B Falke | P. Downes & D. Gardner |
| | G-BLZB | Cameron N-65 balloon | D. Bareford |
| | G-BLZD | Robin R.1180T | J. R. Howard & P. D. Wheatland |
| | G-BLZE | Cessna F.152 | Flairhire Ltd (G-CSSC)/Redhill |
| | G-BLZF | Thunder Ax7-77 balloon | H. M. Savage |
| | G-BLZH | Cessna F.152 | Biggin Hill School of Flying |
| | G-BLZM | Rutan LongEz | Zulu Mike Group |
| | G-BLZN | Bell 206B JetRanger | Helicopter Services |
| | G-BLZP | Cessna F.152 | E. Midlands Flying School Ltd |
| | G-BLZR | Cameron A-140 balloon | Clipper Worldwide Trading Ltd |
| | G-BLZS | Cameron O-77 balloon | M. M. Cobbold |
| | G-BLZT | Short SD3-60 | Air UK Ltd/Norwich |
| | G-BMAA | Douglas DC-9-15 | British Midland Airways Ltd *The Shah Diamond*/(G-BFIH)/E. Midlands |
| | G-BMAB | Douglas DC-9-15 | British Midland Airways Ltd *The Great Mogul Diamond*/E. Midlands |
| | G-BMAC | Douglas DC-9-15 | British Midland Airways Ltd *The Eugenie Diamond*/E. Midlands |
| | G-BMAD | Cameron V-77 balloon | F. J. J. Fielder |
| | G-BMAF | Cessna 180F | P. Channon |
| | G-BMAG | Douglas DC-9-15 | British Midland Airways Ltd *The Nassak Diamond*/E. Midlands |
| | G-BMAH | Douglas DC-9-14 | British Midland Airways Ltd *The Florentine Diamond*/E. Midlands |
| | G-BMAI | Douglas DC-9-14 | British Midland Airways Ltd *The Star of Este Diamond*/E. Midlands |
| | G-BMAK | Douglas DC-9-30 | British Midland Airways Ltd *The Stewart Diamond*/E. Midlands |
| | G-BMAL | Sikorsky S-76A | Bond Helicopters Ltd |
| | G-BMAM | Douglas DC-9-30 | British Midland Airways Ltd *The Cullinan Diamond*/E. Midlands |
| | G-BMAO | Taylor JT.1 Monoplane | V. A. Wordsworth |
| | G-BMAR | Short SD3-60 | Loganair Ltd (G-BLCR)/Glasgow |
| | G-BMAV | AS.350B Ecureuil | Southern Trust Co Ltd/Jersey |
| | G-BMAX | FRED Srs 2 | D. A. Arkley |
| | G-BMAY | PA-18 Super Cub 135 | Target Technology Ltd |
| | G-BMBB | Cessna F.150L | Dacebow Aviation |
| | G-BMBC | PA-31-350 Navajo Chieftain | Air & General Services Ltd |
| | G-BMBE | PA-46-310P Malibu | Barfax Distributing Co Ltd & Glasdon Group Ltd/Blackpool |
| | G-BMBF | Nord 3202B | F. & H. Aircraft Ltd/Breighton |
| | G-BMBI | PA-31-350 Navajo Chieftain | Ennemix Holdings Ltd/E. Midlands |
| | G-BMBJ | Schempp-Hirth Janus CM | Oxfordshire Sportflying Ltd/Enstone |
| | G-BMBR | Issoire D77-M Motor Iris | G. R. Horner |
| | G-BMBS | Colt 105A balloon | H. G. Davies |
| | G-BMBT | Thunder Ax8-90 balloon | Capital Balloon Club Ltd |
| | G-BMBW | Bensen B.80 | M. Vahdat |
| | G-BMBY | Beech A36 Bonanza | Arthur Webb Engineers Ltd/Birmingham |
| | G-BMBZ | Scheibe SF.25E Super Falke | Buckminster Super Falke Syndicate |
| | G-BMCC | Thunder Ax7-77 balloon | H. N. Harben Ltd |
| | G-BMCD | Cameron V-65 balloon | M. C. Drye |

| Reg. | Type | Owner or Operator | Notes |
|------|------|-------------------|-------|
| G-BMCE | Bensen B.8M | J. Lee | |
| G-BMCG | Grob G.109B | Lagerholm Finnimport Ltd/Booker | |
| G-BMCH | AB-206B JetRanger | Trent Air Services Ltd/Cranfield | |
| G-BMCI | Cessna F.172H | A. B. Davis/Edinburgh | |
| G-BMCJ | PA-31-350 Navajo Chieftain | Chelsea Land (Finance) Ltd | |
| G-BMCK | Cameron O-77 balloon | D. L. Smith | |
| G-BMCM | Grob G.109B | Sonardyne Ltd/Blackbushe | |
| G-BMCN | Cessna F.152 | Lincoln Aero Club Ltd/Sturgate | |
| G-BMCO | Colomban MC.15 Cri-Cri | G. P. Clarke/Enstone | |
| G-BMCS | PA-22 Tri-Pacer 135 | C. J. Weaver | |
| G-BMCV | Cessna F.152 | Leicestershire Aero Club Ltd | |
| G-BMCW | AS.332L Super Puma | Bristow Helicopters Ltd | |
| G-BMCX | AS.332L Super Puma | Bristow Helicopters Ltd | |
| G-BMCZ | Colt 69A balloon | Thunder & Colt Ltd | |
| G-BMDB | SE-5A replica (F235) | D. Biggs | |
| G-BMDC | PA-32-301 Saratoga | Maclaren Aviation/Newcastle | |
| G-BMDD | Slingsby T.29 | A. R. Worters | |
| G-BMDE | Pientenpol Air Camper | D. Silsbury | |
| G-BMDF | Boeing 737-2E7 | Dan-Air Services Ltd/Gatwick | |
| G-BMDG | Cameron O-105 balloon | Buddy Bombard Balloons Ltd | |
| G-BMDH | Cameron O-105 balloon | Buddy Bombard Balloons Ltd | |
| G-BMDI | Thunder Ax8-105Z balloon | Buddy Bombard Balloons Ltd | |
| G-BMDJ | Price Ax7-77S balloon | T. S. Price | |
| G-BMDK | PA-34-220T Seneca III | Triple Oak Ltd | |
| G-BMDO | ARV Super 2 | H. L. Wensley | |
| G-BMDP | Partenavia P.64B Oscar 200 | D. Foey | |
| G-BMDS | Jodel D.120 | D. Stansfield | |
| G-BMDV | Bell 47G-5 | Trent Air Services Ltd/Cranfield | |
| G-BMDW | Dangerous Sports Club/Colt Hoppalong 1 balloon | D. A. C. Kirke | |
| G-BMDY | GA-7 Cougar | P. J. Bristow | |
| G-BMEA | PA-18 Super Cub 95 | C. L. Towell | |
| G-BMEB | Rotorway Scorpion 145 | I. M. Bartlett | |
| G-BMEE | Cameron O-105 balloon | A. G. R. Calder | |
| G-BMEG | SOCATA TB.10 Tobago | G. H. N. & R. V. Chamberlain | |
| G-BMEH | Jodel Special Super Mascaret | W. Coupar Ltd | |
| G-BMEJ | PA-28R Cherokee Arrow 200 | London Flight Centre (Stansted) Ltd | |
| G-BMEK | Mooney M.20K | Atlantic Film Investments Ltd/USA | |
| G-BMET | Taylor JT.1 Monoplane | M. K. A. Blyth | |
| G-BMEU | Isaacs Fury II | A. W. Austin | |
| G-BMEX | Cessna A.150K | S. G. Eldred & N. A. M. Brain | |
| G-BMEZ | Cameron DP-70 airship | Cameron Balloons Ltd | |
| G-BMFD | PA-23 Aztec 250F | Rangemile Ltd (G-BGYY)/Coventry | |
| G-BMFG | Dornier Do.27A-4 (3460) | R. F. Warner | |
| G-BMFH | Dornier Do.27A-4 (3497) | Onderstar Aviation Ltd/Booker | |
| G-BMFI | PZL SZD-45A Ogar | Marrix Ltd/Redhill | |
| G-BMFL | Rand KR-2 | E. W. B. Comber & M. F. Leusby | |
| G-BMFN | QAC Quickie Tri-Q.200 | A. W. Webster | |
| G-BMFP | PA-28-161 Warrior II | T. J. Froggatt & ptnrs/Blackbushe | |
| G-BMFT | H.S.748 Srs 2A | — | |
| G-BMFU | Cameron N-90 balloon | J. J. Rudoni | |
| G-BMFW | Hughes 369E | Ford Helicopters Ltd | |
| G-BMFY | Grob G.109B | P. J. Shearer | |
| G-BMFZ | Cessna F.152 | Cornwall Flying Club Ltd | |
| G-BMGB | PA-28R Cherokee Arrow 200 | Malmesbury Specialist Cars | |
| G-BMGC | Fairey Swordfish Mk II (W5856) | FAA Museum/Yeovilton | |
| G-BMGD | Colt 17A balloon | Airbureau Ltd | |
| G-BMGG | Cessna 152 | EFG Flying Services Ltd/Biggin Hill | |
| G-BMGH | PA-31-325 Turbo Navajo C/R | Jet West Ltd/Exeter | |
| G-BMGP | Hughes 269C | Orion Atlantic Ltd | |
| G-BMGR | Grob G.109B | BMGR Group/Lasham | |
| G-BMGT | Cessna 310R | Air Service Training Ltd/Perth | |
| G-BMGV | Robinson R-22 | D. L. Weldon | |
| G-BMGY | Lake LA-4-200 Buccaneer | M. A. Ashmole (G-BWKS/G-BDDI) | |
| G-BMHA | Rutan Long Ez | S. F. Elvins | |
| G-BMHC | Cessna U.206G | Clacton Aero Club (1988) Ltd | |
| G-BMHI | Cessna F.152 | Skyviews & General Ltd/Leeds | |
| G-BMHJ | Thunder Ax7-65 balloon | M. G. Robinson | |
| G-BMHK | Cameron V-77 balloon | B. J. Workman | |
| G-BMHL | Wittman W.8 Tailwind | T. G. Hoult | |
| G-BMHN | Robinson R-22A | Fulford Builders (York) Ltd | |
| G-BMHR | Grob G.109B | HRN Aviation Ltd | |
| G-BMHS | Cessna F.172M | C. H. Ludar-Smith | |

| Notes | Reg. | Type | Owner or Operator |
|-------|------|------|-------------------|
| | G-BMHT | PA-28RT-201T Turbo Arrow IV | Relay Services Ltd |
| | G-BMHX | Short SD3-60 | Loganair Ltd/Glasgow |
| | G-BMHY | Short SD3-60 | Air Europe Express/Gatwick |
| | G-BMHZ | PA-28RT-201T Turbo Arrow IV | M. A. Grayburn |
| | G-BMIA | Thunder Ax8-90 balloon | A. G. R. Calder |
| | G-BMIB | Bell 206B JetRanger | Lee Aviation Ltd/Booker |
| | G-BMID | Jodel D.120 | P. D. Smoothy |
| | G-BMIF | AS.350B Ecureuil | Colt Car Co Ltd/Staverton |
| | G-BMIG | Cessna 172N | J. R. Nicholls/Conington |
| | G-BMIM | Rutan LongEz | R. M. Smith |
| | G-BMIO | Stoddard-Hamilton Glasair RG | A. H. Carrington |
| | G-BMIP | Jodel D.112 | M. T. Kinch |
| | G-BMIR | Westland Wasp HAS.1 (XT788) | R. Windley |
| | G-BMIS | Monnet Sonerai II | B. A. Bower/Thruxton |
| | G-BMIV | PA-28R-201T Turbo Arrow III | Maurice Mason Ltd |
| | G-BMIW | PA-28-181 Archer II | Oldbus Ltd |
| | G-BMIY | Oldfield Baby Great Lakes | J. B. Scott (G-NOME) |
| | G-BMJA | PA-32R-301 Saratoga SP | Continental Cars (Stansted) Ltd |
| | G-BMJB | Cessna 152 | Bobbington Air Training School Ltd/<br>Halfpenny Green |
| | G-BMJC | Cessna 152 | Cambridge Aero Club Ltd |
| | G-BMJD | Cessna 152 | Fife Airport Management Ltd/<br>Glenrothes |
| | G-BMJG | PA-28R Cherokee Arrow 200 | D. J. D. Ritchie & ptnrs/Elstree |
| | G-BMJL | R. Commander 114 | H. Snelson |
| | G-BMJM | Evans VP-1 | J. A. Mawby |
| | G-BMJN | Cameron O-65 balloon | E. J. A. Machole |
| | G-BMJO | PA-34-220T Seneca III | B. Walker & Co (Dursley) Ltd &<br>John Ward (Holdings) Ltd |
| | G-BMJP | Colt AS-56 airship | Thunder & Colt Ltd |
| | G-BMJR | Cessna T.337H | John Roberts Services Ltd (G-NOVA) |
| | G-BMJS | Thunder Ax7-77 balloon | Anglia Balloon School Ltd |
| | G-BMJT | Beech 76 Duchess | Mike Osborne Properties Ltd |
| | G-BMJW | NA AT-6D Harvard III (EZ259) | J. Woods |
| | G-BMJX | Wallis WA-116X | K. H. Wallis |
| | G-BMJY | Yakolev C18M | R. Lamplough/North Weald |
| | G-BMJZ | Cameron N-90 balloon | Windsor Pharmaceuticals Ltd |
| | G-BMKB | PA-18 Super Cub 135 | C. Marsh |
| | G-BMKC | Piper J-3C-65 Cub (329854) | R. J. H. Springall |
| | G-BMKD | Beech C90A King Air | A. E. Bristow |
| | G-BMKE | PA-28RT-201 Arrow IV | AT Aviation Ltd/Cardiff |
| | G-BMKF | Jodel DR.221 | B. M. R. Clavel & J. M. A. Lassauze |
| | G-BMKG | PA-38-112 Tomahawk | R. J. Hickson |
| | G-BMKH | Colt 105A balloon | Thunder & Colt Ltd |
| | G-BMKI | Colt 21A balloon | Thunder & Colt Ltd |
| | G-BMKJ | Cameron V-77 balloon | R. C. Thursby |
| | G-BMKK | PA-28R Cherokee Arrow 200 | Arrow Aviation |
| | G-BMKM | AB-206B JetRanger 3 | Fizzle Ltd |
| | G-BMKN | Colt 31A balloon | Thunder & Colt Ltd |
| | G-BMKO | PA-28-181 Archer II | Northfield Garage (Cowdenbeath) Ltd |
| | G-BMKP | Cameron V-77 balloon | Jacques W. Soukup Enterprises Ltd |
| | G-BMKR | PA-28-161 Warrior II | Field Flying Group (G-BGKR)/<br>Goodwood |
| | G-BMKV | Thunder Ax7-77 balloon | A. Hornak & M. J. Nadel |
| | G-BMKW | Cameron V-77 balloon | A. C. Garnett |
| | G-BMKX | Cameron 77 Elephant balloon | Cameron Balloons Ltd |
| | G-BMKY | Cameron O-65 balloon | First Reflex Ltd |
| | G-BMLA | Bell UH-1H ★ | Grampian Helicopters International Ltd |
| | G-BMLB | Jodel D.120A | W. O. Brown |
| | G-BMLC | Short SD3-60 Variant 100 | Loganair Ltd/Glasgow |
| | G-BMLH | Mooney M.20C | G. D. Bowd |
| | G-BMLJ | Cameron N-77 balloon | C. J. Dunkley |
| | G-BMLK | Grob G.109B | A. Batters/Rufforth |
| | G-BMLL | Grob G.109B | A. H. R. Stansfield |
| | G-BMLP | Boeing 727-264 | Dan-Air Services Ltd/Gatwick |
| | G-BMLS | PA-28R-201 Arrow III | Faukland Flyers Ltd |
| | G-BMLT | Pietenpol Air Camper | R. A. & F. A. Hawke/Redhill |
| | G-BMLU | Colt 90A balloon | Danish Catering Services Ltd |
| | G-BMLV | Robinson R-22A | Skyline Helicopters Ltd/Booker |
| | G-BMLW | Cameron V-65 balloon | M. L. & L. P. Willoughby |
| | G-BMLX | Cessna F.150L | S. G. P. Foster/Headcorn |
| | G-BMLY | Grob G.109B | P. H. Yarrow & D. G. Margetts |
| | G-BMLZ | Cessna 421C | Jet West Ltd (G-OTAD/G-BEVL)/Exeter |

| Reg. | Type | Owner or Operator | Notes |
|---|---|---|---|
| G-BMMC | Cessna T310Q | Cooper Clegg Ltd | |
| G-BMMD | Rand KR-2 | K. R. Wheatley & R. S. Stoddart-Jones | |
| G-BMMF | FRED Srs 2 | J. M. Jones | |
| G-BMMG | Thunder Ax 7-77 balloon | G. V. Beckwith | |
| G-BMMI | Pazmany PL.4 | M. L. Martin | |
| G-BMMJ | Siren PIK-30 | G-BMMJ Flying Group | |
| G-BMMK | Cessna 182P | M. S. Knight/Goodwood | |
| G-BMML | PA-38-112 Tomahawk | Andrew Dick & Son (Engineers) Ltd | |
| G-BMMM | Cessna 152 | Luton Flight Training | |
| G-BMMN | Thunder Ax8-105 balloon | R. C. Weyda | |
| G-BMMP | Grob G.109B | B. F. Fraser-Smith & B. F. Pearson | |
| G-BMMR | Dornier Do.228-200 | Suckling Airways Ltd/Cambridge | |
| G-BMMU | Thunder Ax8-105 balloon | H. C. Wright | |
| G-BMMV | ICA-Brasov IS-28M2A | T. Cust | |
| G-BMMW | Thunder Ax7-77 balloon | P. A. Georges | |
| G-BMMX | ICA-Brasov IS-28M2A | M. Lee & ptnrs | |
| G-BMMY | Thunder Ax7-77 balloon | Double Glazing Components Ltd | |
| G-BMMZ | Boeing 737-2D6 | Britannia Airways Ltd/Luton | |
| G-BMNF | Beech B200 Super King Air | Bernard Matthews PLC/Norwich | |
| G-BMNL | PA-28R Cherokee Arrow 200 | Airways Aero Associations Ltd/Booker | |
| G-BMNP | PA-38-112 Tomahawk | Seal Executive Aircraft Ltd | |
| G-BMNT | PA-34-220T Seneca III | Airpart Supply Ltd | |
| G-BMNU | Cameron V-77 balloon | B. K. & G. S. Palmer | |
| G-BMNV | SNCAN Stampe SV-4D | Wessex Aviation & Transport Ltd | |
| G-BMNW | PA-31-350 Navajo Chieftain | K. Fletcher/Coventry | |
| G-BMNX | Colt 56A balloon | J. H. Dryden | |
| G-BMNY | Everett gyroplane | G. Jenkis-Lover | |
| G-BMNZ | Cessna U206F | Macpara Ltd/Shobdon | |
| G-BMOE | PA-28R Cherokee Arrow 200 | B. J. Mason/Shoreham | |
| G-BMOF | Cessna U206G | Integrated Hydraulics Ltd | |
| G-BMOG | Thunder Ax7-77A balloon | Anglia Balloon School Ltd | |
| G-BMOH | Cameron N-77 balloon | Legal & General PLC | |
| G-BMOI | Partenavia P.68B | Simmette Ltd | |
| G-BMOJ | Cameron V-56 balloon | S. R. Bridge | |
| G-BMOK | ARV Super 2 | Nik Coates Ltd | |
| G-BMOL | PA-23 Aztec 250D | LDL Enterprises (G-BBSR)/Elstree | |
| G-BMOM | ICA-Brasov IS-28M2A | R. E. Todd | |
| G-BMOO | FRED Srs 2 | N. Purllant | |
| G-BMOP | PA-28R-201T Turbo Arrow III | Coleridge Self Service/Cardiff | |
| G-BMOT | Bensen B.8M | R. S. W. Jones | |
| G-BMOV | Cameron O-105 balloon | C. Gillott | |
| G-BMOW | G.159 Gulfstream 1 | Birmingham European Airways Ltd | |
| G-BMOX | Hovey Beta Bird | A. D. Tatton | |
| G-BMPA | G.159 Gulfstream 1 | Aberdeen Airways Ltd | |
| G-BMPC | PA-28-181 Archer II | Trent Securities Ltd | |
| G-BMPD | Cameron V-65 balloon | G. J. Barton | |
| G-BMPF | OA.7 Optica | Brooklands Aircraft Co Ltd/Old Sarum | |
| G-BMPI | OA.7 Optica | Optica Industries Ltd/Old Sarum | |
| G-BMPL | OA.7 Optica | Hampshire Police Authority (Air Support Unit)/Lee-on-Solent | |
| G-BMPM | OA.7 Optica | Optica Industries Ltd/Old Sarum | |
| G-BMPN | OA.7 Optica | Optica Industries Ltd/Old Sarum | |
| G-BMPO | Cessna 182Q | City Flying Group/Swansea | |
| G-BMPP | Cameron N-77 balloon | Sarnia Balloon Group | |
| G-BMPR | PA-28R-201 Arrow III | AH Flight Services Ltd | |
| G-BMPS | Strojnik S-2A | G. J. Green | |
| G-BMPU | Robinson R-22 | Sloane Helicopters Ltd/Luton | |
| G-BMPY | D.H.82A Tiger Moth | S. M. F. Eisenstein | |
| G-BMRA | Boeing 757-236 | British Airways *Beaumaris Castle*/Heathrow | |
| G-BMRB | Boeing 757-236 | British Airways *Colchester Castle*/Heathrow | |
| G-BMRC | Boeing 757-236 | British Airways *Rochester Castle*/Heathrow | |
| G-BMRD | Boeing 757-236 | British Airways *Bothwell Castle*/Heathrow | |
| G-BMRE | Boeing 757-236 | British Airways *Killyleagh Castle*/Heathrow | |
| G-BMRF | Boeing 757-236 | British Airways *Hever Castle*/Heathrow | |
| G-BMRG | Boeing 757-236 | British Airways *Caerphilly Castle*/Heathrow | |
| G-BMRH | Boeing 757-236 | British Airways *Norwich Castle*/Heathrow | |

| Notes | Reg. | Type | Owner or Operator |
|---|---|---|---|
| | G-BMRI | Boeing 757-236 | British Airways *Tonbridge Castle*/Heathrow |
| | G-BMRJ | Boeing 757-236 | British Airways *Old Wardour Castle*/Heathrow |
| | G-BMSA | Stinson HW.75 Voyager | P. F. Bennison (G-BCUM)/Barton |
| | G-BMSB | V.S.509 Spitfire IX (MJ627) | M. S. Bayliss (G-ASOZ) |
| | G-BMSC | Evans VP-2 | F. R. Donaldson |
| | G-BMSD | PA-28-181 Archer II | Courtridge Ltd |
| | G-BMSE | Valentin Taifun 17E | K. P. O'Sullivan & G. T. Birks/Booker |
| | G-BMSF | PA-38-112 Tomahawk | N. Bradley/Leeds |
| | G-BMSG | Saab 32A Lansen ★ | Aces High Ltd/Cranfield |
| | G-BMSI | Cameron N-105 balloon | Direction Air Conditioning Ltd |
| | G-BMSK | Hoffman H-36 Dimona | J. P. Kovacs |
| | G-BMSL | FRED Srs 3 | A. C. Coombe |
| | G-BMSP | Hughes 369HS | R. Windley |
| | G-BMSR | G.159 Gulfstream 1 | Aberdeen Airways Ltd |
| | G-BMST | Cameron N-31 balloon | Hot Air Balloon Co Ltd |
| | G-BMSU | Cessna 152 | M. T. Tidswell |
| | G-BMSW | Cessna T.210M | Foxgrove Construction Ltd |
| | G-BMSX | PA-30 Twin Comanche 160 | M. Sparks/Bristol |
| | G-BMSY | Cameron A-140 balloon | GT Flying Clubs Ltd |
| | G-BMSZ | Cessna 152 | Aerohire Ltd |
| | G-BMTA | Cessna 152 | Paysure Ltd/Edinburgh |
| | G-BMTB | Cessna 152 | J. A. Pothecary/Shoreham |
| | G-BMTJ | Cessna 152 | Creaton Aviation Services Ltd |
| | G-BMTK | Cessna 152 | N. A. Ali |
| | G-BMTL | Cessna 152 | Agricultural & General Aviation/Bournemouth |
| | G-BMTN | Cameron O-77 balloon | Industrial Services (MH) Ltd |
| | G-BMTO | PA-38-112 Tomahawk | N. A. Ali |
| | G-BMTP | PA-38-112 Tomahawk | R. A. Wakefield |
| | G-BMTR | PA-28-161 Warrior II | London Flight Centre (Stansted) Ltd |
| | G-BMTS | Cessna 172N | Luton Flight Training Ltd |
| | G-BMTU | Pitts S-1E Special | O. R. Howe |
| | G-BMTW | PA-31-350 Navajo Chieftain | Air Northwest Ltd |
| | G-BMTX | Cameron V-77 balloon | J. A. Langley |
| | G-BMTY | Colt 77A balloon | L. D. Ormerod |
| | G-BMUD | Cessna 182P | M. A. Hocking |
| | G-BMUE | Boeing 727-81 | Ali Finance Ltd |
| | G-BMUG | Rutan LongEz | P. Richardson & J. Shanley |
| | G-BMUH | Bensen B.8M-R | J. M. Montgomerie |
| | G-BMUI | Brügger MB.2 Colibri | Carlton Flying Group/Netherthorpe |
| | G-BMUJ | Colt Drachenfisch balloon | Air 2 Air Ltd |
| | G-BMUK | Colt UFO balloon | Air 2 Air Ltd |
| | G-BMUL | Colt Kindermond balloon | Air 2 Air Ltd |
| | G-BMUN | Cameron Harley 78 balloon | Forbes Europe Inc/France |
| | G-BMUO | Cessna A.152 | Redhill Flying Club |
| | G-BMUR | Cameron gas airship | Cameron Balloons Ltd |
| | G-BMUT | PA-34-200T Seneca II | G. G. Long |
| | G-BMUU | Thunder Ax7-77 balloon | Thunder & Colt Ltd |
| | G-BMUZ | PA-28-161 Warrior II | Newcastle-upon-Tyne Aero Club Ltd |
| | G-BMVA | Schiebe SF.25B Falke | R. Brown |
| | G-BMVB | Cessna 152 | Light Planes (Lancashire) Ltd/Barton |
| | G-BMVE | PA-28RT-201 Arrow IV | F. E. Gooding/Biggin Hill |
| | G-BMVG | QAC Quickie Q.1 | P. M. Wright |
| | G-BMVI | Cameron O-105 balloon | Heart of England Balloons |
| | G-BMVJ | Cessna 172N | G & B Aviation Ltd/Coventry |
| | G-BMVK | PA-38-112 Tomahawk | Airways Aero Associations Ltd/Booker |
| | G-BMVL | PA-38-112 Tomahawk | Airways Aero Associations Ltd/Booker |
| | G-BMVM | PA-38-112 Tomahawk | Airways Aero Associations Ltd/Booker |
| | G-BMVO | Cameron O-77 balloon | Warners Motors (Leasing) Ltd |
| | G-BMVS | Cameron 77 SS balloon | Shellrise Ltd |
| | G-BMVT | Thunder Ax7-77A balloon | M. L. & L. P. Willoughby |
| | G-BMVU | Monnet Moni | S. R. Jee |
| | G-BMVV | Rutan Vari-Viggen | G. B. Roberts |
| | G-BMVW | Cameron O-65 balloon | S. P. Richards |
| | G-BMVX | M.S.733 Alcyon Srs 1 | J. D. Read |
| | G-BMVY | Beech B200 Super King Air | A. F. Budge (Aviation) Ltd/Gamston |
| | G-BMVZ | Cameron 66 Cornetto SS balloon | Gone With The Wind Ltd |
| | G-BMWA | Hughes 269C | Southern Air Ltd/Shoreham |
| | G-BMWB | Cessna 421C | Capital Trading Aviation Ltd/Cardiff |
| | G-BMWE | ARV Super 2 | Interair (Aviation) Ltd/Bournemouth |
| | G-BMWF | ARV Super 2 | ARV Aviation Ltd/Sandown |

| Reg. | Type | Owner or Operator | Notes |
|------|------|-------------------|-------|
| G-BMWG | ARV Super 2 | Falstaff Finance Ltd/Sandown | |
| G-BMWJ | ARV Super 2 | ARV Aviation Ltd/Sandown | |
| G-BMWM | ARV Super 2 | Adrianair Ltd | |
| G-BMWN | Cameron 80 SS Temple balloon | Forbes Europe Inc | |
| G-BMWP | PA-34-200T Seneca II | R. H. Steward | |
| G-BMWR | R. Commander 112A | M. Edwards & B. Fields | |
| G-BMWU | Cameron N-42 balloon | The Hot Air Balloon Co Ltd | |
| G-BMWV | Putzer Elster B | E. A. J. Hibberd | |
| G-BMWX | Robinson R-22B | P. D. Bruce | |
| G-BMXA | Cessna 152 | Chamberlain Leasing | |
| G-BMXB | Cessna 152 | Andrewsfield Flying Club Ltd | |
| G-BMXC | Cessna 152 | Vectair Aviation Ltd | |
| G-BMXD | F.27 Friendship Mk 500 | Air UK Ltd *Victor Hugo*/Norwich | |
| G-BMXH | Robinson R-22HP | South West Helicopters Ltd | |
| G-BMXJ | Cessna F.150L | J. W. G. Ellis | |
| G-BMXL | PA-38-112 Tomahawk | Airways Aero Associations Ltd/Booker | |
| G-BMXM | Colt 180A balloon | Thunder & Colt Ltd | |
| G-BMXW | D.H.C.6 Twin Otter 310 | Loganair Ltd/Glasgow | |
| G-BMXX | Cessna 152 | Aerohire Ltd/Halfpenny Green | |
| G-BMXY | Scheibe SF.25B Falke | Marrix Ltd | |
| G-BMYA | Colt 56A balloon | Flying Pictures (Balloons) Ltd | |
| G-BMYC | SOCATA TB.10 Tobago | C. J. Crooks/Southampton | |
| G-BMYD | Beech A36 Bonanza | F. B. Gibbons & Sons Ltd | |
| G-BMYE | BAe 146-200 | British Aerospace PLC (G-WAUS/ G-WISC)/Hatfield | |
| G-BMYF | Bensen B.8M | T. H. G. Russell | |
| G-BMYG | Cessna F.152 | Rolim Ltd/Aberdeen | |
| G-BMYH | Rotorway Executive 133 | J. Netherwood | |
| G-BMYI | AA-5 Traveler | W. C. & S. C. Westran | |
| G-BMYJ | Cameron V-65 balloon | S. M. Antony & R. J. Christopher | |
| G-BMYK | BAe ATP | British Midland Airways Ltd/E. Midlands | |
| G-BMYL | BAe ATP | British Midland Airways Ltd/E. Midlands | |
| G-BMYM | BAe ATP | British Midland Airways Ltd/E. Midlands | |
| G-BMYN | Colt 77A balloon | J. D. Shapland & ptnrs | |
| G-BMYO | Cameron V-65 balloon | N. V. Moreton | |
| G-BMYP | Fairey Gannet AEW.3 (XL502) | R. King | |
| G-BMYR | Robinson R-22 | B. Warrington | |
| G-BMYS | Thunder Ax7-77Z balloon | J. E. Weidema | |
| G-BMYT | Boeing 727-51 | Ali Finance Ltd | |
| G-BMYU | Jodel D.120 | G. Davies | |
| G-BMYV | Bensen B.8M | R. G. Cotman | |
| G-BMYW | Hughes 269C | William Tomkins Ltd | |
| G-BMZA | Air Command 503 Commander | R. W. Husband | |
| G-BMZB | Cameron N-77 balloon | D. C. Eager | |
| G-BMZC | Cessna 421C | Gilchrist Enterprises | |
| G-BMZD | Beech C90 King Air | Colt Transport Ltd | |
| G-BMZE | SOCATA TB.9 Tampico | Air Touring Services Ltd/Biggin Hill | |
| G-BMZF | Mikoyan Gurevich MiG-15 (1420) ★ | FAA Museum/Yeovilton | |
| G-BMZG | QAC Quickie Q.2 | K. W. Brooker | |
| G-BMZH | Cameron A-140 balloon | The Balloon Stable Ltd | |
| G-BMZJ | Colt 400A balloon | Thunder & Colt Ltd | |
| G-BMZM | Rand KR-2 | K. McNaughton | |
| G-BMZN | Everett gyroplane | R. J. Brown | |
| G-BMZO | — | — | |
| G-BMZP | Everett gyroplane | B. C. Norris | |
| G-BMZR | — | — | |
| G-BMZS | Everett gyroplane | C. W. Cload | |
| G-BMZV | Cessna 172P | Mid Shires Aviation Ltd | |
| G-BMZW | Bensen B.8 | P. D. Widdicombe | |
| G-BMZX | Wolf W-II Boredom Fighter (146-11042) | J. J. Penney | |
| G-BMZZ | Stephens Akro Z | P. G. Kynsey & J. Harper/Redhill | |
| G-BNAA | V.806 Viscount | British Air Ferries (G-AOYH)/Southend | |
| G-BNAB | GA-7 Cougar | Brod Gallery (G-BGYP)/Elstree | |
| G-BNAC | Jurca MJ-100 Spitfire | S. E. Richards | |
| G-BNAD | Rand KR-2 | R. A. Davis | |
| G-BNAG | Colt 105A balloon | R. W. Batcholer | |
| G-BNAH | Colt Paper Bag SS balloon | Thrustell Ltd | |
| G-BNAI | Wolf W-II Boredom Fighter (146-11083) | P. J. D. Gronow | |
| G-BNAJ | Cessna 152 | G. Duncan | |

| Notes | Reg. | Type | Owner or Operator |
|-------|------|------|-------------------|
| | G-BNAL | F.27 Friendship Mk 600 | Air UK Ltd/Norwich |
| | G-BNAM | Colt 8A balloon | Thunder & Colt Ltd |
| | G-BNAN | Cameron V-65 balloon | A. M. Lindsay |
| | G-BNAO | Colt AS-105 airship | Heather Flight Ltd |
| | G-BNAP | Colt 240A balloon | Heather Flight Ltd |
| | G-BNAR | Taylor JT.1 Monoplane | C. J. Smith |
| | G-BNAU | Cameron V-65 balloon | J. Buckle |
| | G-BNAV | Rutan Cozy | G. E. Broome |
| | G-BNAW | Cameron V-65 balloon | A. Walker |
| | G-BNAY | Grob G.109B | Microperm Ltd |
| | G-BNBD | Short SD3-60 | Air Europe Express/Gatwick |
| | G-BNBJ | AS.355F-1 Twin Squirrel | Coln Helicopters Ltd |
| | G-BNBL | Thunder Ax7-77 balloon | J. R. Henderson |
| | G-BNBM | Colt 90A balloon | Huntair Ltd |
| | G-BNBN | Replica P-38 Lightning | R. C. Cummings |
| | G-BNBR | Cameron N-90 balloon | Morning Star Motors Ltd |
| | G-BNBU | Bensen B.8MV | D. T. Murchie |
| | G-BNBV | Thunder Ax7-77 balloon | J. M. Robinson |
| | G-BNBW | Thunder Ax7-77 balloon | I. S. & S. W. Watthews |
| | G-BNBY | Beech 95-B55A Baron | C. Wright (G-AXXR) |
| | G-BNBZ | LET L-200D Morava | M. Emery/Redhill |
| | G-BNCA | Lightning F.2A ★ | P. Hoar/Cranfield |
| | G-BNCB | Cameron V-77 balloon | Tyred & Battered Balloon Group |
| | G-BNCC | Thunder Ax7-77 balloon | C. J. Burnhope |
| | G-BNCE | G.159 Gulfstream 1 | Aberdeen Airways Ltd |
| | G-BNCG | QAC Quickie Q.2 | T. F. Francis |
| | G-BNCH | Cameron V-77 balloon | Royal Engineers Balloon Club |
| | G-BNCJ | Cameron N-77 balloon | I. S. Bridge |
| | G-BNCK | Cameron V-77 balloon | G. Randall/W. Germany |
| | G-BNCL | WG.13 Lynx HAS.2 (XX469) | J. E. Wilkie/Blackpool |
| | G-BNCM | Cameron N-77 balloon | S. & A. Stone Ltd |
| | G-BNCN | Glaser-Dirks DG.400 | M. C. Costin |
| | G-BNCO | PA-38-112 Tomahawk | Cambrian Flying Club/Swansea |
| | G-BNCR | PA-28-161 Warrior II | Airways Aero Associations Ltd/Booker |
| | G-BNCS | Cessna 180 | C. Elwell Transport Ltd |
| | G-BNCU | Thunder Ax7-77 balloon | G. C. Scott |
| | G-BNCV | Bensen B.8 | L. W. Cload |
| | G-BNCW | Boeing 767-204 | Britannia Airways Ltd/Luton |
| | G-BNCX | Hunter T.7 | Lovaux Ltd |
| | G-BNCY | F.27 Friendship Mk 500 | Air UK Ltd *Lillie Langtry*/Norwich |
| | G-BNCZ | Rutan LongEz | R. M. Bainbridge/Sherburn |
| | G-BNDD | PA-31-310 Turbo Navajo B | Aviation & Marine Interiors Ltd |
| | G-BNDG | Wallis WA-201/R Srs1 | K. H. Wallis |
| | G-BNDH | Colt 21A balloon | Hot-Air Balloon Co Ltd |
| | G-BNDI | Short SD3-60 Variant 100 | Air Europe Express (G-OBLK)/Gatwick |
| | G-BNDK | Short SD3-60 Variant 100 | Air Europe Express (G-OBHD)/Gatwick |
| | G-BNDM | Short SD3-60 Variant 100 | Birmingham European Airways Ltd |
| | G-BNDN | Cameron V-77 balloon | J. A. Smith |
| | G-BNDO | Cessna 152 II | V. B. Cheesewright |
| | G-BNDP | Brügger MB.2 Colibri | D. A. Peet |
| | G-BNDR | SOCATA TB.10 Tobago | Air Touring Services Ltd/Biggin Hill |
| | G-BNDS | PA-31-350 Navajo Chieftain | Abingway Ltd |
| | G-BNDT | Brügger MB.2 Colibri | Bolkow Flying Group |
| | G-BNDV | Cameron V-77 balloon | R. Jones |
| | G-BNDW | D.H.82A Tiger Moth | N. D. Welch |
| | G-BNDY | Cessna 425-1 | Standard Aviation Ltd/Newcastle |
| | G-BNED | PA-22 Tri-Pacer 135 | P. Storey |
| | G-BNEE | PA-28R-201 Arrow III | Britannic Management (Aviation) Ltd |
| | G-BNEF | PA-31-310 Turbo Navajo B | Pulsegrove Ltd/Shoreham |
| | G-BNEH | BAe 125 Srs 800B | High Speed Flight Ltd |
| | G-BNEI | PA-34-200T Seneca II | A. Bucknole |
| | G-BNEJ | PA-38-112 Tomahawk | V. C. & S. G. Swindell |
| | G-BNEK | PA-38-112 Tomahawk | Seal Executive Aircraft Ltd/E. Midlands |
| | G-BNEL | PA-28-161 Warrior II | J. A. Pothecary/Shoreham |
| | G-BNEN | PA-34-200T Seneca II | Willall Ltd |
| | G-BNEO | Cameron V-77 balloon | Graham Tatum & Sons Ltd |
| | G-BNEP | PA-34-220T Seneca III | Handhorn Ltd/Blackpool |
| | G-BNER | PA-34-200T Seneca II | Compass Peripheral Systems Ltd |
| | G-BNES | Cameron V-77 balloon | G. Wells |
| | G-BNET | Cameron O-84 balloon | J. Bennett & Son (Insurance Brokers) Ltd |
| | G-BNEU | Colt 105A balloon | I. Lilja |
| | G-BNEV | Viking Dragonfly | N. W. Eyre |

| Reg. | Type | Owner or Operator | Notes |
|------|------|-------------------|-------|
| G-BNEX | Cameron O-120 balloon | The Balloon Club Ltd | |
| G-BNEZ | Cessna 421C | M. C. Daniels | |
| G-BNFG | Cameron O-77 balloon | Capital Balloon Club Ltd | |
| G-BNFI | Cessna 150J | M. Jackson | |
| G-BNFK | Cameron 89 Egg SS balloon | Forbes Europe Inc | |
| G-BNFL | WHE Airbuggy | Roger Savage (Photography) (G-AXXN) | |
| G-BNFM | Colt 21A balloon | M. E. Dworksi | |
| G-BNFN | Cameron N-105 balloon | Western Counties Automobile Co Ltd | |
| G-BNFO | Cameron V-77 balloon | D. C. Patrick-Brown | |
| G-BNFP | Cameron O-84 balloon | A. J. & E. J. Clarke | |
| G-BNFR | Cessna 152 II | London Flight Centre (Stansted) Ltd | |
| G-BNFS | Cessna 152 II | London Flight Centre (Stansted) Ltd | |
| G-BNFV | Robin DR.400/120 | FTI Aviation Ltd/Biggin Hill | |
| G-BNFW | H.S.125 Srs 700B | British Aerospace PLC | |
| G-BNFX | Colt 21A balloon | Thunder & Colt Ltd | |
| G-BNFY | Cameron N-77 balloon | Holker Estates Ltd | |
| G-BNGC | Robinson R-22 | T. J. Clark | |
| G-BNGD | Cessna 152 | AV Aviation Ltd | |
| G-BNGE | Auster AOP.6 (TW536) | R. W. W. Eastman | |
| G-BNGH | Boeing 707-321C | Tradewinds Airways Ltd (G-BFZF)/ Stansted | |
| G-BNGJ | Cameron V-77 balloon | Latham Timber Centres (Holdings) Ltd | |
| G-BNGL | Boeing 737-3Y0 | Inter European Airways Ltd/Cardiff | |
| G-BNGM | Boeing 737-3Y0 | Inter European Airways Ltd/Cardiff | |
| G-BNGN | Cameron V-77 balloon | A. R. & L. J. McGregor | |
| G-BNGO | Thunder Ax7-77 balloon | J. S. Finlan | |
| G-BNGP | Colt 77A balloon | Headland Services Ltd | |
| G-BNGR | PA-38-112 Tomahawk | Frontline Aviation Ltd/Teesside | |
| G-BNGS | PA-38-112 Tomahawk | Frontline Aviation Ltd/Teesside | |
| G-BNGT | PA-28-181 Archer II | Aviation Development & Management Ltd | |
| G-BNGV | ARV Super 2 | A. C. Gradidge | |
| G-BNGW | ARV Super 2 | Southern Gas Turbines Ltd | |
| G-BNGX | ARV Super 2 | Southern Gas Turbines Ltd | |
| G-BNGY | ARV Super 2 | N. R. F. McNally (G-BMWL) | |
| G-BNHB | ARV Super 2 | Engine Developments Ltd | |
| G-BNHC | ARV Super 2 | Lombard North Central PLC | |
| G-BNHD | ARV Super 2 | Falstaff Finance Ltd/Sandown | |
| G-BNHE | ARV Super 2 | Falstaff Finance Ltd/Sandown | |
| G-BNHF | Cameron N-31 balloon | P. G. Dunnington | |
| G-BNHG | PA-38-112 Tomahawk | W. J. Lumby & M. R. Walker | |
| G-BNHH | Thunder Ax7-77 balloon | Gee-Tee Signs Ltd | |
| G-BNHI | Cameron V-77 balloon | Phillair | |
| G-BNHJ | Cessna 152 | Ladel Ltd | |
| G-BNHK | Cessna 152 | Osprey Flying Club/Cranfield | |
| G-BNHL | Colt 90 Beer Glass SS balloon | G. V. Beckwith | |
| G-BNHM | Thunder Ax8-105 balloon | Thunder & Colt Ltd | |
| G-BNHN | Colt Aerial Bottle SS balloon | The Balloon Stable Ltd | |
| G-BNHO | Thunder Ax7-77 balloon | M. J. Forster | |
| G-BNHP | Saffrey S.330 balloon | N. H. Ponsford *Alpha II* | |
| G-BNHR | Cameron V-77 balloon | R. L. Rummery | |
| G-BNHS | Thunder Ax7-77 balloon | M. V. Farrant | |
| G-BNHT | Fournier RF-3 | D. Harker | |
| G-BNHV | Thunder Ax10-180 balloon | Thunder & Colt Ltd | |
| G-BNIB | Cameron A-105 balloon | A. G. E. Faulkner | |
| G-BNID | Cessna 152 | Mercia Aircraft Leasing & Sales Ltd/ Coventry | |
| G-BNIE | Cameron O-160 balloon | The Balloon Club Ltd | |
| G-BNIF | Cameron O-56 balloon | D. V. Fowler | |
| G-BNII | Cameron N-90 balloon | DW (Direct Wholesale) PLC | |
| G-BNIJ | SOCATA TB.10 Tobago | Alandi Investments Ltd | |
| G-BNIK | Robin HR.200/120 | W. C. Smeaton/Popham | |
| G-BNIM | PA-38-112 Tomahawk | T. Miller & F. R. H. Parker | |
| G-BNIN | Cameron V-77 balloon | Cloud Nine Balloon Group | |
| G-BNIO | Luscombe 8A Silvaire | P. T. Szluha | |
| G-BNIP | Luscombe 8A Silvaire | D. R. C. Hunter & S. Maric | |
| G-BNIT | Bell 206B JetRanger | Black Isle Helicopters Ltd | |
| G-BNIU | Cameron O-77 balloon | A. J. Matthews & D. S. Dunlop | |
| G-BNIV | Cessna 152 | Aerohire Ltd/Halfpenny Green | |
| G-BNIW | Boeing Stearman PT-17 | Lintally Ltd/E. Midlands | |
| G-BNIX | EMB-110P1 Bandeirante | Aeroservices (E. Midlands) Ltd | |
| G-BNJA | Wag-Aero Wag-a-Bond | D. H. Pattison | |
| G-BNJB | Cessna 152 | Klingair Ltd/Conington | |

| Notes | Reg. | Type | Owner or Operator |
|-------|------|------|-------------------|
| | G-BNJC | Cessna 152 | LAR Aviation Ltd/Shoreham |
| | G-BNJD | Cessna 152 | J. A Pothecary/Shoreham |
| | G-BNJE | Cessna A.152 | Seawing Flying Club Ltd/Southend |
| | G-BNJF | PA-32RT-300 Lance II | T. D. C. Lloyd & B. F. Brown |
| | G-BNJG | Cameron O-77 balloon | A. M. Figiel |
| | G-BNJH | Cessna 152 | Paysure Ltd/Edinburgh |
| | G-BNJJ | Cessna 152 | Merrett Aviation Ltd |
| | G-BNJK | Macavia BAe 748 Turbine Tanker | Macavia International Ltd |
| | G-BNJL | Bensen B.8 | T. G. Ogilvie |
| | G-BNJM | PA-28-161 Warrior II | Frontline Aviation Ltd/Teesside |
| | G-BNJO | QAC Quickie Q.2 | J. D. McKay |
| | G-BNJR | PA-28RT-201T Turbo Arrow IV | North West Aviation Ltd/Liverpool |
| | G-BNJT | PA-28-161 Warrior II | Airways Aero Associations Ltd/Booker |
| | G-BNJU | Cameron 80 Bust SS balloon | Forbes Europe Inc |
| | G-BNJV | Cessna 152 | Alouette Flying Club Ltd/Biggin Hill |
| | G-BNJW | Rutan Cozy | J. Whiting |
| | G-BNJX | Cameron N-90 balloon | Mars UK Ltd |
| | G-BNJZ | Cassutt IIIM | J. E. Cubitt |
| | G-BNKC | Cessna 152 | Herefordshire Aero Club Ltd/Shobdon |
| | G-BNKD | Cessna 172N | Bristol Flying Centre Ltd |
| | G-BNKE | Cessna 172N | Jacques Hall & Co Ltd |
| | G-BNKF | Colt AS-56 airship | Formtrack Ltd |
| | G-BNKG | Alexander Todd Steen Skybolt | Cavendish Aviation Ltd (G-RATS/ G-RHFI) |
| | G-BNKH | PA-38-112 Tomahawk | Goodwood Terrena Ltd |
| | G-BNKI | Cessna 152 | RAF Halton Aeroplane Club Ltd |
| | G-BNKJ | BAe 146-200A | British Aerospace PLC/Hatfield |
| | G-BNKL | Beech 95-58PA Baron | E. L. Klinge/Fairoaks |
| | G-BNKN | G.159 Gulfstream 1 | Birmingham European Airways Ltd |
| | G-BNKO | G.159 Gulfstream 1 | Birmingham European Airways Ltd |
| | G-BNKP | Cessna 152 | Clacton Aero Club (1988) Ltd |
| | G-BNKR | Cessna 152 | Fife Airport Management Ltd |
| | G-BNKS | Cessna 152 | Shropshire Aero Club Ltd/Shobdon |
| | G-BNKT | Cameron O-77 balloon | British Airways PLC |
| | G-BNKV | Cessna 152 | I. C. Adams & Vectair Aviation Ltd |
| | G-BNKW | PA-38-112 Tomahawk | D. M. Maclean |
| | G-BNKX | Robinson R-22 | A. G. Macmillan |
| | G-BNKZ | Hughes 369HS | Reeds Motor Co/Sywell |
| | G-BNLA | Boeing 747-436 | British Airways City of London/ Heathrow |
| | G-BNLB | Boeing 747-436 | British Airways City of Edinburgh/ Heathrow |
| | G-BNLC | Boeing 747-436 | British Airways City of Cardiff/ Heathrow |
| | G-BNLD | Boeing 747-436 | British Airways City of Belfast/ Heathrow |
| | G-BNLE | Boeing 747-436 | British Airways City of Newcastle/ Heathrow |
| | G-BNLF | Boeing 747-436 | British Airways City of Leeds/Heathrow |
| | G-BNLG | Boeing 747-436 | British Airways City of Southampton/ Heathrow |
| | G-BNLH | Boeing 747-436 | British Airways City of Westminster/ Heathrow |
| | G-BNLI | Boeing 747-436 | British Airways City of Sheffield/ Heathrow |
| | G-BNLJ | Boeing 747-436 | British Airways City of Nottingham/ Heathrow |
| | G-BNLK | Boeing 747-436 | British Airways City of Bristol/Heathrow |
| | G-BNLL | Boeing 747-436 | British Airways City of Leicester/ Heathrow |
| | G-BNLM | Boeing 747-436 | British Airways City of Durham/ Heathrow |
| | G-BNLN | Boeing 747-436 | British Airways City of Portsmouth/ Heathrow |
| | G-BNLO | Boeing 747-436 | British Airways City of Dundee/ Heathrow |
| | G-BNLP | Boeing 747-436 | British Airways City of Aberdeen/ Heathrow |
| | G-BNLR | Boeing 747-436 | British Airways City of Hull/Heathrow |
| | G-BNLS | Boeing 747-436 | British Airways City of Chester/ Heathrow |
| | G-BNLT | Boeing 747-436 | British Airways City of Bangor/ Heathrow |

| Reg. | Type | Owner or Operator | Notes |
|------|------|-------------------|-------|
| G-BNLU | Boeing 747-436 | British Airways/Heathrow | |
| G-BNLV | Boeing 747-436 | British Airways/Heathrow | |
| G-BNLW | — | — | |
| G-BNLX | — | — | |
| G-BNLY | — | — | |
| G-BNLZ | — | — | |
| G-BNMA | Cameron O-77 balloon | Flying Colours Balloon Group | |
| G-BNMB | PA-28-151 Warrior | Angelchain Ltd/Manchester | |
| G-BNMC | Cessna 152 | M. L. Jones/Burnaston | |
| G-BNMD | Cessna 152 | T. M. Jones | |
| G-BNME | Cessna 152 | L. V. Atkinson | |
| G-BNMF | Cessna 152 | Aerohire Ltd | |
| G-BNMG | Cameron V-77 balloon | Windsor Life Assurance Co Ltd | |
| G-BNMH | Pietenpol Aircamper | N. M. Hitchman | |
| G-BNMI | Colt Flying Fantasy SS balloon | Air 2 Air Ltd | |
| G-BNMK | Dornier Do.27A-1 | G. Machie | |
| G-BNML | Rand KR-2 | R. J. Smyth | |
| G-BNMM | Bell 206B JetRanger | Veritair Ltd | |
| G-BNMN | PA-28R-201 Arrow III | Sandford Aviation Ltd | |
| G-BNMO | Cessna TR.182RG | G-BNMO Flying Group | |
| G-BNMP | Cessna R.182RG | T. J. Clarke/Cranfield | |
| G-BNMX | Thunder Ax7-77 balloon | S. A. D. Beard | |
| G-BNMZ | Isaacs Fury II | T. E. G. Buckett | |
| G-BNNA | Stolp SA.300 Starduster Too | D. F. Simpson | |
| G-BNNB | PA-34-200 Seneca II | Shoreham Flight Simulation/Bournemouth | |
| G-BNNC | Cameron N-77 balloon | West Country Business Machines Ltd | |
| G-BNNE | Cameron N-77 balloon | The Balloon Stable Ltd | |
| G-BNNF | SA.315B Alouette III Lama | Dollar Air Services Ltd/Coventry | |
| G-BNNG | Cessna T.337D | Somet Ltd (G-COLD) | |
| G-BNNI | Boeing 727-276 | Dan-Air Services Ltd/Gatwick | |
| G-BNNJ | Boeing 737-3Q8 | Dan-Air Services Ltd/Gatwick | |
| G-BNNK | Boeing 737-4Q8 | Dan-Air Services Ltd/Gatwick | |
| G-BNNL | Boeing 737-4Q8 | Dan-Air Services Ltd/Gatwick | |
| G-BNNO | PA-28-161 Warrior II | W. Lancs Aero Club Ltd/Woodvale | |
| G-BNNR | Cessna 152 | Interair (Aviation) Ltd/Bournemouth | |
| G-BNNS | PA-28-161 Warrior II | P. A. Lancaster | |
| G-BNNT | PA-28-151 Warrior | T. Miller & A. K. Hilton | |
| G-BNNU | PA-38-112 Tomahawk | Seal Executive Aircraft Ltd | |
| G-BNNX | PA-28R-201T Turbo Arrow III | C. Dugard Ltd/Shoreham | |
| G-BNNY | PA-28-161 Warrior II | Falcon Flying Services/Biggin Hill | |
| G-BNNZ | PA-28-161 Warrior II | D. Heater/Fairoaks | |
| G-BNOA | PA-38-112 Tomahawk | Aerohire Ltd/Halfpenny Green | |
| G-BNOB | Wittman W.8 Tailwind | M. Robson-Robinson | |
| G-BNOC | EMB-110P1 Bandeirante | —/Southend | |
| G-BNOD | PA-28-161 Warrior II | BAe Flying College/Prestwick | |
| G-BNOE | PA-28-161 Warrior II | BAe Flying College/Prestwick | |
| G-BNOF | PA-28-161 Warrior II | BAe Flying College/Prestwick | |
| G-BNOG | PA-28-161 Warrior II | BAe Flying College/Prestwick | |
| G-BNOH | PA-28-161 Warrior II | BAe Flying College/Prestwick | |
| G-BNOI | PA-28-161 Warrior II | BAe Flying College/Prestwick | |
| G-BNOJ | PA-28-161 Warrior II | BAe Flying College/Prestwick | |
| G-BNOK | PA-28-161 Warrior II | BAe Flying College/Prestwick | |
| G-BNOL | PA-28-161 Warrior II | BAe Flying College/Prestwick | |
| G-BNOM | PA-28-161 Warrior II | BAe Flying College/Prestwick | |
| G-BNON | PA-28-161 Warrior II | BAe Flying College/Prestwick | |
| G-BNOO | PA-28-161 Warrior II | BAe Flying College/Prestwick | |
| G-BNOP | PA-28-161 Warrior II | BAe Flying College/Prestwick | |
| G-BNOR | PA-28-161 Warrior II | BAe Flying College/Prestwick | |
| G-BNOS | PA-28-161 Warrior II | BAe Flying College/Prestwick | |
| G-BNOT | PA-28-161 Warrior II | BAe Flying College/Prestwick | |
| G-BNOU | PA-28-161 Warrior II | BAe Flying College/Prestwick | |
| G-BNOV | PA-28-161 Warrior II | BAe Flying College/Prestwick | |
| G-BNOW | PA-28-161 Warrior II | BAe Flying College/Prestwick | |
| G-BNOX | Cessna R.182 | D. C. Shepherd | |
| G-BNOY | Colt 90A balloon | Huntair Ltd | |
| G-BNPA | Boeing 737-3S3 | Air Europe Ltd/Gatwick | |
| G-BNPB | Boeing 737-3S3 | Air Europe Ltd/Gatwick | |
| G-BNPD | PA-23 Aztec 250E | Cormack (Aircraft Services) Ltd/Glasgow | |
| G-BNPE | Cameron N-77 balloon | Kent Garden Centres Ltd | |
| G-BNPF | Slingsby T.31M | S. Luck & ptnrs | |
| G-BNPH | P.66 Pembroke C.1 (WV740) | R. J. F. Parker/Denham | |

| Notes | Reg. | Type | Owner or Operator |
|---|---|---|---|
| | G-BNPI | Colt 21A balloon | Virgin Atlantic Airways Ltd |
| | G-BNPK | Cameron DP-70 airship | Cameron Balloons Ltd |
| | G-BNPL | PA-38-112 Tomahawk | Tomahawk Aviation Ltd/Leavesden |
| | G-BNPM | PA-38-112 Tomahawk | Papa Mike Aviation Ltd/Leavesden |
| | G-BNPN | PA-28-181 Archer II | Willis Aviation Ltd |
| | G-BNPO | PA-28-181 Archer II | Leavesden Flight Centre Ltd |
| | G-BNPP | Colt 90A balloon | Huntair Ltd |
| | G-BNPT | PA-38-112 Tomahawk II | Cumbernauld Aviation Ltd |
| | G-BNPU | P.66 Pembroke C.1 (XL929) ★ | Chelsea College/Shoreham |
| | G-BNPV | Bowers Flybaby 1A | J. G. Day |
| | G-BNPY | Cessna 152 | Doncaster Aero Club Ltd |
| | G-BNPZ | Cessna 152 | Bristol Flying Centre Ltd |
| | G-BNRA | SOCATA TB.10 Tobago | D. Marriott |
| | G-BNRB | Robin DR.400/180R | Soaring (Oxford) Ltd/Booker |
| | G-BNRC | AB-206A JetRanger | M. & P. Food Products Ltd |
| | G-BNRD | AB-206A JetRanger | M. & P. Food Products Ltd |
| | G-BNRE | AB-206A JetRanger | Aqua Glass Ltd |
| | G-BNRF | PA-28-181 Archer II | G-Air Ltd/Goodwood |
| | G-BNRG | PA-28-161 Warrior II | RAF Brize Norton Flying Club Ltd |
| | G-BNRH | Beech 95-E55 Baron | K. L. Hawes/Elstree |
| | G-BNRI | Cessna U.206G | Flying Tigers Ltd |
| | G-BNRK | Cessna 152 | Redhill Flying Club |
| | G-BNRL | Cessna 152 | J. R. Nicholls/Sibson |
| | G-BNRP | PA-28-181 Archer II | Atomchoice Ltd/Goodwood |
| | G-BNRR | Cessna 172P | Skyhawk Group |
| | G-BNRT | Boeing 737-3T5 | Britannia Airways/Luton |
| | G-BNRU | Cameron V-77 balloon | M. A. Mueller |
| | G-BNRW | Colt 69A balloon | Callers Pegasus Travel Service Ltd |
| | G-BNRX | PA-34-200T Seneca II | Futurama Signs Ltd |
| | G-BNRY | Cessna 182Q | Reefly Ltd |
| | G-BNRZ | Robinson R-22B | W. Jorden-Millers Ltd |
| | G-BNSC | Cessna 550 Citation II | IDS Aircraft Ltd/Heathrow |
| | G-BNSD | Boeing 757-236 | Air Europe/Air Europa (EC-EMA)/NFD (D-AOEA) |
| | G-BNSE | Boeing 757-236 | Air Europe/Air Europa |
| | G-BNSF | Boeing 757-236 | Air Europe/Air Europa (EC-ELS)/NFD (D-AOEB) |
| | G-BNSG | PA-28R-201 Arrow III | Ewdec Technology Ltd |
| | G-BNSH | Sikorsky S-76A | Bond Helicopters Ltd |
| | G-BNSI | Cessna 152 | Interair (Aviation) Ltd |
| | G-BNSL | PA-38-112 Tomahawk II | M. H. Kleiser |
| | G-BNSM | Cessna 152 | Cornwall Flying Club Ltd/Bodmin |
| | G-BNSN | Cessna 152 | M. K. Barnes & G. N. Olson/Bristol |
| | G-BNSO | Slingsby T.67M Mk II | Slingsby Aviation Ltd/Kirkbymoorside |
| | G-BNSP | Slingsby T.67M | Slingsby Aviation Ltd/Kirkbymoorside |
| | G-BNSR | Slingsby T.67M | Slingsby Aviation Ltd/Kirkbymoorside |
| | G-BNSS | Cessna 150M | Interair (Aviation) Ltd |
| | G-BNST | Cessna 172N | E. J. H. Morgan |
| | G-BNSU | Cessna 152 | Channel Aviation Ltd/Bourn |
| | G-BNSV | Cessna 152 | Channel Aviation Ltd/Bourn |
| | G-BNSW | Cessna 152 | One Zero One Three Ltd |
| | G-BNSY | PA-28-161 Warrior II | Carill Aviation Ltd/Southampton |
| | G-BNSZ | PA-28-161 Warrior II | Carill Aviation Ltd |
| | G-BNTC | PA-28RT-201T Turbo Arrow IV | Techspan Aviation Ltd/Booker |
| | G-BNTD | PA-28-161 Warrior II | S. S. Copsey/Ipswich |
| | G-BNTE | FFA AS.202/184A Wren | BAe Flying College Ltd/Prestwick |
| | G-BNTF | FFA AS.202/184A Wren | BAe Flying College Ltd/Prestwick |
| | G-BNTG | FFA AS.202/184A Wren | BAe Flying College Ltd/Prestwick |
| | G-BNTH | FFA AS.202/184A Wren | BAe Flying College Ltd/Prestwick |
| | G-BNTI | FFA AS.202/184A Wren | BAe Flying College Ltd/Prestwick |
| | G-BNTJ | FFA AS.202/184A Wren | BAe Flying College Ltd/Prestwick |
| | G-BNTK | FFA AS.202/184A Wren | BAe Flying College Ltd/Prestwick |
| | G-BNTL | FFA AS.202/184A Wren | BAe Flying College Ltd/Prestwick |
| | G-BNTM | FFA AS.202/184A Wren | BAe Flying College Ltd/Prestwick |
| | G-BNTN | FFA AS.202/184A Wren | BAe Flying College Ltd/Prestwick |
| | G-BNTO | FFA AS.202/184A Wren | BAe Flying College Ltd/Prestwick |
| | G-BNTP | Cessna 172N | Light Planes Lancashire Ltd/Barton |
| | G-BNTS | PA-28RT-201T Turbo Arrow IV | Nasire Ltd |
| | G-BNTT | Beech 76 Duchess | L. & J. Donne |
| | G-BNTU | Cessna 152 | Seal Executive Aviation Ltd |
| | G-BNTV | Cessna 172N | Brandon Aviation/Biggin Hill |
| | G-BNTW | Cameron V-77 balloon | P. R. S. Briault |
| | G-BNTX | Short SD3-30 Variant 100 | Shorts Aircraft Leasing Ltd (G-BKDN) |

| Reg. | Type | Owner or Operator | Notes |
|------|------|-------------------|-------|
| G-BNTY | Short SD3-30 Variant 100 | Shorts Aircraft Leasing Ltd (G-BKDO) | |
| G-BNTZ | Cameron N-77 balloon | Balloon Team | |
| G-BNUC | Cameron O-77 balloon | C. F. Sisson | |
| G-BNUG | Cameron O-105 balloon | Thunder & Colt Ltd | |
| G-BNUH | Cameron O-105 balloon | Thunder & Colt Ltd | |
| G-BNUI | Rutan Vari-Eze | T. N. F. Skead | |
| G-BNUK | Cameron O-84 balloon | Thunder & Colt Ltd | |
| G-BNUL | Cessna 152 | Osprey Air Services Ltd | |
| G-BNUN | Beech 95-58PA Baron | British Midland Airways Ltd/E. Midlands | |
| G-BNUO | Beech 76 Duchess | B. & W. Aircraft Ltd | |
| G-BNUR | Cessna 172E | Newland Ltd | |
| G-BNUS | Cessna 152 | Stapleford Flying Club Ltd | |
| G-BNUT | Cessna 152 Turbo | Stapleford Flying Club Ltd | |
| G-BNUU | PA-44-180T Turbo Seminole | TEL (IOM) Ltd/Ronaldsway | |
| G-BNUV | PA-23 Aztec 250F | L. J. Martin | |
| G-BNUX | Hoffmann H-36 Dimona | K. H. Abel | |
| G-BNUY | PA-38-112 Tomahawk II | AT Aviation Ltd/Cardiff | |
| G-BNUZ | Robinson R-22B | J. L. E. Smith | |
| G-BNVB | AA-5A Cheetah | R. M. Dockeray | |
| G-BNVD | PA-38-112 Tomahawk | Channel Aviation Ltd | |
| G-BNVE | PA-28-181 Archer II | Sound Technology PLC | |
| G-BNVF | Robinson R-22B | Jetbury Ltd | |
| G-BNVG | ARV Super 2 | ARV Aviation Ltd/Sandown | |
| G-BNVH | ARV Super 2 | ARV Aviation Ltd/Sandown | |
| G-BNVI | ARV Super 2 | Adrianair Ltd | |
| G-BNVJ | ARV Super 2 | ARV Aviation Ltd/Sandown | |
| G-BNVT | PA-28R-201T Turbo Arrow III | Commercial Coachbuilders (Strathclyde) Ltd | |
| G-BNVV | Cameron DG-19 gas airship | US Skyship (UK) Ltd | |
| G-BNVW | Dornier Do.28A-1 | Wessex Aviation & Transport Ltd | |
| G-BNVZ | Beech 95-B55 Baron | C. A. Breeze/Barton | |
| G-BNWA | Boeing 767-336ER | British Airways *City of Brussels*/ Heathrow | |
| G-BNWB | Boeing 767-336ER | British Airways *City of Paris*/ Heathrow | |
| G-BNWC | Boeing 767-336ER | British Airways *City of Frankfurt*/ Heathrow | |
| G-BNWD | Boeing 767-336ER | British Airways *City of Copenhagen*/ Heathrow | |
| G-BNWE | Boeing 767-336ER | British Airways *City of Lisbon*/ Heathrow | |
| G-BNWF | Boeing 767-336ER | British Airways *City of Milan*/ Heathrow | |
| G-BNWG | Boeing 767-336ER | British Airways *City of Strasbourg*/ Heathrow | |
| G-BNWH | Boeing 767-336ER | British Airways *City of Rome*/ Heathrow | |
| G-BNWI | Boeing 767-336ER | British Airways *City of Madrid*/ Heathrow | |
| G-BNWJ | Boeing 767-336ER | British Airways *City of Athens*/ Heathrow | |
| G-BNWK | Boeing 767-336ER | British Airways *City of Amsterdam*/ Heathrow | |
| G-BNWL | Boeing 767-336ER | British Airways *City of Luxembourg*/ Heathrow | |
| G-BNWM | Boeing 767-336ER | British Airways *City of Toulouse*/ Heathrow | |
| G-BNWN | — | — | |
| G-BNWO | — | — | |
| G-BNWP | — | — | |
| G-BNWR | — | — | |
| G-BNWS | — | — | |
| G-BNWT | — | — | |
| G-BNWU | — | — | |
| G-BNWV | — | — | |
| G-BNWW | — | — | |
| G-BNWX | — | — | |
| G-BNWY | — | — | |
| G-BNWZ | — | — | |
| G-BNXA | BN-2A Islander | Atlantic Air Transport Ltd/Coventry | |
| G-BNXB | BN-2A Islander | M. E. Mortlock/Parnpisford | |
| G-BNXC | Cessna 152 | Sir W. G. Armstrong-Whitworth Flying Group/Coventry | |

| Notes | Reg. | Type | Owner or Operator |
|-------|------|------|-------------------|
| | G-BNXD | Cessna 172N | Interair (Aviation) Ltd/Bournemouth |
| | G-BNXE | PA-28-161 Warrior II | Rugby Autobody Repairs |
| | G-BNXF | Bell 206B JetRanger | P. Pilkington & K. M. Armitage |
| | G-BNXG | Cameron DP-70 airship | Rexstyle Ltd |
| | G-BNXH | Cessna T.210N | Wilson Feeds Ltd |
| | G-BNXI | Robin DR.400-180R | London Gliding Club Ltd/Dunstable |
| | G-BNXJ | Robinson R-22B | J. D. Marsh |
| | G-BNXK | Nott-Cameron ULD-3 balloon | J. R. P. Nott |
| | G-BNXL | Glaser-Dirks DG.400 | B. A. Eastwell |
| | G-BNXM | PA-18 Super Cub 95 | P. D. Scandrett |
| | G-BNXN | Partenavia P.68B | N. P. W. G. Edmiston |
| | G-BNXO | Colt 21A balloon | Thunder & Colt Ltd |
| | G-BNXR | Cameron O-84 balloon | J. A. & N. J. Ballard Gray |
| | G-BNXS | Cessna 404 | Turnbull Associates |
| | G-BNXT | PA-28-161 Warrior II | Falcon Flying Services/Biggin Hill |
| | G-BNXU | PA-28-161 Warrior II | V. J. Rutherford & P. D. Donoghue |
| | G-BNXV | PA-38-112 Tomahawk | Falcon Flying Services/Biggin Hill |
| | G-BNXW | Boeing 737-33A | Air Europe/Air Europe Scandinavia (LN-NOR) |
| | G-BNXX | SOCATA TB.20 Trinidad | EAC Components Ltd |
| | G-BNXY | Cessna 172M | Biggin Hill School of FLying |
| | G-BNXZ | Thunder Ax7-77 balloon | Hale Hot Air Balloon Group |
| | G-BNYA | Short SD3-30 | Shorts Aircraft Leasing Ltd (G-BKSU) |
| | G-BNYB | PA-28-201T Turbo Dakota | S. R. Culley Developments Ltd |
| | G-BNYD | Bell 206B JetRanger | Sterling Helicopters Ltd |
| | G-BNYJ | Cessna 421B | Charles Robertson (Developments) Ltd |
| | G-BNYK | PA-38-112 Tomahawk | Seal Executive Aircraft Ltd |
| | G-BNYL | Cessna 152 | Seal Executive Aircraft Ltd |
| | G-BNYM | Cessna 172N | G. Manning/Coventry |
| | G-BNYN | Cessna 152 | Redhill Flying Club |
| | G-BNYO | Beech 76 Duchess | Skyhawk Ltd |
| | G-BNYP | PA-28-181 Archer II | R. D. Cooper/Cranfield |
| | G-BNYS | Boeing 767-204 | Britannia Airways Ltd/Luton |
| | G-BNYU | Faithful Ax7-61A balloon | M. L. Faithfull |
| | G-BNYV | PA-38-112 Tomahawk | Channel Aviation Ltd |
| | G-BNYX | Denney Aerocraft Kitfox | R. W. Husband |
| | G-BNYY | PA-28RT-201T Turbo Arrow IV | Kendrick Construction Ltd |
| | G-BNYZ | SNCAN Stampe SV-4E | Tapestry Colour Ltd |
| | G-BNZA | Beech 300LW Super King Air | British Airways/Heathrow |
| | G-BNZB | PA-28-161 Warrior II | Hillvine Ltd |
| | G-BNZC | D.H.C.1 Chipmunk 22 (671) | The Aircraft Restoration Co (G-ROYS)/ Duxford |
| | G-BNZF | Grob G.109B | N. Adam |
| | G-BNZG | PA-28RT-201T Turbo Arrow IV | Trinity Garage (Gainsborough) Ltd |
| | G-BNZJ | Colt 21A balloon | Willowbest Ltd |
| | G-BNZK | Thunder Ax7-77 balloon | Shropshire Lass Group |
| | G-BNZL | Rotorway Scorpion 133 | J. R. Wraight |
| | G-BNZM | Cessna T.210N | Stansted Fluid Power (Products) Ltd |
| | G-BNZO | Rotorway Executive | M. G. Wiltshire |
| | G-BNZR | FRED Srs 2 | R. M. Waugh |
| | G-BNZS | Mooney M.20K | P. E. Sandy |
| | G-BNZV | PA-25 Pawnee 235 | Northumbria Soaring Co Ltd |
| | G-BNZX | — | — |
| | G-BNZZ | PA-28-161 Warrior II | J. P. Alexander/Denham |
| | G-BOAA | Concorde 102 | British Airways (G-N94AA)/Heathrow |
| | G-BOAB | Concorde 102 | British Airways (G-N94AB)/Heathrow |
| | G-BOAC | Concorde 102 | British Airways (G-N81AC)/Heathrow |
| | G-BOAD | Concorde 102 | British Airways (G-N94AD)/Heathrow |
| | G-BOAE | Concorde 102 | British Airways (G-N94AE)/Heathrow |
| | G-BOAF | Concorde 102 | British Airways (G-N94AF/G-BFKX)/ Heathrow |
| | G-BOAG | Concorde 102 | British Airways (G-BFKW)/Heathrow |
| | G-BOAH | PA-28-161 Warrior II | Denham School of Flying Ltd |
| | G-BOAI | Cessna 152 | G. Duncan |
| | G-BOAK | PA-22 Caribbean 150 | I. B. Grace & ptnrs |
| | G-BOAL | Cameron V-65 balloon | A. M. Lindsay |
| | G-BOAM | Robinson R-22B | Bristow Helicopters Ltd/Redhill |
| | G-BOAN | PA-30 Twin Comanche 160B | R. L. C. Appleton |
| | G-BOAO | Thunder Ax7-77 balloon | D. V. Fowler |
| | G-BOAS | Air Command 503 Commander | R. Robinson |
| | G-BOAU | Cameron V-77 balloon | J. Smallwood |
| | G-BOAW | D.H.C.7-110 Dash Seven | British Midland Airways/London City |

| Reg. | Type | Owner or Operator | Notes |
|------|------|-------------------|-------|
| G-BOAX | D.H.C.7-110 Dash Seven | Natural Environment Research Council | |
| G-BOAY | D.H.C.7-110 Dash Seven | British Midland Airways/London City | |
| G-BOAZ | D.H.C.7-102 Dash Seven | Brymon Aviation Ltd | |
| G-BOBA | PA-28R-201 Arrow III | GNJ Engineering Ltd | |
| G-BOBB | Cameron O-120 balloon | J. M. Albury | |
| G-BOBC | BN-2T Islander | Rhine Army Parachute Association (G-BJYZ) | |
| G-BOBD | Cameron O-160 balloon | Heart of England Balloon Club | |
| G-BOBE | Cameron O-160 balloon | Heart of England Balloon Club | |
| G-BOBF | Brügger MB.2 Colibri | R. Bennett | |
| G-BOBG | Jodel D.150 | C. A. Laycock | |
| G-BOBH | Airtour AH-77 balloon | Airtour Balloon Co Ltd | |
| G-BOBJ | PA-38-112 Tomahawk | Surrey & Kent Flying Club (1982) Ltd/ Biggin Hill | |
| G-BOBK | PA-38-112 Tomahawk | Surrey & Kent Flying Club (1982) Ltd/ Biggin Hill | |
| G-BOBL | PA-38-112 Tomahawk | Surrey & Kent Flying Club (1982) Ltd/ Biggin Hill | |
| G-BOBN | Cessna 310R | Edinburgh Air Charter Ltd | |
| G-BOBO | Robinson R-22 | D. J. Saunders | |
| G-BOBR | Cameron N-77 balloon | Loganair Ltd | |
| G-BOBS | Quickie Q.2 | R. R. Stevens/Denham | |
| G-BOBT | Stolp SA.300 Starduster Too | Alcina Aviation | |
| G-BOBU | Colt 90A balloon | Thunder & Colt Ltd | |
| G-BOBV | Cessna F.150M | Osprey Air Services Ltd/Cranfield | |
| G-BOBW | Air & Space 18A gyroplane | M. A. Schumann/Shipdham | |
| G-BOBX | G.159 Gulfstream 1 ★ | Airport Fire Section/Birmingham | |
| G-BOBY | Monnet Sonerai II | R. G. Hallam (stored)/Sleap | |
| G-BOBZ | PA-28-181 Archer II | Trustcomms International Ltd | |
| G-BOCB | H.S.125 Srs 1B/522 | MAGEC Aviation Ltd (G-OMCA/ G-DJMJ/G-AWUF)/Luton | |
| G-BOCC | PA-38-112 Tomahawk | Goodwood Terrena Ltd | |
| G-BOCD | Grob G.115 | Soaring (Oxford) Ltd | |
| G-BOCF | Colt 77A balloon | P. S. J. Mason | |
| G-BOCG | PA-34-200T Seneca II | Airways Flight Training (Exeter) Ltd | |
| G-BOCH | PA-32 Cherokee Six 300 | Basic Vale Ltd | |
| G-BOCI | Cessna 140A | D. Nieman | |
| G-BOCK | Sopwith Triplane (replica) (N6290) | Shuttleworth Trust/O. Warden | |
| G-BOCL | Slingsby T.67C | C.S.E. Aviation Ltd/Kidlington | |
| G-BOCM | Slingsby T.67C | C.S.E. Aviation Ltd/Kidlington | |
| G-BOCN | Robinson R-22B | J. Bignall | |
| G-BOCP | PA-34-220T Seneca III | BAe Flying College Ltd/Prestwick | |
| G-BOCR | PA-34-220T Seneca III | BAe Flying College Ltd/Prestwick | |
| G-BOCS | PA-34-220T Seneca III | BAe Flying College Ltd/Prestwick | |
| G-BOCT | PA-34-220T Seneca III | BAe Flying College Ltd/Prestwick | |
| G-BOCU | PA-34-220T Seneca III | BAe Flying College Ltd/Prestwick | |
| G-BOCV | PA-34-220T Seneca III | BAe Flying College Ltd/Prestwick | |
| G-BOCW | PA-34-220T Seneca III | BAe Flying College Ltd/Prestwick | |
| G-BOCX | PA-34-220T Seneca III | BAe Flying College Ltd/Prestwick | |
| G-BOCY | PA-34-220T Seneca III | BAe Flying College Ltd/Prestwick | |
| G-BOCZ | PA-34-220T Seneca III | BAe Flying College Ltd/Prestwick | |
| G-BODA | PA-28-161 Warrior II | C.S.E. Aviation Ltd/Kidlington | |
| G-BODB | PA-28-161 Warrior II | C.S.E. Aviation Ltd/Kidlington | |
| G-BODC | PA-28-161 Warrior II | C.S.E. Aviation Ltd/Kidlington | |
| G-BODD | PA-28-161 Warrior II | C.S.E. Aviation Ltd/Kidlington | |
| G-BODE | PA-28-161 Warrior II | C.S.E. Aviation Ltd/Kidlington | |
| G-BODF | PA-28-161 Warrior II | C.S.E. Aviation Ltd/Kidlington | |
| G-BODG | Slingsby T.31 Motor Cadet III | H. P. Vox | |
| G-BODH | Slingsby T.31 Motor Cadet III | H. P. Vox | |
| G-BODI | Stoddard-Hamilton Glasair III | Jackson Barr Ltd | |
| G-BODK | Rotorway Scorpion 133 | J. Brannigan | |
| G-BODL | Steen Skybolt | K. E. Armstrong | |
| G-BODM | PA-28 Cherokee 180 | Bristol & Wessex Aeroplane Club Ltd | |
| G-BODN | PA-28R-201 Arrow III | N. M. G. Pearson/Bristol | |
| G-BODO | Cessna 152 | A. R. Sarson | |
| G-BODP | PA-38-112 Tomahawk | N. C. Gray | |
| G-BODR | PA-28-161 Warrior II | Airways Aero Associations Ltd/Booker | |
| G-BODS | PA-38-112 Tomahawk | Ipswich School of Flying Ltd | |
| G-BODT | Jodel D.18 | R. A. Jarvis | |
| G-BODU | Scheibe SF.25C | Monica English Memorial Trust | |
| G-BODW | Bell 206B JetRanger | Wood Hall Helicopters Ltd | |
| G-BODX | Beech 76 Duchess | Neric Ltd | |

| Notes | Reg. | Type | Owner or Operator |
|-------|------|------|-------------------|
| | G-BODY | Cessna 310R | Atlantic Air Transport Ltd/Coventry |
| | G-BODZ | Robinson R-22B | Langley Construction Ltd |
| | G-BOEC | PA-38-112 Tomahawk | R. A. Wakefield |
| | G-BOED | Cameron Opera House SS balloon | Cameron Balloons Ltd |
| | G-BOEE | PA-28-181 Archer II | T. B. Parmenter |
| | G-BOEH | Jodel DR.340 | E. J. & P. E. Horsfall/Blackpool |
| | G-BOEK | Cameron V-77 balloon | A. J. E. Jones |
| | G-BOEM | Aerotek-Pitts S-2A | Walsh Bros (Tunneling) Ltd |
| | G-BOEN | Cessna 172M | P. N. Herold |
| | G-BOER | PA-28-161 Warrior II | Ridgway Aviation Services Ltd/Booker |
| | G-BOES | Cessna FA.152 | J. R. Nicholls (G-FLIP) |
| | G-BOET | PA-28RT-201 Arrow IV | IBEC (Holdings) Ltd (G-IBEC)/Liverpool |
| | G-BOEW | Robinson R-22B | Bristow Helicopters Ltd |
| | G-BOEX | Robinson R-22B | Bristow Helicopters Ltd |
| | G-BOEY | Robinson R-22B | Bristow Helicopters Ltd |
| | G-BOEZ | Robinson R-22B | Bristow Helicopters Ltd |
| | G-BOFA | Robinson R-22 | Panair Ltd |
| | G-BOFB | Sikorsky S-76A | Bond Helicopters Ltd/Bourn |
| | G-BOFC | Beech 76 Duchess | Wickenby Aviation Ltd |
| | G-BOFD | Cessna U.206G | D. M. Penny |
| | G-BOFE | PA-34-200T Seneca II | E. C. English |
| | G-BOFF | Cameron N-77 balloon | Systems-80 Double Glazing Ltd & N. M. Gabriel |
| | G-BOFL | Cessna 152 | Coventry (Civil) Aviation Ltd |
| | G-BOFM | Cessna 152 | Coventry (Civil) Aviation Ltd |
| | G-BOFO | Ultimate 10-200 | I. G. Anderson |
| | G-BOFV | PA-44-180 Seminole | Stapleford Flying Club Ltd |
| | G-BOFW | Cessna A.150M | Three Counties Aero Club Ltd/Blackbushe |
| | G-BOFX | Cessna A.150M | Shropshire Aero Club Ltd |
| | G-BOFY | PA-28 Cherokee 140 | Bristol & Wessex Aeroplane Club Ltd |
| | G-BOFZ | PA-28-161 Warrior II | Bristol & Wessex Aeroplane Club Ltd |
| | G-BOGB | Hawker Tempest II replica | D. L. Riley |
| | G-BOGC | Cessna 152 | Skyviews & General Ltd/Leeds |
| | G-BOGG | Cessna 152 | J. S. & S. Peplow |
| | G-BOGI | Robin DR.400/180 | B. Hodge |
| | G-BOGK | ARV Super 2 | D. R. Trouse |
| | G-BOGL | Thunder Ax7-77 balloon | Thunder & Colt Ltd |
| | G-BOGM | PA-28RT-201T Turbo Arrow IV | RJP Aviation |
| | G-BOGO | PA-32R-301T Saratoga SP | F. L. Hunter |
| | G-BOGP | Cameron V-77 balloon | The Wealden Balloon Group |
| | G-BOGR | Colt 180A balloon | The Balloon Club of Great Britain Ltd |
| | G-BOGS | PA-34-200T Seneca II | Airways Flight Training (Exeter) Ltd |
| | G-BOGT | Colt 77A balloon | The Hot Air Balloon Co Ltd |
| | G-BOGV | Air Command 532 Elite | G. M. Hobman |
| | G-BOGW | Air Command 532 Elite | K. Ashford |
| | G-BOGY | Cameron V-77 balloon | Dante Balloon Group |
| | G-BOHA | PA-28-161 Warrior II | London Flight Centre (Stansted) Ltd |
| | G-BOHB | Cessna 152 | London Flight Centre (Stansted) Ltd |
| | G-BOHC | Boeing 757-236 | Air Europe/Air Europa (EC-ELA) |
| | G-BOHD | Colt 77A balloon | County Garage Ltd |
| | G-BOHE | Cameron O-120 balloon | Blue Sky Balloons Ltd |
| | G-BOHF | Thunder Ax8-84 balloon | Slater Hogg & Howison Ltd |
| | G-BOHG | Air Command 532 Elite | T. E. McDonald |
| | G-BOHH | Cessna 172N | J. S. Baxter |
| | G-BOHI | Cessna 152 | Clacton Aero Club (1988) Ltd |
| | G-BOHJ | Cessna 152 | F. E. P. Holmes |
| | G-BOHL | Cameron A-120 balloon | The Balloon Stable Ltd |
| | G-BOHM | PA-28 Cherokee 180 | M. J. Anthony & B. Keogh |
| | G-BOHN | PA-38-112 Tomahawk | AT Aviation Ltd |
| | G-BOHO | PA-28-161 Warrior II | Air Navigation & Trading Ltd/Blackpool |
| | G-BOHR | PA-28-151 Warrior | L. T. Evans |
| | G-BOHS | PA-38-112 Tomahawk | Falcon Flying Services/Biggin Hill |
| | G-BOHT | PA-38-112 Tomahawk | Falcon Flying Services/Biggin Hill |
| | G-BOHU | PA-38-112 Tomahawk | Falcon Flying Services/Biggin Hill |
| | G-BOHV | Wittman W.8 Tailwind | R. A. Povall |
| | G-BOHW | Van's RV-4 | R. W. H. Cole |
| | G-BOHX | PA-44-180 Seminole | Golden Castle Caravans Ltd |
| | G-BOHY | H.S.748 Srs 2B | British Airways Glen Shee/Glasgow |
| | G-BOHZ | H.S.748 Srs 2B | British Airways Glen Turret/Glasgow |
| | G-BOIA | Cessna 180K | R. E. Styles & ptnrs |
| | G-BOIB | Wittman W.10 Tailwind | P. H. Lewis |

| Reg. | Type | Owner or Operator | Notes |
|------|------|-------------------|-------|
| G-BOIC | PA-28R-201T Turbo Arrow III | M. J. Pearson | |
| G-BOID | Bellanca 7ECA Citabria | Chemtech Ltd | |
| G-BOIF | Beech 95-B55 Baron | Seal Executive Aircraft Ltd | |
| G-BOIG | PA-28-161 Warrior II | D. W. Higgins | |
| G-BOIH | Pitts S-1E Special | S. L. Goldspink | |
| G-BOII | Cessna 172N | Trevair Group/Bournemouth | |
| G-BOIJ | Thunder Ax7-77 balloon | Shropshire Lad Original Ballooning | |
| G-BOIK | Air Command 503 Commander | D. W. Smith | |
| G-BOIL | Cessna 172N | Upperstack Ltd | |
| G-BOIM | Cessna 150M | ARK Ltd | |
| G-BOIN | Bellanca 7ECA Citabria | AV Aviation Ltd | |
| G-BOIO | Cessna 152 | AV Aviation Ltd | |
| G-BOIP | Cessna 152 | Stapleford Flying Club Ltd | |
| G-BOIR | Cessna 152 | Shropshire Aero Club Ltd/Sleap | |
| G-BOIS | PA-31 Turbo Navajo | Compass Aviation Ltd (G-AYNB) | |
| G-BOIT | SOCATA TB.10 Tobago | Air Touring Services Ltd/Biggin Hill | |
| G-BOIU | SOCATA TB.10 Tobago | Portman Welbeck Ltd | |
| G-BOIV | Cesna 150M | F. E. P. Holmes/Andrewsfield | |
| G-BOIW | Cessna 152 | London Flight Centre (Stansted) Ltd | |
| G-BOIX | Cessna 172N | JR Flying Ltd | |
| G-BOIY | Cessna 172N | London Flight Centre (Stansted) Ltd | |
| G-BOIZ | PA-34-200T Seneca II | Northumbria Aviation Ltd | |
| G-BOJB | Cameron V-77 balloon | K. L. Heron & R. M. Trotter | |
| G-BOJD | Cameron V-77 balloon | The Independent Balloon Co Ltd | |
| G-BOJE | PA-28-236 Dakota | Martin & Randle Ltd | |
| G-BOJF | Air Command 532 Elite | P. J. Davies | |
| G-BOJH | PA-28R Cherokee Arrow 200 | Ryders Express Services Ltd/ Birmingham | |
| G-BOJI | PA-28RT-201 Arrow IV | Market Penetration Services Ltd | |
| G-BOJJ | BAe 146-300 | British Aerospace PLC/Hatfield | |
| G-BOJK | PA-34-220T Seneca III | Redhill Flying Club (G-BRUF) | |
| G-BOJL | M.S.885 Super Rallye | J. Rees | |
| G-BOJM | PA-28-181 Archer II | H. Skelton | |
| G-BOJO | Colt 120A balloon | Airbureau Ltd | |
| G-BOJR | Cessna 172P | Exeter Flying Club Ltd | |
| G-BOJS | Cessna 172P | J. D. Beckett/Exeter | |
| G-BOJT | Beech 76 Duchess | Aviation Services (UK) Ltd | |
| G-BOJU | Cameron N-77 balloon | The Hot Air Balloon Co Ltd | |
| G-BOJW | PA-28-161 Warrior II | R. D. Hill & F. R. H. Parker | |
| G-BOJX | PA-28-181 Archer II | Southern Air Ltd/Shoreham | |
| G-BOJY | PA-28-161 Warrior II | Southern Air Ltd/Shoreham | |
| G-BOJZ | PA-28-161 Warrior II | Southern Air Ltd/Shoreham | |
| G-BOKA | PA-28-201T Turbo Dakota | CBG Aviation Ltd/Biggin Hill | |
| G-BOKB | PA-28-161 Warrior II | Southern Air Ltd/Shoreham | |
| G-BOKE | PA-34-200T Seneca II | J. G. Kelwick | |
| G-BOKF | Air Command 532 Elite | P. T. Waldron | |
| G-BOKG | Slingsby T.31 Motor Cadet III | A. M. Witt | |
| G-BOKH | Whittaker MW.7 | M. W. J. Whittaker | |
| G-BOKI | Whittaker MW.7 | R. K. Willcox | |
| G-BOKJ | Whittaker MW.7 | M. N. Gauntlett | |
| G-BOKK | PA-28-161 Warrior II | David Gilliam Ltd | |
| G-BOKL | PA-28-161 Warrior II | BAe Flying College Ltd/Prestwick | |
| G-BOKM | PA-28-161 Warrior II | BAe Flying College Ltd/Prestwick | |
| G-BOKN | PA-28-161 Warrior II | BAe Flying College Ltd/Prestwick | |
| G-BOKO | PA-28-161 Warrior II | BAe Flying College Ltd/Prestwick | |
| G-BOKP | PA-28-161 Warrior II | BAe Flying College Ltd/Prestwick | |
| G-BOKR | PA-28-161 Warrior II | BAe Flying College Ltd/Prestwick | |
| G-BOKS | PA-28-161 Warrior II | BAe Flying College Ltd/Prestwick | |
| G-BOKT | PA-28-161 Warrior II | BAe Flying College Ltd/Prestwick | |
| G-BOKU | PA-28-161 Warrior II | BAe Flying College Ltd/Prestwick | |
| G-BOKW | Bo 208C Junior | R. A. Farrington (G-BITT) | |
| G-BOKX | PA-28-161 Warrior II | W. P. J. Jackson | |
| G-BOKY | Cessna 152 | London Flight Centre (Stansted) Ltd | |
| G-BOLB | Taylorcraft BC-12-65 | G-BOLB Flying Group | |
| G-BOLC | Fournier RF-6B-100 | I. Perry | |
| G-BOLD | PA-38-112 Tomahawk | B. R. Pearson & B. F. Fraser-Smith/ Eaglescott | |
| G-BOLE | PA-38-112 Tomahawk | M. W. Kibble & E. A. Minard | |
| G-BOLF | PA-38-112 Tomahawk | B. R. Pearson & B. F. Fraser-Smith/ Eaglescott | |
| G-BOLG | Bellanca 7KCAB Citabria | B. R. Pearson/Eaglescott | |
| G-BOLI | Cessna 172P | Boli Flying Club | |
| G-BOLJ | GA-7 Cougar | Hastemark Ltd | |

| Notes | Reg. | Type | Owner or Operator |
|-------|------|------|-------------------|
| | G-BOLL | Lake LA-4 Skimmer | T. M. Kidd/Glasgow |
| | G-BOLN | Colt 21A balloon | Airship & Balloon Co Ltd |
| | G-BOLO | Bell 206B JetRanger | Hargreaves Construction Co Ltd/ Shoreham |
| | G-BOLP | Colt 21A balloon | Airship & Balloon Co Ltd |
| | G-BOLR | Colt 21A balloon | Airship & Balloon Co Ltd |
| | G-BOLS | FRED Srs 2 | R. G. Goodburn |
| | G-BOLT | R. Commander 114 | R. D. Rooke/Elstree |
| | G-BOLU | Robin R.3000/120 | Lydair Ltd/Lydd |
| | G-BOLV | Cessna 152 | London Flight Centre (Stansted) Ltd |
| | G-BOLW | Cessna 152 | Seawing Flying Club Ltd/Southend |
| | G-BOLX | Cessna 172N | London Flight Centre (Stansted) Ltd |
| | G-BOLY | Cessna 172N | London Flight Centre (Headcorn) Ltd |
| | G-BOLZ | Rand KR-2 | B. Normington |
| | G-BOMB | Cussutt Racer | P. P. Chapman/Biggin Hill |
| | G-BOML | Hispano HA.1112MIL (—) | R. G. Hanna/Duxford |
| | G-BOMN | Cessna 150F | D. G. Williams |
| | G-BOMO | PA-38-112 Tomahawk | Gloucester & Cheltenham Aviation/ Staverton |
| | G-BOMP | PA-28-181 Archer II | Falcon Flying Services/Biggin Hill |
| | G-BOMS | Cessna 172N | Osprey Air Services Ltd/Cranfield |
| | G-BOMT | Cessna 172N | Herefordshire Aero Club Ltd/Shobdon |
| | G-BOMU | PA-28-181 Archer II | RJ Aviation/Blackbushe |
| | G-BOMY | PA-28-161 Warrior II | Carill Aviation Ltd/Southampton |
| | G-BOMZ | PA-38-112 Tomahawk | B. E. Simpson/Booker |
| | G-BONA | Cessna 172RG | A. Garner/Florida |
| | G-BONC | PA-28RT-201 Arrow IV | Modern Air |
| | G-BOND | Sikorsky S-76A | Bond Helicopters Ltd/Bourn |
| | G-BONE | Pilatus P2-06 (U-142) | D. C. R. Writer |
| | G-BONG | Enstrom F-28A | Spectolal Ltd/Blackbushe |
| | G-BONH | Enstrom F-28A | Blades Helicopters Ltd |
| | G-BONK | Colt 180A balloon | Wye Valley Aviation Ltd |
| | G-BONL | Bell 206B JetRanger 2 | Dollar Air Services Ltd |
| | G-BONO | Cessna 172N | M. Rowe/Sywell |
| | G-BONP | CFM Streak Shadow | CFM Metal-Fax Ltd |
| | G-BONR | Cessna 172N | Atlaslocal Ltd/Biggin Hill |
| | G-BONS | Cessna 172N | N. P. Bendle |
| | G-BONT | Slingsby T.67M Mk II | Slingsby Aviation Ltd/Kirkbymoorside |
| | G-BONU | Slingsby T.67B | Slingsby Aviation Ltd/Kirkbymoorside |
| | G-BONV | Colt 17A balloon | Airship & Balloon Co Ltd |
| | G-BONW | Cessna 152 | Lincoln Aero Club Ltd/Sturgate |
| | G-BONX | Robinson R-22B | Rightbest Ltd |
| | G-BONY | Denney Aerocraft Kitfox | Penny Hydraulics Ltd |
| | G-BONZ | Beech V35B Bonanza | P. M. Coulten |
| | G-BOOB | Cameron N-65 balloon | I. J. Sadler |
| | G-BOOC | PA-18 Super Cub 150 | R. R. & S. A. Marriott |
| | G-BOOD | Slingsby T.31M Motor Tutor | P. J. Titherington |
| | G-BOOE | GA-7 Cougar | G. L. Cailes |
| | G-BOOF | PA-28-181 Archer II | Golf Boof Group |
| | G-BOOG | PA-28RT-201T Turbo Arrow IV | A. W. D. Perkins & J. C. Walton |
| | G-BOOH | Jodel D.112 | D. F. Madams |
| | G-BOOI | Cessna 152 | Stapleford Flying Club Ltd |
| | G-BOOJ | Air Command 532 Elite | G. Snook |
| | G-BOOK | Pitts S-1S Special | A. N. R. Houghton |
| | G-BOOL | Cessna 172N | Biggin Hill School of Flying |
| | G-BOOM | Hunter T.7 | Hunter Wing Ltd/Bournemouth |
| | G-BOON | PA-32RT-300 Lance II | G-BOON Ltd/Luton |
| | G-BOOO | Brugger MB .2 Colibri | D. G. Cole |
| | G-BOOP | Cameron N-90 balloon | The Hot Air Balloon Co Ltd (G-BOMX) |
| | G-BOOS | Colt 240A balloon | Thunder & Colt Ltd |
| | G-BOOT | Colt 240A balloon | Thunder & Colt Ltd |
| | G-BOOU | Cameron N-77 balloon | Aqualisa Products Ltd |
| | G-BOOV | AS.355F-2 Twin Squirrel | Merseyside Police Authority |
| | G-BOOW | Aerosport Scamp | B. I. Turner |
| | G-BOOX | Rutan LongEz | I. R. Thomas & I. R. Wilde |
| | G-BOOZ | Cameron N-77 balloon | J. E. F. Kettley |
| | G-BOPA | PA-28-181 Archer II | J. E. Strutt Ltd |
| | G-BOPB | Boeing 767-204ER | Britannia Airways Ltd *Captain Sir Ross Smith*/Luton |
| | G-BOPC | PA-28-161 Warrior II | Channel Aviation Ltd |
| | G-BOPD | Bede BD-4 | S. T. Dauncey |
| | G-BOPE | Hiller UH-12E | Courtfarm Ltd |
| | G-BOPG | Cessna 182Q | Rajmech Ltd & Charles Hawkins Ltd |

| Reg. | Type | Owner or Operator | Notes |
|------|------|-------------------|-------|
| G-BOPH | Cessna TR.182RG | E. A. L. Sturmer | |
| G-BOPJ | Boeing 737-46B | British Midland Airways Ltd/E. Midlands | |
| G-BOPK | Boeing 737-46B | Air Europe Ltd/Gatwick | |
| G-BOPL | PA-28-161 Warrior II | Cambrian Flying Club/Swansea | |
| G-BOPN | Brooklands OA.7 Optica | Brooklands Aerospace Ltd/Old Sarum | |
| G-BOPT | Grob G.115 | Light Planes Lancashire Ltd/Barton | |
| G-BOPU | Grob G.115 | Light Planes Lancashire Ltd/Barton | |
| G-BOPV | PA-34-200T Seneca II | Tewin Aviation | |
| G-BOPW | Cessna A.152 | Northamptonshire School of Flying Ltd/ Sywell | |
| G-BOPX | Cessna A.152 | Osprey Air Services Ltd/Cranfield | |
| G-BOPZ | Cameron DP-70 airship | The Hot Air Balloon Co Ltd (G-BOMW) | |
| G-BORA | Colt 77A balloon | Cala Homes (Southern) Ltd | |
| G-BORB | Cameron V-77 balloon | M. H. Wolff | |
| G-BORC | Colt 180A balloon | Airship & Balloon Co Ltd | |
| G-BORD | Thunder Ax7-77 balloon | D. D. Owen | |
| G-BORE | Colt 77A balloon | Little Secret Hot-Air Balloon Group | |
| G-BORF | Colt AS-80 Mk II airship | Thunder & Colt Ltd | |
| G-BORG | Campbell Cricket | N. G. Bailey | |
| G-BORH | PA-34-200T Seneca II | Self Adhesive Fixings Ltd/Sandown | |
| G-BORI | Cessna 152 | R. D. Ward | |
| G-BORJ | Cessna 152 | Antler Enterprises Ltd | |
| G-BORK | PA-28-161 Warrior II | J. A. Hilton/Coventry | |
| G-BORL | PA-28-161 Warrior II | D. C. Harry | |
| G-BORM | H.S.748 Srs 2B | Sean T. Hully (Sales) Ltd | |
| G-BORN | Cameron N-77 balloon | Laing Homes Ltd | |
| G-BORO | Cessna 152 | Seal Executive Aircraft Ltd | |
| G-BORP | PA-46-310P Malibu | SMC Aviation Ltd/Southend | |
| G-BORR | Thunder Ax8-90 balloon | W. J. Harris | |
| G-BORS | PA-28-181 Archer II | Modern Air/Panshanger | |
| G-BORT | Colt 77A balloon | I. E. A. Joslyn/Germany | |
| G-BORV | Bell 206B JetRanger 2 | P. V. Doman | |
| G-BORW | Cessna 172P | Briter Aviation Ltd/Coventry | |
| G-BORY | Cessna 150L | Airspeed Aviation Ltd | |
| G-BOSA | Boeing 737-204ADV | Ali Finance Ltd (G-BAZI)/Luton | |
| G-BOSB | Thunder Ax7-77 balloon | M. Gallagher | |
| G-BOSC | Cessna U.206G | A. J. Buczkowski/Cranfield | |
| G-BOSD | PA-34-200T Seneca II | Barnes Olson Aeroleasing Ltd | |
| G-BOSE | PA-28-181 Archer II | A. P. Bath | |
| G-BOSF | Colt 69A balloon | Airship & Balloon Co Ltd | |
| G-BOSG | Colt 17A balloon | Airship & Balloon Co Ltd | |
| G-BOSH | Thunder Ax8-84 balloon | Ace Balloons (Bath) Ltd | |
| G-BOSJ | Nord 3400 | M. F. W. Boyd-Maunsell | |
| G-BOSK | AS.355F-1 Twin Squirrel | McAlpine Helicopters Ltd/Hayes | |
| G-BOSM | Jodel DR.253B | J. Cantellow | |
| G-BOSO | Cessna A.152 | Redhill Flying Club | |
| G-BOSP | PA-28-151 Warrior | F. E. P. Holmes/Andrewsfield | |
| G-BOSR | PA-28 Cherokee 140 | R. D. Cornish | |
| G-BOSU | PA-28 Cherokee 140 | M. A. Roberts | |
| G-BOSV | Cameron V-77 balloon | K. H. Greenaway | |
| G-BOSW | Bell 206B JetRanger | Walsh Aviation | |
| G-BOSY | Robinson R-22B | Cross Lane Properties (Builders) Ltd | |
| G-BOTB | Cessna 152 | Stapleford Flying Club Ltd | |
| G-BOTC | Cessna 152 | Stapleford Flying Club Ltd | |
| G-BOTD | Cameron O-105 balloon | P. J. Beglan | |
| G-BOTE | Thunder Ax8-90 balloon | R. S. Hunjan | |
| G-BOTF | PA-28-151 Warrior | G-BOTF Group/Southend | |
| G-BOTG | Cessna 152 | Donington Aviation Ltd/E. Midlands | |
| G-BOTH | Cessna 182Q | R. H. Durston | |
| G-BOTI | PA-28-151 Warrior | Tango India Flying Group/Biggin Hill | |
| G-BOTK | Cameron O-105 balloon | S. J. Fensome | |
| G-BOTM | Bell 206B JetRanger 2 | R. J. & E. M. Frost | |
| G-BOTN | PA-28-161 Warrior II | W. Lancashire Aero Club Ltd/Woodvale | |
| G-BOTO | Bellanca 7ECA Citabria | G-BOTO Group | |
| G-BOTP | Cessna 150J | R. E. Thorne | |
| G-BOTS | Hughes 269C | Horizon Helicopters | |
| G-BOTT | Rand KR-2 | M. D. Ott & M. R. Hutchins | |
| G-BOTU | Piper J-3C-65 Cub | L. G. Burrell & W. J. Clarke | |
| G-BOTV | PA-32RT-300 Lance II | Robin Lance Aviation Association Ltd | |
| G-BOTW | Cameron V-77 balloon | D. N. Malcolm | |
| G-BOTY | Cessna 150J | T. J. C. Darby & G. Webster | |
| G-BOTZ | Bensen B.80R | C. Jones | |
| G-BOUD | PA-38-112 Tomahawk | K. & C. J. Powell/Southend | |

| Notes | Reg. | Type | Owner or Operator |
|-------|------|------|-------------------|
| | G-BOUE | Cessna 172N | ARK Ltd |
| | G-BOUF | Cessna 172N | Zycomm Electronics Ltd/Burnaston |
| | G-BOUH | Cessna 172RG | M. G. Fountain |
| | G-BOUI | PA-28-236 Dakota | Solvit Software |
| | G-BOUJ | Cessna 150M | P. & M. O'Conner |
| | G-BOUK | PA-34-200T Seneca II | Airtime (Hampshire) Ltd |
| | G-BOUL | PA-34-200T Seneca II | C.S.E. Aviation Ltd/Kidlington |
| | G-BOUM | PA-34-200T Seneca II | C.S.E. Aviation Ltd/Kidlington |
| | G-BOUN | Rand KR-2 | W. J. Allen |
| | G-BOUO | Thunder Ax8-105 balloon | V. D. Ling |
| | G-BOUP | PA-28-161 Warrior II | C.S.E. Aviation Ltd/Kidlington |
| | G-BOUR | PA-28-161 Warrior II | C.S.E. Aviation Ltd/Kidlington |
| | G-BOUS | PA-28RT-201 Arrow IV | Hamilton Compass Aviation Ltd |
| | G-BOUT | Colomban MC.12 Cri-Cri | C. K. Farley |
| | G-BOUU | Everett gyroplane | A. Everett |
| | G-BOUV | Bensen B.8R | P. Wilkinson |
| | G-BOUX | Everett gyroplane | A. Everett |
| | G-BOUY | Bell 206B JetRanger | Clyde Helicopters Ltd/Glasgow |
| | G-BOUZ | Cessna 150G | G. Webster & T. J. C. Darby |
| | G-BOVA | PA-31-310 Turbo Navajo C | Birmingham Aviation Ltd (G-BECP) |
| | G-BOVB | PA-15 Vagabond | Oscar Flying Group/Shoreham |
| | G-BOVC | Everett gyroplane | M. T. Byrne |
| | G-BOVE | Everett gyroplane | A. Everett |
| | G-BOVG | Cessna F.172H | The G-BOVG Group |
| | G-BOVH | PA-28-161 Warrior II | R. W. Tebby |
| | G-BOVK | PA-28-161 Warrior II | Hamilton Compass Aviation Ltd |
| | G-BOVL | SNCAN Stampe SV-4C | T. A. Reed |
| | G-BOVN | Air Command 532 Elite | I. R. Lee |
| | G-BOVP | Air Command 532 Elite | C. K. Park |
| | G-BOVR | Robinson R-22 | P. J. Homan |
| | G-BOVS | Cessna 150M | V. B. Cheesewright |
| | G-BOVT | Cessna 150M | R. G. Moss |
| | G-BOVU | Stoddard-Hamilton Glasair III | W. N. Blair-Hickman |
| | G-BOVV | Cameron V-77 balloon | J. P. Clifford |
| | G-BOVW | Colt 69A balloon | V. Hyland |
| | G-BOVX | Hughes 269C | McIntyre Aviation Ltd/Staverton |
| | G-BOVY | Hughes 269C | R. C. Button |
| | G-BOVZ | Hughes 269C | March Helicopters Ltd/Sywell |
| | G-BOWA | Thunder Ax8-90 balloon | G. & L. Fitzpatrick |
| | G-BOWB | Cameron V-77 balloon | R. C. Stone |
| | G-BOWC | Cessna 150J | G-BOWC Flying Group/Southend |
| | G-BOWD | Cessna F.337G | John Hewitson Ltd (G-BLSB) |
| | G-BOWE | PA-34-200T Seneca II | C.S.E. Aviation Ltd/Kidlington |
| | G-BOWK | Cameron N-90 balloon | S. R. Bridge |
| | G-BOWL | Cameron V-77 balloon | Matrix Computers Ltd |
| | G-BOWM | Cameron V-56 balloon | C. G. Caldecott & G. Pitt |
| | G-BOWN | PA-12 Super Cruiser | F. E. P. Holmes/Andrewsfield |
| | G-BOWO | Cessna R.182 | Kenbal Properties Ltd |
| | G-BOWP | Jodel D.120A | A. G. Gedney & ptnrs/Sibson |
| | G-BOWR | Boeing 737-3Q8 | Britannia Airways Ltd/Luton |
| | G-BOWS | Cessna 150M | Semloh Aviation Services/Andrewsfield |
| | G-BOWT | Stolp SA.300 Starduster Too | F. E. P. Holmes/Andrewsfield |
| | G-BOWU | Cameron O-84 balloon | Raybrake & Co Ltd |
| | G-BOWV | Cameron V-65 balloon | C. P. R. & S. J. Baxter |
| | G-BOWY | PA-28RT-201T Turbo Arrow IV | Littlebird (UK) Ltd/Elstree |
| | G-BOWZ | Benson B.80V | W. M. Day |
| | G-BOXA | PA-28-161 Warrior II | CI Aero Holdings Ltd |
| | G-BOXB | PA-28-161 Warrior II | CI Aero Holdings Ltd |
| | G-BOXC | PA-28-161 Warrior II | CI Aero Holdings Ltd |
| | G-BOXG | Cameron O-77 balloon | S. J. Butler |
| | G-BOXH | Pitts S-1S Special | S. Fenwick |
| | G-BOXJ | Piper J-3C-65 Cub | J. L. Quick & A. J. P. Jackson/Biggin Hill |
| | G-BOXK | Slingsby T.67C | Slingsby Aviation Ltd/Kirkbymoorside |
| | G-BOXN | Robinson R-22B | Conguess Aviation Ltd |
| | G-BOXR | GA-7 Cougar | Campbell Air Services Ltd/Booker |
| | G-BOXS | Hughes 269C | Ford Helicopters Ltd |
| | G-BOXT | Hughes 269C | Elite Helicopters Ltd |
| | G-BOXU | AA-5B Tiger | J. J. Woodhouse |
| | G-BOXV | Pitts S-1S Special | J. N. Carter |
| | G-BOXW | Cassutt Racer Srs IIIM | D. I. Johnson |
| | G-BOXX | Robinson R-22B | Doncaster Helicopter Services |
| | G-BOXY | PA-28-181 Archer II | Sheffield Aero Club Ltd/Netherthorpe |
| | G-BOYA | Cessna A.152 | Denham School of Flying Ltd |

| Reg. | Type | Owner or Operator | Notes |
|------|------|-------------------|-------|
| G-BOYB | Cessna A.152 | Northamptonshire School of Flying Ltd/ Sywell | |
| G-BOYC | Robinson R-22B | K. M. Hiley | |
| G-BOYE | Cessna TR.182RG | S. K. & W. J. Boettcher | |
| G-BOYF | Sikorsky S-76B | Darley Steel Management Co Ltd | |
| G-BOYG | Cessna 421C | Leeds Aviation Ltd | |
| G-BOYH | PA-28-151 Warrior | Superpause Ltd/Booker | |
| G-BOYI | PA-28-161 Warrior II | Rankart Ltd/Kidlington | |
| G-BOYK | Montgomerie-Benson B.8 | H. P. Latham | |
| G-BOYL | Cessna 152 | T. Hayselden (Doncaster) Ltd | |
| G-BOYM | Cameron O-84 balloon | Frontline Distribution Ltd | |
| G-BOYN | Boeing 737-3S3 | Air Europe/Air Europa (EC-ECQ) | |
| G-BOYO | Cameron V-20 balloon | Cameron Balloons Ltd | |
| G-BOYP | Cessna 172N | S. J. Randle & T. W. Crow | |
| G-BOYR | Cessna F.337G | C. M. Vlieland-Boddy/Compton Abbas | |
| G-BOYS | Cameron N-77 balloon | The Independent Balloon Co Ltd | |
| G-BOYT | PA-38-112 Tomahawk | Seal Executive Aircraft Ltd | |
| G-BOYU | Cessna A.150L | Seal Executive Aircraft Ltd | |
| G-BOYV | PA-28R-201T Turbo Arrow III | P. R. Goldsworthy | |
| G-BOYX | Robinson R-22B | R. Towle | |
| G-BOYY | Cameron A-105 balloon | Hoyers (UK) Ltd | |
| G-BOYZ | Laser Z.200 | M. G. Jefferies | |
| G-BOZA | Boeing 737-3L9 | British Airways River Lossie/Heathrow | |
| G-BOZB | Boeing 737-3L9 | British Airways River Wyre/Heathrow | |
| G-BOZI | PA-28-161 Warrior II | Klingair Ltd/Conington | |
| G-BOZJ | Thunder Ax8-105 balloon | G. V. Beckwith | |
| G-BOZK | AS.332L Super Puma | British International Helicopters Ltd | |
| G-BOZL | Bell 206B JetRanger | Ernest George Aviation Ltd | |
| G-BOZM | PA-38-112 Tomahawk | S. J. Green | |
| G-BOZN | Cameron N-77 balloon | Calarel Developments Ltd | |
| G-BOZO | AA-5B Tiger | Becketts Honda Car Centre Ltd | |
| G-BOZP | Beech 76 Duchess | Millhouse Developments Ltd | |
| G-BOZR | Cessna 152 | Interair (Aviation) Ltd/Bournemouth | |
| G-BOZS | Pitts S-1C Special | T. G. Soloman/Shoreham | |
| G-BOZT | PA-28-181 Archer II | Andrews Aviation Ltd | |
| G-BOZU | Sparrow Hawk Mk II | R. V. Phillimore | |
| G-BOZV | CEA DR.340 Major | E. H. Ellis | |
| G-BOZW | Benson B.8M | M. E. Wills | |
| G-BOZX | Robinson R-22B | M. J. Burgess | |
| G-BOZY | Cameron RTW-120 balloon | Pacific Television Enterprises Ltd | |
| G-BOZZ | AA-5B Tiger | P. R. Draper | |
| G-BPAA | Acro Advanced | Acro Engines & Airframes Ltd | |
| G-BPAB | Cessna 150M | A. & B. Aviation/Earls Colne | |
| G-BPAC | PA-28-161 Warror II | G. G. Pratt | |
| G-BPAD | PA-34-200T Seneca II | North West Aviation Ltd/Liverpool | |
| G-BPAE | Cameron V-77 balloon | A. R. Peart & J. E. Astall | |
| G-BPAF | PA-28-161 Warrior II | Hendafern Ltd | |
| G-BPAG | Bellanca 8KCAB Decathlon | The Real Aeroplane Co Ltd | |
| G-BPAH | Colt 69A balloon | International Distillers & Vintners Ltd | |
| G-BPAI | Bell 47F-2A1 | Fizzle Ltd | |
| G-BPAJ | D.H.82A Tiger Moth | P. A. Jackson (G-AOIX) | |
| G-BPAL | D.H.C.1 Chipmunk 22 (WG350) | D. F. Ranger (G-BCYE) | |
| G-BPAM | Jodel D.150A | A. J. Symes-Bullen | |
| G-BPAO | Air Command 503 Commander | D. J. Sagar | |
| G-BPAP | Robinson R-22B | Stag Electronic Design Ltd | |
| G-BPAS | SOCATA TB.20 Trinidad | J. Miskelly | |
| G-BPAU | PA-28-161 Warrior II | Lapwing Flying Group Ltd/Denham | |
| G-BPAV | FRED Srs 2 | P. A. Valentine | |
| G-BPAW | Cessna 150M | Skegness Air Taxi Service Ltd | |
| G-BPAX | Cessna 150M | LAR Aviation Ltd | |
| G-BPAY | PA-28-181 Archer II | C. Juggins/Goodwood | |
| G-BPBA | Benson B.8 | M. E. Green | |
| G-BPBC | Bell 206B JetRanger | Delfino Maritime Ltd | |
| G-BPBG | Cessna 152 | Atlantic Air Transport Ltd/Coventry | |
| G-BPBH | Cessna 152 | B. W. Wells & Burbage Farms Ltd | |
| G-BPBI | Cessna 152 | B. W. Wells & Burbage Farms Ltd | |
| G-BPBJ | Cessna 152 | B. W. Wells & Burbage Farms Ltd | |
| G-BPBK | Cessna 152 | B. W. Wells & Burbage Farms Ltd | |
| G-BPBL | Cessna 152 | B. W. Wells & Burbage Farms Ltd | |
| G-BPBM | PA-28-161 Warrior II | T. Hayselden (Doncaster) Ltd | |
| G-BPBO | PA-28RT-201T Turbo Arrow IV | TEL (IoM) Ltd | |
| G-BPBR | PA-38-112 Tomahawk | A.T. Aviation Ltd/Cardiff | |

| Notes | Reg. | Type | Owner or Operator |
|---|---|---|---|
| | G-BPBU | Cameron V-77 balloon | G. Illing |
| | G-BPBV | Cameron V-77 balloon | J. E. Smith |
| | G-BPBW | Cameron O-105 balloon | R. J. Mansfield |
| | G-BPBX | Cameron V-77 balloon | A. R. M. Hill & C. J. Bell (G-BPCU) |
| | G-BPBY | Cameron V-77 balloon | T. J. & K. A. Brewster (G-BPCS) |
| | G-BPBZ | Thunder Ax7-77 balloon | Wye Valley Aviation Ltd |
| | G-BPCA | BN-2B Islander | Loganair Ltd (G-BLNX)/Glasgow |
| | G-BPCD | BN-2A-26 Islander | Air & General Services Ltd (G-BFNV) |
| | G-BPCE | Stolp SA.300 Starduster Too | R. E. Todd |
| | G-BPCF | Piper J-3C-65 Cub | A. J. Cook |
| | G-BPCG | Colt AS-80 airship | Willowbest Ltd |
| | G-BPCI | Cessna R.172K | B. E. Simpson |
| | G-BPCJ | Cessna 150J | C. R. Hughes & B. E. Simpson |
| | G-BPCK | PA-28-161 Warrior II | C. R. Hughes & B. E. Simpson |
| | G-BPCL | SA Bulldog 120/128 | Isohigh Ltd/Denham |
| | G-BPCM | Rotorway Executive | Normans (Burton-on-Trent) Ltd |
| | G-BPCN | Cameron A-160 balloon | Chard Balloon Co Ltd |
| | G-BPCO | Short SD3-60 Variant 100 | Air Europe Express (G-RMSS/G-BKKU)/ Gatwick |
| | G-BPCR | Mooney M.20K | T. & R. Harris |
| | G-BPCT | Bell 206L-1 LongRanger | Trillionair Ltd |
| | G-BPCV | Montgomerie Bensen MB.8R | J. Fisher |
| | G-BPCW | Slingsby T.31 Motor Cadet III | P. C. Williams |
| | G-BPCX | PA-28-236 Dakota | Visual Phantom Ltd |
| | G-BPCY | PA-34-200T Seneca | Compton Abbas Airfield Ltd |
| | G-BPDA | H.S.748 Srs 2A | Greyhound Financial Services Ltd (G-GLAS) |
| | G-BPDC | PA-46-310P Malibu | D. W. Clark |
| | G-BPDD | Colt 240A balloon | Heather Flight Ltd |
| | G-BPDE | Colt 56A balloon | J. W. Weidema |
| | G-BPDF | Cameron V-77 balloon | Boyson Construction Ltd |
| | G-BPDG | Cameron V-77 balloon | A. & M. A. Dunning |
| | G-BPDJ | Chris Tena Mini Coupe | Air Time Acquisition Ltd |
| | G-BPDK | Sorrell SNS-7 Hyperbipe | A. J. Cable/Barton |
| | G-BPDL | EMB-110P1 Bandeirante | Titan Airways/Stansted |
| | G-BPDM | C.A.S.A. 1.131E Jungmann (E3B-369) | Spanish Acquisition/Shoreham |
| | G-BPDN | PA-28R-201 Arrow III | J. M. C. Crompton |
| | G-BPDR | Schweizer 269C | C.S.E. Aviation Ltd/Kidlington |
| | G-BPDS | PA-28-161 Warrior II | Hendafern Ltd |
| | G-BPDT | PA-28-161 Warrior II | Hendafern Ltd |
| | G-BPDU | PA-28-161 Warrior II | Hendafern Ltd |
| | G-BPDV | Pitts S-1S Special | D. Clarke |
| | G-BPDY | Westland-Bell 47G-3B1 | Fairglobe Ltd |
| | G-BPDZ | Cessna 340A | Gwent Plant Sales |
| | G-BPEA | Boeing 757-236ER | Caledonian Airways Ltd Loch of the Clans/Gatwick |
| | G-BPEB | Boeing 757-236ER | Caledonian Airways Ltd Loch Lomond/ Gatwick |
| | G-BPEC | Boeing 757-236ER | Caledonian Airways Ltd Loch Katrine/ Gatwick |
| | G-BPED | Boeing 757-236ER | Caledonian Airways Ltd Loch Sheil/ Gatwick |
| | G-BPEE | Boeing 757-236ER | Caledonian Airways Ltd Loch Tay/ Gatwick |
| | G-BPEF | — | Caledonian Airways Ltd/Gatwick |
| | G-BPEH | — | Caledonian Airways Ltd/Gatwick |
| | G-BPEI | — | Caledonian Airways Ltd/Gatwick |
| | G-BPEJ | — | Caledonian Airways Ltd/Gatwick |
| | G-BPEK | — | Caledonian Airways Ltd/Gatwick |
| | G-BPEL | PA-28-151 Warrior | M. E. Benterman |
| | G-BPEM | Cessna 150K | C. A. Outhwaite |
| | G-BPEO | Cessna 152 | M. E. Benterman |
| | G-BPER | PA-38-112 Tomahawk | E. Midlands Flying School Ltd |
| | G-BPES | PA-38-112 Tomahawk | Sherwood Flying Club Ltd/Tollerton |
| | G-BPEW | Robinson R-22B | Trade Photographic Services Ltd |
| | G-BPEZ | Colt 77A balloon | Thunder & Colt Ltd |
| | G-BPFA | Knight GK-2 Swallow | G. Knight & D. G. Pridham |
| | G-BPFB | Colt 77A balloon | S. Ingram |
| | G-BPFC | Mooney M.20C | Kington Building Supplies Ltd & RV Engineering Ltd |
| | G-BPFD | Jodel D.112 | K. Manley |
| | G-BPFE | Lightning T.5 (XS452) | Ruanil Investments Ltd/Cranfield |

| Reg. | Type | Owner or Operator | Notes |
|------|------|-------------------|-------|
| G-BPFF | Cameron DP-70 airship | Cameron Balloons Ltd | |
| G-BPFG | SOCATA TB.20 Trinidad | F. T. Arnold | |
| G-BPFH | PA-28-161 Warrior II | M. H. Kleiser | |
| G-BPFI | PA-28-181 Archer II | Dixon Spain Estates Ltd | |
| G-BPFJ | Cameron 90 Can SS balloon | The Hot-Air Balloon Co Ltd | |
| G-BPFK | Bensen B.8M | J. W. Birkett | |
| G-BPFL | Davis DA-2 | C. A. Lightfoot | |
| G-BPFM | Aeronca 7AC Champion | J. Tye | |
| G-BPFS | Short SD3-60 Variant 100 | Birmingham European Airways Ltd (G-REGN/G-OCIA) *City of Newcastle* | |
| G-BPFT | Cameron N-77 balloon | Cameron Balloons Ltd | |
| G-BPFU | H.S.748 Srs 2A | Scottish European Airways Ltd (G-EDIN)/Glasgow | |
| G-BPFV | Boeing 767-204ER | Britannia Airways Ltd/Luton | |
| G-BPFW | Air Command 532 Elite | B. A. Snell | |
| G-BPFX | Colt 21A balloon | The Hot-Air Balloon Co Ltd | |
| G-BPFY | Consolidated PBY-6A Catalina | D. W. Arnold/Biggin Hill | |
| G-BPFZ | Cessna 152 | J. J. Baumhardt/Southend | |
| G-BPGA | Mooney M.20J | Medallionair Ltd | |
| G-BPGB | Cessna 150J | Skegness Air Taxi Service Ltd | |
| G-BPGC | Air Command 532 Elite | E. C. E. Brown | |
| G-BPGD | Cameron V-65 balloon | Gone With The Wind Ltd | |
| G-BPGE | Cessna U.206C | H. J. Owen & T. Bassford | |
| G-BPGF | Thunder Ax7-77 balloon | Dovetail Upholstery Co Ltd | |
| G-BPGH | EAA Acro Sport 2 | Pennine Lightning Film & TV Ltd | |
| G-BPGI | Colt 69A balloon | Thunder & Colt Ltd | |
| G-BPGJ | Colt 31A balloon | Thunder & Colt Ltd | |
| G-BPGK | Aeronca 7AC Champion | T. M. Williams | |
| G-BPGL | PA-28 Cherokee 180 | C. N. Ellerbrook | |
| G-BPGM | Cessna 152 | Westward Airways (Land's End) Ltd | |
| G-BPGN | Cameron 90 Tractor SS balloon | Cameron Balloons Ltd | |
| G-BPGO | Cessna T.210N | K. A. Clarke | |
| G-BPGT | Colt AS-80 airship | Thunder & Co Ltd | |
| G-BPGU | PA-28-181 Archer II | G. Underwood | |
| G-BPGV | Robinson R-22B | Featureford Ltd | |
| G-BPGX | SOCATA TB.9 Tampico | Martin Ltd/Biggin Hill | |
| G-BPGY | Cessna 150H | Three Counties Aero Club Ltd | |
| G-BPGZ | Cessna 150G | D. F. & B. L. Sperring | |
| G-BPHB | PA-28-161 Warrior II | Channel Islands Aero Holdings (Jersey) Ltd | |
| G-BPHD | Cameron N-42 balloon | Legal & General Group PLC | |
| G-BPHE | PA-28-161 Warrior II | Seal Executive Aircraft Ltd | |
| G-BPHF | AB-206A JetRanger | RCR Aviation Ltd/Southampton | |
| G-BPHG | Robin DR.400/180 | K. J. & M. B. White/Redhill | |
| G-BPHH | Cameron V-77 balloon | C. J. Madigan | |
| G-BPHJ | Cameron V-77 balloon | R. G. Davidson | |
| G-BPHK | Whittaker MW.7 | J. G. Beesley | |
| G-BPHL | PA-28-161 Warrior II | Frontline Aviation Ltd | |
| G-BPHM | Beech A36 Bonanza | A. P. Vonk | |
| G-BPHO | Taylorcraft BC-12D | Beeches Auto Services | |
| G-BPHP | Taylorcraft BC-12-65 | A. Liddiard & A. D. Pearce | |
| G-BPHR | D.H.82A Tiger Moth | N. Parry | |
| G-BPHS | Cessna 152 | Rich International Airways Ltd | |
| G-BPHT | Cessna 152 | P. Wood | |
| G-BPHU | Thunder Ax7-77 balloon | G. G. Bacon | |
| G-BPHW | Cessna 140 | H. C. Palmer | |
| G-BPHX | Cessna 140 | Ark Ltd | |
| G-BPHY | Cameron 110 Cow SS balloon | Cameron Balloons Ltd | |
| G-BPHZ | M.S.505 Criquet (TA+RC) | The Aircraft Restoration Co/Duxford | |
| G-BPIB | AB-206A JetRanger | Heliwork Services Ltd | |
| G-BPIC | AB.206B JetRanger 3 | Heliwork Services Ltd | |
| G-BPID | PA-28-161 Warrior II | GB Air Academy Ltd/Goodwood | |
| G-BPIE | Bell 206B JetRanger | Walsh Aviation | |
| G-BPIF | Bensen-Parsons 2 seat | I. L. Griffith | |
| G-BPIH | Rand KR-2 | J. R. Rowley | |
| G-BPII | Denney Aerocraft Kitfox | J. K. Cross | |
| G-BPIJ | Brantly B.2B | R. B. Paine | |
| G-BPIK | PA-38-112 Tomahawk | Cumbernauld Aviation Ltd | |
| G-BPIL | Cessna 310B | W. A Taylor | |
| G-BPIM | Cameron N-77 balloon | Thermalite Ltd | |
| G-BPIN | Glaser-Dirks DG.400 | M. P. Seth-Smith & J. N. Stevenson | |
| G-BPIO | Cessna F.152 II | S. Harcourt | |
| G-BPIP | Slingsby T.31 Motor Cadet III | J. H. Beard | |

| Notes | Reg. | Type | Owner or Operator |
|---|---|---|---|
| | G-BPIR | Scheibe SF.25E Super Falke | Coventry Gliding Club Ltd |
| | G-BPIT | Robinson R-22B | Turnbull Crane Hire Ltd |
| | G-BPIU | PA-28-161 Warrior II | I. R. Jones |
| | G-BPIV | Bristol 149 Bolingbroke Mk IVT | The Aircraft Restoration Co/Duxford |
| | G-BPIX | AA-5A Cheetah | Lowlog Ltd |
| | G-BPIY | Cessna 152 | J. J. Baumhardt |
| | G-BPIZ | AA-5B Tiger | D. A. Horsley |
| | G-BPJA | Beech 95-58 Baron | Morse Computers Ltd |
| | G-BPJB | Schweizer 269C | J. F. Britten |
| | G-BPJC | Robinson R-22B | Leicester Helicopters Ltd |
| | G-BPJD | SOCATA Rallye 110ST | E. Hopper |
| | G-BPJE | Cameron A-105 balloon | J. S. Eckersley |
| | G-BPJF | PA-38-112 Tomahawk | Air Yorkshire Ltd |
| | G-BPJG | PA-18 Super Cub 150 | Trent Valley Aerotowing Ltd |
| | G-BPJH | PA-18 Super Cub 95 | P. J. Heron |
| | G-BPJK | Colt 77A balloon | Akal Ltd |
| | G-BPJL | Cessna 152 | London Flight Centre (Headcorn) Ltd |
| | G-BPJN | Jodel D.18 | J. A. Nugent |
| | G-BPJO | PA-28-161 Cadet | C.S.E. Aviation Ltd/Kidlington |
| | G-BPJP | PA-28-161 Cadet | C.S.E. Aviation Ltd/Kidlington |
| | G-BPJR | PA-28-161 Cadet | C.S.E. Aviation Ltd/Kidlington |
| | G-BPJS | PA-28-161 Cadet | C.S.E. Aviation Ltd/Kidlington |
| | G-BPJT | PA-28-161 Cadet | C.S.E. Aviation Ltd/Kidlington |
| | G-BPJU | PA-28-161 Cadet | C.S.E. Aviation Ltd/Kidlington |
| | G-BPJV | Taylorcraft F-21 | J. G. Waller |
| | G-BPJW | Cessna A.150K | Heathgrange Ltd |
| | G-BPJZ | Cameron O-160 balloon | M. L. Gabb |
| | G-BPKA | Boeing 737-4S3 | Air Europe Ltd/Gatwick |
| | G-BPKB | Boeing 737-4S3 | Air Europe Ltd/Gatwick |
| | G-BPKC | Boeing 737-4S3 | Air Europe Ltd/Gatwick |
| | G-BPKD | Boeing 737-4S3 | Air Europe Ltd/Gatwick |
| | G-BPKE | Boeing 737-4S3 | Air Europe Ltd/Gatwick |
| | G-BPKF | Grob G.115 | Tayside Aviation Ltd/Dundee |
| | G-BPKG | Grob G.115 | Tayside Aviation Ltd/Dundee |
| | G-BPKH | Robinson R-22B | Findon Air Services |
| | G-BPKI | EAA Acro Sport 1 | J. A. Sykes |
| | G-BPKJ | Colt AS-80 Mk II airship | Thunder & Co Ltd |
| | G-BPKK | Denney Aerocraft Kitfox | G-BPKK Group |
| | G-BPKL | Mooney M.20J | Astraflight Ltd |
| | G-BPKM | PA-28-161 Warrior II | M. J. Greasby |
| | G-BPKN | Colt AS-80 Mk II airship | C. Turnbull |
| | G-BPKO | Cessna 140 | R. B. Sporik & M. D. Hughes |
| | G-BPKR | PA-28-151 Warrior | R. R. Harris |
| | G-BPKS | Stolp SA.300 Starduster Too | J. A. Hubner |
| | G-BPKT | Piper J-5A Cub Cruiser | W. A. N. Jenkins |
| | G-BPKU | Bell 206A JetRanger | M. E. Mortlock |
| | G-BPLA | Boeing 737-2K2 | Britannia Airways Ltd *Sir Stanley Matthews*/Luton |
| | G-BPLE | Cameron A-160 balloon | Balloons & Airships International Ltd |
| | G-BPLF | Cameron V-77 balloon | Dalesight Ltd |
| | G-BPLG | Morane-Saulnier M.S.317 | F. A. Anderson |
| | G-BPLH | Jodel DR.1051 | E. J. Horsfall/Blackpool |
| | G-BPLI | Colt 77A balloon | Yanin International Ltd |
| | G-BPLJ | Colt 90A balloon | Thunder & Colt Ltd |
| | G-BPLK | Slingsby T.67C | Slingsby Aviation Ltd/Kirkbymoorside |
| | G-BPLM | AIA Stampe SV-4C | C. J. & K. E. Jenson/Redhill |
| | G-BPLU | Thunder Ax10-160 balloon | Subsearch Ltd |
| | G-BPLV | Cameron V-77 balloon | Jessops (Tailors) Ltd |
| | G-BPLW | Cessna 152 | Eglinton Flying Club Ltd |
| | G-BPLY | Pitts S-2B Special | D. A. Hammant |
| | G-BPLZ | Hughes 369HS | Conguess Aviation Ltd/Conington |
| | G-BPMB | Maule M5-235C Lunar Rocket | P. M. Breton |
| | G-BPMC | Air Command 503 Commander | M. A. Cheshire |
| | G-BPMD | Boeing Stearman A.75L-3 (320) | M. G. Saunders/White Waltham |
| | G-BPME | Cessna 152 | London Flight Centre (Headcorn) Ltd |
| | G-BPMF | PA-28-151 Warrior | Logtrip Ltd |
| | G-BPMG | Bensen B.8MR | P. Doherty |
| | G-BPMH | Schempp-Hirth Nimbus 3DM | Southern Sailplanes |
| | G-BPMI | Colt 56A balloon | Thunder & Colt Ltd |
| | G-BPMJ | Colt 56A balloon | Thunder & Colt Ltd |
| | G-BPML | Cessna 172M | J. M. Gale & R. D. Andrews |
| | G-BPMM | Champion 7ECA Citabria | D. M. Griffiths |
| | G-BPMN | Aerocar Super Coot Model A | P. Napp |

| Reg. | Type | Owner or Operator | Notes |
|------|------|-------------------|-------|
| G-BPMO | Cessna 150M | S. L. Mills | |
| G-BPMP | Douglas C-47A-50-DL | Wesco 113 Ltd/Cranfield | |
| G-BPMR | PA-28-161 Warrior II | McIntyre Aviation/Staverton | |
| G-BPMS | PA-38-112 Tomahawk II | D. W. Higgins/Glasgow | |
| G-BPMU | Nord 3202B | John Durkin Technical Services Ltd (G-BIZJ) | |
| G-BPMV | PA-28-161 Warrior II | J. A. Hilton | |
| G-BPMW | QAC Quickie Q.2 | P. M. Wright (G-OICI/G-OGKN) | |
| G-BPMX | ARV Super 2 | B. Houghton | |
| G-BPMY | Cameron A-120 balloon | British School of Ballooning | |
| G-BPNA | Cessna 150L | B. E. Simpson | |
| G-BPNB | PA-38-112 Tomahawk | R. A. Wakefield | |
| G-BPNC | Rotorway Executive | Executive Helicopter Club Ltd | |
| G-BPND | Boeing 727-2D3 | Dan-Air Services Ltd/Gatwick | |
| G-BPNF | Robinson R-22B | N. S. Madden | |
| G-BPNI | Robinson R-22B | Arrowbury Ltd | |
| G-BPNL | QAC Quickie Q.2 | J. Catley | |
| G-BPNM | Cessna 340A | Western Air Charter Services Ltd | |
| G-BPNN | Bensen B.8MR | M. E. Vahdat | |
| G-BPNO | Zlin Z.326 Trener Master | J. A. S. Bailey & S. T. Logan | |
| G-BPNR | (reserved) | Dan-Air Services Ltd/Gatwick | |
| G-BPNS | Boeing 727-277 | Dan-Air Services Ltd/Gatwick | |
| G-BPNT | BAe 146-300 | Dan-Air Services Ltd/Gatwick | |
| G-BPNU | Thunder Ax7-77 balloon | J. Fenton | |
| G-BPNV | PA-38-112 Tomahawk | Rich International Airways Ltd/Luton | |
| G-BPNX | BAC One-Eleven 304AX | Ali Finance Ltd | |
| G-BPNY | Boeing 727-230 | Dan-Air Services Ltd/Gatwick | |
| G-BPNZ | Boeing 737-4Q8 | Dan-Air Services Ltd/Gatwick | |
| G-BPOA | Gloster Meteor T.7 (WF877) | Aces High Ltd/North Weald | |
| G-BPOB | Sopwith Camel F.1 (replica) (542) | Bianchi Aviation Film Services Ltd/ Booker | |
| G-BPOD | Stolp SA.300 Starduster Too | A. T. Fines | |
| G-BPOE | Colt 77A balloon | Albatross Aviation Ltd | |
| G-BPOF | Robinson R-22B | R. D. Masters | |
| G-BPOL | Pietenpol Air Camper | G. W. Postance | |
| G-BPOM | PA-28-161 Warrior II | B. McIntyre | |
| G-BPON | PA-34-200T Seneca II | London Flight Centre Air Charter Ltd | |
| G-BPOO | Montgomerie Bensen B.8MR | M. E. Vahdat | |
| G-BPOR | Bell 206B JetRanger 2 | Thetford Compactors Finance Ltd | |
| G-BPOS | Cessna 150M | Lanx Engineering Ltd | |
| G-BPOT | PA-28-181 Archer II | Time Software (IoM) Ltd | |
| G-BPOU | Luscombe 8A Silvaire | E. T. Wicks | |
| G-BPOV | Cameron 90 Magazine SS balloon | Forbes Europe Inc | |
| G-BPOX | Enstrom 280C Shark | J. Evans | |
| G-BPOY | Enstrom F-28A | M. & P. Food Products Ltd | |
| G-BPOZ | Enstrom F-28A | M. & P. Food Products Ltd | |
| G-BPPA | Cameron O-65 balloon | Rix Petroleum Ltd | |
| G-BPPB | PA-34-220T Seneca III | A. Smith | |
| G-BPPC | Robinson R-22 Mariner | B. H. Strudwick | |
| G-BPPD | PA-38-112 Tomahawk | AT Aviation Ltd/Cardiff | |
| G-BPPE | PA-38-112 Tomahawk | Norwich School of Flying | |
| G-BPPF | PA-38-112 Tomahawk | A. N. Doughty | |
| G-BPPG | PA-38-112 Tomahawk | AT Aviation Ltd/Cardiff | |
| G-BPPI | Colt 180A balloon | A. Faulkner | |
| G-BPPJ | Cameron A-180 Balloon | H. R. Evans | |
| G-BPPK | PA-28-151 Warrior | First European (Leasing & Finance) Ltd | |
| G-BPPL | Enstrom F-28A | M. & P. Food Products Ltd | |
| G-BPPM | Beech B200 Super King Air | Gama Aviation Ltd/Fairoaks | |
| G-BPPN | Cessna F.182Q | Hunt Norris Ltd | |
| G-BPPO | Luscombe 8A Silvaire | Free Air Flying Group/Goodwood | |
| G-BPPP | Cameron V-77 balloon | P. F. Smart | |
| G-BPPR | Air Command 532 Elite | T. D. Inch | |
| G-BPPS | Mudry CAARP CAP.21 | BAC Aviation Ltd/Earls Colne | |
| G-BPPT | PA-31-350 Navajo Chieftain | Ellan-Vannin Airlines PLC/Bournemouth | |
| G-BPPU | Air Command 532 Elite | J. Hough | |
| G-BPPV | Piper J-3C-65 Cub | G. W. Polson-Brown | |
| G-BPPW | Schweizer 269C | Compass Aviation Ltd | |
| G-BPPX | Schweizer 269C | Lakeside Helicopters Ltd | |
| G-BPPY | Hughes 269B | Compass Aviation Ltd | |
| G-BPPZ | Taylorcraft BC-12D | Zulu Warriors Flying Group | |
| G-BPRA | Aeronca 11AC Chief | J. M. Fforde | |
| G-BPRC | Cameron Elephant SS balloon | Cameron Balloons Ltd | |
| G-BPRD | Pitts S-1C Special | S. L. Robinson | |

| Notes | Reg. | Type | Owner or Operator |
|-------|------|------|-------------------|
| | G-BPRF | AS.355F-1 Twin Squirrel | McAlpine Helicopters Ltd/Hayes |
| | G-BPRH | AS.355F-1 Twin Squirrel | American Aviation Technologies Ltd |
| | G-BPRI | AS.355F-1 Twin Squirrel | American Aviation Technologies Ltd |
| | G-BPRJ | AS.355F-1 Twin Squirrel | G. Greenall |
| | G-BPRL | AS.355F-1 Twin Squirrel | Wood Hall Helicopters Ltd |
| | G-BPRM | Cessna F.172L | Nultree Ltd (G-AZKG) |
| | G-BPRN | PA-28-161 Warrior II | Air Navigation & Trading Co Ltd/ Blackpool |
| | G-BPRO | Cessna A.150K | C. R. Cox |
| | G-BPRP | Cessna 150E | P. G. Powter/Shoreham |
| | G-BPRR | Rand KR-2 | M. W. Albery |
| | G-BPRS | Air Command 532 Elite | B. K. Snoxall |
| | G-BPRT | Piel CP.328 | N. Reddish |
| | G-BPRV | PA-28-161 Warrior II | AT Aviation Ltd/Cardiff |
| | G-BPRX | Aeronca 11AC Chief | P. G. Kavanagh/Barton |
| | G-BPRY | PA-28-161 Warrior II | B. McIntyre |
| | G-BPRZ | Robinson R-22A | H. Melton/Cranfield |
| | G-BPSA | Luscombe 8A Silvaire | K. P. Gorman/Staverton |
| | G-BPSB | Air Command 532 Elite | D. K. Duckworth |
| | G-BPSE | NA AT-6D Harvard (483009) | Aces High Ltd/North Weald |
| | G-BPSH | Cameron V-77 balloon | P. G. Hossack |
| | G-BPSI | Thunder Ax10-160 balloon | Airborne Adventures Ltd |
| | G-BPSJ | Thunder Ax6-56 balloon | Thunder & Colt Ltd |
| | G-BPSK | Montgomerie Bensen B.8M | B. Harrison |
| | G-BPSL | Cessna 177 | I. P. Burnett & ptnrs/White Waltham |
| | G-BPSN | Boeing 757-236 | Air Europe/Air Europa (EC-EHY) |
| | G-BPSO | Cameron N-90 balloon | L. A. Sadler & K. J. Holt |
| | G-BPSP | Cameron 90 Ship SS balloon | Forbes Europe Inc |
| | G-BPSR | Cameron V-77 balloon | K. D. & S. L. Johnson |
| | G-BPSS | Cameron A-120 balloon | J. P. Clifford |
| | G-BPSV | Cessna F.406 Caravan II | Bob Crowe Aircraft Sales Ltd |
| | G-BPSW | Cessna F.406 Caravan II | Directflight Ltd/Norwich |
| | G-BPSX | Cessna F.406 Caravan II | Directflight Ltd/Norwich |
| | G-BPSY | Grob G.115 | Soaring (Oxford) Ltd |
| | G-BPSZ | Cameron N-180 balloon | The Balloon Club Ltd |
| | G-BPTA | Stinson 108-2 | G. W. Polson-Brown |
| | G-BPTB | Boeing Stearman A.75N1 (442) | Aero Vintage Ltd |
| | G-BPTC | Taylorcraft BC-12D | J. R. Surbey |
| | G-BPTD | Cameron V-77 balloon | J. Lippett |
| | G-BPTE | PA-28-181 Archer II | London Flight Centre (Stansted) Ltd |
| | G-BPTF | Cessna 152 | London Flight Centre (Stansted) Ltd |
| | G-BPTG | R. Commander 112TC | A. C. & M. Denny |
| | G-BPTH | Air Command 532 Elite | R. Wheeler |
| | G-BPTI | SOCATA TB.20 Trinidad | Lyndon Scaffolding Hire Ltd/ Birmingham |
| | G-BPTJ | PA-34-200T Seneca II | Air Leasing Ltd |
| | G-BPTL | Cessna 172N | Cleveland Flying School Ltd/Teesside |
| | G-BPTM | Pitts S-1T Special | RPM Aviation Ltd |
| | G-BPTO | Zenith CH.200-AA | B. Philips |
| | G-BPTP | Robinson R-22 | KOI (UK) Ltd/Biggin Hill |
| | G-BPTR | Robinson R-22 | Northern Helicopters Ltd |
| | G-BPTS | C.A.S.A 1.131E Jungmann | Aerobatic Displays Ltd/Booker |
| | G-BPTT | Robin DR.400/120 | The Cotswold Aero Club Ltd/Staverton |
| | G-BPTU | Cessna 152 | Flyteam Aviation Ltd |
| | G-BPTV | Bensen B.8 | L. Chiappi |
| | G-BPTW | Cameron A-160 balloon | Newbury Ballooning Co Ltd |
| | G-BPTX | Cameron O-120 balloon | J. M. Langley |
| | G-BPTZ | Robinson R-22B | Charmaine Aviation |
| | G-BPUA | EAA P-2 Biplane | R. A. Bowes |
| | G-BPUB | Cameron V-31 balloon | M. T. Evans |
| | G-BPUC | QAC Quickie Q.200 | R. Wells |
| | G-BPUD | Ryan PT-22 (I-492) | J. Hewett |
| | G-BPUE | Air Command 532 Elite | R. A. Fazackerly |
| | G-BPUF | Thunder Ax6-56Z balloon | Buf-Puf Balloon Group |
| | G-BPUG | Air Command 532 Elite | T. A. Holmes |
| | G-BPUH | Cameron A-180 balloon | Golf Centres Balloons Ltd |
| | G-BPUI | Air Command 532 Elite | M. A. Turner |
| | G-BPUJ | Cameron N-90 balloon | Touch Panel Products Ltd |
| | G-BPUK | Robinson R-22B | Centaur Software Ltd |
| | G-BPUL | PA-18 Super Cub 150 | Crissair Ltd |
| | G-BPUM | Cessna R.182RG | Ray Cochrane Racing Ltd |
| | G-BPUP | Whittaker MW-7 | J. H. Beard |
| | G-BPUR | Piper J-3L-65 Cub | J3 Group |

| Reg. | Type | Owner or Operator | Notes |
|------|------|-------------------|-------|
| G-BPUS | Rans S.9 | P. M. Shipman | |
| G-BPUU | Cessna 140 | R. Crossland/Exeter | |
| G-BPUW | Colt 90A balloon | Huntair Ltd | |
| G-BPUX | Cessna 150J | P. J. Egan | |
| G-BPUY | Cessna 150K | M. Hewison/Luton | |
| G-BPUZ | Cessna 150M | Premier Plane Leasing Co Ltd | |
| G-BPVA | Cessna 172F | J. E. Stevens | |
| G-BPVC | Cameron V-77 balloon | Courtaulds PLC | |
| G-BPVE | Bleriot 1909 replica | Bianchi Aviation Film Services Ltd/ Booker | |
| G-BPVH | Cub Aircraft J-3C-65 Prospector | D. E. Cooper-Maguire | |
| G-BPVI | PA-32R-301 Saratoga SP | I. E. Humphries/Kidlington | |
| G-BPVJ | Cessna 152 | J. E. Stevens | |
| G-BPVK | Varga 2150A Kachina | H. W. Hall | |
| G-BPVM | Cameron V-77 balloon | Royal Engineers Balloon Club | |
| G-BPVN | PA32R-301T Turbo Saratoga SP | Hero Aviation/Stapleford | |
| G-BPVO | Cassutt Racer IIIM | Lanx Engineering Ltd | |
| G-BPVP | Aerotek Pitts S-2B Special | N. J. Hunt | |
| G-BPVR | Colt Flying Battery SS balloon | Thunder & Colt Ltd | |
| G-BPVT | Thunder Ax7-65 balloon | Anglia Balloon School Ltd | |
| G-BPVU | Thunder Ax7-77 balloon | J. Burlinson | |
| G-BPVV | Cameron V-77 balloon | Abbey Plant Co Ltd | |
| G-BPVW | C.A.S.A. 1.131E Jungmann | S. A. W. Becker/Goodwood | |
| G-BPVX | Cassutt Racer IIIM | A. A. A. White/Barton | |
| G-BPVY | Cessna 172D | Techspan Aviation Ltd/Booker | |
| G-BPVZ | Luscombe 8E Silvaire | N. Huxtable | |
| G-BPWA | PA-28-161 Warrior II | GB Air Academy Ltd | |
| G-BPWB | Sikorsky S-61N | Bristow Helicopters Ltd/Aberdeen | |
| G-BPWC | Cameron V-77 balloon | H. B. Roberts | |
| G-BPWD | Cessna 120 | Peregrine Flying Group | |
| G-BPWE | PA-28-161 Warrior II | AT Aviation Ltd/Cardiff | |
| G-BPWF | PA-28 Cherokee 140 | S. J. Harris | |
| G-BPWG | Cessna 150M | Wickenby Aviation Ltd | |
| G-BPWH | Robinson R-22B | Bravo Aviation Ltd | |
| G-BPWI | Bell 206B JetRanger 2 | Lakeside Helicopters Ltd | |
| G-BPWJ | Beech 200 Super King Air | A. F. Budge (Aviation) Ltd/Gamston | |
| G-BPWK | Sportavia Fournier RF-5B | D. B. Almey | |
| G-BPWM | Cessna 150L | Lanx Engineering Ltd | |
| G-BPWN | Cessna 150L | Premier Plane Leasing Co Ltd | |
| G-BPWO | Cessna 150L | Premier Plane Leasing Co Ltd | |
| G-BPWP | Rutan LongEz | J. F. O'Hara & A. J. Voyle | |
| G-BPWR | Cessna R.172K | A. M. Skelton | |
| G-BPWS | Cessna 172P | B. Taylor | |
| G-BPWT | Cameron DG-19 airship | Airspace Outdoor Advertising Ltd | |
| G-BPWV | Colt 56A balloon | Cooper Exeter Ltd | |
| G-BPWW | Piaggio FWP.149D | American Aviation Technologies Ltd | |
| G-BPWX | Montgomerie Bensen B.8MR | M. S. Lloyd | |
| G-BPWY | Isaacs Fury II | R. J. Knights | |
| G-BPWZ | PA-28-161 Warrior II | Hamilton Compass Aviation Ltd | |
| G-BPXA | PA-28-181 Archer II | Cherokee Flying Group/Netherthorpe | |
| G-BPXB | Glaser-Dirks DG.400 | Glaser-Dirks UK | |
| G-BPXE | Enstrom 280C Shark | N. I. H. Corbin | |
| G-BPXF | Cameron V-65 balloon | D. Pascall | |
| G-BPXG | Colt 42A balloon | Cooper Group Ltd | |
| G-BPXH | Colt 17A balloon | Gone With The Wind Ltd | |
| G-BPXI | PA-23 Aztec 250F | A. R. D. Knott/Elstree | |
| G-BPXJ | PA-28RT-201T Turbo Arrow IV | Grumman Travel (Surrey) Ltd | |
| G-BPXP | Thunder Ax10-160 balloon | Thunder & Colt Ltd | |
| G-BPXX | PA-34-200T Seneca II | Hockstar Ltd | |
| G-BPXY | Aeronca 11AC Chief | S. Hawksworth | |
| G-BPXZ | Cameron V-77 balloon | M. D. Hammond | |
| G-BPYA | Rotorway Executive | Orchard Engineering Co Ltd | |
| G-BPYB | Air Command 532 Elite | P. J. Houtman | |
| G-BPYC | Cessna 310R | Air Service Training Ltd/Perth | |
| G-BPYG | Beech C23 Sundowner | K. A. Aubrey | |
| G-BPYH | Robinson R-22B | Goadby Air Services Ltd | |
| G-BPYI | Cameron O-77 balloon | Macleod Garage Ltd | |
| G-BPYJ | Wittman W.8 Tailwind | J. Dixon | |
| G-BPYK | Thunder Ax7-77 balloon | A. R. Swinnerton | |
| G-BPYL | Hughes 369D | Aly Aviation Ltd/Henstridge | |
| G-BPYN | Piper J-3C-65 Cub | The Aquila Group/White Waltham | |
| G-BPYO | PA-28-181 Archer II | L. Robinson | |
| G-BPYP | Cameron O-105 balloon | Newbury Ballooning Co Ltd | |

| Notes | Reg. | Type | Owner or Operator |
|---|---|---|---|
| | G-BPYR | PA-31-310 Turbo Navajo | Oston Air Finance Ltd (G-ECMA) |
| | G-BPYS | Cameron O-77 balloon | D. J. Goldsmith |
| | G-BPYT | Cameron V-77 balloon | Skylite Aviation Ltd |
| | G-BPYU | Short SD3-30 | Short Bros PLC/Belfast City |
| | G-BPYV | Cameron V-77 balloon | M. E. Weston |
| | G-BPYW | Air Command 532 Elite | W. V. Tatters |
| | G-BPYX | Robinson R-22B | Glentworth Scottish Farms Ltd |
| | G-BPYY | Cameron A-180 balloon | J. A. Barber |
| | G-BPYZ | Thunder Ax7-77 balloon | V. J. Baker |
| | G-BPZA | Luscombe 8A Silvaire | T. P. W. Hyde |
| | G-BPZB | Cessna 120 | C. Grime & J. Cook |
| | G-BPZC | Luscombe 8A Silvaire | C. C. & J. M. Lovell |
| | G-BPZD | SNCAN NC.858S | G. Richards |
| | G-BPZE | Luscombe 8E Silvaire | S. B. Marsden |
| | G-BPZF | PA-46-310P Malibu | Jenrick Engineering Services Ltd |
| | G-BPZG | PA-28R-201T Turbo Arrow III | Salborne Farms Ltd |
| | G-BPZI | Christen Eagle II | R. I. Warren & A. Fines |
| | G-BPZK | Cameron O-120 balloon | D. L. Smith |
| | G-BPZM | PA-28RT-201 Arrow IV | J. H. Kimber (G-ROYW/G-CRTI) |
| | G-BPZN | Cessna T.303 | R. S. Williams & S. B. Danser (G-RSUL) |
| | G-BPZO | Cameron N-90 balloon | Seaward PLC |
| | G-BPZP | Robin DR.400/180R | Booker Gliding Club Ltd |
| | G-BPZS | Colt 105A balloon | The Balloon Club of GB Ltd |
| | G-BPZT | Cameron N-90 balloon | Peter Lane Transport Ltd |
| | G-BPZU | Scheibe SF.25C Falke | G-BPZU Group |
| | G-BPZV | Cessna T.303 | J. N. Carter |
| | G-BPZW | SOCATA TB.20 Trinidad | Air Touring Services Ltd/Biggin Hill |
| | G-BPZX | Cessna 152 | Actioncall Ltd/Netherthorpe |
| | G-BPZY | Pitts S-1C Special | S. T. A. Albu |
| | G-BPZZ | Thunder Ax8-105 balloon | Breachwood Motors Ltd |
| | | | |
| | G-BRAA | Pitts S-1C Special | C. Davidson |
| | G-BRAE | Colt 69A balloon | Jentime Ltd |
| | G-BRAF | V.S.394 Spitfire FR.XVIII (SM969) | D. W. Arnold/Biggin Hill |
| | G-BRAG | Taylor JT.2 Titch | A. R. Greenfield |
| | G-BRAI | — | |
| | G-BRAJ | Cameron V-77 balloon | H. R. Evans |
| | G-BRAK | Cessna 172N | C. D. Brack |
| | G-BRAL | G.159 Gulfstream 1 | Ford Motor Co Ltd/Stansted |
| | G-BRAM | Mikoyan MiG-21PF | Aces High Ltd/North Weald |
| | G-BRAP | Thermal Aircraft 104 | Thermal Aircraft |
| | G-BRAR | Aeronca 7AC Champion | M. E. Pumford & R. N. Owen |
| | G-BRAV | PA-23 Aztec 250E | Hartfield Aviation Ltd (G-BBCM) |
| | G-BRAW | Pitts S-1 Special | P. G. Bond & P. B. Hunter |
| | G-BRAX | Payne Knight Twister 85B | P. G. Bond & P. B. Hunter |
| | G-BRAZ | EMB-120RT Brasilia | Air Exel Ltd/Luton |
| | G-BRBA | PA-28-161 Warrior II | Hendafern Ltd |
| | G-BRBB | PA-28-161 Warrior II | D. P. Hughes |
| | G-BRBC | — | |
| | G-BRBD | PA-28-151 Warrior | B. E. Simpson & C. R. Hughes |
| | G-BRBE | PA-28-161 Warrior II | P. A. Lancaster/Compton Abbas |
| | G-BRBF | Cessna 152 | Seal Executive Aircraft Ltd |
| | G-BRBG | PA-28 Cherokee 180 | D. C. L. Smith |
| | G-BRBH | Cessna 150H | L. C. Macknight/Elstree |
| | G-BRBI | Cessna 172N | L. C. Macknight/Elstree |
| | G-BRBJ | Cessna 172M | L. C. Macknight/Elstree |
| | G-BRBK | Robin DR.400/180 | R. Kemp |
| | G-BRBL | Robin DR.400/180 | Crown Export Services |
| | G-BRBM | Robin DR.400/180 | R. W. Davies/Headcorn |
| | G-BRBN | Pitts S-1S Special | D. R. Evans |
| | G-BRBO | Cameron V-77 balloon | Matrix Computers Ltd |
| | G-BRBP | Cessna 152 | Staverton Flying Services Ltd |
| | G-BRBR | Cameron V-77 balloon | 1066 Balloon Group |
| | G-BRBS | Bensen B.8M | J. Simpson |
| | G-BRBT | Trotter Ax3-20 balloon | R. M. Trotter |
| | G-BRBU | Colt 17A balloon | Airship & Balloon Co Ltd |
| | G-BRBV | Piper J-4A Cub Coupé | J. Pearson |
| | G-BRBW | PA-28 Cherokee 140 | Cherokee Group/Shoreham |
| | G-BRBX | PA-28-181 Archer II | M. J. Ireland |
| | G-BRBY | Robinson R-22B | Adern Aviation Ltd |
| | G-BRBZ | Beech 400 Beechjet | Bass PLC |
| | G-BRCA | Jodel D.112 | D. I. Walker & W. H. Sherlock |

| Reg. | Type | Owner or Operator | Notes |
|------|------|-------------------|-------|
| G-BRCC | Cessna 152 | Anthony Foreman & Co Ltd/Shoreham | |
| G-BRCD | Cessna A.152 | D. E. Simmons/Shoreham | |
| G-BRCE | Pitts S-1C Special | S. J. Perkins & D. Dobson | |
| G-BRCF | Montgomerie-Bensen B.8 | J. S. Walton | |
| G-BRCG | Grob G.109 | Oxfordshire Sportflying Ltd/Enstone | |
| G-BRCI | Pitts S-1 Special | R. N. Crosland | |
| G-BRCJ | Cameron NS-20 balloon | Cameron Balloons Ltd | |
| G-BRCK | Anderson EA-1 Kingfisher | T. Crawford | |
| G-BRCL | Colt Flying Hat SS balloon | Jentime Ltd | |
| G-BRCM | Cessna 172L | S. G. E. Plessis & D. C. C. Handley | |
| G-BRCO | Cameron NS-20 balloon | Flying Pictures Ltd | |
| G-BRCP | Enstrom F-28F | Southern Air Ltd/Shoreham | |
| G-BRCR | Cameron V-77 balloon | E. E. Clark | |
| G-BRCS | Colt 105A balloon | Jentime Ltd | |
| G-BRCT | Denney Aerocraft Kitfox | Wessex Aviation & Transport Ltd | |
| G-BRCV | Aeronca 7AC Champion | H. A. Bridgman | |
| G-BRCW | Aeronca 11AC Chief | A. E. Eastelon | |
| G-BRCX | Colt 105A balloon | Jentime Ltd | |
| G-BRDA | Denney Aerocraft Kitfox | D. Webb & E. J. D. Proctor | |
| G-BRDB | Zenair CH.701 STOL | D. L. Botwell | |
| G-BRDC | Thunder Ax7-77 balloon | A. P. Woolhouse & ptnrs | |
| G-BRDD | Avions Mudry CAP.10B | R. D. Dickson/Gamston | |
| G-BRDE | Thunder Ax7-77 balloon | S. R. Seager | |
| G-BRDF | PA-28-161 Warrior II | W. London Aero Services Ltd/ White Waltham | |
| G-BRDG | PA-28-161 Warrior II | W. London Aero Services Ltd/ White Waltham | |
| G-BRDJ | Luscombe 8A Silvaire | K. Sheppard & I. R. Green | |
| G-BRDL | Bell 206B JetRanger | Clyde Helicopters Ltd | |
| G-BRDM | PA-28-161 Warrior II | W. London Aero Services Ltd/ White Waltham | |
| G-BRDN | M.S.880B Rallye Club | C. R. Owen | |
| G-BRDO | Cessna 177B | H. Stephenson & R. Wells | |
| G-BRDP | Colt Jumbo SS balloon | Thunder & Colt Ltd | |
| G-BRDS | Colt Flying Coke Can SS balloon | Thunder & Colt Ltd | |
| G-BRDT | Cameron DP-70 airship | M. M. Cobbold | |
| G-BRDU | Cameron DG-14 airship | Cameron Balloons Ltd | |
| G-BRDV | Viking Wood Products Spitfire Prototype replica | C. Du Cros | |
| G-BRDW | PA-24 Comanche 180 | I. P. Gibson/Switzerland | |
| G-BREA | Bensen B.8M | R. Firth | |
| G-BREB | Piper J-3C-65 Cub | C. Parr & I. Watts | |
| G-BREC | Colt Flying Chips Bag SS balloon | Thunder & Colt Ltd | |
| G-BREE | Whittaker MW.7 | M. J. Hayman | |
| G-BREG | Colt 21A balloon | Thunder & Colt Ltd | |
| G-BREH | Cameron V-65 balloon | A. E. & L. C. Rogers | |
| G-BREI | Christen Eagle II | J. Brown & D. W. Palfrey | |
| G-BREJ | Schweizer 269C | C.S.E. Aviation Ltd/Kidlington | |
| G-BREK | Piper J-3C-65 Cub | C. Parr & I. Watts | |
| G-BREL | Cameron O-77 balloon | A. J. Moore & D. J. Green | |
| G-BREM | Air Command 532 Elite | Modern Air | |
| G-BREO | Mooney M.20K | Quilon Investments Ltd | |
| G-BREP | PA-28RT-201 Arrow IV | P. G. McQuaid | |
| G-BRER | Aeronca 7AC Champion | A. J. O'Shea | |
| G-BRES | Montgomerie-Bensen B.8 | I. H. C. Branson | |
| G-BRET | — | | |
| G-BREU | Montgomerie-Bensen B.8 | M. A. Hayward | |
| G-BREX | Cameron O-84 balloon | Ovolo Ltd | |
| G-BREY | Taylorcraft BC-12D | BJNS Services | |
| G-BREZ | Cessna 172M | B. J. Tucker | |
| G-BRFA | PA-31-350 Navajo Chieftain | Greenclose Aviation Ltd (G-BREW) | |
| G-BRFB | Rutan LongEz | R. A. Gardiner | |
| G-BRFC | P.57 Sea Prince T.1 (WP321) | Rural Naval Air Service/Bourn | |
| G-BRFD | Bell 206B JetRanger | Farmex Ltd | |
| G-BRFE | Cameron V-77 balloon | N. J. Appleton | |
| G-BRFF | Colt 90A balloon | Zycomm Electronics Ltd | |
| G-BRFH | Colt 90A balloon | Polydron UK Ltd | |
| G-BRFI | Aeronca 7DC Champion | I. J. Boyd & D. J. McCooke | |
| G-BRFJ | Aeronca 11AC Chief | Junipa Sales Aviation Ltd | |
| G-BRFK | Colt Flying Drinks Can SS balloon | Thunder & Colt Ltd | |
| G-BRFL | PA-38-112 Tomahawk | Technology & Marketing Ltd | |
| G-BRFM | PA-28-161 Warrior II | GCJ Moffatt & Co Ltd | |
| G-BRFN | PA-38-112 Tomahawk | Technology & Marketing Ltd | |

| Notes | Reg. | Type | Owner or Operator |
|---|---|---|---|
| | G-BRFO | Cameron V-77 balloon | Hedge Hoppers Balloon Group |
| | G-BRFP | Schweizer 269C | Radstrong Ltd |
| | G-BRFR | Cameron N-105 balloon | Flying Pictures (Balloons) Ltd |
| | G-BRFS | Cameron N-90 balloon | Flying Pictures (Balloons) Ltd |
| | G-BRFT | — | |
| | G-BRFU | Fouga CM.170 Magister | P. F. A. Hoar/Cranfield |
| | G-BRFV | Cessna T.182 | Goddard Kay Rogers & Associates Ltd |
| | G-BRFW | Montgomerie-Bensen B.8 Two Seat | J. M. Montgomerie |
| | G-BRFX | Pazmany PL.4A | D. E. Hills |
| | G-BRGD | Cameron O-84 balloon | J. R. H. & M. A. Ashworth |
| | G-BRGE | Cameron N-90 balloon | Oakfield Farm Products Ltd |
| | G-BRGF | Luscombe 8E Silvaire | C. C. & J. M. Lovell |
| | G-BRGG | Luscombe 8A Silvaire | M. P. & V. H. Weatherby |
| | G-BRGH | FRED Srs 2 | F. G. Hallam |
| | G-BRGI | PA-28 Cherokee 180 | Golf India Aviation Ltd |
| | G-BRGJ | PA-28-151 Warrior | C. Ward |
| | G-BRGL | BAe Jetstream 3109 | British Aerospace PLC/Prestwick |
| | G-BRGN | BAe Jetstream 3102 | British Aerospace PLC (G-BLHC)/ Prestwick |
| | G-BRGO | Air Command 532 Elite | D. A. Wood |
| | G-BRGP | Colt Flying Stork SS balloon | Thunder & Colt Ltd |
| | G-BRGR | BAe Jetstream 3108 | British Aerospace PLC/Prestwick |
| | G-BRGT | PA-32 Cherokee Six 260 | G. W. Cartledge |
| | G-BRGU | Cameron R-60 balloon | Noble Adventures Ltd |
| | G-BRGW | GY-201 Minicab | R. G. White |
| | G-BRGX | Rotorway Executive | D. W. J. Lee |
| | G-BRHA | PA-32RT-300 Lance II | AT Aviation Ltd/Cardiff |
| | G-BRHB | Boeing Stearman B.75N-1 | D. Calabritto |
| | G-BRHC | Cameron V-77 balloon | G. L. Hicks |
| | G-BRHE | — | |
| | G-BRHF | PA-31-350 Navajo Chieftain | Inter European Airways Ltd/Cardiff |
| | G-BRHG | Colt 90A balloon | Bath University Students Union |
| | G-BRHH | Cameron 106 Cow SS balloon | Cameron Ballons Ltd |
| | G-BRHI | Bell 206B JetRanger 3 | Highland Properties Ltd |
| | G-BRHJ | PA-34-200T Seneca II | J. A. Gibbs |
| | G-BRHK | Colt GA-42 airship | Thunder & Colt Ltd |
| | G-BRHL | Montgomerie-Bensen B.8M | N. D. Marshall |
| | G-BRHM | Bensen B.8M | D. P. Clout |
| | G-BRHN | Robinson R-22B | Barhale Surveying Ltd |
| | G-BRHO | PA-34-200 Seneca | First European (Leasing & Finance) Ltd |
| | G-BRHP | Aeronca O-58B Grasshopper (31923) | J. G. Townsend |
| | G-BRHR | PA-38-112 Tomahawk | Hamilton Compass Aviation Ltd |
| | G-BRHS | PA-38-112 Tomahawk | Hamilton Compass Aviation Ltd |
| | G-BRHT | PA-38-112 Tomahawk | Hamilton Compass Aviation Ltd |
| | G-BRHU | Montgomerie-Bensen B.8MR | G. L. & S. R. Moon |
| | G-BRHV | Colt 180A balloon | Timwing Ltd |
| | G-BRHW | D. H. 82A Tiger Moth | P. J. & A. J. Borsberry |
| | G-BRHX | Luscombe 8E Silvaire | J. M. Thorpe & S. W. Watkins |
| | G-BRHY | Luscombe 8E Silvaire | D. Lofts & A. R. W. Taylor |
| | G-BRHZ | Stephens Akro Astro 235 | A. N. Onn & T. R. G. Barnby |
| | G-BRIA | Cessna 310L | Cashfield Ltd/Shobdon |
| | G-BRIB | Cameron N-77 balloon | D. Stitt |
| | G-BRID | Cessna U.206A | Emair Bridlington Ltd |
| | G-BRIE | Cameron N-77 balloon | Vokins Estates Ltd |
| | G-BRIF | Boeing 767-204ER | Britannia Airways Ltd/Air Holland |
| | G-BRIG | Boeing 767-204ER | Britannia Airways Ltd/Luton |
| | G-BRIH | Taylorcraft BC-12D | K. E. Ballington |
| | G-BRII | Zenair CH.600 Zodiac | B. F. Arnall |
| | G-BRIJ | Taylorcraft F-19 | K. E. Ballington |
| | G-BRIK | T.66 Nipper 3 | C. W. R. Piper |
| | G-BRIL | Piper J-5A Cub Cruiser | M. Stow |
| | G-BRIM | Cameron O-160 balloon | Chard Balloon Co Ltd |
| | G-BRIN | SOCATA TB.20 Trinidad | Kendrick Construction Ltd |
| | G-BRIO | Turner Super T-40A | D. McIntyre |
| | G-BRIP | | |
| | G-BRIR | Cameron V-56 balloon | Century Factors Ltd |
| | G-BRIS | Steen Skybolt | Cavendish Aviation Ltd |
| | G-BRIT | Cessna 421C | Chaseside Holdings Ltd |
| | G-BRIV | SOCATA TB.9 Tampico | B. W. Kempster/Cranfield |
| | G-BRIW | Hughes 269C | Belmont Press Ltd |
| | G-BRIY | Taylorcraft DF-65 Tandem Trainer | J. A. Rollason |

| Reg. | Type | Owner or Operator | Notes |
|------|------|-------------------|-------|
| G-BRIZ | D.31 Turbulent | M. C. Hunt | |
| G-BRJA | Luscombe 8A Silvaire | C. C. & J. M. Lovell | |
| G-BRJB | Zenair CH.600 Zodiac | E. G. Brown | |
| G-BRJC | Cessna 120 | N. R. Haines | |
| G-BRJD | Boeing 757-236 | Air Europe Ltd/Air Europa (EC-ESC) | |
| G-BRJE | Boeing 757-236 | Air Europe Ltd/Air Europa (EC-EOL) | |
| G-BRJF | Boeing 757-236 | Air Europe Ltd/Air Europa (EC-EVD)/ Air Europe SpA (I-......) | |
| G-BRJG | Boeing 757-236 | Air Europe Ltd/Gatwick | |
| G-BRJH | Boeing 757-236 | Air Europe Ltd/Gatwick | |
| G-BRJI | Boeing 757-236 | Air Europe Ltd/Air Europa (EC----) | |
| G-BRJJ | Boeing 757-236 | Air Europe Ltd/Air Europa (EC----) | |
| G-BRJK | Luscombe 8A Silvaire | C. J. L. Peat | |
| G-BRJL | PA-15 Vagabond | D. D. Saint | |
| G-BRJM | Cameron A-210 balloon | P. J. D. Kerr | |
| G-BRJN | Pitts S-1C Special | G-BRJN Group | |
| G-BRJO | Bell 206B JetRanger 3 | Alan Mann Helicopters Ltd | |
| G-BRJR | PA-38-112 Tomahawk | MFM Enterprises Ltd/Newcastle | |
| G-BRJT | Cessna 150H | Technology & Marketing Ltd | |
| G-BRJU | PA-28-151 Warrior | Newcastle-Upon-Tyne Aero Club Ltd | |
| G-BRJV | PA-28-161 Cadet | Newcastle-Upon-Tyne Aero Club Ltd | |
| G-BRJW | Bellanca 7GCBC Citabria | H. W. Weston/Staverton | |
| G-BRJX | Rand KR-2 | C. Willcocks | |
| G-BRJY | Rand KR-2 | J. M. Scott | |
| G-BRKA | Luscombe 8F Silvaire | C. H. J. Andrews | |
| G-BRKB | Cameron N-65 balloon | M. C. Bradley/Hong Kong | |
| G-BRKC | J/1 Autocrat | J. W. Conlon | |
| G-BRKD | Piaggio FWP.149D | Operation Ability Ltd | |
| G-BRKE | Hawker Sea Hurricane XIIA (BW853) | AJD Engineering Ltd | |
| G-BRKF | Boeing 737-4S3 | Air Europe Ltd/Gatwick | |
| G-BRKG | Boeing 737-4S3 | Air Europe Ltd/Gatwick | |
| G-BRKH | PA-28-236 Dakota | P. A. Wright & D. Rawlley | |
| G-BRKI | Robinson R-22B | Questspan Ltd/Booker | |
| G-BRKJ | Stoddard-Hamilton Glasair III | R. F. E. Simard | |
| G-BRKK | Aero Designs Star-Lite SL.1 | I. J. Widger | |
| G-BRKL | Cameron H-34 balloon | Cameron Balloons Ltd | |
| G-BRKN | Robinson R-22 Mariner | P. M. Webber/Greece | |
| G-BRKO | Oldfield Baby Great Lakes | C. Wren | |
| G-BRKP | Colt 31A balloon | Thunder & Colt Ltd | |
| G-BRKR | Cessna 182R | A. R. D. Brooker | |
| G-BRKS | Air Command 532 Elite | G. Sandercock | |
| G-BRKT | PA-28-161 Warrior II | Leisure World (Holdings) Ltd | |
| G-BRKV | Cessna 421C | Baron International (Aviation) Ltd | |
| G-BRKW | Cameron V-77 balloon | M. W. A. Shemilt | |
| G-BRKX | Air Command 532 Elite | K. Davis | |
| G-BRKY | Viking Dragonfly Mk II | G. D. Price | |
| G-BRKZ | Air Command 532 Elite | S. C. West | |
| G-BRLA | Piper J-3C-65 Cub | D. Robotham | |
| G-BRLB | Air Command 532 Elite | D. Wilson | |
| G-BRLC | Thunder Ax7-77 balloon | Fuji Photo Film (UK) Ltd | |
| G-BRLD | Robinson R-22B | Future Music (Chelmsford) Ltd | |
| G-BRLE | PA-28-181 Archer II | Charles Clowes (Estates) Co Ltd | |
| G-BRLF | Campbell Cricket | D. Wood | |
| G-BRLG | PA-28RT-201T Turbo Arrow IV | B. Walker & Co (Dursley) Ltd | |
| G-BRLH | Air Command 532 Elite | Childs Garages (Sherborne) Ltd | |
| G-BRLI | Piper J-5A Cub Cruiser | A. E. Poulson | |
| G-BRLJ | Evans VP-2 | R. L. Jones | |
| G-BRLK | Air Command 532 Elite | G. L. Hunt | |
| G-BRLL | Cameron A-105 balloon | Chris Evans Leisure Ltd | |
| G-BRLM | BAe 146-100 | British Aerospace PLC | |
| G-BRLN | BAe 146-100 | British Aerospace PLC | |
| G-BRLO | PA-38-112 Tomahawk | Scotia Safari Ltd/Prestwick | |
| G-BRLP | PA-38-112 Tomahawk | M. Stow | |
| G-BRLR | Cessna 150G | D. C. Maxwell | |
| G-BRLS | Thunder Ax7-77 balloon | M. G. Ferguson & A. J. Nunns | |
| G-BRLT | Colt 77A balloon | D. Bareford | |
| G-BRLU | Cameron H-24 balloon | Airspace Outdoor Advertising Ltd | |
| G-BRLV | CCF Harvard IV (93542) | G. L. Owens/North Weald | |
| G-BRLW | Cessna 150M | Cloudfirst Trading Ltd | |
| G-BRLX | Cameron N-77 balloon | National Power | |
| G-BRLY | BAe ATP | British Aerospace PLC/Woodford | |
| G-BRLZ | Cessna 150G | J. D. Corney | |

| Notes | Reg. | Type | Owner or Operator |
|---|---|---|---|
| | G-BRMA | W.S.51 Dragonfly HR.5 (WG719) ★ | International Helicopter Museum/ Weston-s-Mare |
| | G-BRMB | B.192 Belvedere HC.1 (XG452) ★ | International Helicopter Museum/ Weston-s-Mare |
| | G-BRMC | Stampe SV-4B | E. K. Coventry |
| | G-BRMD | Cameron O-160 balloon | Ballooning Endeavours Ltd |
| | G-BRME | PA-28-181 Archer II | P. Kearney |
| | G-BRMF | Bell 206B JetRanger 3 | Heliwork Services Ltd/Thruxton |
| | G-BRMG | V.S.384 Seafire XVII (5X336) | P. J. Wood |
| | G-BRMH | Bell 206B JetRanger 2 | RMH Stainless Ltd (G-BBUX) |
| | G-BRMI | Cameron V-65 balloon | M. Davies |
| | G-BRMJ | PA-38-112 Tomahawk | P. H. Rogers/Coventry |
| | G-BRMK | PA-38-112 Tomahawk | P. H. Rogers/Coventry |
| | G-BRML | PA-38-112 Tomahawk | P. H. Rogers/Coventry |
| | G-BRMM | Air Command 532 Elite | R. de Serville |
| | G-BRMN | Thunder Ax7-77 balloon | G. Restell & R. Higham |
| | G-BRMO | Robinson R-22B | Delta Helicopters Ltd |
| | G-BRMS | PA-28RT-201 Arrow IV | Fleetbridge Ltd |
| | G-BRMT | Cameron V-31 balloon | R. M. Trotter & K. L. Heron |
| | G-BRMU | Cameron V-77 balloon | K. J. & G. R. Ibbotson |
| | G-BRMV | Cameron O-77 balloon | P. D. Griffiths |
| | G-BRMW | Whittaker MW.7 | M. R. Grunwell |
| | G-BRMY | Short SD3-60 | Short Bros PLC/Belfast City |
| | G-BRMZ | Short SD3-60 | Short Bros PLC/Belfast City |
| | G-BRNA | Short SD3-60 | Short Bros PLC/Belfast City |
| | G-BRNB | Short SD3-60 | Short Bros PLC/Belfast City |
| | G-BRNC | Cessna 150M | Mercia Aircraft Leasing Ltd |
| | G-BRND | Cessna 152 | Mercia Aircraft Leasing Ltd |
| | G-BRNE | Cessna 152 | Mercia Aircraft Leasing Ltd |
| | G-BRNJ | PA-38-112 Tomahawk | S. Eddison |
| | G-BRNK | Cessna 152 | Sheffield Aero Club Ltd/Netherthorpe |
| | G-BRNL | Cessna 172P | Holmes Rental |
| | G-BRNM | Chichester-Miles Leopard | Chichester-Miles Consultants Ltd |
| | G-BRNN | Cessna 152 | Sheffield Aero Club Ltd/Netherthorpe |
| | G-BRNP | Rotorway Executive | C. A. Laycock |
| | G-BRNR | Schweizer 269C | C.S.E. Aviation Ltd/Kidlington |
| | G-BRNS | Avid Flyer | Ladel Ltd |
| | G-BRNT | Robin DR.400/180 | M. J. Cowham |
| | G-BRNU | Robin DR.400/180 | Pranconic Ltd |
| | G-BRNV | PA-28-181 Archer II | S. Williams |
| | G-BRNW | Cameron V-77 balloon | N. Robertson & G. Smith |
| | G-BRNX | PA-22 Tri-Pacer 150 | I. J. Widger & M. K. Faro |
| | G-BRNY | Thunder Ax6-56A balloon | P. A. Clent |
| | G-BRNZ | PA-32 Cherokee Six 300B | Notionfresh Ltd |
| | G-BROB | Cameron V-77 balloon | R. W. Richardson |
| | G-BROE | Cameron N-65 balloon | R. H. Sanderson |
| | G-BROF | Air Command 532 Elite | M. J. Hoskins |
| | G-BROG | Cameron V-65 balloon | R. Kunert |
| | G-BROH | Cameron O-90 balloon | A. & W. Derbyshire |
| | G-BROI | CFM Streak Shadow Srs SA | G. W. Rowbotham |
| | G-BROJ | Colt 31A balloon | Thunder & Colt Ltd |
| | G-BROL | Colt AS-80 Mk II airship | Thunder & Colt Ltd |
| | G-BROM | ICA IS-282MA | Kent Motor Gliding & Soaring Centre |
| | G-BROO | Luscombe 8A Silvaire | B. F. Arnall |
| | G-BROP | Van's RV-4 | K. E. Armstrong |
| | G-BROR | Piper J-3C-65 Cub | Woodside Flying Group/Headcorn |
| | G-BROS | Cameron V-65 balloon | Airship Shop Ltd |
| | G-BROV | Colt 105A balloon | Thunder & Colt Ltd |
| | G-BROW | Colt 90A balloon | Thunder & Colt Ltd |
| | G-BROX | Robinson R-22B | David Gilmour Music Ltd |
| | G-BROY | Cameron V-77 balloon | Zebedee Balloon Service |
| | G-BROZ | PA-18 Super Cub 150 | P. G. Kynsey |
| | G-BRPC | BN-2B-26 Islander | Pilatus BN Ltd/Bembridge |
| | G-BRPE | Cessna 120 | T. W. Greaves |
| | G-BRPF | Cessna 120 | D. Sharp |
| | G-BRPG | Cessna 120 | T. W. Greaves |
| | G-BRPH | Cessna 120 | T. W. Greaves |
| | G-BRPI | Pitts S-1C Special | J. C. Lister |
| | G-BRPJ | Cameron N-90 balloon | Paul Johnson Cars Ltd |
| | G-BRPK | PA-28 Cherokee 140 | Halsmith (Aircraft Sales) Ltd |
| | G-BRPL | PA-28 Cherokee 140 | Archer Flight Hire |
| | G-BRPM | T.66 Nipper 3 | T. C. Horner |

| Reg. | Type | Owner or Operator | Notes |
|------|------|-------------------|-------|
| G-BRPN | Enstrom F-28C | Manchester Helicopter Centre/Barton | |
| G-BRPO | Enstrom 280C | Manchester Helicopter Centre/Barton | |
| G-BRPP | Brookland Hornet | D. E. Cox | |
| G-BRPR | Aeronca O-58B Grasshopper (43-1952) | G. Underwood | |
| G-BRPS | Cessna 177B | C. R. Goforth | |
| G-BRPT | Rans S.10 Sakota | J. G. Beesley | |
| G-BRPU | Beech 76 Duchess | Hamilton Compass Aviation Ltd | |
| G-BRPV | Cessna 152 | Coventry (Civil) Aviation Ltd | |
| G-BRPX | Taylorcraft BC-12D | M. J. Brett | |
| G-BRPY | PA-15 Vagabond | J. P. Esson | |
| G-BRPZ | Luscombe 8A Silvaire | J. D. Rooney/Goodwood | |
| G-BRRA | V.S.361 Spitfire LF.IX | Historic Aircraft Collection Ltd | |
| G-BRRB | Luscombe 8E Silvaire | D. J. Willison | |
| G-BRRD | Scheibe SF.25B Falke | K. E. Ballington | |
| G-BRRE | Colt 77A balloon | P. Patel | |
| G-BRRF | Cameron O-77 balloon | Mid-Bucks Farmers Balloon Group | |
| G-BRRG | Glaser-Dirks DG.500M | A. W. White | |
| G-BRRH | Ayres S2R-T34 Turbo Thrush | Agricultural Aviation Overseas Ltd | |
| G-BRRI | Ayres S2R-T34 Turbo Thrush | Agricultural Aviation Overseas Ltd | |
| G-BRRJ | PA-28RT-201T Turbo Arrow IV | M. & E. Machinery Ltd | |
| G-BRRK | Cessna 182Q | Wallis & Son Ltd | |
| G-BRRL | PA-18 Super Cub 95 | T. J. McRae | |
| G-BRRM | PA-28-161 Cadet | R. H. Sellier | |
| G-BRRN | PA-28-161 Warrior II | C. J. & L. M. Worsley | |
| G-BRRO | Cameron N-77 balloon | Newbury Building Soc | |
| G-BRRP | Pitts S-1S Special | J. E. Sweetman/Hong Kong | |
| G-BRRR | Cameron V-77 balloon | Kent & Sussex Tree Surgeons Ltd | |
| G-BRRS | Pitts S-1C Special | R. C. Atkinson | |
| G-BRRT | C.A.S.A. 1-131E Jungmann | Soaring (Oxford) Ltd | |
| G-BRRU | Colt 90A balloon | Thunder & Colt Ltd | |
| G-BRRW | Cameron O-77 balloon | D. V. Fowler | |
| G-BRRX | Hughes 369HS | M. J. Stanton & T. R. Cole | |
| G-BRRY | Robinson R-22B | Bristow Helicopters Ltd/Redhill | |
| G-BRRZ | Robinson R-22B | Skylem Ltd | |
| G-BRSA | Cameron N-56 balloon | Cameron Balloons Ltd | |
| G-BRSC | Rans S.10 Sakota | R. A. Buckley | |
| G-BRSD | Cameron V-77 balloon | A. B. Stephens | |
| G-BRSE | PA-28-161 Warrior II | Air Service Training Ltd/Perth | |
| G-BRSF | V.S.361 Spitfire F.IX | Sussex Spraying Services Ltd | |
| G-BRSG | PA-28-161 Cadet | Biblio Aviation Ltd/Booker | |
| G-BRSH | C.A.S.A. 1-131E Jungmann | Badsaddle Stables Ltd & Spanhoe Stone Co Ltd | |
| G-BRSI | PA-28-161 Cadet | Biblio Aviation Ltd/Booker | |
| G-BRSJ | PA-38-112 Tomahawk | Seal Executive Aircraft Ltd | |
| G-BRSK | Boeing Stearman N2S-3 (180) | Great Cloud Designs Ltd | |
| G-BRSL | Cameron N-56 balloon | S. Budd | |
| G-BRSM | Cessna 140 | Great Cloud Designs Ltd | |
| G-BRSN | Rand-Robinson KR-2 | K. W. Darby | |
| G-BRSO | CFM Streak Shadow Srs SA | D. J. Smith | |
| G-BRSP | Air Command 532 Elite | D. R. G. Griffith | |
| G-BRSW | Luscombe 8A Silvaire | R. J. Knights | |
| G-BRSX | PA-15 Vagabond | C. Milne-Fowler | |
| G-BRSY | Hatz CB-1 | R. E. Todd | |
| G-BRSZ | MEM RSZ-05/1 balloon | Zebedee Balloon Service | |
| G-BRTA | PA-38-112 Tomahawk | R. A. Wakefield | |
| G-BRTB | Bell 206B JetRanger 2 | Harris Technology Ltd | |
| G-BRTC | Cessna 150G | Thorpe Air Ltd/Goodwood | |
| G-BRTD | Cessna 152 II | Thorpe Air Ltd/Goodwood | |
| G-BRTE | Colt 240A balloon | H. C. J. Williams | |
| G-BRTF | Thunder Ax7-77 balloon | Thunder & Colt Ltd | |
| G-BRTH | Cameron A-180 balloon | The Ballooning Business Ltd | |
| G-BRTI | Robinson R-22B | J. J. Martyn | |
| G-BRTJ | Cessna 150F | Seal Executive Aircraft Ltd | |
| G-BRTK | Boeing Stearman E.75 | Howard Avis (Aviation) Ltd | |
| G-BRTL | Hughes 369E | P. C. Shann Management & Research Ltd | |
| G-BRTM | PA-28-161 Warrior II | Air Service Training Ltd/Perth | |
| G-BRTN | Beech 95-B58 Baron | Colneway Ltd | |
| G-BRTO | Cessna 152 | N. A. Ali | |
| G-BRTP | Cessna 152 | Anglia Aviation Ltd | |
| G-BRTR | Colt GA-42 airship | Thunder & Colt Ltd | |
| G-BRTS | Bell 206B JetRanger 3 | Norwich Aviation Ltd | |

| Notes | Reg. | Type | Owner or Operator |
|---|---|---|---|
| | G-BRTT | Schweizer 269C | Fairthorpe Ltd/Denham |
| | G-BRTU | — | — |
| | G-BRTV | Cameron O-77 balloon | C. Vening |
| | G-BRTW | Glaser-Dirks DG.400 | I. J. Carruthers |
| | G-BRTX | PA-28-151 Warrior | Compton Abbas Airfield Ltd |
| | G-BRTZ | Slingsby T.31 Motor Cadet III | M. N. Martin |
| | G-BRUA | Cessna 152 | Compton Abbas Airfield Ltd |
| | G-BRUB | PA-28-161 Warrior II | Compton Abbas Airfield Ltd |
| | G-BRUC | BAe 146-100 | British Aerospace PLC |
| | G-BRUD | PA-28-181 Archer II | Wilkins & Wilkins Special Auctions Ltd |
| | G-BRUE | Cameron V-77 balloon | B. J. Newman & P. L. Harrison |
| | G-BRUG | Luscombe 8E Silvaire | J. F. & N. W. Barrett |
| | G-BRUH | Colt 105A balloon | D. C. Chipping |
| | G-BRUI | PA-44-180 Seminole | Bath Stone Co Ltd |
| | G-BRUJ | Boeing Stearman A.75N1 | Early Birds Ltd/Staverton |
| | G-BRUL | Thunder Ax8-105 balloon | H. C. J. Williams |
| | G-BRUM | Cessna A.152 | Warwickshire Flying Training Centre |
| | G-BRUN | Cessna 120 | O. C. Brun (G-BRDH) |
| | G-BRUO | Taylor JT.1 Monoplane | P. C. Cardno |
| | G-BRUP | Fairchild M-62A Cornell | C. L. H. Parr |
| | G-BRUR | Grob G.115 | Risestat Ltd |
| | G-BRUS | Cessna 140 | J. C. Greenslade |
| | G-BRUT | Thunder Ax8-90 balloon | Moet & Chandon (London) Ltd |
| | G-BRUU | EAA Biplane Model P.1 | J. C. Greenslade |
| | G-BRUV | Cameron V-77 balloon | T. W. & R. F. Benbrook |
| | G-BRUX | PA-44-180 Seminole | Hambrair Ltd/Tollerton |
| | G-BRUZ | Raven Europe FS-57A balloon | R. H. Etherington |
| | G-BRVA | Nord 3202B-1 | A. G. Martlew (G-BIZL) |
| | G-BRVB | Stolp SA.300 Starduster Too | R. W. Davies |
| | G-BRVC | Cameron N-180 balloon | The Apollo Balloon Co Ltd |
| | G-BRVE | Beech D.17S | Early Birds Ltd/Staverton |
| | G-BRVF | Colt 77A balloon | Airborne Adventures Ltd |
| | G-BRVG | North American SNJ-7 Trojan | Early Birds Ltd/Staverton |
| | G-BRVH | Smyth Model S Sidewinder | I. S. Bellamy |
| | G-BRVI | Robinson R-22B | Burnell Helicopters Ltd |
| | G-BRVJ | Slingsby T.31 Motor Cadet III | D. F. Micklethwait & J. R. Paskins |
| | G-BRVK | Cameron A-210 Balloon | The Balloon Club Ltd |
| | G-BRVL | Pitts S-1C Special | I. Duncan |
| | G-BRVM | — | — |
| | G-BRVN | Thunder Ax7-77 balloon | J. T. Hughes Ltd |
| | G-BRVO | AS.350B Ecureuil | Radstrong Ltd/Booker |
| | G-BRVR | Barnett J4B-2 | Ilkeston Contractors |
| | G-BRVS | Barnett J4B-2 | Ilkeston Contractors |
| | G-BRVT | Pitts S-2B Special | C. J. & M. D. Green |
| | G-BRVU | Colt 77A balloon | H. C. J. Williams |
| | G-BRVV | Colt 56B balloon | S. J. Hollingsworth |
| | G-BRVW | — | — |
| | G-BRVX | Cameron A-210 balloon | Bath Hot Air Balloon Club Ltd |
| | G-BRVY | Thunder Ax8-90 balloon | G. E. Morris |
| | G-BRVZ | Jodel D.117 | J.G. Patton |
| | G-BRWA | Aeronca 7AC Champion | D. D. Smith & J. R. Edwards |
| | G-BRWB | NA T-6G Texan | Aircraft Restorations Ltd/Duxford |
| | G-BRWC | Cessna 152 | T. Hayselden (Doncaster) Ltd |
| | G-BRWD | Robinson R22B | Odanrose Ltd |
| | G-BRWE | AS.332L Super Puma | Bristow Helicopters Ltd |
| | G-BRWF | Thunder Ax7-77 | D. J. Greaves |
| | G-BRWH | Cameron N-77 | R. K. McCulloch |
| | G-BRWI | Short SD3-60 Variant 300 | Short Bros PLC/Belfast City |
| | G-BRWJ | Short SD3-60 Variant 300 | Short Bros PLC/Belfast City |
| | G-BRWK | Short SD3-60 Variant 300 | Short Bros PLC/Belfast City |
| | G-BRWL | Short SD3-60 Variant 300 | Short Bros PLC/Belfast City |
| | G-BRWM | Short SD3-60 Variant 300 | Short Bros PLC/Belfast City |
| | G-BRWN | G.159 Gulfstream 1 | Aberdeen Airways Ltd |
| | G-BRWO | PA-28 Cherokee 140 | Severn Aircraft Co |
| | G-BRWP | CFM Streak Shadow Srs SA | D. F. Gaughan |
| | G-BRWR | Aeronca 11AC Chief | P. G. Peal |
| | G-BRWT | Scheibe SF.25C Falke | Brompton Promotions Ltd |
| | G-BRWU | Luton LA-4A Minor | R. B. Webber & P. K. Pike |
| | G-BRWV | Brügger MB.2 Colibri | S. J. McCollum |
| | G-BRWX | Cessna 172P | D. A. Abels |
| | G-BRWY | Cameron H-34 balloon | G. N. & K. A. Connolly |
| | G-BRWZ | Cameron 90 Macaw SS balloon | Forbes Europe Inc |
| | G-BRXA | Cameron O-120 balloon | A. F. Green |

| Reg. | Type | Owner or Operator | Notes |
|------|------|-------------------|-------|
| G-BRXB | Thunder Ax7-77 balloon | H. Peel | |
| G-BRXC | PA-28-161 Warrior II | Air Service Training Ltd/Perth | |
| G-BRXD | PA-28-181 Archer II | Cloudshire Ltd | |
| G-BRXE | Taylorcraft BC-12D | V. H. Spencer | |
| G-BRXF | Aeronca 11AC Chief | G. G. Pugh/Stapleford | |
| G-BRXG | Aeronca 7AC Champion | X-Ray Golf Flying Group | |
| G-BRXH | Cessna 120 | TSA (Thaddaeus Stewart Associates) Ltd | |
| G-BRXJ | Boeing 737-33A | Air Europe/Air Europe Scandinavia (LN-NOS) | |
| G-BRXK | Soko P-2 Kraguj | Cavok Ltd | |
| G-BRXL | Aeronca 11AC Chief | R. L. Jones | |
| G-BRXN | Montgomerie-Bensen B.8MR | J. C. Aitken | |
| G-BRXO | PA-34-200T Seneca II | Aviation Services Ltd | |
| G-BRXP | SNCAN Stampe SV-4C (modified) | P. G. Kavanagh & D. T. Kaberry | |
| G-BRXS | Howard Special T Minus | H. C. Cox | |
| G-BRXT | BAe 146-200 | British Aerospace PLC | |
| G-BRXU | AS.332L Super Puma | Bristow Helicopters Ltd | |
| G-BRXV | Robinson R-22B | E. Wootton | |
| G-BRXW | PA-24 Comanche 260 | R. J. Lane Pharmaceuticals | |
| G-BRXX | Colt 180A balloon | J. P. Clifford | |
| G-BRXY | Pietenpol Air Camper | A. E. Morris | |
| G-BRXZ | Robinson R-22B | MG Group Ltd | |
| G-BRYA | D.H.C.7-110 Dash Seven | Brymon/Air France *City of Paris/ Plymouth* | |
| G-BRYB | D.H.C.7-110 Dash Seven | Brymon Aviation Ltd *City of Plymouth/ Plymouth* | |
| G-BRYC | D.H.C.7-110 Dash Seven | Brymon/Air France *City of London/ Plymouth* | |
| G-BRYD | D.H.C.7-110 Dash Seven | Brymon Aviation Ltd *City of Exeter/ Plymouth* | |
| G-BRYE | D.H.C.7-102 Dash Seven | Brymon Aviation Ltd *City of Aberdeen/ Plymouth* | |
| G-BRYF | D.H.C.7-102 Dash Seven | Brymon Aviation Ltd (G-BPDX)/ Plymouth | |
| G-BRYG | D.H.C.8-102A Dash Eight | Brymon Aviation Ltd *City of Bristol/ Plymouth* | |
| G-BRYH | D.H.C.8-102A Dash Eight | Brymon Aviation Ltd/Plymouth | |
| G-BRYI | D.H.C.8-301A Dash Eight | Brymon Aviation Ltd/Plymouth | |
| G-BRYJ | D.H.C.8-301A Dash Eight | Brymon Aviation Ltd/Plymouth | |
| G-BRYK | — | Brymon Aviation Ltd | |
| G-BRYM | — | Brymon Aviation Ltd | |
| G-BRYN | SOCATA TB.20 Trinidad | Jones & Bradbourn (Guernsey) Ltd | |
| G-BRYO | — | Brymon Aviation Ltd | |
| G-BRYP | — | Brymon Aviation Ltd | |
| G-BRZA | Cameron O-77 balloon | L. & R. J. Mold | |
| G-BRZB | Cameron A-105 balloon | Headland Services Ltd | |
| G-BRZC | Cameron N-90 balloon | Flying Pictures (Balloons) Ltd | |
| G-BRZD | Hapi Cygnet SF-2A | L. G. Millen | |
| G-BRZE | Thunder Ax7-77 balloon | G. V. Beckwith | |
| G-BRZF | Enstrom 280C | Haversham Helicopters Ltd | |
| G-BRZG | Enstrom F-28A | Incentives Two Ltd | |
| G-BRZI | Cameron N-180 balloon | Pegasus Balloon Co Ltd | |
| G-BRZK | Stinson 108-2 | F. H. Wheeler & P. J. Mills | |
| G-BRZL | Pitts S-1D Special | G. W. Polson-Brown | |
| G-BRZM | Montgomerie-Bensen B.8MR | J. A. Campbell | |
| G-BRZN | Hughes 269B | Tranheli Ltd | |
| G-BRZO | Jodel D.18 | J. D. Anson | |
| G-BRZP | PA-28-161 Warrior II | Air Service Training Ltd/Perth | |
| G-BRZR | PA-22 Tri-Pacer 150 | B. E. Simpson | |
| G-BRZS | Cessna 172P | R. Tarling | |
| G-BRZT | Cameron V-77 balloon | B. Drawbridge | |
| G-BRZU | Colt Flying Cheese SS balloon | Willow Best Ltd | |
| G-BRZV | Colt Flying Apple SS balloon | Thrust Drive Ltd | |
| G-BRZW | Rans S.10 Sakota | D. L. Davies | |
| G-BRZX | Pitts S-1S Special | Cubitt Aviation Ltd | |
| G-BRZY | Saab 91B/2 Safir | Sylmar Aviation & Services Ltd | |
| G-BRZZ | CFM Streak Shadow | P. R. Oakes | |
| G-BSAB | PA-46-350P Malibu Mirage | D. O. Hooper | |
| G-BSAC | BN-2B-26 Islander | Pilatus BN Ltd/Bembridge | |
| G-BSAD | BN-2B-26 Islander | Pilatus BN Ltd/Bembridge | |
| G-BSAE | BN-2B-26 Islander | Pilatus BN Ltd/Bembridge | |

| Notes | Reg. | Type | Owner or Operator |
|---|---|---|---|
| | G-BSAF | BN-2B-26 Islander | Pilatus BN Ltd/Bembridge |
| | G-BSAH | BN-2B-26 Islander | Pilatus BN Ltd/Bembridge |
| | G-BSAI | Stoddard-Hamilton Glasair III | K. J. & P. J. Whitehead |
| | G-BSAJ | C.A.S.A. 1-131E Jungmann | R. J. F. Parker/Denham |
| | G-BSAK | Colt 21A balloon | Airship & Balloon Co Ltd |
| | G-BSAO | Steen Skybolt | S. F. Elvins |
| | G-BSAP | Cameron A-105 balloon | B. J. Petteford |
| | G-BSAR | Air Command 532 Elite | S. A. Ryder |
| | G-BSAS | Cameron V-65 balloon | D. J. Bailey & A. J. McRobie |
| | G-BSAT | PA-28-181 Archer II | A1 Aircraft Ltd/Biggin Hill |
| | G-BSAU | Enstrom F-28F | Southern Air Ltd/Shoreham |
| | G-BSAV | Thunder Ax7-77 balloon | E. A. Evans & ptnrs |
| | G-BSAW | PA-28-161 Warrior II | Carill Aviation Ltd/Southampton |
| | G-BSAX | — | — |
| | G-BSAY | Cessna 172M | D. B. Zabel |
| | G-BSAZ | Denney Aerocraft Kitfox | P. E. Hinkley |
| | G-BSBA | PA-28-161 Warrior II | P. A. Lancaster/White Waltham |
| | G-BSBB | CCF Harvard IV | J. Woodhouse/Thruxton |
| | G-BSBC | CCF Harvard IV | J. Woodhouse/Thruxton |
| | G-BSBD | NA T-6G Texan | J. Woodhouse/Thruxton |
| | G-BSBE | CCF Harvard IV | Pulsgrove Ltd/Thruxton |
| | G-BSBF | CCF Harvard IV | Pulsgrove Ltd/Thruxton |
| | G-BSBG | CCF Harvard IV | Pulsgrove Ltd/Thruxton |
| | G-BSBH | Short SD3-30★ | Ulster Aviation Soc Museum (stored) |
| | G-BSBI | Cameron O-77 balloon | Calibre Motor Co Ltd |
| | G-BSBJ | Bell 206B JetRanger 3 | Air Hanson Sales Ltd/Blackbushe |
| | G-BSBK | Colt 105A balloon | Zebra Balloons |
| | G-BSBM | Cameron N-77 balloon | Nuclear Electric |
| | G-BSBN | Thunder Ax7-77 balloon | B. Pawson |
| | G-BSBO | Marco J-5 | G. R. Horner |
| | G-BSBP | Jodel D.18 | R. T. Pratt |
| | G-BSBR | Cameron V-77 balloon | B. Bromiley |
| | G-BSBT | Piper J-3C-65 Cub | M. B. & L. J. Proudfoot |
| | G-BSBU | Firefly 8B | A. R. Peart |
| | G-BSBV | Rans S.10 Sakota | Sportair UK Ltd |
| | G-BSBW | Bell 206B JetRanger 3 | Danbank Developments Ltd |
| | G-BSBX | Montgomerie-Bensen B.8MR | B. Ibbott |
| | G-BSBY | Cessna 150L | D. F. Harrison |
| | G-BSBZ | Cessna 150M | D. F. Harrison |
| | G-BSCA | Cameron N-90 balloon | Legal & General Group PLC |
| | G-BSCB | Air Command 532 Elite | P. H. Smith |
| | G-BSCC | Colt 105A balloon | A. F. Selby |
| | G-BSCD | Hughes 269C | McIntyre Aviation Ltd |
| | G-BSCE | Robinson R-22B | S. B. Evans |
| | G-BSCF | Thunder Ax7-77 balloon | France Cottage (UK) Ltd |
| | G-BSCG | Denney Aerocraft Kitfox | A. C. & T. G. Pinkstone |
| | G-BSCH | Denney Aerocraft Kitfox | Baldoon Leisure Flying Co Ltd |
| | G-BSCI | Colt 77A balloon | F. W. Farnsworth Ltd |
| | G-BSCK | Cameron H-34 balloon | Flying Pictures (Balloons) Ltd |
| | G-BSCL | Robinson R-22B | Ketton Holdings Ltd |
| | G-BSCM | Denney Aerocraft Kitfox | M. Richardson |
| | G-BSCN | SOCATA TB.20 Trinidad | Air Touring Services Ltd/Biggin Hill |
| | G-BSCO | Thunder Ax7-77 balloon | F. J. Whalley |
| | G-BSCP | Cessna 152 | Doncaster Aero Club Ltd |
| | G-BSCR | Cessna 172M | Halsmith (Aircraft Sales) Ltd |
| | G-BSCS | PA-28-181 Archer II | Halsmith (Aircraft Sales) Ltd |
| | G-BSCU | Colt GA-42 gas airship | Thunder & Colt Ltd |
| | G-BSCV | PA-28-161 Warrior II | Southwood Flying Group/Southend |
| | G-BSCW | Taylorcraft BC-65 | J. W. Heale |
| | G-BSCX | Thunder Ax8-105 balloon | Balloon Flights Club Ltd |
| | G-BSCY | PA-28-151 Warrior | S. G. P. Fowler |
| | G-BSCZ | Cessna 152 | London Flight Centre (Stansted) Ltd |
| | G-BSDA | Taylorcraft BC-12D | L. Perry/White Waltham |
| | G-BSDB | Pitts S-1C Special | M. K. Whitaker |
| | G-BSDC | — | — |
| | G-BSDD | Denney Aerocraft Kitfox | J. Windmill |
| | G-BSDE | Cameron A-105 balloon | G. V. Beckwith |
| | G-BSDF | Cameron N-105 balloon | G. V. Beckwith |
| | G-BSDG | Robin DR.400/180 | Jeff Brown (Aviation Services) |
| | G-BSDH | Robin DR.400/180 | Hamilton Slade Co Ltd |
| | G-BSDI | Corben Junior Ace Model E | J. Pearson |
| | G-BSDJ | — | — |
| | G-BSDK | Piper J-5A Cub Cruiser | J. Pearson |

138

| Reg. | Type | Owner or Operator | Notes |
|------|------|-------------------|-------|
| G-BSDL | SOCATA TB.10 Tobago | Consort Aviation Ltd/Sherburn | |
| G-BSDN | PA-34-200T Seneca II | European Aircraft Services Ltd/Fairoaks | |
| G-BSDO | Cessna 152 | Independent Air Services Ltd | |
| G-BSDP | Cessna 152 | Independent Air Services Ltd | |
| G-BSDR | Boeing Stearman A.75N1 | Early Birds Ltd | |
| G-BSDS | Boeing Stearman E.75 | V. S. E. Norman | |
| G-BSDT | Cameron 0-120 balloon | Cameron Balloons Ltd | |
| G-BSDU | Bell 206B JetRanger 3 | Allied Leisure PLC | |
| G-BSDV | Colt 31A balloon | Airship & Balloon Co Ltd | |
| G-BSDW | Cessna 182P | Kerygma Trust | |
| G-BSDX | Cameron V-77 balloon | M. J. Snow | |
| G-BSDY | Beech 58 Baron | Astra Aviation Ltd | |
| G-BSEA | Thunder Ax7-77 balloon | R. Titterton | |
| G-BSEC | — | — | |
| G-BSED | PA-22 Tri-Pacer 160 | Sylmar Aviation & Services Ltd | |
| G-BSEE | Rans S.9 | P. M. Semler | |
| G-BSEF | PA-28 Cherokee 180 | D. J. R. Chapple | |
| G-BSEG | Ken Brock KB-2 | H. A. Bancroft-Wilson | |
| G-BSEH | Cameron V-77 balloon | G. V. Beckwith | |
| G-BSEI | Cameron N-90 balloon | Flying Pictures (Balloons) Ltd | |
| G-BSEJ | Cessna 150M | Hollyclass Ltd | |
| G-BSEK | Robinson R-22 | Skyline Helicopters Ltd | |
| G-BSEL | Slingsby T.61G Super Falke | RAFGSA/Hullavington | |
| G-BSEM | Cameron 90 Four-Pack SS balloon | Flying Pictures (Balloons) Ltd | |
| G-BSEN | Colt 31A balloon | Thunder & Colt Ltd | |
| G-BSEO | Beech 200 Super King Air | Air Hanson Aircraft Sales Ltd (G-OADT/ G-KBCA) | |
| G-BSEP | Cessna 172 | B. Myers & C. H. Moore/Doncaster | |
| G-BSER | PA-28 Cherokee 160 | Yorkair Ltd/Leeds | |
| G-BSES | Denney Aerocraft Kitfox | M. Albert-Brecht & J. J. M. Donnelly | |
| G-BSET | B.206 Srs 1 Basset | Beagle Basset Ltd/Shoreham | |
| G-BSEU | PA-28-181 Archer II | Halsmith (Aircraft Sales) Ltd | |
| G-BSEV | Cameron O-77 balloon | UK Transplant Co-ordinators Assoc | |
| G-BSEW | Sikorsky S-76A | Bond Helicopters Ltd | |
| G-BSEX | Cameron A-180 balloon | Heart of England Balloons | |
| G-BSEY | Beech A36 Bonanza | K. Phillips Ltd | |
| G-BSEZ | Air Command 532 Elite | D. S. Robinson | |
| G-BSFA | Pulsar | S. A. Gill | |
| G-BSFB | C.A.S.A. 1.131E Jungmann 2000 | R. A. L. Hubbard | |
| G-BSFD | Piper J-3C-65 Cub | E. C. English | |
| G-BSFE | PA-38-112 Tomahawk II | W. S. Robertson | |
| G-BSFF | Robin DR.400/180R | Lasham Gliding Soc Ltd | |
| G-BSFG | BAe Jetstream 3108 | British Aerospace PLC/Prestwick | |
| G-BSFH | BAe Jetstream 3108 | British Aerospace PLC/Prestwick | |
| G-BSFJ | Thunder Ax8-105 balloon | Airborne Adventures Ltd | |
| G-BSFK | PA-28-161 Warrior II | Air Service Training Ltd/Perth | |
| G-BSFM | Cameron 82 Cheese SS balloon | Gone With The Wind Ltd | |
| G-BSFN | SE.313B Alouette II | M & P Food Products Ltd | |
| G-BSFO | Cameron 60 House SS balloon | Clipsal UK Ltd | |
| G-BSFP | Cessna 152 | J. R. Nicholls | |
| G-BSFR | Cessna 152 | Galair Ltd | |
| G-BSFS | SE.313B Alouette II | M & P Food Products Ltd | |
| G-BSFT | PA-31 Turbo Navajo | SFT Aviation Ltd (G-AXYC)/ Bournemouth | |
| G-BSFU | SE.313B Alouette II | M & P Food Products Ltd | |
| G-BSFV | Woods Woody Pusher | M. G. E. Hutton | |
| G-BSFW | PA-15 Vagabond | D. P. Williams | |
| G-BSFX | Denney Aerocraft Kitfox | D. A. McFadyean | |
| G-BSFY | Denney Aerocraft Kitfox | J. R. Howard | |
| G-BSGA | — | — | |
| G-BSGB | Gaertner Ax4 Skyranger balloon | B. Gaertner | |
| G-BSGC | PA-18 Super Cub 95 | G. Churchill | |
| G-BSGD | PA-28 Cherokee 180 | R. J. Cleverley | |
| G-BSGF | Robinson R-22B | Birchwood Boats Solent Ltd | |
| G-BSGG | Denney Aerocraft Kitfox | C. G. Richardson | |
| G-BSGH | Airtour AH-56B balloon | Airtour Balloon Co Ltd | |
| G-BSGI | BAe 146-300 | British Aerospace PLC | |
| G-BSGJ | Monnet Sonerai 2 | A. N. Burrows | |
| G-BSGK | PA-34-200T Seneca II | J. A. Burrett & S. W. Frost | |
| G-BSGL | PA-28-161 Warrior II | 1st European (Leasing & Finance) Ltd | |
| G-BSGM | Cameron V-77 balloon | 5th Regiment Royal Artillery | |
| G-BSGN | PA-28-151 Warrior | 1st European (Leasing & Finance) Ltd | |
| G-BSGP | Cameron N-56 balloon | Haywards Heath Building Soc | |

| Notes | Reg. | Type | Owner or Operator |
|---|---|---|---|
| | G-BSGR | Boeing Stearman E.75 | A. G. Dunkerley |
| | G-BSGS | Rans S.10 Sakota | R. Handley |
| | G-BSGT | Cessna T.210N | B. J. Sharpe/Booker |
| | G-BSGU | Cessna P.206B | B. W. Wells & Burbage Farms Ltd |
| | G-BSGV | Rotorway Executive | R. A. Kingston |
| | G-BSGY | Thunder Ax7-77 balloon | Thunder & Colt Ltd |
| | G-BSGZ | Colt Financial Times SS balloon | Financial Times Ltd |
| | G-BSHA | PA-34-200T Seneca II | Warrior Aircraft Sales & Leasing Ltd |
| | G-BSHB | Colt 69A balloon | Airship & Balloon Co Ltd |
| | G-BSHC | Colt 69A balloon | Airship & Balloon Co Ltd |
| | G-BSHD | Colt 69A balloon | Airship & Balloon Co Ltd |
| | G-BSHE | Cessna 152 | J. A. Pothecary/Shoreham |
| | G-BSHF | Robinson R-22B | R. Richardson |
| | G-BSHH | Luscombe 8E Silvaire | Golf Centres Balloons Ltd |
| | G-BSHI | Luscombe 8F Silvaire | C. C. & J. M. Lovell |
| | G-BSHJ | Luscombe 8E Silvaire | C. R. M. Hart & S. J. Turner |
| | G-BSHK | Denney Aerocraft Kitfox | A. E. Cree & G. J. Cuzzocrea |
| | G-BSHL | H.S.125 Srs 600B | Magec Aviation Ltd (G-BBMD)/Luton |
| | G-BSHM | Slingsby Motor Cadet III | R. R. Hadley |
| | G-BSHN | Cessna 152 | C. Walsh |
| | G-BSHO | Cameron V-77 balloon | T. P. Barlass & D. J. Duckworth |
| | G-BSHP | PA-28-161 Warrior II | Air Service Training Ltd/Perth |
| | G-BSHR | Cessna F.172N | H. Rothwell (G-BFGE)/Blackpool |
| | G-BSHS | Colt 105A balloon | Europa Investments (Management) Ltd |
| | G-BSHT | Cameron V-77 balloon | ECM Construction Ltd |
| | G-BSHV | PA-18 Super Cub 135 | Fen Tigers Flying Group |
| | G-BSHW | — | |
| | G-BSHX | Enstrom F-28A | GB Air Academy Ltd/Goodwood |
| | G-BSHY | EAA Acro Sport 1 | A. W. Hughes & ptnrs |
| | G-BSHZ | Enstrom F-28F | Blades Helicopters Ltd |
| | G-BSIB | PA-28-161 Warrior II | Bobbington Air Training School Ltd |
| | G-BSIC | Cameron V-77 balloon | P. D. Worthy |
| | G-BSIE | Enstrom 280FX | Southern Air Ltd/Shoreham |
| | G-BSIF | Denney Aerocraft Kitfox | Junipa Sales (Aviation) Ltd |
| | G-BSIG | Colt 21A balloon | Thunder & Colt Ltd |
| | G-BSIH | Rutan LongEz | W. S. Allen |
| | G-BSII | PA-34-200T Seneca II | M. Fraser |
| | G-BSIJ | Cameron V-77 balloon | A. S. Jones |
| | G-BSIK | Denney Aerocraft Kitfox | I. A. Davies & B. Barr |
| | G-BSIL | Colt 120A balloon | A. Bolger |
| | G-BSIM | PA-28-181 Archer II | E. Midlands Aircraft Hire Ltd |
| | G-BSIN | Robinson R-22B | Solent Projects Ltd |
| | G-BSIO | Cameron 80 Shed SS balloon | Furness Building Soc |
| | G-BSIP | Cameron V-77 balloon | R. S. Ham |
| | G-BSIR | Cessna 340 | Airmaster Aviation Ltd/Cardiff |
| | G-BSIT | Robinson R-22B | D. J. Foreman |
| | G-BSIU | Colt 90A balloon | Thunder & Colt Ltd |
| | G-BSIW | BAe Jetstream 3100 | British Aerospace PLC/Prestwick |
| | G-BSIY | Schleicher ASK.14 | H. F. Lamprey |
| | G-BSIZ | PA-28-181 Archer II | Firmdale Ltd |
| | G-BSJA | Cameron N-77 balloon | N. Sanders (G-SPAR) |
| | G-BSJB | Bensen B.8 | J. W. Limbrick |
| | G-BSJC | Bell 206B JetRanger 3 | JETC Helicopters |
| | G-BSJD | Colt 160A balloon | Speedarrow Ltd |
| | G-BSJE | Colt 120A balloon | Speedarrow Ltd |
| | G-BSJF | Colt 120A balloon | Speedarrow Ltd |
| | G-BSJG | Colt 120A balloon | Speedarrow Ltd |
| | G-BSJH | Colt 120A balloon | Speedarrow Ltd |
| | G-BSJT | Cessna 152 | Fox Aviation Ltd/E. Midlands |
| | G-BSJU | Cessna 150M | Fox Aviation Ltd/E. Midlands |
| | G-BSJV | Cessna 172N | Fox Aviation Ltd/E. Midlands |
| | G-BSJW | Everett Srs 2 gyroplane | A. R. Willis |
| | G-BSJX | PA-28-161 Warrior II | GB Air Academy Ltd/Goodwood |
| | G-BSJY | Renegade II | J. Hatswell |
| | G-BSJZ | — | |
| | G-BSKA | Cessna 150M | K. J. Farrance |
| | G-BSKB | — | |
| | G-BSKC | PA-38-112 Tomahawk | Serendipity Aircraft Sales Ltd |
| | G-BSKD | Cameron V-77 balloon | P. Thomas |
| | G-BSKE | Cameron O-84 balloon | T. H. Whadden |
| | G-BSKF | Schweizer 269C | J. W. Sandle |
| | G-BSKG | Maule MXT-7-180 | Beeches Auto Services |
| | G-BSKH | Cessna 421C | Bristol & Mendip Estates Ltd |

| Reg. | Type | Owner or Operator | Notes |
|------|------|-------------------|-------|
| G-BSKI | Thunder Ax8-90 balloon | M. J. Gunston & ptners | |
| G-BSKJ | Mooney M.20J | M. C. Wroe | |
| G-BSKK | PA-38-112 Tomahawk | Falcon Flying Services/Biggin Hill | |
| G-BSKL | PA-38-112 Tomahawk | Falcon Flying Services/Biggin Hill | |
| G-BSKM | Cessna 182Q | Bob Crowe Aircraft Sales Ltd/Cranfield | |
| G-BSKN | Grob G.109B | C. S. Faber | |
| G-BSKO | Maule MXT-7-180 | Aeromarine Ltd | |
| G-BSKP | V.S.379 Spitfire F.XIV | Historic Aircraft Collection Ltd | |
| G-BSKR | Rand Robinson KR-2 | T. D. Saveker | |
| G-BSKS | Nieuport 28C-1 | Historic Aircraft Collection Ltd | |
| G-BSKT | Maule MXT-7-180 | D. D. Smith | |
| G-BSKU | Cameron O-84 balloon | Alfred Bagnall & Sons (West) Ltd | |
| G-BSKV | PA-28-181 Archer II | BAe Flying College Ltd/Prestwick | |
| G-BSKW | PA-28-181 Archer II | BAe Flying College Ltd/Prestwick | |
| G-BSKX | PA-28-181 Archer II | BAe Flying College Ltd/Prestwick | |
| G-BSLA | Robin DR.400/180 | A. B. McCoig/Biggin Hill | |
| G-BSLB | Robinson R-22B | J. H. Turkington & Sons (Contractors) Ltd | |
| G-BSLC | Robinson R-22B | Modern Air/Fowlmere | |
| G-BSLD | PA-28RT-201 Arrow IV | Actionwings Ltd | |
| G-BSLE | PA-28-161 Warrior II | Air Service Training Ltd/Perth | |
| G-BSLF | Robinson R-22B | Trainslide Ltd | |
| G-BSLG | Cameron A-180 balloon | Bridges Van Hire Ltd | |
| G-BSLH | C.A.S.A. 1-131E Jungmann 2000 | P. Warden | |
| G-BSLI | Cameron V-77 balloon | V. J. Holmes | |
| G-BSLJ | Denney Aerocraft Kitfox | A. F. Reid | |
| G-BSLK | PA-28-161 Warrior II | R. A. Rose | |
| G-BSLL | AS.355F-2 Twin Squirrel | Star Aviation (G-BOGX) | |
| G-BSLM | PA-28 Cherokee 160 | E. Sussex Aviation/Shoreham | |
| G-BSLN | Thunder Ax10-180 balloon | Albatross Aviation Ltd | |
| G-BSLO | Cameron A-180 balloon | Adventure Balloon Co Ltd | |
| G-BSLR | Schweizer 269C | Cuffroy Ltd | |
| G-BSLT | PA-28-161 Warrior II | Warrior Aircraft Sales & Leasing Ltd | |
| G-BSLU | PA-28 Cherokee 140 | Warrior Aircraft Sales & Leasing Ltd | |
| G-BSLV | Enstrom 280FX | Southern Air Ltd/Shoreham | |
| G-BSLW | Bellanca 7ECA Citabria | E. Sussex Aviation/Shoreham | |
| G-BSLX | WAR Focke-Wulf Fw.190 | E. Sussex Aviation/Shoreham | |
| G-BSLY | Colt AS-80 GD airship | Huntair Ltd | |
| G-BSLZ | BAe 146-300 | British Aerospace PLC | |
| G-BSMA | Colt Flying Open Book SS balloon | Jentime Ltd | |
| G-BSMB | Cessna U.206E | Army Parachute Association/Netheravon | |
| G-BSMD | Nord 1101 Noralpha | Magnificent Obsessions Ltd | |
| G-BSME | Bo 208C Junior | D. J. Hampson | |
| G-BSMF | Avro 652A Anson C.19 (TX183) | G. M. K. Fraser | |
| G-BSMG | Montgomerie-Bensen B.8M | A. C. Timperley | |
| G-BSMH | Colt 240A balloon | Formtrack Ltd | |
| G-BSMI | Schweizer 269C | A. J. Hardy | |
| G-BSMJ | — | — | |
| G-BSMK | Cameron O-84 balloon | J. C. Reavley | |
| G-BSML | Schweizer 269C | Nunkeeling Ltd | |
| G-BSMM | Colt 31A balloon | D. V. Fowler | |
| G-BSMN | CFM Streak Shadow | K. Daniels | |
| G-BSMO | Denney Aerocraft Kitfox | G-BSMO Group | |
| G-BSMP | PA-34-220T Seneca III | Gabriel Enterprises Ltd | |
| G-BSMR | BAe 146-300 | British Aerospace PLC | |
| G-BSMS | Cameron V-77 balloon | C. D. Howes | |
| G-BSMT | Rans S.10 Sakota | N. Woodworth | |
| G-BSMU | Rans S.6 | W. D. Walker (G-MWJE) | |
| G-BSMV | PA-17 Vagabond (modified) | R. D. & S. A. Carswell | |
| G-BSMW | Colt Flying Lager Bottle SS balloon | Wellfarrow Ltd | |
| G-BSMX | Bensen B.8MR | J. S. E. McGregor | |
| G-BSMZ | PA-28-161 Warrior II | Air Service Training Ltd/Perth | |
| G-BSNA | Boeing 757-236 | Air Europe Ltd/Gatwick | |
| G-BSNB | Boeing 757-236 | Air Europe Ltd/Gatwick | |
| G-BSNC | Boeing 757-236 | Air Europe Ltd/Gatwick | |
| G-BSND | Air Command 532 Elite | B. J. Castle | |
| G-BSNE | Luscombe 8A Silvaire | Aerolite Luscombe Group | |
| G-BSNF | Piper J-3C-65 Cub | J. A. Hoblyn | |
| G-BSNG | Cessna 172N | Berry Air/Edinburgh | |
| G-BSNH | Robinson R-22 | Skyline Helicopters Ltd/Booker | |
| G-BSNI | Bensen B.8V | B. D. Gibbs | |

| Notes | Reg. | Type | Owner or Operator |
|---|---|---|---|
| | G-BSNJ | Cameron N-90 balloon | D. P. H. Smith |
| | G-BSNK | — | — |
| | G-BSNL | Bensen B.8MR | T. R. Grief |
| | G-BSNN | Rans S.10 | S. Adams |
| | G-BSNO | Denney Aerocraft Kitfox | A. G. V. McClintock |
| | G-BSNP | PA-28-201T Turbo Arrow III | Stapleford Flying Club Ltd |
| | G-BSNT | Luscombe 8A Silvaire | B. J. Robe |
| | G-BSNU | Colt 105A balloon | Sun Life Assurance Soc PLC |
| | G-BSNV | — | — |
| | G-BSNW | — | — |
| | G-BSNX | PA-28-181 Archer II | Lotus Air |
| | G-BSNY | Bensen B.8M | A. S. Deakin |
| | G-BSNZ | Cameron O-105 balloon | Aire Valley Balloons |
| | G-BSOA | Bell 212 | Bristow Helicopters Ltd (G-BRDY) |
| | G-BSOE | Luscombe 8A Silvaire | S. B. Marsden |
| | G-BSOF | Colt 25A Mk II balloon | Thunder & Colt Ltd |
| | G-BSOG | Cessna 172M | B. Chapman & A. R. Budden |
| | G-BSOI | AS.332L Super Puma | Bristow Helicopters Ltd |
| | G-BSOJ | Thunder Ax7-77 balloon | Jentime Ltd |
| | G-BSOK | PA-28-161 Warrior II | Hamilton Compass Aviation Ltd |
| | G-BSOL | — | — |
| | G-BSOM | Glaser-Dirks DG.400 | G-BSOM Group |
| | G-BSON | Green S.25 | J. J. Green |
| | G-BSOO | Cessna 172F | BC & S Flying Services Ltd |
| | G-BSOR | CFM Streak Shadow Srs SA | J. P. Sorenson |
| | G-BSOT | PA-38-112 Tomahawk II | Cormack (Aircraft Services) Ltd/ Glasgow |
| | G-BSOU | PA-38-112 Tomahawk II | Cormack (Aircraft Services) Ltd/ Glasgow |
| | G-BSOV | PA-38-112 Tomahawk II | Cormack (Aircraft Services) Ltd/ Glasgow |
| | G-BSOW | PA-32R Cherokee Lance 300 | Halsmith (Aircraft Sales) Ltd |
| | G-BSOX | Luscombe 8A Silvaire | D. Gill |
| | G-BSOY | PA-34-220T Seneca III | BAe Flying College Ltd/Prestwick |
| | G-BSOZ | PA-28-161 Warrior II | Moray Flying Club Ltd/Kinloss |
| | G-BSPA | QAC Quickie Q.2 | Paul Martin Wright Ltd |
| | G-BSPB | Thunder Ax8-84 balloon | Nigs Pertwee Ltd |
| | G-BSPC | Jodel D.140C | B. E. Cotton/Headcorn |
| | G-BSPE | Cessna F.172P | P. & M. Jones/Denham |
| | G-BSPF | Cessna T.303 | McDonald Kane Ltd & K. P. Gibbin |
| | G-BSPG | PA-34-200T Seneca II | Fifo Ltd & C. M. Vlieland-Boddy |
| | G-BSPI | PA-28-161 Warrior II | Cloudshire Ltd |
| | G-BSPJ | Bensen B.8 | J. M. Hydes |
| | G-BSPK | Cessna 195A | Great Cloud Designs Ltd |
| | G-BSPL | CFM Streak Shadow Srs SA | D. G. Cook |
| | G-BSPM | PA-28-161 Warrior II | W. London Aero Services Ltd/White Waltham |
| | G-BSPN | PA-28R-201T Turbo Arrow III | R. J. Bickerton |
| | G-BSPO | BN-2B-26 Islander | Pilatus BN Ltd/Bembridge |
| | G-BSPP | BN-2B-26 Islander | Pilatus BN Ltd/Bembridge |
| | G-BSPR | BN-2B-26 Islander | Pilatus BN Ltd/Bembridge |
| | G-BSPS | BN-2B-26 Islander | Pilatus BN Ltd/Bembridge |
| | G-BSPT | BN-2B-26 Islander | Pilatus BN Ltd/Bembridge |
| | G-BSPU | BN-2B-26 Islander | Pilatus BN Ltd/Bembridge |
| | G-BSPW | Avid Flyer C | P. D. Wheatland |
| | G-BSPX | Lancair 320 | C. H. Skelt |
| | G-BSPY | BN-2A Islander | Glassbrush Ltd (G-AXYM) |
| | G-BSPZ | PA-28-161 Warrior II | Air Service Training Ltd/Perth |
| | G-BSRA | Boeing 737-4S3 | Air Europe Ltd/Gatwick |
| | G-BSRB | Boeing 737-4S3 | Air Europe Ltd/Gatwick |
| | G-BSRC | Cessna 150M | D. M. Leonard/Teesside |
| | G-BSRD | Cameron N-105 balloon | J. R. Joiner |
| | G-BSRG | Robinson R-22B | Meridian Helicopters |
| | G-BSRH | Pitts S-1C Special | J. R. Groom/Biggin Hill |
| | G-BSRI | Lancair 235 | G. Lewis |
| | G-BSRJ | Colt AA-1050 balloon | Thunder & Colt Ltd |
| | G-BSRK | ARV Super 2 | S. G. Dallison |
| | G-BSRL | Everett Srs 2 gyroplane | R. F. E. Burley |
| | G-BSRM | SA.365C-1 Dauphin | Nash Group Ltd |
| | G-BSRN | SA.365C-1 Dauphin | Nash Group Ltd |
| | G-BSRP | Rotorway Executive | J. P. Dennison |
| | G-BSRR | Cessna 182Q | Comet Aviation Ltd |
| | G-BSRT | Denney Aerocraft Kitfox | L. A. James |

| Reg. | Type | Owner or Operator | Notes |
|------|------|-------------------|-------|
| G-BSRU | BAe 146-200 | British Aerospace PLC (G-OSKI) | |
| G-BSRV | BAe 146-200 | British Aerospace PLC (G-OSUN) | |
| G-BSRW | Cameron 90 Tiger SS balloon | Cameron Balloons Ltd | |
| G-BSRX | CFM Streak Shadow | CFM Metal-Fax | |
| G-BSRY | Cessna F.406 Caravan II | Field Aircraft Services (Heathrow) Ltd | |
| G-BSRZ | Air Command 532 Elite 2-seat | A. S. G. Crabb | |
| G-BSSA | Luscombe 8E Silvaire | C. C. & J. M. Lovell | |
| G-BSSB | Cessna 150L | C. C. & J. M. Lovell | |
| G-BSSC | PA-28-161 Warrior II | Air Service Training Ltd/Perth | |
| G-BSSD | Cameron O-105 balloon | Gone With The Wind Ltd | |
| G-BSSE | PA-28 Cherokee 140 | Severn Aircraft Co | |
| G-BSSF | Denney Aerocraft Kitfox | D. M. Orrock | |
| G-BSSH | Bell 206L-1 LongRanger | RCR Aviation Ltd | |
| G-BSSI | Rans S.6 | D. A. Farnworth (G-MWJA) | |
| G-BSSJ | FRED Srs 2 | R. F. Jopling | |
| G-BSSK | QAC Quickie Q.2 | D. G. Greatrex | |
| G-BSSN | Air Command 532 Elite 2-seat | D. S. Robinson | |
| G-BSSO | Cameron O-90 balloon | J. N. H. Purvis | |
| G-BSSP | Robin DR.400/180R | Aeromarine Ltd/Southampton | |
| G-BSSR | PA-28-151 Warrior | G. Webster & R. J. Sixsmith | |
| G-BSSS | Cessna 421C | Freshname No77 Ltd | |
| G-BSST | Concorde 002★ | FAA Museum/Yeovilton | |
| G-BSSV | CFM Streak Shadow | A. M. Green | |
| G-BSSW | PA-28-161 Warrior II | MJ Leasing/Cardiff | |
| G-BSSX | PA-28-161 Warrior II | Airpart Supply Ltd/Booker | |
| G-BSSY | Polikarpov Po-2W | Sussex Spraying Services Ltd | |
| G-BSSZ | Thunder Ax8-90 balloon | Capital Balloon Club Ltd | |
| G-BSTA | BAe 146-100STA | British Aerospace PLC (G-BPNP/ G-SSHH/G-OPSA/G-BIAE)/Hatfield | |
| G-BSTC | Aeronca 11AC Chief | B. Bridgman & N. J. Mortimore | |
| G-BSTD | — | — | |
| G-BSTE | AS.355F-2 Twin Squirrel | McAlpine Helicopters Ltd | |
| G-BSTF | Beech 300LW Super King Air | Tim Leacock Aircraft Sales Ltd (G-UBSH) | |
| G-BSTG | Bell 206B JetRanger 2 | Skyline Helicopters Ltd (G-RIKK) | |
| G-BSTH | PA-25 Pawnee 235 | Scottish Gliding Union Ltd | |
| G-BSTI | Piper J-3C-65 Cub | I. Fraser & G. L. Nunn | |
| G-BSTJ | D.H.82A Tiger Moth | R. F. Harvey | |
| G-BSTK | Thunder Ax8-90 balloon | M. Williams | |
| G-BSTL | Rand Robinson KR-2 | T. M. Scale | |
| G-BSTM | Cessna 172L | G-BSTM Group/Cambridge | |
| G-BSTO | Cessna 152 | S. W. Belton | |
| G-BSTP | Cessna 152 | S. W. Belton | |
| G-BSTR | AA-5 Traveler | James Allan (Aviation & Engineering) Ltd | |
| G-BSTS | Schleicher ASW.20L | T. I. Gardiner | |
| G-BSTT | Rans S.6 | M. W. Holmes | |
| G-BSTU | Cessna P.210N | Boomselect Ltd | |
| G-BSTV | PA-32 Cherokee Six 300 | J. V. Hudson | |
| G-BSTW | Luscombe 8A Silvaire | M. D. Souch | |
| G-BSTX | Luscombe 8A Silvaire | J. O. Souch | |
| G-BSTY | Thunder Ax8-90 balloon | J. W. Cato | |
| G-BSTZ | PA-28 Cherokee 140 | H. M. & J. W. Young | |
| G-BSUA | Rans S.6 | P. S. Dopson & A. J. Todd | |
| G-BSUB | Colt 77A balloon | W. Country Marketing & Licensing Ltd | |
| G-BSUD | Luscombe 8A Silvaire | J. M. Jeapes | |
| G-BSUE | Cessna U.206G | R. A. Robinson | |
| G-BSUF | PA-32RT-300 Lance II | MCG Buildings | |
| G-BSUH | Cessna 140 | J. C. Greenslade | |
| G-BSUI | Robinson R-22B | C. T. Norman | |
| G-BSUJ | Brügger MB.2 Colibri | M. A. Farrelly | |
| G-BSUK | Colt 77A balloon | K. J. Foster | |
| G-BSUL | BAe 125 Srs 800B | British Aerospace PLC/Hatfield | |
| G-BSUM | Scheibe SF.27MB | M Syndicate | |
| G-BSUO | Scheibe SF.25C Falke | British Gliding Association Ltd | |
| G-BSUP | Schweizer 269C | Achilles Holdings Ltd | |
| G-BSUR | Rotorway Executive 90 | N. J. Betmell | |
| G-BSUS | Taylor JT.1 Monoplane | R. Parker | |
| G-BSUT | Rans S.6 | P. J. Clegg | |
| G-BSUU | Colt 180A balloon | J. P. Clifford | |
| G-BSUV | Cameron O-77 balloon | R. Moss | |
| G-BSUW | PA-34-200T Seneca II | Computaplane Ltd/Glasgow | |
| G-BSUX | Carlson Sparrow II | J. Stephenson | |

| Notes | Reg. | Type | Owner or Operator |
|-------|------|------|-------------------|
| | G-BSUY | BAe 146-300 | British Aerospace PLC |
| | G-BSUZ | Denney Aerocraft Kitfox | E. T. Wicks |
| | G-BSVA | Christen A.1 Husky | STOL Aviation Ltd |
| | G-BSVB | PA-28-181 Archer II | Redhill Flying Club |
| | G-BSVC | Cameron A-120 balloon | First Class Ballooning Ltd |
| | G-BSVE | Binder CP.301S Smaragd | B. F. Arnall |
| | G-BSVF | PA-28-161 Warrior II | Airways Aero Associations Ltd/Booker |
| | G-BSVG | PA-28-161 Warrior II | Airways Aero Associations Ltd/Booker |
| | G-BSVH | Piper J-3C-65 Cub | Knight Flying Group |
| | G-BSVI | PA-16 Clipper | Knight Flying Group |
| | G-BSVJ | — | — |
| | G-BSVK | Denney Aerocraft Kitfox | K. P. Wordsworth |
| | G-BSVL | Cessna 560 Citation V | P. & G. S. Thomas/Cardiff |
| | G-BSVM | PA-28-161 Warrior II | Falcon Flying Services/Biggin Hill |
| | G-BSVN | Thorp T-18 | J. E. Stevens |
| | G-BSVO | Sikorsky S-61N | Bristow Helicopters Ltd |
| | G-BSVP | PA-23 Aztec 250 | Time Electronics Ltd/Biggin Hill |
| | G-BSVR | Schweizer 269C | Nunkeeling Ltd |
| | G-BSVS | Robin DR.400/100 | Aeromarine Ltd/Southampton |
| | G-BSVT | — | — |
| | G-BSVU | Stemme S.10 | Sonic Aviation Ltd |
| | G-BSVV | PA-38-112 Tomahawk | Tradecliff Ltd |
| | G-BSVW | PA-38-112 Tomahawk | Tradecliff Ltd |
| | G-BSVX | PA-38-112 Tomahawk | Tradecliff Ltd |
| | G-BSVY | PA-38-112 Tomahawk | Tradecliff Ltd |
| | G-BSVZ | Pietenpol Air Camper | A. F. Cashin |
| | G-BSWA | Luscombe 8A Silvaire | C. C. & J. M. Lovell |
| | G-BSWB | Rans S.10 Sakota | F. A. Hewitt |
| | G-BSWC | Boeing Stearman E.75 | R. J. & N. R. Lancaster |
| | G-BSWD | Cameron A-180 balloon | Cameron Balloons Ltd |
| | G-BSWE | PA-18 Super Cub 150 | Stoneacre Aircraft Ltd |
| | G-BSWF | PA-16 Clipper | T. M. Storey |
| | G-BSWG | PA-17 Vagabond | J. P. Taylor |
| | G-BSWH | Cessna 152 | Airspeed Aviation Ltd/Tatenhill |
| | G-BSWI | Rans S.10 Sakota | K. E. Sheppard |
| | G-BSWJ | Cameron O-77 balloon | T. Charlwood |
| | G-BSWK | Robinson R-22B | Clarity Aviation Ltd |
| | G-BSWL | Slingsby T.67F | L. J. McKelvie |
| | G-BSWM | Slingsby T.67F | L. J. McKelvie |
| | G-BSWN | BN-2B-26 Islander | Pilatus BN Ltd/Bembridge |
| | G-BSWO | BN-2B-26 Islander | Pilatus BN Ltd/Bembridge |
| | G-BSWP | BN-2B-26 Islander | Pilatus BN Ltd/Bembridge |
| | G-BSWR | BN-2B-26 Islander | Pilatus BN Ltd/Bembridge |
| | G-BSWS | BN-2B-26 Islander | Pilatus BN Ltd/Bembridge |
| | G-BSWT | BN-2B-26 Islander | Pilatus BN Ltd/Bembridge |
| | G-BSWU | BN-2B-26 Islander | Pilatus BN Ltd/Bembridge |
| | G-BSWV | Cameron N-77 balloon | Leicester Mercury Ltd |
| | G-BSWW | Cameron O-105 balloon | R. B. & R. A. Naylor |
| | G-BSWX | Cameron V-90 balloon | Cameron Balloons Ltd |
| | G-BSWY | Cameron N-77 balloon | Nottingham Building Soc |
| | G-BSWZ | Cameron A-180 balloon | Cameron Balloons Ltd |
| | G-BSXA | PA-28-161 Warrior II | Hillvine Ltd |
| | G-BSXB | PA-28-161 Warrior II | Hillvine Ltd |
| | G-BSXC | PA-28-161 Warrior II | Hillvine Ltd |
| | G-BSXD | Soko P-2 Kraguj | C. J. Pearce |
| | G-BSXE | Bell 206B JetRanger | R. & M. International Helicopters Ltd |
| | G-BSXF | Cameron A-180 balloon | Gone With The Wind Ltd |
| | G-BSXG | Cessna 150K | Midair Aviation Ltd/Bournemouth |
| | G-BSXH | Pitts S-1 Special | A. Howard |
| | G-BSXI | Mooney M.20E | Halsmith (Aircraft Sales) Ltd |
| | G-BSXJ | BAC One-Eleven 401AK | Aviation Finance & Leasing Co Ltd |
| | G-BSXK | BAC One-Eleven 401AK | Aviation Finance & Leasing Co Ltd |
| | G-BSXL | BAe 146-300 | British Aerospace PLC/Hatfield |
| | G-BSXM | Cameron V-77 balloon | C. A. Oxby |
| | G-BSXN | Robinson R-22B | Sloane Helicopters Ltd/Sywell |
| | G-BSXO | Robinson R-22B | Reynard Racing Cars Ltd |
| | G-BSXP | Air Command 532 Elite | B. J. West |
| | G-BSXR | Air Command 532 Elite | T. Wing |
| | G-BSXS | PA-28-181 Archer II | Premier Flight Services Ltd |
| | G-BSXT | Piper J-5A Cub Cruiser | R. G. Trute |
| | G-BSXU | BAC One-Eleven 407AW | Winchester Aircraft Financing Ltd |
| | G-BSXV | BAC One-Eleven 407AW | Winchester Aircraft Financing Ltd |
| | G-BSXW | PA-28-161 Warrior II | MFM Enterprises Ltd |

| Reg. | Type | Owner or Operator | Notes |
|------|------|-------------------|-------|
| G-BSXX | Whittaker MW.7 | H. J. Stanley | |
| G-BSXY | Oldfield Baby Great Lakes | B. Freeman-Jones | |
| G-BSYA | Jodel D.18 | S. Harrison | |
| G-BSYB | Cameron N-120 balloon | Cameron Balloons Ltd | |
| G-BSYD | Cameron A-180 balloon | A. A. Brown | |
| G-BSYE | Cessna 140 | M. K. Whitaker | |
| G-BSYF | Luscombe 8A Silvaire | M. K. Whitaker | |
| G-BSYG | PA-12 Super Cruiser | M. K. Whitaker | |
| G-BSYH | Luscombe 8A Silvaire | C. C. & J. M. Lovell | |
| G-BSYI | AS.355F-1 Twin Squirrel | Lynton Aviation Ltd/Denham | |
| G-BSYJ | Cameron N-77 balloon | Chub Fire Ltd | |
| G-BSYK | PA-38-112 Tomahawk | Joyset Ltd | |
| G-BSYL | PA-38-112 Tomahawk | Joyset Ltd | |
| G-BSYM | PA-38-112 Tomahawk | Joyset Ltd | |
| G-BSYN | BAC One-Eleven 509EW | Dan-Air Services Ltd (G-AWWZ) | |
| G-BSYO | — | — | |
| G-BSYP | Bensen B.8M | A. T. Pocklington | |
| G-BSYR | BAe 146-300 | British Aerospace PLC | |
| G-BSYS | BAe 146-300 | British Aerospace PLC | |
| G-BSYT | BAe 146-300 | British Aerospace PLC | |
| G-BSYU | Robin DR.400/180 | Aeromarine Ltd/Southampton | |
| G-BSYV | Cessna 150M | Ravenair/Manchester | |
| G-BSYW | Cessna 150M | Ravenair/Manchester | |
| G-BSYX | Cessna 152 | Ravenair/Manchester | |
| G-BSYY | PA-28-161 Warrior II | Air Service Training Ltd/Perth | |
| G-BSYZ | PA-28-161 Warrior II | Air Service Training Ltd/Perth | |
| G-BSZA | Boeing 707-351B | Executive Aviation Group Ltd | |
| G-BSZB | Stolp SA.300 Starduster Too | Cambrian Flying Club/Swansea | |
| G-BSZC | Beech C-45H | Great Cloud Designs Ltd | |
| G-BSZD | Robin DR.400/180 | Aeromarine Ltd/Southampton | |
| G-BSZF | Jodel DR.250/160 | J. B. Randle | |
| G-BSZG | Stolp SA.100 Starduster | S. W. Watkins | |
| G-BSZH | Thunder Ax7-77 balloon | M. S. Drinkwater | |
| G-BSZI | Cessna 152 | Eglinton Flying Club Ltd | |
| G-BSZJ | PA-28-181 Archer II | Premier Flight Services Ltd | |
| G-BSZK | BAe Jetstream 3109 | British Aerospace PLC/Prestwick | |
| G-BSZL | Colt 77A balloon | Airship & Balloon Co Ltd | |
| G-BSZM | Bensen B.8 | J. H. H. Turner | |
| G-BSZN | Bucker Bul33D-1 Jungmeister | V. Lindsay | |
| G-BSZO | Cessna 152 | Cloudshire Ltd/Wellesbourne | |
| G-BSZP | Beech 400 Beechjet | Air Hanson Aircraft Sales Ltd/ Farnborough | |
| G-BSZR | PA-28RT-201T Turbo Arrow IV | Venuetime Ltd | |
| G-BSZS | Robinson R-22B | South West Helicopters Ltd | |
| G-BSZT | PA-28-161 Warrior II | N. A. Ali | |
| G-BSZU | Cessna 150F | Midair Aviation Ltd/Bournemouth | |
| G-BSZV | Cessna 150F | Midair Aviation Ltd/Bournemouth | |
| G-BSZW | Cessna 152 | Midair Aviation Ltd/Bournemouth | |
| G-BSZX | Cessna 150M | Midair Aviation Ltd/Bournemouth | |
| G-BSZY | Cameron A-180 balloon | Bryant Group PLC | |
| G-BTAA | EMB-110P1 Bandeirante | Alexandra Aviation Ltd (G-BHJY) | |
| G-BTAB | BAe 125 Srs 800B | Abbey Investments Co Ltd (G-BOOA) | |
| G-BTAD | Macair Merlin | A. T. & M. R. Dowie | |
| G-BTAE | BAe 125 Srs 800B | CIBC Finance PLC | |
| G-BTAF | PA-28-181 Archer II | Enpar (North) Ltd | |
| G-BTAG | Cameron O-77 balloon | H. Phethean & R. A. Shapland | |
| G-BTAH | Bensen B.8A | T. B. Johnson | |
| G-BTAI | BAe Jetstream 3109 | British Aerospace PLC/Prestwick | |
| G-BTAJ | PA-34-200T Seneca II | Ravenair Aircraft Engineering Ltd/ Manchester | |
| G-BTAK | EAA Acro Sport 2 | B. Brown | |
| G-BTAL | Cessna F.152 | Thanet Flying Club/Manston | |
| G-BTAM | PA-28-181 Archer II | Premier Flight Services Ltd | |
| G-BTAO | Cameron A-180 balloon | R. M. Bishop & D. C. La Beaume | |
| G-BTAN | Thunder Ax7-65Z balloon | C. Wilkinson | |
| G-BTAP | PA-38-112 Tomahawk | I. J. McGarrigle | |
| G-BTAR | — | | |
| G-BTAS | — | | |
| G-BTAT | Denny Aerocraft Kitfox | Fast Ford Centre Ltd | |
| G-BTAU | Thunder Ax7-77 balloon | Thunder & Colt Ltd | |
| G-BTAV | Colt 105A balloon | D. C. Chipping | |
| G-BTAW | PA-28-161 Warrior II | Enpar (North) Ltd | |

| Notes | Reg. | Type | Owner or Operator |
|---|---|---|---|
| | G-BTAX | PA-31-350 Navajo Chieftain | Jet West Ltd/Exeter |
| | G-BTAY | — | — |
| | G-BTAZ | Evans VP-2 | G. S. Poulter |
| | G-BTBA | — | — |
| | G-BTBB | Thunder Ax8-105 balloon | Scotia Balloons Ltd |
| | G-BTBC | PA-28-161 Warrior II | B. Powell |
| | G-BTBD | MBB Bo 105D | Nash Group Ltd |
| | G-BTBE | — | — |
| | G-BTBF | Super Koala | E. A. Taylor (G-MWOZ) |
| | G-BTBG | Denny Aerocraft Kitfox | J. Catley |
| | G-BTBH | — | — |
| | G-BTBI | WAR P-47 Thunderbolt (replica) | J. Berry |
| | G-BTBJ | — | — |
| | G-BTBK | Cessna 152 | Mercia Aircraft Leasing & Sales Ltd |
| | G-BTBL | Montgomerie-Bensen B.8MR | J. M. Montgomerie |
| | G-BTBN | Denney Aerocraft Kitfox | Avon Valley Flying Group |
| | G-BTBO | Cameron N-77 balloon | Cameron Balloons Ltd |
| | G-BTBP | Cameron N-90 balloon | Cameron Balloons Ltd |
| | G-BTBR | Cameron DP-80 airship | Cameron Balloons Ltd |
| | G-BTBS | Cameron N-180 balloon | G. Scaife & B. Smith |
| | G-BTBT | PA-32R-301 Saratoga SP | B. Taylor |
| | G-BTBU | PA-18 Super Cub 150 | Stoneacre Aircraft Ltd |
| | G-BTBV | — | — |
| | G-BTBW | Cessna 120 | A. Brinkley |
| | G-BTBX | Piper J-3C-65 Cub | A. Brinkley |
| | G-BTBY | PA-17 Vagabond | M. M. Wallis |
| | G-BTBZ | Cessna 172B | J. W. Rimington |
| | G-BTCA | PA-32R-300 Lance | P. Taylor |
| | G-BTCB | Air Command 582 Sport | G. Scurrah |
| | G-BTCC | F6F-5 Hellcat | Patina Ltd/Duxford |
| | G-BTCD | P-51D-25-NA Mustang | Patina Ltd/Duxford |
| | G-BTCE | Cessna 152 | W. & J. E. Cubitt |
| | G-BTCF | CFM Streak Shadow | P. Crossman |
| | G-BTCG | PA-23 Aztec 250 | Eagle Tugs Ltd (G-AVRX)/Nairobi |
| | G-BTCH | — | — |
| | G-BTCI | PA-17 Vagabond | C. C. & J. M. Lovell |
| | G-BTCJ | Luscombe 8C Silvaire | C. C. & J. M. Lovell |
| | G-BTCK | Cameron A-210 balloon | P. J. D. Kerr & A. J. Street |
| | G-BTCL | Cameron A-210 balloon | P. J. D. Kerr & A. J. Street |
| | G-BTCM | Cameron N-90 balloon | W. I. Hooker |
| | G-BTCN | Cameron A-300 balloon | Cameron Balloons Ltd |
| | G-BTCO | FRED Srs 2 | I. P. Manley |
| | G-BTCP | BAe 146-200 | British Aerospace PLC |
| | G-BTCR | Rans S.10 Sakota | S. H. Barr |
| | G-BTCS | Colt 90A balloon | D. N. Belton |
| | G-BTCT | AS.332L Super Puma | Bristow Helicopters Ltd |
| | G-BTCU | — | — |
| | G-BTCV | Cameron V-90 balloon | Cameron Balloons Ltd |
| | G-BTCW | Cameron A-180 balloon | Bristol Balloons |
| | G-BTCX | Hunter F.4 | Gray Tuplin Ltd |
| | G-BTCY | Hunter F.4 | Gray Tuplin Ltd |
| | G-BTCZ | Cameron 84 Chateau SS balloon | Forbes Europe Inc |
| | G-BTDA | — | — |
| | G-BTDB | Cameron A-180 balloon | Balloon-A-Drome Ltd |
| | G-BTDC | Denney Aerocraft Kitfox | D. Collinson |
| | G-BTDD | CFM Streak Shadow | S. J. Evans |
| | G-BTDE | Cessna C-165 | I. H. Logan |
| | G-BTDF | — | — |
| | G-BTDG | Colt 105A balloon | Thunder & Colt Ltd |
| | G-BTDH | P.56 Provost T.1 | Pulsegrove Ltd/Shoreham |
| | G-BTDI | Robinson R-22B | A. Palmer |
| | G-BTDJ | — | — |
| | G-BTDK | Cessna 421C | RK Carbon Fibre Ltd/Manchester |
| | G-BTDL | D.H.C.2 Beaver 1 | Seaflite Ltd |
| | G-BTDM | D.H.C.2 Beaver 1 | A. F. Allen |
| | G-BTDN | Denney Aerocraft Kitfox | A. B. Butler |
| | G-BTDO | BAe 146-200 | British Aerospace PLC |
| | G-BTDR | Aero Designs Pulsar | R. M. Hughes |
| | G-BTDS | Colt 77A balloon | C. P. Witter Ltd |
| | G-BTDT | — | — |
| | G-BTDU | — | — |
| | G-BTDV | — | — |
| | G-BTDW | — | — |

| Reg. | Type | Owner or Operator | Notes |
|------|------|-------------------|-------|
| G-BTDX | PA-18 Super Cub 150 | Stoneacre Aircraft Ltd | |
| G-BTDY | PA-18 Super Cub 150 | Stoneacre Aircraft Ltd | |
| G-BTDZ | — | — | |
| G-BTEA | Cameron N-105 balloon | Southern Balloon Group | |
| G-BTEE | Cameron O-120 balloon | W. H. & J. P. Morgan | |
| G-BTEG | Taylorcraft BC-65 | Aeroship Ltd | |
| G-BTEH | Colt 77A balloon | Thunder & Colt Ltd | |
| G-BTEI | Everett Srs 3 gyroplane | J. W. Highton | |
| G-BTEL | CFM Streak Shadow | J. E. Eatwell | |
| G-BTEN | Thunder Ax7-77 balloon | T. W. Dawson | |
| G-BTEO | Cameron V-90 balloon | Cameron Balloons Ltd | |
| G-BTEP | Cameron DP-80 airship | Cameron Balloons Ltd | |
| G-BTFC | Cessna F.152 II | Tayside Aviation Ltd/Dundee | |
| G-BTGS | Stolp SA.300 Starduster Too | T. G. Soloman (G-AYMA)/Shoreham | |
| G-BTIE | SOCATA TB.10 Tobago | Rotaters Ltd/Manchester | |
| G-BTIM | PA-28-161 Cadet | London Aviation Ltd/Biggin Hill | |
| G-BTLB | Wassmer WA.52 Europa | M. D. O'Brien/Shoreham | |
| G-BTLE | PA-31-350 Navajo Chieftain | Octavious Hunt Ltd | |
| G-BTLT | Colt 31A balloon | Thunder & Colt Ltd | |
| G-BTNU | BAe 146-300 | Dan-Air Services Ltd (G-BSLS)/Gatwick | |
| G-BTOM | PA-38-112 Tomahawk | R. A. Wakefield | |
| G-BTOW | SOCATA Rallye 180GT | Wallis & Son Ltd | |
| G-BTPA | BAe ATP | British Airways *Strathallan*/Glasgow | |
| G-BTPB | Cameron N-105 balloon | British Telecom PLC | |
| G-BTPC | BAe ATP | British Airways *Strathblane*/Glasgow | |
| G-BTPD | BAe ATP | British Airways *Strathconan*/Glasgow | |
| G-BTPE | BAe ATP | British Airways *Strathdon*/Glasgow | |
| G-BTPF | BAe ATP | British Airways *Strathearn*/Glasgow | |
| G-BTPG | BAe ATP | British Airways *Strathfillan*/Glasgow | |
| G-BTPH | BAe ATP | British Airways *Strathnaver*/Glasgow | |
| G-BTPJ | BAe ATP | British Airways *Strathpeffer*/Glasgow | |
| G-BTSC | Evans VP-2 | B. P. Irish | |
| G-BTSG | Cessna 414A | T. S. Grimshaw Ltd (G-BFTH) | |
| G-BTSL | Cameron Glass SS balloon | M. R. Humphrey & J. R. Clifton | |
| G-BTUC | EMB-312 Tucano | Short Bros PLC/Belfast City | |
| G-BTUG | SOCATA Rallye 180T | Lasham Gliding Soc | |
| G-BTVS | AS.355F-1 Twin Squirrel | BLS Aviation Ltd (G-STVE/G-TOFF/ G-BKJX)/Elstree | |
| G-BTWW | AB-206B JetRanger | Dollar Air Services Ltd/Coventry | |
| G-BTXL | BAe JetStream 3102 | Berlin Regional UK Ltd (G-BLDO) | |

# Out-of-Sequence Registrations

| Notes | Reg. | Type | Owner or Operator |
|---|---|---|---|
| | G-BUBL | Thunder Ax8-105 balloon | Moet & Chandon (London) Ltd |
| | G-BUBU | PA-34-220T Seneca III | Brinor (Holdings) Ltd |
| | G-BUCA | Cessna A.150K | A. Bucknale |
| | G-BUCK | C.A.S.A. 1.131E Jungmann (BU+CK) | Jungmann Flying Group/ White Waltham |
| | G-BUCS | Cessna 150F | A. Bucknale |
| | G-BUCT | Cessna 150L | A. Bucknale |
| | G-BUDS | Rand KR-2 | D. W. Munday |
| | G-BUDY | Colt 17A balloon | Bondbaste Ltd |
| | G-BUEM | C.A.S.A. 1.131E Jungmann | E. K. McEntee (G-BUCC)/White Waltham |
| | G-BUFF | Jodel D.112 | D. J. Buffham/Fenland |
| | G-BUFO | Cameron Wedgwood SS balloon | Airship & Balloon Co Ltd |
| | G-BUKK | Bucker Bu133 Jungmeister | R. H. Reeves |
| | G-BULL | SA Bulldog 120/128 | J. D. Richardson |
| | G-BUMP | PA-28-181 Archer II | M. Dunlop |
| | G-BUND | PA-28R-201T Turbo Arrow III | W. S. Stanley |
| | G-BUNY | Beech 95-B55 Baron | Gama Aviation Ltd |
| | G-BUPI | Cameron V-77 balloon | S. A. Masey (G-BOUC) |
| | G-BURD | Cessna F.172N | RJS Aviation Ltd/Halfpenny Green |
| | G-BURS | Sikorsky S-76A | Lynton Aviation Ltd (G-OHTL) |
| | G-BURT | PA-28-161 Warrior II | I. P. Stockwell |
| | G-BUSB | Airbus A.320-111 | British Airways *Isle of Jersey* |
| | G-BUSC | Airbus A.320-111 | British Airways *Isle of Skye* |
| | G-BUSD | Airbus A.320-111 | British Airways *Isle of Mull* |
| | G-BUSE | Airbus A.320-111 | British Airways *Isle of Scilly* |
| | G-BUSF | Airbus A.320-111 | British Airways *Isle of Man* |
| | G-BUSG | Airbus A.320-211 | British Airways *Isle of Wight* |
| | G-BUSH | Airbus A.320-211 | British Airways *Isle of Jura* |
| | G-BUSI | Airbus A.320-211 | British Airways *Isle of Anglesey* |
| | G-BUSJ | Airbus A.320-211 | British Airways *Island of Sark* |
| | G-BUSK | Airbus A.320-211 | British Airways *Isle of Guernsey* |
| | G-BUSS | Cameron Bus SS balloon | A. Faulkner |
| | G-BUSY | Thunder Ax6-56A balloon | M. Drinkwater |
| | G-BUTL | PA-24 Comanche 250 | D. Buttle (G-ARLB)/Blackbushe |
| | G-BUTT | Cessna FA.150K | P. L. Borek (G-AXSJ) |
| | G-BUYI | Thunder Ax7-77 balloon | Chelmsford Management Ltd |
| | G-BUZI | AS.355F-1 Twin Squirrel | Butane Buzzard Aviation Corporation Ltd |
| | G-BUZZ | AB-206B JetRanger 2 | ICS Worldwide Courier Ltd |
| | G-BVAN | M.S.892E Rallye 150 | C. D. Weiswall |
| | G-BVAX | Colt 77A balloon | Vax Appliances Ltd |
| | G-BVMM | Robin HR.200/100 | M. G. Owen |
| | G-BVMZ | Robin HR.100/210 | Chiltern Handbags (London) Ltd |
| | G-BVPI | Evans VP-1 | C. M. Gibson |
| | G-BVPM | Evans VP-2 | P. Marigold |
| | G-BWAS | PA-31-350 Navajo Chieftain | BWOC Ltd/Bristol |
| | G-BWAY | Beech A36 Bonanza | Briway Transit Systems |
| | G-BWDJ | Jurca MJ.5 Sirocco | A. Burani |
| | G-BWDT | PA-34-220T Seneca II | Budleigh Estates Ltd (G-BKHS) |
| | G-BWEC | Cassutt-Colson Variant | N. R. Thomason & M. P. J. Hill |
| | G-BWFJ | Evans VP-1 | G. F. Kennedy |
| | G-BWHY | Robinson R-22 | R. E. Benke |
| | G-BWIG | G.17S replica | K. Wigglesworth |
| | G-BWJB | Thunder Ax8-105 balloon | Justerini & Brooks Ltd *Whiskey J. & B.* |
| | G-BWKK | Auster AOP.9 (XP279) | A. Hawley |
| | G-BWMA | Colt 105A balloon | Bristol & West Motor Auction Ltd |
| | G-BWMB | Jodel D.119 | K. Jarman & S. Levey |
| | G-BWMP | Gulfstream 695A | R. B. Tyler (Plant) Ltd |
| | G-BWOC | PA-31-350 Navajo Chieftain | BWOC Ltd |
| | G-BWSA | PA-31-350 Navajo Chieftain | Quantum Leasing Ltd (G-BPJX) |
| | G-BWSI | K&S SA.102.5 Cavalier | B. W. Shaw |
| | G-BWTX | PA-42-720 Cheyenne III | Broome & Wellington (Aviation) Ltd |
| | G-BWVE | Bell 206B JetRanger | Willow Vale Electronics Ltd (G-BOSX) |
| | G-BWWJ | Hughes 269C | Dave Nieman Models Ltd (G-BMYZ) |
| | G-BWWW | BAe Jetstream 3102 | British Aerospace PLC/Dunsfold |
| | G-BXAX | Cameron N-77 balloon | Flying Pictures Ltd |
| | G-BXPS | PA-23 Aztec 250C | N. H. Bailey (G-AYLI) |

| Reg. | Type | Owner or Operator | Notes |
|------|------|-------------------|-------|
| G-BXVI | V.S.361 Spitfire F.XVI (RW386) | D. Arnold | |
| G-BXYZ | R. Turbo Commander 690C | British Airports Authority/Gatwick | |
| G-BYAA | Boeing 767-204ER | Britannia Airways Ltd/Air Holland | |
| G-BYAB | Boeing 767-204ER | Britannia Airways Ltd/Luton | |
| G-BYAC | Boeing 767-204ER | Britannia Airways Ltd/Luton | |
| G-BYAD | Boeing 767-204ER | Britannia Airways Ltd/Luton | |
| G-BYAE | Boeing 767-204ER | Britannia Airways Ltd/Luton | |
| G-BYAF | Boeing 767-204ER | Britannia Airways Ltd/Luton | |
| G-BYBB | PA-32RT-300 Lance II | BB Aviation Ltd/Stapleford | |
| G-BYEE | Mooney M.20K | Axe & Status Ltd | |
| G-BYIJ | C.A.S.A. 1-131E Jungmann 2000 | K. B. Palmer | |
| G-BYLL | F.8L Falco | N. J. Langrick/Sherburn | |
| G-BYLS | Bede BD-4 | G. H. Bayliss | |
| G-BYNG | Cessna T.303 | J. M. E. Byng (G-PTWB) | |
| G-BYOL | Cessna 340A | Jetline Ltd | |
| G-BYPS | Cameron 90 Carrots SS balloon | Airship & Balloon Co Ltd | |
| G-BYRD | Mooney M.20K | V. J. Holden/Teesside | |
| G-BYRN | PA-31-350 Navajo Chieftain | Byrne Group PLC (G-YLAN) | |
| G-BYSE | AB-206B JetRanger 2 | Bewise Ltd (G-BFND) | |
| G-BYSL | Cameron O-56 balloon | Charles of the Ritz Ltd | |
| G-BYTE | Robinson R-22B | Datel Electronics Ltd | |
| G-BZAC | Sikorsky S-76A | British International Helicopters Ltd | |
| G-BZBH | Thunder Ax6-65 balloon | R. S. Whittaker & P. E. Sadler | |
| G-BZKK | Cameron V-56 balloon | P. J. Green & C. Bosley *Gemini II* | |
| G-BZZZ | Enstrom F-28C-UK | Owners Abroad Aviation Ltd (G-BBBZ) | |
| G-CALL | PA-23 Aztec 250F | Woodgate Aviation Ltd/Ronaldsway | |
| G-CALV | PA-39 Twin Comanche 160 C/R | J. Calverley (G-AZFO) | |
| G-CAPT | Taylor JT.2 Titch | V. W. B. Davies (G-BTJM) | |
| G-CAXF | Cameron O-77 balloon | R. D. & S. J. Sarjeant | |
| G-CAYN | Dornier Do.228-201 | Cayenne Ltd (G-MLNR) | |
| G-CBEA | BAe Jetstream 3102-01 | Birmingham European Airways Ltd | |
| G-CBIL | Cessna 182K | C. P. Gurley & R. S. Merrell | |
| G-CBJB | Sikorsky S-76A | Bond Helicopters Ltd | |
| G-CBKT | Cameron O-77 balloon | Caledonian Airways Ltd | |
| G-CBOR | Cessna F.172N | J. Seville | |
| G-CCAR | Cameron N-77 balloon | The Colt Car Co Ltd | |
| G-CCCC | Cessna 172H | K. E. Wilson | |
| G-CCCL | Cessna 500 Citation | The Colt Car Co Ltd (G-BEIZ)/Staverton | |
| G-CCDI | Cameron N-77 balloon | Charles Church Developments PLC | |
| G-CCIX | V.S.361 Spitfire LF.IX | Charles Church Displays Ltd (G-BIXP) | |
| G-CCOZ | Monnet Sonerai II | P. R. Cozens | |
| G-CCUB | Piper J-3C-65 Cub | Cormack (Aircraft Services) Ltd | |
| G-CCVV | V.S.379 Spitfire FR.XIV | Charles Church Displays Ltd | |
| G-CDAH | Taylor Sooper Coot A | D. A. Hood | |
| G-CDBS | MBB Bo 105DBS | Bond Helicopters Ltd/Aberdeen | |
| G-CDET | Culver LCA Cadet | H. B. Fox/Booker | |
| G-CDGA | Taylor JT.1 Monoplane | R. M. Larimore | |
| G-CDGL | Saffery S.330 balloon | C. J. Dodd & G. J. Luckett *Penny* | |
| G-CDON | PA-28-161 Warrior II | East Midlands Flying Club PLC | |
| G-CDOS | Beech 95-58 Baron | Astra Aviation Ltd | |
| G-CDRU | C.A.S.A. 1-131E Jungmann | P. Cunniff/White Waltham | |
| G-CEAS | HPR-7 Herald 214 | Channel Express PLC (G-BEBB)/Bournemouth | |
| G-CEGA | PA-34-200T Seneca II | Hendefern Ltd | |
| G-CELL | PA-32R-301 Saratoga SP | CEL Electronics Ltd | |
| G-CERT | Mooney M.20K | Fairline Boats PLC/Conington | |
| G-CETC | Aeronca 15AC Sedan | J. W. Scale | |
| G-CEXP | HPR-7 Herald 209 | Channel Express PLC (G-BFRJ)/Bournemouth | |
| G-CFBI | Colt 56A balloon | G. A. Fisher | |
| G-CFLT | AS.355F-1 Twin Squirrel | Filemart Ltd (G-BNBI) | |
| G-CFLY | Cessna 172F | I. Hughes & B. T. Williams | |
| G-CGHM | PA-28 Cherokee 140 | CGH Managements Ltd/Elstree | |
| G-CHAL | Robinson R-22B | Chalrey Ltd | |
| G-CHAR | Grob G.109B | RAFGSA/Bicester | |
| G-CHAT | Bell 206B JetRanger 2 | Chiltern Hunt Aviation & Transport Ltd (G-KFDF) | |
| G-CHEM | PA-34-200T Seneca II | Everts Balloon Co Ltd | |
| G-CHIK | Cessna F.152 | Stapleford Flying Club Ltd (G-BHAZ) | |
| G-CHIL | Robinson R-22HP | Skyline Helicopters Ltd | |
| G-CHIP | PA-28-181 Archer II | C. M. Hough/Fairoaks | |
| G-CHOK | Cameron V-77 balloon | K. W. Overton | |

| Notes | Reg. | Type | Owner or Operator |
|---|---|---|---|
| | G-CHOP | Westland-Bell 47G-3B1 | Time Choppers Ltd/Chilbolton |
| | G-CHRO | Thunder & Colt Flying Book SS balloon | Chronicle Communications Ltd |
| | G-CHRP | Colt Flying Book SS balloon | Chronicle Communications Ltd |
| | G-CHRR | Colt Flying Book SS balloon | Chronicle Communications Ltd |
| | G-CHSR | BAe 146-200 | Air UK Ltd/Norwich |
| | G-CHTA | AA-5A Cheetah | Rapid Spin Ltd (G-BFRC)/Biggin Hill |
| | G-CHTT | Varga 2150A Kachina | C.H.T. Trace |
| | G-CHUB | Colt N-51 balloon | Chubb Fire Security Ltd |
| | G-CHYL | Robinson R-22B | L. M. Dresher |
| | G-CICI | Cameron R-15 balloon | Ballooning Endeavours Ltd |
| | G-CIII | Oldfield Baby Great Lakes | G. Cooper |
| | G-CINE | Bell 206L-1 LongRanger | Air Ward Aviation Ltd |
| | G-CIPI | AJEP Wittman W.8 Tailwind | G. J. Z. Cipirski (G-AYDU)/Biggin Hill |
| | G-CITI | Cessna 501 Citation | Messenger Group PLC |
| | G-CITY | PA-31-350 Navajo Chieftain | Woodgate Aviation Ltd/Ronaldsway |
| | G-CJBC | PA-28 Cherokee 180 | J. B. Cave/Halfpenny Green |
| | G-CJCI | Pilatus P2-06 (CC+43) | Charles Church Displays Ltd |
| | G-CJET | Learjet 35A | Interflight (Learjet) Ltd (G-SEBE/G-ZIPS/ G-ZONE)/Gatwick |
| | G-CJIM | Taylor JT.1 Monoplane | J. Crawford |
| | G-CJWS | PA-34-200T Seneca II | Lyreb Trading & Manufacturing Co Ltd |
| | G-CKEN | Wombat autogyro | K. H. Durran |
| | G-CLAC | PA-28-161 Warrior II | J. D. Moonie |
| | G-CLAW | EMB-110P1 Bandeirante | — |
| | G-CLEA | PA-28-161 Warrior II | Creative Logistics Enterprises & Aviation Ltd & R. J. Harrison |
| | G-CLEM | Bo 208A2 Junior | A. W. Webster (G-ASWE) |
| | G-CLIK | PA-18 Super Cub 95 | N. J. R. Empson/Ipswich |
| | G-CLIV | PA-28R-201T Turbo Arrow III | C. R. Harrisson |
| | G-CLOS | PA-34-200 Seneca II | Greenclose Aviation Services Ltd/ Bournemouth |
| | G-CLRL | Agusta A.109A-II | Farr PLC (G-EJCB) |
| | G-CLUB | Cessna FRA.150M | J. J. Woodhouse |
| | G-CLUX | Cessna F.172N | J. & K. Aviation/Liverpool |
| | G-CMCM | Robinson R-22B | K. & R. Helicopters Ltd |
| | G-CMDR | R. Commander 114 | J. D. Hallahan & G. C. Bishop |
| | G-CMMP | Boeing 737-3L9 | British Airways *River Colne*/Heathrow |
| | G-CMMR | Boeing 737-3L9 | British Airways *River Orwell*/Heathrow |
| | G-CNIS | Partenavia P.68B | Beechair Ltd (G-BJOF/G-PAUL) |
| | G-CNMF | BAe 146-200 | Air UK Ltd *Vincent Van Gogh*/Norwich |
| | G-COCO | Cessna F.172M | P. C. Sheard & R. C. Larder |
| | G-COIN | Bell 206B JetRanger 2 | British Helicopter Service |
| | G-COKE | Cameron O-65 balloon | M. C. Bradley |
| | G-COLL | Enstrom 280C-UK-2 Shark | Estate Computer Systems Ltd |
| | G-COLR | Colt 69A balloon | Graeme Scaife Productions Ltd |
| | G-COMB | PA-30 Twin Comanche 160B | W. A. L. Mitchell (G-AVBL)/Ronaldsway |
| | G-COMM | PA-23 Aztec 250C | M. G. Wild (G-AZMG) |
| | G-COMP | Cameron N-90 balloon | Computacenter Ltd |
| | G-CONC | Cameron N-90 balloon | British Airways |
| | G-COOK | Cameron N-77 balloon | IAZ (International) Ltd |
| | G-COOP | Cameron N-31 balloon | Aire Valley Balloons |
| | G-COPS | Piper J-3C-65 Cub | W. T. Sproat |
| | G-COPY | AA-5A Cheetah | Emberden Ltd (G-BIEU)/Biggin Hill |
| | G-CORC | Bell 206B JetRanger 2 | Kieron Corcoran Construction Ltd (G-CJHI/G-BBFB) |
| | G-CORD | Slingsby T.66 Nipper 3 | B. A. Wright (G-AVTB) |
| | G-CORK | Air Command 532 Elite | D. N. B. McCorquodale |
| | G-COTT | Cameron 60 SS balloon | Nottingham Hot-Air Balloon Club |
| | G-COWE | Beech C90A King Air | Cowie Aviation Ltd/Newcastle |
| | G-COWI | Cessna 414A | Milegood Ltd (G-MLCS/G-MHGI/ G-BHKK) |
| | G-COWS | ARV Super 2 | D. J. Royce (G-BONB) |
| | G-COWZ | Bell 206B JetRanger | Wight Air Ltd (G-BRDK) |
| | G-COYS | Colt 42A balloon | Thunder & Colt Ltd |
| | G-COZY | Rutan Cozy | J. F. MacKay |
| | G-CPCD | CEA DR.221 | J. C. Jess & ptnrs |
| | G-CPFC | Cessna F.152 | Falcon Flying Services/Biggin Hill |
| | G-CPTL | Short SD3-60 | Shorts Aircraft Financing Ltd (G-BOFI) |
| | G-CPTS | AB-206B JetRanger 2 | A. R. B. Aspinall |
| | G-CRAK | Cameron N-77 balloon | Mobile Windscreens Ltd |
| | G-CRAN | Robin R.1180T | D. S. Watson |
| | G-CRAY | Robinson R-22B | Hecray Ltd |

| Reg. | Type | Owner or Operator | Notes |
|------|------|-------------------|-------|
| G-CRES | Denney Aerocraft Kitfox | R. J. Cresswell | |
| G-CRIC | Colomban MC.15 Cri-Cri | A. J. Maxwell | |
| G-CRIL | R. Commander 112B | Rockwell Aviation Group/Cardiff | |
| G-CRIS | Taylor JT.1 Monoplane | C. R. Steer | |
| G-CRUS | Cessna T.303 | B. A. Groves | |
| G-CRUZ | Cessna T.303 | Bank Farm Ltd | |
| G-CRZY | Thunder Ax8-105 balloon | R. Carr (G-BDLP)/France | |
| G-CSBM | Cessna F.150M | S. Warwickshire Flying School | |
| G-CSCS | Cessna F.172N | Conegate Ltd | |
| G-CSFC | Cessna 150L | Shropshire Aero Club Ltd | |
| G-CSFT | PA-23 Aztec 250D | Ellan-Vannin Airlines PLC (G-AYKU)/ Bournemouth | |
| G-CSJH | BAe 146-200 | Air UK Ltd/Norwich | |
| G-CSNA | Cessna 421C | Knightway Air Charter Ltd/Leeds | |
| G-CSZB | V.807B Viscount | British Air Ferries Viscount Scotland (G-AOXU)/Southend | |
| G-CTCL | SOCATA TB.10 Tobago | Merryfield Leasing Ltd (G-BSIV) | |
| G-CTIX | V.S.509 Spitfire T.IX (PT462) | Charles Church Displays Ltd | |
| G-CTKL | CCF Harvard IV (54137) | G. J. & S. P. Keegan | |
| G-CTRN | Enstrom F-28C-UK | W. E. Taylor & Son Ltd | |
| G-CTRX | H.P.137 Jetstream 200 | Centrax Ltd (G-BCWW/G-AXUN)/Exeter | |
| G-CUBB | PA-18 Super Cub 180 | G. J. Busby/Booker | |
| G-CUBI | PA-18 Super Cub 135 (51-15673) | M. G. Searley | |
| G-CUBJ | PA-18 Super Cub 150 | A. K. Leasing (Jersey) Ltd | |
| G-CUGA | GA-7 Cougar | Frontline Aviation Ltd | |
| G-CULL | Bell 206B JetRanger | Dollar Air Services Ltd (G-BEWY)/ Coventry | |
| G-CURE | Colt 77A balloon | Flying Pictures (Balloons) Ltd | |
| G-CWOT | Currie Wot | D. A. Lord | |
| G-CXCX | Cameron N-90 balloon | Cathay Pacific Airways (London) Ltd | |
| G-CYLS | Cessna T.303 | Gledhill Water Storage Ltd & M. F. Joseph/Blackpool | |
| G-CYMA | GA-7 Cougar | Cyma Petroleum Ltd (G-BKOM)/Elstree | |
| G-CZAR | Cessna 560 Citation V | N. M. Jagger | |
| G-DAAH | PA-28RT-201T Turbo Arrow IV | R. Peplow | |
| G-DACA | P.57 Sea Prince T.1 | P. G. Vallance Ltd | |
| G-DACC | Cessna 401B | Niglon Ltd (G-AYOU)/Birmingham | |
| G-DADS | Hughes 369HS | B. Wronski | |
| G-DAFT | AS.355F-2 Twin Squirrel | Powersense Ltd (G-BNNN)/Hayes | |
| G-DAJB | Boeing 757-2T7 | Monarch Airlines Ltd/Luton | |
| G-DAJW | K & S Jungster 1 | A. J. Walters | |
| G-DAKS | Dakota 3 (TS423) | Aces High Ltd/North Weald | |
| G-DAMI | Robinson R-22B | Aramerco Ltd | |
| G-DAND | SOCATA TB.10 Tobago | Whitemoor Engineering Co Ltd | |
| G-DANN | Stampe SV-4B | I. M. White | |
| G-DARA | PA-34-220T Seneca III | Sunspot Investments Ltd | |
| G-DARL | PA-28 Cherokee 180C | A. R. Liyanage | |
| G-DART | Rollason Beta B2 | M. G. Ollis | |
| G-DASH | R. Commander 112A | Josef D. J. Jons & Co Ltd (G-BDAJ) | |
| G-DASI | Short SD3-60 | Air UK Ltd (G-BKKW)/Norwich | |
| G-DASU | Cameron V-77 balloon | D. & L. S. Litchfield | |
| G-DAVE | Jodel D.112 | D. A. Porter/Sturgate | |
| G-DAVY | Evans VP-2 | D. Morris | |
| G-DBAF | BAC One-Eleven 201AC | British Air Ferries Ltd (G-ASJG)/ Stansted | |
| G-DBAL | H.S.125 Srs 3B | RCR International Ltd (G-BSAA) | |
| G-DBAR | Beech 200 Super King Air | Brown & Root (UK) Ltd | |
| G-DBII | Cessna 560 Citation V | Artix Ltd | |
| G-DBMS | Cessna U.206G | BMS Electrical Services Ltd | |
| G-DCAC | McD Douglas MD-83 | Airtours International Aviation Ltd | |
| G-DCAN | PA-38-112 Tomahawk | Airways Aero Associations Ltd/Booker | |
| G-DCCH | MBB Bo 105D | Devon & Cornwall Police Authority | |
| G-DCFB | Cessna 425 | Foodbrokers Ltd (G-BMSH) | |
| G-DCIO | Douglas DC-10-30 | British Airways Epping Forest/Gatwick | |
| G-DCKK | Cessna F.172N | A. R. Mead/Clacton | |
| G-DCOX | PA-31-310 Turbo Navajo | Skywatch Ltd (G-DIDI)/Birmingham | |
| G-DCSW | PA-32R-301 Saratoga SP | Samworth Bros Ltd | |
| G-DCXL | Jodel D.140C | P. Underhill | |
| G-DDAY | PA-28R-201T Turbo Arrow III | W. Haynes (G-BPDO) | |
| G-DDCD | D.H.104 Dove 8 | C. Daniel (G-ARUM)/Biggin Hill | |
| G-DDMV | NA T-6G Texan | E. A. Morgan | |
| G-DEDE | Cessna 421C | Aviation Sales Co Ltd | |

| Notes | Reg. | Type | Owner or Operator |
|---|---|---|---|
| | G-DELB | Robinson R-22B | Derek Williams (Film Editors) Ltd |
| | G-DELI | Thunder Ax7-77 balloon | Heather Flight Ltd |
| | G-DELL | Robinson R-22B | Delta Helicopters Ltd/Luton |
| | G-DELS | Robin DR.400/180 | W. D. Nightingale |
| | G-DELT | Robinson R-22B | Mortec Services |
| | G-DELY | Cessna TU.206G | G. Dommett |
| | G-DEMO | BN-2T Islander | Pilatus BN Ltd (G-BKEA)/Bembridge |
| | G-DENS | Binder CP.301S Smaragd | W. St G. V. Stoney |
| | G-DENW | PA-44-180 Seminole | D. A. Woodhams |
| | G-DERV | Cameron Truck SS balloon | The Hot Air Balloon Co Ltd |
| | G-DESS | Mooney M.20J | W. E. Newnes |
| | G-DEVN | D.H.104 Devon C.2 | P. Gaston & T. P. Luscombe |
| | G-DEVS | PA-28 Cherokee 180 | P & H Flyers (G-BGVJ)/Blackbushe |
| | G-DEXP | ARV Super 2 | Kintai Developments Ltd |
| | G-DEXY | Beech E90 King Air | Tornado Ltd |
| | G-DFLT | Cessna F.406 Caravan II | Direct Flight Ltd/Norwich |
| | G-DFLY | PA-38-112 Tomahawk | Airways Aero Associations Ltd/Booker |
| | G-DFVA | Cessna R.172K | R. A. Plowright |
| | G-DGDG | Glaser-Dirks DG.400/17 | DG400 Flying Group/Lasham |
| | G-DHCI | D.H.C.1 Chipmunk 22 | C. J. Crooks (G-BBSE) |
| | G-DHSW | Boeing 737-3Y0 | Monarch Airlines/Canadian (C-FPWD) |
| | G-DHTM | D.H.82A Tiger Moth replica | E. G. Waite-Roberts |
| | G-DIAL | Cameron N-90 balloon | A. J. Street |
| | G-DIAN | Extra EA.230 | D. M. Britten |
| | G-DIAT | PA-28 Cherokee 140 | RAF Benevolent Fund's IAT/Bristol & Wessex Aeroplane Club (G-BCGK)/ Lulsgate |
| | G-DICK | Thunder Ax6-56Z balloon | R. D. Sargeant |
| | G-DIME | R. Commander 114 | Badminton Horse Boxes Ltd |
| | G-DINA | AA-5B Tiger | J. D. Poole & ptnrs |
| | G-DIPI | Cameron Tub SS balloon | Airship & Balloon Co Ltd |
| | G-DIPS | Taylor JT.1 Monoplane | B. J. Halls |
| | G-DIPZ | Colt 17A balloon | Airship & Balloon Co Ltd |
| | G-DIRK | Glaser-Dirks DG.400 | D. M. Chalmers |
| | G-DIRT | Thunder Ax7-77Z balloon | R. J. Ngbaronye |
| | G-DISC | Cessna U.206A | I. A. Louttit (G-BGWR)/Exeter |
| | G-DISK | PA-24 Comanche 250 | M. A. McLoughlin (G-APZG)/Booker |
| | G-DISO | Jodel D.150 | P. F. Craven & J. H. Shearer |
| | G-DIVA | Cessna R.172K XPII | R. A. Plowright & J. A. Kaye/ Biggin Hill |
| | G-DIXI | PA-31-350 Navajo Chieftain | Birmingham Aviation Ltd |
| | G-DIZY | PA-28-201T Turbo Arrow III | Precision Engineering (Medway) Ltd |
| | G-DJEM | AS.350B Ecureuil | Maynard & Harris Plastics Ltd (G-ZBAC/ G-SEBI/G-BMCU) |
| | G-DJHB | Beech A23-19 Musketeer | M. Wells & J. H. Prankerd (G-AZZE)/ Lydd |
| | G-DJIM | MHCA-I | J. Crawford |
| | G-DJJA | PA-28-181 Archer II | S. J. Lucas |
| | G-DJLW | H.S.125 Srs 3B/RA | Lindsay Wood Promotions Ltd (G-AVVB) |
| | G-DJNH | Denney Aerocraft Kitfox | D. J. N. Hall |
| | G-DKDP | Grob G.109 | Diss Aviation Ltd/Tibenham |
| | G-DKGF | Viking Dragonfly | K. G. Fathers |
| | G-DLOM | SOCATA TB.20 Trinidad | J. N. A. Adderley/Guernsey |
| | G-DLTA | Slingsby T.67M | Sherwood Flying Club (G-SFTX) |
| | G-DLTI | Robinson R-22B | Springfield Aviation Ltd |
| | G-DMCD | Robinson R-22B | D. E. McDowell |
| | G-DMCH | Hiller UH-12E | D. McK. Carnegie & ptnrs |
| | G-DMCS | PA-28R Cherokee Arrow 200-II | D. L. Johns & F. K. Parker (G-CPAC) |
| | G-DNCS | PA-28R-201T Turbo Arrow III | BRT Arrow Ltd/Barton |
| | G-DNLD | Cameron 97 Donald SS balloon | The Walt Disney Co Ltd |
| | G-DNVT | G.1159C Gulfstream IV | Shell Aircraft Ltd/Heathrow |
| | G-DOCA | Boeing 737-436 | British Airways |
| | G-DOCB | Boeing 737-436 | British Airways |
| | G-DOCC | Boeing 737-436 | British Airways |
| | G-DOCD | Boeing 737-436 | British Airways |
| | G-DOCE | Boeing 737-436 | British Airways |
| | G-DOCF | Boeing 737-436 | British Airways |
| | G-DOCG | Boeing 737-436 | British Airways |
| | G-DOCH | Boeing 737- | British Airways |
| | G-DOCI | Boeing 737- | British Airways |
| | G-DOCJ | Boeing 737- | British Airways |
| | G-DOCK | Boeing 737- | British Airways |

| Reg. | Type | Owner or Operator | Notes |
|------|------|-------------------|-------|
| G-DOCL | Boeing 737- | British Airways | |
| G-DOCM | Boeing 737- | British Airways | |
| G-DOCN | Boeing 737- | British Airways | |
| G-DOCO | Boeing 737- | British Airways | |
| G-DOCP | Boeing 737- | British Airways | |
| G-DOCR | Boeing 737- | British Airways | |
| G-DOCS | Boeing 737- | British Airways | |
| G-DOCT | Boeing 737- | British Airways | |
| G-DOCU | Boeing 737- | British Airways | |
| G-DOCV | Boeing 737- | British Airways | |
| G-DOCW | Boeing 737- | British Airways | |
| G-DOCX | Boeing 737- | British Airways | |
| G-DOCY | | British Airways | |
| G-DOCZ | | British Airways | |
| G-DODD | Cessna F.172P-II | K. Watts/Elstree | |
| G-DODS | PA-46-310P Malibu | HPM Investments Ltd | |
| G-DOFY | Bell 206B JetRanger | Cinnamond Ltd | |
| G-DOGS | Cessna R.182RG | Usoland Ltd | |
| G-DOLR | AS.355F-1 Twin Squirrel | Dollar Air Services Ltd (G-BPVB) | |
| G-DONA | Cessna 152 | P. Wood | |
| G-DONS | PA-28RT-201T Turbo Arrow IV | D. J. Murphy | |
| G-DOOR | M.S.893E Rallye 180GT | Lynair Aviation | |
| G-DOOZ | AS.355F-2 Twin Squirrel | Lynton Aviation Ltd (G-BNSX) | |
| G-DORB | Bell 206B JetRanger 3 | Dorb Crest Homes Ltd | |
| G-DORK | EMB-110P1 Bandeirante | Aero Services (E. Midlands) Ltd | |
| G-DOSH | D.H.C.6 Twin Otter 210 | Scenic Airways Ltd | |
| G-DOVE | Cessna 182Q | P. J. Contracting | |
| G-DOWN | Colt 31A | M. Williams | |
| G-DPPA | Bell 206B JetRanger 3 | Dyfed-Powys Police Authority | |
| G-DRAG | Cessna 152 (tailwheel) | Roger Clark Mechanical Engineering Ltd (G-BRNF) | |
| G-DRAI | Robinson R-22B | D. R. Anthony Builders Ltd | |
| G-DRAW | Colt 77A balloon | Readers Digest Association Ltd | |
| G-DRAY | Taylor JT.1 Monoplane | L. J. Dray | |
| G-DRJC | Boeing 757-2T7 | Monarch Airlines Ltd/Luton | |
| G-DRNT | Sikorsky S-76A | Bond Helicopters Ltd/Aberdeen | |
| G-DROP | Cessna U.206C | A. A. Louttit (G-UKNO/G-BAMN) | |
| G-DRSV | CEA DR.315 (modified) | R. S. Voice | |
| G-DRYI | Cameron N-77 balloon | J. Barbour & Sons Ltd | |
| G-DSAM | AS.350B Ecureuil | PLM Helicopters Ltd | |
| G-DSGN | Robinson R-22B | William Towns Ltd | |
| G-DTOO | PA-38-112 Tomahawk | A. Todd | |
| G-DUCH | Beech 76 Duchess | Carriage Communications Consultancy Ltd | |
| G-DUCK | Grumman G.44 Widgeon | L. E. Usher/Ipswich | |
| G-DUDS | C.A.S.A. 1-131E Jungmann 2000 | D. H. Pattison | |
| G-DUET | Wood Duet | C. Wood | |
| G-DUNN | Zenair CH.250 | A. Dunn | |
| G-DURX | Thunder 77A balloon | V. Trimble | |
| G-DUST | Stolp SA.300 Starduster Too | J. V. George | |
| G-DUVL | Cessna F.172N | A. J. Simpson/Denham | |
| G-DVON | D.H.104 Devon C.2 (VP955) | C. L. Thatcher | |
| G-DWHH | Boeing 737-2T7 | Monarch Airlines Ltd/Luton | |
| G-DWMI | Bell 206L-1 LongRanger | Glenwood Helicopters Ltd/Fairoaks | |
| G-DXRG | Cameron 105 Agfa SS balloon | Cameron Balloons Ltd | |
| G-DYNE | Cessna 414 | Cormair Aviation Ltd/E. Midlands | |
| G-DYOU | PA-38-112 Tomahawk | Airways Aero Associations Ltd/Booker | |
| G-EAGL | Cessna 421C | Humberside Commercial Aviation Ltd | |
| G-EBJI | Hawker Cygnet Replica | A. V. Francis | |
| G-ECAV | Beech 200 Super King Air | GEC Avionics Ltd/Rochester | |
| G-ECBH | Cessna F.150K | Air Fenland Ltd | |
| G-ECGC | Cessna F.172N-II | Leicestershire Aero Club Ltd | |
| G-ECGO | Bo208C Junior | R. S. T. Sears | |
| G-ECHO | Enstrom 280C-UK-2 Shark | ALP Electrical (Maidenhead) Ltd (G-LONS/G-BDIB)/White Waltham | |
| G-ECJM | PA-28R-201T Turbo Arrow III | Anglosky (G-FESL/G-BNRN) | |
| G-ECKO | Colt 180A balloon | T. Donnelly | |
| G-ECOX | Grega GN.1 Air Camper | H. C. Cox | |
| G-EDEN | SOCATA TB.10 Tobago | Group Eden/Elstree | |
| G-EDGE | Jodel D.150 | A. D. Edge | |
| G-EDIT | Beech B95 TravelAir | Warrior Aircraft Sales & Leasing Ltd (G-AXUX) | |

| Notes | Reg. | Type | Owner or Operator |
|---|---|---|---|
| | G-EDNA | PA-38-112 Tomahawk | MSF Aviation Ltd |
| | G-EDOT | Cessna T.337D | A. Brinkley (G-BJIY) |
| | G-EDRY | Cessna T.303 | Pat Eddery Ltd |
| | G-EEEE | Slingsby T.31 Motor Glider | R. F. Selby |
| | G-EEGE | Robinson R-22A | Northern Helicopters Ltd (G-BKZK) |
| | G-EEGL | Christen Eagle II | A. J. Wilson |
| | G-EENY | GA-7 Cougar | Walsh Aviation |
| | G-EEUP | SNCAN Stampe SV-4C | A. M. Wajih |
| | G-EEZE | Rutan Vari-Eze | A. J. Nurse |
| | G-EFTE | Bolkow Bo 207 | Hornet Aviation Ltd |
| | G-EGAP | Sequoia F.8L Falco | E. G. A. Prance |
| | G-EGEE | Cessna 310Q | A. J. Fuller & ptnrs (G-AZVY) |
| | G-EGGS | Robin DR.400/180 | R. Foot |
| | G-EGJA | SOCATA TB.20 Trinidad | D. A. Williamson/Alderney |
| | G-EGLD | PA-28-161 Cadet | J. Appleton |
| | G-EGLE | Christen Eagle II | Myrick Aviation Services Ltd |
| | G-EHAP | Sportavia-Pützer RF.7 | Old Sarum Fornie Group |
| | G-EHBJ | C.A.S.A. 1-131E Jungmann 2000 | Mangreen Holdings Ltd |
| | G-EHIL | Westland-Agusta EH.101 | Westland Helicopters Ltd/Yeovil |
| | G-EHMM | Robin DR.400/180R | Booker Gliding Club Ltd |
| | G-EIIR | Cameron N-77 balloon | Major C. J. T. Davey Silver Jubilee |
| | G-EIST | Robinson R-22B | European Executive Ltd |
| | G-EITE | Luscombe 8A Silvaire | D. L. Eite |
| | G-EIWT | Cessna FR.182RG | P. P. D. Howard-Johnston/ Edinburgh |
| | G-EJET | Cessna 550 Citation II | European Jet Ltd (G-DJBE) |
| | G-EJGO | Z.226HE Trener | N. J. Radford |
| | G-ELAN | Boeing Stearman B.75N-1 (361) | D. J. Ashley |
| | G-ELDG | Douglas DC-9-32 | British Midland Airways Ltd The Orloff Diamond/E. Midlands |
| | G-ELDH | Douglas DC-9-32 | British Midland Airways Ltd/E. Midlands |
| | G-ELDI | Douglas DC-9-32 | British Midland Airways Ltd/E. Midlands |
| | G-ELEC | Westland WG.30 Srs 200 | Westland Helicopters Ltd (G-BKNV)/ Yeovil |
| | G-ELFI | Robinson R-22B | P. J. Paine |
| | G-ELIZ | Denney Aerocraft Kitfox | A. J. Ellis |
| | G-ELOT | Cessna 550 Citation II | Elliotts Brick Ltd |
| | G-ELRA | BAe 125-1000 | British Aerospace PLC |
| | G-EMAK | PA-28R-201 Arrow III | Arrow Aircraft Group/E. Midlands |
| | G-EMAZ | PA-28-181 Archer II | Emmair Ltd |
| | G-EMKM | Jodel D.120A | J. A. Wills |
| | G-EMMA | Cessna F.182Q | Watkiss Group Aviation |
| | G-EMMS | PA-38-112 Tomahawk | G. C. J. Moffatt & Co Ltd/Cardiff |
| | G-EMMY | Rutan Vari-Eze | M. J. Tooze |
| | G-ENAM | Cessna 340A | Benham & Wilcox Ltd |
| | G-ENCE | Partenavia P.68B | P. Davies(G-OROY/G-BFSU) |
| | G-ENIE | Tipsy T.66 Nipper 3 | I. D. Daniels |
| | G-ENII | Cessna F.172M | A. G. Martlew |
| | G-ENIU | PA-24 Comanche 260 | K. S. V. Bass (G-AVJU) |
| | G-ENNA | PA-28-161 Warrior II | A. J. Wood |
| | G-ENNY | Cameron V-77 balloon | B. G. Jones |
| | G-ENOA | Cessna F.172F | M. K. Acors (G-ASZW) |
| | G-ENRY | Cameron N-105 balloon | Numatic International Ltd |
| | G-ENSI | Beech F33A Bonanza | Nesstra Services (UK) Ltd & Special Analysis & Simulation Technology Ltd |
| | G-ENUS | Cameron N-90 balloon | The Hot-Air Balloon Co Ltd |
| | G-EOCO | Boeing 707-338C | Anglo Airlines Ltd/Gatwick |
| | G-EOFF | Taylor JT.2 Titch | G. H. Wylde |
| | G-EORG | PA-38-112 Tomahawk | Airways Aero Association/Booker |
| | G-EPDI | Cameron N-77 balloon | R. Moss & Pegasus Aviation Ltd |
| | G-ERIC | R. Commander 112TC | P. P. Patterson/Newcastle |
| | G-ERIK | Cameron N-77 balloon | Cultural Resource Management Ltd |
| | G-ERIX | Boeing Stearman A75N-1 | E. E. Rix |
| | G-ERMO | ARV Super 2 | M. J. Holdsworth Ltd (G-BMWK) |
| | G-ERMS | Thunder AS-33 airship | B. R. & M. Boyle |
| | G-EROS | Cameron H-34 balloon | Evening Standard Co Ltd |
| | G-ERRY | AA-5B Tiger | P. D. Cullen (G-BFMJ) |
| | G-ERTY | D.H.82A Tiger Moth | R. F. Tolhurst (G-ANDC) |
| | G-ESSX | PA-28-161 Warrior II | S. Harcourt (G-BHYY)/Shoreham |
| | G-ESTE | AA-5A Cheetah | McGeohan Plant Hire & Excavations Ltd (G-GHNC) |
| | G-ETBY | PA-32 Cherokee Six 260 | Brook Shaw Ltd (G-AWCY) |

| Reg. | Type | Owner or Operator | Notes |
|------|------|-------------------|-------|
| G-ETCD | Colt 77A balloon | Philips Electronics Ltd | |
| G-ETDA | PA-28-161 Warrior II | T. Griffiths | |
| G-ETDB | PA-38-112 Tomahawk | R. A. Wakefield | |
| G-ETDC | Cessna 172P | Osprey Air Services Ltd | |
| G-ETIN | Robinson R-22B | Lullingstone Water Ltd | |
| G-EURA | Agusta-Bell 47J-2 | E. W. Schnedlitz (G-ASNV) | |
| G-EURR | Boeing 737-3L9 | Berlin European UK Ltd | |
| G-EVAN | Taylor JT.2 Titch | E. Evans | |
| G-EVER | Robinson R-22B | Everards Brewery Ltd | |
| G-EWBJ | SOCATA TB.10 Tobago | Lydd Air Training Centre Ltd | |
| G-EWEL | Sikorsky S-76A | Ratners Group PLC | |
| G-EWFN | SOCATA TB-20 Trinidad | Trinidair Ltd (G-BRTY) | |
| G-EWIZ | Pitts S-2E Special | R. H. Jago | |
| G-EWUD | Cessna F.172F | Parplon Ltd (G-ESSO/G-ATBK) | |
| G-EXEC | PA-34-200 Seneca | S. J. Green | |
| G-EXEL | EMB-120RT Brasilia | Air Exel (UK) Ltd | |
| G-EXEX | Cessna 404 | Atlantic Air Transport Ltd/Coventry | |
| G-EXIT | M.S.893E Rallye 180GT | G-Exit Ltd/Rochester | |
| G-EXLR | BAe 125-1000 | British Aerospace PLC | |
| G-EXPM | BAC One-Eleven 217EA | European Aviation Ltd | |
| G-EXPR | Colt 90A balloon | Air Canada Ltd | |
| G-EYCO | Robin DR.400/180 | L. M. Gould | |
| G-EYES | Cessna 402C | Atlantic Air Promotions Ltd (G-BLCE)/ Coventry | |
| G-EYRE | Bell 206L-1 LongRanger | Hideroute Ltd (G-STVI) | |
| G-EZEE | Rutan Vari-Eze | D. & M. Schwier | |
| G-EZIO | EMB-120RT Brasilia | — | |
| G-EZOS | Rutan Vari-Eze | O. Smith/Tees-side | |
| G-FABB | Cameron V-77 balloon | V. P. F. Haines | |
| G-FAGN | Robinson R-22B | Fagins Toys Ltd | |
| G-FAIR | SOCATA TB.10 Tobago | Sally Marine Ltd/Guernsey | |
| G-FALC | Aeromere F.8L Falco | P. W. Hunter (G-AROT)/Elstree | |
| G-FALK | Sequoia F.8L Falco 4 | I. Chancellor | |
| G-FANC | Fairchild 24R-46 Argus III | J. I. Hyslop | |
| G-FANG | AA-5A Cheetah | Church & Co | |
| G-FANL | Cessna FR.172K XP-II | J. Woodhouse & Co/Staverton | |
| G-FANN | H.S.125 Srs 600B | Osprey Aviation Ltd (G-BARR) | |
| G-FARM | SOCATA Rallye 235GT | Bristol Cars Ltd | |
| G-FARO | Aero Designs Star-Lite SL.1 | M. K. Faro | |
| G-FARR | Jodel D.150 | G. H. Farr | |
| G-FASL | BAe 125 Srs 800B | Fisons PLC/E. Midlands | |
| G-FAST | Cessna 337G | Seillans Land Investigations Ltd | |
| G-FAVI | Beech E90 King Air | Flightline Ltd (G-OOAG/G-BAVG)/ Southend | |
| G-FAYE | Cessna F.150M | Cheshire Air Training School Ltd/ Liverpool | |
| G-FBMB | Canadair CL.600-2B16 Challenger | Challenger Aviation Ltd | |
| G-FBWH | PA-28R Cherokee Arrow 180 | Servicecentre Systems (Cambs) Ltd | |
| G-FCHJ | Cessna 340A | P. L. & M. J. E. Builder (G-BJLS) | |
| G-FCSP | Robin DR.400/180 | Aeromarine Ltd/Southampton | |
| G-FDGM | Beech B60 Duke | Parissi Air Ltd/Perth | |
| G-FEAD | F.27 Friendship Mk 600 | Federal Express/British Air Ferries/ Southend | |
| G-FEAE | F.27 Friendship Mk 600 | Federal Express/Channel Express (Air Services) Ltd/Bournemouth | |
| G-FEBE | Cessna 340A | W. P. J. Davison | |
| G-FEDL | Hughes 369D | Federal Aviation Ltd | |
| G-FELT | Cameron N-77 balloon | Allan Industries Ltd | |
| G-FENI | Robinson R-22B | I. Fenwick | |
| G-FFBR | Thunder Ax8-105 balloon | Fuji Photo Film (UK) Ltd | |
| G-FFEN | Cessna F.150M | Suffolk Aero Club Ltd/Ipswich | |
| G-FFLT | H.S.125 Srs 600B | Albion Aviation Management Ltd | |
| G-FFOR | Cessna 310R | Air Service Training Ltd (G-BMGF)/Perth | |
| G-FFTI | SOCATA TB.20 Trinidad | Blicqair Ltd | |
| G-FFTN | Bell 206B JetRanger | Fountain Forestry Ltd | |
| G-FFWD | Cessna 310R | Keef & Co Ltd (G-TVKE/G-EURO) | |
| G-FHAS | Scheibe SF.25E Super Falke | Burn Gliding Club Ltd | |
| G-FIAT | PA-28 Cherokee 140 | RAF Benevolent Fund's IAT/Bristol & Wessex Aeroplane Club (G-BBYW)/ Lulsgate | |
| G-FIFI | SOCATA TB.20 Trinidad | D. J. & M. Gower (G-BMWS) | |
| G-FIGA | Cessna 152 | Relstage Trading Ltd | |

| Notes | Reg. | Type | Owner or Operator |
|---|---|---|---|
| | G-FIGB | Cessna 152 | G & B Aviation Ltd |
| | G-FILE | PA-34-200T Seneca | Filemart Ltd |
| | G-FIMI | Bell 206L-1 LongRanger | Lynton Aviation Ltd |
| | G-FIND | Cessna F.406 Caravan II | Atlantic Air Transport Ltd/Coventry |
| | G-FINN | Cameron 90 Reindeer SS balloon | Forbes Europe Inc |
| | G-FINS | AB-206B JetRanger 2 | Specialist Heat Exchangers Ltd (G-FSCL) |
| | G-FIOA | Fokker 100 | Air Europe Ltd/Gatwick |
| | G-FIOB | Fokker 100 | Air Europe Ltd/Gatwick |
| | G-FIOC | Fokker 100 | Air Europe Ltd/Gatwick |
| | G-FIOD | Fokker 100 | Air Europe Ltd/Gatwick |
| | G-FIOE | Fokker 100 | Air Europe Ltd/Gatwick |
| | G-FIOO | Fokker 100 | Air Europe Ltd/Gatwick |
| | G-FIOR | Fokker 100 | Air Europe Ltd/Gatwick |
| | G-FIOS | Fokker 100 | Air Europe Ltd/Gatwick |
| | G-FIOT | Fokker 100 | Air Europe Ltd/Gatwick |
| | G-FIOU | Fokker 100 | Air Europe Ltd/Gatwick |
| | G-FIOV | Fokker 100 | Air Europe Ltd/Gatwick |
| | G-FIOW | Fokker 100 | Air Europe Ltd/Gatwick |
| | G-FIOX | Fokker 100 | Air Europe Ltd/Gatwick |
| | G-FIOY | Fokker 100 | Air Europe Ltd/Gatwick |
| | G-FIOZ | Fokker 100 | Air Europe Ltd/Gatwick |
| | G-FISH | Cessna 310R-II | Bostonair Ltd/Humberside |
| | G-FISK | Pazmany PL-4A | K. S. Woodard |
| | G-FIST | Fieseler Fi.156C Storch | Spoils Kitchen Reject Shops Ltd |
| | G-FIZZ | PA-28-161 Warrior II | Arrow Air Centre Ltd/Shipdham |
| | G-FKKM | PA-28RT-201T Turbo Arrow IV | D. J. Kaye |
| | G-FLAG | Colt 77A balloon | Thunder & Colt Ltd |
| | G-FLAK | Beech 95-E55 Baron | S. R. Flack/Elstree |
| | G-FLAT | Schweizer 269C | M. A. Billings |
| | G-FLCA | Fleet Model 80 Canuck | E. C. Taylor |
| | G-FLCO | Sequoia F.8L Falco | J. B. Mowforth |
| | G-FLEA | SOCATA TB.10 Tobago | Fleair Trading Co/Biggin Hill |
| | G-FLEN | PA-28-161 Warrior II | Flentri Aircraft Leasing/Fairoaks |
| | G-FLIK | Pitts S.1S Special | R. P. Millinship |
| | G-FLIX | Cessna E.310P | Cabledraw Ltd (G-AZFL) |
| | G-FLMS | Colt 600A balloon | Thunder & Colt Ltd |
| | G-FLPI | R. Commander 112A | Tuscany Ltd/Leicester |
| | G-FLRU | BAC One-Eleven 518FG | London European Airways PLC (G-AXMG)/Luton |
| | G-FLTI | Beech F90 King Air | Flightline Ltd/Southend |
| | G-FLUG | Gyroflug SC.01B-160 Speed Canard | ITPS Ltd/Cranfield |
| | G-FLUT | Stitts SA.6B Flut-R-Bug | B. J. Towers |
| | G-FLYA | Mooney M.20J | Symtec Computer Service Ltd |
| | G-FLYI | PA-34-200 Seneca | G. W. Plowman & Sons Ltd (G-BHVO)/Elstree |
| | G-FLYR | AB-206B JetRanger | Kwik Fit Euro Ltd (G-BAKT) |
| | G-FLYV | Slingsby T.67M-200 | Firefly Aerial Promotions Ltd |
| | G-FMAL | AB-206A JetRanger | Global Map Ltd (G-RIAN/G-BHSG) |
| | G-FMAM | PA-28-151 Warrior | Essex Radio PLC (G-BBXV)/Southend |
| | G-FMUS | Robinson R-22 | A. I. Freeman (G-BJBT) |
| | G-FNLD | Cessna 172N | Papa Hotel Flying Group |
| | G-FNLY | Cessna F.172M | London Aviation Ltd (G-WACX/G-BAEX)/Biggin Hill |
| | G-FOCK | WAR Focke-Wulf Fw.190-A | P. R. Underhill |
| | G-FOEL | PA-31-350 Navajo Chieftain | W. R. C. M. Foyle (G-BBXR)/Luton |
| | G-FOGG | Cameron N-90 balloon | J. P. E. Money-Kyrle |
| | G-FOLY | Aerotek Pitts S-2A Modified | A. A. Laing |
| | G-FOOD | Beech B200 Super King Air | Specbridge Ltd/Gamston |
| | G-FORC | SNCAN Stampe SV-4C | G. Pullan |
| | G-FORD | SNCAN Stampe SV-4B | P. Meeson & R. A. J. Spurrell/White Waltham |
| | G-FORE | Bell 47G-4A | Garrick Aviation |
| | G-FOTO | PA-E23 Aztec 250F | A. Gibson (G-BJDH/G-BDXV)/Elstree |
| | G-FOWL | Colt 90A balloon | Chesterfield Cold Storage Ltd |
| | G-FOXA | PA-28-161 Cadet | Leicestershire Aero Club Ltd |
| | G-FOXD | Denney Aerocraft Kitfox | M. Hanley |
| | G-FOXE | Denney Aerocraft Kitfox | K. M. Pinkard |
| | G-FOXG | Denney Aerocraft Kitfox | Kitfox Group |
| | G-FOXI | Denney Aerocraft Kitfox | I. N. Jennison |
| | G-FOXS | Denney Aerocraft Kitfox | S. P. Watkins & C. C. Rea |
| | G-FOXX | Denney Aerocraft Kitfox | R. O. F. Harper |
| | G-FOXZ | Denney Aerocraft Kitfox | M. Smalley & ptnrs |

| Reg. | Type | Owner or Operator | Notes |
|------|------|-------------------|-------|
| G-FPEL | Schweizer 269C | Donovan Ltd | |
| G-FRAA | Dassault Falcon 20F | FR Aviation Ltd/Bournemouth | |
| G-FRAB | Dassault Falcon 20F | FR Aviation Ltd/Bournemouth | |
| G-FRAC | Dassault Falcon 20F | FR Aviation Ltd/Bournemouth | |
| G-FRAD | Dassault Falcon 20E | FR Aviation Ltd (G-BCYF)/Bournemouth | |
| G-FRAE | Dassault Falcon 20E | FR Aviation Ltd/Bournemouth | |
| G-FRAF | Dassault Falcon 20E | FR Aviation Ltd/Bournemouth | |
| G-FRAG | PA-32 Cherokee Six 300E | R. Goodwin & Co Ltd/Southend | |
| G-FRAH | Dassault Falcon 20DC | FR Aviation Ltd/Bournemouth | |
| G-FRAI | Dassault Falcon 20E | FR Aviation Ltd/Bournemouth | |
| G-FRAN | Piper J-3C-90 Cub (480321) | Essex L-4 Group (G-BIXY) | |
| G-FRAS | Dassault Falcon 20C | FR Aviation Ltd/Bournemouth | |
| G-FRAT | Dassault Falcon 20C | FR Aviation Ltd/Bournemouth | |
| G-FRAU | Dassault Falcon 20C | FR Aviation Ltd/Bournemouth | |
| G-FRAV | Dassault Falcon 20ECM | FR Aviation Ltd/Bournemouth | |
| G-FRAW | Dassault Falcon 20ECM | FR Aviation Ltd/Bournemouth | |
| G-FRAX | Cessna 441 | FR Aviation Ltd (G-BMTZ)/ Bournemouth | |
| G-FRAY | Cassutt IIIM (modified) | C. I. Fray | |
| G-FRAZ | Cessna 441 | FR Aviation Ltd/Bournemouth | |
| G-FRCE | H.S. Gnat T.1 | Butane Buzzard Aviation Corporation Ltd | |
| G-FRED | FRED Srs 2 | R. Cox | |
| G-FREE | Pitts S-2A Special | Pegasus Flying Group/Fairoaks | |
| G-FRJB | Britten Sheriff SA-1 ★ | Aeropark/E. Midlands | |
| G-FROZ | Cessna 421C | Mashmor Investments Ltd | |
| G-FRST | PA-44-180T Turbo Seminole | Mondiale Aviation Ltd | |
| G-FRYS | Christen Eagle II | R. W. J. Foster | |
| G-FSDC | Enstrom 280C-UK Shark | Southern Air Ltd (G-BKTG)/Shoreham | |
| G-FSDG | AB-206B JetRanger | Flair (Soft Drinks) Ltd (G-ROOT/G-JETR) | |
| G-FSDH | Hughes 269A | Compass Aviation Ltd | |
| G-FSDT | Hughes 269A | S. G. Oliphant-Hope/Shoreham | |
| G-FSPL | PA-32R Cherokee Lance 300 | J. D. L. Richardson & Goodridge (UK) Ltd | |
| G-FTAX | Cessna 421C | Jet West Ltd (G-BFFM)/Exeter | |
| G-FTFT | Colt Financial Times SS balloon | Financial Times Ltd | |
| G-FTIL | Robin DR.400/180R | Wild Touch Aviazione Ltd/Cardiff | |
| G-FTIM | Robin DR.400/100 | FTI Aviation Ltd/Biggin Hill | |
| G-FTIN | Robin DR.400/100 | FTI Aviation Ltd/Biggin Hill | |
| G-FTIO | Robin DR.400/100 | FTI Aviation Ltd/Biggin Hill | |
| G-FTWO | AS.355F-2 Twin Squirrel | McAlpine Helicopters Ltd (G-OJOR/G-BMUS)/Hayes | |
| G-FUEL | Robin DR.400/180 | R. Darch/Compton Abbas | |
| G-FUGA | Fouga CM.170R Magister | Royalair Services Ltd (G-BSCT) | |
| G-FUJI | Fuji FA.200-180 | G. C. B. Weir | |
| G-FULL | PA-28R Cherokee Arrow 200-II | Fuller Aviation (G-HWAY/G-JULI) | |
| G-FUND | Thunder Ax7-65Z balloon | Soft Sell Ltd | |
| G-FUZY | Cameron N-77 balloon | Allan Industries Ltd | |
| G-FUZZ | PA-18 Super Cub 95 | G. W. Cline | |
| G-FVEE | Monnet Sonerai I | D. R. Sparke | |
| G-FWPW | PA-28-236 Dakota | P. A. & F. C. Winters | |
| G-FWRP | Cessna 421C | Maxfab Ltd | |
| G-FXII | V.S.366 Spitfire F.XII (EN224) | P. R. Arnold | |
| G-FXIV | V.S.379 Spitfire FR.XIV (MV370) | R. Lamplough | |
| G-FZZI | Cameron H-34 balloon | Airship & Balloon Co Ltd | |
| G-FZZY | Colt 69A balloon | Hot-Air Balloon Co Ltd | |
| G-FZZZ | Colt 56A balloon | Hot-Air Balloon Co Ltd | |
| G-GABD | GA-7 Cougar | J. Bett/Glasgow | |
| G-GACA | P.57 Sea Prince T.1 | P. G. Vallance Ltd | |
| G-GAGA | AA-5B Tiger | Daniels Timetrak Ltd (G-BGPG)/Denham | |
| G-GAJB | AA-5B Tiger | G. A. J. Bowles (G-BHZN) | |
| G-GALA | PA-28 Cherokee 180E | M. J. Green (G-AYAP) | |
| G-GALE | PA-34-200T Seneca II | Gale Construction Co Ltd/Norwich | |
| G-GAMA | Beech 95-58 Baron | Gama Aviation Ltd (G-BBSD)/Fairoaks | |
| G-GAME | Cessna T.303 | Street Construction (Wigan) Ltd | |
| G-GANE | Sequoia F.8L Falco | S. J. Gane | |
| G-GANJ | Fournier RF-6B-100 | Soaring Equipment Ltd/Coventry | |
| G-GASC | Hughes 369HS | Crewhall Ltd (G-WELD/G-FROG) | |
| G-GASP | PA-28-181 Archer II | G-GASP Flying Group | |
| G-GASS | Thunder Ax7-77 balloon | Travel Gas (Midlands) Ltd | |
| G-GAUL | Cessna 550 Citation II | The WCRS Group Ltd | |

| Notes | Reg. | Type | Owner or Operator |
|---|---|---|---|
| | G-GAYL | Learjet 35A | Northern Executive Aviation Ltd (G-ZING)/Manchester |
| | G-GAZI | SA.341G Gazelle 1 | Stratton Motor Co (Norfolk) Ltd & UCC International Group Ltd (G-BKLU) |
| | G-GAZZ | SA.341G Gazelle 1 | Stratton Motor Co (Norfolk) Ltd & UCC International Group Ltd |
| | G-GBAO | Robin R.1180TD | J. Kay-Movat |
| | G-GBLR | Cessna F.150L | Blue Max Flying Group |
| | G-GBSL | Beech 76 Duchess | F. B. Miles (G-BGVG) |
| | G-GBUE | Robin DR.400/120A | G. Higgins & ptnrs (G-BPXD) |
| | G-GCAA | PA-28R Cherokee Arrow 200 | Southern Air Ltd/Shoreham |
| | G-GCAB | PA-30 Twin Comanche 180 | Southern Air Ltd/Shoreham |
| | G-GCAL | Douglas DC-10-10 | — |
| | G-GCAT | PA-28 Cherokee 140B | J. J. Feeney & P. H. Marlow (G-BFRH)/Elstree |
| | G-GCCL | Beech 76 Duchess | Multirun Ltd |
| | G-GCKI | Mooney M.20K | G. C. Kent/Tollerton |
| | G-GCNZ | Cessna 150M | Heathgrange Ltd |
| | G-GDAM | PA-18 Super Cub 135 | G. D. A. Martin |
| | G-GDAY | Robinson R-22B | Rebelmile Ltd/Blackpool |
| | G-GDOG | PA-28R Cherokee Arrow 200-II | C. S. B. Large (G-BDXW)/Elstree |
| | G-GEAR | Cessna FR.182Q | B. C. J. Lovrey/White Waltham |
| | G-GEDS | AS.350B Ecureuil | Direct Produce Supplies Ltd (G-HMAN/G-SKIM/G-BIVP) |
| | G-GEEE | Hughes 369HS | B. P. Stein (G-BDOY) |
| | G-GEEP | Robin R.1180T | Organic Concentrates Ltd/Booker |
| | G-GEES | Cameron N-77 balloon | Mark Jarvis *Mark Jarvis* |
| | G-GEEZ | Cameron N-77 balloon | Charnwood Forest Turf Accountants Ltd |
| | G-GEIL | BAe 125 Srs 800B | Heron Management Ltd |
| | G-GEOF | Pereira Osprey 2 | G. Crossley |
| | G-GEUP | Cameron N-77 balloon | D. P. & B. O. Turner |
| | G-GFAB | Cameron N-105 balloon | The Andrew Brownsword Collection Ltd |
| | G-GFCA | PA-28-161 Cadet | Swallow Aviation Ltd/Staverton |
| | G-GFCB | PA-28-161 Cadet | S. F. Tebby & Sons |
| | G-GFCC | PA-28-161 Cadet | Swallow Aviation Ltd/Staverton |
| | G-GFCD | PA-34-220T Seneca III | BWOC Ltd (G-KIDS)/Staverton |
| | G-GFCE | PA-28-161 Warrior II | Swallow Aviation Ltd (G-BNJP)/Staverton |
| | G-GFCF | PA-28-161 Cadet | Swallow Aviation Ltd (G-RHBH)/Staverton |
| | G-GFLY | Cessna F.150L | W. Lancashire Aero Club Ltd/Woodvale |
| | G-GGCC | AB-206B JetRanger 2 | Hampton Printing (Bristol) Ltd (G-BEHG) |
| | G-GGGG | Thunder Ax7-77A balloon | T. A. Gilmour |
| | G-GGOW | Colt 77A balloon | City of Glasgow District Council |
| | G-GHIA | Cameron N-120 balloon | Bristol Street Motors (Cheltenham) Ltd |
| | G-GHIN | Thunder Ax7-77 balloon | G. M. Ghinn |
| | G-GHRW | PA-28RT-201 Arrow IV | Leavesden Flight Centre Ltd (G-ONAB/G-BHAK) |
| | G-GIGI | M.S.893A Rallye Commodore | P. J. C. Phillips (G-AYVX) |
| | G-GILY | Robinson R-22B | Reynard Racing Cars Ltd |
| | G-GINA | AS.350B Ecureuil | Endeavour Aviation Ltd |
| | G-GIRO | Schweizer 269C | F. J. Barnett |
| | G-GJCB | BAe 125 Srs 800B | J. C. Bamford Excavators Ltd |
| | G-GJCD | Robinson R-22B | A. G. Forshaw |
| | G-GLAW | Cameron N-90 balloon | George Law Ltd |
| | G-GLED | Cessna 150M | Firecrest Aviation Ltd/Leavesden |
| | G-GLOR | Cessna 425 | Calmcraft Ltd |
| | G-GLOS | H.P.137 Jetstream 200 | British Aerospace PLC (G-BCGU/G-AXRI) |
| | G-GLOW | AS.355-1 Twin Squirrel | Coalite Group PLC (G-PAPA/G-MCAH/G-CNET) |
| | G-GLUE | Cameron N-65 balloon | L. J. M. Muir & G. D. Hallett |
| | G-GLYN | Boeing 747-211B | British Airways *City of Perth* |
| | G-GMAX | SNCAN Stampe SV-4C | Glidegold Ltd (G-BXNW) |
| | G-GMPA | AS.355F-2 Twin Squirrel | Greater Manchester Police Authority (G-BPOI) |
| | G-GMSI | SOCATA TB.9 Tampico | Subtec Aviation Ltd |
| | G-GNAT | H.S. Gnat T.1 (XS101) | Ruanil Investments Ltd/Cranfield |
| | G-GNSY | HPR-7 Herald 209 | Channel Express PLC (G-BFRK)/Bournemouth |
| | G-GOGO | Hughes 369D | A. W. Alloys Ltd |
| | G-GOLD | Thunder Ax6-56A balloon | Joseph Terry & Sons Ltd |
| | G-GOLF | SOCATA TB.10 Tobago | E. H. Scamell & ptnrs |

| Reg. | Type | Owner or Operator | Notes |
|------|------|-------------------|-------|
| G-GOLO | Robinson R-22B | Croftflight Ltd | |
| G-GOMM | PA-32R Cherokee Lance 300 | A. Kazaz/Leicester | |
| G-GONE | D.H.112 Venom FB.50 | Venom Jet Promotions Ltd/ Bournemouth | |
| G-GOOS | Cessna F.182Q | Roger Clark (Air Transport) Ltd | |
| G-GORE | CFM Streak Shadow | D. N. & E. M. Gore | |
| G-GOSS | Jodel DR.221 | D. Folens | |
| G-GOZO | Cessna R.182 | Transmatic Fyllan Ltd (G-BJZO)/ Cranfield | |
| G-GPMW | PA-28RT-201T Turbo Arrow IV | M. Worrall & G. Patterson | |
| G-GPST | ST.1 | P. J. C. Philips | |
| G-GRAC | GA-7 Cougar | H. J. Dant | |
| G-GRAY | Cessna 172N | Truman Aviation Ltd/Tollerton | |
| G-GREG | Jodel DR.220 2+2 | J. T. Wilson | |
| G-GREN | Cessna T.310R | Lagren International Ltd/France | |
| G-GRID | AS.355F-1 Twin Squirrel | National Grid Co PLC | |
| G-GRIF | R. Commander 112TCA | International Motors Ltd (G-BHXC) | |
| G-GROB | Grob G.109 | G-GROB Ltd | |
| G-GROW | Cameron N-77 balloon | Derbyshire Building Society | |
| G-GRUB | PA-28 Cherokee 180 | Cambourne Insurance Brokers Ltd (G-AYAS) | |
| G-GSFC | Robinson R-22B | G. R. Weller | |
| G-GSML | Enstrom 280C-UK | Guardwell Security Management Ltd (G-BNNV) | |
| G-GTAX | PA-31-350 Navajo Chieftain | Jet West Ltd (G-OIAS)/Exeter | |
| G-GTHM | PA-38-112 Tomahawk | T. Miller | |
| G-GTPL | Mooney M.20K | W. R. Emberton/Spain | |
| G-GUNN | Cessna F.172H | J. G. Gunn (G-AWGC) | |
| G-GUNS | Cameron V-77 balloon | Royal School of Artillery Hot Air Balloon Club | |
| G-GURL | Cameron A-210 balloon | Hot Airlines Ltd | |
| G-GUYI | PA-28-181 Archer II | B. Butler | |
| G-GUYS | PA-34-200T Seneca | H. Jowett & Co Ltd (G-BMWT) | |
| G-GWEN | Cessna F.172M | R. E. Youngsworth (G-GBLP) | |
| G-GWHH | AS.355F Twin Squirrel | Wimpey Homes Holdings Ltd (G-BKUL) | |
| G-GWIL | AS.350B Ecureuil | Talan Ltd | |
| G-GWIN | Bell 206L-3 LongRanger | Southern Counties Estates Ltd | |
| G-GWIT | Cameron O-84 balloon | M. Pearce & V. J. Thorne | |
| G-GWIZ | Colt Clown SS balloon | Oxford Promotions (UK) Ltd | |
| G-GWYN | Cessna F.172M | C. Bosher | |
| G-GYAV | Cessna 172N | Fletcher Bros (Car Hire) Ltd | |
| G-GYMM | PA-28R Cherokee Arrow 200 | D. M. Ball (G-AYWW) | |
| G-GYRO | Bensen B.8 | N. A. Pitcher & A. L. Howell | |
| G-GZDO | Cessna 172N | Cambridge Hall Aviation | |
| G-HAEC | Commonwealth Mustang 22 | R. G. Hanna/Duxford | |
| G-HAGS | Bensen B.8 | R. H. Harris | |
| G-HAIG | Rutan LongEz | P. N. Haigh | |
| G-HAJJ | Glaser-Dirks DG.400 | P. W. Endean | |
| G-HALC | PA-28R Cherokee Arrow 200 | Halcyon Aviation Ltd | |
| G-HALL | PA-22 Tri-Pacer 160 | F. P. Hall (G-ARAH) | |
| G-HALP | SOCATA TB.10 Tobago | D. Halpera (G-BITD)/Elstree | |
| G-HAMA | Beech 200 Super King Air | Gama Aviation Ltd/Fairoaks | |
| G-HAMP | Bellanca 7ACA Champ | R. J. Grimstead | |
| G-HANS | Robin DR.400 2+2 | Headcorn Flying School Ltd | |
| G-HAPR | B.171 Sycamore HR.14 (XG547) ★ | International Helicopter Museum/ Weston-s-Mare | |
| G-HARE | Cameron N-77 balloon | M. F. Glue | |
| G-HART | Cessna 152 | Atlantic Air Transport Ltd/Coventry | |
| G-HASL | AA-5A Cheetah | D.B.G. Ltd (G-BGSL)/(stored) | |
| G-HATZ | Hatz CB-1 | J. Pearson | |
| G-HAUL | Westland WG.30 Srs 300 | Westland Helicopters PLC/Yeovil | |
| G-HAZE | Thunder Ax8-90 balloon | H. A. Ingham | |
| G-HBAC | AS.355F-1 Twin Squirrel | BAC Ltd (G-HJET) | |
| G-HBCO | PA-31-325 Navajo C/R | D. Garner/Manchester | |
| G-HBUG | Cameron N-90 balloon | Datasolve Ltd (G-BRCN) | |
| G-HCRP | McD Douglas MD-83 | Airtours International Aviation Ltd | |
| G-HCTL | PA-31-350 Navajo Chieftain | Field Aircraft Services (Heathrow) Ltd (G-BGOY) | |
| G-HDBA | H.S.748 Srs 2B | British Airways Glen Esk/Glasgow | |
| G-HDBB | H.S.748 Srs 2B | British Airways Glen Eagles/Glasgow | |
| G-HDBC | H.S.748 Srs 2B | British Airways Glen Dronach/Glasgow | |
| G-HDBD | H.S.748 Srs 2B | British Airways/Glasgow | |

| Notes | Reg. | Type | Owner or Operator |
|-------|------|------|-------------------|
| | G-HDEW | PA-32R-301 Saratoga SP | Lord Howard de Walden (G-BRGZ) |
| | G-HEAD | Colt 56 balloon | Colt Balloons Ltd |
| | G-HELI | Saro Skeeter Mk 12 (XM556) ★ | International Helicopter Museum/ Weston-s-Mare |
| | G-HELP | PA-18 Super Cub 95 | J. J. Anziani (G-BKDG)/Booker |
| | G-HELO | Bell 206B JetRanger 2 | Surrey Helicopter Hire Ltd (G-BAZN) |
| | G-HELP | Colt 17A balloon | Airship & Balloon Co Ltd |
| | G-HELX | Cameron N-31 balloon | Hot-Air Balloon Co Ltd |
| | G-HELY | Agusta 109A | Candyfleet Ltd |
| | G-HEMS | SA.365N Dauphin 2 | Express Newspapers PLC |
| | G-HENS | Cameron N-65 balloon | Horrells Dairies Ltd |
| | G-HERA | Robinson R-22B | S. N. H. Boardman-Weston |
| | G-HERB | PA-28R-201 Arrow III | D. I. Weidner |
| | G-HERO | PA-32RT-300 Lance II | R. P. Thomas & C. Moore(G-BOGN) |
| | G-HERS | Jodel D.18 | A. Usherwood |
| | G-HETH | Robinson R-22B | Leach-Lewis Ltd |
| | G-HEVY | Boeing 707-324C | HeavyLift Cargo Airlines Ltd/Stansted |
| | G-HEWI | Piper J-3C-90 Cub | Denham Grasshopper Group (G-BLEN) |
| | G-HEWS | Hughes 369D* | Spares use/Sywell |
| | G-HEWT | Hughes 369D | A. H. Canvin |
| | G-HEYY | Cameron 77 Bear SS balloon | Hot-Air Balloon Co Ltd George |
| | G-HFBM | Curtiss Robin C-2 | Colin Crabbe Holdings Ltd |
| | G-HFCB | Cessna F.150L | Horizon Flying Club Ltd (G-AZVR)/ Ipswich |
| | G-HFCI | Cessna F.150L | Horizon Flying Club Ltd/Ipswich |
| | G-HFCL | Cessna F.152 | Horizon Flying Club Ltd (G-BGLR)/ Ipswich |
| | G-HFCT | Cessna F.152 | Stapleford Flying Club Ltd |
| | G-HFIX | V.S.361 Spitfire HF.IXe (MJ730) | D. W. Pennell (G-BLAS) |
| | G-HFLA | Schweizer 269C | Heliflair Ltd |
| | G-HFLR | Schweizer 269C | Heliflair Ltd |
| | G-HFTG | PA-23 Aztec 250E | Air Navigation & Training Co Ltd (G-BSOB/G-BCJR)/Blackpool |
| | G-HGAS | Cameron V-77 balloon | Handygas Ltd |
| | G-HGPI | SOCATA TB.20 Trinidad | M. J. Jackson/Bournemouth |
| | G-HHUN | Hunter F.4 | Hunter Wing Ltd/Bournemouth |
| | G-HIEL | Robinson R-22B | Hields Aviation |
| | G-HIHI | PA-32R-301 Saratoga SP | Aviation Metals Ltd/Cranfield |
| | G-HILR | Hiller UH-12E | G. & S. G. Neal (Helicopters) Ltd |
| | G-HILS | Cessna F.172H | Heathfield Investments Ltd (G-AWCH) |
| | G-HILT | SOCATA TB.10 Tobago | P. J. Morrison |
| | G-HINT | Cameron N-90 balloon | Hinton Garage Bath Ltd |
| | G-HIRE | GA-7 Cougar | London Aerial Tours Ltd (G-BGSZ)/ Biggin Hill |
| | G-HIVA | Cessna 337A | High Voltage Applications Ltd (G-BAES) |
| | G-HIVE | Cessna F.150M | M. P. Lynn (G-BCXT)/Sibson |
| | G-HLFT | SC.5 Belfast 2 | HeavyLift Cargo Airlines Ltd/Stansted |
| | G-HLIX | Cameron 80 Oil Can balloon | Hot-Air Balloon Co Ltd |
| | G-HMES | PA-28-161 Warrior II | Cleveland Flying School Ltd/Teesside |
| | G-HMJB | PA-34-220T Seneca III | M. Gavaghan |
| | G-HMMM | Cameron N-65 balloon | S. Moss |
| | G-HMPH | Bell 206B JetRanger2 | Mightycraft Ltd (G-BBUY) |
| | G-HNTR | Hunter T.7 | Hunter Wing Ltd/Bournemouth |
| | G-HOCK | PA-28 Cherokee 180 | Arabact Ltd (G-AVSH) |
| | G-HODG | Robinson R-22B | B. Hodge |
| | G-HOFM | Cameron N-56 balloon | Hot-Air Balloon Co Ltd |
| | G-HOHO | Colt Santa Claus SS balloon | Thunder & Colt Ltd |
| | G-HOLT | Taylor JT.1 Monoplane | K. D. Holt |
| | G-HOLY | ST.10 Diplomate | Cavok Ltd/Staverton |
| | G-HOME | Colt 77A balloon | Anglia Balloon School Tardis |
| | G-HONK | Cameron O-105 balloon | T. F. W. Dixon & Son Ltd |
| | G-HOOV | Cameron N-56 balloon | H. R. Evans |
| | G-HOPE | Beech F33A Bonanza | Hurn Aviation Ltd |
| | G-HOPS | Thunder Ax8-90 balloon | Air Hops Ltd |
| | G-HORN | Cameron V-77 balloon | Travel Gas (Midlands) Ltd |
| | G-HOSI | Colt 77A balloon | J. N. Harley (Engineering) Ltd |
| | G-HOST | Cameron N-77 balloon | D. Grimshaw |
| | G-HOTI | Colt 77A balloon | R. Ollier |
| | G-HOTS | Thunder Colt AS-80 airship | Island Airship Ltd |
| | G-HOUL | FRED Srs 2 | D. M. M. Richardson |
| | G-HOUS | Colt 31A balloon | Anglia Balloons Ltd |
| | G-HOVR | Robinson R-22B | Sloane Helicopters Ltd/Sywell |
| | G-HOWE | Thunder Ax7-77 balloon | M. F. Howe |

| Reg. | Type | Owner or Operator | Notes |
|------|------|-------------------|-------|
| G-HPLC | Sikorsky S-76B | Air Hanson Ltd/Blackbushe | |
| G-HPVC | Partenavia P.68B | Airtime (Hampshire) Ltd | |
| G-HRAY | AB-206B JetRanger 3 | Hecray Co Ltd (G-VANG/G-BIZA) | |
| G-HRHI | B.206 Srs 1 Basset | Universal Salvage (Holdings) Ltd | |
| G-HRIO | Robin HR.100/120 | R. L. & G. M. Bagnall | |
| G-HRIS | Cessna P210N | Birmingham Aviation Ltd | |
| G-HRLK | Saab 91D/2 Safir | Sylmar Aviation & Services Ltd (G-BRZY) | |
| G-HRLM | Brügger MB.2 Colibri | R. A. Harris | |
| G-HROI | R. Commander 112A | H. R. Oldland | |
| G-HRZN | Colt 77A balloon | A. J. Spindler | |
| G-HSDW | Bell 206B JetRanger | Winfield Shoe Co Ltd | |
| G-HSHS | Colt 105A balloon | H. & S. Aviation Ltd | |
| G-HTAX | PA-31-350 Navajo Chieftain | Jet West Ltd/Exeter | |
| G-HTPS | SA. 341G Gazelle 1 | ITPS Ltd (G-BRNI) | |
| G-HTRF | Robinson R-22B | Hecray Ltd | |
| G-HUBB | Partenavia P.68B | G-HUBB Ltd | |
| G-HUEY | Bell UH-1H | RAF Benevolent Fund/Odiham | |
| G-HUFF | Cessna 182P | J. R. W. Keates/Biggin Hill | |
| G-HULL | Cessna F.150M | A. D. McLeod | |
| G-HUMF | Robinson R-22B | J. M. Wicks | |
| G-HUMP | Beech 95-B55 Baron | J. H. Humphreys (G-BAMI)/Guernsey | |
| G-HUMT | Bell 206B JetRanger | H. J. Walters | |
| G-HUNN | Hispano HA.1112MIL (+14) | Charles Church Displays Ltd (G-BJZZ) | |
| G-HUNY | Cessna F.150G | T. J. Lynn (G-AVGL) | |
| G-HURI | CCF Hawker Hurricane IIB (Z7381) | Patina Ltd/Duxford | |
| G-HURN | Robinson R-22B | Yorkshire Helicopter Centre Ltd | |
| G-HURR | Hawker Hurricane XII | Autokraft Ltd | |
| G-HURY | Hawker Hurricane IV (KZ321) | D. W. Arnold/Biggin Hill | |
| G-HUTT | Denney Aerocraft Kitfox | M. A. J. Hutt | |
| G-HUWS | Hughes 269C | J. Grant | |
| G-HVRD | PA-31-350 Navajo Chieftain | London Flight Centre Air Charter Ltd (G-BEZU) | |
| G-HVRS | Robinson R-22B | M. P. & A. L. Wilkinson | |
| G-HWBK | Agusta A.109A | Camlet Helicopters Ltd | |
| G-HWKN | PA-31P Pressurised Navajo | Industrial Marketing Group | |
| G-HWKR | Colt 90A balloon | Hawker Siddeley Group PLC | |
| G-HYGA | BAe 125 Srs 800B | Helpfactor Ltd | |
| G-HYLT | PA-32R-301 Saratoga SP | R. G. Moggridge | |
| G-HYPO | Colt 180A balloon | The Balloon Club of GB Ltd | |
| G-IBAC | Beech 95-58 Baron | BAC Aviation Ltd/Southend | |
| G-IBAK | Cessna 421C | MJD Aviation Ltd | |
| G-IBET | Cameron 70 Can SS balloon | M. R. Humphrey & J. R. Clifton | |
| G-IBFW | PA-28R-201 Arrow III | Speedway Car & Van Hire Ltd | |
| G-IBLW | BAe Jetstream 3109 | British Aerospace PLC/Prestwick | |
| G-IBLX | BAe Jetstream 3109 | British Aerospace PLC/Prestwick | |
| G-IBTX | Boeing 737-2M8 | GB Airways Ltd (G-BTEB)/Gatwick | |
| G-IBTY | Boeing 737-2E3 | GB Airways (G-BNZT)/Gatwick | |
| G-IBTZ | Boeing 737-2U4 | GB Airways (G-OSLA)/Gatwick | |
| G-ICED | Cessna 501 Citation | Iceland Frozen Foods PLC/Manchester | |
| G-ICES | Thunder Ax6-56 balloon | — | |
| G-IDDI | Cameron N-77 balloon | Allen & Harris Ltd | |
| G-IDDY | D.H.C.1 Super Chipmunk | A. J. E. Ditheridge (G-BBMS) | |
| G-IDEA | AA-5A Cheetah | Lowlog Ltd (G-BGNO) | |
| G-IDJB | Cessna 150L | R. J. Browne | |
| G-IDWR | Hughes 369HS | Ryburn Air Ltd (G-AXEJ) | |
| G-IEAA | Boeing 737-33A | Inter European Airways Ltd/Cardiff | |
| G-IEAB | Boeing 757-23A | Inter European Airways Ltd/Cardiff | |
| G-IEPF | Robinson R-22B | Airmarch Ltd | |
| G-IESA | Cessna 421C | Primerent Ltd | |
| G-IFIT | PA-31-350 Navajo Chieftain | Cook Aviation Services Ltd (G-NABI/G-MARG) | |
| G-IFLI | AA-5A Cheetah | Biggin Hill School of Flying | |
| G-IFLP | PA-34-200T Seneca II | Golf-Sala Ltd | |
| G-IFTA | PA-31-350 Navajo Chieftain | Interflight (Air Charters) Ltd (G-BAVM)/Gatwick | |
| G-IFTD | Cessna 404 | Interflight (Air Charters) Ltd (G-BKUN)/Gatwick | |
| G-IGAR | PA-31-310 Turbo Navajo C | BWOC Ltd | |
| G-IGON | PA-31-310 Turbo Navajo | Computaplane Ltd/Glasgow | |
| G-IHSA | Robinson R-22B | D. P. Fiske | |
| G-IHSB | Robinson R-22B | Hatfield Development Co Ltd/Ipswich | |

| Notes | Reg. | Type | Owner or Operator |
|---|---|---|---|
| | G-IHSC | Robinson R-22B | Anglo-Norden Ltd/Ipswich |
| | G-IIII | Aerotek Pitts S-2B Special | B. K. Lecomber |
| | G-IIIL | Pitts S-1T Special | Aerobatic Displays Ltd |
| | G-IIIT | Aerotek Pitts S-2A Special | Aerobatic Displays Ltd |
| | G-IIIX | Pitts S-1S Special | Rugby Finance (Midlands) Ltd (G-LBAT/G-UCCI/G-BIYN) |
| | G-IINA | AS.350B-2 Ecureuil | Endeavour Aviation Ltd |
| | G-IIRB | Bell 206B JetRanger 3 | Robard Consultants Ltd |
| | G-IJOE | PA-28RT-201T Turbo Arrow IV | Scotlandair Ltd/Glasgow |
| | G-IKBP | PA-28-161 Warrior II | Hendafern Ltd/Shoreham |
| | G-IKIS | Cessna 210M | A. C. Davison |
| | G-ILES | Cameron O-90 balloon | G. N. Lantos |
| | G-ILLE | Boeing Stearman A.75L3 | M. H. Pendlebury |
| | G-ILLS | H.S.125 Srs 3B | S. Gill (G-AVRF)/Luton |
| | G-ILLY | PA-28-181 Archer II | A. G. & K. M. Spiers |
| | G-ILSE | Corby CJ-1 Starlet | S. Stride |
| | G-ILTS | PA-32 Cherokee Six 300 | Fadmoor Flying Group (G-CVOK) |
| | G-ILYS | Robinson R-22B | Wood Hall Helicopters Ltd |
| | G-IMAG | Colt 77A balloon | Flying Pictures (Balloons) Ltd |
| | G-IMAX | Cameron O-120 balloon | Air 2 Air Ltd |
| | G-IMLH | Bell 206A JetRanger 3 | Subaru (UK) Ltd |
| | G-IMLI | Cessna 310Q | Michael Leonard Interiors Ltd (G-AZYK)/ Blackbushe |
| | G-IMPW | PA-32R-301 Saratoga SP | C. M. Juggins |
| | G-IMPX | R. Commander 112B | P. A. Day |
| | G-IMPY | Avid Flyer C | T. R. C. Griffin |
| | G-INAV | Aviation Composites Mercury | Aviation Composites Co Ltd |
| | G-INCA | Glaser-Dirks DG.400 | H. W. Ober |
| | G-INDC | Cessna T.303 | Howarth Timber (Aircharters) Ltd |
| | G-INGB | Robinson R-22B | Filemart Ltd |
| | G-INMO | PA-31-310 Turbo Navajo | Subaru (UK) Ltd/Coventry |
| | G-INNY | SE-5A Replica (F5459) | R. M. Ordish/Old Sarum |
| | G-INOW | Monnet Moni | T. W. Clark |
| | G-INTC | Robinson R-22B | Intec Project Engineering Ltd |
| | G-IOOI | Robin DR.400/160 | Freshname No 77 Ltd |
| | G-IOSI | Jodel DR.1051 | R. G. E. Simpson & A. M. Alexander |
| | G-IPEC | SIAI-Marchetti S.205-18F | P. J. Warne (G-AVEG) |
| | G-IPJC | PA-28R Cherokee Arrow 200 | PJC Leasing Ltd |
| | G-IPPM | SA.102-5 Cavalier | I. D. Perry & P. S. Murfitt |
| | G-IPRA | Beech A200 Super King Air | Filemart Ltd (G-BGRD) |
| | G-IPSI | Grob G.109B | G-IPSI Ltd (G-BMLO) |
| | G-IPSY | Rutan Vari-Eze | R. A. Fairclough/Biggin Hill |
| | G-IPUT | PA-34-220T Seneca III | J. Cole & R. E. Gilbert/Southend |
| | G-IRIS | AA-5B Tiger | E. I. Bett (G-BIXU) |
| | G-IRLS | Cessna FR.172J | R. C. Chapman |
| | G-IRLY | Colt 90A balloon | Air Canada Ltd |
| | G-ISEB | Agusta A.109A II | Walkfine Ltd (G-IADT/G-HBCA) |
| | G-ISEH | Cessna 182R | SEH (Holdings) Ltd/Ipswich |
| | G-ISIS | D.H.82A Tiger Moth | D. R. & M. Wood (G-AODR) |
| | G-ISLE | Short SD3-60 | Manx Airlines Ltd/(G-BLEG) *King Olaf* (1113-1153) |
| | G-ISMO | Robinson R-22B | Jet Heritage Ltd/Bournemouth |
| | G-ISPY | Colt GA-42 airship | Airship & Balloon Co Ltd |
| | G-ISTT | Thunder Ax8-84 balloon | RAF Halton Hot Air Balloon Club |
| | G-ITDA | PA-32R-301 Saratoga SP | ITD Aviation Ltd |
| | G-ITPS | Pilatus PC-6/B2-H2 Turbo Porter | ITPS Ltd/Cranfield |
| | G-ITTU | PA-23 Aztec 250E | D. Byrne (G-BCSW) |
| | G-IVAC | Airtour AH-77B balloon | M. G. F. White |
| | G-IVAN | Shaw TwinEze | I. Shaw |
| | G-IVAR | Yakovlev Yak-50 | R. N. Goode/White Waltham |
| | G-IVOR | Aeronca 11AC Chief | M. A. Hales/Bourn |
| | G-IXCC | V.S.361 Spitfire LF.IXe | Charles Church Displays Ltd |
| | G-IZMO | Thunder Ax8-90 balloon | Landrell Fabric Engineering Ltd |
| | G-JACT | Partenavia P.68C | JCT 600 Ltd (G-NVIA)/Leeds |
| | G-JADE | Beech 95-58 Baron | S. W. B. Parkinson |
| | G-JAFE | D.H.C.2 Beaver 1 | J. M. Jeapes |
| | G-JAKE | D.H.C.1 Chipmunk 22 | J. M. W. Henstock (G-BBMY)/ Netherthorpe |
| | G-JAKY | PA-31-325 Turbo Navajo C/R | Ace Aviation Ltd/Glasgow |
| | G-JANA | PA-28-181 Archer II | Croaker Aviation/Stapleford |
| | G-JANB | Colt Flying Bottle SS balloon | Justerini & Brooks Ltd |
| | G-JANE | Cessna 340A | John Hewitson Ltd |

| Reg. | Type | Owner or Operator | Notes |
|------|------|-------------------|-------|
| G-JANN | PA-34-220T Seneca III | J. A. Powell | |
| G-JANS | Cessna FR.172J | I. G. Aizlewood/Luton | |
| G-JANT | PA-28-181 Archer II | Janair Aviation Ltd | |
| G-JASM | Robinson R-22A | J. L. Lawrence & ptnrs | |
| G-JASP | PA-23 Turbo Aztec 250E | Landsurcon (Air Survey) Ltd/Staverton | |
| G-JAVA | AA-5A Cheetah | J. A. Pothecary | |
| G-JAZZ | AA-5A Cheetah | Falcon Flying Services/Biggin Hill | |
| G-JBDH | Robin DR.400/180 | J. B. Hoolahan/Biggin Hill | |
| G-JBET | Beech F33A Bonanza | J. Bett/Glasgow | |
| G-JBJB | Colt 69A balloon | Justerini & Brooks Ltd | |
| G-JBPR | Wittman W.10 Tailwind | P. A. Rose & J. P. Broadhurst | |
| G-JBUS | FRED Srs 2 | R. V. Joyce | |
| G-JBWI | Robinson R-22B | N. J. Wagstaff Leasing | |
| G-JCAS | PA-28-181 Archer II | C. A. Sprent | |
| G-JCJC | Colt Flying Jeans SS balloon | J. C. Balloon Co Ltd | |
| G-JCUB | PA-18 Super Cub 135 | Piper Cub Consortium Ltd/Jersey | |
| G-JDEE | SOCATA TB.20 Trinidad | Melville Associates Ltd (G-BKLA) | |
| G-JDHI | Enstrom F-28C-UK | B. J. W. Carter (G-BCOT) | |
| G-JDIX | Mooney M.20B | J. E. Dixon (G-ARTB) | |
| G-JDTI | Cessna 421C | Eastfield Air Ltd/Sturgate | |
| G-JEAA | F.27 Friendship Mk 500F | Jersey European Airways Ltd | |
| G-JEAB | F.27 Friendship Mk 500F | Jersey European Airways Ltd | |
| G-JEAD | F.27 Friendship Mk 500 | Jersey European Airways Ltd | |
| G-JEAE | F.27 Friendship Mk 500 | Jersey European Airways Ltd | |
| G-JEAF | F.27 Friendship Mk 500 | Jersey European Airways Ltd | |
| G-JEAG | F.27 Friendship Mk 500 | Jersey European Airways Ltd | |
| G-JEAH | F.27 Friendship Mk 500 | Jersey European Airways Ltd | |
| G-JEAI | F.27 Friendship Mk 500 | Jersey European Airways Ltd | |
| G-JEAN | Cessna 500 Citation | Foster Associates Ltd | |
| G-JEET | Cessna FA.152 | Luton Flight Training (G-BHMF) | |
| G-JEFF | PA-38-112 Tomahawk | R. J. Alford | |
| G-JENA | Mooney M.20K | P. Leverkuehn/Biggin Hill | |
| G-JENI | Cessna R.182 | R. A. Bentley | |
| G-JENN | AA-5B Tiger | Clamair Aviation Ltd | |
| G-JENS | SOCATA Rallye 100ST | Palmer Pastoral Co Ltd (G-BDEG) | |
| G-JENY | Baby Great Lakes | J. M. C. Pothecary | |
| G-JERS | Robinson R-22B | J. E. R. Seeger | |
| G-JERY | AB-206B JetRanger 2 | J. J. Woodhouse (G-BDBR) | |
| G-JEST | PA-22 Tri-Pacer 160 | Saltair Ltd (G-ARGY) | |
| G-JETA | Cessna 550 Citation II | IDS Aircraft Ltd/Heathrow | |
| G-JETB | Cessna 550 Citation II | IDS Aircraft Ltd (G-MAMA)/Heathrow | |
| G-JETC | Cessna 550 Citation II | Nelson Leasing & Finance Ltd | |
| G-JETE | Cessna 500 Citation | IDS Aircraft Ltd (G-BCKM)/Heathrow | |
| G-JETH | Hawker Sea Hawk FGA.6 ★ | P. G. Vallence Ltd/Charlwood | |
| G-JETI | BAe 125 Srs 800B | Yeates of Leicester Ltd | |
| G-JETL | Learjet 35A | Cameron Hall Developments Ltd | |
| G-JETM | Gloster Meteor T.7 | Aces High Ltd/North Weald | |
| G-JETP | P.84 Jet Provost T.52A (T.4) | Hunter Wing Ltd/Bournemouth | |
| G-JETS | A.61 Terrier 2 | J. E. Tootell (G-ASOM) | |
| G-JETX | Bell 206B JetRanger | Tripgate Ltd | |
| G-JFHL | PA-28-161 Warrior II | C. L. Palmer | |
| G-JFWI | Cessna F.172N | Staryear Ltd | |
| G-JGAL | Beech E90 King Air | Vaux (Aviation) Ltd/Newcastle | |
| G-JGCL | Cessna 414A | M. J. Holt | |
| G-JHAN | Beech B200 Super King Air | John Hanson Services Ltd | |
| G-JHAS | Schweizer 269C | Albany Helicopters Ltd | |
| G-JHEW | Robinson R-22B | Burbage Farms Ltd | |
| G-JHLN | H.S.748 Srs 2A | Merchant Enterprises Ltd | |
| G-JILL | R. Commander 112TCA | Hanover Aviation/Elstree | |
| G-JIMI | Hughes 369D | F. Booker Builders & Contractors Ltd | |
| G-JIMS | Cessna 340A-II | Stagecoach Holdings Ltd (G-PETE) | |
| G-JJAN | PA-28-181 Archer II | Redhill Flying Club | |
| G-JJSG | Learjet 35A | Smurfit Ltd | |
| G-JLCY | Agusta A.109A | John Laing Construction Ltd/Elstree | |
| G-JLEE | AB-206B JetRanger 3 | Lee Aviation Ltd (G-JOKE/G-CSKY/ G-TALY) | |
| G-JLHS | Beech A36 Bonanza | J. L. Hopkins/Guernsey | |
| G-JLMW | Cameron V-77 balloon | The Apollo Balloon Co Ltd | |
| G-JLRW | Beech 76 Duchess | Moorfield Developments Ltd/Elstree | |
| G-JMDD | Cessna 340A | Thoroughbred Technology Ltd | |
| G-JMFW | Taylor JT.1 Monoplane | G. J. M. F. Winder | |
| G-JMHB | Robin DR.400/140 | TMA Associates Ltd/Biggin Hill | |
| G-JMTS | Robin DR.400/180 | Aeromarine Ltd/Southampton | |

| Notes | Reg. | Type | Owner or Operator |
|---|---|---|---|
| | G-JMTT | PA-28R-201T Turbo Arrow III | E. W. Passmore (G-BMHM) |
| | G-JMWT | SOCATA TB.10 Tobago | P. Fleming |
| | G-JOCO | AB-206B JetRanger 2 | Northern Helicopter Services Ltd |
| | G-JODL | Jodel DR.1050M | M. D. Mold |
| | G-JODY | Bell 206B JetRanger 2 | Maztest Motors Ltd |
| | G-JOEY | BN-2A Mk III-2 Trislander | Aurigny Air Services (G-BDGG)/ Guernsey |
| | G-JOIN | Cameron V-65 balloon | Derbyshire Building Society |
| | G-JOLY | Cessna 120 | J. D. Tarrant/Bristol |
| | G-JOND | Beech 95-B55 Baron | John Dee Group Ltd (G-BMVC) |
| | G-JONE | Cessna 172M | A. Pierce |
| | G-JONI | Cessna FA.152 | Luton Flight Training Ltd (G-BFTU) |
| | G-JONN | Bell 206L-1 LongRanger | Harmeston Holdings Ltd |
| | G-JONO | Colt 77A balloon | The Sandcliffe Motor Group |
| | G-JONS | PA-31-350 Navajo Chieftain | Byrne Bros Holdings Ltd |
| | G-JONZ | Cessna 172P | Jonesco (Preston) Ltd |
| | G-JOSH | Cameron N-105 balloon | GT Flying Clubs Ltd |
| | G-JOSY | Enstrom 280FX | S. Oliphant-Hope (G-BSTB) |
| | G-JOYC | Beech F33A Bonanza | Dunmhor Transport Ltd |
| | G-JOYT | PA-28-181 Archer II | S. W. Taylor (G-BOVO)/Redhill |
| | G-JSCL | Rans S.10 Sakota | J. D. Bedford |
| | G-JSMC | McD Douglas MD-83 | Airtours International Aviation Ltd |
| | G-JSSD | SA. Jetstream 3001 | British Aerospace (G-AXJZ)/Prestwick |
| | G-JTCA | PA-23 Aztec 250E | J. D. Tighe (G-BBCU)/Sturgate |
| | G-JTWO | Piper J-2 Cub | A. T. Hooper & C. C. Silk (G-BPZR) |
| | G-JUDE | CEA DR.400/180 | L. R. Marks |
| | G-JUDI | AT-6D Harvard III (FX301) | A. A. Hodgson |
| | G-JUDY | AA-5A Cheetah | Brandon Aviation/Biggin Hill |
| | G-JUIN | Cessna 303 | Michael Newman Aviation Ltd/Denham |
| | G-JUNG | C.A.S.A. 1.131E Jungmann 1000 | K. H. Wilson |
| | G-JURG | R. Commander 114A | Jurgair Ltd |
| | G-JVAJ | PA-31T1 Cheyenne | Jacques Vert PLC |
| | G-JVJA | Partenavia P.68C | Twinflite Aviation Ltd (G-BMEI) |
| | G-JVMR | Partenavia P.68B | Sonardyne Ltd (G-JCTI/G-OJOE)/ Blackbushe |
| | G-JWDS | Cessna F.150G | London Aerial Tours Ltd (G-AVNB) |
| | G-JWFT | Robinson R-22B | Tukair Aircraft Charter |
| | G-JWIV | Jodel DR.1051 | R. A. Bragger |
| | G-JWSD | Robinson R-22B | J. W. Sparrow Developments Ltd |
| | G-KADY | Rutan Long Ez | M. W. Caddy |
| | G-KAFE | Cameron N-65 balloon | Hot-Air Balloon Co Ltd |
| | G-KAIR | PA-28-181 Archer II | Academy Lithoplates Ltd/Aldergrove |
| | G-KARI | Fuji FA.200-160 | I. Mansfield & F. M. Fiore (G-BBRE) |
| | G-KARY | Fuji FA.200-180AO | C. J. Zetter (G-BEYP) |
| | G-KASS | H.S.125 Srs 3B | Eroten Ltd (G-AVPE) |
| | G-KATE | Westland WG.30 Srs 100 | British International Helicopters Ltd/ Aberdeen |
| | G-KATH | Cessna P.210N | Wilson-Air Ltd |
| | G-KATS | PA-28 Cherokee 140 | Ipswich School of Flying Ltd (G-BIRC) |
| | G-KBPI | PA-28-161 Warrior II | K. B. Page (Aviation) Ltd (G-BFSZ)/ Shoreham |
| | G-KCAS | Beech 95-B55 Baron | M. J. & J. D. Crymble |
| | G-KCIG | Sportavia RF-5B | Exeter Sperber Syndicate Ltd |
| | G-KDET | PA-28-161 Cadet | Rapidspin Ltd/Biggin Hill |
| | G-KDFF | Scheibe SF.25E Super Falke | M. Lee & K. Dudley |
| | G-KDIX | Jodel D.9 Bebe | D. J. Wells |
| | G-KEAA | Beech 65-70 Queen Air | Kent Executive Aviation Ltd (G-REXP/ G-AYPC) |
| | G-KEAB | Beech 65-B80 Queen Air | Kent Executive Aviation Ltd (G-BSSL/ G-BFEP) |
| | G-KEAC | Beech 65-A80 Queen Air | Kent Executive Aviation Ltd (G-REXY/ G-AVNG) |
| | G-KEEN | Stolp SA.300 Starduster Too | Holland Aerobatics Ltd |
| | G-KEMC | Grob G.109 | Eye-Fly Ltd |
| | G-KENB | Air Command 503 Commander | K. Brogden |
| | G-KENI | Rotorway Executive | K. Hassall |
| | G-KENN | Robinson R-22B | Cromwell Charter/Southampton |
| | G-KERC | SNCAN NC.854S | E. H. Gould |
| | G-KERY | PA-28 Cherokee 180 | Kerrytype Ltd (G-ATWO)/Goodwood |
| | G-KEYB | Cameron O-84 balloon | B. P. Key |
| | G-KEYS | PA-23 Aztec 250F | Wards Aviation Ltd |
| | G-KEYY | Cameron N-77 balloon | Business Design Group Ltd (G-BORZ) |

| Reg. | Type | Owner or Operator | Notes |
|------|------|-------------------|-------|
| G-KFIT | Beech F90 King Air | Kwik Fit Euro Ltd (G-BHUS)/Edinburgh | |
| G-KFOX | Denney Aerocraft Kitfox | J. Hannibal | |
| G-KFZI | KFZ-1 Tigerfalke | L. R. Williams | |
| G-KHRE | M.S.893E Rallye 150SV | B. Proctor/Dunkeswell | |
| G-KIAM | Grob G.109B | D. T. Hulme | |
| G-KILY | Robinson R-22A | Julians Supermarket Ltd | |
| G-KIMB | Robin DR.340/140 | R. M. Kimbell | |
| G-KINE | AA-5A Cheetah | G. W. Plowman Ltd | |
| G-KING | PA-38-112 Tomahawk | M. Hunter | |
| G-KINK | Cessna 340 | Hulbert of Dudley (Holdings) Ltd (G-PLEV) | |
| G-KIRK | Piper J-3C-65 Cub | M. J. Kirk | |
| G-KISS | Rand KR-2 | E. A. Rooney | |
| G-KITE | PA-28-181 Archer II | World Business Publications Ltd/Elstree | |
| G-KITF | Denney Aerocraft Kitfox | Junipa Sales Aviation Ltd | |
| G-KITI | Pitts S-2E Special | P. A. Grant | |
| G-KITY | Denney Aerocraft Kitfox | Kitfox KFM Group | |
| G-KIWI | Cessna 404 Titan | Aviation Beauport Ltd (G-BHNI) | |
| G-KJET | Beech B90 King Air | Hawk Aviation Ltd (G-AXFE) | |
| G-KKDL | SOCATA TB.20 Trinidad | Kimber Kempster Contractors Ltd (G-BSHU) | |
| G-KLAY | Enstrom 280C Shark | Percivalls Ltd (G-BGZD) | |
| G-KLIK | Air Command 532 Elite | Roger Martin (Photography) | |
| G-KMAC | Bell 206B JetRanger | Specbridge Ltd | |
| G-KNAP | PA-28-161 Warrior II | R. E. Knapton (G-BIUX)/Kidlington | |
| G-KNIT | Robinson R-22B | BHM Knitwear Ltd | |
| G-KNOW | PA-32 Cherokee Six 300 | P. H. Knowland | |
| G-KODA | Cameron O-77 balloon | United Photofinishers Ltd | |
| G-KOLI | PZL-110 Koliber 150 | S. Coast Aviation Ltd/Shoreham | |
| G-KOLY | Enstrom F-28C-UK | Midland Trailers Ltd (G-WWUK/G-BFFN) | |
| G-KOOL | D.H.104 Devon C.2 ★ | E. Surrey Technical College/nr Redhill | |
| G-KORN | Cameron 70 Brentzen SS balloon | Cameron Balloons Ltd | |
| G-KOTA | PA-28-236 Dakota | Klingair Ltd/Conington | |
| G-KRII | Rand KR-2 | M. R. Cleveley | |
| G-KRIS | Maule M5-235C Lunar Rocket | M. G. Pickering | |
| G-KROO | BAC One-Eleven 217EA | European Aviation Ltd | |
| G-KTEE | Cameron V-77 balloon | D. C. & N. P. Bull | |
| G-KUKU | Pfalzkuku (BS676) | A. D. Lawrence | |
| G-KUTU | Quickie Q2 | J. Parkinson & ptnrs | |
| G-KWAX | Cessna 182E Skylane | A. R. Carrillo/Bournemouth | |
| G-KWIK | Partenavia P.68B | Travelair UK Ltd | |
| G-KYAK | Yakolev C-11 (00) | R. Lamplough/Duxford | |
| G-KYIN | Cessna 421C | Sulair Services Ltd (G-OAKS) | |
| G-LACA | PA-28-161 Warrior II | Light Planes (Lancashire) Ltd/Barton | |
| G-LACB | PA-28-161 Warrior II | Light Planes (Lancashire) Ltd/Barton | |
| G-LACR | Denney Aerocraft Kitfox | C. M. Rose | |
| G-LADE | PA-32 Cherokee Six 300E | A. G. & D. Webb | |
| G-LADN | PA-28-161 Warrior II | E. C. Clark (G-BOLK)/Biggin Hill | |
| G-LADS | R. Commander 114 | D. F. Soul | |
| G-LAGR | Cameron N-90 balloon | Bass & Tennent Sales Ltd | |
| G-LAKE | Lake LA.250 | Stanford Ltd | |
| G-LAKI | Jodel DR.1050 | V. Panteli | |
| G-LAMB | Beech C90 King Air | Lascar Electronics Ltd | |
| G-LAMS | Cessna F.152 | J. J. Baumhardt/Southend | |
| G-LANA | SOCATA TB.10 Tobago | Aero-Go Systems Ltd | |
| G-LANC | Avro 683 Lancaster X (KB889) ★ | Imperial War Museum/Duxford | |
| G-LAND | Robinson R-22B | Charter Group PLC | |
| G-LANE | Cessna F.172N | G. C. Bantin | |
| G-LANG | Denney Aerocraft Kitfox | J. W. Lang | |
| G-LARK | Helton Lark 95 | J. Fox | |
| G-LASH | Monnet Sonerai II | A. Lawson | |
| G-LASR | Stoddard-Hamilton Glasair II | P. Taylor | |
| G-LASS | Rutan Vari-Eze | G. Lewis/Liverpool | |
| G-LATC | EMB-110P1 Bandeirante | Business Air Ltd | |
| G-LAZR | Cameron O-77 balloon | Laser Civil Engineering Ltd | |
| G-LBMM | PA-28-161 Warrior II | M. C. Lawton | |
| G-LBRC | PA-28RT-201 Arrow IV | R. Chown | |
| G-LCIO | Colt 240A balloon | Star Micronics UK Ltd | |
| G-LCOK | Colt 69A balloon | Hot-Air Balloon Co Ltd (G-BLWI) | |
| G-LDYS | Colt 56A balloon | A. Green | |
| G-LEAM | PA-28-236 Dakota | Blessvale Fabrications Ltd (G-BHLS) | |

| Notes | Reg. | Type | Owner or Operator |
|---|---|---|---|
| | G-LEAN | Cessna FR.182 | JGH Services Ltd (G-BGAP)/Biggin Hill |
| | G-LEAP | BN-2B Islander | Army Parachute Association (G-BLND)/ Netheravon |
| | G-LEAR | Learjet 35A | Northern Executive Aviation Ltd/ Manchester |
| | G-LEAU | Cameron N-31 balloon | Balloon Stable Ltd |
| | G-LECA | AS.355F-1 Twin Squirrel | S. W. Electricity Board (G-BNBK)/Bristol |
| | G-LEDN | Short SD3-30 Variant 100 | Janes Aviation Ltd (G-BIOF)/Blackpool |
| | G-LEEM | PA-28R Cherokee Arrow 200-II | J. Phelan & J. M. O'Grady (G-BJXW) |
| | G-LEES | Glaser-Dirks DG.400 | T. B. Sargeant & C. A. Marren |
| | G-LEGO | Cameron O-77 balloon | C. H. Pearce Construction PLC |
| | G-LEGS | Short SD3-60 | Manx Airlines Ltd (G-BLEF)/*King Magnus Barefoot (1098-1103)* |
| | G-LEIC | Cessna FA.152 | Leicestershire Aero Club Ltd |
| | G-LEIS | Bell 206-1 LongRanger | C.S.E. Aviation Ltd/Kidlington |
| | G-LEND | Cameron N-77 balloon | Southern Finance Co Ltd |
| | G-LENN | Cameron V-56 balloon | Anglia Balloon School Ltd |
| | G-LENS | Thunder Ax7-77Z balloon | Big Yellow Balloon Group |
| | G-LEON | PA-31-350 Navajo Chieftain | Chauffair Ltd/Blackbushe |
| | G-LEOS | Robin DR.400/120 | J. L. da Costa Sayago & P. A. Milne |
| | G-LEPF | Fairchild 24R-46A Argus III | J. M. Greenland |
| | G-LEPI | Colt 160A balloon | Thunder & Colt Ltd |
| | G-LEVI | Aeronca 7AC Champion | L. Perry & J. P. A. Pumphrey |
| | G-LEXI | Cameron N-77 balloon | R. H. Welch |
| | G-LEZE | Rutan Long Ez | K. G. M. Loyal & ptnrs |
| | G-LFCA | Cessna F.152 | Mercia Aircraft Leasing & Sales Ltd/ Coventry |
| | G-LFIX | V.S.509 Spitfire T.IX (ML407) | Jet Air Ltd/Goodwood |
| | G-LFSA | PA-38-112 Tomahawk | Liverpool Flying School Ltd (G-BSFC) |
| | G-LFSI | PA-28 Cherokee 140 | Liverpool Flying School Ltd (G-AYKV) |
| | G-LIAN | Robinson R-22B | Cotwell Air Services |
| | G-LIBS | Hughes 369HS | Griffair Ltd |
| | G-LICK | Cessna 172N | Dacebow Ltd (G-BNTR) |
| | G-LIDE | PA-31-350 Navajo Chieftain | Woodgate Executive Air Charter Ltd |
| | G-LIFE | Thunder Ax6-56Z balloon | M. J. & J. Evans |
| | G-LIGG | Cessna F.182Q | Navair Ltd (G-THAM) |
| | G-LIMA | R. Commander 114 | Tricolore Ltd/Biggin Hill |
| | G-LINC | Hughes 369HS | Fairglobe Ltd |
| | G-LIOA | Lockheed 10A Electra ★ (NC5171N) | Science Museum/Wroughton |
| | G-LION | PA-18 Super Cub 135 (542457 R-167) | A. W. Kennedy |
| | G-LIOT | Cameron O-77 balloon | D. Eliot |
| | G-LIPP | BN-2T Turbine Islander | Rhine Army Parachute Association (G-BKJG) |
| | G-LISA | Steen Skybolt | T. C. Humphreys |
| | G-LITE | R. Commander 112A | Rhoburt Ltd/Manchester |
| | G-LIZA | Cessna 340A | M. D. Joy (G-BMDM) |
| | G-LIZI | PA-28 Cherokee 160 | G. & E. A. Newman (G-ARRP)/Redhill |
| | G-LIZY | Westland Lysander III (V9300) ★ | G. A. Warner/Duxford |
| | G-LJET | Learjet 35A | Tiger Aviation Ltd/Gatwick |
| | G-LOAG | Cameron N-77 balloon | Matthew Gloag & Son Ltd |
| | G-LOAN | Cameron N-77 balloon | Newbury Building Soc |
| | G-LOCH | Piper J-3C-90 Cub | J. M. Greenland |
| | G-LOGS | Robinson R-22B | M. Chantler & ptnrs |
| | G-LOND | V.806 Viscount | Caicos International Airways Ltd (G-AOYI) |
| | G-LONG | Bell 206L LongRanger | Air Hanson Ltd/Brooklands |
| | G-LOOP | Pitts S-1C Special | B. G. Salter |
| | G-LORD | PA-34-200T Seneca II | C. R. Lord |
| | G-LORI | H.S.125 Srs 403B | Re-Enforce Trading Co Ltd (G-AYOJ) |
| | G-LORY | Thunder Ax4-31Z balloon | A. J. Moore |
| | G-LOSM | Gloster Meteor NF.11 (WM167) | Hunter Wing Ltd/Bournemouth |
| | G-LOSS | Cameron N-77 balloon | J. A. Kershaw |
| | G-LOTI | Bleriot XI (replica) | M. L. Beach |
| | G-LOUP | Partenavia P.68B | M. H. Wolff (G-OCAL/G-BGMY) |
| | G-LOVX | Cessna 441 Conquest | Hustlepon Ltd/Suckling Airways (G-BLCJ) |
| | G-LOWA | Colt 77A balloon | The Hot-Air Balloon Co Ltd |
| | G-LOWE | Monnet Sonerai II | J. L. Kinch |
| | G-LOYA | Cessna FR.172J | T. R. Scorer (G-BLVT) |
| | G-LOYD | SA.341G Gazelle 1 | Appollo Manufacturing (Derby) Ltd (G-SFTC) |

| Reg. | Type | Owner or Operator | Notes |
|------|------|-------------------|-------|
| G-LPGO | Cameron V-77 balloon | J. Walter Thompson Co Ltd | |
| G-LRII | Bell 206L LongRanger | Carroll Aircraft Operational Services Ltd | |
| G-LSFI | AA-5A Cheetah | Norfolk Flight Centre (G-BGSK)/Norwich | |
| G-LSHI | Colt 77A balloon | Lambert Smith Hampton Ltd | |
| G-LSLH | Schweizer 269C | Homewood Park Ltd | |
| G-LSMI | Cessna F.152 | Andrewsfield Flying Club Ltd | |
| G-LTNG | Lightning T.5 (XS451) | Lightning Flying Club | |
| G-LUAR | SOCATA TB.10 Tobago | CB Air Ltd | |
| G-LUBE | Cameron N-77 balloon | A. C. K. Rawson | |
| G-LUCA | Thunder Ax7-77Z balloon | Lucas Aerospace Ltd | |
| G-LUCE | Cameron A-210 balloon | Independent Balloon Co Ltd | |
| G-LUCK | Cessna F.150M | T. J. C. Darby | |
| G-LUCS | Colt 90A balloon | Lucas Aerospace Ltd | |
| G-LUGG | Colt 21A balloon | The Hot-Air Balloon Co Ltd | |
| G-LUKE | Rutan LongEz | S. G. Busby | |
| G-LULU | Grob G.109 | Strathtay Flying Group | |
| G-LUNA | PA-32RT-300T Turbo Lance II | E. Cliffe/Norwich | |
| G-LUSC | Luscombe 8E Silvaire | M. Fowler | |
| G-LUSI | Luscombe 8E Silvaire | R. J. Walker & J. Wrayton/O. Sarum | |
| G-LUST | Luscombe 8E Silvaire | M. Griffiths | |
| G-LUXE | BAe 146-300 | British Aerospace PLC (G-SSSH)/ Hatfield | |
| G-LYDD | PA-31 Turbo Navajo | Earlyexact Ltd (G-BBDU)/Lydd | |
| G-LYNN | PA-32RT-300 Lance II | Crosswind Aviation Ltd (G-BGNV)/Leeds | |
| G-LYNX | Westland WG.13 Lynx | Westland Helicopters Ltd/Yeovil | |
| G-LYTE | Thunder Ax7-77 balloon | A. S. Morton | |
| G-MAAC | Advanced Airship Corporation ANR-1 | Advanced Airship Corporation Ltd | |
| G-MABI | Cessna F.150L | Herefordshire Aero Club Ltd (G-BGOJ)/ Shobdon | |
| G-MACH | SIAI-Marchetti SF.260 | Cheyne Motors Ltd/Popham | |
| G-MACK | PA-28R Cherokee Arrow 200 | JF Packaging | |
| G-MAFF | BN-2T Islander | FR Aviation Ltd/(G-BJEO)/Bournemouth | |
| G-MAFI | Dornier Do.228-200 | FR Aviation Ltd/Bournemouth | |
| G-MAGG | Pitts S-1SE Special | C. A. Boardman | |
| G-MAGS | Cessna 340A | Tunstall Group PLC | |
| G-MAGY | AS.350B Ecureuil | Quantel Ltd (G-BIYC) | |
| G-MAIR | PA-34-200T Seneca II | Emmair Ltd/Kidlington | |
| G-MALA | PA-28-181 Archer II | H. Burtwhistle & Son (G-BIIU) | |
| G-MALC | AA-5 Traveler | C. B. Drew (G-BCPM) | |
| G-MALK | Cessna F.172N | K. M. Drewitt & J. G. Jackson/Liverpool | |
| G-MALS | Mooney M.20K-231 | C. J. Davy/Biggin Hill | |
| G-MALT | Colt Flying Hop balloon | The Hot-Air Balloon Co Ltd | |
| G-MAMO | Cameron V-77 balloon | The Marble Mosaic Co Ltd | |
| G-MANN | SA.341G Gazelle 1 | Robert Fraser & Partners Ltd (G-BKLW) | |
| G-MANT | Cessna 210L | CHJW Group (G-MAXY)/Coventry | |
| G-MANX | FRED Srs 2 | T. A. Timms | |
| G-MARC | AS.350B Ecureuil | Gabriel Enterprises Ltd (G-BKHU) | |
| G-MARE | Schweizer 269C | The Earl of Caledon | |
| G-MARR | Cessna 421C | Jacmil Ltd (G-JTIE/G-RBBE) | |
| G-MARS | Beech 400 Beechjet | Havilland Air Ltd (G-RSRS) | |
| G-MARY | Cassutt Special 1 | J. Chadwick/Redhill | |
| G-MASH | Westland Bell 47G-4A | Defence Products Ltd (G-AXKU) | |
| G-MASL | Mooney M.20J | Beta Trading Ltd | |
| G-MATE | Moravan Zlin Z.50LS | V. S. E. Norman | |
| G-MATI | Stolp SA.300 Starduster Too | M. R. Clark & J. McM. Rosser/ Newcastle | |
| G-MATP | BAe ATP | British Aerospace PLC/Woodford | |
| G-MATS | Colt GA-42 airship | Flying Pictures (Airships) Ltd | |
| G-MATT | Robin R.2160 | Sierra Flying Group (G-BKRC)/ Newcastle | |
| G-MATZ | PA-28 Cherokee 140 | Midland Air Training School (G-BASI) | |
| G-MAUK | Colt 77A balloon | Airship & Balloon Co Ltd | |
| G-MAVI | Robinson R-22B | Moorgate Aviation | |
| G-MAWL | Maule M4-210C Rocket | D. Group | |
| G-MAXI | PA-34-200T Seneca II | C. W. Middlemass | |
| G-MAYO | PA-28-161 Warrior II | Jermyk Engineering/Fairoaks | |
| G-MCAR | PA-32 Cherokee Six 300D | Miller Aerial Spraying Ltd (G-LADA/G-AYWK)/Wickenby | |
| G-MCBP | AIA Stampe SV-4C | Stampe Flying Group (G-BALA) | |
| G-MCKE | Boeing 757-28A | Monarch Airlines Ltd/Luton | |
| G-MCOX | Fuji FA.200-180AO | W. Surrey Engineering (Shepperton) Ltd | |

| Notes | Reg. | Type | Owner or Operator |
|---|---|---|---|
| | G-MCPI | Bell 206B JetRanger 3 | D. A. C. Pipe (G-ONTB) |
| | G-MCPL | PA-28-161 Warrior II | MCP Ltd |
| | G-MDAC | PA-28-181 Archer II | B. R. Mckay/Bournemouth |
| | G-MDAS | PA-31-310 Turbo Navajo C | Universal Data Technology Ltd (G-BCJZ) |
| | G-MDII | McD Douglas MD-11 | Air Europe Ltd/Gatwick |
| | G-MDKD | Robinson R-22B | D. K. Duckworth |
| | G-MDTV | Cameron N-105 balloon | Ideas Factory |
| | G-MEAN | Agusta A.109A | Castle Air Charters Ltd (G-BRYL/G-ROPE/G-OAMH) |
| | G-MEAT | Robinson R-22B | St Merryn Meat Ltd |
| | G-MEBC | Cessna 310-1 | P. H. Johnson (G-ROGA/G-ASVV) |
| | G-MEDC | Beech 95-58 Baron | Aircare (Southwest) Ltd |
| | G-MEGA | PA-28R-201T Turbo Arrow III | Travelworth Ltd |
| | G-MELD | AA-5A Cheetah | Fletcher Aviation Ltd (G-BHCB)/ Blackbushe |
| | G-MELI | Air & Space 18A gyroplane | M. Richardson |
| | G-MELT | Cessna F.172H | Vectair Aviation Ltd (G-AWTI) |
| | G-MELV | SOCATA Rallye 235E | Wallis & Sons Ltd (G-BIND) |
| | G-MEME | PA-28R-201 Arrow III | Henry J. Clare Ltd |
| | G-MERC | Colt 56A balloon | Castles Northgate Ltd |
| | G-MERI | PA-28-181 Archer II | Scotia Safari Ltd/Glasgow |
| | G-MERL | PA-28RT-201 Arrow IV | M. Giles |
| | G-MERV | PA-28-161 Warrior II | M. N. Choules |
| | G-META | Bell 222 | The Metropolitan Police/Lippitts Hill |
| | G-METB | Bell 222 | The Metropolitan Police/Lippitts Hill |
| | G-METC | Bell 222 | The Metropolitan Police (G-JAMC)/ Lippitts Hill |
| | G-METP | Short SD3-30 | — (G-METO/G-BKIE)/Southend |
| | G-MEUP | Cameron A-120 balloon | N. J. Tovey |
| | G-MFAL | Gulfstream Commander 690D | Marlborough Fine Art (London) Ltd |
| | G-MFHL | Robinson R-22B | MFH Ltd |
| | G-MFMF | Bell 206B JetRanger 3 | S.W. Electricity Board (G-BJNJ)/Bristol |
| | G-MFMM | Scheibe SF.25C Falke | S. T. Evans & ptnrs |
| | G-MHBD | Cameron O-105 balloon | K. Hull |
| | G-MHCA | Enstrom F-28C-UK | Trimcares Ltd (G-SHWW/G-SMUJ/ G-BHTF) |
| | G-MHCC | Bell 206B JetRanger 2 | LRC Helicopters Ltd |
| | G-MHIH | H.S. 125 Srs 700B | Queens Moat Houses PLC (G-BKAA) |
| | G-MHSL | MBB Bo 105DBS/4 | MBB Helicopter Systems Ltd |
| | G-MICH | Robinson R-22B | A. I. Freeman (G-BNKY) |
| | G-MICK | Cessna F.172N | S. Grant & ptnrs |
| | G-MICY | Everett Srs 1 gyroplane | D. M. Hughes |
| | G-MIDG | Midget Mustang | G. A. Stanley |
| | G-MIGI | Colt 105a balloon | MI Group Ltd |
| | G-MIKE | Brookland Hornet | M. H. J. Goldring |
| | G-MIKY | Cameron 90 Mickey SS balloon | The Walt Disney Co Ltd |
| | G-MILE | Cameron N-77 balloon | Miles Air Ltd |
| | G-MILK | SOCATA TB.10 Tobago | G. Whincup |
| | G-MILL | PA-32-301T Turbo Saratoga | S. S. Bernholt |
| | G-MIMI | SOCATA TB.20 Trinidad | T. J. & P. S. Gower/Biggin Hill |
| | G-MINI | Currie Wot | D. Collinson |
| | G-MINT | Pitts S-1S Special | T. G. Sanderson/Tollerton |
| | G-MINX | Bell 47G-4A | R. F. Warner |
| | G-MIOO | Miles GM.100 Student 2 ★ | M. Woodley (G-APLK)/(stored) Cranfield |
| | G-MISS | Taylor JT.2 Titch | A. Brennan |
| | G-MIST | Cessna T.210K | K. A. Summers (G-AYGM) |
| | G-MITS | Cameron N-77 balloon | Colt Car Co Ltd |
| | G-MITZ | Cameron N-77 balloon | Colt Car Co Ltd |
| | G-MKAY | Cessna 172N | Limbros Demolition Ltd |
| | G-MKEE | EAA Acro Sport | G. M. McKee |
| | G-MKIX | V.S.361 Spitfire F.IX (NH238) | D. W. Arnold |
| | G-MKVB | V.S.349 Spitfire LF.VB (BM597) | T. Routis |
| | G-MKXI | V.S.365 Spitfire PR.XI (PL985) | C. P. B. Horsley |
| | G-MLAS | Cessna 182E | Parachute jump trainer/St Merryn |
| | G-MLBU | PA-46-310P Malibu | Northern Scaffold Group Ltd |
| | G-MLFF | PA-23 Aztec 250E | Brands Hatch Circuit Ltd (G-WEBB/G-BJBU) |
| | G-MLGL | Colt 21A balloon | Colt Balloons Ltd |
| | G-MLWI | Thunder Ax7-77 balloon | M. L. & L. P. Willoughby |
| | G-MOAC | Beech F33A Bonanza | Chalkfarm Productions Ltd |
| | G-MOAT | Beech 200 Super King Air | Thurston Aviation (Stansted) Ltd |
| | G-MOFF | Cameron O-77 balloon | D. M. Moffat |

| Reg. | Type | Owner or Operator | Notes |
|------|------|-------------------|-------|
| G-MOGG | Cessna F.172N | J. G. James (G-BHDY) | |
| G-MOGI | AA-5A Cheetah | I. D. & C. R. Stait (G-BFMU) | |
| G-MOGY | Robinson R-22B | Reachmain Ltd | |
| G-MOHR | Cameron 105 Sarotti balloon | Cameron Balloons Ltd | |
| G-MOLE | Taylor JT.2 Titch | S. R. Mowle | |
| G-MOLY | PA-23 Apache 160 | R. R. & M-A. T. Thorogood/St Just | |
| G-MONA | M.S.880B Rallye Club | G. L. Thomas | |
| G-MONB | Boeing 757-2T7 | Monarch Airlines Ltd/Luton | |
| G-MONC | Boeing 757-2T7 | Monarch Airlines Ltd/Luton | |
| G-MOND | Boeing 757-2T7 | Monarch Airlines Ltd/Luton | |
| G-MONE | Boeing 757-2T7 | Monarch Airlines Ltd/Luton | |
| G-MONF | Boeing 737-3Y0 | Monarch Airlines/Canadian (C-FPWE) | |
| G-MONG | Boeing 737-3Y0 | Monarch Airlines/Canadian (C-FPWG) | |
| G-MONH | Boeing 737-3Y0 | Monarch Airlines Ltd/Euro Berlin | |
| G-MONI | Monnet Moni | R. J. Baron | |
| G-MONJ | Boeing 757-2T7 | Monarch Airlines Ltd/Luton | |
| G-MONK | Boeing 757-2T7 | Monarch Airlines Ltd/Luton | |
| G-MONL | Boeing 737-3Y0 | Monarch Airlines Ltd/Euro Berlin | |
| G-MONM | Boeing 737-3Y0 | Monarch Airlines Ltd/Euro Berlin | |
| G-MONN | Boeing 737-33A | Monarch Airlines Ltd/Euro Berlin | |
| G-MONO | Taylor JT.1 Monoplane | A. J. Holmes | |
| G-MONP | Boeing 737-33A | Monarch Airlines Ltd/Luton | |
| G-MONT | Boeing 737-33A | Monarch Airlines Ltd/Euro Berlin | |
| G-MONU | Boeing 737-33A | Monarch Airlines Ltd/Euro Berlin | |
| G-MOON | Mooney M.20K | M. A. Eccles | |
| G-MORL | Maule MX-7-180 | R. E. & K. Baker | |
| G-MOTH | D.H.82A Tiger Moth (K2567) | M. C. Russell/Duxford | |
| G-MOTO | PA-24 Comanche 160 | C. C. Letchford & A. J. Redknapp (G-EDHE/G-ASFH) | |
| G-MOUL | Maule M6-235 | Aeromarine Ltd | |
| G-MOUR | H.S. Gnat T.1 | D. J. Gilmour | |
| G-MOUS | Cameron 90 Mickey SS balloon | The Walt Disney Co Ltd | |
| G-MOVE | PA-60 Aerostar 601P | Red Dragon Travel Ltd/Cardiff | |
| G-MOVI | PA-32R-301 Saratoga SP | Peter Walker (Heritage) Ltd (G-MARI) | |
| G-MOZY | D.H.98 (replica) | J. Beck & G. L. Kemp | |
| G-MOZZ | Avions Mudry CAP.10B | Brandzone Ltd | |
| G-MPBH | Cessna FA.152 | Metropolitan Police Flying Club (G-FLIC/G-BILV) | |
| G-MPCU | Cessna 402B | Atlantic Air Transport Ltd/Coventry | |
| G-MPWH | Rotorway Executive | MPW Aviation Ltd | |
| G-MPWI | Robin HR.100/210 | Propwash Investments Ltd/Cardiff | |
| G-MPWT | PA-34-220T Seneca III | MPW Aviation Ltd | |
| G-MRPP | PA-34-220T Seneca III | P. E. Pearce | |
| G-MRST | PA-28RT-201 Arrow IV | Winchfield Enterprises Ltd | |
| G-MRTY | Cameron N-77 balloon | R. A. & P. G. Vale | |
| G-MSDJ | AS.350B-1 Ecureuil | Denis Ferranti Hoverknights Ltd (G-BPOH) | |
| G-MSFC | PA-38-112 Tomahawk | Sherwood Flying Club Ltd/Tollerton | |
| G-MSFY | H.S.125 Srs 700B | Mohamed Said Fakhry/Heathrow | |
| G-MTLE | Cessna 501 Citation | Talan Ltd (G-GENE) | |
| G-MUFF | AS.355F-1 Twin Squirrel | Lynton Aviation Ltd (G-CORR) | |
| G-MUIR | Cameron V-65 balloon | L. C. M. Muir | |
| G-MULL | Douglas DC-10-30 | British Airways *New Forest*/Gatwick | |
| G-MUNI | Mooney M.20J | Aeromarine Ltd/Southampton | |
| G-MURF | AA-5B Tiger | D. Murphy (G-JOAN/G-BFML) | |
| G-MUSI | Robinson R-22B | F. M. Usher-Smith | |
| G-MUSO | Rutan LongEz | M. Moran | |
| G-MXVI | V.S.361 Spitfire LF.XVIe | Myrick Aviation Services Ltd | |
| G-NAAS | AS.355F-1 Twin Squirrel | McAlpine Helicopters Ltd (G-BPRG) | |
| G-NAAT | H.S. Gnat T.1 | Hunter Wing Ltd/Bournemouth | |
| G-NABS | Robinson R-22B | Arian Helicopters Ltd | |
| G-NACA | Norman NAC.2 Freelance 180 | Aeronortec Ltd | |
| G-NACI | Norman NAC.1 Srs 100 | Aeronortec Ltd | |
| G-NACL | Norman NAC.6 Fieldmaster | Legistshelfco Ltd (G-BNEG)/Cardiff | |
| G-NACM | Norman NAC.6 Fieldmaster | Legistshelfco Ltd/Cardiff | |
| G-NACN | Norman NAC.6 Fieldmaster | Legistshelfco Ltd/Cardiff | |
| G-NACO | Norman NAC.6 Fieldmaster | Legistshelfco Ltd/Cardiff | |
| G-NACP | Norman NAC.6 Fieldmaster | Legistshelfco Ltd/Cardiff | |
| G-NAIL | Cessna 340A | Parelarch Ltd (G-DEXI) | |
| G-NALI | Cessna 152 | N. A. Ali (G-BHVM) | |
| G-NASH | AA-5A Cheetah | M. J. Dant/Southampton | |

| Notes | Reg. | Type | Owner or Operator |
|-------|------|------|-------------------|
| | G-NATT | R. Commander 114A | Northgleam Ltd |
| | G-NATX | Cameron O-65 balloon | A. Faulkner |
| | G-NATY | H. S. Gnat T.1 | Jet Heritage Ltd/Bournemouth |
| | G-NAVO | PA-31-325 Navajo C/R | Mega Yield Ltd (G-BMPV) |
| | G-NAVY | D.H.104 Sea Devon C.20 (XJ348) | Hayward & Green Ltd (G-AMXX)/ Shoreham |
| | G-NAZO | PA-31-310 Navajo B | Pathway Holdings Ltd (G-AZIM) |
| | G-NBDD | Robin DR.400/180 | D. Dufton/Sherburn |
| | G-NBSI | Cameron N-77 balloon | Nottingham Hot-Air Balloon Club |
| | G-NCUB | Piper J-3C-65 Cub | N. Thomson (G-BGXV)/Norwich |
| | G-NDGC | Grob G.109 | C. H. Appleyard |
| | G-NDNI | NDN-1 Firecracker | Norman Marsh Aircraft Ltd |
| | G-NEAL | PA-32 Cherokee Six 260 | Midland Aircraft Maintenance Ltd (G-BFPY) |
| | G-NEEL | Rotorway Executive 90 | P. N. Haigh |
| | G-NEEP | Bell 206B JetRanger | Dollar Air Services Ltd/Coventry |
| | G-NEGS | Thunder Ax7-77 balloon | R. Holden |
| | G-NEIL | Thunder Ax3 balloon | Islington Motors (Trowbridge) Ltd |
| | G-NEPB | Cameron N-77 balloon | The Post Office |
| | G-NEUS | Brügger MB.2 Colibri | G. E. Smeaton |
| | G-NEVL | Learjet 35A | Atlantic Learjet Sales Ltd |
| | G-NEWR | PA-31-350 Navajo Chieftain | Eastern Air Executive Ltd/Sturgate |
| | G-NEWS | Bell 206B JetRanger 3 | Peter Press Ltd |
| | G-NEWT | Beech 35 Bonanza | D. W. Mickleburgh (G-APVW) |
| | G-NGBI | AA-5B Tiger | Filemart Ltd (G-JAKK/G-BHWI)/ Biggin Hill |
| | G-NGRM | Spezio DAL.1 | P. A. Crawford |
| | G-NHRH | PA-28 Cherokee 140 | H. Dodd |
| | G-NHVH | Maule M5-235C Lunar Rocket | Commercial Go-Karts Ltd/Exeter |
| | G-NICH | Robinson R-22B | Panair Ltd |
| | G-NICK | PA-18 Super Cub 95 | J. G. O'Donnell & I. Woolacott |
| | G-NICO | Robinson R-22B | N. G. Cook |
| | G-NIFR | Beech 76 Duchess | J. J. Baumhardt |
| | G-NIGB | Boeing 747-211B | British Airways *City of Gloucester* |
| | G-NIGE | Luscombe 8E Silvaire | Pullmerit Ltd (G-BSHG) |
| | G-NIGS | Thunder Ax7-65 balloon | A. N. F. Pertwee |
| | G-NIKD | Cameron O-120 balloon | D. S. King |
| | G-NIKE | PA-28-181 Archer II | Key Properties Ltd/White Waltham |
| | G-NIKY | PA-31-350 Navajo Chieftain | Subtec Aviation Ltd (G-BPAR)/Shoreham |
| | G-NINA | PA-28-161 Warrior II | Bailey Aviation Ltd (G-BEUC) |
| | G-NIOS | PA-32R-301 Saratoga SP | Metafin Holdings Ltd |
| | G-NISR | R. Commander 690A | Z. I. Bilbeisi |
| | G-NITA | PA-28 Cherokee 180 | Universal Air Services Ltd (G-AVVG) |
| | G-NIUK | Douglas DC-10-30 | British Airways *Cairn Edward Forest*/ Gatwick |
| | G-NJAG | Cessna 207 | G. H. Nolan Ltd |
| | G-NJSH | Robinson R-22B | T. F. Hawes |
| | G-NNAC | PA-18 Super Cub 135 | P. A. Wilde |
| | G-NOBI | Spezio Sport HES-1 | M. R. Clark |
| | G-NOBY | Rand KR-2 | N. P. Rieser |
| | G-NODE | AA-5B Tiger | Curd & Green Ltd/Elstree |
| | G-NONI | AA-5 Traveler | D. R. Ranger (G-BBDA) |
| | G-NORD | SNCAN NC.854 | H. J. Taggart |
| | G-NORS | Cessna 425 | Arrowbridge Ltd/Gamston |
| | G-NOTT | Nott ULD-2 balloon | J. R. P. Nott |
| | G-NOVO | Colt AS-56 airship | Rowntree Mackintosh Confectionery Ltd |
| | G-NRDC | NDN-6 Fieldmaster | The Norman Aeroplane Co Ltd/Cardiff |
| | G-NROA | Boeing 727-217 | Dan-Air Services Ltd (G-BKNG)/Gatwick |
| | G-NSTG | Cessna F.150F | N. S. T. Griffin (G-ATNI)/Blackpool |
| | G-NTBI | Bell 206B JetRanger 3 | E. Midlands Helicopters Ltd |
| | G-NTOO | SA.365N-2 Dauphin 2 | Bond Helicopters Ltd |
| | G-NTWO | SA.365N-2 Dauphin 2 | Bond Helicopters Ltd |
| | G-NUIG | Beech C90-1 King Air | Norwich Union Fire Insurance Soc (G-BKIP) |
| | G-NUTZ | AS.355F-1 Twin Squirrel | Lake & Elliot Helicopters Ltd (G-BLRI) |
| | G-NWPR | Cameron N-77 balloon | Post Office N.W. Postal Board |
| | G-NYTE | Cessna F.337G | County Garage Ltd (G-BATH) |
| | G-NZGL | Cameron O-105 balloon | P. G. & P. M. Vale |
| | G-NZSS | Boeing Stearman N2S-5 (343251) | Pacific Shelf 331 Ltd |
| | G-OAAC | Airtour AH-77B balloon | Army Air Corps |
| | G-OAAL | PA-38-112 Tomahawk | Cumbernauld Aviation Ltd |

| Reg. | Type | Owner or Operator | Notes |
|------|------|-------------------|-------|
| G-OAAS | Short SD3-60 Variant 100 | Aurigny Air Services Ltd (G-BLIL)/ Guernsey | |
| G-OABC | Colt 69A balloon | Airship & Balloon Co Ltd | |
| G-OABG | Hughes 369E | A. B. Gee of Ripley | |
| G-OABI | Cessna 421C | Blue Star Ship Management Ltd | |
| G-OACE | Valentin Taifun 17E | Aero Club Enstone | |
| G-OADY | Beech 76 Duchess | M. T. Dawson | |
| G-OAEL | AA-5A Cheetah | Light Aircraft Group | |
| G-OAEX | Short SD3-60 | Air Europe Express (G-SALU/G-BKZR)/ Gatwick | |
| G-OAFB | Beech 200 Super King Air | A. F. Budge Ltd/Gamston | |
| G-OAFC | Airtour 56AH balloon | P. J. Donnellan & L. A. Watts | |
| G-OAFT | Cessna 152 | L. E. Steynor (G-BNKM) | |
| G-OAFY | SA.341G Gazelle 1 | R. J. Best (G-SFTH/G-BLAP) | |
| G-OAHF | Boeing 757-27B | Britannia Airways Ltd/Luton | |
| G-OAHI | Boeing 757-27B | Britannia Airways Ltd/Luton | |
| G-OAHK | Boeing 757-23A | Britannia Airways Ltd/Luton | |
| G-OAJF | BAe 146-300 | British Aerospace PLC/Hatfield | |
| G-OAJH | AA-5A Cheetah | BLS Aviation (G-KILT/G-BJFA)/ Elstree | |
| G-OAJS | Airbus A.300-605R | Monarch Airlines Ltd/Luton | |
| G-OAKC | PA-31-350 Navajo Chieftain | Air Kilroe Ltd (G-WSSC)/Manchester | |
| G-OAKJ | BAe Jetstream 3200 | Air Kilroe Ltd (G-BOTJ)/Manchester | |
| G-OAKL | Beech 200 Super King Air | Air Kilroe Ltd (G-BJZG)/Manchester | |
| G-OAKM | Beech 200 Super King Air | Air Kilroe Ltd (G-BCUZ)/Manchester | |
| G-OAKZ | Beech C90A King Air | Barratt Developments Ltd | |
| G-OALD | SOCATA TB.20 Trinidad | Mike Little Preparations Ltd | |
| G-OALF | Dornier Do.228-201K | Region Airways Ltd (G-MLDO)/ Southend | |
| G-OALM | McD Douglas MD-11 | Air Europe Ltd/Gatwick | |
| G-OAMG | Bell 206B JetRanger 3 | Millfields Estate Ltd | |
| G-OAMY | Cessna 152 | Warwickshire Flying Training Centre Ltd/Birmingham | |
| G-OANC | PA-28-161 Warrior II | Woodvale Aviation Co Ltd (G-BFAD) | |
| G-OANT | PA-23 Aztec 250 | Air Navigation & Trading Ltd (G-TRFM)/ Blackpool | |
| G-OAPR | Brantly B.2B | Helicopter International Magazine/ Weston-s-Mare | |
| G-OAPW | Glaser-Dirks DG.400 | A. P. Walsh | |
| G-OARV | ARV Super 2 | H. Pound | |
| G-OASH | Robinson R-22B | A. S. Hawkridge | |
| G-OATC | PA-31-310 Turbo Navajo C | Roger Clark Mechanical Engineering Ltd (G-OJPW/G-BGCC) | |
| G-OATP | BAe ATP | Manx Airlines Ltd (G-BZWW)/ *King Godred Crovan 1079-1095/* Ronaldsway | |
| G-OATS | PA-38-112 Tomahawk | Truman Aviation Ltd/Tollerton | |
| G-OATV | Cameron V-77 balloon | Gone With The Wind Ltd | |
| G-OAUS | Sikorsky S-76A | Darley Stud Management Co Ltd | |
| G-OAVX | Beech 200 Super King Air | AVX Ltd (G-IBCA/G-BMCA)/Blackbushe | |
| G-OAWY | Cessna 340A | Industrial Alum Ltd | |
| G-OBAA | Beech B200 Super King Air | BAA PLC | |
| G-OBAL | Mooney M.20J | Britannia Airways Ltd/Luton | |
| G-OBAT | Cessna F.152 | J. J. Baumhardt | |
| G-OBBC | Colt 90A balloon | R. A. & M. A. Riley | |
| G-OBEA | BAe Jetstream 3102-01 | Birmingham European Airways Ltd | |
| G-OBED | PA-34-200T Seneca II | V. J. Holden/Newcastle | |
| G-OBEL | Cessna 500 Citation | Gator Aviation Ltd (G-BOGA) | |
| G-OBEY | PA-23 Aztec 250C | Creaton Aircraft Services (G-BAAJ) | |
| G-OBHX | Cessna F.172H | Jones Aviation Sales Ltd (G-AWMU) | |
| G-OBIL | Robinson R-22B | F. C. Noakes & M. R. Tideswell | |
| G-OBIP | Robinson R-22B | D. W. Wetherell | |
| G-OBLC | Beech 76 Duchess | F. J. Duckworth Ltd | |
| G-OBMA | Boeing 737-33A | British Midland Airways Ltd/E. Midlands | |
| G-OBMB | Boeing 737-33A | British Midland Airways Ltd/E. Midlands | |
| G-OBMC | Boeing 737-33A | British Midland Airways Ltd/E. Midlands | |
| G-OBMD | Boeing 737-33A | British Midland Airways Ltd/E. Midlands | |
| G-OBMF | Boeing 737-4Y0 | British Midland Airways Ltd/E. Midlands | |
| G-OBMG | Boeing 737-4Y0 | British Midland Airways Ltd/E. Midlands | |
| G-OBMH | Boeing 737-33A | British Midland Airways Ltd/E. Midlands | |
| G-OBMJ | Boeing 737-33A | British Midland Airways Ltd/E. Midlands | |
| G-OBMS | Cessna F.172N | D. Beverley & W. F. van Schoten | |
| G-OBMW | AA-5 Traveler | Fretcourt Ltd (G-BDPV) | |

| Notes | Reg. | Type | Owner or Operator |
|-------|------|------|-------------------|
| | G-OBOH | Short SD3-60 | Jersey European Airways (G-BNDJ) |
| | G-OBPG | Brantly B.2B | A. C. Dent (G-AWIO) |
| | G-OBSF | AA-5A Cheetah | Lowlog Ltd (G-ODSF/G-BEUW) |
| | G-OBSV | Partenavia P.68B Observer | Skywatch Ltd/Birmingham |
| | G-OBUD | Colt 69A balloon | Hot-Air Balloon Co Ltd |
| | G-OCAN | Cessna 340A | Ripley Aviation Ltd |
| | G-OCAP | Bell 206B JetRanger 3 | Capital Computers (G-OACS) |
| | G-OCAR | Colt 77A balloon | M. D. Cookson |
| | G-OCAT | Eiri PIK-20E | W. A. D. Thorp/Doncaster |
| | G-OCBA | H.S.125 Srs 3B | CB Helicopters (G-MRFB/G-AZVS) |
| | G-OCBB | Bell 206B JetRanger 2 | CG Group Ltd (G-BASE) |
| | G-OCBC | Cameron A-120 balloon | Corporate Balloon Co |
| | G-OCCA | PA-32R-301 Saratoga SP | CC Aviation Ltd (G-BRIX)/Elstree |
| | G-OCCC | BAe 125 Srs 800B | Consolidated Contractors International |
| | G-OCDS | Aviamilano F.8L Falco II | P. G. Greenslade & P. J. Collins (G-VEGL) |
| | G-OCGJ | Robinson R-22B | The Levitt Group Ltd |
| | G-OCHL | Bell 206B JetRanger 2 | Southern Air Ltd/Shoreham |
| | G-OCJK | Schweizer 269C | M. D. Thorpe |
| | G-OCJR | SA.341G Gazelle 1 | Reeds Motor Co (G-BRGS) |
| | G-OCND | Cameron O-77 balloon | D. P. H. Smith & Dalby |
| | G-OCNW | BAC One-Eleven 201AC | British Air Ferries (G-ASJH)/Stansted |
| | G-OCPC | Cessna FA.152 | Westward Airways (Lands End) Ltd/ St Just |
| | G-OCPL | AA-5A Cheetah | Walsh Aviation Ltd (G-RCPW/G-BERM) |
| | G-OCTA | BN-2A Mk III-2 Trislander | GB Airways Ltd (G-BCXW)/Gibraltar |
| | G-OCTI | PA-32 Cherokee Six 260 | J. K. Sharkey (G-BGZX)/Elstree |
| | G-OCTU | PA-28-161 Cadet | J. P. Alexander |
| | G-OCUB | Piper J-3C-90 Cub | C. A. Foss & P. A. Brook/Shoreham |
| | G-OCWC | AA-5A Cheetah | BLS Aviation Ltd (G-WULL)/Elstree |
| | G-ODAH | Aerotek-Pitts S.2A Special | S. E. Marples (G-BDKS) |
| | G-ODAM | AA-5A Cheetah | D. Hilditch/Elstree |
| | G-ODAY | Cameron N-56 balloon | C. O. Day (Estate Agents) |
| | G-ODEL | Falconar F-11-3 | G. F. Brummell |
| | G-ODEN | PA-28-161 Cadet | J. Appleton |
| | G-ODER | Cameron O-77 balloon | W. H. Morgan |
| | G-ODHL | Cameron N-77 balloon | DHL International (UK) Ltd |
| | G-ODIL | Bell 206B JetRanger | Assetglobal Ltd |
| | G-ODIR | PA-23 Aztec 250D | Air Direct Ltd (G-AZGB)/Southampton |
| | G-ODIY | Colt 69A balloon | Flying Pictures (Balloons) Ltd |
| | G-ODJP | Robinson R-22 | Hawkspire Ltd |
| | G-ODLG | D.H.114 Heron 2 | D. Liddle-Grainger (G-ARKU) |
| | G-ODLY | Cessna 310J | R. J. Huband (G-TUBY/G-ASZZ) |
| | G-ODMC | AS.350B-1 Ecureuil | D. M. Coombs (G-BPVF) |
| | G-ODMM | PA-31-350 Navajo Chieftain | Birmingham Aviation Ltd |
| | G-ODNP | Cessna 310R | Bostonair Ltd/Humberside |
| | G-ODSC | Enstrom 280FX | Heliflair Ltd (G-BSDZ)/Shoreham |
| | G-OEAC | Mooney M.20J | Trifik Services Ltd |
| | G-OECH | AA-5A Cheetah | G. W. Plowman & Sons Ltd (G-BKBE) |
| | G-OEDB | PA-38-112 Tomahawk | Air Delta Bravo Ltd (G-BGGJ)/Elstree |
| | G-OEDP | Cameron N-77 balloon | M. J. Betts & Eastern Counties Newspapers |
| | G-OEEC | Short SD3-60 Variant 100 | Shorts Aircraft Financing Ltd (G-BPKY) |
| | G-OEGG | Cameron 65 Egg SS balloon | Airship & Balloon Co Ltd |
| | G-OESX | PA-23 Aztec 250E | Greenacre Services Ltd (G-BAJX) |
| | G-OEZE | Rutan Vari-Eze | S. Stride & ptnrs |
| | G-OFCM | Cessna F172L | F. C. M Aviation Ltd (G-AZUN)/Guernsey |
| | G-OFER | PA-18 Super Cub 150 | M. S. W. Meagher |
| | G-OFHJ | Cessna 441 | Tilling Associates Ltd (G-HSON) |
| | G-OFIT | SOCATA TB.10 Tobago | G. S.M. Brain (G-BRIU) |
| | G-OFIZ | Cameron 80 Can SS balloon | Airship & Balloon Co Ltd |
| | G-OFLI | Colt 105A balloon | Virgin Atlantic Airways Ltd |
| | G-OFLT | EMB-110P1 Bandeirante | Flightline Ltd (G-MOBL)/Southend |
| | G-OFLY | Cessna 210L | A. P. Mothew/Stapleford |
| | G-OFOR | Thunder Ax3 balloon | A. Walker |
| | G-OFOX | Denney Aerocraft Kitfox | P. R. Skeels |
| | G-OFRB | Everett gyroplane | F. R. Blennerhassett |
| | G-OFRH | Cessna 421C | Rogers Aviation Sales Ltd (G-NORX)/ Cranfield |
| | G-OFTI | PA-28 Cherokee 140 | FTI Aviation Ltd (G-BRKU)/Biggin Hill |
| | G-OFUN | Valentin Taifun 17E | J. A. Sangster/Booker |
| | G-OGAR | PZL SZD-45A Ogar | K. E. Ballington |
| | G-OGAS | Westland WG.30 Srs 100 | British International Helicopters Ltd (G-BKNW)/Aberdeen |

| Reg. | Type | Owner or Operator | Notes |
|------|------|-------------------|-------|
| G-OGCA | PA-28-161 Warrior II | GC Aviation/Newtownards | |
| G-OGDA | AS.350B Ecureuil | Lomas Helicopters Ltd (G-PLMD/G-NIAL) | |
| G-OGEM | PA-28-181 Archer II | GEM Rewinds Ltd | |
| G-OGET | PA-39 Twin Comanche 160 C/R | P. G. Kitchingman (G-AYXY) | |
| G-OGGS | Thunder Ax8-84 balloon | G. Gamble & Sons (Quorn) Ltd | |
| G-OGIL | Short SD3-30 Variant 100 | Gill Aviation Ltd (G-BITV)/Newcastle | |
| G-OGJS | Puffer Cozy | G. J. Stamper | |
| G-OGOA | AS.350B Ecureuil | Lomas Helicopters (Training) Ltd (G-PLMD/G-NIAL) | |
| G-OGOB | Schweizer 269C | Lomas Helicopters (Training) Ltd (G-GLEE/G-BRUW) | |
| G-OGOS | Everett Autogyro | L. W. Sampson | |
| G-OGRV | PA-31-350 Navajo Chieftain | Grosvenor Aviation Services Ltd (G-BMPX) | |
| G-OGTS | Air Command 532 Elite | GTS Engineering (Coventry) Ltd | |
| G-OHCA | SC.5 Belfast (XR363) | HeavyLift Cargo Airlines Ltd/Southend | |
| G-OHEA | H.S.125 Srs 3B/RA | Rogers Aviation Sales Ltd (G-AVRG)/ Cranfield | |
| G-OHER | Extra EA.300 | L. C. A. Knapp | |
| G-OHHL | Robinson R-22B | Hillar Helicopters Ltd | |
| G-OHIM | Extra EA.300 | R. N. Goode | |
| G-OHMS | AS.355F-1 Twin Squirrel | S.W. Electricity PLC | |
| G-OHOT | V.813 Viscount | British Air Ferries Ltd (G-BMAT/G-AZLT)/Southend | |
| G-OIAN | M.S.880B Rallye Club | Ian Richard Transport Services Ltd | |
| G-OIBM | R. Commander 114 | South Coast Computers Ltd (G-BLVZ) | |
| G-OIBO | PA-28 Cherokee 180 | M. J. & J. E. Moxley (G-AVAZ) | |
| G-OICS | Bell 206A JetRanger | Lotwatch Ltd | |
| G-OIDW | Cessna F.150GF | I. D. Wakeling | |
| G-OIEA | PA-31P Pressurised Navajo | Inter European Airways Ltd (G-BBTW)/Cardiff | |
| G-OIMC | Cessna 152 | E. Midlands Flying School Ltd | |
| G-OING | AA-5A Cheetah ★ | Abraxas Aviation Ltd (G-BFPD)/Denham | |
| G-OINK | Piper J-3C-65 Cub | A. R. Harding (G-BILD/G-KERK) | |
| G-OIOI | EH Industries EH.101 | Westland Helicopters Ltd/Yeovil | |
| G-OIOW | Hughes 369D | Magnum Helicopters (UK) Ltd | |
| G-OISF | Fuji FA.200-180 | Ipswich School of Flying Ltd (G-BAPT) | |
| G-OISO | Cessna FRA.150L | Crisptime Ltd (G-BBJW) | |
| G-OITN | AS.355F-1 Twin Squirrel | Independent Television News Ltd | |
| G-OJAC | Mooney M.20J | Mistral Aviation Ltd | |
| G-OJAE | Hughes 269C | Jade Air Engineering Ltd/Shoreham | |
| G-OJAK | Robinson R-22B | Formwork & Scaffold Systems (GB) Ltd | |
| G-OJAV | BN-2A Mk III-2 Trislander | Janes Aviation Ltd (G-BDOS)/Blackpool | |
| G-OJBA | Beech B200 Super King Air | M1 Machinery Ltd/Luton | |
| G-OJCB | AB-206B JetRanger 2 | G. Day Aviation Ltd | |
| G-OJCW | PA-32RT-300 Lance II | M. J. Metham/Blackbushe | |
| G-OJDC | Thunder Ax7-77 balloon | J. Crosby | |
| G-OJEE | Bede BD-4 | G. Hodges | |
| G-OJET | BAe 146-100 | Manx Airlines Ltd (G-BRJS/G-OBAF/ G-SCHH)/Ronaldsway | |
| G-OJFR | Bell 206B JetRanger | B. E. E. Smith | |
| G-OJGA | Beech 200 Super King Air | RM Aviation Ltd/Leavesden | |
| G-OJIM | PA-28R-201T Turbo Arrow III | Motomecca Spares Ltd | |
| G-OJJB | Mooney M.20K | Jeff Brown (Aviation Services) | |
| G-OJMR | Airbus A.300-605R | Monarch Airlines Ltd/Luton | |
| G-OJON | Taylor JT.2 Titch | J. H. Fell | |
| G-OJPI | Robinson R-22B | John Battleday at Kirton Farms Ltd | |
| G-OJSY | Short SD3-60 | Jersey European/Business Air (G-BKKT) | |
| G-OJUG | PA-31-350 Navajo Chieftain | Air International (Manchester) Ltd (G-SCOT) | |
| G-OJVC | J/1N Alpha | M. C. Boddington & P. D. Castle (G-AHCL)/Sywell | |
| G-OJVH | Cessna F.150H | Yorkshire Light Aircraft Ltd (G-AWJZ)/ Leeds | |
| G-OJVI | Robinson R-22B | JV Investments Ltd (G-OJVJ) | |
| G-OJWS | PA-28-161 Warrior II | J. W. Sharman | |
| G-OKAG | PA-28R Cherokee Arrow 180 | Panorama Design Consultants Ltd | |
| G-OKAT | AS.350B Ecureuil | Tom Walkinshaw Racing Ltd (G-BGIM) | |
| G-OKAY | Pitts S-1E Special | Aerial & Aerobatic Service/Booker | |
| G-OKCC | Cameron N-90 balloon | Kerridge Computer Co Ltd | |
| G-OKEN | PA-28R-201T Turbo Arrow III | K. Hassall | |
| G-OKIT | Rotorway Executive | C. W. Thomas | |

| Notes | Reg. | Type | Owner or Operator |
|---|---|---|---|
| | G-OKSP | Cessna 500 Citation | Osiwel Ltd/Leavesden |
| | G-OKYA | Cameron V-77 balloon | 14/20 Kings Hussars |
| | G-OKYM | PA-28 Cherokee 140 | D. Hotham (G-AVLS) |
| | G-OLAF | Beech C90 King Air | Westair Flying Services Ltd (G-BFVX)/ Blackpool |
| | G-OLAU | Robinson R-22B | P. M. Green |
| | G-OLBA | Short SD3-60 Variant 100 | Shorts Aircraft Financing Ltd (G-BOFG) |
| | G-OLBC | PA-23 Aztec 250 | Metronote Business Group Ltd (G-BHCT)/Denham |
| | G-OLCA | BAe 146-200 | Loganair Ltd/Glasgow |
| | G-OLCB | BAe 146-200 | Loganair Ltd/Glasgow |
| | G-OLCC | BAe ATP | Loganair Ltd/Glasgow |
| | G-OLCD | BAe ATP | Loganair Ltd/Glasgow |
| | G-OLDN | Bell 206L LongRanger | A. G. M. Davis (G-TBCA/G-BFAL) |
| | G-OLDY | Luton LA-5 Major | M. P. & A. P. Sargent |
| | G-OLEE | Cessna F.152 | Warwickshire Flying Training Centre Ltd/Birmingham |
| | G-OLES | Partenavia P.68C | D. Henrikson (G-JAJV) |
| | G-OLFC | PA-38-112 Tomahawk | T. F. L. Hayes (G-BGZG) |
| | G-OLFR | H.S. 125 Srs 403B | Osprey Aviation Ltd (G-BRXR/G-AXYJ)/ Dunsfold |
| | G-OLFS | M.S.880B Rallye Club | M. A. Kempson (G-AYYZ)/Dunkeswell |
| | G-OLFT | R. Commander 114 | B. C. Richens (G-WJMN)/Redhill |
| | G-OLGW | Short SD3-60 Variant 100 | Shorts Aircraft Financing Ltd (G-BOFK) |
| | G-OLIE | Robinson R-22B | Optionbuild Ltd (G-BOUW) |
| | G-OLIZ | Robinson R-22B | H. Pelham |
| | G-OLLE | Cameron O-84 balloon | N. A. Robertson |
| | G-OLLI | Cameron O-31 SS balloon | N. A. Robertson |
| | G-OLLY | PA-31-350 Navajo Chieftain | Compass Aviation Ltd (G-BCES) |
| | G-OLMA | Partenavia P.68B | C. M. Evans (G-BGBT) |
| | G-OLRT | Robinson R-22B | Lambourne Racehorse Transport Ltd |
| | G-OLSC | Cessna 182A | London Skydiving Centre Ltd (G-ATNU)/Cranfield |
| | G-OLSF | PA-28-161 Cadet | BLS Aviation Ltd/Elstree |
| | G-OLTN | Short SD3-60 Variant 100 | Shorts Aircraft Financing Ltd (G-BOFH) |
| | G-OLUM | Robinson R-22B | P. A. Fraser |
| | G-OLVR | FRED Srs 2 | A. R. Oliver |
| | G-OMAC | Cessna FR.172E | R. Knox & R. Conway |
| | G-OMAF | Dornier Do.228-200 | FR Aviation Ltd/Bournemouth |
| | G-OMAR | PA-34-220T Seneca III | Redhill Flying Club |
| | G-OMAT | PA-28 Cherokee 140 | Midland Air Training School (G-JIMY/ G-AYUG)/Coventry |
| | G-OMAX | Brantly B.2B | P. D. Benmax (G-AVJN) |
| | G-OMCL | Cessna 550 Citation II | Quantel Ltd/Biggin Hill |
| | G-OMDH | Hughes 369E | Stilgate Ltd/Booker |
| | G-OMEC | AB-206B JetRanger 3 | Star Construction Group Ltd (G-OBLD) |
| | G-OMED | AA-5B Tiger | Caslon Ltd (G-BERL)/Elstree |
| | G-OMGB | H.S. 125 Srs 600B | Magec Aviation Ltd (G-BKBM/G-BCCL)/ Luton |
| | G-OMHC | PA-28RT-201 Arrow IV | M. H. Cundley/Redhill |
| | G-OMHS | AS.355FD-1 Twin Squirrel | S. W. Electricity PLC |
| | G-OMJB | Bell 206B JetRanger | Martin Brundle (Overseas) Ltd |
| | G-OMMC | Mooney M.20J | A. D. Russell/Bourn |
| | G-OMNI | PA-28R Cherokee Arrow 200D | G. H. Lee |
| | G-OMOB | Robinson R-22B | Triple Oak Ltd/Booker |
| | G-OMOG | AA-5A Cheetah | Popham Flight (G-BHWR) |
| | G-OMPS | PA-28-161 Warrior II | Mircoprose Ltd (G-BOHP) |
| | G-OMRB | Cameron V-77 balloon | M. R. Bayne |
| | G-OMRG | Hoffmann H.36 Dimona | MRG Systems Ltd (G-BLHG) |
| | G-ONAF | Naval Aircraft Factory N3N-1 | P. M. H. Threadway |
| | G-ONCL | Colt 77A balloon | Delphi Marketing Ltd |
| | G-ONEA | Beech 200 Super King Air | Northern Executive Aviation Ltd/ Manchester |
| | G-ONHH | Forney F-1A Aircoupe | H. Dodd (G-ARHA) |
| | G-ONOR | Cessna 425 | Rockville Investments (Jersey) Ltd (G-BKSA) |
| | G-ONOW | Bell 206A JetRanger 2 | Hadley Green Garage Ltd (G-AYMX) |
| | G-ONPI | Thunder Ax10-160 balloon | Ballooning World Ltd |
| | G-ONTA | Hughes 369D | Solid State Logic Ltd |
| | G-ONZO | Cameron N-77 balloon | J. A. Kershaw |
| | G-OOAA | Boeing 737-4YO | Air 2000 |
| | G-OOAB | Boeing 737-4YO | Air 2000 Ltd/Manchester |
| | G-OODE | SNCAN Stampe SV-4C (G) | The Biplane Co Ltd (G-AZNN) |

| Reg. | Type | Owner or Operator | Notes |
|------|------|-------------------|-------|
| G-OODI | Pitts S-1D Special | R. N. Goode (G-BBBU)/White Waltham | |
| G-OODS | Extra EA.230 | R. N. Goode | |
| G-OODW | PA-28-181 Archer II | Goodwood Terrena Ltd | |
| G-OOFI | Cameron N-77 balloon | I. Fishwick | |
| G-OOFY | Rollason Beta | G. Staples | |
| G-OOGA | GA-7 Cougar | Trent Air Services Ltd/Cranfield | |
| G-OOLE | Cessna 172M | Bostonair Ltd (G-BOSI)/Humberside | |
| G-OONE | Mooney M.20J | N. Skipworth/Booker | |
| G-OONI | Thunder Ax7-77 balloon | Fivedata Ltd | |
| G-OONS | AB-206B JetRanger | Bellini Aviation Ltd | |
| G-OONY | PA-28-161 Warrior II | D. A. Field & P. B. Jenkins | |
| G-OOOA | Boeing 757-28A | Air 2000/Canada 3000 (C-FOOA) | |
| G-OOOB | Boeing 757-28A | Air 2000/Canada 3000 (C-FOOB) | |
| G-OOOC | Boeing 757-28A | Air 2000/Canada 3000 (C-....) | |
| G-OOOD | Boeing 757-28A | Air 2000/Canada 3000 (C-FXOD) | |
| G-OOOG | Boeing 757-23A | Air 2000 Ltd/Manchester | |
| G-OOOH | Boeing 757-23A | Air 2000 Ltd/Manchester | |
| G-OOOI | Boeing 757-23A | Air 2000 Ltd/Manchester | |
| G-OOOJ | Boeing 757-23A | Air 2000 Ltd/Manchester | |
| G-OOOM | Boeing 757-225 | Air 2000 Ltd/Manchester | |
| G-OOOO | Mooney M.20J | Michael Jackson Motors Ltd | |
| G-OOSE | Rutan Vari-Eze | J. A. Towers | |
| G-OOXP | Pulsar XP | GW Associates Ltd | |
| G-OPAC | Robinson R-22B | Crest Engineering Ltd | |
| G-OPAG | PA-34-200 Seneca II | Parker & Heard Ltd (G-BNGB) | |
| G-OPAL | Robinson R-22B | Service Graphics Ltd | |
| G-OPAM | Cessna F.152 | Stapleford Flying Club Ltd (G-BFZS) | |
| G-OPAT | Beech 76 Duchess | Ray Holt (Land Drainage) Ltd/(G-BHAO) | |
| G-OPED | Partenavia P.68B | Pedley Woodwork Ltd/(G-BFKP) | |
| G-OPFC | BAe 125-1000 | British Aerospace PLC | |
| G-OPIG | ARV Super 2 | D. Davidson (G-BMSJ) | |
| G-OPIK | Eiri PIK-20E | K. & S. C. A. Dudley | |
| G-OPIT | CFM Streak Shadow Srs SA | L. W. Opit | |
| G-OPIX | Cessna 180K | Steve Bicknell Productions Ltd | |
| G-OPJC | Cessna 152 | PJC Leasing Ltd/Stapleford | |
| G-OPJD | PA-28RT-201T Turbo Arrow IV | North West Aviation Ltd | |
| G-OPKF | Cameron 90 Bowler SS balloon | Flying Pictures (Balloons) Ltd | |
| G-OPOL | H.S.125 Srs F3B/RA | MAGEC Aviation Ltd (G-BXPU/G-IBIS/ G-AXPU)/Luton | |
| G-OPOP | Enstrom 280C-UK-2 Shark | Crewhall Ltd (G-OFED) | |
| G-OPPL | AA-5A Cheetah | London School of Flying Ltd (G-BGNN)/ Elstree | |
| G-OPRO | MDH Hughes 369E | Prodrive Ltd | |
| G-OPSF | PA-38-112 Tomahawk | Panshanger School of Flying (G-BGZI) | |
| G-OPST | Cessna 182R | Lota Ltd/Shoreham | |
| G-OPUP | B.121 Pup 2 | P. W. Hunter (G-AXEU) | |
| G-OPWL | Bell 206B JetRanger 3 | PWL Records Ltd (G-BPCZ) | |
| G-ORAF | CFM Streak Shadow | G. A. & S. M. Taylor | |
| G-ORAY | Cessna F.182Q II | C. Robinson (G-BHDN)/Blackpool | |
| G-ORBY | Sukhoi Su-26MX | R. N. Goode/White Waltham | |
| G-ORCE | Cessna 550 Citation II | Oracle Corporation UK Ltd (G-MINE) | |
| G-ORCL | Cessna 421C | Oracle Corporation UK Ltd | |
| G-ORDN | PA-31R Cherokee Arrow 200-II | A. S. & A. M. Gordon (G-BAJT) | |
| G-ORED | BN-2T Islander | The Red Devils (G-BJYW)/Farnborough | |
| G-OREG | BN-2A Mk III-1 Trislander | Channel Air Shuttle Ltd (G-OAVVW/G-AZLJ) | |
| G-ORFC | Jurca MJ.5 Sirocco | D. J. Phillips | |
| G-ORGI | Hawker Hurricane IIB | Charles Church Displays Ltd | |
| G-ORJW | Laverda F.8L Falco Srs 4 | W. R. M. Sutton | |
| G-ORMB | Robinson R-22B | R. M. Bailey | |
| G-ORME | Bell 206B JetRanger | Dollar Air Services Ltd/Coventry | |
| G-ORMP | Cessna 414A | Ascham Aviation/Bournemouth | |
| G-OROB | Robinson R-22B | Corniche Helicopters (G-TBFC) | |
| G-OROD | PA-18 Super Cub 150 | R. J. O. Walker | |
| G-ORON | Cameron 77A balloon | A. M. Rocliffe | |
| G-ORPR | Cameron O-77 balloon | Outright PR Ltd | |
| G-ORSJ | D.H.114 Heron 2 | D. Liddle-Grainger (G-ARKW) | |
| G-ORTC | Bell 206B JetRanger 2 | Fitview Ltd (G-BPNG) | |
| G-ORTM | Glaser-Dirks DG.400 | I. M. Stromberg/Barton | |
| G-ORVB | McCulloch J-2 | R. V. Bowles (G-BLGI/G-BKKL) | |
| G-ORZZ | Robinson R-22B | Sloane Helicopters Ltd/Sywell | |
| G-OSAB | Enstrom 280FX | Southern Air Ltd/Shoreham | |
| G-OSAL | Cessna 421C | Cityshare Ltd | |

| Notes | Reg. | Type | Owner or Operator |
|---|---|---|---|
| | G-OSCC | PA-32 Cherokee Six 300 | Plant Aviation Ltd (G-BGFD)/Elstree |
| | G-OSDI | Beech 95-58 Baron | Archer Aviation Ltd (G-BHFY) |
| | G-OSEA | BN-2B-26 Islander | W. T. Johnson & Sons (Huddersfield) Ltd |
| | G-OSEB | Bell 222 | Air Hanson Sales Ltd (G-BNDA) |
| | G-OSEE | Robinson R-22B | Aquaprint Ltd |
| | G-OSFC | Cessna F.152 | Stapleford Flying Club Ltd (G-BIVJ) |
| | G-OSHA | Hughes 269C | Starline Helicopters Ltd |
| | G-OSHB | Hughes 269B | Starline Helicopters Ltd |
| | G-OSHC | Hughes 269C | Starline Helicopters Ltd/Biggin Hill |
| | G-OSHL | Robinson R-22B | Sloane Helicopters Ltd |
| | G-OSIX | PA-32 Cherokee Six 260 | Strata Surveys Ltd (G-AZMO) |
| | G-OSKY | Cessna 172M | G-OSKY (1990) |
| | G-OSLO | Schwiezer 269C | IMM Ltd |
| | G-OSMC | Cessna 550 Citation II | SMC Aviation Ltd |
| | G-OSNB | Cessna 550 Citation II | Scottish & Newcastle Breweries PLC (G-JFRS) |
| | G-OSND | Cessna FRA.150M | J. J. Baumhardt (G-BDOU)/Southend |
| | G-OSOO | Hughes 369E | Malcolm Wilson (Motorsport) Ltd |
| | G-OSPI | Robinson R-22B | L. R. Pond/Denham |
| | G-OSRF | Cessna 421C | Marginslot Ltd/Elstree |
| | G-OSST | Colt 77A balloon | British Airways PLC |
| | G-OSSY | PA-28-181 Archer II | Bryan Goss Motorcycles Ltd/ Bournemouth |
| | G-OSUE | Bell 206B JetRanger 3 | British Car Auctions (Aviation) Ltd (G-BKBY) |
| | G-OTAL | ARV Super 2 | J. R. Nutter & S. Cole (G-BNGZ) |
| | G-OTAM | Cessna 172M | T. W. Woods |
| | G-OTAX | PA-31-350 Navajo Chieftain | Jet West Ltd/Exeter |
| | G-OTEL | Thunder Ax8-90 balloon | Stakis Hotels & Inns Ltd |
| | G-OTHE | Enstrom 280C-UK Shark | The Engineering Co Ltd (G-OPJT/ G-BKCO) |
| | G-OTIM | Bensen B.8MV | T. J. Deane |
| | G-OTMC | Beech 400 Beechjet | Tarmac Aviation Ltd |
| | G-OTOE | Aeronca 7AC Champion | J. M. Gale (G-BRWW) |
| | G-OTOW | Cessna 175BX | G-OTOW Flying Group (G-AROC) |
| | G-OTRG | Cessna TR.182RG | A. Hopper |
| | G-OTSB | BN-2A Mk III-2 Trislander | Aurigny Air Services Ltd (G-BDTO) |
| | G-OTSL | Agusta A.109A Srs II | Direct Smooth Ltd |
| | G-OTSW | Pitts S-1E Special | R. A. Bowes (G-BLHE) |
| | G-OTUG | PA-18 Super Cub 150 | B. Walker & Co (Dursley) Ltd |
| | G-OTVS | BN-2T Islander | Headcorn Parachute Club Ltd (G-BPBN/ G-BCMY) |
| | G-OTWO | Rutan Defiant | D. G. Foreman |
| | G-OUAE | Cameron 90 Wimmi Airbus SS balloon | Airship & Balloon Co Ltd |
| | G-OULD | Gould Mk I balloon | C. A. Gould |
| | G-OUSA | Colt 105A balloon | Continental Airlines Inc |
| | G-OUVI | Cameron O-105 balloon | Windsor Pharmaceuticals Ltd |
| | G-OVAA | Colt Jumbo SS balloon | Airship & Balloon Co Ltd |
| | G-OVAN | SC.7 Skyvan 3 Variant 100 | Peterborough Parachute Centre (G-AYZA)/Sibson |
| | G-OVAX | Colt AS-80 Mk II airship | Vax Appliances Ltd |
| | G-OVFM | Cessna 120 | Storyteller Cassettes Ltd |
| | G-OVFR | Cessna F.172N | C. & A. Jenkins Ltd |
| | G-OVMC | Cessna F.152 II | Staverton Flying Services Ltd |
| | G-OVNE | Cessna 401A | M. A. Billings/Ipswich |
| | G-OVNR | Robinson R-22B | Davron Aviation |
| | G-OWAC | Cessna F.152 | Barnes Olson Aeroleasing Ltd (G-BHEB) |
| | G-OWAK | Cessna F.152 | Falcon Flying Services (G-BHEA) |
| | G-OWAR | PA-28-161 Warrior II | Biblio Aviation Ltd/Denham |
| | G-OWEL | Colt 105A balloon | Autohaus of Aylesbury Ltd |
| | G-OWEN | K & S Jungster | R. C. Owen |
| | G-OWIN | BN-2A-8 Islander | UK Parachute Services Ltd (G-AYXE) |
| | G-OWIZ | Luscombe 8A Silvaire | J. Wilson & J. V. George |
| | G-OWNR | Beech 200 Super King Air | Owners Abroad Group PLC/Luton |
| | G-OWVA | PA-28 Cherokee 140 | Woodvale Aviation Co Ltd |
| | G-OWWF | Colt 2500A balloon | Virgin Atlantic Airways Ltd |
| | G-OWYN | Aviamilano F.14 Nibbio | J. R. Wynn |
| | G-OXEC | Cessna 500 Citation | IF Aviation Ltd |
| | G-OXTC | PA-23 Aztec 250D | Falcon Flying Services (G-AZOD)/ Biggin Hill |

| Reg. | Type | Owner or Operator | Notes |
|------|------|-------------------|-------|
| G-OXVI | V.S.361 Spitfire LF.XVIe | BAC Aviation Ltd | |
| G-OYAK | Yakovlev C-11 | E. K. Coventry | |
| G-OZOI | Cessna R.182 | Velcourt (East) Ltd (G-ROBK) | |
| G-OZUP | Colt 77A balloon | Yanin International Ltd | |
| G-PACE | Robin R.1180T | Millicron Instruments Ltd/Coventry | |
| G-PACK | Cessna 152 | Gray Tuplin Ltd/Denham | |
| G-PACY | Rutan Vari-Viggen | E. Pace | |
| G-PADI | Cameron V-77 balloon | T. R. Duffell | |
| G-PALS | Enstrom 280C-UK-2 Shark | Sonus Wholesale Audio Products | |
| G-PAMI | AS.355F-1 Twin Squirrel | Lynton Aviation Ltd (G-BUSA) | |
| G-PAMS | PA-60 Aerostar 601P | Averglen Ltd (G-GAIR) | |
| G-PAPU | Beech 58PA Baron | ADL Aviation Ltd (G-NIPU) | |
| G-PARA | Cessna 207 | Paraski/Swansea | |
| G-PARI | Cessna 172RG Cutlass | Applied Signs Ltd | |
| G-PARS | Evans VP-2 | A. Parsfield | |
| G-PART | Partenavia P.68B | Phlight Avia Ltd/Coventry | |
| G-PASA | MBB Bo 105D | Medical Aviation Services Ltd (G-BGWP)/Shoreham | |
| G-PASB | MBB Bo 105D | Medical Aviation Services Ltd (G-BDMC)/Shoreham | |
| G-PASC | MBB Bo 105DBS/4 | Police Aviation Services Ltd (G-BNPS) | |
| G-PASD | MBB Bo 105DBS/4 | Police Aviation Services Ltd (G-BNRS) | |
| G-PASE | AS.355F-1 Twin Squirrel | Police Aviation Services Ltd | |
| G-PASW | BN-2A Islander | Police Aviation Services Ltd (G-AXXJ) | |
| G-PASX | MBB Bo 105DBS/4 | Police Aviation Services Ltd | |
| G-PASY | BN-2A-26 Islander | Medical Aviation Services Ltd (G-BPCB/G-BEXA/G-MALI-G-DIVE)/Shoreham | |
| G-PASZ | BN-2A-26 Islander | Medical Aviation Services Ltd (G-BPCD/G-BFNV)/Shoreham | |
| G-PATY | Colt Flying Sausage balloon | Colt Balloons Ltd | |
| G-PAWL | PA-28 Cherokee 140 | A. M. & D. Fitton (G-AWEU) | |
| G-PAWS | AA-5A Cheetah | J. Tolhurst | |
| G-PAXX | PA-20 Pacer 135 | D. W. & M. R. Grace | |
| G-PBBT | Cameron N-56 balloon | British Telecom PLC | |
| G-PBHF | Robinson R-22B | Broughton-Hall Security Fencing | |
| G-PBWH | BAe 125 Srs 800B | Lynton Aviation Ltd | |
| G-PCUB | PA-18 Super Cub 135 | M. J. Wilson/Redhill | |
| G-PDHJ | Cessna T.182R | P. G. Vallance | |
| G-PDOC | PA-44-180 Seminole | Medicare (G-PVAF) | |
| G-PDON | WMB.2 Windtracker balloon | P. Donnellan | |
| G-PDSI | Cessna 172N | Quick Logic Ltd | |
| G-PEAL | Aerotek Pitts S-2A | Hallmark Aerobatics Ltd | |
| G-PEAT | Cessna 421B | Forest City Export Ltd (G-BBIJ)/Manchester | |
| G-PEEL | BAe ATP | Manx Airlines Ltd/*King Scmerled (1158-1164)* | |
| G-PEET | Cessna 401A | Air & General Services Ltd | |
| G-PEGG | Colt 90A balloon | Michael Pegg Partnership Ltd | |
| G-PEGI | PA-34-200T Seneca II | Tayflite Ltd | |
| G-PEKT | SOCATA TB.20 Trinidad | Pektron Ltd | |
| G-PELE | Cameron 80 Pele SS balloon | Cameron Balloons Ltd | |
| G-PENN | AA-5B Tiger | Compair | |
| G-PENY | Sopwith LC-1T Triplane (5492) | J. S. Penny | |
| G-PERL | Robinson R-22B | R. Fawcett | |
| G-PERR | Cameron 60 bottle balloon | The Balloon Stable Ltd | |
| G-PERS | Colt Soapbox SS balloon | G. V. Beckwith | |
| G-PEST | Hawker Tempest II | Autokraft Ltd | |
| G-PETR | PA-28 Cherokee 140 | E. W. Keeble/Ipswich (G-BCJL) | |
| G-PFAA | EAA Biplane Model P | P. E. Barker | |
| G-PFAB | Colomban MC.15 Cri-Cri | P. Fabish | |
| G-PFAC | FRED Srs 2 | G. R. Yates | |
| G-PFAD | Wittman W.8 Tailwind | M. R. Stamp | |
| G-PFAE | Taylor JT.1 Monoplane | G. Johnson | |
| G-PFAF | FRED Srs 2 | M. S. Perkins | |
| G-PFAG | Evans VP-1 | P. A. Evans | |
| G-PFAH | Evans VP-1 | J. A. Scott | |
| G-PFAI | Clutton EC.2 Easy Too | G. W. Cartledge | |
| G-PFAL | FRED Srs 2 | J. McD. Robinson | |
| G-PFAM | FRED Srs 2 | W. C. Rigby | |
| G-PFAN | Avro 558 (replica) | N. P. Harrison | |
| G-PFAO | Evans VP-1 | P. W. Price | |

| Notes | Reg. | Type | Owner or Operator |
|---|---|---|---|
| | G-PFAP | Currie Wot/SE-5A (C1904) | J. M. Alcock |
| | G-PFAR | Isaacs Fury II (K2059) | C. J. Repik |
| | G-PFAS | GY-20 Minicab | J. Sproston & F. W. Speed |
| | G-PFAT | Monnet Sonerai II | H. B. Carter |
| | G-PFAU | Rand KR-2 | D. E. Peace |
| | G-PFAV | D.31 Turbulent | B. A. Luckins |
| | G-PFAW | Evans VP-1 | R. F. Shingler |
| | G-PFAX | FRED Srs 2 | A. J. Dunston |
| | G-PFAY | EAA Biplane | A. K. Lang & A. L. Young |
| | G-PHIL | Brookland Hornet | A. J. Philpotts |
| | G-PHTG | SOCATA TB.10 Tobago | T&G Engineering Co Ltd |
| | G-PIAF | Thunder Ax7-65 balloon | Ballooning Adventures Ltd |
| | G-PICS | Cessna 182F | Astral Aerial Surveys Ltd (G-ASHO) |
| | G-PICT | Colt 180A balloon | Scotia Balloons |
| | G-PIEL | CP.301A Emeraude | P. R. Thorne (G-BARY) |
| | G-PIES | Thunder Ax7-77Z balloon | Pork Farms Ltd |
| | G-PIGS | SOCATA Rallye 150ST | Boonhill Flying Group (G-BDWB) |
| | G-PIKK | PA-28 Cherokee 140 | L. P. & I. Keegan (G-AVLA) |
| | G-PIKN | Extra EA.230 | R. J. Pickin |
| | G-PINE | Thunder Ax8-90 balloon | J. A. Pine |
| | G-PINT | Cameron 65 SS balloon | Charles Wells Ltd |
| | G-PIPE | Cameron N-56 SS balloon | Carreras Rothmans Ltd |
| | G-PIPS | Van's RV-4 | C. J. Marsh |
| | G-PITS | Pitts S-2AE | D. Rolfe |
| | G-PITZ | Pitts S.2A Special | R. P. Synge & C. England |
| | G-PIXS | Cessna 336 | Astral Aerial Surveys Ltd |
| | G-PJCB | Agusta A.109A-II | J. C. Bamford Excavators Ltd |
| | G-PJMD | Hughes 369D | Dodici Ltd (G-BMJV) |
| | G-PKBD | Douglas DC-9-32 | British Midland Airways Ltd *Jubilee Diamond*/E. Midlands |
| | G-PKBE | Douglas DC-9-32 | British Midland Airways Ltd *Excelsior Diamond*/E. Midlands |
| | G-PKBM | Douglas DC-9-32 | British Midland Airways Ltd *The Tiffany Diamond*/E. Midlands |
| | G-PLAN | Cessna F.150L | Jones Aviation Ltd/Blackpool |
| | G-PLAS | GA-7 Cougar | S. J. A. Smith (G-BGHL)/Biggin Hill |
| | G-PLAX | AS.355F-1 Twin Squirrel | Plaxton PLC (G-BPMT) |
| | G-PLAY | Robin R.2100A | Cotswold Aero Club Ltd/Staverton |
| | G-PLEE | Cessna 182Q | W. J. & M. Barnes |
| | G-PLIV | Pazmany PL.4 | B. P. North |
| | G-PLMA | AS.350B Ecureuil | PLM Helicopters Ltd (G-BMMA) |
| | G-PLMB | AS.350B Ecureuil | PLM Helicopters Ltd (G-BMMB) |
| | G-PLMC | AS.350B Ecureuil | PLM Helicopters Ltd (G-BKUM) |
| | G-PLME | AS.350B-1 Ecureuil | PLM Helicopters Ltd (G-BONN) |
| | G-PLOW | Hughes 269B | Sulby Aerial Surveys Ltd (G-AVUM) |
| | G-PLUS | PA-34-200T Seneca II | C. G. Strasser/Jersey |
| | G-PLYD | SOCATA TB.20 Trinidad | Crocker Air Services/Biggin Hill |
| | G-PMAM | Cameron V-65 balloon | P. A. Meecham |
| | G-PMCN | Monnet Sonerai II | P. J. McNamee |
| | G-PMNL | Extra EA.230 | Aerobatic Displays Ltd/Booker |
| | G-PNAV | PA-31P Pressurised Navajo | Tech Air (Cambridge) Ltd |
| | G-PNNY | Cessna 500 Citation | Merlin Marine Aviation (Jersey) Ltd |
| | G-POAV | SA.365N-1 Dauphin 2 | The Peninsular & Oriental Steam Navigation Co Ltd (G-BOPI) |
| | G-POLE | Rutan LongEz | A. M. Dutton |
| | G-POLO | PA-31-350 Navajo Chieftain | Aircam Technical Services /Teesside |
| | G-POLY | Cameron N-77 balloon | Empty Wallets Balloon Group |
| | G-POND | Oldfield Baby Great Lakes | N. Davis |
| | G-PONY | Colt 31A balloon | Ace Balloons (Bath) Ltd |
| | G-POOH | Piper J-3C-65 Cub | P. & H. Robinson |
| | G-POOL | ARV Super 2 | Falstaff Finance Ltd (G-BNHA) |
| | G-POPE | Eiri PIK-20E-1 | C. J. Hadley |
| | G-POPI | SOCATA TB.10 Tobago | Rocol Aviation Ltd (G-BKEN) |
| | G-POPS | PA-34-220T Seneca III | Ryde International PLC |
| | G-PORK | AA-5B Tiger | Regishire Ltd (G-BFHS) |
| | G-PORT | Bell 206B JetRanger 3 | C. Clark |
| | G-POSH | Colt 56A balloon | Columna Ltd (G-BMPT) |
| | G-POSN | BAe 125 Srs 800B | P&O Containers (Assets) Ltd |
| | G-POST | EMB-110P1 Bandeirante | Region Airways Ltd/Southend |
| | G-POWL | Cessna 182R | Glasdon Group Ltd/Blackpool |
| | G-PPLH | Robinson R-22B | Henderson Financial Management Ltd |
| | G-PPLI | Pazmany PL.1 | G. Anderson |
| | G-PPPE | Colt 77A balloon | Thunder & Colt Ltd |

| Reg. | Type | Owner or Operator | Notes |
|------|------|-------------------|-------|
| G-PRAG | Brügger MB.2 Colibri | R. J. Hodder & ptnrs | |
| G-PRCS | BAe 146-200QC | Princess Air Ltd/Southend | |
| G-PRIM | PA-38-112 Tomahawk | Braddock Ltd | |
| G-PRIN | BAe 146-200QC | Princess Air PLC/Southend | |
| G-PRIT | Cameron N-90 balloon | J. M. Albury | |
| G-PRMC | H.S.125 Srs 700B | RMC Group Services Ltd (G-BFSP)/ Biggin Hill | |
| G-PROP | AA-5A Cheetah | Blackbushe School of Flying Ltd (G-BHKU) | |
| G-PROV | P.84 Jet Provost T.52A (T.4) | Hunter Wing Ltd/Bournemouth | |
| G-PRTT | Cameron N-31 balloon | J. M. Albury | |
| G-PRUE | Cameron O-84 balloon | Lalondes Residential Ltd | |
| G-PRXI | V.S.365 Spitfire PR.XI (PL983) | D. W. Arnold/Biggin Hill | |
| G-PSCI | Bell 206B JetRanger 3 | Scammell Properties Ltd (G-BOKD) | |
| G-PSVS | Beech 95-58 Baron | Stesco Ltd/Guernsey | |
| G-PTER | Beech C90 King Air | Moseley Group (PSV) Ltd (G-BIEE) | |
| G-PTRE | SOCATA TB.20 Trinidad | Openmid Ltd | |
| G-PTWO | Pilatus P2-05 (RF+16) | C. M. Lee | |
| G-PUBS | Colt 56 SS balloon | The Balloonatics | |
| G-PUDD | Robinson R-22B | Pique Holdings PLC | |
| G-PUFF | Thunder Ax7-77A balloon | Intervarsity Balloon Club *Puffin II* | |
| G-PULS | Aero Designs Pulsar | M. J. McBride | |
| G-PUMA | AS.332L Super Puma | Bond Helicopters Ltd | |
| G-PUMB | AS.332L Super Puma | Bond Helicopters Ltd | |
| G-PUMD | AS.332L Super Puma | Bond Helicopters Ltd | |
| G-PUME | AS.332L Super Puma | Bond Helicopters Ltd | |
| G-PUMG | AS.332L Super Puma | Bond Helicopters Ltd | |
| G-PUMH | AS.332L Super Puma | Bond Helicopters Ltd | |
| G-PUMI | AS.332L Super Puma | Bond Helicopters Ltd | |
| G-PUMJ | AS.332L Super Puma | Bond Helicopters Ltd (G-BLZJ) | |
| G-PUMK | AS.332L Super Puma | Bond Helicopters Ltd | |
| G-PUML | AS.332L Super Puma | Bond Helicopters Ltd | |
| G-PUNK | Thunder Ax8-105 balloon | G. E. Harris | |
| G-PURE | Cameron 70 Can SS balloon | The Hot-Air Balloon Co Ltd | |
| G-PURR | AA-5A Cheetah | D. T. Smith (G-BJDN) | |
| G-PURS | Rotorway Executive | J. E. Houseman | |
| G-PUSH | Rutan LongEz | E. G. Peterson | |
| G-PUSI | Cessna T.303 | W. R. Swinburn Ltd | |
| G-PUSS | Cameron N-77 balloon | London Life Association Ltd | |
| G-PVAM | Port Victoria 7 Grain Kitten replica | A. J. Manning | |
| G-PYRO | Cameron N-65 balloon | N. A. Mitchell | |
| G-RAAD | Mooney M.20L | As-Al Ltd | |
| G-RACA | P.57 Sea Prince T.1 | D. A. Cotton | |
| G-RACH | Robinson R-22B | T. C. Barry | |
| G-RADE | Cessna 210L | D. O. Seton (G-CENT)/Bourn | |
| G-RAEM | Rutan LongEz | G. F. H. Singleton | |
| G-RAFA | Grob G.115 | RAF College Flying Club Ltd/Cranwell | |
| G-RAFB | Grob G.115 | RAF College Flying Club Ltd/Cranwell | |
| G-RAFC | Robin R.2112 | Noel Penny Turbines Ltd | |
| G-RAFE | Thunder Ax7-77 balloon | A. J. W. Rose | |
| G-RAFF | Learjet 35A | Graff Aviation Ltd/Heathrow | |
| G-RAFG | Slingsby T.67C | S. J. Donkin | |
| G-RAFT | Rutan LongEz | MAC Communications Ltd | |
| G-RAFW | Mooney M.20E | G. C. Smith (G-ATHW)/Southend | |
| G-RAIL | Colt 105A balloon | Ballooning World Ltd | |
| G-RAIN | Maule M5-235C Lunar Rocket | D. S. McKay & J. A. Rayment | |
| G-RALE | SA.341G Gazelle 1 | Malcolm Wilson (Motorsport) Ltd (G-SFTG) | |
| G-RALI | Hughes 369HS | Kallas Ltd (G-BLKO) | |
| G-RAMI | Bell 206B JetRanger | R. & M. International Helicopters Ltd | |
| G-RAMP | Piper J-3C-65 Cub | K. N. Whittall | |
| G-RAMS | PA-32R-301 Saratoga SP | Peacock & Archer Ltd/Manchester | |
| G-RAND | Rand KR-2 | R. L. Wharmby | |
| G-RANS | Rans S.10 Sakota | J. D. Weller | |
| G-RANY | Cessna 421C | Booth Plant & Equipment Ltd (G-BHLA) | |
| G-RANZ | Rans S-10 Sakota | B. A. Phillips | |
| G-RAPA | BN-2T Islander | Joint Services Parachute Centre | |
| G-RAPE | Colt 300A balloon | O. T. Holmes & R. J. Barr | |
| G-RAPH | Cameron O-77 balloon | P. H. Jenkins | |
| G-RAPP | Cameron H-34 balloon | Cameron Balloons Ltd | |
| G-RARE | Thunder Ax5-42 SS balloon | International Distillers & Vintners Ltd | |
| G-RASC | Evans VP-2 | R. A. Codling | |

| Notes | Reg. | Type | Owner or Operator |
|---|---|---|---|
| | G-RASS | Bell 206L-1 LongRanger 1 | Arlington Securities Ltd (G-JLBI) |
| | G-RATE | AA-5A Cheetah | GP Services (G-BIFF) |
| | G-RAVL | H.P.137 Jetstream Srs 200 | Cranfield Institute of Technology (G-AWVK) |
| | G-RAYS | Zenair CH.250 | R. E. Delves |
| | G-RBIN | Robin DR.400/2+2 | Headcorn Flying School Ltd |
| | G-RBOS | Colt AS-105 airship ★ | Science Museum/Wroughton |
| | G-RBOW | Thunder Ax-7-65 balloon | P. G. & S. D. Viney |
| | G-RBUT | Hughes 369HS | R. C. Button |
| | G-RCMF | Cameron V-77 balloon | Mouldform Ltd |
| | G-RCYI | PA-28-161 Cadet | G. G. L. Thomas |
| | G-RDCI | R. Commander 112A | A. C. Hendriksen (G-BFWG) |
| | G-RDON | WMB.2 Windtracker balloon | P. J. Donnellan (G-BICH) |
| | G-READ | Colt 77A balloon | CB Helicopters Ltd |
| | G-REAP | Pitts S-1S Special | S. Howes |
| | G-REAT | GA-7 Cougar | Autair Helicopters Ltd |
| | G-REBI | Colt 90A balloon | United Friendly Insurance PLC (G-BOYD) |
| | G-REBL | Hughes 269B | Rebelmile Ltd |
| | G-RECK | PA-28 Cherokee 140B | Phoenix Aviation Services Ltd (G-AXJW) |
| | G-REEK | AA-5A Cheetah | Velopend Ltd |
| | G-REEN | Cessna 340 | E. & M. Green (G-AZYR)/Guernsey |
| | G-REES | Jodel D.140C | M. D. S. Hood/Redhill |
| | G-REFI | Enstrom 280C-UK | Nash & Partners Ltd |
| | G-REGA | EMB-110P1 Bandeirante | Region Airways Ltd/Southend |
| | G-REGS | Thunder Ax7-77 balloon | M. E. Gregory |
| | G-REID | Rotorway Scorpion 133 | J. Reid (G-BGAW) |
| | G-REIS | PA-28R-201T Turbo Arrow III | G. Webster & J. D. Caudwell |
| | G-RENO | SOCATA TB.10 Tobago | Lamond Ltd |
| | G-RENT | Robinson R-22B | Rentatruck Self Drive Ltd |
| | G-REPM | PA-38-112 Tomahawk | Nultree Ltd |
| | G-REST | Beech P35 Bonanza | C. R. Taylor (G-ASFJ) |
| | G-RETA | C.A.S.A. 1.131 Jungmann | J. S. Allison/Denham |
| | G-REVS | Bell 206B JetRanger | J. C. Palmer (G-AWOL) |
| | G-REXS | PA-28-181 Archer II | Channel Islands Aero Holdings (Jersey) Ltd |
| | G-REZE | Rutan VariEze | S. D. Brown & S. P. Evans |
| | G-RFIL | Colt 77A balloon | Regency Films International Ltd |
| | G-RFSB | Sportavia RF-5B | S. W. Brown |
| | G-RGII | Cessna 172RG | North West Aviation Ltd |
| | G-RGUS | Fairchild 24R-46A Argus 3 (44-83184) | R. C. Handcraff/Shoreham |
| | G-RHCC | PA-31-350 Navajo Chieftain | Delta Commerical Ltd |
| | G-RHCN | Cessna FR.182RG | R. H. C. Neville |
| | G-RHHT | PA-32RT-300 Lance II | P. Maxwell-Brown |
| | G-RICH | Cessna F.152 | Stanton Aircraft Management Ltd |
| | G-RICK | Beech 95-B55 Baron | R. M. S. Holland (G-BAAG) |
| | G-RIDE | Stephens Akro | R. Mitchell/Coventry |
| | G-RIFA | SA.341G Gazelle 1 | Griffair Ltd (G-ORGE/G-BBHU) |
| | G-RIGB | Thunder Ax7-77 balloon | Antrum & Andrews Ltd |
| | G-RIGS | PA-60 Aerostar 601P | Rigs Design Services Ltd/Fairoaks |
| | G-RILL | Cessna 421C | Maxwell Restaurants Ltd (G-BGZM)/Elstree |
| | G-RILY | Monnet Sonerai II | N. Highton/Henstridge |
| | G-RIND | Cessna 335 | ATA Grinding Processes/Leavesden |
| | G-RING | Cessna FR.182RG | Oxford Aviation Co Ltd |
| | G-RINO | Thunder Ax7-77 balloon | Rino Balloon Team |
| | G-RIOO | Beech B200 Super King Air | Belaire Factoring Ltd |
| | G-RISE | Cameron V-77 balloon | D. L. Smith |
| | G-RIST | Cessna 310R-II | Air Service Training Ltd (G-DATS)/Perth |
| | G-RITA | Cessna 340A | C. Good |
| | G-RJAH | Boeing Stearman A.75N1 | R. J. Horne |
| | G-RJMI | AA-5A Cheetah | Aircraft Investments (UK) Ltd |
| | G-RJMS | PA-28R-201 Arrow III | Robin James Ltd |
| | G-RJWW | Maule M5-235C Lunar Rocket | Paw Flying Services Ltd (G-BRWG) |
| | G-RLFI | Cessna FA.152 | Tayside Aviation Ltd (G-DFTS)/Dundee |
| | G-RLMC | Cessna 421C | Richard Lawson Motor Co Ltd |
| | G-RMAM | Musselwhite MAM.1 | M. A. Musselwhite |
| | G-RMGN | AS.355F-1 Twin Squirrel | VIP Marine & Aviation Ltd (G-BMCY) |
| | G-RNAS | D.H.104 Sea Devon C.20 (XK896) | D. W. Hermiston-Hooper/Staverton |
| | G-RNGR | AB-206B JetRanger 3 | Unicorn Software Ltd |

| Reg. | Type | Owner or Operator | Notes |
|------|------|-------------------|-------|
| G-RNIE | Cameron 70 Ball SS balloon | Airship & Balloon Co Ltd | |
| G-RNLI | V.S. Walrus 1 | R. E. Melton | |
| G-RNRM | Cessna A.185F | RN & R. Marines Sport Parachute Association | |
| G-RNTV | PA-30 Twin Comanche 160C | J. L. Vaughan (G-AXDL) | |
| G-ROAR | Cessna 401 | H. W. Weston (G-BZFL/G-AWSF)/ Staverton | |
| G-ROBB | Grob G.109B | A. P. Mayne | |
| G-ROBI | Grob G.109B | A. W. McGarrigle/Cardiff | |
| G-ROBN | Robin R.1180T | J. G. Beaumont | |
| G-ROBO | Robinson R-22B | Cabair Air Taxis Ltd/Elstree | |
| G-ROBS | Robinson R-22B | Corniche Helicopters (G-BPDH) | |
| G-ROBY | Colt 17A balloon | Airship & Balloon Co Ltd | |
| G-ROCH | Cessna T.303 | R. S. Bentley | |
| G-ROCK | Thunder Ax7-77 balloon | The Long Rake Spar Co Ltd | |
| G-ROCR | Schweizer 269C | ROC Robinson Ltd | |
| G-RODD | Cessna 310R II | R. J. Herbert Engineering Ltd (G-TEDD/ G-MADI) | |
| G-RODI | Isaacs Fury (K3731) | M. R. Baker/Shoreham | |
| G-RODS | A-Bell 206B JetRanger 2 | Crook & Son (G-NOEL/G-BCWN) | |
| G-ROGG | Robinson R-22B | Catto Helicopters | |
| G-ROGR | Bell 206A JetRanger | Crook & Son (G-AXMM) | |
| G-ROLA | PA-34-200T Seneca | Highsteeple Ltd | |
| G-ROLF | PA-32R-301 Saratoga SP | R. W. Burchardt/Gamston | |
| G-ROLL | Pitts S-2A Special | RPM Aviation Ltd/Guernsey | |
| G-ROLO | Robinson R-22B | Osprey Helicopters Ltd | |
| G-ROMA | Hughes 369S | Harris Technology Ltd (G-ROPI/G-ONPP) | |
| G-RONG | PA-28R Cherokee Arrow 200-II | W. R. Griffiths | |
| G-RONI | Cameron V-77 balloon | R. E. Simpson | |
| G-RONT | Enstrom F-28A | R. Thomas (G-BDAW) | |
| G-RONW | FRED Srs 2 | K. Atkinson | |
| G-ROOF | Brantly B.2B | S. Lee (G-AXSR) | |
| G-ROOK | Cessna F.172P | Crop Aviation (UK) Ltd | |
| G-RORO | Cessna 337B | C. Keane (G-AVIX) | |
| G-RORY | Piaggio FW P.149D | R. McCarthy (G-TOWN)/Booker | |
| G-ROSE | Evans VP-1 | W. K. Rose | |
| G-ROSI | Thunder Ax7-77 balloon | Scotia Balloons Ltd | |
| G-ROSS | Practavia Pilot Sprite | F. M. T. Ross | |
| G-ROTA | Bensen B.8 | D. Ellerton | |
| G-ROTI | Luscombe 8A Silvaire | A. L. Chapman & ptnrs | |
| G-ROTS | CFM Streak Shadow Srs SA | H. R. Cayzer | |
| G-ROUP | Cessna F.172M | Stapleford Flying Club Ltd (G-BDPH) | |
| G-ROUS | PA-34-200T Seneca II | C.S.E. Aviation Ltd/Kidlington | |
| G-ROUT | Robinson R-22B | Hooley Bridge Helicopter Services | |
| G-ROVE | PA-18 Super Cub 135 | Brailsford Aviation Ltd | |
| G-ROWL | AA-5B Tiger | Aviation Simulation/Biggin Hill | |
| G-ROWN | Beech 200 Super King Air | Chauffair Ltd (G-BHLC) | |
| G-ROWS | PA-28-151 Warrior | Mustarrow Ltd | |
| G-ROYI | PA-32R-301 Saratoga | R. L. West (G-BMEY) | |
| G-ROYL | Taylor JT.1 Monoplane | R. L. Wharmby | |
| G-ROYY | Robinson R-22B | Tudor Motorcycles | |
| G-ROZY | Cameron R.36 balloon | Jacques W. Soukup Ltd | |
| G-RPAH | Rutan Vari-Eze | B. Hanson | |
| G-RPEZ | Rutan LongEz | B. A. Fairston & D. Richardson | |
| G-RRRR | Privateer Motor Glider | R. F. Selby | |
| G-RRSG | Thunder Ax7-77 balloon | M. T. Stevens | |
| G-RRTM | Sikorsky S-70C | Rolls-Royce PLC/Filton | |
| G-RTHL | Leivers Special | R. Leivers | |
| G-RUBB | AA-5B Tiger | J. M. Summerfield/Elstree | |
| G-RUBI | Thunder Ax7-77 balloon | Anglia Balloon School Ltd | |
| G-RUBY | PA-28RT-201T Turbo Arrow IV | N. A. Ayub (G-BROU) | |
| G-RUDD | Cameron V-65 balloon | N. A. Apsey | |
| G-RUGB | Cameron 89 Egg SS balloon | The Hot-Air Balloon Co Ltd | |
| G-RUIA | Cessna F.172M | F. Daly | |
| G-RUMN | AA-1A Trainer | M. A. Hales/Cranfield | |
| G-RUMP | Robinson R-22B | I. P. Crane | |
| G-RUNT | Cassutt Racer IIIM | S. B. Jones | |
| G-RUSS | Cessna 172N | Leisure Lease/Southend | |
| G-RWIN | Rearwin 175 | G. Kay | |
| G-RWWW | W.S.55 Whirlwind HCC.12 | R. Windley | |
| G-SAAB | R. Commander 112TC | S. Richmen (G-BEFS) | |
| G-SAAM | Cessna T.182R | Hopstop Ltd (G-TAGL)/Elstree | |

181

| Notes | Reg. | Type | Owner or Operator |
|-------|------|------|-------------------|
| | G-SABA | PA-28R-201T Turbo Arrow III | G. I. Cooper (G-BFEN) |
| | G-SACA | Cessna 152 II | LAR Aviation Ltd (G-HOSE)/Shoreham |
| | G-SACB | Cessna F.152 II | Westward Airways (Land's End) Ltd (G-BFRB)/St Just |
| | G-SACD | Cessna F.172H | Northbrook College of Design & Technology (G-AVCD)/Shoreham |
| | G-SACE | Cessna F.150L | LAR Aviation Ltd (G-AZLK)/Shoreham |
| | G-SACF | Cessna 152 II | T. M. & M. L. Jones |
| | G-SACI | PA-28-161 Warrior II | Southern Aero Club/Shoreham |
| | G-SACO | PA-28-161 Warrior II | Southern Aero Club/Shoreham |
| | G-SACR | PA-28-161 Cadet | Sherburn Aero Club Ltd |
| | G-SACS | PA-28-161 Cadet | Sherburn Aero Club Ltd |
| | G-SACT | PA-28-161 Cadet | Sherburn Aero Club Ltd |
| | G-SACU | PA-28-161 Cadet | Sherburn Aero Club Ltd |
| | G-SACV | PA-28-161 Cadet | Sherburn Aero Club Ltd |
| | G-SACZ | PA-28-161 Warrior II | Southern Aero Club/Shoreham |
| | G-SAFE | Cameron N-77 balloon | Nottingham Hot Air Balloon Club |
| | G-SAGA | Grob G.109B | G-GROB Ltd/Booker |
| | G-SAGE | Luscombe 8A Silvaire | S. J. Sage (G-AKTL) |
| | G-SAHI | Trago Mills SAH-1 | Orca Aircraft Ltd |
| | G-SAIR | Cessna 421C | Air Support Aviation Services Ltd |
| | G-SALA | PA-32 Cherokee Six 300E | Stonebold Ltd |
| | G-SALI | Cessna 421C | Rapid 3864 Ltd/Luton |
| | G-SALL | Cessna F.150L (Tailwheel) | J. A. Millar-Craig & M. R. Shelton |
| | G-SALY | Hawker Sea Fury FB.11 (WJ288) | D. W. Arnold/Duxford |
| | G-SAMA | PA-31-350 Navajo Chieftain | Asseman Ltd |
| | G-SAMG | Grob G.109B | RAFGSA/Bicester |
| | G-SAMM | Cessna 340A | M. R. Cross |
| | G-SAMS | M.S.880B Rallye Club | M. T. Lewis |
| | G-SAMZ | Cessna 150D | N. E. Sames (G-ASSO) |
| | G-SANB | Beech E90 King Air | Scottish & Newcastle Breweries PLC (G-BGNU) |
| | G-SAND | Schweizer 269C | Aerocroft Ltd |
| | G-SARA | PA-28-181 Archer II | R. H. Ford/Elstree |
| | G-SARN | BN-2A Mk III-2 Trislander | Oston Air Finance Ltd (G-BEFO) |
| | G-SARO | Saro Skeeter Mk 12 | F. F. Chamberlain |
| | G-SASU | AS.355F-1 Twin Squirrel | Gulf & UK Industrial Consultants Ltd (G-BSSM/G-BMTC/G-BKUK) |
| | G-SATI | Cameron 105 Sphere balloon | Cameron Balloons Ltd |
| | G-SATO | PA-23 Aztec 250E | P. L. Creffield (G-BCXP)/Southend |
| | G-SAUF | Colt 90A balloon | K. H. Medau |
| | G-SAVE | PA-31-350 Navajo Chieftain | Merrixair Ltd/Exeter |
| | G-SBAS | Beech B200 Super King Air | Bond Helicopters Ltd/Aberdeen |
| | G-SBUS | BN-2A-26 Islander | Isles of Scilly Skybus Ltd (G-BMMH)/St Just |
| | G-SCAH | Cameron V-77 balloon | S. C. A. Howarth |
| | G-SCAN | Vinten-Wallis WA-116/100 | K. H. Wallis |
| | G-SCAT | Cessna F.150F | Cheshire Air Training School (Merseyside) Ltd (G-ATRN)/Liverpool |
| | G-SCFO | Cameron O-77 balloon | M. K. Grigson |
| | G-SCHH | BAe 146-100 | British Aerospace PLC/Hatfield |
| | G-SCHU | AS.355F-1 Twin Squirrel | McAlpine Helicopters Ltd/Hayes |
| | G-SCPL | PA-28 Cherokee 140 | Hillvine Ltd (G-BPVL)/Staverton |
| | G-SCTT | HPR-7 Herald 210 | Channel Express Group PLC (G-ASPJ)/Bournemouth |
| | G-SCUB | PA-18 Super Cub 135 (542447) | N. D. Needham Farms |
| | G-SCUH | Boeing 737-3Q8 | Dan-Air Services Ltd/Gatwick |
| | G-SDEV | D.H.104 Sea Devon C.20 | P. C. Gill & W. Gentle |
| | G-SEAB | Republic RC-3 Seabee | G. Cormack/Glasgow |
| | G-SEAH | Hawker Sea Hawk FB.3 | Jet Heritage Ltd/Bournemouth |
| | G-SEAN | Bell 206L-3 LongRanger | The Berkeley Leisure Group Ltd |
| | G-SEAS | PA-31-310 Navajo C | Sea Surveillance Ltd |
| | G-SEAT | Colt 42 balloon | Virgin Atlantic Airways |
| | G-SEBB | Brügger MB.2 Colibri | M. Riddin |
| | G-SEED | Piper J-3C-65 Cub | J. H. Seed |
| | G-SEEK | Cessna T.210N | Melrose Pigs Ltd |
| | G-SEGO | Robinson R-22B | G. Seago |
| | G-SEJW | PA-28-161 Warrior II | Truman Aviation Ltd/Tollerton |
| | G-SELL | Robin DR.400/180 | L. S. Thorne |
| | G-SEPT | Cameron N-105 balloon | Deproco UK Ltd |
| | G-SETA | AS.355F-1 Twin Squirrel | McAlpine Helicopters Ltd (G-NEAS/G-CMMM/G-BNBJ) |

**G-SEVA — G-SMAF**

| Reg. | Type | Owner or Operator | Notes |
|------|------|-------------------|-------|
| G-SEVA | SE-5A replica (F141) | I. D. Gregory | |
| G-SEVE | Cessna 172N | S. Patterson | |
| G-SEWL | PA-28-151 Warrior | A. R. Sewell & Sons/Andrewsfield | |
| G-SEXY | AA-1 Yankee | H. Morris (G-AYLM) | |
| G-SFHR | PA-23 Aztec 250F | E. L. Becker & J. Harper (G-BHSO) | |
| G-SFRY | Thunder Ax7-77 balloon | R. J. Fry | |
| G-SFTD | SA.341G Gazelle 1 | Blades Helicopters Ltd/Goodwood | |
| G-SFTS | NDN-1T Turbo Firecracker | Marinco Ltd | |
| G-SFTZ | Slingsby T.67M Firefly | Specialist Flying Training Ltd/Carlisle | |
| G-SHAA | Enstrom 280-UK | Manchester Helicopter Centre/Barton | |
| G-SHAW | PA-30 Twin Comanche 160B | CCR Holding Co Ltd | |
| G-SHCC | AB-206B JetRanger | Humphrey Mining Services Ltd | |
| G-SHDD | Enstrom F-28C | Durston Air Services Ltd (G-BNBS) | |
| G-SHED | PA-28-181 Archer II | S. V. Smeeth (G-BRAU) | |
| G-SHEL | Cameron O-56 balloon | The Shell Company of Hong Kong Ltd | |
| G-SHFL | Cameron N-77 balloon | M. C. Bradley/Hong Kong | |
| G-SHGG | Enstrom 280C Shark | Haversham Helicopters Ltd | |
| G-SHIP | PA-23 Aztec 250F ★ | Midland Air Museum/Coventry | |
| G-SHIV | GA-7 Cougar | Trent Air Services Ltd/Cranfield | |
| G-SHKK | Hughes 269A | Starline Helicopters Ltd | |
| G-SHNN | Enstrom 280C | Farm Supply Co (Thirsk) Ltd | |
| G-SHOO | Hughes TH-55A | Starline Helicopters Ltd | |
| G-SHOT | Cameron V-77 balloon | Bucks Hot-Air Balloon Group | |
| G-SHOW | M.S.733 Alycon | Vintage Aircraft Team/Cranfield | |
| G-SHPP | Hughes TH-55A | R. P. Bateman & A. C. Braithwaite | |
| G-SHRR | AB-206B JetRanger 2 | Vamplas Glass Design Ltd (G-FSDA/ G-AWJW) | |
| G-SHSS | Enstrom 280C-UK Shark | Free Flight Aviation Ltd (G-BENO) | |
| G-SHST | Colt 180A balloon | G. V. Beckwith | |
| G-SHUG | PA-28R-201T Turbo Arrow III | N. E. Rennie | |
| G-SHUU | Enstrom 280C-UK-2 Shark | H. Ingham (G-OMCP/G-KENY/G-BJFG) | |
| G-SHVV | Bell 206B JetRanger 2 | Starline Helicopters Ltd/Booker | |
| G-SHZZ | Bell 206B JetRanger 3 | Starline Helicopters Ltd (G-BNUW) | |
| G-SIGN | PA-39 Twin Comanche 160 C/R | Comanche Travel Ltd/Elstree | |
| G-SING | Beech B60 Duke | Sasha Fashions International Ltd/ Leavesden | |
| G-SIPA | SIPA 903 | T. J. McRae (G-BGBM) | |
| G-SITE | AS.355F-1 Twin Squirrel | Charter Group PLC (G-BPHC) | |
| G-SITU | Partenavia P.68C | Air Sarnia Ltd (G-NEWU/G-BHJX)/ Guernsey | |
| G-SIXC | Douglas DC-6A | Atlantic Air Transport Ltd/Coventry | |
| G-SIXX | Colt 77A balloon | G. E. Harris & S. C. Kinsey | |
| G-SJAB | PA-39 Twin Comanche 160 C/R | Foyle Flyers Ltd | |
| G-SJGM | Cessna 182R | Crystal Air Ltd | |
| G-SKAN | Cessna F.172M | Aircraft Rentals Humberside Ltd (G-BFKT) | |
| G-SKIL | Cameron N-77 balloon | Flying Pictures (Balloons) Ltd | |
| G-SKIP | Cameron N-77 balloon | Skipton Building Soc | |
| G-SKKA | PA-31 Turbo Navajo | J. J. Baumhardt (G-FOAL/G-RMAE/ G-BAEG) | |
| G-SKKB | PA-31 Turbo Navajo | J. J. Baumhardt (G-BBDS)/Southend | |
| G-SKKC | Cessan 404 | J. J. Baumhardt (G-OHUB)/Southend | |
| G-SKSA | Airship Industries SKS.500 | Airship Industries Ltd/Cardington | |
| G-SKSB | Airship Industries SKS.500 | Airship Industries Ltd/Cardington | |
| G-SKSC | Airship Industries SKS.600 | Airship Industries Ltd/Cardington | |
| G-SKSF | Airship Industries SKS.600 | Airship Industries Ltd/Cardington | |
| G-SKSG | Airship Industries SKS.600/03 | Airship Industries Ltd/Cardington | |
| G-SKYE | Cessna TU.206G | RAF Sport Parachute Association | |
| G-SKYH | Cessna 172N | Elgor Hire Purchase & Credit Ltd/ Southend | |
| G-SKYI | Air Command 532 Elite | Skyrider Aviation Ltd | |
| G-SKYM | Cessna F.337E | Bencray Ltd (G-AYHW) (stored)/ Blackpool | |
| G-SKYS | Cameron O-84 balloon | J. R. Christopher | |
| G-SLAC | Cameron N-77 balloon | The Scottish Life Assurance Co | |
| G-SLCI | Thunder Ax8-90 balloon | S. L. Cuhat | |
| G-SLEA | Mudry/CAARP CAP.10B | P. D. Southerington/Sturgate | |
| G-SLII | Cameron O-90 balloon | S. L. Cuhat | |
| G-SLIK | Taylor JT.2 Titch | J. A. Jennings | |
| G-SLIM | Colt 56A balloon | Hot-Air Balloon Co Ltd | |
| G-SLOT | Cessna 340A | Bristol Uniforms Ltd | |
| G-SLYN | PA-28-161 Warrior II | G. E. Layton | |
| G-SMAF | Sikorsky S-76A | Fayair (Jersey) 1984 Ltd | |

| Notes | Reg. | Type | Owner or Operator |
|-------|------|------|-------------------|
| | G-SMHK | Cameron D-38 airship | San Miguel Brewery Ltd |
| | G-SMIG | Cameron O-65 balloon | Hong Kong Balloon & Airship Club |
| | G-SMJJ | Cessna 414A | Gull Air Ltd/Guernsey |
| | G-SMTH | PA-28 Cherokee 140 | G. N. Smith (G-AYJS) |
| | G-SNAP | Cameron V-77 balloon | N. A. Apsey |
| | G-SNAX | Colt 69A balloon | Derwent Valley Foods Ltd |
| | G-SNDY | Piper J-3C-65 Cub | R. R. K. Mayall |
| | G-SNOB | Beech A.36 Bonanza | R. I. Craddock (G-BEIK) |
| | G-SNOW | Cameron V-77 balloon | M. J. Snow |
| | G-SOAR | Eiri PIK-20E | P. Rees |
| | G-SOAS | PA-60 Aerostar 601P | Kenilgate Ltd |
| | G-SOFA | Cameron N-65 balloon | GT Flying Club Ltd |
| | G-SOFI | PA-60 Aerostar 601P (Machen Superstar II) | Allzones Travel Ltd/Biggin Hill |
| | G-SOFS | F.27 Friendship Mk 200 | Secretary of State for Scotland & Department of Agriculture and Fisheries (G-BLML)/Edinburgh |
| | G-SOFT | Thunder Ax7-77 balloon | Bristol Software Factory Ltd |
| | G-SOLA | Aero Designs Star-Lite SL.1 | P. Clifton & A. Clarke |
| | G-SOLD | Robinson R-22A | Travel Management Ltd |
| | G-SOLO | Pitts S-2S Special | Fyat Ltd/Booker |
| | G-SONA | SOCATA TB.10 Tobago | J. Greenwood (G-BIBI) |
| | G-SONY | Aero Commander 200D | General Airline Ltd (G-BGPS) |
| | G-SOOE | Hughes 369E | Arrow Aviation Co Ltd/Manchester |
| | G-SOOS | Colt 21A balloon | The Independent Balloon Co Ltd |
| | G-SOOT | PA-28 Cherokee 180 | Streamline Aviation (G-AVNM)/ E. Midlands |
| | G-SOUL | Cessna 310R | Atlantic Air Transport Ltd/Coventry |
| | G-SPEY | AB-206B JetRanger 3 | Castle Air Charters Ltd (G-BIGO) |
| | G-SPIN | Pitts S-2A Special | R. N. Goode/White Waltham |
| | G-SPIT | V.S.379 Spitfire FR.XIV (MV363) | B. J. S. Grey (G-BGHB)/Duxford |
| | G-SPOL | MBB Bo 105CBS/4 | Clyde Helicopters Ltd |
| | G-SSBS | Colting Ax77 balloon | K. J. & M. E. Gregory |
| | G-SSFT | PA-28-161 Warrior II | SFT Aviation Ltd (G-BHIL)/Bournemouth |
| | G-SSJT | Cessna 210L | J. Taylor |
| | G-SSOZ | Cessna 550 Citation II | Arrows Aviation Co Ltd |
| | G-SSRS | Cessna 172N | B. Powell |
| | G-SSWV | Sportavia Fournier RF-5B | J. L. Collins & J. A. Melville |
| | G-STAG | Cameron O-65 balloon | Holker Estates Ltd |
| | G-STAK | Bell 206B JetRanger 2 | Tyringham Charter & Group Services Ltd (G-BNIS) |
| | G-STAN | F.27 Friendship Mk.200 | Air UK *Jimmy Saville OBE*/Norwich |
| | G-STAP | Cessna FA.152 | Stapleford Flying Club Ltd |
| | G-STAT | Cessna U.206F | SMK Engineers Ltd |
| | G-STEF | Hughes 369HS | D. J. L. Wood (G-BKTK) |
| | G-STEP | Schweizer 269C | M. D. Thorpe |
| | G-STEV | Jodel DR.221 | S. W. Talbot/Long Marston |
| | G-STMI | Robinson R-22B | Orchard Property Developments Ltd |
| | G-STMP | SNCAN Stampe SV-4A | W. R. Partridge |
| | G-STOX | Bell 206B JetRanger 2 | Tickstop Ltd (G-BNIR) |
| | G-STOY | Robinson R-22B | Tickstop Ltd |
| | G-STRK | CFM Streak Shadow Srs SA | M. E. Dodd |
| | G-STST | Bell 206B JetRanger 3 | Petrochemical Supplies Ltd |
| | G-STVN | HPR-7 Herald 210 | Channel Express Group PLC/ Bournemouth |
| | G-STWO | ARV Super 2 | Falstaff Finance Ltd |
| | G-STYL | Pitts S-1S Special | B. MacMillan |
| | G-SULL | PA-32R-301 Saratoga SP | B. R. Chaplin |
| | G-SULY | Monnet Moni | M. J. Sullivan |
| | G-SUNI | Bell 206B JetRanger 3 | Sunley Holdings PLC |
| | G-SUPA | PA-18 Super Cub 150 | Yorkshire Gliding Club (Pty) Ltd/ Sutton Bank |
| | G-SURG | PA-30 Twin Comanche 160B | A. R. Taylor (G-VIST/G-AVHZ) |
| | G-SUSI | Cameron V-77 balloon | H. S. & C. J. Dryden |
| | G-SUSY | P-51D-25-NA Mustang (472773) | Charles Church Displays Ltd |
| | G-SUTT | Hughes 369E | Southern Air Ltd (G-OEPF/G-OMJH) |
| | G-SUZI | Beech 95-B55 Baron | Directfield Ltd (G-BAXR) |
| | G-SUZY | Taylor JT.1 Monoplane | E. J. Blackoe |
| | G-SVHA | Partenavia P.68B | David Martin Couriers Ltd |
| | G-SVIV | SNCAN Stampe SV-4C | A. J. Clarry & S. F. Bancroft |
| | G-SVJM | AS.355F-1 Twin Squirrel | UB Air Ltd & Jensen & Nicholson Ltd (G-BOPS) |
| | G-SWEB | Cameron N-90 balloon | Air 2 Air Ltd |

| Reg. | Type | Owner or Operator | Notes |
|------|------|-------------------|-------|
| G-SWFT | Beech 200 Super King Air | Airswift Ltd (G-SIBE/G-MCEO/G-BILY) | |
| G-SWIF | V.S.541 Swift F.7 | Jet Heritage Ltd/Bournemouth | |
| G-SWIM | Taylor Coot Amphibian(modified) | P. C. J. Farries | |
| G-SWOT | Currie Super Wot | R. A. Bowes | |
| G-SWPR | Cameron N-56 balloon | A. Brown | |
| G-SYFW | Focke-Wulf Fw.190 replica (2+1) | M. R. Parr | |
| | | | |
| G-TACK | Grob G.109B | Oval (275) Ltd/Bristol | |
| G-TAFF | C.A.S.A. 1.131 Jungmann | Custompac Ltd (G-BFNE) ˙ | |
| G-TAFY | Piper J-3F-65 Cub | C. P. Goodley | |
| G-TAGS | PA-28-161 Warrior II | Air Service Training Ltd/Perth | |
| G-TAIL | Cessna 150J | Routair Aviation Services Ltd/Southend | |
| G-TAIR | PA-34-200T Seneca II | Wessex Mouldings Ltd | |
| G-TALI | AS.355F-1 Twin Squirrel | The Duke of Westminster | |
| G-TAMY | Cessna 421B | Malcolm Enamellers (Midlands) Ltd | |
| G-TAPE | PA-23 Aztec 250D | Merlix Ltd (G-AWVW) | |
| G-TART | PA-28-236 Dakota | Withercourt Ltd | |
| G-TATT | GY-20 Minicab | L. Tattershall | |
| G-TAXI | PA-23 Aztec 250E | Yorkair Ltd/Leeds | |
| G-TAYI | Grob G.115 | Tayside Aviation Ltd (G-DODO)/Dundee | |
| G-TBAG | Renegade II | M. R. Tetley | |
| G-TBIO | SOCATA TB.10 Tobago | H. M. Fenn & J. E. Hailes | |
| G-TBIX | MDH Hughes 369E | Weetabix Ltd/Sywell | |
| G-TBSL | Colt 90A balloon ˙ | Tubesales (UK) Ltd | |
| G-TBXX | SOCATA TB.20 Trinidad | JDM Electrical & Mechanical Services Ltd/Denham | |
| G-TBZO | SOCATA TB.20 Trinidad | G. Brookes | |
| G-TCAR | Robin HR.100/210 | Gibad Aviation Ltd | |
| G-TCMP | Robinson R-22B | Pulsegrove Ltd/Shoreham | |
| G-TCTC | PA-28RT-201 Arrow IV | Scorpion Vehicle Security Systems Ltd | |
| G-TCUB | Piper J-3C-65 Cub | N. R. Windley | |
| G-TDAD | SOCATA TB.20 Trinidad | Air Touring Services Ltd/Biggin Hill | |
| G-TDFS | IMCO Callair A.9 | Dollarhigh Ltd (G-AVZA) | |
| G-TEAA | Boeing 737-3Y0 | TEA UK Ltd/Birmginham | |
| G-TEAB | Boeing 737-3Y0 | TEA UK Ltd/Birmingham | |
| G-TEAC | AT-6C Harvard IIA (EX280) | E. C. English/Bourn | |
| G-TEAD | Boeing 737-33A | TEA UK Ltd/Birmingham | |
| G-TECH | R. Commander 114 | P. A. Reed (G-BEDH)/Denham | |
| G-TECK | Cameron V-77 balloon | G. M. N. Spencer | |
| G-TEDS | SOCATA TB.10 Tobago | E. W. Lyon (G-BHCO) | |
| G-TEDY | Evans VP-1 | C. J. D. Edwards (G-BHGN) | |
| G-TEES | Cessna F.152 | Cleveland Flying School Ltd (G-BIUI)/Teesside | |
| G-TEFC | PA-28 Cherokee 140 | A. J. Cornish | |
| G-TEFH | Cessna 500 Citation | Birmingham Aviation Ltd (G-BCII) | |
| G-TELL | Cessna 421C | Holding & Barnes Ltd | |
| G-TELY | Agusta A.109A-II | Castle Air Charters Ltd | |
| G-TEMI | BN-2T Islander | Pilatus BN Ltd (G-BJYX)/Bembridge | |
| G-TEMP | PA-28 Cherokee 180 | W. D. Hubble (G-AYBK) | |
| G-TEMT | Hawker Tempest II | Autokraft Ltd | |
| G-TENT | J/1N Alpha | R. Callaway-Lewis (G-AKJU) | |
| G-TERI | Beech F33A Bonanza | T. & D. E. Beanland/Jersey | |
| G-TERY | PA-28-181 Archer II | T. Barlow (G-BOXZ)/Barton | |
| G-TESS | Quickie Q.2 | D. Evans | |
| G-TEST | PA-34-200 Seneca | Stapleford Flying Club Ltd (G-BLCD) | |
| G-TEWS | PA-28 Cherokee 140 | M. J. & M. J. Tew (G-KEAN/G-AWTM) | |
| G-TFCI | Cessna FA.152 | Tayside Aviation Ltd/Dundee | |
| G-TFRB | Air Command 532 Elite | F. R. Blennerhassett | |
| G-TFUN | Valentin Taifun 17E | M. R. Shelton | |
| G-TGAS | Cameron O-160 balloon | R. S. Hunjan | |
| G-TGER | AA-5B Tiger | A. Wuensche (G-BFZP) | |
| G-THAN | Cessna F.406 Caravan II | Air Thanet Ltd/Manston | |
| G-THCL | Cessna 550 Citation II | Tower House Consultants Ltd | |
| G-THEA | Boeing Stearman E.75 | L. M. Walton | |
| G-THGS | SA. 365N-1 Dauphin 2 | HeavyLift Cargo Airlines Ltd (G-BPOJ) | |
| G-THOM | Thunder Ax6-56 balloon | T. H. Wilson | |
| G-THOR | Thunder Ax8-105 balloon | N. C. Faithful *Turncoat* | |
| G-THOS | Thunder Ax7-77 balloon | Thos Wood & Son (Builders) Ltd | |
| G-THSL | PA-28R-201 Arrow III | G. Fearnley/Southend | |
| G-THUR | Beech 200 Super King Air | Thurston Aviation (Stansted) Ltd | |
| G-TIBC | Cameron A-180 balloon | The Independent Balloon Co Ltd | |
| G-TICK | Cameron V-77 balloon | T. J. Tickler | |
| G-TIDS | Jodel D.150 | J. B. Dovey/Ipswich | |

| Notes | Reg. | Type | Owner or Operator |
|-------|------|------|-------------------|
| | G-TIFT | Colt 90A balloon | Norwest Holst Construction Ltd |
| | G-TIGA | D.H.82A Tiger Moth | Truman Aviation Ltd (G-AOEG) |
| | G-TIGB | AS.332L Super Puma | Bristow Helicopters Ltd (G-BJXC) |
| | G-TIGC | AS.332L Super Puma | Bristow Helicopters Ltd (G-BJYH) |
| | G-TIGE | AS.332L Super Puma | Bristow Helicopters Ltd (G-BJYJ) |
| | G-TIGF | AS.332L Super Puma | Bristow Helicopters Ltd |
| | G-TIGG | AS.332L Super Puma | Bristow Helicopters Ltd |
| | G-TIGH | AS.332L Super Puma | Bristow Helicopters Ltd |
| | G-TIGI | AS.332L Super Puma | Bristow Helicopters Ltd |
| | G-TIGJ | AS.332L Super Puma | Bristow Helicopters Ltd |
| | G-TIGK | AS.332L Super Puma | Bristow Helicopters Ltd |
| | G-TIGL | AS.332L Super Puma | Bristow Helicopters Ltd |
| | G-TIGM | AS.332L Super Puma | Bristow Helicopters Ltd |
| | G-TIGO | AS.332L Super Puma | Bristow Helicopters Ltd |
| | G-TIGP | AS.332L Super Puma | Bristow Helicopters Ltd |
| | G-TIGR | AS.332L Super Puma | Bristow Helicopters Ltd |
| | G-TIGS | AS.332L Super Puma | Bristow Helicopters Ltd |
| | G-TIGT | AS.332L Super Puma | Bristow Helicopters Ltd |
| | G-TIGU | AS.332L Super Puma | Bristow Helicopters Ltd |
| | G-TIGW | AS.332L Super Puma | Bristow Helicopters Ltd |
| | G-TIGZ | AS.332L Super Puma | British International Helicopters Ltd |
| | G-TIII | Aerotek Pitts S-2A | Aerobatic Displays Ltd (G-BGSE)/Booker |
| | G-TILE | Robinson R-22B | S. Lee |
| | G-TILL | Robinson R-22B | G. Till |
| | G-TIMB | Rutan Vari-Eze | T. M. Bailey (G-BKXJ) |
| | G-TIME | Ted Smith Aerostar 601P | J. J. Donn |
| | G-TIMJ | Rand KR-2 | N. Seaton |
| | G-TIMK | PA-28-181 Archer II | T. Baker |
| | G-TIMW | PA-28 Cherokee 140C | W. H. Sanders (G-AXSH) |
| | G-TINA | SOCATA TB.10 Tobago | A. Lister |
| | G-TINS | Cameron N-90 balloon | Bass & Tennent Sales Ltd |
| | G-TISH | PA-31-310 Turbo Navajo | Air Transport Centre Ltd (G-BFKJ) |
| | G-TJET | Lockheed T-33A-1-LO | Aces High Ltd/North Weald |
| | G-TKPZ | Cessna 310R | Auxili-Air Aviation Ltd (G-BRAH)/ Humberside |
| | G-TKYO | Boeing 747-212B | Virgin Atlantic Airways Ltd *Maiden Japan* |
| | G-TLOL | Cessna 421C | Littlewoods Organisation Ltd/ Liverpool |
| | G-TLTD | Cessna 182Q | Gray Tuplin Ltd |
| | G-TMJH | Hughes 369E | Annoville Ltd |
| | G-TMMC | AS.355F-1 Twin Squirrel | The Colt Car Co Ltd (G-JLCO) |
| | G-TNTA | BAe 146-200QT | TNT Roadfreight (UK) Ltd |
| | G-TNTB | BAe 146-200QT | TNT Roadfreight (UK) Ltd |
| | G-TNTD | BAe 146-200QT | TNT Express (UK) Ltd (G-BOMJ) |
| | G-TNTE | BAe 146-300QT | TNT Express (UK) Ltd (G-BRPW)/Luton |
| | G-TNTF | BAe 146-300QT | TNT Express (UK) Ltd (G-BRZI)/Luton |
| | G-TOAD | Jodel D.140B | Mothballs Ltd |
| | G-TOAK | SOCATA TB.20 Trinidad | Self Adhesive Fixings Ltd |
| | G-TOBE | PA-28R Cherokee Arrow 200 | J. Bradley & Barry Ltd (G-BNRO) |
| | G-TOBI | Cessna F.172K | G. Hall (G-AYVB) |
| | G-TODD | ICA IS-28M2A | C. I. Roberts & C. D. King |
| | G-TOFT | Colt 90A balloon | Norwest Holst Construction Ltd |
| | G-TOGA | PA-32-301 Saratoga | Toga Flying Four Group |
| | G-TOMI | H.S.125 Srs 600B | Falcon Jet Centre Ltd (G-BBEP/G-BJOY)/Heathrow |
| | G-TOMO | BAC One-Eleven 487GK | Anglo Cargo Airlines Ltd/Manston |
| | G-TOMS | PA-38-112 Tomahawk | R. J. Alford |
| | G-TOMY | Mitsubishi Mu.300 Diamond | Lynton Aviation Ltd |
| | G-TONE | Pazmany PL.4 | J. A. Walmsley |
| | G-TONI | Cessna 421C | M. Scott |
| | G-TOOL | Thunder Ax8-105 balloon | W. J. Honey |
| | G-TOTO | Cessna F.177RG | C. R. & J. Cox (G-OADE/G-AZKH) |
| | G-TOTY | Robinson R-22B | Northern Helicopters Ltd |
| | G-TOUR | Robin R.2112 | Barnes Martin Ltd |
| | G-TOYS | Enstrom 280C-UK-2 Shark | J. J. Martyn (G-BISE) |
| | G-TPHK | BAe 125 Srs 800B | Tiphook PLC (G-FDSL)/Biggin Hill |
| | G-TPII | Colt 21A balloon | Airship & Balloon Co Ltd |
| | G-TRAK | Edgley EA.7 Optica | Brooklands Aerospace Group PLC (G-BLFC)/Old Sarum |
| | G-TRCO | PA-23 Aztec 250E | R. Dorrien-Smith (G-OCFS/G-BBFU) |
| | G-TREE | Bell 206B JetRanger | LGH Aviation Ltd |
| | G-TRIC | D.H.C.1 Chipmunk 22A | D. M. Barnett (G-AOSZ) |

| Reg. | Type | Owner or Operator | Notes |
|------|------|-------------------|-------|
| G-TRIK | Bell 206B JetRanger 2 | Annabelle Casion Ltd (G-BMWY) | |
| G-TRIM | Monnet Moni | J. E. Bennell | |
| G-TRIN | SOCATA TB.20 Trinidad | Air Touring Services Ltd/Biggin Hill | |
| G-TRIP | PA-32R-301 Saratoga SP | C. P. Lockyer (G-HOSK) | |
| G-TRIV | Colt Trivial Pursuit SS balloon | Airship & Balloon Co Ltd | |
| G-TRIX | V.S.509 Spitfire T.IX (PV202) | R. J. F. Parker | |
| G-TROP | Cessna 310R | R. P. Nash/Norwich | |
| G-TRUC | Cassutt Speed One | J. A. H. Chadwick | |
| G-TRUK | Stoddard-Hamilton Glasair RG | Archer Engineering (Leeds) Ltd | |
| G-TRUX | Colt 77A balloon | Highway Truck Rental Ltd | |
| G-TSAM | BAe 125 Srs 800B | British Aerospace PLC/Hatfield | |
| G-TSFT | PA-28-161 Warrior II | SFT Aviation Ltd (G-BLDJ)/ Bournemouth | |
| G-TSGJ | PA-28-181 Archer II | Golf Juliet Flying Club | |
| G-TSIX | AT-6C Harvard IIA | D. Taylor/E. Midlands | |
| G-TTAM | Taylor JT.2 Titch | A. J. Manning | |
| G-TTEL | PA-E23 Aztec 250D | Target Technology Electronics Ltd (G-BBXE) | |
| G-TTHC | Robinson R-22B | Tyne-Tees Helicopter Centre Ltd/ Teesside | |
| G-TTWO | Colt 56A balloon | P. N. Tilney | |
| G-TUBE | Hughes 369E | Apex Tubulars Ltd | |
| G-TUBS | Beech 65-80 Queen Air | A. H. Bowers (G-ASKM)/Staverton | |
| G-TUDR | Cameron V-77 balloon | Jacques W. Soukup Ltd | |
| G-TUGG | PA-18 Super Cub 150 | Ulster Gliding Club Ltd | |
| G-TUKE | Robin DR.400/160 | Tukair/Headcorn | |
| G-TURB | D.31 Turbulent | A. Ryan-Fecitt | |
| G-TURK | Cameron 80 Sultan SS balloon | Forbes Europe Inc | |
| G-TURN | Steen Skybolt | M. Hammond | |
| G-TURP | SA.341G Gazelle 1 | Lenval Essex Ltd (G-BKLS) | |
| G-TVMM | Cessna 310Q | F. G. Quartermaine (G-CETA/G-BBIM) | |
| G-TVSI | Campbell Cricket | W. H. Beevers (G-AYHH) | |
| G-TVTV | Cameron TV-90 SS balloon | Cameron Balloons Ltd | |
| G-TWEL | PA-28-181 Archer II | Universal Salvage (Holdings) Ltd | |
| G-TWEY | Colt 69A balloon | British Telecom Thamesway | |
| G-TWIN | PA-44-180 Seminole | Leavesden Flight Centre Ltd | |
| G-TWIZ | R. Commander 114 | B. C. & P. M. Cox/Biggin Hill | |
| G-TWOB | BN-2B-26 Islander | Pilatus BN Ltd (G-BKJJ)/Bembridge | |
| G-TYGA | AA-5B Tiger | Hovemere Ltd (G-BHNZ)/Biggin Hill | |
| G-TYRE | Cessna F.172M | Staverton Flying Services Ltd | |
| G-TZAR | PA-46-350P Malibu Mirage | Czar Aviation Ltd | |
| G-UARD | Sequoia F.8L Falco | A. J. Baggarley | |
| G-UDAY | Robinson R-22B | Oakover Holdings Ltd | |
| G-UERN | BN-2B-26 Islander | Air Sarnia Ltd (G-BHXI)/Guernsey | |
| G-UEST | Bell 206B JetRanger 2 | Air Hilstone Ltd (G-ROYB/G-BLWU) | |
| G-UFLY | Cessna F.150H | Westair Flying Services Ltd (G-AVVY)/ Blackpool | |
| G-UIDE | Jodel D.120 | S. T. Gilbert/Popham | |
| G-UIET | BAe ATP | Manx Airlines Ltd/Ronaldsway | |
| G-UILD | Grob G.109B | Runnymede Consultants Ltd | |
| G-UKAC | BAe 146-300 | Air UK Ltd/Norwich | |
| G-UKAG | BAe 146-300 | Air UK Ltd/Stansted | |
| G-UKCA | H.S.125 Srs 700B | Magec Aviation Ltd/Luton | |
| G-UKHP | BAe 146-300 | Air UK Ltd/Norwich | |
| G-UKID | BAe 146-300 | Air UK Ltd/Norwich | |
| G-UKJF | BAe 146-100 | Air UK Ltd/Norwich | |
| G-UKLA | Boeing 737-4Y0 | Air UK Leisure Ltd *St Andrew*/Stansted | |
| G-UKLB | Boeing 737-4Y0 | Air UK Leisure Ltd *St Bernard*/Stansted | |
| G-UKLC | Boeing 737-42C | Air UK Leisure Ltd *St Christopher*/ Stansted | |
| G-UKLD | Boeing 737-42C | Air UK Leisure Ltd *St David*/Stansted | |
| G-UKLE | Boeing 737-4Y0 | Air UK Leisure Ltd *St Edmund*/Stansted | |
| G-UKLF | Boeing 737-42C | Air UK Leisure Ltd *St Francis*/Stansted | |
| G-UKLG | Boeing 737-42C | Air UK Leisure Ltd *St George*/Stansted | |
| G-UKNZ | Colt Flying Harp SS balloon | Flying Pictures Ltd | |
| G-UKPC | BAe 146-100 | Air UK Ltd (G-BKXZ)/Norwich | |
| G-UKRB | Colt 105A balloon | Airship & Balloon Co Ltd | |
| G-UKSC | BAe 146-300 | Air UK Ltd/Norwich | |
| G-UMBO | Thunder Ax7-77A balloon | Virgin Atlantic Airways Ltd | |
| G-UNIK | AB-206B JetRanger 2 | RCR Aviation Ltd (G-TPPH/G-BCYP) | |
| G-UPCC | Robinson R-22B | E. C. Cooke (G-MUSS) | |
| G-UPDN | Cameron V-65 balloon | R. J. O. Evans | |

| Notes | Reg. | Type | Owner or Operator |
|---|---|---|---|
| | G-UPPP | Colt 77A balloon | M. Williams |
| | G-UPPY | Cameron DP-80 balloon | Cameron Balloons Ltd |
| | G-UPUP | Cameron V-77 balloon | M. White |
| | G-UROP | Beech 95-B55 Baron | Pooler International Ltd |
| | G-URRR | Air Command 582 Sport | L. Armes |
| | G-USAF | NA T-28C Trojan | M. B. Walker |
| | G-USAM | Cameron Uncle Sam balloon | Jacques W. Soukup Enterprises Ltd |
| | G-USGB | Colt 105A balloon | Thunder & Colt Ltd |
| | G-USIL | Thunder Ax7-77 balloon | Solarmoor Ltd |
| | G-USMC | Cameron 90 Chestie SS balloon | Jacques W. Soukup Enterprises Ltd |
| | G-USSR | Cameron 90 Doll SS balloon | Cameron Balloons Ltd |
| | G-USSY | PA-28-181 Archer II | Thruxton Helicopter & Equipment Sales |
| | G-USTI | Cameron H-34 balloon | Allen & Harris Ltd |
| | G-USTV | Messerschmitt Bf.109G-2 | Imperial War Museum/Duxford |
| | G-USTY | FRED Srs 2 | K. Jones |
| | G-UTSI | Rand KR-2 | K. B. Gutridge |
| | G-UTSY | PA-28R-201 Arrow III | D. G. Perry/Stapleford |
| | G-UTZY | SA.341G Gazelle 1 | Davinci Aviation Ltd (G-BKLV) |
| | G-UZEL | SA.341G Gazelle 1 | Rutland Properties Ltd (G-BRNH) |
| | | | |
| | G-VAGA | PA-15 Vagabond | E. J. McEntee/White Waltham |
| | G-VAJT | M.S.894E Rallye 220GT | R. W. B. Rolfe |
| | G-VARG | Varga 2150A Kachina | J. Hannibal/Halfpenny Green |
| | G-VAUK | PA-31-350 Navajo Chieftain | John Mowlem & Co PLC (G-GWEA) |
| | G-VAUN | Cessna 340 | F. E. Peacock & Son (Thorney) Ltd |
| | G-VCJH | Robinson R-22B | Great Northern Helicopters Ltd |
| | G-VCSI | Rotorway Executive | Qual-Rect Ltd |
| | G-VELA | SIAI-Marchetti S.205-22R | D. P. & P. A. Dawson |
| | G-VENI | D.H.112 Venom FB.50 | Source Premium & Promotional Consultants Ltd |
| | G-VERT | Bell 222 | Arlington Securities PLC (G-JLBZ/ G-BNDB) |
| | G-VEZE | Rutan Vari-Eze | P. J. Henderson |
| | G-VGIN | Boeing 747-243B | Virgin Atlantic Airways Ltd *Scarlet Lady/* Gatwick |
| | G-VHFA | PA-23 Aztec 250 | Hartfield Aviation Ltd (G-BZFE/G-AZFE) |
| | G-VICK | PA-31 Turbo Navajo | Skywatch Ltd (G-AWED)/Birmingham |
| | G-VIDI | D.H.112 Venom FB.50 (WE402) | Source Premium & Promotional Consultants Ltd |
| | G-VIEW | Vinten-Wallis WA-116/100 | K. H. Wallis |
| | G-VIII | V. S. Spitfire LF.VIII (MT719) | Reynard Racing Cars Ltd/Duxford |
| | G-VIKE | Bellanca 1730A Viking | Peter Dolan & Co Ltd |
| | G-VIPS | Learjet 35A | Executive Air Charter Ltd (G-SOVN/ G-PJET)/Biggin Hill |
| | G-VIRG | Boeing 747-287B | Virgin Atlantic Airways Ltd *Maiden Voyager/*Gatwick |
| | G-VISA | Cessna A.152 | K. W. Felton |
| | G-VIST | PA-30 Twin Comanche 160B | Vist Aviation (G-AVHZ) |
| | G-VITE | Robin R.1180T | G-VITE Flying Group |
| | G-VIVA | Thunder Ax7-65 balloon | J. G. Spearing |
| | G-VIXN | D.H.110 Sea Vixen FAW.2 (XS587) ★ | P. G. Vallance Ltd |
| | G-VIZZ | Sportavia RS.180 Sportsman | Executive Air Sport Ltd/Exeter |
| | G-VJAI | GA-7 Cougar | United Breweries (International) Ltd (G-OCAB/G-BICF)/Elstree |
| | G-VJAY | H.S.125 Srs F400B | Jensen & Nicholson (S) Pte Ltd (G-AYLG) |
| | G-VJCB | Agusta A.109A II | J. C. Bamford Excavators Ltd (G-BOUA) |
| | G-VJCT | Partenavia P.68C | Montrose Leasing Ltd |
| | G-VJET | Avro 698 Vulcan B.2 (XL426) | R. E. Jacobsen |
| | G-VJFK | Boeing 747-238B | Virgin Atlantic Airways Ltd/Gatwick |
| | G-VJIM | Colt 77 Jumbo Jim SS balloon | Airship & Balloon Co Ltd |
| | G-VLAD | Yakolev Yak-50 | R. Goode/Staverton |
| | G-VLAX | Boeing 747-238B | Virgin Atlantic Airways Ltd/Gatwick |
| | G-VMAX | Mooney M.20K | Glidegold Ltd |
| | G-VMDE | Cessna P.210N | Royton Express Deliveries (Welwyn) Ltd |
| | G-VMIA | Boeing 747-123 | Virgin Atlantic Airways Ltd (G-HIHO)/ Gatwick |
| | G-VNOM | D.H.112 Venom FB.50 | A. Topen/Cranfield |
| | G-VODA | Cameron N-77 balloon | Racal Telecom PLC |
| | G-VOID | PA-28RT-201 Arrow IV | R. B. H. Vetch |
| | G-VOLT | Cameron N-77 balloon | National Power |
| | G-VOYG | Boeing 747-283B | Virgin Atlantic Airways Ltd (G-BMGS)/ Gatwick |

| Reg. | Type | Owner or Operator | Notes |
|------|------|-------------------|-------|
| G-VPII | Evans VP-2 | V. D. J. Hitchings (G-EDIF) | |
| G-VPLC | Beech 200 Super King Air | Vickers Shipbuilding & Engineering Ltd | |
| G-VPTO | Evans VP-2 | J. Cater | |
| G-VRES | Beech A200 Super King Air | Northern Executive Aviation Ltd/ Manchester | |
| G-VRGN | Boeing 747-212B | Virgin Atlantic Airways Ltd *Maid of Honour*/Gatwick | |
| G-VSEL | Beech 200 Super King Air | Vickers Shipbuilding & Engineering Ltd (G-SONG/G-BKTI)/Barrow | |
| G-VSOP | Cameron 60 SS balloon | J. R. Parkington & Co Ltd | |
| G-VTAX | PA-31-350 Navajo Chieftain | Jet West Ltd/Exeter | |
| G-VTII | D.H.115 Vampire T.11 (WZ507) | J. Turnbull & ptnrs/Cranfield | |
| G-VTOL | H.S. Harrier T52★ | Brooklands Museum of Aviation/ Weybridge | |
| G-VULC | Avro 698 Vulcan B.2 (XM655) | R. E. Jacobsen | |
| G-VVBK | PA-34-200T Seneca II | Videovision Air (G-BSBS/G-BDRI) | |
| G-WAAC | Cameron N-56 balloon | Newbury Ballooning Co Ltd | |
| G-WACA | Cessna F.152 | Wycombe Air Centre Ltd | |
| G-WACB | Cessna F.152 | Wycombe Air Centre Ltd | |
| G-WACC | Cessna F.152 | Wycombe Air Centre Ltd | |
| G-WACE | Cessna F.152 | Wycombe Air Centre Ltd | |
| G-WACF | Cessna 152 | Wycombe Air Centre Ltd | |
| G-WACG | Cessna F.152 | Wycombe Air Centre Ltd | |
| G-WACH | Cessna FA.152 | Wycombe Air Centre Ltd | |
| G-WACI | Beech 76 Duchess | Wycombe Air Centre Ltd | |
| G-WACJ | Beech 76 Duchess | Wycombe Air Centre Ltd | |
| G-WACK | Short SD3-60 Variant 100 | Loganair Ltd (G-BMAJ)/Glasgow | |
| G-WACL | Cessna F.172N | Wycombe Air Centre Ltd (G-BHGG) | |
| G-WACO | Waco UPF.7 | RGV (Aircraft Services) & Co/Staverton | |
| G-WACP | PA-28 Cherokee 180 | Hartmann Ltd (G-BBPP)/Booker | |
| G-WACR | PA-28 Cherokee 180 | Wycombe Air Centre Ltd (G-BCZF) | |
| G-WACS | Cessna F.152 | Hartmann Ltd/Booker | |
| G-WACT | Cessna F.152 II | Hartmann Ltd (G-BKFT)/Booker | |
| G-WACU | Cessna FA.152 | Hartmann Ltd (G-BJZU)/Booker | |
| G-WACV | Cessna 182N | Deeperton Ltd (G-AZEA)/Booker | |
| G-WACW | Cessna 172P | Wycombe Air Centre Ltd | |
| G-WACY | Cessna F.172P | Wycombe Air Centre Ltd | |
| G-WACZ | Cessna F.172M | Wycombe Air Centre Ltd (G-BCUK) | |
| G-WAGI | Robinson R-22B | J. Wagstaff | |
| G-WAIT | Cameron V-77 balloon | G. & D. A. Waite | |
| G-WALL | Beech 95-58PA Baron | C. D. Weiswall/Elstree | |
| G-WALS | Cessna A.152 | Redhill Flying Club | |
| G-WARD | Taylor JT.1 Monoplane | G. D. & P. J. Ward | |
| G-WARE | PA-28-161 Warrior II | W. J. Ware | |
| G-WARI | PA-28-161 Warrior II | Garrick Aviation | |
| G-WARK | Schweizer 269C | Warwickshire Constabulary | |
| G-WARR | PA-28-161 Warrior II | M. Rumbol | |
| G-WASH | Noble 1250 balloon | Noble Adventures Ltd | |
| G-WASP | Brantly B.2B | W. C. Evans & M. L. Morris (G-ASXE) | |
| G-WATS | PA-34-220T Seneca III | Walker Air Training Services Ltd (G-BOVJ) | |
| G-WATT | Cameron Cooling Tower SS balloon | National Power | |
| G-WATZ | PA-28-151 Warrior | Walker Air Training Services Ltd | |
| G-WBAT | Wombat gyroplane | C. D. Julian (G-BSID) | |
| G-WBPR | BAe 125 Srs 800B | Trusthouse Forte PLC/Heathrow | |
| G-WBTS | Falconair F-11 | W. C. Brown (G-BDPL) | |
| G-WCAT | Colt Flying Mitt SS balloon | Interline Develoments Ltd | |
| G-WCEI | M.S.894E Rallye 220GT | T. W. Pullin (G-BAOC) | |
| G-WDEB | Thunder Ax-7-77 balloon | W. de Bock | |
| G-WEEZ | Mooney M.20J | Aeromarine Ltd | |
| G-WELI | Cameron N-77 balloon | A. K. F. Violett | |
| G-WELL | Beech E90 King Air | CEGA Aviation Ltd/Goodwood | |
| G-WELS | Cameron N-65 balloon | Charles Wells Ltd | |
| G-WEND | PA-28RT-201 Arrow IV | Warwickshire Flying Training Centre Ltd/Birmingham | |
| G-WERY | SOCATA TB.20 Trinidad | Wery Flying Group/Sherburn | |
| G-WEST | Agusta A.109A | Westland Helicopters Ltd/Yeovil | |
| G-WESX | CFM Streak Shadow | Wessex Aviation Ltd | |
| G-WETI | Cameron N-31 balloon | C. A. Butter & J. J. T. Cooke | |
| G-WGCS | PA-18 Super Cub 95 | T. M. Storey/Shoreham | |

| Notes | Reg. | Type | Owner or Operator |
|---|---|---|---|
| | G-WGEL | Boeing 737-2U4 | Dan-Air Services Ltd (G-ILFC/G-BOSL)/ Gatwick |
| | G-WGSC | Pilatus PC-6/B2-H4 Turbo Porter | D. M. Penny |
| | G-WHIM | Colt 77A balloon | D. L. Morgan |
| | G-WHIR | Montgomerie Bensen B.8MR | A. P. Barden (G-BROT) |
| | G-WHIZ | Pitts S-1 Special | K. M. McLeod |
| | G-WHIZ† | V.701 Viscount ★ | Saltwell Park (G-AMOE)/Gateshead |
| | G-WHIZ† | V.732 Viscount (fuselage only) ★ | Wales Aircraft Museum (G-ANRS)/ Cardiff |
| | G-WHRL | Schweizer 269C | Wessex Whirlybirds Ltd |
| | G-WICH | FRED Srs 2 | R. H. Hearn |
| | G-WICK | Partenavia P.68B | Strix Ltd & ptnrs (G-BGFZ) |
| | G-WIEN | Rans S.10 Sakota | N. P. Rieser |
| | G-WILD | Pitts S-1T Special | G. H. Wilson |
| | G-WILI | PA-32R-301 Saratoga SP | Minster Enterprises Ltd |
| | G-WILK | Beech B200 Super King Air | Wilkes Asset Management Ltd (G-BOBM)/Leeds |
| | G-WILO | Bell 206B JetRanger | Candyfleet Ltd |
| | G-WILY | Rutan LongEz | P. D. Bruce |
| | G-WIMP | Colt 56A balloon | C. Wolstenholme *Wimp* |
| | G-WINE | Thunder Ax7-77Z balloon | R. Brooker |
| | G-WINK | AA-5B Tiger | D. G. Winks |
| | G-WIRE | AS.355F-1 Twin Squirrel | National Grid Co PLC (G-CEGB/G/BLJL) |
| | G-WIRL | Robinson R-22B | T. Goring |
| | G-WISK | Schweizer 269C | Freightflow International Ltd |
| | G-WITE | Cessna 414A | Orkney Property Services (G-LOVO/ G-KENT) |
| | G-WIZO | PA-34-220T Seneca III | Landhurst Leasing PLC |
| | G-WIZZ | AB-206B JetRanger 2 | Crest Engineering Ltd |
| | G-WLAD | BAC One-Eleven 304AX | Ali Finance Ltd (G-ATPI) |
| | G-WMCC | BAe Jetstream 3102-01 | Birmingham European Airways Ltd (G-TALL) |
| | G-WMPA | AS.355F-2 Twin Squirrel | W. Midlands Police Authority/ Birmingham |
| | G-WOLD | Scheibe SF.25E Falke | Wolds Gliding Club Ltd (G-BOVM) Pocklington Ltd |
| | G-WOLF | PA-28 Cherokee 140 | P. R. Wernham |
| | G-WOOD | Beech 95-B55A Baron | T. D. Broadhurst (G-AYID) |
| | G-WOSP | Bell 206B JetRanger 3 | Gleneagles Helicopter Services (Scotland) Ltd |
| | G-WOTG | BN-2T Islander | RAF Sport Parachute Association (G-BJYT) |
| | G-WOTS | PA-34-200T Seneca II | Walker Air Training Services Ltd (G-SEVL) |
| | G-WPLC | Beech 200 Super King Air | Whitbread & Co PLC |
| | G-WRCF | Beech 200 Super King Air | W. R. C. M. Foyle/Luton |
| | G-WREN | Pitts S-2A Special | P. R. Rutterford/Redhill |
| | G-WRFM | Enstrom 280C-UK Shark | Trimlook Ltd (G-CTSI/G-BKIO) |
| | G-WRIT | Thunder Ax7-77A balloon | J. Edge |
| | G-WRLD | Cameron R-15 balloon | Cameron Balloons Ltd |
| | G-WRMN | Glaser-Dirks DG.400 | W. R. McNair |
| | G-WROX | PA-31-350 Navajo Chieftain | Levenmere Ltd (G-BNZI) |
| | G-WSEC | Enstrom F-28C | J. Mills (G-BONF) |
| | G-WSFT | PA-23 Aztec 250F | SFT Aviation Ltd (G-BTHS)/ Bournemouth |
| | G-WSKY | Enstrom 280C-UK-2 Shark | Footlea Ltd (G-BEEK) |
| | G-WSSL | PA-31-350 Navajo Chieftain | Compass Aviation Ltd |
| | G-WTFA | Cessna F.182P | David Martin Couriers Ltd |
| | G-WULF | WAR Focke-Wulf Fw.190 (08) | P. C. Logsdon |
| | G-WWII | V.S. 379 Spitfire XIV (SM832) | Charles Church Displays Ltd |
| | G-WYCH | Cameron 90 Witch SS balloon | Jacques W. Soukup Enterprises Ltd |
| | G-WYMP | Cessna F.150J | L. Scattergood & R. Hall (G-BAGW) |
| | G-WYNN | Rand KR-2 | W. Thomas |
| | G-WYNT | Cameron N-56 balloon | Jacques W. Soukup Enterprises Ltd |
| | G-WYPA | MBB Bo 105DBS/4 | W. Yorkshire Police Authority |
| | G-WYTE | Bell 47G-2A-1 | CKS Air Ltd/Southend |
| | G-WYZZ | Air Command 532 Elite | C. H. Gem (G-BPAK) |
| | G-WZZZ | Colt AS-56 airship | Hot-Air Balloon Co Ltd |
| | G-XALP | Schweizer 269C | R. F. Jones |
| | G-XCUB | PA-18 Super Cub 150 | M. C. Barraclough |
| | G-XIIX | Robinson R-22B | Defence Products Ltd |
| | G-XMAF | G.1159A Gulfstream 3 | Fayair (Jersey) 1984 Ltd |

| Reg. | Type | Owner or Operator | Notes |
|------|------|-------------------|-------|
| G-XRAY | Rand KR-2 | R. S. Smith | |
| G-XRMC | BAe 125 Srs 800B | RMC Group Services Ltd | |
| G-XSFT | PA-23 Aztec 250F | SFT Aviation Ltd (G-CPPC/G-BGBH)/ Bournemouth | |
| G-XTRA | Extra EA.230 | Firebird Aerobatics Ltd/Booker | |
| G-XXIV | AB-206B JetRanger 3 | Defence Products Ltd | |
| G-YAWW | PA-28R-201T Turbo Arrow III | Barton Aviation Ltd | |
| G-YBAA | Cessna FR.172J | J. Blackburn | |
| G-YEOM | PA-31-350 Navajo Chieftain | Foster Yeoman Ltd/Exeter | |
| G-YEWS | Rotorway Executive | D. G. Pollard | |
| G-YIII | Cessna F.150L | Skyviews & General Ltd/Sherburn | |
| G-YNOT | D.62B Condor | T. Littlefair (G-AYFH) | |
| G-YOGI | Robin DR.400/140B | R. M. Gosling (G-BDME) | |
| G-YORK | Cessna F.172M | H. G. Keighley/Sherburn | |
| G-YOTT | Cessna 425 | E. & M. Green (G-NORC)/Guernsey | |
| G-YPSY | Andreasson BA-4B | H. P. Burrill | |
| G-YROB | Air Command 532 Elite | R. R. Mainstone | |
| G-YROI | Air Command Commander 532 | W. B. Lumb | |
| G-YROS | Bensen B.80-D | C. Tuxworth | |
| G-YROY | Montgomerie Bensen B.8MR | R. D. Armishaw | |
| G-YSFT | PA-23 Aztec 250F | SFT Aviation Ltd (G-BEJT)/ Bournemouth | |
| G-YSKY | PA-31-350 Navajo Chieftain | J. J. Baumhardt/Southend | |
| G-YTWO | Cessna F.172M | Sherburn Aero Club Ltd | |
| G-YUCS | PA-32R-301 Saratoga SP | Eastman Securities Ltd (G-BSOL) | |
| G-YUGO | H.S.125 Srs 1B/R-522 | Burtonwood Development Ltd (G-ATWH) | |
| G-YULL | PA-28 Cherokee 180E | Lansdowne Chemical Co (G-BEAJ)/ Kidlington | |
| G-YUPI | Cameron N-90 balloon | West Country Marketing & Advertising Ltd | |
| G-ZADT | Colt 77A balloon | ADT Auctions Ltd (G-ZBCA) | |
| G-ZAPA | Cessna 404 Titan | Titan Airways Ltd/Stansted | |
| G-ZAPB | Cessna 404 Titan | Artac Airchartering Services Ltd (G-HIGS/G-ODAS) | |
| G-ZAPC | Short SD3-30 Variant 100 | Titan Airways Ltd (G-RNMO/G-BFZW)/ Stansted | |
| G-ZARA | Nord 3400 | D. E. Bain & ptnrs | |
| G-ZARI | AA-5B Tiger | P. L. Pilch (G-BHVY)/Biggin Hill | |
| G-ZAZA | PA-18 Super Cub 95 | Airbourne Taxi Services Ltd | |
| G-ZELL | SA.341G Gazelle 1 | Don Shead Ltd | |
| G-ZERO | AA-5B Tiger | Snowadem Ltd/Luton | |
| G-ZFDB | AS.355F-1 Twin Squirrel | Haydon-Baillie Naval & Aircraft Museum (G-BLEV)/Southampton | |
| G-ZIGG | Robinson R-22B | Nivison Holdings Ltd | |
| G-ZIPI | Robin DR.400/180 | Stahl Engineering Co Ltd/Headcorn | |
| G-ZIPP | Cessna E.310Q | Bank Farm Ltd (G-BAYU) | |
| G-ZLIN | Z.526 Trener Master | R. P. Hallam | |
| G-ZSFT | PA-23 Aztec 250 | SFT Aviation Ltd (G-SALT/G-BGTH)/ Bournemouth | |
| G-ZSOL | Zlin Z.50L | A. J. E. Ditheridge | |
| G-ZULU | PA-28-161 Warrior II | Denham School of Flying Ltd | |
| G-ZUMP | Cameron N-77 balloon | Allen & Harris Ltd | |

# Toy Balloons

| Notes | Reg. | Type | Owner or Operator |
|-------|------|------|-------------------|
|  | G-FYAK | European E.21 | J. E. Christopher |
|  | G-FYAN | Williams | M. D. Williams |
|  | G-FYAO | Williams | M. D. Williams |
|  | G-FYAT | Osprey Mk 4D | L. A. Cotgrove |
|  | G-FYAU | Williams MK 2 | M. D. Williams |
|  | G-FYAV | Osprey Mk 4E2 | C. D. Egan & C. Stiles |
|  | G-FYAZ | Osprey Mk 4D2 | M. A. Roblett |
|  | G-FYBA | Portswood Mk XVI | C. R. Rundle |
|  | G-FYBD | Osprey Mk 1E | M. Vincent |
|  | G-FYBE | Osprey Mk 4D | M. Vincent |
|  | G-FYBF | Osprey Mk V | M. Vincent |
|  | G-FYBG | Osprey Mk 4G2 | M. Vincent |
|  | G-FYBH | Osprey Mk 4G | M. Vincent |
|  | G-FYBI | Osprey Mk 4H | M. Vincent |
|  | G-FYBP | European E.84PW | D. Eaves |
|  | G-FYBR | Osprey Mk 4G2 | A. J. Pugh |
|  | G-FYBU | Portswood Mk XVI | M. A. Roblett |
|  | G-FYBX | Portswood Mk XVI | I. Chadwick |
|  | G-FYCC | Osprey Mk 4G2 | A. Russell |
|  | G-FYCL | Osprey Mk 4G | P. J. Rogers |
|  | G-FYCN | Osprey Mk 4D | C. F. Chipping |
|  | G-FYCO | Osprey Mk 4B | C. F. Chipping |
|  | G-FYCP | Osprey Mk 1E | C. F. Chipping |
|  | G-FYCR | Osprey MK 4D | C. F. Chipping |
|  | G-FYCT | Osprey Mk 4D | S. T. Wallbank |
|  | G-FYCU | Osprey Mk 4D | G. M. Smith |
|  | G-FYCV | Osprey Mk 4D | M. Thomson |
|  | G-FYCW | Osprey Mk 4D | M. L. Partridge |
|  | G-FYCZ | Osprey Mk 4D2 | P. Middleton |
|  | G-FYDC | European EDH-1 | D. Eaves & H. Goddard |
|  | G-FYDD | Osprey Mk 4D | A. C. Mitchell |
|  | G-FYDF | Osprey Mk 4D | K. A. Jones |
|  | G-FYDI | Williams Westwind Two | M. D. Williams |
|  | G-FYDK | Williams Westwind Two | M. D. Williams |
|  | G-FYDM | Williams Westwind Four | M. D. Williams |
|  | G-FYDN | European 8C | P. D. Ridout |
|  | G-FYDO | Osprey Mk 4D | N. L. Scallan |
|  | G-FYDP | Williams Westwind Three | M. D. Williams |
|  | G-FYDS | Osprey Mk 4D | N. L. Scallan |
|  | G-FYDW | Osprey Mk 4B | R. A. Balfre |
|  | G-FYEB | Rango Rega | N. H. Ponsford |
|  | G-FYEG | Osprey Mk 1C | P. E. Prime |
|  | G-FYEI | Portswood Mk XVI | A. Russell |
|  | G-FYEJ | Rango NA.24 | N. H. Ponsford |
|  | G-FYEK | Unicorn UE.1C | D. & D. Eaves |
|  | G-FYEL | European E.84Z | D. Eaves |
|  | G-FYEO | Eagle Mk 1 | M. E. Scallon |
|  | G-FYEV | Osprey Mk 1C | M. E. Scallen |
|  | G-FYEZ | Firefly Mk 1 | M. E. & N. L. Scallan |
|  | G-FYFA | European E.84LD | D. Goddard & D. Eaves |
|  | G-FYFG | European E.84DE | D. Eaves |
|  | G-FYFH | European E.84DS | D. Eaves |
|  | G-FYFI | European E.84DS | M. Stelling |
|  | G-FYFJ | Williams Westland 2 | M. D. Williams |
|  | G-FYFK | Williams Westland 2 | D. Feasey |
|  | G-FYFN | Osprey Saturn 2 | J. & M. Woods |
|  | G-FYFT | Rango NA-32BC | Rango Kite & Balloon Co |
|  | G-FYFV | Saffrey Grand Edinburgh | I. G. & G. M. McIntosh |
|  | G-FYFW | Rango NA-55 | Rango Kite & Balloon Co |
|  | G-FYFY | Rango NA-55RC | A. M. Lindsay |
|  | G-FYGA | Rango NA-50RC | Rango Kite & Balloon Co |
|  | G-FYGB | Rango NA-105RC | Rango Kite & Balloon Co |
|  | G-FYGC | Rango NA-42B | L. J. Wardle |
|  | G-FYGG | Buz-B20 | D. P. Busby & S. Spink |
|  | G-FYGH | Busby Buz B.20W | D. P. Busby |
|  | G-FYGI | Rango NA-55RC | Advertair Ltd |

G-ANEZ  DH82A Tiger Moth.  AJW

G-BEKG    HS748 srs 1 of British Independent Airways.    AJW

G-BPDL Embraer EMB-110P1 Bandeirante of Titan Airways. *PRM*

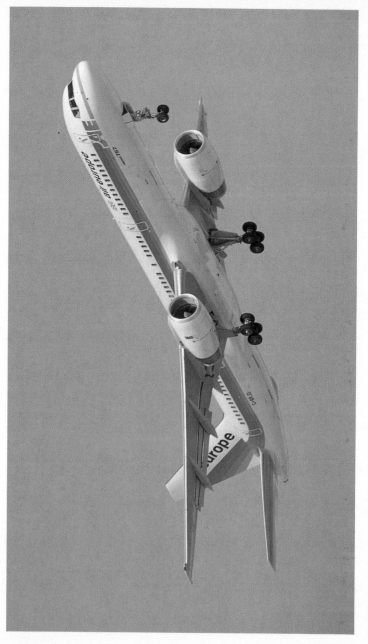

G-BRJD   Boeing 757-236 belonging to Air Europe.   AJW

G-CAYN Dornier 228-201 of Cayenne Ltd.  *ADB*

G-HPLC   Sikorsky S-76B helicopter owned by Hanson PLC.   *PRM*

G-JEAI   Fokker F-27-500 in the colours of Jersey European Airways.   *Austin J. Brown/Aviation Picture Library*

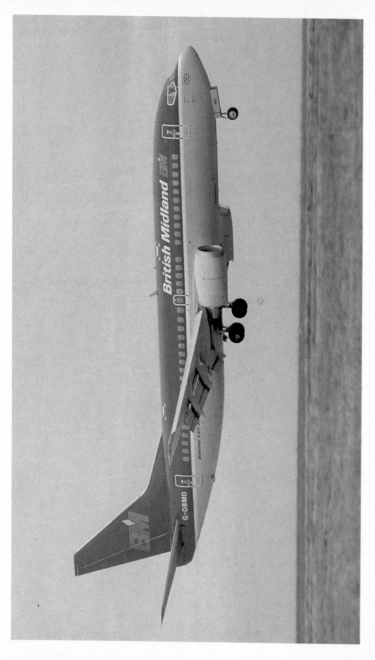

G-OBMD Boeing 737-300 of British Midland. *AJW*

G-RAIN   Maule M5-235C Lunar Rocket.   *PRM*

G-VLAD and G-IVAR   Yak-50s of the Vladivar aerobatic team.   *PRM*

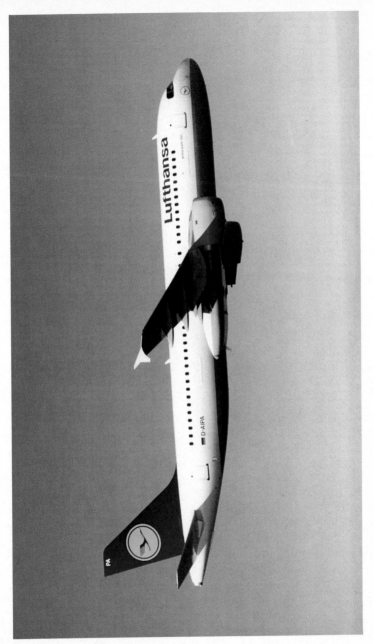

D-AIPA Airbus A320-200 of German carrier Lufthansa. *Airbus*

D-BEAT   DHC Dash 8 srs 300 belonging to DLT.   *PRM*

HB-IHK   Douglas DC-10-30 of Swiss carrier Balair.   AJW

LZ-BTD   Tupolev Tu-154B of Balkan Bulgarian Airlines.   *AJW*

OY-STI   SE210 Caravelle 10B of Danish airline Sterling Airways.   *AJW*

VH-OJA    Boeing 747-400 of Australian flag-carrier Qantas.    *PRM*

# Microlights

| Reg. | Type | Owner or Operator | Notes |
|------|------|-------------------|-------|
| G-MBAA | Hiway Skytrike Mk 2 | M. J. Aubrey | |
| G-MBAB | Hovey Whing-Ding II | R. F. Morton | |
| G-MBAD | Weedhopper JC-24A | M. Stott | |
| G-MBAF | R. J. Swift 3 | C. G. Wrzesien | |
| G-MBAJ | Chargus T.250 | V. F. Potter | |
| G-MBAL | Hiway Demon | I. M. Munster | |
| G-MBAM | Skycraft Scout 2 | J. P. & C. J. Carney | |
| G-MBAN | American Aerolights Eagle | R. W. Millward | |
| G-MBAP | Rotec Rally 2B | P. D. Lucas | |
| G-MBAR | Skycraft Scout | L. Chiappi | |
| G-MBAS | Typhoon Tripacer 250 | T. J. Birkbeck | |
| G-MBAU | Hiway Skytrike | R. E. Tallack | |
| G-MBAW | Pterodactyl Ptraveller | J. C. K. Soardifield | |
| G-MBAZ | Rotec Rally 2B | Western Skysports Ltd | |
| G-MBBA | Ultraflight Lazair | A. J. Taylor | |
| G-MBBB | Skycraft Scout 2 | A. J. & B. Chalkley | |
| G-MBBG | Weedhopper JC-24B | A. J. Plumbridge & G. E. Kershaw | |
| G-MBBH | Flexiform Sealander 160 | D. A. Campbell | |
| G-MBBI | Ultraflight Mirage | G. A. Squires | |
| G-MBBJ | Hiway Demon Trike | E. B. Jones | |
| G-MBBM | Eipper Quicksilver MX | J. Brown | |
| G-MBBN | Eagle Microlight | S. Taylor & D. Williams | |
| G-MBBT | Ultrasports Tripacer 330 | The Post Office | |
| G-MBBU | Southdown Savage | D. Ward & B. J. Holloway | |
| G-MBBW | Flexiform Hilander | R. J. Hamilton & W. J. Shaw | |
| G-MBBX | Chargus Skytrike | J. R. Breislin | |
| G-MBBY | Flexiform Sealander | P. M. Fidell & H. M. Johnson | |
| G-MBBZ | Volmer Jensen VJ-24W | D. G. Cook | |
| G-MBCA | Chargus Cyclone T.250 | E. M. Jelonek | |
| G-MBCD | La Mouette Atlas | M. G. Dean | |
| G-MBCE | American Aerolights Eagle | I. H. Lewis | |
| G-MBCF | Pterodactyl Ptraveler | T. C. N. Carroll | |
| G-MBCG | Ultrasports Tripacer T.250 | A. G. Parkinson | |
| G-MBCI | Hiway Skytrike | P. A. Kilburn | |
| G-MBCJ | Mainair Sports Tri-Flyer | R. A. Smith | |
| G-MBCK | Eipper Quicksilver MX | P. Rowbotham | |
| G-MBCL | Hiway Demon Triflyer | B. R. Underwood & P. J. Challis | |
| G-MBCM | Hiway Demon 175 | J. J. Bishop | |
| G-MBCN | Hiway Super Scorpion | M. J. Hadland | |
| G-MBCO | Flexiform Sealander Buggy | P. G. Kavanagh | |
| G-MBCR | Ultraflight Mirage | B. N. Bower | |
| G-MBCU | American Aerolights Eagle | J. L. May | |
| G-MBCV | Hiway Skytrike | C. J. Greasley | |
| G-MBCW | Hiway Demon 175 | C. Foster & S. B. Elwis | |
| G-MBCX | Airwave Nimrod 165 | M. J. Ashley-Rogers | |
| G-MBCZ | Chargus Skytrike 160 | R. M. Sheppard | |
| G-MBDC | Skyhook Cutlass | R. M. Tunstall | |
| G-MBDD | Skyhook Skytrike | D. Hancock | |
| G-MBDE | Flexiform Skytrike | A. R. Cantrill & K. Michael | |
| G-MBDF | Rotec Rally 2B | J. R. & B. T. Jordan | |
| G-MBDG | Eurowing Goldwing | N. W. Beadle & ptnrs | |
| G-MBDH | Hiway Demon Triflyer | A. T. Delaney | |
| G-MBDI | Flexiform Sealander | K. Bryan | |
| G-MBDJ | Flexiform Sealander Triflyer | J. W. F. Hargrave | |
| G-MBDM | Southdown Sigma Trike | A. R. Prentice | |
| G-MBDN | Hornet Atlas | P. J. Kidson | |
| G-MBDO | Flexiform Sealander Trike | M. J. Ashey-Rogers | |
| G-MBDR | U.A.S. Stormbuggy | S. J. M. Morling | |
| G-MBDU | Chargus Titan 38 | G. C. Brooke | |
| G-MBDW | Ultrasports Tripacer Skytrike A | J. T. Meager | |
| G-MBDX | Electraflyer Eagle | Ardenco Ltd | |
| G-MBDZ | Eipper Quicksilver MX | H. Glover | |
| G-MBEA | Hornet Nimrod | M. Holling | |
| G-MBEB | Hiway Skytrike 250 Mk II | K. D. Napier & ptnrs | |
| G-MBED | Chargus Titan 38 | G. G. Foster | |
| G-MBEE | Hiway Super Scorpion Skytrike 160 | J. N. Horner | |
| G-MBEG | Eipper Quicksilver MX | T. V. Wood | |

| Notes | Reg. | Type | Owner or Operator |
|-------|------|------|-------------------|
| | G-MBEJ | Electraflyer Eagle | D. J. Royce & C. R. Gale |
| | G-MBEN | Eipper Quicksilver MX | A. A. McKenzie |
| | G-MBEP | American Aerolights Eagle | R. W. Lavender |
| | G-MBES | Skyhook Cutlass | Skyhook Sailwings Ltd |
| | G-MBET | MEA Mistral Trainer | B. H. Stephens |
| | G-MBEU | Hiway Demon T.250 | R. C. Smith |
| | G-MBEV | Chargus Titan 38 | N. Hooper |
| | G-MBFA | Hiway Skytrike 250 | P. S. Jones |
| | G-MBFE | American Aerolights Eagle | P. W. Cole |
| | G-MBFF | Southern Aerosports Scorpion | H. Redwin |
| | G-MBFG | Skyhook Sabre | M. Williamson |
| | G-MBFJ | Chargus Typhoon T.250 | R. J. B. Perry |
| | G-MBFK | Hiway Demon | D. W. Stamp |
| | G-MBFM | Hiway Hang Glider | G. P. Kimmons & T. V. O. Mahony |
| | G-MBFU | Ultrasports Tripacer | T. H. J. Prowse |
| | G-MBFX | Hiway Skytrike 250 | I. R. Ogden |
| | G-MBFY | Mirage II | J. P. Metcalf |
| | G-MBFZ | M. S. S. Goldwing | I. T. Barr |
| | G-MBGA | Solar Wings Typhoon | R. W. Hutchinson & C. Payne-Culpan |
| | G-MBGB | American Aerolights Eagle | J. C. Miles |
| | G-MBGF | Twamley Trike | T. B. Woolley |
| | G-MBGJ | Hiway Skytrike Mk 2 | B. C. Norris & J. R. Edwards |
| | G-MBGK | Electra Flyer Eagle | R. J. Osbourne |
| | G-MBGP | Solar Wings Typhoon Skytrike | C. A. Mitchell |
| | G-MBGR | Eurowing Goldwing | G. A. J. Salter |
| | G-MBGS | Rotec Rally 2B | P. C. Bell |
| | G-MBGT | American Aerolights Eagle | D. C. Lloyd |
| | G-MBGV | Skyhook Cutlass | D. M. Parsons |
| | G-MBGW | Hiway Skytrike | G. W. R. Cooke |
| | G-MBGX | Southdown Lightning | T. Knight |
| | G-MBGY | Hiway Demon Skytrike | W. Hopkins |
| | G-MBHA | Trident Trike | P. Jackson |
| | G-MBHC | Chargus Lightning T.250 | R. E. Worth |
| | G-MBHD | Hiway Vulcan Trike | D. Kiddy |
| | G-MBHE | American Aerolights Eagle | D. J. Lewis |
| | G-MBHH | Flexiform Sealander Skytrike | K. L. Smith |
| | G-MBHJ | Hornet Skyhook Cutlass | M. J. Ashcroft |
| | G-MBHK | Flexiform Skytrike | E. Barfoot |
| | G-MBHP | American Aerolights Eagle II | P. V. Trollope & H. Caldwell |
| | G-MBHT | Chargus T.250 | S. F. Dawe |
| | G-MBHW | American Aerolights Eagle | M. A. Alker |
| | G-MBHX | Pterodactyl Ptraveller | F. D. C. Luddington & P. J. Dunmore |
| | G-MBHZ | Pterodactyl Ptraveller | J. C. K. Scardfield |
| | G-MBIA | Flexiform Sealander Skytrike | I. P. Cook |
| | G-MBIC | Maxair Hummer | G. C. Calow |
| | G-MBID | American Aerolights Eagle | D. A. Campbell |
| | G-MBII | Hiway Skytrike | K. D. Beeton |
| | G-MBIO | American Aerolights Eagle Z Drive | B. J. C. Hill |
| | G-MBIT | Hiway Demon Skytrike | Kuernaland (UK) Ltd |
| | G-MBIU | Hiway Super Scorpion | M. E. Wills |
| | G-MBIV | Flexiform Skytrike | M. D. Knowlson & R. A. Pendleton |
| | G-MBIW | Hiway Demon Tri-Flyer Skytrike | Computer Mart Ltd |
| | G-MBIY | Ultra Sports | P. G. Overall |
| | G-MBIZ | Mainair Tri-Flyer | E. F. Clapham & ptnrs |
| | G-MBJA | Eurowing Goldwing | W. D. Gordon |
| | G-MBJD | American Aerolights Eagle | R. W. F. Boarder |
| | G-MBJE | Airwave Nimrod | M. E. Glanvill |
| | G-MBJF | Hiway Skytrike Mk II | C. H. Bestwick |
| | G-MBJG | Airwave Nimrod | D. H. George |
| | G-MBJI | Southern Aerosports Scorpion | Robert Montgomery Ltd |
| | G-MBJK | American Aerolights Eagle | B. W. Olley |
| | G-MBJL | Airwave Nimrod | A. G. Lowe |
| | G-MBJM | Striplin Lone Ranger | C. K. Brown |
| | G-MBJN | Electraflyer Eagle | M. M. Wallace |
| | G-MBJO | Birdman Cherokee | C. A. James & T. T. Parr |
| | G-MBJP | Hiway Skytrike | R. C. Crowley |
| | G-MBJR | American Aerolights Eagle | M. P. Skelding |
| | G-MBJS | Mainair Tri-Flyer | T. W. Taylor |
| | G-MBJT | Hiway Skytrike II | R. A. Kennedy |
| | G-MBJZ | Eurowing Catto CP.16 | Neville Chamberlain Ltd |
| | G-MBKA | Mistral Trainer | G. H. Liddle |
| | G-MBKC | Southdown Lightning | R. I. Deakin |

| Reg. | Type | Owner or Operator | Notes |
|------|------|-------------------|-------|
| G-MBKD | Chargus T.250 | P. Kerr | |
| G-MBKG | Batchelor-Hunt Skytrike | C. Leighton-Thomas | |
| G-MBKH | Southdown Skytrike | S. T. D. Hands | |
| G-MBKS | Hiway Skytrike 160 | G. R. Briggs | |
| G-MBKT | Mitchell Wing B.10 | T. Beckett | |
| G-MBKU | Hiway Demon Skytrike | A. P. Whitehead | |
| G-MBKV | Eurowing Goldwing | Entertainment Film Productions Ltd | |
| G-MBKW | Pterodactyl Ptraveller | A. J. Glynn | |
| G-MBKZ | Hiway Skytrike | S. I. Harding | |
| G-MBLA | Flexiform Skytrike | G. C. Reid | |
| G-MBLB | Eipper Quicksilver MX | Southern Microlight Centre Ltd | |
| G-MBLD | Flexiform Striker | F. A. Craig | |
| G-MBLF | Hiway Demon 195 Tri Pacer | A. P. Rostron | |
| G-MBLH | Flexwing Tri-Flyer 330 | N. S. Davison | |
| G-MBLJ | Eipper Quicksilver MX | Flylight South East | |
| G-MBLK | Southdown Puma | P. Davies | |
| G-MBLM | Hiway Skytrike | K. A. Maughan | |
| G-MBLN | Pterodactyl Ptraveller | F. D. C. Luddington | |
| G-MBLO | Sealander Skytrike | A. R. Fawkes | |
| G-MBLR | Ultrasports Tripacer | M. N. Asquith | |
| G-MBLS | MEA Mistral | I. D. Stokes | |
| G-MBLU | Southdown Lightning L.195 | C. R. Franklin | |
| G-MBLV | Ultrasports Hybrid | J. C. T. Williamson | |
| G-MBLY | Flexiform Sealander Trike | C. Smith | |
| G-MBLZ | Southern Aerosports Scorpion | J. P. Bennett-Snewin | |
| G-MBME | American Aerolights Eagle Z Drive | Perme Westcott Flying Club | |
| G-MBMG | Rotec Rally 2B | J. R. Pyper | |
| G-MBMJ | Mainair Tri-Flyer | P. A. Gardner | |
| G-MBMO | Hiway Skytrike 160 | S. G. Isaac | |
| G-MBMR | Ultrasports Tripacer Typhoon | L. Mills | |
| G-MBMS | Hornet | R. L. Smith | |
| G-MBMT | Mainair Tri-Flyer | T. R. Yeomans | |
| G-MBMU | Eurowing Goldwing | P. R. Wason | |
| G-MBMW | Solar Wings Typhoon | R. Harrison | |
| G-MBMZ | Sealander Tripacer | T. D. Otho-Briggs | |
| G-MBNA | American Aerolights Eagle | N. D. Hall | |
| G-MBNF | American Aerolights Eagle | D. Read | |
| G-MBNG | Hiway Demon Skytrike | D. I. Robertson | |
| G-MBNH | Southern Airsports Scorpion | R. F. Thomas | |
| G-MBNJ | Eipper Quicksilver MX | C. Lamb | |
| G-MBNK | American Aerolights Eagle | R. Moss | |
| G-MBNL | Hiway Skytrike C.2 | K. V. Shail & H. W. Preston | |
| G-MBNN | Southern Microlight Gazelle P.160N | N. A. Pitcher | |
| G-MBNT | American Aerolights Eagle | M. D. O'Brien | |
| G-MBNY | Steer Terror Fledge II | M. J. Steer | |
| G-MBNZ | Hiway Skytrike Demon | J. E. Brown | |
| G-MBOA | Flexiform Hilander | A. F. Stafford | |
| G-MBOD | American Aerolights Eagle | M. A. Ford & ptnrs | |
| G-MBOE | Solar Wing Typhoon Trike | W. Turner & C. Ferrie | |
| G-MBOF | Pakes Jackdaw | L. G. Pakes | |
| G-MBOH | Microlight Engineering Mistral | N. A. Bell | |
| G-MBOK | Dunstable Microlight | W. E. Brooks | |
| G-MBOM | Hiway Hilander | P. H. Beaumont | |
| G-MBON | Eurowing Goldwing Canard | A. H. Dunlop | |
| G-MBOR | Chotia 460B Weedhopper | D. J. Whysall | |
| G-MBOT | Hiway 250 Skytrike | I. C. Campbell | |
| G-MBOU | Wheeler Scout | P. Stark | |
| G-MBOV | Southdown Lightning Trike | J. McV. Macdonald | |
| G-MBOX | American Aerolights Eagle | J. S. Paine | |
| G-MBPA | Weedhopper Srs 2 | C. H. & P. B. Smith | |
| G-MBPC | American Aerolights Eagle | Aerial Imaging Systems Ltd | |
| G-MBPD | American Aerolights Eagle | R. G. Harris & K. Hall | |
| G-MBPE | Ultrasports Trike | K. L. Turner | |
| G-MBPG | Hunt Skytrike | W. Shaw | |
| G-MBPJ | Moto-Delta | J. B. Jackson | |
| G-MBPL | Hiway Demon | B. J. Merrett | |
| G-MBPM | Eurowing Goldwing | F. W. McCann | |
| G-MBPN | American Aerolights Eagle | N. O. G. & P. C. Wooler | |
| G-MBPO | Volnik Arrow | N. A. Seymour | |
| G-MBPP | American Aerolights Eagle | R. C. Colbeck | |
| G-MBPS | Gryphon Willpower | J. T. Meager | |

| Notes | Reg. | Type | Owner or Operator |
|---|---|---|---|
| | G-MBPU | Hiway Demon | R. Scott |
| | G-MBPW | Weedhopper | P. G. Walton |
| | G-MBPX | Eurowing Goldwing | W. R. Haworth & V. C. Cannon |
| | G-MBPY | Ultrasports Tripacer 330 | P. J. Sutton |
| | G-MBPZ | Flexiform Striker | C. Harris |
| | G-MBRB | Electraflyer Eagle 1 | R. C. Bott |
| | G-MBRD | American Aerolights Eagle | D. G. Fisher |
| | G-MBRE | Wheeler Scout | C. A. Foster |
| | G-MBRF | Weedhopper 460C | L. R. Smith |
| | G-MBRH | Ultraflight Mirage Mk II | R. W. F. Boarder |
| | G-MBRK | Huntair Pathfinder | F. M. Sharland |
| | G-MBRM | Hiway Demon | T. M. Clarke |
| | G-MBRO | Hiway Skytrike 160 | P. F. Bett |
| | G-MBRS | American Aerolights Eagle | R. W. Chatterton |
| | G-MBRV | Eurowing Goldwing | J. H. G. Lywood & A. A. Boyle |
| | G-MBRZ | Hiway Vulcan 250 | D. J. Jackson |
| | G-MBSA | Ultraflight Mirage II | T. N. Thomlinson |
| | G-MBSC | Ultraflight Mirage II | R. P. Warren |
| | G-MBSD | Southdown Puma DS | D. J. Whysall |
| | G-MBSF | Ultraflight Mirage II | A. J. Horne |
| | G-MBSG | Ultraflight Mirage II | P. E. Owen |
| | G-MBSN | American Aerolights Eagle | D. Duckworth |
| | G-MBSR | Southdown Puma DS | J. G. H. Featherstone |
| | G-MBSS | Ultrasports Puma 2 | W. G. Lindsay & Air Westward Co Ltd |
| | G-MBST | Mainair Gemini Sprint | D. F. Coles |
| | G-MBSW | Ultraflight Mirage II | G. Clare |
| | G-MBSX | Ultraflight Mirage II | W. H. Sherlock |
| | G-MBTA | UAS Storm Buggy 5 Mk 2 | N. & D. McEwan |
| | G-MBTB | Davies Tri-Flyer S | P. Wharton |
| | G-MBTC | Weedhopper | P. C. Lovegrove |
| | G-MBTF | Mainair Tri-Flyer Skytrike | P. A. Lawson & D. C. E. Titcombe |
| | G-MBTG | Mainair Gemini | L. J. Fisher |
| | G-MBTH | Whittaker MW.4 | MWA Flying Group |
| | G-MBTI | Hovey Whing Ding | A. Carr & R. Saddington |
| | G-MBTJ | Solar Wings Microlight | H. A. Comber |
| | G-MBTO | Mainair Tri-Flyer 250 | P. G. Griffin |
| | G-MBTS | Hovey WD-II Whing-Ding | T. G. Solomon |
| | G-MBTW | Raven Vector 600 | W. I. Fuller |
| | G-MBTZ | Huntair Pathfinder | G. M. Hayden |
| | G-MBUA | Hiway Demon | R. J. Nicholson |
| | G-MBUB | Horne Sigma Skytrike | O. D. H. Hill |
| | G-MBUC | Huntair Pathfinder | Huntair Ltd |
| | G-MBUD | Wheeler Scout Mk III | R. J. Adams |
| | G-MBUE | MBA Tiger Cub 440 | N. M. Cuthbertson |
| | G-MBUH | Hiway Skytrike | G. T. Cairns |
| | G-MBUI | Wheeler Scout Mk I | G. C. Martin |
| | G-MBUK | Mainair 330 Tri Pacer | D. G. Matthews |
| | G-MBUL | American Aerolights Eagle | Nottingham Offshore Marine |
| | G-MBUO | Southern Aerosports Scorpion | I. C. Vanner |
| | G-MBUP | Hiway Skytrike | P. Hamilton |
| | G-MBUT | UAS Storm Buggy | J. N. Wrigley |
| | G-MBUZ | Wheeler Scout Mk II | A. B. Cameron |
| | G-MBVA | Volmer Jensen VJ-23E | D. P. Eichorn |
| | G-MBVC | American Aerolights Eagle | E. M. Salt |
| | G-MBVH | Mainair Triflyer Striker | S. Wigham |
| | G-MBVJ | Skyhook Trike | A. H. Milne |
| | G-MBVK | Ultraflight Mirage II | C. W. Grant |
| | G-MBVL | Southern Aerosports Scorpion | R. H. Wentham |
| | G-MBVP | Mainair Triflyer 330 Striker | R. R. Brougham |
| | G-MBVR | Rotec Rally 2B | A. C. W. Day |
| | G-MBVS | Hiway Skytrike | M. A. Brown |
| | G-MBVT | American Aerolights Eagle | D. Cracknell |
| | G-MBVU | Flexiform Sealander Triflyer | D. Laverick |
| | G-MBVV | Hiway Skytrike | G. Hayton |
| | G-MBVW | Skyhook TR.2 | M. Jobling |
| | G-MBVY | Eipper Quicksilver MX | J. Moss |
| | G-MBWA | American Aerolights Eagle | S. Pizzey |
| | G-MBWB | Hiway Skytrike | C. K. Board |
| | G-MBWD | Rotec Rally 2B | A. Craw |
| | G-MBWE | American Aerolights Eagle | R. H. Tombs |
| | G-MBWF | Mainair Triflyer Striker | J. B. Brierley |
| | G-MBWG | Huntair Pathfinder | S. M. Pascoe |
| | G-MBWH | Designability Duet I | Designability Ltd |

| Reg. | Type | Owner or Operator | Notes |
|------|------|-------------------|-------|
| G-MBWL | Huntair Pathfinder | D. A. Izod & R. C. Wright | |
| G-MBWM | American Aerolights Eagle | J. N. B. Mourant | |
| G-MBWN | American Aerolights Eagle | J. N. B. Mourant | |
| G-MBWO | Hiway Demon Skytrike | J. T. W. J. Edwards | |
| G-MBWP | Ultrasports Trike | C. Riley | |
| G-MBWR | Hornet | G. Edwards | |
| G-MBWT | Huntair Pathfinder | D. G. Gibson | |
| G-MBWU | Hiway Demon Skytrike | R. M. Lister | |
| G-MBWW | Southern Aerosports Scorpion | D. Batters | |
| G-MBWX | Southern Aerosports Scorpion | Twinflight Ltd | |
| G-MBWY | American Aerolights Eagle | J. P. Donovan | |
| G-MBXB | Southdown Sailwings Puma | K. I. Pryce | |
| G-MBXE | Hiway Skytrike | T. A. Harlow | |
| G-MBXF | Hiway Skytrike | R. Ford | |
| G-MBXH | Southdown Sailwings Puma | M. Sorbie | |
| G-MBXI | Hiway Skytrike | P. J. Davis | |
| G-MBXJ | Hiway Demon Skytrike | S. Ward | |
| G-MBXK | Ultrasports Puma | P. J. Brookman | |
| G-MBXO | Sheffield Trident | M. I. Watson | |
| G-MBXP | Hornet Skytrike | K. Wales | |
| G-MBXR | Hiway Skytrike 150 | C. Shutt | |
| G-MBXT | Eipper Quicksilver MX2 | B. J. Gordon | |
| G-MBXW | Hiway Skytrike | M. Owens | |
| G-MBXX | Ultraflight Mirage II | Westward Airways (Lands End) Ltd | |
| G-MBYD | American Aerolights Eagle | J. M. Hutchinson | |
| G-MBYE | Eipper Quicksilver MX | M. J. Beeby | |
| G-MBYF | Skyhook TR2 | E. J. Larnder | |
| G-MBYH | Maxair Hummer | A. Edwards | |
| G-MBYI | Ultraflight Lazair | A. M. Fleming | |
| G-MBYJ | Hiway Super Scorpion IIC | R. Flaum | |
| G-MBYL | Huntair Pathfinder 330 | J. S. S. Calder & R. Tyler | |
| G-MBYM | Eipper Quicksilver MX | J. Wibberley | |
| G-MBYO | American Aerolights Eagle | B. J. & M. G. Ferguson | |
| G-MBYR | American Aerolights Eagle | A. J. Cook | |
| G-MBYS | Ultraflight Mirage II | I. M. Willsher | |
| G-MBYT | Ultraflight Mirage II | L. J. Perring | |
| G-MBYU | American Aerolights Eagle | F. L. Wiseman | |
| G-MBYX | American Aerolights Eagle | N. P. Austen | |
| G-MBYY | Southern Aerosports Scorpion | D. J. Lovell | |
| G-MBZA | Ultrasports Tripacer 330 | S. P. de Montfalcon | |
| G-MBZB | Hiway Skytrike | M. W. Hurst & B. Emery | |
| G-MBZF | American Aerolights Eagle | G. Calder & A. C. Bernard | |
| G-MBZG | Twinflight Scorpion 2 seat | H. T. Edwards | |
| G-MBZH | Eurowing Goldwing | J. Spavins | |
| G-MBZI | Eurowing Goldwing | G. M. Hayden | |
| G-MBZK | Ultrasports Tripacer 250 | M. T. Pearce | |
| G-MBZL | Weedhopper | A. R. Prior | |
| G-MBZM | UAS Storm Buggy | S. Comber & A. Crabtree | |
| G-MBZN | Ultrasports Puma | A. Brown | |
| G-MBZO | Mainair Triflyer 330 | J. Baxendale | |
| G-MBZP | Skyhook TR2 | Army Hang Gliding School | |
| G-MBZT | Solarwings Skytrike | S. Hetherton | |
| G-MBZU | Skyhook Sabre C | G. N. Beyer-Kay | |
| G-MBZV | American Aerolights Eagle | M. H. & G. C. Davies | |
| G-MBZZ | Southern Aerosports Scorpion | P. J. Harlow | |
| | | | |
| G-MGAG | Aviasud Mistral | A. I. Grant | |
| G-MGOO | Renegade Spirit UK Ltd | A. R. Max | |
| G-MGUY | CFM Shadow Srs BD | Aerolite Flight Parks Ltd | |
| | | | |
| G-MJAA | Ultrasports Tripacer | M. P. Carr & D. Baker | |
| G-MJAB | Ultrasports Skytrike | I. W. Kemsley | |
| G-MJAD | Eipper Quicksilver MX | J. McCullough | |
| G-MJAE | American Aerolights Eagle | T. B. Wooley | |
| G-MJAF | Ultrasports Puma 440 | D. M. Waddle | |
| G-MJAG | Skyhook TR1 | D. J. Wright & L. Florence | |
| G-MJAH | American Aerolights Eagle | R. L. Arscott | |
| G-MJAI | American Aerolights Eagle | A. L. Griffiths | |
| G-MJAJ | Eurowing Goldwing | J. S. R. Moodie | |
| G-MJAL | Wheeler Scout 3 | G. W. Wickington | |
| G-MJAM | Eipper Quicksilver MX | J. C. Larkin | |
| G-MJAN | Hiway Skytrike | G. M. Sutcliffe | |
| G-MJAO | Hiway Skytrike | T. Le Gassicke | |

| Notes | Reg. | Type | Owner or Operator |
|-------|------|------|-------------------|
| | G-MJAP | Hiway 160 | A. L. Flude |
| | G-MJAR | Chargus Titan | Quest Air Ltd |
| | G-MJAV | Hiway Demon Skytrike 244cc | J. N. J. Roberts |
| | G-MJAX | American Aerolights Eagle | J. P. Simpson & C. W. Mellard |
| | G-MJAY | Eurowing Goldwing | C. Tuxworth |
| | G-MJAZ | Aerodyne Vector 610 | B. Fussell |
| | G-MJBF | Southdown Puma 330 | C. Jacobs |
| | G-MJBH | American Aerolights Eagle | P. Smith |
| | G-MJBK | Swallow AeroPlane Swallow B | M. A. Newbould |
| | G-MJBL | American Aerolights Eagle | B. W. Olley |
| | G-MJBN | American Aerolights Eagle | D. Darke |
| | G-MJBS | Ultralight Stormbuggy | G. I. Sargeant |
| | G-MJBT | Eipper Quicksilver MX | G. A. Barclay |
| | G-MJBV | American Aerolights Eagle | B. H. Stephens |
| | G-MJBX | Pterodactyl Ptraveller | R. E. Hawkes |
| | G-MJBZ | Huntair Pathfinder | J. C. Rose |
| | G-MJCA | Skyhook Sabre | B. G. Axworthy |
| | G-MJCB | Hornet 330 | A. C. Aspden & ptnrs |
| | G-MJCC | Ultrasports Puma | S. Barrass |
| | G-MJCD | Sigma Tetley Skytrike | N. L. Betts & B. Tetley |
| | G-MJCE | Ultrasports Tripacer | C. M. Theakstone |
| | G-MJCF | Maxair Hummer | R. G. Banfield |
| | G-MJCG | S.M.C. Flyer Mk 1 | E. N. Skinner |
| | G-MJCH | Ultraflight Mirage II | R. Sherwin |
| | G-MJCI | Kruchek Firefly 440 | E. Kepka |
| | G-MJCJ | Hiway Spectrum | J. F. Mayes |
| | G-MJCK | Southern Aerosports Scorpion | S. L. Moss |
| | G-MJCL | Eipper Quicksilver MX | R. F. Witt |
| | G-MJCN | S.M.C. Flyer Mk 1 | C. W. Merriam |
| | G-MJCP | Huntair Pathfinder | R. C. Wright |
| | G-MJCT | Hiway Skytrike | E. W. Barker |
| | G-MJCU | Tarjani | T. A. Sayer |
| | G-MJCW | Hiway Super Scorpion | M. G. Sheppard |
| | G-MJCY | Eurowing Goldwing | A. E. Dewdeswell |
| | G-MJCZ | Southern Aerosports Scorpion 2 | C. Baldwin |
| | G-MJDA | Hornet Trike Executive | J. Hainsworth |
| | G-MJDB | Birdman Cherokee | W. G. Farr |
| | G-MJDE | Huntair Pathfinder | L. G. Horne |
| | G-MJDG | Hornet Supertrike | P. F. Rose |
| | G-MJDH | Huntair Pathfinder | J. A. Joynes |
| | G-MJDI | Southern Flyer Mk 1 | N. P. Day |
| | G-MJDJ | Hiway Skytrike Demon | A. J. Cowan |
| | G-MJDK | American Aerolights Eagle | P. A. McPherson & ptnrs |
| | G-MJDO | Southdown Puma 440 | G. R. Wright |
| | G-MJDP | Eurowing Goldwing | J. R. Ledbrook & F. C. James |
| | G-MJDR | Hiway Demon Skytrike | D. R. Redmile |
| | G-MJDU | Eipper Quicksilver MX2 | J. Brown |
| | G-MJDW | Eipper Quicksilver MX | Remus International Ltd |
| | G-MJDX | Moyes Mega II | P. H. Davies |
| | G-MJDY | Ultrasports Solarwings | S. A. Barnes |
| | G-MJEC | Ultrasports Puma | M. C. Gardner |
| | G-MJEE | Mainair Triflyer Trike | M. F. Eddington |
| | G-MJEF | Gryphon 180 | F. C. Coulson |
| | G-MJEG | Eurowing Goldwing | G. J. Stamper |
| | G-MJEJ | American Aerolights Eagle | J. Cole |
| | G-MJEK | Hiway Demon 330 Skytrike | J. Grant |
| | G-MJEL | GMD-01 Trike | G. M. Drinkell |
| | G-MJEO | American Aerolights Eagle | A. M. Shaw |
| | G-MJEP | Pterodactyl Ptraveller | G. H. Liddle |
| | G-MJER | Flexiform Striker | D. S. Simpson |
| | G-MJET | Stratos Prototype 3 Axis 1 | Stratos Aviation Ltd |
| | G-MJEX | Eipper Quicksilver MX | M. J. Sundaram |
| | G-MJEY | Southdown Lightning | P. M. Coppola |
| | G-MJFB | Flexiform Striker | B. Tetley |
| | G-MJFD | Ultrasports Tripacer | R. N. O. Kingsbury |
| | G-MJFF | Huntair Pathfinder | F. E. Hardy |
| | G-MJFG | Eurowing Goldwing | J. G. Aspinall & H. R. Marsden |
| | G-MJFH | Eipper Quicksilver MX | I. H. Lewis |
| | G-MJFI | Flexiform Striker | J. E. Harris |
| | G-MJFJ | Hiway Skytrike 250 | J. S. Woollatt |
| | G-MJFK | Flexiform Skytrike Dual | J. J. Woollen |
| | G-MJFL | Mainair Tri-Flyer 440 | J. Phillips |
| | G-MJFM | Huntair Pathfinder | J. T. Houghton |

| Reg. | Type | Owner or Operator | Notes |
|------|------|-------------------|-------|
| G-MJFP | American Aerolights Eagle | R. C. Colbeck | |
| G-MJFS | American Aerolights Eagle | A. L. Griffiths | |
| G-MJFV | Ultrasports Tripacer | Hatfield Polytechnic Students Union | |
| G-MJFX | Skyhook TR-1 | M. R. Dean | |
| G-MJGC | Hornet | P. C. & S. J. Turnbull | |
| G-MJGD | Huntair Pathfinder | A. Carling | |
| G-MJGE | Eipper Quicksilver MX | D. Brown | |
| G-MJGG | Skyhook TR-1 | R. Pritchard | |
| G-MJGI | Eipper Quicksilver MX | J. M. Hayer & J. R. Wilman | |
| G-MJGL | Chargus Titan 38 | J. Houston & J. R. Appleton | |
| G-MJGM | Hiway Demon 195 Skytrike | J. M. Creasey | |
| G-MJGN | Greenslade Monotrike | P. G. Greenslade | |
| G-MJGO | Barnes Avon Skytrike | B. R. Barnes | |
| G-MJGR | Hiway Demon Skytrike | L. V. Strickland & P. H. Howell | |
| G-MJGT | Skyhook Cutlass Trike | T. Silvester | |
| G-MJGV | Eipper Quicksilver MX2 | D. Beer | |
| G-MJGW | Solar Wings Trike | D. J. D. Beck | |
| G-MJGX | Ultrasports Puma 250 | R. F. McKay | |
| G-MJHA | Hiway Skytrike 250 Mk II | A. G. Bird | |
| G-MJHC | Ultrasports Tripacer 330 | S. Galley | |
| G-MJHE | Hiway Demon Skytrike | S. Pickering | |
| G-MJHF | Skyhook Sailwing Trike | R. A. Watering | |
| G-MJHK | Hiway Demon 195 | J. C. Bowden | |
| G-MJHM | Ultrasports Trike | D. B. Markham | |
| G-MJHN | American Aerolights Eagle | P. K. Ewens | |
| G-MJHO | Shilling Bumble Bee Srs 1 | A. C. Thorne | |
| G-MJHP | American Aerolights Eagle | K. Garnett & ptnrs | |
| G-MJHR | Southdown Lightning | B. R. Barnes | |
| G-MJHU | Eipper Quicksilver MX | P. J. Hawcock & ptnrs | |
| G-MJHV | Hiway Demon 250 | A. G. Griffiths | |
| G-MJHW | Ultrasports Puma 1 | R. C. Barnett | |
| G-MJHX | Eipper Quicksilver MX | P. D. Lucas | |
| G-MJHZ | Southdown Sailwings | C. G. Ponsford | |
| G-MJIA | Flexiform Striker | R. M. Jamison | |
| G-MJIB | Hornet 250 | S. H. Williams | |
| G-MJIC | Ultrasports Puma 330 | R. J. Ridgway | |
| G-MJID | Southdown Sailwings Puma DS | P. Jarman | |
| G-MJIE | Hornet 330 | C. J. Dalby | |
| G-MJIF | Mainair Triflyer | R. J. Payne | |
| G-MJIG | Hiway Demon Skytrike | E. Dauncey | |
| G-MJIH | Ultrasports Tripacer | J. L. Bakewell | |
| G-MJIJ | Ultrasports Tripacer 250 | D. H. Targett | |
| G-MJIK | Southdown Sailwings Lightning | J. F. Chithalan | |
| G-MJIL | Bremner Mitchell B.10 | D. S. & R. M. Bremner | |
| G-MJIN | Hiway Skytrike | P. W. Harding | |
| G-MJIO | American Aerolights Eagle | R. Apps & J. Marshall | |
| G-MJIR | Eipper Quicksilver MX | H. Feeney | |
| G-MJIS | American Aerolights Eagle | E. Gee | |
| G-MJIT | Hiway Skytrike | F. A. Mileham & D. W. B. Hatch | |
| G-MJIU | Eipper Quicksilver MX | O. W. A. Church | |
| G-MJIV | Pterodactyl Ptraveller | G. E. Fowles | |
| G-MJIY | Flexiform Voyage | R. J. Sims | |
| G-MJIZ | Southdown Lightning | J. J. Crudington | |
| G-MJJA | Huntair Pathfinder | J. M. Watkins & R. D. Bateman | |
| G-MJJB | Eipper Quicksilver MX | T. V. Thorp | |
| G-MJJD | Birdman Cherokee | B. J. Sanderson | |
| G-MJJF | Sealey | L. G. Thomas & R. D. Thomasson | |
| G-MJJJ | Moyes Knight | R. J. Broomfield | |
| G-MJJK | Eipper Quicksilver MX2 | M. J. O'Malley | |
| G-MJJL | Solar Wings Storm | P. Wharton | |
| G-MJJM | Birdman Cherokee Mk 1 | R. J. Wilson | |
| G-MJJN | Ultrasports Puma | J. Cooper | |
| G-MJJO | Flexiform Skytrike Dual | Kington Mead Flying Group | |
| G-MJJS | Swallow AeroPlane Swallow B | A. J. Marshall | |
| G-MJJU | Hiway Demon | I. C. Willetts | |
| G-MJJV | Wheeler Scout | C. G. Johes | |
| G-MJJX | Hiway Skytrike | P. C. Millward | |
| G-MJJY | Tirith Firefly | Tirith Microplane Ltd | |
| G-MJJZ | Hiway Demon 175 Skytrike | B. C. Williams | |
| G-MJKA | Skyhook Sabre Trike | A. P. Nikitits | |
| G-MJKB | Striplin Skyranger | A. P. Booth | |
| G-MJKC | Mainair Triflyer 330 Striker | W. H. Prince | |
| G-MJKE | Mainair Triflyer 330 | R. E. D. Bailey | |

| Notes | Reg. | Type | Owner or Operator |
|---|---|---|---|
| | G-MJKF | Hiway Demon | S. D. Hill |
| | G-MJKG | John Ivor Skytrike | R. C. Wright |
| | G-MJKH | Eipper Quicksilver MX II | E. H. E. Nunn |
| | G-MJKI | Eipper Quicksilver MX | D. R. Gibbons |
| | G-MJKJ | Eipper Quicksilver MX | Aerolite Aviation Co Ltd |
| | G-MJKO | Goldmarque 250 Skytrike | M. J. Barry |
| | G-MJKP | Hiway Super Scorpion | M. Horsfall |
| | G-MJKR | Rotec Rally 2B | J. R. Darlow & J. D. Whitcock |
| | G-MJKS | Mainair Triflyer | P. C. Collins |
| | G-MJKU | Hiway Demon 175 | D. L. Barrett |
| | G-MJKV | Hornet | D. Hodgson |
| | G-MJKX | Ultralight Skyrider Phantom | E. A. Matty |
| | G-MJKY | Hiway Skytrike | J. G. McGlinchey |
| | G-MJLA | Ultrasports Puma 2 | C. A. R. Hay |
| | G-MJLB | Ultrasports Puma 2 | Breen Aviation Ltd |
| | G-MJLD | Wheeler Scout Mk III | M. Buchanan-Jones |
| | G-MJLF | Southern Microlight Trike | C. Moore |
| | G-MJLH | American Aerolights Eagle 2 | A. Cussins |
| | G-MJLI | Hiway Demon Skytrike | A. J. P. Farmer |
| | G-MJLJ | Flexiform Sealander | Questair Ltd |
| | G-MJLL | Hiway Demon Skytrike | D. Hines |
| | G-MJLM | Mainair Triflyer 250 | C. Wong |
| | G-MJLO | Goldmarque Skytrike | K. G. Steer |
| | G-MJLR | Skyhook SK-1 | T. Moore |
| | G-MJLS | Rotec Rally 2B | G. Messenger |
| | G-MJLT | American Aerolights Eagle | P. de Vere Hunt |
| | G-MJLU | Skyhook | C. A. Shayes |
| | G-MJLY | American Aerolights Eagle | A. H. Read |
| | G-MJMA | Hiway Demon | R. I. Simpson |
| | G-MJMB | Weedhopper | J. E. Brown |
| | G-MJME | Ultrasports Tripacer Mega II | A. D. Cranfield |
| | G-MJMM | Chargus Vortex | R. J. Gray |
| | G-MJMP | Eipper Quicksilver MX | S. A. S. McCulloch |
| | G-MJMR | Solar Wings Typhoon | J. C. S. Jones |
| | G-MJMS | Hiway Skytrike | G. J. Foard |
| | G-MJMT | Hiway Demon Skytrike | N. J. Brunskill |
| | G-MJMW | Eipper Quicksilver MX2 | S. E. Borrow |
| | G-MJMX | Ultrasports Tripacer | D. Myles |
| | G-MJNB | Hiway Skytrike | G. Hammond |
| | G-MJNE | Hornet Supreme Dual Trike | Hornet Microlights |
| | G-MJNH | Skyhook Cutlass Trike | M. E. James |
| | G-MJNK | Hiway Skytrike | E. W. Barker |
| | G-MJNL | American Aerolights Eagle | W. A. H. Vick |
| | G-MJNM | American Aerolights Double Eagle | B. H. Stephens |
| | G-MJNN | Ultraflight Mirage II | Breen Aviation Ltd |
| | G-MJNO | American Aerolights Double Eagle | R. S. Martin & J. L. May |
| | G-MJNP | American Aerolights Eagle | D. J. Jackson |
| | G-MJNR | Ultralight Solar Buggy | D. J. Smith |
| | G-MJNS | Swallow AeroPlane Swallow B | S. M. Pickard |
| | G-MJNT | Hiway Skytrike | F. Tyreman |
| | G-MJNU | Skyhook Cutlass | R. W. Taylor |
| | G-MJNV | Eipper Quicksilver MX | W. Toulmin |
| | G-MJNY | Skyhook Sabre Trike | P. Ratcliffe |
| | G-MJOA | Chargus T.250 Vortex | S. F. Chave |
| | G-MJOC | Huntair Pathfinder | A. J. Glynn |
| | G-MJOD | Rotec Rally 2B | A. J. Capel & K. D. Halsey |
| | G-MJOE | Eurowing Goldwing | R. J. Osbourne |
| | G-MJOG | American Aerolights Eagle | J. B. Rush |
| | G-MJOI | Hiway Demon | S. J. Walker |
| | G-MJOJ | Flexiform Skytrike | D. Haynes |
| | G-MJOK | Mainair Triflyer 250 | S. H. Choules |
| | G-MJOL | Skyhook Cutlass | G. Singh |
| | G-MJOM | Southdown Puma 40F | J. G. Crawford |
| | G-MJOO | Southdown Puma 40F | D. J. England |
| | G-MJOR | Solair Phoenix | T. V. Wood |
| | G-MJOS | Southdown Lightning 170 | C. W. Payne |
| | G-MJOU | Hiway Demon 175 | H. Phipps |
| | G-MJOV | Solar Wings Typhoon | I. R. Hoad |
| | G-MJOW | Eipper Quicksilver MX | P. N. Haigh |
| | G-MJPA | Rotec Rally 2B | R. Boyd |
| | G-MJPC | American Aerolights Double Eagle | D. M. Jackson |

| Reg. | Type | Owner or Operator | Notes |
|------|------|-------------------|-------|
| G-MJPD | Hiway Demon Skytrike | P. D. Lee | |
| G-MJPE | Hiway Demon Skytrike | D. Hill | |
| G-MJPG | American Aerolights Eagle 430R | N. R. Macrae | |
| G-MJPI | Flexiform Striker | D. A. Watkins | |
| G-MJPJ | Flexiform Dual Trike 440 | M. D. Phillips & ptnrs | |
| G-MJPK | Hiway Vulcan | R. G. Darcy | |
| G-MJPO | Eurowing Goldwing | M. Merryman | |
| G-MJPS | American Aerolights Eagle 430R | Peter Symonds & Co | |
| G-MJPT | Dragon | Fly-In Ltd | |
| G-MJPU | Solar Wings Typhoon | B. G. Birkett | |
| G-MJPV | Eipper Quicksilver MX | J. J. James | |
| G-MJRA | Hiway Demon | E. Jones | |
| G-MJRE | Hiway Demon | P. A. Smith | |
| G-MJRG | Ultrasports Puma | P. Brockway | |
| G-MJRH | Hiway Skytrike | N. C. Hopwood | |
| G-MJRI | American Aerolights Eagle | N. N. Brown | |
| G-MJRK | Flexiform Striker | P. J. & G. Long | |
| G-MJRL | Eurowing Goldwing | G. A. J. Salter | |
| G-MJRN | Flexiform Striker | K. Handley | |
| G-MJRO | Eurowing Goldwing | S. P. Reeve | |
| G-MJRP | Mainair Triflyer 330 | A. Hulme | |
| G-MJRR | Striplin Skyranger Srs 1 | J. R. Reece | |
| G-MJRS | Eurowing Goldwing | R. V. Hogg | |
| G-MJRT | Southdown Lightning DS | R. J. Perry | |
| G-MJRU | MBA Tiger Cub 440 | D. V. Short | |
| G-MJRX | Ultrasports Puma II | E. M. Woods | |
| G-MJSA | Mainair 2-Seat Trike | W. O. Wright | |
| G-MJSE | Skyrider Airsports Phantom | Cranfield Vertigo Ventures Ltd | |
| G-MJSF | Skyrider Airsports Phantom | Skyrider Airsports | |
| G-MJSL | Dragon 200 | S. C. Weston | |
| G-MJSO | Hiway Skytrike | M. T. Connah | |
| G-MJSP | MBA Super Tiger Cub 440 | J. W. E. Romain | |
| G-MJSS | American Aerolights Eagle | G. N. S. Farrant | |
| G-MJST | Pterodactyl Ptraveler | C. H. J. Goodwin | |
| G-MJSU | MBA Tiger Cub | R. J. Adams | |
| G-MJSV | MBA Tiger Cub | D. A. Izod | |
| G-MJSY | Eurowing Goldwing | A. J. Rex | |
| G-MJSZ | D.H. Wasp | P. S. Cotterell | |
| G-MJTC | Solar Wings Typhoon | V. C. Readhead | |
| G-MJTD | Gardner T-M Scout | D. Gardner | |
| G-MJTE | Skyrider Airsports Phantom | B. J. M. Albiston | |
| G-MJTF | Gryphon Wing | A. T. Armstrong | |
| G-MJTH | S.M.D. Gazelle | I. R. Down | |
| G-MJTI | Huntair Pathfinder II | B. Gunn | |
| G-MJTL | Aerostructure Pipistrelle 2B | J. McD. Robinson & C. G. McCrae | |
| G-MJTM | Aerostructure Pipistrelle 2B | Southdown Aero Services Ltd | |
| G-MJTN | Eipper Quicksilver MX | N. F. Cuthbert | |
| G-MJTO | Jordan Duet Srs 1 | J. R. Jordan | |
| G-MJTP | Flexiform Striker | R. D. A. Henderson | |
| G-MJTR | Southdown Puma DS Mk 1 | P. Soanes | |
| G-MJTU | Skyhook Cutlass 185 | P. D. Wade | |
| G-MJTW | Eurowing Trike | W. G. Lindsay | |
| G-MJTX | Skyrider Phantom | Haywood Design | |
| G-MJTY | Huntair Pathfinder | C. H. Smith | |
| G-MJTZ | Skyrider Airsports Phantom | A. I. Stott | |
| G-MJUB | MBA Tiger Cub 440 | C. C. Butt | |
| G-MJUC | MBA Tiger Cub 440 | G. A. Costelloe | |
| G-MJUE | Southdown Wild Cat II | W. M. A. Alladin | |
| G-MJUH | MBA Tiger Cub 440 | J. E. Carr | |
| G-MJUI | Flexiform Striker | L. M. & R. E. Bailey | |
| G-MJUJ | Eipper Quicksilver Mk II | J. F. A. Cooke | |
| G-MJUK | Eipper Quicksilver MX II | J. C. M. Haigh | |
| G-MJUL | Southdown Puma Sprint | M. L. Harris | |
| G-MJUM | Flexiform Striker | C. C. Horton | |
| G-MJUO | Eipper Quicksilver MX II | A. Hamilton | |
| G-MJUP | Weedhopper B | R. A. P. Cox | |
| G-MJUR | Skyrider Airsports Phantom | J. Hannibal | |
| G-MJUS | MBA Tiger Cub 440 | B. Jenks | |
| G-MJUT | Eurowing Goldwing | D. L. Eite | |
| G-MJUU | Eurowing Goldwing | A. J. Rollin | |
| G-MJUW | MBA Tiger Cub 440 | H. F. Robertson | |

| Notes | Reg. | Type | Owner or Operator |
|---|---|---|---|
| | G-MJUX | Skyrider Airsports Phantom | C. M. Tomkins |
| | G-MJUY | Eurowing Goldwing | J. E. M. Barnatt-Millns |
| | G-MJUZ | Dragon Srs 150 | J. R. Fairweather |
| | G-MJVA | Skyrider Airsports Phantom | Skyrider Airsports |
| | G-MJVC | Hiway Skytrike | J. H. Stage |
| | G-MJVE | Hybred Skytrike | R. C. Smith |
| | G-MJVF | CFM Shadow | D. G. Cook |
| | G-MJVG | Hiway Skytrike | D. Bridges |
| | G-MJVJ | Flexiform Striker Dual | R. Nay |
| | G-MJVL | Flexiform Striker | H. Phipps |
| | G-MJVM | Dragon 150 | A. Fairweather |
| | G-MJVN | Ultrasports Puma 440 | O. R. Pluck |
| | G-MJVP | Eipper Quicksilver MX II | G. J. Ward & G. Hawkins |
| | G-MJVR | Flexiform Striker | D. R. Sutton |
| | G-MJVT | Eipper Quicksilver MX | A. M. Reid |
| | G-MJVU | Eipper Quicksilver MX II | F. J. Griffith |
| | G-MJVV | Hornet Supreme Dual | P. M. Gilfoyle |
| | G-MJVW | Airwave Nimrod | T. P. Mason |
| | G-MJVY | Dragon Srs 150 | J. C. Craddock |
| | G-MJVZ | Hiway Demon Tripacer | M. G. & M. L. Sadler |
| | G-MJWB | Eurowing Goldwing | F. C. Claydon |
| | G-MJWD | Solar Wings Typhoon XL | E. Daleki |
| | G-MJWE | Hiway Demon | S. R. Loomes |
| | G-MJWI | Flexiform Striker | R. W. Twamley |
| | G-MJWJ | MBA Tiger Cub 440 | H. A. Bromiley |
| | G-MJWK | Huntair Pathfinder | M. R. Swaffield |
| | G-MJWN | Flexiform Striker | A. K. & V. B. Johnson |
| | G-MJWO | Hiway Skytrike | A. Gray |
| | G-MJWR | MBA Tiger Cub 440 | M. G. &. M. W. Sadler |
| | G-MJWS | Eurowing Goldwing | J. W. Salter |
| | G-MJWU | Maxair Hummer TX | J. Bagnall |
| | G-MJWV | Southdown Puma MS | R. J. Gray |
| | G-MJWW | MBA Super Tiger Cub 440 | P. J. Ward |
| | G-MJWX | Flexiform Striker | W. A. Bibby |
| | G-MJWY | Flexiform Striker | M. B. Horan |
| | G-MJWZ | Ultrasports Panther XL | T. V. Ward |
| | G-MJXA | Flexiform Striker | C. A. Palmer |
| | G-MJXB | Eurowing Goldwing | R. B. McCornish |
| | G-MJXD | MBA Tiger Cub 440 | W. L. Rogers |
| | G-MJXE | Hiway Demon | H. Sykes |
| | G-MJXF | MBA Tiger Cub 440 | N. P. Day |
| | G-MJXJ | MBA Tiger Cub 440 | P. J. Wright |
| | G-MJXM | Hiway Skytrike | G. S. & P. W. G. Carter |
| | G-MJXR | Huntair Pathfinder II | J. F. H. James |
| | G-MJXS | Huntair Pathfinder II | A. E. Sawyer |
| | G-MJXT | Phoenix Falcon 1 | Phoenix Aircraft Co |
| | G-MJXV | Flexiform Striker | H. L. Clarke |
| | G-MJXX | Flexiform Striker Dual | H. A. Ward |
| | G-MJXY | Hiway Demon Skytrike | P. E. A. Dook |
| | G-MJXZ | Hiway Demon | O. Wood |
| | G-MJYA | Huntair Pathfinder | Ultrasports Ltd |
| | G-MJYC | Ultrasports Panther XL Dual 440 | R. E. Grey |
| | G-MJYD | MBA Tiger Cub 440 | R. A. Budd |
| | G-MJYF | Mainair Gemini Flash | R. Young |
| | G-MJYG | Skyhook Orion Canard | Skyhook Sailwings Ltd |
| | G-MJYI | Mainair Triflyer | B. L. Wallond |
| | G-MJYJ | MBA Tiger Cub 440 | M. F. Collett |
| | G-MJYL | Airwave Nimrod | J. D. Needham |
| | G-MJYM | Southdown Puma Sprint | Breen Aviation Ltd |
| | G-MJYP | Mainair Triflyer 440 | Mainair Sports Ltd |
| | G-MJYR | Catto CP.16 | M. Hindley |
| | G-MJYS | Southdown Puma Sprint | G. Breen |
| | G-MJYT | Southdown Puma Sprint | G. Breen |
| | G-MJYV | Mainair Triflyer 2 Seat | D. A. McFadyean |
| | G-MJYW | Wasp Gryphon III | P. D. Lawrence |
| | G-MJYX | Mainair Triflyer | R. K. Birlison |
| | G-MJYY | Hiway Demon | N. Smith |
| | G-MJYZ | Flexiform Striker | S. C. Beesley |
| | G-MJZA | MBA Tiger Cub | D. W. Bedford |
| | G-MJZB | Flexiform Striker Dual | K. R. Gillett |
| | G-MJZC | MBA Tiger Cub 440 | P. G. Walton |
| | G-MJZD | Mainair Gemini Flash | A. R. Gaivoto |
| | G-MJZE | MBA Tiger Cub 440 | D. Ridley & ptnrs |

| Reg. | Type | Owner or Operator | Notes |
|------|------|-------------------|-------|
| G-MJZF | La Mouette Atlas 16 | W. R. Crew | |
| G-MJZG | Mainair Triflyer 440 | K. C. Bennett | |
| G-MJZH | Southdown Lightning 195 | P. H. Risdale | |
| G-MJZI | Eurowing Goldwing | A. J. Sharpe | |
| G-MJZJ | Hiway Cutlass Skytrike | G. D. H. Sandlin | |
| G-MJZK | Southdown Puma Sprint 440 | R. J. Osbourne | |
| G-MJZL | Eipper Quicksilver MX II | S. R. Jackson | |
| G-MJZO | Flexiform Striker | M. G. Rawsthorne | |
| G-MJZP | MBA Tiger Cub 440 | Herts & Cambs Biplanes Ltd | |
| G-MJZT | Flexiform Striker | J. Whitehouse | |
| G-MJZU | Flexiform Striker | R. G. Hooker | |
| G-MJZW | Eipper Quicksilver MX II | W. Smith & ptnrs | |
| G-MJZX | Maxair Hummer TX | R. J. Folwell | |
| G-MJZZ | Skyhook Cutlass | P. E. Penrose | |
| | | | |
| G-MMAC | Dragon Srs 150 | Hargrave Microlite Club | |
| G-MMAE | Dragon Srs 150 | B. P. Walmisley | |
| G-MMAG | MBA Tiger Cub 440 | W. R. Tull | |
| G-MMAH | Eipper Quicksilver MX II | R. G. Cook | |
| G-MMAI | Dragon Srs 150 | T. W. Dukes | |
| G-MMAJ | Mainair Tri-Flyer 440 | D. A. Frank & M. J. Moon | |
| G-MMAK | MBA Tiger Cub 440 | G. E. Heritage | |
| G-MMAL | Flexiform Striker Dual | C. A. Rathbone | |
| G-MMAM | MBA Tiger Cub 440 | I. M. Bartlett | |
| G-MMAN | Flexiform Striker | K. Southam | |
| G-MMAO | Southdown Puma Sprint | J. C. A. Smith | |
| G-MMAP | Hummer TX | J. S. Millard | |
| G-MMAR | Southdown Puma Sprint MS | J. R. North | |
| G-MMAS | Southdown Sprint | J. V. George | |
| G-MMAT | Southdown Puma Sprint MS | Mainair Sports Ltd | |
| G-MMAU | Flexiform Rapier | R. Hemsworth | |
| G-MMAW | Mainair Rapier | G. B. Hutchison | |
| G-MMAX | Flexiform Striker | A. Smolarz | |
| G-MMAZ | Southdown Puma Sprint | A. R. Smith | |
| G-MMBA | Hiway Super Scorpion | B. J. Hampshire | |
| G-MMBB | American Aerolights Eagle | M. R. Starling | |
| G-MMBC | Hiway Super Scorpion | A. T. Grain | |
| G-MMBD | Spectrum 330 | J. Hollings | |
| G-MMBE | MBA Tiger Cub 440 | R. J. B. Jordan & R. W. Pearce | |
| G-MMBF | American Aerolights Eagle | N. V. Middleton | |
| G-MMBH | MBA Super Tiger Cub 440 | C. H. Jennings & J. F. Howesman | |
| G-MMBJ | Solar Wings Typhoon | D. W. Beach | |
| G-MMBK | American Aerolights Eagle | B. M. Quinn | |
| G-MMBL | Southdown Puma | B. J. Farrell | |
| G-MMBN | Eurowing Goldwing | W. G. Reynolds | |
| G-MMBS | Flexiform Striker | P. Thompson | |
| G-MMBT | MBA Tiger Cub 440 | F. F. Chamberlain | |
| G-MMBU | Eipper Quicksilver MX II | S. J. Wills | |
| G-MMBV | Huntair Pathfinder | P. J. Bishop | |
| G-MMBW | MBA Tiger Cub 440 | J. C. Miles | |
| G-MMBX | MBA Tiger Cub 440 | G. Clark | |
| G-MMBY | Solar Wings Panther | T. Harper | |
| G-MMBZ | Solar Wings Typhoon P | C. W. Lark | |
| G-MMCD | Southdown Lightning DS | I. K. Wilson | |
| G-MMCE | MBA Tiger Cub 440 | M. K. Dring | |
| G-MMCF | Solar Wings Panther 330 | N. Birkin | |
| G-MMCG | Eipper Quicksilver MX I | L. W. Farrow | |
| G-MMCI | Southdown Puma Sprint | R. J. Webb | |
| G-MMCJ | Flexiform Striker | P. Hayes | |
| G-MMCM | Southdown Puma Sprint | J. G. Kane | |
| G-MMCN | Solar Wings Storm | A. P. S. Presland | |
| G-MMCO | Southdown Sprint | B. F. & C. Jones | |
| G-MMCP | Southdown Lightning | T. C. Saunders | |
| G-MMCR | Eipper Quicksilver MX | T. L. & B. L. Holland | |
| G-MMCS | Southdown Puma Sprint | R. G. Calvert | |
| G-MMCV | Solar Wings Typhoon III | J. Doogan | |
| G-MMCX | MBA Super Tiger Cub 440 | D. Harkin | |
| G-MMCY | Flexiform Striker | K. E. Preston | |
| G-MMCZ | Flexiform Striker | T. D. Adamson | |
| G-MMDB | La Mouette Atlas | K. A. Martin | |
| G-MMDC | Eipper Quicksilver MXII | M. Risdale & C. Lamb | |
| G-MMDD | Huntair Pathfinder | M. R. Starling | |
| G-MMDE | Solar Wings Typhoon | S. G. Rule | |

| Notes | Reg. | Type | Owner or Operator |
|---|---|---|---|
| | G-MMDF | Southdown Lightning Phase II | P. Kelly |
| | G-MMDG | Eurowing Goldwing | Edgim Ltd |
| | G-MMDH | Manta Fledge 2B | C. R. Brewitt |
| | G-MMDI | Hiway Super Scorpion | R. E. Hodge |
| | G-MMDJ | Solar Wings Typhoon | I. Love |
| | G-MMDK | Flexiform Striker | G. Forster |
| | G-MMDN | Flexiform Striker | M. G. Griffiths |
| | G-MMDO | Southdown Sprint | S. Stevens |
| | G-MMDP | Southdown Sprint | J. D. Bridgewater & C. H. Prince |
| | G-MMDR | Huntair Pathfinder II | C. Dolling |
| | G-MMDS | Ultrasports Panther XLS | L. A. Bastin |
| | G-MMDT | Flexiform Striker | W. J. C. M. Baker |
| | G-MMDU | MBA Tiger Cub 440 | W. K. Harris |
| | G-MMDV | Ultrasports Panther | T. M. Evans |
| | G-MMDW | Pterodactyl Pfledgling | J. Fletcher |
| | G-MMDX | Solar Wings Typhoon | E. J. Lloyd |
| | G-MMDY | Southdown Puma Sprint | A. J. Perry |
| | G-MMDZ | Flexiform Dual Strike | D. C. Seager-Thomas |
| | G-MMEB | Hiway Super Scorpion | V. Q. Robertshaw |
| | G-MMEE | American Aerolights Eagle | G. R. Bell & J. D. Bailey |
| | G-MMEF | Hiway Super Scorpion | R. H. Evans |
| | G-MMEG | Eipper Quicksilver MX | W. K. Harris |
| | G-MMEI | Hiway Demon | W. H. Shakeshaft |
| | G-MMEJ | Flexiform Striker | J. E. Chisholm |
| | G-MMEK | Solar Wings Typhoon XL2 | T. A. Baker |
| | G-MMEL | Solar Wings Typhoon XL2 | D. O. Hilton |
| | G-MMEM | Solar Wings Typhoon XL2 | Wyndham Wade Ltd |
| | G-MMEN | Solar Wings Typhoon XL2 | I. M. Rapley |
| | G-MMEP | MBA Tiger Cub 440 | P. M. Yeoman & D. Freestone-Barks |
| | G-MMES | Southdown Puma Sprint | B. J. Sanderson |
| | G-MMET | Skyhook Sabre TR-1 Mk II | A. B. Greenbank |
| | G-MMEU | MBS Tiger Cub 440 | R. Taylor |
| | G-MMEW | MBA Tiger Cub 440 | V. N. Baker |
| | G-MMEX | Solar Wings Sprint | E. Bayliss |
| | G-MMEY | MBA Tiger Cub 440 | M. G. Selley |
| | G-MMEZ | Southdown Puma Sprint | I. G. Reason |
| | G-MMFB | Flexiform Striker | M. V. Adams |
| | G-MMFC | Flexiform Striker | K. A. Maughan |
| | G-MMFD | Flexiform Striker | M. E. & W. L. Chapman |
| | G-MMFE | Flexiform Striker | W. Camm |
| | G-MMFG | Flexiform Striker | M. G. Dean & M. J. Hadland |
| | G-MMFI | Flexiform Striker | A. J. Wood |
| | G-MMFJ | Flexiform Striker | A. R. Broughton-Tompkins |
| | G-MMFK | Flexiform Striker | S. W. England |
| | G-MMFL | Flexiform Striker | T. C. Bradley |
| | G-MMFM | Piranha Srs 200 | E. L. Williams |
| | G-MMFN | MBA Tiger Cub 440 | J. A. Hunt |
| | G-MMFS | MBA Tiger Cub 440 | D. K. Webb |
| | G-MMFW | Skyhook Cutlass | W. Chapel |
| | G-MMFX | MBA Tiger Cub 440 | J. W. E. Romain |
| | G-MMFY | Flexiform Dual Striker | S. W. Tizard |
| | G-MMFZ | AES Sky Ranger | H. A. Ward |
| | G-MMGA | Bass Gosling | G. J. Bass |
| | G-MMGB | Southdown Puma Sprint | G. Breen |
| | G-MMGC | Southdown Puma Sprint | Innovative Air Services Ltd |
| | G-MMGD | Southdown Puma Sprint | I. Hughes |
| | G-MMGE | Hiway Super Scorpion | M. K. Haddon |
| | G-MMGF | MBA Tiger Cub 440 | L. P. Durrant |
| | G-MMGL | MBA Tiger Cub 440 | A. R. Cornelius |
| | G-MMGN | Southdown Puma Sprint | H. Stieker |
| | G-MMGO | MBA Tiger Cub 440 | T. J. Court |
| | G-MMGP | Southdown Puma Sprint | H. Lorimer |
| | G-MMGR | Flexiform Dual Striker | G. P. Jones |
| | G-MMGS | Solar Wings Panther Dual | G. D. Featherstone |
| | G-MMGT | Solar Wings Typhoon | J. A. Hunt |
| | G-MMGU | Flexiform Sealander | C. J. Meadows |
| | G-MMGV | Whittaker MW.5 Sorcerer Srs A | G. N. Haffey & G. M. Hislop |
| | G-MMGX | Southdown Puma | G. S. Mitchell |
| | G-MMGY | Dean Piranha 1000 | M. G. Dean |
| | G-MMHA | Skyhook TR-1 Pixie | P. J. & A. St J. Hollis |
| | G-MMHB | Skyhook TR-1 Pixie | D. M. Pollard |
| | G-MMHD | Hiway Demon 175 | R. D. Midgley |
| | G-MMHE | Southdown Puma Sprint MS | J. Mayer |

| Reg. | Type | Owner or Operator | Notes |
|------|------|-------------------|-------|
| G-MMHF | Southdown Puma Sprint | B. R. Claughton | |
| G-MMHG | Solar Wings Storm | W. T. Price | |
| G-MMHJ | Flexiform Hilander | B. Whittingham | |
| G-MMHK | Hiway Super Scorpion | R. Pearson | |
| G-MMHL | Hiway Super Scorpion | E. H. Jenkins | |
| G-MMHM | Goldmarque Gyr | G. J. Foard | |
| G-MMHP | Hiway Demon | P. Bedford | |
| G-MMHR | Southdown Puma Sprint DS | C. A. Eagles | |
| G-MMHS | SMD Viper | C. J. Meadows | |
| G-MMHT | Flexiform Viper | T. G. F. Trenchard | |
| G-MMHX | Hornet Invader 440 | Hornet Microlights | |
| G-MMHY | Hornet Invader 440 | W. Finlay | |
| G-MMHZ | Solar Wings Typhoon XL | S. J. Pain | |
| G-MMIB | MEA Mistral | G. W. Hockley | |
| G-MMIC | Luscombe Vitality | Luscombe Aircraft Ltd | |
| G-MMID | Flexiform Dual Striker | D. H. Brown | |
| G-MMIE | MBA Tiger Cub 440 | A. B. Eadon-Mills | |
| G-MMIF | Wasp Gryphon | F. Coulson | |
| G-MMIH | MBA Tiger Cub 440 | W. A. Taylor | |
| G-MMII | Southdown Puma Sprint 440 | T. C. Harrold | |
| G-MMIJ | Ultrasports Tripacer | R. W. Evans | |
| G-MMIL | Eipper Quicksilver MX II | C. K. Brown | |
| G-MMIM | MBA Tiger Cub 440 | D. A. Small | |
| G-MMIO | Huntair Pathfinder II | C. Slater | |
| G-MMIP | Hiway Vulcan | A. A. Cale | |
| G-MMIR | Mainair Tri-Flyer 440 | N. Fielding | |
| G-MMIS | Hiway Demon | M. P. Wing | |
| G-MMIV | Southdown Puma Sprint | J. S. Walton | |
| G-MMIW | Southdown Puma Sprint | A. P. & D. K. Robinson | |
| G-MMIX | MBA Tiger Cub 440 | M. J. Butler & C. Bell | |
| G-MMIY | Eurowing Goldwing | R. J. Wood | |
| G-MMIZ | Southdown Lightning II | M. A. Cooper | |
| G-MMJC | Southdown Sprint | P. G. Marshall | |
| G-MMJD | Southdown Puma Sprint | N. G. Tibbenham | |
| G-MMJE | Southdown Puma Sprint | F. N. M. Sergeant | |
| G-MMJF | Ultrasports Panther Dual 440 | D. H. Stokes | |
| G-MMJG | Mainair Tri-Flyer 440 | A. D. Stewart | |
| G-MMJH | Southdown Puma Sprint | A. R. Lawrence & T. J. Weston | |
| G-MMJI | Southdown Puma Sprint | N. J. Holt | |
| G-MMJJ | Solar Wings Typhoon | R. J. Wood | |
| G-MMJK | Hiway Demon | J. B. C. Brown & M. L. Jones | |
| G-MMJL | Flexiform 1+1 Sealander | J. C. B. Leech | |
| G-MMJM | Southdown Puma Sprint | R. J. Sanger | |
| G-MMJN | Eipper Quicksilver MX II | R. M. Gunn | |
| G-MMJO | MBA Tiger Cub 440 | R. J. Adams | |
| G-MMJS | MBA Tiger Cub | Woodgate Air Services Ltd | |
| G-MMJT | Southdown Puma Sprint MS | W. F. Murray | |
| G-MMJU | Hiway Demon | D. Whiteside | |
| G-MMJV | MBA Tiger Cub 440 | K. Bannister | |
| G-MMJW | Southdown Puma Sprint | C. L. S. Boswell | |
| G-MMJY | MBA Tiger Cub 440 | Peterson Clarke Sports Ltd | |
| G-MMJZ | Skyhook Pixie | J. H. Cooling | |
| G-MMKA | Ultrasports Panther Dual | R. S. Wood | |
| G-MMKB | Ultralight Flight Mirage II | K. G. Wigley | |
| G-MMKC | Southdown Puma Sprint MS | J. Potts | |
| G-MMKD | Southdown Puma Sprint | R. H. Harris | |
| G-MMKE | Birdman Chinook WT-11 | D. M. Jackson | |
| G-MMKF | Ultrasports Panther Dual 440 | G. Ellis | |
| G-MMKG | Solar Wings Typhoon XL | G. P. Lane | |
| G-MMKH | Solar Wings Typhoon XL | D. E. Home & M. Baylis | |
| G-MMKI | Ultrasports Panther 330 | Lightflight Aviation | |
| G-MMKJ | Ultrasports Panther 330 | D. A. Poole | |
| G-MMKK | Mainair Flash | J. C. Bowden | |
| G-MMKL | Mainair Flash | S. Allinson | |
| G-MMKM | Flexiform Dual Striker | A. C. Snowling | |
| G-MMKO | Southdown Puma Sprint | G. Breen | |
| G-MMKP | MBA Tiger Cub 440 | J. W. Beaty | |
| G-MMKR | Southdown Lightning DS | R. I. Lowe | |
| G-MMKS | Southdown Lightning 195 | J. Cameron | |
| G-MMKT | MBA Tiger Cub 440 | K. N. Townsend | |
| G-MMKU | Southdown Puma Sprint MS | J. T. Hearle | |
| G-MMKV | Southdown Puma Sprint | J. Walsom | |
| G-MMKW | Solar Wings Storm | P. M. & R. Dewhurst | |

| Notes | Reg. | Type | Owner or Operator |
|---|---|---|---|
| | G-MMKY | Jordan Duet | C. H. Smith |
| | G-MMKZ | Ultrasports Puma 440 | J. V. Clewer |
| | G-MMLB | MBA Tiger Cub 440 | A. Newton |
| | G-MMLD | Solar Wings Typhoon S | N. P. Moran |
| | G-MMLE | Eurowing Goldwing SP | D. Lamberty |
| | G-MMLF | MBA Tiger Cub 440 | D. J. Flower & S. Bell |
| | G-MMLG | Solar Wings Typhoon S4 XL | R. M. Cornwell |
| | G-MMLH | Hiway Demon | P. M. Hendry & D. J. Lukery |
| | G-MMLI | Solar Wings Typhoon S | J. D. Grey |
| | G-MMLJ | — | — |
| | G-MMLK | MBA Tiger Cub 440 | W. B. Nolson |
| | G-MMLL | Midland Ultralights Sirocco | Midland Ultralights Ltd |
| | G-MMLM | MBA Tiger Cub 440 | J. Scholefield |
| | G-MMLN | Skyhook Pixie | P. G. G. Taylor |
| | G-MMLO | Skyhook Pixie | T. G. Hilton |
| | G-MMLP | Southdown Sprint | S. F. K. Blakeman |
| | G-MMLU | — | — |
| | G-MMLV | Southdown Puma 330 | R. A. C. Brewster |
| | G-MMLW | — | — |
| | G-MMLX | Ultrasports Panther | J. A. Stark |
| | G-MMLY | — | — |
| | G-MMLZ | Mainair Tri-Flyer | D. A. Whiteside |
| | G-MMMB | Mainair Tri-Flyer | D. M. Rusbridge |
| | G-MMMD | Flexiform Dual Striker | C. P. Sales |
| | G-MMMG | Eipper Quicksilver MXL | W. Murphy |
| | G-MMMH | Hadland Willow | M. J. Hadland |
| | G-MMMI | Southdown Lightning | J. Knighton |
| | G-MMMJ | Southdown Sprint | R. R. Wolfenden |
| | G-MMMK | Hornet Invader | R. R. Wolfenden |
| | G-MMML | Dragon 150 | R. G. Huntley |
| | G-MMMN | Ultrasports Panther Dual 440 | T. L. Travis |
| | G-MMMP | Flexiform Dual Striker | K. P. Southwell |
| | G-MMMR | Flexiform Striker | M. A. Rigler |
| | G-MMMS | MBA Tiger Cub 440 | F. J. Griffith |
| | G-MMMT | Hornet Sigma | B. O'Connell |
| | G-MMMU | Skyhook Cutlass CD | F. J. Lightburn |
| | G-MMMV | Skyhook Cutlass Dual | R. R. Wolfenden |
| | G-MMMW | Flexiform Striker | K. & M. Spedding |
| | G-MMMX | Hornet Nimrod | R. Patrick |
| | G-MMNA | Eipper Quicksilver MX II | K. R. Daly |
| | G-MMNB | Eipper Quicksilver MX | J. T. Lindop |
| | G-MMNC | Eipper Quicksilver MX | K. R. Daly |
| | G-MMND | Eipper Quicksilver MX II-Q2 | J. E. Holloway |
| | G-MMNE | Eipper Quicksilver MX II | W. Murphy |
| | G-MMNF | Hornet | C. Hudson |
| | G-MMNG | Solar Wings Typhoon XL | R. Simpson |
| | G-MMNN | Buzzard | E. W. Sherry |
| | G-MMNP | Ultrasports Panther 250 | J. M. Baird |
| | G-MMNS | Mitchell U-2 Super Wing | D. J. Baldwin |
| | G-MMNT | Flexiform Striker | A. C. Coutts |
| | G-MMNU | Ultrasports Panther | R. F. Aves |
| | G-MMNW | Mainair Tri-Flyer 330 | T. Jackson |
| | G-MMNX | Solar Wings Panther XL | B. Montsern |
| | G-MMNZ | — | — |
| | G-MMOA | — | — |
| | G-MMOB | Southdown Sprint | D. Woolcock |
| | G-MMOD | MBA Tiger Cub 440 | G. W. de Lancey Aitchison |
| | G-MMOF | MBA Tiger Cub 440 | A. M. Witt |
| | G-MMOG | Huntair Pathfinder | R. G. Maguire |
| | G-MMOH | Solar Wings Typhoon XL | T. H. Scott |
| | G-MMOI | MBA Tiger Cub 440 | J. S. Smith & P. R. Talbot |
| | G-MMOJ | — | — |
| | G-MMOK | Solar Wings Panther XL | R. F. Foster |
| | G-MMOL | Skycraft Scout R3 | P. D. G. Weller |
| | G-MMOO | Southdown Storm | S. Bourne |
| | G-MMOW | Mainair Gemini Flash | M. T. Pearce |
| | G-MMOX | Mainair Gemini Flash | J. K. Allen & G. Newby |
| | G-MMOY | Mainair Gemini Sprint | Mainair Sports Ltd |
| | G-MMPD | Mainair Tri-Flyer | A. R. J. Dorling |
| | G-MMPE | Eurowing Goldwing | K. J. Jones |
| | G-MMPG | Southdown Puma | J. M. Hodgins |
| | G-MMPH | Southdown Puma Sprint | J. E. Mills |
| | G-MMPI | Pterodactyl Ptraveller | G. P. Smith & A. W. Burton |

| Reg. | Type | Owner or Operator | Notes |
|------|------|-------------------|-------|
| G-MMPJ | Mainair Tri-Flyer 440 | K. R. Pickering | |
| G-MMPL | Flexiform Dual Striker | P. D. Lawrence | |
| G-MMPN | Chargus T250 | S. M. Powrie | |
| G-MMPO | Mainair Gemini Flash | H. B. Baker | |
| G-MMPR | Dragon 150 | P. N. B. Rosenfeld | |
| G-MMPT | SMD Gazelle | J. R. Hall | |
| G-MMPU | Ultrasports Tripacer 250 | J. T. Halford | |
| G-MMPW | Airwave Nimrod | D. A. Smith | |
| G-MMPX | Ultrasports Panther Dual 440 | M. T. Jones | |
| G-MMPZ | Teman Mono-Fly | J. W. Highton | |
| G-MMRA | Mainair Tri-Flyer 250 | S. R. Criddle | |
| G-MMRC | Southdown Lightning | J. C. Dodin & L. A. Ithier | |
| G-MMRD | Skyhook Cutlass CD | C. & R. A. White | |
| G-MMRF | MBA Tiger Cub 440 | R. Gardner | |
| G-MMRH | Hiway Demon | J. S. McCaig | |
| G-MMRI | Skyhook Sabre | G. M. Wrigley | |
| G-MMRJ | Solar Wings Panther XL | D. E. Jones | |
| G-MMRK | Ultrasports Panther XL | K. G. Seeley | |
| G-MMRL | Solar Wings Panther XL | R. G. Thomas | |
| G-MMRM | — | | |
| G-MMRN | Southdown Puma Sprint | A. G. Jones | |
| G-MMRO | Mainair Gemini 440 | P. R. Grady | |
| G-MMRP | Mainair Gemini | M. A. Pugh | |
| G-MMRR | Southdown Panther 250 | D. D. & A. R. Young | |
| G-MMRT | Southdown Puma Sprint | V. Brierley | |
| G-MMRU | Tirith Firebird FB-2 | Tirith Microplane Ltd | |
| G-MMRV | MBA Tiger Cub 440 | C. J. R. V. Baker | |
| G-MMRW | Flexiform Dual Striker | M. D. Hinge | |
| G-MMRX | Willmot J.W.1 | N. J. Willmot | |
| G-MMRY | Chargus T.250 | D. L. Edwards & ptnrs | |
| G-MMRZ | Ultrasports Panther Dual 440 | A. J. Baigrie & K. A. Calder | |
| G-MMSA | Ultrasports Panther XL | D. W. Taylor | |
| G-MMSC | Mainair Gemini | A. B. Jones | |
| G-MMSE | Eipper Quicksilver MX | P. Rowbotham | |
| G-MMSF | — | | |
| G-MMSG | Solar Wings Panther XL | R. D. E. Baskerville | |
| G-MMSH | Solar Wings Panther XL | I. J. Drake | |
| G-MMSM | Mainair Gemini Flash | A. W. Birchley | |
| G-MMSN | Mainair Gemini | S. J. G. Harris | |
| G-MMSO | Mainair Tri-Flyer 440 | D. Morley | |
| G-MMSP | Mainair Gemini Flash | B. J. Robe | |
| G-MMSR | MBA Tiger Cub 440 | D. J. Rees | |
| G-MMSS | Solar Wings Panther 330 | J. H. Cooling | |
| G-MMST | Southdown Puma Sprint | I. Davis | |
| G-MMSU | American Aerolights Eagle B | C. Bilham | |
| G-MMSV | Southdown Puma Sprint | S. D. Dando | |
| G-MMSW | MBA Tiger Cub 440 | D. R. Hemmings | |
| G-MMSZ | Medway Half Pint | Lancaster Partners (Holdings) Ltd | |
| G-MMTA | Ultrasports Panther XL | R. J. & M. H. Fry | |
| G-MMTC | Ultrasports Panther Dual | J. M. Butler | |
| G-MMTD | Mainair Tri-Flyer 330 | E. I. Armstrong | |
| G-MMTE | Mainair Gemini | B. F. Crick | |
| G-MMTF | Southdown Puma Sprint | P. J. K. Scriven | |
| G-MMTG | Mainair Gemini | R. P. W. Johnstone | |
| G-MMTH | Southdown Puma Sprint | R. G. Tomlinson | |
| G-MMTI | Southdown Puma Sprint | G. Sinnott | |
| G-MMTJ | Southdown Puma Sprint | B. P. Barker | |
| G-MMTK | Medway Hybred | J. F. Nicholls | |
| G-MMTL | Mainair Gemini | Baxby Microlights Ltd | |
| G-MMTM | Mainair Tri-Flyer 440 | C. Z. Anderson | |
| G-MMTO | Mainair Tri-Flyer | R. G. Swales | |
| G-MMTR | Ultrasports Panther | R. T. Bray | |
| G-MMTS | Solar Wings Panther XL | T. A. Dockrell | |
| G-MMTT | Solar Wings Panther XL | A. C. Snowling | |
| G-MMTV | American Aerolights Eagle | P. J. Scott | |
| G-MMTX | Mainair Gemini 440 | R. L. Mann | |
| G-MMTY | Fisher FP.202U | B. E. Maggs | |
| G-MMTZ | Eurowing Goldwing | R. B. D. Baker | |
| G-MMUA | Southdown Puma Sprint | J. T. Houghton | |
| G-MMUB | Ultrasports Tripacer 250 | P. G. Thompson | |
| G-MMUC | Mainair Gemini 440 | H. Edwards | |
| G-MMUE | Mainair Gemini Flash | I. R. Russell | |
| G-MMUF | Mainair Gemini | C. J. Ellison | |

| Notes | Reg. | Type | Owner or Operator |
|---|---|---|---|
| | G-MMUG | Mainair Tri-Flyer | K. C. Rutland |
| | G-MMUH | Mainair Tri-Flyer | J. P. Nicklin |
| | G-MMUJ | Southdown Puma Sprint 440 | T. A. Hinton |
| | G-MMUK | Mainair Tri-Flyer | B. R. Kirk |
| | G-MMUL | Ward Elf E.47 | M. Ward |
| | G-MMUM | MBA Tiger Cub 440 | D. B. Coulson |
| | G-MMUN | Ultrasports Panther Dual XL | K. S. Smith |
| | G-MMUO | Mainair Gemini Flash | R. A. Watering |
| | G-MMUP | Airwave Nimrod 140 | R. J. Bickham |
| | G-MMUS | Mainair Gemini | R. M. Findlay |
| | G-MMUU | ParaPlane PM-1 | Colt Balloons Ltd |
| | G-MMUV | Southdown Puma Sprint | D. C. Read |
| | G-MMUW | Mainair Gemini Flash | J. C. K. Scardifield |
| | G-MMUX | Mainair Gemini | H. C. Walker |
| | G-MMUY | Mainair Gemini Flash | W. A. Bibby |
| | G-MMVA | Southdown Puma Sprint | P. J. Callis & M. Aylett |
| | G-MMVC | Ultrasports Panther XL | E. R. Holton |
| | G-MMVG | MBA Tiger Cub 440 | C. W. Grant |
| | G-MMVH | Southdown Raven | M. Dold |
| | G-MMVI | Southdown Puma Sprint | R. J. Wheeler & M. J. Trenberth |
| | G-MMVJ | Southdown Puma Sprint | S. L. Robbins |
| | G-MMVL | Ultrasports Panther XL-S | B. Milton |
| | G-MMVM | Whiteley Orion 1 | P. N. Whiteley |
| | G-MMVN | Solar Wings Typhoon | D. C. Davies |
| | G-MMVO | Southdown Puma Sprint | R. W. Jennings |
| | G-MMVP | Mainair Gemini Flash | G. R. Protheroe |
| | G-MMVR | Hiway Skytrike 1 | B. P. Barker |
| | G-MMVS | Skyhook Pixie | G. Bilham |
| | G-MMVT | Mainair Gemini Flash | Aircraft Microlight Services |
| | G-MMVU | Mainair Gemini Flash | R. Wheeler |
| | G-MMVW | Skyhook Pixie | R. Keighley |
| | G-MMVX | Southdown Puma Sprint | D. J. Reynolds |
| | G-MMVY | American Aerolights Eagle | R. Savva |
| | G-MMVZ | Southdown Puma Sprint | M. R. Bayliss |
| | G-MMWA | Mainair Gemini Flash | A. & K. Worthington |
| | G-MMWC | Eipper Quicksilver MXII | P. W. Cole & L. R. Mudge |
| | G-MMWF | Hiway Skytrike 250 | J. R. Du Plessis |
| | G-MMWG | Greenslade Mono-Trike | L. J. Perring |
| | G-MMWH | Southdown Puma Sprint 440 | J. R. Bowman |
| | G-MMWI | Southdown Lightning | A. W. Cove |
| | G-MMWJ | Pterodactyl Ptraveler | G. A. Harman |
| | G-MMWK | Hiway Demon | G. Sinclair |
| | G-MMWL | Eurowing Goldwing | D. J. White |
| | G-MMWM | — | — |
| | G-MMWN | Ultrasports Tripacer | J. M. Balfe |
| | G-MMWO | Ultrasports Panther XL | P. F. J. Rogers |
| | G-MMWP | American Aerolights Eagle | C. E. Tait |
| | G-MMWR | — | — |
| | G-MMWS | Mainair Tri-Flyer | R. J. Wilson |
| | G-MMWT | CFM Shadow | H. R. Block |
| | G-MMWX | Southdown Puma Sprint | G. Hill |
| | G-MMWY | Skyhook Pixie | N. M. Cuthbertson |
| | G-MMWZ | Southdown Puma Sprint | R. J. J. Wesson |
| | G-MMXB | — | — |
| | G-MMXC | Mainair Gemini Flash | C. R. Maybury |
| | G-MMXD | Mainair Gemini Flash | D. Lund |
| | G-MMXE | Mainair Gemini Flash | Aircraft Microlight Services |
| | G-MMXG | Mainair Gemini Flash | S. D. Hill |
| | G-MMXH | Mainair Gemini Flash | I. C. Willetts |
| | G-MMXI | Horizon Prototype | Horizon Aerosails Ltd |
| | G-MMXJ | Mainair Gemini Flash | R. Meredith-Hardy |
| | G-MMXK | Mainair Gemini Flash | N. S. Brown |
| | G-MMXL | Mainair Gemini Flash | D. Yates |
| | G-MMXM | Mainair Gemini Flash | R. Perrett |
| | G-MMXN | Southdown Puma Sprint | K. F. Hefford & A. Wright |
| | G-MMXO | Southdown Puma Sprint | D. J. Tasker |
| | G-MMXP | Southdown Puma Sprint | D. M. Humphreys |
| | G-MMXR | Southdown Puma DS | M. J. Brooks |
| | G-MMXT | Mainair Gemini Flash | P. N. Cruise |
| | G-MMXU | Mainair Gemini Flash | T. J. Franklin |
| | G-MMXV | Mainair Gemini Flash | A. V. Szolin |
| | G-MMXW | Mainair Gemini | A. Hodgson |
| | G-MMXX | Mainair Gemini | S. & S. Warburton-Pitt |

| Reg. | Type | Owner or Operator | Notes |
|------|------|-------------------|-------|
| G-MMXY | – | – | |
| G-MMXZ | Eipper Quicksilver MXII | C. J. Padro | |
| G-MMYA | Solar Wings Pegasus XL | Solar Wings Ltd | |
| G-MMYB | Solar Wings Pegasus XL | Solar Wings Ltd | |
| G-MMYD | CFM Shadow Srs B | CFM Metal-Fax Ltd | |
| G-MMYE | – | – | |
| G-MMYF | Southdown Puma Sprint | D. O. Crane | |
| G-MMYG | – | – | |
| G-MMYH | – | – | |
| G-MMYI | Southdown Puma Sprint | R. J. Ripley | |
| G-MMYJ | Southdown Puma Sprint | R. K. Seddon | |
| G-MMYK | Southdown Puma Sprint | C. L. Gore | |
| G-MMYL | Cyclone 70 | J. T. Halford | |
| G-MMYM | – | – | |
| G-MMYN | Ultrasports Panther XL | G. M. R. Walters & H. Clarke | |
| G-MMYO | Southdown Puma Sprint | K. J. Taylor | |
| G-MMYP | – | – | |
| G-MMYR | Eipper Quicksilver MXII | M. Reed | |
| G-MMYS | Southdown Puma Sprint | Enstone Microlight Centre | |
| G-MMYT | Southdown Puma Sprint | I. S. Stamp | |
| G-MMYU | Southdown Puma Sprint | I. Parr | |
| G-MMYV | Webb Trike | A. P. Fenn | |
| G-MMYX | Mitchell U-2 | R. A. Codling | |
| G-MMYY | Southdown Puma Sprint | J. C. & A. M. Rose | |
| G-MMYZ | Southdown Puma Sprint | N. Crisp | |
| G-MMZA | Mainair Gemini Flash | D. French | |
| G-MMZB | Mainair Gemini Flash | M. A. Nolan | |
| G-MMZC | Mainair Gemini Flash | G. T. Johnston | |
| G-MMZE | Mainair Gemini Flash | S. D. Pain | |
| G-MMZF | Mainair Gemini Flash | A. R. Rhodes | |
| G-MMZG | Ultrasports Panther XL-S | G. D. Fogg | |
| G-MMZH | Ultrasports Tripacer | R. Bacon | |
| G-MMZI | Medway 130SX | P. M. Lang | |
| G-MMZJ | Mainair Gemini Flash | A. C. Williams | |
| G-MMZK | Mainair Gemini Flash | J. D. O. Gill | |
| G-MMZL | Mainair Gemini Flash | R. F. Aves | |
| G-MMZM | Mainair Gemini Flash | R. E. D. Bailey | |
| G-MMZN | Mainair Gemini Flash | W. K. Dalus | |
| G-MMZO | Microflight Spectrum | Microflight Aircraft Ltd | |
| G-MMZP | Ultrasports Panther XL | B. Richardson | |
| G-MMZR | Southdown Puea Sprint | A. McDermid | |
| G-MMZS | Eipper Quicksilver MX1 | J. T. Halford | |
| G-MMZU | Southdown Puma DS | E. Clark | |
| G-MMZV | Mainair Gemini Flash | J. F. Bishop | |
| G-MMZW | Southdown Puma Sprint | T. & M. Bowyer | |
| G-MMZX | Southdown Puma Sprint | D. P. G. Sarll | |
| G-MMZY | Ultrasports Tripacer 330 | G. P. Gibson | |
| G-MMZZ | Maxair Hummer | Microflight Ltd | |
| | | | |
| G-MNAA | Striplin Sky Ranger | Ingleby Microlight Flying Club | |
| G-MNAC | Mainair Gemini Flash | D. Holliday | |
| G-MNAD | Mainair Gemini Flash | J. M. Bain | |
| G-MNAE | Mainair Gemini Flash | A. D. Gilbert | |
| G-MNAF | Solar Wings Panther XL | D. T. Smith | |
| G-MNAG | Hiway Skytrike 1 | R. J. Grogan | |
| G-MNAH | Solar Wings Panther XL | B. S. Buddery | |
| G-MNAI | Ultrasports Panther XL-S | R. G. Cameron | |
| G-MNAJ | Solar Wings Panther XL-S | C. Laverty | |
| G-MNAK | Solar Wings Panther XL-S | R. B. Bisset & G. W. Craig | |
| G-MNAL | MBA Tiger Cub 440 | Ace Aero Ltd | |
| G-MNAM | Solar Wings Panther XL-S | J. Batchelor | |
| G-MNAN | Solar Wings Panther XL-S | J. W. F. Hargrave | |
| G-MNAO | Solar Wings Panther XL-S | J. Caudle | |
| G-MNAP | – | – | |
| G-MNAR | Solar Wings Panther XL-S | B. R. Cannon | |
| G-MNAT | Solar Wings Pegasus XL-R | Solar Wings Ltd | |
| G-MNAU | Solar Wings Pegasus XL-R | R. J. Ridgway | |
| G-MNAV | Southdown Puma Sprint | C. G. Deeley | |
| G-MNAW | Solar Wings Pegasus XL-R | G. D. Woodcock & D. Thorn | |
| G-MNAX | Solar Wings Pegasus XL-R | C. J. Yea | |
| G-MNAY | Ultrasports Panther XL-S | N. Baumber | |
| G-MNAZ | Solar Wings Pegasus XL-R | S. J. Baker | |
| G-MNBA | Solar Wings Pegasus XL-R | K. S. Daniels | |

| Notes | Reg. | Type | Owner or Operator |
|---|---|---|---|
| | G-MNBB | Solar Wings Pegasus XL-R | M. Sims |
| | G-MNBC | Solar Wings Pegasus XL-R | K. Wade |
| | G-MNBD | Mainair Gemini Flash | G. J. & G. G. Norris |
| | G-MNBE | Southdown Puma Sprint | J. P. Bleakley & J. M. Travers |
| | G-MNBF | Mainair Gemini Flash | H. G. Denton |
| | G-MNBG | Mainair Gemini Flash | D. A. Riggs & A. B. Shepherd |
| | G-MNBH | Southdown Puma Sprint | M. N. Cowley |
| | G-MNBI | Ultrasports Panther XL | M. G. J. Bridges |
| | G-MNBJ | Skyhook Pixie | G. M. Mansfield |
| | G-MNBK | Hiway Skytrike | J. D. Swinbank |
| | G-MNBL | American Aerolights Z Eagle | J. H. Telford |
| | G-MNBM | Southdown Puma Sprint | M. W. Hurst |
| | G-MNBN | Mainair Gemini Flash | S. Allinson |
| | G-MNBP | Mainair Gemini Flash | R. Whitby |
| | G-MNBR | Mainair Gemini Flash | N. A. P. Gregory |
| | G-MNBS | Mainair Gemini Flash | J. G. Crawford |
| | G-MNBT | Mainair Gemini Flash | D. W. Barnes |
| | G-MNBU | Mainair Gemini Flash | K. L. Turner |
| | G-MNBV | Mainair Gemini Flash | K. Gay |
| | G-MNBW | Mainair Gemini Flash | B. D. Bastin & D. R. Howells |
| | G-MNBY | Mainair Gemini | J. A. Hindley |
| | G-MNCA | Hiway Demon 175 | C. & P. G. Kett |
| | G-MNCB | Mainair Gemini Flash | K. B. O'Regan |
| | G-MNCD | Harmsworth Trike | A. D. Cranfield |
| | G-MNCF | Mainair Gemini Flash | A. W. Abraham |
| | G-MNCG | Mainair Gemini Flash | K. Ainscow & A. Horrocks |
| | G-MNCH | Lancashire Micro Trike 330 | D. M. Travis |
| | G-MNCI | Southdown Puma Sprint | M. T. G. Payne |
| | G-MNCJ | Mainair Gemini Flash | G. P. Hodgson |
| | G-MNCK | Southdown Puma Sprint | D. J. Gibbs |
| | G-MNCL | Southdown Puma Sprint | N. M. Lassman |
| | G-MNCM | CFM Shadow Srs B | P. B. Merritt |
| | G-MNCO | Eipper Quicksilver MXII | S. Lawton |
| | G-MNCP | Southdown Puma Sprint | J. G. Sealey |
| | G-MNCR | Flexiform Striker | I. M. Stamp |
| | G-MNCS | Skyrider Airsports Phantom | P. D. Lucas |
| | G-MNCU | Medway Hybred | K. M. Taylor |
| | G-MNCV | Medway Typhoon XL | M. Pryke |
| | G-MNCW | Hornet Dual Trainer | D. L. Bowtell & J. B. Harper |
| | G-MNCX | Mainair Gemini Flash | G. C. James |
| | G-MNCZ | Solar Wings Pegasus XL-T | Solar Wings Ltd |
| | G-MNDA | Thruster TST | Thruster Aircraft (UK) Ltd |
| | G-MNDB | Southdown Puma Sprint | C. P. H. Cherry |
| | G-MNDC | Mainair Gemini Flash | P. J. Hepburn |
| | G-MNDD | Mainair Scorcher Solo | G. N. Hatchett |
| | G-MNDE | Medway Half Pint | T. E. Owen |
| | G-MNDF | Mainair Gemini Flash | R. Meredith-Hardy |
| | G-MNDG | Southdown Puma Sprint | D. S. Marshall |
| | G-MNDH | Hiway Skytrike | N. R. Holloway |
| | G-MNDI | MBA Tiger Cub 440 | F. Clarke |
| | G-MNDM | Mainair Gemini Flash | J. H. Bradbury |
| | G-MNDO | Mainair Flash | R. G. Grundy |
| | G-MNDP | Southdown Puma Sprint | P. T. Braithwaite |
| | G-MNDU | Midland Sirocco 377GB | L. G. Horne |
| | G-MNDV | Midland Sirocco 377GB | L. J. Dutch |
| | G-MNDW | Midland Sirocco 377GB | G. van der Gaag |
| | G-MNDY | Southdown Puma Sprint | M. A. Ford |
| | G-MNDZ | Southdown Puma Sprint | D. A. Fiddler |
| | G-MNEF | Mainair Gemini Flash | C. Parkinson |
| | G-MNEG | Mainair Gemini Flash | MNEG Group |
| | G-MNEH | Mainair Gemini Flash | I. Rawson |
| | G-MNEI | Medway Hybred 440 | A. J. Tyler |
| | G-MNEK | Medway Half Pint | M. I. Dougall |
| | G-MNEL | Medway Half Pint | D. R. Young |
| | G-MNEM | Solar Wings Pegasus Dual | P. F. Crosby |
| | G-MNEN | Southdown Puma Sprint | A. J. Mann |
| | G-MNEO | Southdown Raven | Lawlor Car Service |
| | G-MNEP | Aerostructure Pipstrelle P.2B | M. R. Guerard |
| | G-MNER | CFM Shadow Srs B | D. Roberts |
| | G-MNET | Mainair Gemini Flash | S. W. Barker |
| | G-MNEV | Mainair Gemini Flash | A. A. White |
| | G-MNEW | Mainair Tri-Flyer | D. C. Hibbitt |
| | G-MNEX | Mainair Gemini Flash | A. Holc |

| Reg. | Type | Owner or Operator | Notes |
|------|------|-------------------|-------|
| G-MNEY | Mainair Gemini Flash | R. H. Faux | |
| G-MNEZ | Skyhook TR1 Mk 2 | M. J. Kaye | |
| G-MNFA | Solar Wings Typhoon | R. Lewis-Evans | |
| G-MNFB | Southdown Puma Sprint | C. Lawrence | |
| G-MNFC | Midland Ultralights Sirocco 377GB | D. J. Cole | |
| G-MNFE | Mainair Gemini Flash | C. H. Spencer | |
| G-MNFF | Mainair Gemini Flash | C. H. Spencer | |
| G-MNFG | Southdown Puma Sprint | K. D. Beeton | |
| G-MNFH | Mainair Gemini Flash | A. Stevenson | |
| G-MNFI | Medway Half Pint | M. I. J. Hewett | |
| G-MNFJ | Mainair Gemini Flash | S. C. Marshall | |
| G-MNFK | Mainair Gemini Flash | S. Quinn | |
| G-MNFL | AMF Chevron | P. W. Wright | |
| G-MNFM | Mainair Gemini Flash | M. L. Copland | |
| G-MNFN | Mainair Gemini Flash | J. R. Martin | |
| G-MNFP | Mainair Gemini Flash | S. Farnsworth & P. Howarth | |
| G-MNFR | Wright Tri-Flyer | R. L. Arscott | |
| G-MNFT | Mainair Gemini Flash | P. Brewster | |
| G-MNFV | Ultrasports Trike | M. M. Bowyer | |
| G-MNFW | Medway Hybred 44XL | E. Lewis | |
| G-MNFX | Southdown Puma Sprint | A. M. Shaw | |
| G-MNFY | Hornet 250 | M. O'Hearne | |
| G-MNFZ | Southdown Puma Sprint | R. C. Colbeck | |
| G-MNGA | Aerial Arts Chaser 110SX | J. F. Chitalan | |
| G-MNGB | Mainair Gemini Flash | R. Harrison | |
| G-MNGD | Quest Air Services | P. R. Davey | |
| G-MNGF | Solar Wings Pegasus | D. R. Stapleton | |
| G-MNGG | Solar Wings Pegasus XL-R | R. Carson | |
| G-MNGH | Skyhook Pixie | A. R. Smith | |
| G-MNGJ | Skyhook Zipper | Skyhook Sailwings Ltd | |
| G-MNGK | Mainair Gemini Flash | J. A. Shepherdson | |
| G-MNGL | Mainair Gemini Flash | S. W. Tallamy & G. Cusden | |
| G-MNGM | Mainair Gemini Flash | J. E. Caffull & D. R. Beale | |
| G-MNGN | Mainair Gemini Flash | T. B. Margetts | |
| G-MNGO | Solar Wings Storm | S. Adams | |
| G-MNGR | Southdown Puma Sprint | M. A. Cooper | |
| G-MNGS | Southdown Puma 330 | C. R. Mortlock & B. P. Cooke | |
| G-MNGT | Mainair Gemini Flash | I. K. Wilson | |
| G-MNGU | Mainair Gemini Flash | P. K. Dean | |
| G-MNGW | Mainair Gemini Flash | E. H. E. Nunn | |
| G-MNGX | Southdown Puma Sprint | R. J. Morris | |
| G-MNGY | Hiway Skytrike 160 | D. Braddick | |
| G-MNGZ | Mainair Gemini Flash | G. T. Snoddon | |
| G-MNHB | Solar Wings Pegasus XL-R | S. G. Pine | |
| G-MNHC | Solar Wings Pegasus XL-R | W. R. Pryce | |
| G-MNHD | Solar Wings Pegasus XL-R | P. D. Stiles | |
| G-MNHE | Solar Wings Pegasus XL-R | E. C. Crellin | |
| G-MNHF | Solar Wings Pegasus XL-R | J. Cox | |
| G-MNHG | Solar Wings Pegasus XL-R | Sure Chemicals Ltd | |
| G-MNHH | Solar Wings Panther XL-S | F. J. Williams | |
| G-MNHI | Solar Wings Pegasus XL-R | P. G. Pickett | |
| G-MNHJ | Solar Wings Pegasus XL-R | S. J. Wood | |
| G-MNHK | Solar Wings Pegasus XL-R | Battalion Grenadier Guards Microlight Group | |
| G-MNHL | Solar Wings Pegasus XL-R | I. D. Evans | |
| G-MNHM | Solar Wings Pegasus XL-R | M. P. Tyson | |
| G-MNHN | Solar Wings Pegasus XL-R | J. Nicholson | |
| G-MNHP | Solar Wings Pegasus XL-R | P. N. Bailey & D. M. Smith | |
| G-MNHR | Solar Wings Pegasus XL-R | M. F. Eddington | |
| G-MNHS | Solar Wings Pegasus XL-R | G. King | |
| G-MNHT | Solar Wings Pegasus XL-R | T. T. Parr | |
| G-MNHU | Solar Wings Pegasus XL-R | C. Pidler | |
| G-MNHV | Solar Wings Pegasus XL-R | G. R. Organ | |
| G-MNHW | Medway Half Pint | S. G. Argo | |
| G-MNHX | Solar Wings Typhoon S4 | R. Blackwell | |
| G-MNHZ | Mainair Gemini Flash | J. R. Hewson | |
| G-MNIA | Mainair Gemini Flash | A. E. Dix | |
| G-MNIB | American Aerolights Eagle 215B | C. R. Cattell | |
| G-MNID | Mainair Gemini Flash | K. Lowery | |
| G-MNIE | Mainair Gemini Flash | P. Eden & B. Weinrabe | |
| G-MNIF | Mainair Gemini Flash | D. Yarr | |
| G-MNIG | Mainair Gemini Flash | I. S. Everett | |

| Notes | Reg. | Type | Owner or Operator |
|---|---|---|---|
| | G-MNIH | Mainair Gemini Flash | I. C. Lomax |
| | G-MNII | Mainair Gemini Flash | R. F. Finnis |
| | G-MNIL | Southdown Puma Sprint | G. J. Langston |
| | G-MNIM | Maxair Hummer | K. Wood |
| | G-MNIN | Designability Duet | S. Osmond |
| | G-MNIO | Mainair Gemini Flash | M. A. Hayward |
| | G-MNIP | Mainair Gemini Flash | G. S. Bulpitt |
| | G-MNIR | Skyhook Pixie 130 | I. G. Cole |
| | G-MNIS | CFM Shadow Srs B | R. W. Payne |
| | G-MNIT | Aerial Arts 130SX | M. J. Edmett |
| | G-MNIU | Solar Wings Pegasus Photon | K. Roberts |
| | G-MNIV | Solar Wings Typhoon | D. Tipping |
| | G-MNIW | Airwave Nimrod 165 | J. A. McIntosh & R. W. Mitchell |
| | G-MNIX | Mainair Gemini Flash | J. P. Gilbert |
| | G-MNIY | Skyhook Pixie Zipper | Skyhook Sailwings Ltd |
| | G-MNIZ | Mainair Gemini Flash | J. F. Hampson |
| | G-MNJA | Southdown Lightning Skytrike | E. G. Cameron |
| | G-MNJB | Southdown Raven | D. Millar |
| | G-MNJC | MBA Tiger Cub 440 | J. G. Carpenter |
| | G-MNJD | Southdown Puma Sprint | J. B. Duffus |
| | G-MNJE | Southdown Puma Sprint | D. L. Morris |
| | G-MNJF | Dragon 150 | L. R. Jillings |
| | G-MNJG | Mainair Tri-Flyer | J. M. Spatcher |
| | G-MNJH | Solar Wings Pegasus Flash | C. P. Course |
| | G-MNJI | Solar Wings Pegasus Flash | M. J. O'Connor |
| | G-MNJJ | Solar Wings Pegasus Flash | C. W. Lowe |
| | G-MNJK | Solar Wings Pegasus Flash | C. Green |
| | G-MNJL | Solar Wings Pegasus Flash | G. H. Cork |
| | G-MNJM | Solar Wings Pegasus Flash | N. Jefferson |
| | G-MNJN | Solar Wings Pegasus Flash | D. J. Pay |
| | G-MNJO | Solar Wings Pegasus Flash | S. J. Farrant & Sons Ltd |
| | G-MNJP | Solar Wings Pegasus Flash | R. J. Butler |
| | G-MNJR | Solar Wings Pegasus Flash | J. Stokes |
| | G-MNJS | Southdown Puma Sprint | C. E. Bates |
| | G-MNJT | Southdown Raven | W. G. Reynolds |
| | G-MNJU | Mainair Gemini Flash | N. V. Wnekowski |
| | G-MNJV | Medway Half Pint | R. J. Grogan |
| | G-MNJW | Mitchell Wing B10 | J. D. Webb |
| | G-MNJX | Medway Hybred 44XL | H. A. Stewart |
| | G-MNJY | Medway Half Pint | P. M. Stoney |
| | G-MNJZ | Aerial Arts Alpha 130SX | I. M. Grayland |
| | G-MNKA | Solar Wings Pegasus Photon | T. E. Edmond |
| | G-MNKB | Solar Wings Pegasus Photon | M. E. Gilbert |
| | G-MNKC | Solar Wings Pegasus Photon | H. C. Mowthorpe |
| | G-MNKD | Solar Wings Pegasus Photon | E. H. Jenkins |
| | G-MNKG | Solar Wings Pegasus Photon | T. W. Thompson |
| | G-MNKH | Solar Wings Pegasus Photon | A. G. Drury |
| | G-MNKI | Solar Wings Pegasus Photon | Solar Wings Ltd |
| | G-MNKJ | Solar Wings Pegasus Photon | G. Townshend |
| | G-MNKK | Solar Wings Pegasus Photon | K. S. Marine |
| | G-MNKL | Mainair Gemini Flash | R. Thorpe |
| | G-MNKM | MBA Tiger Cub 440 | L. J. Forinton |
| | G-MNKN | Skycraft Scout Mk III | E. A. Diamond |
| | G-MNKO | Solar Wings Pegasus Flash | J. D. Gray |
| | G-MNKP | Solar Wings Pegasus Flash | C. Hasell |
| | G-MNKR | Solar Wings Pegasus Flash | C. Broadley |
| | G-MNKS | Solar Wings Pegasus Flash | M. J. Sinnett & A. Howarth |
| | G-MNKT | Solar Wings Typhoon S4 | P. I. Parsons |
| | G-MNKU | Southdown Puma Sprint | R. W. Jones |
| | G-MNKV | Solar Wings Pegasus Flash | J. H. Kempton |
| | G-MNKW | Solar Wings Pegasus Flash | M. & M. S. Adams |
| | G-MNKX | Solar Wings Pegasus Flash | P. Samal |
| | G-MNKY | Southdown Raven | G. A. Harman |
| | G-MNKZ | Southdown Raven | A. E. Silvey |
| | G-MNLB | Southdown Raven X | J. C. Longmore |
| | G-MNLC | Southdown Raven | P. M. Coppola |
| | G-MNLE | Southdown Raven X | N. C. Fox |
| | G-MNLH | Romain Cobra Biplane | J. W. E. Romain |
| | G-MNLI | Mainair Gemini Flash | F. M. Pearce |
| | G-MNLK | Southdown Raven | G. C. Weighell |
| | G-MNLL | Southdown Raven | S. Barrass |
| | G-MNLM | Southdown Raven | A. P. White |
| | G-MNLN | Southdown Raven | M. C. Druce |

| Reg. | Type | Owner or Operator | Notes |
|------|------|-------------------|-------|
| G-MNLO | Southdown Raven | D. Kiddy | |
| G-MNLP | Southdown Raven | G. M. Mansfield | |
| G-MNLS | Southdown Raven | L. P. Geer | |
| G-MNLU | Southdown Raven | I. E. Spencer | |
| G-MNLV | Southdown Raven | J. Murphy | |
| G-MNLW | Medway Halt Pint | C. F. Medgett | |
| G-MNLX | Mainair Gemini Flash | J. Gamlen | |
| G-MNLY | Mainair Gemini Flash | P. Orritt & ptnrs | |
| G-MNLZ | Southdown Raven | E. L. Jenkins | |
| G-MNMA | Solar Wings Pegasus Flash | J. C. B. Halford | |
| G-MNMB | Solar Wings Pegasus Flash | M. Wells | |
| G-MNMC | Southdown Puma MS | R. E. Symonds | |
| G-MNMD | Southdown Raven | E. M. Woods & D. Little | |
| G-MNME | Hiway Skytrike | W. T. Church | |
| G-MNMF | Maxair Hummer TX | M. I. Smith | |
| G-MNMG | Mainair Gemini Flash | N. A. M. Beyer-Kay | |
| G-MNMH | Mainair Gemini Flash | W. R. & P. T. Bielby | |
| G-MNMI | Mainair Gemini Flash | T. E. McDonald | |
| G-MNMJ | Mainair Gemini Flash | P. Wareing | |
| G-MNMK | Solar Wings Pegasus XL-R | Knowles Transport Ltd | |
| G-MNML | Southdown Puma Sprint | M. J. Hammond | |
| G-MNMM | Aerotech MW.5 Sorcerer | D. B. White | |
| G-MNMN | Medway Microlights Hybred 44 | R. Skene | |
| G-MNMO | Mainair Gemini Flash | M. W. Walsh | |
| G-MNMR | Solar Wings Typhoon 180 | B. D. Jackson | |
| G-MNMS | Wheeler Scout | M. I. Smith | |
| G-MNMT | Southdown Raven | Hornet Microlights | |
| G-MNMU | Southdown Raven | P. A. Winfield | |
| G-MNMV | Mainair Gemini Flash | D. Sutherland | |
| G-MNMW | Aerotech MW.6 Merlin | E. F. Clapham & ptnrs | |
| G-MNMY | Cyclone 70 | Cyclone Hovercraft Ltd | |
| G-MNNA | Southdown Raven | D. & G. D. Palfrey | |
| G-MNNB | Southdown Raven | P. C. Knight | |
| G-MNNC | Southdown Raven | S. J. M. Morling | |
| G-MNND | Solar Wings Pegasus Flash | M. J. Matthews | |
| G-MNNE | Mainair Gemini Flash | B. L. Benson | |
| G-MNNF | Mainair Gemini Flash | KT Airsports Ltd | |
| G-MNNG | Solar Wings Photon | M. N. Hudson | |
| G-MNNI | Mainair Gemini Flash | P. J. Dean | |
| G-MNNJ | Mainair Gemini Flash | M. J. W. Thake | |
| G-MNNK | Mainair Gemini Flash | J. R. Appleton | |
| G-MNNL | Mainair Gemini Flash | D. Wilson & A. Bielawski | |
| G-MNNM | Mainair Scorcher Solo | M. R. Parr | |
| G-MNNN | Southdown Raven | F. Byford & S. Hooker | |
| G-MNNO | Southdown Raven | J. R. Poolman | |
| G-MNNP | Mainair Gemini Flash | K. J. Regan | |
| G-MNNR | Mainair Gemini Flash | Milequip Computer Systems | |
| G-MNNS | Eurowing Goldwing | D. Johnstone & R. J. Wood | |
| G-MNNT | Medway Microlights Hybred | P. Cockett | |
| G-MNNU | Mainair Gemini Flash | S. P. Willis | |
| G-MNNV | Mainair Gemini Flash | A. K. Wilkinson | |
| G-MNNY | Solar Wings Pegasus Flash | Southwest Airsports Ltd | |
| G-MNNZ | Solar Wings Pegasus Flash | P. A. R. Hicks | |
| G-MNPA | Solar Wings Pegasus Flash | E. J. Blyth | |
| G-MNPB | Solar Wings Pegasus Flash | A. G. Dyer | |
| G-MNPC | Mainair Gemini Flash | B. F. Crick | |
| G-MNPD | Midland Ultralights 130SX | C. Jones | |
| G-MNPF | Mainair Gemini Flash | M. G. A. Wood | |
| G-MNPG | Mainair Gemini Flash | P. Kirton | |
| G-MNPH | Flexiform Dual Striker | D. L. Aspinall | |
| G-MNPI | Southdown Pipistrelle 2C | R. Riley | |
| G-MNPL | Ultrasports Panther 330 | P. N. Long | |
| G-MNPP | Romain Cobra Biplane | J. W. E. Romain | |
| G-MNPR | Hiway Demon 175 | L. R. B. Howitz | |
| G-MNPV | Mainair Scorcher Solo | G. W. Doswell | |
| G-MNPW | AMF Chevron | AMF Microlight Ltd | |
| G-MNPX | Mainair Gemini Flash | M. A. Hodgson | |
| G-MNPY | Mainair Scorcher Solo | R. N. O. Kingsbury | |
| G-MNPZ | Mainair Scorcher Solo | Mainair Sports Ltd | |
| G-MNRA | CFM Shadow Srs B | CFM Metal-Fax Ltd | |
| G-MNRD | Ultraflight Lazair | D. W. & M. F. Briggs | |
| G-MNRE | Mainair Scorcher Solo | B. R. Chamberlain | |
| G-MNRF | Mainair Scorcher Solo | W. C. Yates | |

| Notes | Reg. | Type | Owner or Operator |
|-------|------|------|-------------------|
| | G-MNRG | Mainair Scorcher Solo | G. A. Tungatt |
| | G-MNRI | Hornet Dual Trainer | D. A. Robinson |
| | G-MNRJ | Hornet Dual Trainer | S. R. Morris & ptnrs |
| | G-MNRK | Hornet Dual Trainer | J. R. Pritchard |
| | G-MNRL | Hornet Dual Trainer | Hornet Microlights |
| | G-MNRM | Hornet Dual Trainer | R. I. Cannon |
| | G-MNRN | Hornet Dual Trainer | Hornet Microlights |
| | G-MNRP | Southdown Raven | C. Moore |
| | G-MNRR | Southdown Raven X | J. G. Jennings |
| | G-MNRS | Southdown Raven | P. H. E. & P. G. Woodliffe-Thomas |
| | G-MNRT | Midland Ultralights Sirocco | R. F. Hinton |
| | G-MNRU | Midland Ultralights Sirocco | Midland Ultralights Ltd |
| | G-MNRW | Mainair Gemini Flash II | L. A. Maynard |
| | G-MNRX | Mainair Gemini Flash II | J. Greenhalgh |
| | G-MNRY | Mainair Gemini Flash | M. A. Lomas |
| | G-MNRZ | Mainair Scorcher Solo | J. N. Wrigley |
| | G-MNSA | Mainair Gemini Flash | L. M. Retallick |
| | G-MNSB | Southdown Puma Sprint | A. C. Cale |
| | G-MNSD | Solar Wings Typhoon | W. Read & A. J. Lloyd |
| | G-MNSE | Mainair Gemini Flash | J. S. Mather |
| | G-MNSF | Hornet Dual Trainer | R. Pattrick |
| | G-MNSH | Solar Wings Pegasus Flash II | P. J. Gwatkin |
| | G-MNSI | Mainair Gemini Flash | A. Jones |
| | G-MNSJ | Mainair Gemini Flash | M. L. Plant Insulations Ltd |
| | G-MNSK | Hiway Skytrike | E. B. Jones |
| | G-MNSL | Southdown Raven X | P. B. Robinson |
| | G-MNSM | Hornet Demon | A. R. Glenn |
| | G-MNSN | Solar Wings Pegasus Flash II | P. R. Waite |
| | G-MNSO | Solar Wings Pegasus Flash II | P. W. Giesler |
| | G-MNSP | Aerial Arts 130SX | C. J. Upton-Taylor |
| | G-MNSR | Mainair Gemini Flash | J. Brown |
| | G-MNSS | American Aerolights Eagle | G. P. Jones |
| | G-MNST | Vector 600 | M. Quigley |
| | G-MNSV | CFM Shadow Srs B | P. J. W. Rowell |
| | G-MNSW | Southdown Raven X | P. J. Barton |
| | G-MNSX | Southdown Raven X | J. D. Thompson |
| | G-MNSY | Southdown Raven X | R. D. Hatton |
| | G-MNSZ | Noble Hardman Snowbird | Noble Hardman Aviation Ltd |
| | G-MNTB | Solar Wings Typhoon S4 | P. Timms |
| | G-MNTC | Southdown Raven X | J. R. Brabbs |
| | G-MNTD | Aerial Arts Chaser 110SX | H. Phipps |
| | G-MNTE | Southdown Raven X | D. Kiddy |
| | G-MNTF | Southdown Raven X | J. P. Kynaston |
| | G-MNTG | Southdown Raven X | D. Thorpe |
| | G-MNTH | Mainair Gemini Flash | S. M. Hargreaves |
| | G-MNTI | Mainair Gemini Flash | R. T. Strathie |
| | G-MNTK | CFM Shadow Srs B | M. I. M. Smith |
| | G-MNTL | Arbee Wasp Gryphon | D. K. Liddard |
| | G-MNTM | Southdown Raven X | M. W. Hurst |
| | G-MNTN | Southdown Raven X | J. Hall |
| | G-MNTO | Southdown Raven X | J. T. Nunn |
| | G-MNTP | CFM Shadow Srs B | G. E. Gould |
| | G-MNTS | Mainair Gemini Flash II | K. J. Cole |
| | G-MNTT | Medway Half Pint | Lancaster Partners (Holdings) Ltd |
| | G-MNTU | Mainair Gemini Flash II | P. F. Lynch |
| | G-MNTV | Mainair Gemini Flash II | K. L. Turner |
| | G-MNTW | Mainair Gemini Flash II | M. E. Hemming-Allen |
| | G-MNTX | Mainair Gemini Flash II | C. W. Thomas |
| | G-MNTY | Southdown Raven X | T. E. Baxter |
| | G-MNTZ | Mainair Gemini Flash II | Weston Furnishers |
| | G-MNUA | Mainair Gemini Flash II | R. T. R. Morwood |
| | G-MNUB | Mainair Gemini Flash II | R. V. Emerson |
| | G-MNUC | Solar Wings Pegasus Flash II | K. D. Calvert |
| | G-MNUD | Solar Wings Pegasus Flash II | P. G. Ford |
| | G-MNUE | Solar Wings Pegasus Flash II | S. Rands |
| | G-MNUF | Mainair Gemini Flash II | C. Hannaby |
| | G-MNUG | Mainair Gemini Flash II | A. F. Stafford |
| | G-MNUH | Southdown Raven X | A. L. Flude |
| | G-MNUI | Skyhook Cutlass Dual | M. Holling |
| | G-MNUJ | Solar Wings Pegasus Photon | W. G. Farr |
| | G-MNUK | Midland Ultralights SX130 | B. G. Colvin |
| | G-MNUL | Midland Ultralights SX130 | D. H. Griffin |
| | G-MNUM | Southdown Puma Sprint MS | B. Rawlance |

| Reg. | Type | Owner or Operator | Notes |
|------|------|-------------------|-------|
| G-MNUO | Mainair Gemini Flash II | B. J. Bishop | |
| G-MNUP | Mainair Gemini Flash II | W. Grieveson & P. Smith | |
| G-MNUR | Mainair Gemini Flash II | J. C. Greves | |
| G-MNUS | Mainair Gemini Flash II | C. D. Hannam | |
| G-MNUT | Southdown Raven X | J. O. Gent | |
| G-MNUU | Southdown Raven X | M. J. W. Holding | |
| G-MNUV | Southdown Raven X | D. Houghton | |
| G-MNUW | Southdown Raven X | B. A. McDonald | |
| G-MNUX | Solar Wings Pegasus XL-R | N. Smith | |
| G-MNUY | Mainair Gemini Flash II | R. M. Cornwell | |
| G-MNUZ | Mainair Gemini Flash II | G. Brunton | |
| G-MNVA | Solar Wings Pegasus XL-R | P. M. Aslin | |
| G-MNVB | Solar Wings Pegasus XL-R | J. R. Deverell | |
| G-MNVC | Solar Wings Pegasus XL-R | T. Davies | |
| G-MNVE | Solar Wings Pegasus XL-R | M. Aris | |
| G-MNVF | Solar Wings Pegasus Flash II | A. Rooker | |
| G-MNVG | Solar Wings Pegasus Flash II | D. J. Ward | |
| G-MNVH | Solar Wings Pegasus Flash II | I. M. Wilsher | |
| G-MNVI | CFM Shadow Srs B | D. R. C. Pugh | |
| G-MNVJ | CFM Shadow Srs B | V. C. Redhead | |
| G-MNVK | CFM Shadow Srs B | G. W. Sisson | |
| G-MNVL | Medway Half Pint | N. J. Frost | |
| G-MNVM | Southdown Raven X | R. Turnbull | |
| G-MNVN | Southdown Raven X | L. D. Wright | |
| G-MNVO | Hovey Whing-Ding II | C. Wilson | |
| G-MNVP | Southdown Raven X | R. A. Keene | |
| G-MNVR | Mainair Gemini Flash II | Multiscope Ltd | |
| G-MNVS | Mainair Gemini Flash II | D. P. Ballard & W. G. Prout | |
| G-MNVT | Mainair Gemini Flash II | ACB Hydraulics | |
| G-MNVU | Mainair Gemini Flash II | W. R. Marsh | |
| G-MNVV | Mainair Gemini Flash II | J. C. Lane | |
| G-MNVW | Mainair Gemini Flash II | J. C. Munro-Hunt | |
| G-MNVY | Solar Wings Pegasus Photon | P. Kelly | |
| G-MNVZ | Solar Wings Pegasus Photon | J. J. Russ | |
| G-MNWA | Southdown Raven X | A. Reynolds | |
| G-MNWB | Thruster TST | H. E. Hewitt | |
| G-MNWC | Mainair Gemini Flash II | B. Dungworth | |
| G-MNWD | Mainair Gemini Flash | I. Cummins | |
| G-MNWF | Southdown Raven X | Southdown International Ltd | |
| G-MNWG | Southdown Raven X | G. Handyside | |
| G-MNWH | Aerial Arts 130SX | P. N. & A. M. Keohane | |
| G-MNWI | Mainair Gemini Flash II | B. Bennison | |
| G-MNWJ | Mainair Gemini Flash II | J. C. Lucas | |
| G-MNWK | CFM Shadow Srs B | R. E. Petford | |
| G-MNWL | Aerial Arts 130SX | Arbiter Services Ltd | |
| G-MNWM | CFM Shadow Srs B | J. E. Laidler | |
| G-MNWN | Mainair Gemini Flash II | W. Murphy & I. G. Cole | |
| G-MNWO | Mainair Gemini Flash II | P. B. Kerr | |
| G-MNWP | Solar Wings Pegasus Flash II | G. Ferguson | |
| G-MNWR | Medway Hybred 44LR | C. J. Draper | |
| G-MNWT | Southdown Raven | M. J. Kenton | |
| G-MNWU | Solar Wings Pegasus Flash II | F. J. E. Browshill & W. Parkin | |
| G-MNWV | Solar Wings Pegasus Flash II | A. G. & P. J. Dover | |
| G-MNWW | Solar Wings Pegasus XL-R | B. R. Cannell | |
| G-MNWX | Solar Wings Pegasus XL-R | J. A. Crofts & G. M. Birkett | |
| G-MNWY | CFM Shadown Srs B | M. H. Player | |
| G-MNWZ | Mainair Gemini Flash II | J. Park | |
| G-MNXA | Southdown Raven X | D. Coging | |
| G-MNXB | Solar Wings Photon | F. S. Ogden | |
| G-MNXC | Aerial Arts 110SX | J. E. Sweetingham | |
| G-MNXD | Southdown Raven | G. M. Davies | |
| G-MNXE | Southdown Raven X | H. L. Dyson | |
| G-MNXF | Southdown Raven | D. E. Gwenin | |
| G-MNXG | Southdown Raven X | M. A. & E. M. Miller | |
| G-MNXI | Southdown Raven X | A. M. Yates | |
| G-MNXJ | Medway Half Pint | M. Dougall | |
| G-MNXK | Medway Half Pint | G. J. Bass | |
| G-MNXM | Medway Hybred 44XLR | C. J. Draper | |
| G-MNXN | Medway Hybred 44XLR | J. Rodger & J. Dinwoodey | |
| G-MNXO | Medway Hybred 44XLR | R. A. Clarke | |
| G-MNXP | Solar Wings Pegasus Flash II | M. R. D. Bridgewater | |
| G-MNXR | Mainair Gemini Flash II | B. J. Crockett | |
| G-MNXS | Mainair Gemini Flash II | F. T. Rawlings | |

| Notes | Reg. | Type | Owner or Operator |
|---|---|---|---|
| | G-MNXT | Mainair Gemini Flash II | N. W. Barnett |
| | G-MNXU | Mainair Gemini Flash II | F. R. Curtis |
| | G-MNXW | Mainair Gemini Flash II | P. Hayes |
| | G-MNXX | CFM Shadow Srs BD | F. J. Luckhurst |
| | G-MNXY | Whittaker MW.5 Sorcerer | Cyclone Hovercraft Ltd |
| | G-MNXZ | Whittaker MW.5 Sorcerer | M. N. Gauntlett |
| | G-MNYA | Solar Wings Pegasus Flash II | B. O. Dowsett |
| | G-MNYB | Solar Wings Pegasus XL-R | J. G. Robinson |
| | G-MNYC | Solar Wings Pegasus XL-R | C. Smith |
| | G-MNYD | Aerial Arts 110SX Chaser | B. Richardson |
| | G-MNYE | Aerial Arts 110SX Chaser | N. J. Brunskill |
| | G-MNYF | Aerial Arts 110SX Chaser | B. Richardson |
| | G-MNYG | Southdown Raven | J. D. Aston |
| | G-MNYH | Southdown Puma Sprint | E. K. Battersea |
| | G-MNYI | Southdown Raven X | P. T. Knight |
| | G-MNYJ | Mainair Gemini Flash II | J. G. Jones |
| | G-MNYK | Mainair Gemini Flash II | C. D. Hannam & J. W. Taylor |
| | G-MNYL | Southdown Raven X | R. Barringer |
| | G-MNYM | Southdown Raven X | M. Timwey |
| | G-MNYO | Southdown Raven X | Aerotech International Ltd |
| | G-MNYP | Southdown Raven X | A. G. Davies |
| | G-MNYS | Southdown Raven X | M. R. Dickens |
| | G-MNYT | Solar Wings Pegasus XL-R | G. E. Cripps |
| | G-MNYU | Solar Wings Pegasus XL-R | P. D. Bethal & R. M. Lusty |
| | G-MNYV | Solar Wings Pegasus XL-R | B. M. Quinn |
| | G-MNYW | Solar Wings Pegasus XL-R | M. P. Waldock |
| | G-MNYX | Solar Wings Pegasus XL-R | Dartsprint Ltd |
| | G-MNYY | Solar Wings Pegasus Flash II | S. A. Jaques |
| | G-MNYZ | Solar Wings Pegasus Flash | F. C. Claydon |
| | G-MNZA | Solar Wings Pegasus Flash II | A. D. Fennell & S. P. Cholmondeley |
| | G-MNZB | Mainair Gemini Flash II | C. J. Millership |
| | G-MNZC | Mainair Gemini Flash II | C. J. Whittaker |
| | G-MNZD | Mainair Gemini Flash II | P. W. Sandwith |
| | G-MNZE | Mainair Gemini Flash II | A. I. Grant |
| | G-MNZF | Mainair Gemini Flash II | R. A. Knight |
| | G-MNZG | Aerial Arts 110SX | C. F. Grainger |
| | G-MNZH | AMF Chevron 2-32 | AMF Microlight Ltd |
| | G-MNZI | Prone Power Typhoon 2 | R. J. Folwell |
| | G-MNZJ | CFM Shadow Srs BD | T. E. P. Eves & A. Rotherey |
| | G-MNZK | Solar Wings Pegasus XL-R | G. Twomlow |
| | G-MNZL | Solar Wings Pegasus XL-R | M. A. Concannon |
| | G-MNZM | Solar Wings Pegasus XL-R | Solar Wings Ltd |
| | G-MNZN | Solar Wings Pegasus Flash II | Solar Wings Ltd |
| | G-MNZO | Solar Wings Pegasus Flash II | D. Johnson & K. B. Woods |
| | G-MNZP | CFM Shadow Srs B | S. N. Freestone & J. G. Wakefield |
| | G-MNZR | CFM Shadown Srs BD | Microlight Aircraft |
| | G-MNZS | Aerial Arts 130SX | R. Scott |
| | G-MNZU | Eurowing Goldwing | H. B. Baker |
| | G-MNZV | Southdown Raven X | P. J. Walker |
| | G-MNZW | Southdown Raven X | P. G. Greenslade |
| | G-MNZX | Southdown Raven X | M. D. Phillips |
| | G-MNZY | Striker Tri-Flyer 330 | P. W. Fieldman |
| | G-MNZZ | CFM Shadow Srs B | N. G. Souter |
| | | | |
| | G-MTAA | Solar Wings Pegasus XL-R | B. Dossett |
| | G-MTAB | Mainair Gemini Flash II | K. C. Dodd |
| | G-MTAC | Mainair Gemini Flash II | J. Edwards |
| | G-MTAD | Mainair Gemini Skyflash | Mainair Sports Ltd |
| | G-MTAE | Mainair Gemini Flash II | S. W. Tallamy |
| | G-MTAF | Mainair Gemini Flash II | P. A. Long |
| | G-MTAG | Mainair Gemini Flash II | A. Gibson |
| | G-MTAH | Mainair Gemini Flash II | C. T. Tennison |
| | G-MTAI | Solar Wings Pegasus XL-R | M. E. Bates Engineering |
| | G-MTAJ | Solar Wings Pegasus XL-R | N. R. Holloway |
| | G-MTAK | Solar Wings Pegasus XL-R | P. J. Kirkpatrick |
| | G-MTAL | Solar Wings Photon | I. Munro |
| | G-MTAM | Solar Wings Pegasus Flash | J. P. Scales |
| | G-MTAN | Bragg Dual Seat | I. Ellithorn |
| | G-MTAO | Solar Wings Pegasus XL-R | D. J. Crow |
| | G-MTAP | Southdown Raven X | D. B. McCalvey |
| | G-MTAR | Mainair Gemini Flash II | J. Sharman |
| | G-MTAS | Whittaker MW.5 Sorcerer | E. A. Henman |
| | G-MTAT | Solar Wings Pegasus XL-R | D. Graham |

| Reg. | Type | Owner or Operator | Notes |
|------|------|-------------------|-------|
| G-MTAU | Solar Wings Pegasus XL-R | R. E. Howard | |
| G-MTAV | Solar Wings Pegasus XL-R | A. W. Scott | |
| G-MTAW | Solar Wings Pegasus XL-R | T. Cameron | |
| G-MTAX | Solar Wings Pegasus XL-R | W. Vos | |
| G-MTAY | Solar Wings Pegasus XL-R | S. A. McLatchie | |
| G-MTAZ | Solar Wings Pegasus XL-R | H. W. Banham | |
| G-MTBA | Solar Wings Pegasus XL-R | M. Stanton | |
| G-MTBB | Southdown Raven X | C. M. Raven | |
| G-MTBC | Mainair Gemini Flash II | M. J. Coomber | |
| G-MTBD | Mainair Gemini Flash II | A. M. Smyth | |
| G-MTBE | CFM Shadow Srs BD | S. Delia | |
| G-MTBF | Mirage Mk II | G. A. Squires | |
| G-MTBG | Mainair Gemini Flash II | N. Spencer-Baryn | |
| G-MTBH | Mainair Gemini Flash II | G. E. Cole | |
| G-MTBI | Mainair Gemini Flash II | D. J. Bowie | |
| G-MTBJ | Mainair Gemini Flash II | K. M. Jones | |
| G-MTBK | Southdown Raven X | R. C. Barnett | |
| G-MTBL | Solar Wings Pegasus XL-R | R. N. Whiting | |
| G-MTBM | Airwave Nimrod | B. R. Beer | |
| G-MTBN | Southdown Raven X | A. J. Crosby-Jones | |
| G-MTBO | Southdown Raven X | A. Miller | |
| G-MTBP | Aerotech MW.5 Sorcerer | R. Thompson | |
| G-MTBR | Aerotech MW.5 Sorcerer | C. D. Hatcher | |
| G-MTBS | Aerotech MW.5 Sorcerer | J. M. Benton | |
| G-MTBT | Aerotech MW.5 Sorcerer | N. W. Finn-Kelcey & D. J. Adams | |
| G-MTBU | Solar Wings Pegasus XL-R | Building Profiles Ltd | |
| G-MTBV | Solar Wings Pegasus XL-R | G. A. Smith | |
| G-MTBW | Mainair Gemini Flash II | R. & M. A. Nicklin | |
| G-MTBX | Mainair Gemini Flash II | S. R. Kerr | |
| G-MTBY | Mainair Gemini Flash II | A. R. Hawkins | |
| G-MTBZ | Southdown Raven X | R. A. Bates | |
| G-MTCA | CFM Shadow Srs B | E. Dawson | |
| G-MTCB | Snowbird Mk III | Noble Hardman Aviation Ltd | |
| G-MTCC | Mainair Gemini Flash II | R. C. Barker | |
| G-MTCD | Southdown Raven X | R. I. Young | |
| G-MTCE | Mainair Gemini Flash II | M. H. & R. J. Fry | |
| G-MTCG | Solar Wings Pegasus XL-R | R. W. Allen | |
| G-MTCH | Solar Wings Pegasus XL-R | R. E. H. Harris | |
| G-MTCJ | Aerial Arts Avenger | I. M. Grayland | |
| G-MTCK | Solar Wings Pegasus Flash | P. J. Sutton | |
| G-MTCL | Southdown Raven X | W. Nonforth | |
| G-MTCM | Southdown Raven X | J. C. & A. M. Rose | |
| G-MTCN | Solar Wings Pegasus XL-R | R. W. H. de Serville | |
| G-MTCO | Solar Wings Pegasus XL-R | A. J. Nesom | |
| G-MTCP | Aerial Arts Chaser 110SX | D. Cannon | |
| G-MTCR | Solar Wings Pegasus XL-R | K. Pratt | |
| G-MTCT | CFM Shadow Srs BD | G. R. Cooper & G. N. Heaton | |
| G-MTCU | Mainair Gemini Flash II | F. L. Arnold & W. D. Haigh | |
| G-MTCV | Microflight Spectrum | Microflight Aircraft Ltd | |
| G-MTCW | Mainair Gemini Flash | M. R. Starling | |
| G-MTCX | Solar Wings Pegasus XL-R | N. B. Morley | |
| G-MTCY | Southdown Raven X | Airbourne Aviation Ltd | |
| G-MTCZ | Ultrasports Tripacer 250 | R. Parkin | |
| G-MTDA | Hornet Dual Trainer | H. Lang | |
| G-MTDB | Owen Pola Mk 1 | P. E. Owen | |
| G-MTDC | Owen Pola Mk 1 | P. E. Owen | |
| G-MTDD | Aerial Arts Chaser 110SX | R. Bacon | |
| G-MTDE | American Aerolights 110SX | M. J. Slater | |
| G-MTDF | Mainair Gemini Flash II | B. D. Cudlip | |
| G-MTDG | Solar Wings Pegasus XL-R | R. N. Stead | |
| G-MTDH | Solar Wings Pegasus XL-R | D. B. Casley-Smith | |
| G-MTDI | Solar Wings Pegasus XL-R | W. Wood | |
| G-MTDJ | Medway Hybred 44XL | J. A. Slocombe & C. D. Gates | |
| G-MTDK | Aerotech MW.5 Sorcerer | A. R. Bradley | |
| G-MTDL | Solar Wings Pegasus XL-R | A. D. Janaway | |
| G-MTDM | Mainair Gemini Flash II | J. F. Cawley | |
| G-MTDN | Ultraflight Lazair IIIE | R. D. Good | |
| G-MTDO | Eipper Quicksilver MXII | D. L. Ham | |
| G-MTDP | Solar Wings Pegasus XL-R | S. P. Mcandy | |
| G-MTDR | Mainair Gemini Flash II | G. Penson | |
| G-MTDS | Solar Wings Photon | D. K. Harvey | |
| G-MTDT | Solar Wings Pegasus XL-R | M. T. Jones | |
| G-MTDU | CFM Shadow Srs BD | M. Jones | |

| Notes | Reg. | Type | Owner or Operator |
|-------|------|------|-------------------|
| | G-MTDV | Solar Wings Pegasus XL-R | N. Shaw |
| | G-MTDW | Mainair Gemini Flash II | S. R. Leeper |
| | G-MTDX | CFM Shadow Srs BD | M. P. Chetwynd-Talbot |
| | G-MTDY | Mainair Gemini Flash II | S. Penoyre |
| | G-MTDZ | Eipper Quicksilver MXII | Survival Anglia Ltd |
| | G-MTEA | Solar Wings Pegasus XL-R | F. H. Shaw |
| | G-MTEB | Solar Wings Pegasus XL-R | M. Boagey |
| | G-MTEC | Solar Wings Pegasus XL-R | R. W. Glover |
| | G-MTED | Solar Wings Pegasus XL-R | D. Marsh |
| | G-MTEE | Solar Wings Pegasus XL-R | S. M. Dewson |
| | G-MTEF | Solar Wings Pegasus XL-R | B. D. Waller |
| | G-MTEG | Mainair Gemini Flash II | HRH Sheikh Omar Bin Saqr Al Qassimi Ras Al Khaimah |
| | G-MTEH | Mainair Gemini Flash II | S. J. Green |
| | G-MTEJ | Mainair Gemini Flash II | A. P. Pitchforth |
| | G-MTEK | Mainair Gemini Flash II | A. Carter |
| | G-MTEL | Mainair Gemini Flash II | J. W. Townsend |
| | G-MTEM | Mainair Gemini Flash II | S. J. Pullan |
| | G-MTEN | Mainair Gemini Flash II | S. Mersay |
| | G-MTEO | Midland Ultralight Sirocco 337 | J. Brown |
| | G-MTER | Solar Wings Pegasus XL-R | W. G. Bond |
| | G-MTES | Solar Wings Pegasus XL-R | I. Callaghan |
| | G-MTET | Solar Wings Pegasus XL-R | S. J. D. Ridgway |
| | G-MTEU | Solar Wings Pegasus XL-R | N. Hyde |
| | G-MTEV | Solar Wings Pegasus XL-R | J. S. & M. R. Fuller |
| | G-MTEW | Solar Wings Pegasus XL-R | B. T. Bott & R. Holley |
| | G-MTEX | Solar Wings Pegasus XL-R | R. A. Barrett |
| | G-MTEY | Mainair Gemini Flash II | S. A. Rennison |
| | G-MTEZ | Ultraflight Lazair IIIE | M. J. Ford |
| | G-MTFA | Solar Wings Pegasus XL-R | W. J. M. Lowe |
| | G-MTFB | Solar Wings Pegasus XL-R | D. M. Hepworth |
| | G-MTFC | Medway Hybred 44XLR | Speed Couriers Ltd |
| | G-MTFE | Solar Wings Pegasus XL-R | B. A. Coombe |
| | G-MTFF | Mainair Gemini Flash II | T. N. Taylor |
| | G-MTFG | AMF Chevvron 232 | AMF Microflight Ltd |
| | G-MTFH | Aerotech MW.5B Sorcerer | R. C. H. Russell |
| | G-MTFI | Mainair Gemini Flash II | R. A. P. Swainston |
| | G-MTFJ | Mainair Gemini Flash II | G. Souch & M. D. Peacock |
| | G-MTFL | AMF Lazair IIIE | P. J. Turrell |
| | G-MTFM | Solar Wings Pegasus XL-R | D. J. Still & A. J. Hickey |
| | G-MTFN | Aerotech MW.5 Sorcerer | G. E. Jewitt |
| | G-MTFO | Solar Wings Pegasus XL-R | D. W. Maxwell |
| | G-MTFP | Solar Wings Pegasus XL-R | J. G. Allison |
| | G-MTFR | Solar Wings Pegasus XL-R | V. & D. Concannon |
| | G-MTFS | Solar Wings Pegasus XL-R | T. J. Acton |
| | G-MTFT | Solar Wings Pegasus XL-R | A. C. Tyler |
| | G-MTFU | CFM Shadow Series BD | G. R. Eastwood |
| | G-MTFX | Mainair Gemini Flash | M. B. Rutherford & S. Maurice |
| | G-MTFY | CFM Shadow Srs BD | CFM Metal-Fax Ltd |
| | G-MTFZ | CFM Shadow Srs BD | R. P. Stonor |
| | G-MTGA | Mainair Gemini Flash | H. R. Bethune & S. P. Watkins |
| | G-MTGB | Thruster TST Mk 1 | G. Arthur |
| | G-MTGC | Thruster TST Mk 1 | D. A. Izod |
| | G-MTGD | Thruster TST Mk 1 | Cumbria Microlights |
| | G-MTGE | Thruster TST Mk 1 | R. Gowler |
| | G-MTGF | Thruster TST Mk 1 | A. J. B. Shaw |
| | G-MTGH | Mainair Gemini Flash IIA | D. Shackleton |
| | G-MTGI | Solar Wings Pegasus XL-R | J. P. Davis |
| | G-MTGJ | Solar Wings Pegasus XL-R | C. M. Council |
| | G-MTGK | Solar Wings Pegasus XL-R | I. A. Smith |
| | G-MTGL | Solar Wings Pegasus XL-R | G-MTGL Flying Group |
| | G-MTGM | Solar Wings Pegasus XL-R | B. M. Marsh |
| | G-MTGO | Mainair Gemini Flash | D. E. Price |
| | G-MTGP | Thruster TST Mk 1 | S. M. Hart & K. Garnett |
| | G-MTGR | Thruster TST Mk 1 | S. A. Wood |
| | G-MTGS | Thruster TST Mk 1 | G. & G. E. F. Warren |
| | G-MTGT | Thruster TST Mk 1 | R. H. Y. Farrer |
| | G-MTGU | Thruster TST Mk 1 | K. A. Stewart & A. Donowho |
| | G-MTGV | CFM Shadow Srs BD | S. A. Wood |
| | G-MTGX | Hornet Dual Trainer | W. D. Holmes |
| | G-MTGY | Southdown Lightning | P. J. S. Ritchie |
| | G-MTHB | Aerotech MW.5B Sorcerer | D. B. White |
| | G-MTHC | Raven X | P. A. Arnold & N. A. Rathbone |

| Reg. | Type | Owner or Operator | Notes |
|------|------|-------------------|-------|
| G-MTHD | Hiway Demon 195 | C. H. Middleton | |
| G-MTHF | Solar Wings Pegasus XL-R | W. R. Keene | |
| G-MTHG | Solar Wings Pegasus XL-R | M. P. Jackson | |
| G-MTHH | Solar Wings Pegasus XL-R | A. E. Goodwin & M. R. Fidler | |
| G-MTHI | Solar Wings Pegasus XL-R | N. Jones | |
| G-MTHJ | Solar Wings Pegasus XL-R | B. R. Ward & P. A. Simpson | |
| G-MTHK | Solar Wings Pegasus XL-R | B. P. Somerville-Large | |
| G-MTHL | Solar Wings Pegasus XL-R | S. R. S. Evans | |
| G-MTHM | Solar Wings Pegasus XL-R | D. Cameron | |
| G-MTHN | Solar Wings Pegasus XL-R | C. Cheeseman | |
| G-MTHO | Solar Wings Pegasus XL-R | P. Cotton | |
| G-MTHP | Solar Wings Pegasus XL-R | J. S. Wright | |
| G-MTHS | CFM Shadow Srs BD | M. P. Wells | |
| G-MTHT | CFM Shadow Srs BD | N. F. L. Agar | |
| G-MTHU | Hornet Dual Trainer | D. M. Couling & P. Myers | |
| G-MTHV | CFM Shadow Srs BD | P. Walker | |
| G-MTHW | Mainair Gemini Flash II | J. W. Barr | |
| G-MTHX | Mainair Gemini Flash IIA | L. G. G. Faulkner | |
| G-MTHY | Mainair Gemini Flash IIA | M. Stevenson | |
| G-MTHZ | Mainair Gemini Flash IIA | A. P. S. John | |
| G-MTIA | Mainair Gemini Flash IIA | M. Callum | |
| G-MTIB | Mainair Gemini Flash IIA | M. Morris | |
| G-MTIC | Mainair Gemini Flash IIA | P. Whitney | |
| G-MTID | Southdown Raven X | R. G. Feathersby | |
| G-MTIE | Solar Wings Pegasus XL-R | A. Swanson | |
| G-MTIF | Solar Wings Pegasus XL-R | P. H. Risdale | |
| G-MTIG | Solar Wings Pegasus XL-R | A. R. Gouge | |
| G-MTIH | Solar Wings Pegasus XL-R | A. M. Brumpton | |
| G-MTII | Solar Wings Pegasus XL-R | J. D. Pitkethly | |
| G-MTIJ | Solar Wings Pegasus XL-R | D. O'Gorman | |
| G-MTIK | Southdown Raven X | B. W. Atkinson | |
| G-MTIL | Mainair Gemini Flash IIA | J. T. Aldersley | |
| G-MTIM | Mainair Gemini Flash IIA | R. A. Wylde | |
| G-MTIN | Mainair Gemini Flash IIA | B. J. Avery | |
| G-MTIO | Solar Wings Pegasus XL-R | M. A. Coe | |
| G-MTIP | Solar Wings Pegasus XL-R | W. Shaw | |
| G-MTIR | Solar Wings Pegasus XL-R | G. J. Boulton | |
| G-MTIS | Solar Wings Pegasus XL-R | T. M. Stiles | |
| G-MTIT | Solar Wings Pegasus XL-R | Solar Wings Ltd | |
| G-MTIU | Solar Wings Pegasus XL-R | D. Chisholm | |
| G-MTIV | Solar Wings Pegasus XL-R | R. P. Wilkinson | |
| G-MTIW | Solar Wings Pegasus XL-R | P. P. Willmott | |
| G-MTIX | Solar Wings Pegasus XL-R | S. Pickering | |
| G-MTIY | Solar Wings Pegasus XL-R | R. J. Tonkin | |
| G-MTIZ | Solar Wings Pegasus XL-R | W. J. Clayton | |
| G-MTJA | Mainair Gemini Flash IIA | R. T. Oldroyd | |
| G-MTJB | Mainair Gemini Flash IIA | K. Lewis | |
| G-MTJC | Mainair Gemini Flash IIA | S. M. Vickers | |
| G-MTJD | Mainair Gemini Flash IIA | Vinmar Holdings Ltd | |
| G-MTJE | Mainair Gemini Flash IIA | A. W. & B. W. Austin | |
| G-MTJF | Mainair Gemini Flash IIA | G. R. Cox | |
| G-MTJG | Medway Hybred 44XLR | M. Anthony | |
| G-MTJH | Solar Wings Pegasus Flash | C. L. Parker | |
| G-MTJI | Raven X | E. J. Macpherson | |
| G-MTJK | Mainair Gemini Flash IIA | R. C. White | |
| G-MTJL | Mainair Gemini Flash IIA | M. E. Newbold | |
| G-MTJM | Mainair Gemini Flash IIA | M. E. Jeffreys | |
| G-MTJN | Midland Ultralights Sirocco 377GB | R. Harris | |
| G-MTJP | Medway Hybred 44XLR | W. A. Stevens | |
| G-MTJR | Solar Wings Pegasus XL-R | Pegasus Skylink Ltd | |
| G-MTJS | Solar Wings Pegasus XL-Q | A. C. Macdonald | |
| G-MTJT | Mainair Gemini Flash IIA | D. T. A. Rees | |
| G-MTJV | Mainair Gemini Flash IIA | N. Charles & J. Richards | |
| G-MTJW | Mainair Gemini Flash IIA | J. D. Smith | |
| G-MTJX | Hornet Dual Trainer | F. M. Hurst | |
| G-MTJY | Mainair Gemini Flash IIA | S. J. Smith | |
| G-MTJZ | Mainair Gemini Flash IIA | A. R. Max | |
| G-MTKA | Thruster TST Mk 1 | S. McKenzie & S. Cordova | |
| G-MTKB | Thruster TST Mk 1 | A. Troughton | |
| G-MTKD | Thruster TST Mk 1 | I. K. Ratcliffe | |
| G-MTKE | Thruster TST Mk 1 | M. P. Allinson | |
| G-MTKG | Solar Wings Pegasus XL-R | S. J. Beecroft | |

| Notes | Reg. | Type | Owner or Operator |
|-------|------|------|-------------------|
| | G-MTKH | Solar Wings Pegasus XL-R | S. C. Jeffs & R. D. Gearing |
| | G-MTKI | Solar Wings Pegasus XL-R | M. J. Calnan |
| | G-MTKJ | Solar Wings Pegasus XL-R | R. Croucher |
| | G-MTKK | Solar Wings Pegasus XL-R | J. L. Rawlings |
| | G-MTKL | — | — |
| | G-MTKM | Gardner T-M Scout S.2 | D. Gardner |
| | G-MTKN | Mainair Gemini Flash IIA | A. J. Taylor |
| | G-MTKO | Mainair Gemini Flash IIA | Microflight Sales Ltd |
| | G-MTKP | Solar Wings Pegasus XL-R | R. Feist |
| | G-MTKR | CFM Shadow Srs BD | C. R. James |
| | G-MTKS | CFM Shadow Srs BD | R. B. Milton |
| | G-MTKU | CFM Shadow Srs BD | S. Marriott |
| | G-MTKV | Mainair Gemini Flash | S. M. Garrod |
| | G-MTKW | Mainair Gemini Flash IIA | A. J. Lavin |
| | G-MTKX | Mainair Gemini Flash IIA | L. D. Britzman |
| | G-MTKY | Mainair Gemini Flash IIA | R. A. Brierley-Jones |
| | G-MTKZ | Mainair Gemini Flash IIA | D. Naylor |
| | G-MTLA | Mainair Gemini Flash IIA | J. R. Fairweather & K. C. Wigley & Co Ltd |
| | G-MTLB | Mainair Gemini Flash IIA | D. N. Bacon |
| | G-MTLC | Mainair Gemini Flash IIA | R. J. Alston |
| | G-MTLD | Mainair Gemini Flash IIA | D. J. Wood |
| | G-MTLE | See main Register | — |
| | G-MTLG | Solar Wings Pegasus XL-R | C. J. Dodwell |
| | G-MTLH | Solar Wings Pegasus XL-R | B. S. Waite |
| | G-MTLI | Solar Wings Pegasus XL-R | M. McKay |
| | G-MTLJ | Solar Wings Pegasus XL-R | T. D. P. Gates |
| | G-MTLK | Raven X | Raven Aircraft International Ltd |
| | G-MTLL | Mainair Gemini Flash IIA | M. F. Shaw & M. J. Bird |
| | G-MTLM | Thruster TST Mk 1 | D. Roberts |
| | G-MTLN | Thruster TST Mk 1 | C. Less |
| | G-MTLO | Thruster TST Mk 1 | G. H. V. Thomas |
| | G-MTLP | Thruster TST Mk 1 | D. S. Worman |
| | G-MTLR | Thruster TST Mk 1 | I. Bartlett |
| | G-MTLS | Solar Wings Pegasus XL-R | K. M. Simmons |
| | G-MTLT | Solar Wings Pegasus XL-R | P. Rayson |
| | G-MTLU | Solar Wings Pegasus XL-R | E. Gordon & M. Stott |
| | G-MTLV | Solar Wings Pegasus XL-R | D. E. Watson |
| | G-MTLW | Solar Wings Pegasus XL-R | S. R. Sutch |
| | G-MTLX | Medway Hybred 44XLR | P. M. Feasey |
| | G-MTLY | Solar Wings Pegasus XL-R | I. Johnston |
| | G-MTLZ | Whittaker MW.5 Sorceror | E. H. Gould |
| | G-MTMA | Mainair Gemini Flash IIA | A. Butt & D. H. Wood |
| | G-MTMB | Mainair Gemini Flash IIA | J. Cunliffe |
| | G-MTMC | Mainair Gemini Flash IIA | A. R. Johnson |
| | G-MTMD | Whittaker MW.6 Merlin | K. Kerr |
| | G-MTME | Solar Wings Pegasus XL-R | M. T. Finch |
| | G-MTMF | Solar Wings Pegasus XL-R | J. T. M. Smith |
| | G-MTMG | Solar Wings Pegasus XL-R | C. W. & P. E. F. Suckling |
| | G-MTMH | Solar Wings Pegasus XL-R | I. D. Bell-Berry |
| | G-MTMI | Solar Wings Pegasus XL-R | J. S. Hogg |
| | G-MTMJ | Maxair Hummer | M. J. Makin |
| | G-MTMK | Raven X | T. M. Tootill |
| | G-MTML | Mainair Gemini Flash IIA | S. M. Cawthra |
| | G-MTMM | CFM Shadow Srs BD | W. Friend |
| | G-MTMO | Raven X | P. G. Driver |
| | G-MTMP | Hornet Dual Trainer/Raven | P. Thompson |
| | G-MTMR | Hornet Dual Trainer/Raven | D. J. Smith |
| | G-MTMS | Hornet Dual Trainer/Raven | Hornet Microlights Ltd |
| | G-MTMT | Mainair Gemini Flash IIA | C. Briggs |
| | G-MTMU | Mainair Gemini Flash IIA | D. J. Robinson |
| | G-MTMV | Mainair Gemini Flash IIA | I. S. Atkinson |
| | G-MTMW | Mainair Gemini Flash IIA | D. M. Law |
| | G-MTMX | CFM Shadow Srs BD | G. A. S. Hulkes |
| | G-MTMY | CFM Shadow Srs BD | P. A. James |
| | G-MTMZ | CFM Shadow Srs BD | C. A. Keens |
| | G-MTNB | Raven X | R. Coar |
| | G-MTNC | Mainair Gemini Flash IIA | A. P. Fenn |
| | G-MTND | Medway Hybred 44XLR | Butty Boys Flying Group |
| | G-MTNE | Medway Hybred 44XLR | P. Sawday |
| | G-MTNF | Medway Hybred 44XLR | S. R. Groves |
| | G-MTNG | Mainair Gemini Flash IIA | S. Lichtenstein |
| | G-MTNH | Mainair Gemini Flash IIA | B. W. Drake |

| Reg. | Type | Owner or Operator | Notes |
|------|------|-------------------|-------|
| G-MTNI | Mainair Gemini Flash IIA | K. P. Widdowson | |
| G-MTNJ | Mainair Gemini Flash IIA | R. H. Hunt | |
| G-MTNK | Weedhopper JC-24B | K. J. Tomlinson | |
| G-MTNL | Mainair Gemini Flash IIA | G. C. Baird | |
| G-MTNM | Mainair Gemini Flash IIA | C. J. Janson | |
| G-MTNN | Mainair Gemini Flash IIA | G. F. Cutler | |
| G-MTNO | Solar Wings Pegasus XL-Q | A. F. Batchelor | |
| G-MTNP | Solar Wings Pegasus XL-Q | G. G. Roberts | |
| G-MTNR | Thruster TST Mk 1 | G. E. Collard | |
| G-MTNS | Thruster TST Mk 1 | I. D. Stokes | |
| G-MTNT | Thruster TST Mk 1 | R. Holt | |
| G-MTNU | Thruster TST Mk 1 | D. G. Marwick | |
| G-MTNV | Thruster TST Mk 1 | J. B. Russell | |
| G-MTNW | Thruster TST Mk 1 | P. J. Ward & ptnrs | |
| G-MTNX | Mainair Gemini Flash II | C. J. & R. J. Lines | |
| G-MTNY | Mainair Gemini Flash IIA | P. T. Knight | |
| G-MTNZ | Solar Wings Pegasus XL-Q | J. V. Clewer | |
| G-MTOA | Solar Wings Pegasus XL-R | R. A. Bird | |
| G-MTOB | Solar Wings Pegasus XL-R | R. F. Walbank | |
| G-MTOC | Solar Wings Pegasus XL-R | D. Jordan | |
| G-MTOD | Solar Wings Pegasus XL-R | G. G. Clayton | |
| G-MTOE | Solar Wings Pegasus XL-R | J. R. Ravenhill | |
| G-MTOF | Solar Wings Pegasus XL-R | C. Stebbings | |
| G-MTOG | Solar Wings Pegasus XL-R | J. C. Owens | |
| G-MTOH | Solar Wings Pegasus XL-R | H. Cook | |
| G-MTOI | Solar Wings Pegasus XL-R | J. Grotian | |
| G-MTOJ | Solar Wings Pegasus XL-R | P. R. A. Walker | |
| G-MTOK | Solar Wings Pegasus XL-R | A. D. Stanyer | |
| G-MTOL | Solar Wings Pegasus XL-R | I. Colborn | |
| G-MTOM | Solar Wings Pegasus XL-R | A. J. Macfie | |
| G-MTON | Solar Wings Pegasus XL-R | J. W. & P. Manifold | |
| G-MTOO | Solar Wings Pegasus XL-R | G. W. Bulmer | |
| G-MTOP | Solar Wings Pegasus XL-R | P. J. Anderson | |
| G-MTOR | Solar Wings Pegasus XL-R | Solar Wings Ltd | |
| G-MTOS | Solar Wings Pegasus XL-R | M. J. Gillespie | |
| G-MTOT | Solar Wings Pegasus XL-R | J. H. Sparks | |
| G-MTOU | Solar Wings Pegasus XL-R | M. Harris | |
| G-MTOV | Solar Wings Pegasus XL-R | J. M. Wragg | |
| G-MTOW | Solar Wings Pegasus XL-R | M. W. Oliver | |
| G-MTOX | Solar Wings Pegasus XL-R | Solar Wings Ltd | |
| G-MTOY | Solar Wings Pegasus XL-R | P. W. Haines | |
| G-MTOZ | Solar Wings Pegasus XL-R | K. Wright | |
| G-MTPA | Mainair Gemini Flash IIA | J. Nimmo | |
| G-MTPB | Mainair Gemini Flash IIA | M. P. Middleton | |
| G-MTPC | Raven X | R. L. Cross | |
| G-MTPE | Solar Wings Pegasus XL-R | J. A. Flock & G. Clark | |
| G-MTPF | Solar Wings Pegasus XL-R | P. A. West | |
| G-MTPG | Solar Wings Pegasus XL-R | D. L. Hadley | |
| G-MTPH | Solar Wings Pegasus XL-R | G. R. Hall | |
| G-MTPI | Solar Wings Pegasus XL-R | I. J. Alexander | |
| G-MTPJ | Solar Wings Pegasus XL-R | E. J. Larnder | |
| G-MTPK | Solar Wings Pegasus XL-R | B. Harding | |
| G-MTPL | Solar Wings Pegasus XL-R | D. Stott | |
| G-MTPM | Solar Wings Pegasus XL-R | P. R. Brooker | |
| G-MTPN | Solar Wings Pegasus XL-Q | C. G. Johns | |
| G-MTPO | Solar Wings Pegasus XL-Q | M. G. & S. A. Collins | |
| G-MTPP | Solar Wings Pegasus XL-Q | R. T. Curant | |
| G-MTPR | Solar Wings Pegasus XL-R | M. Castle | |
| G-MTPS | Solar Wings Pegasus XL-Q | P. R. Snowden | |
| G-MTPT | Thruster TST Mk Mk 1 | G. S. Langdon | |
| G-MTPU | Thruster TST Mk 1 | N. H. McCue | |
| G-MTPV | Thruster TST Mk 1 | S. J. Fretwell | |
| G-MTPW | Thruster TST Mk 1 | K. Handley & J. J. Naughton | |
| G-MTPX | Thruster TST Mk 1 | B. J. Gordon | |
| G-MTPY | Thruster TST Mk 1 | A. N. Wicks | |
| G-MTPZ | Solar Wings Pegasus XL-R | M. R. P. McCarthy | |
| G-MTRA | Mainair Gemini Flash IIA | E. N. Alms | |
| G-MTRB | Mainair Gemini Flash IIA | N. F. Schlank | |
| G-MTRC | Midlands Ultralights Sirocco 377GB | J. Bagnall | |
| G-MTRD | Midlands Ultralights Sirocco 377GB | A. K. Pomroy | |
| G-MTRE | Whittaker MW.6 Merlin | M. J. Batchelor | |

| Notes | Reg. | Type | Owner or Operator |
|---|---|---|---|
| | G-MTRF | Mainair Gemini Flash IIA | J. McGaughran |
| | G-MTRG | Mainair Gemini Flash IIA | M. S. Glynn |
| | G-MTRH | Hiway Demon | D. C. P. Cardey |
| | G-MTRJ | AMF Chevvron 232 | Chartersteps Ltd |
| | G-MTRK | Hornet Dual Trainer | P. M. Gilfoyle |
| | G-MTRL | Hornet Dual Trainer | J. McAlpine |
| | G-MTRM | Solar Wings Pegasus XL-R | D. Dugdale |
| | G-MTRN | Solar Wings Pegasus XL-R | T. G. M. White |
| | G-MTRO | Solar Wings Pegasus XL-R | D. G. Burrows |
| | G-MTRP | Solar Wings Pegasus XL-R | D. W. Cardy |
| | G-MTRR | Solar Wings Pegasus XL-R | D. T. Hutchinson |
| | G-MTRS | Solar Wings Pegasus XL-R | R. H. Braithwaite |
| | G-MTRT | Raven X | D. Hines |
| | G-MTRU | Solar Wings Pegasus XL-Q | A. Barnish |
| | G-MTRV | Solar Wings Pegasus XL-Q | C. Leighton-Thomas |
| | G-MTRW | Raven X | S. MacGill |
| | G-MTRX | Whittaker MW.5 Sorceror | W. Turner |
| | G-MTRY | Noble Hardman Snowbird IV | D. A. Riggs |
| | G-MTRZ | Mainair Gemini Flash IIA | N. Buckley |
| | G-MTSA | Mainair Gemini Flash IIA | Microflight Tuition & Sales Ltd |
| | G-MTSB | Mainair Gemini Flash IIA | C. E. Walley |
| | G-MTSC | Mainair Gemini Flash IIA | A. A. Ridgway |
| | G-MTSD | Raven X | D. Turner |
| | G-MTSE | Flexiform Striker | D. Laverick |
| | G-MTSF | Aerial Arts Chaser 110SX | D. Dixon |
| | G-MTSG | CFM Shadow Srs BD | J. W. E. Pearson |
| | G-MTSH | Thruster TST Mk 1 | M. Hanna |
| | G-MTSI | Thruster TST Mk 1 | C. Yarrow |
| | G-MTSJ | Thruster TST Mk 1 | A. Kingston |
| | G-MTSK | Thruster TST Mk 1 | J. S. Pyke & J. K. Druce |
| | G-MTSL | Thruster TST Mk 1 | J. R. Hammett |
| | G-MTSM | Thruster TST Mk 1 | D. R. Cox |
| | G-MTSN | Solar Wings Pegasus XL-R | A. J. Blackwell |
| | G-MTSO | Solar Wings Pegasus XL-R | P. A. Mercer |
| | G-MTSP | Solar Wings Pegasus XL-R | S. P. Christian |
| | G-MTSR | Solar Wings Pegasus XL-R | N. H. Dyer |
| | G-MTSS | Solar Wings Pegasus XL-R | H. T. Edmonds |
| | G-MTST | Thruster TST Mk 1 | S. J. Pullan |
| | G-MTSU | Solar Wings Pegasus XL-R | S. M. Saint |
| | G-MTSV | Solar Wings Pegasus XL-R | T. Phillips |
| | G-MTSX | Solar Wings Pegasus XL-R | G. P. Jones |
| | G-MTSY | Solar Wings Pegasus XL-R | B. Alexander |
| | G-MTSZ | Solar Wings Pegasus XL-R | P. A. S. Claxton |
| | G-MTTA | Solar Wings Pegasus XL-R | D. Verdon |
| | G-MTTB | Solar Wings Pegasus XL-R | T. L. Wells |
| | G-MTTC | Solar Wings Pegasus XL-R | C. J. Jakes |
| | G-MTTD | Solar Wings Pegasus XL-R | R. Purdham |
| | G-MTTE | Solar Wings Pegasus XL-R | Solar Wings Ltd |
| | G-MTTF | Aerotech MW.6 Merlin | V. E. Booth |
| | G-MTTG | Excalibur TriPacer 250 | D. R. Hawkins |
| | G-MTTH | CFM Shadow Srs BD | C. T. H. Pattison |
| | G-MTTI | Mainair Gemini Flash IIA | S. M. Savage |
| | G-MTTK | Southdown Lightning DS | D. E. Oakley |
| | G-MTTL | Hiway Sky-Trike | R. D. Layton |
| | G-MTTM | Mainair Gemini Flash IIA | Milequip Computer Systems |
| | G-MTTN | Ultralight Flight Phantom | H. R. Duggins |
| | G-MTTO | Mainair Gemini Flash IIA | R. Painter |
| | G-MTTP | Mainair Gemini Flash IIA | C. Bodill |
| | G-MTTR | Mainair Gemini Flash IIA | M. Richardson |
| | G-MTTS | Mainair Gemini Flash IIA | J. B. Bailey |
| | G-MTTU | Solar Wings Pegasus XL-R | N. V. Middleton |
| | G-MTTW | Mainair Gemini Flash IIA | M. J. Kaye |
| | G-MTTX | Solar Wings Pegasus XL-Q | P. G. Moss |
| | G-MTTY | Solar Wings Pegasus XL-Q | I. E. McCambridge & M. R. Teader |
| | G-MTTZ | Solar Wings Pegasus XL-Q | J. Haskett |
| | G-MTUA | Solar Wings Pegasus XL-R | D. W. Suttill |
| | G-MTUB | Thruster TST Mk 1 | S. R. Pike & K. Fagan |
| | G-MTUC | Thruster TST Mk 1 | W. H. J. Knowles |
| | G-MTUD | Thruster TST Mk 1 | K. J. Lywood |
| | G-MTUE | Thruster TST Mk 1 | A. Troughton |
| | G-MTUF | Thruster TST Mk 1 | D. R. G. Whitelaw |
| | G-MTUG | Thruster TST Mk 1 | A. G. Procter |
| | G-MTUH | Solar Wings Pegasus XL-R | Solar Wings Ltd |

| Reg. | Type | Owner or Operator | Notes |
|------|------|-------------------|-------|
| G-MTUI | Solar Wings Pegasus XL-R | B. J. Keylock | |
| G-MTUJ | Solar Wings Pegasus XL-R | R. C. Taplin | |
| G-MTUK | Solar Wings Pegasus XL-R | D. L. Pickover | |
| G-MTUL | Solar Wings Pegasus XL-R | S. H. James | |
| G-MTUN | Solar Wings Pegasus XL-Q | B. J. Gordon & D. L. Smith | |
| G-MTUO | Solar Wings Pegasus XL-Q | J. N. Whelan | |
| G-MTUP | Solar Wings Pegasus XL-Q | G. T. Gooch & T. A. Patricot | |
| G-MTUR | Solar Wings Pegasus XL-Q | M. D. Travers | |
| G-MTUS | Solar Wings Pegasus XL-Q | D. G. Mayling | |
| G-MTUT | Solar Wings Pegasus XL-Q | R. P. Tinsley | |
| G-MTUU | Mainair Gemini Flash IIA | G. O. Manners | |
| G-MTUV | Mainair Gemini Flash IIA | P. A. Lee | |
| G-MTUX | Medway Hybred 44XLR | P. A. R. Wilson | |
| G-MTUY | Solar Wings Pegasus XL-Q | Viscount Lowther | |
| G-MTUZ | Hornet Dual Trainer | Pegasus Skylink Ltd | |
| G-MTVA | Solar Wings Pegasus XL-R | Solar Wings Ltd | |
| G-MTVB | Solar Wings Pegasus XL-R | K. Wildish | |
| G-MTVC | Solar Wings Pegasus XL-R | A. J. Jenkins | |
| G-MTVE | Solar Wings Pegasus XL-R | Solar Wings Ltd | |
| G-MTVF | Solar Wings Pegasus XL-R | Solar Wings Ltd | |
| G-MTVG | Mainair Gemini Flash IIA | D. A. Whitworth | |
| G-MTVH | Mainair Gemini Flash IIA | P. I. Frost | |
| G-MTVI | Mainair Gemini Flash IIA | R. A. McDowell | |
| G-MTVJ | Mainair Gemini Flash IIA | D. M. Pearson | |
| G-MTVK | Solar Wings Pegasus XL-R | L. M. Brass | |
| G-MTVL | Solar Wings Pegasus XL-R | S. L. Grand | |
| G-MTVM | Solar Wings Pegasus XL-R | G. S. Cridland | |
| G-MTVN | Solar Wings Pegasus XL-R | A. R. Emerson | |
| G-MTVO | Solar Wings Pegasus XL-R | W. I. Burnet | |
| G-MTVP | Thruster TST Mk 1 | P. R. Jenson | |
| G-MTVR | Thruster TST Mk 1 | S. F. Vint & ptnrs | |
| G-MTVS | Thruster TST Mk 1 | K. Fletcher | |
| G-MTVT | Thruster TST Mk 1 | C. E. Brown | |
| G-MTVU | Thruster TST Mk 1 | R. T. Hall & G. L. Head | |
| G-MTVV | Thruster TST Mk 1 | A. Hipkin | |
| G-MTVX | Solar Wings Pegasus XL-Q | P. Bennett & N. G. Duncombe | |
| G-MTVY | Solar Wings Pegasus XL-Q | K. Handley | |
| G-MTVZ | Powerchute Raider | British Powerchute Schools | |
| G-MTWA | Solar Wings Pegasus XL-R | D. P. Maltby | |
| G-MTWB | Solar Wings Pegasus XL-R | D. L. Watson | |
| G-MTWC | Solar Wings Pegasus XL-R | B. D. W. Steen | |
| G-MTWD | Solar Wings Pegasus XL-R | C. F. Two | |
| G-MTWE | Solar Wings Pegasus XL-R | A. Thomas | |
| G-MTWF | Mainair Gemini Flash IIA | G. A. Clayton | |
| G-MTWG | Mainair Gemini Flash IIA | S. Meadowcroft | |
| G-MTWH | CFM Shadow Srs BD | V. A. Hutchinson | |
| G-MTWI | — | — | |
| G-MTWJ | — | — | |
| G-MTWK | CFM Shadow Srs Bd | R. C. Fendick & J. A. Pritchard | |
| G-MTWL | CFM Shadow Srs BD | M. L. Gray | |
| G-MTWM | CFM Shadow Srs BD | B. R. Johnson | |
| G-MTWN | CFM Shadow Srs BD | R. K. Waddams | |
| G-MTWO | Weedhopper JC-24B | A. J. Glynn | |
| G-MTWP | CFM Shadow Srs BD | L. J. Chapman | |
| G-MTWR | Mainair Gemini Flash IIA | C. Foster | |
| G-MTWS | Mainair Gemini Flash IIA | G. V. Nash & J. G. Lees | |
| G-MTWW | Solar Wings Typhoon | C. W. Payne | |
| G-MTWX | Mainair Gemini Flash IIA | S. G. Meylan & C. R. Fells | |
| G-MTWY | Thruster TST Mk 1 | D. R. Smith | |
| G-MTWZ | Thruster TST Mk 1 | G. F. Beabey | |
| G-MTXA | Thruster TST Mk 1 | J. F. Boyce | |
| G-MTXB | Thruster TST Mk 1 | M. Watson | |
| G-MTXC | Thruster TST Mk 1 | J. A. Huntley | |
| G-MTXD | Thruster TST Mk 1 | J. D. Smith | |
| G-MTXE | Hornet Dual Trainer | B. Berry | |
| G-MTXG | Solar Wings Pegasus XL-Q | P. Wright | |
| G-MTXH | Solar Wings Pegasus XL-Q | D. J. Moseley | |
| G-MTXI | Solar Wings Pegasus XL-Q | R. B. Best | |
| G-MTXJ | Solar Wings Pegasus XL-Q | A. R. Brough & ptnrs | |
| G-MTXK | Solar Wings Pegasus XL-Q | J. McConnachie | |
| G-MTXL | Noble Hardman Snowbird Mk IV | D. Calo & R. Bailey | |
| G-MTXM | Mainair Gemini Flash IIA | A. S. Birch | |
| G-MTXO | Whittaker MW.6 | J. G. Vaughan | |

| Notes | Reg. | Type | Owner or Operator |
|-------|------|------|-------------------|
| | G-MTXP | Mainair Gemini Flash IIA | L. D. Esposti |
| | G-MTXR | CFM Shadow Srs BD | J. C. Carpenter |
| | G-MTXS | Mainair Gemini Flash IIA | Mapa Construction Ltd |
| | G-MTXT | MBA Tiger Cub 440 | A. F. Stafford |
| | G-MTXU | Noble Hardman Snowbird Mk IV | Davlin Microlights Ltd |
| | G-MTXV | Noble Hardman Snowbird Mk IV | J. M. & M. C. Edwards |
| | G-MTXW | Noble Hardman Snowbird Mk IV | W. Murphy |
| | G-MTXY | Hornet Dual Trainer | Hornet Microlights |
| | G-MTXZ | Mainair Gemini Flash IIA | W. T. J. Bridgwater |
| | G-MTYA | Solar Wings Pegasus XL-Q | D. Christy |
| | G-MTYC | Solar Wings Pegasus XL-Q | Timeshare Bourse Ltd |
| | G-MTYD | Solar Wings Pegasus XL-Q | F. E. Treveil |
| | G-MTYE | Solar Wings Pegasus XL-Q | G. C. Weighell |
| | G-MTYF | Solar Wings Pegasus XL-Q | J. Hyde |
| | G-MTYG | Solar Wings Pegasus XL-Q | D. C. Fellows |
| | G-MTYH | Solar Wings Pegasus XL-Q | O. R. Pluck |
| | G-MTYI | Solar Wings Pegasus XL-Q | K. J. Berrisford |
| | G-MTYK | Solar Wings Pegasus XL-Q | K. Wade |
| | G-MTYL | Solar Wings Pegasus XL-Q | T. P. Roche |
| | G-MTYM | Solar Wings Pegasus XL-Q | D. R. Cowieson |
| | G-MTYN | Solar Wings Pegasus XL-Q | K. Hann |
| | G-MTYO | Solar Wings Pegasus XL-Q | G. P. Wilkins |
| | G-MTYP | Solar Wings Pegasus XL-Q | C. Stallard |
| | G-MTYR | Solar Wings Pegasus XL-Q | C. J. Hill |
| | G-MTYS | Solar Wings Pegasus XL-Q | Airplay (UK) Ltd |
| | G-MTYT | Solar Wings Pegasus XL-Q | A. J. B. Winter |
| | G-MTYU | Solar Wings Pegasus XL-Q | G. J. Parker |
| | G-MTYV | Raven X | A. Reynolds |
| | G-MTYW | Raven X | The Hon J. Nivison |
| | G-MTYX | Raven X | M. J. Knight |
| | G-MTYY | Solar Wings Pegasus XL-R | A. Makepeace |
| | G-MTZA | Thruster TST Mk 1 | M. W. Stevens |
| | G-MTZB | Thruster TST Mk 1 | P. Milne |
| | G-MTZC | Thruster TST Mk 1 | P. J. Gribben |
| | G-MTZD | Thruster TST Mk 1 | A. J. Monkcom |
| | G-MTZE | Thruster TST Mk 1 | J. L. Phipps |
| | G-MTZF | Thruster TST Mk 1 | B. J. Gordon |
| | G-MTZG | Mainair Gemini Flash IIA | A. Arnold & C. D. Stokes |
| | G-MTZH | Mainair Gemini Flash IIA | D. C. Hughes |
| | G-MTZI | Solar Wings Pegasus XL-R | G. A. Breen |
| | G-MTZJ | Solar Wings Pegasus XL-R | P. J. Burns |
| | G-MTZK | Solar Wings Pegasus XL-R | P. R. Claridge |
| | G-MTZL | Mainair Gemini Flash IIA | M. L. Smith |
| | G-MTZM | Mainair Gemini Flash IIA | Brend Design Ltd |
| | G-MTZN | Mainair Gemini Flash IIA | R. Almond |
| | G-MTZO | Mainair Gemini Flash IIA | Pegasus Building Preservation |
| | G-MTZP | Solar Wings Pegasus XL-Q | J. E. Gooch |
| | G-MTZR | Solar Wings Pegasus XL-Q | S. S. Dixon |
| | G-MTZS | Solar Wings Pegasus XL-Q | S. G. Beeson |
| | G-MTZT | Solar Wings Pegasus XL-Q | S. Solley |
| | G-MTZU | Solar Wings Pegasus XL-Q | R. A. Morris & H. F. Breakwell |
| | G-MTZV | Mainair Gemini Flash IIA | G. J. Donnellon |
| | G-MTZW | Mainair Gemini Flash IIA | R. Mason |
| | G-MTZX | Mainair Gemini Flash IIA | I. K. Cleeton |
| | G-MTZY | Mainair Gemini Flash IIA | K. Dale |
| | G-MTZZ | Mainair Gemini Flash IIA | P. J. Clegg |
| | G-MVAA | Mainair Gemini Flash IIA | N. S. Payne |
| | G-MVAB | Mainair Gemini Flash IIA | M. J. Burton |
| | G-MVAC | CFM Shadow Srs BD | J. V. Thompson |
| | G-MVAD | Mainair Gemini Flash IIA | K. A. Lindley |
| | G-MVAE | — | |
| | G-MVAF | Southdown Puma Sprint | W. G. Harling |
| | G-MVAG | Thruster TST Mk 1 | N. P. Thomson |
| | G-MVAH | Thruster TST Mk 1 | D. C. Mant |
| | G-MVAI | Thruster TST Mk 1 | J. Parker |
| | G-MVAJ | Thruster TST Mk 1 | T. S. Mangat |
| | G-MVAK | Thruster TST Mk 1 | J. W. Freeman |
| | G-MVAL | Thruster TST Mk 1 | Altec Syndicate |
| | G-MVAM | CFM Shadow Srs BD | H. Grindrod & ptnrs |
| | G-MVAN | CFM Shadow Srs BD | A. M. C. Batten |
| | G-MVAO | Mainair Gemini Flash IIA | T. Gate |
| | G-MVAP | Mainair Gemini Flash IIA | T. J. Hattin |

| Reg. | Type | Owner or Operator | Notes |
|------|------|-------------------|-------|
| G-MVAR | Solar Wings Pegasus XL-R | K. H. Creeo | |
| G-MVAS | Solar Wings Pegasus XL-R | G. A. Breen | |
| G-MVAT | Solar Wings Pegasus XL-R | T. D. Grieve | |
| G-MVAU | Solar Wings Pegasus XL-R | R. & J. A. Rhodes | |
| G-MVAV | Solar Wings Pegasus XL-R | P. G. Gardner | |
| G-MVAW | Solar Wings Pegasus XL-Q | N. J. Stoneman | |
| G-MVAX | Solar Wings Pegasus XL-Q | I. Griffiths | |
| G-MVAY | Solar Wings Pegasus XL-Q | E. W. Jones | |
| G-MVAZ | Solar Wings Pegasus XL-Q | Solar Wings Ltd | |
| G-MVBA | Solar Wings Pegasus XL-Q | Solar Wings Ltd | |
| G-MVBB | CFM Shadow Srs BD | R. Garrod | |
| G-MVBC | Aerial Arts Tri-Flyer 130SX | D. Beer | |
| G-MVBD | Mainair Gemini Flash IIA | A. L. Ruben | |
| G-MVBE | Mainair Scorcher | P. R. Sexton | |
| G-MVBF | Mainair Gemini Flash IIA | A. K. Rupai | |
| G-MVBG | Mainair Gemini Flash IIA | A. P. Sherrott | |
| G-MVBH | Mainair Gemini Flash IIA | I. D. Robertson | |
| G-MVBI | Mainair Gemini Flash IIA | E. R. Wilson | |
| G-MVBJ | Solar Wings Pegasus XL-R | R. Rae | |
| G-MVBK | Mainair Gemini Flash IIA | J. R. Holloway | |
| G-MVBL | Mainair Gemini Flash IIA | J. P. Fitzmaurice | |
| G-MVBM | Mainair Gemini Flash IIA | D. R. Davies | |
| G-MVBN | Mainair Gemini Flash IIA | U. K. S. Lawson & S. W. J. Garthwaite | |
| G-MVBO | Mainair Gemini Flash IIA | A. B. French | |
| G-MVBP | Thruster TST Mk 1 | A. B. Wilson | |
| G-MVBR | Thruster TST Mk 1 | E. J. & J. E. Garner | |
| G-MVBS | Thruster TST Mk 1 | J. S. Yates | |
| G-MVBT | Thruster TST Mk 1 | C. A. Mordlock | |
| G-MVBW | CFM Shadow Srs BD | J. K. England Ltd | |
| G-MVBX | Solar Wings Pegasus XL-R | J. A. Lord | |
| G-MVBY | Solar Wings Pegasus XL-R | J. D. Sings | |
| G-MVBZ | Solar Wings Pegasus XL-R | A. G. Butler | |
| G-MVCA | Solar Wings Pegasus XL-R | R. Walker | |
| G-MVCB | Solar Wings Pegasus XL-R | G. T. Clipstone | |
| G-MVCC | CFM Shadow Srs BD | H. J. Passall | |
| G-MVCD | Medway Hybred 44XLR | D. M. Pollard | |
| G-MVCE | Mainair Gemini Flash IIA | J. H. Stothert | |
| G-MVCF | Mainair Gemini Flash IIA | J. L. Hamer | |
| G-MVCH | Noble Hardman Snowbird Mk IV | Slipstream Aviation Ltd | |
| G-MVCI | Noble Hardman Snowbird Mk IV | A. R. Wells | |
| G-MVCJ | Noble Hardman Snowbird Mk IV | D. Golding & ptnrs | |
| G-MVCL | Solar Wings Pegasus XL-Q | D. J. Hill | |
| G-MVCM | Solar Wings Pegasus XL-Q | C. H. Wood | |
| G-MVCN | Solar Wings Pegasus XL-Q | D. J. Harber | |
| G-MVCO | Solar Wings Pegasus XL-Q | P. S. Flynn | |
| G-MVCP | Solar Wings Pegasus XL-Q | P. E. Leicester | |
| G-MVCR | Solar Wings Pegasus XL-Q | H. D. J. Niece | |
| G-MVCS | Solar Wings Pegasus XL-Q | J. J. Sparrow | |
| G-MVCT | Solar Wings Pegasus XL-Q | B. N. Wilson | |
| G-MVCU | Solar Wings Pegasus XL-Q | A. D. Stewart | |
| G-MVCV | Solar Wings Pegasus XL-Q | G. Bye | |
| G-MVCW | CFM Shadow Srs BD | R. A. Smith | |
| G-MVCY | Mainair Gemini Flash IIA | R. Lloyd & A. W. Jones | |
| G-MVCZ | Mainair Gemini Flash IIA | Microflight Tuition & Sales Ltd | |
| G-MVDA | Mainair Gemini Flash IIA | C. J. Robson | |
| G-MVDB | Medway Hybred 44XLR | R. M. Summers | |
| G-MVDC | Medway Hybred 44XLR | P. Hudson | |
| G-MVDD | Thruster TST Mk 1 | S. A. Wood | |
| G-MVDE | Thruster TST Mk 1 | R. H. Davis | |
| G-MVDF | Thruster TST Mk 1 | A. J. Smith & W. R. Muir | |
| G-MVDG | Thruster TST Mk 1 | D. G. Smith & ptnrs | |
| G-MVDH | Thruster TST Mk 1 | M. L. Roberts | |
| G-MVDI | Thruster TST Mk 1 | G. S. Adams | |
| G-MVDJ | Medway Hybred 44XLR | A. Dring | |
| G-MVDK | Aerial Arts Chaser S | B. F. Crick | |
| G-MVDL | Aerial Arts Chaser S | S. J. Walker | |
| G-MVDM | Aerial Arts Chaser S | B. R. Shepperd | |
| G-MVDN | Aerial Arts Chaser S | Oban Divers Ltd | |
| G-MVDO | Aerial Arts Chaser S | F. P. Latham | |
| G-MVDP | Aerial Arts Chaser S | Airplay (UK) Ltd | |
| G-MVDR | Aerial Arts Chaser S | R. J. Bonwick | |
| G-MVDS | Hiway Skytrike | P. Butler | |
| G-MVDT | Mainair Gemini Flash IIA | D. C. Stephens | |

| Notes | Reg. | Type | Owner or Operator |
|-------|------|------|-------------------|
| | G-MVDU | Solar Wings Pegasus XL-R | T. B. Jenkins |
| | G-MVDV | Solar Wings Pegasus XL-R | D. A. Preston |
| | G-MVDW | Solar Wings Pegasus XL-R | R. P. Brown |
| | G-MVDX | Solar Wings Pegasus XL-R | J. A. Haggie |
| | G-MVDY | Solar Wings Pegasus XL-R | H. M. Read |
| | G-MVDZ | Solar Wings Pegasus XL-R | A. J. Tillman |
| | G-MVEA | Solar Wings Pegasus XL-R | A. J. Jackson |
| | G-MVEB | Solar Wings Pegasus XL-R | S. P. Hollis |
| | G-MVEC | Solar Wings Pegasus XL-R | J. J. A. K. Smith |
| | G-MVED | Solar Wings Pegasus XL-R | D. R. Piggott |
| | G-MVEE | Medway Hybred 44XLR | D. Evans |
| | G-MVEF | Solar Wings Pegasus XL-R | E. J. Blyth |
| | G-MVEG | Solar Wings Pegasus XL-R | J. M. Wassmer |
| | G-MVEH | Mainair Gemini Flash IIA | J. I. Greenshields |
| | G-MVEI | CFM Shadow Srs BD | T. J. McKean |
| | G-MVEJ | Mainair Gemini Flash IIA | M. G. Jones |
| | G-MVEK | Mainair Gemini Flash IIA | J. R. Spinks |
| | G-MVEL | Mainair Gemini Flash IIA | L. R. H. D'Eath |
| | G-MVEN | CFM Shadow Srs BD | T. J. T. Dorricott |
| | G-MVEO | Mainair Gemini Flash IIA | J. C. R. Gubbins |
| | G-MVEP | Mainair Gemini Flash IIA | P. Harper |
| | G-MVER | Mainair Gemini Flash IIA | G. K. Hoult |
| | G-MVES | Mainair Gemini Flash IIA | A. W. Fish |
| | G-MVET | Mainair Gemini Flash IIA | B. T. Fehily |
| | G-MVEV | Mainair Gemini Flash IIA | S. L. Roobottom |
| | G-MVEW | Mainair Gemini Flash IIA | N. A. Dye |
| | G-MVEX | Solar Wings Pegasus XL-Q | J. S. Hamilton |
| | G-MVEY | Solar Wings Pegasus XL-Q | Airplay (UK) Ltd |
| | G-MVEZ | Solar Wings Pegasus XL-Q | P. W. Millar |
| | G-MVFA | Solar Wings Pegasus XL-Q | C. C. Hill |
| | G-MVFB | Solar Wings Pegasus XL-Q | M. O. Bloy |
| | G-MVFC | Solar Wings Pegasus XL-Q | S. C. Goozee |
| | G-MVFD | Solar Wings Pegasus XL-Q | P. G. Barnes |
| | G-MVFE | Solar Wings Pegasus XL-Q | D. Young |
| | G-MVFF | Solar Wings Pegasus XL-Q | C. L. Ross |
| | G-MVFG | Solar Wings Pegasus XL-Q | R. F. Cooper |
| | G-MVFH | CFM Shadow Srs BD | RS Roof Trusses Ltd |
| | G-MVFJ | Thruster TST Mk 1 | Kestrel Flying Group |
| | G-MVFK | Thruster TST Mk 1 | J. E. L. Goodall |
| | G-MVFL | Thruster TST Mk 1 | R. O. Smith & D. Osborne |
| | G-MVFM | Thruster TST Mk 1 | J. D. Wainwright |
| | G-MVFN | Thruster TST Mk 1 | J. P. Jenkins |
| | G-MVFO | Thruster TST Mk 1 | G-MVFO Group |
| | G-MVFP | Solar Wings Pegasus XL-R | P. Woodcock |
| | G-MVFR | Solar Wings Pegasus XL-R | A. N. F. Stewart |
| | G-MVFS | Solar Wings Pegasus XL-R | G. W. Millar |
| | G-MVFT | Solar Wings Pegasus XL-R | J. E. Halsall |
| | G-MVFU | Solar Wings Pegasus XL-R | J. E. Glendinning |
| | G-MVFV | Solar Wings Pegasus XL-R | J. R. Hairsine |
| | G-MVFW | Solar Wings Pegasus XL-R | J. H. Cranfield |
| | G-MVFX | Solar Wings Pegasus XL-R | G. D. Sanders Ltd |
| | G-MVFY | Solar Wings Pegasus XL-R | J. Kinson |
| | G-MVFZ | Solar Wings Pegasus XL-R | C. D. Muir |
| | G-MVGA | Aerial Arts Chaser S | Cyclone Hovercraft Ltd |
| | G-MVGB | Medway Hybred 44XLR | M. A. Perry |
| | G-MVGC | AMF Chevvron 232 | C. J. L. Hunt |
| | G-MVGD | AMF Chevvron 232 | Calvert Holdings Ltd |
| | G-MVGE | AMF Chevvron 232 | K. G. Baker |
| | G-MVGF | Aerial Arts Chaser S | N. St. L. Evans |
| | G-MVGG | Aerial Arts Chaser S | M. I. Hubbard |
| | G-MVGH | Aerial Arts Chaser S | P. Kelly |
| | G-MVGI | Aerial Arts Chaser S | B. J. Lyford |
| | G-MVGJ | Aerial Arts Chaser S | P. J. McNamee |
| | G-MVGK | Aerial Arts Chaser S | C. F. Grainger |
| | G-MVGL | Medway Hybred 44XLR | S. Tensch |
| | G-MVGM | Mainair Gemini Flash IIA | J. L. Bruton |
| | G-MVGN | Solar Wings Pegasus XL-R | T. Holford |
| | G-MVGO | Solar Wings Pegasus XL-R | A. P. Slade |
| | G-MVGP | Solar Wings Pegasus XL-R | C. A. Taylor |
| | G-MVGR | Solar Wings Pegasus XL-R | G. C. Manley |
| | G-MVGS | Solar Wings Pegasus XL-R | M. H. Woodward |
| | G-MVGT | Solar Wings Pegasus XL-Q | Cloudbase Airsports Ltd |
| | G-MVGU | Solar Wings Pegasus XL-Q | D. K. Fuller |

| Reg. | Type | Owner or Operator | Notes |
|------|------|-------------------|-------|
| G-MVGV | Solar Wings Pegasus XL-Q | D. M. Lane | |
| G-MVGW | Solar Wings Pegasus XL-Q | G. A. Breen | |
| G-MVGX | Solar Wings Pegasus XL-Q | N. D. White | |
| G-MVGY | Medway Hybred 44XL | M. F. Evanson | |
| G-MVGZ | Ultraflight Lazair IIIE | M. F. Briggs | |
| G-MVHA | Aerial Arts Chaser S | R. Meredith-Hardy | |
| G-MVHB | Powerchute Raider | Powerchute Systems International Ltd | |
| G-MVHC | Powerchute Raider | K. N. Dewhurst | |
| G-MVHD | CFM Shadow Srs BD | Wessex Aviation Ltd | |
| G-MVHE | Mainair Gemini Flash IIA | S. A. Clarehugh | |
| G-MVHF | Mainair Gemini Flash IIA | D. Haslam | |
| G-MVHG | Mainair Gemini Flash IIA | E. P. Howard | |
| G-MVHH | Mainair Gemini Flash IIA | F. Beeson | |
| G-MVHI | Thruster TST Mk 1 | P. D. Gill | |
| G-MVHJ | Thruster TST Mk 1 | I. S. Rolfe | |
| G-MVHK | Thruster TST Mk 1 | A. L. Rowland | |
| G-MVHL | Thruster TST Mk 1 | M. W. & J. C. Hanley | |
| G-MVHM | Whittaker MW.5 Sorcerer | J. F. Bakewell | |
| G-MVHN | Aerial Arts Chaser S | K. J. Regan | |
| G-MVHO | Solar Wings Pegasus XL-Q | C. J. Dale | |
| G-MVHP | Solar Wings Pegasus XL-Q | V. E. J. Smith | |
| G-MVHR | Solar Wings Pegasus XL-Q | A. W. Reed | |
| G-MVHS | Solar Wings Pegasus XL-Q | A. E. Goodwin | |
| G-MVHT | Solar Wings Pegasus XL-Q | O. J. J. Rogers | |
| G-MVHU | Solar Wings Pegasus XL-Q | H. J. Aldridge | |
| G-MVHV | Solar Wings Pegasus XL-Q | C. James & A. West | |
| G-MVHW | Solar Wings Pegasus XL-Q | Airplay (UK) Ltd | |
| G-MVHX | Solar Wings Pegasus XL-Q | S. N. Dalton & N. M. S. Walters | |
| G-MVHY | Solar Wings Pegasus XL-Q | D. J. Gardner | |
| G-MVHZ | Hornet Dual Trainer | A. R. Hogg | |
| G-MVIA | Solar Wings Pegasus XL-R | B. Curtis | |
| G-MVIB | Mainair Gemini Flash IIA | LSA Systems Ltd | |
| G-MVIC | Mainair Gemini Flash IIA | W. A. Emmerson | |
| G-MVID | Aerial Arts Chaser S | G. P. Wilkins | |
| G-MVIE | Aerial Arts Chaser S | T. M. Stiles | |
| G-MVIF | Medway Hybred 44XLR | S. M. Hall | |
| G-MVIG | CFM Shadow Srs B | M. P. & P. A. G. Harper | |
| G-MVIH | Mainair Gemini Flash IIA | J. H. Tope | |
| G-MVIL | Noble Hardman Snowbird Mk IV | R. M. G. Sunderland | |
| G-MVIM | Noble Hardman Snowbird Mk IV | R. H. Whitaker | |
| G-MVIN | Noble Hardman Snowbird Mk IV | J. C. Larkin | |
| G-MVIO | — | | |
| G-MVIP | AMF Chevvron 232 | Chilbolton Flying Club | |
| G-MVIR | Thruster TST Mk 1 | P. G. Forder | |
| G-MVIS | Thruster TST Mk 1 | Taylor Project Services | |
| G-MVIU | Thruster TST Mk 1 | G. J. Chater | |
| G-MVIV | Thruster TST Mk 1 | M. J. Gordon | |
| G-MVIW | Thruster TST Mk 1 | H. K. Wooler | |
| G-MVIX | Mainair Gemini Flash IIA | C. Laverty | |
| G-MVIY | Mainair Gemini Flash IIA | G. Brown | |
| G-MVIZ | Mainair Gemini Flash IIA | A. J. Lloyd | |
| G-MVJA | Mainair Gemini Flash IIA | M. P. Chadney | |
| G-MVJB | Mainair Gemini Flash IIA | H. Mason | |
| G-MVJC | Mainair Gemini Flash IIA | D. Clarke | |
| G-MVJD | Solar Wings Pegasus XL-R | A. Nichols | |
| G-MVJE | Mainair Gemini Flash IIA | S. J. Whistance | |
| G-MVJF | Aerial Arts Chaser S | B. J. Marshall | |
| G-MVJG | Aerial Arts Chaser S | P. Johnson | |
| G-MVJH | Aerial Arts Chaser S | J. P. Wild | |
| G-MVJI | Aerial Arts Chaser S | P. M. Dewhurst | |
| G-MVJJ | Aerial Arts Chaser S | C. R. Marriott | |
| G-MVJK | Aerial Arts Chaser S | R. F. Miller | |
| G-MVJL | Mainair Gemini Flash IIA | M. A. & S. J. Wood | |
| G-MVJM | Microflight Spectrum | Microflight Aircraft Ltd | |
| G-MVJN | Solar Wings Pegasus XL-Q | J. W. Wall | |
| G-MVJO | Solar Wings Pegasus XL-Q | S. J. T. Bonham | |
| G-MVJP | Solar Wings Pegasus XL-Q | R. E. Thatcher | |
| G-MVJR | Solar Wings Pegasus XL-Q | I. D. Rutherford | |
| G-MVJS | Solar Wings Pegasus XL-Q | M. Howe | |
| G-MVJT | Solar Wings Pegasus XL-Q | I. K. Donkin | |
| G-MVJU | Solar Wings Pegasus XL-Q | J. A. Lord | |
| G-MVJV | Solar Wings Pegasus XL-Q | J. G. Davies | |
| G-MVJW | Solar Wings Pegasus XL-Q | R. Dainty & D. W. Stamp | |

227

| Notes | Reg. | Type | Owner or Operator |
|-------|------|------|-------------------|
| | G-MVJX | Solar Wings Pegasus XL-Q | S. J. Gregg |
| | G-MVJZ | Birdman Cherokee | N. E. Birch |
| | G-MVKA | Medway Hybred 44XLR | P. M. Standen |
| | G-MVKB | Medway Hybred 44XLR | T. Rankin |
| | G-MVKC | Mainair Gemini Flash IIA | M. J. Trevillion |
| | G-MVKE | Solar Wings Pegasus XL-R | B. Wardell & N. Butterfield |
| | G-MVKF | Solar Wings Pegasus XL-R | A. Harper |
| | G-MVKG | Solar Wings Pegasus XL-R | C. S. Smith |
| | G-MVKH | Solar Wings Pegasus XL-R | K. Anderson |
| | G-MVKI | Solar Wings Pegasus XL-R | J. Walker |
| | G-MVKJ | Solar Wings Pegasus XL-R | P. S. Nicholls |
| | G-MVKK | Solar Wings Pegasus XL-R | S. White |
| | G-MVKL | Solar Wings Pegasus XL-R | J. T. Powell-Tuck |
| | G-MVKM | Solar Wings Pegasus XL-R | D. S. Corbett |
| | G-MVKN | Solar Wings Pegasus XL-Q | R. J. Pattinson & R. M. Wisely |
| | G-MVKO | Solar Wings Pegasus XL-Q | T. G. Ledbury |
| | G-MVKP | Solar Wings Pegasus XL-Q | C. Leonard |
| | G-MVKR | Solar Wings Pegasus XL-Q | Micro Air Sales Ltd |
| | G-MVKS | Solar Wings Pegasus XL-Q | K. S. Wright |
| | G-MVKT | Solar Wings Pegasus XL-Q | A. R. L. Hewison |
| | G-MVKU | Solar Wings Pegasus XL-Q | R. Hemsworth |
| | G-MVKV | Solar Wings Pegasus XL-Q | Wiltshire Microlight Centre Ltd |
| | G-MVKW | Solar Wings Pegasus XL-Q | A. T. Scott |
| | G-MVKX | Solar Wings Pegasus XL-Q | J. W. Holland |
| | G-MVKY | Aerial Arts Chaser S | A. L. Rogers |
| | G-MVKZ | Aerial Arts Chaser S | R. J. Bowering |
| | G-MVLA | Aerial Arts Chaser S | R. Thorpe |
| | G-MVLB | Aerial Arts Chaser S | C. R. Read |
| | G-MVLC | Aerial Arts Chaser S | B. R. Barnes |
| | G-MVLD | Aerial Arts Chaser S | T. G. Elmhirst |
| | G-MVLE | Aerial Arts Chaser S | D. T. Smith |
| | G-MVLF | Aerial Arts Chaser S | R. Blenkley |
| | G-MVLG | Aerial Arts Chaser S | D. Little |
| | G-MVLH | Aerial Arts Chaser S | S. J. M. Morling |
| | G-MVLI | — | |
| | G-MVLJ | CFM Shadow Srs B | W. J. F. Maclean |
| | G-MVLL | Mainair Gemini Flash IIA | L. E. Comben |
| | G-MVLM | Solar Wings Pegasus Bandit | Solar Wings Ltd |
| | G-MVLP | CFM Shadow Srs BD | R. F. Bridgland |
| | G-MVLR | Mainair Gemini Flash IIA | K. Akister |
| | G-MVLS | Aerial Arts Chaser S | E. W. P. van Zeller |
| | G-MVLT | Aerial Arts Chaser S | C. R. Thorne |
| | G-MVLU | Aerial Arts Chaser S | M. J. Aubrey |
| | G-MVLW | Aerial Arts Chaser S | J. C. Goodchild |
| | G-MVLX | Solar Wings Pegasus XL-Q | P. W. M. Powell |
| | G-MVLY | Solar Wings Pegasus XL-Q | I. Glover |
| | G-MVLZ | Solar Wings Pegasus XL-Q | G. E. Phillips |
| | G-MVMA | Solar Wings Pegasus XL-Q | D. J. Baker |
| | G-MVMB | Solar Wings Pegasus XL-Q | S. Nimmo |
| | G-MVMC | Solar Wings Pegasus XL-Q | R. G. Goodwin |
| | G-MVMD | Powerchute Raider | D. W. Gurner |
| | G-MVME | Thruster TST Mk 1 | M. A. Dobson |
| | G-MVMF | — | — |
| | G-MVMG | Thruster TST Mk 1 | R. H. Bicker |
| | G-MVMI | Thruster TST Mk 1 | M. T. Brandler |
| | G-MVMJ | Thruster TST Mk 1 | D. R. Augarde & S. Vining |
| | G-MVMK | Medway Hybred 44XLR | D. J. Lewis |
| | G-MVML | Aerial Arts Chaser S | P. R. Leach |
| | G-MVMM | Aerial Arts Chaser S | J. McDowall |
| | G-MVMN | Mainair Gemini Flash IIA | C. C. Mercer |
| | G-MVMO | Mainair Gemini Flash IIA | R. C. Colclough |
| | G-MVMP | Eipper Quicksilver MXII | R. Daltrey |
| | G-MVMR | Mainair Gemini Flash IIA | P. W. Ramage |
| | G-MVMT | Mainair Gemini Flash IIA | Independent Financial Advisory |
| | G-MVMU | Mainair Gemini Flash IIA | M. J. A. New & A. Clift |
| | G-MVMV | Mainair Gemini Flash IIA | M. Spearing |
| | G-MVMW | Mainair Gemini Flash IIA | M. H. Wright |
| | G-MVMX | Mainair Gemini Flash IIA | L. Gregory |
| | G-MVMY | Mainair Gemini Flash IIA | J. B. P. Hay |
| | G-MVMZ | Mainair Gemini Flash IIA | J. Hollings |
| | G-MVNA | Powerchute Raider | C. N. Bond |
| | G-MVNB | Powerchute Raider | G. A. W. Ivey |
| | G-MVNC | Powerchute Raider | W. R. Hanley |

| Reg. | Type | Owner or Operator | Notes |
|------|------|-------------------|-------|
| G-MVND | Powerchute Raider | R. A. I. Hamilton | |
| G-MVNE | Powerchute Raider | Powerchute Systems International Ltd | |
| G-MVNF | Powerchute Raider | R. Harding | |
| G-MVNG | Powerchute Raider | Powerchute Systems International Ltd | |
| G-MVNI | Powerchute Raider | T. Willett | |
| G-MVNJ | Powerchute Raider | Powerchute Systems International Ltd | |
| G-MVNK | Powerchute Raider | B. Cartwright | |
| G-MVNL | Powerchute Raider | Powerchute Systems International Ltd | |
| G-MVNM | Mainair Gemini Flash IIA | K. B. Pownall | |
| G-MVNN | Whittaker MW.5 (K) Sorcerer | K. N. Dando | |
| G-MVNO | Aerotech MW.5 (K) Sorcerer | R. L. Wadley | |
| G-MVNP | Aerotech MW.5 (K) Sorcerer | J. C. Neale | |
| G-MVNR | Aerotech MW.5 (K) Sorcerer | M. A. J. Hutt | |
| G-MVNS | Aerotech MW.5 (K) Sorcerer | R. D. Chiles | |
| G-MVNT | Whittaker MW.5 (K) Sorcerer | P. E. Blyth | |
| G-MVNU | Aerotech MW.5 Sorcerer | G. A. Archer | |
| G-MVNV | — | — | |
| G-MVNW | Mainair Gemini Flash IIA | A. Weatherall | |
| G-MVNX | Mainair Gemini Flash IIA | M. G. Welch | |
| G-MVNY | Mainair Gemini Flash IIA | M. K. Buckland | |
| G-MVNZ | Mainair Gemini Flash IIA | I. Jones | |
| G-MVOA | Aerial Arts Alligator | M. R. Pierce | |
| G-MVOB | Mainair Gemini Flash IIA | J. G. Venn | |
| G-MVOD | Aerial Arts Chaser 110SX | R. Bacon | |
| G-MVOE | Solar Wings Pegasus XL-R | Micro Air Sales Ltd | |
| G-MVOF | Mainair Gemini Flash IIA | Winning Format Television Ltd | |
| G-MVOG | Huntair Pathfinder Mk 1 | P. P. Trangmar | |
| G-MVOH | CFM Shadow Srs B | P. P. Trangmar | |
| G-MVOI | Noble Hardman Snowbird Mk IV | T. W. Dukes | |
| G-MVOJ | Noble Hardman Snowbird Mk IV | Davlin Microlights Ltd | |
| G-MVOK | Noble Hardman Snowbird Mk IV | B. M. Akin | |
| G-MVOL | Noble Hardman Snowbird Mk IV | Swansea Snowbird Fliers | |
| G-MVOM | Medway Hybred 44XLR | R. J. Baker | |
| G-MVON | Mainair Gemini Flash IIA | A. D. Langtree | |
| G-MVOO | AMF Chevvron 232 | A. Hipkin | |
| G-MVOP | Aerial Arts Chaser S | D. Thorpe | |
| G-MVOR | Mainair Gemini Flash IIA | M. E. O'Brien | |
| G-MVOS | Southdown Raven | P. J. Brookman | |
| G-MVOT | Thruster TST Mk 1 | Hornet Group | |
| G-MVOU | Thruster TST Mk 1 | A. T. Murray | |
| G-MVOV | Thruster TST Mk 1 | J. N. Webster | |
| G-MVOW | Thruster TST Mk 1 | C. W. Judge | |
| G-MVOX | Thruster TST Mk 1 | W. R. H. Thomas | |
| G-MVOY | Thruster TST Mk 1 | R. V. Buxton | |
| G-MVPA | Mainair Gemini Flash IIA | T. Anderson | |
| G-MVPB | Mainair Gemini Flash IIA | G. M. Prowling | |
| G-MVPC | Mainair Gemini Flash IIA | A. Howarth | |
| G-MVPD | Mainair Gemini Flash IIA | J. Lynch | |
| G-MVPE | Mainair Gemini Flash IIA | E. A. Wrathall & H. N. Houghton | |
| G-MVPF | Medway Hybred 44XLR | M. K. O'Donnell | |
| G-MVPG | Medway Hybred 44XLR | A. P. Hussey | |
| G-MVPH | Whittaker MW.6 Merlin | E. A. Henman | |
| G-MVPI | Mainair Gemini Flash IIA | C. & P. Squibbs | |
| G-MVPJ | Rans S.5 | Sportair UK Ltd | |
| G-MVPK | CFM Shadow Srs B | G. Dalton | |
| G-MVPL | Medway Hybred 44XLR | Speed Missile Ski Co Ltd | |
| G-MVPM | Whittaker MW.6 Merlin | C. Crabb & P. I. Marsh | |
| G-MVPN | Whittaker MW.6 Merlin | A. M. Field | |
| G-MVPO | Mainair Gemini Flash IIA | A. H. & C. I. King | |
| G-MVPR | Solar Wings Pegasus XL-Q | A. W. Turner | |
| G-MVPS | Solar Wings Pegasus XL-Q | T. J. M. Bonham | |
| G-MVPT | Solar Wings Pegasus XL-Q | Solar Wings Ltd | |
| G-MVPU | Solar Wings Pegasus XL-Q | B. J. Gordon | |
| G-MVPV | Solar Wings Pegasus XL-Q | J. Leden | |
| G-MVPW | Solar Wings Pegasus XL-R | C. Phillips | |
| G-MVPX | Solar Wings Pegasus XL-Q | P. Sutton | |
| G-MVPY | Solar Wings Pegasus XL-Q | C. N. Jarvis | |
| G-MVPZ | Rans S.5 | P. S. Cottrell | |
| G-MVRA | Mainair Gemini Flash IIA | T. N. Jerry | |
| G-MVRB | Mainair Gemini Flash IIA | R. E. D. Bailey | |
| G-MVRC | Mainair Gemini Flash IIA | R. E. D. Bailey | |
| G-MVRD | Mainair Gemini Flash IIA | D. Sugden | |
| G-MVRE | CFM Shadow Srs BD | L. Kellner | |

| Notes | Reg. | Type | Owner or Operator |
|-------|------|------|-------------------|
| | G-MVRF | Rotec Rally 2B | A. I. Edwards |
| | G-MVRG | Aerial Arts Chaser S | A. V. Newton |
| | G-MVRH | Solar Wings Pegasus XL-Q | S. W. Hill |
| | G-MVRI | Solar Wings Pegasus XL-Q | M. F. Quinn |
| | G-MVRJ | Solar Wings Pegasus XL-Q | G. S. Ungless |
| | G-MVRK | Solar Wings Pegasus XL-Q | S. J. Edwards & P. V. Lewis |
| | G-MVRL | Aerial Arts Chaser S | D. Bannister |
| | G-MVRM | Mainair Gemini Flash IIA | C. S. Simmons |
| | G-MVRN | Rans S.4 Coyote | C. Briggs |
| | G-MVRO | CFM Shadow Srs BD | CFM Metal-Fax |
| | G-MVRP | CFM Shadow Srs BD | Quantum Leasing Ltd |
| | G-MVRR | CFM Shadow Srs BD | J. C. Duncan |
| | G-MVRT | CFM Shadow Srs BD | Wessex Aviation Ltd |
| | G-MVRU | Solar Wings Pegasus XL-Q | D. E. & S. Wall |
| | G-MVRV | Powerchute Kestrel | Powerchute Systems International Ltd |
| | G-MVRW | Solar Wings Pegasus XL-Q | R. A. P. Mules |
| | G-MVRX | Solar Wings Pegasus XL-Q | M. Everest |
| | G-MVRY | Medway Hybred 44XLR | A. T. Hart |
| | G-MVRZ | Medway Hybred 44XLR | D. A. Slater |
| | G-MVSA | Solar Wings Pegasus XL-Q | R. A. Johns |
| | G-MVSB | Solar Wings Pegasus XL-Q | P. G. Angus |
| | G-MVSC | Solar Wings Pegasus XL-Q | K. Pritchard |
| | G-MVSD | Solar Wings Pegasus XL-Q | A. D. Kinch |
| | G-MVSE | Solar Wings Pegasus XL-Q | J. A. Robinson & L. Bennett |
| | G-MVSG | Aerial Arts Chaser S | C. G. Thomson |
| | G-MVSI | Medway Hybred 44XLR | J. Nivison |
| | G-MVSJ | Aviasud Mistral 532 | R. E. D. Bailey |
| | G-MVSK | Aerial Arts Chaser S | D. R. Wells |
| | G-MVSL | Aerial Arts Chaser S | A. St. J. Hollis |
| | G-MVSM | Midland Ultralights Sirocco | J. A. Hambleton |
| | G-MVSN | Mainair Gemini Flash IIA | R. N. Scarr |
| | G-MVSO | Mainair Gemini Flash IIA | M. Watkins |
| | G-MVSP | Mainair Gemini Flash IIA | D. M. McGee |
| | G-MVSR | Medway Hybred 44XLR | S. M. Stanwix |
| | G-MVSS | Hornet RS-ZA | Hornet Microlights Ltd |
| | G-MVST | Mainair Gemini Flash IIA | T. Westerman |
| | G-MVSU | Microflight Spectrum | W. R. J. Wallis |
| | G-MVSV | Mainair Gemini Flash IIA | P. Kneeshaw |
| | G-MVSW | Solar Wings Pegasus XL-Q | D. A. Gandle |
| | G-MVSX | Solar Wings Pegasus XL-Q | I. D. Overthrow & R. Johnson |
| | G-MVSY | Solar Wings Pegasus XL-Q | R. W. Wotton |
| | G-MVSZ | Solar Wings Pegasus XL-Q | J. L. Brown |
| | G-MVTA | Solar Wings Pegasus XL-Q | E. Findley |
| | G-MVTB | — | — |
| | G-MVTC | Mainair Gemini Flash IIA | H. B. Blamires |
| | G-MVTD | Whittaker MW.6 Merlin | J. S. Yates |
| | G-MVTE | Whittaker MW.6 Merlin | D. S. Bremer & T. Willford |
| | G-MVTF | Aerial Arts Chaser S | J. Collyer |
| | G-MVTG | Solar Wings Pegasus XL-Q | J. C. O'Donnell |
| | G-MVTH | Solar Wings Pegasus XL-Q | C. A. Taylor |
| | G-MVTI | Solar Wings Pegasus XL-Q | T. M. Adcock |
| | G-MVTJ | Solar Wings Pegasus XL-Q | R. S. Arroyo |
| | G-MVTK | Solar Wings Pegasus XL-Q | C. W. Curtain |
| | G-MVTL | Aerial Arts Chaser S | R. J. Grainger |
| | G-MVTM | Aerial Arts Chaser S | C. C. W. Mates |
| | G-MVUA | Mainair Gemini Flash IIA | Cash-Weigh Ltd |
| | G-MVUB | Thruster T.300 | Uniform Bravo Group |
| | G-MVUC | Medway Hybred 44XLR | D. H. Griffin |
| | G-MVUD | Medway Hybred 44XLR | J. Nivison |
| | G-MVUE | Solar Wings Pegasus XL-Q | C. I. D. Garrison |
| | G-MVUF | Solar Wings Pegasus XL-Q | P. A. Crowe & L. M. Groves |
| | G-MVUG | Solar Wings Pegasus XL-Q | R. B. Milton |
| | G-MVUH | Solar Wings Pegasus XL-Q | J. Thomas |
| | G-MVUI | Solar Wings Pegasus XL-Q | C. J. Tomlin |
| | G-MVUJ | Solar Wings Pegasus XL-Q | P. de Fraine |
| | G-MVUK | Solar Wings Pegasus XL-Q | P. M. Lynn |
| | G-MVUL | Solar Wings Pegasus XL-Q | G-MVUL Group |
| | G-MVUM | Solar Wings Pegasus XL-Q | I. M. Munster |
| | G-MVUN | Solar Wings Pegasus XL-Q | J. & K. I. Greenaway |
| | G-MVUO | AMF Chevvron 232 | C. A. Mordlock |
| | G-MVUP | Aviasud Mistral | D. M. Whitham |
| | G-MVUR | Hornet ZA | C. Churchyard |
| | G-MVUS | Aerial Arts Chaser S | P. D. Atkinson |

| Reg. | Type | Owner or Operator | Notes |
|------|------|-------------------|-------|
| G-MVUT | Aerial Arts Chaser S | K. C. Rutland | |
| G-MVUU | Hornet R-ZA | P. Barrow | |
| G-MVVF | Medway Hybred 44XLR | T. Kendall & ptnrs | |
| G-MVVG | Medway Hybred 44XLR | C. Smith | |
| G-MVVH | Medway Hybred 44XLR | M. S. Henson | |
| G-MVVI | Medway Hybred 44XLR | A. Bourner | |
| G-MVVJ | Medway Hybred 44XLR | D. Sinclair | |
| G-MVVK | Solar Wings Pegasus XL-R | M. Kellaway | |
| G-MVVM | Solar Wings Pegasus XL-R | C. Ackroyd | |
| G-MVVN | Solar Wings Pegasus XL-Q | A. A. Taddei | |
| G-MVVP | Solar Wings Pegasus XL-Q | J. S. & D. J. Melville | |
| G-MVVR | Medway Hybred 44XLR | J. McMillan & A. A. Ellman | |
| G-MVVS | Southdown Puma Sprint | P. A. Harris | |
| G-MVVT | CFM Shadow Srs BD | B. J. W. Birchall | |
| G-MVVU | Aerial Arts Chaser S | P. M. Wisniewski | |
| G-MVVW | Aerial Arts Chaser S | W. Myers | |
| G-MVVX | Powerchute Raider | Powerchute Systems International Ltd | |
| G-MVVY | Powerchute Raider | Powerchute Systems International Ltd | |
| G-MVVZ | Powerchute Raider | Powerchute Systems International Ltd | |
| G-MVWA | Powerchute Raider | Powerchute Systems International Ltd | |
| G-MVWB | Powerchute Raider | Powerchute Systems International Ltd | |
| G-MVWD | Powerchute Raider | Powerchute Systems International Ltd | |
| G-MVWE | Powerchute Raider | Powerchute Systems International Ltd | |
| G-MVWF | Powerchute Raider | Powerchute Systems International Ltd | |
| G-MVWG | Powerchute Raider | Powerchute Systems International Ltd | |
| G-MVWH | Powerchute Raider | Powerchute Systems International Ltd | |
| G-MVWI | Powerchute Raider | Powerchute Systems International Ltd | |
| G-MVWJ | Powerchute Raider | Powerchute Systems International Ltd | |
| G-MVWK | Powerchute Raider | Powerchute Systems International Ltd | |
| G-MVWL | Powerchute Raider | Powerchute Systems International Ltd | |
| G-MVWM | Powerchute Raider | Powerchute Systems International Ltd | |
| G-MVWN | Thruster T.300 | P. J. Reed | |
| G-MVWO | Thruster T.300 | M. L. Smith | |
| G-MVWP | Thruster T.300 | D. R. G. Whitelaw & W. G. Miller | |
| G-MVWR | Thruster T.300 | D. Goillon | |
| G-MVWS | Thruster T.300 | Superavian Ltd | |
| G-MVWU | Medway Hybred 44XLR | J. R. A. Dickinson | |
| G-MVWV | Medway Hybred 44XLR | F. Davies | |
| G-MVWW | Aviasud Mistral 532 | C. A. Mordlock | |
| G-MVWX | Microflight Spectrum | F. Credland | |
| G-MVWY | – | – | |
| G-MVWZ | Aviasud Mistral | A. Konieczek & B. Kirkland | |
| G-MVXA | Whittaker MW.6 Merlin | I. Brewster | |
| G-MVXB | Mainair Gemini Flash IIA | G. J. Stallard | |
| G-MVXC | Mainair Gemini Flash IIA | Humberside Aggregates & Excavations Ltd | |
| G-MVXD | Medway Hybred 44XLR | I. A. Stamp | |
| G-MVXE | Medway Hybred 44XLR | A. M. Brittle | |
| G-MVXF | Weedhopper JC-31A | R. A. Sammons | |
| G-MVXG | Aerial Arts Chaser S | T. David | |
| G-MVXH | Microflight Spectrum | Microflight Aircraft Ltd | |
| G-MVXI | Medway Hybred 44XLR | M. K. Evenett | |
| G-MVXJ | Medway Hybred 44XLR | P. J. Wilks | |
| G-MVXK | Medway Hybred 44XLR | H. P. Owen | |
| G-MVXL | Thruster TST Mk 1 | Southwest Airsports Ltd | |
| G-MVXM | Medway Hybred 44XLR | T. Thomson | |
| G-MVXN | Aviasud Mistral | NE Granite Co Ltd | |
| G-MVXO | Aerial Arts Chaser S | J. Nivison | |
| G-MVXP | Aerial Arts Chaser S | J. Nivison | |
| G-MVXR | Mainair Gemini Flash IIA | G. M. Douglas | |
| G-MVXS | Mainair Gemini Flash IIA | C. Johnson | |
| G-MVXT | Mainair Gemini Flash IIA | J. R. North | |
| G-MVXU | Aviasud Mistral | S. J. Fretwell | |
| G-MVXV | Aviasud Mistral | F. D. Bennett & M. H. Silversides | |
| G-MVXW | Rans S.4 Coyote | D. Hedley-Goddard | |
| G-MVXX | AMF Chevvron 232 | B. M. Akin | |
| G-MVXY | AMF Paracat 1-24 | AMF Microflight Ltd | |
| G-MVXZ | Minimax | P. Harvey | |
| G-MVYA | Aerial Arts Chaser S | J. I. Greenshields | |
| G-MVYB | Solar Wings Pegasus XL-Q | R. V. L. Mitchell | |
| G-MVYC | Solar Wings Pegasus XL-Q | S. Wileman | |
| G-MVYD | Solar Wings Pegasus XL-Q | P. J. Preece | |
| G-MVYE | Thruster TST Mk 1 | B. C. Allen | |

| Notes | Reg. | Type | Owner or Operator |
|-------|------|------|-------------------|
| | G-MVYF | Hornet R-ZA | Hornet Microlights Ltd |
| | G-MVYG | Hornet R-ZA | N. J. Stoneman |
| | G-MVYH | Hornet R-ZA | D. Reay |
| | G-MVYI | Hornet R-ZA | L. Mullin |
| | G-MVYJ | Hornet R-ZA | R. Williamson |
| | G-MVYK | Hornet R-ZA | K. W. E. Brunnekant |
| | G-MVYL | Hornet R-ZA | Hornet Microlights Ltd |
| | G-MVYM | Hornet R-ZA | D. M. Smith |
| | G-MVYN | Hornet R-ZA | G. Moscrop |
| | G-MVYO | Hornet R-ZA | R. W. Swain & C. K. Ford |
| | G-MVYP | Medway Hybred 44XLR | Industrial Foam Systems Ltd |
| | G-MVYR | Medway Hybred 44XLR | A. MacDonald |
| | G-MVYS | Mainair Gemini Flash IIA | J. E. Walewdowski |
| | G-MVYT | Noble Hardman Snowbird Mk IV | D. T. A. Rees |
| | G-MVYU | Noble Hardman Snowbird Mk IV | R. W. J. Nunn |
| | G-MVYV | Noble Hardman Snowbird Mk IV | The Snowbird Aeroplane Co Ltd |
| | G-MVYW | Noble Hardman Snowbird Mk IV | T. J. Hattin |
| | G-MVYX | — | — |
| | G-MVYY | Aerial Arts Chaser S508 | P. A. R. Hicks |
| | G-MVYZ | CFM Shadow Srs BD | Erindale Products Ltd |
| | G-MVZA | Thruster T.300 | L. J. Rys |
| | G-MVZB | Thruster T.300 | Southwest Airsports Ltd |
| | G-MVZC | Thruster T.300 | N. A. Wilson |
| | G-MVZD | Thruster T.300 | M. L. Smith |
| | G-MVZE | Thruster T.300 | C. E. Brookes |
| | G-MVZF | Thruster T.300 | P. C. Bell |
| | G-MVZG | Thruster T.300 | M. L. Smith |
| | G-MVZH | Thruster T.300 | T. M. Clark |
| | G-MVZI | Thruster T.300 | R. R. R. Whittern |
| | G-MVZJ | Solar Wings Pegasus XL-Q | G. J. Gordon |
| | G-MVZK | Challenger II | K. B. Tolley |
| | G-MVZL | Solar Wings Pegasus XL-Q | G. J. Pearce |
| | G-MVZM | Aerial Arts Chaser S | D. S. North |
| | G-MVZN | Aerial Arts Chaser S | A. C. Tyler |
| | G-MVZO | Medway Hybred 44XLR | P. Smith |
| | G-MVZP | Renegade Spirit UK | G. S. Hollingsworth |
| | G-MVZR | Aviasud Mistral | W. G. Dunn |
| | G-MVZS | Mainair Gemini Flash IIA | W. Hoolachan |
| | G-MVZT | Solar Wings Pegasus XL-Q | R. P. S. Elcomb |
| | G-MVZU | Solar Wings Pegasus XL-Q | R. D. Proctor |
| | G-MVZV | Solar Wings Pegasus XL-Q | S. R. Bowsher |
| | G-MVZW | Hornet R-ZA | M. L. Smith |
| | G-MVZX | Renegade Spirit UK | G. Holmes |
| | G-MVZY | Aerial Arts Chaser S | N. W. O'Brien |
| | G-MVZZ | AMF Chevvron 232 | Lancaster Partners (Holdings) Ltd |
| | G-MWAA | Medway Hybred 44XLR | D. J. Clark |
| | G-MWAB | Mainair Gemini Flash IIA | P. A. Nicholson |
| | G-MWAC | Solar Wings Pegasus XL-Q | T. D. Spencer |
| | G-MWAD | Solar Wings Pegasus XL-Q | N. Wannop |
| | G-MWAE | CFM Shadow Srs BD | D. J. Adams |
| | G-MWAF | Solar Wings Pegasus XL-R | B. A. Wisniewski |
| | G-MWAG | Solar Wings Pegasus XL-R | K. J. Wilson |
| | G-MWAH | Hornet RS-ZA | Skylink Systems Ltd |
| | G-MWAI | Solar Wings Pegasus XL-R | E. K. Battersea |
| | G-MWAJ | Renegade Spirit UK | J. D. Hall |
| | G-MWAK | Solar Wings Pegasus XL-Q | P. Grant |
| | G-MWAL | Solar Wings Pegasus XL-Q | S. E. J. McLaughlin |
| | G-MWAM | Thruster T.300 | M. Rudd |
| | G-MWAN | Thruster T.300 | I. R. Banbury |
| | G-MWAO | Thruster T.300 | N. F. Simpson |
| | G-MWAP | Thruster T.300 | S. P. Read |
| | G-MWAR | Thruster T.300 | G. J. Pill |
| | G-MWAS | Thruster T.300 | E. B. Landsler |
| | G-MWAT | Solar Wings Pegasus XL-Q | S. C. Beale |
| | G-MWAU | Mainair Gemini Flash IIA | Mainair Sports Ltd |
| | G-MWAV | Solar Wings Pegasus XL-R | S. R. D. Slaughter |
| | G-MWAW | Whittaker MW.6 Merlin | P. Palmer |
| | G-MWBH | Hornet RS-ZA | R. N. Stead |
| | G-MWBI | Medway Hybred 44XLR | C. J. Draper |
| | G-MWBJ | Medway Sprint | C. J. Draper |
| | G-MWBK | Solar Wings Pegasus XL-Q | D. G. Benson |
| | G-MWBL | Solar Wings Pegasus XL-Q | D. L. Robson |

| Reg. | Type | Owner or Operator | Notes |
|------|------|-------------------|-------|
| G-MWBM | Hornet RS-ZA | D. J. A. Bradley | |
| G-MWBN | Hornet RS-ZA | D. J. Stafford | |
| G-MWBO | Rans S.4 | M. R. H. D'Eath | |
| G-MWBP | Hornet RS-ZA | J. B. & S. Brierley | |
| G-MWBR | Hornet RS-ZA | R. D. Andrews | |
| G-MWBS | Hornet RS-ZA | Hornet Microlights Ltd | |
| G-MWBT | Hornet RS-ZA | Hornet Microlights Ltd | |
| G-MWBU | Hornet RS-ZA | Hornet Microlights Ltd | |
| G-MWBV | Hornet RS-ZA | Hornet Microlights Ltd | |
| G-MWBW | Hornet RS-ZA | Hornet Microlights Ltd | |
| G-MWBX | Hornet RS-ZA | Hornet Microlights Ltd | |
| G-MWBY | Hornet RS-ZA | W. Burgess | |
| G-MWBZ | Hornet RS-ZA | Hornet Microlights Ltd | |
| G-MWCA | Hornet RS-ZA | Hornet Microlights Ltd | |
| G-MWCB | Solar Wings Pegasus XL-Q | J. S. Hamilton | |
| G-MWCC | Solar Wings Pegasus XL-R | R. H. Tait | |
| G-MWCD | – | | |
| G-MWCE | Mainair Gemini Flash IIA | B. A. Tooze | |
| G-MWCF | Solar Wings Pegasus XL-R | D. V. Lawrence | |
| G-MWCG | Microflight Spectrum | P. J. Collicutt | |
| G-MWCH | Rans S.6 | Sportair UK Ltd | |
| G-MWCI | Powerchute Kestrel | E. G. Bray | |
| G-MWCJ | Powerchute Kestrel | K. M. Hall | |
| G-MWCK | Powerchute Kestrel | N. H. Tolley | |
| G-MWCL | Powerchute Kestrel | G. F. Snith | |
| G-MWCM | Powerchute Kestrel | G. E. Lockyer | |
| G-MWCN | Powerchute Kestrel | A. C. Simpson | |
| G-MWCO | Powerchute Kestrel | T. F. Bakker | |
| G-MWCP | Powerchute Kestrel | British Powerchute Schools | |
| G-MWCR | Southdown Puma Sprint | S. F. Chave | |
| G-MWCS | Powerchute Kestrel | Powerchute Systems International Ltd | |
| G-MMCT | Powerchute Kestrel | Powerchute Systems International Ltd | |
| G-MWCU | Solar Wings Pegasus XL-R | A. C. Bell | |
| G-MWCV | Solar Wings Pegasus XL-Q | G. M. Rollinson | |
| G-MWCW | Mainair Gemini Flash IIA | B. C. Jones | |
| G-MWCX | Medway Hybred 44XLR | K. W. Wilkes | |
| G-MWCY | Medway Hybred 44XLR | S. T. Martin | |
| G-MWCZ | Medway Hybred 44XLR | A. Baskerville | |
| G-MWDA | Jakeway Powered Parachute | R. T. Jakeway | |
| G-MWDB | CFM Shadow Srs BD | D. V. Brunt | |
| G-MWDC | Solar Wings Pegasus XL-R | A. N. Edwards | |
| G-MWDD | Solar Wings Pegasus XL-Q | T. P. Toth | |
| G-MWDE | Hornet RS-ZA | Baxby Microlights Ltd | |
| G-MWDF | Hornet RS-ZA | Skylink Systems Ltd | |
| G-MWDG | Hornet RS-ZA | Skylink Systems Ltd | |
| G-MWDH | Hornet RS-ZA | Skylink Systems Ltd | |
| G-MWDI | Hornet RS-ZA | R. J. Perrin | |
| G-MWDJ | Mainair Gemini Flash IIA | B. Cowburn | |
| G-MWDK | Solar Wings Pegasus XL-R | R. C. Barkworth | |
| G-MWDL | Solar Wings Pegasus XL-R | R. Frost | |
| G-MWDM | Renegade Spirit UK | R. G. Humphries | |
| G-MWDN | CFM Shadow Srs BD | P. M. & S. A. Harrison | |
| G-MWDO | Spencer Cub | Spencer Aviation | |
| G-MWDP | Thruster TST Mk 1 | R. D. Andrews | |
| G-MWDR | Thruster T.300 | Thruster Aircraft (UK) Ltd | |
| G-MWDS | Thruster T.300 | Superavian Ltd | |
| G-MWDT | Thruster T.300 | Thruster Aircraft (UK) Ltd | |
| G-MWDU | Thruster T.300 | Thruster Aircraft (UK) Ltd | |
| G-MWDV | Thruster T.300 | Thruster Aircraft (UK) Ltd | |
| G-MWDW | Thruster T.300 | Thruster Aircraft (UK) Ltd | |
| G-MWDX | Thruster T.300 | Thruster Aircraft (UK) Ltd | |
| G-MWDY | Thruster T.300 | Thruster Aircraft (UK) Ltd | |
| G-MWDZ | Eipper Quicksilver MXL II | W. Murphy | |
| G-MWEA | Mosler Motors N.3 Pup | Meridian Ultralights Ltd | |
| G-MWEB | – | – | |
| G-MWEC | – | – | |
| G-MWED | – | – | |
| G-MWEE | Solar Wings Pegasus XL-Q | R. J. Sharp | |
| G-MWEF | Solar Wings Pegasus XL-Q | T. A. Earley | |
| G-MWEG | Solar Wings Pegasus XL-Q | R. Donaldson | |
| G-MWEH | Solar Wings Pegasus XL-Q | G. S. Wheatley | |
| G-MWEI | Mainair Gemini Flash IIA | R. E. Price | |
| G-MWEK | Whittaker MW.5 Sorcerer | J. T. Francis | |

| Notes | Reg. | Type | Owner or Operator |
|---|---|---|---|
| | G-MWEL | Mainair Gemini Flash IIA | B. L. Benson |
| | G-MWEM | Medway Hybred 44XLR | J. K. Newell |
| | G-MWEN | CFM Shadow Srs BD | A. M. Pepper |
| | G-MWEO | Whittaker MW.5 Sorcerer | C. D. Wills |
| | G-MWEP | Rans S.4 | K. E. Wedl |
| | G-MWER | Solar Wings Pegasus XL-Q | S. V. Stojanovic |
| | G-MWES | Rans S.4 | R. W. Sage & I. Fleming |
| | G-MWET | Hornet RS-ZA | I. Ellithorn |
| | G-MWEU | Hornet RS-ZA | Hornet Microlights Ltd |
| | G-MWEV | Hornet RS-ZA | Hornet Microlights Ltd |
| | G-MWEW | Hornet RS-ZA | Hornet Microlights Ltd |
| | G-MWEX | Hornet RS-ZA | Hornet Microlights Ltd |
| | G-MWEY | Hornet RS-ZA | R. Basnett |
| | G-MWEZ | CFM Shadow Srs CD | L. G. Cook |
| | G-MWFA | Solar Wings Pegasus XL-R | A. W. Edwards |
| | G-MWFB | CFM Shadow Srs BD | G. W. F. Webb |
| | G-MWFC | Team Minimax | M. H. D. Soltau |
| | G-MWFD | Team Minimax | J. Riley |
| | G-MWFE | Robin 330/Lightning 195 | N. J. Cole |
| | G-MWFF | Rans S.4 | A. J. Haworth |
| | G-MWFG | Powerchute Kestrel | P. M. Blench |
| | G-MWFH | Powerchute Kestrel | Valley Canoe Products Ltd |
| | G-MWFI | Powerchute Kestrel | R. W. Topping |
| | G-MWFJ | Powerchute Kestrel | Powerchute Systems International Ltd |
| | G-MWFK | Powerchute Kestrel | M. L. Hitchcock |
| | G-MWFL | Powerchute Kestrel | P. D. Jones |
| | G-MWFN | Powerchute Kestrel | J. A. Whitamore |
| | G-MWFO | Solar Wings Pegasus XL-R | R. Barton |
| | G-MWFP | Solar Wings Pegasus XL-R | C. J. Flavin |
| | G-MWFR | Solar Wings Pegasus Quasar | Solar Wings Ltd |
| | G-MWFS | Solar Wings Pegasus XL-Q | A. McCredie |
| | G-MWFT | MBA Tiger Cub 440 | S. R. Giles |
| | G-MWFU | Quad City Challenger II UK | BFC (Aviation) Ltd |
| | G-MWFV | Quad City Challenger II UK | BFC (Aviation) Ltd |
| | G-MWFW | Rans S.4 | G. R. Hillary |
| | G-MWFX | Quad City Challenger II UK | I. M. Walton |
| | G-MWFY | Quad City Challenger II UK | P. J. Ladd |
| | G-MWFZ | Quad City Challenger II UK | A. Slade |
| | G-MWGA | Rans S.5 | M. A. C. Stephenson |
| | G-MWGB | Medway Hybred 44XLR | J. Nivison |
| | G-MWGC | Medway Hybred 44XLR | H. G. Martin |
| | G-MWGD | Medway Hybred 44XLR | D. Cassidy |
| | G-MWGE | Medway Hybred 44XLR | R. D. Homden |
| | G-MWGF | Renegade Spirit UK | J. A. Cuthbertson |
| | G-MWGG | Mainair Gemini Flash IIA | R. Potter |
| | G-MWGH | — | — |
| | G-MWGI | Whittaker MW.5 (K) Sorcerer | D. H. Griffin |
| | G-MWGJ | Whittaker MW.5 (K) Sorcerer | R. J. Freestone |
| | G-MWGK | Whittaker MW.5 (K) Sorcerer | J. A. Roberts (G-MWLV) |
| | G-MWGL | Solar Wings Pegasus XL-Q | C. E. Bell |
| | G-MWGM | Solar Wings Pegasus XL-Q | Wiltshire Microlight Centre |
| | G-MWGN | Rans S.4 | B. H. Ashman |
| | G-MWGO | Aerial Arts Chaser 110SX | B. Nicholson |
| | G-MWGP | Renegade Spirit UK | B. Bayley |
| | G-MWGR | Solar Wings Pegasus XL-Q | O. W. Achurch |
| | G-MWGS | Powerchute Kestrel | Powerchute Systems International Ltd |
| | G-MWGT | Powerchute Kestrel | Powerchute Systems International Ltd |
| | G-MWGU | Powerchute Kestrel | Powerchute Systems International Ltd |
| | G-MWGV | Powerchute Kestrel | Powerchute Systems International Ltd |
| | G-MWGW | Powerchute Kestrel | Powerchute Systems International Ltd |
| | G-MWGY | Powerchute Kestrel | Powerchute Systems International Ltd |
| | G-MWGZ | Powerchute Kestrel | Powerchute Systems International Ltd |
| | G-MWHC | Solar Wings Pegasus XL-Q | R. A. Rawes |
| | G-MWHD | Microflight Spectrum | E. J. Blyth |
| | G-MWHE | Microflight Spectrum | P. R. B. Truscott |
| | G-MWHF | Solar Wings Pegasus XL-Q | B. R. Underwood |
| | G-MWHG | Solar Wings Pegasus XL-Q | T. M. Cooper |
| | G-MWHH | Team Minimax | B. F. Crick |
| | G-MWHI | Mainair Gemini Flash IIA | R. E. D. Bailey |
| | G-MWHJ | Solar Wings Pegasus XL-Q | A. J. Bacon |
| | G-MWHK | Renegade Spirit UK | J. P. Leigh |
| | G-MWHL | Solar Wings Pegasus XL-Q | T. G. Jackson |
| | G-MWHM | Whittaker MW.6 Merlin | D. W. & M. L. Squire |

| Reg. | Type | Owner or Operator | Notes |
|------|------|-------------------|-------|
| G-MWHO | Mainair Gemini Flash IIA | A. W. Brandsom | |
| G-MWHP | Rans S.6 | J. F. Bickerstaffe | |
| G-MWHR | Mainair Gemini Flash IIA | S. K. Grzybowski | |
| G-MWHS | AMF Chevvron 232 | C. J. A. Porter | |
| G-MWHT | Solar Wings Pegasus Quasar | D. K. Ross | |
| G-MWHU | Solar Wings Pegasus Quasar | N. J. Pugh | |
| G-MWHV | Solar Wings Pegasus Quasar | M. A. Lee & E. Whittle | |
| G-MWHW | Solar Wings Pegasus XL-Q | A. Cox | |
| G-MWHX | Solar Wings Pegasus XL-Q | Swansea Air Sport | |
| G-MWHY | Mainair Gemini Flash IIA | A. G. Rossiter | |
| G-MWHZ | Trion J-1 | J. Wibberley | |
| G-MWIA | Mainair Gemini Flash IIA | J. Brewer | |
| G-MWIB | Aviasud Mistral | N. W. Finn-Kelcey | |
| G-MWIC | Whittaker MW.5 Sorcerer | I. P. Croft | |
| G-MWID | Solar Wings Pegasus XL-Q | A. J. Pike | |
| G-MWIE | Solar Wings Pegasus XL-Q | S. G. Taylor | |
| G-MWIF | Rans S.6 | M. G. K. Prout | |
| G-MWIG | Mainair Gemini Flash IIA | J. P. Witcher | |
| G-MWIH | Mainair Gemini Flash IIA | Mainair Sports Ltd | |
| G-MWII | Medway Hybred 44XLR | D. A. Bowdidge | |
| G-MWIJ | Medway Hybred 44XLR | L. Bartosik | |
| G-MWIK | Medway Hybred 44XLR | M. W. Whapham | |
| G-MWIL | Medway Hybred 44XLR | D. C. Fairbrass | |
| G-MWIM | Solar Wings Pegasus Quasar | E. C. Crellin & H. R. Bethune | |
| G-MWIN | Mainair Gemini Flash IIA | M. Lockyer | |
| G-MWIO | Rans S.4 | G. Ferguson | |
| G-MWIP | Whittaker MW.6 Merlin | D. Beer & B. J. Merrett | |
| G-MWIR | Solar Wings Pegasus XL-Q | J. S. Seddon-Harvey | |
| G-MWIS | Solar Wings Pegasus XL-Q | R. C. Trelease | |
| G-MWIT | Solar Wings Pegasus XL-Q | G. F. Ryland | |
| G-MWIU | Solar Wings Pegasus XL-Q | M. J. Mawle | |
| G-MWIV | Mainair Gemini Flash IIA | B. O'Grady | |
| G-MWIW | Solar Wings Pegasus Quasar | L. W. Evans | |
| G-MWIX | Solar Wings Pegasus Quasar | T. D. Neal | |
| G-MWIY | Solar Wings Pegasus Quasar | D. J. Payne | |
| G-MWIZ | CFM Shadow Srs BD | CFM Metal-Fax | |
| G-MWJB | — | | |
| G-MWJC | Solar Wings Pegasus Quasar | L. G. Vincent | |
| G-MWJD | Solar Wings Pegasus Quasar | A. J. Blackwell | |
| G-MWJF | CFM Shadow Srs BD | A. J. Briars | |
| G-MWJG | Solar Wings Pegasus XL-R | M. J. Piggott | |
| G-MWJH | Solar Wings Pegasus Quasar | A. W. Reed | |
| G-MWJI | Solar Wings Pegasus Quasar | B. J. Crockett | |
| G-MWJJ | Solar Wings Pegasus Quasar | G. R. & J. A. Pritchard | |
| G-MWJK | Solar Wings Pegasus Quasar | V. E. J. Smith | |
| G-MWJL | AMF Chevvron 232 | Chevron Microlight Tuition (Swansea) Ltd | |
| G-MWJM | AMF Chevvron 232 | BA Chevvron Group | |
| G-MWJN | Solar Wings Pegasus XL-Q | R. J. Williamson | |
| G-MWJO | Solar Wings Pegasus XL-Q | R. L. Gilmore | |
| G-MWJP | Medway Hybred 44XLR | A. Milton | |
| G-MWJR | Medway Hybred 44XLR | J. Stokes | |
| G-MWJS | Solar Wings Pegasus Quasar | N. C. Turner | |
| G-MWJT | Solar Wings Pegasus Quasar | T. D. Otho-Briggs | |
| G-MWJU | Solar Wings Pegasus Quasar | S. Baker | |
| G-MWJV | Solar Wings Pegasus Quasar | G. S. Cass | |
| G-MWJW | Whittaker MW.5 Sorcerer | J. D. Webb | |
| G-MWJX | Medway Puma Sprint | A. Tristram | |
| G-MWJY | Mainair Gemini Flash IIA | G. C. Hobson | |
| G-MWJZ | CFM Shadow Srs CD | C. C. I. Burnett | |
| G-MWKA | Renegade Spirit UK | Downlands Flying Group | |
| G-MWKB | Hornet R-ZA | Hornet Microlights Ltd | |
| G-MWKC | Hornet R-ZA | Hornet Microlights Ltd | |
| G-MWKD | Hornet R-ZA | Hornet Microlights Ltd | |
| G-MWKE | Hornet R-ZA | Hornet Microlights Ltd | |
| G-MWKF | Hornet R-ZA | Hornet Microlights Ltd | |
| G-MWKG | Hornet R-ZA | Hornet Microlights Ltd | |
| G-MWKH | Hornet R-ZA | Hornet Microlights Ltd | |
| G-MWKI | Hornet R-ZA | Hornet Microlights Ltd | |
| G-MWKJ | Hornet R-ZA | Hornet Microlights Ltd | |
| G-MWKK | Hornet R-ZA | Hornet Microlights Ltd | |
| G-MWKL | Hornet R-ZA | Hornet Microlights Ltd | |
| G-MWKM | Hornet R-ZA | Hornet Microlights Ltd | |

| Notes | Reg. | Type | Owner or Operator |
|---|---|---|---|
| | G-MWKN | Hornet R-ZA | Hornet Microlights Ltd |
| | G-MWKO | Solar Wings Pegasus XL-Q | M. A. Baldwin |
| | G-MWKP | Solar Wings Pegasus XL-Q | Solar Wings Ltd |
| | G-MWKR | Hornet R-ZA | Hornet Microlights Ltd |
| | G-MWKS | Hornet R-ZA | Hornet Microlights Ltd |
| | G-MWKT | Hornet R-ZA | Hornet Microlights Ltd |
| | G-MWKU | Hornet R-ZA | Hornet Microlights Ltd |
| | G-MWKV | Hornet R-ZA | Hornet Microlights Ltd |
| | G-MWKW | Microflight Spectrum | Corbett Farms Ltd |
| | G-MWKX | Microflight Spectrum | S. A. Clarehugh |
| | G-MWKY | Solar Wings Pegasus XL-Q | B. Allen |
| | G-MWKZ | Solar Wings Pegasus XL-Q | Steelform Fabrications (High Wycombe) Ltd |
| | G-MWLA | Rans S.4 | S. H. Williams |
| | G-MWLB | Medway Hybred 44XLR | E. Clarke |
| | G-MWLC | Medway Hybred 44XLR | G. J. Slater |
| | G-MWLD | CFM Shadow Srs BD | Tom Palmer (Scotland) Ltd |
| | G-MWLE | Solar Wings Pegasus XL-R | F. G. Bassill |
| | G-MWLF | Solar Wings Pegasus XL-R | Solar Wings Ltd |
| | G-MWLG | Solar Wings Pegasus XL-R | Solar Wings Ltd |
| | G-MWLH | Solar Wings Pegasus XL-R | S. Pluckrose |
| | G-MWLI | Solar Wings Pegasus Quasar | Solar Wings Ltd |
| | G-MWLJ | Solar Wings Pegasus Quasar | C. G. Rouse |
| | G-MWLK | Solar Wings Pegasus Quasar | A. W. Buchan |
| | G-MWLL | Solar Wings Pegasus XL-Q | Hereford Airsports Ltd |
| | G-MWLM | Solar Wings Pegasus XL-Q | R. J. Hawkins |
| | G-MWLN | Whittaker MW.6-S Fatboy Flyer | S. J. Field |
| | G-MWLO | Whittaker MW.6 Merlin | G. W. Peacock |
| | G-MWLP | Mainair Gemini Flash IIA | J. W. Harrison |
| | G-MWLR | Mainair Gemini Flash IIA | J. H. Bradbury |
| | G-MWLS | Medway Hybred 44XLR | Airbourne Aviation Ltd |
| | G-MWLT | Mainair Gemini Flash IIA | J. M. Coate |
| | G-MWLU | Solar Wings Pegasus XL-R | M. D. Morris |
| | G-MWLW | Team Minimax | W. T. Kirk |
| | G-MWLX | Mainair Gemini Flash IIA | W. G. Dent |
| | G-MWLY | Rans S.4 | A. Bulling |
| | G-MWLZ | Rans S.4 | T. E. G. Buckett |
| | G-MWMA | Powerchute Kestrel | Powerchute Systems International Ltd |
| | G-MWMB | Powerchute Kestrel | Powerchute Systems International Ltd |
| | G-MWMC | Powerchute Kestrel | Powerchute Systems International Ltd |
| | G-MWMD | Powerchute Kestrel | Powerchute Systems International Ltd |
| | G-MWME | Powerchute Kestrel | Powerchute Systems International Ltd |
| | G-MWMF | Powerchute Kestrel | Powerchute Systems International Ltd |
| | G-MWMG | Powerchute Kestrel | Powerchute Systems International Ltd |
| | G-MWMH | Powerchute Kestrel | Powerchute Systems International Ltd |
| | G-MWMI | Solar Wings Pegasus Quasar | A. Z. Saleem |
| | G-MWMJ | Solar Wings Pegasus Quasar | Solar Wings Ltd |
| | G-MWMK | Solar Wings Pegasus Quasar | Solar Wings Ltd |
| | G-MWML | Solar Wings Pegasus Quasar | Solar Wings Ltd |
| | G-MWMM | Mainair Gemini Flash IIA | M. R. Lovegrove |
| | G-MWMN | Solar Wings Pegasus XL-Q | S. A. Wemyss-Holden |
| | G-MWMO | Solar Wings Pegasus XL-Q | Solar Wings Ltd |
| | G-MWMP | Solar Wings Pegasus XL-Q | Solar Wings Ltd |
| | G-MWMR | Solar Wings Pegasus XL-R | Solar Wings Ltd |
| | G-MWMS | Mainair Gemini Flash | K. J. Cruikshank |
| | G-MWMT | Mainair Gemini Flash IIA | J. L. Wakefield |
| | G-MWMU | CFM Shadow Srs CD | D. Reeve |
| | G-MWMV | Solar Wings Pegasus XL-R | Solar Wings Ltd |
| | G-MWMW | Renegade Spirit UK | M. W. & J. C. Hanley |
| | G-MWMX | Mainair Gemini Flash IIA | G. H. & N. H. Kirk |
| | G-MWMY | Mainair Gemini Flash IIA | L. Elley |
| | G-MWMZ | Solar Wings Pegasus XL-Q | Solar Wings Ltd |
| | G-MWNA | Solar Wings Pegasus XL-Q | Solar Wings Ltd |
| | G-MWNB | Solar Wings Pegasus XL-Q | Solar Wings Ltd |
| | G-MWNC | Solar Wings Pegasus XL-Q | Solar Wings Ltd |
| | G-MWND | Tiger Cub Developments RL.5A | Tiger Cub Developments Ltd |
| | G-MWNE | Mainair Gemini Flash IIA | Mainair Sports Ltd |
| | G-MWNF | Renegade Spirit UK | D. J. White |
| | G-MWNG | Solar Wings Pegasus XL-Q | Solar Wings Ltd |
| | G-MWNH | – | – |
| | G-MWNI | – | – |
| | G-MWNJ | – | – |
| | G-MWNK | Solar Wings Pegasus Quasar | Solar Wings Ltd |

| Reg. | Type | Owner or Operator | Notes |
|------|------|-------------------|-------|
| G-MWNL | Solar Wings Pegasus Quasar | Solar Wings Ltd | |
| G-MWNM | Solar Wings Pegasus Quasar | Solar Wings Ltd | |
| G-MWNN | Solar Wings Pegasus Quasar | Solar Wings Ltd | |
| G-MWNO | AMF Chevvron 232 | R. W. Chatterton | |
| G-MWNP | AMF Chevvron 232 | D. G. Titterton | |
| G-MWNR | Renegade Spirit UK | RJR Flying Group | |
| G-MWNS | Mainair Gemini Flash IIA | M. A. Farr | |
| G-MWNT | Mainair Gemini Flash IIA | Mainair Sports Ltd | |
| G-MWNU | Mainair Gemini Flash IIA | P. J. Anderson | |
| G-MWNV | Powerchute Kestrel | Powerchute Systems International Ltd | |
| G-MWNW | Powerchute Kestrel | Powerchute Systems International Ltd | |
| G-MWNX | Powerchute Kestrel | Powerchute Systems International Ltd | |
| G-MWNY | Powerchute Kestrel | Powerchute Systems International Ltd | |
| G-MWNZ | Powerchute Kestrel | Powerchute Systems International Ltd | |
| G-MWOA | Powerchute Kestrel | Powerchute Systems International Ltd | |
| G-MWOB | Powerchute Kestrel | Powerchute Systems International Ltd | |
| G-MWOC | Powerchute Kestrel | Powerchute Systems International Ltd | |
| G-MWOD | Powerchute Kestrel | Powerchute Systems International Ltd | |
| G-MWOE | Powerchute Kestrel | Powerchute Systems International Ltd | |
| G-MWOF | Microflight Spectrum | P. R. B. Truscott | |
| G-MWOG | — | — | |
| G-MWOH | Solar Wings Pegasus XL-R | Solar Wings Ltd | |
| G-MWOI | Solar Wings Pegasus XL-R | Solar Wings Ltd | |
| G-MWOJ | Mainair Gemini Flash IIA | A. D. & J. S. Forster | |
| G-MWOK | Mainair Gemini Flash IIA | R. Stevenson | |
| G-MWOL | Mainair Gemini Flash IIA | I. V. Watters | |
| G-MWOM | — | — | |
| G-MWON | CFM Shadow Srs CD | J. S. Aspinwall | |
| G-MWOO | Renegade Spirit UK | A. Hipkin | |
| G-MWOP | Solar Wings Pegasus Quasar | Solar Wings Ltd | |
| G-MWOR | Solar Wings Pegasus XL-Q | Solar Wings Ltd | |
| G-MWOS | — | — | |
| G-MWOT | Icarus Covert Insertion & Recovery Vehicle | Icarus Aircraft Ltd | |
| G-MWOU | Medway Hybred 44XLR | Medway Microlights Ltd | |
| G-MWOV | — | — | |
| G-MWOW | CFM Shadow Srs B | Global Aviation Projects Ltd | |
| G-MWOX | — | — | |
| G-MWOY | — | — | |
| G-MWPL | MBA Tiger Cub 440 | P. A. Lee | |
| G-MWPR | Whittaker MW.6 Merlin | P. J. S. Ritchie | |
| G-MWPW | AMF Chevvron 232 | P. Wulff | |
| G-MWRS | Ultravia Super Pelican | Embermere Ltd | |
| G-MWTF | Mainair Gemini | G. D. C. Buyers | |
| G-MWVI | Whittaker MW.6 Merlin | B. H. & P. M. Gilmore | |
| G-MYAA | CFM Shadow Srs CD | M. L. Plant | |
| G-MYCC | Renegade Spirit UK | B. C. M. Collisson | |
| G-MYCD | CFM Shadow Srs CD | CITR Ltd | |
| G-MYDS | Quad City Challenger II UK | D. D. Smith | |
| G-MYGS | Whittaker MW.5 (K) Sorcerer | G. Stewart | |
| G-MYKE | CFM Shadow Srs BD | M. Hughes | |
| G-MYNA | CFM Shadow Srs BD | N. H. Martin | |
| G-MYPG | Solar Wings Pegasus XL-Q | P. Gibbs | |
| G-MYRK | Renegade Spirit UK | J. Brown | |
| G-MYST | Aviasud Mistral | M J. McBride | |
| G-MYTH | CFM Shadow Srs BD | E. G. Shimmin | |
| G-MZDP | AMF Chevvron 232 | AMF Microflight Ltd | |
| G-MZIP | Renegade Spirit UK | A. L. Nightingale & C. S. Warr | |
| G-MZOO | Renegade Spirit UK | T. Green | |
| G-MZRS | CFM Shadow Srs CD | M. P. Wilkinson | |
| G-MZZZ | Whitaker MW.6-S Fatboy Flyer | P. M. N. Richardson | |

| Serial carried | Civil identity | Serial carried | Civil identity |
|---|---|---|---|
| 2+1 (Luftwaffe) | G-SYFW | 430823 | N1042B |
| 8 (Luftwaffe) | G-WULF | 454467 (J-44 USAAF) | G-BILI |
| 14 (Luftwaffe) | G-BJAX | 454537 (J-04 USAAF) | G-BFDL |
| 23 (USAAC) | N49272 | 461748 | G-BHDK |
| 26 (US) | G-BAVO | 463221 (G4-5 USAAF) | N51JJ |
| 45 (Aeronavale) | G-BHFG | 472216 HO-L USAAF | G-BIXL |
| 75 | G-AFDX | 472773 (AJ-C USAF) | G-SUSY |
| 92 (Moroccan AF) | G-BJGW | 479766 (D-63 USAAF) | G-BKHG |
| 120 (Fr AF) | G-AZGC | 480015 (USAAF) | G-AKIB |
| 152/17 | G-ATJM | 480133 (B-44 USAAF) | G-BDCD |
| 157 (Fr AF) | G-AVEB | 480321 (H-44 USAAF) | G-FRAN |
| 168 | G-BFDE | 480480 (USAAF) | G-BECN |
| 177 (Irish AC) | G-BLIW | 483009 (USAF) | G-BPSE |
| 178 (Irish AC) | G-BKOS | 485784 (YB-E) | G-BEDF |
| 180 (USN) | G-BRSK | 41-33275 (USAAC CE) | G-BICE |
| 192 (Fr AF) | G-BKPT | 43-1952 (USAAC) | G-BRPR |
| 320 (USAAC) | G-BPMD | 44-30861 | N9089Z |
| 361 (USN) | G-ELAN | 44-30925 | N9494Z |
| 385 (RCAF) | G-BGPB | 44-79609 (PR USAAF) | G-BHXY |
| 422-15 | G-AVJO | 44-80594 (USAAF) | G-BEDJ |
| 425/17 | G-BEFR | 44-83184 | G-RGUS |
| 442 (USN) | G-BPTB | 45-49192 | N47DD |
| 542 | G-BPOB | 511371 (USAAF VF-S) | NL1051S |
| 671 (RCAF) | G-BNZC | 542447 | G-SCUB |
| 855 (USAAC) | N56421 | 542457 | G-LION |
| 1164 (USAAC) | G-BKGL | 542474 (R-184) | G-PCUB |
| 1420 (Polish AF) | G-BMZF | 51-15227 (USN) | G-BKRA |
| 2009 | G-BEFR | 51-15673 (USAF) | G-CUBI |
| 2345 | G-ATVP | 54-21261 (USAF) | N33VC |
| 2807 (VE-111 USN) | G-BHTH | 607327 (09-L USAAF) | G-ARAO |
| 3066 | G-AETA | A16-199 (SF-R RAAF) | G-BEOX |
| 3460 | G-BMFG | A8226 | G-BIDW |
| 3497 | G-BMFH | B1807 | G-EAVX |
| 4253/18 | G-BFPL | B4863 | G-BLXT |
| 5492 | G-PENY | B6291 | G-ASOP |
| 5894 | G-BFVH | B6401 | G-AWYY |
| 7198/18 | G-AANJ | B7270 | G-BFCZ |
| 7797 (USAAF) | G-BFAF | C1904 (Z) | G-PFAP |
| 8449M | G-ASWJ | C4994 | G-BLWM |
| 16693 (693 RCAF) | G-BLPG | D88 | G-AWXZ |
| 18393 (C.A.F.) | G-BCYK | D5397/17 | G-BFXL |
| 20385 (385 RCAF) | G-BGPB | D7889 | G-AANM |
| 31923 (USAAC) | G-BRHP | D8096 (D) | G-AEPH |
| 53319 (USN) | N3966A | E-15 (RNethAF) | G-BIYU |
| 54137 (USN 69) | G-CTKL | E3B-369 (781-32 Span AF) | G-BPDM |
| 56321 (U-AB RNorAF) | G-BKPY | E449 | G-EBJE |
| 88297 | N8297 | E6452 | G-AXNW |
| 88439 (USN) | N55JP | EM-01 (Spanish AF) | G-AAOR |
| 93542 (LTA-542 USAF) | G-BRLV | F141 | G-SEVA |
| 115042 (TA-042 USAF) | G-BGHU | F235 | G-BMDB |
| 115302 (TP USAAF) | G-BJTP | F904 | G-EBIA |
| 18-2001 (USAAF) | G-BIZV | F938 | G-EBIC |
| 121714 | NX700HL | F939 (6) | G-EBIB |
| 133722 | NX1337A | F943 | G-BIHF |
| 226671 (MX-X USAAF) | NX47DD | F943 | G-BKDT |
| 231983 (USAAF) | F-BDRS | F5447 (N) | G-BKER |
| 236800 (A-44 USAAF) | G-BHPK | F5459 | G-INNY |
| 315509 (USAAF) | G-BHUB | F8010 | G-BDWJ |
| 329417 (USAAF) | G-BDHK | F8614 | G-AWAU |
| 329471 (F-44 USAAF) | G-BGXA | G-48-1 (Class B) | G-ALSX |
| 329601 (D-44 USAAF) | G-AXHR | H2311 | G-ABAA |
| 329854 (A-72 USAAF) | G-BMKC | H5199 | G-ADEV |
| 329934 (B-72 USAAF) | G-BCPH | — (I-492 USAAC) | G-BPUD |
| 330485 (C-44 USAAF) | G-AJES | J-1605 (Swiss AF) | G-BLID |
| 343251 (USAAC) | G-NZSS | J-1758 (Swiss AF) | G-BLSD |
| 413048 (E-39 USAAF) | G-BCXJ | J9941 (57) | G-ABMR |
| 414151 (HO-M USAAF) | NL314BG | — (K-33 USAAF) | G-BJLH |
| 429366 (USAAF) | N9115Z | K1786 | G-AFTA |

| Serial carried | Civil identity | Serial carried | Civil identity |
|---|---|---|---|
| K1930 | G-BKBB | BW853 | G-BRKE |
| K2050 | G-ASCM | DE208 | G-AGYU |
| K2059 | G-PFAR | DE363 | G-ANFC |
| K2567 | G-MOTH | DE623 | G-ANFI |
| K2568 | G-APMM | DE992 | G-AXXV |
| K2572 | G-AOZH | DF128 (RCO-U) | G-AOJJ |
| K3215 | G-AHSA | DF155 | G-ANFV |
| K3731 | G-RODI | DF198 | G-BBRB |
| K4235 | G-AHMJ | DG590 | G-ADMW |
| K5414 (XV) | G-AENP | DR613 | G-AFJB |
| L2301 | G-AIZG | EM720 | G-AXAN |
| N1854 | G-AIBE | EM903 | G-APBI |
| N2308 (HP-B) | G-AMRK | EN224 | G-FXII |
| N4877 (VX-F) | G-AMDA | EX280 | G-TEAC |
| N5180 | G-EBKY | EZ259 | G-BMJW |
| N5182 | G-APUP | FE992 | G-BDAM |
| N5195 | G-ABOX | FH153 | G-BBHK |
| N6290 | G-BOCK | FR870 | NL1009N |
| N6452 | G-BIAU | FS728 | G-BAFM |
| N6466 | G-ANKZ | FT239 | G-BIWX |
| N6532 | G-ANTS | FT391 | G-AZBN |
| N6847 | G-APAL | FX301 (FD-NQ) | G-JUDI |
| N6848 | G-BALX | HB275 | N5063N |
| N6965 | G-AJTW | HB751 | G-BCBL |
| N6985 | G-AHMN | HM580 | G-ACUU |
| N9191 | G-ALND | JV928 (Y) | G-BLSC |
| N9238 | G-ANEL | KB889 | G-LANC |
| N9389 | G-ANJA | KB976 (LQ-K) | G-BCOH |
| N9510 | G-AOEL | KG874 (YS-L) | G-DAKS |
| P5865 (LE-W) | G-BKCK | KL161 | N88972 |
| P6382 | G-AJRS | KZ321 | G-HURY |
| R-163 (RNethAF) | G-BIRH | LB294 | G-AHWJ |
| R-167 (RNethAF) | G-LION | LB312 | G-AHXE |
| R1914 | G-AHUJ | LB375 | G-AHGW |
| R4907 | G-ANCS | LF858 | G-BLUZ |
| R4959 | G-ARAZ | LZ766 | G-ALCK |
| R5086 | G-APIH | MD497 | G-ANLW |
| S1287 | G-BEYB | MH434 | G-ASJV |
| S1579 | G-BBVO | MJ627 | G-BMSB |
| S3398 (2) | G-BFYO | MJ730 (HT-W) | G-HFIX |
| T5424 | G-AJOA | ML407 (OU-V) | G-LFIX |
| T5493 | G-ANEF | ML417 (2I-T) | G-BJSG |
| T5672 | G-ALRI | MP425 | G-AITB |
| T5854 | G-ANKK | MT438 | G-AREI |
| T5879 | G-AXBW | MT719 (YB-J) | G-VIII |
| T6099 | G-AOGR | MV154 | G-BKMI |
| T6313 | G-AHVU | MV363 | G-SPIT |
| T6645 | G-AIIZ | MV370 (AV-L) | G-FXIV |
| T6818 | G-ANKT | MW100 | G-AGNV |
| T7281 | G-ARTL | NF875 (603/CH) | G-AGTM |
| T7404 | G-ANMV | NH238 (D-A) | G-MKIX |
| T7909 | G-ANON | NJ695 | G-AJXV |
| T7997 | G-AOBH | NJ703 | G-AKPI |
| T9707 | G-AKKR | NJ719 | G-ANFU |
| T9738 | G-AKAT | NP181 | G-AOAR |
| U-0247 (Class B identity) | G-AGOY | NP184 | G-ANYP |
| U-142 (Swiss AF) | G-BONE | NP303 | G-ANZJ |
| V1075 | G-AKPF | NX611 | G-ASXX |
| V3388 | G-AHTW | NZ5628 | N240CA |
| V9281 (RU-M) | G-BCWL | PL983 | G-PRXI |
| V9300 | G-LIZY | PL985 | G-MKXI |
| V9441 (AR-A) | G-AZWT | PT462 | G-CTIX |
| W5856 | G-BMGC | PV202 | G-TRIX |
| Z2033 | G-ASTL | RG333 | G-AIEK |
| Z7015 | G-BKTH | RG333 | G-AKEZ |
| Z7197 | G-AKZN | RH377 | G-ALAH |
| Z7258 | G-AHGD | RL962 | G-AHED |
| Z7381 (XR-T) | G-HURI | RM221 | G-ANXR |
| AP507 (KX-P) | G-ACWP | RM689 (MN-E) | G-ALGT |
| AR213 (PR-D) | G-AIST | RN218 (N) | G-BBJI |
| AR501 (NN-D) | G-AWII | RR299 (HT-E) | G-ASKH |
| BM597 | G-MKVB | RT486 | G-AJGJ |
| BS676 (K-U) | G-KUKU | RT520 | G-ALYB |

| Serial carried | Civil identity | Serial carried | Civil identity |
|---|---|---|---|
| RW386 | G-BXVI | WT933 | G-ALSW |
| SM832 | G-WWII | WV198 | G-BJWY |
| SM969 | G-BRAF | WV493 | G-BDYG |
| SX336 | G-BRMG | WV686 | G-BLFT |
| TA634 (8K-K) | G-AWJV | WV740 | G-BNPH |
| TA719 | G-ASKC | WV783 | G-ALSP |
| TE566 | G-BLCK | WW397 (N-E) | G-BKHP |
| TJ569 | G-AKOW | WZ507 | G-VTII |
| TJ672 | G-ANIJ | WZ662 | G-BKVK |
| TS423 | G-DAKS | WZ711 | G-AVHT |
| TW439 | G-ANRP | WZ868 (H) | G-BCIW |
| TW467 | G-ANIE | WZ876 | G-BBWN |
| TW536 (TS-V) | G-BNGE | XB733 | G-ATBF |
| TW591 | G-ARIH | XF597 (AH) | G-BKFW |
| TW641 | G-ATDN | XF690 | G-BGKA |
| TX183 | G-BSMF | XF785 | G-ALBN |
| VF516 | G-ASMZ | XF836 (J-G) | G-AWRY |
| VF548 | G-ASEG | XF877 (JX) | G-AWVF |
| VL348 | G-AVVO | XG452 | G-BRMB |
| VL349 | G-AWSA | XG547 | G-HAPR |
| VM360 | G-APHV | XJ348 | G-NAVY |
| VP955 | G-DVON | XJ389 | G-AJJP |
| VP962 | G-BLRB | XJ763 | G-BKHA |
| VR192 | G-APIT | XK417 | G-AVXY |
| VR249 | G-APIY | XK482 | G-BJWC |
| VR259 | G-APJB | XK896 | G-RNAS |
| VS356 | G-AOLU | XL426 | G-VJET |
| VS610 | G-AOKL | XL502 | G-BMYP |
| VS623 | G-AOKZ | XL717 | G-AOXG |
| VX118 | G-ASNB | XL809 | G-BLIX |
| VZ728 | G-AGOS | XL929 | G-BNPU |
| WA576 | G-ALSS | XM553 | G-AWSV |
| WA577 | G-ALST | XM556 | G-HELI |
| WB531 | G-BLRN | XM575 | G-BLMC |
| WB585 (RCU-X) | G-AOSY | XM655 | G-VULC |
| WB588 (D) | G-AOTD | XM685 | G-AYZJ |
| WB660 | G-ARMB | XN351 | G-BKSC |
| WB703 | G-ARMC | XN435 | G-BGBU |
| WB763 | G-BBMR | XN437 | G-AXWA |
| WD286 (J) | G-BBND | XN441 | G-BGKT |
| WD305 | G-ARGG | XN637 | G-BKOU |
| WD363 (5) | G-BCIH | XP279 | G-BWKK |
| WD379 (K) | G-APLO | XP282 | G-BGTC |
| WD413 | G-BFIR | XP328 | G-BKHC |
| WE402 | G-VIDI | XP355 | G-BEBC |
| WE569 | G-ASAJ | XR240 | G-BDFH |
| WF877 | G-BPOA | XR241 | G-AXRR |
| WG307 | G-BCYJ | XR267 | G-BJXR |
| WG316 | G-BCAH | XR269 | G-BDXY |
| WG348 | G-BBMV | XR363 | G-OHCA |
| WG350 | G-BPAL | XR944 | G-ATTB |
| WG422 (16) | G-BFAX | XS101 | G-GNAT |
| WG472 | G-AOTY | XS451 | G-LTNG |
| WG719 | G-BRMA | XS452 (BT) | G-BPFE |
| WJ237 (113/O) | G-BLTG | XS587 | G-VIXN |
| WJ288 (029) | G-SALY | XT788 (442) | G-BMIR |
| WJ358 | G-ARYD | XW635 | G-AWSW |
| WJ945 | G-BEDV | +14 (Luftwaffe) | G-HUNN |
| WK522 | G-BCOU | 14+ (Luftwaffe) | G-BJAX |
| WK611 | G-ARWB | F+IS (Luftwaffe) | G-BIRW |
| WK622 | G-BCZH | BU+CK (Luftwaffe) | G-BUCK |
| WK628 | G-BBMW | CC+43 (Luftwaffe) | G-CJCI |
| WL626 | G-BHDD | 1Z+EK (Luftwaffe) | N9012P |
| WM167 | G-LOSM | LG+01 (Luftwaffe) | G-AYSJ |
| WP321 (750/CU) | G-BRFC | NJ+C11 (Luftwaffe) | G-ATBG |
| WP788 | G-BCHL | RF+16 (Luftwaffe) | G-PTWO |
| WP790 | G-BBNC | TA+RC (Luftwaffe) | G-BPHZ |
| WP800 (2) | G-BCXN | VK+AZ (Luftwaffe) | G-BFHG |
| WP808 | G-BDEU | ZA+WN (Luftwaffe) | G-AZMH |
| WP835 | G-BDCB | 6J+PR | G-AWHB |
| WP857 (24) | G-BDRJ | 97+04 (Luftwaffe) | G-APVF |
| WP903 | G-BCGC | ⓪ (Russian AF) | G-KYAK |
| WP971 | G-ATHD | — (Luftwaffe) | G-BOML |
| WP977 | G-BHRD | 146-11042 (7) | G-BMZX |
| WR410 (N) | G-BLKA | 146-11083 (5) | G-BNAI |

# Overseas Airliner Registrations

(Aircraft included in this section are those most likely to be seen at UK and major European airports on scheduled or charter services.)

## A6 (United Arab Emirates)

| Reg. | Type | Owner or Operator | Notes |
|---|---|---|---|
| A6-EKA | Airbus A.310-304 | Emirate Airlines | |
| A6-EKB | Airbus A.310-304 | Emirate Airlines | |
| A6-EKC | Airbus A.300-605R | Emirate Airlines | |
| A6-EKD | Airbus A.300-605R | Emirate Airlines | |
| A6-EKE | Airbus A.300-605R | Emirate Airlines | |
| A6-EKF | Airbus A.300-605R | Emirate Airlines | |

## A40 (Oman)

| | | | |
|---|---|---|---|
| A40-GF | Boeing 767-3P6ER (601) | Gulf Air | |
| A40-GG | Boeing 767-3P6ER (602) | Gulf Air | |
| A40-GH | Boeing 767-3P6ER (603) | Gulf Air | |
| A40-GI | Boeing 767-3P6ER (604) | Gulf Air | |
| A40-GJ | Boeing 767-3P6ER (605) | Gulf Air | |
| A40-GK | Boeing 767-3P6ER (606) | Gulf Air | |
| A40-GL | Boeing 767-3P6ER | Gulf Air | |
| A40-GM | Boeing 767-3P6ER | Gulf Air | |
| A40-GN | Boeing 767-3P6ER | Gulf Air | |
| A40-GO | Boeing 767-3P6ER | Gulf Air | |
| A40-GP | Boeing 767-3P6ER | Gulf Air | |
| A40-GR | Boeing 767-3P6ER | Gulf Air | |
| A40-TA | L-1011-385 TriStar 200 (105) | Gulf Air | |
| A40-TB | L-1011-385 TriStar 200 (106) | Gulf Air | |
| A40-TT | L-1011-385 TriStar 200 (107) | Gulf Air | |
| A40-TV | L-1011-385 TriStar 200 (108) | Gulf Air | |
| A40-TW | L-1011-385 TriStar 200 (101) | Gulf Air | |
| A40-TX | L-1011-385 TriStar 200 (102) | Gulf Air | |
| A40-TY | L-1011-385 TriStar 200 (103) | Gulf Air | |
| A40-TZ | L-1011-385 TriStar 200 (104) | Gulf Air | |

## AP (Pakistan)

| | | | |
|---|---|---|---|
| AP-AXA | Boeing 707-340C | Pakistan International Airlines | |
| AP-AXG | Boeing 707-340C | Pakistan International Airlines | |
| AP-AYV | Boeing 747-282B | Pakistan International Airlines | |
| AP-AYW | Boeing 747-282B | Pakistan International Airlines | |
| AP-AZW | Boeing 707-351B | Pakistan International Airlines | |
| AP-BAK | Boeing 747-240B (SCD) | Pakistan International Airlines | |
| AP-BAT | Boeing 747-240B (SCD) | Pakistan International Airlines | |
| AP-BBK | Boeing 707-323C | Pakistan International Airlines | |
| AP-BCL | Boeing 747-217B | Pakistan International Airlines | |
| AP-BCM | Boeing 747-217B | Pakistan International Airlines | |
| AP-BCN | Boeing 747-217B | Pakistan International Airlines | |
| AP-BCO | Boeing 747-217B | Pakistan International Airlines | |

## B (China/Taiwan)

| | | | |
|---|---|---|---|
| B-160 | Boeing 747-209F | China Airlines | |
| B-161 | Boeing 747-409 | China Airlines | |
| B-162 | Boeing 747-409 | China Airlines | |
| B-163 | Boeing 747-409 | China Airlines | |
| B-164 | Boeing 747-409 | China Airlines | |
| B-165 | Boeing 747-409 | China Airlines | |
| B-198 | Boeing 747-2R7F (SCD) | China Airlines | |
| B-1862 | Boeing 747SP-09 | China Airlines | |
| B-1864 | Boeing 747-209B (SCD) | China Airlines | |
| B-1866 | Boeing 747-209B | China Airlines | |
| B-1880 | Boeing 747SP-09 | China Airlines | |
| B-1886 | Boeing 747-209B | China Airlines | |
| B-1888 | Boeing 747-209B | China Airlines | |

| Notes | Reg. | Type | Owner or Operator |
|-------|------|------|-------------------|
| | B-1894 | Boeing 747-209F (SCD) | China Airlines |
| | B-2404 | Boeing 707-3J6B | CAAC/Air China |
| | B-2406 | Boeing 707-3J6B | CAAC/Air China |
| | B-2414 | Boeing 707-3J6C | CAAC/Air China |
| | B-2416 | Boeing 707-3J6C | CAAC/Air China |
| | B-2420 | Boeing 707-3J6C | CAAC/Air China |
| | B-2442 | Boeing 747SP-J6 | CAAC/Air China |
| | B-2444 | Boeing 747SP-J6 | CAAC/Air China |
| | B-2446 | Boeing 747-2J6B (SCD) | CAAC/Air China |
| | B-2448 | Boeing 747-2J6B (SCD) | CAAC/Air China |
| | B-2450 | Boeing 747-2J6B | CAAC/Air China |
| | B-2452 | Boeing 747SP-J6 | CAAC/Air China |
| | B-2454 | Boeing 747SP-27 | CAAC/Air China |
| | B-2456 | Boeing 747-4J6 | CAAC/Air China |
| | B-2458 | Boeing 747-4J6 | CAAC/Air China |
| | B-2460 | Boeing 747-4J6 | CAAC/Air China |
| | B-2462 | Boeing 747-2J6F | CAAC/Air China |

**Note:** China Airlines also operates N4508H and N4522V, both Boeing 747SP-09s.

# C5 (Gambia)

**Note:** Gambia Airways operates one DC-8-55 on lease.

# C9 (Mozambique)

| | | | |
|---|---|---|---|
| C9-BAE | Ilyushin IL-62M | | Linhas Aéreas de Mocambique (LAM) *Mozambique* |

**Note:** LAM also operates DC-10-30 F-GDJK on lease from UTA.

# C-F and C-G (Canada)

| | Reg. | Type | Owner or Operator |
|---|------|------|-------------------|
| | C-FBCA | Boeing 747-475 (883) | Canadian Airlines International |
| | C-FBEF | Boeing 767-233ER (617) | Air Canada |
| | C-FBEG | Boeing 767-233ER (618) | Air Canada |
| | C-FBEM | Boeing 767-233ER (619) | Air Canada |
| | C-FCAB | Boeing 767-375ER (631) | Canadian Airlines International |
| | C-FCAE | Boeing 767-375ER (632) | Canadian Airlines International |
| | C-FCAF | Boeing 767-375ER (633) | Canadian Airlines International |
| | C-FCAG | Boeing 767-375ER (634) | Canadian Airlines International |
| | C-FCAJ | Boeing 767-375ER (635) | Canadian Airlines International |
| | C-FCAU | Boeing 767-375ER (636) | Canadian Airlines International |
| | C-FCPO | Douglas DC-8-63 (801) | Worldways Canada |
| | C-FCPP | Douglas DC-8-63 (802) | Worldways Canada |
| | C-FCPQ | Douglas DC-8-63 (803) | Worldways Canada |
| | C-FCPS | Douglas DC-8-63 (804) | Worldways Canada |
| | C-FCRA | Boeing 747-475 (882) | Canadian Airlines International |
| | C-FCRB | Douglas DC-10-30 (910) | Canadian Airlines International *Empress of Tokyo* |
| | C-FCRD | Douglas DC-10-30 (912) | Canadian Airlines International *Empress of Lisbon* |
| | C-FCRE | Douglas DC-10-30 (911) | Canadian Airlines International *Empress of Canada* |
| | C-FCWW | Douglas DC-8-55F | ACS of Canada |
| | C-FDJC | Boeing 747-1D1 (399) | Nationair |
| | C-FDWW | Douglas DC-8-55F | ACS of Canada *Gilles Roudeau* |
| | C-FIWW | Douglas DC-8-55F | ACS of Canada |
| | C-FOCA | Boeing 767-375ER (640) | Canadian Airlines International |
| | C-FOOA | Boeing 757-28A | Canada 3000/Air 2000 (G-OOOA) |
| | C-FOOB | Boeing 757-28A | Canada 3000/Air 2000 (G-OOOB) |
| | C-FOOE | Boeing 757-28A | Canada 3000 Airlines |
| | C-FPCA | Boeing 767-375ER (637) | Canadian Airlines International |
| | C-FTCA | Boeing 767-375ER (638) | Canadian Airlines International |
| | C-FTIK | Douglas DC-8-73AF (867) | Air Canada |
| | C-FTIO | Douglas DC-8-73AF (871) | Air Canada |
| | C-FTIQ | Douglas DC-8-73AF (873) | Air Canada |
| | C-FTIR | Douglas DC-8-73AF (874) | Air Canada |
| | C-FTIS | Douglas DC-8-73AF (875) | Air Canada |

| Reg. | Type | Owner or Operator | Notes |
|------|------|-------------------|-------|
| C-FTNA | L.1011-385 TriStar 100 (501) | Air Transat | |
| C-FTNB | L.1011-385 TriStar 100 (549) | Air Transat | |
| C-FTNC | L.1011-385 TriStar 100 (503) | Air Transat | |
| C-FTOC | Boeing 747-133 (303) | Air Canada | |
| C-FTOD | Boeing 747-133 (304) | Air Canada | |
| C-FTOE | Boeing 747-133 (305) | Air Canada | |
| C-FXCA | Boeing 767-375ER (639) | Canadian Airlines International | |
| C-FXOD | Boeing 757-28A | Canada 3000/Air 2000 (G-OOOD) | |
| C-FXOF | Boeing 757-28A | Canada 3000 Airlines | |
| C-GAGA | Boeing 747-233B (SCD) (306) | Air Canada | |
| C-GAGB | Boeing 747-233B (SCD) (307) | Air Canada | |
| C-GAGC | Boeing 747-238B (SCD) (308) | Air Canada | |
| C-GAGF | L.1011-385 TriStar 500 (551) | Air Canada | |
| C-GAGG | L.1011-385 TriStar 500 (552) | Air Canada | |
| C-GAGH | L.1011-385 TriStar 500 (553) | Air Canada | |
| C-GAGI | L.1011-385 TriStar 500 (554) | Air Canada | |
| C-GAGJ | L.1011-385 TriStar 500 (555) | Air Canada | |
| C-GAGK | L.1011-385 TriStar 500 (556) | Air Canada | |
| C-GAUY | Boeing 767-233 (609) | Air Canada | |
| C-GAVA | Boeing 767-233 (610) | Air Canada | |
| C-GAVC | Boeing 767-233ER (611) | Air Canada | |
| C-GAVF | Boeing 767-233ER (612) | Air Canada | |
| C-GCPC | Douglas DC-10-30 (901) | Canadian Airlines International *Empress of Amsterdam* | |
| C-GCPD | Douglas DC-10-30 (902) | Canadian Airlines International *Empress of British Colombia* | |
| C-GCPE | Douglas DC-10-30ER (903) | Canadian Airlines International *Empress of Buenos Aires* | |
| C-GCPF | Douglas DC-10-30ER (904) | Canadian Airlines International *Empress of Santiago* | |
| C-GCPG | Douglas DC-10-30ER (905) | Canadian Airlines International *Empress of Fiji* | |
| C-GCPH | Douglas DC-10-30ER (906) | Canadian Airlines International *Empress of Lima* | |
| C-GCPI | Douglas DC-10-30ER (907) | Canadian Airlines International *Empress of Auckland* | |
| C-GCPJ | Douglas DC-10-30 (908) | Canadian Airlines International *Empress of Rome* | |
| C-GDSP | Boeing 767-233ER (613) | Air Canada | |
| C-GDSS | Boeing 767-233ER (614) | Air Canada | |
| C-GDSU | Boeing 767-233ER (615) | Air Canada | |
| C-GDSY | Boeing 767-233ER (616) | Air Canada | |
| C-GIES | L.1011-385 TriStar 50 (101) | Worldways Canada | |
| C-GIFE | L.1011-385 TriStar 50 (102) | Worldways Canada | |
| C-GLCA | Boeing 767-375ER | Canadian Airlines International | |
| C-GMWW | Boeing 747-475 (881) | Canadian Airlines International *Maxwell Ward* | |
| C- | Boeing 767-375ER | Canadian Airlines International | |
| C- | Boeing 767-375ER | Canadian Airlines International | |
| C-GMXB | Douglas DC-8-61 (801) | Nationair | |
| C-GMXD | Douglas DC-8-61 (805) | Nationair | |
| C-GMXL | Douglas DC-8-61 (808) | Nationair | |
| C-GMXQ | Douglas DC-8-61 (802) | Nationair | |
| C-GMXR | Douglas DC-8-62 (803) | Nationair | |
| C-GMXY | Douglas DC-8-62 (804) | Nationair | |
| C-GNXC | Boeing 757-28A (501) | Nationair | |
| C-GNXI | Boeing 757-28A (502) | Nationair | |
| C-G | Boeing 747-128 | Nationair | |
| C-GQBA | Douglas DC-8-63 (806) | Nationair | |
| C-GQBF | Douglas DC-8-63 (807) | Nationair | |
| C-GSCA | Boeing 767-375ER | Canadian Airlines International | |
| C-GTSZ | L.1011-385 TriStar 100 | Air Transat | |

**Note:** Airline fleet number carried on aircraft is shown in parenthesis.

# CCCP (Russia)

All aircraft listed are operated by Aeroflot. The registrations are prefixed by CCCP in each case.

| Notes | Reg. | Type | Notes | Reg. | Type |
|---|---|---|---|---|---|
| | 65020 | Tu-134A | | 65639 | Tu-134 |
| | 65024 | Tu-134A | | 65642 | Tu-134 |
| | 65027 | Tu-134A | | 65644 | Tu-134 |
| | 65028 | Tu-134A | | 65645 | Tu-134A |
| | 65035 | Tu-134A | | 65646 | Tu-134A |
| | 65036 | Tu-134A | | 65647 | Tu-134A |
| | 65038 | Tu-134A | | 65648 | Tu-134A |
| | 65040 | Tu-134A | | 65649 | Tu-134A |
| | 65042 | Tu-134A | | 65650 | Tu-134A |
| | 65044 | Tu-134A | | 65651 | Tu-134A |
| | 65048 | Tu-134A | | 65652 | Tu-134A |
| | 65049 | Tu-134A | | 65653 | Tu-134A |
| | 65050 | Tu-134A | | 65654 | Tu-134A |
| | 65051 | Tu-134A | | 65655 | Tu-134A |
| | 65064 | Tu-134A | | 65656 | Tu-134A |
| | 65072 | Tu-134A | | 65657 | Tu-134A |
| | 65073 | Tu-134A | | 65658 | Tu-134A |
| | 65076 | Tu-134A | | 65659 | Tu-134A |
| | 65077 | Tu-134A | | 65660 | Tu-134A |
| | 65079 | Tu-134A | | 65661 | Tu-134A |
| | 65087 | Tu-134A | | 65662 | Tu-134A |
| | 65089 | Tu-134A | | 65663 | Tu-134A |
| | 65107 | Tu-134A | | 65664 | Tu-134A |
| | 65119 | Tu-134A | | 65665 | Tu-134A |
| | 65134 | Tu-134A | | 65666 | Tu-134A |
| | 65135 | Tu-134A | | 65667 | Tu-134A |
| | 65139 | Tu-134A | | 65669 | Tu-134A |
| | 65145 | Tu-134A | | 65680 | Tu-134A-3 |
| | 65550 | Tu-134A | | 65692 | Tu-134-3 |
| | 65551 | Tu-134A | | 65697 | Tu-134A |
| | 65552 | Tu-134A-3 (VIP) | | 65710 | Tu-134A |
| | | | | 65717 | Tu-134A-3 |
| | 65553 | Tu-134A | | 65739 | Tu-134A |
| | 65554 | Tu-134A | | 65757 | Tu-134A |
| | 65555 | Tu-134A | | 65758 | Tu-134A |
| | 65601 | Tu-134 | | 65765 | Tu-134A |
| | 65602 | Tu-134 | | 65769 | Tu-134A-3 |
| | 65603 | Tu-134 | | 65770 | Tu-134A-3 |
| | 65604 | Tu-134 | | 65772 | Tu-134A |
| | 65605 | Tu-134 | | 65777 | Tu-134A-3 |
| | 65606 | Tu-134 | | 65780 | Tu-134A |
| | 65607 | Tu-134 | | 65781 | Tu-134A-3 |
| | 65608 | Tu-134 | | 65782 | Tu-134A |
| | 65609 | Tu-134 | | 65783 | Tu-134A-3 |
| | 65610 | Tu-134 | | 65784 | Tu-134A-3 |
| | 65611 | Tu-134 | | 65785 | Tu-134A-3 |
| | 65612 | Tu-134 | | 65786 | Tu-134A-3 |
| | 65613 | Tu-134 | | 65790 | Tu-134A-3 |
| | 65614 | Tu-134 | | 65791 | Tu-134A |
| | 65615 | Tu-134 | | 65794 | Tu-134A |
| | 65616 | Tu-134 | | 65801 | Tu-134A |
| | 65617 | Tu-134 | | 65802 | Tu-134A |
| | 65618 | Tu-134 | | 65815 | Tu-134A |
| | 65619 | Tu-134 | | 65835 | Tu-134A |
| | 65620 | Tu-134 | | 65837 | Tu-134A |
| | 65621 | Tu-134 | | 65851 | Tu-134A |
| | 65625 | Tu-134 | | 65854 | Tu-134A |
| | 65627 | Tu-134 | | 65862 | Tu-134A |
| | 65628 | Tu-134 | | 65864 | Tu-134A |
| | 65629 | Tu-134 | | 65872 | Tu-134A |
| | 65630 | Tu-134 | | 65888 | Tu-134A |
| | 65631 | Tu-134 | | 65891 | Tu-134A |
| | 65632 | Tu-134 | | 65892 | Tu-134A |
| | 65633 | Tu-134 | | 65893 | Tu-134A |
| | 65634 | Tu-134 | | 65894 | Tu-134A |
| | 65635 | Tu-134 | | 65904 | Tu-134A |
| | 65636 | Tu-134 | | 65905 | Tu-134A-3 |
| | 65637 | Tu-134 | | 65911 | Tu-134A-3 |

| Reg. | Type | Notes | Reg. | Type | Notes |
|------|------|-------|------|------|-------|
| 65912 | Tu-134A-3 | | 85064 | Tu-154A | |
| 65916 | Tu-134A | | 65072 | Tu-134A | |
| 65919 | Tu-134A | | 65073 | Tu-134A | |
| 65921 | Tu-134A-3 | | 85065 | Tu-154A | |
| 65923 | Tu-134A | | 85066 | Tu-154A | |
| 65926 | Tu-134A | | 85067 | Tu-154C | |
| 65935 | Tu-134A | | 85068 | Tu-154B | |
| 65939 | Tu-134A | | 85069 | Tu-154A | |
| 65951 | Tu-134A | | 85070 | Tu-154A | |
| 65953 | Tu-134A | | 85071 | Tu-154A | |
| 65954 | Tu-134A | | 85072 | Tu-154A | |
| 65955 | Tu-134A | | 85074 | Tu-154A | |
| 65956 | Tu-134A | | 85075 | Tu-154B | |
| 65965 | Tu-134A | | 85076 | Tu-154A | |
| 65967 | Tu-134A-3 | | 85078 | Tu-154A | |
| 65971 | Tu-134A | | 85079 | Tu-154A | |
| 65972 | Tu-134A | | 85080 | Tu-154A | |
| 65973 | Tu-134A | | 85081 | Tu-154C | |
| 65974 | Tu-134A | | 85082 | Tu-154A | |
| 65976 | Tu-134A | | 85083 | Tu-154A | |
| | | | 85084 | Tu-154A | |
| 85001 | Tu-154 | | 85085 | Tu-154A | |
| 85002 | Tu-154 | | 85086 | Tu-154A | |
| 85003 | Tu-154 | | 85087 | Tu-154A | |
| 85004 | Tu-154 | | 85088 | Tu-154A | |
| 85005 | Tu-154 | | 85089 | Tu-154A | |
| 85006 | Tu-154 | | 85090 | Tu-154A | |
| 85007 | Tu-154 | | 85091 | Tu-154A | |
| 85008 | Tu-154 | | 85092 | Tu-154B-1 | |
| 85009 | Tu-154 | | 85093 | Tu-154A | |
| 85010 | Tu-154 | | 85094 | Tu-154A | |
| 85011 | Tu-154 | | 85096 | Tu-154B-2 | |
| 85012 | Tu-154 | | 85097 | Tu-154B-1 | |
| 85013 | Tu-154 | | 85098 | Tu-154A | |
| 85014 | Tu-154 | | 85099 | Tu-154A | |
| 85015 | Tu-154 | | 85100 | Tu-154A | |
| 85016 | Tu-154 | | 85101 | Tu-154A | |
| 85017 | Tu-154 | | 85103 | Tu-154A | |
| 85018 | Tu-154 | | 85104 | Tu-154A | |
| 85019 | Tu-154 | | 85105 | Tu-154A | |
| 85020 | Tu-154 | | 85106 | Tu-154B-2 | |
| 85021 | Tu-154 | | 85107 | Tu-154A | |
| 85022 | Tu-154 | | 85108 | Tu-154A | |
| 85024 | Tu-154 | | 85109 | Tu-154B-1 | |
| 85025 | Tu-154B-2 | | 85110 | Tu-154A | |
| 85028 | Tu-154B | | 85111 | Tu-154A | |
| 85029 | Tu-154 | | 85112 | Tu-154A | |
| 85030 | Tu-154 | | 85113 | Tu-154A | |
| 85031 | Tu-154 | | 85114 | Tu-154A | |
| 85032 | Tu-154 | | 85115 | Tu-154A | |
| 85033 | Tu-154B | | 85116 | Tu-154A | |
| 85034 | Tu-154 | | 85117 | Tu-154A | |
| 85035 | Tu-154 | | 85118 | Tu-154B | |
| 85037 | Tu-154 | | 85119 | Tu-154A | |
| 85038 | Tu-154 | | 85120 | Tu-154B | |
| 85039 | Tu-154 | | 85121 | Tu-154B | |
| 85040 | Tu-154 | | 85122 | Tu-154B | |
| 85041 | Tu-154 | | 85123 | Tu-154B | |
| 85042 | Tu-154 | | 85124 | Tu-154B | |
| 85043 | Tu-154 | | 85125 | Tu-154B | |
| 85044 | Tu-154 | | 85129 | Tu-154B | |
| 85049 | Tu-154 | | 85130 | Tu-154B | |
| 85050 | Tu-154 | | 85131 | Tu-154B | |
| 85051 | Tu-154 | | 85132 | Tu-154B | |
| 85052 | Tu-154 | | 85133 | Tu-154B | |
| 85055 | Tu-154 | | 85134 | Tu-154B | |
| 85056 | Tu-154 | | 85135 | Tu-154B | |
| 85057 | Tu-154 | | 85136 | Tu-154B | |
| 85059 | Tu-154A | | 85137 | Tu-154B | |
| 85060 | Tu-154A | | 85138 | Tu-154B | |
| 85061 | Tu-154A | | 85139 | Tu-154B | |
| 85062 | Tu-154C | | 85140 | Tu-154B | |
| 85063 | Tu-154C | | 85141 | Tu-154B | |

| Notes | Reg. | Type | Notes | Reg. | Type |
|-------|------|------|-------|------|------|
| | 85142 | Tu-154B | | 85221 | Tu-154B |
| | 85143 | Tu-154B | | 85222 | Tu-154B |
| | 85145 | Tu-154B | | 85223 | Tu-154B |
| | 85146 | Tu-154B | | 85226 | Tu-154B |
| | 85147 | Tu-154B | | 85227 | Tu-154B |
| | 85148 | Tu-154B | | 85228 | Tu-154B |
| | 85149 | Tu-154B | | 85229 | Tu-154B-1 |
| | 85150 | Tu-154B | | 85230 | Tu-154B-1 |
| | 85151 | Tu-154B | | 85231 | Tu-154B-1 |
| | 85152 | Tu-154B | | 85232 | Tu-154B-1 |
| | 85153 | Tu-154B | | 85233 | Tu-154B-1 |
| | 85154 | Tu-154B | | 85234 | Tu-154B-1 |
| | 85155 | Tu-154B | | 85235 | Tu-154B-1 |
| | 85156 | Tu-154B | | 85236 | Tu-154B-1 |
| | 85157 | Tu-154B | | 85237 | Tu-154B-1 |
| | 85158 | Tu-154B | | 85238 | Tu-154B-1 |
| | 85160 | Tu-154B | | 85240 | Tu-154B-1 |
| | 85162 | Tu-154B | | 85241 | Tu-154B-1 |
| | 85163 | Tu-154B | | 85242 | Tu-154B-1 |
| | 85164 | Tu-154B | | 85243 | Tu-154B-1 |
| | 85165 | Tu-154B | | 85244 | Tu-154B-1 |
| | 85166 | Tu-154B | | 85245 | Tu-154B-1 |
| | 85167 | Tu-154B | | 85246 | Tu-154B-1 |
| | 85168 | Tu-154B | | 85247 | Tu-154B-1 |
| | 85169 | Tu-154B | | 85248 | Tu-154B-1 |
| | 85170 | Tu-154B | | 85249 | Tu-154B-1 |
| | 85171 | Tu-154B | | 85250 | Tu-154B-1 |
| | 85172 | Tu-154B | | 85251 | Tu-154B-1 |
| | 85173 | Tu-154B | | 85252 | Tu-154B-1 |
| | 85174 | Tu-154B | | 85253 | Tu-154B-1 |
| | 85176 | Tu-154B | | 85255 | Tu-154B-1 |
| | 85177 | Tu-154B | | 85256 | Tu-154B-1 |
| | 85178 | Tu-154B | | 85257 | Tu-154B-1 |
| | 85179 | Tu-154B | | 85259 | Tu-154B-1 |
| | 85180 | Tu-154B | | 85260 | Tu-154B-1 |
| | 85181 | Tu-154B | | 85261 | Tu-154B-1 |
| | 85182 | Tu-154B | | 85263 | Tu-154B-1 |
| | 85183 | Tu-154B | | 85264 | Tu-154B-1 |
| | 85184 | Tu-154B | | 85265 | Tu-154B-1 |
| | 85185 | Tu-154B | | 85266 | Tu-154B-1 |
| | 85186 | Tu-154B | | 85267 | Tu-154B-1 |
| | 85187 | Tu-154B | | 85268 | Tu-154B-1 |
| | 85188 | Tu-154B | | 85269 | Tu-154B-1 |
| | 85189 | Tu-154B | | 85270 | Tu-154B-1 |
| | 85190 | Tu-154B | | 85271 | Tu-154B-1 |
| | 85191 | Tu-154B | | 85272 | Tu-154B-1 |
| | 85192 | Tu-154B | | 85273 | Tu-154B-1 |
| | 85193 | Tu-154B | | 85274 | Tu-154B-1 |
| | 85194 | Tu-154B | | 85275 | Tu-154B-1 |
| | 85195 | Tu-154B | | 85276 | Tu-154B-1 |
| | 85196 | Tu-154B | | 85277 | Tu-154B-1 |
| | 85197 | Tu-154B | | 85279 | Tu-154B-1 |
| | 85198 | Tu-154B | | 85280 | Tu-154B-1 |
| | 85199 | Tu-154B | | 85281 | Tu-154B-1 |
| | 85200 | Tu-154B | | 85282 | Tu-154B-1 |
| | 85201 | Tu-154B | | 85283 | Tu-154B-1 |
| | 85202 | Tu-154B | | 85284 | Tu-154B-1 |
| | 85203 | Tu-154B | | 85285 | Tu-154B-1 |
| | 85204 | Tu-154B | | 85286 | Tu-154B-1 |
| | 85205 | Tu-154B | | 85287 | Tu-154B-1 |
| | 85206 | Tu-154B | | 85288 | Tu-154B-1 |
| | 85207 | Tu-154B | | 85289 | Tu-154B-1 |
| | 85210 | Tu-154B | | 85290 | Tu-154B-1 |
| | 85211 | Tu-154B | | 85291 | Tu-154B-1 |
| | 85212 | Tu-154B | | 85292 | Tu-154B-2 |
| | 85213 | Tu-154B | | 85293 | Tu-154B-1 |
| | 85214 | Tu-154B | | 85294 | Tu-154B-1 |
| | 85215 | Tu-154B | | 85295 | Tu-154B-1 |
| | 85216 | Tu-154B | | 85296 | Tu-154B-1 |
| | 85217 | Tu-154B | | 85297 | Tu-154B-1 |
| | 85218 | Tu-154B | | 85298 | Tu-154B-1 |
| | 85219 | Tu-154B | | 85299 | Tu-154B-1 |
| | 85220 | Tu-154B | | 85300 | Tu-154B-2 |
| | | | | 85301 | Tu-154B-2 |

| Reg. | Type | Notes | Reg. | Type | Notes |
|------|------|-------|------|------|-------|
| 85302 | Tu-154B-2 | | 85380 | Tu-154B-2 | |
| 85303 | Tu-154B-2 | | 85381 | Tu-154B-2 | |
| 85304 | Tu-154B-2 | | 85382 | Tu-154B-2 | |
| 85305 | Tu-154B-2 | | 85383 | Tu-154B-2 | |
| 85306 | Tu-154B-2 | | 85384 | Tu-154B-2 | |
| 85307 | Tu-154B-2 | | 85385 | Tu-154B-2 | |
| 85308 | Tu-154B-2 | | 85386 | Tu-154B-2 | |
| 85309 | Tu-154B-2 | | 85387 | Tu-154B-2 | |
| 85310 | Tu-154B-2 | | 85388 | Tu-154B-2 | |
| 85311 | Tu-154B-2 | | 85389 | Tu-154B-2 | |
| 85312 | Tu-154B-2 | | 85390 | Tu-154B-2 | |
| 85313 | Tu-154B-2 | | 85391 | Tu-154B-2 | |
| 85314 | Tu-154B-2 | | 85392 | Tu-154B-2 | |
| 85315 | Tu-154B-2 | | 85393 | Tu-154B-2 | |
| 85316 | Tu-154B-2 | | 85394 | Tu-154B-2 | |
| 85317 | Tu-154M | | 85395 | Tu-154B-2 | |
| 85318 | Tu-154B-2 | | 85396 | Tu-154B-2 | |
| 85319 | Tu-154B-2 | | 85397 | Tu-154B-2 | |
| 85321 | Tu-154B-2 | | 85398 | Tu-154B-2 | |
| 85322 | Tu-154B-2 | | 85399 | Tu-154B-2 | |
| 85323 | Tu-154B-2 | | 85400 | Tu-154B-2 | |
| 85324 | Tu-154B-2 | | 85401 | Tu-154B-2 | |
| 85327 | Tu-154B-2 | | 85402 | Tu-154B-2 | |
| 85328 | Tu-154B-2 | | 85403 | Tu-154B-2 | |
| 85329 | Tu-154B-2 | | 85404 | Tu-154B-2 | |
| 85330 | Tu-154B-2 | | 85405 | Tu-154B-2 | |
| 85331 | Tu-154B-2 | | 85406 | Tu-154B-2 | |
| 85332 | Tu-154B-2 | | 85407 | Tu-154B-2 | |
| 85333 | Tu-154B-2 | | 85409 | Tu-154B-2 | |
| 85334 | Tu-154B-2 | | 85410 | Tu-154B-2 | |
| 85335 | Tu-154B-2 | | 85411 | Tu-154B-2 | |
| 85336 | Tu-154B-2 | | 85412 | Tu-154B-2 | |
| 85337 | Tu-154B-2 | | 85414 | Tu-154B-2 | |
| 85338 | Tu-154B-2 | | 85416 | Tu-154B-2 | |
| 85339 | Tu-154B-2 | | 85417 | Tu-154B-2 | |
| 85340 | Tu-154B-2 | | 85418 | Tu-154B-2 | |
| 85341 | Tu-154B-2 | | 85419 | Tu-154B-2 | |
| 85343 | Tu-154B-2 | | 85421 | Tu-154B-2 | |
| 85344 | Tu-154B-2 | | 85423 | Tu-154B-2 | |
| 85345 | Tu-154B-2 | | 85424 | Tu-154B-2 | |
| 85346 | Tu-154B-2 | | 85425 | Tu-154B-2 | |
| 85347 | Tu-154B-2 | | 85426 | Tu-154B-2 | |
| 85348 | Tu-154B-2 | | 85427 | Tu-154B-2 | |
| 85349 | Tu-154B-2 | | 85429 | Tu-154B-2 | |
| 85350 | Tu-154B-2 | | 85430 | Tu-154B-2 | |
| 85351 | Tu-154B-2 | | 85431 | Tu-154B-2 | |
| 85352 | Tu-154B-2 | | 85432 | Tu-154B-2 | |
| 85353 | Tu-154B-2 | | 85433 | Tu-154B-2 | |
| 85354 | Tu-154B-2 | | 85434 | Tu-154B-2 | |
| 85355 | Tu-154B-2 | | 85435 | Tu-154B-2 | |
| 85356 | Tu-154B-2 | | 85436 | Tu-154B-2 | |
| 85357 | Tu-154B-2 | | 85437 | Tu-154B-2 | |
| 85358 | Tu-154B-2 | | 85438 | Tu-154B-2 | |
| 85359 | Tu-154B-2 | | 85439 | Tu-154B-2 | |
| 85360 | Tu-154B-2 | | 85440 | Tu-154B-2 | |
| 85361 | Tu-154B-2 | | 85441 | Tu-154B-2 | |
| 85362 | Tu-154B-2 | | 85442 | Tu-154B-2 | |
| 85363 | Tu-154B-2 | | 85443 | Tu-154B-2 | |
| 85364 | Tu-154B-2 | | 85444 | Tu-154B-2 | |
| 85365 | Tu-154B-2 | | 85445 | Tu-154B-2 | |
| 85366 | Tu-154B-2 | | 85446 | Tu-154B-2 | |
| 85367 | Tu-154B-2 | | 85448 | Tu-154B-2 | |
| 85368 | Tu-154B-2 | | 85449 | Tu-154B-2 | |
| 85369 | Tu-154B-2 | | 85450 | Tu-154B-2 | |
| 85370 | Tu-154B-2 | | 85451 | Tu-154B-2 | |
| 85371 | Tu-154B-2 | | 85452 | Tu-154B-2 | |
| 85372 | Tu-154B-2 | | 85453 | Tu-154B-2 | |
| 85373 | Tu-154B-2 | | 85454 | Tu-154B-2 | |
| 85374 | Tu-154B-2 | | 85455 | Tu-154B-2 | |
| 85375 | Tu-154B-2 | | 85456 | Tu-154B-2 | |
| 85376 | Tu-154B-2 | | 85457 | Tu-154B-2 | |
| 85377 | Tu-154B-2 | | 85458 | Tu-154B-2 | |
| 85378 | Tu-154B-2 | | | | |
| 85379 | Tu-154B-2 | | | | |

| Notes | Reg. | Type | Notes | Reg. | Type |
|-------|------|------|-------|------|------|
| | 85459 | Tu-154B-2 | | 85540 | Tu-154B-2 |
| | 85460 | Tu-154B-2 | | 85542 | Tu-154B-2 |
| | 85461 | Tu-154B-2 | | 85545 | Tu-154B-2 |
| | 85462 | Tu-154B-2 | | 85546 | Tu-154B-2 |
| | 85463 | Tu-154B-2 | | 85547 | Tu-154B-2 |
| | 85464 | Tu-154B-2 | | 85548 | Tu-154B-2 |
| | 85465 | Tu-154B-2 | | 85549 | Tu-154B-2 |
| | 85466 | Tu-154B-2 | | 85550 | Tu-154B-2 |
| | 85467 | Tu-154B-2 | | 85551 | Tu-154B-2 |
| | 85468 | Tu-154B-2 | | 85552 | Tu-154B-2 |
| | 85469 | Tu-154B-2 | | 85553 | Tu-154B-2 |
| | 85470 | Tu-154B-2 | | 85554 | Tu-154B-2 |
| | 85471 | Tu-154B-2 | | 85555 | Tu-154B-2 |
| | 85472 | Tu-154B-2 | | 85556 | Tu-154B-2 |
| | 85475 | Tu-154B-2 | | 85557 | Tu-154B-2 |
| | 85476 | Tu-154B-2 | | 85558 | Tu-154B-2 |
| | 85477 | Tu-154B-2 | | 85559 | Tu-154B-2 |
| | 85478 | Tu-154B-2 | | 85560 | Tu-154B-2 |
| | 85479 | Tu-154B-2 | | 85561 | Tu-154B-2 |
| | 85480 | Tu-154B-2 | | 85562 | Tu-154B-2 |
| | 85481 | Tu-154B-2 | | 85563 | Tu-154B-2 |
| | 85482 | Tu-154B-2 | | 85565 | Tu-154B-2 |
| | 85485 | Tu-154B-2 | | 85566 | Tu-154B-2 |
| | 85486 | Tu-154B-2 | | 85567 | Tu-154B-2 |
| | 85487 | Tu-154B-2 | | 85568 | Tu-154B-2 |
| | 85489 | Tu-154B-2 | | 85570 | Tu-154B-2 |
| | 85490 | Tu-154B-2 | | 85571 | Tu-154B-2 |
| | 85491 | Tu-154B-2 | | 85572 | Tu-154B-2 |
| | 85492 | Tu-154B-2 | | 85573 | Tu-154B-2 |
| | 85494 | Tu-154B-2 | | 85574 | Tu-154B-2 |
| | 85495 | Tu-154B-2 | | 85575 | Tu-154B-2 |
| | 85496 | Tu-154B-2 | | 85577 | Tu-154B-2 |
| | 85497 | Tu-154B-2 | | 85578 | Tu-154B-2 |
| | 85498 | Tu-154B-2 | | 85579 | Tu-154B-2 |
| | 85499 | Tu-154B-2 | | 85580 | Tu-154B-2 |
| | 85500 | Tu-154B-2 | | 85581 | Tu-154B-2 |
| | 85501 | Tu-154B-2 | | 85582 | Tu-154B-2 |
| | 85502 | Tu-154B-2 | | 85583 | Tu-154B-2 |
| | 85503 | Tu-154B-2 | | 85584 | Tu-154B-2 |
| | 85504 | Tu-154B-2 | | 85585 | Tu-154B-2 |
| | 85505 | Tu-154B-2 | | 85586 | Tu-154B-2 |
| | 85506 | Tu-154B-2 | | 85587 | Tu-154B-2 |
| | 85507 | Tu-154B-2 | | 85588 | Tu-154B-2 |
| | 85508 | Tu-154B-2 | | 85589 | Tu-154B-2 |
| | 85509 | Tu-154B-2 | | 85590 | Tu-154B-2 |
| | 85510 | Tu-154B-2 | | 85591 | Tu-154B-2 |
| | 85511 | Tu-154B-2 | | 85592 | Tu-154B-2 |
| | 85512 | Tu-154B-2 | | 85593 | Tu-154B-2 |
| | 85513 | Tu-154B-2 | | 85594 | Tu-154B-2 |
| | 85514 | Tu-154B-2 | | 85595 | Tu-154B-2 |
| | 85515 | Tu-154B-2 | | 85596 | Tu-154B-2 |
| | 85516 | Tu-154B-2 | | 85597 | Tu-154B-2 |
| | 85518 | Tu-154B-2 | | 85598 | Tu-154B-2 |
| | 85519 | Tu-154B-2 | | 85600 | Tu-154B-2 |
| | 85520 | Tu-154B-2 | | 85601 | Tu-154B-2 |
| | 85521 | Tu-154B-2 | | 85602 | Tu-154B-2 |
| | 85522 | Tu-154B-2 | | 85603 | Tu-154B-2 |
| | 85523 | Tu-154B-2 | | 85604 | Tu-154B-2 (VIP) |
| | 85524 | Tu-154B-2 | | 85605 | Tu-154B-2 |
| | 85525 | Tu-154C-2 | | 85606 | Tu-154B-2 |
| | 85526 | Tu-154B-2 | | 85607 | Tu-154B-2 |
| | 85527 | Tu-154B-2 | | 85608 | Tu-154B-2 |
| | 85528 | Tu-154B-2 | | 85609 | Tu-154M |
| | 85529 | Tu-154B-2 | | 85610 | Tu-154M |
| | 85530 | Tu-154B-2 | | 85611 | Tu-154M |
| | 85532 | Tu-154B-2 | | 85612 | Tu-154M |
| | 85533 | Tu-154B-2 | | 85613 | Tu-154M |
| | 85534 | Tu-154B-2 | | 85614 | Tu-154M |
| | 85535 | Tu-154B-2 | | 85615 | Tu-154M |
| | 85536 | Tu-154B-2 | | 85616 | Tu-154M |
| | 85537 | Tu-154B-2 | | 85617 | Tu-154M |
| | 85538 | Tu-154B-2 | | 85618 | Tu-154M |
| | 85539 | Tu-154B-2 | | 85619 | Tu-154M |
| | | | | 85621 | Tu-154M |

| Reg. | Type | Notes | Reg. | Type | Notes |
|------|------|-------|------|------|-------|
| 85622 | Tu-154M | | 86003 | IL-86 | |
| 85623 | Tu-154M | | 86004 | IL-86 | |
| 85624 | Tu-154M | | 86005 | IL-86 | |
| 85625 | Tu-154M | | 86006 | IL-86 | |
| 85626 | Tu-154M | | 86007 | IL-86 | |
| 85627 | Tu-154M | | 86008 | IL-86 | |
| 85628 | Tu-154M | | 86009 | IL-86 | |
| 85629 | Tu-154M | | 86010 | IL-86 | |
| 85630 | Tu-154M | | 86011 | IL-86 | |
| 85631 | Tu-154M | | 86012 | IL-86 | |
| 85632 | Tu-154M | | 86013 | IL-86 | |
| 85633 | Tu-154M | | 86014 | IL-86 | |
| 85634 | Tu-154M | | 86015 | IL-86 | |
| 85635 | Tu-154M | | 86016 | IL-86 | |
| 85636 | Tu-154M | | 86017 | IL-86 | |
| 85637 | Tu-154M | | 86018 | IL-86 | |
| 85638 | Tu-154M | | 86050 | IL-86 | |
| 85639 | Tu-154M | | 86051 | IL-86 | |
| 85640 | Tu-154M | | 86052 | IL-86 | |
| 85641 | Tu-154M | | 86053 | IL-86 | |
| 85642 | Tu-154M | | 86054 | IL-86 | |
| 85643 | Tu-154M | | 86055 | IL-86 | |
| 85644 | Tu-154M | | 86056 | IL-86 | |
| 85645 | Tu-154M | | 86057 | IL-86 | |
| 85646 | Tu-154M | | 86058 | IL-86 | |
| 85647 | Tu-154M | | 86059 | IL-86 | |
| 85648 | Tu-154M | | 86060 | IL-86 | |
| 85649 | Tu-154M | | 86061 | IL-86 | |
| 85650 | Tu-154M | | 86062 | IL-86 | |
| 85651 | Tu-154M | | 86063 | IL-86 | |
| 85652 | Tu-154M | | 86064 | IL-86 | |
| 85653 | Tu-154M | | 86065 | IL-86 | |
| 85654 | Tu-154M | | 86066 | IL-86 | |
| 85655 | Tu-154M | | 86067 | IL-86 | |
| 85656 | Tu-154M | | 86068 | IL-86 | |
| 85657 | Tu-154M | | 86069 | IL-86 | |
| 85658 | Tu-154M | | 86070 | IL-86 | |
| 85659 | Tu-154M | | 86071 | IL-86 | |
| 85660 | Tu-154M | | 86072 | IL-86 | |
| 85661 | Tu-154M | | 86073 | IL-86 | |
| 85662 | Tu-154M | | 86074 | IL-86 | |
| 85663 | Tu-154M | | 86075 | IL-86 | |
| 85665 | Tu-154M | | 86076 | IL-86 | |
| 85666 | Tu-154M | | 86077 | IL-86 | |
| 85667 | Tu-154M | | 86078 | IL-86 | |
| 85668 | Tu-154M | | 86079 | IL-86 | |
| 85669 | Tu-154M | | 86080 | IL-86 | |
| 85670 | Tu-154M | | 86081 | IL-86 | |
| 85671 | Tu-154M | | 86082 | IL-86 | |
| 85672 | Tu-154M | | 86083 | IL-86 | |
| 85674 | Tu-154M | | 86084 | IL-86 | |
| 85675 | Tu-154M | | 86085 | IL-86 | |
| 85676 | Tu-154M | | 86086 | IL-86 | |
| 85677 | Tu-154M | | 86087 | IL-86 | |
| 85678 | Tu-154M | | 86088 | IL-86 | |
| 85679 | Tu-154M | | 86089 | IL-86 | |
| 85680 | Tu-154M | | 86090 | IL-86 | |
| 85681 | Tu-154M | | 86091 | IL-86 | |
| 85682 | Tu-154M | | 86092 | IL-86 | |
| 85683 | Tu-154M | | 86093 | IL-86 | |
| 85684 | Tu-154M | | 86094 | IL-86 | |
| 85685 | Tu-154M | | 86095 | IL-86 | |
| 85686 | Tu-154M | | 86096 | IL-86 | |
| 85687 | Tu-154M | | 86097 | IL-86 | |
| 85688 | Tu-154M | | 86098 | IL-86 | |
| 85689 | Tu-154M | | 86099 | IL-86 | |
| 85690 | Tu-154M | | 86100 | IL-86 | |
| 85691 | Tu-154M | | 86101 | IL-86 | |
| 85692 | Tu-154M | | 86102 | IL-86 | |
| 85693 | Tu-154M | | 86103 | IL-86 | |
| 85694 | Tu-154M | | 86104 | IL-86 | |
| 85695 | Tu-154M | | 86105 | IL-86 | |
| 86000 | IL-86 | | 86106 | IL-86 | |
| 86002 | IL-86 | | 86107 | IL-86 | |

| Notes | Reg. | Type | Notes | Reg. | Type |
|-------|------|------|-------|------|------|
| | 86108 | IL-86 | | 86511 | IL-62M |
| | 86109 | IL-86 | | 86512 | IL-62M |
| | 86110 | IL-86 | | 86513 | IL-62M |
| | 86111 | IL-86 | | 86514 | IL-62M |
| | 86112 | IL-86 | | 86515 | IL-62M |
| | 86113 | IL-86 | | 86516 | IL-62M |
| | 86114 | IL-86 | | 86517 | IL-62MK |
| | 86115 | IL-86 | | 86518 | IL-62M |
| | 86116 | IL-86 | | 86519 | IL-62M |
| | 86117 | IL-86 | | 86520 | IL-62MK |
| | 86118 | IL-86 | | 86521 | IL-62M |
| | 86119 | IL-86 | | 86522 | IL-62M |
| | 86120 | IL-86 | | 86523 | IL-62M |
| | | | | 86524 | IL-62M |
| | 86450 | IL-62 | | 86527 | IL-62MK |
| | 86451 | IL-62 | | 86528 | IL-62MK |
| | 86452 | IL-62M | | 86529 | IL-62MK |
| | 86453 | IL-62M | | 86530 | IL-62MK |
| | 86454 | IL-62M | | 86531 | IL-62M |
| | 86455 | IL-62M | | 86532 | IL-62MK |
| | 86456 | IL-62M | | 86533 | IL-62M |
| | 86457 | IL-62M | | 86534 | IL-62MK |
| | 86458 | IL-62M | | 86535 | IL-62M |
| | 86459 | IL-62M | | 86536 | IL-62M (VIP) |
| | 86460 | IL-62 | | 86537 | IL-62M (VIP) |
| | 86461 | IL-62 | | 86538 | IL-62M (VIP) |
| | 86462 | IL-62M | | 86539 | IL-62MK (VIP) |
| | 86463 | IL-62M | | 86540 | IL-62M (VIP) |
| | 86464 | IL-62M | | 86555 | IL-62M (VIP) |
| | 86465 | IL-62M | | 86558 | IL-62M |
| | 86466 | IL-62MK | | 86605 | IL-62 |
| | 86467 | IL-62MK | | 86606 | IL-62 |
| | 86468 | IL-62MK (VIP) | | 86607 | IL-62M |
| | 86469 | IL-62M | | 86608 | IL-62 |
| | 86471 | IL-62M | | 86609 | IL-62 |
| | 86472 | IL-62M | | 86610 | IL-62 |
| | 86473 | IL-62M | | 86611 | IL-62 |
| | 86474 | IL-62M | | 86612 | IL-62 |
| | 86475 | IL-62M | | 86613 | IL-62 |
| | 86476 | IL-62M | | 86614 | IL-62 |
| | 86477 | IL-62M | | 86615 | IL-62 |
| | 86478 | IL-62M | | 86616 | IL-62 |
| | 86479 | IL-62M | | 86617 | IL-62 |
| | 86480 | IL-62M | | 86618 | IL-62M |
| | 86481 | IL-62M | | 86619 | IL-62M |
| | 86482 | IL-62M | | 86620 | IL-62M |
| | 86483 | IL-62M | | 86621 | IL-62M |
| | 86484 | IL-62M | | 86622 | IL-62M |
| | 86485 | IL-62M | | 86623 | IL-62M |
| | 86486 | IL-62M | | 86624 | IL-62M |
| | 86487 | IL-62M | | 86648 | IL-62 |
| | 86488 | IL-62M | | 86649 | IL-62 |
| | 86489 | IL-62M | | 86650 | IL-62 |
| | 86490 | IL-62M | | 86652 | IL-62 |
| | 86491 | IL-62M | | 86653 | IL-62 |
| | 86492 | IL-62M | | 86654 | IL-62 |
| | 86493 | IL-62M | | 86655 | IL-62 |
| | 86494 | IL-62M | | 86656 | IL-62M |
| | 86495 | IL-62M | | 86657 | IL-62 |
| | 86496 | IL-62M | | 86658 | IL-62M |
| | 86497 | IL-62M | | 86659 | IL-62M |
| | 86498 | IL-62M | | 86661 | IL-62 |
| | 86499 | IL-62M | | 86662 | IL-62 |
| | 86500 | IL-62M | | 86663 | IL-62 |
| | 86501 | IL-62M | | 86664 | IL-62 |
| | 86502 | IL-62M | | 86665 | IL-62 |
| | 86503 | IL-62M | | 86666 | IL-62 |
| | 86504 | IL-62M | | 86667 | IL-62 |
| | 86505 | IL-62M | | 86668 | IL-62 |
| | 86506 | IL-62M | | 86669 | IL-62 |
| | 86507 | IL-62M | | 86670 | IL-62 |
| | 86508 | IL-62M | | 86672 | IL-62 |
| | 86509 | IL-62M | | 86673 | IL-62M |
| | 86510 | IL-62M | | 86674 | IL-62 |

| Reg. | Type | Notes | Reg. | Type | Notes |
|------|------|-------|------|------|-------|
| 86675 | IL-62 | | 86694 | IL-62 | |
| 86676 | IL-62 | | 86695 | IL-62 | |
| 86677 | IL-62 | | 86696 | IL-62 | |
| 86678 | IL-62 | | 86697 | IL-62 | |
| 86679 | IL-62 | | 86698 | IL-62 | |
| 86680 | IL-62 | | 86699 | IL-62 | |
| 86681 | IL-62 | | 86700 | IL-62M | |
| 86682 | IL-62 | | 86701 | IL-62M | |
| 86683 | IL-62 | | 86702 | IL-62M | |
| 86684 | IL-62 | | 86703 | IL-62M | |
| 86685 | IL-62 | | 86704 | IL-62M | |
| 86686 | IL-62 | | 86705 | IL-62M | |
| 86687 | IL-62 | | 86706 | IL-62M | |
| 86688 | IL-62 | | 86708 | IL-62MK | |
| 86689 | IL-62 | | 86709 | IL-62MK | |
| 86690 | IL-62 | | 86710 | IL-62MK | |
| 86691 | IL-62 | | 86711 | IL-62M | |
| 86692 | IL-62M | | 86712 | IL-62M | |
| 86693 | IL-62M | | | | |

# CN (Morocco)

| Reg. | Type | Owner or Operator | Notes |
|------|------|-------------------|-------|
| CN-CCF | Boeing 727-2B6 | Royal Air Maroc *Fez* | |
| CN-CCG | Boeing 727-2B6 | Royal Air Maroc *L'Oiseau de la Providence* | |
| CN-CCH | Boeing 727-2B6 | Royal Air Maroc *Marrakech* | |
| CN-CCW | Boeing 727-2B6 | Royal Air Maroc *Agadir* | |
| CN-RMB | Boeing 707-351C | Royal Air Maroc *Tangier* | |
| CN-RMC | Boeing 707-351C | Royal Air Maroc *Casablanca* | |
| CN-RME | Boeing 747-2B6B (SCD) | Royal Air Maroc | |
| CN-RMF | Boeing 737-4B6 | Royal Air Maroc | |
| CN-RMG | Boeing 737-4B6 | Royal Air Maroc | |
| CN-RMH | Boeing 737-2T5 | Royal Air Maroc | |
| CN-RMI | Boeing 737-2B6 | Royal Air Maroc *El Ayounne* | |
| CN-RMJ | Boeing 737-2B6 | Royal Air Maroc *Oujda* | |
| CN-RMK | Boeing 737-2B6 | Royal Air Maroc *Smara* | |
| CN-RML | Boeing 737-2B6 | Royal Air Maroc | |
| CN-RMM | Boeing 737-2B6C | Royal Air Maroc | |
| CN-RMN | Boeing 737-2B6C | Royal Air Maroc | |
| CN-RMO | Boeing 727-2B6 | Royal Air Maroc | |
| CN-RMP | Boeing 727-2B6 | Royal Air Maroc | |
| CN-RMQ | Boeing 727-2B6 | Royal Air Maroc | |
| CN-RMR | Boeing 727-2B6 | Royal Air Maroc | |
| CN-RMS | Boeing 747SP-44 | Royal Air Maroc | |
| CN-RMT | Boeing 757-2B6 | Royal Air Maroc | |
| CN-RMU | Boeing 737-53A | Royal Air Maroc | |
| CN-RMZ | Boeing 757-2B6 | Royal Air Maroc | |
| CN- | Boeing 737-5B6 | Royal Air Maroc | |
| CN- | Boeing 737-5B6 | Royal Air Maroc | |

# CS (Portugal)

| | | | |
|------|------|-------|---|
| CS-TBS | Boeing 727-282 | TAP — Air Portugal *Lisboa* | |
| CS-TBW | Boeing 727-282 | TAP — Air Portugal *Coimbra* | |
| CS-TBX | Boeing 727-282 | TAP — Air Portugal *Faro* | |
| CS-TBY | Boeing 727-282 | TAP — Air Portugal *Amadora* | |
| CS-TEA | L.1011-385 TriStar 500 | TAP — Air Portugal *Luis de Camoes* | |
| CS-TEB | L.1011-385 TriStar 500 | TAP — Air Portugal *Infante D. Henrique* | |
| CS-TEC | L.1011-385 TriStar 500 | TAP — Air Portugal *Gago Coutinho* | |
| CS-TED | L.1011-385 TriStar 500 Gusmao | TAP — Air Portugal *Bartolomeu de* | |
| CS-TEE | L.1011-385 TriStar 500 de Lisboa | TAP — Air Portugal *St Antonio* | |
| CS-TEF | L.1011-385 TriStar 500 | TAP — Air Portugal *Fernando Pessoa* | |
| CS-TEG | L.1011-385 TriStar 500 | TAP — Air Portugal *Eca de Queriroz* | |
| CS-TEH | Airbus A.310-304 | TAP — Air Portugal *Bartolomeu Dias* | |
| CS-TEI | Airbus A.310-304 | TAP — Air Portugal *Farnao de Magalhaes* | |
| CS-TEJ | Airbus A.310-304 | TAP — Air Portugal *Pedro Nunes* | |
| CS-TEK | Boeing 737-282 | TAP — Air Portugal *Ponta Delgada* | |

| Notes | Reg. | Type | Owner or Operator |
|---|---|---|---|
| | CS-TEL | Boeing 737-282 | TAP — Air Portugal *Funchal* |
| | CS-TEM | Boeing 737-282 | TAP — Air Portugal *Setubal* |
| | CS-TEN | Boeing 737-282 | TAP — Air Portugal *Braga* |
| | CS-TEO | Boeing 737-282 | TAP — Air Portugal *Evora* |
| | CS-TEP | Boeing 737-282 | TAP — Air Portugal *Oporto* |
| | CS-TEQ | Boeing 737-282C | TAP — Air Portugal *Vila Real* |
| | CS-TER | Boeing 737-230 | TAP — Air Portugal *Aveiro* |
| | CS-TES | Boeing 737-230 | TAP — Air Portugal *Viana do Castelo* |
| | CS-TET | Boeing 737-2K9 | Air Atlantis *Viseu* |
| | CS-TEU | Boeing 737-2K9 | Air Atlantis *Porto Santo* |
| | CS-TEV | Boeing 737-230 | Air Atlantis |
| | CS-TEW | Airbus A.310-304 | TAP — Air Portugal |
| | CS-T | Airbus A.310-304 | TAP — Air Portugal |
| | CS-T | Airbus A.310-304 | TAP — Air Portugal |
| | CS-TIA | Boeing 737-382 | TAP — Air Portugal *Madeira* |
| | CS-TIB | Boeing 737-382 | TAP — Air Portugal *Acores* |
| | CS-TIC | Boeing 737-382 | TAP — Air Portugal *Algarve* |
| | CS-TID | Boeing 737-382 | TAP — Air Portugal |
| | CS-TIE | Boeing 737-382 | TAP — Air Portugal |
| | CS-TIF | Boeing 737-3K9 | Air Atlantis |
| | CS-TIG | Boeing 737-3K9 | Air Atlantis |
| | CS-TIH | Boeing 737-3K9 | Air Atlantis |
| | CS-TIR | Boeing 737-3K2 | Air Atlantis |
| | CS-T | Boeing 737-382 | Air Atlantis |
| | CS-T | Boeing 737-382 | Air Atlantis |
| | CS-T | Boeing 737-382 | Air Atlantis |
| | CS-TKA | Boeing 727-2J4RE | Air Columbus *Cristovao Colombo* |
| | CS-T | Boeing 727-2J4RE | Air Columbus |
| | CS-TMB | Boeing 737-291 | Air Sul |
| | CS-TMC | Boeing 737-291 | Air Sul |
| | CS-TPA | Fokker 100 | Portugalia |
| | CS-TPB | Fokker 100 | Portugalia |
| | CS-TPC | Fokker 100 | Portugalia |

# CU (Cuba)

| | CU-T1208 | Ilyushin IL-62M | Cubana *Capt Wifredo Perez* |
|---|---|---|---|
| | CU-T1209 | Ilyushin IL-62M | Cubana |
| | CU-T1215 | Ilyushin IL-62M | Cubana |
| | CU-T1216 | Ilyushin IL-62M | Cubana |
| | CU-T1217 | Ilyushin IL-62M | Cubana |
| | CU-T1218 | Ilyushin IL-62M | Cubana |
| | CU-T1225 | Ilyushin IL-62M | Cubana |
| | CU-T1226 | Ilyushin IL-62M | Cubana |
| | CU-T1252 | Ilyushin IL-62M | Cubana |
| | CU-T1259 | Ilyushin IL-62M | Cubana |
| | CU-T1280 | Ilyushin IL-62M | Cubana |
| | CU-T | Airbus A.310-304 | Cubana (*leased from TEA France*) |

**Note:** Cubana also operates an Airbus A.310 on lease from TEA France

# D (Germany)

| | D-AARS | F.27 Friendship Mk 600 | FTG Air Service |
|---|---|---|---|
| | D-AAST | S.E.210 Caravelle 10R | Aero Lloyd |
| | D-ABAK | S.E.210 Caravelle 10R | Aero Lloyd |
| | D-ABEA | Boeing 737-330 | Lufthansa *Saarbrücken* |
| | D-ABEB | Boeing 737-330 | Lufthansa |
| | D-ABEC | Boeing 737-330 | Lufthansa |
| | D-ABED | Boeing 737-330 | Lufthansa |
| | D-ABEE | Boeing 737-330 | Lufthansa |
| | D-ABEF | Boeing 737-330 | Lufthansa |
| | D-ABEH | Boeing 737-330 | Lufthansa |
| | D-ABFA | Boeing 737-230 | Lufthansa *Regensburg* |
| | D-ABFB | Boeing 737-230 | Lufthansa *Flensburg* |
| | D-ABFC | Boeing 737-230 | Lufthansa *Würzburg* |
| | D-ABFD | Boeing 737-230 | Lufthansa *Bamberg* |
| | D-ABFF | Boeing 737-230 | Lufthansa *Gelsenkirchen* |
| | D-ABFH | Boeing 737-230 | Lufthansa *Pforzheim* |
| | D-ABFK | Boeing 737-230 | Lufthansa *Wuppertal* |

| Reg. | Type | Owner or Operator | Notes |
|------|------|-------------------|-------|
| D-ABFL | Boeing 737-230 | Lufthansa *Coburg* | |
| D-ABFM | Boeing 737-230 | Lufthansa *Osnabrück* | |
| D-ABFN | Boeing 737-230 | Lufthansa *Kempten* | |
| D-ABFP | Boeing 737-230 | Lufthansa *Offenbach* | |
| D-ABFR | Boeing 737-230 | Lufthansa *Solingen* | |
| D-ABFS | Boeing 737-230 | Lufthansa *Oldenburg* | |
| D-ABFU | Boeing 737-230 | Lufthansa *Mülheim a.d.R* | |
| D-ABFW | Boeing 737-230 | Lufthansa *Wolfsburg* | |
| D-ABFX | Boeing 737-230 | Lufthansa *Tübingen* | |
| D-ABFY | Boeing 737-230 | Lufthansa *Göttingen* | |
| D-ABFZ | Boeing 737-230 | Lufthansa *Wilhelmshaven* | |
| D-ABGE | Boeing 737-230F | Lufthansa/German Cargo | |
| D-ABHA | Boeing 737-230 | Lufthansa *Koblenz* | |
| D-ABHB | Boeing 737-230 | Lufthansa *Goslar* | |
| D-ABHC | Boeing 737-230 | Lufthansa *Friedrichshafen* | |
| D-ABHE | Boeing 737-230F | Lufthansa/German Cargo | |
| D-ABHF | Boeing 737-230 | Lufthansa *Heilbronn* | |
| D-ABHH | Boeing 737-230 | Lufthansa *Marburg* | |
| D-ABHI | Boeing 727-230 | Lufthansa *Mönchengladbach* | |
| D-ABHK | Boeing 737-230 | Lufthansa *Bayreuth* | |
| D-ABHL | Boeing 737-230 | Lufthansa *Worms* | |
| D-ABHM | Boeing 737-230 | Lufthansa *Landshut* | |
| D-ABHN | Boeing 737-230 | Lufthansa *Trier* | |
| D-ABHP | Boeing 737-230 | Lufthansa *Erlangen* | |
| D-ABHR | Boeing 737-230 | Lufthansa *Darmstadt* | |
| D-ABHS | Boeing 737-230 | Lufthansa *Remscheid* | |
| D-ABHU | Boeing 737-230 | Lufthansa *Konstanz* | |
| D-ABHW | Boeing 737-230 | Lufthansa *Baden Baden* | |
| D-ABIA | Boeing 737-530 | Lufthansa *Regensburg* | |
| D-ABIB | Boeing 737-530 | Lufthansa *Wuppertal* | |
| D-ABIC | Boeing 737-530 | Lufthansa *Coburg* | |
| D-ABID | Boeing 737-530 | Lufthansa *Osnabrück* | |
| D-ABIE | Boeing 737-530 | Lufthansa *Kempten* | |
| D-ABIF | Boeing 737-530 | Lufthansa | |
| D-ABIH | Boeing 737-530 | Lufthansa | |
| D-ABII | Boeing 737-530 | Lufthansa | |
| D-ABIK | Boeing 737-530 | Lufthansa | |
| D-ABIL | Boeing 737-530 | Lufthansa | |
| D-ABIM | Boeing 737-530 | Lufthansa | |
| D-ABIN | Boeing 737-530 | Lufthansa | |
| D-ABIO | Boeing 737-530 | Lufthansa | |
| D-ABIP | Boeing 737-530 | Lufthansa | |
| D-ABIR | Boeing 737-530 | Lufthansa | |
| D-ABIS | Boeing 737-530 | Lufthansa | |
| D-ABIT | Boeing 737-530 | Lufthansa | |
| D-ABIU | Boeing 737-530 | Lufthansa | |
| D-ABIW | Boeing 737-530 | Lufthansa | |
| D-ABIX | Boeing 737-530 | Lufthansa | |
| D-ABIY | Boeing 737-530 | Lufthansa | |
| D-ABIZ | Boeing 737-530 | Lufthansa | |
| D-ABJA | Boeing 737-530 | Lufthansa | |
| D-ABJB | Boeing 737-530 | Lufthansa | |
| D-ABJC | Boeing 737-530 | Lufthansa | |
| D-ABJD | Boeing 737-530 | Lufthansa | |
| D-ABJE | Boeing 737-530 | Lufthansa | |
| D-ABJF | Boeing 737-530 | Lufthansa | |
| D-ABJH | Boeing 737-530 | Lufthansa | |
| D-ABJI | Boeing 737-530 | Lufthansa | |
| D-ABJK | Boeing 737-530 | Lufthansa | |
| D-ABJL | Boeing 737-530 | Lufthansa | |
| D-ABJM | Boeing 737-530 | Lufthansa | |
| D-ABJN | Boeing 737-530 | Lufthansa | |
| D-ABJP | Boeing 737-530 | Lufthansa | |
| D-ABJR | Boeing 737-530 | Lufthansa | |
| D-ABJS | Boeing 737-530 | Lufthansa | |
| D-ABJT | Boeing 737-530 | Lufthansa | |
| D-ABJU | Boeing 737-530 | Lufthansa | |
| D-ABKE | Boeing 727-230 | Lufthansa *Mannheim* | |
| D-ABKH | Boeing 727-230 | Lufthansa *Karlsruhe* | |
| D-ABKI | Boeing 727-230 | Lufthansa *Bremerhaven* | |
| D-ABKM | Boeing 727-230 | Lufthansa *Hagen* | |
| D-ABKN | Boeing 727-230 | Lufthansa *Ulm* | |
| D-ABKP | Boeing 727-230 | Lufthansa *Krefeld* | |

| Notes | Reg. | Type | Owner or Operator |
|---|---|---|---|
| | D-ABKQ | Boeing 727-230 | Lufthansa *Mainz* |
| | D-ABKR | Boeing 727-230 | Lufthansa *Bielefeld* |
| | D-ABKT | Boeing 727-230 | Lufthansa *Aachen* |
| | D-ABMA | Boeing 737-230 | Lufthansa *Idar-Oberstein* |
| | D-ABMB | Boeing 737-230 | Lufthansa *Ingolstadt* |
| | D-ABMC | Boeing 737-230 | Lufthansa *Norderstedt* |
| | D-ABMD | Boeing 737-230 | Lufthansa *Paderborn* |
| | D-ABME | Boeing 737-230 | Lufthansa *Schweinfurt* |
| | D-ABMF | Boeing 737-230 | Lufthansa *Verden* |
| | D-ABNA | Boeing 757-230 | Condor Flugdienst/Sudflug |
| | D-ABNB | Boeing 757-230 | Condor Flugdienst/Sudflug |
| | D-ABNC | Boeing 757-230 | Condor Flugdienst/Sudflug |
| | D-ABND | Boeing 757-230 | Condor Flugdienst/Sudflug |
| | D-ABNE | Boeing 757-230 | Condor Flugdienst/Sudflug |
| | D-ABNF | Boeing 757-230 | Condor Flugdienst/Sudflug |
| | D-AB | Boeing 757-230 | Condor Flugdienst/Sudflug |
| | D-AB | Boeing 757-230 | Condor Flugdienst/Sudflug |
| | D-AB | Boeing 767-330ER | Condor Flugdienst/Sudflug |
| | D-AB | Boeing 767-330ER | Condor Flugdienst/Sudflug |
| | D-AB | Boeing 767-330ER | Condor Flugdienst/Sudflug |
| | D-ABNX | Boeing 757-2J4ER | Condor/Air Holland (PH-AHL) |
| | D-ABPI | Boeing 727-230 | Lufthansa *Münster* |
| | D-ABQI | Boeing 727-230 | Lufthansa *Hildesheim* |
| | D-ABRI | Boeing 727-230 | Lufthansa *Esslingen* |
| | D-ABTA | Boeing 747-430 (SCD) | Lufthansa |
| | D-ABTB | Boeing 747-430 (SCD) | Lufthansa |
| | D-ABTC | Boeing 747-430 (SCD) | Lufthansa |
| | D-ABTD | Boeing 747-430 (SCD) | Lufthansa *Hamburg* |
| | D-ABTE | Boeing 747-430 | Lufthansa |
| | D-ABTF | Boeing 747-430 | Lufthansa |
| | D-ABTH | Boeing 747-430 | Lufthansa |
| | D-ABVA | Boeing 747-430 | Lufthansa *Berlin* |
| | D-ABVB | Boeing 747-430 | Lufthansa *Bonn* |
| | D-ABVC | Boeing 747-430 | Lufthansa *Baden-Wuertemberg* |
| | D-ABVD | Boeing 747-430 | Lufthansa/Condor Flugdienst |
| | D-ABVE | Boeing 747-430 | Lufthansa |
| | D-ABVF | Boeing 747-430 | Lufthansa |
| | D-ABVH | Boeing 747-430 | Lufthansa |
| | D-ABVK | Boeing 747-430 | Lufthansa |
| | D-ABWA | Boeing 737-330 | Condor Flugdienst *Claus Gillmann* |
| | D-ABWB | Boeing 737-330 | Condor Flugdienst |
| | D-ABWC | Boeing 737-330 | Condor Flugdienst |
| | D-ABWD | Boeing 737-330 | Condor Flugdienst/Lufthansa |
| | D-ABWE | Boeing 737-330 | Condor Flugdienst/Lufthansa |
| | D-ABWF | Boeing 737-330 | Condor Flugdienst/Lufthansa |
| | D-ABWH | Boeing 737-330 | Condor Flugdienst/Lufthansa |
| | D-ABXA | Boeing 737-330 | Lufthansa *Giessen* |
| | D-ABXB | Boeing 737-330 | Lufthansa *Passau* |
| | D-ABXC | Boeing 737-330 | Lufthansa *Delmenhorst* |
| | D-ABXD | Boeing 737-330 | Lufthansa *Siegen* |
| | D-ABXE | Boeing 737-330 | Lufthansa *Hamm* |
| | D-ABXF | Boeing 737-330 | Lufthansa *Minden* |
| | D-ABXH | Boeing 737-330 | Lufthansa *Cuxhaven* |
| | D-ABXI | Boeing 737-330 | Lufthansa *Berchtesgaden* |
| | D-ABXK | Boeing 737-330 | Lufthansa *Ludwigsburg* |
| | D-ABXL | Boeing 737-330 | Lufthansa *Neuss* |
| | D-ABXM | Boeing 737-330 | Lufthansa *Herford* |
| | D-ABXN | Boeing 737-330 | Lufthansa *Böblingen* |
| | D-ABXO | Boeing 737-330 | Lufthansa *Schwäbisch-Gmünd* |
| | D-ABXP | Boeing 737-330 | Lufthansa *Fulda* |
| | D-ABXR | Boeing 737-330 | Lufthansa *Celle* |
| | D-ABXS | Boeing 737-330 | Lufthansa *Sindelfingen* |
| | D-ABXT | Boeing 737-330 | Lufthansa *Reutlingen* |
| | D-ABXU | Boeing 737-330 | Lufthansa *Seeheim-Jugenheim* |
| | D-ABXW | Boeing 737-330 | Lufthansa *Hanau* |
| | D-ABXX | Boeing 737-330 | Lufthansa *Bad Homberg v.d. Höhe* |
| | D-ABXY | Boeing 737-330 | Lufthansa *Hof* |
| | D-ABXZ | Boeing 737-330 | Lufthansa *Bad Morgentheim* |
| | D-ABYJ | Boeing 747-230B (SCD) | Lufthansa *Hessen* |
| | D-ABYK | Boeing 747-230B (SCD) | Lufthansa *Rheinland-Pfalz* |
| | D-ABYL | Boeing 747-230B (SCD) | Lufthansa *Saarland* |
| | D-ABYM | Boeing 747-230B (SCD) | Lufthansa *Schleswig-Holstein* |
| | D-ABYO | Boeing 747-230F (SCD) | Lufthansa *America* |

| Reg. | Type | Owner or Operator | Notes |
|------|------|-------------------|-------|
| D-ABYP | Boeing 747-230B | Lufthansa *Niedersachen* | |
| D-ABYQ | Boeing 747-230B | Lufthansa *Bremen* | |
| D-ABYR | Boeing 747-230B (SCD) | Lufthansa *Nordrhein-Westfalen* | |
| D-ABYS | Boeing 747-230B (SCD) | Lufthansa *Bayern* | |
| D-ABYT | Boeing 747-230F (SCD) | German Cargo | |
| D-ABYU | Boeing 747-230F (SCD) | Lufthansa *Asia* | |
| D-ABYW | Boeing 747-230F (SCD) | German Cargo | |
| D-ABYX | Boeing 747-230B (SCD) | Lufthansa *Köln* | |
| D-ABYY | Boeing 747-230B (SCD) | Lufthansa *München* | |
| D-ABYZ | Boeing 747-230B (SCD) | Lufthansa *Frankfurt* | |
| D-ABZA | Boeing 747-230B (SCD) | Lufthansa *Düsseldorf* | |
| D-ABZB | Boeing 747-230F (SCD) | Lufthansa *Europa* | |
| D-ABZC | Boeing 747-230B (SCD) | Lufthansa *Hannover* | |
| D-ABZD | Boeing 747-230B | Lufthansa *Kiel* | |
| D-ABZE | Boeing 747-230B (SCD) | Lufthansa *Stuttgart* | |
| D-ABZF | Boeing 747-230F (SCD) | Lufthansa *Africa* | |
| D-ABZH | Boeing 747-230B | Lufthansa *Bonn* | |
| D-ABZI | Boeing 747-230F (SCD) | Lufthansa *Australia* | |
| D-ACBA | Boeing 737-505 | Lufthansa | |
| D-ACBB | Boeing 737-505 | Lufthansa | |
| D-ACBC | Boeing 737-505 | Lufthansa | |
| D-ACVK | S.E.210 Caravelle 10R | Aero Lloyd *Otto Trump* | |
| D-ADAO | Douglas DC-10-30 | Lufthansa *Leverkusen* | |
| D-ADCO | Douglas DC-10-30 | Lufthansa | |
| D-ADDO | Douglas DC-10-30 | Lufthansa *Duisburg* | |
| D-ADEP | F.27 Friendship Mk 600 | Ratioflug | |
| D-ADFO | Douglas DC-10-30 | Lufthansa *Fürth* | |
| D-ADGO | Douglas DC-10-30 | Lufthansa | |
| D-ADHO | Douglas DC-10-30 | Lufthansa | |
| D-ADJO | Douglas DC-10-30 | Lufthansa *Essen* | |
| D-ADKO | Douglas DC-10-30 | Lufthansa | |
| D-ADLO | Douglas DC-10-30 | Lufthansa *Nurnberg* | |
| D-ADMO | Douglas DC-10-30 | Lufthansa *Dortmund* | |
| D-ADPO | Douglas DC-10-30 | Condor Flugdienst | |
| D-ADQO | Douglas DC-10-30 | Condor Flugdienst | |
| D-ADSO | Douglas DC-10-30 | Condor Flugdienst | |
| D-ADUA | Douglas DC-8-73AF | German Cargo | |
| D-ADUC | Douglas DC-8-73AF | German Cargo | |
| D-ADUE | Douglas DC-8-73AF | German Cargo | |
| D-ADUI | Douglas DC-8-73AF | German Cargo | |
| D-ADUO | Douglas DC-8-73AF | German Cargo | |
| D-AERE | L.1011-385 TriStar 1 | LTU | |
| D-AERI | L.1011-385 TriStar 1 | LTU | |
| D-AERL | L.1011-385 TriStar 500 | LTU | |
| D-AERM | L.1011-385 TriStar 1 | LTU | |
| D-AERN | L.1011-385 TriStar 200 | LTU | |
| D-AERP | L.1011-385 TriStar 1 | LTU | |
| D-AERT | L.1011-385 TriStar 500 | LTU | |
| D-AERU | L.1011-385 TriStar 100 | LTU | |
| D-AERV | L.1011-385 TriStar 500 | LTU | |
| D-AERY | L.1011-385 TriStar 1 | LTU | |
| D-A | McD Douglas MD-11 | LTU | |
| D-A | McD Douglas MD-11 | LTU | |
| D-A | McD Douglas MD-11 | LTU | |
| D-A | McD Douglas MD-11 | LTU | |
| D-AFEH | F.27 Friendship Mk 600 | Ratioflug/Federal Express | |
| D-AFEM | F.27 Friendship Mk 600 | Ratioflug/Federal Express | |
| D-AFKA | Fokker 50 | D.L.T. | |
| D-AFKB | Fokker 50 | D.L.T. | |
| D-AFKC | Fokker 50 | D.L.T. | |
| D-AFKD | Fokker 50 | D.L.T. | |
| D-AFKE | Fokker 50 | D.L.T. | |
| D-AFKF | Fokker 50 | D.L.T. | |
| D-AFKG | Fokker 50 | D.L.T. | |
| D-AFKH | Fokker 50 | D.L.T. | |
| D-AFKI | Fokker 50 | D.L.T. | |
| D-AFKJ | Fokker 50 | D.L.T. | |
| D-AFKK | Fokker 50 | D.L.T. | |
| D-AFKL | Fokker 50 | D.L.T. | |
| D-AFKM | Fokker 50 | D.L.T. | |
| D-AFKN | Fokker 50 | D.L.T. | |
| D-AFKO | Fokker 50 | D.L.T. | |
| D-AFKP | Fokker 50 | D.L.T. | |

| Notes | Reg. | Type | Owner or Operator |
|---|---|---|---|
| | D-AFTG | F.27 Friendship Mk 600 | FTG Air Service |
| | D-AGEA | Boeing 737-35B | Germania |
| | D-AGEB | Boeing 737-35B | Germania |
| | D-AGEC | Boeing 737-35B | Deutsche Ferienflugdienste (DFD) |
| | D-AGED | Boeing 737-35B | Deutsche Ferienflugdienste (DFD) |
| | D-AGEE | Boeing 737-35B | Germania |
| | D-AGEG | Boeing 737-35B | Germania |
| | D-AGWC | McD Douglas MD-83 | Aero Lloyd |
| | D-AHLA | Airbus A.310-304 | Hapag-Lloyd |
| | D-AHLB | Airbus A.310-304 | Hapag-Lloyd |
| | D-AHLC | — | — |
| | D-AHLD | Boeing 737-5K5 | Hapag-Lloyd |
| | D-AHLE | Boeing 737-5K5 | Hapag-Lloyd |
| | D-AHLF | Boeing 737-5K5 | Hapag-Lloyd |
| | D-AHLG | Boeing 737-2K5 | Hapag-Lloyd/Air Aruba |
| | D-AHLH | Boeing 737-2K5 | Hapag-Lloyd/Air Aruba |
| | D-AHLI | Boeing 737-5K5 | Hapag-Lloyd |
| | D-AHLJ | Boeing 737-4K5 | Hapag-Lloyd |
| | D-AHLK | Boeing 737-4K5 | Hapag-Lloyd |
| | D-AHLL | Boeing 737-4K5 | Hapag-Lloyd |
| | D-AHLM | Boeing 727-81 | Hapag-Lloyd |
| | D-AHLN | Boeing 737-5K5 | Hapag-Lloyd |
| | D-AHLO | Boeing 737-4K5 | Hapag-Lloyd |
| | D-AHLP | Boeing 737-4K5 | Hapag-Lloyd |
| | D-AHLQ | Boeing 737-4K5 | Hapag-Lloyd |
| | D-AHLR | Boeing 737-4K5 | Hapag-Lloyd |
| | D-AHLS | Boeing 727-89 | Hapag-Lloyd |
| | D-AHLV | Airbus A.310-204 | Hapag-Lloyd |
| | D-AHLW | Airbus A.310-204 | Hapag-Lloyd |
| | D-AHLX | Airbus A.310-204 | Hapag-Lloyd |
| | D-AHLZ | Airbus A.310-204 | Hapag-Lloyd |
| | D-AIAH | Airbus A.300-603 | Lufthansa *Lindau/Bodenzee* |
| | D-AIAI | Airbus A.300-603 | Lufthansa *Erbach/Odenwald* |
| | D-AIAK | Airbus A.300-603 | Lufthansa *Kronberg im Taunus* |
| | D-AIAL | Airbus A.300-603 | Lufthansa *Stade* |
| | D-AIAM | Airbus A.300-603 | Lufthansa *Rosenheim* |
| | D-AIAN | Airbus A.300-603 | Lufthansa *Nördlingen* |
| | D-AIAP | Airbus A.300-603 | Lufthansa *Donauwörth* |
| | D-AIAR | Airbus A.300-603 | Lufthansa *Bingen* |
| | D-AIAS | Airbus A.300-603 | Lufthansa *Moenchengladbach* |
| | D-AIAT | Airbus A.300-603 | Lufthansa |
| | D-AIAU | Airbus A.300-603 | Lufthansa |
| | D-AICA | Airbus A.310-203 | Lufthansa *Neustadt an der Weinstrausse* |
| | D-AICB | Airbus A.310-203 | Lufthansa *Garmisch-Partenkirchen* |
| | D-AICC | Airbus A.310-203 | Lufthansa *Kaiserslauten* |
| | D-AICD | Airbus A.310-203 | Lufthansa *Detmold* |
| | D-AICF | Airbus A.310-203 | Lufthansa *Rüdesheim am Rhein* |
| | D-AICH | Airbus A.310-203 | Lufthansa *Lüneburg* |
| | D-AICK | Airbus A.310-203 | Lufthansa *Westerland-Sylt* |
| | D-AICL | Airbus A.310-203 | Lufthansa *Rothenburg ob der Tauber* |
| | D-AICM | Airbus A.310-203 | Lufthansa |
| | D-AICN | Airbus A.310-203 | Lufthansa *Lubeck* |
| | D-AICP | Airbus A.310-203 | Lufthansa *Bremerhaven* |
| | D-AICR | Airbus A.310-203 | Lufthansa *Freudenstadt* |
| | D-AICS | Airbus A.310-203 | Lufthansa *Recklinghausen* |
| | D-AIDA | Airbus A.310-304 | Condor Flugdienst |
| | D-AIDB | Airbus A.310-304 | Lufthansa *Fürth* |
| | D-AIDC | Airbus A.310-304 | Condor Flugdienst |
| | D-AIDD | Airbus A.310-304 | Lufthansa *Emden* |
| | D-AIDE | Airbus A.310-304 | Lufthansa *Speyer* |
| | D-AIDF | Airbus A.310-304 | Lufthansa *Aschaffenburg* |
| | D-AIDH | Airbus A.310-304 | Lufthansa *Wetzlar* |
| | D-AIDI | Airbus A.310-304 | Lufthansa *Fellbach* |
| | D-AIDK | Airbus A.310-304 | Lufthansa *Donaueschingen* |
| | D-AIDL | Airbus A.310-304 | Lufthansa |
| | D-AIDM | Airbus A.300-304 | Lufthansa |
| | D-AIDN | Airbus A.300-304 | Lufthansa |
| | D-AIPA | Airbus A.320-211 | Lufthansa *Buxtehude* |
| | D-AIPB | Airbus A.320-211 | Lufthansa *Heidelberg* |
| | D-AIPC | Airbus A.320-211 | Lufthansa *Braunschweig* |
| | D-AIPD | Airbus A.320-211 | Lufthansa *Freiburg* |
| | D-AIPE | Airbus A.320-211 | Lufthansa *Kassel* |
| | D-AIPF | Airbus A.320-211 | Lufthansa *Leipzig* |

# OVERSEAS AIRLINERS

| Reg. | Type | Owner or Operator | Notes |
|------|------|-------------------|-------|
| D-AIPH | Airbus A.320-211 | Lufthansa *Munster* | |
| D-AIPK | Airbus A.320-211 | Lufthansa *Wiesbaden* | |
| D-AIPL | Airbus A.320-211 | Lufthansa *Ludwigshafen* | |
| D-AIPM | Airbus A.320-211 | Lufthansa *Troisdorf* | |
| D-AIPN | Airbus A.320-211 | Lufthansa *Kulmbach* | |
| D-AIPP | Airbus A.320-211 | Lufthansa *Starnberg* | |
| D-AIPR | Airbus A.320-211 | Lufthansa *Kaufbeuren* | |
| D-AIPS | Airbus A.320-211 | Lufthansa *Augsberg* | |
| D-AIPT | Airbus A.320-211 | Lufthansa | |
| D-AIPU | Airbus A.320-211 | Lufthansa | |
| D-AIPW | Airbus A.320-211 | Lufthansa | |
| D-AIPX | Airbus A.320-211 | Lufthansa | |
| D-AIPY | Airbus A.320-211 | Lufthansa | |
| D-AIPZ | Airbus A.320-211 | Lufthansa | |
| D-AIQA | Airbus A.320-211 | Lufthansa | |
| D-AIQC | Airbus A.320-211 | Lufthansa | |
| D-AIQD | Airbus A.320-211 | Lufthansa | |
| D-AIQE | Airbus A.320-211 | Lufthansa | |
| D-AIQF | Airbus A.320-211 | Lufthansa | |
| D-AIQH | Airbus A.320-211 | Lufthansa | |
| D-AIQK | Airbus A.320-211 | Lufthansa | |
| D-ALLA | Douglas DC-9-32 | Aero Lloyd | |
| D-ALLB | Douglas DC-9-32 | Aero Lloyd | |
| D-ALLC | Douglas DC-9-32 | Aero Lloyd | |
| D-ALLD | McD Douglas MD-83 | Aero Lloyd | |
| D-ALLE | McD Douglas MD-83 | Aero Lloyd | |
| D-ALLF | McD Douglas MD-83 | Aero Lloyd | |
| D-ALLG | McD Douglas MD-87 | Aero Lloyd | |
| D-ALLH | McD Douglas MD-87 | Aero Lloyd | |
| D-ALLI | McD Douglas MD-87 | Aero Lloyd | |
| D-ALLJ | McD Douglas MD-87 | Aero Lloyd | |
| D-ALLK | McD Douglas MD-83 | Aero Lloyd | |
| D-ALLL | McD Douglas MD-83 | Aero Lloyd | |
| D-ALLM | McD Douglas MD-83 | Aero Lloyd | |
| D-ALLN | McD Douglas MD-83 | Aero Lloyd | |
| D-ALLO | McD Douglas MD-83 | Aero Lloyd | |
| D-ALLP | McD Douglas MD-83 | Aero Lloyd | |
| D-ALLQ | McD Douglas MD-83 | Aero Lloyd | |
| D-ALLR | McD Douglas MD-83 | Aero Lloyd | |
| D-AL | McD Douglas MD-83 | Aero Lloyd | |
| D-AL | McD Douglas MD-83 | Aero Lloyd | |
| D-AMUM | Boeing 757-2G5 | LTU-Sud | |
| D-AMUN | Boeing 767-3G5ER | LTU-Sud | |
| D-AMUR | Boeing 767-3G5ER | LTU-Sud | |
| D-AMUS | Boeing 767-3G5ER | LTU-Sud | |
| D-AMUU | Boeing 757-225 | LTU-Sud | |
| D-AMUV | Boeing 757-2G5ER | LTU-Sud | |
| D-AMUW | Boeing 757-2G5ER | LTU-Sud | |
| D-AMUX | Boeing 757-2G5ER | LTU-Sud | |
| D-AMUY | Boeing 757-2G5ER | LTU-Sud | |
| D-AMUZ | Boeing 757-2G5 | LTU-Sud | |
| D-ANTJ | BAe 146-200QT | NFD/TNT Express Europe | |
| D-AOAA | Airbus A.310-304 | Interflug | |
| D-AOAB | Airbus A.310-304 | Interflug | |
| D-AOAC | Airbus A.310-304 | Interflug | |
| D-AOAD | Ilyushin IL-62M | Interflug | |
| D-AOAE | Ilyushin IL-62MK | Interflug | |
| D-AOAF | Ilyushin IL-62MK | Interflug | |
| D-AOAG | Ilyushin IL-62M | Interflug | |
| D-AOAH | Ilyushin IL-62M | Interflug | |
| D-AOAI | Ilyushin IL-62MK | Interflug | |
| D-AOAJ | Ilyushin IL-62M | Interflug | |
| D-AOAK | Ilyushin IL-62M | Interflug | |
| D-AOAL | Ilyushin IL-62M | Interflug | |
| D-AOAM | Ilyushin IL-62M | Interflug | |
| D-AOAN | Ilyushin IL-62M | Interflug | |
| D-AOAO | Ilyushin IL-18V | Interflug | |
| D-AOAP | Ilyushin IL-18D | Interflug | |
| D-AOAQ | Ilyushin IL-18V | Interflug | |
| D-AOAR | Ilyushin IL-18D | Interflug | |
| D-AOAS | Ilyushin IL-18D | Interflug | |
| D-AOAT | Ilyushin IL-18D | Interflug | |
| D-AOAU | Ilyushin IL-18D | Interflug | |

| Notes | Reg. | Type | Owner or Operator |
|---|---|---|---|
| | D-AOBA | Tupolev Tu-134A | Interflug |
| | D-AOBC | Tupolev Tu-134A | Interflug |
| | D-AOBD | Tupolev Tu-134A | Interflug |
| | D-AOBE | Tupolev Tu-134A | Interflug |
| | D-AOBF | Tupolev Tu-134A | Interflug |
| | D-AOBG | Tupolev Tu-134A | Interflug |
| | D-AOBH | Tupolev Tu-134A | Interflug |
| | D-AOBI | Tupolev Tu-134A | Interflug |
| | D-AOBJ | Tupolev Tu-134A | Interflug |
| | D-AOBK | Tupolev Tu-134A | Interflug |
| | D-AOBL | Tupolev Tu-134A | Interflug |
| | D-AOBM | Tupolev Tu-134A-1 | Interflug |
| | D-AOBN | Tupolev Tu-134A | Interflug |
| | D-AOBO | Tupolev Tu-134A | Interflug |
| | D-AOBP | Tupolev Tu-134A | Interflug |
| | D-AOBQ | Tupolev Tu-134A | Interflug |
| | D-AOBR | Tupolev Tu-134A | Interflug |
| | D-AOBS | Tupolev Tu-134A | Interflug |
| | D-AOEA | Boeing 757-236 | NFD/Air Europe (G-BNSD) |
| | D-AOEB | Boeing 757-236ER | NFD/Air Euorpe (G-BNSF) |
| | D-A | Boeing 757-236 | NFD/Air Europe (G-....) |
| | D-BAAA | Aerospatiale ATR-42-300 | Nürnberger Flugdienst (NFD) |
| | D-BAKA | F.27 Friendship Mk 100 | WDL/FTG Air Service |
| | D-BAKI | F.27 Friendship Mk 100 | WDL/FTG Air Service |
| | D-BAKO | F.27 Friendship Mk 100 | WDL |
| | D-BAKU | F.27 Friendship Mk 200 | WDL |
| | D-BBBB | Aerospatiale ATR-42-300 | Nürnberger Flugdienst (NFD) |
| | D-BCCC | Aerospatiale ATR-42-300 | Nürnberger Flugdienst (NFD) |
| | D-BCRM | Aerospatiale ATR-42-300QC | R.F.G. |
| | D-BCRN | Aerospatiale ATR-42-300QC | R.F.G. |
| | D-BCRO | Aerospatiale ATR-42-300QC | R.F.G. |
| | D-BCRP | Aerospatiale ATR-42-300QC | R.F.G. |
| | D-BC | Aerospatiale ATR-42-300QC | R.F.G. |
| | D-BDDD | Aerospatiale ATR-42-300 | Nürnberger Flugdienst (NFD) |
| | D-BEAT | D.H.C. 8-301 Dash Eight | Contactair/D.L.T. |
| | D-BEEE | Aerospatiale ATR-42-300 | Nürnberger Flugdienst (NFD) |
| | D-BELT | D.H.C.8-301 Dash Eight | Contactair/D.L.T. |
| | D-BERT | D.H.C.8-102 Dash Eight | Contactair/D.L.T. |
| | D-BEST | D.H.C.8-102 Dash Eight | Contactair/D.L.T. |
| | D-BEYT | D.H.C.8-301 Dash Eight | Contactair/D.L.T. |
| | D-BFFF | Aerospatiale ATR-42-300 | Nürnberger Flugdienst (NFD) |
| | D-BGGG | Aerospatiale ATR-42-300 | Nürnberger Flugdienst (NFD) |
| | D-BHHH | Aerospatiale ATR-42-300 | Nürnberger Flugdienst (NFD) |
| | D-BIII | Aerospatiale ATR-42-300 | Nürnberger Flugdienst (NFD) |
| | D-BJJJ | Aerospatiale ATR-42-300 | Nürnberger Flugdienst (NFD) |
| | D- | Aerospatiale ATR-72 | Nürnberger Flugdienst (NFD) |
| | D-BOBL | D.H.C.8-301 Dash Eight | Hamburg Airlines |
| | D-BOBO | D.H.C.8-102 Dash Eight | Hamburg Airlines |
| | D-BOBY | D.H.C.8-102 Dash Eight | Hamburg Airlines |
| | D-CABD | Swearingen SA227AC Metro III | Nürnberger Flugdienst (NFD) |
| | D-CABE | Swearingen SA227AC Metro III | Nürnberger Flugdienst (NFD) |
| | D-CABF | Swearingen SA227AC Metro III | Nürnberger Flugdienst (NFD) |
| | D-CABG | Swearingen SA227AC Metro III | Nürnberger Flugdienst (NFD) |
| | D-CABH | Swearingen SA227AC Metro III | Nürnberger Flugdienst (NFD) |
| | D-CABI | Swearingen SA227AC Metro III | Nürnberger Flugdienst (NFD) |
| | D-CALY | Dornier Do.228-212 | Ratioflug |
| | D-CARA | Beech 1900 | Sudavia |
| | D-CBOL | Dornier Do.228-202 | Ratioflug |
| | D-CCCC | Douglas DC-3 | Classic Wings |
| | D-CDIA | Saab SF.340A | Delta Air |
| | D-CDIB | Saab SF.340A | Delta Air |
| | D-CDIC | Saab SF.340A | Delta Air |
| | D-CDID | Saab SF.340A | Delta Air |
| | D-CDIE | Saab SF.340A | Delta Air |
| | D-CDIF | Saab SF.340A | Delta Air |
| | D-CDIZ | Dornier Do.228-201 | Delta Air |
| | D-CESA | Beech 1900C | Sudavia |
| | D-CHOF | Dornier Do.228-201 | Nürnberger Flugdienst (NFD) |
| | D-CIRB | Beech 1900C-1 | Interot Air Service |
| | D-CISA | Beech 1900C | Interot Air Service |
| | D-CKVW | Swearingen SA227AC Metro III | Nürnberger Flugdienst (NFD) |
| | D-CMUC | Dornier Do.228-201 | Ratioflug |
| | D-CMUL | Dornier Do.228-202 | Ratioflug |

| Reg. | Type | Owner or Operator | Notes |
|---|---|---|---|
| D-CONA | BAe Jetstream 3102 | Contactair | |
| D-CONU | BAe Jetstream 3102 | Contactair | |
| D-ICRJ | Swearingen SA226TC Metro II | R.F.G. | |
| D-ICRK | Swearingen SA226TC Metro II | R.F.G. | |
| D-ICRL | Swearingen SA226TC Metro II | R.F.G. | |
| D-IHCW | Swearingen SA226TC Metro II | R.F.G. | |

**Note:** Hamburg Airlines also operates a Fokker 100 registered F-OGQA and R.F.G. employs three SF.340s which retain the marks N109TA, N110TA and N120TA.

# EC (Spain)

| Reg. | Type | Owner or Operator |
|---|---|---|
| EC-BIG | Douglas DC-9-32 | Iberia Villa de Madrid |
| EC-BIH | Douglas DC-9-32 | Aviaco Ciudad de Barcelona |
| EC-BIJ | Douglas DC-9-32 | Iberia Ciudad de Santa Cruz de Tenerife |
| EC-BIK | Douglas DC-9-32 | Aviaco Castillo de Guanapa |
| EC-BIL | Douglas DC-9-32 | Viva Air |
| EC-BIM | Douglas DC-9-32 | Iberia Ciudad de Santander |
| EC-BIN | Douglas DC-9-32 | Iberia Palma de Mallorca |
| EC-BIO | Douglas DC-9-32 | Iberia Villa de Bilbao |
| EC-BIP | Douglas DC-9-32 | Aviaco Castillo de Monteagudo |
| EC-BIQ | Douglas DC-9-32 | Aviaco Castillo de Argueso |
| EC-BIR | Douglas DC-9-32 | Iberia Ciudad de Valencia |
| EC-BIS | Douglas DC-9-32 | Iberia Ciudad de Alicante |
| EC-BIT | Douglas DC-9-32 | Iberia Ciudad de San Sebastian |
| EC-BIU | Douglas DC-9-32 | Viva Air |
| EC-BPF | Douglas DC-9-32 | Viva Air |
| EC-BPG | Douglas DC-9-32 | Iberia Ciudad de Vigo |
| EC-BPH | Douglas DC-9-32 | Iberia Ciudad de Gerona |
| EC-BQT | Douglas DC-9-32 | Iberia Ciudad de Murcia |
| EC-BQU | Douglas DC-9-32 | Iberia Ciudad de La Coruna |
| EC-BQV | Douglas DC-9-32 | Iberia Ciudad de Ibiza |
| EC-BQX | Douglas DC-9-32 | Iberia Ciudad de Valladolid |
| EC-BQY | Douglas DC-9-32 | Aviaco Ciudad de Cordoba |
| EC-BQZ | Douglas DC-9-32 | Iberia Ciudad de Santa Cruz de La Palma |
| EC-BRQ | Boeing 747-256B | Iberia Calderon de la Barca |
| EC-BYD | Douglas DC-9-32 | Aviaco Ciudad de Arrecife de Lanzarote |
| EC-BYE | Douglas DC-9-32 | Aviaco Ciudad de Mahon |
| EC-BYF | Douglas DC-9-32 | Iberia Ciudad de Granada |
| EC-BYG | Douglas DC-9-32 | Aviaco Ciudad de Pamplona |
| EC-BYH | Douglas DC-9-32 | Aviaco Castillo de Butron |
| EC-BYI | Douglas DC-9-32 | Iberia Ciudad de Vitoria |
| EC-BYJ | Douglas DC-9-32 | Iberia Ciudad de Salamanca |
| EC-CAI | Boeing 727-256 | Iberia Castilla la Neuva |
| EC-CAJ | Boeing 727-256 | Iberia Cataluna |
| EC-CAK | Boeing 727-256 | Iberia Aragon |
| EC-CBA | Boeing 727-256 | Iberia Vascongadas |
| EC-CBB | Boeing 727-256 | Iberia Valencia |
| EC-CBC | Boeing 727-256 | Iberia Navarra |
| EC-CBD | Boeing 727-256 | Iberia Murcia |
| EC-CBE | Boeing 727-256 | Iberia Leon |
| EC-CBF | Boeing 727-256 | Iberia Gran Canaria |
| EC-CBG | Boeing 727-256 | Iberia Extremadura |
| EC-CBH | Boeing 727-256 | Iberia Galicia |
| EC-CBI | Boeing 727-256 | Iberia Asturias |
| EC-CBJ | Boeing 727-256 | Iberia Andalucia |
| EC-CBK | Boeing 727-256 | Iberia Baleares |
| EC-CBL | Boeing 727-256 | Iberia Tenerife |
| EC-CBM | Boeing 727-256 | Iberia Castilla La Vieja |
| EC-CBO | Douglas DC-10-30 | Iberia Costa del Sol |
| EC-CBP | Douglas DC-10-30 | Iberia Costa Dorada |
| EC-CEZ | Douglas DC-10-30 | Iberia Costa del Azahar |
| EC-CFA | Boeing 727-256 | Iberia Jerez Xeres Sherry |
| EC-CFB | Boeing 727-256 | Iberia Rioja |
| EC-CFC | Boeing 727-256 | Iberia Tarragona |
| EC-CFD | Boeing 727-256 | Iberia Montilla-Moriles |
| EC-CFE | Boeing 727-256 | Iberia Penedes |
| EC-CFF | Boeing 727-256 | Iberia Valdepenas |
| EC-CFG | Boeing 727-256 | Iberia La Mancha |
| EC-CFH | Boeing 727-256 | Iberia Priorato |
| EC-CFI | Boeing 727-256 | Iberia Carinena |

| Notes | Reg. | Type | Owner or Operator |
|-------|------|------|-------------------|
| | EC-CFK | Boeing 727-256 | Iberia *Riberio* |
| | EC-CGN | Douglas DC-9-32 | Aviaco *Martin Alonso Pinzon* |
| | EC-CGO | Douglas DC-9-32 | Aviaco *Pedro Alonso Nino* |
| | EC-CGP | Douglas DC-9-32 | Aviaco *Juan Sebastian Elcano* |
| | EC-CGQ | Douglas DC-9-32 | Aviaco *Alonso de Ojeda* |
| | EC-CGR | Douglas DC-9-32 | Aviaco *Francisco de Orellana* |
| | EC-CID | Boeing 727-256 | Iberia *Malaga* |
| | EC-CIE | Boeing 727-256 | Iberia *Esparragosa* |
| | EC-CLB | Douglas DC-10-30 | Iberia *Costa Blanca* |
| | EC-CLD | Douglas DC-9-32 | Aviaco *Hernando de Soto* |
| | EC-CLE | Douglas DC-9-32 | Aviaco *Jaun Ponce de Leon* |
| | EC-CSJ | Douglas DC-10-30 | Iberia *Costa de la Luz* |
| | EC-CSK | Douglas DC-10-30 | Iberia *Cornisa Cantabrica* |
| | EC-CTR | Douglas DC-9-34CF | Cargosur |
| | EC-CTS | Douglas DC-9-34CF | Cargosur |
| | EC-CTT | Douglas DC-9-34CF | Cargosur |
| | EC-CTU | Douglas DC-9-34CF | Cargosur |
| | EC-DCC | Boeing 727-256 | Iberia *Albarino* |
| | EC-DCD | Boeing 727-256 | Iberia *Chacoli* |
| | EC-DCE | Boeing 727-256 | Iberia *Mentrida* |
| | EC-DDV | Boeing 727-256 | Iberia *Acueducto de Segovia* |
| | EC-DDX | Boeing 727-256 | Iberia *Monasterio de Poblet* |
| | EC-DDY | Boeing 727-256 | Iberia *Cuevas de Altamira* |
| | EC-DDZ | Boeing 727-256 | Iberia *Murallas de Avila* |
| | EC-DEA | Douglas DC-10-30 | Iberia *Rias Gallegas* |
| | EC-DGB | Douglas DC-9-34 | Aviaco *Castillo de Javier* |
| | EC-DGC | Douglas DC-9-34 | Aviaco *Castillo de Sotomayor* |
| | EC-DGD | Douglas DC-9-34 | Aviaco *Castillo de Arcos* |
| | EC-DGE | Douglas DC-9-34 | Aviaco *Castillo de Bellver* |
| | EC-DHZ | Douglas DC-10-30 | Iberia *Costas Canarias* |
| | EC-DIA | Boeing 747-256B | Iberia *Tirso de Molina* |
| | EC-DIB | Boeing 747-256B | Iberia *Cervantes* |
| | EC-DLC | Boeing 747-256B (SCD) | Iberia *Francisco de Quevedo* |
| | EC-DLD | Boeing 747-256B (SCD) | Iberia *Lupe de Vega* |
| | EC-DLE | Airbus A.300B4-120 | Iberia *Doana* |
| | EC-DLF | Airbus A.300B4-120 | Iberia *Canadas del Teide* |
| | EC-DLG | Airbus A.300B4-120 | Iberia *Tablas de Daimiel* |
| | EC-DLH | Airbus A.300B4-120 | Iberia *Aigues Tortes* |
| | EC-DNP | Boeing 747-256B | Iberia *Juan Ramon Jimenez* |
| | EC-DNQ | Airbus A.300B4-120 | Iberia *Islas Cies* |
| | EC-DNR | Airbus A.300B4-120 | Iberia *Ordesa* |
| | EC-ECO | McD Douglas MD-83 | Air Sur |
| | EC-ECQ | Boeing 737-3S3 | Air Europa/Air Europe (G-BOYN) |
| | EC-ECR | Boeing 737-3Y0 | Air Europa |
| | EC-ECS | Boeing 737-375 | Air Europa |
| | EC-EEK | Boeing 747-256B (SCD) | Iberia *Garcia Lorca* |
| | EC-EFU | McD Douglas MD-83 | Lineas Aereas Canarias *Isla de Lanzarote* |
| | EC-EFX | Boeing 757-2G5 | LTE International Airways |
| | EC-EGH | Boeing 757-2G5 | LTE International Airways *Bluebird II* |
| | EC-EHA | Boeing 737-3L9 | Air Europa |
| | EC-EHT | McD Douglas MD-83 | Spanair *Sunrise* |
| | EC-EHX | Boeing 737-3A4 | Viva Air |
| | EC-EHY | Boeing 757-236 | Air Europa/Air Europe (G-BPSN) |
| | EC-EID | Boeing 737-3T0 | Universair |
| | EC-EIG | McD Douglas MD-83 | Spanair *Sunlight* |
| | EC-EII | Boeing 737-3Q8 | Viva Air |
| | EC-EIK | McD Douglas MD-83 | Aviaco |
| | EC-EIR | Boeing 737-3Q8 | Viva Air |
| | EC- | McD Douglas MD-83 | Oasis International Airlines |
| | EC-EJQ | McD Douglas MD-83 | Spanair *Sunshine* |
| | EC-EJU | McD Douglas MD-83 | Spanair *Sunbird* |
| | EC-EJZ | McD Douglas MD-83 | Lineas Aereas Canarias |
| | EC-EKM | McD Douglas MD-83 | Lineas Aereas Canarias |
| | EC-ELA | Boeing 757-236 | Air Europa/Air Europe (G-BOHC) |
| | EC-ELJ | Boeing 737-3Q8 | Viva Air |
| | EC-ELM | Douglas DC-8-62F | Cargosur |
| | EC-ELS | Boeing 757-236 | Air Europa/Air Europe (G-BNSF) |
| | EC-ELT | BAe 146-200QT | Pan Air Lineas Aéreas/TNT |
| | EC-ELY | Boeing 737-3K9 | Viva Air |
| | EC-EMA | Boeing 757-236 | Air Europa/Air Europe (G-BNSD) |
| | EC-EMD | Douglas DC-8-62F | Cargosur |
| | EC-EMG | McD Douglas MD-83 | Lineas Aereas Canarias |

| Reg. | Type | Owner or Operator | Notes |
|------|------|-------------------|-------|
| EC-EMI | Boeing 737-4Y0 | Nortjet *Alava* | |
| EC-EMT | McD Douglas MD-83 | Aviaco *Puerta de Alcala* | |
| EC-EMX | Douglas DC-8-62F | Cargosur | |
| EC-EMY | Boeing 737-4Y0 | Nortjet *Guipuzcoa* | |
| EC-ENQ | Boeing 757-2G5 | LTE International Airways *Bluebird III* | |
| EC-EOL | Boeing 757-236 | Air Europa/Air Europe (G-BRJE) | |
| EC-EOM | McD Douglas MD-83 | Oasis International Airlines | |
| EC-EON | Airbus A.300B4 | Iberia | |
| EC-EOO | Airbus A.300B4 | Iberia | |
| EC-EOY | McD Douglas MD-83 | Oasis International Airlines | |
| EC-EOZ | McD Douglas MD-83 | Spanair | |
| EC-EPA | BAe 146-200QT | Pan Air Lineas Aéreas/TNT | |
| EC-EPL | McD Douglas MD-83 | Spanair | |
| EC-EPM | McD Douglas MD-83 | Oasis International Airlines | |
| EC-EPN | Boeing 737-4Y0 | Nortjet | |
| EC-EQI | Douglas DC-8-62F | Cargosur | |
| EC-ESC | Boeing 757-236ER | Air Europa/Air Europe (G-BRJD) | |
| EC-ESJ | McD Douglas MD-83 | Spanair *Sunflower* | |
| EC-EST | Boeing 737-3L9 | Air Europa | |
| EC-ETB | Boeing 737-4Y0 | Futura International Airways | |
| EC-ETZ | Boeing 757-225 | LTE International Airways | |
| EC- | Boeing 757-236 | Air Europa/Air Europe (G-BRJI) | |
| EC- | Boeing 757-236 | Air Europa/Air Europe (G-BRJJ) | |
| EC-EUB | McD Douglas MD-87 | Iberia *Arrecife de Lanzarote* | |
| EC-EUC | McD Douglas MD-87 | Iberia *Ciudad de Burgos* | |
| EC-EUD | McD Douglas MD-87 | Iberia *Ciudad de Toledo* | |
| EC-EUE | McD Douglas MD-87 | Iberia *Ciudad de Sevilla* | |
| EC-EUF | McD Douglas MD-83 | Aviaco | |
| EC-EUG | McD Douglas MD-87 | Iberia | |
| EC-EUL | McD Douglas MD-87 | Iberia *Ciudad de Cadiz* | |
| EC-EUU | F.27 Friendship Mk 600 | Pan Air Lineas Aéreas/TNT | |
| EC-EUZ | McD Douglas MD-83 | Aviaco | |
| EC-EVB | McD Douglas MD-87 | Iberia | |
| EC-EVC | Boeing 757-236 | Air Europa | |
| EC-EVD | Boeing 757-236 | Air Europa/Air Europe (G-BRJF) | |
| EC-EVU | McD Douglas MD-83 | Aviaco | |
| EC-EVY | McD Douglas MD-82 | Spanair | |
| EC-EXF | McD Douglas MD-87 | Iberia *Ciudad de Pamplona* | |
| EC-EXG | McD Douglas MD-87 | Iberia *Ciudad de Almeria* | |
| EC-EXM | McD Douglas MD-87 | Iberia *Ciudad de Zaragoza* | |
| EC-EXN | McD Douglas MD-87 | Iberia *Ciudad de Badajoz* | |
| EC-EXR | McD Douglas MD-87 | Iberia *Ciudad de Oviedo* | |
| EC-EXT | McD Douglas MD-87 | Iberia *Ciudad de Albacete* | |
| EC-EXX | McD Douglas MD-83 | Oasis International Airlines | |
| EC-EXY | Boeing 737-4Y0 | Futura International Airways | |
| EC-EYB | McD Douglas MD-87 | Iberia *Ciudad de Onis* | |
| EC- | Boeing 737-4Y0 | Futura International Airways | |
| EC- | Boeing 767-300ER | Spanair | |
| EC- | Boeing 767-300ER | Spanair | |
| EC-EYP | McD Douglas MD-82 | Air Sur | |
| EC-EYS | Douglas DC-9-15MC | Air Sur | |
| EC-EYX | McD Douglas MD-87 | Iberia *Ciudad de Caceres* | |
| EC-EYY | McD Douglas MD-87 | Iberia | |
| EC-EYZ | McD Douglas MD-87 | Iberia | |
| EC- | Airbus A.320-211 | Iberia | |
| EC- | Airbus A.320-211 | Iberia | |
| EC- | Airbus A.320-211 | Iberia | |
| EC- | Airbus A.320-211 | Iberia | |
| EC- | Airbus A.320-211 | Iberia | |
| EC- | Airbus A.320-211 | Iberia | |
| EC- | Airbus A.320-211 | Iberia | |
| EC- | Airbus A.320-211 | Iberia | |
| EC- | Airbus A.320-211 | Iberia | |
| EC- | Airbus A.320-211 | Iberia | |
| EC- | Airbus A.320-211 | Iberia | |
| EC- | Airbus A.320-211 | Iberia | |
| EC- | Airbus A.320-211 | Iberia | |
| EC- | Airbus A.320-211 | Iberia | |
| EC- | Airbus A.320-211 | Iberia | |

# EI (Republic of Ireland)

Including complete current Irish Civil Register

| Reg. | Type | Owner or Operator |
|------|------|-------------------|
| EI-ABI | D.H.84 Dragon | Aer Lingus *Iolar* (EI-AFK) |
| EI-ADV | PA-12 Super Cruiser | R. E. Levis |
| EI-AFF | B.A. Swallow 2 ★ | J. McCarthy |
| EI-AFN | B.A. Swallow 2 ★ | J. McCarthy |
| EI-AGB | Miles M.38 Messenger 4 ★ | J. McLoughlin |
| EI-AGD | Taylorcraft Plus D ★ | H. Wolf |
| EI-AGJ | J/1 Autocrat | W. G. Rafter |
| EI-AHA | D.H.82A Tiger Moth ★ | J. H. Maher |
| EI-AHR | D.H.C.1 Chipmunk 22 ★ | C. Lane |
| EI-AKM | Piper J-3C-65 Cub | Setanta Flying Group |
| EI-ALH | Taylorcraft Plus D | N. Reilly |
| EI-ALP | Avro 643 Cadet | J. C. O'Loughlin |
| EI-ALU | Avro 631 Cadet | M. P. Cahill (*stored*) |
| EI-AMK | J/1 Autocrat | Irish Aero Club |
| EI-AMO | J/1B Aiglet | R. Hassett (*stored*) |
| EI-AND | Cessna 175A | M. A. Cooke |
| EI-ANT | Champion 7ECA Citabria | S. Donohoe |
| EI-ANY | PA-18 Super Cub 95 | T. Joyce & ptnrs |
| EI-AOB | PA-28 Cherokee 140 | J. Surdival & ptnrs |
| EI-AOK | Cessna F.172G | R. J. Cloughley & N. J. Simpson |
| EI-AOO | Cessna 150E | R. Hassett (*stored*) |
| EI-AOP | D.H.82A Tiger Moth ★ | Institute of Technology/Dublin |
| EI-AOS | Cessna 310B | Joyce Aviation Ltd |
| EI-APF | Cessna F.150F | L. O. Kennedy |
| EI-APS | Schleicher ASK.14 | G. W. Connolly & M. Slazenger |
| EI-ARH | Currie Wot/S.E.5 Replica | L. Garrison |
| EI-ARM | Currie Wot/S.E.5 Replica | L. Garrison |
| EI-ARW | Jodel D.R.1050 | P. Walsh & P. Ryan |
| EI-ASD | Boeing 737-248C | Aer Lingus *St Ide* |
| EI-ASE | Boeing 737-248C | Aer Lingus *St Fachtna* |
| EI-ASG | Boeing 737-248 | Aer Lingus *St Cormack* |
| EI-ASH | Boeing 737-248 | Aer Lingus *St Eugene* |
| EI-ASI | Boeing 747-148 | Aer Lingus *St Colmcille* |
| EI-ASJ | Boeing 747-148 | Aer Lingus *St Patrick* |
| EI-ASL | Boeing 737-248C | Aer Lingus *St Killian* |
| EI-AST | Cessna F.150H | Liberty Flying Group |
| EI-ATC | Cessna 310G | Iona National Airways Ltd |
| EI-ATJ | B.121 Pup 1 | Wexford Aero Club |
| EI-ATK | PA-28 Cherokee 140 | Mayo Flying Club Ltd |
| EI-ATS | M.S.880B Rallye Club | O. Bruton & G. Farrar |
| EI-AUC | Cessna FA.150K Aerobat | Twentieth Air Training Co Ltd |
| EI-AUE | M.S.880B Rallye Club | Kilkenny Flying Club Ltd |
| EI-AUG | M.S.894 Rallye Minerva 220 | K. O'Leary |
| EI-AUJ | M.S.880B Rallye Club | P. Mulhall |
| EI-AUM | J/1 Autocrat | J. G. Rafter |
| EI-AUO | Cessna FA.150K Aerobat | Kerry Aero Club |
| EI-AUS | J/5F Aiglet Trainer | T. Stephens & T. Lennon |
| EI-AUT | Forney F-1A Aircoupe | Joyce Aviation Ltd |
| EI-AUV | PA-23 Aztec 250C | Shannon Executive Aviation |
| EI-AUY | Morane-Saulnier M.S.502 | G. Warner/Duxford |
| EI-AVB | Aeronca 7AC Champion | P. Ryan |
| EI-AVC | Cessna F.337F | 337 Flying Group |
| EI-AVM | Cessna F.150L | P. Kearney |
| EI-AVN | Hughes 369HM | Helicopter Maintenance Ltd |
| EI-AVW | J/1N Alpha | A. Bailey |
| EI-AWE | Cessna F.150M | Third Flight Group |
| EI-AWH | Cessna 210J | Cork Flying Club Ltd |
| EI-AWP | D.H.82A Tiger Moth | A. Lyons |
| EI-AWU | Malmo MFI-9 Junior | M. R. Nesbitt & S. Duignan |
| EI-AWU | M.S.880B Rallye Club | Longford Aviation Ltd |
| EI-AWW | Cessna 414 | Shannon Executive Aviation Ltd |
| EI-AYA | M.S.880B Rallye Club | D. Bothwell & ptnrs |
| EI-AYB | GY-80 Horizon 180 | Westwing Flying Group |
| EI-AYD | AA-5 Traveler | P. Howick & ptnrs |
| EI-AYF | Cessna FRA.150L | Garda Flying Club |
| EI-AYI | M.S.880B Rallye Club | J. McNamara |
| EI-AYK | Cessna F.172M | S. T. Scully |
| EI-AYL | A.109 Airedale | J. Ronan |

| Reg. | Type | Owner or Operator | Notes |
|------|------|-------------------|-------|
| EI-AYN | BN-2A Islander | Aer Arran | |
| EI-AYO | Douglas DC-3A ★ | Science Museum, Wroughton | |
| EI-AYR | Schleicher ASK-16 | Kilkenny Airport Ltd | |
| EI-AYS | PA-22 Colt 108 | M. Skelly & R. Hall | |
| EI-AYV | M.S.892A Rallye Commodore 150 | P. Murtagh | |
| EI-AYW | PA-23 Aztec 250 | Chutehall International Ltd | |
| EI-AYY | Evans VP-1 | M. Donoghue | |
| EI-BAF | Thunder Ax6-56 balloon | W. G. Woollett | |
| EI-BAJ | SNCAN Stampe SV-4C | Dublin Tiger Group | |
| EI-BAO | Cessna F.172G | Kingdom Air Ltd | |
| EI-BAR | Thunder Ax8-105 balloon | J. Burke & V. Hourihane | |
| EI-BAS | Cessna F.172M | Falcon Aviation Ltd | |
| EI-BAT | Cessna F.150M | J. Barrow | |
| EI-BAV | PA-22 Colt 108 | J. Davy | |
| EI-BAY | Cameron V-77 balloon | F. N. Lewis | |
| EI-BBC | PA-28 Cherokee 180C | B. Healy | |
| EI-BBD | Evans VP-1 | Volksplane Group | |
| EI-BBE | Champion 7FC Tri-Traveler (tailwheel) | P. Forde & D. Connaire | |
| EI-BBG | M.S.880B Rallye Club | Weston Ltd | |
| EI-BBI | M.S.892 Rallye Commodore | Kilkenny Airport Ltd | |
| EI-BBJ | M.S.880B Rallye Club | Weston Ltd | |
| EI-BBK | A.109 Airedale | H. S. Igoe | |
| EI-BBL | R. Commander 690A | Earl of Granard | |
| EI-BBM | Cameron O-65 balloon | Dublin Ballooning Club | |
| EI-BBN | Cessna F.150M | Sligo N.W. Aero Club | |
| EI-BBO | M.S.893E Rallye 180GT | J. G. Lacey & ptnrs | |
| EI-BBV | Piper J-3C-65 Cub | F. Cronin | |
| EI-BCE | BN-2A-26 Islander | Aer Arann | |
| EI-BCF | Bensen B.8M | T. A. Brennan | |
| EI-BCH | M.S.892A Rallye Commodore 150 | The Condor Group | |
| EI-BCJ | F.8L Falco 1 Srs 3 | D. Kelly | |
| EI-BCK | Cessna F.172K | H. Caulfield | |
| EI-BCL | Cessna 182P | Iona National Airways | |
| EI-BCM | Piper J-3C-65 Cub | Kilmoon Flying Group | |
| EI-BCN | Piper J-3C-65 Cub | Snowflake Flying Group | |
| EI-BCO | Piper J-3C-65 Cub | J. Molloy | |
| EI-BCP | D.628 Condor | A. Delaney | |
| EI-BCR | Boeing 737-281 | Aer Lingus St Oliver Plunkett | |
| EI-BCS | M.S.880B Rallye Club | J. Murphy | |
| EI-BCT | Cessna 411A | Avmark (Ireland) Ltd | |
| EI-BCU | M.S.880B Rallye Club | Weston Ltd | |
| EI-BCW | M.S.880B Rallye Club | Kilkenny Flying Club | |
| EI-BCY | Beech 200 Super King Air (232) | Minister of Defence | |
| EI-BDH | M.S.880B Rallye Club | Munster Wings Ltd | |
| EI-BDK | M.S.880B Rallye Club | Limerick Flying Club Ltd | |
| EI-BDL | Evans VP-2 | J. Duggan | |
| EI-BDM | PA-23 Aztec 250D ★ | Industrial Training School | |
| EI-BDP | Cessna 182P | S. Bruton | |
| EI-BDR | PA-28 Cherokee 180 | K. Bickerdyke | |
| EI-BDY | Boeing 737-2E1 | Aer Lingus Teo St Brigid | |
| EI-BEA | M.S.880B Rallye 100ST | Weston Ltd | |
| EI-BEB | Boeing 737-248 | Aer Lingus Teo St Eunan | |
| EI-BEC | Boeing 737-248 | Aer Lingus Teo St Fiacre | |
| EI-BED | Boeing 747-130 | Aer Linte Eireann Teo St Kieran | |
| EI-BEE | Boeing 737-281 | Aer Lingus Teo St Cronin | |
| EI-BEI | — | Aer Lingus Teo | |
| EI-BEJ | — | Aer Lingus Teo | |
| EI-BEK | Short SD3-60 | Aer Lingus Commuter Ltd St Eithne | |
| EI-BEL | Short SD3-60 | Aer Lingus Commuter Ltd St Aoife | |
| EI-BEN | Piper J-3C-65 Cub | J. J. Sullivan | |
| EI-BEO | Cessna 310Q | Iona National Airways | |
| EI-BEP | M.S.892A Rallye Commodore 150 | H. Lynch & J. O'Leary | |
| EI-BEY | Naval N3N-3 ★ | Huntley & Huntley Ltd | |
| EI-BFF | Beech A.23 Musketeer | E. Hopkins | |
| EI-BFH | Bell 212 | Irish Helicopters Ltd | |
| EI-BFI | M.S.880B Rallye 100ST | J. O'Neill | |

263

| Notes | Reg. | Type | Owner or Operator |
|---|---|---|---|
| | EI-BFJ | Beech A.200 Super King Air (234) | Minister of Defence |
| | EI-BFM | M.S.893E Rallye 235GT | J. K. Group |
| | EI-BFO | Piper J-3C-90 Cub | M. Slattery |
| | EI-BFP | M.S.800B Rallye 100ST | Weston Ltd |
| | EI-BFR | M.S.880B Rallye 100ST | G. P. Moorhead |
| | EI-BFS | FRED Srs 2 | G. J. McGlennon |
| | EI-BFV | M.S.880B Rallye 100T | Ormond Flying Club |
| | EI-BGA | SOCATA Rallye 100ST | J. J. Frew |
| | EI-BGB | M.S.880B Rallye Club | Limerick Flying Club |
| | EI-BGD | M.S.880B Rallye Club | N. Kavanagh |
| | EI-BGG | M.S.892E Rallye 150GT | M. J. Hanlon |
| | EI-BGH | Cessna F.172N | Iona National Airways |
| | EI-BGJ | Cessna F.152 | Hibernian Flying Club |
| | EI-BGO | Canadair CL-44D-4J ★ | Irish Airports Authority/Dublin |
| | EI-BGP | Cessna 414A | Iona National Airways |
| | EI-BGS | M.S.893E Rallye 180GT | M. Farrelly |
| | EI-BGT | Colt 77A balloon | K. Haugh |
| | EI-BGU | M.S.880B Rallye Club | M. F. Neary |
| | EI-BHB | M.S.887 Rallye 125 | Hotel Bravo Flying Club |
| | EI-BHC | Cessna F.177RG | P. V. Maguire |
| | EI-BHF | M.S.892A Rallye Commodore 150 | B. Mullen |
| | EI-BHI | Bell 206B JetRanger 2 | J. Mansfield |
| | EI-BHK | M.S.880B Rallye Club | J. Lawlor & B. Lyons |
| | EI-BHL | Beech E90 King Air | Stewart Singlam Fabrics Ltd |
| | EI-BHM | Cessna 337E | The Ross Flying Group |
| | EI-BHN | M.S.893A Rallye Commodore 180 | K. O'Driscoll & ptnrs |
| | EI-BHP | M.S.893A Rallye Commodore 180 | G. Atkinson |
| | EI-BHT | Beech 77 Skipper | Waterford Aero Club |
| | EI-BHV | Champion 7EC Traveler | Condor Group |
| | EI-BHW | Cessna F.150F | R. Sharpe |
| | EI-BHY | SOCATA Rallye 150ST | D. Killian |
| | EI-BIB | Cessna F.152 | Galway Flying Club |
| | EI-BIC | Cessna F.172N | Oriel Flying Group Ltd |
| | EI-BID | PA-18 Super Cub 95 | D. MacCarthy |
| | EI-BIF | SOCATA Rallye 235E | Empire Enterprises Ltd |
| | EI-BIG | Zlin 526 | P. von Lonkhuyzen |
| | EI-BIJ | AB-206B JetRanger 2 | Celtic Helicopters Ltd |
| | EI-BIK | PA-18 Super Cub 180 | Dublin Gliding Club |
| | EI-BIM | M.S.880B Rallye Club | D. Millar |
| | EI-BIO | Piper J-3C-65 Cub | Monasterevin Flying Club |
| | EI-BIR | Cessna F.172M | B. Harrison & ptnrs |
| | EI-BIS | Robin R.1180TD | Robin Aiglon Group |
| | EI-BIT | M.S.887 Rallye 125 | City Aviation Ltd |
| | EI-BIU | Robin R.2112A | Wicklow Flying Group |
| | EI-BIV | Bellanca 8KCAB Citabria | Aerocrats Flying Group |
| | EI-BIW | M.S.880B Rallye Club | E. J. Barr |
| | EI-BJA | Cessna FRA.150L | Blackwater Flying Group |
| | EI-BJC | Aeronca 7AC Champion | R. J. Bentley |
| | EI-BJG | Robin R.1180 | N. Hanley |
| | EI-BJJ | Aeronca 15AC Sedan | A. A. Alderdice & S. H. Boyd |
| | EI-BJK | M.S.880B Rallye 110ST | T. Lennon |
| | EI-BJL | Cessna 550 Citation II | Helicopter Maintenance Ltd |
| | EI-BJM | Cessna A.152 | Leinster Aero Club |
| | EI-BJO | Cessna R.172K | P. Hogan & G. Ryder |
| | EI-BJS | AA-5B Tiger | P. Morrisey |
| | EI-BJW | D.H.104 Dove 6 ★ | Waterford Museum |
| | EI-BKC | Aeronca 115AC Sedan | G. Treacy |
| | EI-BKD | Mooney M.20J | Limerick Warehousing Ltd |
| | EI-BKF | Cessna F.172H | M. & M. C. Veale |
| | EI-BKK | Taylor JT.1 Monoplane | Waterford Aero Club |
| | EI-BKM | Zenith CH.200 | D. van de Braam |
| | EI-BKN | M.S.880B Rallye 100ST | Weston Ltd |
| | EI-BKS | Eipper Quicksilver | Irish Microlight Ltd |
| | EI-BKT | AB-206B JetRanger 3 | Irish Helicopters Ltd |
| | EI-BKU | M.S.892A Rallye Commodore 150 | Limerick Flying Club |
| | EI-BLB | SNCAN Stampe SV-4C | J. E. Hutchinson & R. A. Stafford |
| | EI-BLD | Bolkow Bo 105C | Irish Helicopters Ltd |
| | EI-BLE | Eipper Microlight | R. P. St George-Smith |

| Reg. | Type | Owner or Operator | Notes |
|------|------|-------------------|-------|
| EI-BLG | AB-206B JetRanger 3 | Monarch Property Services Ltd | |
| EI-BLN | Eipper Quicksilver MX | O. J. Conway & B. Daffy | |
| EI-BLO | Catto CP.16 | R. W. Hall | |
| EI-BLR | PA-34-200T Seneca II | R. Paris | |
| EI-BLU | Evans VP-1 | S. Pallister | |
| EI-BLY | Sikorsky S-61N | Irish Helicopters Ltd | |
| EI-BMA | M.S.880B Rallye Club | W. Rankin & M. Kelleher | |
| EI-BMB | M.S.880B Rallye 100T | Clyde Court Development Ltd | |
| EI-BMC | Hiway Demon Skytrike | S. Pallister | |
| EI-BMF | Laverda F.8L Falco | M. Slazenger & H. McCann | |
| EI-BMH | M.S.880B Rallye Club | N. J. Bracken | |
| EI-BMI | SOCATA TB.9 Tampico | Weston Ltd | |
| EI-BMJ | M.S.880B Rallye 100T | Weston Ltd | |
| EI-BMK | Cessna 310Q | Iona National Airways Ltd | |
| EI-BML | PA-23 Aztec 250 | Bruton Aircraft Engineering Ltd | |
| EI-BMM | Cessna F.152 II | Iona National Airways Ltd | |
| EI-BMN | Cessna F.152 II | Iona National Airways Ltd | |
| EI-BMO | Robin R.2160 | L. Gavin & pntrs | |
| EI-BMS | Cessna F.177RG | A. M. Smyth | |
| EI-BMU | Monnet Sonerai II | P. Forde & D. Connaire | |
| EI-BMV | AA-5 Traveler | R. C. Cunningham | |
| EI-BMW | Vulcan Air Trike | L. Maddock | |
| EI-BNA | Douglas DC-8-63CF | Aer Turas Teo | |
| EI-BNB | Lake LA-4-200 Buccaneer | L. McNamara & M. Ledwith | |
| EI-BNC | Cessna F.152 | Iona National Airlines | |
| EI-BND | Conroy CL-44-0 | HeavyLift Cargo Airlines Ltd/Stansted | |
| EI-BNF | Goldwing Canard | T. Morelli | |
| EI-BNG | M.S.892A Rallye Commodore 150 | Shannon Executive Aviation | |
| EI-BNH | Hiway Skytrike | M. Martin | |
| EI-BNJ | Evans VP-2 | G. A. Cashman | |
| EI-BNK | Cessna U.206F | Irish Parachute Club Ltd | |
| EI-BNL | Rand KR-2 | K. Hayes | |
| EI-BNP | Rotorway 133 | R. L. Renfroe | |
| EI-BNT | Cvjetkovic CA-65 | B. Tobin & P. G. Ryan | |
| EI-BNU | M.S.880B Rallye Club | P. A. Doyle | |
| EI-BOA | Pterodactyl Ptraveller | A. Murphy | |
| EI-BOE | SOCATA TB.10 Tobago | P. Byron & ptnrs | |
| EI-BOH | Eipper Quicksilver | J. Leech | |
| EI-BOK | PA-23 Aztec 250E | K. A. O'Connor | |
| EI-BOM | Boeing 737-2T4 | Air Tara Ltd (leased to Delta A/L) | |
| EI-BON | Boeing 737-2T4 | Air Tara Ltd (leased to Delta A/L) | |
| EI-BOO | PA-23 Aztec 250C | P. Mercer | |
| EI-BOR | Bell 222 | Westair Ltd | |
| EI-BOT | AS.350B Ecureuil | J. J. Kelly | |
| EI-BOV | Rand KR-2 | G. O'Hara & G. Callan | |
| EI-BOX | Duet | K. Riccius | |
| EI-BPB | PA-28R Cherokee Arrow 200 | Rathcoole Flying Club | |
| EI-BPD | Short SD3-60 | Aer Lingus Commuter Ltd St Finbarr | |
| EI-BPE | Viking Dragonfly | G. Bracken | |
| EI-BPI | EMB-110P1 Bandeirante | Iona National Airways Ltd | |
| EI-BPJ | Cessna 182A | J. Matthews & V. McCarthy | |
| EI-BPL | Cessna F.172K | Phoenix Flying | |
| EI-BPM | AS.350B Ecureuil | Helicopter Maintenance Ltd | |
| EI-BPO | Puma Skytrike | A. Morelli | |
| EI-BPP | Quicksilver MX | J. A. Smith | |
| EI-BPS | PA-30 Twin Comanche 160 | Group Air | |
| EI-BPT | Skyhook Sabre | T. McGrath | |
| EI-BPU | Hiway Demon | A. Channing | |
| EI-BRH | Mainair Gemini Flash | F. Warren & T. McGrath | |
| EI-BRK | Flexiform Trike | L. Maddock | |
| EI-BRM | Cessna 172Q | Iona National Airways | |
| EI-BRO | Cessna F.152 | Iona National Airways | |
| EI-BRP | Canadair CL-44J | HeavyLift Cargo Airlines Ltd/Stansted | |
| EI-BRS | Cessna P.172D | D. & M. Hillery | |
| EI-BRT | Flexwing M17727 | M. J. McCrystal | |
| EI-BRU | Evans VP-1 | R. Smith & T. Coughlan | |
| EI-BRV | Hiway Demon | M. Garvey & C. Tully | |
| EI-BRW | Ultralight Deltabird | A. & E. Aerosports | |
| EI-BRX | Cessna FRA.150L | P. O'Donnell | |
| EI-BSB | Jodel D.112 | W. Kennedy | |
| EI-BSC | Cessna F.172N | S. Phelan | |
| EI-BSD | Enstrom F-28A | Clark Aviation | |
| EI-BSF | H.S.748 Srs 1 | Ryanair Ltd (withdrawn) | |

| Notes | Reg. | Type | Owner or Operator |
|---|---|---|---|
| | EI-BSG | Bensen B.80 | J. Todd |
| | EI-BSK | SOCATA TB.9 Tampico | Weston Ltd |
| | EI-BSL | PA-34-220T Seneca | E. L. Symons |
| | EI-BSN | Cameron O-65 balloon | W. Woollett |
| | EI-BSO | PA-28 Cherokee 140B | D. Rooney |
| | EI-BSP | Short SD3-60 | Aer Lingus Commuter Ltd *St Senan* |
| | EI-BSQ | Thundercolt Ax6-56Z balloon | D. Hooper |
| | EI-BSR | Lake LA.4-200 Buccaneer | Derg Developments Ltd |
| | EI-BST | Bell 206B JetRanger | Celtic Helicopters Ltd |
| | EI-BSU | Champion 7KCAB | R. Bentley |
| | EI-BSV | SOCATA TB.20 Trinidad | J. Condron |
| | EI-BSW | Solar Wings Pegasus XL-R | E. Fitzgerald |
| | EI-BSX | Piper J-3C-65 Cub | J. & T. O'Dwyer |
| | EI-BTC | McD Douglas MD-82 | Irish Aerospace Ltd (*leased in US*) |
| | EI-BTD | McD Douglas MD-82 | Irish Aerospace Ltd (*leased in US*) |
| | EI-BTF | Boeing 737-3Y0 | Air Tara Ltd (*leased to Corse Air*) |
| | EI-BTN | L.1101-385 TriStar 1 | Air Tara Ltd (*leased to Air America*) |
| | EI-BTS | Boeing 747-283B | Air Tara Ltd (*leased to Philippine A/L*) |
| | EI-BTT | Boeing 737-3Y0 | Air Tara Ltd (*leased to Corse Air*) |
| | EI-BTX | McD Douglas MD-82 | Air Tara Ltd (*leased to AeroMexico*) |
| | EI-BTY | McD Douglas MD-82 | Air Tara Ltd |
| | EI-BUA | Cessna 172M | Skyhawks Flying Club |
| | EI-BUC | Jodel D.9 Bebe | L. Maddock |
| | EI-BUD | Boeing 737-348 | Aer Lingus *St Lawrance O'Toole* |
| | EI-BUE | Boeing 737-348 | Aer Lingus *St Ciara* |
| | EI-BUF | Cessna 210N | 210 Group |
| | EI-BUG | SOCATA ST.10 Diplomate | Diplomat Air Ltd |
| | EI-BUH | Lake LA.4-200 Buccaneer | Derg Aviation (Group) Ltd |
| | EI-BUJ | M.S.892A Rallye Commodore 150 | S. Bruton |
| | EI-BUL | MW-5 Sorcerer | J. Conlon |
| | EI-BUM | Cessna 404 | Iona National Airways Ltd |
| | EI-BUN | Beech 76 Duchess | S. Ryle |
| | EI-BUO | Lavery Sea Hawker | C. Lavery & C. Donaldson |
| | EI-BUQ | — | Ryanair Ltd |
| | EI-BUR | PA-38-112 Tomahawk | Leoni Aviation Ltd |
| | EI-BUS | PA-38-112 Tomahawk | Leoni Aviation Ltd |
| | EI-BUT | M.S.893A Commodore 180 | T. Keating |
| | EI-BUU | Solar Wings Pegasus XL-R | R. L. T. Hudson |
| | EI-BUV | Cessna 172RG | J. J. Spollen |
| | EI-BUW | Noble Hardman Snowbird IIIA | T.I.F.C. & I.S. Ltd |
| | EI-BUX | Agusta A.109A | Orring Ltd |
| | EI-BUY | Cessna 551 Citation 2 | Tool & Mould Steel (Ireland) Ltd |
| | EI-BUZ | Robinson R-22 | Leoni Aviation Ltd |
| | EI-BVA | Cessna 404 Titan | Iona National Airways Ltd |
| | EI-BVB | Whittaker MW.6 Merlin | R. England |
| | EI-BVC | Cameron N-65 balloon | E. Shepherd |
| | EI-BVE | Jodel D.9 Bebe | J. Greene |
| | EI-BVF | Cessna F.172N | First Phantom Group |
| | EI-BVG | BAC One-Eleven 525FT | Ryanair Ltd |
| | EI-BVH | RomBac One-Eleven 561RC | Ryanair Ltd *The Spirit of Tara* |
| | EI-BVI | BAC One-Eleven 525FT | Ryanair Ltd |
| | EI-BVJ | AMF Chevvron 232 | W. T. King & S. G. Dunne |
| | EI-BVK | PA-38 Tomahawk | Shannon Executive Aviation |
| | EI-BVM | Short SD3-60 | Aer Lingus Commuter Ltd *St Maeve* |
| | EI-BVN | Bell 206B Jet Ranger 3 | Helicopter Hire (Ireland) Ltd |
| | EI-BVP | Cessna T.303 | Iona National Airways Ltd |
| | EI-BVQ | Cameron Can SS balloon | T. McCormack |
| | EI-BVS | Cessna 172RG | P. Bruno |
| | EI-BVT | Evans VP-2 | J. J. Sullivan |
| | EI-BVU | Cessna 152 | Iona National Airways Ltd |
| | EI-BVW | Cessna 152 | Iona National Airways Ltd |
| | EI-BVX | EMB-110P1 Bandeirante | Iona National Airways Ltd |
| | EI-BVY | Zenith 200AA-RW | J. Matthews & ptnrs |
| | EI-BVZ | Scheibe SF.25B Falke | D. Lamb & ptnrs |
| | EI-BWD | McD Douglas MD-83 | Air Tara Ltd (*leased to BWIA*) |
| | EI-BWF | Boeing 747-283B | Air Tara Ltd (*leased to Philippine A/L*) |
| | EI-BWJ | BAC One-Eleven 210AC | Air Tara Ltd |
| | EI-BWM | BAC One-Eleven 201AC | Air Tara Ltd |
| | EI-BWN | BAC One-Eleven 203AE | Air Tara Ltd |
| | EI-BWO | BAC One-Eleven 203AE | Air Tara Ltd |
| | EI-BWP | BAC One-Eleven 203AE | Air Tara Ltd |
| | EI-BWS | BAC One-Eleven 201AC | Air Tara Ltd |
| | EI-BWT | BAC One-Eleven 414ED | Air Tara Ltd |

| Reg. | Type | Owner or Operator | Notes |
|------|------|-------------------|-------|
| EI-BXA | Boeing 737-448 | Aer Lingus Teo *St Conleth* | |
| EI-BXB | Boeing 737-448 | Aer Lingus Teo *St Gall* | |
| EI-BXC | Boeing 737-448 | Aer Lingus Teo *St Brendan* | |
| EI-BXD | Boeing 737-448 | Aer Lingus Teo | |
| EI-BXE | Boeing 737-548 | Aer Lingus Teo *St Columba* | |
| EI-BXF | Boeing 737-548 | Aer Lingus Teo *St Albert* | |
| EI-BXG | Boeing 737-548 | Aer Lingus Teo *St Munchen* | |
| EI-BXH | Boeing 737-548 | Aer Lingus Teo *St Phelim* | |
| EI-BXI | Boeing 737-448 | Aer Lingus Teo *St Finnian* | |
| EI-BXJ | Boeing 737-548 | Aer Lingus Teo *St Jarlath* | |
| EI-BXK | — | Aer Lingus Teo | |
| EI-BXL | — | Aer Lingus Teo | |
| EI-BXM | — | Aer Lingus Teo | |
| EI-BXN | Microlight | C. O'Donaghue | |
| EI-BXO | Fouga CM.170 Magister | G. W. Connolly | |
| EI-BXP | PA-23 Aztec 250E | Aer Arran | |
| EI-BXR | Aerospatiale ATR-42-300 | Ryanair Ltd | |
| EI-BXS | Aerospatiale ATR-42-300 | Ryanair Ltd | |
| EI-BXT | D.62B Condor | J. Sweeney | |
| EI-BXU | PA-28-161 Warrior II | W. T. King | |
| EI-BXX | AB-206B JetRanger | Leoni Aviation Ltd | |
| EI-BXY | Boeing 737-2S3 | Aer Lingus Teo *St Canice* | |
| EI-BXZ | Flexiwing | R. England | |
| EI-BYA | Thruster TST Mk 1 | E. Fagan | |
| EI-BYB | Robinson R-22B | Robinson Group | |
| EI-BYC | Bensen B.8MR | C. Kirwan | |
| EI-BYD | Cessna 150J | Kestrel Flying Group | |
| EI-BYE | PA-31-350 Navajo Chieftain | EI-Air Exports Ltd | |
| EI-BYF | Cessna 150M | Kestrel Flying Group | |
| EI-BYG | SOCATA TB.9 Tampico | Weston Ltd | |
| EI-BYH | Cessna 340A | Claddagh Air Carriers | |
| EI-BYJ | Bell 206B JetRanger | Celtic Helicopters Ltd | |
| EI-BYK | PA-23 Aztec 250E | M. F. Hilary | |
| EI-BYL | Zenith CH.250 | A. Corcoran & J. Martin | |
| EI-BYM | Cessna 500 Citation | Leoni Aviation Ltd | |
| EI-BYN | Cessna 550 Citation II | J. Mansfield | |
| EI-BYO | Aerospatiale ATR-42-300 | Ryanair Ltd | |
| EI-BYP | Aerospatiale ATR-42-300 | Ryanair Ltd | |
| EI-BYQ | Aerospatiale ATR-42-300 | Ryanair Ltd | |
| EI-BYS | Robinson R-22B | G. V. Maloney | |
| EI-BYT | AS.350B Ecureuil | Helicopter Hire | |
| EI-BYV | Hughes 369D | Irish Helicopters Ltd | |
| EI-BYW | Thruster 3 Axis | S. P. McCaffrey | |
| EI-BYX | Champion 7GCAA | J. Keane & P. Gallagher | |
| EI-BYY | Piper J-3C-85 Cub | A. J. Haines | |
| EI-BYZ | PA-44-180 Seminole | European College of Aeronautics | |
| EI-BZA | Boeing 747-283B | Air Tara Ltd (*leased to Philippine A/L*) | |
| EI-BZB | Airbus A.300C4 | GPA Finance (*leased to Philippine A/L*) | |
| EI-BZD | Douglas DC-10-30 | GPA Finance Ltd (*leased to Garuda*) | |
| EI-BZE | Boeing 737-3Y0 | GPA Group Ltd (*leased to Philippine A/L*) | |
| EI-BZF | Boeing 737-3Y0 | GPA Group Ltd (*leased to Philippine A/L*) | |
| EI-BZH | Boeing 737-3Y0 | GPA Group Ltd (*leased to Philippine A/L*) | |
| EI-BZI | Boeing 737-3Y0 | GPA Group Ltd (*leased to Philippine A/L*) | |
| EI-BZJ | Boeing 737-3Y0 | GPA Group Ltd (*leased to Philippine A/L*) | |
| EI-BZK | Boeing 737-3Y0 | GPA Group Ltd (*leased to Philippine A/L*) | |
| EI-BZL | Boeing 737-3Y0 | GPA Group Ltd (*leased to Philippine A/L*) | |
| EI-BZM | Boeing 737-3Y0 | GPA Group Ltd (*leased to Philippine A/L*) | |
| EI-BZN | Boeing 737-3Y0 | GPA Group Ltd (*leased to Philippine A/L*) | |
| EI-BZU | Douglas DC-8-71 | GPA Group Ltd (*leased to Kenya Airways*) | |
| EI-BZZ | Douglas DC-9-15 | GPA Finance Ltd (*stored*) | |
| EI-CAA | Cessna Fr.172J | K. O'Connor | |
| EI-CAB | Grob G.115 | European College of Aeronautics | |
| EI-CAC | Grob G.115 | European College of Aeronautics | |
| EI-CAD | Grob G.115 | European College of Aeronautics | |
| EI-CAE | Grob B.115 | European College of Aeronautics | |
| EI-CAF | Bell 206B JetRanger 2 | Irish Helicopters Ltd | |
| EI-CAG | PA-31 Navajo | Leoni Aviation Ltd | |
| EI-CAH | G.1159C Gulfstream 4 | Ardesir Ltd | |
| EI-CAJ | O'Leary Biplane | J. O. Leary | |
| EI-CAK | Douglas DC-8-63AF | Aer Turas Teo | |
| EI-CAL | Boeing 767-3Y0ER | Aer Lingus Teo *St Kevin* | |
| EI-CAM | Boeing 767-3Y0ER | Aer Lingus Teo *St Ibar* | |

| Notes | Reg. | Type | Owner or Operator |
|---|---|---|---|
| | EI-CAN | Aerotech MW.5 Sorcerer | J. Conlon |
| | EI-CAO | Cameron O-84 balloon | K. Haugh |
| | EI-CAP | Cessna R.182RG | P. Byrne |
| | EI-CAR | Schweizer 269C | Island Helicopters Ltd |
| | EI-CAU | AMF Chevvron 232 | H. Sydner |
| | EI-CAV | — | — |
| | EI-CAW | — | — |
| | EI-CAX | Cessna P.210N | — |
| | EI-CAY | Mooney M.20C | Other Worlds Ltd |
| | EI-CAZ | — | Ranger Flights Ltd |
| | EI-CBA | Douglas DC-9-15 | GPA Finance Ltd (*stored*) |
| | EI-CBB | Douglas DC-9-15 | GPA Finance Ltd (*stored*) |
| | EI-CBC | Aerospatiale ATR-72 | Air Tara Ltd |
| | EI-CBD | Aerospatiale ATR-72 | Air Tara Ltd |
| | EI-CBF | Aerospatiale ATR-42-300 | Air Tara Ltd (*leased to Trans World Express*) |
| | EI-CBG | Douglas DC-9-51 | GPA Finance Ltd (*leased to Hawaiian*) |
| | EI-CBH | Douglas DC-9-51 | GPA Finance Ltd (*leased to Hawaiian*) |
| | EI-CBI | Douglas DC-9-51 | Air Tara Ltd (*leased to Hawaiian*) |
| | EI-CBJ | — | — |
| | EI-CBK | Aerospatiale ATR-42-300 | Air Tara Ltd |
| | EI-CBL | Boeing 737-2K6 | Air Tara Ltd |
| | EI-CBM | L-1011-385 TriStar 100 | Air Tara Ltd |
| | EI-CBN | McD Douglas MD-83 | Air Tara Ltd |
| | EI-CBO | McD Douglas MD-83 | Air Sur |
| | EI-CCA | Beech 19A Musketeer | J. Donoher |
| | EI-CCB | PA-44-180 Seminole | European College of Aeronautics |
| | EI-CCC | — | — |
| | EI-CCD | Grob G.115A | European College of Aeronautics |
| | EI-CCE | — | — |
| | EI-CCF | — | — |
| | EI-CCG | Robinson R-22B | Leoni Aviation Ltd |
| | EI-CCH | — | — |
| | EI-CCI | AA-5 Traveler | J. Crowe |
| | EI-CCJ | Cessna 152 | Irish Aero Club |
| | EI-CCK | Cessna 152 | Irish Aero Club |
| | EI-CCL | Cessna 152 | Irish Aero Club |
| | EI-CCM | Cessna 152 | Irish Aero Club |
| | EI-CCN | Grob G.115A | European College of Aeronautics |
| | EI-CCO | — | — |
| | EI-CCP | — | — |
| | EI-CCR | — | — |
| | EI-CCS | Enstrom 280C-UK | Orring Ltd |
| | EI-CCT | — | — |
| | EI-CCU | BAC One-Eleven 531FS | Ryanair Ltd |
| | EI-CCV | — | — |
| | EI-CCW | BAC One-Eleven 509EW | Ryanair Ltd (G-BSYN) |
| | EI-CCX | BAC One-Eleven 531FS | Ryanair Ltd |
| | EI-CCY | — | — |
| | EI-CCZ | — | — |
| | EI-CGO | Douglas DC-8-63AF | Aer Turas Teo |
| | EI-CHL | Bell 206B JetRanger 3 | Celtic Helicopters Ltd |
| | EI-EDR | PA-28R Cherokee Arrow 200 | Victor Mike Flying Group Ltd |
| | EI-FDX | Cessna 208 | Iona National Airways (FedEx) |
| | EI-FKA | Fokker 50 | Aer Lingus Commuter *St Fionnan* |
| | EI-FKB | Fokker 50 | Aer Lingus Commuter *St Fergal* |
| | EI-FKC | Fokker 50 | Aer Lingus Commuter *St Fidelma* |
| | EI-FKD | Fokker 50 | Aer Lingus Commuter *St Flannan* |
| | EI-FKE | Fokker 50 | Aer Lingus Commuter |
| | EI-FKF | Fokker 50 | Aer Lingus Commuter |
| | EI-LJG | Canadair CL.601-3A Challenger | Ven Air |
| | EI-LMG | Bell 206L-3 LongRanger | Ven Air |
| | EI-SNN | Cessna 650 Citation III | Westair Aviation Ltd |
| | EI-XMA | Robinson R-22B | Leoni Aviation Ltd |

# EL (Liberia)

| | EL-AJC | Boeing 707-430 ★ | Airport Fire Services/Bournemouth |
|---|---|---|---|
| | EL-AJO | Douglas DC-8-55F | Liberia World Airways |
| | EL-AJQ | Douglas DC-8-54F | Liberia World Airways |
| | EL-AJT | Boeing 707-344B | Liberia World Airways |

| Reg. | Type | Owner or Operator | Notes |
|------|------|-------------------|-------|
| EL-AKA | Boeing 707-123B | Omega Air | |
| EL-JNS | Boeing 707-323C | Transway Air International | |
| EL-ZGS | Boeing 707-309C | Jet Cargo Liberia | |

## EP (Iran)

| | | | |
|------|------|-------------------|-------|
| EP-IAA | Boeing 747SP-86 | Iran Air *Fars* | |
| EP-IAB | Boeing 747SP-86 | Iran Air *Kurdistan* | |
| EP-IAC | Boeing 747SP-86 | Iran Air *Khuzestan* | |
| EP-IAD | Boeing 747SP-86 | Iran Air *Rushdie* | |
| EP-IAG | Boeing 747-286B (SCD) | Iran Air *Azarabadegan* | |
| EP-IAH | Boeing 747-286B (SCD) | Iran Air *Khorasan* | |
| EP-IAM | Boeing 747-186B | Iran Air | |

## ET (Ethiopia)

| | | | |
|------|------|-------------------|-------|
| ET-AIE | Boeing 767-260ER | Ethiopian Airlines | |
| ET-AIF | Boeing 767-260ER | Ethiopian Airlines | |
| ET-AIV | Boeing 707-327C | Ethiopian Airlines | |
| ET-AIZ | Boeing 767-260ER | Ethiopian Airlines | |
| ET-AJS | Boeing 757-260PF | Ethiopian Airlines | |
| ET-AJX | Boeing 757-260PF | Ethiopian Airlines | |
| ET-AJY | Boeing 757-260PF | Ethiopian Airlines | |
| ET-AJZ | Boeing 707-385C | Ethiopian Airlines | |

## F (France)

| | | | |
|------|------|-------------------|-------|
| F-BGNR | V.708 Viscount ★ | Air Service Training Ltd/Perth | |
| F-BIUK | F.27 Friendship Mk 100 | Uni-Air | |
| F-BJEN | S.E.210 Caravelle 10B | Air Charter/Europe Aero Service | |
| F-BJTU | S.E.210 Caravelle 10B | Aero France International | |
| F-BLHX | Nord 262A | Compagnie Air Littoral | |
| F-BMKS | S.E.210 Caravelle 10B | Jet Europe/Europe Aero Service | |
| F-BOJA | Boeing 727-228 | Air France | |
| F-BOJD | Boeing 727-228 | Air France | |
| F-BPJK | Boeing 727-228 | Air France | |
| F-BPJL | Boeing 727-228 | Air France | |
| F-BPJO | Boeing 727-228 | Air France | |
| F-BPJP | Boeing 727-228 | Air France | |
| F-BPJQ | Boeing 727-228 | Air Charter | |
| F-BPJR | Boeing 727-228 | Air France | |
| F-BPJS | Boeing 727-228 | Air France | |
| F-BPJT | Boeing 727-228 | Air Charter/Europe Aero Service | |
| F-BPJU | Boeing 727-214 | Air Charter | |
| F-BPJV | Boeing 727-214 | Airbus Industrie | |
| F-BPPA | Aero Spacelines Super Guppy-201 | *Airbus Skylink 2* | |
| F-BPUA | F.27 Friendship Mk 500 | Air France | |
| F-BPUB | F.27 Friendship Mk 500 | Air France | |
| F-BPUC | F.27 Friendship Mk 500 | Air France | |
| F-BPUD | F.27 Friendship Mk 500 | Air France | |
| F-BPUE | F.27 Friendship Mk 500 | Air France | |
| F-BPUF | F.27 Friendship Mk 500 | Air France | |
| F-BPUG | F.27 Friendship Mk 500 | Air France | |
| F-BPUH | F.27 Friendship Mk 500 | Air France | |
| F-BPUI | F.27 Friendship Mk 500 | Air France | |
| F-BPUJ | F.27 Friendship Mk 500 | Air France | |
| F-BPUK | F.27 Friendship Mk 500 | Air France | |
| F-BPUL | F.27 Friendship Mk 500 | Air France | |
| F-BPVA | Boeing 747-128 | Air France | |
| F-BPVB | Boeing 747-128 | Air France | |
| F-BPVC | Boeing 747-128 | Air France/Air Inter | |
| F-BPVD | Boeing 747-128 | Air France | |
| F-BPVE | Boeing 747-128 | Air France | |
| F-BPVF | Boeing 747-128 | Air France | |
| F-BPVG | Boeing 747-128 | Air France | |
| F-BPVH | Boeing 747-128 | Air France | |

| Notes | Reg. | Type | Owner or Operator |
|---|---|---|---|
| | F-BPVJ | Boeing 747-128 | Air France |
| | F-BPVK | Boeing 747-128 | Air France |
| | F-BPVL | Boeing 747-128 | Air France |
| | F-BPVM | Boeing 747-128 | Air France |
| | F-BPVN | Boeing 747-128 | Air France |
| | F-BPVO | Boeing 747-228F (SCD) | Air France |
| | F-BPVP | Boeing 747-128 | Air France |
| | F-BPVQ | Boeing 747-128 | Air France |
| | F-BPVR | Boeing 747-228F (SCD) | Air France |
| | F-BPVS | Boeing 747-228B (SCD) | Air France |
| | F-BPVT | Boeing 747-228B (SCD) | Air France |
| | F-BPVU | Boeing 747-228B (SCD) | Air France |
| | F-BPVV | Boeing 747-228F (SCD) | Air France |
| | F-BPVX | Boeing 747-228B (SCD) | Air France |
| | F-BPVY | Boeing 747-228B | Air France |
| | F-BPVZ | Boeing 747-228F (SCD) | Air France |
| | F-BRUN | Beech 99 | T.A.T./Uni-Air |
| | F-BSUM | F.27 Friendship Mk 500 | Air France |
| | F-BSUN | F.27 Friendship Mk 500 | Air France |
| | F-BSUO | F.27 Friendship Mk 500 | Air France |
| | F-BTDB | Douglas DC-10-30 | Union de Transports Aériens (UTA) |
| | F-BTDC | Douglas DC-10-30 | Union de Transports Aériens (UTA) |
| | F-BTDD | Douglas DC-10-30 | Union de Transports Aériens (UTA) |
| | F-BTDE | Douglas DC-10-30 | Union de Transports Aériens (UTA) |
| | F-BTDG | Boeing 747-3B3 (SCD) | Union de Transports Aériens (UTA) |
| | F-BTDH | Boeing 747-3B3 (SCD) | Union de Transports Aériens (UTA) |
| | F-BTGV | Aero Spacelines Super Guppy-201 | Airbus Industrie |
| | | | *Airbus Skylink 1* |
| | F-BTMA | Beech 99 | T.A.T./Uni-Air |
| | F-BTMD | Mercure 100 | Air Inter |
| | F-BTMJ | Beech 99A | T.A.T./Uni-Air |
| | F-BTMK | Beech 99A | T.A.T./Uni-Air |
| | F-BTOA | S.E.210 Caravelle 12 | Industries Air Charter |
| | F-BTOC | S.E.210 Caravelle 12 | Air Inter |
| | F-BTOE | S.E.210 Caravelle 12 | Air Inter |
| | F-BTSC | Concorde 101 | Air France |
| | F-BTSD | Concorde 101 | Air France |
| | F-BTTA | Mercure 100 | Air Inter |
| | F-BTTB | Mercure 100 | Air Inter |
| | F-BTTC | Mercure 100 | Air Inter |
| | F-BTTD | Mercure 100 | Air Inter |
| | F-BTTE | Mercure 100 | Air Inter |
| | F-BTTF | Mercure 100 | Air Inter |
| | F-BTTG | Mercure 100 | Air Inter |
| | F-BTTH | Mercure 100 | Air Inter |
| | F-BTTI | Mercure 100 | Air Inter |
| | F-BTTJ | Mercure 100 | Air Inter |
| | F-BUAE | Airbus A.300B2 | Air Inter |
| | F-BUAF | Airbus A.300B2 | Air Inter |
| | F-BUAG | Airbus A.300B2 | Air Inter |
| | F-BUAH | Airbus A.300B2 | Air Inter |
| | F-BUAI | Airbus A.300B2 | Air Inter |
| | F-BUAJ | Airbus A.300B2 | Air Inter |
| | F-BUAK | Airbus A.300B2 | Air Inter |
| | F-BUAL | Airbus A.300B4 | Air Inter |
| | F-BUAM | Airbus A.300B2 | Air Inter |
| | F-BUAN | Airbus A.300B2 | Air Inter |
| | F-BUAO | Airbus A.300B2 | Air Inter |
| | F-BUAP | Airbus A.300B2 | Air Inter |
| | F-BUAQ | Airbus A.300B4 | Air Inter |
| | F-BUAR | Airbus A.300B4 | Air Inter |
| | F-BUTI | F.28 Fellowship 1000 | T.A.T. |
| | F-BVFA | Concorde 101 | Air France |
| | F-BVFB | Concorde 101 | Air France |
| | F-BVFC | Concorde 101 | Air France (*stored*) |
| | F-BVFD | Concorde 101 | Air France (*stored*) |
| | F-BVFF | Concorde 101 | Air France |
| | F-BVFJ | Nord 262A | T.A.T. |
| | F-BVGA | Airbus A.300B2 | Air France |
| | F-BVGB | Airbus A.300B2 | Air France |
| | F-BVGC | Airbus A.300B2 | Air France |
| | F-BVGD | Airbus A.300B2 | Air Inter |
| | F-BVGE | Airbus A.300B2 | Air Inter |
| | F-BVGF | Airbus A.300B2 | Air Inter |

# OVERSEAS AIRLINERS

| Reg. | Type | Owner or Operator | Notes |
|------|------|-------------------|-------|
| F-BVGG | Airbus A.300B4 | Air France | |
| F-BVGH | Airbus A.300B4 | Air France | |
| F-BVGI | Airbus A.300B4 | Air Charter | |
| F-BVGJ | Airbus A.300B4 | Air France | |
| F-BVGL | Airbus A.300B4 | Air France | |
| F-BVGM | Airbus A.300B4 | Air France | |
| F-BVGN | Airbus A.300B4 | Air France | |
| F-BVGO | Airbus A.300B4 | Air France | |
| F-BVGP | Airbus A.300B4 | Air France | |
| F-BVGQ | Airbus A.300B4 | Air France | |
| F-BVGR | Airbus A.300B4 | Air France | |
| F-BVGS | Airbus A.300B4 | Air Charter | |
| F-BVGT | Airbus A.300B4 | T.A.T./Uni-Air | |
| F-BVJL | Beech 99A | Air Jet | |
| F-BYAB | F.27 Friendship Mk 600 | | |
| | | | |
| F-GATS | EMB-110P2 Bandeirante | Compagnie Air Littoral *Hérault* | |
| F-GBBR | F.28 Fellowship 1000 | T.A.T./Air France | |
| F-GBBS | F.28 Fellowship 1000 | T.A.T./Air France | |
| F-GBBT | F.28 Fellowship 1000 | T.A.T./Air France | |
| F-GBBX | F.28 Fellowship 1000 | T.A.T./Air France | |
| F-GBEA | Airbus A.300B2 | Air Inter | |
| F-GBEB | Airbus A.300B2 | Air Inter | |
| F-GBEC | Airbus A.300B2 | Air France | |
| F-GBEI | Nord 262B | Compagnie Air Littoral | |
| F-GBEJ | Nord 262B | Compagnie Air Littoral | |
| F-GBEK | Nord 262A | Compagnie Air Littoral | |
| F-GBGA | EMB-110P2 Bandeirante | Brit Air | |
| F-GBME | EMB-110P2 Bandeirante | Compagnie Air Littoral | |
| F-GBMF | EMB-110P2 Bandeirante | Compagnie Air Littoral | |
| F-GBMG | EMB-110P2 Bandeirante | Brit Air | |
| F-GBOX | Boeing 747-2B3F (SCD) | Union de Transports Aériens (UTA) | |
| F-GBRM | EMB-110P2 Bandeirante | Brit Air | |
| F-GBRQ | FH.227B Friendship | T.A.T. | |
| F-GBRU | F.27J Friendship | ACE Transvalair | |
| F-GBRV | F.27J Friendship | T.A.T./ACE Transvalair | |
| F-GBTO | Swearingen SA.226TC Metro II | Compagnie Air Littoral | |
| F-GBYA | Boeing 737-228 | Air France | |
| F-GBYB | Boeing 737-228 | Air France/Air Charter | |
| F-GBYC | Boeing 737-228 | Air France | |
| F-GBYD | Boeing 737-228 | Air France | |
| F-GBYE | Boeing 737-228 | Air France | |
| F-GBYF | Boeing 737-228 | Air France | |
| F-GBYG | Boeing 737-228 | Air France | |
| F-GBYH | Boeing 737-228 | Air France | |
| F-GBYI | Boeing 737-228 | Air France | |
| F-GBYJ | Boeing 737-228 | Air France | |
| F-GBYK | Boeing 737-228 | Air France | |
| F-GBYL | Boeing 737-228 | Air France | |
| F-GBYM | Boeing 737-228 | Air France | |
| F-GBYN | Boeing 737-228 | Air France | |
| F-GBYO | Boeing 737-228 | Air France | |
| F-GBYP | Boeing 737-228 | Air France | |
| F-GBYQ | Boeing 737-228 | Air France | |
| F-GCBA | Boeing 747-228B | Air France | |
| F-GCBB | Boeing 747-228B | Air France | |
| F-GCBD | Boeing 747-228B (SCD) | Air France | |
| F-GCBF | Boeing 474-228B | Air France | |
| F-GCBG | Boeing 747-228B | Air France | |
| F-GCBH | Boeing 747-228B (SCD) | Air France | |
| F-GCBI | Boeing 747-228B (SCD) | Air France | |
| F-GCBJ | Boeing 747-228B (SCD) | Air France | |
| F-GCBK | Boeing 747-228F (SCD) | Air France | |
| F-GCBL | Boeing 747-228F | Air France | |
| F-GCBM | Boeing 747-228F | Air France/UTA | |
| F-GCDA | Boeing 727-228 | Air France | |
| F-GCDB | Boeing 727-228 | Air France | |
| F-GCDC | Boeing 727-228 | Air France | |
| F-GCDD | Boeing 727-228 | Air France | |
| F-GCDE | Boeing 727-228 | Air France | |
| F-GCDF | Boeing 727-228 | Air France | |
| F-GCDG | Boeing 727-228 | Air France | |
| F-GCDH | Boeing 727-228 | Air France | |
| F-GCDI | Boeing 727-228 | Air France | |

| Notes | Reg. | Type | Owner or Operator |
|-------|------|------|-------------------|
| | F-GCFC | FH.227B Friendship | T.A.T. |
| | F-GCFE | Swearingen SA.226TC Metro II | Compagnie Air Littoral |
| | F-GCGH | FH.227B Friendship | T.A.T. |
| | F-GCGQ | Boeing 727-227 | Europe Aero Service *Normandie* |
| | F-GCJL | Boeing 737-222 | Euralair/Air Charter |
| | F-GCJO | FH.227B Friendship | ACE Transvalair |
| | F-GCJV | F.27 Friendship Mk 400 | Air Jet |
| | F-GCLA | EMB-110P1 Bandeirante | Aigle Azur |
| | F-GCLL | Boeing 737-222 | Euralair/Air Charter |
| | F-GCLO | FH.227B Friendship | T.A.T./ACE Transvalair |
| | F-GCLQ | FH.227B Friendship | T.A.T. |
| | F-GCMQ | EMB-110P2 Bandeirante | Compagnie Air Littoral *Provence* |
| | F-GCMV | Boeing 727-2X3 | Air Charter |
| | F-GCMX | Boeing 727-2X3 | Air Charter |
| | F-GCPT | FH.227B Friendship | T.A.T. |
| | F-GCPU | FH.227B Friendship | T.A.T. |
| | F-GCPV | FH.227B Friendship | T.A.T. |
| | F-GCPX | FH.227B Friendship | T.A.T. |
| | F-GCPY | FH.227B Friendship | T.A.T. |
| | F-GCPZ | FH.227B Friendship | T.A.T. |
| | F-GCSL | Boeing 737-222 | Euralair/Air Charter |
| | F-GCVJ | S.E.210 Caravelle 12 | Air Inter |
| | F-GCVK | S.E.210 Caravelle 12 | Air Inter |
| | F-GCVL | S.E.210 Caravelle 12 | Air Inter |
| | F-GDAQ | L.100-30 Hercules | Jet Fret |
| | F-GDCI | EMB-110P2 Bandeirante | Compagnie Air Littoral *Comté de Nice* |
| | F-GDFC | F.28 Fellowship 4000 | T.A.T./Air France |
| | F-GDFD | F.28 Fellowship 4000 | T.A.T./Air France |
| | F-GDFY | S.E.210 Caravelle 10B | Air Charter/Europe Aero Service |
| | F-GDFZ | S.E.210 Caravelle 10B | Air Charter/Europe Aero Service |
| | F-GDJK | Douglas DC-10-30 | Lineas Aereas de Mocambique (LAM) |
| | F-GDJM | Douglas DC-8-62CF | Minerve |
| | F-GDJU | S.E.210 Caravelle 10B | Europe Aero Service *Lorraine* |
| | F-GDMR | Swearingen SA.226TC Metro II | Compagnie Air Littoral |
| | F-GDPP | Douglas DC-3 | ACE Transvalair |
| | F-GDRM | Douglas DC-8-73 | Minerve |
| | F-GDSG | UTA Super Guppy | Airbus Industrie *Airbus Skylink 3* |
| | F-GDSK | F.28 Fellowship 4000 | T.A.T./Air France |
| | F-GDUS | F.28 Fellowship 2000 | T.A.T. |
| | F-GDUT | F.28 Fellowship 2000 | T.A.T./Air France |
| | F-GDUU | F.28 Fellowship 2000 | T.A.T. |
| | F-GDUV | F.28 Fellowship 2000 | T.A.T. |
| | F-GDUY | F.28 Fellowship 4000 | T.A.T./Air France |
| | F-GDUZ | F.28 Fellowship 4000 | T.A.T./Air France |
| | F-GDXL | Aerospatiale ATR-42-300 | Brit Air |
| | F-GDXT | F.27J Friendship | Stellair |
| | F-GEAI | UTA Super Guppy | Airbus Industrie *Airbus Skylink 4* |
| | F-GEBU | Swearingen SA.226TC Metro II | Compagnie Air Littoral |
| | F-GECK | F.28 Fellowship 1000 | T.A.T./Air France |
| | F-GEDR | EMB-110 P1 Bandeirante | Stellair |
| | F-GEGD | Aerospatiale ATR-42-300 | Compagnie Air Littoral/Air France |
| | F-GEGE | Aerospatiale ATR-42-300 | Compagnie Air Littoral/Air France |
| | F-GEGF | Aerospatiale ATR-42-300 | Compagnie Air Littoral/Air France |
| | F-GELG | Saab SF.340A | Brit Air/Air France |
| | F-GELP | S.E.210 Caravelle | Europe Aero Service/Air Charter |
| | F-GEMA | Airbus A.310-203 | Air France |
| | F-GEMB | Airbus A.310-203 | Air France |
| | F-GEMC | Airbus A.310-203 | Air France |
| | F-GEMD | Airbus A.310-203 | Air France |
| | F-GEME | Airbus A.310-203 | Air France/Air Inter |
| | F-GEMF | Airbus A.310-203 | Air France |
| | F-GEMG | Airbus A.310-203 | Air France |
| | F-GEMN | Airbus A.310-304 | Air France |
| | F-GEMO | Airbus A.310-304 | Air France |
| | F-GEMP | Airbus A.310-304 | Air France |
| | F-GEMQ | Airbus A.310-304 | Air France |
| | F-GEOM | Douglas DC-3C | Stellair |
| | F-GEPC | S.E. 210 Caravelle 10B3 | Aero France International |
| | F-GERV | Swearingen SA226TC Metro II | Air Vendee |
| | F-GESM | Douglas DC-8-73CF | Minerve |
| | F-GETA | Boeing 747-3B3 (SCD) | Union de Transports Aériens (UTA) |
| | F-GETB | Boeing 747-3B3 (SCD) | Union de Transports Aériens (UTA)/ Aeromaritime |
| | F-GEXA | Boeing 747-4B3 | Union de Transports Aeriens (UTA) |

| Reg. | Type | Owner or Operator | Notes |
|------|------|-------------------|-------|
| F-GEXB | Boeing 747-4B3 | Union de Transports Aeriens (UTA) | |
| F-GEXI | Boeing 737-2L9 | Air Charter/Europe Aero Service | |
| F-GEXJ | Boeing 737-2Q8 | Air Charter/Europe Aero Service | |
| F-GEXX | F.28 Fellowship 1000 | T.A.T. | |
| F-GEXZ | F.27J Friendship | Stellair | |
| F-GFAE | D.H.C.6 Twin Otter 310 | T.A.T. | |
| F-GFAF | D.H.C.6 Twin Otter 310 | T.A.T. | |
| F-GFAG | D.H.C.6 Twin Otter 310 | T.A.T./Uni-Air | |
| F-GFBA | S.E.210 Caravelle 10B | Europe Aero Service | |
| F-GFBZ | Saab SF.340A | Brit Air | |
| F-GFEN | EMB-120 Brasilia | Compagnie Air Littoral/Air France | |
| F-GFEO | EMB-120 Brasilia | Compagnie Air Littoral/Air France | |
| F-GFEP | EMB-120 Brasilia | Compagnie Air Littoral/Air France | |
| F-GFEQ | EMB-120 Brasilia | Compagnie Air Littoral/Air France | |
| F-GFER | EMB-120 Brasilia | Compagnie Air Littoral/Air France | |
| F-GFES | Aerospatiale ATR-42-300 | Compagnie Air Littoral/Air France | |
| F-GFHZ | F.27J Friendship | Air Corse | |
| F-GFIJ | Swearingen SA226TC Metro II | Compagnie Air Littoral | |
| F-GFIK | Swearingen SA226TC Metro II | Compagnie Air Littoral | |
| F-GFIN | EMB-120 Brasilia | Compagnie Air Littoral/Air France | |
| F-GFJH | Aerospatiale ATR-42-300 | Brit Air/Air France | |
| F-GFJP | Aerospatiale ATR-42-300 | Brit Air/Air France | |
| F-GFJS | F.27 Friendship Mk 600 | Air Jet | |
| F-GFJU | Swearingen SA226TC Metro II | T.A.T. | |
| F-GFJV | Swearingen SA226TC Metro II | T.A.T. | |
| F-GFJX | Swearingen SA226TC Metro II | T.A.T. | |
| F-GFKA | Airbus A.320-111 | Air France *Ville de Paris* | |
| F-GFK | Airbus A.320-111 | Air France | |
| F-GFKB | Airbus A.320-111 | Air France *Ville de Rome* | |
| F-GFKD | Airbus A.320-111 | Air France *Ville de Londres* | |
| F-GFKE | Airbus A.320-111 | Air France *Ville de Bonn* | |
| F-GFKF | Airbus A.320-111 | Air France *Ville de Madrid* | |
| F-GFKG | Airbus A.320-111 | Air France *Ville d'Amsterdam* | |
| F-GFKH | Airbus A.320-211 | Air France *Ville de Bruxelles* | |
| F-GFKI | Airbus A.320-211 | Air France *Ville de Lisbonne* | |
| F-GFKJ | Airbus A.320-211 | Air France *Ville de Copenhagen* | |
| F-GFKK | Airbus A.320-211 | Air France *Ville d'Athenes* | |
| F-GFKL | Airbus A.320-211 | Air France *Ville de Dublin* | |
| F-GFKM | Airbus A.320-211 | Air France *Ville de Luxembourg* | |
| F-GFKN | Airbus A.320-211 | Air France | |
| F-GFKO | Airbus A.320-211 | Air France | |
| F-GFKP | Airbus A.320-211 | Air France | |
| F-GFKQ | Airbus A.320-211 | Air France | |
| F-GFKR | Airbus A.320-211 | Air France | |
| F-GFKS | Airbus A.320-211 | Air France | |
| F-GFKT | Airbus A.320-211 | Air France | |
| F-GFKU | Airbus A.320-211 | Air France | |
| F-GFKV | Airbus A.320-211 | Air France | |
| F-GFLV | Boeing 737-2K5 | Air Charter/Air France | |
| F-GFLX | Boeing 737-2K5 | Air Charter/Air France | |
| F-GFTB | EMB-120RT Brasilia | Air Exel | |
| F-GFUA | Boeing 737-33A | Aeromaritime | |
| F-GFUD | Boeing 737-33A | Aeromaritime | |
| F-GFUE | Boeing 737-3B3 | Aeromaritime | |
| F-GFUF | Boeing 737-3B3 | Aeromaritime | |
| F-GFUG | Boeing 737-4B3 | Aeromaritime | |
| F-GFUH | Boeing 737-4B3 | Aeromaritime | |
| F-GFUK | Boeing 747-2D3B | Union de Transports Aériens (UTA) | |
| F-G | Boeing 767-37EER | Aeromaritime | |
| F-G | Boeing 767-3Q8ER | Aeromaritime | |
| F-G | Boeing 767-3Q8ER | Aeromaritime | |
| F-GFVI | Boeing 737-230C | ICS Inter Ciel Service | |
| F-GFVJ | Boeing 737-230C | ICS Inter Ciel Service | |
| F-GFVK | Boeing 737-242C | ICS Inter Ciel Service | |
| F-GFVR | Boeing 737-2Q5C | ICS Inter Ciel Service | |
| F-GFYL | Boeing 737-2A9C | Euralair/Air Charter | |
| F-GFYM | H.S.748 Srs 2A | Kel-Air | |
| F-GFYN | Aerospatiale ATR-42-300 | Compagnie Air Littoral/Air France | |
| F-GFYZ | EMB-110P1 Bandeirante | Compagnie Air Littoral | |
| F-GFZB | McD Douglas MD-83 | Air Liberte | |
| F-GFZE | L.382G Hercules | ICS Inter Ciel Service | |
| F-GGAV | Dornier Do.228-201 | Air Vendee | |
| F-GGEA | Airbus A.320-111 | Air Inter | |

| Notes | Reg. | Type | Owner or Operator |
|-------|------|------|-------------------|
| | F-GGEB | Airbus A.320-111 | Air Inter |
| | F-GGEC | Airbus A.320-111 | Air Inter |
| | F-GGED | Airbus A.320-111 | Air Inter |
| | F-GGEE | Airbus A.320-111 | Air Inter |
| | F-GGEF | Airbus A.320-111 | Air Inter |
| | F-GGEG | Airbus A.320-111 | Air Inter |
| | F-GGFI | Boeing 737-210C | T.A.T. |
| | F-GGFJ | Boeing 737-248C | T.A.T. |
| | F-GGGR | Boeing 727-2H3 | Europe Aero Service Alsace |
| | F-GGGV | Dornier Do.228-202 | Air Vendee |
| | F-GGKD | S.E.210 Caravelle 10B | Air Service Nantes |
| | F-GGLK | Aerospatiale ATR-42-300 | T.A.T. |
| | F-GGLR | Aerospatiale ATR-42-300 | Brit Air/Air France |
| | F-GGMA | McD Douglas MD-83 | Minerve |
| | F-GGMB | McD Douglas MD-83 | Minerve |
| | F-GGMC | McD Douglas MD-83 | Minerve |
| | F-GGMD | McD Douglas MD-83 | Minerve |
| | F-GGME | McD Douglas MD-83 | Minerve |
| | F-GG | McD Douglas MD-83 | Minerve |
| | F-GGML | Boeing 737-53A | Euralair International/Air France |
| | F-GGMZ | Douglas DC-10-30 | Minerve |
| | F-GGPA | Boeing 737-242C | T.A.T. |
| | F-GGPB | Boeing 737-242C | T.A.T. |
| | F-GGPC | Boeing 737-204C | T.A.T. |
| | F-GGPN | FH.227B Friendship | Uni-Air |
| | F-GGSV | Swearingen SA226TC Metro II | Air Vendee |
| | F-GGSZ | F.27J Friendship | Air Corse |
| | F-GGTD | EMB-120RT Brasilia | Air Exel |
| | F-GGTE | EMB-120RT Brasilia | Air Exel |
| | F-GGVP | Boeing 737-2K2C | ICS Inter Ciel Service |
| | F-GGVQ | Boeing 737-2K2C | ICS Inter Ciel Service |
| | F-GHBM | Boeing 747-283B | Minerve |
| | F-GHDB | Saab SF.340A | Brit Air/Air France |
| | F-GHEB | McD Douglas MD-83 | Air Liberte |
| | F-GHEC | McD Douglas MD-83 | Air Liberte |
| | F-GHED | McD Douglas MD-83 | Air Liberte |
| | F-GHEF | Airbus A.300-622R | Air Liberte |
| | F-GHEG | Airbus A.300-622R | Air Liberte |
| | F-GHEH | McD Douglas MD-83 | Air Liberte |
| | F-GHEI | McD Douglas MD-83 | Air Liberte |
| | F-GHEJ | Airbus A.310-304 | Air Liberte |
| | F-GHEK | McD Douglas MD-83 | Air Liberte |
| | F-GHGD | Boeing 767-27EER | Aeromaritime |
| | F-GHGE | Boeing 767-27EER | Aeromaritime |
| | F-GHGF | Boeing 767-3Q8ER | Aeromaritime |
| | F-GHGG | Boeing 767-3Q8ER | Aeromaritime |
| | F-GHGM | Airbus A.310-304 | Europe Aero Service |
| | F-GHIA | EMB-120RT Brasilia | Compagnie Air Littoral |
| | F-GHIB | EMB-120RT Brasilia | Compagnie Air Littoral |
| | F-GHJE | Aerospatiale ATR-42-300 | Brit Air |
| | F-GHKA | H.S.748 Srs 2A | Kel-Air |
| | F-GHKL | H.S.748 Srs 2A | Kel-Air |
| | F-GHKM | S.E.210 Caravelle 10B | Air Toulouse |
| | F-GHKN | S.E.210 Caravelle 10B | Air Toulouse |
| | F-GHKO | S.E.210 Caravelle 10B | Air Toulouse |
| | F-GHME | Aerospatiale ATR-42-300 | Brit Air |
| | F-GHMI | Saab SF.340A | Brit Air/Air France |
| | F-GHMJ | Saab SF.340A | Brit Air |
| | F-GHMK | Saab SF.340A | Brit Air |
| | F-GHOI | Douglas DC-10-30 | Union de Transports Aériens (UTA) |
| | F-GHOL | Boeing 737-53C | Euralair International/Air France |
| | F-GHPH | Aerospatiale ATR-72 | Brit Air |
| | F-GHPI | Aerospatiale ATR-42-300 | Brit Air |
| | F-GHPK | Aerospatiale ATR- | Brit Air |
| | F-GHPS | Aerospatiale ATR-42-300 | Brit Air |
| | F-GHPV | Aerospatiale ATR-72 | Brit Air |
| | F-GHPX | Aerospatiale ATR-72 | Brit Air |
| | F-GHPY | Aerospatiale ATR-72 | Brit Air |
| | F-GHPZ | Aerospatiale ATR-42-300 | Brit Air |
| | F-GHQA | Airbus A.320-211 | Air Inter |
| | F-GHQB | Airbus A.320-211 | Air Inter |
| | F-GHQC | Airbus A.320-211 | Air Inter |
| | F-GHQD | Airbus A.320-211 | Air Inter |
| | F-GHQE | Airbus A.320-211 | Air Inter |

| Reg. | Type | Owner or Operator | Notes |
|------|------|-------------------|-------|
| F-GHQF | Airbus A.320-211 | Air Inter | |
| F-GHRC | F.27 Friendship Mk 600 | Air Jet | |
| F-GHUL | Boeing 737-53C | Euralair | |
| F-GHVA | Swearingen SA227AC Metro III | Air Vendee | |
| F-GHVC | Swearingen SA227AC Metro III | Air Vendee | |
| F-GHVD | Swearingen SA227AC Metro III | Air Vendee | |
| F-GHVE | Swearingen SA227AC Metro III | Air Vendee | |
| F-GHVF | Swearingen SA227AT Merlin IV | Air Vendee | |
| F-GHVG | Swearingen SA227AC Metro III | Air Vendee | |
| F-GHVL | Boeing 737-53C | Euralair | |
| F-GHVS | Saab SF.340B | Air Vendee | |
| F-GHXB | F.27J Friendship | Air Service Nantes | |
| F-GHXK | Boeing 737-2A1 | Europe Aero Service *J-L Heng* | |
| F-GHXL | Boeing 737-2S3 | Europe Aero Service/Air Charter | |
| F-GHXM | Boeing 737-53A | Europe Aero Service/Air Charter | |
| F-GHXN | Boeing 737-53A | Europe Aero Service | |
| F-GIAH | F.28 Fellowship 1000 | T.A.T. | |
| F-GIAI | F.28 Fellowship 1000 | T.A.T. | |
| F-GIAJ | F.28 Fellowship 1000 | T.A.T. | |
| F-GIAK | F.28 Fellowship 1000 | T.A.T. | |
| F-GIDM | Fokker 100 | Compagnie Air Littoral | |
| F-GIDN | Fokker 100 | Compagnie Air Littoral | |
| F-GIDO | Fokker 100 | Compagnie Air Littoral | |
| F-GIDP | Fokker 100 | Compagnie Air Littoral | |
| F-GIDQ | Fokker 100 | Compagnie Air Littoral | |
| F-GIDT | Fokker 100 | Compagnie Air Littoral | |
| F-GIHR | F.27J Friendship | Uni-Air *La Mongié* | |
| F-GIJS | Airbus A.300B4 | Air Inter | |
| F-GIJT | Airbus A.300B4 | Air Inter | |
| F-GIJU | Airbus A.300B4 | Air Inter | |
| F-GIMH | F.28 Fellowship 1000 | T.A.T./Air France | |
| F-GIOA | Fokker 100 | T.A.T./Air France | |
| F-GIOB | Fokker 100 | T.A.T./Air France | |
| F-GIOC | Fokker 100 | T.A.T. | |
| F-GIOD | Fokker 100 | T.A.T. | |
| F-GIOE | Fokker 100 | T.A.T. | |
| F-GIOF | Fokker 100 | T.A.T. | |
| F-GIOG | Fokker 100 | T.A.T. | |
| F-GIOH | Fokker 100 | T.A.T. | |
| F-GIPD | F.27A Friendship | Uni-Air | |
| F-GIRC | Aerospatiale ATR-42-300 | T.A.T. | |
| F-GISA | Boeing 747-428 (SCD) | Air France | |
| F-GISB | Boeing 747-428 (SCD) | Air France | |
| F-GISC | Boeing 747-428 (SCD) | Air France | |
| F-GITA | Boeing 747-428 | Air France | |
| F-GITB | Boeing 747-428 | Air France | |
| F-GITC | Boeing 747-428 | Air France | |
| F-GIVJ | Boeing 707-311C | Pan Europe Air | |
| F-GJAK | EMB-120RT Brasilia | Compagnie Air Littoral | |
| F-GJDL | Boeing 737-210C | Air Charter/Euralair | |
| F-GJDM | S.E.210 Caravelle 10B | STAIR | |
| F-GJNA | Boeing 737-528 | Air France | |
| F-GJNB | Boeing 737-528 | Air France | |
| F-GJNC | Boeing 737-528 | Air France | |
| F-GJND | Boeing 737-528 | Air France | |
| F-GJNE | Boeing 737-528 | Air France | |
| F-GJNF | Boeing 737-528 | Air France | |
| F-GJNG | Boeing 737-528 | Air France | |
| F-GJNH | Boeing 737-528 | Air France | |
| F-GJNI | Boeing 737-528 | Air France | |
| F-GJNJ | Boeing 737-528 | Air France | |
| F-GJNK | Boeing 737-528 | Air France | |
| F-GJNL | Boeing 737-528 | Air France | |
| F-GKCI | Boeing 707-369C | Pan Europe Air | |
| F-GKCS | Boeing 707-369C | Pan Europe Air | |
| F-GKCT | Boeing 707-369C | Pan Europe Air | |
| F-GKJC | F.27 Friendship Mk 600 | Air Jet | |
| F-GKLA | Saab SF.340B | Alsavia/Air France | |
| F-GKNA | Aerospatiale ATR-42-300 | T.A.T. | |
| F-GKNB | Aerospatiale ATR-42-300 | T.A.T. | |
| F-GKNC | Aerospatiale ATR-42-300 | T.A.T. | |
| F-GKND | Aerospatiale ATR-42-300 | T.A.T. | |
| F-GKTA | Boeing 737-3M8 | TEA France | |

| Notes | Reg. | Type | Owner or Operator |
|-------|------|------|-------------------|
| | F-GKTB | Boeing 737-3M8 | TEA France |
| | F-G | Boeing 737-3MB | TEA France |
| | F-G | Boeing 737-3MB | TEA France |
| | F-G | Airbus A.310-307 | TEA France/Cubana |
| | F-GPAN | Boeing 747-2B3F (SCD) | Air France |
| | F-GTNT | BAe 146-200QT | Euralair/TNT |
| | F-GTNU | BAe 146-200QT | Euralair/TNT |
| | F-ODJG | Boeing 747-2Q2B | Air Gabon |
| | F-ODLX | Douglas DC-10-30 | Air Outre Mer |
| | F-ODLY | Douglas DC-10-30 | Air Outre Mer |
| | F-ODLZ | Douglas DC-10-30 | Air Outre Mer |
| | F-ODSV | Airbus A.310-304 | Somali Airlines (*to become* 6O-SHH) |
| | F-ODVD | Airbus A.310-304 | Royal Jordanian Airline *Prince Hashem* |
| | F-ODVE | Airbus A.310-304 | Royal Jordanian Airline *Princess Iman* |
| | F-ODVF | Airbus A.310-304 | Royal Jordanian Airline *Princess Raiyah* |
| | F-ODVG | Airbus A.310-304 | Royal Jordanian Airline *Prince Faisal* |
| | F-ODVH | Airbus A.310-304 | Royal Jordanian Airline *Prince Hamazeh* |
| | F-ODVI | Airbus A.310-304 | Royal Jordanian Airline *Princess Haya* |
| | F-OGQA | Fokker 100 | Hamburg Airlines |

Note: Air France also operates a 747 which retains the US identity N4508E. UTA also operates one DC-10-30 registered N54649.

## HA (Hungary)

| | | | |
|---|---|---|---|
| | HA-LBI | Tupolev Tu-134A-3 | Malev |
| | HA-LBK | Tupolev Tu-134A-3 | Malev |
| | HA-LBN | Tupolev Tu-134A-3 | Malev |
| | HA-LBO | Tupolev Tu-134A-3 | Malev |
| | HA-LBP | Tupolev Tu-134A-3 | Malev |
| | HA-LBR | Tupolev Tu-134A-3 | Malev |
| | HA-LCA | Tupolev Tu-154B-2 | Malev |
| | HA-LCB | Tupolev Tu-154B-2 | Malev |
| | HA-LCE | Tupolev Tu-154B-2 | Malev |
| | HA-LCG | Tupolev Tu-154B-2 | Malev |
| | HA-LCH | Tupolev Tu-154B-2 | Malev |
| | HA-LCM | Tupolev Tu-154B-2 | Malev |
| | HA-LCN | Tupolev Tu-154B-2 | Malev |
| | HA-LCO | Tupolev Tu-154B-2 | Malev |
| | HA-LCP | Tupolev Tu-154B-2 | Malev |
| | HA-LCR | Tupolev Tu-154B-2 | Malev |
| | HA-LCU | Tupolev Tu-154B-2 | Malev |
| | HA-LCV | Tupolev Tu-154B-2 | Malev |
| | HA-LEA | Boeing 737-2QB | Malev |
| | HA-LEB | Boeing 737-2M8 | Malev |
| | HA-LEC | Boeing 737-2T5 | Malev |
| | HA-LED | Boeing 737-3Y0 | Malev |
| | HA-LEF | Boeing 737-3Y0 | Malev |
| | HA-LEG | Boeing 737-3Y0 | Malev |
| | HA-TAB | BAe 146-200QT | TNT/Malev |

## HB (Switzerland)

| | | | |
|---|---|---|---|
| | HB-AHB | Saab SF.340A | Crossair |
| | HB-AHC | Saab SF.340A | Crossair |
| | HB-AHD | Saab SF.340A | Crossair |
| | HB-AHE | Saab SF.340A | Crossair |
| | HB-AHH | Saab SF.340A | Crossair |
| | HB-AHI | Saab SF.340A | Crossair |
| | HB-AHK | Saab SF.340A | Crossair |
| | HB-AHL | Saab SF.340A | Crossair/Business Air |
| | HB-AHM | Saab SF.340A | Crossair |
| | HB-AHN | Saab SF.340A | Crossair |
| | HB-AHO | Saab SF.340A | Crossair |
| | HB-AHR | Saab SF.340A | Crossair |
| | HB-AHS | Saab SF.340A | Crossair |
| | HB-AHT | Saab SF.340A | Crossair |
| | HB-AKA | Saab SF.340B | Crossair |

| Reg. | Type | Owner or Operator | Notes |
|------|------|-------------------|-------|
| HB-AKB | Saab SF.340B | Crossair | |
| HB-AKC | Saab SF.340B | Crossair | |
| HB-AKD | Saab SF.340B | Crossair | |
| HB-AKE | Saab SF.340B | Crossair | |
| HB-AKF | Saab SF.340B | Crossair | |
| HB-AKG | Saab SF.340B | Crossair | |
| HB-AKH | Saab SF.340B | Crossair | |
| HB-AKI | Saab SF.340B | Crossair | |
| HB-AKK | Saab SF.340B | Crossair | |
| HB-AKL | Saab SF.340B | Crossair | |
| HB-AKM | Saab SF.340B | Crossair | |
| HB-AKN | Saab SF.340B | Crossair | |
| HB-AKO | Saab SF.340B | Crossair | |
| HB-IAN | Fokker 50 | Crossair | |
| HB-IAO | Fokker 50 | Crossair | |
| HB-IAP | Fokker 50 | Crossair | |
| HB-IAR | Fokker 50 | Crossair | |
| HB-IAS | Fokker 50 | Crossair | |
| HB-IBF | Douglas DC-8-63 | African Safari Airways | |
| HB-ICJ | S.E.210 Caravelle 10B | Air City | |
| HB-IGC | Boeing 747-357 (SCD) | Swissair *Bern* | |
| HB-IGD | Boeing 747-357 (SCD) | Swissair *Basel* | |
| HB-IGG | Boeing 747-357 (SCD) | Swissair *Ticino* | |
| HB-IHC | Douglas DC-10-30 | Swissair *Obwalden* | |
| HB-IHE | Douglas DC-10-30 | Swissair *Vaud* | |
| HB-IHF | Douglas DC-10-30 | Swissair *Nidwalden* | |
| HB-IHG | Douglas DC-10-30 | Swissair *Graubünden* | |
| HB-IHH | Douglas DC-10-30 | Swissair *Schaffhausen* | |
| HB-IHI | Douglas DC-10-30 | Swissair *Fribourg* | |
| HB-IHK | Douglas DC-10-30 | Balair | |
| HB-IHL | Douglas DC-10-30ER | Swissair *Thurgau* | |
| HB-IHM | Douglas DC-10-30ER | Swissair *Valais-Wallis* | |
| HB-IHN | Douglas DC-10-30ER | Swissair *St Gallen* | |
| HB-IHO | Douglas DC-10-30ER | Swissair *Uri* | |
| HB-IHP | Douglas DC-10-30 | Swissair | |
| HB-IIA | Boeing 737-3M8 | TEA Basle | |
| HB-IIB | Boeing 737-3M8 | TEA Basle | |
| HB-IKD | S.E. 210 Caravelle 10B3 | Air City | |
| HB-IKK | McD Douglas MD-82 | Alisarda (Italy) | |
| HB-IKL | McD Douglas MD-82 | Alisarda (Italy) | |
| HB-INA | McD Douglas MD-81 | Swissair *Höri* | |
| HB-INB | McD Douglas MD-82 | Balair | |
| HB-INC | McD Douglas MD-81 | Swissair *Lugano* | |
| HB-IND | McD Douglas MD-81 | Swissair *Bachenbülach* | |
| HB-INE | McD Douglas MD-81 | Swissair *Rümlang* | |
| HB-INF | McD Douglas MD-81 | Swissair *Appenzell a.Rh.* | |
| HB-ING | McD Douglas MD-81 | Swissair *Winkel* | |
| HB-INH | McD Douglas MD-81 | Swissair *Winterthur* | |
| HB-INI | McD Douglas MD-81 | Swissair *Kloten* | |
| HB-INK | McD Douglas MD-81 | Swissair *Opfikon* | |
| HB-INL | McD Douglas MD-81 | Swissair *Jura* | |
| HB-INM | McD Douglas MD-81 | Swissair *Lausanne* | |
| HB-INN | McD Douglas MD-81 | Swissair *Bülach* | |
| HB-INO | McD Douglas MD-81 | Swissair *Bellinzona* | |
| HB-INP | McD Douglas MD-81 | Swissair *Oberglatt* | |
| HB-INR | McD Douglas MD-82 | Balair | |
| HB-INS | McD Douglas MD-81 | Swissair *Meyrin* | |
| HB-INT | McD Douglas MD-81 | Swissair *Grand-Saconnex* | |
| HB-INU | McD Douglas MD-81 | Swissair *Vernier* | |
| HB-INV | McD Douglas MD-81 | Swissair *Dubendorf* | |
| HB-INW | McD Douglas MD-82 | Balair | |
| HB-INX | McD Douglas MD-81 | Swissair *Wallisellen* | |
| HB-INY | McD Douglas MD-81 | Swissair *Bassersdorf* | |
| HB-INZ | McD Douglas MD-81 | Swissair *Regensdorf* | |
| HB-IPA | Airbus A.310-221 | Swissair *Aargau* | |
| HB-IPB | Airbus A.310-221 | Swissair *Neuchatel* | |
| HB-IPC | Airbus A.310-221 | Swissair *Schwyz* | |
| HB-IPD | Airbus A.310-221 | Swissair *Solothurn* | |
| HB-IPE | Airbus A.310-221 | Swissair *Basel-Land* | |
| HB-IPF | Airbus A.310-322 | Swissair *Glarus* | |
| HB-IPG | Airbus A.310-322 | Swissair *Zug* | |
| HB-IPH | Airbus A.310-322 | Swissair *Appenzell i. Rh* | |

| Notes | Reg. | Type | Owner or Operator |
|---|---|---|---|
| | HB-IPI | Airbus A.310-322 | Swissair *Luzern* |
| | HB-IPK | Airbus A.310-322 | Balair |
| | HB-IPL | Airbus A.310-325 | Balair |
| | HB-IPM | Airbus A.310-325 | Balair |
| | HB-IPN | Airbus A.310-325 | Balair |
| | HB-ISB | Douglas DC-3C | Classic Air |
| | HB-ISC | Douglas DC-3C | Classic Air |
| | HB-ISG | F.27 Friendship Mk 200 | Sunshine Aviation |
| | HB-ISH | F.27 Friendship Mk 200 | Sunshine Aviation *Locarno* |
| | HB-ISX | McD Douglas MD-81 | Swissair *Binningen* |
| | HB-ISZ | McD Douglas MD-83 | Balair |
| | HB-IUA | McD Douglas MD-87 | CTA |
| | HB-IUB | McD Douglas MD-87 | CTA |
| | HB-IUC | McD Douglas MD-87 | CTA |
| | HB-IUD | McD Douglas MD-87 | CTA |
| | HB-IUG | McD Douglas MD-81 | Swissair |
| | HB-IUH | McD Douglas MD-81 | Swissair |
| | HB-IVA | Fokker 100 | Swissair *Aarau* |
| | HB-IVB | Fokker 100 | Swissair *Biel/Bienne* |
| | HB-IVC | Fokker 100 | Swissair *Chur* |
| | HB-IVD | Fokker 100 | Swissair *Dietlikon* |
| | HB-IVE | Fokker 100 | Swissair *Baden* |
| | HB-IVF | Fokker 100 | Swissair *Sion* |
| | HB-IVG | Fokker 100 | Swissair *Genthod* |
| | HB-IVH | Fokker 100 | Swissair *Stadel* |
| | HB-IV | Fokker 100 | Swissair |
| | HB-IV | Fokker 100 | Swissair |
| | HB-IWA | McD Douglas MD-11 | Swissair *Obwalden* |
| | HB-IWB | McD Douglas MD-11 | Swissair *Graubünden* |
| | HB-IWC | McD Douglas MD-11 | Swissair *Vaud* |
| | HB-IWD | McD Douglas MD-11 | Swissair *Thurgau* |
| | HB-IWE | McD Douglas MD-11 | Swissair *Nidwalden* |
| | HB-IWF | McD Douglas MD-11 | Swissair *Schafthausen* |
| | HB-IWG | McD Douglas MD-11 | Swissair *Valais* |
| | HB-IWH | McD Douglas MD-11 | Swissair *St Gallen* |
| | HB-IWI | McD Douglas MD-11 | Swissair *Uri* |
| | HB-IWK | McD Douglas MD-11 | Swissair *Fribourg* |
| | HB-IWL | McD Douglas MD-11 | Swissair *Appenzell* |
| | HB-IWM | McD Douglas MD-11 | Swissair *Jura* |
| | HB-IXB | BAe 146-200A | Crossair *Jumbolino* |
| | HB-IXC | BAe 146-200A | Crossair |
| | HB-IXD | BAe 146-200A | Crossair |
| | HB-IXF | BAe 146-200 | Crossair |
| | HB-IXG | BAe 146-200 | Crossair |
| | HB-IXH | BAe 146-200 | Crossair |
| | HB-IXK | BAe 146-200 | Crossair |

**Note:** Swissair also operates two Boeing 747-357s which retain their US registrations N221GE and N221GF and are named *Genève* and *Zurich* respectively.

# HK (Colombia)

| | HK-2980X | Boeing 747-259B (SCD) | Avianca *Cartagena de Indias* |
|---|---|---|---|

# HL (Korea)

| | HL7315 | Douglas DC-10-30 | Korean Air |
|---|---|---|---|
| | HL7316 | Douglas DC-10-30 | Korean Air |
| | HL7317 | Douglas DC-10-30 | Korean Air |
| | HL7431 | Boeing 707-321C | Korean Air |
| | HL7435 | Boeing 707-321B | Korean Air |
| | HL7440 | Boeing 747-230B | Korean Air |
| | HL7441 | Boeing 747-230F | Korean Air |
| | HL7443 | Boeing 747-2B5B | Korean Air |
| | HL7447 | Boeing 747-230B | Korean Air |
| | HL7451 | Boeing 747-2B5F (SCD) | Korean Air |
| | HL7452 | Boeing 747-2B5F (SCD) | Korean Air |
| | HL7453 | Boeing 747-212B | Korean Air |
| | HL7454 | Boeing 747-2B5B | Korean Air |

| Reg. | Type | Owner or Operator | Notes |
|------|------|-------------------|-------|
| HL7458 | Boeing 747-2B5B | Korean Air | |
| HL7459 | Boeing 747-2B5F (SCD) | Korean Air | |
| HL7463 | Boeing 747-2B5B | Korean Air | |
| HL7464 | Boeing 747-2B5B | Korean Air | |
| HL7468 | Boeing 747-3B5 | Korean Air | |
| HL7469 | Boeing 747-3B5 | Korean Air | |
| HL7470 | Boeing 747-3B5 (SCD) | Korean Air | |
| HL7471 | Boeing 747-273C | Korean Air | |
| HL7474 | Boeing 747-2S4F (SCD) | Korean Air | |
| HL7475 | Boeing 747-2B5F (SCD) | Korean Air | |
| HL7476 | Boeing 747-2B5F (SCD) | Korean Air | |
| HL7477 | Boeing 747-4B5 | Korean Air | |
| HL7478 | Boeing 747-4B5 | Korean Air | |
| HL7479 | Boeing 747-4B5 | Korean Air | |
| HL7480 | Boeing 747-4B5 (SCD) | Korean Air | |
| HL7481 | Boeing 747-4B5 | Korean Air | |
| HL7482 | Boeing 747-4B5 (SCD) | Korean Air | |

## HS (Thailand)

| Reg. | Type | Owner or Operator | Notes |
|------|------|-------------------|-------|
| HS-TGA | Boeing 747-2D7B | Thai Airways International *Visuthakasatriya* | |
| HS-TGB | Boeing 747-2D7B | Thai Airways International *Sirisobhakya* | |
| HS-TGC | Boeing 747-2D7B | Thai Airways International *Dararasmi* | |
| HS-TGD | Boeing 747-3D7 | Thai Airways International *Suchada* | |
| HS-TGE | Boeing 747-3D7 | Thai Airways International *Chutamat* | |
| HS-TGF | Boeing 747-2D7B | Thai Airways International *Phimara* | |
| HS-TGG | Boeing 747-2D7B | Thai Airways International *Sriwanna* | |
| HS-TGH | Boeing 747-4D7 | Thai Airways International | |
| HS-TGJ | Boeing 747-4D7 | Thai Airways International | |
| HS-TGS | Boeing 747-2D7B | Thai Airways International *Chainarai* | |
| HS-TMA | Douglas DC-10-30ER | Thai Airways International *Kwanmuang* | |
| HS-TMB | Douglas DC-10-30ER | Thai Airways International *Thepalai* | |
| HS-TMC | Douglas DC-10-30ER | Thai Airways International *Sri Ubon* | |

## HZ (Saudi Arabia)

| Reg. | Type | Owner or Operator | Notes |
|------|------|-------------------|-------|
| HZ-AHA | L.1011-385 TriStar 200 | Saudia — Saudi Arabian Airlines | |
| HZ-AHB | L.1011-385 TriStar 200 | Saudia — Saudi Arabian Airlines | |
| HZ-AHC | L.1011-385 TriStar 200 | Saudia — Saudi Arabian Airlines | |
| HZ-AHD | L.1011-385 TriStar 200 | Saudia — Saudi Arabian Airlines | |
| HZ-AHE | L.1011-385 TriStar 200 | Saudia — Saudi Arabian Airlines | |
| HZ-AHF | L.1011-385 TriStar 200 | Saudia — Saudi Arabian Airlines | |
| HZ-AHG | L.1011-385 TriStar 200 | Saudia — Saudi Arabian Airlines | |
| HZ-AHH | L.1011-385 TriStar 200 | Saudia — Saudi Arabian Airlines | |
| HZ-AHI | L.1011-385 TriStar 200 | Saudia — Saudi Arabian Airlines | |
| HZ-AHJ | L.1011-385 TriStar 200 | Saudia — Saudi Arabian Airlines | |
| HZ-AHL | L.1011-385 TriStar 200 | Saudia — Saudi Arabian Airlines | |
| HZ-AHM | L.1011-385 TriStar 200 | Saudia — Saudi Arabian Airlines | |
| HZ-AHN | L.1011-385 TriStar 200 | Saudia — Saudi Arabian Airlines | |
| HZ-AHO | L.1011-385 TriStar 200 | Saudia — Saudi Arabian Airlines | |
| HZ-AHP | L.1011-385 TriStar 200 | Saudia — Saudi Arabian Airlines | |
| HZ-AHQ | L.1011-385 TriStar 200 | Saudia — Saudi Arabian Airlines | |
| HZ-AHR | L.1011-385 TriStar 200 | Saudia — Saudi Arabian Airlines | |
| HZ-AIA | Boeing 747-168B | Saudia — Saudi Arabian Airlines | |
| HZ-AIB | Boeing 747-168B | Saudia — Saudi Arabian Airlines | |
| HZ-AIC | Boeing 747-168B | Saudia — Saudi Arabian Airlines | |
| HZ-AID | Boeing 747-168B | Saudia — Saudi Arabian Airlines | |
| HZ-AIE | Boeing 747-168B | Saudia — Saudi Arabian Airlines | |
| HZ-AIF | Boeing 747SP-68 | Saudia — Saudi Arabian Airlines | |
| HZ-AIG | Boeing 747-168B | Saudia — Saudi Arabian Airlines | |
| HZ-AIH | Boeing 747-168B | Saudia — Saudi Arabian Airlines | |
| HZ-AII | Boeing 747-168B | Saudia — Saudi Arabian Airlines | |
| HZ-AIJ | Boeing 747SP-68 | Saudia — Saudi Arabian Airlines | |
| HZ-AIK | Boeing 747-368 | Saudia — Saudi Arabian Airlines | |
| HZ-AIL | Boeing 747-368 | Saudia — Saudi Arabian Airlines | |
| HZ-AIM | Boeing 747-368 | Saudia — Saudi Arabian Airlines | |
| HZ-AIN | Boeing 747-368 | Saudia — Saudi Arabian Airlines | |
| HZ-AIO | Boeing 747-368 | Saudia — Saudi Arabian Airlines | |

| Notes | Reg. | Type | Owner or Operator |
|-------|------|------|-------------------|
| | HZ-AIP | Boeing 747-368 | Saudia — Saudi Arabian Airlines |
| | HZ-AIQ | Boeing 747-368 | Saudia — Saudi Arabian Airlines |
| | HZ-AIR | Boeing 747-368 | Saudia — Saudi Arabian Airlines |
| | HZ-AIS | Boeing 747-368 | Saudia — Saudi Arabian Airlines |
| | HZ-AIT | Boeing 747-368 | Saudia — Saudi Arabian Airlines |
| | HZ-AIU | Boeing 747-268F | Saudia — Saudi Arabian Airlines |
| | HZ-AJA | Airbus A.300-620 | Saudia — Saudi Arabian Airlines |
| | HZ-AJB | Airbus A.300-620 | Saudia — Saudi Arabian Airlines |
| | HZ-AJC | Airbus A.300-620 | Saudia — Saudi Arabian Airlines |
| | HZ-AJD | Airbus A.300-620 | Saudia — Saudi Arabian Airlines |
| | HZ-AJE | Airbus A.300-620 | Saudia — Saudi Arabian Airlines |
| | HZ-AJF | Airbus A.300-620 | Saudia — Saudi Arabian Airlines |
| | HZ-AJG | Airbus A.300-620 | Saudia — Saudi Arabian Airlines |
| | HZ-AJH | Airbus A.300-620 | Saudia — Saudi Arabian Airlines |
| | HZ-AJI | Airbus A.300-620 | Saudia — Saudi Arabian Airlines |
| | HZ-AJJ | Airbus A.300-620 | Saudia — Saudi Arabian Airlines |
| | HZ-AJK | Airbus A.300-620 | Saudia — Saudi Arabian Airlines |

**Note:** Saudia also operates other aircraft on lease.

# I (Italy)

| Notes | Reg. | Type | Owner or Operator |
|-------|------|------|-------------------|
| | I-ATIJ | Douglas DC-9-32 | Aero Trasporti Italiani (ATI) *Marche* |
| | I-ATIQ | Douglas DC-9-32 | Aero Trasporti Italiani (ATI) *Friuli Venezia Giulia* |
| | I-ATIY | Douglas DC-9-32 | Aero Trasporti Italiani (ATI) *Lombardia* |
| | I-ATJB | Douglas DC-9-32 | Aero Trasporti Italiani (ATI) *Calabria* |
| | I-BUSB | Airbus A.300B4 | Alitalia *Tiziano* |
| | I-BUSC | Airbus A.300B4 | Alitalia *Botticelli* |
| | I-BUSD | Airbus A.300B4 | Alitalia *Caravaggio* |
| | I-BUSF | Airbus A.300B4 | Alitalia *Tintoretto* |
| | I-BUSG | Airbus A.300B4 | Alitalia *Canaletto* |
| | I-BUSH | Airbus A.300B4 | Alitalia *Mantegua* |
| | I-BUSJ | Airbus A.300B4 | Alitalia *Tiepolo* |
| | I-BUSL | Airbus A.300B4 | Alitalia *Pinturicchia* |
| | I-BUSM | Airbus A.300B2 | Alitalia *Raffaello* |
| | I-BUSN | Airbus A.300B2 | Alitalia |
| | I-BUSP | Airbus A.300B4 | Alitalia |
| | I-BUSQ | Airbus A.300B4 | Alitalia *Michelangelo* |
| | I-BUSR | Airbus A.300B4 | Alitalia |
| | I-BUST | Airbus A.300B4 | Alitalia |
| | I-DACM | McD Douglas MD-82 | Aero Trasporti Italiani (ATI) *La Spezia* |
| | I-DACN | McD Douglas MD-82 | Aero Trasporti Italiani (ATI) *Rieti* |
| | I-DACP | McD Douglas MD-82 | Aero Trasporti Italiani (ATI) *Padova* |
| | I-DACQ | McD Douglas MD-82 | Aero Trasporti Italiani (ATI) *Taranto* |
| | I-DACR | McD Douglas MD-82 | Aero Trasporti Italiani (ATI) *Carrara* |
| | I-DACS | McD Douglas MD-82 | Alitalia *Valtellina* |
| | I-DACT | McD Douglas MD-82 | Alitalia *Maratea* |
| | I-DACU | McD Douglas MD-82 | Aero Trasporti Italiani (ATI) *Fabriano* |
| | I-DACV | McD Douglas MD-82 | Aero Trasporti Italiani (ATI) *Riccione* |
| | I-DACW | McD Douglas MD-82 | Alitalia *Vieste* |
| | I-DACX | McD Douglas MD-82 | Aero Trasporti Italiani (ATI) *Piacenza* |
| | I-DACY | McD Douglas MD-82 | Alitalia *Novara* |
| | I-DACZ | McD Douglas MD-82 | Aero Trasporti Italiani (ATI) *Castelfidardo* |
| | I-DAND | McD Douglas MD-82 | Alitalia *Bolzano* |
| | I-DANF | McD Douglas MD-82 | Aero Trasporti Italiani (ATI *Vicenza* |
| | I-DANG | McD Douglas MD-82 | Alitalia |
| | I-DANH | McD Douglas MD-82 | Alitalia |
| | I-DANL | McD Douglas MD-82 | Alitalia |
| | I-DANM | McD Douglas MD-82 | Alitalia |
| | I-DANP | McD Douglas MD-82 | Alitalia |
| | I-DANQ | McD Douglas MD-82 | Alitalia |
| | I-DANR | McD Douglas MD-82 | Alitalia |
| | I-DANU | McD Douglas MD-82 | Alitalia |
| | I-DANV | McD Douglas MD-82 | Alitalia |
| | I-DANW | McD Douglas MD-82 | Alitalia |
| | I-DAVA | McD Douglas MD-82 | Aero Trasporti Italiani (ATI) *Cuneo* |
| | I-DAVB | McD Douglas MD-82 | Alitalia *Ferrara* |

| Reg. | Type | Owner or Operator | Notes |
|------|------|-------------------|-------|
| I-DAVC | McD Douglas MD-82 | Aero Trasporti Italiani (ATI) *Lucca* | |
| I-DAVD | McD Douglas MD-82 | Aero Trasporti Italiani (ATI) *Mantova* | |
| I-DAVF | McD Douglas MD-82 | Aero Trasporti Italiani (ATI) *Oristano* | |
| I-DAVG | McD Douglas MD-82 | Aero Trasporti Italiani (ATI) *Pesaro* | |
| I-DAVH | McD Douglas MD-82 | Aero Trasporti Italiani (ATI) *Salerno* | |
| I-DAVI | McD Douglas MD-82 | Alitalia *Assisi* | |
| I-DAVJ | McD Douglas MD-82 | Alitalia *Parma* | |
| I-DAVK | McD Douglas MD-82 | Alitalia *Pompei* | |
| I-DAVL | McD Douglas MD-82 | Aero Trasporti Italiani (ATI) *Reggio Calabria* | |
| I-DAVM | McD Douglas MD-82 | Alitalia *Caserta* | |
| I-DAVN | McD Douglas MD-82 | Aero Trasporti Italiani (ATI) *Volterra* | |
| I-DAVP | McD Douglas MD-82 | Aero Trasporti Italiani (ATI) *Gorizia* | |
| I-DAVR | McD Douglas MD-82 | Aero Trasporti Italiani (ATI) | |
| I-DAVS | McD Douglas MD-82 | Aero Trasporti Italiani (ATI) | |
| I-DAVT | McD Douglas MD-82 | Aero Trasporti Italiani (ATI) | |
| I-DAVU | McD Douglas MD-82 | Aero Trasporti Italiani (ATI) | |
| I-DAVV | McD Douglas MD-82 | Aero Trasporti Italiani (ATI) | |
| I-DAVW | McD Douglas MD-82 | Aero Trasporti Italiani (ATI) *Camerino* | |
| I-DAVX | McD Douglas MD-82 | Aero Trasporti Italiani (ATI) *Asti* | |
| I-DAVZ | McD Douglas MD-82 | Aero Trasporti Italiani (ATI) *Brescia* | |
| I-DAWA | McD Douglas MD-82 | Alitalia *Roma* | |
| I-DAWB | McD Douglas MD-82 | Alitalia *Cagliari* | |
| I-DAWC | McD Douglas MD-82 | Alitalia *Campobasso* | |
| I-DAWD | McD Douglas MD-82 | Alitalia *Catanzaro* | |
| I-DAWE | McD Douglas MD-82 | Alitalia *Milano* | |
| I-DAWF | McD Douglas MD-82 | Alitalia *Firenze* | |
| I-DAWG | McD Douglas MD-82 | Alitalia *L'Aquila* | |
| I-DAWH | McD Douglas MD-82 | Alitalia *Palermo* | |
| I-DAWI | McD Douglas MD-82 | Alitalia *Ancona* | |
| I-DAWJ | McD Douglas MD-82 | Alitalia *Genova* | |
| I-DAWL | McD Douglas MD-82 | Alitalia *Perugia* | |
| I-DAWM | McD Douglas MD-82 | Alitalia *Potenza* | |
| I-DAWO | McD Douglas MD-82 | Alitalia *Bari* | |
| I-DAWP | McD Douglas MD-82 | Alitalia *Torino* | |
| I-DAWQ | McD Douglas MD-82 | Alitalia *Trieste* | |
| I-DAWR | McD Douglas MD-82 | Alitalia *Venezia* | |
| I-DAWS | McD Douglas MD-82 | Alitalia *Aosta* | |
| I-DAWT | McD Douglas MD-82 | Aero Trasporti Italiani (ATI) *Napoli* | |
| I-DAWU | McD Douglas MD-82 | Alitalia *Bologna* | |
| I-DAWV | McD Douglas MD-82 | Aero Trasporti Italiani (ATI) *Trento* | |
| I-DAWW | McD Douglas MD-82 | Aero Trasporti Italiani (ATI) *Riace* | |
| I-DAWY | McD Douglas MD-82 | Aero Trasporti Italiani (ATI) *Agrigento* | |
| I-DAWZ | McD Douglas MD-82 | Aero Trasporti Italiani (ATI) *Avellino* | |
| I-DEMC | Boeing 747-243B (SCD) | Alitalia *Taormina* | |
| I-DEMD | Boeing 747-243B (SCD) | Alitalia *Cortina d'Ampezzo* | |
| I-DEMF | Boeing 747-243B (SCD) | Alitalia *Portofino* | |
| I-DEMG | Boeing 747-243B | Alitalia *Cervinia* | |
| I-DEML | Boeing 747-243B | Alitalia *Sorrento* | |
| I-DEMN | Boeing 747-243B | Alitalia *Portocervo* | |
| I-DEMP | Boeing 747-243B | Alitalia *Capri* | |
| I-DEMR | Boeing 747-243F (SCD) | Alitalia *Stresa* | |
| I-DEMS | Boeing 747-243B | Alitalia *Monte Argentario* | |
| I-DEMT | Boeing 747-243B (SCD) | Alitalia *Monte Catini* | |
| I-DEMV | Boeing 747-243B | Alitalia *Sestriere* | |
| I-DEMW | Boeing 747-243B (SCD) | Alitalia *Spoleto* | |
| I-DEMY | Boeing 747-230B | Alitalia | |
| I-DIBR | Douglas DC-9-32 | Alitalia *Isola di Capri* | |
| I-DIBS | Douglas DC-9-32 | Alitalia *Isola d'Elba* | |
| I-DIBT | Douglas DC-9-32 | Alitalia *Isola di Murano* | |
| I-DIBU | Douglas DC-9-32 | Alitalia *Isola di Pantellaria* | |
| I-DIBV | Douglas DC-9-32 | Alitalia *Isola d'Ischia* | |
| I-DIBW | Douglas DC-9-32 | Alitalia *Isola del Giglio* | |
| I-DIBX | Douglas DC-9-32 | Alitalia *Isola di Giannutri* | |
| I-DIBY | Douglas DC-9-32 | Alitalia *Isola di Panarea* | |
| I-DIBZ | Douglas DC-9-32 | Alitalia *Isola di Lipari* | |
| I-DIKM | Douglas DC-9-32 | Alitalia *Isola di Positano* | |
| I-DIKP | Douglas DC-9-32 | Alitalia *Isola di Marettimo* | |
| I-DIKR | Douglas DC-9-32 | Alitalia *Piemonte* | |
| I-DIZE | Douglas DC-9-32 | Alitalia *Isola della Meloria* | |
| I-DUPA | McD Douglas MD-11C | Alitalia *Teatro alla Scala* | |
| I-DUPB | McD Douglas MD-11C | Alitalia *Valli dei Templi* | |
| I-DUPE | McD Douglas MD-11C | Alitalia *Arena di Verona* | |

| Notes | Reg. | Type | Owner or Operator |
|---|---|---|---|
| | I-DUPI | McD Douglas MD-11C | Alitalia *Fontona di Trevi* |
| | I-DUPO | McD Douglas MD-11C | Alitalia *Canal Grande* |
| | I-DUPU | McD Douglas MD-11C | Alitalia *Ponte Vecchio* |
| | I-JETA | Boeing 737-229 | Ital Jet |
| | I-RIBC | Douglas DC-9-32 | Alitalia *Isola di Lampedusa* |
| | I-RIBD | Douglas DC-9-32 | Alitalia *Isola di Montecristo* |
| | I-RIBJ | Douglas DC-9-32 | Alitalia *Isola della Capraia* |
| | I-RIBN | Douglas DC-9-32 | Alitalia *Isola della Palmaria* |
| | I-RIBQ | Douglas DC-9-32 | Alitalia *Isola di Pianosa* |
| | I-RIKS | Douglas DC-9-32 | Aero Trasporti Italiani (ATI) *Basilicata* |
| | I-RIKT | Douglas DC-9-32 | Aero Trasporti Italiani (ATI) *Trento Alto Adige* |
| | I-RIKV | Douglas DC-9-32 | Alitalia *Isola di Vulcano* |
| | I-RIKZ | Douglas DC-9-32 | Alitalia *Isola di Linosa* |
| | I-RIZA | Douglas DC-9-32 | Alitalia *Isola di Palmorola* |
| | I-RIZB | Douglas DC-9-32 | Alitalia |
| | I-RIZC | Douglas DC-9-32 | Aero Trasporti Italiani (ATI) *Molise* |
| | I-RIZF | Douglas DC-9-32 | Alitalia *Isola di Spargi* |
| | I-RIZG | Douglas DC-9-32 | Alitalia *Isola di Nisida* |
| | I-RIZH | Douglas DC-9-32 | Alitalia *Isola di Ponza* |
| | I-RIZJ | Douglas DC-9-32 | Aero Trasporti Italiani (ATI) *Umbria* |
| | I-RIZK | Douglas DC-9-32 | Alitalia *Toscana* |
| | I-RIZL | Douglas DC-9-32 | Alitalia *Romagna* |
| | I-RIZP | Douglas DC-9-32 | Alitalia *Veneto* |
| | I-RIZQ | Douglas DC-9-32 | Alitalia *Erice* |
| | I-RIZS | Douglas DC-9-32 | Aero Trasporti Italiani (ATI) *Compania* |
| | I-RIZU | Douglas DC-9-32 | Aero Trasporti Italiani (ATI) *Valle d'Aosta* |
| | I-RIZV | Douglas DC-9-32 | Aero Trasporti Italiani (ATI) *Lazio* |
| | I-RIZX | Douglas DC-9-32 | Alitalia *Isola di Procida* |
| | I-RIZY | Douglas DC-9-32 | Alitalia *Isola di Alicudi* |
| | I-SMEA | Douglas DC-9-51 | Alisarda |
| | I-SMEE | Douglas DC-9-51 | Alisarda |
| | I-SMEI | Douglas DC-9-51 | Alisarda |
| | I-SMEJ | Douglas DC-9-51 | Alisarda |
| | I-SMEO | Douglas DC-9-51 | Alisarda |
| | I-SMEP | McD Douglas MD-82 | Alisarda |
| | I-SMET | McD Douglas MD-82 | Alisarda |
| | I-SMEU | Douglas DC-9-51 | Alisarda |
| | I-SMEV | McD Douglas MD-82 | Alisarda |
| | I-TEAA | Boeing 737-3M8 | TEA Italy |
| | I-TEAE | Boeing 737-3M8 | TEA Italy |
| | I-TNTC | BAe 146-200QT | Mistral Air/TNT |

**Note:** Alisarda also uses two DC-9-82s which retain their Swiss registrations HB-IKK and HB-IKL.

# JA (Japan)

| | JA0803 | Boeing 747-446 | Japan Airlines |
|---|---|---|---|
| | JA0804 | Boeing 747-446 | Japan Airlines |
| | JA0805 | Boeing 747-446 | Japan Airlines |
| | JA0806 | Boeing 747-446 | Japan Airlines |
| | JA0807 | Boeing 747-446 | Japan Airlines |
| | JA8071 | Boeing 747-446 | Japan Airlines |
| | JA8072 | Boeing 747-446 | Japan Airlines |
| | JA8073 | Boeing 747-446 | Japan Airlines |
| | JA8074 | Boeing 747-446 | Japan Airlines |
| | JA8075 | Boeing 747-446 | Japan Airlines |
| | JA8076 | Boeing 747-446 | Japan Airlines |
| | JA8077 | Boeing 747-446 | Japan Airlines |
| | JA8078 | Boeing 747-446 | Japan Airlines |
| | JA8079 | Boeing 747-446 | Japan Airlines |
| | JA8080 | Boeing 747-446 | Japan Airlines |
| | JA8081 | Boeing 747-446 | Japan Airlines |
| | JA8082 | Boeing 747-446 | Japan Airlines |
| | JA8083 | Boeing 747-446 | Japan Airlines |
| | JA8084 | Boeing 747-446 | Japan Airlines |

| Reg. | Type | Owner or Operator | Notes |
|------|------|-------------------|-------|
| JA8085 | Boeing 747-446 | Japan Airlines | |
| JA8086 | Boeing 747-446 | Japan Airlines | |
| JA8087 | Boeing 747-446 | Japan Airlines | |
| JA8104 | Boeing 747-246B | Japan Airlines | |
| JA8105 | Boeing 747-246B | Japan Airlines | |
| JA8106 | Boeing 747-246B | Japan Airlines | |
| JA8107 | Boeing 747-146F (SCD) | Japan Airlines | |
| JA8108 | Boeing 747-246B | Japan Airlines | |
| JA8110 | Boeing 747-246B | Japan Airlines | |
| JA8111 | Boeing 747-246B | Japan Airlines | |
| JA8112 | Boeing 747-146A | Japan Airlines | |
| JA8113 | Boeing 747-246B | Japan Airlines | |
| JA8114 | Boeing 747-246B | Japan Airlines | |
| JA8115 | Boeing 747-146A | Japan Airlines | |
| JA8116 | Boeing 747-146A | Japan Airlines | |
| JA8122 | Boeing 747-246B | Japan Airlines | |
| JA8123 | Boeing 747-246F (SCD) | Japan Airlines | |
| JA8125 | Boeing 747-246B | Japan Airlines | |
| JA8130 | Boeing 747-246B | Japan Airlines | |
| JA8131 | Boeing 747-246B | Japan Airlines | |
| JA8132 | Boeing 747-246F | Japan Airlines | |
| JA8140 | Boeing 747-246B | Japan Airlines | |
| JA8141 | Boeing 747-246B | Japan Airlines | |
| JA8144 | Boeing 747-246F (SCD) | Japan Airlines | |
| JA8149 | Boeing 747-246B | Japan Airlines | |
| JA8150 | Boeing 747-246B | Japan Airlines | |
| JA8151 | Boeing 747-246F (SCD) | Japan Airlines | |
| JA8154 | Boeing 747-246B | Japan Airlines | |
| JA8155 | Boeing 747-246B | Japan Airlines | |
| JA8160 | Boeing 747-221F (SCD) | Japan Airlines | |
| JA8161 | Boeing 747-246B | Japan Airlines | |
| JA8162 | Boeing 747-246B | Japan Airlines | |
| JA8163 | Boeing 747-346 | Japan Airlines | |
| JA8165 | Boeing 747-221F (SCD) | Japan Airlines | |
| JA8166 | Boeing 747-346 | Japan Airlines | |
| JA8169 | Boeing 747-246B | Japan Airlines | |
| JA8171 | Boeing 747-246F (SCD) | Japan Airlines | |
| JA8173 | Boeing 747-346 | Japan Airlines | |
| JA8174 | Boeing 747-281B | All Nippon Airways | |
| JA8175 | Boeing 747-281B | All Nippon Airways | |
| JA8177 | Boeing 747-346 | Japan Airlines | |
| JA8178 | Boeing 747-346 | Japan Airlines | |
| JA8179 | Boeing 747-346 | Japan Airlines | |
| JA8180 | Boeing 747-246F (SCD) | Japan Airlines | |
| JA8181 | Boeing 747-281B | All Nippon Airways | |
| JA8182 | Boeing 747-281B | All Nippon Airways | |
| JA8185 | Boeing 747-346 | Japan Airlines | |
| JA8190 | Boeing 747-281B | All Nippon Airways | |
| JA8192 | Boeing 747-2D3B | All Nippon Airways | |
| JA8535 | Douglas DC-10-40 | Japan Airlines | |
| JA8538 | Douglas DC-10-40 | Japan Airlines | |
| JA8541 | Douglas DC-10-40 | Japan Airlines | |
| JA8542 | Douglas DC-10-40 | Japan Airlines | |
| JA8543 | Douglas DC-10-40 | Japan Airlines | |
| JA8545 | Douglas DC-10-40 | Japan Airlines | |
| JA8547 | Douglas DC-10-40 | Japan Airlines | |

**e:** Japan Airlines also operates a Boeing 747-246F which retains its US registration N211JL and two 747-346s N212JL and N213JL.

## (Jordan)

| | | | |
|------|------|-------------------|-------|
| JY-ADP | Boeing 707-3D3C | Royal Jordanian Airline *Mafreq* | |
| JY-AEC | Boeing 707-384C | Royal Jordanian Airline *Um Qais* | |
| JY-AGA | L.1011-385 TriStar 500 | Royal Jordanian Airline *Amman* | |
| JY-AGB | L.1011-385 TriStar 500 | Royal Jordanian Airline/Air Lanka *Princess Alia* | |
| JY-AGC | L.1011-385 TriStar 500 | Royal Jordanian Airline *Princes Zein* | |
| JY-AGD | L.1011-385 TriStar 500 | Royal Jordanian Airline *Prince Ali* | |

| Notes | Reg. | Type | Owner or Operator |
|-------|------|------|-------------------|
| | JY-AGE | L.1011-385 TriStar 500 | Royal Jordanian Airline *Princess Aysha* |
| | JY-AJK | Boeing 707-384C | Royal Jordanian Airline *City of Jerash* |
| | JY-HKJ | L.1011-385 TriStar 500 | Jordan Government |

**Note:** Royal Jordanian also operates six A.310-304s registered F-ODVD, F-ODVE, F-ODVF, F-ODVG, F-ODVH and F-ODVI. The marks JY-CAD, JY-CAE, JY-CAF, JY-CAG, JY-CAH and JY-CAI respectively have been reserved for them.

# LN (Norway)

| | | | |
|------|------|------|------|
| LN-AKA | F.27 Friendship Mk 200 | Busy Bee | |
| LN-AKB | F.27 Friendship Mk 200 | Busy Bee | |
| LN-AKC | F.27 Friendship Mk 200 | Busy Bee | |
| LN-AKD | F.27 Friendship Mk 200 | Busy Bee | |
| LN-BBA | Fokker 50 | Busy Bee | |
| LN-BBB | Fokker 50 | Busy Bee | |
| LN-BBC | Fokker 50 | Busy Bee | |
| LN-BBD | Fokker 50 | Busy Bee | |
| LN-BBE | Fokker 50 | Busy Bee | |
| LN-BRA | Boeing 737-405 | Braathens SAFE *Eirik Blodoeks* | |
| LN-BRB | Boeing 737-405 | Braathens SAFE *Inge Bardson* | |
| LN-BRC | Boeing 737-505 | Braathens SAFE | |
| LN-BRD | Boeing 737-505 | Braathens SAFE | |
| LN-BRE | Boeing 737-405 | Braathens SAFE | |
| LN-BRG | Boeing 737-505 | Braathens SAFE | |
| LN-BRI | Boeing 737-405 | Braathens SAFE | |
| LN-BRK | Boeing 737-505 | Braathens SAFE | |
| LN-BRL | Boeing 737-296 | Braathens SAFE/*Sigurd Munn* | |
| LN-BRM | Boeing 737-505 | Braathens SAFE | |
| LN-BRN | Boeing 737-505 | Braathens SAFE | |
| LN-BRO | Boeing 737-505 | Braathens SAFE | |
| LN-BRP | Boeing 737-505 | Braathens SAFE | |
| LN-BRQ | Boeing 737-405 | Braathens SAFE | |
| LN-BWG | Convair 580 | — | |
| LN-BWN | Convair 580 | — | |
| LN-FOG | L-188AF Electra | Fred Olsen Airtransport/TNT | |
| LN-FOH | L-188AF Electra | Fred Olsen Airtransport/TNT | |
| LN-FOI | L-188CF Electra | Fred Olsen Airtransport/TNT | |
| LN-KLK | Convair 440 | Norsk Metropolitan Fly Klubb | |
| LN-KOC | EMB-120RT Brasilia | Norsk Air | |
| LN-KOD | EMB-120RT Brasilia | Norsk Air | |
| LN-KOE | EMB-120RT Brasilia | Norsk Air | |
| LN-MOA | Cessna 441 Conquest | Morefly | |
| LN-MOB | Beech 200 Super King Air | Morefly | |
| LN-NOR | Boeing 737-33A | Air Europe Scandinavia/Air Europe (G-BNXW) *City of Stavanger* | |
| LN-NOS | Boeing 737-33A | Air Europe Scandinavia/Air Europe (G-BRXJ) *City of Trondheim* | |
| LN-NPB | Boeing 737-2R4C | Busy Bee | |
| LN-NPC | F-27 Friendship Mk 100 | Busy Bee | |
| LN-NPD | F-27 Friendship Mk 100 | Busy Bee | |
| LN-NPI | F.27 Friendship Mk 100 | Busy Bee | |
| LN-NPM | F.27 Friendship Mk 100 | Busy Bee | |
| LN-RCB | Boeing 767-383ER | S.A.S. *Astrid Viking* | |
| LN-RCC | Boeing 767-283ER | S.A.S. *Freydis Viking* | |
| LN-RCD | Boeing 767-383ER | S.A.S. *Gyda Viking* | |
| LN-RCE | Boeing 767-383ER | S.A.S. *Aase Viking* | |
| LN-RKC | Douglas DC-10-30 | S.A.S. *Leif Viking* | |
| LN-RLA | Douglas DC-9-41 | S.A.S. *Are Viking* | |
| LN-RLB | Douglas DC-9-41 | S.A.S. *Arne Viking* | |
| LN-RLD | Douglas DC-9-41 | S.A.S. *Torleif Viking* | |
| LN-RLE | McD Douglas MD-81 | S.A.S. *Trygve Viking* | |
| LN-RLF | McD Douglas MD-82 | S.A.S. *Finn Viking* | |
| LN-RLG | McD Douglas MD-82 | S.A.S. *Trond Viking* | |
| LN-RLH | Douglas DC-9-41 | S.A.S. *Einar Viking* | |
| LN-RLN | Douglas DC-9-41 | S.A.S. *Halldor Viking* | |
| LN-RLP | Douglas DC-9-41 | S.A.S. *Froste Viking* | |
| LN-RLR | McD Douglas MD-82 | S.A.S. *Kettil Viking* | |
| LN-RLS | Douglas DC-9-41 | S.A.S. *Asmund Viking* | |
| LN-RLT | Douglas DC-9-41 | S.A.S. *Audun Viking* | |
| LN-RLU | Douglas DC-9-41 | S.A.S. *Eivind Viking* | |

| Reg. | Type | Owner or Operator | Notes |
|------|------|-------------------|-------|
| LN-RLX | Douglas DC-9-41 | S.A.S. *Sote Viking* | |
| LN-RLZ | Douglas DC-9-41 | S.A.S. *Bodvar Viking* | |
| LN-RMA | McD Douglas MD-81 | S.A.S. *Hasting Viking* | |
| LN-RMB | McD Douglas MD-83 | S.A.S. *Erik Viking* | |
| LN-RMD | McD Douglas MD-82 | S.A.S. *Fenge Viking* | |
| LN-RMF | McD Douglas MD-83 | S.A.S. *Torgny Viking* | |
| LN-RMG | McD Douglas MD-87 | S.A.S. *Snorre Viking* | |
| LN-RMH | McD Douglas MD-87 | S.A.S. *Solmund Viking* | |
| LN-RMJ | McD Douglas MD-81 | S.A.S. *Rand Viking* | |
| LN-RMK | McD Douglas MD-87 | S.A.S. *Ragnhild Viking* | |
| LN-RML | McD Douglas MD-81 | S.A.S. *Aud Viking* | |
| LN-RMM | McD Douglas MD-81 | S.A.S. *Blenda Viking* | |
| LN-RNB | Fokker 50 | S.A.S. Commuter *Bardufoss* | |
| LN-RNC | Fokker 50 | S.A.S. Commuter *Evenes* | |
| LN-RND | Fokker 50 | S.A.S. Commuter *Lakselv* | |
| LN-RNE | Fokker 50 | S.A.S. Commuter *Alta* | |
| LN-RNF | Fokker 50 | S.A.S. Commuter *Kirkenes* | |
| LN-RNG | Fokker 50 | S.A.S. Commuter *Bodö* | |
| LN-RNH | Fokker 50 | S.A.S. Commuter *Trondheim* | |
| LN-R | Fokker 50 | S.A.S. Commuter | |
| LN-R | Fokker 50 | S.A.S. Commuter | |
| LN-SUA | Boeing 737-205 | Braathens SAFE *Halvdan Svarte* | |
| LN-SUE | F.27 Friendship Mk 100 | Busy Bee | |
| LN-SUF | F.27 Friendship Mk 100 | Busy Bee | |
| LN-SUL | F.27 Friendship Mk 100 | Busy Bee | |
| LN-SUU | Boeing 737-205 | Braathens SAFE *Harald Hardrade* | |
| LN-SUZ | Boeing 737-205 | Braathens SAFE *Olav Kyrre* | |
| LN-WND | Douglas DC-3 | Dakota Norway | |

**Note:** Braathens also operates the Boeing 737-205s N73FS, N73TH, N197QQ, N197SS, N890FS, N891FS, N7031A and N7031F (ex-LN-SUB, -SUK, -SUI, -SUD, -SUQ, -SUJ, -SUH and -SUM respectively) plus N197AL and N197JQ.

# LV (Argentina)

| | | | |
|------|------|-------------------|-------|
| LV-MLO | Boeing 747-287B | Aerolineas Argentinas | |
| LV-MLP | Boeing 747-287B | Aerolineas Argentinas | |
| LV-MLR | Boeing 747-287B | Aerolineas Argentinas | |
| LV-OEP | Boeing 747-287B | Aerolineas Argentinas | |
| LV-OHV | Boeing 747SP-27 | Aerolineas Argentinas | |
| LV-OOZ | Boeing 747-287B | Aerolineas Argentinas | |
| LV-OPA | Boeing 747-287B | Aerolineas Argentinas | |

# LX (Luxembourg)

| | | | |
|------|------|-------------------|-------|
| LX-ACV | Boeing 747-271C (SCD) | Cargolux *City of Esch/Alzette* | |
| LX-BCV | Boeing 747-271C (SCD) | Cargolux | |
| LX-ECV | Boeing 747-271C (SCD) | Cargolux *City of Luxembourg* | |
| LX-FCV | Boeing 747-121 | Lionair | |
| LX-GCV | Boeing 747-121 | Lionair | |
| LX-LGA | F.27 Friendship Mk 100 | Luxair *Prince Henri* | |
| LX-LGB | F.27 Friendship Mk 100 | Luxair *Prince Jean* | |
| LX-LGC | Fokker 50 | Luxair *Prince Guillaume* | |
| LX-LGD | Fokker 50 | Luxair *Prince Felix* | |
| LX-LGE | Fokker 50 | Luxair | |
| LX- | Fokker 50 | Luxair | |
| LX-LGH | Boeing 737-2C9 | Luxair *Prince Guillaume* | |
| LX-LGI | Boeing 737-2C9 | Luxair *Princess Marie-Astrid* | |
| LX-LGN | Boeing 737-229 | Luxair | |
| LX-LGX | Boeing 747SP-44 | Luxair | |

# LZ (Bulgaria)

| | | | |
|------|------|-------------------|-------|
| LZ-BAB | Antonov AN-12 | Balkan Bulgarian Airlines | |
| LZ-BAC | Antonov AN-12 | Balkan Bulgarian Airlines | |
| LZ-BAE | Antonov AN-12 | Balkan Bulgarian Airlines | |
| LZ-BAF | Antonov AN-12 | Balkan Bulgarian Airlines | |
| LZ-BEA | Ilyushin IL-18D | Balkan Bulgarian Airlines | |

| Notes | Reg. | Type | Owner or Operator |
|-------|------|------|-------------------|
| | LZ-BEI | Ilyushin IL-18V | Balkan Bulgarian Airlines |
| | LZ-BEK | Ilyushin IL-18V | Balkan Bulgarian Airlines |
| | LZ-BEL | Ilyushin IL-18V | Balkan Bulgarian Airlines |
| | LZ-BEO | Ilyushin IL-18D | Balkan Bulgarian Airlines |
| | LZ-BEU | Ilyushin IL-18V | Balkan Bulgarian Airlines |
| | LZ-BOA | Boeing 737-53A | Balkan Bulgarian Airlines |
| | LZ-BOB | Boeing 737-53A | Balkan Bulgarian Airlines |
| | LZ-BOC | Boeing 737-53A | Balkan Bulgarian Airlines |
| | LZ-BTA | Tupolev Tu-154B | Balkan Bulgarian Airlines |
| | LZ-BTC | Tupolev Tu-154B | Balkan Bulgarian Airlines |
| | LZ-BTD | Tupolev Tu-154B | Balkan Bulgarian Airlines |
| | LZ-BTE | Tupolev Tu-154B | Balkan Bulgarian Airlines |
| | LZ-BTF | Tupolev Tu-154B | Balkan Bulgarian Airlines |
| | LZ-BTG | Tupolev Tu-154B | Balkan Bulgarian Airlines |
| | LZ-BTH | Tupolev Tu-154M | Balkan Bulgarian Airlines |
| | LZ-BTI | Tupolev Tu-154M | Balkan Bulgarian Airlines |
| | LZ-BTK | Tupolev Tu-154B | Balkan Bulgarian Airlines |
| | LZ-BTL | Tupolev Tu-154B | Balkan Bulgarian Airlines |
| | LZ-BTM | Tupolev Tu-154B | Balkan Bulgarian Airlines |
| | LZ-BTO | Tupolev Tu-154B-1 | Balkan Bulgarian Airlines |
| | LZ-BTP | Tupolev Tu-154B-1 | Balkan Bulgarian Airlines |
| | LZ-BTQ | Tupolev Tu-154M | Balkan Bulgarian Airlines |
| | LZ-BTR | Tupolev Tu-154B-2 | Balkan Bulgarian Airlines |
| | LZ-BTS | Tupolev Tu-154B-2 | Balkan Bulgarian Airlines |
| | LZ-BTT | Tupolev Tu-154B-2 | Balkan Bulgarian Airlines |
| | LZ-BTU | Tupolev Tu-154B-2 | Balkan Bulgarian Airlines |
| | LZ-BTV | Tupolev Tu-154B-2 | Balkan Bulgarian Airlines |
| | LZ-BTW | Tupolev Tu-154M | Balkan Bulgarian Airlines |
| | LZ-BTX | Tupolev Tu-154M | Balkan Bulgarian Airlines |
| | LZ-BTY | Tupolev Tu-154M | Balkan Bulgarian Airlines |
| | LZ-BTZ | Tupolev Tu-154M | Balkan Bulgarian Airlines |
| | LZ-INK | Ilyushin IL-76TD | Metro Cargo *Lugano* |
| | LZ-MIG | Tupolev Tu-154M | Varna International Airways (VIA) |
| | LZ-MIK | Tupolev Tu-154M | Varna International Airways (VIA) |
| | LZ-MIL | Tupolev Tu-154M | Varna International Airways (VIA) |
| | LZ-TUA | Tupolev Tu-134 | Balkan Bulgarian Airlines |
| | LZ-TUC | Tupolev Tu-134 | Balkan Bulgarian Airlines |
| | LZ-TUD | Tupolev Tu-134 | Balkan Bulgarian Airlines |
| | LZ-TUE | Tupolev Tu-134 | Balkan Bulgarian Airlines |
| | LZ-TUG | Tupolev Tu-134A-3 | Balkan Bulgarian Airlines |
| | LZ-TUK | Tupolev Tu-134A | Balkan Bulgarian Airlines |
| | LZ-TUL | Tupolev Tu-134A-3 | Balkan Bulgarian Airlines |
| | LZ-TUM | Tupolev Tu-134A-3 | Balkan Bulgarian Airlines |
| | LZ-TUN | Tupolev Tu-134A-3 | Balkan Bulgarian Airlines |
| | LZ-TUO | Tupolev Tu-134 | Balkan Bulgarian Airlines |
| | LZ-TUP | Tupolev Tu-134A | Balkan Bulgarian Airlines |
| | LZ-TUS | Tupolev Tu-134A | Balkan Bulgarian Airlines |
| | LZ-TUT | Tupulev Tu-134A-3 | Balkan Bulgarian Airlines |
| | LZ-TUU | Tupolev Tu-134A-3 | Balkan Bulgarian Airlines |
| | LZ-TUV | Tupolev Tu-134A-3 | Balkan Bulgarian Airlines |
| | LZ-TUZ | Tupolev Tu-134A-3 | Balkan Bulgarian Airlines |

# N (USA)

| Notes | Reg. | Type | Owner or Operator |
|-------|------|------|-------------------|
| | N11AB | Boeing 737-4Y0 | Air Berlin |
| | N14AZ | Boeing 707-336C | Seagreen Air Transport |
| | N18AZ | Boeing 707-351C | Seagreen Air Transport |
| | N20UA | Douglas DC-8-61 | United Aviation Services |
| | N21AZ | Boeing 707-351C | Seagreen Air Transport |
| | N22UA | Douglas DC-8-61 | United Aviation Services |
| | N23UA | Douglas DC-8-61 | United Aviation Services |
| | N26UA | Douglas DC-8-61 | United Aviation Services |
| | N27UA | Douglas DC-8-61 | United Aviation Services |
| | N29AZ | Boeing 707-323C | Seagreen Air Transport |
| | N29UA | Douglas DC-8-61 | United Aviation Services |
| | N30UA | Douglas DC-8-61 | United Aviation Services |
| | N47UA | Douglas DC-8-61 | United Aviation Services |
| | N48UA | Douglas DC-8-61 | United Aviation Services |
| | N67AB | Boeing 737-3Y0 | Air Berlin |
| | N73FS | Boeing 737-205 | Braathens SAFE *Magnus den Gode* |
| | N73TH | Boeing 737-205 | Braathens SAFE *Magnus Erlingsson* |

| Reg. | Type | Owner or Operator | Notes |
|------|------|-------------------|-------|
| N104WA | Douglas DC-10-30CF | World Airways | |
| N105WA | Douglas DC-10-30CF | World Airways | |
| N106WA | Douglas DC-10-30CF | World Airways | |
| N107WA | Douglas DC-10-30CF | World Airways | |
| N108BV | Boeing 707-323C | HeavyLift Cargo Airlines Ltd/Stansted | |
| N108WA | Douglas DC-10-30CF | World Airways | |
| N109TA | Saab SF.340A | R.F.G. | |
| N110TA | Saab SF.340A | R.F.G. | |
| N112WA | Douglas DC-10-30CF | World Airways | |
| N116KB | Boeing 747-312 | Singapore Airlines | |
| N117KC | Boeing 747-312 | Singapore Airlines | |
| N118KD | Boeing 747-312 | Singapore Airlines | |
| N119KE | Boeing 747-312 | Singapore Airlines | |
| N120KF | Boeing 747-312 | Singapore Airlines | |
| N120TA | Saab SF.340A | R.F.G. | |
| N121KG | Boeing 747-312 | Singapore Airlines | |
| N122KH | Boeing 747-312 | Singapore Airlines | |
| N123KJ | Boeing 747-312 | Singapore Airlines | |
| N124KK | Boeing 747-312 | Singapore Airlines | |
| N125KL | Boeing 747-312 | Singapore Airlines | |
| N133JC | Douglas DC-10-40 | Northwest Airlines/Sun Country | |
| N133TW | Boeing 747-156 | Trans World Airlines | |
| N134TW | Boeing 747-156 | Trans World Airlines | |
| N137AA | Douglas DC-10-30 | American Airlines | |
| N138AA | Douglas DC-10-30 | American Airlines | |
| N139AA | Douglas DC-10-30 | American Airlines | |
| N140AA | Douglas DC-10-30 | American Airlines | |
| N141AA | Douglas DC-10-30 | American Airlines | |
| N141US | Douglas DC-10-40 | Northwest Airlines | |
| N142AA | Douglas DC-10-30 | American Airlines | |
| N143AA | Douglas DC-10-30 | American Airlines | |
| N144AA | Douglas DC-10-30 | American Airlines | |
| N145US | Douglas DC-10-40 | Northwest Airlines | |
| N146US | Douglas DC-10-40 | Northwest Airlines | |
| N147US | Douglas DC-10-40 | Northwest Airlines | |
| N148US | Douglas DC-10-40 | Northwest Airlines | |
| N149US | Douglas DC-10-40 | Northwest Airlines | |
| N150US | Douglas DC-10-40 | Northwest Airlines | |
| N151US | Douglas DC-10-40 | Northwest Airlines | |
| N152US | Douglas DC-10-40 | Northwest Airlines | |
| N153US | Douglas DC-10-40 | Northwest Airlines | |
| N154US | Douglas DC-10-40 | Northwest Airlines | |
| N155US | Douglas DC-10-40 | Northwest Airlines | |
| N156US | Douglas DC-10-40 | Northwest Airlines | |
| N157US | Douglas DC-10-40 | Northwest Airlines | |
| N158US | Douglas DC-10-40 | Northwest Airlines | |
| N159US | Douglas DC-10-40 | Northwest Airlines | |
| N160US | Douglas DC-10-40 | Northwest Airlines | |
| N161US | Douglas DC-10-40 | Northwest Airlines | |
| N162US | Douglas DC-10-40 | Northwest Airlines | |
| N163AA | Douglas DC-10-30 | American Airlines | |
| N164AA | Douglas DC-10-30 | American Airlines | |
| N171DN | Boeing 767-332ER | Delta Air Lines | |
| N171UA | Boeing 747-422 | United Airlines *Spirit of Seattle II* | |
| N172DN | Boeing 767-332ER | Delta Air Lines | |
| N172UA | Boeing 747-422 | United Airlines | |
| N173DN | Boeing 767-332ER | Delta Air Lines | |
| N173UA | Boeing 747-422 | United Airlines | |
| N174DN | Boeing 767-332ER | Delta Air Lines | |
| N174UA | Boeing 747-422 | United Airlines | |
| N175DN | Boeing 767-332ER | Delta Air Lines | |
| N175UA | Boeing 747-422 | United Airlines | |
| N176DN | Boeing 767-332ER | Delta Air Lines | |
| N176UA | Boeing 747-422 | United Airlines | |
| N177DN | Boeing 767-332ER | Delta Air Lines | |
| N177UA | Boeing 747-422 | United Airlines | |
| N178DN | Boeing 767-332ER | Delta Air Lines | |
| N178UA | Boeing 747-422 | United Airlines | |
| N179DN | Boeing 767-332ER | Delta Air Lines | |
| N179UA | Boeing 747-422 | United Airlines | |
| N180UA | Boeing 747-422 | United Airlines | |
| N181UA | Boeing 747-422 | United Airlines | |
| N182UA | Boeing 747-422 | United Airlines | |

| Notes | Reg. | Type | Owner or Operator |
|-------|------|------|-------------------|
| | N183UA | Boeing 747-422 | United Airlines |
| | N184UA | Boeing 747-422 | United Airlines |
| | N185AT | L-1011 TriStar 50 | American Trans Air/Air Afrique |
| | N185UA | Boeing 747-422 | United Airlines |
| | N186AT | L.1011 TriStar 50 | American Trans Air |
| | N187AT | L.1011 TriStar 50 | American Trans Air |
| | N188AT | L.1011 TriStar 50 | American Trans Air |
| | N189AT | L.1011 TriStar 50 | American Trans Air |
| | N190AT | L.1011 TriStar 50 | American Trans Air |
| | N191AT | L.1011 TriStar 50 | American Trans Air |
| | N192AT | L.1011 TriStar 50 | American Trans Air |
| | N193AT | L.1011 TriStar 50 | American Trans Air |
| | N195AT | L.1011 TriStar 50 | American Trans Air |
| | N197AL | Boeing 737-2E1 | Braathens SAFE |
| | N197JQ | Boeing 737-217 | Braathens SAFE |
| | N197QQ | Boeing 737-205 | Braathens SAFE *Haakon den Gode* |
| | N199SS | Boeing 737-205 | Braathens SAFE *Olav Tryggvason* |
| | N202AE | Boeing 747-2B4B (SCD) | Middle East Airlines |
| | N203AE | Boeing 747-2B4B (SCD) | Middle East Airlines |
| | N204AE | Boeing 747-2B4B | Middle East Airlines |
| | N211JL | Boeing 747-221F | Japan Air Lines |
| | N212JL | Boeing 747-346 | Japan Air Lines |
| | N213JL | Boeing 747-346 | Japan Air Lines |
| | N221GE | Boeing 747-357 | Swissair *Genève* |
| | N221GF | Boeing 747-357 | Swissair *Zurich* |
| | N301FE | Douglas DC-10-30AF | Federal Express |
| | N301TW | Boeing 747-282B | Trans World Airlines |
| | N302FE | Douglas DC-10-30AF | Federal Express |
| | N302TW | Boeing 747-282B | Trans World Airlines |
| | N303FE | Douglas DC-10-30AF | Federal Express |
| | N303TW | Boeing 747-257B | Nationair |
| | N304FE | Douglas DC-10-30AF | Federal Express |
| | N304TW | Boeing 747-257B | — |
| | N305FE | Douglas DC-10-30AF | Federal Express *John David* |
| | N305TW | Boeing 747-284B | Trans World Airlines |
| | N306FE | Douglas DC-10-30AF | Federal Express *John Peter* |
| | N307FE | Douglas DC-10-30AF | Federal Express *Erin Lee* |
| | N308FE | Douglas DC-10-30AF | Federal Express *Ann* |
| | N309FE | Douglas DC-10-30AF | Federal Express *Stacey* |
| | N310FE | Douglas DC-10-30AF | Federal Express *John Shelby* |
| | N311FE | Douglas DC-10-30AF | Federal Express *Abe* |
| | N312FE | Douglas DC-10-30AF | Federal Express *Angela* |
| | N313FE | Douglas DC-10-30AF | Federal Express *Brandon Parks* |
| | N314FE | Douglas DC-10-30AF | Federal Express *Caitlin-Ann* |
| | N315FE | Douglas DC-10-30AF | Federal Express *Kevin* |
| | N316FE | Douglas DC-10-30AF | Federal Express |
| | N319AA | Boeing 767-223ER | American Airlines |
| | N320AA | Boeing 767-223ER | American Airlines |
| | N321AA | Boeing 767-223ER | American Airlines |
| | N322AA | Boeing 767-223ER | American Airlines |
| | N323AA | Boeing 767-223ER | American Airlines |
| | N324AA | Boeing 767-223ER | American Airlines |
| | N325AA | Boeing 767-223ER | American Airlines |
| | N327AA | Boeing 767-223ER | American Airlines |
| | N328AA | Boeing 767-223ER | American Airlines |
| | N329AA | Boeing 767-223ER | American Airlines |
| | N330AA | Boeing 767-223ER | American Airlines |
| | N332AA | Boeing 767-223ER | American Airlines |
| | N334AA | Boeing 767-223ER | American Airlines |
| | N335AA | Boeing 767-223ER | American Airlines |
| | N336AA | Boeing 767-223ER | American Airlines |
| | N338AA | Boeing 767-223ER | American Airlines |
| | N339AA | Boeing 767-223ER | American Airlines |
| | N343HA | L.188 Electra | Channel Express Group PLC/ Bournemouth |
| | N345HC | Douglas DC-10-30ER | Finnair |
| | N347HA | L.188 Electra | Channel Express Group PLC/ Bournemouth |
| | N351AA | Boeing 767-323ER | American Airlines |
| | N352AA | Boeing 767-323ER | American Airlines |
| | N353AA | Boeing 767-323ER | American Airlines |
| | N354AA | Boeing 767-323ER | American Airlines |
| | N355AA | Boeing 767-323ER | American Airlines |

| Reg. | Type | Owner or Operator | Notes |
|------|------|-------------------|-------|
| N355WS | L.188 Electra | Air Bridge Carriers/World Airlines Gambia | |
| N356WS | Douglas DC-8-54F | TPI International Airways | |
| N357AA | Boeing 767-323ER | American Airlines | |
| N358AA | Boeing 767-323ER | American Airlines | |
| N359AA | Boeing 767-323ER | American Airlines | |
| N360AA | Boeing 767-323ER | American Airlines | |
| N360WS | L.188 Electra | Air Bridge Carriers/World Airlines Gambia | |
| N361AA | Boeing 767-323ER | American Airlines | |
| N362AA | Boeing 767-323ER | American Airlines | |
| N363AA | Boeing 767-323ER | American Airlines | |
| N366AA | Boeing 767-323ER | American Airlines | |
| N368AA | Boeing 767-323ER | American Airlines | |
| N369AA | Boeing 767-323ER | American Airlines | |
| N370AA | Boeing 767-323ER | American Airlines | |
| N371AA | Boeing 767-323ER | American Airlines | |
| N372AA | Boeing 767-323ER | American Airlines | |
| N373AA | Boeing 767-323ER | American Airlines | |
| N374AA | Boeing 767-323ER | American Airlines | |
| N391EA | Douglas DC-10-30 | Continental Airlines | |
| N417DG | Douglas DC-10-30 | Aeromexico *Ciudad de Mexico* | |
| N441J | Douglas DC-8-63CF | Arrow Air | |
| N457PC | Boeing 707-323B | Independent Air | |
| N470EV | Boeing 747-273C | Evergreen International Airlines | |
| N471EV | Boeing 747-273C | Evergreen International Airlines | |
| N472EV | Boeing 747-131 | Evergreen International Airlines | |
| N473EV | Boeing 747-121F (SCD) | Evergreen International Airlines | |
| N474EV | Boeing 747-121 | Evergreen International Airlines | |
| N475EV | Boeing 747-121F (SCD) | Evergreen International Airlines | |
| N476EV | Boeing 747-121 | Evergreen International Airlines | |
| N | Boeing 747-146F | Evergreen International Airlines | |
| N521SJ | L-100-20 Hercules | Southern Air Transport | |
| N522SJ | L-100-20 Hercules | Southern Air Transport | |
| N526SJ | Boeing 707-338C | Southern Air Transport | |
| N527SJ | Boeing 707-321C | Southern Air Transport | |
| N601FE | McD Douglas MD-11F | Federal Express | |
| N601FF | Boeing 747-127 | Tower Air *Sam* | |
| N601TW | Boeing 767-231ER | Trans World Airlines | |
| N601UA | Boeing 767-222ER | United Airlines | |
| N601US | Boeing 747-151 | Northwest Airlines | |
| N602FE | McDouglas MD-11F | Federal Express | |
| N602FF | Boeing 747-124 | Tower Air | |
| N602TW | Boeing 767-231ER | Trans World Airlines | |
| N602UA | Boeing 767-222ER | United Airlines | |
| N602US | Boeing 747-151 | Northwest Airlines | |
| N603FE | McD Douglas MD-11F | Federal Express | |
| N603FF | Boeing 747-130 | Tower Air *Suzie* | |
| N603TW | Boeing 767-231ER | Trans World Airlines | |
| N603UA | Boeing 767-222ER | United Airlines | |
| N603US | Boeing 747-151 | Northwest Airlines | |
| N604FE | McD Douglas MD-11F | Federal Express | |
| N604FF | Boeing 747-121 | Tower Air | |
| N604TW | Boeing 767-231ER | Trans World Airlines | |
| N604UA | Boeing 767-222ER | United Airlines | |
| N604US | Boeing 747-151 | Northwest Airlines | |
| N605FE | McD Douglas MD-11F | Federal Express | |
| N605PE | Boeing 747-243B (021) | Continental Airlines *(to become N33021)* | |
| N605TW | Boeing 767-231ER | Trans World Airlines | |
| N605UA | Boeing 767-222ER | United Airlines | |
| N605US | Boeing 747-151 | Northwest Airlines | |
| N606FE | McD Douglas MD-11F | Federal Express | |
| N606TW | Boeing 767-231ER | Trans World Airlines | |
| N606UA | Boeing 767-222ER | United Airlines | |
| N606US | Boeing 747-151 | Northwest Airlines | |
| N607FE | McD Douglas MD-11F | Federal Express | |
| N607PE | Boeing 747-238B (022) | Continental Airlines *(to become N50022)* | |
| N607TW | Boeing 767-231ER | Trans World Airlines | |
| N607UA | Boeing 767-222ER | United Airlines | |
| N607US | Boeing 747-151 | Northwest Airlines | |
| N608FE | McD Douglas MD-11F | Federal Express | |
| N608PE | Boeing 747-238B (023) | Continental Airlines *(to become N10023)* | |
| N608TW | Boeing 767-231ER | Trans World Airlines | |

| Notes | Reg. | Type | Owner or Operator |
|---|---|---|---|
| | N608UA | Boeing 767-222ER | United Airlines |
| | N608US | Boeing 747-151 | Northwest Airlines |
| | N609PE | Boeing 747-238B (024) | Continental Airlines *(to become N10024)* |
| | N609TW | Boeing 767-231ER | Trans World Airlines |
| | N609UA | Boeing 767-222ER | United Airlines |
| | N609US | Boeing 747-151 | Northwest Airlines |
| | N610TW | Boeing 767-231ER | Trans World Airlines |
| | N610UA | Boeing 767-222ER | United Airlines |
| | N610US | Boeing 747-151 | Northwest Airlines |
| | N611UA | Boeing 767-222ER | United Airlines |
| | N611US | Boeing 747-251B | Northwest Airlines |
| | N612UA | Boeing 767-222ER | United Airlines |
| | N612US | Boeing 747-251B | Northwest Airlines |
| | N613UA | Boeing 767-222ER | United Airlines |
| | N613US | Boeing 747-251B | Northwest Airlines |
| | N614UA | Boeing 767-222ER | United Airlines |
| | N614US | Boeing 747-251B | Northwest Airlines |
| | N615UA | Boeing 767-222ER | United Airlines |
| | N615US | Boeing 747-251B | Northwest Airlines |
| | N616US | Boeing 747-251F (SCD) | Northwest Airlines |
| | N617UA | Boeing 767-222ER | United Airlines |
| | N617US | Boeing 747-251F (SCD) | Northwest Airlines |
| | N618UA | Boeing 767-222ER | United Airlines |
| | N618US | Boeing 747-251F (SCD) | Northwest Airlines |
| | N619UA | Boeing 767-222ER | United Airlines |
| | N619US | Boeing 747-251F (SCD) | Northwest Airlines |
| | N620FE | Boeing 747-133 | Federal Express |
| | N620UA | Boeing 767-222ER | United Airlines |
| | N620US | Boeing 747-135 | Northwest Airlines |
| | N621FE | Boeing 747-133 | Federal Express |
| | N621US | Boeing 747-135 | Northwest Airlines |
| | N622US | Boeing 747-251B | Northwest Airlines |
| | N623FE | Boeing 747-132F (SCD) | Federal Express |
| | N623US | Boeing 747-251B | Northwest Airlines |
| | N624FE | Boeing 747-132F (SCD) | Federal Express |
| | N624US | Boeing 747-251B | Northwest Airlines |
| | N625FE | Boeing 747-132F (SCD) | Federal Express |
| | N625US | Boeing 747-251B | Northwest Airlines |
| | N626FE | Boeing 747-121F (SCD) | Federal Express |
| | N626US | Boeing 747-251B | Northwest Airlines |
| | N627FE | Boeing 747-121F (SCD) | Federal Express |
| | N627US | Boeing 747-251B | Northwest Airlines |
| | N628FE | Boeing 747-121F (SCD) | Federal Express |
| | N628US | Boeing 747-251B | Northwest Airlines |
| | N629FE | Boeing 747-123F | Federal Express |
| | N629US | Boeing 747-251F (SCD) | Northwest Airlines |
| | N630FE | Boeing 747-124F | Federal Express |
| | N630US | Boeing 747-2J9F | Northwest Airlines |
| | N631FE | Boeing 747-245F (SCD) | Federal Express |
| | N631US | Boeing 747-251B | Northwest Airlines |
| | N632FE | Boeing 747-249F (SCD) | Federal Express |
| | N632US | Boeing 747-251B | Northwest Airlines |
| | N633FE | Boeing 747-249F | Federal Express |
| | N633US | Boeing 747-227B | Northwest Airlines |
| | N634FE | Boeing 747-245F (SCD) | Federal Express |
| | N634US | Boeing 747-227B | Northwest Airlines |
| | N635FE | Boeing 747-245F (SCD) | Federal Express |
| | N635US | Boeing 747-227B | Northwest Airlines |
| | N636FE | Boeing 747-249F (SCD) | Federal Express |
| | N636US | Boeing 747-251B | Northwest Airlines |
| | N637US | Boeing 747-251B | Northwest Airlines |
| | N638FE | Boeing 747-245F (SCD) | Federal Express |
| | N638US | Boeing 747-251B | Northwest Airlines |
| | N639FE | Boeing 747-2R7F (SCD) | Federal Express |
| | N639US | Boeing 747-251F (SCD) | Northwest Airlines |
| | N640FE | Boeing 747-245F (SCD) | Federal Express |
| | N640US | Boeing 747-251F (SCD) | Northwest Airlines |
| | N641FE | Boeing 747-245F (SCD) | Federal Express |
| | N645US | Boeing 767-201ER | USAir *Pride of Piedmont* |
| | N646US | Boeing 767-201ER | USAir *City of London* |
| | N647US | Boeing 767-201ER | USAir *City of Charlotte* |
| | N648US | Boeing 767-201ER | USAir *City of Tampa* |
| | N649US | Boeing 767-201ER | USAir *City of Los Angeles* |

| Reg. | Type | Owner or Operator | Notes |
|------|------|-------------------|-------|
| N650TW | Boeing 767-205ER | Trans World Airlines | |
| N650US | Boeing 767-201ER | USAir *Pride of Baltimore* | |
| N651US | Boeing 767-2B7ER | USAir | |
| N652PA | Boeing 747-121 | Pan Am *Clipper Mermaid* | |
| N652US | Boeing 767-2B7ER | USAir | |
| N653PA | Boeing 747-121 (SCD) | Pan Am *Clipper Unity* | |
| N653US | Boeing 767-2B7ER | USAir | |
| N655PA | Boeing 747-121 (SCD) | Pan Am *Clipper Sea Serpent* | |
| N656PA | Boeing 747-121 | Evergreen International Airlines/Pan Am | |
| N657PA | Boeing 747-121 | Evergreen International Airlines/Pan Am | |
| N659PA | Boeing 747-121 | Pan Am *Clipper Voyager* | |
| N661AV | Douglas DC-8-63AF | Arrow Air | |
| N661US | Boeing 747-451 | Northwest Airlines | |
| N662US | Boeing 747-451 | Northwest Airlines | |
| N663US | Boeing 747-451 | Northwest Airlines | |
| N664US | Boeing 747-451 | Northwest Airlines | |
| N665US | Boeing 747-451 | Northwest Airlines | |
| N666US | Boeing 747-451 | Northwest Airlines | |
| N667US | Boeing 747-451 | Northwest Airlines | |
| N668US | Boeing 747-451 | Northwest Airlines | |
| N669F | L.188 Electra | Air Bridge Carriers/EMS International | |
| N669US | Boeing 747-451 | Northwest Airlines | |
| N670US | Boeing 747-451 | Northwest Airlines | |
| N671UP | Boeing 747-123F (SCD) | United Parcel Service | |
| N672UP | Boeing 747-123F (SCD) | United Parcel Service | |
| N673UP | Boeing 747-123F (SCD) | United Parcel Service | |
| N674UP | Boeing 747-123F (SCD) | United Parcel Service | |
| N675UP | Boeing 747-123F (SCD) | United Parcel Service | |
| N676UP | Boeing 747-123F (SCD) | United Parcel Service | |
| N723PA | Boeing 747-212B | Pan Am *Clipper China Clipper II* | |
| N724DA | L.1011-385 TriStar 200 | Delta Air Lines | |
| N724PA | Boeing 747-212B | Pan Am *Clipper Fairwind* | |
| N725PA | Boeing 747-132 (SCD) | Pan Am *Clipper Mandarin* | |
| N726PA | Boeing 747-212B (SCD) | Pan Am *Clipper Belle of the Skies* | |
| N727PA | Boeing 747-212B | Pan Am *Clipper Cathay* | |
| N728PA | Boeing 747-212B (SCD) | Pan Am *Clipper Water Witch* | |
| N728Q | Boeing 707-321B | Independent Air | |
| N729PA | Boeing 747-212B (SCD) | Pan Am *Clipper Wild Wave* | |
| N730PA | Boeing 747-212B (SCD) | Pan Am *Clipper Gem of the Ocean* | |
| N733PA | Boeing 747-121 | Pan Am *Clipper Pride of the Sea* | |
| N734PA | Boeing 747-121 (SCD) | Pan Am *Clipper Champion of the Seas* | |
| N735PA | Boeing 747-121 | Pan Am *Clipper Spark of the Ocean* | |
| N736DY | L.1011-385 TriStar 250 | Delta Air Lines | |
| N737D | L.1011-385 TriStar 250 | Delta Air Lines | |
| N737PA | Boeing 747-121 | Pan Am *Clipper Ocean Herald* | |
| N740DA | L.1011-385 TriStar 250 | Delta Air Lines | |
| N740PA | Boeing 747-121 | Pan Am *Clipper Ocean Pearl* | |
| N741DA | L.1011-385 TriStar 250 | Delta Air Lines | |
| N741PA | Boeing 747-121 | Pan Am *Clipper Special Olympian* | |
| N741PR | Boeing 747-2F6B | Philippine Airlines | |
| N742PA | Boeing 747-121 | Pan Am *Clipper Neptune's Car* | |
| N742PR | Boeing 747-2F6B | Philippine Airlines | |
| N743PA | Boeing 747-121 (SCD) | Pan Am *Clipper Black Sea* | |
| N743PR | Boeing 747-2F6B | Philippine Airlines | |
| N744PA | Boeing 747-121 | Pan Am *Clipper Ocean Spray* | |
| N744PR | Boeing 747-2F6B | Philippine Airlines | |
| N747PA | Boeing 747-121 (SCD) | Pan Am *Clipper Juan T. Trippe* | |
| N748PA | Boeing 747-121 | Pan Am *Clipper Crest of the Wave* | |
| N749PA | Boeing 747-121 | Pan Am *Clipper Dashing Wave* | |
| N750AT | Boeing 757-212ER | American Trans Air | |
| N750PA | Boeing 747-121 | Pan Am *Clipper Neptune's Favorite* | |
| N751AT | Boeing 757-212ER | American Trans Air | |
| N751DA | L-1011-385 TriStar 500 | Delta Air Lines | |
| N752AT | Boeing 757-212ER | American Trans Air | |
| N752DA | L.1011-385 TriStar 500 | Delta Air Lines | |
| N753DA | L.1011-385 TriStar 500 | Delta Air Lines | |
| N754DL | L.1011-385 TriStar 500 | Delta Air Lines | |
| N755DL | L.1011-385 TriStar 500 | Delta Air Lines | |
| N756DR | L.1011-385 TriStar 500 | Delta Air Lines | |
| N757AT | Boeing 757-212ER | American Trans Air | |
| N | Boeing 757-2Q8ER | American Trans Air | |
| N | Boeing 757-2Q8ER | American Trans Air | |
| N759DA | L.1011-385 TriStar 500 | Delta Air Lines | |

| Notes | Reg. | Type | Owner or Operator |
|-------|------|------|-------------------|
| | N760DH | L.1011-385 TriStar 500 | Delta Air Lines |
| | N761DA | L.1011-385 TriStar 500 | Delta Air Lines |
| | N762BE | L.1011-385 TriStar 1 | Hawaiian Air *Waikiki* |
| | N762DA | L.1011-385 TriStar 500 | Delta Air Lines |
| | N763BE | L.1011-385 TriStar 1 | Hawaiian Air *Maui* |
| | N763DL | L.1011-385 TriStar 500 | Delta Air Lines |
| | N764BE | L.1011-385 TriStar 1 | Hawaiian Air *Wahwaii* |
| | N765BE | L.1011-385 TriStar 1 | Hawaiian Air *Kauai* |
| | N766BE | L.1011-385 TriStar 1 | Hawaiian Air *Oahu* |
| | N772CA | Douglas DC-8-62 | Rich International Airways |
| | N791AL | Douglas DC-8-62AF | Arrow Air |
| | N791FT | Douglas DC-8-73AF | Emery Worldwide |
| | N792FT | Douglas DC-8-73AF | Emery Worldwide |
| | N795FT | Douglas DC-8-73AF | Emery Worldwide |
| | N796AL | Douglas DC-8-63AF | Emery Worldwide |
| | N796FT | Douglas DC-8-73AF | Emery Worldwide |
| | N797AL | Douglas DC-8-63AF | Emery Worldwide |
| | N798AL | Douglas DC-8-62CF | Arrow Air |
| | N801CK | Douglas DC-8-55F | Connie Kalitta Services |
| | N801DL | McD Douglas MD-11 | Delta Air Lines |
| | N801PA | Airbus A.310-222 | Pan Am *Clipper Berlin* |
| | N801UP | Douglas DC-8-73AF | United Parcel Service |
| | N802BN | Douglas DC-8-62AF | Arrow Air |
| | N802CK | Douglas DC-8-54F | Connie Kalitta Services |
| | N802DL | McD Douglas MD-11 | Delta Air Lines |
| | N802PA | Airbus A.310-222 | Pan Am *Clipper Frankfurt* |
| | N802UP | Douglas DC-8-73AF | United Parcel Service |
| | N803CK | Douglas DC-8-54F | Connie Kalitta Services |
| | N803DL | McD Douglas MD-11 | Delta Air Lines |
| | N803PA | Airbus A.310-222 | Pan Am *Clipper Munich* |
| | N804CK | Douglas DC-8-51F | Connie Kalitta Services |
| | N804DL | McD Douglas MD-11 | Delta Air Lines |
| | N804PA | Airbus A.310-222 | Pan Am *Clipper Hamburg* |
| | N804UP | Douglas DC-8-73AF | United Parcel Service |
| | N805CK | Douglas DC-8-51F | Connie Kalitta Services |
| | N805DL | McD Douglas MD-11 | Delta Air Lines |
| | N805PA | Airbus A.310-222 | Pan Am *Clipper Miles Standish* |
| | N805UP | Douglas DC-8-73CF | United Parcel Service |
| | N806DL | McD Douglas MD-11 | Delta Air Lines |
| | N806PA | Airbus A.310-222 | Pan Am *Clipper Betsy Ross* |
| | N806UP | Douglas DC-8-73AF | United Parcel Service |
| | N807CK | Douglas DC-8-55F | Connie Kalitta Services |
| | N807DL | McD Douglas MD-11 | Delta Air Lines |
| | N807PA | Airbus A.310-222 | Pan Am *Clipper Kit Carson* |
| | N807UP | Douglas DC-8-73AF | United Parcel Service |
| | N808CK | Douglas DC-8-55F | Connie Kalitta Services |
| | N808DL | McD Douglas MD-11 | Delta Air Lines |
| | N808UP | Douglas DC-8-73AF | United Parcel Service |
| | N809CK | Douglas DC-8-73AF | Connie Kalitta Services |
| | N809DL | McD Douglas MD-11 | Delta Air Lines |
| | N809UP | Douglas DC-8-73AF | United Parcel Service |
| | N810CK | Douglas DC-8-52F | Connie Kalitta Services |
| | N810UP | Douglas DC-8-71AF | United Parcel Service |
| | N811CK | Douglas DC-8-63AF | Connie Kalitta Services |
| | N811PA | Airbus A.310-324 | Pan Am *Clipper Constitution* |
| | N812PA | Airbus A.310-324 | Pan Am *Clipper Freedom* |
| | N812UP | Douglas DC-8-73AF | United Parcel Service |
| | N813PA | Airbus A.310-324 | Pan Am *Clipper Great Republic* |
| | N814PA | Airbus A.310-324 | Pan Am *Clipper Liberty Bell* |
| | N815EV | Douglas DC-8-73CF | Evergreen International Airlines |
| | N815PA | Airbus A.310-324 | Pan Am *Clipper Mayflower* |
| | N816EV | Douglas DC-8-73CF | Evergreen International Airlines |
| | N816PA | Airbus A.310-324 | Pan Am *Clipper Meteor* |
| | N817EV | Douglas DC-8-62AF | Evergreen International Airlines |
| | N817PA | Airbus A.310-324 | Pan Am *Clipper Midnight Sun* |
| | N818PA | Airbus A.310-324 | Pan Am *Clipper Morning Star* |
| | N818UP | Douglas DC-8-73AF | United Parcel Service |
| | N819PA | Airbus A.310-324 | Pan Am *Clipper Northern Light* |
| | N819UP | Douglas DC-8-73AF | United Parcel Service |
| | N820PA | Airbus A.310-324 | Pan Am *Clipper Plymouth Rock* |
| | N820TC | Douglas DC-8-63 | Trans Continental Airlines |
| | N821PA | Airbus A.310-324 | Pan Am *Clipper Queen of the Skies* |
| | N821TC | Douglas DC-8-61 | Trans Continental Airlines |

| Reg. | Type | Owner or Operator | Notes |
|------|------|-------------------|-------|
| N822PA | Airbus A.310-324 | Pan Am *Clipper Victory* | |
| N823PA | Airbus A.310-324 | Pan Am | |
| N824PA | Airbus A.310-324 | Pan Am | |
| N831TW | Boeing 727-31 | Trans World Airlines | |
| N836UP | Douglas DC-8-73AF | United Parcel Service | |
| N839TW | Boeing 727-31 | Trans World Airlines | |
| N840UP | Douglas DC-8-73AF | United Parcel Service | |
| N844TW | Boeing 727-31 | Trans World Airlines | |
| N848TW | Boeing 727-31 | Trans World Airlines | |
| N851UP | Douglas DC-8-73AF | United Parcel Service | |
| N852UP | Douglas DC-8-73AF | United Parcel Service | |
| N855TW | Boeing 727-31 | Trans World Airlines | |
| N859TW | Boeing 727-31 | Trans World Airlines | |
| N865F | Douglas DC-8-63AF | Emery Worldwide | |
| N866UP | Douglas DC-8-73AF | United Parcel Service | |
| N867BX | Douglas DC-8-63AF | Burlington Express | |
| N867UP | Douglas DC-8-73AF | United Parcel Service | |
| N868BX | Douglas DC-8-63AF | Burlington Express | |
| N868UP | Douglas DC-8-73AF | United Parcel Service | |
| N869BX | Doulgas DC-8-63AF | Burlington Express | |
| N870BX | Doulgas DC-8-63AF | Burlington Express | |
| N870SJ | Douglas DC-8-71 | Southern Air Transport | |
| N870TV | Douglas DC-8-73AF | Emery Worldwide | |
| N874UP | Douglas DC-8-73AF | United Parcel Service | |
| N880UP | Douglas DC-8-73AF | United Parcel Service | |
| N889TW | Boeing 727-31 | Trans World Airlines | |
| N890FS | Boeing 737-205 | Braathens SAFE *Hakon Sverresson* | |
| N891FS | Boeing 737-205 | Braathens SAFE *Magnus Barfot* | |
| N894UP | Douglas DC-8-73AF | United Parcel Service | |
| N901SJ | L.100-30 Hercules | Southern Air Transport | |
| N902PA | Boeing 747-132 | Pan Am *Clipper Seaman's Bride* | |
| N902SJ | L.100-30 Hercules | Southern Air Transport | |
| N903SJ | L.100-30 Hercules | Southern Air Transport | |
| N904SJ | L.100-30 Hercules | Southern Air Transport | |
| N906R | Douglas DC-8-63AF | Emery Worldwide | |
| N907SJ | L.100-30 Hercules | Southern Air Transport | |
| N908SJ | L.100-30 Hercules | Southern Air Transport | |
| N910SJ | L.100-30 Hercules | Southern Air Transport | |
| N911SJ | L.100-30 Hercules | Southern Air Transport | |
| N912SJ | L.100-30 Hercules | Southern Air Transport | |
| N916SJ | L.100-30 Hercules | Southern Air Transport | |
| N918SJ | L.100-30 Hercules | Southern Air Transport | |
| N919SJ | L.100-30 Hercules | Southern Air Transport | |
| N920SJ | L.100-30 Hercules | Southern Air Transport | |
| N921R | Douglas DC-8-63AF | Emery Worldwide | |
| N921SJ | L.100-30 Hercules | Southern Air Transport | |
| N923SJ | L.100-30 Hercules | Southern Air Transport | |
| N929R | Douglas DC-8-63AF | Emery Worldwide | |
| N950R | Douglas DC-8-63AF | Emery Worldwide | |
| N951R | Douglas DC-8-63AF | Emery Worldwide | |
| N952R | Douglas DC-8-63AF | Emery Worldwide | |
| N957R | Douglas DC-8-63AF | Emery Worldwide | |
| N959R | Douglas DC-8-63AF | Emery Worldwide | |
| N961R | Douglas DC-8-73AF | Emery Worldwide | |
| N964R | Douglas DC-8-63AF | Emery Worldwide | |
| N990CF | Douglas DC-8-62AF | Emery Worldwide | |
| N993CF | Douglas DC-8-62AF | Emery Worldwide | |
| N994CF | Douglas DC-8-62AF | Emery Worldwide | |
| N995CF | Douglas DC-8-62AF | Emery Worldwide | |
| N996CF | Douglas DC-8-62AF | Emery Worldwide | |
| N997CF | Douglas DC-8-62AF | Emery Worldwide | |
| N998CF | Douglas DC-8-62AF | Emery Worldwide | |
| N1295E | Boeing 747-306 | K.L.M. *The Ganges* | |
| N1298E | Boeing 747-306 | K.L.M. *The Indus* | |
| N1309E | Boeing 747-306 | K.L.M. *Admiral Richard E. Byrd* | |
| N1738D | L.1011-385 TriStar 250 | Delta Air Lines | |
| N1739D | L.1011-385 TriStar 250 | Delta Air Lines | |
| N1750B | McD Douglas MD-11 | American Airlines | |
| N1751A | McD Douglas MD-11 | American Airlines | |
| N1752K | McD Douglas MD-11 | American Airlines | |
| N1753 | McD Douglas MD-11 | American Airlines | |
| N1754 | McD Douglas MD-11 | American Airlines | |
| N1755 | McD Douglas MD-11 | American Airlines | |

| Reg. | Type | Owner or Operator |
|------|------|-------------------|
| N1756 | McD Douglas MD-11 | American Airlines |
| N1757A | McD Douglas MD-11 | American Airlines |
| N1758B | McD Douglas MD-11 | American Airlines |
| N1759 | McD Douglas MD-11 | American Airlines |
| N1760A | McD Douglas MD-11 | American Airlines |
| N1761R | McD Douglas MD-11 | American Airlines |
| N1762B | McD Douglas MD-11 | American Airlines |
| N1763 | McD Douglas MD-11 | American Airlines |
| N1764B | McD Douglas MD-11 | American Airlines |
| N1805 | Douglas DC-8-62 | Rich International Airways |
| N1808E | Douglas DC-8-62 | Rich International Airways |
| N2215Y | Boeing 707-351C | HeavyLift Cargo Airlines Ltd/Stansted |
| N2674U | Douglas DC-8-73AF | Emery Worldwide |
| N3016Z | Douglas DC-10-30 | Zambia Airways *Nkwazi* |
| N3024W | Douglas DC-10-30 | Nigeria Airways |
| N3140D | L.1011-385 TriStar 500 (598) | B.W.I.A. |
| N4508E | Boeing 747-228F | Air France |
| N4508H | Boeing 747SP-09 | China Airlines |
| N4522V | Boeing 747SP-09 | China Airlines |
| N4548M | Boeing 747-306 | K.L.M. *Sir Frank Whittle* |
| N4551N | Boeing 747-306 | K.L.M. *Sir Geoffrey de Havilland* |
| N4703U | Boeing 747-122 (SCD) | Pan Am *Clipper Nautilus* |
| N4704U | Boeing 747-122 | Pan Am *Clipper Belle of the Sea* |
| N4710U | Boeing 747-122 | Pan Am *Clipper Sea Lark* |
| N4711U | Boeing 747-122 (SCD) | Pan Am *Clipper Witch of the Waves* |
| N4712U | Boeing 747-122 (SCD) | Pan Am *Clipper Tradewind* |
| N4730 | Boeing 727-235 | Pan Am *Clipper Fidelity* |
| N4731 | Boeing 727-235 | Pan Am *Clipper Alert* |
| N4732 | Boeing 727-235 | Pan Am *Clipper Challenger* |
| N4733 | Boeing 727-235 | Pan Am *Clipper Charger* |
| N4734 | Boeing 727-235 | Pan Am *Clipper Charmer* |
| N4735 | Boeing 727-235 | Pan Am *Clipper Daring* |
| N4736 | Boeing 727-235 | Pan Am *Clipper Dashaway* |
| N4738 | Boeing 727-235 | Pan Am *Clipper Electric* |
| N4739 | Boeing 727-235 | Pan Am *Clipper Electric Spark* |
| N4740 | Boeing 727-235 | Pan Am *Clipper Endeavour* |
| N4741 | Boeing 727-235 | Pan Am *Clipper Defender* |
| N4742 | Boeing 727-235 | Pan Am *Clipper Friendship Force* |
| N4743 | Boeing 727-235 | Pan Am *Clipper Good Hope* |
| N4745 | Boeing 727-235 | Pan Am *Clipper Invincible* |
| N4746 | Boeing 727-235 | Pan Am *Clipper Intrepid* |
| N4747 | Boeing 727-235 | Pan Am *Clipper Lookout* |
| N4748 | Boeing 727-235 | Pan Am *Clipper Progressive* |
| N4749 | Boeing 727-235 | Pan Am *Clipper Quick Step* |
| N4750 | Boeing 727-235 | Pan Am *Clipper Royal* |
| N4751 | Boeing 727-235 | Pan Am *Clipper Competitor* |
| N4752 | Boeing 727-235 | Pan Am *Clipper Surprise* |
| N4753 | Boeing 727-235 | Pan Am *Clipper Undaunted* |
| N4754 | Boeing 727-235 | Pan Am *Clipper Resolute* |
| N4934Z | Douglas DC-8-63 | Hawaiian Air |
| N5535 | L.188 Electra | Channel Express Group PLC/ Bournemouth |
| N5539 | L.188 Electra | Channel Express Group PLC/ Bournemouth |
| N7031A | Boeing 737-205 | Braathens SAFE *Sigurd Jorsalfar* |
| N7031F | Boeing 737-205 | Braathens SAFE *Magnus Lagaboter* |
| N7035T | L.1011-385 TriStar 100 | Trans World Airlines |
| N7036T | L.1011-385 TriStar 100 | Trans World Airlines |
| N7043U | Douglas DC-8-63AF | Arrow Air |
| N7232X | Boeing 707-331B | Independent Air |
| N7375A | Boeing 767-323ER | American Airlines |
| N8034T | L.1011-385 TriStar 100 | Trans World Airlines |
| N8228P | Douglas DC-10-30 | Aeromexico *Castillo de Chapultepec* |
| N8968U | Douglas DC-8-62AF | Arrow Air |
| N8969U | Douglas DC-8-62 | Hawaiian Air |
| N8970U | Douglas DC-8-62 | Hawaiian Air |
| N8973U | Douglas DC-8-62 | Hawaiian Air |
| N9670 | Boeing 747-123 (SCD) | Pan Am *Clipper Empress of the Skies* |
| N9674 | Boeing 747-123 | Pan Am *Clipper Beacon Light* |
| N10023 | Boeing 747-238B | Continental Airlines (ex-N608PE) |
| N10024 | Boeing 747-238B | Continental Airlines (ex-N609PE) |
| N12061 | Douglas DC-10-30 | Continental Airlines *Richard M. Adams* |
| N12064 | Douglas DC-10-30 | Continental Airlines |

## OVERSEAS AIRLINERS

| Reg. | Type | Owner or Operator | Notes |
|------|------|-------------------|-------|
| N13066 | Douglas DC-10-30 | Continental Airlines | |
| N14062 | Douglas DC-10-30 | Continental Airlines | |
| N14063 | Douglas DC-10-30 | Continental Airlines | |
| N17010 | Boeing 747-143 | Continental Airlines | |
| N17011 | Boeing 747-143 | Continental Airlines | |
| N17025 | Boeing 747-238B | Continental Airlines | |
| N17125 | Boeing 747-136 | Trans World Airlines | |
| N17126 | Boeing 747-136 | Trans World Airlines | |
| N19072 | Douglas DC-10-30 | Continental Airlines | |
| N31018 | L.1011-385 TriStar 50 | Trans World Airlines | |
| N31019 | L.1011-385 TriStar 50 | Trans World Airlines | |
| N31021 | L.1011-385 TriStar 50 | Trans World Airlines | |
| N31022 | L.1011-385 TriStar 50 | American Trans Air | |
| N31023 | L.1011-385 TriStar 50 | Trans World Airlines | |
| N31024 | L.1011-385 TriStar 50 | Trans World Airlines | |
| N31029 | L.1011-385 TriStar 100 | Trans World Airlines | |
| N31030 | L.1011-385 TriStar 100 | Trans World Airlines | |
| N31031 | L.1011-385 TriStar 100 | Trans World Airlines | |
| N31032 | L.1011-385 TriStar 100 | Trans World Airlines | |
| N31033 | L.1011-385 TriStar 100 | Trans World Airlines | |
| N33021 | Boeing 747-243B | Continental Airlines (ex-N605PE) | |
| N39356 | Boeing 767-323ER | American Airlines | |
| N39364 | Boeing 767-323ER | American Airlines | |
| N39365 | Boeing 767-323ER | American Airlines | |
| N39367 | Boeing 767-323ER | American Airlines | |
| N41020 | L.1011-385 TriStar | Transworld Air Transport | |
| N50022 | Boeing 747-238B | Continental Airlines (ex-N607PE) | |
| N53110 | Boeing 747-131 | Trans World Airlines | |
| N53116 | Boeing 747-131 | Trans World Airlines | |
| N54649 | Douglas DC-10-30 | U.T.A. | |
| N68060 | Douglas DC-10-30 | Continental Airlines *Robert F. Six* | |
| N68065 | Douglas DC-10-30 | Continental Airlines *Robert P. Gallaway* | |
| N78019 | Boeing 747-230B | Continental Airlines | |
| N81025 | L.1011-385 TriStar 100 | Trans World Airlines | |
| N81026 | L.1011-385 TriStar 100 | Trans World Airlines | |
| N81027 | L.1011-385 TriStar 50 | Trans World Airlines | |
| N81028 | L.1011-385 TriStar 100 | Trans World Airlines | |
| N93104 | Boeing 747-131 | Trans World Airlines | |
| N93105 | Boeing 747-131 | Trans World Airlines | |
| N93106 | Boeing 747-131 | Trans World Airlines | |
| N93107 | Boeing 747-131 | Trans World Airlines | |
| N93108 | Boeing 747-131 | Trans World Airlines | |
| N93109 | Boeing 747-131 | Trans World Airlines | |
| N93117 | Boeing 747-131 | Trans World Airlines | |
| N93119 | Boeing 747-131 | Trans World Airlines | |

**Note:** Changes are likely amongst the transatlantic carriers during 1991, bringing a reduction in the number of Pan Am and TWA aircraft in Europe but these will be replaced by those of United and American Airlines.

## OD (Lebanon)

| Reg. | Type | Owner or Operator | Notes |
|------|------|-------------------|-------|
| OD-AFD | Boeing 707-3B4C | Middle East Airlines | |
| OD-AFE | Boeing 707-3B4C | Middle East Airlines | |
| OD-AFM | Boeing 720-023B | Middle East Airlines | |
| OD-AFN | Boeing 720-023B | Middle East Airlines | |
| OD-AFY | Boeing 707-327C | Trans Mediterranean Airways | |
| OD-AFZ | Boeing 720-023B | Middle East Airlines | |
| OD-AGB | Boeing 720-023B | Middle East Airlines | |
| OD-AGD | Boeing 707-323C | Trans Mediterranean Airways | |
| OD-AGF | Boeing 720-047B | Middle East Airlines | |
| OD-AGO | Boeing 707-321C | Trans Mediterranean Airways | |
| OD-AGP | Boeing 707-321C | Trans Mediterranean Airways | |
| OD-AGS | Boeing 707-331C | Trans Mediterranean Airways | |
| OD-AGU | Boeing 707-347C | Middle East Airlines | |
| OD-AGV | Boeing 707-347C | Middle East Airlines | |
| OD-AGX | Boeing 707-327C | Trans Mediterranean Airways | |
| OD-AGY | Boeing 707-327C | Trans Mediterranean Airways | |
| OD-AHC | Boeing 707-323C | Middle East Airlines | |
| OD-AHD | Boeing 707-323C | Middle East Airlines | |
| OD-AHE | Boeing 707-323C | Middle East Airlines | |
| OD-AHF | Boeing 707-323B | Middle East Airlines | |

**Note:** MEA also uses the 747s N202AE, N203AE and N204AE when not on lease.

| Notes | Reg. | Type | Owner or Operator |
|-------|------|------|-------------------|

# OE (Austria)

| | OE-ILF | Boeing 737-3Z9 | Lauda Air *Bob Marley* |
|---|---|---|---|
| | OE-ILG | Boeing 737-3Z9 | Lauda Air *John Lennon* |
| | OE-ILH | Boeing 737-4Z9 | Lauda Air |
| | OE-LAA | Airbus A.310-324 | Austrian Airlines *New York* |
| | OE-LAB | Airbus A.310-324 | Austrian Airlines *Tokyo* |
| | OE-LAC | Airbus A.310-324 | Austrian Airlines |
| | OE-LAD | Airbus A.310-324 | Austrian Airlines |
| | OE-LAU | Boeing 767-3Z9ER | Lauda Air *Johann Strauss* |
| | OE-LAV | Boeing 767-3Z9ER | Lauda Air *Mozart* |
| | OE- | Boeing 767-3Z9ER | Lauda Air |
| | OE-LDP | McD Douglas MD-81 | Austrian Airlines *Niederösterreich* |
| | OE-LDR | McD Douglas MD-81 | Austrian Airlines *Wien* |
| | OE-LDS | McD Douglas MD-81 | Austrian Airlines *Burgenland* |
| | OE-LDT | McD Douglas MD-81 | Austrian Airlines *Kärnten* |
| | OE-LDU | McD Douglas MD-81 | Austrian Airlines *Steiermark* |
| | OE-LDV | McD Douglas MD-81 | Austrian Airlines *Oberösterreich* |
| | OE-LDW | McD Douglas MD-81 | Austrian Airlines *Salzburg* |
| | OE-LDX | McD Douglas MD-81 | Austrian Airlines *Tirol* |
| | OE-LDY | McD Douglas MD-81 | Austrian Airlines *Vorarlberg* |
| | OE-LDZ | McD Douglas MD-81 | Austrian Airlines *Graz* |
| | OE-LLM | D.H.C.8-103 Dash Eight | Tyrolean Airways |
| | OE-LLN | D.H.C.8-103 Dash Eight | Tyrolean Airways *Stadt Linz* |
| | OE-LLO | D.H.C.8-103 Dash Eight | Tyrolean Airways |
| | OE-LLP | D.H.C.8-103 Dash Eight | Tyrolean Airways *Stadt Klagenfurt* |
| | OE-LLR | D.H.C.8-103 Dash Eight | Tyrolean Airways *Stadt Graz* |
| | OE-LLS | D.H.C.7-102 Dash Seven | Tyrolean Airways *Stadt Innsbruck* |
| | OE-LLU | D.H.C.7-102 Dash Seven | Tyrolean Airways *Stadt Wien* |
| | OE-LMA | McD Douglas MD-82 | Austrian Airlines *Linz* |
| | OE-LMB | McD Douglas MD-82 | Austrian Airlines *Eisenstadt* |
| | OE-LMC | McD Douglas MD-82 | Austrian Airlines *Baden* |
| | OE-LMD | McD Douglas MD-83 | Austrian Airlines |
| | OE-LMK | McD Douglas MD-87 | Austrian Airlines *St Pölten* |
| | OE-LML | McD Douglas MD-87 | Austrian Airlines *Salzburg* |
| | OE-LMM | McD Douglas MD-87 | Austrian Airlines *Innsbruck* |
| | OE-LMN | McD Douglas MD-87 | Austrian Airlines *Klagenfurt* |
| | OE-LMO | McD Douglas MD-87 | Austrian Airlines *Bregenz* |

# OH (Finland)

| | OH-LAA | Airbus A.300B4-203 | Kar-Air |
|---|---|---|---|
| | OH-LAB | Airbus A.300B4-203 | Kar-Air |
| | OH-LGA | McD Douglas MD-11 | Finnair |
| | OH-LGB | McD Douglas MD-11 | Finnair |
| | OH-LHA | Douglas DC-10-30ER | Finnair *Iso Antti* |
| | OH-LHB | Douglas DC-10-30ER | Finnair |
| | OH-LHD | Douglas DC-10-30ER | Finnair |
| | OH-LHE | Douglas DC-10-30ER | Finnair |
| | OH-LMA | McD Douglas MD-87 | Finnair |
| | OH-LMB | McD Douglas MD-87 | Finnair |
| | OH-LMC | McD Douglas MD-87 | Finnair |
| | OH-LMG | McD Douglas MD-83 | Finnair |
| | OH-LMH | McD Douglas MD-83 | Finnair |
| | OH-LMN | McD Douglas MD-82 | Finnair |
| | OH-LMO | McD Douglas MD-82 | Finnair |
| | OH-LMP | McD Douglas MD-82 | Finnair |
| | OH-LMR | McD Douglas MD-83 | Finnair |
| | OH-LMS | McD Douglas MD-83 | Finnair |
| | OH-LMT | McD Douglas MD-82 | Finnair |
| | OH-LMU | McD Douglas MD-83 | Finnair |
| | OH-LMV | McD Douglas MD-83 | Finnair |
| | OH-LMW | McD Douglas MD-82 | Finnair |
| | OH-LMX | McD Douglas MD-82 | Finnair |
| | OH-LMY | McD Douglas MD-82 | Finnair |
| | OH-LMZ | McD Douglas MD-82 | Finnair |
| | OH-LNB | Douglas DC-9-41 | Finnair |
| | OH-LNC | Douglas DC-9-41 | Finnair |
| | OH-LND | Douglas DC-9-41 | Finnair |
| | OH-LNE | Douglas DC-9-41 | Finnair |

| Reg. | Type | Owner or Operator | Notes |
|------|------|-------------------|-------|
| OH-LNF | Douglas DC-9-41 | Finnair | |
| OH-LYN | Douglas DC-9-51 | Finnair | |
| OH-LYO | Douglas DC-9-51 | Finnair | |
| OH-LYP | Douglas DC-9-51 | Finnair | |
| OH-LYR | Douglas DC-9-51 | Finnair | |
| OH-LYS | Douglas DC-9-51 | Finnair | |
| OH-LYT | Douglas DC-9-51 | Finnair | |
| OH-LYU | Douglas DC-9-51 | Finnair | |
| OH-LYV | Douglas DC-9-51 | Finnair | |
| OH-LYW | Douglas DC-9-51 | Finnair | |
| OH-LYX | Douglas DC-9-51 | Finnair | |
| OH-LYY | Douglas DC-9-51 | Finnair | |
| OH-LYZ | Douglas DC-9-51 | Finnair | |

**Note:** Finnair also operates a DC-10-30ER which retains its US registration N345HC.

# OK (Czechoslovakia)

| Reg. | Type | Owner or Operator | Notes |
|------|------|-------------------|-------|
| OK-CFC | Tupolev Tu-134A | Ceskoslovenske Aerolinie | |
| OK-CFE | Tupolev Tu-134A | Ceskoslovenske Aerolinie | |
| OK-CFG | Tupolev Tu-134A | Ceskoslovenske Aerolinie | |
| OK-CFH | Tupolev Tu-134A | Ceskoslovenske Aerolinie | |
| OK-DFI | Tupolev Tu-134A | Ceskoslovenske Aerolinie | |
| OK-EBG | Ilyushin IL-62 | Ceskoslovenske Aerolinie *Banska Bystrica* | |
| OK-EFJ | Tupolev Tu-134A | Ceskoslovenske Aerolinie | |
| OK-EFK | Tupolev Tu-134A | Ceskoslovenske Aerolinie | |
| OK-FBF | Ilyushin IL-62 | Ceskoslovenske Aerolinie | |
| OK-GBH | Ilyushin IL-62 | Ceskoslovenske Aerolinie *Usti Nad Labem* | |
| OK-HFL | Tupolev Tu-134A | Ceskoslovenske Aerolinie | |
| OK-HFM | Tupolev Tu-134A | Ceskoslovenske Aerolinie | |
| OK-IFN | Tupolev Tu-134A | Ceskoslovenske Aerolinie | |
| OK-JBI | Ilyushin IL-62M | Ceskoslovenske Aerolinie *Plzen* | |
| OK-JBJ | Ilyushin IL-62M | Ceskoslovenske Aerolinie *Hradec Kralové* | |
| OK-KBK | Ilyushin IL-62M | Ceskoslovenske Aerolinie *Ceske Budejovice* | |
| OK-KBN | Ilyushin IL-62M | Ceskoslovenske Aerolinie | |
| OK-OBL | Ilyushin IL-62M | Ceskoslovenske Aerolinie *Ostrava* | |
| OK-PBM | Ilyushin IL-62M | Ceskoslovenske Aerolinie | |
| OK-SCA | Tupolev Tu-154M | Ceskoslovenske Aerolinie *Mesto Piestany* | |
| OK-TCB | Tupolev Tu-154M | Ceskoslovenske Aerolinie | |
| OK-TCC | Tupolev Tu-154M | Ceskoslovenske Aerolinie *Teplice* | |
| OK-TCD | Tupolev Tu-154M | Ceskoslovenske Aerolinie | |
| OK-UCE | Tupolev Tu-154M | Ceskoslovenske Aerolinie | |
| OK-UCF | Tupolev Tu-154M | Ceskoslovenske Aerolinie | |
| OK-VAA | Airbus A.310-304 | Ceskoslovenske Aerolinie | |
| OK-VCG | Tupolev Tu-154M | Ceskoslovenske Aerolinie | |
| OK-WAB | Airbus A.310-304 | Ceskoslovenske Aerolinie | |

# OO (Belgium)

| Reg. | Type | Owner or Operator | Notes |
|------|------|-------------------|-------|
| OO- | Boeing 737-429 | Sobelair | |
| OO-CDE | Boeing 707-365C | Belgian International Air Cargo | |
| OO-DHB | Convair Cv.580 | European Air Transport (DHL) | |
| OO-DHC | Convair Cv.580 | European Air Transport (DHL) | |
| OO-DHD | Convair Cv.580 | European Air Transport (DHL) | |
| OO-DHE | Convair Cv.580 | European Air Transport (DHL) | |
| OO-DHF | Convair Cv.580 | European Air Transport (DHL) | |
| OO-DHG | Convair Cv.580 | European Air Transport (DHL) | |
| OO-DHH | Convair Cv.580 | European Air Transport (DHL) | |
| OO-DHI | Convair Cv.580 | European Air Transport (DHL) | |
| OO-DHJ | Convair Cv.580 | European Air Transport (DHL) | |
| OO-DHK | Boeing 727-31F | European Air Transport (DHL) | |
| OO-DHL | Convair Cv.580 | European Air Transport (DHL) | |
| OO-DHM | Boeing 727-31F | European Air Transport (DHL) | |

| Notes | Reg. | Type | Owner or Operator |
|-------|------|------|-------------------|
| | OO-DHN | Boeing 727-31F | European Air Transport (DHL) |
| | OO-DHO | Boeing 727-31F | European Air Transport (DHL) |
| | OO-DJA | F.28 Fellowship 3000 | Delta Air Transport |
| | OO-DJB | F.28 Fellowship 4000 | Delta Air Transport |
| | OO-DJC | BAe 146-200 | Delta Air Transport |
| | OO-DJD | BAe 146-200 | Delta Air Transport |
| | OO-DJE | BAe 146-200 | Delta Air Transport |
| | OO-DJF | BAe 146-200 | Delta Air Transport |
| | OO-DTF | EMB-120RT Brasilia | Delta Air Transport |
| | OO-DTG | EMB-120RT Brasilia | Delta Air Transport |
| | OO-DTH | EMB-120RT Brasilia | Delta Air Transport |
| | OO-DTI | EMB-120RT Brasilia | Delta Air Transport |
| | OO-DTJ | EMB-120RT Brasilia | Delta Air Transport |
| | OO-DTK | EMB-120RT Brasilia | Delta Air Transport |
| | OO-DTL | EMB-120RT Brasilia | Delta Air Transport |
| | OO-EEE | Beech 99A | European Expedite |
| | OO-FEA | F.27 Friendship Mk 600 | Flanders Airlines/Federal Express |
| | OO-FEF | F.27 Friendship Mk 600 | Flanders Airlines/Federal Express |
| | OO-FEG | F.27 Friendship Mk 600 | Flanders Airlines/Federal Express |
| | OO-FFF | Swearingen SA227AC Metro III | Transport International Aérien |
| | OO-GGG | Swearingen SA227AC Metro III | Transport International Aérien |
| | OO-HUB | Convair Cv.580 | European Air Transport (DHL) |
| | OO-ILH | Boeing 737-4Q8 | Air Belgium |
| | OO-ILI | Boeing 757-23A | Air Belgium |
| | OO-JPA | Swearingen SA226AT Merlin IVA | European Air Transport |
| | OO-JPI | Swearingen SA226TC Metro II | European Air Transport |
| | OO-JPN | Swearingen SA226AT Merlin IVA | European Air Transport |
| | OO-LTF | Boeing 737-3M8 | Trans European Airways |
| | OO-LTG | Boeing 737-3M8 | Trans European Airways |
| | OO-LTH | Boeing 737-3M8 | Trans European Airways |
| | OO-LTI | Boeing 737-3M8 | Trans European Airways |
| | OO-LTM | Boeing 737-3M8 | Trans European Airways |
| | OO-LTN | Boeing 737-3M8 | Trans European Airways |
| | OO-PHC | Boeing 737-248 | Skyjet |
| | OO-PHE | Boeing 737-248 | Skyjet |
| | OO-RXM | Saab SF.340B | Air Exel Belgium |
| | OO-SBJ | Boeing 737-46B | Sobelair *Juliette* |
| | OO- | Boeing 737-429 | Sobelair |
| | OO-SBQ | Boeing 737-229 | Sobelair |
| | OO-SBT | Boeing 737-229 | Sobelair |
| | OO-SBZ | Boeing 737-329 | Sobelair |
| | OO-SCA | Airbus A.310-222 | Sabena |
| | OO-SCB | Airbus A.310-222 | Sabena |
| | OO-SCC | Airbus A.310-322 | Sabena |
| | OO-SDB | Boeing 737-229 | Trans European Airways |
| | OO-SDC | Boeing 737-229 | Trans European Airways |
| | OO-SDD | Boeing 737-229 | Sabena |
| | OO-SDE | Boeing 737-229 | Sabena |
| | OO-SDF | Boeing 737-229 | Sabena |
| | OO-SDG | Boeing 737-229 | Sabena |
| | OO-SDJ | Boeing 737-229C | Sabena |
| | OO-SDK | Boeing 737-229C | Sabena |
| | OO-SDL | Boeing 737-229 | Sabena |
| | OO-SDM | Boeing 737-229 | Sabena |
| | OO-SDN | Boeing 737-229 | Sabena |
| | OO-SDO | Boeing 737-229 | Sabena |
| | OO-SDP | Boeing 737-229C | Sabena |
| | OO-SDR | Boeing 737-229C | Sabena |
| | OO-SDV | Boeing 737-329 | Sabena |
| | OO-SDW | Boeing 737-329 | Sabena |
| | OO-SDX | Boeing 737-329 | Sabena |
| | OO-SDY | Boeing 737-329 | Sabena |
| | OO-SGA | Boeing 747-129A (SCD) | Sabena |
| | OO-SGC | Boeing 747-329 (SCD) | Sabena |
| | OO-SGD | Boeing 747-329 (SCD) | Sabena |
| | OO-SLA | Douglas DC-10-30CF | Sabena |
| | OO-SLB | Douglas DC-10-30CF | Sabena |
| | OO-SLC | Douglas DC-10-30CF | Sabena |
| | OO-SLD | Douglas DC-10-30CF | Sabena |
| | OO-SLE | Douglas DC-10-30CF | Sabena |
| | OO-SVL | F.27 Friendship Mk 100 | Flanders Airlines |
| | OO-SVM | F.27 Friendship Mk 100 (SCD) | Flanders Airlines |
| | OO-SVN | F.27 Friendship Mk 100 | Flanders Airlines |

| Reg. | Type | Owner or Operator | Notes |
|------|------|-------------------|-------|
| OO-SYA | Boeing 737-329 | Sabena | |
| OO-SYB | Boeing 737-329 | Sabena | |
| OO-TEF | Airbus A.300B1 | Trans European Airways *Aline* | |
| OO-VGC | Swearingen SA226AT Merlin IV | Flanders Airlines | |
| OO-VGD | Swearingen SA226AT Merlin IV | Flanders Airlines | |
| OO-VGH | Convair Cv.580 | European Air Transport (DHL) | |

# OY (Denmark)

| Reg. | Type | Owner or Operator | Notes |
|------|------|-------------------|-------|
| OY-APF | F.27 Friendship Mk 500 | Business Flight | |
| OY-BDD | Nord 262A-21 | Cimber Air | |
| OY-BHT | EMB-110P2 Bandeirante | Muk Air | |
| OY-BNM | EMB-110P2 Bandeirante | Muk Air | |
| OY-BVF | F.27 Friendship Mk 600 | Business Flight | |
| OY-BVG | Beech 1900C-1 | Business Flight | |
| OY-BVH | F.27 Friendship Mk 200 | Business Flight | |
| OY-BVI | Beech 1900C-1 | Business Flight | |
| OY-BYN | Swearingen SA226TC Metro II | Muk Air | |
| OY-BZW | Swearingen SA226TC Metro II | Business Flight | |
| OY-CCL | F.27 Friendship Mk.600 | Starair | |
| OY-CCR | F.27 Friendship Mk 600 | Alkair | |
| OY-CIB | Aerospatiale ATR-42-300 | Cimber Air | |
| OY-CIC | Aerospatiale ATR-42-300 | Cimber Air | |
| OY-CID | Aerospatiale ATR-42-300 | Cimber Air/D.L.T. | |
| OY-CIE | Aerospatiale ATR-42-300 | Cimber Air/D.L.T. | |
| OY-CIF | Aerospatiale ATR-42-300 | Cimber Air/D.L.T. | |
| OY-CNA | Airbus A.300B4 | Conair | |
| OY-CNK | Airbus A.300B4 | Conair | |
| OY-CNL | Airbus A.300B4 | Conair | |
| OY- | Airbus A.320-211 | Conair | |
| OY- | Airbus A.320-211 | Conair | |
| OY- | Airbus A.320-211 | Conair | |
| OY- | Airbus A.320-211 | Conair | |
| OY- | Airbus A.320-211 | Conair | |
| OY- | Airbus A.320-211 | Conair | |
| OY-CPG | EMB-110P1 Bandeirante | Sun-Air International | |
| OY-CRP | H.P. 137 Jetstream 1 | Newair | |
| OY-CRR | H.P. 137 Jetstream 1 | Newair | |
| OY-CRS | H.P. 137 Jetstream 1 | Newair | |
| OY-CRT | H.P. 137 Jetstream 1 | Newair | |
| OY-DDA | Douglas DC-3 | Danish Air Lines | |
| OY-FEG | F.27 Friendship Mk 600 | Starair/Federal Express | |
| OY-KAE | Fokker 50 | S.A.S. Commuter *Hans* | |
| OY-KAF | Fokker 50 | S.A.S. Commuter *Sigvat* | |
| OY-KAG | Fokker 50 | S.A.S. Commuter *Odensis* | |
| OY-KAH | Fokker 50 | S.A.S. Commuter *Bjorn* | |
| OY-KAI | Fokker 50 | S.A.S. Commuter *Skjold* | |
| OY-KAK | Fokker 50 | S.A.S. Commuter *Turid* | |
| OY-KDB | Douglas DC-10-30 | S.A.S. *Frode Viking* | |
| OY-KDH | Boeing 767-383ER | S.A.S. *Tyra Viking* | |
| OY-KDI | Boeing 767-383ER | S.A.S. *Yrsa Viking* | |
| OY-KDK | Boeing 767-383ER | S.A.S. *Helga Viking* | |
| OY-KDL | Boeing 767-383ER | S.A.S. | |
| OY-KDN | Boeing 767-383ER | S.A.S. *Ulf Viking* | |
| OY-KGA | Douglas DC-9-41 | S.A.S. *Heming Viking* | |
| OY-KGC | Douglas DC-9-41 | S.A.S. *Helge Viking* | |
| OY-KGD | Douglas DC-9-21 | S.A.S. *Ubbe Viking* | |
| OY-KGE | Douglas DC-9-21 | S.A.S. *Orvar Viking* | |
| OY-KGF | Douglas DC-9-21 | S.A.S. *Rolf Viking* | |
| OY-KGG | Douglas DC-9-41 | S.A.S. *Sune Viking* | |
| OY-KGI | Douglas DC-9-41 | S.A.S. *Bent Viking* | |
| OY-KGK | Douglas DC-9-41 | S.A.S. *Ebbe Viking* | |
| OY-KGL | Douglas DC-9-41 | S.A.S. *Angantyr Viking* | |
| OY-KGM | Douglas DC-9-41 | S.A.S. *Arnfinn Viking* | |
| OY-KGN | Douglas DC-9-41 | S.A.S. *Gram Viking* | |
| OY-KGO | Douglas DC-9-41 | S.A.S. *Holte Viking* | |
| OY-KGP | Douglas DC-9-41 | S.A.S. *Torbern Viking* | |
| OY-KGR | Douglas DC-9-41 | S.A.S. *Holger Viking* | |
| OY-KGS | Douglas DC-9-41 | S.A.S. *Hall Viking* | |
| OY-KGT | McD Douglas MD-81 | S.A.S. *Hake Viking* | |
| OY-KGY | McD Douglas MD-81 | S.A.S. *Rollo Viking* | |

| Notes | Reg. | Type | Owner or Operator |
|-------|------|------|-------------------|
| | OY-KGZ | McD Douglas MD-81 | S.A.S. *Hagbard Viking* |
| | OY-KHC | McD Douglas MD-81 | S.A.S. *Faste Viking* |
| | OY-KHE | McD Douglas MD-82 | S.A.S. *Saxo Viking* |
| | OY-KHF | McD Douglas MD-87 | S.A.S. *Ragnar Viking* |
| | OY-KHG | McD Douglas MD-81 | S.A.S. *Alle Viking* |
| | OY-KHI | McD Douglas MD-87 | S.A.S. *Torkel Viking* |
| | OY-KHK | McD Douglas MD-81 | S.A.S. *Roald Viking* |
| | OY-KHL | McD Douglas MD-81 | S.A.S. *Knud Viking* |
| | OY-KHM | McD Douglas MD-81 | S.A.S. *Mette Viking* |
| | OY-KHN | McD Douglas MD-81 | S.A.S. *Dan Viking* |
| | OY-KHO | McD Douglas MD-81 | S.A.S. *Dana Viking* |
| | OY-KHP | McD Douglas MD-81 | S.A.S. *Arild Viking* |
| | OY-KIA | Douglas DC-9-21 | S.A.S. *Guttorm Viking* |
| | OY-KIB | Douglas DC-9-21 | S.A.S. *Gunder Viking* |
| | OY-KIC | Douglas DC-9-21 | S.A.S. *Siger Viking* |
| | OY-KID | Douglas DC-9-21 | S.A.S. *Rane Viking* |
| | OY-KIE | Douglas DC-9-21 | S.A.S. *Skate Viking* |
| | OY-KIF | Douglas DC-9-21 | S.A.S. *Svipdag Viking* |
| | OY-MAA | Boeing 737-5L9 | Maersk Air |
| | OY-MAB | Boeing 737-5L9 | Maersk Air |
| | OY-MAC | Boeing 737-5L9 | Maersk Air |
| | OY-MAD | Boeing 737-5L9 | Maersk Air |
| | OY-MMD | Boeing 737-3L9 | Maersk Air *Vaermland* |
| | OY-MME | Boeing 737-3L9 | Maersk Air |
| | OY-MMF | Boeing 737-3L9 | Maersk Air |
| | OY-MMG | Fokker 50 | Maersk Air |
| | OY-MMH | Fokker 50 | Maersk Air |
| | OY-MMI | Fokker 50 | Maersk Air |
| | OY-MMJ | Fokker 50 | Maersk Air |
| | OY-MMS | Fokker 50 | Maersk Air |
| | OY-MMT | Fokker 50 | Maersk Air |
| | OY-MMU | Fokker 50 | Maersk Air/D.L.T. |
| | OY-MMV | Fokker 50 | Maersk Air/D.L.T. |
| | OY-MMW | Boeing 737-3L9 | Maersk Air |
| | OY-MMY | Boeing 737-3L9 | Maersk Air |
| | OY-MMZ | Boeing 737-3L9 | Maersk Air |
| | OY-MUA | EMB-110P1 Bandeirante | Muk Air |
| | OY-MUB | Short SD3-30 | Muk Air |
| | OY-MUF | F.27J Friendship | Muk Air |
| | OY-SAT | Boeing 727-2J4 | Sterling Airways |
| | OY-SAU | Boeing 727-2J4 | Sterling Airways |
| | OY-SBE | Boeing 727-2J4 | Sterling Airways |
| | OY-SBF | Boeing 727-2J4 | Sterling Airways |
| | OY-SBG | Boeing 727-2J4 | Sterling Airways |
| | OY-SBH | Boeing 727-2B7 | Sterling Airways |
| | OY-SBI | Boeing 727-270 | Sterling Airways |
| | OY-SBN | Boeing 727-2B7 | Sterling Airways |
| | OY-SBO | Boeing 727-2K3 | Sterling Airways |
| | OY-SHE | Boeing 757-27B | Sterling Airways/Air Holland (PH-AHE) |
| | OY-S | Boeing 757-2J2 | Sterling Airways |
| | OY-S | Boeing 757-2J4 | Sterling Airways |
| | OY-S | Boeing 757-2J4 | Sterling Airways |
| | OY-SRA | F.27 Friendship Mk 600 | Starair |
| | OY-SRB | F.27 Friendship Mk 600 | Alkair |
| | OY-SRR | F.27 Friendship Mk 600 | Starair |
| | OY-SRZ | F.27 Friendship Mk 600 | Starair |
| | OY-STD | S.E.210 Caravelle 10B | Sterling Airways |
| | OY-STI | S.E.210 Caravelle 10B | Sterling Airways |
| | OY-STM | S.E.210 Caravelle 10B | Sterling Airways |
| | OY-SUJ | Cessna 500 Citation | Sun Air |
| | OY-SVG | Cessna 500 Citation | Sun Air |
| | OY-TOV | Nord 262A-30 | Cimber Air |

# PH (Netherlands)

| | | | |
|---|---|---|---|
| | PH-AGA | Airbus A.310-203 | K.L.M. *Rembrandt* |
| | PH-AGB | Airbus A.310-203 | K.L.M. *Jeroen Bosch* |
| | PH-AGC | Airbus A.310-203 | K.L.M. *Albert Cuyp* |
| | PH-AGD | Airbus A.310-203 | K.L.M. *Marinus Ruppert* |
| | PH-AGE | Airbus A.310-203 | K.L.M. *Jan Steen* |
| | PH-AGF | Airbus A.310-203 | K.L.M. *Frans Hals* |

| Reg. | Type | Owner or Operator | Notes |
|---|---|---|---|
| PH-AGG | Airbus A.310-203 | K.L.M. *Vincent van Gogh* | |
| PH-AGH | Airbus A.310-203 | K.L.M. *Peiter de Hoogh* | |
| PH-AGI | Airbus A.310-203 | K.L.M. *Jan Toorop* | |
| PH-AGK | Airbus A.310-203 | K.L.M. *Johannes Vermeer* | |
| PH-AHE | Boeing 757-27B | Air Holland/Sterling Airways (OY-SHE) | |
| PH-AHL | Boeing 757-27B | Air Holland/Condor (D-ABNX) | |
| PH-AHM | Boeing 767-204ER | Air Holland | |
| PH-AHN | Boeing 767-204ER | Air Holland | |
| PH-BDA | Boeing 737-306 | K.L.M. *Willem Barentz* | |
| PH-BDB | Boeing 737-306 | K.L.M. *Olivier van Noort* | |
| PH-BDC | Boeing 737-306 | K.L.M. *Cornelis De Houteman* | |
| PH-BDD | Boeing 737-306 | K.L.M. *Anthony van Diemen* | |
| PH-BDE | Boeing 737-306 | K.L.M. *Abel J. Tasman* | |
| PH-BDG | Boeing 737-306 | K.L.M. *Michiel A. D. Ruyter* | |
| PH-BDH | Boeing 737-306 | K.L.M. *Petrus Plancius* | |
| PH-BDI | Boeing 737-306 | K.L.M. *Maarten H. Tromp* | |
| PH-BDK | Boeing 737-306 | K.L.M. *Jan H. van Linschoten* | |
| PH-BDL | Boeing 737-306 | K.L.M. *Piet Heyn* | |
| PH-BDN | Boeing 737-306 | K.L.M. *Willem van Ruysbroeck* | |
| PH-BDO | Boeing 737-306 | K.L.M. *Jacob van Heemskerck* | |
| PH-BDP | Boeing 737-306 | K.L.M. *Jacob Rogeveen* | |
| PH-BDR | Boeing 737-406 | K.L.M. *Willem C. Schouten* | |
| PH-BDS | Boeing 737-406 | K.L.M. *Jorris van Spilbergen* | |
| PH-BDT | Boeing 737-406 | K.L.M. *Gerrit de Veer* | |
| PH-BDU | Boeing 737-406 | K.L.M. *Marco Polo* | |
| PH-BDW | Boeing 737-406 | K.L.M. *Leifur Eirksson* | |
| PH-BDY | Boeing 737-406 | K.L.M. *Vasco da Gama* | |
| PH-BDZ | Boeing 737-406 | K.L.M. | |
| PH-BFA | Boeing 747-406 | K.L.M. *City of Atlanta* | |
| PH-BFB | Boeing 747-406 | K.L.M. *City of Bangkok* | |
| PH-BFC | Boeing 747-406 (SCD) | K.L.M. *City of Calgary* | |
| PH-BFD | Boeing 747-406 (SCD) | K.L.M. *City of Dubai* | |
| PH-BFE | Boeing 747-406 (SCD) | K.L.M. *City of Melbourne* | |
| PH-BFF | Boeing 747-406 (SCD) | K.L.M. *City of Freetown* | |
| PH-BFG | Boeing 747-406 | K.L.M. *City of Guayaquil* | |
| PH-BFH | Boeing 747-406 (SCD) | K.L.M. *City of Hong Kong* | |
| PH-BFI | Boeing 747-406 | K.L.M. *City of Jakarta* | |
| PH-BFK | Boeing 747-406 | K.L.M. *City of Karachi* | |
| PH-BFL | Boeing 747-406 | K.L.M. *City of Lima* | |
| PH-BFM | Boeing 747-406 | K.L.M. *City of Mexico* | |
| PH-BFN | Boeing 747-406 | K.L.M. *City of Nairobi* | |
| PH-BFO | Boeing 747-406 | K.L.M. | |
| PH-BFP | Boeing 747-406 | K.L.M. | |
| PH-BTA | Boeing 737-406 | K.L.M. | |
| PH-BTB | Boeing 737-406 | K.L.M. | |
| PH-BTC | Boeing 737-406 | K.L.M. | |
| PH-BTD | Boeing 737-406 | K.L.M. | |
| PH-BTE | Boeing 737-406 | K.L.M. | |
| PH-BTF | Boeing 737-406 | K.L.M. | |
| PH-BUH | Boeing 747-306 (SCD) | K.L.M. *Dr Albert Plesman* | |
| PH-BUI | Boeing 747-306 (SCD) | K.L.M. *Wilbur Wright* | |
| PH-BUK | Boeing 747-306 (SCD) | K.L.M. *Louis Blèriot* | |
| PH-BUL | Boeing 747-306 (SCD) | K.L.M. *Charles A. Lindbergh* | |
| PH-BUM | Boeing 747-306 (SCD) | K.L.M. *Sir Charles E. Kingsford-Smith* | |
| PH-BUN | Boeing 747-306 (SCD) | K.L.M. *Anthony H. G. Fokker* | |
| PH-BUO | Boeing 747-306 | K.L.M. *Missouri* | |
| PH-BUW | Boeing 747-306 (SCD) | K.L.M. *Leonardo da Vinci* | |
| PH-CHB | F.28 Fellowship 4000 | K.L.M. CityHopper *Birmingham* | |
| PH-CHD | F.28 Fellowship 4000 | K.L.M. CityHopper *Maastricht* | |
| PH-CHF | F.28 Fellowship 4000 | K.L.M. CityHopper *Guernsey* | |
| PH-CHN | F.28 Fellowship 4000 | K.L.M. CityHopper | |
| PH-DDA | Douglas DC-3 | Dutch Dakota Association | |
| PH-DTA | Douglas DC-10-30 | K.L.M. *Johann Sebastian Bach* | |
| PH-DTB | Douglas DC-10-30 | K.L.M. *Ludwig van Beethoven* | |
| PH-DTC | Douglas DC-10-30 | K.L.M. *Frédéric François Chopin* | |
| PH-DTD | Douglas DC-10-30 | K.L.M. *Maurice Ravel* | |
| PH-DTL | Douglas DC-10-30 | K.L.M. *Edvard Hagerup Grieg* | |
| PH-FKT | F-27 Friendship Mk 600 | Schreiner Airways | |
| PH-FWS | EMB-110P1 Bandeirante | Freeway Air | |
| PH-FWT | EMB-110P1 Bandeirante | Freeway Air | |
| PH-FXA | Dornier Do.228 | Flexair | |
| PH-HVG | Boeing 737-3K2 | Transavia *Wubbo Ockels* | |
| PH-HVJ | Boeing 737-3K2 | Transavia *Nelli Cooman* | |

| Notes | Reg. | Type | Owner or Operator |
|---|---|---|---|
| | PH-HVK | Boeing 737-3K2 | Transavia *Evert van Benthern* |
| | PH-HVM | Boeing 737-3K2 | Transavia |
| | PH-HVN | Boeing 737-3K2 | Transavia |
| | PH-HVT | Boeing 737-3K2 | Transavia |
| | PH-HVV | Boeing 737-3K2 | Transavia |
| | PH-HVW | Boeing 737-3K2 | Transavia |
| | PH-KFD | F.27 Friendship Mk 200 | K.L.M. CityHopper *Jan Moll* |
| | PH-KFE | F.27 Friendship Mk 600 | K.L.M. CityHopper *Jan Dellaert* |
| | PH-KFG | F.27 Friendship Mk 200 | K.L.M. CityHopper *Koos Abspoel* |
| | PH-KFI | F.27 Friendship Mk 500 | K.L.M. CityHopper *Bremen* |
| | PH-KFK | F.27 Friendship Mk 500 | K.L.M. CityHopper *Zestienhoven* |
| | PH-KFL | F.27 Friendship Mk 500 | K.L.M. CityHopper |
| | PH-KSA | Saab SF.340B | K.L.M. CityHopper |
| | PH-KSB | Saab SF.340B | K.L.M. CityHopper |
| | PH-KSC | Saab SF.340B | K.L.M. CityHopper |
| | PH-KSD | Saab SF.340B | K.L.M. CityHopper |
| | PH-KSE | Saab SF.340B | K.L.M. CityHopper |
| | PH-KSF | Saab SF.340B | K.L.M. CityHopper |
| | PH-KSG | Saab SF.340B | K.L.M. CityHopper |
| | PH-KSH | Saab SF.340B | K.L.M. CityHopper |
| | PH-KSI | Saab SF.340B | K.L.M. CityHopper |
| | PH-KSK | Saab SF.340B | K.L.M. CityHopper |
| | PH-KSL | Saab SF.340B | K.L.M. CityHopper |
| | PH-KSM | Saab SF.340B | K.L.M. CityHopper |
| | PH-KVA | Fokker 50 | K.L.M. CityHopper |
| | PH-KVB | Fokker 50 | K.L.M. CityHopper |
| | PH-KVC | Fokker 50 | K.L.M. CityHopper |
| | PH-KVD | Fokker 50 | K.L.M. CityHopper |
| | PH-KVE | Fokker 50 | K.L.M. CityHopper |
| | PH-KVF | Fokker 50 | K.L.M. CityHopper |
| | PH-KVG | Fokker 50 | K.L.M. CityHopper |
| | PH-KVH | Fokker 50 | K.L.M. CityHopper |
| | PH-KVI | Fokker 50 | K.L.M. CityHopper |
| | PH-KVK | Fokker 50 | K.L.M. CityHopper |
| | PH-MBN | Douglas DC-10-30CF | Martinair *Anthony Ruys* |
| | PH-MBP | Douglas DC-10-30CF | Martinair *Hong Kong* |
| | PH-MBT | Douglas DC-10-30CF | K.L.M. *George Gershwin* |
| | PH-MBZ | Douglas DC-9-82 | Martinair *Prinses Juiliana* |
| | PH-MCA | Airbus A.310-203 | Martinair *Prins Bernhard* |
| | PH-MCB | Airbus A.310-203CF | Martinair *Prins Maurits* |
| | PH-MCD | Douglas DC-9-82 | Martinair *Lucien Ruys* |
| | PH-MCE | Boeing 747-21AC (SCD) | Martinair *Prins van Oranje* |
| | PH-MCF | Boeing 747-21AC (SCD) | Martinair *Prins Claus* |
| | PH-MCG | Boeing 767-31AER | Martinair *Prins Johan Friso* |
| | PH-MCH | Boeing 767-31AER | Martinair *Prins Constantijn* |
| | PH-MCI | Boeing 767-31AER | Martinair |
| | PH-MCK | Boeing 767-31AER | Martinair/K.L.M. |
| | PH-SAD | F.27 Friendship Mk 200 | K.L.M. CityHopper *Evert van Dijk* |
| | PH-SDH | D.H.C.8-102 Dash Eight | Schreiner Airways |
| | PH-SDI | D.H.C.8-301A Dash Eight | Schreiner Airways |
| | PH-SDJ | D.H.C.8-301A Dash Eight | Schreiner Airways/Sabena |
| | PH-SFA | F.27 Friendship Mk 400 | Schreiner Airways |
| | PH-SFB | F.27 Friendship Mk 400 | Schreiner Airways |
| | PH-SFE | F.27 Friendship Mk 300 | Schreiner Airways |
| | PH-SFI | F.27 Friendship Mk 500 | Schreiner Airways |
| | PH-SHE | L.100-30 Hercules | Schreiner Airways |
| | PH-TFA | Boeing 757-2K2 | Transavia |
| | PH-TFB | Boeing 757-2K2 | Transavia |
| | PH-TVH | Boeing 737-222 | Transavia *Neil Armstrong* |
| | PH-TVR | Boeing 737-2K2 | Transavia/K.L.M. |
| | PH-TVS | Boeing 737-2K2 | Transavia |
| | PH-TVX | Boeing 737-2K2 | Transavia/K.L.M. |

**Note:** K.L.M. also operates Boeing 747-306s N1295E, N1298E, N1309E, N4548M and N4551N.

# PK (Indonesia)

| | | | |
|---|---|---|---|
| | PK-GIA | Douglas DC-10-30 | Garuda Indonesian Airways |
| | PK-GIB | Douglas DC-10-30 | Garuda Indonesian Airways |
| | PK-GIC | Douglas DC-10-30 | Garuda Indonesian Airways |
| | PK-GID | Douglas DC-10-30 | Garuda Indonesian Airways |

| Reg. | Type | Owner or Operator | Notes |
|---|---|---|---|
| PK-GIE | Douglas DC-10-30 | Garuda Indonesian Airways | |
| PK-GIF | Douglas DC-10-30 | Garuda Indonesian Airways | |
| PK-GSA | Boeing 747-2U3B | Garuda Indonesian Airways | |
| PK-GSB | Boeing 747-2U3B | Garuda Indonesian Airways | |
| PK-GSC | Boeing 747-2U3B | Garuda Indonesian Airways | |
| PK-GSD | Boeing 747-2U3B | Garuda Indonesian Airways | |
| PK-GSE | Boeing 747-2U3B | Garuda Indonesian Airways | |
| PK-GSF | Boeing 747-2U3B | Garuda Indonesian Airways | |
| PK-PLR | L.100-30 Hercules | HeavyLift Cargo Airlines | |
| PK-PLU | L.100-30 Hercules | HeavyLift Cargo Airlines | |
| PK-PLV | L.100-30 Hercules | HeavyLift Cargo Airlines | |
| PK-PLW | L.100-30 Hercules | HeavyLift Cargo Airlines | |

**Note:** The DC-10-30 EI-BZD is also operated by Garuda.

# PP (Brazil)

| Reg. | Type | Owner or Operator |
|---|---|---|
| PK-PLW | L.100-30 Hercules | Heavylift Cargo Airlines |
| PP-VMA | Douglas DC-10-30 | VARIG |
| PP-VMB | Douglas DC-10-30 | VARIG |
| PP-VMD | Douglas DC-10-30 | VARIG |
| PP-VMQ | Douglas DC-10-30 | VARIG |
| PP-VMS | Douglas DC-10-30 | VARIG |
| PP-VMT | Douglas DC-10-30F | VARIG Cargo |
| PP-VMU | Douglas DC-10-30F | VARIG Cargo |
| PP-VMV | Douglas DC-10-30 | VARIG |
| PP-VMW | Douglas DC-10-30 | VARIG |
| PP-VMX | Douglas DC-10-30 | VARIG |
| PP-VMY | Douglas DC-10-30 | VARIG |
| PP-VMZ | Douglas DC-10-30 | VARIG |
| PP-VNA | Boeing 747-2L5B (SCD) | VARIG |
| PP-VNB | Boeing 747-2L5B (SCD) | VARIG |
| PP-VNC | Boeing 747-2L5B (SCD) | VARIG |
| PP-VNH | Boeing 747-341 (SCD) | VARIG |
| PP-VNI | Boeing 747-341 (SCD) | VARIG |
| PP-VOA | Boeing 747-341 | VARIG |
| PP-VOB | Boeing 747-341 | VARIG |
| PP-VOC | Boeing 747-341 | VARIG |

# RP (Philippines)
**Note:** Philippine Airlines operates four Boeing 747-2F6Bs which retain their U.S. identities N741PR, N742PR, N743PR and N744PR and three 747-283Bs registered EI-BTS, EI-BWF and EI-BZA.

# S2 (Bangladesh)

| Reg. | Type | Owner or Operator |
|---|---|---|
| S2-ACO | Douglas DC-10-30 | Bangladesh Biman *City of Hazrat-Shar Makhdoom (R.A.)* |
| S2-ACP | Douglas DC-10-30 | Bangladesh Biman *City of Dhaka* |
| S2-ACQ | Douglas DC-10-30 | Bangladesh Biman *City of Hz Shah Jalal (R.A.)* |
| S2-ACR | Douglas DC-10-30 | Bangladesh Biman *The New Era* |

# S7 (Seychelles)

| Reg. | Type | Owner or Operator |
|---|---|---|
| S7-AAS | Boeing 767-2Q8ER | Air Seychelles *Aldabra* |

# SE (Sweden)

| Reg. | Type | Owner or Operator |
|---|---|---|
| SE-CFP | Douglas DC-3 | Flygande Veteraner *Fridtjof Viking* |
| SE-DAK | Douglas DC-9-41 | S.A.S. *Ragnvald Viking* |
| SE-DAL | Douglas DC-9-41 | S.A.S. *Algot Viking* |
| SE-DAM | Douglas DC-9-41 | S.A.S. *Starkad Viking* |
| SE-DAN | Douglas DC-9-41 | S.A.S. *Alf Viking* |

| Notes | Reg. | Type | Owner or Operator |
|---|---|---|---|
| | SE-DAO | Douglas DC-9-41 | S.A.S. *Asgaut Viking* |
| | SE-DAP | Douglas DC-9-41 | S.A.S. *Torgils Viking* |
| | SE-DAR | Douglas DC-9-41 | S.A.S. *Agnar Viking* |
| | SE-DAS | Douglas DC-9-41 | S.A.S. *Garder Viking* |
| | SE-DAU | Douglas DC-9-41 | S.A.S. *Hadding Viking* |
| | SE-DAW | Douglas DC-9-41 | S.A.S. *Gotrik Viking* |
| | SE-DAX | Douglas DC-9-41 | S.A.S. *Helsing Viking* |
| | SE-DBM | Douglas DC-9-41 | S.A.S. *Ossur Viking* |
| | SE-DBT | Douglas DC-9-41 | S.A.S. *Agne Viking* |
| | SE-DBU | Douglas DC-9-41 | S.A.S. *Hjalmar Viking* |
| | SE-DBW | Douglas DC-9-41 | S.A.S. *Adils Viking* |
| | SE-DBX | Douglas DC-9-41 | S.A.S. *Arnljot Viking* |
| | SE-DDP | Douglas DC-9-41 | S.A.S. *Brun Viking* |
| | SE-DDR | Douglas DC-9-41 | S.A.S. *Atle Viking* |
| | SE-DDS | Douglas DC-9-41 | S.A.S. *Alrik Viking* |
| | SE-DDT | Douglas DC-9-41 | S.A.S. *Amund Viking* |
| | SE-DEI | BAe 146-200QT | Malmö Aviation/TNT |
| | SE-DFR | McD Douglas MD-81 | S.A.S. *Ingsald Viking* |
| | SE-DFS | McD Douglas MD-82 | S.A.S. *Gaut Viking* |
| | SE-DFT | McD Douglas MD-82 | S.A.S. *Assur Viking* |
| | SE-DFU | McD Douglas MD-82 | S.A.S. *Isulv Viking* |
| | SE-DFX | McD Douglas MD-82 | S.A.S. *Ring Viking* |
| | SE-DFY | McD Douglas MD-81 | S.A.S. *Ottar Viking* |
| | SE-DGA | F.28 Fellowship 1000 | Linjeflyg |
| | SE-DGB | F.28 Fellowship 1000 | Linjeflyg |
| | SE-DGD | F.28 Fellowship 4000 | Linjeflyg |
| | SE-DGE | F.28 Fellowship 4000 | Linjeflyg |
| | SE-DGF | F.28 Fellowship 4000 | Linjeflyg |
| | SE-DGG | F.28 Fellowship 4000 | Linjeflyg |
| | SE-DGH | F.28 Fellowship 4000 | Linjeflyg |
| | SE-DGI | F.28 Fellowship 4000 | Linjeflyg |
| | SE-DGK | F.28 Fellowship 4000 | Linjeflyg |
| | SE-DGL | F.28 Fellowship 4000 | Linjeflyg |
| | SE-DGM | F.28 Fellowship 4000 | Linjeflyg |
| | SE-DGN | F.28 Fellowship 4000 | Linjeflyg |
| | SE-DGO | F.28 Fellowship 4000 | Linjeflyg |
| | SE-DGP | F.28 Fellowship 4000 | Linjeflyg |
| | SE-DGR | F.28 Fellowship 4000 | Linjeflyg |
| | SE-DGS | F.28 Fellowship 4000 | Linjeflyg *Svea* |
| | SE-DGT | F.28 Fellowship 4000 | Linjeflyg *Tora* |
| | SE-DGU | F.28 Fellowship 4000 | Linjeflyg *Ulla* |
| | SE-DGX | F.28 Fellowship 4000 | Linjeflyg *Kryss* |
| | SE-DHA | S.E.210 Caravelle 10B3 | Transwede |
| | SE-DHB | McD Douglas MD-83 | Transwede |
| | SE-DHC | McD Douglas MD-83 | Transwede |
| | SE-DHD | McD Douglas MD-83 | Transwede |
| | SE-DHG | McD Douglas MD-87 | Transwede |
| | SE-DHI | McD Douglas MD-87 | Transwede |
| | SE-DHN | McD Douglas MD-83 | Transwede |
| | SE-DHS | Douglas DC-10-10 | Scanair *Baloo* |
| | SE-DHT | Douglas DC-10-10 | Scanair *Dumbo* |
| | SE-DHU | Douglas DC-10-10 | Scanair *Bamse* |
| | SE-DHX | Douglas DC-10-10 | Scanair |
| | SE-DHY | Douglas DC-10-10 | Scanair *Snoopy* |
| | SE-DHZ | Douglas DC-10-10 | Scanair *Moby Dick* |
| | SE-DIA | McD Douglas MD-81 | S.A.S. *Ulvrik Viking* |
| | SE-DIB | McD Douglas MD-87 | S.A.S. *Varin Viking* |
| | SE-DIC | McD Douglas MD-87 | S.A.S. *Grane Viking* |
| | SE-DID | McD Douglas MD-82 | S.A.S. *Spjute Viking* |
| | SE-DIE | McD Douglas MD-82 | S.A.S. *Stenkil Viking* |
| | SE-DIF | McD Douglas MD-87 | S.A.S. *Hjorulv Viking* |
| | SE-DIH | McD Douglas MD-87 | S.A.S. *Slagfinn Viking* |
| | SE-DII | McD Douglas MD-81 | S.A.S. *Askold Viking* |
| | SE-DIK | McD Douglas MD-82 | S.A.S. *Stenkil Viking* |
| | SE-DIL | McD Douglas MD-81 | S.A.S. *Tord Viking* |
| | SE-DIM | BAe 146-300QT | Malmö Aviation /TNT |
| | SE-DIN | McD Douglas MD-81 | S.A.S. *Eskil Viking* |
| | SE-DIP | McD Douglas MD-81 | S.A.S. *Jarl Viking* |
| | SE-DIR | McD Douglas MD-81 | S.A.S. *Nora Viking* |
| | SE-DIS | McD Douglas MD-81 | S.A.S. *Sigmund Viking* |
| | SE-DIT | BAe 146-300QT | Malmö Aviation/TNT |
| | SE-DIU | McD Douglas MD-87 | S.A.S. |
| | SE-DIX | McD Douglas MD-81 | S.A.S. *Anund Viking* |

| Reg. | Type | Owner or Operator | Notes |
|------|------|-------------------|-------|
| SE-DIY | McD Douglas MD-81 | S.A.S. | |
| SE-DKG | Boeing 737-205 | Transwede | |
| SE-DKH | Boeing 737-205 | Transwede | |
| SE-DKO | Boeing 767-383ER | S.A.S. *Ingegerd Viking* | |
| SE-DKP | Boeing 767-283ER | S.A.S. *Sigrid Viking* | |
| SE-DKT | Boeing 767-383ER | S.A.S. *Svea Viking* | |
| SE-DKU | Boeing 767-383ER | S.A.S. *Tor Viking* | |
| SE-DLA | Boeing 737-3Q8 | Linjeflyg | |
| SE-DLC | Douglas DC-9-41 | S.A.S. *Eillv Viking* | |
| SE-DLN | Boeing 737-3Y0 | Transwede | |
| SE-DLO | Boeing 737-3Y0 | Transwede | |
| SE-DLP | Boeing 737-205 | Transwede/Sultan Air | |
| SE-DLS | McD Douglas MD-83 | Transwede | |
| SE-DLU | McD Douglas MD-83 | Transwede | |
| SE- | Boeing 737-5Q8 | Transwede | |
| SE- | Boeing 737-5Q8 | Transwede | |
| SE-DNA | Boeing 737-59D | Linjeflyg | |
| SE-DNB | Boeing 737-59D | Linjeflyg | |
| SE-DNC | Boeing 737-53A | Linjeflyg *Skane* | |
| SE-DND | Boeing 737-59D | Linjeflyg | |
| SE-DNE | Boeing 737-59D | Linjeflyg | |
| SE-DNF | Boeing 737-59D | Linjeflyg | |
| SE-DNG | Boeing 737-59D | Linjeflyg | |
| SE-DNH | Boeing 737-59D | Linjeflyg | |
| SE- | Boeing 737-5Q8 | Linjeflyg | |
| SE- | Boeing 737-5Q8 | Linjeflyg | |
| SE-DPA | Boeing 737-33A | Falcon Aviation | |
| SE-DPB | Boeing 737-33A | Falcon Aviation | |
| SE-DPC | Boeing 737-33A | Falcon Aviation | |
| SE-IVR | L-188CF Electra | Falcon Cargo | |
| SE-IVS | L-188CF Electra | Falcon Cargo | |
| SE-IVT | L-188CF Electra | Falcon Cargo | |
| SE-IVY | V.815 Viscount | Baltic Airlines (*stored*) | |
| SE-IZU | L-188CF Electra | Falcon Cargo | |
| SE-KBP | FH.227E Friendship | Malmö Aviation | |
| SE-KBR | FH.227E Friendship | Malmö Aviation | |
| SE-K | F.27J Friendship | Malmö Aviation | |
| SE-KGA | FH.227B Friendship | Malmö Aviation | |
| SE-KGB | FH.227B Friendship | Malmö Aviation | |
| SE-KGC | F.27 Friendship Mk 600 | Malmö Aviation/TNT | |
| SE-LFA | Fokker 50 | S.A.S. Commuter *Jorund* | |
| SE-LFB | Fokker 50 | S.A.S. Commuter *Sture* | |
| SE-LFC | Fokker 50 | S.A.S. Commuter *Ylva* | |
| SE-LFK | Fokker 50 | S.A.S. Commuter *Alvar* | |
| SE-LFN | Fokker 50 | S.A.S. Commuter *Edmund* | |
| SE-LFO | Fokker 50 | S.A.S. Commuter *Folke* | |
| SE-LFP | Fokker 50 | S.A.S. Commuter *Ingemar* | |
| SE-LFR | Fokker 50 | S.A.S. Commuter *Vagn* | |
| SE-LFS | Fokker 50 | S.A.S. Commuter *Vigge* | |

# SP (Poland)

| | | | |
|------|------|-------------------|-------|
| SP-LBA | Ilyushin IL-62M | Polskie Linie Lotnicze (LOT) *Juliusz Sowacki* | |
| SP-LBB | Ilyushin IL-62M | Polskie Linie Lotnicze (LOT) *Jgnacy Paderewski* | |
| SP-LBC | Ilyushin IL-62M | Polskie Linie Lotnicze (LOT) *Joseph Conrad-Korzeniowski* | |
| SP-LBD | Ilyushin IL-62M | Polskie Linie Lotnicze (LOT) *General Wladystaw Sikorski* | |
| SP-LBE | Ilyushin IL-62M | Polskie Linie Lotnicze (LOT) *Stanislaw Moniuszho* | |
| SP-LBF | Ilyushin IL-62M | Polskie Linie Lotnicze (LOT) *Fryderyk Chopin* | |
| SP-LBH | Ilyushin IL-62M | Polskie Linie Lotnicze (LOT) | |
| SP-LCA | Tupolev Tu-154M | Polskie Linie Lotnicze (LOT) | |
| SP-LCB | Tupolev Tu-154M | Polskie Linie Lotnicze (LOT) | |
| SP-LCC | Tupolev Tu-154M | Polskie Linie Lotnicze (LOT) | |
| SP-LCD | Tupolev Tu-154M | Polskie Linie Lotnicze (LOT) | |
| SP-LCE | Tupolev Tu-154M | Polskie Linie Lotnicze (LOT) | |
| SP-LCF | Tupolev Tu-154M | Polskie Linie Lotnicze (LOT) | |

| Notes | Reg. | Type | Owner or Operator |
|-------|------|------|-------------------|
| | SP-LCG | Tupolev Tu-154M | Polskie Linie Lotnicze (LOT) |
| | SP-LCH | Tupolev Tu-154M | Polskie Linie Lotnicze (LOT) |
| | SP-LCI | Tupolev Tu-154M | Polskie Linie Lotnicze (LOT) |
| | SP-LCK | Tupolev Tu-154M | Polskie Linie Lotnicze (LOT) |
| | SP-LCL | Tupolev Tu-154M | Polskie Linie Lotnicze (LOT) |
| | SP-LCM | Tupolev Tu-154M | Polskie Linie Lotnicze (LOT) |
| | SP-LCN | Tupolev Tu-154M | Polskie Linie Lotnicze (LOT) |
| | SP-LCO | Tupolev Tu-154M | Polskie Linie Lotnicze (LOT) |
| | SP-LHA | Tupolev Tu-134A | Polskie Linie Lotnicze (LOT) |
| | SP-LHB | Tupolev Tu-134A | Polskie Linie Lotnicze (LOT) |
| | SP-LHC | Tupolev Tu-134A | Polskie Linie Lotnicze (LOT) |
| | SP-LHD | Tupolev Tu-134A | Polskie Linie Lotnicze (LOT) |
| | SP-LHE | Tupolev Tu-134A | Polskie Linie Lotnicze (LOT) |
| | SP-LHF | Tupolev Tu-134A | Polskie Linie Lotnicze (LOT) |
| | SP-LHG | Tupolev Tu-134A | Polskie Linie Lotnicze (LOT) |
| | SP-LHI | Tupolev Tu-134A | Polskie Linie Lotnicze (LOT) |
| | SP-LOA | Boeing 767-25DER | Polskie Linie Lotnicze (LOT) *Gneizao* |
| | SP-LOB | Boeing 767-25DER | Polskie Linie Lotnicze (LOT) *Kracow* |
| | SP-LPA | Boeing 767-35DER | Polskie Linie Lotnicze (LOT) *Warszawa* |
| | SP-LSD | Ilyushin IL-18V | Polskie Linie Lotnicze (LOT) |
| | SP-LSF | Ilyushin IL-18E | Polskie Linie Lotnicze (LOT) |
| | SP-LSG | Ilyushin IL-18E | Polskie Linie Lotnicze (LOT) |
| | SP-LSI | Ilyushin IL-18D | Polskie Linie Lotnicze (LOT) |
| | SP-LSK | Ilyushin IL-18V | Polskie Linie Lotnicze (LOT) |

# ST (Sudan)

| Notes | Reg. | Type | Owner or Operator |
|-------|------|------|-------------------|
| | ST-AFA | Boeing 707-3J8C | Sudan Airways |
| | ST-AFB | Boeing 707-3J8C | Sudan Airways |
| | ST-AIX | Boeing 707-369C | Sudan Airways |
| | ST-AKW | Boeing 707-330C | Sudan Airways |
| | ST-ALP | Boeing 707-338C | Trans Arabian Air Transport |
| | ST-DRS | Boeing 707-368C | Sudan Airways |
| | ST-NSR | Boeing 707-330B | Sudan Airways |

# SU (Egypt)

| Notes | Reg. | Type | Owner or Operator |
|-------|------|------|-------------------|
| | SU-AOU | Boeing 707-366C | EgyptAir *Khopho* |
| | SU-APD | Boeing 707-366C | EgyptAir *Khafrah* |
| | SU-AVX | Boeing 707-366C | EgyptAir *Tutankhamun* |
| | SU-AVY | Boeing 707-366C | EgyptAir *Akhenaton* |
| | SU-AVZ | Boeing 707-366C | EgyptAir *Mena* |
| | SU-AXK | Boeing 707-366C | EgyptAir *Seti I* |
| | SU-BCB | Airbus A.300B4 | EgyptAir *Osiris* |
| | SU-BCC | Airbus A.300B4 | EgyptAir *Nout* |
| | SU-BDF | Airbus A.300B4 | EgyptAir *Hathor* |
| | SU-BDG | Airbus A.300B4 | EgyptAir *Aton* |
| | SU-DAA | Boeing 707-351C | ZAS Airline of Egypt |
| | SU-DAC | Boeing 707-336C | ZAS Airline of Egypt |
| | SU-DAN | Airbus A.300B4 | ZAS Airline of Egypt |
| | SU-D | Douglas DC-9-83 | ZAS Airline of Egypt |
| | SU-D | Douglas DC-9-83 | ZAS Airline of Egypt |
| | SU-GAB | Airbus A.300B4 | EgyptAir *Amun* |
| | SU-GAC | Airbus A.300B4 | EgyptAir *Horus* |
| | SU-GAH | Boeing 767-266ER | EgyptAir *Nefertiti* |
| | SU-GAI | Boeing 767-266ER | EgyptAir *Nefertari* |
| | SU-GAJ | Boeing 767-266ER | EgyptAir *Tiye* |
| | SU-GAL | Boeing 747-366 (SCD) | EgyptAir *Hatshepsut* |
| | SU-GAM | Boeing 747-366 (SCD) | EgyptAir *Cleopatra* |
| | SU-GAO | Boeing 767-366ER | EgyptAir |
| | SU-GAP | Boeing 767-366ER | EgyptAir *Thutmosis III* |
| | SU-GAR | Airbus A.300-622R | EgyptAir *Zoser* |
| | SU-GAS | Airbus A.300-622R | EgyptAir *Cheops* |
| | SU-GAT | Airbus A.300-622R | EgyptAir *Chephren* |
| | SU-GAU | Airbus A.300-622R | EgyptAir *Mycerinus* |
| | SU- | Airbus A.300-622R | EgyptAir |
| | SU- | Airbus A.300-622R | EgyptAir |

| Reg. | Type | Owner or Operator | Notes |
|------|------|-------------------|-------|
| SU- | Airbus A.300-622R | EgyptAir | |
| SU- | Airbus A.300-622R | EgyptAir | |
| SU- | Airbus A.300-622R | EgyptAir | |

**Note:** ZAS Airline also operates a DC-9-33 which retains the registration YU-AHW.

# SX (Greece)

| Reg. | Type | Owner or Operator |
|------|------|-------------------|
| SX-BCA | Boeing 737-284 | Olympic Airways *Apollo* |
| SX-BCB | Boeing 737-284 | Olympic Airways *Hermes* |
| SX-BCC | Boeing 737-284 | Olympic Airways *Hercules* |
| SX-BCD | Boeing 737-284 | Olympic Airways *Hephaestus* |
| SX-BCE | Boeing 737-284 | Olympic Airways *Dionysus* |
| SX-BCF | Boeing 737-284 | Olympic Airways *Poseidon* |
| SX-BCG | Boeing 737-284 | Olympic Airways *Phoebus* |
| SX-BCH | Boeing 737-284 | Olympic Airways *Triton* |
| SX-BCI | Boeing 737-284 | Olympic Airways *Proteus* |
| SX-BCK | Boeing 737-284 | Olympic Airways *Nereus* |
| SX-BCL | Boeing 737-284 | Olympic Airways *Isle of Thassos* |
| SX- | Boeing 737-484 | Olympic Airways |
| SX- | Boeing 737-484 | Olympic Airways |
| SX- | Boeing 737-484 | Olympic Airways |
| SX- | Boeing 737-484 | Olympic Airways |
| SX- | Boeing 737-484 | Olympic Airways |
| SX- | Boeing 737-484 | Olympic Airways |
| SX-BEB | Airbus A.300B4 | Olympic Airways *Odysseus* |
| SX-BEC | Airbus A.300B4 | Olympic Airways *Achilleus* |
| SX-BED | Airbus A.300B4 | Olympic Airways *Telemachus* |
| SX-BEE | Airbus A.300B4 | Olympic Airways *Nestor* |
| SX-BEF | Airbus A.300B4 | Olympic Airways *Ajax* |
| SX-BEG | Airbus A.300B4 | Olympic Airways *Diomedes* |
| SX-BEH | Airbus A.300B4 | Olympic Airways *Peleus* |
| SX-BEI | Airbus A.300B4 | Olympic Airways *Neoptolemos* |
| SX-CBA | Boeing 727-284 | Olympic Airways *Mount Olympus* |
| SX-CBB | Boeing 727-284 | Olympic Airways *Mount Pindos* |
| SX-CBC | Boeing 727-284 | Olympic Airways *Mount Parnassus* |
| SX-CBD | Boeing 727-284 | Olympic Airways *Mount Helicon* |
| SX-CBE | Boeing 727-284 | Olympic Airways *Mount Athos* |
| SX-CBF | Boeing 727-284 | Olympic Airways *Mount Taygetus* |
| SX-CBG | Boeing 727-230 | Olympic Airways |
| SX-CBH | Boeing 727-230 | Olympic Airways *Mount Vermio* |
| SX-CBI | Boeing 727-230 | Olympic Airways *Mount Dirfis* |
| SX-DBC | Boeing 707-384C | Olympic Airways *City of Knossos* |
| SX-DBE | Boeing 707-384B | Olympic Airways *City of Pella* |
| SX-OAB | Boeing 747-284B | Olympic Airways *Olympic Eagle* |
| SX-OAC | Boeing 747-212B | Olympic Airways *Olympic Spirit* |
| SX-OAD | Boeing 747-212B | Olympic Airways *Olympic Flame* |
| SX-OAE | Boeing 747-212B | Olympic Airways *Olympic Peace* |

# TC (Turkey)

| Reg. | Type | Owner or Operator |
|------|------|-------------------|
| TC-ABA | S.E.210 Caravelle 10B1R | Istanbul Airlines *Mine* |
| TC-ADA | Boeing 737-4Y0 | Istanbul Airlines |
| TC- | Boeing 737-4Y0 | Istanbul Airlines |
| TC-AFB | Boeing 727-228 | Noble Air *Vatan* |
| TC-AFC | Boeing 727-228 | Noble Air *Ulus* |
| TC-AFD | Boeing 727-230 | Noble Air *Girne* |
| TC-AFE | Boeing 727-230 | Noble Air *Yesilada* |
| TC-AFF | Boeing 727-200 | Noble Air |
| TC-AFG | Boeing 727-231 | Noble Air |
| TC-AFK | Boeing 737-4Y0 | Pegasus Airlines |
| TC-AFL | Boeing 737-4Y0 | Pegasus Airlines |
| TC-AGA | Boeing 737-4Y0 | Istanbul Airlines |
| TC-AKA | S.E.210 Caravelle 10B1R | Istanbul Airlines *Gül* |
| TC-ALA | S.E.210 Caravelle 10B1R | Istanbul Airlines *Orkide* |
| TC-ASA | S.E.210 Caravelle 10B1R | Istanbul Airlines *Nergis* |
| TC-ATA | Boeing 737-4Y0 | Istanbul Airlines |
| TC-ATU | Boeing 727-76 | TUR European Airways |
| TC- | Boeing 737-3Y0 | Istanbul Airlines |
| TC- | Boeing 737-3Y0 | Istanbul Airlines |

| Notes | Reg. | Type | Owner or Operator |
|-------|------|------|-------------------|
| | TC-GHA | Boeing 707-324C | Golden Horn *Zafer* |
| | TC-GHB | Boeing 707-324C | Golden Horn *Falih* |
| | TC-GRA | Tupolev Tu-154M | Greenair *Cappadocia* |
| | TC-GRB | Tupolev Tu-154M | Greenair *Perestroika* |
| | TC-GRC | Tupolev Tu-154M | Greenair *Fenerbahce* |
| | TC-GRD | Tupolev Tu-134A-3 | Greenair *Besiktas* |
| | TC-GRE | Tupolev Tu-134A-3 | Greenair *Galatasary* |
| | TC-JAB | Douglas DC-9-32 | Türk Hava Yollari (THY) *Bogazici* |
| | TC-JAD | Douglas DC-9-32 | Türk Hava Yollari (THY) *Anadolu* |
| | TC-JAE | Douglas DC-9-32 | Türk Hava Yollari (THY) *Trakya* |
| | TC-JAF | Douglas DC-9-32 | Türk Hava Yollari (THY) *Ege* |
| | TC-JAG | Douglas DC-9-32 | Türk Hava Yollari (THY) *Akdeniz* |
| | TC-JAK | Douglas DC-9-32 | Türk Hava Yollari (THY) *Karadeniz* |
| | TC-JAL | Douglas DC-9-32 | Türk Hava Yollari (THY) *Halic* |
| | TC-JBF | Boeing 727-2F2 | Türk Hava Yollari (THY) *Adana* |
| | TC-JBG | Boeing 727-2F2 | Cyprus Turkish Airlines |
| | TC-JBJ | Boeing 727-2F2 | Türk Hava Yollari (THY) *Diyarbakir* |
| | TC-JBK | Douglas DC-9-32 | Türk Hava Yollari (THY) *Aydin* |
| | TC-JBL | Douglas DC-9-32 | Türk Hava Yollari (THY) *Gediz* |
| | TC-JBM | Boeing 727-2F2 | Türk Hava Yollari (THY) *Menderes* |
| | TC-JCA | Boeing 727-2F2 | Türk Hava Yollari (THY) *Edirne* |
| | TC-JCB | Boeing 727-2F2 | Türk Hava Yollari (THY) *Kars* |
| | TC-JCD | Boeing 727-2F2 | Türk Hava Yollari (THY) *Sinop* |
| | TC-JCE | Boeing 727-2F2 | Türk Hava Yollari (THY) *Hatay* |
| | TC-JCK | Boeing 727-243 | Türk Hava Yollari (THY) *Erciyes* |
| | TC-JCL | Airbus A.310-203 | Türk Hava Yollari (THY) *Seyhan* |
| | TC-JCM | Airbus A.310-203 | Türk Hava Yollari (THY) *Ceyhan* |
| | TC-JCN | Airbus A.310-203 | Türk Hava Yollari (THY) *Dicle* |
| | TC-JCO | Airbus A.310-203 | Türk Hava Yollari (THY) *Firat* |
| | TC-JCR | Airbus A.310-203 | Türk Hava Yollari (THY) *Kizilirmak* |
| | TC-JCS | Airbus A.310-203 | Türk Hava Yollari (THY) *Yesilirmak* |
| | TC-JCU | Airbus A.310-203 | Türk Hava Yollari (THY) *Sakarya* |
| | TC-JCV | Airbus A.310-304 | Türk Hava Yollari (THY) *Aras* |
| | TC-JCY | Airbus A.310-304 | Türk Hava Yollari (THY) *Coruh* |
| | TC-JCZ | Airbus A.310-304 | Türk Hava Yollari (THY) *Ergene* |
| | TC-JDA | Airbus A.310-304 | Türk Hava Yollari (THY) *Aksu* |
| | TC-JDB | Airbus A.310-304 | Türk Hava Yollari (THY) *Goksu* |
| | TC-JDC | Airbus A.310-304 | Türk Hava Yollari (THY) *Meric* |
| | TC-J | Airbus A.310-304 | Türk Hava Yollari (THY) |
| | TC-JFA | Boeing 727-264 | Türk Hava Yollari (THY) *Ortaköy* |
| | TC-JFB | Boeing 727-264 | Türk Hava Yollari (THY) *Vaniköy* |
| | TC- | Boeing 747-212B | Türk Hava Yollari (THY) |
| | TC-JUS | Boeing 737-2Q8 | Sultan Air |
| | TC-JUT | Boeing 737-217 | Sultan Air |
| | TC-MAB | Douglas DC-8-61 | Birgenair |
| | TC-SUN | Boeing 737-3Y0 | Sun Express |
| | TC-SUP | Boeing 737-3Y0 | Sun Express |
| | TC-SUR | Boeing 737-3Y0 | Sun Express |
| | TC-TUR | Boeing 727-230 | TUR European Airways |

**Note:** Sultan Air also operates Boeing 737s on lease from Transwede.

# TF (Iceland)

| | TF-ABJ | Boeing 737-201C | Atlanta Icelandic/Finnair Cargo |
|-------|------|------|-------------------|
| | TF-ABT | Boeing 737-205C | Atlanta Icelandic *Spirit of Nome 1924 Alaska* |
| | TF- | L-1011-385 TriStar | Atlanta Icelandic |
| | TF-FIA | Boeing 737-408 | Icelandair *Aldis* |
| | TF-FIB | Boeing 737-408 | Icelandair *Eydis* |
| | TF-FIC | Boeing 737-408 | Icelandair *Vedis* |
| | TF-FIH | Boeing 757-208ER | Icelandair *Haldis* |
| | TF-FII | Boeing 757-208ER | Icelandair *Fanndis* |
| | TF-FLM | F.27 Friendship Mk 200 | Icelandair |
| | TF-FLN | F.27 Friendship Mk 200 | Icelandair |
| | TF-FLO | F.27 Friendship Mk 200 | Icelandair |
| | TF-FLP | F.27 Friendship Mk 200 | Icelandair |
| | TF-FLS | F.27 Friendship Mk 200 | Icelandair |

# TJ (Cameroon)

| Reg. | Type | Owner or Operator | Notes |
|------|------|-------------------|-------|
| TJ-CAB | Boeing 747-2H7B (SCD) | Cameroon Airlines *Mont Cameroun* | |

# TR (Gabon)

| | | | |
|------|------|-------------------|-------|
| TR-LBV | L-100-30 Hercules | Air Gabon Cargo | |

**Note:** Air Gabon operates Boeing 747-2Q2B F-ODJG on lease which will become TR-LXK.

# TS (Tunisia)

| | | |
|------|------|------|
| TS-IMA | Airbus A.300B4 | Tunis-Air *Amilcar* |
| TS-IMB | Airbus A.320-211 | Tunis-Air *Fahrat Hached* |
| TS-IMC | Airbus A.320-211 | Tunis-Air *7 Novembre* |
| TS- | Airbus A.320-211 | Tunis-Air |
| TS-IOC | Boeing 737-2H3 | Tunis-Air *Salammbo* |
| TS-IOD | Boeing 737-2H3C | Tunis-Air *Bulla Regia* |
| TS-IOE | Boeing 737-2H3 | Tunis-Air *Zarzis* |
| TS-IOF | Boeing 737-2H3 | Tunis-Air *Sousse* |
| TS-JHN | Boeing 727-2H3 | Tunis-Air *Carthago* |
| TS-JHQ | Boeing 727-2H3 | Tunis-Air *Tozeur-Nefta* |
| TS-JHR | Boeing 727-2H3 | Tunis-Air *Bizerte* |
| TS-JHS | Boeing 727-2H3 | Tunis-Air *Kairouan* |
| TS-JHT | Boeing 727-2H3 | Tunis-Air *Sidi Bousaid* |
| TS-JHU | Boeing 727-2H3 | Tunis-Air *Hannibal* |
| TS-JHV | Boeing 727-2H3 | Tunis-Air *Jugurtha* |
| TS-JHW | Boeing 727-2H3 | Tunis-Air *Ibn Khaldoun* |

# TU (Ivory Coast)

| | | |
|------|------|------|
| TU-TAL | Douglas DC-10-30 | Air Afrique *Libreville* |
| TU-TAM | Douglas DC-10-30 | Air Afrique |
| TU-TAN | Douglas DC-10-30 | Air Afrique *Niamey* |
| TU-TAO | Airbus A.300B4-203 | Air Afrique *Nouackchott* |
| TU-TAS | Airbus A.300B4-203 | Air Afrique *Bangui* |
| TU-TAT | Airbus A.300B4-203 | Air Afrique |
| TU-TCF | Douglas DC-8-63CF | Air Afrique *Ndjamena* |

# V2 (Antigua)

**Note:** Seagreen Air Transport operates four Boeing 707s registered N14AZ, N18AZ, N21AZ and N29AZ.

# V5 (Namibia)

| | | |
|------|------|------|
| V5-SPF | Boeing 747SP | Air Namibia |

# V8 (Brunei)

| | | |
|------|------|------|
| V8-RBA | Boeing 757-2M6ER | Royal Brunei Airlines |
| V8-RBB | Boeing 757-2M6ER | Royal Brunei Airlines |
| V8-RBC | Boeing 757-2M6ER | Royal Brunei Airlines |
| V8-RBD | Boeing 767-284ER | Royal Brunei Airlines |

# VH (Australia)

| | | |
|------|------|------|
| VH-EBA | Boeing 747-238B | Qantas Airways *City of Ipswich* |
| VH-EBB | Boeing 747-238B | Qantas Airways *City of Newcastle* |
| VH-EBJ | Boeing 747-238B | Qantas Airways *City of Newcastle* |
| VH-EBK | Boeing 747-238B | Qantas Airways *City of Sale* |
| VH-EBL | Boeing 747-238B | Qantas Airways *City of Ballart* |

| Notes | Reg. | Type | Owner or Operator |
|---|---|---|---|
| | VH-EBM | Boeing 747-238B | Qantas Airways *City of Grosford* |
| | VH-EBN | Boeing 747-238B | Qantas Airways *City of Albury* |
| | VH-EBO | Boeing 747-238B | Qantas Airways *City of Elizabeth* |
| | VH-EBP | Boeing 747-238B | Qantas Airways *City of Adelaide* |
| | VH-EBQ | Boeing 747-238B | Qantas Airways *City of Bunbury* |
| | VH-EBR | Boeing 747-238B | Qantas Airways *City of Hobart* |
| | VH-EBS | Boeing 747-238B | Qantas Airways *City of Longreach* |
| | VH-EBT | Boeing 747-338 | Qantas Airways *City of Wagga Wagga* |
| | VH-EBU | Boeing 747-338 | Qantas Airways *City of Warrnambool* |
| | VH-EBV | Boeing 747-338 | Qantas Airways *Geraldton* |
| | VH-EBW | Boeing 747-338 | Qantas Airways *City of Brisbane* |
| | VH-EBX | Boeing 747-338 | Qantas Airways *City of Perth* |
| | VH-EBY | Boeing 747-338 | Qantas Airways *City of Darwin* |
| | VH-OJA | Boeing 747-438 | Qantas Airways *City of Canberra* |
| | VH-OJB | Boeing 747-438 | Qantas Airways *City of Sydney* |
| | VH-OJC | Boeing 747-438 | Qantas Airways *City of Melbourne* |
| | VH-OJD | Boeing 747-438 | Qantas Airways *City of Brisbane* |
| | VH-OJE | Boeing 747-438 | Qantas Airways *City of Adelaide* |
| | VH-OJF | Boeing 747-438 | Qantas Airways *City of Perth* |
| | VH-OJG | Boeing 747-438 | Qantas Airways *City of Hobart* |
| | VH-OJH | Boeing 747-438 | Qantas Airways *City of Darwin* |
| | VH-OJI | Boeing 747-438 | Qantas Airways *Longreach* |
| | VH-OJJ | Boeing 747-438 | Qantas Airways *Winton* |
| | VH-OJK | Boeing 747-438 | Qantas |
| | VH-OJL | Boeing 747-438 | Qantas |
| | VH-OJM | Boeing 747-438 | Qantas |

# VR-H (Hong Kong)

| Notes | Reg. | Type | Owner or Operator |
|---|---|---|---|
| | VR-HIA | Boeing 747-267B | Cathay Pacific Airways |
| | VR-HIB | Boeing 747-267B | Cathay Pacific Airways |
| | VR-HIC | Boeing 747-267B | Cathay Pacific Airways |
| | VR-HID | Boeing 747-267B | Cathay Pacific Airways |
| | VR-HIE | Boeing 747-267B | Cathay Pacific Airways |
| | VR-HIF | Boeing 747-267B | Cathay Pacific Airways |
| | VR-HIH | Boeing 747-267B | Cathay Pacific Airways |
| | VR-HII | Boeing 747-367 | Cathay Pacific Airways |
| | VR-HIJ | Boeing 747-367 | Cathay Pacific Airways |
| | VR-HIK | Boeing 747-367 | Cathay Pacific Airways |
| | VR-HKG | Boeing 747-267B | Cathay Pacific Airways |
| | VR-HKK | Boeing 707-336C | Air Hong Kong |
| | VR-HKL | Boeing 707-321C | Air Hong Kong |
| | VR-HOL | Boeing 747-367 | Cathay Pacific Airways |
| | VR-HOM | Boeing 747-367 | Cathay Pacific Airways |
| | VR-HON | Boeing 747-367 | Cathay Pacific Airways |
| | VR-HOO | Boeing 747-467 | Cathay Pacific Airways |
| | VR-HOP | Boeing 747-467 | Cathay Pacific Airways |
| | VR-HOR | Boeing 747-467 | Cathay Pacific Airways |
| | VR-HOS | Boeing 747-467 | Cathay Pacific Airways |
| | VR-HOT | Boeing 747-467 | Cathay Pacific Airways |
| | VR-HOU | Boeing 747-467 | Cathay Pacific Airways |
| | VR-HOW | Boeing 747-467 | Cathay Pacific Airways |
| | VR-HOV | Boeing 747-467 | Cathay Pacific Airways |
| | VR-HOY | Boeing 747-467 | Cathay Pacific Airways |
| | VR-HVX | Boeing 747-267F (SCD) | Cathay Pacific Airways |
| | VR-HVY | Boeing 747-236F (SCD) | Cathay Pacific Airways *Hong Kong Jumbo* |
| | VR-HVZ | Boeing 747-267F (SCD) | Cathay Pacific Airways |

# VT (India)

| Notes | Reg. | Type | Owner or Operator |
|---|---|---|---|
| | VT-EBE | Boeing 747-237B | Air-India *Emperor Shahjehan* |
| | VT-EBN | Boeing 747-237B | Air-India *Emperor Rajendra Chola* |
| | VT-EBO | Boeing 747-237B | Air-India *Emperor Nikramaditya* |
| | VT-EDU | Boeing 747-237B | Air-India *Emperor Akbar* |
| | VT-EFJ | Boeing 747-237B | Air-India *Emperor Chandragupta* |
| | VT-EFU | Boeing 747-237B | Air-India *Emperor Krishna Deva* |
| | VT-EGA | Boeing 747-237B | Air-India *Emperor Samudra Gupto* |
| | VT-EGB | Boeing 747-237B | Air-India *Emperor Mahendra Varman* |

| Reg. | Type | Owner or Operator | Notes |
|---|---|---|---|
| VT-EGC | Boeing 747-237B | Air-India *Emperor Harsha Vardhuma* | |
| VT-EJG | Airbus A.310-304 | Air-India *Vamuna* | |
| VT-EJH | Airbus A.310-304 | Air-India *Tista* | |
| VT-EJI | Airbus A.310-304 | Air-India *Saraswati* | |
| VT-EJJ | Airbus A.310-304 | Air-India *Beas* | |
| VT-EJK | Airbus A.310-304 | Air-India *Gomti* | |
| VT-EJL | Airbus A.310-304 | Air-India *Sabarmati* | |
| VT-ENQ | Boeing 747-212B | Air-India *Himalaya* | |
| VT-EPW | Boeing 747-337 (SCD) | Air-India *Shivaji* | |
| VT-EPX | Boeing 747-337 (SCD) | Air-India *Narasimha Varman* | |
| VT-EQS | Airbus A.310-304 | Air-India *Krishna* | |
| VT-EQT | Airbus A.310-304 | Air-India | |

**Note:** Air-India Cargo operates Douglas DC-8s and Boeing 747s on lease from various airlines.

# XA (Mexico)

| | | | |
|---|---|---|---|
| XA-AMR | Douglas DC-10-30 | Aeromexico | |
| XA-RIY | Douglas DC-10-30 | Aeromexico *Jose Marie Morelos* | |

**Note:** Aeromexico also operates DC-10-30s N8228P *Castillo de Chapultepec* and N417DG *Ciudad de Mexico.*

# XT (Burkina Faso)

| | | | |
|---|---|---|---|
| XT-ABX | Boeing 707-336C | Naganagani | |

# YI (Iraq)

| | | |
|---|---|---|
| YI-AGE | Boeing 707-370C | Iraqi Airways |
| YI-AGF | Boeing 707-370C | Iraqi Airways |
| YI-AGG | Boeing 707-370C | Iraqi Airways |
| YI-AGK | Boeing 727-270 | Iraqi Airways *Ninevah* |
| YI-AGL | Boeing 727-270 | Iraqi Airways *Basrah* |
| YI-AGM | Boeing 727-270 | Iraqi Airways |
| YI-AGN | Boeing 747-270C (SCD) | Iraqi Airways *Tigris* |
| YI-AGO | Boeing 747-270C (SCD) | Iraqi Airways *Euphrates* |
| YI-AGP | Boeing 747-270C (SCD) | Iraqi Airways *Shat-al-Arab* |
| YI-AGQ | Boeing 727-270 | Iraqi Airways *Ataameem* |
| YI-AGR | Boeing 727-270 | Iraqi Airways *Babylon* |
| YI-AGS | Boeing 727-270 | Iraqi Airways |
| YI-AKO | Ilyushin IL-76M | Iraqi Airways |
| YI-AKP | Ilyushin IL-76M | Iraqi Airways |
| YI-AKQ | Ilyushin IL-76M | Iraqi Airways |
| YI-AKS | Ilyushin IL-76M | Iraqi Airways |
| YI-AKT | Ilyushin IL-76M | Iraqi Airways |
| YI-AKU | Ilyushin IL-76M | Iraqi Airways |
| YI-AKV | Ilyushin IL-76M | Iraqi Airways |
| YI-AKW | Ilyushin IL-76M | Iraqi Airways |
| YI-AKX | Ilyushin IL-76M | Iraqi Airways |
| YI-ALL | Ilyushin IL-76M | Iraqi Airways |
| YI-ALO | Ilyushin IL-76M | Iraqi Airways |
| YI-ALP | Ilyushin IL-76M | Iraqi Airways |
| YI-ALQ | Ilyushin IL-76MD | Iraqi Airways |
| YI-ALR | Ilyushin IL-76MD | Iraqi Airways |
| YI-ALS | Ilyushin IL-76MD | Iraqi Airways |
| YI-ALT | Ilyushin IL-76MD | Iraqi Airways |
| YI-ALU | Ilyushin IL-76MD | Iraqi Airways |
| YI-ALV | Ilyushin IL-76MD | Iraqi Airways |
| YI-ALW | Ilyushin IL-76MD | Iraqi Airways |
| YI-ALX | Ilyushin IL-76MD | Iraqi Airways |
| YI-ANA | Ilyushin IL-76MD | Iraqi Airways |
| YI-ANB | Ilyushin IL-76MD | Iraqi Airways |
| YI-ANC | Ilyushin IL-76MD | Iraqi Airways |
| YI-AND | Ilyushin IL-76MD | Iraqi Airways |
| YI-ANE | Ilyushin IL-76MD | Iraqi Airways |
| YI-ANF | Ilyushin IL-76MD | Iraqi Airways |
| YI-ANG | Ilyushin IL-76MD | Iraqi Airways |

| Notes | Reg. | Type | Owner or Operator |
|---|---|---|---|
| | YI-ANH | Ilyushin IL-76MD | Iraqi Airways |
| | YI-ANI | Ilyushin IL-76MD | Iraqi Airways |
| | YI-ANJ | Ilyushin IL-76MD | Iraqi Airways |
| | YI-ANK | Ilyushin IL-76MD | Iraqi Airways |
| | YI-ANL | Ilyushin IL-76MD | Iraqi Airways |

## YK (Syria)

| | | | |
|---|---|---|---|
| | YK-AGA | Boeing 727-294 | Syrian Arab Airlines *October 6* |
| | YK-AGB | Boeing 727-294 | Syrian Arab Airlines *Damascus* |
| | YK-AGC | Boeing 727-294 | Syrian Arab Airlines *Palmyra* |
| | YK-AHA | Boeing 747SP-94 | Syrian Arab Airlines *16 Novembre* |
| | YK-AHB | Boeing 747SP-94 | Syrian Arab Airlines *Arab Solidarity* |
| | YK-AIA | Tupolev Tu-154M | Syrian Arab Airlines |
| | YK-AIB | Tupolev Tu-154M | Syrian Arab Airlines |
| | YK-AIC | Tupolev Tu-154M | Syrian Arab Airlines |
| | YK-ATA | Ilyushin IL-76M | Syrian Arab Airlines |
| | YK-ATB | Ilyushin IL-76M | Syrian Arab Airlines |
| | YK-ATC | Ilyushin IL-76M | Syrian Arab Airlines |
| | YK-ATD | Ilyushin IL-76M | Syrian Arab Airlines |

## YR (Romania)

| | | | |
|---|---|---|---|
| | YR-ABA | Boeing 707-3K1C | Tarom |
| | YR-ABC | Boeing 707-3K1C | Tarom |
| | YR-ABM | Boeing 707-321C | Tarom |
| | YR-ABN | Boeing 707-321C | Tarom |
| | YR-ADA | Antonov 26 | Tarom |
| | YR-ADB | Antonov 26 | Tarom |
| | YR-ADC | Antonov 26 | Tarom |
| | YR-ADE | Antonov 26 | Tarom |
| | YR-ADG | Antonov 26 | Tarom |
| | YR-ADH | Antonov 26 | Tarom |
| | YR-ADJ | Antonov 26 | Tarom |
| | YR-ADK | Antonov 26 | Tarom |
| | YR-ADL | Antonov 26 | Tarom |
| | YR-ADM | Antonov 26 | Tarom |
| | YR-ADN | Antonov 26 | Tarom |
| | YR- | Airbus A.310-325 | Tarom |
| | YR- | Airbus A.310-325 | Tarom |
| | YR- | Airbus A.310-325 | Tarom |
| | YR-BCE | BAC One-Eleven 424EU | Tarom |
| | YR-BCF | BAC One-Eleven 424EU | Liniile Aeriene Romane (LAR) |
| | YR-BCG | BAC One-Eleven 401AK | Tarom |
| | YR-BCH | BAC One-Eleven 402AP | Tarom |
| | YR-BCI | BAC One-Eleven 525FT | Tarom |
| | YR-BCJ | BAC One-Eleven 525FT | Tarom |
| | YR-BCK | BAC One-Eleven 525FT | Tarom |
| | YR-BCN | BAC One-Eleven 525FT | Tarom |
| | YR-BCO | BAC One Eleven 525FT | Tarom |
| | YR-BCQ | BAC One-Eleven 525FT | Tarom |
| | YR-BRA | RomBac One-Eleven 561RC | Tarom |
| | YR-BRC | RomBac One-Eleven 561RC | Tarom |
| | YR-BRD | RomBac One-Eleven 561RC | Tarom |
| | YR-BRE | RomBac One-Eleven 561RC | Tarom |
| | YR-BRF | RomBac One-Eleven 561RC | Tarom |
| | YR-BRH | RomBac One-Eleven 561RC | Tarom |
| | YR-IMA | Ilyushin IL-18D | Tarom |
| | YR-IMC | Ilyushin IL-18V | Tarom |
| | YR-IMD | Ilyushin IL-18V | Tarom |
| | YR-IME | Ilyushin IL-18V | Tarom |
| | YR-IMF | Ilyushin IL-18V | Tarom |
| | YR-IMG | Ilyushin IL-18V | Tarom |
| | YR-IMH | Ilyushin IL-18V | Tarom |
| | YR-IMJ | Ilyushin IL-18D | Tarom |
| | YR-IML | Ilyushin IL-18D | Tarom |
| | YR-IMM | Ilyushin IL-18D | Tarom |
| | YR-IMZ | Ilyushin IL-18V | Tarom |

| Reg. | Type | Owner or Operator | Notes |
|------|------|-------------------|-------|
| YR-IRA | Ilyushin IL-62 | Tarom | |
| YR-IRB | Ilyushin IL-62 | Tarom | |
| YR-IRC | Ilyushin IL-62 | Tarom | |
| YR-IRD | Ilyushin IL-62M | Tarom | |
| YR-IRE | Ilyushin IL-62M | Tarom | |
| YR-TPA | Tupolev Tu-154B | Tarom | |
| YR-TPB | Tupolev Tu-154B | Tarom | |
| YR-TPC | Tupolev Tu-154B | Tarom | |
| YR-TPD | Tupolev Tu-154B | Tarom | |
| YR-TPE | Tupolev Tu-154B-1 | Tarom | |
| YR-TPF | Tupolev Tu-154B-1 | Tarom | |
| YR-TPG | Tupolev Tu-154B-1 | Tarom | |
| YR-TPI | Tupolev Tu-154B-2 | Tarom | |
| YR-TPK | Tupolev Tu-154B-2 | Tarom | |
| YR-TPL | Tupolev Tu-154B-2 | Tarom | |

# YU (Yugoslavia)

| Reg. | Type | Owner or Operator | Notes |
|------|------|-------------------|-------|
| YU-AGE | Boeing 707-340C | Jugoslovenski Aerotransport | |
| YU-AGG | Boeing 707-340C | Jugoslovenski Aerotransport | |
| YU-AHJ | Douglas DC-9-32 | Adria Airways | |
| YU-AHN | Douglas DC-9-32 | Jugoslovenski Aerotransport | |
| YU-AHU | Douglas DC-9-32 | Jugoslovenski Aerotransport | |
| YU-AHV | Douglas DC-9-32 | Jugoslovenski Aerotransport | |
| YU-AHW | Douglas DC-9-33RC | Adria Airways *(leased to ZAS Airline of Egypt)* | |
| YU-AHX | Tupolev Tu-134A-3 | Aviogenex *Beograd* | |
| YU-AHY | Tupolev Tu-134A-3 | Aviogenex *Zagreb* | |
| YU-AJA | Tupolev Tu-134A-3 | Aviogenex *Titograd* | |
| YU-AJD | Tupolev Tu-134A-3 | Aviogenex *Skopje* | |
| YU-AJF | Douglas DC-9-32 | Adria Airways | |
| YU-AJH | Douglas DC-9-32 | Jugoslovenski Aerotransport | |
| YU-AJI | Douglas DC-9-32 | Jugoslovenski Aerotransport | |
| YU-AJJ | Douglas DC-9-32 | Jugoslovenski Aerotransport | |
| YU-AJK | Douglas DC-9-32 | Jugoslovenski Aerotransport | |
| YU-AJL | Douglas DC-9-32 | Jugoslovenski Aerotransport | |
| YU-AJM | Douglas DC-9-32 | Jugoslovenski Aerotransport | |
| YU-AJZ | McD Douglas MD-81 | Adria Airways | |
| YU-AKB | Boeing 727-2H9 | Jugoslovenski Aerotransport | |
| YU-AKD | Boeing 727-2L8 | Aviogenex *Split* | |
| YU-AKE | Boeing 727-2H9 | Jugoslovenski Aerotransport | |
| YU-AKF | Boeing 727-2H9 | Jugoslovenski Aerotransport | |
| YU-AKG | Boeing 727-2H9 | Jugoslovenski Aerotransport | |
| YU-AKH | Boeing 727-2L8 | Aviogenex *Dubrovnik* | |
| YU-AKI | Boeing 727-2H9 | Jugoslovenski Aerotransport | |
| YU-AKJ | Boeing 727-2H9 | Jugoslovenski Aerotransport | |
| YU-AKK | Boeing 727-2H9 | Jugoslovenski Aerotransport | |
| YU-AKL | Boeing 727-2H9 | Jugoslovenski Aerotransport | |
| YU-AKM | Boeing 727-243 | Aviogenex *Pula* | |
| YU-AMA | Douglas DC-10-30 | Jugoslovenski Aerotransport *Nikola Tesla* | |
| YU-AMB | Douglas DC-10-30 | Jugoslovenski Aerotransport *Edvard Rusijan* | |
| YU-AMC | Douglas DC-10-30 | Jugoslovenski Aerotransport | |
| YU-AMD | Douglas DC-10-30 | Jugoslovenski Aerotransport | |
| YU-ANB | McD Douglas MD-82 | Adria Airways | |
| YU-ANC | McD Douglas MD-82 | Adria Airways | |
| YU-AND | Boeing 737-3H9 | Jugoslovenski Aerotransport | |
| YU-ANF | Boeing 737-3H9 | Jugoslovenski Aerotransport | |
| YU-ANG | McD Douglas MD-82 | Adria Airways | |
| YU-ANH | Boeing 737-3H9 | Jugoslovenski Aerotransport | |
| YU-ANI | Boeing 737-3H9 | Jugoslovenski Aerotransport | |
| YU-ANJ | Boeing 737-3H9 | Jugoslovenski Aerotransport | |
| YU-ANK | Boeing 737-3H9 | Jugoslovenski Aerotransport | |
| YU-ANL | Boeing 737-3H9 | Jugoslovenski Aerotransport | |
| YU-ANO | McD Douglas MD-82 | Adria Airways | |
| YU-ANP | Boeing 737-2K3 | Aviogenex *Zadar* | |
| YU-ANU | Boeing 737-2K3 | Aviogenex *Tivat* | |
| YU-ANV | Boeing 737-3H9 | Jugoslovenski Aerotransport | |
| YU-ANW | Boeing 737-3H9 | Jugoslovenski Aerotransport | |

| Notes | Reg. | Type | Owner or Operator |
|-------|------|------|-------------------|
| | YU-AOA | Airbus A.320-231 | Adria Airways |
| | YU-AOB | Airbus A.320-231 | Adria Airways |
| | YU-AOC | Airbus A.320-231 | Adria Airways |
| | YU-AOD | Airbus A.320-231 | Adria Airways |
| | YU-AOE | Airbus A.320-231 | Adria Airways |
| | YU-AOF | Boeing 737-2K5 | Aviogenex |
| | YU-AOG | Boeing 737-2K5 | Aviogenex |

## YV (Venezuela)

| | YV-134C | Douglas DC-10-30 | Viasa |
|--|---------|------------------|-------|
| | YV-135C | Douglas DC-10-30 | Viasa |
| | YV-136C | Douglas DC-10-30 | Viasa |
| | YV-137C | Douglas DC-10-30 | Viasa |
| | YV-138C | Douglas DC-10-30 | Viasa |

## Z (Zimbabwe)

| | Z-WKR | Boeing 707-330B | Air Zimbabwe |
|--|-------|-----------------|--------------|
| | Z-WKS | Boeing 707-330B | Air Zimbabwe |
| | Z-WKU | Boeing 707-330B | Air Zimbabwe |
| | Z-WKV | Boeing 707-330B | Air Zimbabwe |
| | Z-WMJ | Douglas DC-8-55F | Affretair *Captain Jack Malloch* |
| | Z-WPE | Boeing 767-2N0ER | Air Zimbabwe *Victoria Falls* |
| | Z-WPF | Boeing 767-2N0ER | Air Zimbabwe |
| | Z-WSB | Douglas DC-8-55F | Affretair |

## ZK (New Zealand)

| | ZK-NBS | Boeing 747-419 | Air New Zealand *Mataatua* |
|--|--------|----------------|----------------------------|
| | ZK-NBT | Boeing 747-419 | Air New Zealand |
| | ZK-N | Boeing 747-419 | Air New Zealand |
| | ZK-NZV | Boeing 747-219B | Air New Zealand *Aotea* |
| | ZK-NZW | Boeing 747-219B | Air New Zealand *Tainui* |
| | ZK-NZX | Boeing 747-219B | Air New Zealand *Takitimu* |
| | ZK-NZY | Boeing 747-219B | Air New Zealand *Te Arawa* |
| | ZK-NZZ | Boeing 747-219B | Air New Zealand *Tokomaru* |

## ZP (Paraguay)

| | ZP-CCE | Boeing 707-321B | Lineas Aéreas Paraguayas |
|--|--------|-----------------|--------------------------|
| | ZP-CCF | Boeing 707-321B | Lineas Aéreas Paraguayas |
| | ZP-CCG | Boeing 707-321B | Lineas Aéreas Paraguayas |
| | ZP-CCH | Douglas DC-8-63 | Lineas Aéreas Paraguayas |

## ZS (South Africa)

| | ZS-SAL | Boeing 747-244B | South African Airways *Tafelberg* |
|--|--------|-----------------|-----------------------------------|
| | ZS-SAM | Boeing 747-244B | South African Airways *Drakensberg* |
| | ZS-SAN | Boeing 747-244B | South African Airways *Lebombo* |
| | ZS-SAO | Boeing 747-244B | South African Airways *Magaliesberg* |
| | ZS-SAP | Boeing 747-244B | South African Airways *Swartberg* |
| | ZS-SAR | Boeing 747-244B (SCD) | South African Airways *Waterberg* |
| | ZS-SAT | Boeing 747-344 | South African Airways *Johannesburg* |
| | ZS-SAU | Boeing 747-344 | South African Airways *Cape Town* |
| | ZS-SAV | Boeing 747-444 | South African Airways |
| | ZS-SAW | Boeing 747-444 | South African Airways |
| | ZS-SPE | Boeing 747SP-44 | South African Airways *Hantam* |

# 3B (Mauritius)

| Reg. | Type | Owner or Operator | Notes |
|------|------|-------------------|-------|
| 3B-NAG | Boeing 747SP-44 | Air Mauritius *Chateau du Reduit* | |
| 3B-NAJ | Boeing 747SP-44 | Air Mauritius *Chateau Mon Plaisir* | |
| 3B-NAK | Boeing 767-23BER | Air Mauritius *City of Curepipe* | |
| 3B-NAL | Boeing 767-23BER | Air Mauritius *City of Port Louis* | |
| 3B-NAQ | Boeing 747SP-27 | Air Mauritius *Chateau Benares* | |

# 3D (Swaziland)

| | | |
|------|------|------|
| 3D-ASB | Boeing 707-323C | Air Swazi Cargo |
| 3D-ASC | Boeing 707-344C | Air Swazi Cargo |

# 4R (Sri Lanka)

| | | |
|------|------|------|
| 4R-ULA | L.1011-385 TriStar 500 | Air Lanka |
| 4R-ULB | L.1011-385 TriStar 500 | Air Lanka |
| 4R-ULC | L.1011-385 TriStar 100 | Air Lanka *City of Jayawardanapura* |
| 4R-ULE | L.1011-385 TriStar 50 | Air Lanka *City of Ratnapura* |

**Note:** Air Lanka also operates TriStar JY-AGB on lease.

# 4W (Yemen)

| | | |
|------|------|------|
| 4W-ACF | Boeing 727-2N8 | Yemeni Airways |
| 4W-ACG | Boeing 727-2N8 | Yemeni Airways |
| 4W-ACH | Boeing 727-2N8 | Yemeni Airways |
| 4W-ACI | Boeing 727-2N8 | Yemeni Airways |
| 4W-ACJ | Boeing 727-2N8 | Yemeni Airways |

# 4X (Israel)

| | | |
|------|------|------|
| 4X-ABN | Boeing 737-258 | El Al/Arkia |
| 4X-ABO | Boeing 737-258 | El Al/Arkia |
| 4X-ATG | Boeing 707-323B | Arkia |
| 4X-ATX | Boeing 707-358C | El Al/Arkia |
| 4X-ATY | Boeing 707-358C | El Al/Arkia |
| 4X-AXA | Boeing 747-258B | El Al |
| 4X-AXB | Boeing 747-258B | El Al |
| 4X-AXC | Boeing 747-258B | El Al |
| 4X-AXD | Boeing 747-258C | El Al |
| 4X-AXF | Boeing 747-258C | El Al |
| 4X-AXG | Boeing 747-258F (SCD) | El Al |
| 4X-AXH | Boeing 747-258B | El Al |
| 4X-AXQ | Boeing 747-238B | El Al |
| 4X-AXZ | Boeing 747-124F (SCD) | El Al |
| 4X-EAA | Boeing 767-258 | El Al |
| 4X-EAB | Boeing 767-258 | El Al |
| 4X-EAC | Boeing 767-258ER | El Al |
| 4X-EAD | Boeing 767-258ER | El Al |
| 4X-EBL | Boeing 757-258 | El Al |
| 4X-EBM | Boeing 757-258 | El Al |
| 4X-EBR | Boeing 757-258 | El Al |
| 4X-EBS | Boeing 757-258ER | El Al |
| 4X-EBT | Boeing 757-258ER | El Al |

# 5A (Libya)

| | | |
|------|------|------|
| 5A-DAI | Boeing 727-224 | Libyan Arab Airlines |
| 5A-DAK | Boeing 707-3L5C | Libyan Arab Airlines |
| 5A-DIA | Boeing 727-2L5 | Libyan Arab Airlines |

| Notes | Reg. | Type | Owner or Operator |
|---|---|---|---|
| | 5A-DIB | Boeing 727-2L5 | Libyan Arab Airlines |
| | 5A-DIC | Boeing 727-2L5 | Libyan Arab Airlines |
| | 5A-DID | Boeing 727-2L5 | Libyan Arab Airlines |
| | 5A-DIE | Boeing 727-2L5 | Libyan Arab Airlines |
| | 5A-DIF | Boeing 727-2L5 | Libyan Arab Airlines |
| | 5A-DIG | Boeing 727-2L5 | Libyan Arab Airlines |
| | 5A-DIH | Boeing 727-2L5 | Libyan Arab Airlines |
| | 5A-DII | Boeing 727-2L5 | Libyan Arab Airlines |
| | 5A-DIX | Boeing 707-348C | Libyan Arab Airlines |
| | 5A-DIY | Boeing 707-348C | Libyan Arab Airlines |
| | 5A-DJM | Boeing 707-321B | Libyan Arab Airlines |
| | 5A-DJU | Boeing 707-351C | Libyan Arab Airlines |

**Note:** Services to the UK suspended.

# 5B (Cyprus)

| | | | |
|---|---|---|---|
| | 5B-DAG | BAC One Eleven 537GF | Cyprus Airways |
| | 5B-DAH | BAC One Eleven 537GF | Cyprus Airways |
| | 5B-DAJ | BAC One Eleven 537GF | Cyprus Airways |
| | 5B-DAQ | Airbus A.310-203 | Cyprus Airways |
| | 5B-DAR | Airbus A.310-203 | Cyprus Airways |
| | 5B-DAS | Airbus A.310-203 | Cyprus Airways |
| | 5B-DAT | Airbus A.320-231 | Cyprus Airways |
| | 5B-DAU | Airbus A.320-231 | Cyprus Airways |
| | 5B-DAV | Airbus A.320-231 | Cyprus Airways |
| | 5B-DAW | Airbus A.320-231 | Cyprus Airways |
| | 5B-DAX | Airbus A.310-204 | Cyprus Airways |
| | 5B-DAY | Boeing 707-338C | Avistar |
| | 5B- | Airbus A.320-231 | Cyprus Airways |
| | 5B- | Airbus A.320-231 | Cyprus Airways |
| | 5B- | Airbus A.320-231 | Cyprus Airways |
| | 5B- | Airbus A.320-231 | Cyprus Airways |

# 5N (Nigeria)

| | | | |
|---|---|---|---|
| | 5N-ABK | Boeing 707-3F9C | Nigeria Airways |
| | 5N-ANN | Douglas DC-10-30 | Nigeria Airways *Yunkari* |
| | 5N-ANO | Boeing 707-3F9C | Nigeria Airways |
| | 5N-AOK | BAC One-Eleven 320AZ | Okada Air |
| | 5N-AOM | BAC One-Eleven 420EL | Okada Air |
| | 5N-AOP | BAC One-Eleven 320AZ | Okada Air |
| | 5N-AOQ | Boeing 707-355C | Okada Air |
| | 5N-AOS | BAC One-Eleven 420EL | Okada Air |
| | 5N-AOT | BAC One-Eleven 320AZ | Okada Air |
| | 5N-AOW | BAC One-Eleven 402AP | Okada Air |
| | 5N-AOZ | BAC One-Eleven 320AZ | Okada Air |
| | 5N-ARQ | Boeing 707-338C | DAS Air Cargo |
| | 5N-ASY | Boeing 707-351C | EAS Cargo |
| | 5N- | Boeing 707-351C | EAS Cargo |
| | 5N-ATY | Douglas DC-8-55F | Flash Airlines |
| | 5N-ATZ | Douglas DC-8-55F | Flash Airlines |
| | 5N-AUE | Airbus A.310-222 | Nigeria Airways *River Yobe* |
| | 5N-AUF | Airbus A.310-222 | Nigeria Airways |
| | 5N-AUH | Airbus A.310-222 | Nigeria Airways *Rima River* |
| | 5N-AVO | S.E.210 Caravelle III | Inter Continental Airlines |
| | 5N-AVP | S.E.210 Caravelle III | Inter Continental Airlines |
| | 5N-AVQ | S.E.210 Caravelle III | Inter Continental Airlines |
| | 5N-AVX | BAC One-Eleven 424EU | G.A.S. Air |
| | 5N-AWE | Douglas DC-8-55F | Kabo Air |
| | 5N-AWO | Boeing 707-321C | G.A.S. Air |
| | 5N-AXQ | BAC One-Eleven 432FD | Okada Air |
| | 5N-AXT | BAC One-Eleven 432FD | Okada Air |
| | 5N-AYR | BAC One-Eleven 409AY | Okada Air |
| | 5N-AYS | BAC One-Eleven 416EK | Okada Air |
| | 5N-AYT | BAC One-Eleven 416EK | Okada Air |
| | 5N-AYU | BAC One-Eleven 401AK | Okada Air |
| | 5N-AYV | BAC One-Eleven 408EF | Okada Air |
| | 5N-AYW | BAC One-Eleven 416EK | Okada Air |

**Note:** Nigeria Airways operates a DC-10-30 which retains its US identity N3024W (5N-AUI reserved)

# 5R (Madagascar)

| Reg. | Type | Owner or Operator | Notes |
|------|------|-------------------|-------|
| 5R-MFT | Boeing 747-2B2B (SCD) | Air Madagascar *Tolom Piavotana* | |

# 5X (Uganda)

| | | | |
|------|------|-------------------|-------|
| 5X-DAR | Boeing 707-321C | DAS Air Cargo | |
| 5X-JEF | Boeing 707-379C | DAS Air Cargo *John Joe* | |
| 5X-UCF | L-100-30 Hercules | Uganda Air Cargo *The Silver Lady* | |
| 5X-UCM | Boeing 707-324C | Uganda Air Cargo | |

# 5Y (Kenya)

| | | | |
|------|------|-------------------|-------|
| 5Y-AXG | Boeing 707-321C | African Express Airways | |
| 5Y-AXK | Boeing 707-320C | African Express Airways | |
| 5Y-BBI | Boeing 707-351B | Kenya Airways | |
| 5Y-BBJ | Boeing 707-351B | Kenya Airways | |
| 5Y-BBX | Boeing 720-047B | Kenya Airways | |
| 5Y-BEL | Airbus A.310-304 | Kenya Airways *Nyayo Star* | |
| 5Y-BEN | Airbus A.310-304 | Kenya Airways *Harambee Star* | |
| 5Y-BFT | Airbus A310-304 | Kenya Airways *Uhuru Star* | |
| 5Y-BGI | Boeing 757-23A | Kenya Airways *Jamhuri Star* | |
| 5Y-BHF | Boeing 757-23A | Kenya Airways *Taifa Star* | |
| 5Y-BHG | Boeing 757-23A | Kenya Airways *Umoja Star* | |
| 5Y-ZEB | Douglas DC-8-63 | African Safari Airways | |

**Note:** African Safari also operates DC-8-63 which carries the registration HB-IBF. Kenya Airways operates DC-8-71 EI-BZU on lease

# 6O (Somalia)

| | | | |
|------|------|-------------------|-------|
| 6O-SBT | Boeing 707-330B | Somali Airlines | |
| 6O-SHH | Airbus A.310-304 | Somali Airlines | |

**Note:** The A.310 may retain its French identity F-ODSV

# 6Y (Jamaica)

**Note:** Air Jamaica operates its UK services jointly with British Airways.

# 7T (Algeria)

| | | | |
|------|------|-------------------|-------|
| 7T-VEA | Boeing 727-2D6 | Air Algerie *Tassili* | |
| 7T-VEB | Boeing 727-2D6 | Air Algerie *Hoggar* | |
| 7T-VED | Boeing 737-2D6C | Air Algerie *Atlas Saharien* | |
| 7T-VEE | Boeing 737-2D6C | Air Algerie *Oasis* | |
| 7T-VEF | Boeing 737-2D6 | Air Algerie *Saoura* | |
| 7T-VEG | Boeing 737-2D6 | Air Algerie *Monts des Ouleds Neils* | |
| 7T-VEH | Boeing 727-2D6 | Air Algerie *Lalla Khadidja* | |
| 7T-VEI | Boeing 727-2D6 | Air Algerie *Djebel Amour* | |
| 7T-VEJ | Boeing 737-2D6 | Air Algerie *Chrea* | |
| 7T-VEK | Boeing 737-2D6 | Air Algerie *Edough* | |
| 7T-VEL | Boeing 737-2D6 | Air Algerie *Akfadou* | |
| 7T-VEM | Boeing 727-2D6 | Air Algerie *Mont du Ksall* | |
| 7T-VEN | Boeing 737-2D6 | Air Algerie *La Soummam* | |
| 7T-VEO | Boeing 737-2D6 | Air Algerie *La Titteri* | |
| 7T-VEP | Boeing 737-2D6 | Air Algerie *Mont du Tessala* | |
| 7T-VEQ | Boeing 737-2D6 | Air Algerie *Le Zaccar* | |
| 7T-VER | Boeing 737-2D6 | Air Algerie *Le Souf* | |
| 7T-VES | Boeing 737-2D6C | Air Algerie *Le Tadmaït* | |
| 7T-VET | Boeing 727-2D6 | Air Algerie *Georges du Rhumel* | |
| 7T-VEU | Boeing 727-2D6 | Air Algerie *Djurdjura* | |

| Notes | Reg. | Type | Owner or Operator |
|-------|------|------|-------------------|
| | 7T-VEV | Boeing 727-2D6 | Air Algerie |
| | 7T-VEW | Boeing 727-2D6 | Air Algerie |
| | 7T-VEX | Boeing 727-2D6 | Air Algerie *Djemila* |
| | 7T-VEY | Boeing 737-2D6 | Air Algerie *Rhoufi* |
| | 7T-VEZ | Boeing 737-2T4 | Air Algerie *Monts du Daia* |
| | 7T-VJA | Boeing 737-2T4 | Air Algerie *Monts des Babors* |
| | 7T-VJB | Boeing 737-2T4 | Air Algerie *Monts des Bibons* |
| | 7T-VJC | Airbus A.310-203 | Air Algerie |
| | 7T-VJD | Airbus A.310-203 | Air Algerie |
| | 7T-VJE | Airbus A.310-203 | Air Algerie |
| | 7T-VJF | Airbus A.310-203 | Air Algerie |
| | 7T-VJG | Boeing 767-3D6 | Air Algerie |
| | 7T-VJH | Boeing 767-3D6 | Air Algerie |
| | 7T-VJI | Boeing 767-3D6 | Air Algerie |

# 9G (Ghana)

| | | | |
|---|---|---|---|
| | 9G-ANA | Douglas DC-10-30 | Ghana Airways |
| | 9G-RCA | Boeing 707-351C | Rainbow Cargo Airlines |

**Note:** Phoenix Aviation operate a Boeing 707 registered SX-DBO.

# 9H (Malta)

| | | | |
|---|---|---|---|
| | 9H-ABA | Boeing 737-2Y5 | Air Malta *Manuel de Vilhena* |
| | 9H-ABB | Boeing 737-2Y5 | Air Malta *Phillipe Villiers de L'isle Adam* |
| | 9H-ABC | Boeing 737-2Y5 | Air Malta *Claude de la Sengle* |
| | 9H-ABE | Boeing 737-2Y5 | Air Malta *Alof de Wignacourt* |
| | 9H-ABF | Boeing 737-2Y5 | Air Malta *Manuel Pinto* |
| | 9H-ABG | Boeing 737-2Y5 | Air Malta *Jean de Lavalette* |
| | 9H-ABP | Airbus A.320-211 | Air Malta *Nicholas de Cottoner* |

**Note:** Air Malta also operates other aircraft on lease during the summer.

# 9J (Zambia)

| | | | |
|---|---|---|---|
| | 9J-AFL | Douglas DC-8-71 | Zambia Airways |
| | 9J-AFN | Douglas DC-10-30 | Zambia Airways |
| | 9J-AFO | Boeing 757-23APF | Zambia Airways |

**Note:** Zambia Airways operates DC-10-30 N3016Z *Nkwazi* on lease.

# 9K (Kuwait)

| Reg. | Type | Owner or Operator | Notes |
|------|------|-------------------|-------|
| 9K-ADA | Boeing 747-269B (SCD) | Kuwait Airways *Al Sabahiya* | |
| 9K-ADB | Boeing 747-269B (SCD) | Kuwait Airways *Al Jaberiya* | |
| 9K-ADC | Boeing 747-269B (SCD) | Kuwait Airways *Al Murbarakiya* | |
| 9K-ADD | Boeing 747-269B (SCD) | Kuwait Airways *Al Salmiya* | |
| 9K-AHA | Airbus A.310-222 | Kuwait Airways *Al-Jahra* | |
| 9K-AHB | Airbus A.310-222 | Kuwait Airways *Gharnada* | |
| 9K-AHC | Airbus A.310-222 | Kuwait Airways *Kadhma* | |
| 9K-AHD | Airbus A.310-222 | Kuwait Airways *Failaka* | |
| 9K-AHE | Airbus A.310-222 | Kuwait Airways *Burghan* | |
| 9K-AHF | Airbus A.300-620C | Kuwait Airways *Wafra* | |
| 9K-AHG | Airbus A.300-620C | Kuwait Airways *Wara* | |
| 9K-AHI | Airbus A.300-620C | Kuwait Airways *Ali-Rawdhatain* | |
| 9K-AIA | Boeing 767-269ER | Kuwait Airways *Alriggah* | |
| 9K-AIB | Boeing 767-269ER | Kuwait Airways *Algrain* | |
| 9K-AIC | Boeing 767-269ER | Kuwait Airways *Garouh* | |

**Note:** Many of Kuwait's fleet were seized by Iraq in August 1990.

# 9M (Malaysia)

| Reg. | Type | Owner or Operator | Notes |
|------|------|-------------------|-------|
| 9M-MHI | Boeing 747-236B | Malaysian Airline System | |
| 9M-MHJ | Boeing 747-236B | Malaysian Airline System | |
| 9M-MHK | Boeing 747-3H6 (SCD) | Malaysian Airline System | |
| 9M-MHL | Boeing 747-4H6 (SCD) | Malaysian Airline System | |
| 9M-MHM | Boeing 747-4H6 (SCD) | Malaysian Airline System | |
| 9M-MHN | Boeing 747-4H6 (SCD) | Malaysian Airline System | |
| 9M-M | Boeing 747-4H6 | Malaysian Airline System | |

# 9N (Nepal)

| | | | |
|------|------|-------------------|-------|
| 9N-ACA | Boeing 757-2F8 | Royal Nepal Airlines | |
| 9N-ACB | Boeing 757-2F8C | Royal Nepal Airlines | |

# 9Q (Zaïre)

| | | | |
|------|------|-------------------|-------|
| 9Q-CBW | Boeing 707-329C | Scibe Airlift Zaire | |
| 9Q-CGO | Boeing 707-321C | Air Charter Service | |
| 9Q-CLG | Douglas DC-8-63CF | Air Zaire *Domaine de la Nsélé* | |
| 9Q-CLI | Douglas DC-10-30 | Air Zaire *Mont Ngaliema* | |
| 9Q-CMD | Boeing 707-441 | BCF Aviation *Munia Matapa* | |
| 9Q-CSB | Boeing 707-373C | Sicotra Aviation | |
| 9Q-CTK | Boeing 707-436 | Air Charter Service | |
| 9Q-CVG | Boeing 707-329C | Katale Aero Transport *Sebutana* | |
| 9Q-CVH | Douglas DC-8-55F | Katale Aero Transport | |

# 9V (Singapore)

| | | | |
|------|------|-------------------|-------|
| 9V-SKA | Boeing 747-312 | Singapore Airlines | |
| 9V-SKM | Boeing 747-312 (SCD) | Singapore Airlines | |
| 9V-SKN | Boeing 747-312 (SCD) | Singapore Airlines | |
| 9V-SKP | Boeing 747-312 (SCD) | Singapore Airlines | |
| 9V-SKQ | Boeing 747-212F (SCD) | Singapore Airlines | |
| 9V-SMA | Boeing 747-412 | Singapore Airlines | |
| 9V-SMB | Boeing 747-412 | Singapore Airlines | |
| 9V-SMC | Boeing 747-412 | Singapore Airlines | |
| 9V-SMD | Boeing 747-412 | Singapore Airlines | |
| 9V-SME | Boeing 747-412 | Singapore Airlines | |
| 9V-SMF | Boeing 747-412 | Singapore Airlines | |
| 9V-SMG | Boeing 747-412 | Singapore Airlines | |
| 9V-SMH | Boeing 747-412 | Singapore Airlines | |
| 9V-SMJ | Boeing 747-412 | Singapore Airlines | |
| 9V-SMK | Boeing 747-412 | Singapore Airlines | |
| 9V-SML | Boeing 747-412 | Singapore Airlines | |
| 9V-SMM | Boeing 747-412 | Singapore Airlines | |
| 9V-SMN | Boeing 747-412 | Singapore Airlines | |
| 9V-SQO | Boeing 747-212B | Singapore Airlines | |
| 9V-SQP | Boeing 747-212B | Singapore Airlines | |
| 9V-SQQ | Boeing 747-212B | Singapore Airlines | |
| 9V-SQR | Boeing 747-212B | Singapore Airlines | |
| 9V-SQS | Boeing 747-212B | Singapore Airlines | |

**Note:** Singapore Airlines also operates Boeing 747-312 N116KB, N117KC, N118KD, N119KE, N120KF, N121KG, N122KH, N123KJ, N124KK and N125KL.

# 9XR (Rwanda)

| | | | |
|------|------|-------------------|-------|
| 9XR-JA | Boeing 707-328C | Air Rwanda | |

# 9Y (Trinidad and Tobago)

| Notes | Reg. | Type | Owner or Operator |
|---|---|---|---|
| | 9Y-TGJ | L.1011 TriStar 500 | B.W.I.A. *Flamingo* |
| | 9Y-TGN | L.1011 TriStar 500 | B.W.I.A. |
| | 9Y-THA | L.1011 TriStar 500 (597) | B.W.I.A. |

**Note:** B.W.I.A. also operates a TriStar 500 which retains its US registration N3140D.

# Overseas Registrations

Aircraft included in this section are those based in the UK but which retain their non-British identities.

| Reg | Type | Owner or Operator | Notes |
|-----|------|-------------------|-------|
| A40-AB | V.1103 VC10 ★ | Brooklands Museum (G-ASIX) | |
| CF-EQS | Boeing-Stearman PT-17 ★ | Imperial War Museum/Duxford | |
| CF-KCG | Grumman TBM-3E Avenger AS.3 ★ | Imperial War Museum/Duxford | |
| CS-ACQ | Fleet 80 Canuck ★ | Visionair Ltd (stored)/Coventry | |
| D-HMQV | Bolkow Bo 102 ★ | International Helicopter Museum/ Weston-s-Mare | |
| D-IFSB | D.H.104 Dove 6★ | Mosquito Aircraft Museum | |
| F-BDRS | Boeing B-17G (231965) ★ | Imperial War Museum/Duxford | |
| F-BMCY | Potez 840* | Sumburgh Fire Service | |
| N1MF | Cessna 421B | Pelmont Aviation Inc/Cranfield | |
| N2FU | Learjet 35A | Motor Racing Developments Inc | |
| N14KH | Christen Eagle II | R. Frohmayer | |
| N15AW | Cessna 500 Citation | A. W. Alloys Ltd | |
| N15SC | Learjet 35A | Sea Containers Associates/Luton | |
| N18E | Boeing 247D ★ | Science Museum/Wroughton | |
| N18V | Beech D.17S Traveler (PB1) | R. Lamplough | |
| N33VC | Lockheed T-33A (54-21261) | Old Flying Machine Co/Duxford | |
| N47DD | Republic P-47D Thunderbolt (45-49192)★ | Imperial War Museum/Duxford | |
| N49UR | Canadair CL.601 Challenger | Kingson Corporation | |
| N51JJ | P-51 Mustang (463221) | B. J. S. Grey/Duxford | |
| N55JP | FG-1D Corsair (88439) | D. W. Arnold/Biggin Hill | |
| N59NA | Douglas C-47A | Aces High Ltd (G-AKNB)/North Weald | |
| N71AF | R. Commander 680W | Metropolitan Aviation | |
| N152JS | Fokker DR.1 (replica) | A. E. Hutton/North Weald | |
| N153JS | Nieuport 24 (replica) | A. E. Hutton/North Weald | |
| N154JS | Airco D.H.5 (replica) | A. E. Hutton/North Weald | |
| N158C | S.24 Sandringham (VH-BRC) ★ | Southampton Hall of Aviation | |
| N167F | P-51D Mustang (473877) | RLS 51 Ltd/Duxford | |
| N179P | Vought F4U-7 Corsair | D. W. Arnold/Biggin Hill | |
| N230ET | PA-30 Twin Comanche 160 | P. Bayliss (G-ATET) | |
| N232J | Hawker Sea Fury FB.11 | R. Lamplough/North Weald | |
| N240CA | F-4U-4B Corsair (NZ5628) | R. Hanna/Duxford | |
| N260QB | Pitts S-2S Special | D. Baker | |
| N416FS | F-100F Super Sabre | Flight Refuelling Ltd/Bournemouth | |
| N417FS | F-100F Super Sabre | Flight Refuelling Ltd/Bournemouth | |
| N418FS | F-100F Super Sabre | Flight Refuelling Ltd/Bournemouth | |
| N425EE | Cessna 425 | J. W. MacDonald | |
| N444M | Grumman G.44 Widgeon (1411) | M. Dunkerley/Biggin Hill | |
| N490CC | Cessna 551 Citation II | A. W. Alloys Ltd | |
| N500LN | Howard 500 | D. Baker | |
| N505MH | P-38L Lightning | D. W. Arnold/Biggin Hill | |
| N535SM | R. Commander 680 | J. E. Tuberty | |
| N750M | Grumman G.44 Widgeon★ | L. E. Usher | |
| N804CC | G.159 Gulfstream 1 | American Trans Air/Gatwick | |
| N900FR | Dassault Falcon 20DC | Flight Refuelling Ltd/Bournemouth | |
| N900MD | Learjet 36A | MMFI/Gatwick | |
| N901FR | Dassault Falcon 20DC | Flight Refuelling Ltd/Bournemouth | |
| N902FR | Dassault Falcon 20DC | Flight Refuelling Ltd/Bournemouth | |
| N903FR | Dassault Falcon 20DC | Flight Refuelling Ltd/Bournemouth | |
| N904FR | Dassault Falcon 20DC | Flight Refuelling Ltd/Bournemouth | |
| N905FR | Dassault Falcon 20DC | Flight Refuelling Ltd/Bournemouth | |
| N906FR | Dassault Falcon 20DC | Flight Refuelling Ltd/Bournemouth | |
| N907FR | Dassault Falcon 20DC | Flight Refuelling Ltd/Bournemouth | |
| N908FR | Dassault Falcon 20DC | Flight Refuelling Ltd/Bournemouth | |
| N909FR | Dassault Falcon 20DC | Flight Refuelling Ltd/Bournemouth | |
| N999PJ | M.S.760 Paris 2 | Aces High Ltd/North Weald | |
| N1042B | B-25J Mitchell (430823) | Aces High Ltd/North Weald | |
| N1344 | Ryan PT-22 | H. Mitchell | |
| N1447Q | Cessna 150L | US Embassy Flying Club | |
| N1755C | Cessna 180 | Alconbury Aero Club | |
| N2700 | Fairchild C-119G | Aces High Ltd (G-BLSW)/North Weald | |
| N2929N | PA-28-151 Warrior | R. Lobell | |
| N3600X | Dassault Falcon 10 | Xerox Corporation/Heathrow | |
| N3851Q | Cessna 172K | Bentwaters Aero Club/Woodbridge | |
| N3966A | TBM-3E Avenger (53319) | A. Haig-Thomas/North Weald | |
| N3983N | Agusta A.109A | NSM Aviation | |

| Notes | Reg. | Type | Owner or Operator |
|---|---|---|---|
| | N4306Z | PA-28 Cherokee 140 | USAF Aero Club/Upper Heyford |
| | N4565L | Douglas DC.3 | Hibernian Dakota Flight Ltd/Ipswich |
| | N4712V | Boeing Stearman PT-13D | Wessex Aviation & Transport Ltd |
| | N4727V | Spad S.VII (S4523) | Imperial War Museum/Duxford |
| | N4806E | Douglas A-26C Invader ★ | R. & R. Cadman/Southend |
| | N5063N | Beech D.18S (HB275) | Harvard Formation Team (G-BKGM) |
| | N5237V | Boeing B-17G (483868) ★ | RAF Bomber Command Museum/Hendon |
| | N5246 | Nieuport 28 | A. Graham-Enock |
| | N5824H | PA-38 Tomahawk | Lakenheath Aero Club |
| | N6178C | F7F-3 Tigercat | Planesailing Air Displays/Duxford |
| | N6268 | Travel Air Model 2000 | Personal Plane Services Ltd |
| | N6526D | P-51D Mustang ★ | RAF Museum/Henlow |
| | N6827C | TBM-3E Avenger (X-2) | R. Hanna/Duxford |
| | N7614C | B-25J Mitchell | Imperial War Museum/Duxford |
| | N7777G | L.749A Constellation ★ | Science Museum (G-CONI)/Wroughton |
| | N8155E | Mooney M.20A | D. Skans |
| | N8297 | FG-1D Corsair (88297) | The Fighter Collection/Duxford |
| | N9012P | C.A.S.A. 352L (1Z+EK) | Junkers Ju.52/3M Flight |
| | N9089Z | TB-25J Mitchell (44-30861)★ | Aces High Ltd (G-BKXW)/North Weald |
| | N9115Z | TB-25N Mitchell (429366) ★ | RAF Bomber Command Museum/ Hendon |
| | N9494Z | TB-25N Mitchell (44-30925) | Visionair Ltd |
| | N9606H | Fairchild M.62A Cornell ★ | Rebel Air Museum/Earls Colne |
| | N9950 | P-40N Kittyhawk | D. W. Arnold/Biggin Hill |
| | N15798 | CCF Harvard IV(Zero) | Old Flying Machine Co/Duxford |
| | N26178 | Cessna 550 Citation II | A. W. Alloys Ltd |
| | N26634 | PA-24 Comanche 250 | P. Biggs (G-BFKR) |
| | N30228 | Piper J-3C-65 Cub | C. Morris |
| | N33600 | Cessna L-19A Bird Dog (111989) ★ | Museum of Army Flying/ Middle Wallop |
| | N43069 | PA-28-161 Warrior II | Lakenheath Aero Club |
| | N43401 | PA-28-161 Warrior II | Cabair/Elstree |
| | N49272 | Ryan PT-23 (23) | H. Mitchell |
| | N50993 | Ryan PT-22 | V. S. E. Norman |
| | N52113 | Bell P-63C Kingcobra | D. W. Arnold/Biggin Hill |
| | N54558 | Cessna F.152 | J. J. Baumhardt |
| | N54922 | Boeing Stearman N25-4 | Yugo Cars |
| | N56028 | Ryan PT-22 | V. S. E. Norman |
| | N56421 | Ryan PT-22 (855) | PT Flight/Cosford |
| | N58566 | BT-13 Valiant | PT Flight/Cosford |
| | N70290 | B.121 Pup | Lakenheath Aero Club |
| | N88972 | B-25D-30-ND Mitchell (KL161) | Fighter Collection/Duxford |
| | N90005 | G.1159A Gulfstream 3 | Siebe PLC |
| | N91342 | PA-38-112 Tomahawk | Lakenheath Aero Club |
| | N91437 | PA-38-112 Tomahawk | Lakenheath Aero Club |
| | N91457 | PA-38-112 Tomahawk | Lakenheath Aero Club |
| | N91590 | PA-38-112 Tomahawk | Lakenheath Aero Club |
| | N91764 | Cessna 152 II (tailwheel) | Wessex Aviation & Transport Ltd |
| | N96240 | Beech D.18S | J. Hawke (G-AYAH) |
| | N99153 | T-28C Trojan ★ | Norfolk & Suffolk Aviation Museum/ Flixton |
| | N99225 | Dornier Do.24T-3 (HD.5-1) ★ | RAF Museum/Hendon |
| | NC88ZK | Boeing-Stearman PT-17 | R. Hanna/Duxford |
| | NC5171N | Lockheed 10A Electra ★ | Science Museum (G-LIOA)/Wroughton |
| | NC15214 | Waco UKC-S | P. H. McConnell/White Waltham |
| | NC16403 | Cessna C.34 Airmaster | Kennet Aircraft Ltd (G-BSEB) |
| | NL314BG | P-51D Mustang (414151) | D. W. Arnold/Biggin Hill |
| | NL1009N | P-40N Kittyhawk (FR870) | B. J. S. Grey/Duxford |
| | NL1051S | P-51D-25-NA Mustang (511371) | Myrick Aviation/Southend |
| | NL9494Z | TB-25N Mitchell (151632) | Visionair Ltd |
| | NX11SN | Yakolev C-11 | Old Flying Machine Co/Duxford |
| | NX47DD | Republic P-47D Thunderbolt (226671) | The Fighter Collection/Duxford |
| | NX100TF | F6F-5K Hellcat | The Fighter Collection/Duxford |
| | NX700HL | F8F-2B Bearcat (121714) | B. J. S. Grey/Duxford |
| | NX1337A | F4U-7 Corsair (133722) | L. M. Walton/Duxford |
| | NX49092 | F4U-4 Corsair | D. W. Arnold/Biggin Hill |
| | VH-BRC | See N158C | |
| | VH-SNB | D.H.84 Dragon ★ | Museum of Flight/E. Fortune |
| | VH-UTH | GAL Monospar ST-12 ★ | Newark Air Museum (stored) |
| | VR-BEP | WS.55 Whirlwind 3 ★ | East Midlands Aeropark (G-BAMH) |
| | VR-BET | WS.55 Whirlwind 3 ★ | International Helicopter Museum (G-ANJV)/ Weston-s-Mare |

| Reg. | Type | Owner or Operator | Notes |
|------|------|-------------------|-------|
| VR-BEU | WS.55 Whirlwind 3 ★ | International Helicopter Museum (G-ATKV)/ Weston-s-Mare | |
| VR-BHN | Boeing 727-30 | Jade Air Leasing | |
| VR-BJI | Lockheed Jetstar | Denis Vanguard International Ltd | |
| VR-CBE | Boeing 727-46 | Resebury Corporation | |
| VR-CBI | BAC One-Eleven 401 | Bryan Aviation Ltd | |
| 5N-ABW | Westland Widgeon 2 ★ | International Helicopter Museum (G-AOZE)/Weston-s-Mare | |

# Radio Frequencies

The frequencies used by the larger airfields/airports are listed below. Abbreviations used: TWR — Tower, APP — Approach, A/G — Air-ground advisory. It is possible for changes to be made from time to time with the frequencies allocated which are all quoted in Megahertz (MHz).

| Airfield | TWR | APP | A/G |
|---|---|---|---|
| Aberdeen | 118.1 | 120.4 | |
| Aldergrove | 118.3 | 120.0 | |
| Alderney | 125.35 | | |
| Andrewsfield | | | 130.55 |
| Barton | | | 122.7 |
| Barrow | | | 123.2 |
| Belfast City | 130.75 | 130.85 | |
| Bembridge | | | 123.25 |
| Biggin Hill | 134.8 | 129.4 | |
| Birmingham | 118.3 | 120.5 | |
| Blackbushe | | | 122.3 |
| Blackpool | 118.4 | 135.95 | |
| Bodmin | | | 122.7 |
| Booker | | | 126.55 |
| Bourn | | | 129.8 |
| Bournemouth | 125.6 | 119.75 | |
| Bristol | 133.85 | 132.4 | |
| Cambridge | 122.2 | 123.6 | |
| Cardiff | 121.2 | 125.85 | |
| Carlisle | | | 123.6 |
| Compton Abbas | | | 122.7 |
| Conington | | | 123.0 |
| Coventry | 119.25 | 119.25 | |
| Cranfield | 123.2 | 122.85 | |
| Denham | | | 130.72 |
| Doncaster | | | 122.9 |
| Dundee | 122.9 | 122.9 | |
| Dunkeswell | | | 123.47 |
| Dunsfold | 124.32 | 122.55 | |
| Duxford | | | 123.5 |
| East Midlands | 124.0 | 119.65 | |
| Edinburgh | 118.7 | 121.2 | |
| Elstree | | | 122.4 |
| Exeter | 119.8 | 128.15 | |
| Fairoaks | | | 123.42 |
| Felthorpe | | | 123.5 |
| Fenland | | | 122.925 |
| Filton | 124.95 | 122.725 | |
| Gamston | | | 130.47 |
| Gatwick | 124.22 | 128.57 | |
| Glasgow | 118.8 | 119.1 | |
| Goodwood | 120.65 | 122.45 | |
| Guernsey | 119.95 | 128.65 | |
| Halfpenny Green | | | 123.0 |
| Hatfield | 130.8 | 123.35 | |
| Haverfordwest | | | 122.2 |
| Hawarden | 124.95 | 123.35 | |
| Hayes Heliport | | | 123.65 |
| Headcorn | | | 122.0 |
| Heathrow | 118.7 | 119.2 | |
| | 118.5 | 119.5 | |
| Hethel | | | 122.35 |
| Hucknall | | | 130.8 |
| Humberside | 118.55 | 123.15 | |
| Ingoldmells | | | 130.45 |

| Airfield | TWR | APP | A/G |
|---|---|---|---|
| Inverness | 122.6 | 122.6 | |
| Ipswich | 118.32 | | |
| Jersey | 119.45 | 120.3 | |
| Kidlington | 118.875 | 130.3 | |
| Land's End | 130.7 | | |
| Leavesden | 122.15 | 122.15 | |
| Leeds | 120.3 | 123.75 | |
| Leicester | | | 122.25 |
| Liverpool | 118.1 | 119.85 | |
| London City | 118.07 | 128.05 | |
| Long Marston | | | 130.1 |
| Luton | 120.2 | 128.75 | |
| Lydd | 120.7 | 120.7 | |
| Manchester | 118.625 | 119.4 | |
| Manston | 128.775 | 126.35 | |
| Netherthorpe | | | 123.5 |
| Newcastle | 119.7 | 126.35 | |
| North Denes | | | 120.45 |
| Norwich | 118.9 | 119.35 | |
| Panshanger | | | 120.25 |
| Perth | 119.8 | 122.3 | |
| Plymouth | 122.6 | 133.55 | |
| Popham | | | 129.8 |
| Prestwick | 118.15 | 120.55 | |
| Redhill | | | 123.22 |
| Rochester | | | 122.25 |
| Ronaldsway | 118.9 | 120.85 | |
| Sandown | | | 123.5 |
| Seething | | | 122.6 |
| Sherburn | | | 122.6 |
| Shipdham | | | 123.05 |
| Shobdon | | | 123.5 |
| Shoreham | 125.4 | 123.15 | |
| Sibson | | | 122.3 |
| Sleap | | | 122.45 |
| Southampton | 118.2 | 128.85 | |
| Southend | 127.725 | 128.95 | |
| Stansted | 118.15 | 125.55 | |
| Stapleford | | | 122.8 |
| Staverton | 125.65 | 125.65 | |
| Sumburgh | 118.25 | 123.15 | |
| Swansea | 119.7 | 119.7 | |
| Swanton Morley | | | 123.5 |
| Sywell | | | 122.7 |
| Teesside | 119.8 | 118.85 | |
| Thruxton | | | 130.45 |
| Tollerton | | | 122.8 |
| Wellesbourne | | | 130.45 |
| West Malling | 130.875 | | 130.42 |
| White Waltham | | | 122.6 |
| Wick | 119.7 | | |
| Wickenby | | | 122.45 |
| Woodford | 126.92 | 130.05 | |
| Yeovil | 125.4 | 130.8 | |

Three-letter flight codes are now in general use. Those listed below identify both UK and overseas carriers appearing in the book.

| Code | Airline | | Code | Airline | | Code | Airline | |
|------|---------|--|------|---------|--|------|---------|--|
| AAF | Aigle Azur | F | CPX | Cathay Pacific | VR-H | LCN | Lin. Ae. Canarias | EC |
| AAG | Air Atlantique | G | CRL | Corse Air | F | LDA | Lauda Air | OE |
| AAL | American A/L | N | CRX | Crossair | HB | LGL | Luxair | LX |
| AAN | Oasis | EC | CSA | Czech A/L | OK | LIB | Air Liberte | F |
| AAW | Aberdeen A/W | G | CTA | CTA | HB | LIN | Linjeflyg | SE |
| ABB | Air Belgium | OO | CYP | Cyprus A/W | 5B | LIR | Lionair | LX |
| ABR | Air Bridge | G | DAH | Air Algerie | 7T | LIT | Air Littoral | F |
| ACA | Air Canada | C | DAL | Delta A/L | N | LKA | Alkair | OY |
| ACF | Air Charter Intl | F | DAN | Dan-Air | G | LOG | Loganair | G |
| ACY | Air City | HB | DAT | Delta Air Transport | OO | LON | Ryanair Europe | G |
| ADR | Adria A/W | YU | DLH | Lufthansa | D | LOT | Polish A/L (LOT) | SP |
| AEA | Air Europa | EC | DLT | DLT | D | LTE | LTE | EC |
| AEE | Air Europe Express | G | DMA | Maersk Air | OY | LTS | LTU Sud | D |
| AEF | Aero Lloyd | D | DQI | Cimber Air | OY | LTU | LTU | D |
| AFL | Aeroflot | CCCP | EAF | Emery Worldwide | N | MAH | Malev | HA |
| AFM | Affretair | Z | EGY | Egypt Air | SU | MAS | Malaysian A/L | 9M |
| AFR | Air France | F | EIA | Evergreen Intl | N | MAU | Air Mauritius | 3B |
| AGX | Aviogenex | YU | EIN | Aer Lingus | EI | MEA | Middle East A/L | OD |
| AHD | Air Holland | PH | ELY | El Al | 4X | MIN | Minerve | F |
| AHK | Air Hong Kong | VR-H | ENJ | Nortjet | EC | MNX | Manx A/L | G |
| AIA | Air Atlantis | CS | ETH | Ethiopian A/L | ET | MON | Monarch A/L | G |
| AIC | Air-India | VT | EUI | Euralair | F | MOR | Morefly | LN |
| ALK | Air Lanka | 4R | EXS | Channel Express | G | MPH | Martinair | PH |
| AMC | Air Malta | 9H | EXX | Air Exel UK | F | MSO | Somali A/L | 6O |
| AMM | Air 2000 | G | EYT | Europe Aero Service | F | NAD | Nobleair | TC |
| AMT | American Trans Air | N | FDE | Federal Express | N | NCR | Air Sur | EC |
| ANA | All Nippon A/W | JA | FGT | Fairflight | G | NEX | Northern Executive | G |
| ANC | Anglo Cargo | G | FIN | Finnair | OH | NFD | NFD | D |
| ANZ | Air New Zealand | ZK | FOB | Ford | G | NGA | Nigeria A/W | 5N |
| AOE | A/L of Europe | G | FOF | Fred Olsen | LN | NSA | Nile Safaris | ST |
| APW | Arrow Air | N | FXY | Flexair | PH | NWA | Northwest A/L | N |
| ATI | ATI | I | GBL | GB Airways | G | NXA | Nationair | C |
| ATT | Aer Turas | EI | GEC | German Cargo | D | OAL | Olympic A/L | SX |
| AUA | Austrian A/L | OE | GFA | Gulf Air | A40 | OYC | Conair | OY |
| AUR | Aurigny A/S | G | GFG | Germania | D | PAA | Pan Am | N |
| AVA | Avianca | HK | GHA | Ghana A/W | 9G | PAL | Philippine A/L | RP |
| AVD | Air Vendee | F | GIA | Garuda | PK | PGA | Portugalia | CS |
| AYC | Aviaco | EC | GIL | Gill Air | G | PGT | Pegasus | TC |
| AZA | Alitalia | I | GMP | Transwede | SE | PIA | Pakistan Intl | AP |
| AZI | Air Zimbabwe | Z | GNT | Business Air | G | PRN | Princess Air | G |
| AZR | Air Zaïre | 9Q | GRN | Greenair | TC | QFA | Qantas | VH |
| BAF | British Air Ferries | G | HAL | Hawaiian Air | N | QKL | Aeromaritime | F |
| BAL | Britannia A/L | G | HLA | HeavyLift | G | QSC | African Safaris | 5Y |
| BAW | British Airways | G | HLF | Hapag-Lloyd | D | RAM | Royal Air Maroc | CN |
| BBB | Balair | HB | IAW | Iraqi A/W | YI | RBA | Royal Brunei | V8 |
| BBC | Bangladesh Biman | S2 | IBE | Iberia | EC | RFG | RFG | D |
| BCS | European A/T | OO | ICE | Icelandair | TF | RGL | Regionair | G |
| BEA | Birmingham European | G | IEA | Inter European | G | RIA | Rich Intl | N |
| BEE | Busy Bee | LN | IFL | Interflug | D | RJA | Royal Jordanian | JY |
| BER | Air Berlin | N | IKA | Tradewinds | G | RNA | Royal Nepal A/L | 9N |
| BIC | Belgian Intl Air Cargo | OO | INS | Instone A/L | G | ROT | Tarom | YR |
| BIH | British Intl Heli | G | IRA | Iran Air | EP | RWD | Air Rwanda | 9XR |
| BKT | Caledonian | G | ISL | Eagle Air | TF | RYR | Ryanair | EI |
| BMA | British Midland | G | ISS | Alisarda | I | SAA | South African A/W | ZS |
| BRA | Braathens | LN | ITF | Air Inter | F | SAB | Sabena | OO |
| BRY | Brymon A/W | G | IYE | Yemen A/W | 4W | SAS | SAS | SE OY LN |
| BWA | BWIA | 9Y | JAL | Japan A/L | JA | SAW | Sterling A/W | OY |
| BXH | British Independent | G | JAT | JAT | YU | SAY | Suckling A/W | G |
| BZH | Brit Air | F | JEA | Jersey European A/W | G | SDI | Saudi | HZ |
| CCA | CAAC | B | KAC | Kuwait A/W | 9K | SEY | Air Seychelles | S7 |
| CDN | Canadian A/L Intl | C | KAL | Korean Air | HL | SIA | Singapore A/L | 9V |
| CFG | Condor | D | KAR | Kar-Air | OH | SJM | Southern A/T | N |
| CIC | Celtic Air | G | KIS | Contactair | D | SLA | Sierra Leone A/W | 9L |
| CLX | Cargolux | LX | KLM | KLM | PH | SLA | Sobelair | OO |
| CMM | Canada 3000 A/L | C | KQA | Kenya A/W | 5Y | SPP | Spanair | EC |
| CNB | Air Columbus | CS | LAA | Libyan Arab A/L | 5A | STR | Stellair | F |
| COA | Continental A/L | N | LAZ | Bulgarian A/W | LZ | SUD | Sudan A/W | ST |

| | | | | | | |
|---|---|---|---|---|---|---|
| SWE | Swedair | SE | TRA | Transavia | PH | |
| SWR | Swissair | HB | TSC | Air Transat | C | |
| SYR | Syrian Arab | YK | TSW | TEA Basle | HB | |
| TAP | Air Portugal | CS | TUK | TEA UK | G | |
| TAR | Tunis Air | TS | TWA | TWA | N | |
| TAT | TAT | F | TYR | Tyrolean | OE | |
| TCN | Trans Continental | N | UAE | Emirates A/L | A6 | |
| TEA | Trans European A/W | OO | UAL | United A/L | N | |
| THA | Thai A/W Intl | HS | UGA | Uganda A/L | 5X | |
| THG | Thurston | G | UKA | Air UK | G | |
| THY | Turkish A/L | TC | UKL | Air UK Leisure | G | |
| TMA | Trans Mediterranean | OD | UNA | Universair | EC | |
| TOT | Titan A/W | G | UPA | Air Foyle | G | |
| TOW | Tower Air | N | UPS | United Parcels | N | |

| | | |
|---|---|---|
| URO | Euroair | G |
| USA | USAir | N |
| UTA | UTA | F |
| UYC | Cameroon A/L | TJ |
| VIA | Viasa | YV |
| VIR | Virgin Atlantic | G |
| VIV | Viva Air | EC |
| VKG | Scanair | SE OY LN |
| VRG | Varig | PP |
| WDL | WDL | D |
| WOA | World A/W | N |
| WWC | Worldways | C |
| ZAC | Zambia A/W | 9J |
| ZAS | ZAS A/L of Egypt | SU |

# British Aircraft Preservation Council Register

The British Aircraft Preservation Council was formed in 1967 to co-ordinate the works of all bodies involved in the preservation, restoration and display of historical aircraft. Membership covers the whole spectrum of national, Service, commercial and voluntary groups, and meetings are held regularly at the bases of member organisations. The Council is able to provide a means of communication, helping to resolve any misunderstandings or duplication of effort. Every effort is taken to encourage the raising of standards of both organisation and technical capacity amongst the member groups to the benfit of everyone interested in aviation. To assist historians, the B.A.P.C. register has been set up and provides an identity for those aircraft which do not qualify for a Service serial or inclusion in the UK Civil Register.

Aircraft on the current B.A.P.C. Register are as follows:

| Reg. | Type | Owner or Operator | Notes |
|---|---|---|---|
| 6 | Roe Triplane Type IV (replica) | Greater Manchester Museum of Science & Technology | |
| 7 | Southampton University MPA | Southampton Hall of Aviation | |
| 8 | Dixon ornithopter | The Shuttleworth Trust | |
| 9 | Humber Monoplane (replica) | Airport Terminal/Birmingham | |
| 10 | Hafner R.II Revoplane | Museum of Army Flying/Middle Wallop | |
| 12 | Mignet HM.14 | Museum of Flight/E. Fortune | |
| 13 | Mignet HM.14 | Brimpex Metal Treatments | |
| 14 | Addyman standard training glider | N. H. Ponsford | |
| 15 | Addyman standard training glider | The Aeroplane Collection Ltd | |
| 16 | Addyman ultra-light aircraft | N. H. Ponsford | |
| 17 | Woodhams Sprite | The Aeroplane Collection Ltd | |
| 18 | Killick MP Gyroplane | N. H. Ponsford | |
| 19 | Bristol F.2b | Brussels Air Museum | |
| 20 | Lee-Richards annular biplane (replica) | Newark Air Musem | |
| 21 | Thruxton Jackaroo | M. J. Brett | |
| 22 | Mignet HM.14 (G-AEOF) | Aviodome/Schiphol, Holland | |
| 25 | Nyborg TGN-III glider | Midland Air Museum | |
| 27 | Mignet HM.14 | M. J. Abbey | |
| 28 | Wright Flyer (replica) | Bygone Times Antique Warehouse/ Eccleston | |
| 29 | Mignet HM.14 (replica) (G-ADRY) | Brooklands Museum of Aviation/ Weybridge | |
| 32 | Crossley Tom Thumb | Midland Air Museum | |
| 33 | DFS.108-49 Grunau Baby IIb | Russavia Collection | |
| 34 | DFS.108-49 Grunau Baby IIb | D. Elsdon | |
| 35 | EoN primary glider | Russavia Collection | |
| 36 | Fieseler Fi.103 (V-1) (replica) | Kent Battle of Britain Museum/Hawkinge | |
| 37 | Blake Bluetit | The Shuttleworth Trust | |
| 38 | Bristol Scout replica (A1742) | Historical Aircraft Museum/RAF St Athan | |
| 40 | Bristol Boxkite (replica) | Bristol City Museum | |
| 41 | B.E.2C (replica) (6232) | Historical Aircraft Museum/RAF St Athan | |
| 42 | Avro 504 (replica) (H1968) | Historical Aircraft Museum/RAF St Athan | |
| 43 | Mignet HM.14 | Lincolnshire Aviation Museum | |
| 44 | Miles Magister (L6906) | Berkshire Aviation Group (G-AKKY)/ Woodley | |
| 45 | Pilcher Hawk (replica) | Stanford Hall Museum | |
| 46 | Mignet HM.14 | Alan McKechnie Racing Ltd | |
| 47 | Watkins Monoplane | Historical Aircraft Museum/RAF St Athan | |
| 48 | Pilcher Hawk (replica) | Glasgow Museum of Transport | |
| 49 | Pilcher Hawk | Royal Scottish Museum/Edinburgh | |
| 50 | Roe Triplane Type 1 | Science Museum/S. Kensington | |
| 51 | Vickers Vimy IV | Science Museum/S. Kensington | |
| 52 | Lilienthal glider | Science Museum Store/Hayes | |
| 53 | Wright Flyer (replica) | Science Museum/S. Kensington | |
| 54 | JAP-Harding monoplane | Science Museum/S. Kensington | |
| 55 | Levavasseur Antoinette VII | Science Museum/S. Kensington | |
| 56 | Fokker E.III (210/16) | Science Museum/S. Kensington | |
| 57 | Pilcher Hawk (replica) | Science Museum/S. Kensington | |
| 58 | Yokosuka MXY-7 Ohka II (15-1585) | FAA Museum/Yeovilton | |

| Notes | Reg. | Type | Owner or Operator |
|---|---|---|---|
| | 59 | Sopwith Camel (replica) (D3419) | Historical Aircraft Museum/RAF St Athan |
| | 60 | Murray M.1 helicopter | The Aeroplane Collection Ltd |
| | 61 | Stewart man-powered ornithopter | Lincolnshire Aviation Museum |
| | 62 | Cody Biplane (304) | Science Museum/S. Kensington |
| | 63 | Hurricane (replica) (L1592) | Torbay Aircraft Museum |
| | 64 | Hurricane (replica) (P3059) | Kent Battle of Britain Museum/Hawkinge |
| | 65 | Spitfire (replica) (QV-K) | Kent Battle of Britain Museum/Hawkinge |
| | 66 | Bf 109 (replica) (1480) | Kent Battle of Britain Museum/Hawkinge |
| | 67 | Bf 109 (replica) (14) | Midland Air Museum |
| | 68 | Hurricane (replica) (H3426) | Midland Air Museum |
| | 69 | Spitfire (replica) (QV-K) | Torbay Aircraft Museum |
| | 70 | Auster AOP.5 (TJ398) | Aircraft Preservation Soc of Scotland |
| | 71 | Spitfire (replica) (P9390) | Norfolk & Suffolk Aviation Museum |
| | 72 | Hurricane (replica) (V7767) | N. Weald Aircraft Restoration Flight |
| | 73 | Hurricane (replica) | Queens Head/Bishops Stortford |
| | 74 | Bf 109 (replica) (6) | Torbay Aircraft Museum |
| | 75 | Mignet HM.14 (G-AEFG) | Nigel Ponsford |
| | 76 | Mignet HM.14 (G-AFFI) | Yorkshire Air Museum/Elvington |
| | 77 | Mignet HM.14 (replica) (G-ADRG) | Cotswold Aircraft Restoration Group |
| | 79 | Fiat G.46-4 (MM53211) | British Air Reserve/Lympne |
| | 80 | Airspeed Horsa (TL659) | Museum of Army Flying |
| | 81 | Hawkridge Dagling | Russavia Collection |
| | 82 | Hawker Hind (Afghan) | RAF Museum/Hendon |
| | 83 | Kawasaki Ki-100-1b | Aerospace Museum/Cosford |
| | 84 | Nakajima Ki-46 (Dinah III) | Historical Aircraft Museum/RAF St Athan |
| | 85 | Weir W-2 autogyro | Museum of Flight/E. Fortune |
| | 86 | de Havilland Tiger Moth (replica) | Yorkshire Aircraft Preservation Soc |
| | 87 | Bristol Babe (replica) (G-EASQ) | Bomber County Museum/Hemswell |
| | 88 | Fokker Dr 1 (replica) (102/18) | Fleet Air Arm Museum |
| | 89 | Cayley glider (replica) | Greater Manchester Museum of Science & Technology |
| | 90 | Colditz Cock (replica) | Torbay Aircraft Museum |
| | 91 | Fieseler Fi 103 (V.1) | Lashenden Air Warfare Museum |
| | 92 | Fieseler Fi 103 (V.1) | Historical Aircraft Museum/RAF St Athan |
| | 93 | Fieseler Fi 103 (V.1) | Imperial War Museum/Duxford |
| | 94 | Fieseler Fi 103 (V.1) | Aerospace Museum/Cosford |
| | 95 | Gizmer autogyro | F. Fewsdale |
| | 96 | Brown helicopter | NE Aircraft Museum |
| | 97 | Luton L.A.4A Minor | NE Aircraft Museum |
| | 98 | Yokosuka MXY-7 Ohka II | Greater Manchester Museum of Science & Technology |
| | 99 | Yokosuka MXY-7 Ohka II | Aerospace Museum/Cosford |
| | 100 | Clarke glider | RAF Museum/Hendon |
| | 101 | Mignet HM.14 | Lincolnshire Aviation Museum |
| | 103 | Pilcher glider (replica) | Personal Plane Services Ltd |
| | 105 | Blériot XI (replica) | Aviodome/Schiphol, Holland |
| | 106 | Blériot XI (164) | RAF Museum/Hendon |
| | 107 | Blériot XXVII (433) | RAF Museum/Hendon |
| | 108 | Fairey Swordfish IV (HS503) | RAF Museum/Henlow store |
| | 109 | Slingsby Kirby Cadet TX.1 | RAF Museum/Henlow store |
| | 110 | Fokker D.VII replica (static) (5125) | — |
| | 111 | Sopwith Triplane replica (static) (N5492) | FAA Museum/Yeovilton |
| | 112 | D.H.2 replica (static) (5964) | Museum of Army Flying/Middle Wallop |
| | 113 | S.E.5A replica (static) (B4863) | — |
| | 114 | Vickers Type 60 Viking (static) | Brooklands Museum of Aviation/Weybridge |
| | 115 | Mignet HM.14 | Essex Aviation Group/Andrewsfield |
| | 116 | Santos-Dumont Demoiselle (replica) | Cornwall Aero Park/Helston |
| | 117 | B.E.2C (replica) | N. Weald Aircraft Restoration Flight |
| | 118 | Albatros D.V. (replica) | N. Weald Aircraft Restoration Flight |
| | 119 | Bensen B.7 | N.E. Aircraft Museum |
| | 120 | Mignet HM.14 (G-AEJZ) | Bomber County Museum/Hemswell |
| | 121 | Mignet HM.14 (G-AEKR) | S. Yorks Aviation Soc |
| | 122 | Avro 504 (replica) | British Broadcasting Corp |
| | 123 | Vickers FB.5 Gunbus (replica) | A. Topen (*stored*)/Cranfield |
| | 124 | Lilienthal Glider Type XI (replica) | Science Museum/S. Kensington |
| | 125 | Clay Cherub (G-BDGP) | B. R. Clay |
| | 126 | D.31 Turbulent (static) | Midland Air Museum store |

| Reg. | Type | Owner or Operator | Notes |
|------|------|-------------------|-------|
| 127 | Halton Jupiter MPA | Shuttleworth Trust | |
| 128 | Watkinson Cyclogyroplane Mk IV | International Helicopter Museum/ Weston-s-Mare | |
| 129 | Blackburn 1911 Monoplane (replica) | Cornwall Aero Park/Helston store | |
| 130 | Blackburn 1912 Monoplane (replica) | Cornwall Aero Park/Helston store | |
| 131 | Pilcher Hawk (replica) | C. Paton | |
| 132 | Blériot XI (G-BLXI) | EMK Aeroplane Co Ltd | |
| 133 | Fokker Dr 1 (replica) (425/17) | Torbay Aircraft Museum | |
| 134 | Pitts S-2A static (G-RKSF) | Torbay Aircraft Museum | |
| 135 | Bristol M.1C (replica) (C4912) | Leisure Sport Ltd/Thorpe Park | |
| 136 | Deperdussin Seaplane (replica) | Leisure Sport Ltd/Thorpe Park | |
| 137 | Sopwith Baby Floatplane (replica) (8151) | Leisure Sport Ltd/Thorpe Park | |
| 138 | Hansa Brandenburg W.29 Floatplane (replica) (2292) | Leisure Sport Ltd/Thorpe Park | |
| 139 | Fokker Dr 1 (replica) 150/17 | Leisure Sport Ltd/Thorpe Park | |
| 140 | Curtiss R3C-2 Floatplane (replica) | Leisure Sport Ltd/Thorpe Park | |
| 141 | Macchi M.39 Floatplane (replica) | Planes of Fame Museum/Chino, US | |
| 142 | SE-5A (replica) (F5459) | Cornwall Aero Park/Helston | |
| 143 | Paxton MPA | R. A. Paxton/Staverton | |
| 144 | Weybridge Mercury MPA | Cranwell Gliding Club | |
| 145 | Oliver MPA | D. Oliver (stored)/Warton | |
| 146 | Pedal Aeronauts Toucan MPA | Shuttleworth Trust | |
| 147 | Bensen B.7 | Norfolk & Suffolk Aviation Museum | |
| 148 | Hawker Fury II (replica) (K7271) | Aerospace Museum/Cosford | |
| 149 | Short S.27 (replica) | FAA Museum (stored)/Yeovilton | |
| 150 | SEPECAT Jaguar GR.1 (replica) (XX724) | RAF Exhibition Flight | |
| 151 | SEPECAT Jaguar GR.1 (replica) (XZ363) | RAF Exhibition Flight | |
| 152 | BAe Hawk T.1 (replica) (XX163) | RAF Exhibition Flight | |
| 153 | Westland WG.33 | International Helicopter Museum/ Weston-s-Mare | |
| 154 | D.31 Turbulent | Lincolnshire Aviation Museum | |
| 155 | Panavia Tornado GR.1 (replica) (ZA600) | RAF Exhibition Flight | |
| 156 | Supermarine S-6B (replica) (S1595) | Leisure Sport Ltd | |
| 157 | Waco CG-4A | Pennine Aviation Museum | |
| 158 | Fieseler Fi 103 (V.1) | Joint Bomb Disposal School/Chattenden | |
| 159 | Yokosuka MXY-7 Ohka II | Joint Bomb Disposal School/Chattenden | |
| 160 | Chargus 108 hang glider | Museum of Flight/E. Fortune | |
| 161 | Stewart Ornithopter Coppelia | Bomber County Museum | |
| 162 | Goodhart Newbury Manflier MPA | Science Museum/Wroughton | |
| 163 | AFEE 10/42 Rotabuggy (replica) | Museum of Army Flying/Middle Wallop | |
| 164 | Wight Quadruplane Type 1 (replica) | Wessex Aviation Soc/Wimborne | |
| 165 | Bristol F.2b (E2466) | RAF Museum/Hendon | |
| 167 | S.E.5A replica | Newark Air Museum | |
| 168 | D.H.60G Moth static replica (G-AAAH) | Hilton Hotel/Gatwick | |
| 169 | SEPECAT Jaguar GR.1 (static replica) (XX110) | No 1 S. of T.T. RAF Halton | |
| 170 | Pilcher Hawk (replica) | A. Gourlay/Strathallan | |
| 171 | BAe Hawk T.1 (replica) (XX297) | RAF Exhibition Flight/Abingdon | |
| 172 | Chargus Midas Super 8 hang glider | Science Museum/Wroughton | |
| 173 | Birdman Promotions Grasshopper | Science Museum/Wroughton | |
| 174 | Bensen B.7 | Science Museum/Wroughton | |
| 175 | Volmer VJ-23 Swingwing | Greater Manchester Museum of Science & Technology | |
| 176 | SE-5A (replica) (A4850) | S. Yorkshire Aircraft Preservation Soc | |
| 177 | Avro 504K (replica) (G1381) | Brooklands Museum of Aviation/ Weybridge | |
| 178 | Avro 504K (replica) (E373) | Bygone Times Antique Warehouse/ Eccleston | |
| 179 | Sopwith Camel (replica) | N. Weald Aircraft Restoration Flight | |
| 180 | McCurdy Silver Dart (replica) | RAF Museum/Cardington | |

| Notes | Reg. | Type | Owner or Operator |
|-------|------|------|-------------------|
| | 181 | RAF B.E.2b (replica) | RAF Museum/Cardington |
| | 182 | Wood Ornithopter | Greater Manchester Museum of Science & Technology |
| | 183 | Zurowski ZP.1 | Newark Air Museum |
| | 184 | Spitfire IX (replica) (EN398) | Aces High Ltd/North Weald |
| | 185 | Waco CG-4A (243809) | Museum of Army Flying/Middle Wallop |
| | 186 | D.H.82B Queen Bee (K3584) | Mosquito Aircraft Museum |
| | 187 | Roe Type 1 biplane (replica) | Brooklands Museum of Aviation/ Weybridge |
| | 188 | McBroom Cobra 88 | Science Museum/Wroughton |
| | 189 | Bleriot XI (replica) | — |
| | 190 | Spitfire (replica) | Biggin Hill Museum |
| | 191 | BAe Harrier GR.5 (replica) (ZD472) | RAF Exhibition Flight |
| | 192 | Weedhopper JC-24 | The Aeroplane Collection |
| | 193 | Hovey WD-11 Whing Ding | The Aeroplane Collection |
| | 194 | Santos Dumont Demoiselle (replica) | Brooklands Museum of Aviation/ Weybridge |
| | 195 | Moonraker 77 hang glider | Museum of Flight/E. Fortune |
| | 196 | Sigma 2M hang glider | Museum of Flight/E. Fortune |
| | 197 | Cirrus III hang glider | Museum of Flight/E. Fortune |
| | 198 | Fieseler Fi.103 (V-1) | Imperial War Museum/Lambeth |
| | 199 | Fieseler Fi.103 (V-1) | Science Museum/S. Kensington |
| | 200 | Benson B.7 | K. Fern Collection/Stoke |
| | 204 | McBroom Hang Glider | The Aeroplane Collection |
| | 208 | SE-5A (replica) | Prince's Mead Shopping Precinct/ Farnborough |

**Note:** Registrations/Serials carried are mostly false identities. MPA = Man Powered Aircraft.

# Future Allocations Log (In-Sequence)

The grid provides the facility to record future in-sequence registrations as they are issued or seen. To trace a particular code, refer to the left hand column which contains the three letters following the G prefix. The final letter can be found by reading across the columns headed A to Z. For example, the box for G-BTHD is located five rows down (BTH) and then four across to the D column.

| G- | A | B | C | D | E | F | G | H | I | J | K | L | M | N | O | P | R | S | T | U | V | W | X | Y | Z |
|----|---|---|---|---|---|---|---|---|---|---|---|---|---|---|---|---|---|---|---|---|---|---|---|---|---|
| BTD | | | | | | | | | | | | | | | | | | | | | | | | | |
| BTE | | | | | | | | | | | | | | | | | | | | | | | | | |
| BTF | | | | | | | | | | | | | | | | | | | | | | | | | |
| BTG | | | | | | | | | | | | | | | | | | | | | | | | | |
| BTH | | | | | | | | | | | | | | | | | | | | | | | | | |
| BTI | | | | | | | | | | | | | | | | | | | | | | | | | |
| BTJ | | | | | | | | | | | | | | | | | | | | | | | | | |
| BTK | | | | | | | | | | | | | | | | | | | | | | | | | |
| BTL | | | | | | | | | | | | | | | | | | | | | | | | | |
| BTM | | | | | | | | | | | | | | | | | | | | | | | | | |
| BTN | | | | | | | | | | | | | | | | | | | | | | | | | |
| BTO | | | | | | | | | | | | | | | | | | | | | | | | | |
| BTP | | | | | | | | | | | | | | | | | | | | | | | | | |
| BTR | | | | | | | | | | | | | | | | | | | | | | | | | |
| BTS | | | | | | | | | | | | | | | | | | | | | | | | | |
| BTT | | | | | | | | | | | | | | | | | | | | | | | | | |
| BTU | | | | | | | | | | | | | | | | | | | | | | | | | |
| BTV | | | | | | | | | | | | | | | | | | | | | | | | | |
| BTW | | | | | | | | | | | | | | | | | | | | | | | | | |
| BTX | | | | | | | | | | | | | | | | | | | | | | | | | |
| BTY | | | | | | | | | | | | | | | | | | | | | | | | | |
| BTZ | | | | | | | | | | | | | | | | | | | | | | | | | |
| BUA | | | | | | | | | | | | | | | | | | | | | | | | | |
| BUB | | | | | | | | | | | | | | | | | | | | | | | | | |
| BUC | | | | | | | | | | | | | | | | | | | | | | | | | |
| BUD | | | | | | | | | | | | | | | | | | | | | | | | | |
| BUE | | | | | | | | | | | | | | | | | | | | | | | | | |
| BUF | | | | | | | | | | | | | | | | | | | | | | | | | |
| BUG | | | | | | | | | | | | | | | | | | | | | | | | | |
| BUH | | | | | | | | | | | | | | | | | | | | | | | | | |
| BUI | | | | | | | | | | | | | | | | | | | | | | | | | |
| BUJ | | | | | | | | | | | | | | | | | | | | | | | | | |
| BUK | | | | | | | | | | | | | | | | | | | | | | | | | |
| BUL | | | | | | | | | | | | | | | | | | | | | | | | | |
| BUM | A | B | C | D | E | F | G | H | I | J | K | L | M | N | O | P | R | S | T | U | V | W | X | Y | Z |

Credit: *Wal Gandy*

This grid can be used to record out-of-sequence registrations as they are issued or seen. The first column is provided for the ranges prefixed with G-B, ie from G-BUxx to G-BZxx. The remaining columns cover the sequences from G-Cxxx to G-Zxxx and in this case it is necessary to insert the last three letters in the appropriate section.

| G-B | G-C | G-E | G-G | G-J | G-L | G-N | G-O | G-P | G-S | G-U |
|-----|-----|-----|-----|-----|-----|-----|-----|-----|-----|-----|
|  |  |  |  |  |  |  |  |  |  |  |
|  |  |  |  |  |  |  |  |  |  |  |
|  |  |  |  |  |  |  |  |  |  |  |
|  |  |  |  |  |  |  |  |  |  |  | G-V |
|  | G-D | G-F | G-H |  | G-M | G-O |  |  |  |  |
|  |  |  |  |  |  |  |  |  |  |  |
|  |  |  |  |  |  |  |  |  |  |  |
|  |  |  |  | G-K |  |  |  |  |  |  |
|  |  |  |  |  |  |  |  |  |  | G-W |
|  |  |  |  |  |  |  |  |  |  |  |
|  |  |  |  |  |  |  |  |  |  |  |
|  |  |  |  |  |  |  |  | G-R |  |  |
|  |  |  |  |  |  |  |  |  | G-T |  |
|  |  |  |  |  |  |  |  |  |  | G-X |
|  |  |  |  |  |  |  |  |  |  |  |
| G-C | G-E | G-G | G-I | G-L | G-N |  |  |  |  |  |
|  |  |  |  |  |  |  |  |  |  | G-Y |
|  |  |  |  |  |  |  |  |  |  |  |
|  |  |  |  |  |  |  |  |  |  |  |
|  |  |  |  |  |  |  |  |  |  | G-Z |
|  |  |  |  |  |  |  |  |  |  |  |

# Overseas Airliner Registration Log

This grid may be used to record airliner registrations not included in the main section.

| Reg | Type | Operator |
|-----|------|----------|
|     |      |          |
|     |      |          |
|     |      |          |
|     |      |          |
|     |      |          |
|     |      |          |
|     |      |          |
|     |      |          |
|     |      |          |
|     |      |          |
|     |      |          |
|     |      |          |
|     |      |          |
|     |      |          |
|     |      |          |
|     |      |          |
|     |      |          |
|     |      |          |
|     |      |          |
|     |      |          |
|     |      |          |
|     |      |          |
|     |      |          |
|     |      |          |
|     |      |          |
|     |      |          |
|     |      |          |
|     |      |          |
|     |      |          |
|     |      |          |
|     |      |          |
|     |      |          |
|     |      |          |
|     |      |          |
|     |      |          |
|     |      |          |
|     |      |          |
|     |      |          |
|     |      |          |
|     |      |          |
|     |      |          |

# Addenda

**Cancellations**

G-ARIW, G-AWPX, G-BATU, G-BAWB, G-BEIH, G-BKBB, G-BKCD, G-BKKI, G-BKNJ, G-BLRB, G-BNOC, G-BPFU, G-BPMS, G-BSGZ, G-BSOA, G-BSTF, G-BSTW, G-BSVU, G-BSXZ G-BSYN, G-BTAO, G-CLAW, G-GRUB, G-IBLW, G-LAMB, G-MWGS, G-PRMC, G-SALY, G-SARN, G-SKSF, G-TRCO.

**New overseas registrations**

| Notes | Reg. | Type | Owner or Operator |
|---|---|---|---|
| | C-FIJR | L.188 Electra | Air Bridge Carriers/E. Midlands |
| | C-FNWY | L.188 Electra | Air Bridge Carriers/E. Midlands |
| | D-AISY | F.27 Friendship Mk 600 | Ratioflug |
| | EC-EXH | Boeing 757-236 | Air Europa |
| | EC-EZA | McD Douglas MD-87 | Iberia |
| | F-GKTD | Airbus A.310-304 | TEA France |
| | F-GKTE | Airbus A.310-304 | TEA France |
| | I-ATSC | BAe 146-300 | Sagittair |
| | I-ATSD | BAe 146-300 | Sagittair |
| | OO-DJG | BAe 146-200 | Delta Air Transport |
| | OO-DJH | BAe 146-200 | Delta Air Transport |
| | OO-PHF | Boeing 737-222 | Skyjet |
| | OO-PHG | Boeing 737-222 | Skyjet |
| | N803UP | Douglas DC-8-73CF | United Parcel Service |
| | N811UP | Douglas DC-8-73CF | United Parcel Service |
| | N13067 | Douglas DC-10-30 | Continental Airlines (ex N391EA) |
| | TC-JDE | Boeing 737-4Y0 | Türk Hava Yollari (THY) |
| | TC-JDF | Boeing 737-4Y0 | Türk Hava Yollari (THY) |
| | TC-JDG | Boeing 737-4Y0 | Türk Hava Yollari (THY) |
| | TC-JDH | Boeing 737-4Y0 | Türk Hava Yollari (THY) |

**Cancellations**

CS-TBY, D-AOAD, D-AOAE, EI-BZZ, EI-CCI, F-GCGH, F-GCLQ, F-GCPV, N355WS, N391EA, OO-PHE, OY-CCR.

# Notes